M000288788

ALGORITHMS

SEQUENTIAL, PARALLEL, AND DISTRIBUTED

Kenneth A. Berman and Jerome L. Paul
University of Cincinnati

THOMSON

COURSE TECHNOLOGY

THOMSON

COURSE TECHNOLOGY

Algorithms: Sequential, Parallel, and Distributed

by Kenneth A. Berman and Jerome L. Paul

Senior Acquisitions Editor:
Amy Yarnevich

Senior Product Manager:
Alyssa Pratt

Editorial Assistant:
Jenny Smith

Senior Marketing Manager:
Karen Seitz

Production Editor:
Jennifer Harvey

Designer:
Pre-Press Company, Inc.

Cover Design:
Laura Rickenbach

Cover Image:
Ray Paul

Compositor:
Pre-Press Company, Inc.

Printer:
Quebecor World Taunton

COPYRIGHT © 2005 Course Technology, a division of Thomson Learning, Inc. Thomson Learning™ is a trademark used herein under license.

Printed in the United States of America

1 2 3 4 5 6 7 8 9 BM 06 05 04 03 02

For more information, contact Course Technology, 25 Thomson Place, Boston, Massachusetts, 02210.

Or find us on the World Wide Web at: www.course.com

ALL RIGHTS RESERVED. No part of this work covered by the copyright hereon may be reproduced or used in any form or by any means—graphic, electronic, or mechanical, including photocopying, recording, taping, Web distribution, or information storage and retrieval systems—without the written permission of the publisher.

For permission to use material from this text or product, contact us by

Tel (800) 730-2214

Fax (800) 730-2215

www.thomsonrights.com

Disclaimer

Course Technology reserves the right to revise this publication and make changes from time to time in its content without notice.

ISBN 0-534-42057-5

TABLE OF CONTENTS

PART V SPECIAL TOPICS 629

PREFACE

The objectives of this book are to provide a solid foundation for the classical theory of sequential algorithms and to cover some of the most important recent algorithmic developments, including the rapidly advancing theory of parallel and distributed algorithms. The book is intended to serve as a text for a core upper-division undergraduate course or first-year graduate course in the design and analysis of algorithms.

While parts of the book are revised and updated versions of text taken from the authors' previous book, *Fundamentals of Sequential and Parallel Algorithms*, we have added a significant amount of new material, including an introduction to Internet and distributed algorithms. Also, the material on parallel algorithms that was integrated throughout the previous book has now been moved to a separate part on parallel and distributed algorithms. This separation enables the instructor to cover as little or as much of the parallel material as desired. Another new feature is the inclusion of a number of appendices containing ancillary material, such as a review of mathematical prerequisites. Placing this material in appendices keeps the text more sharply focused on algorithmic issues.

One of the major goals of this book is to provide the reader with a large toolkit of fundamental sequential, parallel, and distributed algorithmic solutions to frequently encountered problems, such as searching and sorting; matrix manipulations; constructing minimum spanning trees and shortest paths in networks; scientific computations, including the Fast Fourier Transform; and data compression and security, among others. Another major goal is to provide the reader with the mathematical tools necessary to analyze the correctness and efficiency of algorithms and to be able to judge how close an algorithm is to being optimal for a given problem. With these tools, the reader can choose the best algorithm to use in a given circumstance from among several algorithms that might be available for the problem. Another goal of this book is to enable the reader to recognize problems that might be NP-hard and to search for algorithms that work well on average or for an approximate solution that works well even in the worst case. Perhaps the most important goal, however, is to enhance the reader's ability to create new algorithms or modify existing algorithms for solving new problems.

Fueled by the rapid expansion of parallel computers and distributed networks such as the Internet, ad hoc mobile computing networks, wireless communication networks, peer-to-peer networks, and computation grids, the theory of parallel and distributed algorithms has now taken a central position in computer science and engineering. Many of the classical problems solved in the sequential environment now appear in the parallel and distributed environment. In addition, new problems arise, such as packet-routing and message-passing problems in distributed networks, searching and relevancy ranking of pages on the World Wide Web, and reliability and security issues relating to communication in large-scale networks. In view of the recent advances in computer and network technology, all students of computer science and computer engineering should be exposed to the theory of parallel and distributed algorithms as part of their undergraduate training.

When designing a parallel or distributed algorithm, many issues arise that were not present in the sequential setting. For example, the type of architecture, the communication model, the number of processors available, synchronization issues, and so forth must be considered when designing a parallel or distributed algorithm. Paradigms and tools developed for sequential algorithms can often be applied in parallel and distributed settings but usually need to be modified and combined with new tools to be implemented and to efficiently solve problems in those settings. For example, exploiting the obvious parallelism implicit in the divide-and-conquer paradigm is usually just the first step in designing a parallel algorithm for a problem. Acceptable speedup usually occurs only when additional tools and strategies are developed to achieve further parallelism. New tools in the distributed setting include flooding and broadcasting, gathering, leader election, termination detection, and so forth. Although the primary focus of this text remains the core material in a traditional undergraduate sequential algorithms course, parallel and distributed algorithms are covered in sufficient detail to prepare the student for independent study or for taking a more advanced graduate course devoted entirely to these topics.

Organization of the Book

The book is divided into five parts, with appendices that review the prerequisite material and supplemental material. We feel that this division allows for a natural flow of the topics and gives the instructor the flexibility to adapt the material easily to fit a variety of course objectives. Part I provides the foundation for the theory of algorithms. Part II introduces the student to the various classical sequential design strategies. Because of the importance of graph and network algorithms in parallel and distributed computing, we devote Part III to this topic. Part IV introduces the student to parallel and distributed algorithms, as well as searching and the Internet. Finally, Part V contains a number of special topics, each of which constitutes a major application area in the theory of algorithms.

Part I begins with a brief history of the subject of algorithms, including a discussion of some algorithms that have been around for quite a long time. We introduce some guidelines for algorithm design, including recursion, and provide some familiar examples as illustrations. The fundamental measures of sequential algorithms are defined, including best-case, worst-case, and average complexity of an algorithm. The notion of the asymptotic order of these measures is also introduced. We illustrate these measures by analyzing some of the most familiar algorithms, such as exponentiation, searching, and sorting. We also discuss the important issues of establishing the correctness of an algorithm and of deciding whether more-efficient algorithms should be sought. Some straightforward lower bounds are established to show the student how to determine how close an algorithm is to exhibiting optimal behavior. Because trees are so important in the design and analysis of algorithms, we devote a chapter to their mathematical properties, how they are implemented, and some of their fundamental uses, such as in maintaining search trees and priority queues. We close Part I with a discussion of the average behavior of algorithms.

Fortunately, the subject of algorithms does not consist of a large collection of ad hoc methods, each tailored to specific problems, without any unifying principles. Although ad hoc methods may have characterized the early development of algorithm design, as the study of algorithms progressed, certain major design strategies emerged. Part II is devoted to classical major design strategies for algorithms, including the greedy method, divide-and-conquer, dynamic programming, and backtracking and branch-and-bound. These strategies are also used for algorithm design throughout the remainder of the book. Other major design strategies of more recent origin, such as heuristic search and probabilistic methods, are covered in Part V.

Although graph and network algorithms have been part of the core material in sequential algorithms for some time, they have taken on special significance with the emergence of parallel computers and various distributed networks such as the Internet. To set the stage for the study of parallel and distributed algorithms, we devote Part III to the basic theory of graph and network algorithms. The minimum spanning tree and shortest-path algorithms discussed here use strategies developed in Part II. Placing these algorithms in one place not only serves to unify the treatment of graph and network algorithms but also reinforces the importance of recognizing when one of the major design strategies is applicable for a given problem. In addition to minimum spanning trees and shortest-path algorithms, we discuss graph connectivity, fault-tolerant routing schemes, and network flow algorithms, topics of major significance in distributed networks.

In Part IV, we introduce the student to the theory of parallel and distributed algorithms. The parallel treatment includes a discussion of both the shared memory (PRAM) model and the distributed memory model as implemented by various interconnection network models (meshes, hypercubes, and so forth). We introduce pseudocode for parallel algorithms in both the PRAM and interconnection network models, and we discuss how basic searching and sorting algorithms are implemented on these models. We stress how to recognize when sequential strategies for solving these problems might be adapted to the parallel setting and what modifications and new tools might be necessary. We then introduce some of these new tools for parallel design strategies, including parallel prefix computations, pointer jumping, and parallel matrix operations.

In the distributed treatment of Part IV, we consider three main areas: searching and ranking algorithms for the Internet, cluster computation using message passing, and algorithms suitable for distributed networks. Our model for message passing in the single-program, multiple-data (SPMD) model of distributed computing closely follows the Message Passing Interface (MPI) model that has become the standard for cluster-based computing. (In Appendix F, we show how our pseudocode for message passing easily translates into actual MPI programs implementing some of our algorithms.) We discuss synchronous and asynchronous message passing, including how to avoid deadlock. The computation/communication alternation model is introduced, and its implementation using the master-worker paradigm is discussed.

In the chapter on distributed network algorithms, which is typified by the lack of a central control mechanism (except for lock-step synchronization of rounds in the synchronized setting), we also develop pseudocode for synchronous and asynchronous distributed algorithms. We solve some fundamental distributed network problems such as flooding and broadcasting, leader election, performing global operations, and computing shortest paths and minimum spanning trees. Here again, solutions to these problems are often facilitated by our previous discussions of sequential algorithms, as well as by solving the problems in the parallel environment.

In Part V, we cover a collection of special topics, all of which are active research areas today. We give enough of an introduction to these topics to allow the student to investigate them in further detail, either independently or in courses entirely devoted to one or more of the topics.

Appendix A reviews some mathematical prerequisites that are needed for algorithm analysis. Appendix B reviews linear data structures and includes a discussion of removing recursion. Appendix C discusses interpolating asymptotic behavior. Appendix D discusses random walks on digraphs, Markov chains, and eigenvalues. Appendix E includes a review of the results from elementary probability theory necessary to analyze the average behavior of algorithms, as well as to discuss probabilistic algorithms. Appendix F contains a brief introduction to MPI programming, including a translation into MPI code of the pseudocode for some of the distributed algorithms discussed in Chapter 18. Finally, Appendix G gives pseudocode conventions that we use for sequential and parallel algorithms.

In addition to the selected references and suggestions for further reading at the end of each chapter, we include a bibliography at the end of the book. An Instructor's Manual containing a full set of solutions is accessible only to instructors adopting the text. This supplement can be downloaded from www.course.com.

Possible Course Coverage

The inclusion of an extended treatment of parallel and distributed algorithms, together with a number of special topics, provides enough material to serve as the basis for a two-semester course in algorithms. However, the material in the first two parts, together with a selection of topics from the remaining parts, gives the instructor sufficient flexibility to readily adapt the material to a one-semester course.

In Part I, much of the material in Chapters 1 through 4 can be quickly reviewed or made a reading assignment for those students already familiar with elementary data structures and algorithms. However, some important material on exponentiation, the mathematical properties of binary trees, union and find algorithms, and correctness proofs included in the first four chapters should be covered, as these concepts are used often in the text and may not be included in the student's background. Chapter 5 covers some special topics in sorting, such as radix and external sorting, which are not needed in the remainder of the text. The first three sections of Chapter 6 should be covered, as material there forms the basis for the analysis of the average behavior of algorithms.

Most of Part II on major design strategies should be covered, as the examples have been chosen to be important representatives of the strategies. These design strategies are the basis of many algorithms throughout the text, and the instructor may wish to include some additional examples when covering Part II. For example, standard greedy algorithms for minimum spanning trees and shortest-path trees in graphs are placed in Part III on graph and network algorithms, but these topics certainly could be covered as part of Chapter 7 on the greedy method. Also, the Fast Fourier Transform is discussed in Chapter 22 but could also be included in the study of the divide-and-conquer strategy in Chapter 8.

In Part III, we would expect that Chapters 11 and 12 would be covered in their entirety, whereas topics could be selected from the remaining chapters depending on time and preference.

Part IV contains a number of topics in parallel and distributed algorithms. It is entirely possible to study these chapters independently. For some examples in distributed algorithms, it is useful, but not necessary, to have seen a parallel version of the algorithm. However, our descriptions of the distributed algorithms, such as even-odd sorting, are complete and mostly self-contained. Also, our discussion of Internet algorithms is largely independent of the rest of the material in Part IV.

Finally, Part V contains a collection of special topics that are also independent of one another. We would expect that most instructors would cover at least part of Chapter 26 on NP-complete problems. The instructor can then pick and choose from the remaining topics as time allows. For example, string-matching algorithms, covered in Chapter 20, have taken on new significance with the emergence of the Internet. Chapter 24 gives an introduction to probabilistic algorithms, which is an important area of research today with many applications. The Fast Fourier Transform, certainly one of the most important algorithms for scientific applications, is the topic of Chapter 22. All these topics are covered in sufficient depth to prepare the student for further investigations.

Acknowledgments

We wish to thank the many students whose suggestions and corrections over the years contributed to our first book and the current book. Special thanks go to Michal Kouril for his suggestions and careful reading of Chapter 18 and his testing of the MPI code in Appendix F. We also wish to thank our colleagues for their suggestions, including Fred Annexstein, Yizong Cheng, John Franco, Ken Meyer, John Schlipf, and Dieter Schmidt.

The material in this and the previous book have undergone a number of external reviews, which have been invaluable. The reviewers of the first book include Andrew Astromoff, Theodore Brown, Donald Burlingame, Adair Dingle, Barry Donahue, Rex Dwyer, Keith Harrow, T. C. Hu, David John, Arkady Kanevsky, Sampath Kannan, Sheau-Doug Lang, Udi Manber, Harold Martin, Tim McGuire, Jerry Potter, Michael Quinn, Robert Roos, Richard Salter, Cliff Shaffer, Greg Starling, Robert Tarjan, David Teague, Roger Wainright, and Lynn Ziegler.

The reviewers of the second book include:

Stefano Lonardi, University of California, Riverside
Steven Janke, Colorado College
Roy P. Pargas, Clemson Colllege
Lorin Schwiebert, Wayne State University

We would like to thank Kallie Swanson of Brooks/Cole who originally signed us up for this project. We would also like to thank Alyssa Pratt and Amy Yarnevich of Course Technology, Jennifer Harvey of Pre-Press Company, and Barbara McGowran, our copyeditor, for their highly professional and invaluable technical support throughout the production of this book. It has been a pleasure to work with them.

We cannot overstate our debt of gratitude to our wives, Peiyan and Ruta, for their constant encouragement, love, and support. Without their considerable sacrifices, this book would not have been possible. We dedicate this book to them and to our children, Rachel and Sarah, and Ray and Renee.

K. A. B. and *J. L. P*

PART ONE

INTRODUCTION TO ALGORITHMS

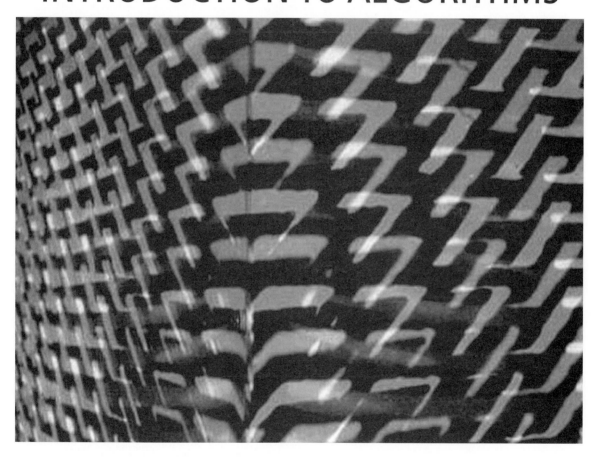

CHAPTER 1

INTRODUCTION AND PRELIMINARIES

The use of algorithms did not begin with the introduction of computers. In fact, people have been using algorithms as long as they have been solving problems systematically. Informally, we can describe an algorithm as a finite sequence of rules that solves a problem. Although a completely rigorous definition of an algorithm uses the notion of a Turing Machine, the following definition will suffice for our purposes.

DEFINITION 1.1   An *algorithm* is a complete, step-by-step procedure for solving a specific problem. Each step must be unambiguously expressed in terms of a finite number of rules and guaranteed to terminate in a finite number of applications of the rules. Typically, a rule calls for the execution of one or more operations.

A *sequential* algorithm performs operations one at a time, in sequence, whereas a *parallel* or *distributed* algorithm can perform many operations simultaneously.

In this text, the operations allowed in a sequential algorithm are restricted to the instructions found in a typical high-level procedural computer language. These instructions are, for example, arithmetical operations, logical comparisons, and transfers of control. A parallel or distributed algorithm allows the same operations as a sequential algorithm (in addition to communication operations among processors), but a given operation can be performed on multiple data instances simultaneously. For instance, a parallel algorithm might add 1 to each element in an array of numbers in a single parallel step.

An important consideration in algorithm design is what models and architectures will implement the algorithm. We discuss the various models later in this chapter. In addition, we provide some historical background for the study of sequential, parallel, and distributed algorithms and give a brief trace of how algorithms have developed from ancient times to the present.

1.1   Algorithms from Ancient to Modern Times

The algorithms discussed in this section solve some classical problems in arithmetic. Some algorithms commonly executed on today's computers were originally developed more than three thousand years ago. The examples we present illustrate the fact that the most straightforward algorithm for solving a given problem often is not the most efficient.

1.1.1 Evaluating Powers

An ancient problem in arithmetic is the efficient evaluation of integer powers of a number x. The naive approach to evaluating x^n is to repeatedly multiply x by itself $n - 1$ times, yielding the following algorithm

```
function NaivePowers(x, n)
Input:   x (a real number), n (a positive integer)
Output: x^n
    Product ← x
    for i ← 1 to n − 1 do
        Product ← Product * x
    endfor
    return(Product)
end NaivePowers
```

Clearly, *NaivePowers* performs $n - 1$ multiplications; for example, to compute x^{32}, *NaivePowers* uses 31 multiplications. However, after a little thought, we could have computed x^{32} using only 5 multiplications by successive squaring operations, yielding: $x^2, x^4, x^8, x^{16}, x^{32}$. Notice that this simple successive squaring works only for exponents that are a power of 2. In fact, we can do much better than the naive algorithm for general n by using an algorithm that has been known for more than two millennia and was referenced in Pingala's Hindu classic *Chandah-sutra*, circa 200 B.C. To see how this algorithm might arise, consider the problem of computing x^{108}. By repeatedly applying the simple (recurrence) formula

$$x^n = \begin{cases} (x^{n/2})^2 & n \text{ even} \\ x(x^{(n-1)/2})^2 & n \text{ odd} \end{cases}$$

we obtain the following collection of reductions:

$$x^{108} = (x^{54})^2, x^{54} = (x^{27})^2, x^{27} = x(x^{13})^2, x^{13} = x(x^6)^2, x^6 = (x^3)^2,$$
$$x^3 = x(x^1)^2, x^1 = x(x^0)^2.$$

Now we can compute x^{108} by working our way through these reductions from right to left, involving the sequence of powers (on the left side of the equalities): 1, 3, 6, 13, 27, 54, 108. Note that when we compute the next power of x, we simply square the previous power of x if the exponent is even, and we multiply the square of the previous power of x by x if the exponent is odd. We can easily determine whether the exponent is even or odd by using its binary (base 2) expansion and checking whether the least significant binary digit is 0 or 1. Writing the exponents in binary, we obtain the sequence 1, 11, 110, 1101, 11011, 110110, 1101100. Taking the least significant digit in each number in the sequence is equivalent to scanning the last binary number in the sequence (that is, the original number 108) from left to right, which is why this method is called *left-to-right binary exponentiation*. In practice, we can always omit the first step (which always yields x) and start our scan from the second most significant digit.

The left-to-right binary method of computing x^{108} required only 9 multiplications, as opposed to the 107 multiplications required by the naive method. For a general positive integer n, left-to-right binary exponentiation requires between $\log_2 n$ and $2\log_2 n$ multiplications (see Exercise 1.1). For a large n, the difference between the $n - 1$ multiplications required by *NaivePowers* and the maximum of $2\log_2 n$ multiplications required by the left-to-right binary method is dramatic. For example, 10^{83} is estimated to be more than the number of atoms in the known universe, but $\log_2 10^{83}$ is smaller than 276. Figure 1.1 illustrates the dramatic difference between n and $\log_2 n$.

FIGURE 1.1

Table of values of
$\log_2 n$ versus $n-1$

$n = 2^m$	$m = \log_2 n$	$n - 1$
1	0	0
2	1	1
16	4	15
128	7	127
1,024	10	1,023
1,048,576	20	1,048,575
562,949,953,421,312	49	562,949,953,421,311

Another method for computing x^n is called *right-to-left binary exponentiation* because it requires scanning the binary expansion of n from right to left. The method was mentioned by al-Kashi in A.D.1427 and is similar to a method used by the Egyptians for multiplication as early as 2000 B.C. To illustrate this method, let us consider again the problem of computing x^{108}. Because $x^{108} = x^{64} x^{44}$, the problem reduces to computing the two powers x^{64} and x^{44} and multiplying them together. We can compute x^{64} by repeatedly squaring x. To compute x^{44}, we scan the binary representation 101100 of 44 (which is simply the binary representation 1101100 of 108 stripped of its most significant digit) from right to left and accumulate the product of the corresponding powers of x. More precisely, we see from the binary representation of 44 that $x^{44} = x^4 x^8 x^{32}$, so we can compute the relevant powers in this factorization of x^{44} and accumulate their product in the same loop used to repeatedly square x. Moreover, knowing when to accumulate a given power of x is completely determined by whether or not there is a 1 occurring in the corresponding binary digit position of n in our right-to-left scan.

The following pseudocode for the function *Powers* that computes x^n for a general positive integer n is a straightforward implementation of the right-to-left binary method. If $s = \lfloor \log_2 n \rfloor$ and $p = 2^s$, then $x^n = x^p x^{n-p}$. The **while** loop in *Powers* computes x^p by simple squaring (using the variable *Pow*) and computes x^{n-p} by using the variable *AccumPow* to accumulate the factors of x^{n-p} based on whether the current value of n is even or odd (note that repeatedly replacing n by **floor**$(n/2)$ amounts to performing a right-to-left scan of the binary expansion of n). A formal proof of the correctness of *Powers* appears in Chapter 2.

```
function Powers(x, n)
Input:    x (a real number), n (a positive integer)
Output:   x^n
    AccumPow ← 1
    Pow ← x
    while n > 1 do
        if odd(n) then AccumPow ← AccumPow*Pow endif
        n ← floor(n/2)
```

> *Pow ← Pow∗Pow*
> **endwhile**
> *Pow ← AccumPow∗Pow*
> **return**(*Pow*)
> **end** *Powers*

Because it does not explicitly require the binary expansion of *n*, right-to-left binary exponentiation is somewhat easier to program than the left-to-right binary method. We leave it as an exercise to show that both methods require the same number of multiplications.

It turns out that *Powers* is the iterative version of a recursive method based on the formula

$$x^n = \begin{cases} (x^2)^{n/2} & n \text{ even} \\ x(x^2)^{(n-1)/2} & n \text{ odd} \end{cases}$$

which is simply the previous formula for x^n with the order of exponentiation interchanged. Both formulas lead to immediate implementations as recursive functions for computing x^n. We discuss this further in Chapter 2.

Both right-to-left and left-to-right binary exponentiation illustrate that the simplest algorithm for solving a problem is often much less efficient than a more clever but perhaps more complicated algorithm. We state this as an important key fact for algorithm design.

Key Fact

The simplest algorithm for solving a problem is often not the most efficient. Therefore, when designing an algorithm, do not settle for just any algorithm that works.

REMARKS

The binary methods for exponentiation do not always yield the minimum number of multiplications. For example, computing x^{15} by either of these methods requires six multiplications. However, it can be done using only five multiplications (see Exercise 1.3).

The binary methods allow computers to perform the multiplications required to compute x^n, where *n* is an integer with hundreds of binary digits. However, for such values of *n*, the successive powers of *x* being computed grow exponentially, quickly exceeding the storage capacity of any computer that could ever be built. In practice—for example, in Internet security communication protocols that involve computing x^n for *n* having hundreds of digits—the exponential growth of the successive powers is avoided by always reducing the powers modulo some fixed integer *p* at each stage (called *modular exponentiation*).

1.1.2 The Euclidean Algorithm

One of the oldest problems in number theory is determining the *greatest common divisor* of two positive integers a and b, or $\gcd(a,b)$, which is the largest positive integer k that divides both a and b with no remainder. The problem of calculating $\gcd(a,b)$ was already known to the mathematicians of ancient Greece. A naive algorithm computes the prime factorization of a and b and collects common prime powers whose product is then equal to $\gcd(a,b)$. However, for large a and b, computing the prime factorizations is very time consuming, even on today's fastest computers. A more efficient algorithm was published in *Euclid's Elements* (circa 300 B.C.) and was a refinement of an algorithm known 200 years earlier. The earlier algorithm was based on the observation that for $a \geq b$, an integer divides both a and b if, and only if, it divides $a - b$ and b. Thus,

$$\gcd(a,b) = \gcd(a - b,b), \quad a \geq b, \quad \gcd(a,a) = a \qquad \textbf{(1.1.1)}$$

Formula (1.1.1) yields the following algorithm for computing $\gcd(a,b)$:

```
function NaiveGCD(a, b)
Input:    a, b (two positive integers)
Output:  gcd(a, b) (the greatest common divisor of a and b)
    while a ≠ b do
        if a > b then
            a ← a − b
        else
            b ← b − a
        endif
    endwhile
    return(a)
end NaiveGCD
```

After each iteration of the while loop in *NaiveGCD*, the larger of the previous values of a and b is replaced by a strictly smaller positive number. Hence, *GCD* eventually terminates, having calculated the greatest common divisor of the original a and b.

Euclid's gcd algorithm refines the algorithm *NaiveGCD* by utilizing the fact that if $a > b$ and $a - b$ is still greater than b, then $a - b$ in turn is replaced by $a - 2b$, and so forth. Hence, if a is not a multiple of b, then a is eventually replaced by $r = a - qb$, where r is the remainder and q is the quotient when a is divided by b. Thus, all the successive subtractions can be replaced by the single invocation $a \bmod b$, where **mod** is the built-in function defined by

$$a \bmod b = a - b \left\lfloor \frac{a}{b} \right\rfloor, a \text{ and } b \text{ integers, } b \neq 0,$$

where for a given positive real number x, $\lfloor x \rfloor$ denotes the largest integer less than or equal to x. For example, when calculating gcd(108,8), the 13 subtractions executed by the algorithm *NaiveGCD* $(108 - 8, 100 - 8, 92 - 8, \ldots, 12 - 8)$ can be replaced by the single calculation $108 \bmod 8 = 4$.

The preceding discussion leads to an algorithm based on the following formula:

$$\gcd(a, b) = \gcd(b, a \bmod b). \tag{1.1.2}$$

Note that when a is a multiple of b, $\gcd(a,b) = b$, and $a \bmod b = 0$. So the usual convention $\gcd(b,0) = b$ shows that Formula (1.1.2) remains valid when a is a multiple of b.

Euclid's description of the gcd algorithm based on (1.1.2) was complicated by the fact that the algebraic concept of zero was not yet formalized. The following is a modern version of Euclid's algorithm:

```
function EuclidGCD(a, b)
Input:   a, b (two nonnegative integers)
Output:  gcd(a, b) (the greatest common divisor of a and b)
    while b ≠ 0 do
        Remainder ← a mod b
        a ← b
        b ← Remainder
    endwhile
    return(a)
end EuclidGCD
```

The following illustrates *EuclidGCD* for input $a = 10724$, $b = 864$:

$$\gcd(10724,864) = \gcd(864,356) = \gcd(356,152) = \gcd(152,52) = \gcd(52,48)$$
$$= \gcd(48,4) = \gcd(4,0) = 4.$$

The problem of computing $\gcd(a,b)$ has very important applications to modern computing, particularly as it occurs in cryptography and commonly used data security systems (see Chapter 18). It turns out that the **while** loop of *EuclidGCD* never executes more than roughly $\log_2(\max\{a,b\})$ times, so the algorithm can be executed rapidly even when the integers a and b have hundreds of digits each.

1.1.3 Babylonian Square Roots

Another mathematical problem gained special significance in the sixth century B.C. when the Pythagorean school of geometers made the startling discovery that the length of the hypotenuse of a right triangle with legs both equal to 1 cannot be expressed as the ratio of two integers. This conclusion is equivalent to saying that $\sqrt{2}$ is not a rational number and therefore its decimal expansion can never be completely calculated. Long before the discovery of irrational numbers, people were interested in calculating the square root of a given positive number a to any desired degree of accuracy. A square root algorithm was already known to the Babylonians by 1500 B.C. and is perhaps the first nontrivial mathematical algorithm.

The Babylonian method for calculating $\sqrt{a}$ is based on averaging two points on either side of $\sqrt{a}$. The Babylonians may have discovered this algorithm by considering the problem of laying out a square plot of a given area. For example, for an area of 5, they may have considered, as a first approximation, a rectangular plot of dimensions 1 by 5. If they replaced one dimension by the average of the previous two dimensions, they would obtain a "more square" plot of dimension 3 by 5/3. If they next replaced one of the new dimensions by the average of 3 and 5/3, the dimensions of the plot would be 7/3 by 5/(7/3) (roughly 2.33 by 2.14). More repetitions of this technique lead to plots having sides that are better and better approximations to $\sqrt{5}$ (see Figure 1.2).

FIGURE 1.2

Increasingly better approximations of $\sqrt{5}$

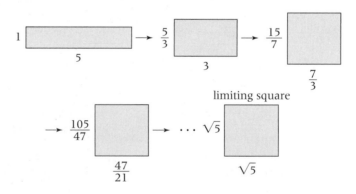

We can use the Babylonian square root algorithm to calculate the square root of any positive number a. Start with an initial guess $x = x_1$ for $\sqrt{a}$; any guess will do, but a good initial guess leads to more rapid convergence. We calculate successive approximations $x_2, x_3, \ldots, \sqrt{a}$ using the formula

$$x_i = \frac{x_{i-1} + (a/x_{i-1})}{2}, \quad i = 2, 3, \ldots$$

We write the Babylonian square root algorithm as a function whose input parameters are the number a and a positive real number *error* measuring the desired accuracy for computing $\sqrt{a}$. For simplicity, we use a as our initial approximation of $\sqrt{a}$.

```
function BabylonianSQRT(a, error)
Input:    a (a positive number), errorr (a positive real number)
Output: √a accurate to within error
    x ← a
    while |x − a/x| > error do
        x ← (x + a/x)/2
    endwhile
    return(x)
end BabylonianSQRT
```

Finding square roots is a special instance of the problem of determining the approximate roots of a polynomial (note that $\sqrt{a}$ is the positive root of the polynomial $x^2 - a$). More generally, suppose $f(x)$ is a real-valued function, and we wish to find a value of x (called a *zero of f*) such that $f(x) = 0$. If f is a continuous function, then the intermediate value theorem of calculus guarantees that a zero occurs in any closed interval $[a, b]$ where $f(a)$ and $f(b)$ have opposite signs. An algorithm (called the *bisection method*) for determining a zero of f proceeds by bisecting such an interval $[a, b]$ in half, then narrowing the search for a zero to one of the two subintervals where a sign change of f occurs. By repeating this process n times, an approximation to a zero is computed that is no more than $(b - a)/2^n$ from an actual zero. We leave the pseudocode for the bisection method to the exercises.

For the case when $f(x)$ is a differentiable function, a more efficient method for finding zeros of f was developed by Sir Isaac Newton in the 17th century. Newton's method is based on constructing the tangent line to the graph of f at an initial guess, say x_1, of a zero of f. The point x_2 where this tangent line crosses the x-axis is taken as the second approximation to a zero of f. This process is then repeated at x_2, yielding a third approximation, x_3 (see Figure 1.3). Successive iterations yield points x_4, x_5, and so on, given by the formula (see Exercise 1.16)

$$x_i = x_{i-1} - \frac{f(x_{i-1})}{f'(x_{i-1})}, i = 2, 3, \ldots \qquad \textbf{(1.1.3)}$$

FIGURE 1.3

Newton's method for finding a zero of a differentiable function f

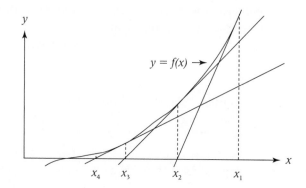

Curiously, when applied to the polynomial $x^2 - a$, Newton's method yields exactly the Babylonian square root algorithm. In general, certain conditions need to be imposed on the function f and starting point x_1 to guarantee that the points x_i given by Formula (1.1.3) actually converge to a zero.

1.1.4 Evaluating Polynomials

A basic problem in mathematics is evaluating a polynomial $p(x) = a_n x^n + a_{n-1} x^{n-1} + \cdots + a_1 x + a_0$ at a particular value v of x. The most straightforward solution to the problem is to compute each term $a_i x^i$ independently, where $i = 1, \ldots, n$, and sum the individual terms. However, when computing each power v^i, where $i = 1, \ldots, n$, it is more efficient to obtain v^i by multiplying the already calculated v^{i-1} by v. This simple observation leads to the following algorithm:

```
function PolyEval(a[0:n], v)
Input:   a[0:n] (an array of real numbers), v (a real number)
Output: the value of the polynomial aₙxⁿ + aₙ₋₁xⁿ⁻¹ + ⋯ + a₁x + a₀ at x = v
    Sum ← a[0]
    Product ← 1
    for i ← 1 to n do
        Product ← Product * v
        Sum ← Sum + a[i] * Product
    endfor
    return(Sum)
end PolyEval
```

PolyEval clearly does $2n$ multiplications and n additions, which might seem the best we can do. However, there is a simple algorithm for polynomial evaluation that cuts the number of multiplications in half. Although the algorithm is called Horner's rule because W. G. Horner popularized it in 1819, the algorithm was actually devised by Sir Isaac Newton in 1699. Horner's rule for polynomial evaluation is based on a clever parenthesizing of the polynomial. For example, a fourth-degree polynomial $a_4x^4 + a_3x^3 + a_2x^2 + a_1x + a_0$ is rewritten as

$$(((a_4 * x + a_3) * x + a_2) * x + a_1) * x + a_0.$$

This rewriting can be done for a polynomial of *any* degree n, yielding the following algorithm:

```
function HornerEval(a[0:n], v)
Input:   a[0:n] (an array of real numbers), v (a real number)
Output: the value of the polynomial aₙxⁿ + aₙ₋₁xⁿ⁻¹ + ⋯ + a₁x + a₀ at x = v
    Sum ← a[n]
    for i ← n − 1 downto 0 do
        Sum ← Sum * v + a[i]
    endfor
    return(Sum)
end HornerEval
```

Clearly, *HornerEval* performs n multiplications and n additions when evaluating a polynomial of degree n. It can be proved that any algorithm for evaluating an nth-degree polynomial that uses only multiplications or divisions and additions or subtractions must perform at least n multiplications or divisions and at least n additions or subtractions. Hence, *HornerEval* is an optimal algorithm for evaluating polynomials.

Algorithms for various other mathematical problems have been developed over the years. These old algorithms were mostly concerned with algebraic rules for calculating numbers and solving arithmetic equations. Indeed, the word *algorithm* itself is taken from the name of the ninth-century Arabic mathematician and astronomer Al-Khowarizmi, who wrote a famous book (*Al Jabr*, circa A.D. 825) on the manipulation of numbers and equations. One of Al-Khowarizmi's accomplishments was to convert Jewish calendar dates to Islamic dates. In fact, many early algorithms involved calendars and fixing the days for feasts.

1.2 Toward a Modern Theory of Algorithms

1.2.1 Early Computation Devices

Until the 20th century, the study of algorithms was largely done on an ad hoc basis, and no general theory of algorithms had emerged. However, as early as 1834, Charles Babbage had already conceived the mechanical implementation of algorithms, as evidenced by his work on the Analytical Engine. Babbage intended this machine to be a general-purpose mechanical device for doing mathematical computations, in contrast to his earlier special-purpose Difference Engine. Unlike the Difference Engine, the Analytical Engine was never built. However, it is clear from Babbage's writings that he recognized that a set of punched cards for controlling his engine would constitute a representation of an algorithm. The algorithmic nature of the Analytical Engine was further discussed in the writings of Ada Augusta Byron, Countess of Lovelace. Countess Lovelace actually wrote algorithms suitable for implementation on the Analytical Engine. She is considered to be the first computer programmer (the modern programming language Ada is named in her honor).

1.2.2 A Formal Theory of Algorithms

The formal mathematical concept of an algorithm was precisely formulated by mathematicians in the 1930s. Perhaps the most influential work in this area was done by the English mathematician Alan Turing, who described a simple but very general theoretical model (called a Turing Machine) of the mechanism by which computing machines can solve problems. Turing also described the stored-program paradigm that is the basis of modern general-purpose computers. This paradigm is usually attributed to John von Neumann, who formally demonstrated the practicality of encoding instructions to a "real" computer in the same (binary) language used for the data it processed, with both instructions and data being stored in the computer's memory. Of course, the advent of the electronic computer in the 1940s ushered in a veritable explosion of interest in the subject of algorithms.

1.2.3 Advent of Electronic Computers

Early computers were all single-processor (serial) machines and could only accept programs that implemented sequential algorithms. General algorithm design strategies for sequential algorithms then evolved, forming a theoretical framework for algorithmic problem solving. Effective computer implementation of algorithms led to the creation of the theory of data structures. The theory of structured programming set guidelines for translating algorithms into code having a high degree of modularity and easily understood logical flow. Modern programming languages were designed to support these data structures and structured programming concepts.

Using appropriate algorithms, computers can solve problems that were once inaccessible. Space travel, robotics, graphics, simulations of large and complex systems, satellite communications, and medical imaging such as CAT scans have all been made possible by the development of efficient algorithms implemented on computers with large memories and extremely fast processors.

1.3 Computing in the Third Millennium

In the early 1980s, the computing industry began developing and marketing parallel computers, a system containing tens, hundreds, or even thousands of homogenous processors working together in a tightly synchronized environment under the control of a central processor. The advent of parallel computers was accompanied by the rapid development of parallel algorithms that exploited this parallelism. Recent years have seen the emergence of grids or clusters of computers, often with processors of various speeds and capacities, working largely asynchronously and communicating with one another over a distributed network using message passing. The distributed computing paradigm, in turn, has been accompanied by the development of the field of distributed algorithms. Even more recently, new paradigms such as DNA computing and quantum computing have emerged with exciting prospects. For example, quantum algorithms have been designed that outperform an algorithm implemented on a classical computer. However, building quantum computers having more than just a few qubits remains an unsolved problem today. In this book, we address all these computing paradigms, emphasizing sequential computation but also devoting Part IV to parallel and distributed computation. We begin with a brief discussion of the high-level properties of the computer architectures that we will assume for the various computing environments.

1.3.1 Serial Computing

The sequential algorithms presented in this book are suitable for implementation on a serial computer having a single processor (CPU) capable of executing all the standard arithmetic operations, logical branching instructions, assignment statements, comparison operations, calls and returns from functions and procedures, and so forth. We assume an internal random access memory, meaning that the CPU can read from or write to any of the memory locations with equal speed. Further, when we perform an operation such as a comparison between two elements in a list, we assume, unless otherwise specified, that this comparison takes unit time, independent of the size of the elements being compared. Because our main concern is with high-level design strategies, we assume that we have sufficient internal memory to store all the variables used by the algorithm. Thus, we make only occasional use of external memory devices accessed by **read** and **write** statements, operations that we assume require rather more time than does accessing internal memory. A serial computer operating under all these assumptions is commonly known as a *random access machine*. We will use the term *RAM* to denote both a random access machine as well as its random access memory.

1.3.2 Parallel Computing

While a single-processor computer can only execute one instruction at a time, a parallel computer with p processors $P_1, \ldots, P_p$ can execute p instructions simultaneously, with each processor operating on (possibly) different data. In this text, we assume that each processor P_i is as powerful as that available in a serial (single-processor) machine and that all the processors are homogeneous, with identical processing capabilities and speed. We also assume that the processors are all subject to a central control, with instructions executed synchronously in lockstep fashion subject to coordination by the central control. Models of parallel computation that restrict the processors to performing the *same* instruction on multiple data are called single-instruction, multiple-data (SIMD) machines. Parallel computers that allow *different* instructions to be performed at the same time on multiple data are called multiple-instruction, multiple-data (MIMD) machines. The serial computer can be viewed in this terminology as a single-instruction, single-data (SISD) machine. In this text, we assume the SIMD machine, for which algorithms are simpler to design and analyze than for the MIMD model. Besides, an MIMD machine can always be simulated by an SIMD model (albeit with a slowdown) in a canonical way.

The notion of RAM memory for serial computers can be extended to parallel computers primarily in two very different forms: *shared* memory and *distributed* memory. The shared-memory model assumes that *all* processors have equal access to a single shared RAM memory. Parallel computers based on this model are referred to as *parallel random access machines,* or *PRAMs*. PRAMs fall into three main categories, depending on how conflicts are resolved when two processors attempt to read or write from the same memory location simultaneously. The distributed-memory model assumes that each processor has its own local memory, and information is passed between processors by sending messages along an interconnection network. However, in a single (parallel) communication step, communication can only take place between processors that are adjacent (directly connected) in the interconnection network. Thus, if information is to be communicated between nonadjacent processors, it must be routed along a path in the interconnection network. Parallel algorithms must be designed according to the particular type of PRAM or interconnection network model used.

1.3.3 The Internet

The emergence of the Internet toward the end of the last century, accompanied by the user-friendly interface known as the World Wide Web (WWW), has revolutionized the manner in which information is gathered, shared, processed, and communicated among the millions of users connected over this network. For example, a query submitted to one of the many Internet search engines currently available will bring to the user a list of perhaps hundreds or even thousands of Web pages containing information matching the query. Moreover, the user will usually receive the list in a fraction of a second. What makes this astonishing speed possible? In addition to the communication speed and bandwidth capabilities of the Internet, together with storage and computation resources allowing the creation of vast (inverted) index files mapping words and phrases to Web pages containing them, the answer lies in the use of extremely efficient algorithms. Not only do these algorithms find Web pages containing the query, but they also present the pages ranked according to their relevancy to the query. Most users find the information they were looking for in the first two or three Web pages listed by the search engine.

Along with rapid search algorithms, the Internet uses data compression algorithms to dramatically reduce the size of text, audio, and image files transmitted to users. Further, encryption algorithms allow secure transmission of credit card numbers for online purchases, fund transfers between financial institutions, military communications, and a host of other data transmissions for which security is a prime concern.

The Internet has also given rise to a computing paradigm known as *grid computing*. In one model of grid computing, the unused cycles of several thousand personal computers (PCs) around the world connected to the Internet are harnessed and brought to bear to solve computationally or data intensive problems. The number of PCs worldwide is approaching half a billion, and the most modern have the computing power of an early 1990s supercomputer. Moreover, most PCs are idle much of the time. Grid computing environments have been set up to tap into the enormous potential computing power of these idle cycles. For example, the SETI@home project is a grid enlisting half a million PCs around the world for the purpose of analyzing data from the Arecibo radio telescope for possible signs of extraterrestrial intelligent life. This type of data intensive problem is well suited to searching for idle cycles because it tolerates high communication latency; that is, processors need not cooperate in real time to do useful work. Many other computing grids have been set up by national and international governmental agencies to serve the needs of scientific researchers, and major computer companies are investing heavily in grid computing to exploit its vast commercial potential.

1.3.4 Distributed Computing

Distributed computing encompasses a wide variety of architectures and paradigms. We limit our discussion in this book to algorithms suitable for a distributed collection of possibly heterogeneous processors, each with a local memory and all connected by a network supporting communication among processors using message passing. In contrast to our model for parallel algorithms, our distributed algorithms model has no central control; rather, the processors proceed independently of one another in a mostly asynchronous manner. Of course, explicit enforcement of some synchronization is often needed to implement a distributed algorithm. For example, one processor might not be able to proceed with a computation until it receives a result from another processor.

The distributed computing environment we have assumed includes the rapidly emerging field of cluster computing, as typically implemented using Beowulf clusters and supported by high-level parallel message-passing languages such as MPI and PVM. Fundamental instructions for Beowulf clusters contain various versions of send and receive messages, including instructions for broadcasting and gathering information from all or a specified subcollection of the processors. Processors can execute programs requiring tight synchronization or proceed in a primarily asynchronous manner. Because communication among processors is much slower than local processor computations, the number of communication steps is an important measure of efficiency for algorithms implemented in a cluster.

1.3.5 Quantum Computing

In all the computers we have discussed so far, information is stored in memory (or memories) using classical 0/1 bits that, at any given instance, are in either state 0 or state 1. Thus, although a register of n bits has 2^n possible configurations, only one configuration can be stored in the register at a time. In the quantum computing environment, computers store information using *qubits*, which, unlike classical bits, can be put in a superposition state that essentially encodes both 0 and 1 simultaneously. More generally, n qubits together could store a superposition of all the 2^n possible values—a possibility known as *quantum parallelism*. With quantum parallelism, encoding an exponential amount of information is possible in a linear amount of quantum storage. Further, quantum parallelism can be exploited by allowing inputs to a quantum computer to be put in a superposition state that encodes all possible input values. The result of a quantum computation on such an initial state would be a superposition of all the corresponding output values. However, there is a big catch: whenever we actually examine a qubit to determine its value, we obtain either 0 or 1. In other words, whenever we measure the state of n qubits, we obtain only one of the 2^n possible output values, even though 2^n possible output values were present in a superposition state. Moreover, in general, we cannot be sure which of the 2^n possible output values will result from the measurement. The trick in quantum computation is to cleverly arrange the superposition of the input so as to make the measurement of the output value after execution by the quantum algorithm likely to be the desired result.

The possibility of quantum computation was first observed by Richard Feynman in the early 1980s when he noted that certain quantum mechanical effects cannot be simulated efficiently on a classical computer. Interest in quantum computing took off in 1994 when Peter Shor described a polynomial-time quantum algorithm for factoring integers. The existence of efficient factoring algorithms is particularly significant because the lack of a known polynomial-time factoring algorithm for classical computers is the basis for computer security schemes like RSA data encryption, which is widely used for Internet security. If quantum computers can actually be built, the current method of data security for Internet applications will be broken. Further impetus to quantum computation was given by Lov Grover, who developed a quantum algorithm that searches for an element in an unordered list of n items in $n^{1/2}$ steps (in the worst case) compared with the n steps (in the worst case) required by any algorithm for a serial computer.

Currently, quantum computers with about 10 qubits are being built, and the practicality of building quantum computers containing hundreds of qubits is still questionable. If, or when, such computers do become a reality, the theory of quantum computation will truly come into its own, together with the concomitant need to design algorithms that exploit quantum parallelism. Writing algorithms for quantum computers will require techniques that are somewhat different from those required to write algorithms for classical computers. Therefore, we do not discuss quantum computation further except as it relates to the Fast Fourier Transform, discussed in Chapter 22.

1.4 Closing Remarks

This chapter presented some historical problems and algorithms designed to solve them. These examples have illustrated that often the most straightforward, simple algorithm is not the most efficient solution to a problem. Designing more efficient algorithms frequently requires using data structures that are more sophisticated than those used in this chapter. The next chapter will give a review of some standard data structures, and we will introduce other data structures as needed throughout the text.

We informally discussed measuring the performance of an algorithm in this chapter. Chapter 2 will define performance measures by introducing best-case, worst-case, and average complexities of an algorithm. To describe the asymptotic nature of these complexities, Chapter 3 discusses asymptotic growth rates of functions.

Until relatively recently, when only single-processor computers were available, algorithms had to be approached from a sequential point of view. Toward the end of the last century, computers using hundreds and even thousands of processors were built, thereby supporting parallel algorithms. Today, with the emergence of the Internet and other distributed computing environments (grids, clusters), new paradigms of distributed computing are becoming increasingly important. A major challenge facing computer scientists today is the design of algorithms and algorithm strategies that exploit parallel and distributed computation.

References and Suggestions for Further Reading

Three classical textbooks on the theory of algorithms, including details on the early development of algorithms:

Knuth, D. E. *The Art of Computer Programming*. Vol. 1, *Fundamental Algorithms*. 3rd ed. Reading, MA: Addison-Wesley, 1997.

———. *The Art of Computer Programming*. Vol. 2, *Seminumerical Algorithms*. 3rd ed. Reading, MA: Addison-Wesley, 1998.

———. *The Art of Computer Programming*. Vol. 3, *Sorting and Searching*. 2nd ed. Reading, MA: Addison-Wesley, 1998.

Boyer, C. B., I. Asimov, and U. C. Merzbach. *A History of Mathematics*. New York: Wiley, 1991. A comprehensive and enjoyable book on the history of mathematics, including some of the early mathematical algorithms.

Two recent books on the history of algorithms:

Chabert, Jean-Luc, ed. *A History of Algorithms: From the Pebble to the Microchip*. Translated by Chris Weeks. Berlin and New York: Springer, 1999.

Berlinski, D. *The Advent of the Algorithm*. New York: Harcourt, 2000.

IEEE Annals of the History of Computing. A journal entirely devoted to the history of computing.

EXERCISES

1.1 Trace the action of the left-to-right binary method to compute:

a. x^{123}

b. x^{64}

c. x^{65}

d. x^{711}

1.2 Repeat Exercise 1.1 for the right-to-left binary method.

1.3 Show that computing x^{15} by either the right-to-left binary method or the left-to-right binary method requires six multiplications, and demonstrate that it can be done using only five multiplications.

1.4 For a general positive integer n, show that the left-to-right binary method for computing requires between $\log_2 n$ and $2\log_2 n$ multiplications.

1.5 Give pseudocode for implementing the left-to-right binary method when

a. the number is input as a binary number.

b. the number is input as a decimal number.

1.6 Show that the right-to-left binary method requires the same number of multiplications as the left-to-right binary method.

1.7 Trace the action of the algorithm *NaiveGCD* for the following input pairs.

a. (24,108)

b. (23,108)

c. (89,144)

d. (1953,1937)

1.8 Repeat Exercise 1.7 for the algorithm *EuclidGCD*.

1.9 The *least common multiple* of two positive integers a and b, lcm(a,b), is the smallest integer divisible by both a and b. For example, lcm$(12,20) = 60$. Give a formula for lcm(a,b) in terms of gcd(a,b).

1.10 Let a and b be positive integers, and let $g = \gcd(a,b)$. Then g can be expressed as an integer linear combination of a and b; that is, there exists integers s and t (not necessarily positive) such that $sa + tb = g$. (We will see uses for this in Chapter 17 in connection with the RSA public key cryptosystem.)

a. Design and give pseudocode for an *extended Euclid's algorithm*, which inputs integers a and b and outputs integers g, s, t such that $g = sa + tb$.

b. Prove that g is the smallest integer that can be expressed as an integer linear combination of a and b.

1.11 Trace the action of the algorithm *BabylonianSQRT* for the following input values of a and *error* = 0.001:

a. $a = 6$

b. $a = 23$

c. $a = 16$

1.12 A continuous function $f(x)$ such that $f(a)$ and $f(b)$ have opposite signs must have a zero (a point x such that $f(x) = 0$) in the interval (a, b). By checking whether $f(a)$ and $f((a + b)/2)$ have opposite signs, we can determine whether the zero occurs in the subinterval $[a, (a + b)/2]$ or the subinterval $[(a + b)/2, b]$. The *bisection method* for approximating a zero of $f(x)$ is based on repeating this process until a zero is obtained to within a predescribed error. Give pseudocode for the bisection method algorithm *Bisec*($f(x),a,b,error$) for finding an approximation to a zero of a continuous function $f(x)$ in the interval $[a, b]$ accurate to within *error*.

1.13   a. Show how to use the bisection method of Exercise 1.12 to compute $\sqrt{c}$.

     b. For $c = 6$ and *error* = 0.00001, compare the efficiency (number of iterations) of *BabylonianSQRT* for computing $\sqrt{c}$ with the bisection method algorithm on the interval $[1, 6]$. (You might want to write a program for this.)

1.14   For each of the following, do three iterations of the bisection method:

     a. $f(x) = x^3 - 6$, initial interval $[1, 3]$

     b. $f(x) = x^3 - 26$, initial interval $[1, 3]$

     c. $f(x) = 2^x - 10$, initial interval $[3, 5]$

1.15   Show that Newton's method reduces to *BabylonianSQRT* in the special case when $f(x) = x^2 - a$.

1.16   Use calculus and the description given in Figure 1.3 to derive Newton's formula (1.1.3).

1.17   Trace the action of Horner's rule for the polynomial $7x^5 - 3x^3 + 2x^2 + x - 5$.

1.18   In practice, when writing a program requiring interactive input of numeric data, it is useful to check whether the user has entered any "bad characters" (that is, characters not corresponding to a digit between 0 and 9, inclusive). To prevent the program from crashing, we can input the data as a character string, test for bad characters, and convert the character string to an integer if no bad characters are found. Devise an algorithm based on Horner's rule for converting a string of alphanumeric digits to its numeric value. Assume a function *ConvertDigit* exists for converting an alphanumeric digit to its integer equivalent (for example, *ConvertDigit* ('5') = 5). Also assume that the alphanumeric digits are input one at a time in an *online* fashion, so that the total number of digits is not known in advance.

1.19   To evaluate a polynomial degree n at v and $-v$, we could simply call *HornerEval* twice, involving $2n$ multiplications and $2n$ additions. Describe a modification of *HornerEval* that solves this particular evaluation problem using only $n + 1$ multiplications and $n + 1$ additions. A generalization of this process is the basis of the Fast Fourier Transform (see Chapter 22).

CHAPTER 2

DESIGN AND ANALYSIS FUNDAMENTALS

In this chapter, we introduce the basic concepts of algorithm design and analysis. We begin by presenting general guidelines for algorithm design and analysis. We then describe one of the most fundamental design strategy tools, recursion. In addition, we outline the major design strategies underlying most of the algorithms discussed in this text. We will return to these design strategies in more detail in Part II. Finally, we discuss algorithm analysis, focusing particularly on basic comparison-based algorithms.

Algorithm analysis is the measurement of the performance, or complexity, of an algorithm in terms of its time and space requirements. Here we focus on analyzing the time complexity of an algorithm; thus, when using the term *complexity*, we mean time complexity, unless we specify otherwise.

We measure the complexity of an algorithm by identifying a basic operation and then counting how many times the algorithm performs that basic operation for an input of size n. However, the number of basic operations performed by an algorithm usually varies for inputs of a given size. Thus, we use the concepts of best-case, worst-case, and average complexity of an algorithm. Occasionally, we measure the complexity of an algorithm by considering several different operations performed by the algorithm and amortizing the performance over all these operations.

Determining the exact number of basic operations performed is often difficult. In practice, it is usually sufficient to obtain an asymptotic approximation of the number of basic operations performed. In the next chapter we will introduce the standard notation for order and asymptotic growth rate of functions.

2.1 Guidelines for Algorithm Design

Designing an algorithm for solving a complicated problem may require dividing the problem into several subproblems and finding algorithms to solve them. In the standard top-down approach to algorithm design, we outline the major steps to a solution and then perform a process of stepwise refinement to simpler and more manageable building blocks. Therefore, the key to solving a complex problem boils down to finding algorithms for the building-block problems, such as evaluating polynomials, computing powers, searching, sorting, and so forth, which are conceptually self-contained. The algorithms for solving such building-block problems are the focus of this text.

The following is a set of general guidelines for designing and analyzing an algorithm that solves a given problem:

1. Formulate the problem, taking into account the resources available, such as the amount of memory and, in a parallel or distributed environment, the number of processors.
2. Identify the appropriate abstract data types to model the problem.
3. Identify parts of the problem that can be solved by known (possibly modified) algorithms (in other words, don't reinvent the wheel). Using an ad hoc method or one of the major design strategies, find algorithms for the remaining parts of the problem.
4. Verify the correctness of the algorithms and analyze their performance.
5. Decide whether searching for more efficient algorithms is necessary.

 ## 2.2 Recursion

Recursion is one of the most powerful tools in algorithm design and analysis. In many situations, the solution to a given problem can be expressed naturally in terms of a solution (or solutions) to a smaller or simpler input (or set of inputs) to the same problem. This expression often takes the form of a *recurrence relation,*

which includes an *initial condition* stating the solutions known initially. In a recurrence relation, the solution to a given input is related to the solution to an input (or set of inputs) that is closer to an input (or inputs) whose solution is known initially. Exploiting such recurrence relations is the essence of *recursive* algorithmic strategy. Recurrence relations not only yield elegant algorithms for solving many problems but also arise frequently in the analysis of the complexity of algorithms, as we will discuss in the next chapter.

Recursive algorithms are implemented in programming languages such as C++, Java, and Fortran as recursive functions or procedures. Simply stated, a recursive function or procedure is one that references itself in the code. When any function or procedure is called, an implicit stack is used to save such things as the current values stored in registers, variables, and a return address to be used on resolution of the call. This overhead can be significant for recursive calls because the algorithm may generate many unresolved calls. The overhead associated with recursion can be somewhat reduced by simulating the recursion using an explicitly implemented stack in the algorithm (see Appendix B for more details on this simulation).

When only one recursive reference is in the code, it is called *single-reference* recursion. A recursive function or procedure may contain several recursive reference statements in the code and still be single-reference recursion. For example, the following code for a function *f* contains two recursive call statements (and no others):

```
if condition A then
     call f with given parameters
else
     call f with other parameters
endif
```

This is still considered single-reference recursion because only one of the two recursive references is executed by any given *current* call of the function *f*. The recursive function *PowersRec* in the next example contains this type of construction. A recursive function or procedure that not only contains two or more recursive references in the code but also executes at least two of these references in a given *current* call is referred to as *multiple-reference* recursion. The recursive sorting algorithms mergesort and quicksort, which we describe later in the chapter, are examples of multiple-reference recursion.

To understand the power of recursion in formulating solutions to problems, we reconsider the problem of computing x^n for a positive integer n. In Chapter 1, we presented the algorithm *Powers* for computing x^n and mentioned that *Powers* is actually the iterative version of the recursive *PowersRec*, which is based on the following recurrence relation:

$$x^n = \begin{cases} (x^2)^{n/2} & \text{if } n \text{ is even,} \\ x(x^2)^{(n-1)/2} & \text{otherwise,} \end{cases} \quad \textbf{init. cond.} \; x^1 = x. \quad \textbf{(2.1.1)}$$

The following pseudocode for *PowersRec* is based directly on Formula (2.1.1):

```
function PowersRec(x, n) recursive
Input:   x (a real number), n (a positive integer)
Output: xⁿ
    if n = 1 then
        Pow ← x              //initial condition
    else
        if even(n) then    //n even
            Pow ← PowersRec(x * x, n/2)
        else               //n odd
            Pow ← x * PowersRec(x * x, (n − 1)/2)
        endif
    endif
    return(Pow)
end PowersRec
```

For input (x,n), similar to the left-to-right and right-to-left binary methods, *PowersRec* performs between $\lfloor \log_2 n \rfloor$ and $2\lfloor \log_2 n \rfloor$ multiplications (see Exercise 2.1). Similar to many recursive algorithms, the correctness of *PowersRec* seems obvious because it is based directly on the obviously correct recurrence relation. We will give a formal proof of the correctness of *PowersRec* in Chapter 3.

The recursive algorithm *PowersRec* is an elegant solution to the problem at hand. We will provide many more examples of the power and elegance of recursion throughout the text. In fact, recursion is the basis of two important general design strategies, divide-and-conquer and dynamic programming.

2.3   Data Structures and Algorithm Design

The performance of an algorithm often depends on how the data is organized, or the *data structure*. One way to determine a data structure is by implementing an abstract data type (ADT), which is a defined collection of data and the operations to be performed on the data.

Many algorithms discussed in this text use the list as their primary abstract data type. Operations associated with the list include insertion, deletion, and accessing a particular element in the list. For convenience, when describing algorithms, we often implement the list ADT as an array. Although in a number of practical situations, a linked-list implementation would improve performance, the array implementation of a list has the important advantage of allowing quick and *direct* access to any element of the list. However, using an array does have some disadvantages. For example, inserting an element at position *i* of a list stored in index positions 0, ... , *n* – 1 of an array requires *n* – *i* array assignments. Deleting an element also requires many array assignments. Another disadvantage relates to inefficient use of space. A particular list may occupy only a small portion of an array that has been declared to handle much larger lists. A linked list avoids these disadvantages at the expense of direct access.

We assume that readers are familiar with the operations of inserting and deleting elements in a linked list, and with stacks (LIFO lists) and queues (FIFO lists) and their linked-list and array implementations. A review of linear data structures is given in Appendix B. In Chapter 4, we will discuss the very important tree ADT in detail and describe some fundamental mathematical properties of trees. Trees are the basis for a number of important data structures, such as balanced search trees for rapid key searching, heaps for maintaining priority queues, forests for maintaining disjoint sets, tries for efficient storing and retrieving of character strings, and so forth. Various other data structures will be introduced throughout the text as appropriate in the design of efficient algorithms.

Modern software design incorporates the notion of object-oriented programming, in which data and associated functions are encapsulated into a single entity called an *object*. An object is an instance of a class, which implements an ADT. Many modern programming languages, such as C++, Java, and C#, support classes and objects in an object-oriented programming environment. Because this text emphasizes a high-level understanding of algorithms, the pseudocode used will not explicitly mention classes and objects. For example, we represent a list of size *n* as $L[0:n-1]$. We typically will implement the list as an array or linked list, without explicitly defining a list class, with associated member functions for insertion, deletion, and so forth. By doing so, we keep the focus on the algorithmic issues without the encumbrance of object-oriented details.

2.4 Major Design Strategies

The study of algorithms has led to the formulation of *major design strategies*, which underly a large percentage of the algorithms in common use today. Here we provide a brief overview of each strategy; in Part 2, we will discuss the major design strategies in more detail.

2.4.1 Divide-and-Conquer

Divide-and-conquer is essentially a special case of recursion in which a given problem is divided into two or more subproblems of exactly the same type, and the solution to the problem is expressed in terms of the solutions to the subproblems. The sorting algorithm mergesort is a good example. Given a list to sort, mergesort divides the list in half, recursively sorts the first half and second half, respectively, and then calls a procedure, which we will call *Merge,* to merge the two sorted sublists into a sorting of the entire list. Divide-and-conquer is not only perhaps the most important design strategy for sequential algorithms, but it works equally well for parallel algorithms because separate processors can be assigned the tasks of solving the subproblems. Of course, this simple parallelization usually does not give sufficient speedup, and further parallelization is required. For example, in mergesort, good speedup requires finding a parallel merging procedure that has good speedup over the sequential procedure *Merge.*

2.4.2 Dynamic Programming

Like divide-and-conquer, the dynamic programming technique builds a solution to a problem from solutions to subproblems, but dynamic programming requires that all the smallest subproblems be solved before proceeding on to the next smallest subproblems. For example, a dynamic programming algorithm for sorting could be based on a "bottom-up" version of mergesort, with the two-element sublists $L[0:1]$, $L[2:3]$, ... , $L[n-2:n-1]$ sorted first, then the four-element sublists $L[0:3]$, $L[4:7]$, ... , $L[n-4:n-1]$ sorted (again, using *Merge*), and so forth. Dynamic programming is usually applied to the problem of optimizing an objective function, where the optimal solution must be built up from optimal solutions to subproblems. The strategy's efficiency results from eliminating suboptimal subproblems while moving up to larger subproblems.

2.4.3 The Greedy Method

The greedy method solves optimization problems by making locally optimal choices and hoping that these choices lead to a globally optimal solution. As an example, we consider the familiar problem of making change (in U.S. pennies, nickels, dimes, and quarters) using the smallest number of coins. The greedy solution is to first use as many coins of the largest denomination (that is, quarters) as possible, then use as many coins of the next largest denomination, and so forth. This method always works for the U.S. coin denominations and is usually very efficient. However, its correctness in a given situation must always be proved. As an obvious example, if there were no nickels, the greedy method would make 30 cents change using 6 coins, 1 quarter and 5 pennies, when 3 dimes suffice.

2.4.4 Backtracking and Branch-and-Bound

Backtracking and branch-and-bound refer to strategies to solve problems that have associated state-space trees. Backtracking searches the state-space tree using a depth-first search, whereas branch-and-bound uses a breadth-first search. Both search strategies apply to problems whose solutions depend on making a series of decisions. The state-space tree for the problem simply models all possible decisions that can be made at each stage. For example, in a state-space tree modeling a board game such as checkers, a node represents a player's move, and the children of that node consist of all legal moves available to the player. For example, in the famous traveling salesman problem (TSP), there are n cities, and a salesman, starting from a given city, wishes to visit all $n - 1$ remaining cities and return in the minimum total distance. The starting city is the root of the state-space tree, a given node represents the cities the salesman has already visited, and the children of that node consist of all the cities he has not yet visited.

Normally, because the state-space tree is quite large, examining each of its nodes is not feasible. For example, the state-space tree for the TSP has $(n - 1)!$ nodes. However, the efficiency of the searches is heightened by the use of bounding functions that cut off large subtrees of the state-space tree that are determined to hold no solutions. For example, in the TSP, an algorithm could keep track of the best tour generated so far in searching the state-space tree and cut-off any partial tour whose distance exceeds the distance of the currently best tour.

2.5 Analyzing Algorithm Performance

> *When you can measure what you are speaking about and can express it in numbers, you know something about it. But when you cannot measure it, when you cannot express it in numbers, your knowledge is of a meager and unsatisfactory kind.*
>
> **—Lord Kelvin**

Recall that to analyze the complexity of an algorithm, we usually identify a basic operation and count how many times the algorithm performs that operation. Algorithm analysis based on a suitably chosen operation is not dependent on a particular computer yet yields measurements similar to those gained by analyzing

FIGURE 2.1

Algorithm
complexity as a
function of input
size n

Problem	Input of size n	Basic operation
Searching a list	lists with n elements	comparison
Sorting a list	lists with n elements	comparison
Multiplying two matrices	two n-by-n matrices	multiplication
Prime factorization	n-digit number	division
Evaluating a polynomial	polynomial of degree n	multiplication
Traversing a tree	tree with n nodes	accessing a node
Towers of Hanoi	n disks	moving a disk

the algorithm's run-time behavior on various computers. Basic operations for some sample algorithms are shown in Figure 2.1.

We measure the complexity of an algorithm as a function of the *input size n* to the algorithm. For example, when searching or sorting a list, the input size is the number of elements in the list; when evaluating a polynomial, the input size is either the degree of the polynomial or the number of nonzero coefficients in the polynomial; when multiplying two square n-by-n matrices, the input size is n; when testing whether an integer is a prime, the input size is the number of digits of the integer; when traversing a tree, the input size is the number of nodes in the tree; and so forth (see Figure 2.1).

We need to be careful about what we take for the measure of input size. For example, we consider the problem of computing x^p for an arbitrary positive integer p. The naive algorithm takes $p - 1$ multiplications, so if we take $n = p$ as the input size, we would have an algorithm that performs $n - 1$ multiplications, which is linear in the input size. However, since $n = p$ is a single number (not the size of an aggregate such as a list), it is a deceptive measure of the size of the input. For example, in modern security schemes such as RSA, the power p of x^p can have hundreds of binary digits. In such cases, the naive algorithm performing $p - 1$ multiplications would not complete in real time, even for a 64-digit number. From the point of view of storing such a p, it is a relatively small number (for example, a 128-digit binary number requires only 128 bits). However, to perform $p - 1 \geq 2^{127} - 1$ multiplications would take hundreds of years on even the fastest computer.

When analyzing the complexity of an algorithm computing x^p, what is typically taken as the measure of the input size is the number of digits n of p in its base two representation; that is, n is approximately equal to $\log_2 p$. The inefficiency of the naive method then becomes apparent, because the number of multiplications performed is approximately equal to 2^n, which is exponential in the input size.

For some algorithms, the number of basic operations performed is the same for any input of size n. However, for many algorithms, the number of basic operations performed can differ for two inputs of the same size. For the latter algorithms, we talk about *best-case, worst-case,* and *average complexity* as functions of the input size n. The formal definitions of these complexities require the specification of the set of inputs of size n to an algorithm. An *input I* to an algorithm is the data, such as numbers, character strings, and records, on which the operations of the algorithm are performed. Let $\mathcal{I}_n$ denote the set of all inputs of size n to an algorithm. The second column of Figure 2.1 shows what is typically considered to be $\mathcal{I}_n$ for various types of problems and their associated algorithms. For $I \in \mathcal{I}_n$, let $\tau(I)$ denote the number of basic operations performed when the algorithm is executed with input I.

DEFINITION 2.5.1 **Best-Case Complexity** The *best-case complexity* of an algorithm is the function $B(n)$ such that $B(n)$ equals the *minimum* value of $\tau(I)$, where I varies over all inputs of size n. That is,

$$B(n) = \min\{\tau(I) \mid I \in \mathcal{I}_n\}. \qquad (2.5.1)$$

The best-case complexity $B(n)$ is typically easy to compute but is not a particularly useful measure of the performance of the algorithm. In fact, $B(n)$ is usually only of use as a lower bound for the average complexity $A(n)$ of the algorithm. Far more important than $B(n)$ is the worst-case complexity $W(n)$.

DEFINITION 2.5.2 **Worst-Case Complexity** The *worst-case complexity* of an algorithm is the function $W(n)$ such that $W(n)$ equals the *maximum* value of $\tau(I)$, where I varies over all inputs of size n. That is,

$$W(n) = \max\{\tau(I) \mid I \in \mathcal{I}_n\}. \qquad (2.5.2)$$

In practice, a given algorithm is usually run repeatedly with varying inputs of size n. Thus, another important measure of the performance of an algorithm is its *average complexity $A(n)$*, defined as the *expected* number $E[\tau]$ of basic operations performed. Average complexity $A(n)$ *depends on the probability distribution imposed on the sample space* $\mathcal{I}_n$ (see Appendix E for definitions of the terms used in this section). For now, we assume that $\mathcal{I}_n$ is a finite set and that each input $I \in \mathcal{I}_n$ has probability $p(I)$ of occurring as the input to the algorithm. An important special case is when each input is equally likely (the *uniform distribution*), in which case $p(I) = 1/|\mathcal{I}_n|$.

DEFINITION 2.5.3 **Average Complexity** The *average complexity* of an algorithm with finite input set $\mathscr{I}_n$ is defined as

$$A(n) = \sum_{I \in \mathscr{I}_n} \tau(I)p(I) = E[\tau]. \qquad (2.5.3)$$

Formula (2.5.3) for $A(n)$ is rarely used directly because it is simply too cumbersome to examine each term in $\mathscr{I}_n$ directly. Also, the growth of the summation as a function of the input size n is usually hard to estimate, much less calculate exactly. Thus, when analyzing the average complexity of a given algorithm, we usually seek closed-form expressions or estimates for $A(n)$, or formulas that allow some gathering of terms in Formula (2.5.3). For example, let p_i denote the probability that the algorithm performs exactly i basic operations; that is $p_i = p(\tau = i)$. Then

$$A(n) = E[\tau] = \sum_{i=1}^{W(n)} ip_i. \qquad (2.5.4)$$

Formula (2.5.4) is often useful in practice and follows from Formula (2.5.3) by simply gathering up, for each i between 1 and $W(n)$, all the inputs I such that $p(I) = i$.

Frequently, there is a natural way to assign a probability distribution on $\mathscr{I}_n$. For example, when analyzing comparison-based sorting algorithms, it is common to assume that each of the $n!$ permutations (or orderings) of a list of size n is equally likely to be input to the algorithm. The average complexity of any comparison-based sorting algorithm is then the sum of the number of comparisons generated by each of the $n!$ permutations divided by $n!$. In practice, it is not feasible to examine each permutation individually because $n!$ simply grows too fast. Fortunately, there are techniques that allow us to calculate this average without resorting to permutation-by-permutation analysis.

Often it is possible to find a recurrence relation expressing $A(n)$ in terms of one or more of the values $A(m)$ with $m < n$. Of course, if the algorithm itself is written recursively, then the recurrence relation is usually easy to find. In general, finding a recurrence relation for $A(n)$ involves using the technique of partitioning the algorithm or the input space.

2.5.1 Multiple-Variable Input Size

In all the problems mentioned so far, the input size was a function of a single variable n (see Figure 2.1). However, sometimes the input size is most naturally a function of two or more variables. For example, suppose we want to find efficient sorting algorithms for lists of size n with repeated elements. The input size is then a function of n and the number m of *distinct* elements in the list, where $1 \leq m \leq n$. In such cases, best-case, worst-case, and average complexities are functions of the two variables n and m.

In this chapter, we illustrate the calculation of $B(n)$ and $W(n)$ for a number of important examples. We limit our discussion of $A(n)$ to a couple of examples but will return to the topic in Chapter 6.

2.6 Analyzing Some Basic Comparison-Based Algorithms

A *comparison-based* algorithm searches or sorts a list by comparing list elements and then making decisions based on the comparisons. The only a priori assumption a comparison-based algorithm makes about the nature of the list elements is their relative order. We can often reduce or transform the sample space of a comparison-based algorithm to a simpler sample space without affecting the average complexity. For example, the lists $(\sqrt{5},1.3,4,2)$, $(108,23,123,55)$, (Mary,Ann,Pete,Joe), and $(30.2,\pi,111.23,12)$ of size 4 can all be regarded as having the same ordering (third largest, first largest, fourth largest, second largest) as the permutation $(3,1,4,2)$. Putting each list into increasing order requires the same number of comparisons from the comparison-based sorting algorithm. Therefore, we can reduce our input space for a comparison-based algorithm to the set of all permutations on the n integers 1, 2, ... , n. This amounts to making two lists in $\mathscr{I}_n$ equivalent if they have the same ordering.

To illustrate the computation of $B(n)$, $W(n)$, and $A(n)$, we consider some basic comparison-based algorithms for searching, finding a maximum element, and sorting lists of size n. Searching lists is one of the most common tasks performed by computers. If no preconditioning (such as sorting) of the list is assumed, then there is no better algorithm than a linear search, which is based on a sequential (linear) scan of the list. On the other hand, for sorted lists, several searching algorithms are much more efficient, such as a binary search. Our first algorithm analyses involve linear search and binary search algorithms, which illustrate well the computations of $B(n)$, $W(n)$, and $A(n)$.

The linear search and binary search algorithms are based on making comparisons between a search element and the key field of the list elements. For simplicity, in our pseudocode for the linear search and binary search algorithms, we do not actually identify the key field of a list element but instead reference the entire list element.

2.6.1 Linear Search

We implement a linear search as a function that returns the first position in a list (array of size n) $L[0{:}n-1]$ if the search element X occurs or returns -1 if X is not in the list.

```
function LinearSearch(L[0:n − 1], X)
Input:   L[0:n − 1] (a list of size n), X (a search item)
Output: returns index of first occurrence of X in the list, or −1 if X is not in the list
   for i ← 0 to n − 1 do
      if X = L[i] then
         return(i)
      endif
   endfor
   return(-1)
end LinearSearch
```

The basic operation of *LinearSearch* is the comparison of the search element to a list element. Clearly, *LinearSearch* performs only one comparison when the input X is the first element in the list, so the best-case complexity is $B(n) = 1$. The most comparisons are performed when X is not in the list or when X occurs in the last position only. Thus, the worst-case complexity of *LinearSearch* is $W(n) = n$.

To simplify the discussion of the average behavior of *LinearSearch*, we assume that the search element X is in the list $L[0{:}n-1]$ and is equally likely to be found in any of the n positions. Note that i comparisons are performed when X is found at position i in the list. Thus, the probability that *LinearSearch* performs i comparisons is given by $p_i = 1/n$. Substituting these probabilities into (2.5.4) yields

$$A(n) = \sum_{i=1}^{W(n)} ip_i = \sum_{i=1}^{n} i\frac{1}{n} = \left(\frac{n(n+1)}{2}\right)\frac{1}{n} = \frac{n+1}{2}. \qquad \textbf{(2.6.1)}$$

Formula (2.6.1) is intuitively correct because under our assumptions, X is equally likely to be found in either half of the list. To see that Formula (2.6.1) truly reflects average behavior, suppose that we run *LinearSearch* m times (m large) with a fixed list $L[0{:}n-1]$ and with search element X being randomly chosen as one of the list elements. Let m_i denote the number of runs in which X was found at position i. Then the total number of comparisons performed over the m runs is given by $1m_1 + 2m_2 + \dots + nm_n$. Dividing this expression by m gives the average number $A_m(n)$ of comparisons over the entire m runs, as follows:

$$A_m(n) = 1\left(\frac{m_1}{m}\right) + 2\left(\frac{m_2}{m}\right) + \dots + n\left(\frac{m_n}{m}\right). \qquad \textbf{(2.6.2)}$$

Note that for large values of m, the ratios m_i/m occurring in Formula (2.6.2) approach the probability p_i that X occurs in the ith position. Because we have assumed that X is equally likely to be found in any of the n positions, each m_i is approximately equal to m/n. Hence, substituting $m_i = m/n$ into Formula (2.6.2) yields

$$A_m(n) \approx \frac{1 + 2 + \cdots + n}{n} = \frac{n + 1}{2} = A(n). \qquad \textbf{(2.6.3)}$$

To summarize, *LinearSearch* has best-case, worst-case, and average complexities 1, n, and $(n + 1)/2$, respectively. The best-case complexity is a constant independent of the input size n, whereas the worst-case and average complexities are both linear functions of n. For simplicity, we say that *LinearSearch* has *constant* best-case complexity and *linear* worst-case and average complexities.

We calculated $A(n)$ for *LinearSearch* under the assumption that the search element X is in the list. In Chapter 6, we will examine a more general situation where we assume that X is in the list with probability p, $0 \le p \le 1$.

2.6.2 Binary Search

LinearSearch assumes nothing about the order of the elements in the list; in fact, it is an optimal algorithm when no special order is assumed. However, *LinearSearch* is not the algorithm to use when searching ordered lists, at least when direct access to each list element is possible (as with an array implementation of the list). For example, if you are looking up the word *riddle* in a dictionary, and you initially open the dictionary to the page containing the word *middle*, then you know you only need to search for the word in the pages that follow. Similarly, if you are looking up the word *fiddle* instead of *riddle*, then you need only search for the word in the pages preceding the page containing *middle*. This simple observation is the basis of *BinarySearch*.

The objective of a binary search is to successively cut in half the range of indices in the list where the search element X might be found. We assume that the list is sorted in nondecreasing order. By comparing X with the element $L[mid]$ in the middle of the list, we can determine whether X might be found in the first half of the list or the second half. We have three possibilities:

$$X = L[mid], \quad X \text{ is found;}$$
$$X < L[mid], \quad \text{search for } X \text{ in } L[0{:}mid - 1];$$
$$X > L[mid], \quad \text{search for } X \text{ in } L[mid + 1{:}n - 1].$$

This process is repeated (if necessary) for the relevant "half list." Thus, the number of elements in a sublist where X might be found is being cut roughly in half for each repetition. When we cut a sublist $L[low:high]$ in half, if the size of the sublist is even, then we take the midpoint index to be the smaller of the two middle indices, so that $mid = \lfloor (low + high)/2 \rfloor$. The following pseudocode implements a binary search as a function with the same parameters and output as *LinearSearch*, except that the list is assumed to be sorted in nondecreasing order:

```
function BinarySearch(L[0:n − 1], X)
Input:   L[0:n − 1] (an array of n list elements, sorted in nondecreasing order)
         X (a search item)
Output: returns the index of an occurrence of X in the list, or −1 if X is not in the list
    Found ← .false.
    low ← 0
    high ← n − 1
    while .not. Found .and. low ≤ high do
        mid ← ⌊(low + high)/2⌋
        if X = L[mid] then
            Found ← .true.
        else
          if X < L[mid] then
             high ← mid − 1
          else
             low ← mid + 1
          endif
        endif
    endwhile
    if Found then
        return(mid)
    else
        return(−1)
    endif
end BinarySearch
```

As with *LinearSearch*, we use comparison of X to a list element as our basic operation when analyzing *BinarySearch*. The best-case complexity of *Binary-Search* is 1, which occurs when X is found in the midpoint position $\lfloor (n − 1)/2 \rfloor$ of $L[0:n − 1]$. The worst-case complexity is equal to twice the longest string of midpoints (values of *mid*) that the algorithm ever generated for an input X. In particular, if we assume that $n = 2^k − 1$ for some positive integer k, then such a string is generated by searching for $X = L[0]$. We then compare X successively to the midpoints $2^{k-1} − 1, 2^{k-2} − 1, \ldots, 0$, so that this longest string has length k. To express k in terms of n, we note that $n + 1 = 2^k$, so we have $k = \log_2(n + 1)$. We leave it as an exercise to verify that for any n, the length of the longest string of midpoints ever generated is $\lceil \log_2(n + 1) \rceil$, so that $W(n) = 2\lceil \log_2(n + 1) \rceil$.

The average performance of *BinarySearch* will be discussed in Chapter 6. Also in Chapter 6, we will discuss a variant of *BinarySearch* that does not test for equality and thereby improves its average and worst-case performances.

2.6.3 Interpolation Search

Although *BinarySearch* assumes that the list $L[0:n – 1]$ is in increasing order, it always compares the search element X to the midpoint index entry in the current sublist $L[low:high]$, ignoring the fact that the value of X might suggest a better place to look. An interpolation search computes an index value in the range between *low* and *high* that, on average, is more likely to be nearer to where X might occur than is the midpoint index. For example, when looking up the word *algorithm* in the dictionary, we would certainly be closer if we opened up the dictionary to a page near the beginning of the dictionary rather than a page in the middle.

An interpolation search computes the index i in the current range *low:high* for comparing $L[i]$ to X by making the assumption that the values in the original list $L[0:n – 1]$ are not only increasing but also lie approximately along a straight line joining the points $(0,L[0])$ to $(n – 1,L[n – 1])$; note that we are interpreting the list values in L as numbers, which can always be assumed with proper conversions. Assuming the "linearity" of the data is essential to the efficiency of an interpolation search but is not essential to its correctness.

Unfortunately, an interpolation search makes n comparisons in the worst case (see Exercise 2.27). However, under suitable assumptions of randomness for the elements of the list $L[0:n – 1]$, it can be shown that the average performance $A(n)$ of an interpolation search is approximately $\log_2(\log_2 n)$, a very slow growing function indeed (see Exercise 2.29). The proof of this average behavior is beyond the scope of this book.

The value for the index i used by an interpolation search (instead of *mid* used by *BinarySearch*) is computed by simply finding the point (i,X) along the line joining $(low,L[low])$ to $(high,L[high])$ corresponding to the search element X. More precisely, i is determined from the equation

$$(X – L[low])/(i – low) = (L(high) – L(low))/(high – low). \quad \textbf{(2.6.4)}$$

Note that even though the entire list $L[0:n – 1]$ may not be approximately linear, a given sublist might be. Thus, recalculating the value of i for each sublist helps make an interpolation search very efficient on average. We leave the pseudocode for an interpolation search and its worst-case analysis to the exercises.

2.6.4 Finding the Maximum and Minimum Elements in a List

We now consider the problem of finding the maximum (or minimum) value of an element in a list $L[0:n-1]$ of size n. We can find the maximum value using a variation of *LinearSearch* to keep track and update the maximum value encountered as we scan the list.

```
function Max(L[0:n − 1])
Input:   L[0:n − 1] (a list of size n)
Output: returns the maximum value occurring in L[0:n − 1]
    MaxValue ← L[0]
    for i ← 1 to n − 1 do
        if L[i] > MaxValue then
            MaxValue ← L[i]    //update MaxValue
        endif
    endfor
    return(MaxValue)
end Max
```

When analyzing the function *Max*, we choose a comparison between list elements ($L[i] > MaxValue$) as our basic operation. The only other operation performed by *Max* is updating *MaxValue*. However, for any input list, the number of comparisons between list elements clearly dominates the number of updates of *MaxValue*, which justifies our choice of basic operation.

Note that *Max* performs $n-1$ comparisons for any input list of size n. Thus, the best-case, worst-case, and average complexities of *Max* all equal $n-1$. In Chapter 3, we will use lower-bound theory to show that any comparison-based algorithm for finding the maximum value of an element in a list of size n must perform at least $n-1$ comparisons for any input, so that *Max* is an optimal algorithm.

To find the minimum value in a list, we can use an analogous algorithm *Min*. Sometimes it is useful to determine *both* the maximum and the minimum values in a list $L[0:n-1]$. An algorithm *MaxMin1* for solving this problem successively invokes *Max* and *Min*. Clearly, *MaxMin1* has best-case, worst-case, and average complexities all equal to $2n-2$. The following algorithm based on a single sequential scan through the list results in some improvement to the best-case and average complexities:

```
procedure MaxMin2(L[0:n − 1], MaxValue, MinValue)
Input:   L[0:n − 1] (a list of size n)
Output: MaxValue, MinValue (maximum and minimum values occurring in L[0:n − 1])
      MaxValue ← L[0]
      MinValue ← L[0]
      for i ← 1 to n − 1 do
          if L[i] > MaxValue then
              MaxValue ← L[i]
          else
              if L[i] < MinValue then
                  MinValue ← L[i]
              endif
          endif
      endfor
end MaxMin2
```

MaxMin2 performs a minimum of $n − 1$ comparisons when the list $L[0:n − 1]$ is in strictly increasing order, so that *MaxMin2* has best-case complexity $B(n) = n − 1$. *MaxMin2* performs a maximum of $2(n − 1)$ comparisons when $L[0]$ has the maximum value in the list $L[0:n − 1]$. Thus, *MaxMin2* has the same worst-case complexity as *MaxMin1*—namely, $W(n) = 2n − 2$.

The average complexity $A(n)$ of *MaxMin2* lies between $B(n) = n − 1$ and $W(n) = 2n − 2$. Unfortunately, it turns out that the average complexity $A(n)$ of *MaxMin2* is approximately equal to $2n − \ln n$, which is closer to the worst-case complexity (see Chapter 6). Is there an algorithm with better average complexity? In fact, there is. We now design an algorithm *MaxMin3* whose worst-case complexity is $\lceil 3n/2 \rceil − 2$, which turns out to be *optimal* (see Chapter 25). To facilitate our discussion of the algorithm *MaxMin3*, we introduce the following procedure *MM*, which solves the max-min problem for a list of size 2.

```
procedure MM(A, B, MaxValue, MinValue)
Input:   A, B
Output: MaxValue, MinValue (the maximum and minimum of A and B)
      if A ≥ B then
          MaxValue ← A
          MinValue ← B
      else
          MaxValue ← B
          MinValue ← A
      endif
end MM
```

Procedure *MaxMin3* works by pairing elements (except for one element when n is odd) in the list $L[0:n-1]$ and computing the maximum and minimum for each pair, yielding $\lceil n/2 \rceil$ potential maxima and $\lceil n/2 \rceil$ potential minima.

```
procedure MaxMin3(L[0:n − 1], MaxValue, MinValue)
Input:   L[0:n − 1] (a list of size n)
Output: MaxValue, MinValue (the maximum and minimum values in L[0:n − 1])
    if even(n) then // n is even
        MM(L[0], L[1], MaxValue, MinValue)
        for i ← 2 to n − 2 by 2 do
            MM(L[i], L[i + 1], b, a)
            if a < MinValue then MinValue ← a endif
            if b > MaxValue then MaxValue ← b endif
        endfor
    else            //n is odd
        MaxValue ← L[0]; MinValue ← L[0];
        for i ← 1 to n − 2 by 2 do
            MM(L[i], L[i + 1], b, a)
            if a < MinValue then MinValue ← a endif
            if b > MaxValue then MaxValue ← b endif
        endfor
    endif
end MaxMin3
```

For n even, $L[0]$ and $L[1]$ are compared, and then the first **for** loop of *MaxMin3* performs $3(n-2)/2$ comparisons. For n odd, there is no initial comparison, and the second **for** loop performs $3(n-1)/2$ comparisons. Thus, the best-case, worst-case, and average complexities of *MaxMin3* for input size n are all equal to $\lceil 3n/2 \rceil - 2$.

We now design and analyze some basic comparison-based sorting algorithms. We start with the simple sorting algorithm insertionsort. While insertionsort is not efficient (in the worst case) for large lists, we shall see that it does have its uses.

2.6.5 Insertionsort

Array Implementation of Insertionsort   Insertionsort sorts a given list $L[0:n-1]$ by successively inserting the list element $L[i]$ into its proper place in the sorted list $L[0:i]$, $i = 1, \ldots, n-1$. It works like a card player who inserts a newly dealt card into a previously dealt and ordered hand that was already put in order. The card player starts a scan at one end of the hand and stops at a place where the new card can be inserted and still maintain an ordered hand. This scan can start at either the low end of the hand (forward scan), or at the high end of the hand (backward scan). The card player has no reason (other than a personality quirk) to prefer one scan over the other. However, with insertionsort, there are several reasons for preferring one scan over the other, depending on the situation.

Given the list $L[0:n-1]$, clearly the sublist consisting of only the element $L[0]$ is a sorted list. Suppose (possibly after reindexing) we have a list L where the sublist $L[0:i-1]$ is already sorted. We can obtain a sorted sublist $L[0:i]$ by inserting the element $L[i]$ in its proper position. In a backward scan, we successively compare $L[i]$ with $L[i-1]$, $L[i-2]$, and so forth, until a list element $L[position]$ is found that is not larger than $L[i]$. We can then insert $L[i]$ at $L[position+1]$. In a forward scan, we successively compare $L[i]$ with $L[0]$, $L[1]$, and so forth, until a list element $L[position]$ is found that is not smaller than $L[i]$. $L[i]$ can then be inserted at $L[position]$.

Figure 2.2 demonstrates the action of the backward scan version of insertionsort for a list of size 6.

FIGURE 2.2

Action of
InsertionSort
(backward scan)
for a list of size 6

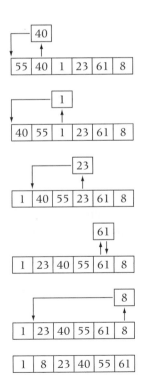

The following pseudocode for insertionsort uses a backward scan.

procedure *InsertionSort*($L[0{:}n-1]$)
Input: $L[0{:}n-1]$ (a list of size n)
Output: $L[0{:}n-1]$ (sorted in nondecreasing order)
   for $i \leftarrow 1$ **to** $n-1$ **do** //insert $L[i]$ in its proper position in $L[0{:}i-1]$
         Current $\leftarrow L[i]$
         position $\leftarrow i-1$
             while *position* ≥ 1 **.and.** *Current* $< L[position]$ **do**
                            //*Current* must precede $L[position]$
                    $L[position+1] \leftarrow L[position]$ //bump up $L[position]$
                    position $\leftarrow$ *position* -1
             endwhile
                            //*position* $+1$ is now the proper position for *Current* $= L[i]$
             $L[position+1] \leftarrow$ *Current*
      endfor
end InsertionSort

When analyzing *InsertionSort*, we choose comparison between list elements (*Current* $< L[position]$) as our basic operation. For any input list of size n, the outer loop of *InsertionSort* is executed $n-1$ times. If the input list is already sorted in nondecreasing order, then the inner loop is iterated only once for each iteration of the outer loop. Hence, the best-case complexity of *InsertionSort* is given by

$$B(n) = n - 1. \qquad\qquad \textbf{(2.6.5)}$$

The worst-case complexity occurs when the inner loop performs the maximum number of comparisons for each value of the outer loop variable i. For a given i, this occurs when $L[i]$ must be compared to each element $L[i-1]$, $L[i-2]$, ... , $L[0]$, so that $i-1$ comparisons are performed in the inner loop. This, in turn, occurs when the list is in strictly decreasing order. Since i varies from 1 to $n-1$, we have

$$W(n) = 1 + 2 + \cdots + (n-1) = \frac{n(n-1)}{2}. \qquad\qquad \textbf{(2.6.6)}$$

Thus, $W(n)$ for *InsertionSort* is quadratic in the input size n.

In Chapter 6, we will show that the average complexity $A(n)$ for *InsertionSort* is about half of $W(n)$ and therefore is also quadratic in n. We can see why this is true, intuitively, when we recognize it is reasonable that when inserting the $(i+1)^{st}$ element $L[i]$ into its proper position in the list $L[0]$, ... , $L[i-1]$, on average $i/2$ comparisons will be made. Hence, it is reasonable that $A(n)$ should be about $1 + (1/2)[2 + 3 + \cdots + n - 1] = 1 + (1/2)[n(n-1)/2 - 1]$.

Because of its quadratic complexity, *InsertionSort* is impractical to use for sorting general large lists. However, *InsertionSort* does have five advantages:

1. *InsertionSort* works quickly on small lists. Thus, *InsertionSort* is often used as a threshold sorting algorithm used in conjunction with other sorting algorithms like mergesort or quicksort.

2. *InsertionSort* works quickly on large lists that are close to being sorted in the sense that no element has many larger elements occurring before it in the list. This property of *InsertionSort* makes it useful in connection with other sorts such as *ShellSort* (see Chapter 5).

3. *InsertionSort* is amenable to implementation as an on-line sorting algorithm. In an *on-line* sorting algorithm, the entire list is not input to the algorithm in advance; rather, elements are added to the list over time. On-line sorting algorithms are required to maintain the dynamic list in sorted order.

4. *InsertionSort* is an in-place sorting algorithm. A sorting algorithm with input parameter $L[0:n-1]$ is called *in-place* if only a constant amount of memory is used (for temporary variables, loop control variables, sentinels, and so forth) in addition to that needed for L.

5. *InsertionSort* is a *stable* sorting algorithm in the sense that it maintains the relative order of repeated elements. More precisely, an algorithm that sorts a list $L[0:n-1]$ into nondecreasing order is called stable if, given any two elements $L[i]$, $L[j]$, with $i < j$ and $L[i] = L[j]$, the final positions i', j' of $L[i]$, $L[j]$, respectively, satisfy $i' < j'$.

Stable algorithms are useful when we want to sort the elements in a list of records according to primary and secondary keys in the records, but where the sorts on these two keys take place independently. For example, suppose we have records comprising a list of names and addresses sorted alphabetically according to name. For purposes of bulk mailing, we now wish to sort the list according to the zip code key in each record. However, within a given zip code, we wish to maintain the alphabetical order. Clearly, a stable sorting algorithm is required.

Why should we use a linear scan to find the correct position to insert the list element $L[i]$ into the already sorted list $L[0:i]$? Wouldn't a binary search to find this position drastically reduce the number of comparisons made by the algorithm? For example, a binary search would reduce the worst-case complexity of *InsertionSort* from $n(n-1)/2$ to approximately $n\log_2 n$. The catch is that this altered version would not reduce the number of array reassignments needed to insert $L[i]$, so a quadratic number of array reassignments would still be made in the worst case. Thus, even though the altered *InsertionSort* is still comparison-based, the number of comparisons made would no longer be a true measure of the complexity of the algorithm. Another drawback of the binary search version of *InsertionSort* is that some of the advantages of *InsertionSort* listed earlier would be lost. For example, the binary search version of *InsertionSort* would no longer be stable and would not necessarily work quickly on large lists that are close to being sorted.

An *adjacent-key* comparison-based sorting algorithm makes comparisons only between elements that occupy *adjacent* positions in the list. These elements are interchanged if they are out of order. *InsertionSort* is essentially an adjacent-key comparison sort, because the comparison between $L[position]$ and *current* can be thought of as an assignment of *current* to $L[position]$ and then a comparison between $L[position]$ and $L[position-1]$. For reasons of efficiency, we chose not to make the actual assignment until the correct position for insertion was determined. Another well-known adjacent-key sorting algorithm is *BubbleSort* (see Exercise 2.36).

In the next chapter we show that the worst-case complexity of *any* adjacent-key comparison-based sorting algorithm is at least $n(n-1)/2$. In view of this result, *InsertionSort* actually has optimal worst-case complexity for an adjacent-key comparison-based sort.

Linked-List Implementation of Insertionsort We now implement insertionsort using a linked list rather than an array. To find the correct position to insert an element X, a forward scan of the linked list is performed using the pointer *Place*. This scan first compares X to the first element in the list. If X is not larger than this element, then the new node containing X is inserted at the beginning of the list. Otherwise, the scan continues down the list until the last element in the list smaller than X is pointed to by *Place*. The new node can then be placed immediately after the node containing this latter element.

We illustrate the linked version of insertion sort in Figure 2.3 for the same list of elements used in Figure 2.2 (the pseudocode for this linked version is left as an exercise). In Figure 2.3, we assume that the elements are placed in nodes and inserted into the sorted linked list immediately after they are input. To improve upon the $n(n-1)/2$ comparisons made by insertionsort in the worst case, we must not always compare keys in adjacent positions.

Key Fact

If we want to design comparison-based sorting algorithms with worst-case complexities smaller than $n(n-1)/2$, we must look for design strategies that compare nonadjacent (farapart) elements in the list.

FIGURE 2.3

Action of the linked
version of
InsertionSort
for *L*[0:5]:
55 40 1 23 61 8

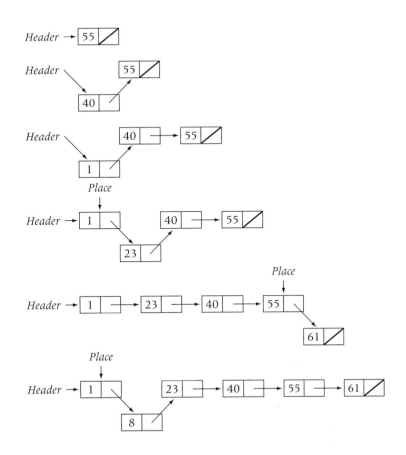

We now give an example, mergesort, of a comparison-based sorting algorithm that only performs about $n\log_2 n$ comparisons in the worst case.

2.6.6 Mergesort

Mergesort is a classical example of an algorithm based on the divide-and-conquer design strategy. Mergesort was already in use in the earliest electronic computers. In fact, it was one of the stored programs implemented by von Neumann in 1945. Given *L*[*low*:*high*], a sublist of the list *L*[0:*n* – 1], let *x* be any index between *low* and *high*. Let *A*, *B*, and *C* denote the sublists *L*[*low*:*x*], *L*[*x*+1:*high*], and *L*[*low*:*high*], respectively. The problem of sorting *C* can be solved by first sorting *A* (recursive call), then sorting *B* (another recursive call), and finally calling the procedure *Merge*, which merges the sorted lists *A* and *B* to obtain a sorted list *C*. The following recursive code for the procedure *MergeSort* implements these steps. Note in *MergeSort* that we have chosen *x* to be the midpoint of *low* and *high*. The list *L*[0:*n* – 1] is sorted by calling *MergeSort* and passing 0 to *low* and *n* – 1 to *high*.

```
procedure MergeSort(L[0:n − 1], low, high) recursive
Input:   L[0:n − 1] (an array of n list elements)
         low, high (indices of L[0:n − 1])
Output: L[low:high] (subarray sorted in nondecreasing order)
   if low < high then
        mid ← ⌊(low + high)/2⌋
        MergeSort(L[0:n − 1], low, mid)
        MergeSort(L[0:n − 1], mid+1, high)
        Merge(L[0:n − 1], low, mid, high)
   endif
end MergeSort
```

In the following pseudocode for the procedure *Merge* called by *MergeSort*, an auxiliary array *Temp* is used to aid in the merging process. *Merge* utilizes two pointers *CurPos1* and *CurPos2*, which refer to the current positions in the already sorted sublists $L[low:x]$ and $L[x+1:high]$, respectively. *Merge* also uses a third pointer *Counter*, which points to the next available position in *Temp*. *CurPos1*, *CurPos2*, and *Counter* are initialized to *low*, $x + 1$, and *low*, respectively. During each iteration of the **while** loop in *Merge*, the elements in the positions *CurPos1* and *CurPos2* are compared, and the smaller element is written to the position *Counter* in *Temp*. Then *Counter* and either *CurPos1* or *CurPos2*, depending on which one points to the element just written to *Temp*, are incremented by 1. When one of the sublists has been completely written to *Temp*, the remaining elements in the other sublist are written to *Temp*. Then *Temp* contains a sorting of $L[low:high]$, and the algorithm terminates after copying $Temp[low:high]$ to $L[low:high]$. The pseudocode for *Merge* follows:

```
procedure Merge(L[0:n − 1], low, x, high)
Input:   L[0:n − 1] (an array of n list elements),
         low, x, high (indices of array L[0:n − 1]; sublists L[low:x], L[x+1:high] are
                       assumed to be sorted in nondecreasing order)
Output: L[low:high] (sublist sorted in nondecreasing order)
   CurPos1 ← low                            //initialize pointers
   CurPos2 ← x + 1
   Counter ← low
   while CurPos1 ≤ x .and. CurPos2 ≤ high do //while elements remain
        if L[CurPos1] ≤ L[CurPos2] then       //to be written in both
           Temp[Counter] ← L[CurPos1]         //sublists, merge to Temp
           CurPos1 ← CurPos1 + 1
        else
           Temp[Counter] ← L[CurPos2]
           CurPos2 ← CurPos2 + 1
        endif
```

```
            Counter ← Counter + 1
        endwhile
        if CurPos1 > x then              //copy remaining elements
            for k ← CurPos2 to high do   //in appropriate sublist //to Temp
                    Temp[Counter] ← L[k]
                    Counter ← Counter + 1
            endfor
        else
            for k ← CurPos1 to x do
                    Temp[Counter] ← L[k]
                    Counter ← Counter + 1
            endfor
        endif
        for k ← low to high do           //copy Temp[low:high] to L[low:high]
            L[k] ← Temp[k]
        endfor
    end Merge
```

The tree of recursive calls to *MergeSort* is illustrated in Figure 2.4. A node in the tree is labeled by the values *low*, *mid*, and *high* involved in the call to *Merge*. (In leaf nodes, *mid* is not computed, as indicated by the symbol *.) Initially, *low* = 0 and *high* = 9. The path around the tree shown in Figure 2.4 indicates how the recursion resolves. Following this path amounts to a postorder traversal of the tree (see Chapter 4), where visiting a node corresponds to a call to *Merge*.

We now analyze the complexity of *MergeSort*, beginning with the worst-case complexity. Note that each call to *Merge* for merging two sublists of sizes m_1 and m_2 performs at most $m_1 + m_2 - 1$ comparisons. When we consider the tree of

FIGURE 2.4

Recursive calls to *MergeSort* for lists of size 10

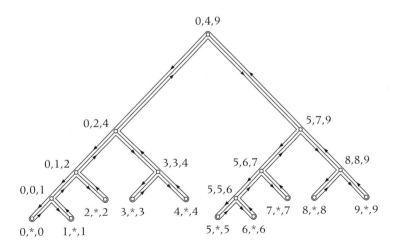

recursive calls to *MergeSort* for a list of size n (see Figure 2.4), we see that the leaf nodes do not generate calls to *Merge*, whereas each internal node generates a single call to *Merge*. At each level of the tree, the total number of comparisons made by all the calls to *Merge* is at most n. The depth of the tree of recursive calls is $\lceil \log_2 n \rceil$ (see Exercise 2.38). It follows that *MergeSort* performs at most $n\lceil \log_2 n \rceil$ comparisons for any list of size n, so that $W(n) \leq n\lceil \log_2 n \rceil$.

To find $B(n)$, we note that each call to *Merge* for merging two sublists of sizes m_1 and m_2, respectively, performs at least $\min\{m_1, m_2\}$ comparisons. We again consider the tree of recursive calls to *MergeSort* for a list of size n. Except for the last two levels, at each level of the tree of recursive calls, the total number of comparisons made by all the calls to *Merge* is at least $n/2$. It follows that *MergeSort* performs at least $(n/2)(\lceil \log_2 n \rceil - 1)$ comparisons for any list of size n, so that $B(n) \geq (n/2)(\lceil \log_2 n \rceil - 1)$. Thus, we have

$$(n/2)(\lceil \log_2 n \rceil - 1) \leq B(n) \leq A(n) \leq W(n) \leq n\lceil \log_2 n \rceil.$$

Because $B(n)$, $A(n)$, and $W(n)$ are all squeezed between functions that are very close to $(n/2)\log_2 n$ and $n\log_2 n$, for asymptotic analysis purposes (where we ignore the effect of positive multiplicative constants), we simply say that these quantities have $n\log n$ complexity (see Chapter 3). Notice that we have omitted the base in the log because change of base formulas show that logarithm functions to two different bases differ by a constant. It turns out that this type of complexity is optimal for $A(n)$ and $W(n)$ for *any* comparison-based sorting algorithm.

By examining Figure 2.4, we can easily come up with a bottom-up version of *MergeSort*. At the bottom level of the tree, we are merging sublists of single adjacent elements in the list. However, as the path around the tree indicates, for a given input list $L[0:n-1]$, *MergeSort* sorts the list $L[0:mid]$ before going on to any of the sublists of $L[mid+1, n-1]$. By contrast, a bottom-up version begins by dividing the list into pairs of adjacent elements, $L[0]:L[1]$, $L[2]:L[3]$, and so forth. Next, these adjacent pairs are merged yielding the sorted lists $L[0:1]$, $L[2:3]$, and so forth. The process is repeated by merging the adjacent pairs of sorted two-element sublists, $L[0:1]:L[2:3]$, $L[4:5]:L[6:7]$, and so forth. Continuing this process, we arrive at the root having sorted the entire list $L[0:n-1]$.

Figure 2.5 shows a tree representing this bottom-up merging of adjacent sublists. Each node represents a call to *Merge* with the indicated values of *low*, *mid*, and *high*. An asterisk (*) denotes the nodes in which a call to *Merge* is not made. Note that the sublists and resulting tree are quite different from the sublists generated by the tree of recursive calls of *MergeSort* given in Figure 2.4. All the calls to *Merge* for a given level are completed before we go up to the next level. The pseudocode for the nonrecursive version of *MergeSort* based on Figure 2.5 is left to the exercises.

FIGURE 2.5

Bottom-up nonrecursive *MergeSort* for a list of size 10

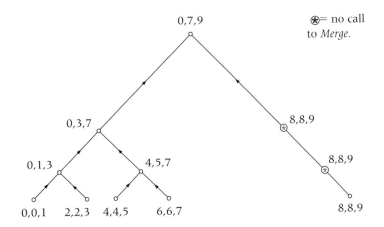

2.6.7 Quicksort

We now discuss the comparison-based sorting algorithm quicksort, discovered by C. A. R. Hoare in 1962. Quicksort is often the sorting algorithm of choice because of its good average behavior. Like mergesort, quicksort, is based on dividing a list into two sublists (actually two sublists of a rearrangement of the original list), and then sorting the sublists recursively. The difference between the two sorting strategies is that mergesort does most of the work in the combine (merge) step, whereas quicksort does most of the work in the divide step. Quicksort is also an in-place sort, as opposed to mergesort, which used an auxiliary array for merging (in-place versions of mergesort can be written, but they are complicated).

In quicksort, the division into sublists is based on rearranging the list $L[low:high]$ with respect to a suitably chosen *pivot element x*. The list $L[low:high]$ is rearranged so that every list element in $L[low:high]$ preceding x (having smaller index than the index of x) is not larger, and every element following x in $L[low:high]$ is not smaller. For example, for the list (23,55,11,17,53,4) and pivot element $x = 23$, the rearrangement might be (17,11,4,23,55,53). After the rearrangement, the pivot element x occupies a proper position in a sorting of the list. Thus, if the sublists on either side of x are sorted recursively, then the entire list will be sorted with no need to invoke an algorithm for combining the sorted sublists.

Procedure *QuickSort* sorts $L[low:high]$ into nondecreasing order by first calling an algorithm *Partition* that rearranges the list with respect to pivot element $x = L[low]$, as previously described. *Partition* assumes that the element $L[high+1]$ is defined and is at least as large as $L[low]$. The output parameter *position* of *Partition* returns the index where x is placed. To sort the entire list $L[0:n-1]$, *QuickSort* would be called initially with $low = 0$ and $high = n-1$.

```
procedure QuickSort(L[0:n − 1], low, high) recursive
Input:   L[0:n − 1] (an array of n list elements)
         low, high (indices of L[0:n − 1])
//for convenience, L[n] is assumed to have the sentinel value +∞}
Output: L[low:high] sorted in nondecreasing order
    if high > low then
        Partition(L[0:n − 1], low, high, position)
        QuickSort(L[0:n − 1], low, position − 1)
        QuickSort(L[0:n − 1], position+1, high)
    endif
end QuickSort
```

The algorithm *Partition* is based on the following clever interplay between two moving variables *moveright* and *moveleft*, which contain the indices of elements in L and are initialized to $low + 1$ and $high$, respectively.

```
while moveright < moveleft do
    moveright moves to the right (one index at a time) until it assumes the index of a
    list element not smaller than x, then it stops.
    moveleft moves to the left (one index at a time) until it assumes the index of a list
    element not larger than x, then it stops.
    if moveright < moveleft then
            interchange L[moveright] and L[moveleft]
    endif
endwhile
```

To guarantee that *moveright* actually finds an element not smaller than x, we assume that $L[high+1]$ is defined and is not smaller than $L[low]$. As commented in the pseudocode, this is arranged by introducing a sentinel value $L[n] = +\infty$. We leave it as an exercise to check that the condition $L[high+1] \geq L[low]$ is then automatically guaranteed for all subsequent calls to *Partition* by *QuickSort*. Of course, *Partition* could be written with explicit checking that *moveright* does not run off the list. However, this checking requires additional comparisons, and we prefer to implement the preconditioning. Figure 2.6 illustrates the movement of *moveright* (*mr*) and *moveleft* (*ml*) for a sample list $L[0:6]$. The pseudocode for *Partition* follows:

```
procedure Partition(L[0:n − 1], low, high, position)
Input:   L[0:n − 1] (an array of n list elements)
         low, high (indices of L[0:n − 1])
         //L[high+1] is assumed defined and ≥ L[low]
```

Output: a rearranged sublist $L[low:high]$ such that
　　　　$L[i] \leq L[position]$, $low \leq i \leq position$,
　　　　$L[i] \geq L[position]$, $position \leq i \leq high$
　　　　where, originally, $L[low] = L[position]$
　　　　position (the position of a proper placement of the original element $L[low]$
　　　　　　　in the list $L[low:high]$)
moveright ← *low*
moveleft ← *high* + 1
x ← $L[low]$
while *moveright* < *moveleft* **do**
　repeat
　　moveright ← *moveright* + 1
　until $L[moveright] \geq x$
　repeat
　　moveleft ← *moveleft* − 1
　until $L[moveleft] \leq x$
　if *moveright* < *moveleft* **then**
　　interchange($L[moveright],L[moveleft]$)
　endif
endwhile
position ← *moveleft*
$L[low]$ ← $L[position]$
$L[position]$ ← *x*
end *Partition*

		0	1	2	3	4	5	6	7
Initially:	index	0	1	2	3	4	5	6	7
	list element	23	9	23	52	15	19	47	+∞
		mr							*ml*
	Rearrange Step			19			23		
1st iteration:		23	9	23	52	15	19	47	+∞
				mr			*ml*		
					15	52			
2nd iteration:		23	9	19	52	15	23	47	+∞
					mr	*ml*			
3rd iteration:		23	9	19	15	52	23	47	+∞
					ml	*mr*			
	Place Step	15			23				
After completion of		23	9	19	15	52	23	47	+∞
Partition:					*position* = 3				

To analyze the performance of *QuickSort*, we again use list comparisons as our basic operation for analysis, where *QuickSort* is originally called with a list $L[0:n-1]$ of distinct elements, and $L[n] = +\infty$. A call to *Partition* with $L[low:high]$ performs exactly $high - low + 2$ comparisons, and this forms the basis of our analysis. We first consider the worst-case complexity.

Unfortunately, the worst-case performance of *QuickSort* occurs for a list that is already in order. In this case, the recursive calls to *QuickSort* are always with the empty list $L[low:low-1]$ and the list $L[low+1:high]$ (see Figure 2.7b). Thus,

....

FIGURE 2.7

Tree of recursive calls for *QuickSort:* (a) best-case behavior; (b) worst-case behavior

....

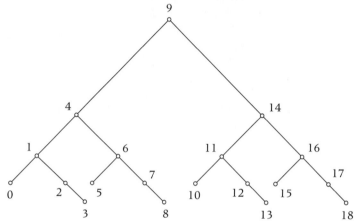

(a) Tree of recursive calls for best-case behavior of *QuickSort* for a list of size 19. Internal nodes are labeled with pivot elements in a call to *Partition*. Leaf nodes are labeled with single-element sublists that result in immediate returns. For simplicity, we do not show leaf nodes corresponding to calls to *QuickSort* with empty lists.

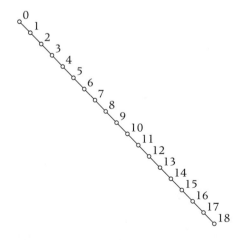

(b) Tree of recursive calls for worst-case behavior of *QuickSort* for a list of size 19, with nodes labeled using the same convention as in (a).

the number of comparisons performed is given by $W(n) = (n + 1) + n + \cdots + 3$ $= (n + 2)(n + 1)/2 - 3$, so that *QuickSort* has quadratic worst-case performance. Note that a decreasing list also generates worst-case performance for *QuickSort*.

The quadratic worst-case performance is disappointing, but quicksort is popular because of its $n\log n$ average behavior. We can expect this behavior because it is reasonable that, on average, the call to *Partition* results in dividing a given sublist into sublists of roughly equal size. In other words, for an average input, the tree of recursive calls would have a balanced nature similar to that of mergesort, producing roughly $\log_2 n$ levels with no more than $n + 1$ comparisons made by the calls to *Partition* on each level. In Chapter 6, we will prove that quicksort does indeed have $O(n\log n)$ average complexity.

R E M A R K S

For simplicity, we chose the pivot element in *QuickSort* to be the first list element. A common alternative is to have the pivot element be the median of the three elements in positions *low,*(*low + high*)*/2*, and *high*. Using this *median of three rule* avoids the bad behavior exhibited by lists that are close to being sorted.

There are many different ways to design an algorithm that accomplishes the same thing as our version of *Partition*. One such alternative version is explored in Exercise 2.46.

Some improvements to *QuickSort* should be made before using it in practice. In particular, *QuickSort* as written generates $n - 1$ unresolved recursive calls (that is, $n - 1$ successive pushes of unresolved activation records) in the worst case. These $n - 1$ successive pushes will no doubt cause stack overflow when run on many computers for even modestly large values of n (that is, even for values of n for which a quadratic number of comparisons will still complete in a reasonable time). Thus, it is important to rewrite *QuickSort* to reduce the number of unresolved recursive calls.

To reduce the number of successive recursive calls, we first note that *QuickSort* is tail recursive (see Appendix B). However, simply removing the tail recursion will result in a version that still generates $n - 1$ unresolved recursive calls for a decreasing list (although an increasing list now generates recursive calls only with empty sublists, so there is only one activation record on the stack generated by recursive calls at any given point in the execution for such lists). The problem is that we are always making a recursive call with the sublist to the left of the partition element, and the size of that sublist is only reduced by one in the worst case. What we need to do is make the recursive call with the smaller of the two sublists on either side of the partition element, redefine the relevant parameter (*low* or *high*) for the larger sublist, and branch to the beginning of the code. This will reduce the number of unresolved recursive activation records on the stack to at most $\lceil \log_2 n \rceil$. Moreover, now both the worst cases of increasing or decreasing lists will only make recursive calls with empty sublists. In practice, it would also be best to remove the recursion altogether by explicitly implementing the stack to simulate the recursion, since we only need to push on the stack the two indices delineating the subarray to be sorted. We leave the code for this altered version of *QuickSort* and its analysis to the exercises.

2.7 Closing Remarks

For most of the algorithms in this text, our analysis of complexity consists of identifying a basic operation and then determining the best-case, worst-case, and average complexities with respect to that basic operation. Occasionally, it is important to measure the complexity of an algorithm in terms of more than one operation. This is especially true for algorithms that involve maintaining several data structures, some of which may be altered by insertion or deletion of elements during the performance of the algorithm. *Amortized* analysis of an algorithm involves computing the maximum total number of all operations on the various data structures performed during the course of the algorithm for an input of size n. Usually, this amortized total is smaller than the number obtained by adding together the worst-case complexities of each individual operation for inputs of size n. Indeed, for an input in which one operation achieves its worst-case complexity, another operation often performs much less than its worst-case complexity, so a trade-off occurs for any input. When designing algorithms for which amortized analysis is appropriate, it then becomes a strategy to exploit this trade-off among the various operations.

In this chapter, we gave an overview of some major issues surrounding the design and analysis of algorithms. This overview sets the stage for the material in the rest of the text. We introduced and analyzed several important classical algorithms. Some of these algorithms were truly old, such as algorithms for exponentiation. Others, such as mergesort and quicksort, date to the period following soon after the advent of the electronic computer. In the remainder of the text, we will consider algorithms of more recent origin, including algorithms that have become important to the efficient functioning of the Internet. Part IV will be devoted to algorithms having specific applications, such as search engines for the Internet. Part V will introduce parallel and distributed algorithms, including algorithms implemented on the rapidly emerging cluster-computing environment based on the message-passing communication paradigm. Among the special topics we will discuss in Part VI are probabilistic algorithms, which often provide the most practical algorithms for solving prime testing and other important problems. Part VI will also introduce the Fast Fourier Transform, which allows dynamic imaging techniques such as CAT scans to take place in real time and forms the basis for some algorithms on quantum computers that outperform anything possible on a classical computer. We finish Part VI with the subject of NP-complete problems and discuss a number of important problems in this fundamental class. We also discuss some of the NP-complete problems that have efficient approximate solutions.

References and Suggestions for Further Reading

Two classical texts on data structures and algorithms:

Aho, A. V., J. E. Hopcroft, and J. D. Ullman. *Data Structures and Algorithms.* Reading, MA: Addison-Wesley, 1983.

Horowitz, E., and S. Sahni. *Fundamentals of Data Structures in Pascal.* 3rd ed. San Francisco: Computer Science Press, 1990.

A formal treatment of removing recursion is given in these texts:

Horowitz E., and S. Sahni. *Fundamentals of Computer Algorithms.* Rockville, MD: Computer Science Press, 1978.

Kruse, R. L. *Data Structures and Program Design.* Englewood Cliffs, NJ: Prentice Hall, 1984.

Cormen, T. H., C. E. Leiserson, R. L. Rivest, and C. Stein. *Introduction to Algorithms.* 2nd ed. Cambridge, MA: MIT Press, 2001. A very comprehensive introduction to the theory of algorithms.

Baase, S., and A. Van Gelder. *Computer Algorithms: Introduction to the Design and Analysis.* 3rd ed. Reading, MA: Addison-Wesley, 2000. A good discussion of measuring the complexity of algorithms in terms of the average and worse-case number of basic operations performed.

Carrano, F. M., and J. J. Pritchard. *Data Abstraction and Problem Solving with C++, Walls and Mirrors.* 3rd ed. Boston: Addison-Wesley, 2002. A good reference for elementary data structures and their implementation in an object-oriented programming language.

Tarjan, R. E. "Amortized Computational Complexity." *SIAM Journal on Applied and Discrete Mathematics* 14 (November 1985): 862–874. A good reference for the amortized analysis of algorithms.

EXERCISES

Section 2.2 Recursion

2.1 Give pseudocode for a recursive function that outputs the maximum value in a list of size n.

2.2 Give pseudocode for a recursive function that tests whether or not an input string of size n is a palindrome (that is, reads the same backward and forward).

2.3 a. Design a recursive algorithm whose input is a decimal integer and whose output is the binary representation of the input.

b. Design a recursive algorithm that computes the reverse of the result in (a)—that is, converts a binary integer to its decimal equivalent.

2.4 Show that for input (x,n), *PowersRec* performs between $\lfloor \log_2 n \rfloor$ and $2\lfloor \log_2 n \rfloor$ multiplications.

2.5 One of the most famous sequences in computer science (and nature) is the Fibonacci sequence, which is defined by the recurrence

$$fib(n) = fib(n-1) + fib(n-2), \text{ init. cond. } fib(0) = 0, fib(1) = 1.$$

In Appendix D, we find an exact formula for the nth Fibonacci number:

$$fib(n) = \frac{1}{\sqrt{5}}\left[\left(\frac{1+\sqrt{5}}{2}\right)^n - \left(\frac{1-\sqrt{5}}{2}\right)^n\right].$$

Without using this formula, argue that

$$(1.5)^{n-2} \le fib(n) \le 2^{n-1}, \ n \ge 1.$$

2.6 Consider the following function *Fib* for computing the nth Fibonacci number based directly on the recursive definition given in the previous question:

```
function Fib(n) recursive
Input:   n (a nonnegative integer)
Output: the nth Fibonacci number
    if n ≤ 1 then
        return(n)
    else
        return(Fib(n − 1) + Fib(n − 2))
    endif
end Fib
```

a. Show that *Fib* is extremely inefficient because it performs many redundant recalculations. How many times is *fib*(*k*) computed by *Fib* when *Fib* is invoked with input *n*, *k* = 0, 1, ... , *n*?

b. Rewrite *Fib* so that it is still recursive but uses a table to avoid redundant calculations.

c. Rewrite *Fib* as a purely iterative function.

2.7 For the pair (89,144) given in Exercise 1.7, the algorithms *NaiveGCD* and *EuclidGCD* perform identical calculations. This phenomenon holds for infinitely many pairs of integers. One such collection can be obtained as successive pairs in the Fibonacci sequence *fib*(*n*).

a. Verify that (except for the last step) *NaiveGCD* and *EuclidGCD* perform identically on any input pair (*fib*(*n* − 1),*fib*(*n*)).

b. Obtain a formula for the number of steps required by *EuclidGCD* to compute gcd(*fib*(*n* − 1),*fib*(*n*)).

2.8 Show that the longest number of steps required by *EuclidGCD* for a pair of integers each having *m* digits or less is achieved by a suitable pair (*fib*(n − 1),*fib*(*n*)).

2.9 Prove by induction that

$$fib(1) + fib(2) + \cdots + fib(n) = fib(n + 2) - 1.$$

2.10 a. Prove by induction that

$$\begin{pmatrix} fib(n) \\ fib(n + 1) \end{pmatrix} = \begin{pmatrix} 0 & 1 \\ 1 & 1 \end{pmatrix}^n \begin{pmatrix} 0 \\ 1 \end{pmatrix},$$

where *fib*(*n*) denotes the nth Fibonacci number.

b. Briefly describe how the formula in (a) can be employed to design an algorithm for computing *fib*(*n*) using only at most $8\log_2 n$ multiplications.

2.11 Consider the famous Towers of Hanoi puzzle (see Appendix B). Prove by induction that the minimum number of moves needed to solve the Towers of Hanoi puzzle is $2^n - 1$ (thus, the solution given in Appendix B is optimal).

Section 2.3 Data Structures and Algorithm Design

2.12 Given a linked list, create a linked list with the same elements but in the reverse direction.

2.13 a. Give pseudocode for the push and pop operations on a stack implemented using an array.

b. Repeat (a) for a linked-list implementation.

2.14 A *circular queue* is implemented using a circular array *Queue*[0:*Max* – 1] and two pointers (indices), *Front* and *Rear*. We view the elements *Queue*[0], *Queue*[1], ... , *Queue*[*Max* – 1] as positioned around a circle in a counterclockwise fashion. Initially, we have *Front* = *Rear* = 0. For non-empty queues, the variable *Rear* points to the position of the element at the rear of the queue. However, *Front* points one position counterclockwise from the element at the front of the queue. An element in variable *x* is enqueued by the two statements

$$Rear \leftarrow (Rear + 1) \bmod Max$$
$$Queue[Rear] \leftarrow x,$$

and an element is dequeued and assigned to *x* by the two statements

$$Front \leftarrow (Front + 1) \bmod Max$$
$$x \leftarrow Queue[Front].$$

Figure 2.8 shows how the circular array *Queue* with *Max* = 6 is updated as a given sequence of enqueues and dequeues are performed.

FIGURE 2.8

Circular array
Queue[0:5]: after a
sequence of
enqueues and
dequeues

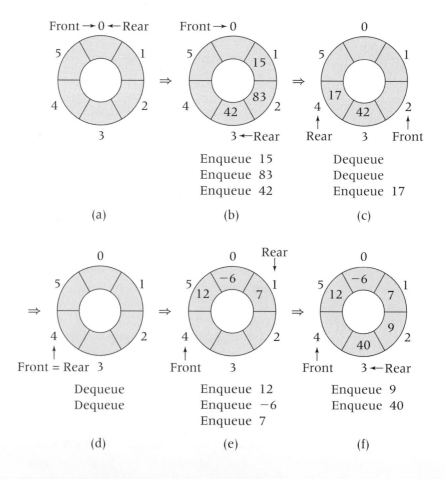

If the queue is empty, then *Rear* = *Front*. If the queue is full, in the sense that the entire array *Queue* is filled, then it is also the case that *Rear* = *Front*. The question then is how to distinguish between the two situations. One way is to introduce a Boolean variable that tags the queue as being empty or full. However, maintaining such a variable could lead to a noticeable increase in the computing time because the procedures for implementing a queue are usually called repetitively. Another solution is to consider the queue full when every position of the array *Queue* but one is filled with elements of the queue. (Of course, this wastes a single memory location in the array *Queue*, but this is hardly significant.)

a. Give pseudocode for procedures *EnqueueCirc* and *DequeueCirc* for enqueueing and dequeueing an element using the latter implementation of a circular queue.

b. Starting with an empty circular queue *Queue*[0:8], show the final state of *Queue*[0:8] and the values of *Rear* and *Front* after the following sequence of enqueues and dequeues:

enqueue 23, enqueue 108, enqueue 55, dequeue, enqueue 61, dequeue, dequeue, dequeue, enqueue 44, enqueue 21, dequeue

2.15 Give pseudocode for inserting and deleting into a linked list implemented using two arrays, $L[0:n-1]$ and $Next[0:n-1]$.

Section 2.5 Analyzing Algorithm Performance

2.16 Design an algorithm that tests whether or not two input lists of size n have at least one element in common. Give formulas for $B(n)$ and $W(n)$ for your algorithm.

2.17 Design and analyze an algorithm that emulates a single elimination tournament (NCAA basketball, Wimbledon tennis, and so forth) to find the maximum element in a list of size n. For simplicity, you may assume that n is a power of two (tournaments arrange this by giving byes when n is not a power of two).

2.18 Design a (simple) algorithm whose input is a text string T of size n and a pattern string P of size m, and determines whether P occurs as a substring of T. Give formulas for $B(n,m)$ and $W(n,m)$.

Section 2.6 Analyzing Some Basic Comparison-Based Algorithms

2.19 a. Write a procedure that finds both the largest and second largest elements in the list $L[0:n-1]$ of size n. You should find a more efficient algorithm than simply performing two scans through the list.

b. Determine $B(n)$ and $W(n)$ for the algorithm in (a). (In Chapter 25, we will give an optimal algorithm for solving this problem that has worst-case complexity $W(n) = n + \lceil \log_2 n \rceil - 2$.)

2.20 Calculate the average complexity $A(n)$ of *LinearSearch*, where both of the following two conditions hold about the input list $L[0:n - 1]$ and search element X.

- The probability that X occurs in the list is 2/3.

- Given that X occurs in the list, X is twice as likely to occur in the first half of the list (positions 1 through $\lfloor n/2 \rfloor$) as in the second half. Further, if X occurs in the first half of the list, it is equally likely to occur in any position in the first half. A similar assumption is made about the second half.

2.21 Trace the action of *BinarySearch*, including listing the value of *Low*, *High*, and *Mid* after each iteration, for the list (2,3,5,7,11,13,17,19,23,29,31,37) for each of the following search elements X:

a. $X = 3$

b. $X = 24$

c. $X = 108$

d. $X = 13$

2.22 Show that *BinarySearch* has worst-case complexity $\lceil \log_2(n + 1) \rceil$ for any n.

2.23 Describe a modification of *BinarySearch* that returns an index in the list after which the search element can be inserted and still maintain an ordered list (or zero if the search element is smaller than any element in the list).

2.24 Design a recursive version of *BinarySearch*.

2.25 Design and analyze a variant of *BinarySearch* that performs a single check for equality between the search element and a list element.

2.26 Suppose $L[0:n - 1]$ is a sorted list of distinct integers. Design and prove correct an algorithm similar to *BinarySearch* that finds an index i such that $L[i] = i$ or returns 0 if no such index exists.

2.27 Give pseudocode for an interpolation search, and analyze its worst-case complexity.

2.28 Give pseudocode for a recursive version of an interpolation search.

2.29 It has been estimated that there are fewer than 10^{83} atoms in the known universe. Show that $\log_2(\log_2 10^{83}) < 9$.

2.30 Design and analyze a forward scan version of *InsertionSort* in which the list is implemented using an array. Discuss the drawbacks of the forward scan version compared with the backward scan version.

2.31 Show that *InsertionSort* is a *stable* sorting algorithm.

2.32 a. Design a linked list version of *InsertionSort*.

b. Give the stable (but slightly less efficient) version of the algorithm in (a).

2.33 a. Design a recursive version of *InsertionSort*.

b. Design a recursive linked-list version of *InsertionSort*.

2.34 The sorting algorithm *SelectionSort* is based on the simple idea of successively selecting the largest element in a sublist $L[0:n-i]$ and interchanging this element with the element in position $n-i$, where $i = 1, \ldots, n-1$.

a. Give pseudocode for *SelectionSort*.

b. Analyze the complexity of *SelectionSort*.

2.35 Design a recursive version of *SelectionSort* as described in the previous exercise.

2.36 There is another well-known sorting algorithm called *BubbleSort*, which, like *SelectionSort*, results in the ith largest element being placed in its proper position at the completion of the ith pass. The two algorithms differ in the manner in which this largest element is determined. During the ith pass, *BubbleSort* passes sequentially through the sublist $L[0:n-i]$, comparing adjacent elements in the sublist and interchanging (swapping) them if they are out of order. Because this sequential pass through the sublist starts at the *beginning* of the sublist, after the ith pass we are guaranteed that the ith largest element will have "bubbled" to the end of the sublist $L[0:n-i]$, its proper place. In *BubbleSort*, this occurs automatically as a consequence of the interchange process, as opposed to *SelectionSort's* method of actually determining the position in the sublist where the ith largest element occurred. Note that if no swapping occurred on the ith pass, the list has been sorted. This suggests including a flag to detect this condition.

a. Give the pseudocode for *BubbleSort*.

b. Determine the best-case and worst-case complexities of *BubbleSort*.

c. Design and analyze an improvement to *BubbleSort* based on keeping track of the last positions where swaps occur in each pass and where the passes are made alternately in different directions.

2.37 Give the appropriately labeled tree of recursive calls to *MergeSort* for lists of size 18 (see Figure 2.4).

2.38 Show that the tree of recursive calls for *MergeSort* has depth $\lceil \log_2 n \rceil$. Conclude that *MergeSort* performs at most $n \lceil \log_2 n \rceil$ comparisons for any list of size n.

2.39 Design a nonrecursive version of *MergeSort* based on Figure 2.4.

2.40 Given a list $L[0:n-1]$, one way of maintaining a sorted order of L is to use an auxiliary array $Link[0:n-1]$. The array $Link[0:n-1]$ serves as a linked list determining the next highest element in L, so the elements of L can be given in nondecreasing order by

$L[Start]$, $L[Link[Start]]$, $L[Link[Link[Start]]]$, and so forth. Then $Link^{n-1}[Start]$ is the index of the largest element in L, and we set $Link[Link^{n-1}[Start]]$ = $Link^n[Start] = 0$ to signal the end of the linked list. Design a version of MergeSort that uses the auxiliary array Link.

*2.41 Develop an in-place version of *MergeSort* — that is, a version that does not use an auxiliary array and uses only a few additional bookkeeping variables.

2.42 a. Give pseudocode for a version of *QuickSort* that incorporates the median of three rule.

b. Show that the worst-case performance of the *QuickSort* in part (a) remains quadratic.

2.43 It is useful to analyze how much stacking is generated by the recursion in *QuickSort*.

a. Show that *QuickSort* may have as many as $n - 1$ unresolved recursive calls active, so that the size of the stack can be as large as $n - 1$.

b. Give pseudocode for a modification of *QuickSort* for which the size of the stack is at most $\lceil \log_2 n \rceil$. Verify your result.

2.44 Give a nonrecursive version of *QuickSort* (using explicit stack operations).

2.45 Give a stable version of *QuickSort* that avoids making extraneous interchanges of elements having identical values.

2.46 Several variants of the algorithm *Partition* are used in *QuickSort*. Design and analyze one such variant based on the following strategy for partitioning an array. The elements in the array minus the pivot element p (which we take to be the first element in the array) are dynamically divided into three contiguous blocks, B_1, B_2, and B_3, where each element in B_1 is less than p, each element in B_2 is greater than or equal to p, and the status of the elements in B_3 is yet to be decided. Initially, B_1 and B_2 are empty (so that B_3 is everything in the subarray except p). The algorithm performs $n - 1$ steps, where each step consists of placing the first element of B_3 into either B_1 or B_2 as appropriate.

MATHEMATICAL TOOLS FOR ALGORITHM ANALYSIS

Determining the complexities of an algorithm exactly is often difficult. In practice, it is usually sufficient to find asymptotic approximations to algorithmic complexities. To describe asymptotic behavior, this chapter introduces and uses standard notation for the order and growth rate of functions. The chapter also presents tools for classifying the growth rate of a given function compared with that of commonly occurring growth rates such as logarithmic, linear, quadratic, and so forth.

In Chapter 2, we discussed the importance of recursion as a design strategy. In this chapter, we describe how most recursive algorithms immediately yield recurrence relations for their complexities, and we illustrate this by giving an alternative proof of the worst-case complexity of *MergeSort*. We also give a general formula for solving some of the more commonly occurring recurrence relations that arise in algorithm analysis.

Proving the correctness of an algorithm is perhaps even more fundamental to its analysis than determining its efficiency. Mathematical induction is the primary tool used to establish correctness. For recursive algorithms, induction on the input size is usually the relevant tool. For algorithms involving loops, the most relevant tool is establishing loop invariants (again, using induction). Both techniques are discussed in this chapter.

A function $L(n)$ is called a lower bound for, say, the worst case $W(n)$ of a problem Q, if *any* algorithm solving Q must perform at least $L(n)$ basic operations for some problem instance of Q of size n. Establishing lower bounds is an important tool in algorithm analysis because they can be used to determine how close a given algorithm is to being optimal for the problem. In this chapter, we use some simple counting arguments to establish lower bounds for such important problems as finding the maximum in a list and sorting a list using a comparison-based sorting algorithm. In Chapter 25, we will use more sophisticated tools to establish lower bounds for various other problems. Unfortunately, for many important problems, the gap between a known lower bound for the problem and the performance of the best known algorithm solving the problem is wide indeed. We close this chapter with a discussion of an important class of such problems, known as NP-complete problems. Typically, a known lower bound for an NP-complete problem is a polynomial of low degree, whereas the best known algorithm solving the problem has exponential (or at least super-polynomial) complexity. However, nobody knows whether the NP-complete problems are truly difficult or whether, despite more than 30 years of searching by the best minds in theoretical computer science, we simply have not yet found the key to solving any of them with a polynomial-complexity algorithm.

3.1   Asymptotic Behavior of Functions

Suppose $f(n) = 400n + 23$ and $g(n) = 2n^2 - 1$ are the worst-case complexities for two algorithms, A and B, respectively, that solve the same problem. Which exhibits better worst-case performance? If $n \leq 200$, then $f(n)$ is greater than $g(n)$, so algorithm B outperforms algorithm A. On the other hand, if $n > 200$, the reverse is true. When analyzing the complexity of an algorithm, we usually consider the behavior of the algorithm as the input size n approaches infinity (asymptotic behavior) to be most important. Thus, we would consider algorithm A to have better worst-case behavior.

For the purposes of algorithm analysis, the asymptotic behavior (*order*) of a function $f(n)$ not only ignores small values of n but also does not distinguish between $f(n)$ and $cf(n)$, where c is a positive constant. For example, *InsertionSort* performs $n^2/2 - n/2$ comparisons in the worst case for an input of size n. However, $n^2/2 - n/2$ and n^2 are considered to be asymptotically equivalent measures of the complexity of an algorithm. This is reasonable because for large n, the quadratic

	n	$n/2$	$n^2/2$	$(n^2/2) - (n/2)$	n^2
	10	5	50	45	100
	1,000	500	500,000	499,500	1,000,000
	10,000	5,000	50,000,000	49,995,000	100,000,000
	100,000	50,000	5,000,000,000	4,999,950,000	10,000,000,000

FIGURE 3.1

Table comparing linear and quadratic growth

term $n^2/2$ completely dominates the linear term $n/2$ (see Figure 3.1), so the $n/2$ term can safely be ignored.

Of course, there is a significant difference between n^2 and $n^2/2$, but there are two reasons for ignoring the factor $1/2$. The first is that the total number of operations performed by *InsertionSort* (comparisons, array reassignments, loop control updates, and so forth) is bounded by a constant multiple of the number of basic operations (comparisons). The second reason involves the feasibility of running the algorithm on a particular computer in a reasonable amount of time. We can assume that it is feasible to perform n^2 operations if, and only if, it is feasible to perform $n^2/2$ operations. For example, today's fastest computers can perform close to a billion operations a second. For an input size of $n = 1,000,000,000$, these computers would take more than 3 centuries to perform n^2 operations and more than 1.5 centuries to perform $n^2/2$ operations. On the other hand, for an input size of $n = 1,000,000$, today's fastest computers can do $n^2/2$ operations in less than 10 minutes and n^2 operations in less than 20 minutes (both of which represent a feasible amount of time in most situations).

Therefore, we say that the worst-case complexity of *InsertionSort* has order n^2.

We now introduce asymptotic notation that formalizes the notion of the order of a function.

3.1.1 Asymptotic Order

Our notion of order is restricted to real-valued functions $f(n): \mathbb{N} \to \mathbb{R}$ defined on the nonnegative integers that are *eventually* positive, so that there exists an integer n_0 (depending on f) such that $f(n) > 0$ for all $n > n_0$. Let $\mathscr{F}$ denote the set of all such functions. Given any function $g(n) \in \mathscr{F}$, we define $\Theta(g(n))$ to be the set of all functions $f(n) \in \mathscr{F}$ that grow at the same rate as $g(n)$ in the sense that they are eventually "squeezed" between two constant multiples of $g(n)$. As shown in Figure 3.2, even though $f(n)$ and $g(n)$ are only assumed to be defined on the nonnegative integers, we have drawn them as defined over the reals to aid in the visualization. In general, when graphing functions $f(n) \in \mathscr{F}$, we will invariably extend $f(n)$ to a function defined on the reals for the same reason.

FIGURE 3.2

$f(n) \in \Theta(g(n))$

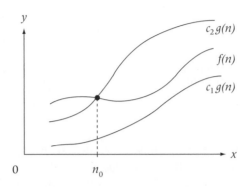

DEFINITION 3.1.1 Given a function $g(n) \in \mathscr{F}$, we define $\Theta(g(n))$ to be the set of all functions $f(n) \in \mathscr{F}$ having the property that there exist positive constants c_1, c_2, and n_0 such that for all $n \geq n_0$,

$$c_1 g(n) \leq f(n) \leq c_2 g(n). \tag{3.1.1}$$

If $f(n) \in \Theta(g(n))$, we say that $f(n)$ *is big theta of* $g(n)$.

REMARKS

1. When a function $f(n)$ is given by a formula, it is standard to identify the function with the formula for the function. For example, if $f(n)$ is given by the formula $f(n) = n^3 + 2n\log_2 n - 3$, then we simply refer to $f(n)$ as the function $n^3 + 2n\log_2 n - 3$. This allows us to say $n^3 + 2n\log_2 n - 3 \in \Theta(n^3)$, $3\sqrt{n} + \log_2 n + 108 \in \Theta(\sqrt{n})$, $864 \in \Theta(1)$, and so forth.
2. It is fairly common in the literature to use the notation $f(n) = \Theta(g(n))$ instead of $f(n) \in \Theta(g(n))$. The same is true for the sets $O(g(n))$ and $\Omega(g(n))$ defined later in Definitions 3.1.3 and 3.1.4.

Proposition 3.1.1 states that Θ determines an *equivalence relation* (see Exercise 3.20) on the set $\mathscr{F}$.

Proposition 3.1.1

Θ determines an equivalence relation on $\mathscr{F}$ —that is, for $f(n), g(n) \in \mathscr{F}$,

1. $f(n) \in \Theta(f(n))$ (Θ is reflexive).
2. $f(n) \in \Theta(g(n)) \Rightarrow g(n) \in \Theta(f(n))$ (Θ is symmetric).
3. $f(n) \in \Theta(g(n))$ and $g(n) \in \Theta(h(n)) \Rightarrow f(n) \in \Theta(h(n))$ (Θ is transitive). ■

The fact that Θ determines an equivalence relation on the set $\mathscr{F}$ shows that the following definition of *order* is well defined.

DEFINITION 3.1.2 Two functions f and g have the *same order* if $f(n) \in \Theta(g(n))$.

Note that the reflexive, symmetric, and transitive properties of Θ can be expressed as follows:

1. f has the same order as itself.
2. If f has the same order as g, then g has the same order as f.
3. If f has the same order as g, and g has the same order as h, then f has the same order as h.

Using these properties of Θ, it follows (see Exercise 3.10) that f and g have the same order if and only if $\Theta(f(n)) = \Theta(g(n))$. Thus, $\Theta(f(n))$ can also be denoted by $\Theta(g(n))$ for any function $g(n) \in \Theta(f(n))$. When describing the order of a function $f(n)$, we usually choose a representative in the set (class) $\Theta(f(n))$ having the "simplest" form. For example, we have

$$\Theta\left((8n^3 + n)^{1/2} + \log_2 n\right) = \Theta(2n^{3/2} + 6n\ln n) = \Theta(n^{3/2}) = \Theta(n^{3/2} + 23n^{1/3})$$
$$= \Theta\left(\frac{n^3 + n + 1}{4n^2 + \ln n}\right).$$

Because $n^{3/2}$ has the simplest form of any function in its Θ-class, we denote this class by $\Theta(n^{3/2})$. Also, we say that any $f \in \Theta(n^{3/2})$ has order $n^{3/2}$.

For purposes of algorithm analysis, we are usually interested in a function whose domain is a subset of the positive integers (and whose input size is integral). However, often such a function is given by an expression involving n that is also meaningful when extended over the domain of nonnegative real numbers x. Then we sketch the graph of f over the reals instead of over just the integers (see Figure 3.3). When the extension to the reals of the domain of f yields a

FIGURE 3.3

Average comlexity for *LinearSearch:* $A(n) = n/2 + 1/2 \in \Theta(n)$

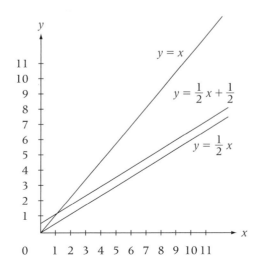

differentiable function, we can use various theorems from calculus to help analyze the asymptotic behavior of f.

3.1.2 Ilustrations of Orders of Complexity

Many of the algorithms arising in computer science have linear, quadratic, cubic, logarithmic, exponential, or $n\log n$ complexities. We now illustrate the use of asymptotic notation for measuring the complexity of some algorithms we have already discussed. For example, recall that *LinearSearch* has average complexity $A(n) = n/2 + 1/2$ when the search element X is assumed to be in the list. As shown in Figure 3.3, $A(n) = n/2 + 1/2$ is squeezed between $n/2$ and n, so that $A(n) \in \Theta(n)$.

As our second example, recall that the algorithm *InsertionSort* has worst-case complexity $W(n) = n^2/2 - n/2$. As seen in Figure 3.4, $n^2/2 - n/2$ is squeezed between $n^2/3$ and n^2, for $n \geq n_0 = 3$. Thus, $W(n) \in \Theta(n^2)$.

FIGURE 3.4

Worst-case
complexity for
InsertionSort:
$W(n) = n^2/2 - n/2$
$\in \Theta(n^2)$

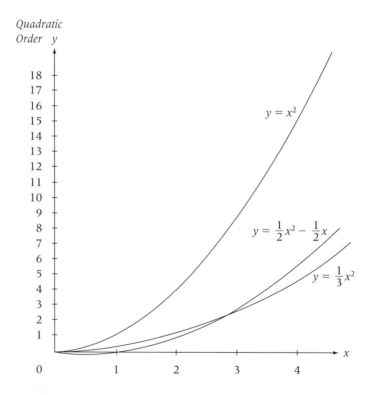

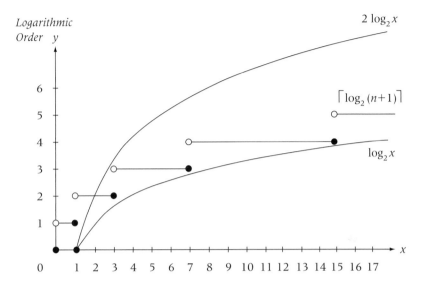

FIGURE 3.5

Worst-case
complexity for
BinarySearch:
$W(n) = \lceil \log_2$
$(n + 1) \rceil$
$\in \Theta(\log_2 n)$

Our third example illustrates logarithmic order. Recall that *BinarySearch* has worst-case complexity $W(n) = \lceil \log_2(n + 1) \rceil$. As seen in Figure 3.5, $\lceil \log_2(n + 1) \rceil$ is squeezed between $\log_2 n$ and $2\log_2 n$, for $n \geq n_0 = 2$. Thus, $W(n) \in \Theta(\log_2 n)$.

Logarithms, usually with base 2, occur frequently in the analysis of algorithms—*BinarySearch*, for example. However, when using asymptotic notation, we drop the base because the logarithm to one base is merely a constant multiple of the logarithm to another base. For instance, in

$$\log_a n = (\log_a b)(\log_b n),$$

$\log_a b$ is a constant that does not depend on n. Letting $c_1 = c_2 = \log_a b$ and $n_0 = 1$, it follows from Definition 3.1.1 that $\log_a n \in \Theta(\log_b n)$, so that $\Theta(\log_a n) = \Theta(\log_b n)$. Thus, we usually denote this Θ-class simply by $\Theta(\log n)$.

Our fourth example illustrates exponential order. Consider the algorithm *Towers* given in Appendix B for solving the Towers of Hanoi puzzle. We show in the next section that *Towers* performs $2^n - 1$ moves for n disks. As illustrated in Figure 3.6, $2^n - 1$ is squeezed between $(1/2)2^n$ and 2^n. We say that *Towers* has *exponential* complexity because $2^n - 1 \in \Theta(2^n)$. More generally, the complexity $t(n)$ of an algorithm is said to be exponential if there exist bases a and b, where $b \geq a > 1$, and positive constants c_1, c_2, and n_0 such that

$$c_1 a^n \leq t(n) \leq c_2 b^n, \text{ for all } n \geq n_0.$$

....

FIGURE 3.6

Complexity of
Towers:
$2^n - 1 \in \Theta(2^n)$

....

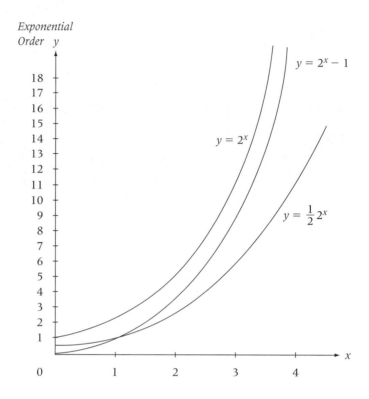

3.1.3 The Asymptotic Relations O and Ω

The set $\Theta(g(n))$ consists of functions $f(n)$ that grow at the same rate (up to a multiplicative constant) as g, meaning that the functions are eventually bounded above and below by constant multiples of $g(n)$. We obtain a (strictly) larger class of functions, denoted by $O(g(n))$, by requiring only that every $f(n)$ eventually be bounded *above* by a constant multiple of $g(n)$, so that f grows no faster than g. Similarly, we obtain a class $\Omega(g(n))$ containing $\Theta(g(n))$ by requiring only that f eventually be bounded *below* by a constant multiple of $g(n)$, so that f grows at least as fast as g.

DEFINITION 3.1.3 Given a function $g(n) \in \mathcal{F}$, we define $O(g(n))$ to be the set of all functions $f(n) \in \mathcal{F}$ having the property that there exist positive constants c and n_0 such that for all $n \geq n_0$,

$$f(n) \leq cg(n). \tag{3.1.2}$$

If $f(n) \in O(g(n))$, we say that $f(n)$ *is big oh of* $g(n)$ (see Figure 3.7).

FIGURE 3.7

$f(n) \in O(g(n))$

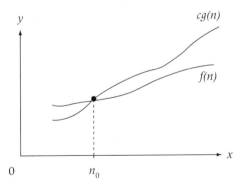

FIGURE 3.7

$f(n) \in O(g(n))$

DEFINITION 3.1.4 Given a function $g(n) \in \mathcal{F}$, we define $\Omega(g(n))$ to be the set of all functions $f(n) \in \mathcal{F}$ having the property that there exist positive constants c and n_0 such that for all $n \geq n_0$,

$$cg(n) \leq f(n). \tag{3.1.3}$$

If $f(n) \in \Omega(g(n))$, we say that $f(n)$ *is big omega of* $g(n)$ (see Figure 3.8).

Big oh is often used as an upper bound on the performance of a particular algorithm for solving a problem, whereas big omega is often used as a lower bound for the complexity of the problem itself.

It is easy to verify that the set $\Theta(g(n))$ consists precisely of functions that are in both sets $O(g(n))$ and $\Omega(g(n))$—that is,

$$\Theta(g(n)) = \Omega(g(n)) \cap O(g(n)). \tag{3.1.4}$$

FIGURE 3.8

$f(n) \in \Omega(g(n))$

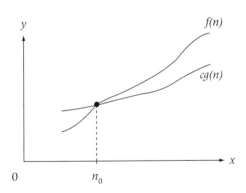

....
FIGURE 3.9

Venn diagram for
$O(n^2)$, $\Theta(n^2)$, and
$\Omega(n^2)$ and sample
set members
....

Set $\mathscr{F}$ of all (eventually positive)
functions $f\colon \mathbb{N} \to \mathbb{R}$

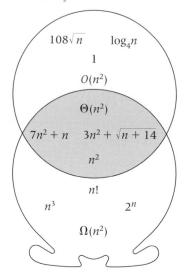

Sample members of the sets $O(n^2)$, $\Theta(n^2)$, and $\Omega(n^2)$ are illustrated in Figure 3.9. Proposition 3.1.2 states some useful properties of the sets O, Θ, and Ω.

Proposition 3.1.2 The following properties hold for $f(n), g(n) \in \mathscr{F}$.

1. Given any positive constant c, $\Omega(f(n)) = \Omega(cf(n))$, $\Theta(f(n)) = \Theta(cf(n))$, and $O(f(n)) = O(cf(n))$.
2. $f(n) \in \Theta(g(n)) \Leftrightarrow f(n) \in O(g(n))$ and $f(n) \in \Omega(g(n))$.
3. $f(n) \in O(g(n)) \Leftrightarrow O(f(n)) \subseteq O(g(n))$.
4. $O(f(n)) = O(g(n)) \Leftrightarrow \Omega(f(n)) = \Omega(g(n)) \Leftrightarrow \Theta(f(n)) = \Theta(g(n))$.
5. $f(n) \in O(g(n)) \Leftrightarrow g(n) \in \Omega(f(n))$.

The proof of Proposition 3.1.2 is left to the exercises. ■

It is common to use the notation

$$f(n) = g(n) + O(h(n)),$$

when $f(n) - g(n) \in O(h(n))$. Similar notation is used for Θ and Ω. For example, if $f(n) = 3n^3 + 4n^2 + 23n - 108$, then we could write

$$f(n) = 3n^3 + O(n^2).$$

FIGURE 3.10

Order of best-case, average, and worst-case complexities

Algorithm	B(n)	A(n)	W(n)
HornerEval	n	n	n
Towers	2^n	2^n	2^n
LinearSearch	1	n	n
BinarySearch	1	$\log n$	$\log n$
Max, Min, MaxMin	n	n	n
InsertionSort	n	n^2	n^2
MergeSort	$n \log n$	$n \log n$	$n \log n$
HeapSort	$n \log n$	$n \log n$	$n \log n$
QuickSort	$n \log n$	$n \log n$	n^2

The table in Figure 3.10 summarizes the order of the best-case, average, and worst-case complexities for most of the algorithms we have discussed so far. The table also includes the sorting algorithm *HeapSort*, which we will discuss in the next chapter.

3.1.4 Hierarchy of Orders

The table in Figure 3.1 indicates that linear complexity is in some sense smaller than quadratic complexity. The question remains, however, whether it might still be true that $n^2 \in O(n)$. Suppose the answer were yes. Then by definition of $O(n)$, there would exist positive constants c and n_0 such that $n^2 \leq cn$, for all $n \geq n_0$. But this implies that $n \leq c$ for all $n \geq n_0$, which is a contradiction. Since $n^2 \notin O(n)$, it follows from property (2) of Proposition 3.1.2 that $n^2 \notin \Theta(n)$, so that n and n^2 have different orders.

Since $n \in O(n^2)$, it follows from property (3) of Proposition 3.1.2 that $O(n)$ is strictly contained in $O(n^2)$—that is, $O(n) \subset O(n^2)$. This makes it natural to say that n has *smaller order* that n^2 and motivates the following general definition of hierarchy of orders.

DEFINITION 3.1.5 Given functions $f(n)$ and $g(n)$, we say that $f(n)$ has *smaller order than* $g(n)$ if $O(f(n))$ is *strictly* contained in $O(g(n))$—that is, $O(f(n)) \subset O(g(n))$.

REMARK

In the literature, the notation $O(f(n)) < O(g(n))$ is sometimes used in place of the more precise $O(f(n)) \subset O(g(n))$.

Some of the most frequently encountered functions in the analysis of algorithms are 1, $\log n$, $\sqrt{n}$, n, $n\log n$, n^2, n^3, 2^n, $n2^n$, and $n!$. These functions form an increasing chain in the hierarchy of orders:

$$O(1) \subset O(\log n) \subset O(\sqrt{n}) \subset O(n) \subset O(n\log n)$$
$$\subset O(n^2) \subset O(n^3) \subset O(2^n) \subset O(n2^n) \subset O(n!).$$

This hierarchy is illustrated by the Venn diagram in Figure 3.11. Although the figure might suggest otherwise, not every order is comparable to all others. The orders of two functions $f(n)$ and $g(n)$ are not comparable if $f(n) \notin O(g(n))$ and $g(n) \notin O(f(n))$. For example, consider the functions $f(n) = n^3$ and $g(n) = n^4(n \bmod 2) + n^2$. We leave it as an exercise to verify that $O(f(n))$ and $O(g(n))$ are not comparable by showing that neither is a subset of the other. This is illustrated in the Venn diagram in Figure 3.12, which includes sample members of $O(f(n))$ and $O(g(n))$. We also leave it as an exercise to find strictly increasing functions whose orders are not comparable.

FIGURE 3.11

An increasing chain in the hierarchy of orders

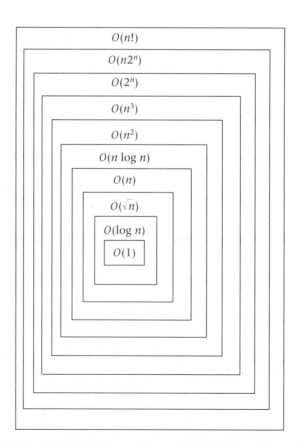

FIGURE 3.12

Incomparable
orders. Sample
functions are shown
in each region.

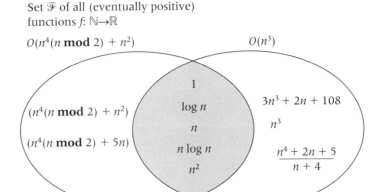

3.1.5 Establishing Order Relationships

We now discuss some techniques for establishing the order relationship between two functions $f(n)$ and $g(n)$. Sometimes we can do this directly from the definitions of Θ, O, Ω. For example, in Proposition 3.1.3, we show that a polynomial of degree k is in $\Theta(n^k)$. We assume that the leading coefficient of the polynomial is positive to ensure that the polynomial is eventually positive (and hence belongs to $\mathscr{F}$).

Proposition 3.1.3   Let $P(n) = a_k n^k + a_{k-1} n^{k-1} + \cdots + a_1 n + a_0$ be any polynomial of degree k, $a_k > 0$. Then

$$P(n) \in \Theta(n^k).$$

PROOF

By property (2) of Proposition 3.1.2, it is sufficient to show that $P(n) \in O(n^k)$ and $P(n) \in \Omega(n^k)$. We first show that $P(n) \in O(n^k)$.

$$
\begin{aligned}
P(n) &= a_k n^k + a_{k-1} n^{k-1} + \cdots + a_1 n + a_0 \\
&\leq a_k n^k + |a_{k-1}| n^k + \cdots + |a_1| n^k + |a_0| n^k \\
&\leq (a_k + |a_{k-1}| + \cdots + |a_1| + |a_0|) n^k
\end{aligned}
$$

Thus, if $c = a_k + |a_{k-1}| + \cdots + |a_1| + |a_0|$, then $P(n) \leq cn^k$ for all $n \geq n_0 = 1$, so that $P(n) \in O(n^k)$. We now show that $P(n) \in \Omega(n^k)$.

$$P(n) = a_k n^k + a_{k-1} n^{k-1} + \cdots + a_1 n + a_0$$

$$\geq a_k n^k - |a_{k-1}| n^{k-1} - \cdots - |a_1| n - |a_0|$$

$$= \left(\frac{a_k}{2}\right) n^k + \left[\left(\frac{a_k}{2}\right) n^k - |a_{k-1}| n^{k-1} - \cdots - |a_1| n - |a_0|\right]$$

$$\geq \left(\frac{a_k}{2}\right) n^k + \left[\left(\frac{a_k}{2}\right) n^k - (|a_{k-1}| n^{k-1} + \cdots + |a_1| n^{k-1} + |a_0| n^{k-1})\right]$$

$$= \left(\frac{a_k}{2}\right) n^k + \left[\left(\frac{a_k}{2}\right) n - (|a_{k-1}| + \cdots + |a_1| + |a_0|)\right] n^{k-1}$$

If $c = a_k/2$ and $n_0 = (|a_{k-1}| + \cdots + |a_1| + |a_0|)(2/a_k)$, the term inside the bracket in the last equation is nonnegative for all $n \geq n_0$; thus, $P(n) \geq cn^k$ for all $n \geq n_0$. This shows that $P(n) \in \Omega(n^k)$, completing the proof of Proposition 3.1.3.   ■

The complexity $t(n)$ of an algorithm is said to be *polynomial* if $t(n) \in O(n^k)$ for some nonnegative integer k. This implies that logarithmic, linear, quadratic, and $n\log n$ functions are all examples of polynomial complexity, but we usually use the more precise terminologies to describe these commonly occurring complexities. In complexity theory, an algorithm exhibiting polynomial complexity is usually regarded as "good." However, there are many important problems for which only super-polynomial algorithms are known. The complexity $t(n)$ of an algorithm is said to be *super-polynomial* if $t(n) \in \Omega(n^k)$ for *every* nonnegative integer k.

Exponential complexities are super-polynomial; however, there are (infinitely) many complexities between polynomial and exponential complexities. One such example is $n^{\ln n}$ (see Exercise 3.7).

Proving directly from the definition of Θ that a polynomial of degree k belongs to $\Theta(n^k)$ was not too difficult. It would be more difficult, for example, to prove directly from the definition that $2n^{3/2} + 6n\ln n \in \Theta(n^{3/2})$. Proposition 3.1.4 provides a useful test for comparing the orders of two functions $f, g \in \mathcal{F}$ when the limit of the ratio $f(n)/g(n)$ exists as n approaches infinity.

Proposition 3.1.4   **The Ratio Limit Theorem**

Let $f(n), g(n) \in \mathcal{F}$. If the limit of the ratio $f(n)/g(n)$ exists as n approaches infinity, then f and g are comparable. Moreover, assuming $L = \lim_{n \to \infty} f(n)/g(n)$ exists, then the following results hold:

1. $0 < L < \infty \Rightarrow f(n) \in \Theta(g(n))$ (*f* and *g* have the same order).
2. $L = 0 \Rightarrow O(f(n)) \subset O(g(n))$ (*f* has a *smaller* order than *g*).
3. $L = \infty \Rightarrow O(g(n)) \subset O(f(n))$ (*f* has a *larger* order than *g*).

PROOF

The definition of $\lim_{n\to\infty} f(n)/g(n) = L$ states that for any given real number $\varepsilon > 0$, there exists an integer N_ε (depending on ε) such that for all $n \geq N_\varepsilon$, $|f(n)g(n) - L| < \varepsilon$, or equivalently,

$$(L - \varepsilon)g(n) < f(n) < (L + \varepsilon)g(n), \quad \text{for all } n \geq N_\varepsilon. \tag{3.1.5}$$

Case 1: $0 < L < \infty$. We are free to choose ε to be any positive real number. In particular, we can choose $\varepsilon = L/2$. Setting $c_1 = L/2$, $c_2 = 3L/2$, and $n_0 = N_{L/2}$ and substituting these values into Formula (3.1.5) yields

$$c_1 g(n) < f(n) < c_2 g(n), \quad \text{for all } n \geq n_0. \tag{3.1.6}$$

Hence, $f(n) \in \Theta(g(n))$.

Case 2: $L = 0$. Substituting $L = 0$ into Formula (3.1.5), for *any* positive real number ε, we have

$$f(n) < \varepsilon g(n), \quad \text{for all } n \geq N_\varepsilon. \tag{3.1.7}$$

It follows immediately that $f(n) \in O(g(n))$. To prove that $O(f(n)) \subset O(g(n))$, it is necessary to show that $f(n) \notin \Omega(g(n))$. Assume to the contrary that there exist constants c and n_0 such that

$$cg(n) \leq f(n), \quad \text{for all } n \geq n_0. \tag{3.1.8}$$

Substituting $\varepsilon = c$ in Formula (3.1.7) yields $f(n) < cg(n)$ for all $n \geq N_c$. Thus, for any integer n larger than the maximum of n_0 and N_c, $f(n) < cg(n)$ and $cg(n) \leq f(n)$, which is a contradiction. Hence, $f(n) \notin \Omega(g(n))$, which implies that $O(f(n)) \subset O(g(n))$.

Case 3: $L = \infty$. For this case, the proof that $O(g(n)) \subset O(f(n))$ is left as an exercise. ■

REMARK

A partial converse to case 2 of Proposition 3.1.4 is true: If $O(f(n)) \subset O(g(n))$ and $\lim_{n\to\infty} f(n)/g(n)$ exists, then this limit must be zero. It is easy to construct examples where $O(f(n)) \subset O(g(n))$ but $\lim_{n\to\infty} f(n)/g(n)$ does not exist (see Exercise 3.18). This remark also applies to the other two cases of Proposition 3.1.4.

The condition $\lim_{n\to\infty} f(n)/g(n) = 0$ is so useful in mathematics that the following special notation is used to denote the corresponding relation on the set of real-valued functions.

DEFINITION 3.1.6 Given the function $g(n)$, we define $o(g(n))$ to be the set of all the functions $f(n)$ having the property that

$$\lim_{n\to\infty}\frac{f(n)}{g(n)} = 0.$$

If $f(n) \in o(g(n))$, we say that $f(n)$ *is little oh of* $g(n)$.

REMARK

In the mathematical literature, $f(n) \in o(g(n))$ is usually written $f(n) = o(g(n))$.

DEFINITION 3.1.7 Given the function $g(n)$, we define $\sim(g(n))$ to be the set of all functions $f(n)$ having the property that

$$\lim_{n\to\infty}\frac{f(n)}{g(n)} = 1.$$

If $f(n) \in \sim(g(n))$, then we say that $f(n)$ is strongly asymptotic to $g(n)$ and denote this by writing $f(n) \sim g(n)$.

Proposition 3.1.5 follows immediately from the ratio limit theorem and the definitions of o and $\sim$.

Proposition 3.1.5 Let $f(n), g(n) \in \mathcal{F}$. Then

1. $f(n) \sim g(n) \Rightarrow f(n) \in \Theta(g(n))$
2. $f(n) \in o(g(n)) \Rightarrow O(f(n)) \subset O(g(n))$. ■

We illustrate Proposition 3.1.5 by proving the following stronger version of Proposition 3.1.3 concerning the asymptotic behavior of polynomials.

Proposition 3.1.6 Let $P(n) = a_k n^k + \cdots + a_1 n + a_0$ be any polynomial of degree k, $a_k > 0$. Then

$$P(n) \sim a_k n^k$$

PROOF

Consider the ratio $(a_k n^k + \cdots + a_0)/a_k n^k$ as n approaches infinity:

$$\lim_{n \to \infty} \frac{(a_k n^k + \cdots + a_0)}{a_k n^k}$$

$$= \lim_{n \to \infty} \left(1 + \frac{a_{k-1}}{a_k n} + \cdots + \frac{a_1}{a_k n^{k-1}} + \frac{a_0}{a_k n^k} \right) = 1.$$

Proposition 3.1.6 now follows immediately from property (1) of the ratio limit theorem. ■

For example, because the binomial coefficient $C(n,k)$ is a polynomial of degree k with leading coefficient $1/k!$, it follows that $C(n,k) \sim n^k/k!$.

Applying Propositions 3.1.4 and 3.1.5 requires calculating $\lim_{n \to \infty} f(n)/g(n)$, which might be difficult to do directly. When calculating $\lim_{n \to \infty} f(n)/g(n)$, a powerful tool from calculus, known as L'Hôpital's rule, is often helpful. Application of L'Hôpital's rule requires extending $f(n)$ and $g(n)$ to functions $f(x)$ and $g(x)$, respectively, both of which are differentiable for sufficiently large real numbers x.

3.1.6 L'Hôpital's Rule

Let $f(x)$ and $g(x)$ be functions that are differentiable for sufficiently large real numbers x. If $\lim_{x \to \infty} f(x) = \infty$ and $\lim_{x \to \infty} g(x) = \infty$, then

$$\lim_{n \to \infty} \frac{f(x)}{g(x)} = \lim_{n \to \infty} \frac{f'(x)}{g'(x)}.$$

We now apply the ratio limit theorem to an example that makes use of L'Hôpital's rule. We show that $2n^{3/2} + 6n \ln n \in \Theta(n^{3/2})$ by considering the ratio $(2n^{3/2} + 6n \ln n)/n^{3/2}$ as n approaches infinity. We have

$$\lim_{x \to \infty} \frac{(2x^{3/2} + 6x \ln x)}{x^{3/2}} = 2 + 6 \lim_{x \to \infty} \frac{\ln x}{x^{1/2}}$$

$$= 2 + 6 \lim_{x \to \infty} \frac{1/x}{(1/2)x^{-1/2}} \qquad \text{(by L'Hôpital's rule)}$$

$$= 2 + 12 \lim_{x \to \infty} \frac{1}{x^{1/2}} = 2 + 0 = 2.$$

In our second illustration, we show that any polynomial has smaller order than any exponential function.

Proposition 3.1.7 For any nonnegative real constants k and a, with $a > 1$,

$$O(n^k) \subset O(a^n).$$

PROOF

Consider the ratio n^k/a^n. Repeated applications of L'Hôpital's rule yields

$$\lim_{n \to \infty} \frac{n^k}{a^n} = \lim_{n \to \infty} \frac{kn^{k-1}}{(\ln a)a^n}$$

$$= \lim_{n \to \infty} \frac{k(k-1)n^{k-2}}{(\ln a)^2 a^n}$$

$$\vdots$$

$$= \lim_{n \to \infty} \frac{k!}{(\ln a)^k a^n} = 0.$$

Hence, $n^k \in O(a^n)$. Proposition 3.1.7 now follows from the ratio limit theorem. ■

3.1.7 Asymptotic Notation for Functions of Several Variables

Occasionally, the input size of an algorithm is a function of two or more variables as opposed to a single variable n. For example, in the case of graph algorithms, the input size is often measured in terms of the number of vertices n and the number of edges m in the graph. In the case of algorithms for searching or sorting lists, we sometimes measure the input size in terms of the total number n of *list* elements and the number m of *distinct* elements. One such algorithm is *BingoSort* (see Chapter 5), which performs order mn comparisons in the average and worst cases and $n + m^2$ comparisons in the best case. Adequate description of this behavior clearly requires that the complexity be measured as a function of *both* n and m. Hence, we describe the best-case, worst-case, and average complexities as functions $B(n,m)$, $W(n,m)$, and $A(n,m)$, respectively.

We do not give a formal theory of order for functions of two or more variables but rely on an analogy with the theory developed for single-variable functions. For example, given a real-valued function $g(n,m)$ of two nonnegative variables n and m, we say that $g(n,m)$ is *eventually nonnegative* if there exists a positive number n_0 such that $g(n,m) \geq 0$ whenever $n \geq n_0$ and $m \geq n_0$. Similarly, the set $O(g(n,m))$ consists of those eventually nonnegative functions $f(n,m)$ that are eventually bounded above by a constant multiple of $g(n,m)$. More precisely, $f(n,m) \in O(g(n,m))$ if and only if there exist positive integers c and n_0, such that $f(n,m) \leq cg(n,m)$ for all $n,m \geq n_0$. The sets $\Theta(g(n,m))$ and $\Omega(g(n,m))$ are defined similarly. The notions also extend to functions of more than two variables.

3.2 Asymptotic Order Formulae for Three Important Series

In this section, we determine the asymptotic order for three mathematical series that occur often in algorithm analysis—namely, the sum of powers $S(n,k) = 1^k + 2^k + \cdots + n^k$, where k is a nonnegative integer; the sum of logarithms $L(b,n) = \log_b 1 + \log_b 2 + \cdots + \log_b n = \log_b(n!)$; and the harmonic series $H(n) = 1 + 1/2 + \cdots + 1/n$. We will present important applications of all of these formulas throughout the text.

3.2.1 Sums of Powers

$S(n,1) = 1 + 2 + \cdots + n$ is certainly one of the most frequently occurring series in algorithm analysis. For example, it comes up later in this chapter in the analysis of adjacent-key comparison sorting. On the other hand, $S(n,k)$, $k > 1$, occurs only occasionally—for example, when establishing the average complexity of the algorithm *ProbeLinSrch* for searching a link-ordered list (see Chapter 6).

In Proposition 3.2.1, we derive the recurrence relation, Formula (3.2.1), that does not yield an explicit formula for $S(n,k)$ for a general k but nevertheless can be used to show that $S(n,k)$ is a polynomial in n of degree $k + 1$. It is interesting that Pascal knew about this recurrence relation and in fact published it in a slightly more general form (see Exercise 3.33).

Proposition 3.2.1 Given any nonnegative k, $S(n,k) = 1^k + 2^k + \cdots + n^k$ satisfies the recurrence relation

$$S(n,k) = \frac{1}{k+1}\left[(n+1)^{k+1} - 1 - \left(\binom{k+1}{0}S(n,0) + \binom{k+1}{1}S(n,1)\right.\right.$$

$$\left.\left. + \cdots + \binom{k+1}{k-1}S(n,k-1)\right)\right] \text{ init. cond. } S(n,0)) = n. \textbf{(3.2.1)}$$

PROOF

The following proof amounts to interchanging the order of summation, using the binomial theorem, and noting the resulting telescoping sum.

$$\sum_{j=0}^{k}\binom{k+1}{j}S(n,j) = \sum_{j=0}^{k}\binom{k+1}{j}\sum_{i=1}^{n}i^j$$

$$= \sum_{i=1}^{n}\sum_{j=0}^{k}\binom{k+1}{j}i^j \text{ (by interchanging the order of summation)}$$

$$= \sum_{i=1}^{n}[(1+i)^{k+1} - i^{k+1}] \text{ (by the binomial theorem)}$$

$$= (1+n)^{k+1} - 1 \text{ (by "telescoping sum").} \qquad \textbf{(3.2.2)}$$

Formula (3.2.1) follows immediately from Formula (3.2.2) by isolating the term $S(n,k)$. ■

To illustrate Formula (3.2.1), we can apply it to obtain an explicit formula for $S_1(n)$ and $S_2(n)$. Substituting $k = 1$ in (3.2.1), we obtain

$$S(n,1) = \frac{1}{2}\left[(n + 1)^2 - 1 - \binom{2}{0}S(n,0)\right] = \frac{1}{2}(n^2 + 2n - n) = \frac{1}{2}n(n + 1).$$

Substituting $k = 2$ in (3.2.1), we obtain

$$S(n,2) = \frac{1}{3}\left[(n + 1)^3 - 1 - \left(\binom{3}{0}S(n,0) + \binom{3}{1}S(n,1)\right)\right]$$

$$= \frac{1}{3}[(n + 1)^3 - 1 - (n + 3n(n + 1)/2)]$$

$$= \frac{1}{3}[n^3 + 3n^2/2 + n/2] = \frac{1}{6}n(n + 1)(2n + 1).$$

The exact value of $S(n,k)$ is not as important as its asymptotic growth rate, as determined from Proposition 3.2.2.

Proposition 3.2.2 $S(n,k) = 1^k + 2^k + \cdots + n^k$ is a polynomial in n of degree $k + 1$ with leading (highest degree) coefficient $1/(k + 1)$.

PROOF

The proof proceeds by induction (strong form, see Appendix C) on k.

Basis step: $S(n,0) = 1^0 + 2^0 + \cdots + n^0 = n$, a polynomial of degree $0 + 1$ with leading coefficient $1/(0+1)$.

Induction step: Given a positive integer k, assume $S(n,j)$ is a polynomial in n with leading coefficient $1/(j + 1)$ for all positive integers $j < k$. We must show that $S(n,k)$ is a polynomial in n of degree $k + 1$ with leading coefficient $1/(k + 1)$. From Formula (3.2.1),

$$S(n,k) = \frac{(n + 1)^{k+1}}{k + 1} + P_k(n), \tag{3.2.3}$$

where

$$P_k(n) = \frac{-1}{k + 1}\left(1 + \binom{k + 1}{0}S(n,0) + \binom{k + 1}{1}S(n,1)\right.$$

$$\left. + \cdots + \binom{k + 1}{k + 1}S(n,k - 1)\right).$$

The strong form of our induction step implies that $P_k(n)$ is a polynomial in n of degree k. By the binomial theorem, $(n + 1)^{k + 1}$ is a polynomial in n of degree $k + 1$ with leading coefficient 1. Proposition 3.2.2 follows from this latter observation and Formula (3.2.3). ■

Various other properties of $S(n,k)$ that follow easily from (3.2.1) and induction are developed in the exercises. For example, based on (3.2.1), it is straightforward to give a recurrence relation for the coefficients of the polynomial representing $S(n,k)$. These coefficients are known as *Bernoulli numbers* $B(j,k)$, where $B(j,k)$ is the coefficient of n^j in the polynomial representing $S(n,k)$. For example, $B(0,k) = 0$ and $B(k,k+1) = 1/(k+1)$ when $k \geq 0$, $B(k,k) = 1/2$ when $k \geq 1$, and $B(k-1,k) = k/12$ when $k \geq 2$.

Because $S(n,k) = 1^k + 2^k + \cdots + n^k$ is a polynomial of degree $k + 1$ with (highest order) leading coefficient $1/(k + 1)$, it follows from Proposition 3.1.6 that $S(n,k) \sim n^k/(k + 1)$.

3.2.2 Sums of Logarithms

The sum $L(b,n) = \log_b 1 + \log_b 2 + \cdots + \log_b n = \log_b(n!)$ is another frequently occurring series in algorithm analysis. For example, we show later in this chapter that $L(2,n)$ is a lower bound for the worst-case complexity of any comparison-based sorting algorithm.

Recall that for any real constants a and $b > 1$, $\log_a n \in \Theta(\log_b n)$; thus, we can use *any* base when representing this Θ-class. For convenience, we denote this class simply by $\Theta(\log n)$. Similarly, it is clear that $L(a,n) \in \Theta(L(b,n))$, so again, we can use *any* base when representing this Θ-class. Thus, for convenience of notation, we drop the base and simply write

$$L(n) = \log(n!) = \log 1 + \log 2 + \cdots + \log n.$$

| **Proposition 3.2.3** | $\log(n!) \in \Theta(n\log n)$. |

PROOF

Clearly, $L(n) \in O(n\log n)$ because

$$\log 1 + \log 2 + \cdots + \log n \leq \log n + \log n + \cdots + \log n = n\log n.$$

It remains to show that $L(n) \in \Omega(n\log n)$. Let $m = \lfloor n/2 \rfloor$. We have

$$\begin{aligned} L(n) &= (\log 1 + \log 2 + \cdots + \log m) + [\log(m + 1) + \log(m + 2) + \cdots + \log n] \\ &\geq \log(m + 1) + \log(m + 2) + \cdots + \log n \\ &\geq \log(m + 1) + \log(m + 1) + \cdots + \log(m + 1) \\ &= (n - m)\log(m + 1) \\ &\geq (n/2)\log(n/2) = (n/2)(\log n - \log 2). \end{aligned}$$

Clearly, $(n/2)(\log n - \log 2) \geq (n/2)[\log n - (1/2)\log n]$ for all $n \geq n_0$, where n_0 is sufficiently large (the constant n_0 depends on the base chosen). Thus, $L(n) \geq (1/4)(n\log n)$, $n \geq n_0$, so that $L(n) \in \Omega(n\log n)$. ■

3.2.3 The Harmonic Series

Our third example, the harmonic series $H(n) = 1 + 1/2 + \cdots + 1/n$, also occurs frequently in algorithm analysis. For example, $H(n)$ will occur in the average analysis of *QuickSort* given in Chapter 6.

Proposition 3.2.4

$H(n) \sim \ln n$. Thus, $H(n) \in \Theta(\log n)$.

PROOF

By definition, $\int_1^n 1/x\,dx = \ln n$, so that $\ln n$ is the area bounded above by the graph of $1/x$ and bounded below by the interval $1 \le x \le n$ on the x-axis. We see from Figure 3.13 that this area is larger than the sum of the areas of the rectangles R_i, $i = 1, \ldots, n - 1$, where the base of R_i is the interval (of unit length) $i \le x \le i + 1$, and the height of R_i equals $1/(i + 1)$. Clearly, this area is smaller than the sum of the areas of the rectangles R_i^*, $i = 1, \ldots, n - 1$, where R_i^* has the same base as R but has height $1/i$. Thus,

$$H(n) - 1 \le \int_1^n \frac{1}{x}\,dx \le H(n) - \frac{1}{n}. \tag{3.2.4}$$

FIGURE 3.13

$H(n) - 1 \le$

$\int_1^n 1/x\,dx \le$

$H(n) - 1/n$

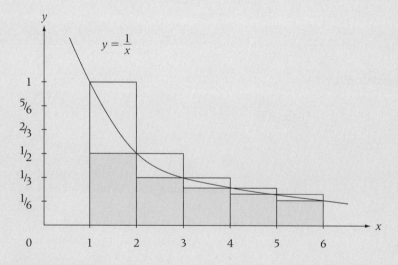

Proposition 3.2.4 follows after dividing each of the three terms in Formula (3.2.4) by $H(n)$ and taking the limit as n approaches infinity. The two outside limits are 1, so the middle limit must exist and also be 1. Showing that the outside limits are 1 amounts to showing that $\lim_{n \to \infty} H(n) = \infty$ (see Exercise 3.28). ■

3.3 Recurrence Relations for Complexity

A recurrence relation typically expresses the value of a function at an input n in terms of the value of the function at a smaller value or values of the input to the function. For example, when analyzing the performance of an algorithm based on a recursive strategy (whether or not the algorithm is expressed explicitly as a recursive algorithm), often we can immediately give a recurrence relation for its complexity for inputs of size n, because the recurrence relation works by repeating the algorithm's operations on an input or inputs of smaller size. Recurrence relations are so natural in determining the complexity of algorithms based on a recursive strategy that we state this as a key fact.

Key Fact

When analyzing the worst-case complexity $W(n)$ of a algorithm based on a recursive strategy, a recurrence relation should immediately emerge because the worst case usually requires that the algorithm perform the repeated operations with smaller input sizes that exhibit worst-case performance. The same is true for the best-case complexity $B(n)$ and the average complexity $A(n)$, although finding (and solving) a recurrence for $A(n)$ is usually more challenging.

To illustrate this key fact, we first consider a binary search. For an input list generating worst-case behavior, a binary search always begins comparing to the midpoint element and then looks for the search element in the larger sublist, which has size $\lceil n/2 \rceil$. Hence, we obtain the following recurrence for $W(n)$:

$$W(n) = W(\lceil n/2 \rceil) + 1, \quad \textbf{init. cond. } W(1) = 1. \qquad \textbf{(3.3.1)}$$

The occurrence of the ceiling function $\lceil \ \rceil$ in Formula (3.3.1) makes it cumbersome to solve. However, if we assume that $n = 2^k$, the relation becomes

$$W(n) = W(n/2) + 1, \quad \textbf{init. cond. } W(1) = 1. \qquad \textbf{(3.3.2)}$$

The recurrence in Formula (3.3.2) can be solved by the method of *repeated substitution* (also called *unwinding*). First, we substitute $n/2$ for n to get

$W(n/2) = W((n/2)/2) + 1$, and then we can use $W((n/2)/2) + 1$ to replace $W(n/2)$. Repeating this substitution process we obtain

$$W(n) = W\left(\frac{n}{2}\right) + 1$$

$$= \left(W\left(\frac{(n/2)}{2}\right) + 1\right) + 1 = W\left(\frac{n}{2^2}\right) + 2$$

$$= \left(W\left(\frac{(n/2^2)}{2}\right) + 1\right) + 2 = W\left(\frac{n}{2^3}\right) + 3$$

$$\vdots$$

$$= \left(W\left(\frac{(n/2^{k-1})}{2}\right) + 1\right) + k - 1 = W\left(\frac{n}{2^k}\right) + k = W(1) + k = 1 + k.$$

Because $k = \log_2 n$, we have

$$W(n) = 1 + \log_2 n, \quad n = 2^k. \tag{3.3.3}$$

We now show how we can use Formula (3.3.3) to obtain an approximation for $W(n)$, for any general n, that is accurate to within a single comparison. Given any positive integer n, there exists a positive integer j such that

$$2^{j-1} \le n < 2^j. \tag{3.3.4}$$

Clearly, $W(m) \le W(n)$ for $m \le n$. Thus,

$$W(2^{j-1}) \le W(n) \le W(2^j). \tag{3.3.5}$$

By Formula (3.3.3), $W(2^{j-1}) = j$ and $W(2^j) = j + 1$. Substituting these results into Formula (3.3.5) yields

$$j \le W(n) \le j + 1. \tag{3.3.6}$$

By taking base-2 logarithms in Formula (3.3.4), we obtain

$$j - 1 \le \log_2 n < j. \tag{3.3.7}$$

Combining Formulas (3.3.6) and (3.3.7) yields

$$\log_2 n < W(n) \le 2 + \log_2 n, \quad n \ge 1. \tag{3.3.8}$$

Because $W(n)$ is an integer, Formula (3.3.8) implies

$$1 + \lfloor \log_2 n \rfloor \leq W(n) \leq 2 + \lfloor \log_2 n \rfloor, \quad n \geq 1. \qquad \textbf{(3.3.9)}$$

It follows from Formula (3.3.9) that $W(n) \in \Theta(\log n)$.

For many of the algorithms that we will analyze using recurrence relations, we will make the simplifying assumption that n is a power of some base b. For most functions that we will encounter, the asymptotic behavior of the function is determined by its behavior at the powers of the base b. In other words, we can "interpolate" the asymptotic behavior between powers of b. We give a general condition for functions for which this interpolation is possible in Appendix D.

As a second illustration of the key fact, we consider the worst-case complexity of *MergeSort*. Again, we assume that $n = 2^k$ for some nonnegative integer k. Since the worst-case complexity of *Merge* is $n - 1$, $W(n)$ satisfies the following recurrence relation:

$$W(n) = 2W\left(\frac{n}{2}\right) + n - 1, \quad W(1) = 0. \qquad \textbf{(3.3.10)}$$

Unwinding the recurrence relation in Formula (3.3.10), we obtain

$$W(n) = 2\left(2W\left(\frac{n}{2^2}\right) + \frac{n}{2} - 1\right) + n - 1 = 2^2 W\left(\frac{n}{2^2}\right) + 2n - (1 + 2)$$

$$= 2^2\left(2W\left(\frac{n}{2^3}\right) + \frac{n}{2^2} - 1\right) + 2n - (1 + 2) = 2^3 W\left(\frac{n}{2^3}\right) + 3n - (1 + 2 + 2^2)$$

$$\vdots$$

$$= 2^k W(1) + kn - (1 + 2 + 2^2 + \cdots + 2^{k-1}) = kn - (2^k - 1).$$

Because $k = \log_2 n$, we have

$$W(n) = n\log_2 n - n + 1, \quad \text{for } n = 2^k, \quad k = 0, 1, 2, \ldots \qquad \textbf{(3.3.11)}$$

Now that we have established a formula for $W(n)$ when n is a power of 2, similar to the situation for binary search we can interpolate the asymptotic behavior of $W(n)$ for all n, and conclude that $W(n) \in \Theta(n\log n)$.

Note that the recurrence relations for binary search and *MergeSort* related $W(n)$ to $W(n/2)$. More generally, whenever the recursive strategy for an algorithm repeats the algorithm's operations on an input size that is a fixed fraction n/b of the original input size n, such as in divide-and-conquer strategies, then the recurrence relations for $W(n)$ will be in terms of $W(n/b)$. Thus, we now consider the general solution to recurrence relations that relate the nth term to the $(n/b)^{\text{th}}$ term.

3.3.1 Solving Linear Recurrence Relations Relating the nth Term to the $(n/b)^{th}$ Term

As mentioned in the previous section, the following general recurrence relation arises often when analyzing divide-and-conquer algorithms:

$$t(n) = at\left(\frac{n}{b}\right) + f(n), \quad t(1) = c_1, n = b^k, b > 1, k = 0, 1, 2, ... \textbf{(3.3.12)}$$

The recurrence relation in Formula (3.3.12) can be solved by repeated substitution. The recurrence is stated for powers of a base b. Unwinding (3.3.12), we obtain

$$t(n) = at\left(\frac{n}{b}\right) + f(n)$$
$$= a\left(at\left(\frac{n}{b^2}\right) + f\left(\frac{n}{b}\right)\right) + f(n) = a^2t\left(\frac{n}{b^2}\right) + af\left(\frac{n}{b}\right) + f(n).$$
$$\vdots \hspace{5cm} \textbf{(3.3.13)}$$
$$= a^k c_1 + a^{k-1}f\left(\frac{n}{b^{k-1}}\right) + a^{k-2}f\left(\frac{n}{b^{k-2}}\right) + \cdots + af\left(\frac{n}{b}\right) + f(n)$$
$$= a^k c_1 + \sum_{i=0}^{k-1} a^i f\left(\frac{n}{b^i}\right), \quad \text{where } k = \log_b n.$$

Two special cases of Formula (3.3.13) that arise often are when $f(n) = c$ and when $f(n) = cn$. Consider the case $f(n) = c$. First, suppose that $a \neq 1$. Substituting $f(n) = c$ into (3.3.13) and simplifying using the identities

$$\sum_{i=0}^{k-1} a^i = \frac{a^k - 1}{a - 1} \quad \text{and} \quad a^k = (b^{\log_b a})^k = (b^k)^{\log_b a} = n^{\log_b a}$$

yields

$$t(n) = c_1 a^k + c\sum_{i=0}^{k-1} a^i$$
$$= c_1 a^k + c\frac{a^k - 1}{a - 1}$$
$$= \left(c_1 + \frac{c}{a - 1}\right)a^k - \frac{c}{a - 1} \hspace{2cm} \textbf{(3.3.14)}$$
$$= \left(c_1 + \frac{a}{a - 1}\right)n^{\log_b a} - \frac{c}{a - 1}.$$

We leave it as an exercise to show that when $a = 1$, $t(n) = c_1 + c\log_b n$.

Now consider the case $f(n) = cn$. Substituting $f(n) = cn$ into Formula (3.3.13) and setting $a = b$ immediately yields

$$t(n) = c_1 n + cn\log_b n, \; n = 1, b, b^2, \ldots.$$

Substituting $f(n) = cn$ in the case $a \neq b$ and simplifying yields

$$t(n) = c_1 a^k + cn \sum_{i=0}^{k-1}\left(\frac{a}{b}\right)^i$$

$$= c_1 a^k + cn\frac{(a/b)^k - 1}{(a/b) - 1} \quad \left(\text{using the identity } \sum_{i=0}^{k-1}x^i = \frac{x^k - 1}{x - 1}\right)$$

$$= c_1 n^{\log_b a} + c\frac{n^{\log_b a} - n}{(a/b) - 1} \quad (\text{substituting } a^k = n^{\log_b a} \text{ and } b^k = n).$$

Thus, in the case where $f(n) = cn$, Formula (3.3.13) simplifies to

$$t(n) = \begin{cases} c_1 n + cn\log_b n, \; a = b, \\ c_1 n^{\log_b a} + c\dfrac{n^{\log_b a} - n}{(a/b) - 1}, a \neq b, \end{cases} \quad n = 1, b, b^2, \ldots \quad \textbf{(3.3.15)}$$

Using the fact that the functions n, $n\log n$, and $n^{\log_a b}$ are sufficiently well-behaved functions (Θ-invariant under scaling, see Appendix D), the next two propositions follow from Formulas (3.3.14) and (3.3.15), respectively.

Proposition 3.3.1 If $t(n)$ is eventually nondecreasing and satisfies the recurrence relation $t(n) = at(n/b) + c$, with initial condition $t(1) = c_1$, where a, b, c, and c_1 are positive constants and $b > 1$, then

$$t(n) \in \begin{cases} \Theta(n^{\log_b a}), a \neq 1, \\ \Theta(\log n), a = 1. \end{cases} \quad \textbf{(3.3.16)} \quad ■$$

Proposition 3.3.2 If $t(n)$ is eventually nondecreasing and satisfies the recurrence relation $t(n) = at(n/b) + cn$, with initial condition $t(1) = c_1$, where a, b, c, and c_1 are positive constants and $b > 1$, then

$$t(n) \in \begin{cases} \Theta(n), a < b \\ \Theta(n\log n), a = b, \\ \Theta(n^{\log_b a}), a > b. \end{cases} \quad \textbf{(3.3.17)} \quad ■$$

3.3.2 Solving Linear Recurrence Relations Relating the nth Term to the $(n-1)^{st}$ Term

Another type of recurrence relation that often arises when analyzing algorithms relates $W(n)$ to $W(n - 1)$. For example, consider the algorithm *InsertionSort* discussed in the previous chapter. For an input list $L[0:n - 1]$, the action of *InsertionSort* can be viewed as first executing *InsertionSort* with input list $L[0:n - 2]$, followed by inserting $L[n - 1]$ into the previously sorted list $L[0:n - 2]$. This observation immediately yields the following recurrence relation for $W(n)$:

$$W(n) = W(n - 1) + n - 1, \quad \textbf{init. cond. } W(1) = 0. \qquad \textbf{(3.3.18)}$$

An explicit formula for $W(n)$ is easily obtained by repeated substitution into Formula (3.3.18) as follows:

$$\begin{aligned}
W(n) &= W(n - 1) + n - 1 \\
&= (W(n - 2) + n - 2) + n - 1 \\
&= (W(n - 3) + n - 3) + n - 2 + n - 1 \\
&\;\;\vdots \\
&= W(1) + 1 + 2 + \cdots + n - 1 \\
&= n^2/2 - n/2.
\end{aligned}$$

Thus, $W(n) \in \Theta(n^2)$.

The recurrence relation in Formula (3.3.18) is a special case of the following more general recurrence relation, which can be solved by a simple repeated substitution (unwinding):

$$t(n) = at(n - 1) + f(n), \quad \textbf{init. cond. } t(1) = b, \qquad \textbf{(3.3.19)}$$

where a and b are positive constants.

Repeated substitution into Formula (3.3.19) yields

$$\begin{aligned}
t(n) &= at(n - 1) + f(n) \\
&= a(at(n - 2) + f(n - 1)) + f(n) = a^2 t(n - 2) + af(n - 1) + f(n) \\
&= a^2(at(n - 3) + f(n - 2)) + af(n - 1) + f(n) \\
&= a^3 t(n - 3) + a^2 f(n - 2) + af(n - 1) + f(n) \qquad \textbf{(3.3.20)} \\
&\;\;\vdots \\
&= a^{n-1}b + \sum_{i=2}^{n} a^{n-i} f(i).
\end{aligned}$$

Because Formula (3.3.19) involves a general function $f(n)$, the solution for $t(n)$ given in Formula (3.3.20) is a summation over n terms. For algorithm analysis, it is desirable to obtain a simple closed-form formula for the exact value of this summation, or at least for its order. For many algorithms considered in this text, such closed-form formulas can be derived using the standard formulas for arithmetic series, geometric series, sum of logarithms, harmonic series, and so forth. For example, suppose $f(n) = c$, where c is constant with respect to n. By substituting $f(n) = c$ in (3.3.20) and applying the standard formula for the geometric series $1 + r + r^2 + \cdots + r^{k-1} = (r^k - 1)/(r - 1)$, for $r \neq 1$ (see Appendix A), we get

$$t(n) = at(n - 1) + f(n)$$
$$= a^{n-1}b + \sum_{i=2}^{n} a^{n-i}f(i).$$
$$= a^{n-1}b + c\sum_{i=2}^{n} a^{n-i} \qquad \text{(3.3.21)}$$
$$= a^{n-1}b + c(a^{n-1} - 1)/(a - 1)$$
$$\in \Theta(a^n).$$

To illustrate this formula in use, we consider the number $t(n)$ of moves performed by *Towers* for n disks (see Appendix B). We can easily verify that $t(n)$ satisfies the following recurrence relation:

$$t(n) = 2t(n - 1) + 1, \quad \textbf{init. cond.} \ t(1) = 1.$$

Substituting $a = 2$, $b = 1$, and $c = 1$ in Formula (3.3.21), we obtain

$$t(n) = 2t(n - 1) + 1$$
$$= 2^{n-1}1 + (2^{n-1} - 1)$$
$$= 2^n - 1.$$

Thus, the Towers of Hanoi puzzle requires an exponential number of steps to solve. Using mathematical induction (Exercise 2.27), it is easily proved that *Towers* solves the Towers of Hanoi puzzle using the fewest possible moves.

The special case of (3.3.19) where $f(n) = cn$ is left to the exercises.

3.4 Mathematical Induction and Proving the Correctness of Algorithms

Even more basic than the need to analyze the efficiency of an algorithm is the need to determine whether the algorithm is correct. Indeed, an efficient algorithm is not particularly useful if it doesn't always produce the desired results. Proving algorithms are correct is most often done through mathematical induction (see Appendix C), which we usually perform using one or both of the following techniques:

1. Induction on the input size of the algorithm.
2. Induction to establish one or more loop invariants. Typically, a loop invariant is stated as an assertion concerning the value of a variable after each

iteration of a given loop, and the final value of the variable helps establish the correctness of the algorithm.

Induction on the input size is particularly relevant for an algorithm based on a recursive strategy, because the recursive execution of the operations usually involves smaller inputs where the induction hypothesis applies. Moreover, usually the strong form of induction is required because the recursion involves input sizes that can be smaller than 1 less than the size of the original input. For the purposes of induction, it is important to know what should be considered as the input size. For example, to implement the recursion of an algorithm like *MergeSort* or *QuickSort* for sorting a list $L[0:n-1]$, we include the additional input parameters *low* and *high*. The correct output for these algorithms is a sorting of $L[low:high]$ (so that $L[0:n-1]$ is sorted when called originally with $low = 0$ and $high = n-1$). Hence, the input size is $k = high - low + 1$.

PROOF OF CORRECTNESS OF *MERGESORT* IF *MERGE* IS CORRECT

Basis step: $k \leq 1$. *MergeSort* is clearly correct in the case of a one-element or empty sublist because the algorithm simply returns without any further action.

Induction step: Given an integer k such that $1 < k \leq n$, *assume* that *MergeSort* is correct for all sublists with $high - low + 1 < k$, and consider a sublist with $high - low + 1 = k$. Then *mid* is assigned the value, and *MergeSort* makes two recursive calls, with sublists $L[low:mid - 1]$ and $L[mid + 1:high]$. Both of these sublists have smaller size than k, so by our induction hypothesis, *MergeSort* sorts these sublists in increasing order. Hence, *MergeSort* is correct if *Merge* is correct.   ■

The proof that *Merge* is correct uses loop invariants and will be developed in the exercises. We now illustrate loop invariants by proving *HornerEval* is correct.

PROOF OF CORRECTNESS OF *HORNEREVAL*

We establish the correctness of *HornerEval* by using induction to show that the following loop invariant condition holds after the kth pass of the loop in *HornerEval*, $k = 0, 1, \ldots, n$:

Sum has the value $a[n]*v^k + a[n-1]*v^{k-1} + \cdots + a[n-k+1]*v + a[n-k]$.

Basis step: Before the loop is entered, *Sum* is assigned the value $a[n]$, so that the claim is true for $k = 0$.

Induction step: Assuming that the claim is true for $k < n$, we show that it is also true for $k + 1$. By assumption, the value of *Sum* after the kth pass is

$$a[n]*v^k + a[n-1]*v^{k-1} + \cdots + a[n-k+1]*v + a[n-k].$$

Now the $(k + 1)^{st}$ pass corresponds to the loop variable i having the value $n - k - 1$. Thus, after this pass, *Sum* has the value

$$(a[n]*v^k + a[n - 1]*v^{k-1} + \cdots + a[n - k + 1]*v + a[n - k])*v + a[n - k - 1]$$
$$= a[n]*v^{k+1} + a[n - 1]*v^k + \cdots + a[n - k + 1]*v^2 + a[n - k]*v + a[n - k - 1].$$

Hence, our claim is true for $k + 1$. By induction, our claim is therefore proved for all $k = 0, 1, \ldots, n$. The correctness of *HornerEval* now follows from our claim, since the algorithm terminates after the nth pass with the correct evaluation of the polynomial at v. ■

Our next illustration is proof of the correctness of the recursive algorithm *PowersRec* and its iterative version, *Powers*, both of which compute x^n for the input positive integer n and real number x. We prove *PowersRec* is correct by the strong form of induction on the exponent n (as we have mentioned, the input size to *PowersRec* is really $\log_2 n$, but this does not matter in the context of this proof). We then offer two proofs of the correctness of *Powers*; the first proof uses induction on n and is more elegant (and more subtle) than the second proof, which uses loop invariants. However, both proofs are rather more difficult than any of the other proofs that we present in this section.

PROOF OF CORRECTNESS OF *POWERSREC*

Basis step: $n = 1$. When $n = 1$, clearly *PowersRec* correctly returns x.

Induction step: We assume that *PowersRec* is correct for all exponents $1 \le k < n$, and consider an input with $k = n$. Assume first that n is even. Then *PowersRec* is recursively invoked with input parameters $x * x$ and $n/2$, which, by induction assumption, results in the return of $(x * x)^{n/2} = x^n$. This result is then returned by *PowersRec*, so the algorithm is correct when n is even. If n is odd, then *PowersRec* is recursively invoked with input parameters $x * x$ and $(n - 2)/2$, which, by induction assumption, results in the return of $(x * x)^{(n-1)/2} = x^{n-1}$. But then *PowersRec* returns $x * x^{n-1} = x^n$, so the algorithm is correct in this case also. ■

FIRST PROOF OF CORRECTNESS OF *POWERS* (INDUCTION ON *n*)

Basis step: $n = 1$. First *AccumPow* is initialized to 1 and *Pow* to x. Then, when $n = 1$, the while loop in *Powers* is skipped, and $x = AccumPow * Pow$ is correctly returned.

Induction step: We assume that *Powers* is correct for all exponents $1 \le k < n$ and consider an input with $k = n$. Suppose that n is even. Then, after the first iteration of the **while** loop, $AccumPow = 1$, $Pow = x * x$, and n is replaced by $n/2$. Thereafter, the action of the **while** loop is the same as when *Powers* is invoked with $x * x$ and $n/2$. Thus, by induction assumption, *Powers* returns $(x * x)^{n/2} = x^n$, which is correct.

Now suppose n is odd. After the first iteration of the **while** loop, *AccumPow* $= x$, *Pow* $= x * x$, and n is replaced by $n/2$. Thereafter, the action of the **while** loop is the same as when *Powers* is invoked with $x * x$ and $n/2$, except that the variable *AccumPow* is initialized to x instead of 1. In other words, *Powers* returns $x * Powers(x * x,(n - 1)/2)$. Hence, by induction assumption, *Powers* returns $x(x * x)^{(n-1)/2} = x^n$. ■

SECOND PROOF OF CORRECTNESS OF *POWERS* (LOOP INVARIANTS)

This proof relies heavily on the binary expansion $b_s b_{s-1} \ldots b_1 b_0$ of n, where $s = \lfloor \log_2 n \rfloor$ and $b_s = 1$. Then, letting $p = 2^s$, we have $x^n = x^p x^{n-p}$. The **while** loop in *Powers* computes x^p by simple squaring (using the variable *Pow*). The **while** loop computes $x^{n-p} = \displaystyle\prod_{b_k \neq 0, 0 \leq k \leq s-1} x^{2^k}$ by accumulating (using the variable *AccumPow*) the product of the appropriate factors x^{2^k} of x^{n-p} based on whether the current value of n is even or odd. We prove the correctness of *Powers* by establishing the following three loop invariants of the **while** loop. After i iterations of the **while** loop, $0 \leq i \leq s$, and the following loop invariants hold:

1. $n = b_s b_{s-1} \ldots b_i$ (in binary)
2. $Pow = x^{2^i}$
3. $AccumPow = \displaystyle\prod_{b_k \neq 0, 0 \leq k \leq i-1} x^{2^k}$

We assume that the product given in (3) is 1 when $b_k = 0$ for $0 \leq k \leq i$. We establish the validity of all three loop invariants using simple induction on i.

Basis step: $i = 0$. Before the **while** loop is entered, n, *Pow*, and *AccumPow* each have the values given by (1), (2), and (3), respectively.

Induction step: Assume that the loop invariants (1), (2), and (3) hold after $i - 1$ iterations of the **while** loop, and consider the state of the variables after the ith iteration. By induction hypothesis, $n = b_s b_{s-1} \ldots b_{i-1}$ (in binary) after the $(i - 1)^{\text{st}}$ iteration of the **while** loop. During the ith iteration, n is replaced by $n/2$. Since division by 2 in binary merely amounts to dropping the least significant binary digit, it follows that $n = b_s b_{s-1} \ldots b_i$ (in binary), so that loop invariant (1) holds. By induction hypothesis, $Pow = x^{2^{i-1}}$ after the $(i - 1)^{\text{st}}$ iteration of the **while** loop. During the ith iteration, *Pow* is replaced by $Pow * Pow = x^{2^{i-1}} * x^{2^{i-1}} = x^{2^i}$, so that loop invariant (2) holds. Finally, by induction hypothesis, *AccumPow* $=$

$\prod_{b_k \neq 0, 0 \leq k \leq i-2} x^{2^k}$, after the $(i-1)^{\text{st}}$ iteration of the **while** loop. During the ith iteration, *AccumPow* is multiplied by $Pow = x^{2^{i-1}}$ if $n = b_s b_{s-1} \ldots b_i$ is odd (i.e., if $b_i = 1$), otherwise *AccumPow* is unchanged. Hence, after the ith iteration, $AccumPow = \prod_{b_k \neq 0, 0 \leq k \leq i-1} x^{2^k}$, so that loop invariant (3) holds. Thus, we have established the validity of all three loop invariants.

With loop invariant (1), the **while** loop will execute exactly s times and then be exited, with $Pow = x^{2^s} = x^p$ and $AccumPow = \prod_{b_k \neq 0, 0 \leq k \leq s-1} x^{2^k} = x^{n-p}$ by loop invariants (2) and (3), respectively. Then *Powers* returns the value $Pow * AccumPow = x^p * x^{n-p} = x^n$. ■

3.5 Establishing Lower Bounds for Problems

Once we have found one or more algorithms solving a given problem, it is important to know whether these algorithms are the best possible. Lower-bound theory aids us in answering this question. The purpose of lower-bound theory is to obtain (as sharp as possible) lower bounds for the complexities of *any* algorithm that solves the problem. An algorithm whose complexity equals a lower bound that has been established is an optimal algorithm for the problem, and the lower bound is sharp. This sharp lower bound is the *complexity of the problem*. For example, we have no better algorithm for polynomial evaluation than *HornerEval*, because any correct algorithm for evaluating an nth-degree polynomial must perform at least n multiplications.

In this section, we introduce lower-bound theory by determining sharp lower bounds for a comparison-based searching algorithm to find the maximum value in a list of size n and for sorting a list of size n using an adjacent-key comparison-based sorting algorithm. A lower bound of $n - 1$ for the best-case, worst-case, and average complexities of any comparison-based algorithm for finding the maximum is established using a simple counting technique. Lower bounds of $n(n-1)/2$ for the worst-case complexity and $n(n-1)/4$ for the average complexity of an adjacent-key comparison-based sorting algorithm are obtained using simple properties of permutations. In the next section, we establish a lower bound of $(n/2)\log_2 n - n/2$ for the worst-case complexity of *any* comparison-based sorting algorithm. More sophisticated strategies for establishing lower bounds, such as comparison trees and adversary arguments, will be given in Chapter 25.

3.5.1 Lower Bound for Finding the Maximum

Consider the problem of using a comparison-based algorithm to find the maximum value of an element in a list $L[0{:}n - 1]$ of size n. Clearly, each list element must participate in at least one comparison, so that $\lceil n/2 \rceil$ is trivially a lower bound for the problem. We now use a simple counting argument to show that any comparison-based algorithm for finding the maximum value of an element in a list of size n must perform at least $n - 1$ comparisons for any input. The algorithm *Max* that makes a simple linear scan of of the list has best-case, worst-case, and average complexities all equaling $n - 1$, so that *Max* is an optimal algorithm.

For convenience, suppose we focus on lists that contain *distinct* elements. When a comparison-based algorithm compares two distinct elements X and Y, we say that X *wins* the comparison if $X > Y$, otherwise X *loses*. Thus, each comparison generates exactly one loss, and this is the unit of work that we associate with the comparison. Now we simply count the number of total losses that must occur if the algorithm is to correctly determine the maximum element. We claim that any comparison-based algorithm must generate at least $n - 1$ units of work. More precisely, we claim that each of the $n - 1$ elements that is *not* the maximum must lose at least one comparison. For example, suppose an input list $L[0{:}n - 1]$ causes the algorithm to terminate with two list elements $L[i]$ and $L[j]$, both of which never lost a comparison. Assume for definiteness that the algorithm declares $L[i]$ to be the maximum. Now consider the input list $L'[0{:}n - 1]$, which is identical to L except that $L'[j]$ is increased so that it is larger than $L[i]$ and remains different from any other list element. By the definition of comparison-based algorithms, our algorithm performs *identically* on L and L'. To see this, note that the algorithm could only perform differently when making comparisons involving $L'[j]$. However, $L[j]$ won all its comparisons, and because $L'[j] \geq L[j]$, so did $L'[j]$. Thus, the algorithm must again declare $L'[i] = L[i]$ to be the maximum element in L', which is a contradiction.

Thus, we have established that any comparison-based algorithm for finding the maximum element in a list of size n (of distinct elements) must perform at least $n - 1$ comparisons. Since *Max* performs $n - 1$ comparisons for *any* input list of size n, it is an optimal algorithm for the problem, as summarized in Proposition 3.5.1.

Proposition 3.5.1 The problem of finding the maximum element in a list of size n using a comparison-based algorithm has worst-case, best-case, and average complexities all equal to $n - 1$. Moreover, *Max* is an optimal algorithm for the problem. ■

3.5.2 Lower Bounds for Adjacent-Key Comparison Sorting

We now consider the problem of sorting a list using an adjacent-key comparison-based algorithm. As discussed earlier, we can view the sorting algorithm *InsertionSort* as an adjacent-key comparison sort. Recall that *InsertionSort* has worst-case complexity $W(n) = n(n - 1)/2$. In this section, we show that *any* adjacent-key comparison sort performs at least $n(n - 1)/2$ comparisons to sort a list $L[0:n - 1]$ of size n in the worst case. Hence, *InsertionSort* achieves optimal worst-case complexity for an adjacent-key comparison-based sort.

We may assume without loss of generality that the input lists of size n to the algorithm are chosen from the set of all permutations of the set of integers $\{1, 2, \ldots, n\}$. We associate with each permutation a combinatorial entity called an *inversion* of the permutation and show that the maximum number of inversions in a permutation on n symbols is given by $n(n - 1)/2$. Since interchanging adjacent list elements (keys) removes at most one inversion, the maximum number of inversions then serves as a lower bound for the problem of adjacent-key comparison-based sorting.

Proposition 3.5.2 A lower bound for the worst-case complexity $W(n)$ of any adjacent-key comparison-based sorting algorithm is $n(n - 1)/2$.

PROOF

Given a permutation π of $\{1, 2, \ldots, n\}$, an *inversion* of π is a pair $(\pi(a),\pi(b))$, $a, b \in \{1, 2, \ldots, n\}$, where $a < b$ but $\pi(a) > \pi(b)$. Figure 3.14 illustrates the inversions corresponding to the six permutations of $\{1, 2, 3\}$.

FIGURE 3.14

All permutations of $\{1,2,3\}$ and their associated inversions

$$\begin{pmatrix} 1 & 2 & 3 \\ \pi(1) & \pi(2) & \pi(3) \end{pmatrix}$$

Representation of a permutation π

$$\begin{pmatrix} 1\ 2\ 3 \\ 1\ 2\ 3 \end{pmatrix} \quad \begin{pmatrix} 1\ 2\ 3 \\ 1\ 3\ 2 \end{pmatrix} \quad \begin{pmatrix} 1\ 2\ 3 \\ 2\ 1\ 3 \end{pmatrix} \quad \begin{pmatrix} 1\ 2\ 3 \\ 2\ 3\ 1 \end{pmatrix} \quad \begin{pmatrix} 1\ 2\ 3 \\ 3\ 1\ 2 \end{pmatrix} \quad \begin{pmatrix} 1\ 2\ 3 \\ 3\ 2\ 1 \end{pmatrix}$$

none (3,2) (2,1) (2,1), (3,1) (3,1), (3,2) (3,2),(3,1),(2,1)

Note that any sorting algorithm must ultimately remove all inversions. Further, by definition, a comparison of list elements used by an adjacent-key comparison-based sorting algorithm considers only inversions of the form $(\pi(i),\pi(i + 1))$. Removing any such inversion (by interchanging $\pi(i)$ and $\pi(i + 1)$) results in a decrease of exactly one inversion (see Exercise 3.49). Thus, the worst-case complexity of any adjacent-key comparison-based sorting algorithm is bounded below by the maximum number of inversions in a permutation of $\{1, 2, \ldots, n\}$.

Consider the permutation corresponding to a list sorted in decreasing order—that is, the permutation $\pi(i) = n - i + 1$, $i = 1, \ldots, n$. Clearly, every pair $(\pi(i), \pi(j))$, $1 \leq i < j \leq n$, is an inversion of π. The number of such pairs is given by $\binom{n}{2} = n(n - 1)/2$ (see Chapter 1), establishing the lower bound given in Proposition 3.5.2. ■

Since *InsertionSort* performs $n(n - 1)/2$ comparisons in the worst case, it follows from Proposition 3.5.2 that *InsertionSort* is an (exactly) optimal worst-case adjacent-key comparison-based sorting algorithm.

We now consider a lower bound for the average behavior of adjacent-key comparison-based sorting algorithms. Proposition 3.5.3 gives us a lower bound that is only half of that found for the worst case.

Proposition 3.5.3 A lower bound for the average complexity $A(n)$ of any adjacent-key comparison-based sorting algorithm is $n(n - 1)/4$.

PROOF

For any input permutation π, a sorting algorithm must ultimately remove all the inversions in π, so that the average complexity of any adjacent-key comparison sorting algorithm is bounded below by the average number of inversions $\iota(n)$ in a permutation of $\{1, 2, \ldots, n\}$. We now give a quick proof of the formula $\iota(n) = n(n - 1)/4$, from which Proposition 3.5.3 follows. Given any permutation π of $\{1, 2, \ldots, n\}$, its *reverse* permutation π_{rev} is defined by $\pi_{\text{rev}}(i) = \pi(n - i + 1)$, $i \in \{1, 2, \ldots, n\}$. Note that given any $x, y \in N_n$, where $x > y$, the pair (x,y) occurs as an inversion in *exactly one* of the permutations π, π_{rev} (see Figure 3.15b). Thus, the permutations π, π_{rev} have a total of exactly $n(n - 1)/2$ inversions between them. We can sum the number of inversions over all permutations of $\{1, 2, \ldots, n\}$ by summing over each (unordered) pair $\{\pi, \pi_{\text{rev}}\}$, thereby obtaining $(n!/2)(n(n - 1)/2)$ inversions altogether. The average is then obtained by dividing this latter number by $n!$, yielding $\iota(n) = n(n - 1)/4$. ■

In Chapter 6, we will show that the average complexity $A(n)$ of *InsertionSort* is given by $A(n) = n^2/4 + 3n/4 - H(n)$, where $H(n)$ is the harmonic series $1 + 2 + \cdots + 1/n$. Hence, $A(n)$ is asymptotically very close to $n^2/4$. Thus, by Proposition 3.5.3, *InsertionSort* has basically optimal average complexity.

$$\begin{pmatrix} 1\ 2\ 3 \\ 1\ 2\ 3 \end{pmatrix} \quad \begin{pmatrix} 1\ 2\ 3 \\ 1\ 3\ 2 \end{pmatrix} \quad \begin{pmatrix} 1\ 2\ 3 \\ 2\ 1\ 3 \end{pmatrix} \quad \begin{pmatrix} 1\ 2\ 3 \\ 2\ 3\ 1 \end{pmatrix} \quad \begin{pmatrix} 1\ 2\ 3 \\ 3\ 1\ 2 \end{pmatrix} \quad \begin{pmatrix} 1\ 2\ 3 \\ 3\ 2\ 1 \end{pmatrix}$$

none (3,2) (2,1) (2,1),(3,1) (3,1),(3,2) (3,2),(3,1),(2,1)

(a) All permutations of {1,2,3} and their inversions

$$\left\{ \begin{pmatrix} 1\ 2\ 3 \\ 1\ 2\ 3 \end{pmatrix}, \begin{pmatrix} 1\ 2\ 3 \\ 3\ 2\ 1 \end{pmatrix} \right\} \quad \left\{ \begin{pmatrix} 1\ 2\ 3 \\ 1\ 3\ 2 \end{pmatrix}, \begin{pmatrix} 1\ 2\ 3 \\ 2\ 3\ 1 \end{pmatrix} \right\} \quad \left\{ \begin{pmatrix} 1\ 2\ 3 \\ 2\ 1\ 3 \end{pmatrix}, \begin{pmatrix} 1\ 2\ 3 \\ 3\ 1\ 2 \end{pmatrix} \right\}$$

none (3,2),(3,1),(2,1) (3,2) (2,1),(3,1) (2,1) (3,1),(3,2)

(b) Partition of the permutations of {1,2,3} into pairs $\{\pi, \pi_{rev}\}$, with each pair
$\{\pi, \pi_{rev}\}$ yielding a full set of inversions

3.5.3 Lower Bound for Comparison-Based Sorting in General

In the previous section, we proved that adjacent-key comparison-based sorting
algorithms must perform at least $n(n-1)/2$ comparisons in the worst case for
inputs of size n, and $n(n-1)/4$ comparisons on average. Similar arguments
show that for any *fixed* positive integer k, if a comparison-based algorithm
always makes comparisons between list elements that occupy positions no more than k
indices apart, then the worst case and average performance remains quadratic in
the input size n (see Exercise 3.45). Thus, to improve on quadratic performance,
we need to compare list elements that are far apart (that is, the difference between index positions of some of the compared elements must *grow* as a function
of the input size). Of course, it is easy to design a comparison-based algorithm
that does compare distant elements but whose performance is still quadratic.
What we need is a clever way to use a comparison-based sorting algorithm like
MergeSort. But the question arises as to how good we can do in general with
comparison-based sorting. The answer for the worst-case complexity is found in
Proposition 3.5.4.

Proposition 3.5.4 A lower bound for the worst-case complexity $W(n)$ of any comparison-based
sorting algorithm is $\log_2 n! \in \Omega(n \log n)$.

PROOF

Given any comparison-based algorithm having worst-case complexity $m = W(n)$, we define a sequence of m partitions $C_1, \dots, C_m$ of the set of all permutations of $\{1, \dots, n\}$ as follows. C_1 is a bipartition of the set of permutations of
$\{1, \dots, n\}$ into two sets S_0 and S_1, where a permutation π is placed in S_0 if,
when input to the algorithm, the elements compared in the first comparison

are in order and placed in S_1 if they are out of order (determining an inversion). Inductively, assuming $C_1, \ldots, C_k$ have been defined, we define C_{k+1} to be a refinement of C_k as follows. Consider any set S in C_k. We partition S into two sets X and Y by placing a permutation $\pi \in S$ in Y if the algorithm performs at least $k + 1$ comparisons with π as input and if the elements that are compared in the $(k + 1)^{st}$ comparison are out of order, and letting X be the set of remaining permutations in S. If any of the resulting sets of C_{k+1} are empty, we simply remove them.

After m comparisons, the algorithm has terminated for each input permutation. We now show that each set in C_m contains exactly one permutation. Suppose, to the contrary, that some set S of C_m contains two permutations π_1 and π_2. Then, because the algorithm is comparison-based, it can easily be shown by induction that, for each comparison performed by the algorithm, precisely the same list positions were compared with input π_1 as with input π_2 and the relative order of these elements was the same. It follows that π_1 and π_2 must be the same permutation (a contradiction). Thus, since there are $n!$ permutations, by the pigeon hole principle, $|C_m| \geq n!$. Clearly, $|C_m| \leq 2^m$, so we have

$$2^m \geq |C_m| \geq n! \Rightarrow m \geq \log_2 n! \in \Omega(n\log n). \qquad ■$$

Other proofs of this lower bound will be given in Chapter 25. *MergeSort* is an example of a sorting algorithm whose worst-case performance is $O(n\log n)$, so it exhibits order-optimal behavior in the worst case. *MergeSort* is also order optimal on average because, as we will show in Chapter 25, $\Omega(n\log n)$ is also a lower bound for the average behavior of comparison-based sorting. Because *QuickSort* has quadratic worst-case complexity, it is not order optimal in the worst case. However, it is often used because its average complexity belongs to $O(n\log n)$, so it has order-optimal average complexity and performs well in practice.

3.6 Hard Problems

A curious fact in algorithm theory is that for most problems of practical importance, the best-known solution is either an algorithm with small-degree polynomial (worst-case) complexity, or an algorithm whose complexity grows faster than *any* polynomial (that is, they are *super-polynomial*). An example of the latter problem is the famous Traveling Salesman Problem (TSP), which we introduced in Chapter 2. The TSP asks for a minimum-length tour of a given set of n cities from a given starting city. Because $(n - 1)!$ tours are possible, even for a relatively small value of n, it is computationally infeasible to find an optimal (minimum-distance) tour by a brute force examination of each tour. While better algorithms exist for the TSP than brute force examination, all known algorithms are super-polynomial. The TSP has many important applications, and whole books have been written about the problem. However, finding an algorithm having polynomial complexity solving TSP, or proving that no such algorithm exists, remains a mystery (it is generally believed that there is no polynomial algorithm for TSP).

Another problem for which no polynomial algorithm has been found is the problem of factoring an integer n. The fact that factoring is generally believed to be a truly hard (that is, requiring a super-polynomial algorithm) problem is the basis for the most widely used Internet security encryption schemes. Yet another problem that appears to be hard is the so-called *discrete logarithm problem*, which, for a given positive base b, asks for the value of n if the value of b^n is known.

The fact that the discrete logarithm problem is computationally difficult, yet the inverse problem of computing b^n is computationally easy, leads to important applications in cryptography. For example, consider the following problem: Alice and Bob wish to send confidential information to one another over some communication medium (such as e-mail, telephone conversation, or fax). However, they know that Eve Dropper has the ability to monitor all communication sent over this medium. Moreover, Alice and Bob have not shared in advance any secret information that could be used for encrypting information. We now describe a communication protocol based on exponentiation modulo p that Alice and Bob can use to share secrets.

Alice and Bob first send messages, monitored by Eve, in which they agree to use a conventional cryptographic system for communication. The cryptographic system, also known by Eve, requires Alice and Bob to exchange a secret key value, which is an arbitrary positive integer. The question arises, can Alice and Bob publicly (that is, known to Eve) exchange information that allows them to efficiently determine a key but at the same time makes it infeasible for Eve to discern the value of this key?

The answer lies in the notion of *one-way* functions. One-way functions are efficiently computable, but their inverses are infeasible to compute. In 1976, Diffie and Hellman first pointed out the utility of one-way functions in cryptology and identified exponentiation modulo p, where p is an integer with, for example, several hundred decimal digits. We now describe how efficient exponentiation yields an effective method of exchanging a secret key.

Alice and Bob send messages agreeing on the value of p, as well as on an integer b between 2 and $p - 1$. Of course, then Eve also knows the values of p and b. Next, Alice and Bob randomly choose integers m and n, respectively, between 1 and $p - 1$. Alice does not know n, and Bob does not know m (Eve knows neither n nor m). Using a modification of *PowersRec* called *PowersRecMod* in which all calculations are carried out modulo p (see Exercise 3.52b), Alice then calculates and sends the integer b^m **mod** p to Bob. Similarly, Bob calculates and sends the integer b^n **mod** p to Alice. Here comes the secret: Using *PowersRecMod* again, Alice calculates $(b^n$ **mod** $p)^m$ **mod** p, and Bob calculates $(b^m$ **mod** $p)^n$ **mod** p. Lo and behold, they have just calculated the same number, b^{mn} **mod** p, which is the secret key they now share.

Because Eve has monitored all exchanges between Alice and Bob, she now knows p, b, b^m **mod** p, and b^n **mod** p. Thus, theoretically Eve can determine the secret key, b^{mn} **mod** p, by calculating m from her knowledge of b^m **mod** p and then calculating $(b^n$ **mod** $p)^m$ **mod** p. The problem of determining m from the known values of b, p, and b^m **mod** p is a special case of the discrete logarithm problem. The naive algorithm solving the discrete logarithm problem computes b^i **mod** p to b^m **mod** p as i takes on successive values 1, 2, 3, $\cdots$, until i reaches a value such that b^i **mod** $p = b^m$ **mod** p. Because this would take $p/2$ iterations on average, the naive algorithm is obviously infeasible. (Recall that p is an integer having more than a hundred digits!) Although there are better algorithms for the discrete logarithm problem, unfortunately for Eve, no efficient algorithm is known.

The algorithm *PowersRecMod* that Alice and Bob used to calculate powers of b requires special techniques for multiplying large integers. A classical divide-and-conquer method for multiplying large integers will be discussed in Chapter 8. Since all calculations are reduced modulo p, *PowersRecMod* always multiplies or squares numbers less than p, so that each such operation takes time bounded above by a constant $C(p)$ depending only on p. Thus, if Alice and Bob choose p, m, and n having 200 decimal digits each, then they can exchange their secret key after performing 3,000 multiplications of 200-digit numbers and 3,000 reductions of a 400-digit number modulo p. All these computations can be done within a reasonable time.

There are literally thousands of important problems such as the three we have just mentioned that are generally believed to be hard (since nobody has found polynomial solutions for any of them), but which have not been proven to be hard (that is, super-polynomial lower bounds have not been found for any of these problems). Settling the question of whether these problems are truly hard is the most important open question in theoretical computer science today.

Interestingly, the problem of factoring and finding the discrete logarithm have both been shown to admit polynomial quantum algorithms, but, as we have already mentioned, the open question here is whether or not quantum computers of sufficiently large size will ever be practical.

3.7 NP-Complete Problems

A decision problem is a problem having a yes or no answer to its inputs. For example, the prime-testing problem is the decision problem that asks whether a given integer n is prime. Many optimization problems have associated decision problem versions obtained by adding a (goodness measure) parameter and asking whether there is a solution as good as the parameter. For example, in the TSP, one could add the parameter k to the problem and ask whether or not there exists a tour whose total length is not greater than k. Of course, if the optimization problem is solved, the associated decision version is also solved immediately (by comparing the length of the optimal tour to the parameter k). Sometimes, given a solution to a general decision problem, we can find a polynomial procedure to solve the optimization problem. For example, a polynomial procedure exists for the TSP if all the distances between cities are integers of bounded size.

For the class of decision problems called NP (for nondeterministic polynomial), we can construct candidate solutions to "yes" instances in polynomial time and then check a given candidate to see if it is a solution in polynomial time. For example, given the TSP with parameter k, a candidate solution is simply a permutation of the $n - 1$ cities to be visited, and we can construct this permutation in linear time. Moreover, checking whether or not the length of the tour corresponding to this permutation is not larger than k can clearly be done in linear time because it amounts to adding n numbers.

The class of decision problems having a polynomial deterministic solutions to all instances is called class P. Note that it is clear that P $\subseteq$ NP because we can consider the candidate solution to "yes" instances of a given problem to be the solution constructed by the algorithm in polynomial time. Since allowing nondeterminism (perfect guessing) should help, we would expect that P $\neq$ NP, but this important question remains unsolved despite the efforts of the best theoretical computer scientists over more than the last 30 years.

The class of NP-complete problems are the problems in NP that, roughly speaking, are as hard to solve (up to polynomial factors) as any other problem in NP. Somewhat more precisely, problem A is as hard to solve as problem B if there is a mapping t from the inputs of size n to problem B to the inputs of size at most $p(n)$ to problem A for a suitable polynomial p, such that t is constructible in polynomial time (and space), and such that an input I to problem B is a "yes" instance if and only if $t(I)$ is a "yes" instance to problem A. We say that problem B is polynomially *reducible* to problem A. A problem A in NP is NP-*complete* if *every* problem in NP is reducible to A. It is certainly not obvious that NP-complete problems exist. But, if NP-complete problems exist, and if any one of them belongs to P, then every NP problem belongs to P (which would imply that P $=$ NP, an equality generally believed to be false). It turns out that the decision version of TSP is NP-complete.

REMARK

We call a problem *NP-hard* if solving it in polynomial time would imply that P=NP. An NP-hard problem is not necessarily a decision problem. For example, because the decision version of TSP is NP-complete, TSP is NP-hard.

The first NP-complete problem was found by Stephen Cook, who showed in 1970 that the problem of determining whether or not the variables in a given Boolean expression can be assigned values (true or false) in such a way as to make the Boolean expression true (called a satisfying assignment) is NP=complete. L. A. Levin found another example at about the same time. Since then, thousands of problems have been shown to be NP-complete. Many NP-complete problems have important applications, so it is frustrating not to know whether they are all super-polynomial in complexity. However, it is true that some important special cases of a given NP-complete problem can be solved, or in some useful sense approximately solved, in polynomial time. We will discuss NP-complete problems and approximation algorithms in detail in Chapters 26 and 27, respectively.

Interestingly, prime testing was not known to be in P until 2002, when it was shown to be solvable by a sixth-degree polynomial in the size of the input. Good probabilistic algorithms for prime testing have been known for some time (see Chapter 24), and these algorithms still are more efficient in practice than the recently found deterministic polynomial-time algorithm. However, showing the prime testing is in P was nevertheless a major achievement.

3.8 Closing Remarks

An algorithm's complexity is often described in the literature in terms of belonging to an O-class, since an O-class bound for $W(n)$ also gives a bound on the computing time for any input of size n. Also, the O-class value for complexity of an algorithm automatically applies to the problem itself. Another reason for using the O-class notation is that it might yield a much simpler measure of the complexity of an algorithm than the more exact order formula using Θ. For example, consider the naive algorithm for testing whether an integer m is prime by successively testing the potential divisors 2, 3, ... , $m^{1/2}$. This algorithm performs only one division when m is even but $m^{1/2}$ divisions when m is prime. Thus, the algorithm performs $O(m^{1/2})$ divisions; that is, it has $O((\sqrt{2})^n)$ complexity when the input size is the number of binary digits n of m. In this case, the Θ-class for the exact worst-case complexity contains no simply expressible function.

The asymptotic classes O, Θ, and Ω do not take into account the size of the constants involved. In practice, the constants sometimes do matter. For example, there are algorithms known for solving certain problems that have linear order but for which the explicit constants involved are so large that the algorithms are totally impractical to implement. Of course, for a sufficiently large input size n, a linear algorithm will outperform, say, a quadratic algorithm, but the quadratic algorithm might have sufficiently small associated explicit and implicit constants that it outperforms the linear algorithm for any input size n small enough to be of practical interest. The linear algorithm in such cases is then mostly of theoretical interest but nevertheless important: It gives hope that a linear algorithm with reasonably small constants can be found.

In this chapter, we discussed the most commonly occurring recurrence relations that relate $t(n)$ to a single term $t(m)$ for $m < n$. There are occasions, such as the recurrence for the Fibonacci numbers or the average complexity of quicksort, where $t(n)$ is related to more than one term $t(m)$ for $m < n$. In Appendix D, we will show how generating functions can be used to solve linear recurrence relations involving more than a single term. In Chapter 6, we will show how the full history recurrence relation for the average complexity of quicksort can actually be reduced to a single-term recurrence that can be solved by repeated substitution.

References and Suggestions for Further Reading

de Bruijn, N. G. *Asymptotic Methods in Analysis.* Amsterdam: North Holland, 1961.

A good classical reference for the use of asymptotic methods in mathematics. In the early 1970s, asymptotic notation became widely used in computer science papers relating to the analysis algorithms. The standard forms for asymptotic notation was proposed by Knuth and further refined by Brassard.

Brassard, G. "Crusade for a Better Notation," *SIGACT News* 17, no.1 (1985): 60–64.

Knuth, D. E. "Big Omicron and Big Omega and Big Theta." *SIGACT News* 8, no. 2 (April–June 1976): 18–24.

EXERCISES

Section 3.1 Asymptotic Behavior of Functions

3.1 Prove each of the following directly from the definition of Θ:

a. $100,000,000 \in \Theta(1)$

b. $n^2/2 + 2n - 5 \in \Theta(n^2)$

c. $\log_{10}(n^2) \in \Theta(\log_2 n)$

3.2 Prove each of the following directly from the definitions of O and Ω:

a. $17n^{1/6} \in O(n^{1/5})$

b. $1000n^2 \in O(n^2)$

c. $n/1000 - 500 \in \Omega(n)$

d. $30n\log_2 n - 23 \in \Omega(n)$

e. $O(n!) \subset O((n + 1)!)$

3.3 Repeat Exercise 3.1 using the ratio limit theorem (Proposition 3.1.4).

3.4 Repeat Exercise 3.2 using the ratio limit theorem (Proposition 3.1.4).

3.5 Using the ratio limit theorem (Proposition 3.1.4) and (possibly) L'Hôpital's rule (Definition 3.17), prove each of the following:

a. $(n^3 + n)/(2n + \ln n) \in \Theta(n^2)$

b. $O(n^4) \subset O(3^n)$

c. $n2^n + n^9 \in O(e^n)$

d. $n^{1/2} \in \Omega((\log n)^4)$

e. $n^{\log_2 n} \in O(2^n)$

3.6 Using the ratio limit theorem (Proposition 3.1.4), prove the following:

$$O(108) \subset O(\ln n) \subset O(n) \subset O(n\ln n) \subset O(n^2) \subset O(n^3) \subset O(2^n) \subset O(3^n)$$

3.7 For any constants k and $b > 1$, show that

$$O(n^k) \subset O(n^{\ln n}) \subset O(b^n).$$

3.8 Prove property (1) of Proposition 3.1.2: For any positive constant c,

$$\Omega(f(n)) = \Omega(cf(n)), \Theta(f(n)) = \Theta(cf(n)), \text{ and } O(f(n)) = O(cf(n)).$$

3.9 Prove property (2) of Proposition 3.1.2:

$$f(n) \in \Theta(g(n)) \Leftrightarrow f(n) \in \Omega(g(n)) \cap O(g(n)).$$

3.10 Show that $f(n) \in \Theta(g(n))$ if and only if $\Theta(f(n)) = \Theta(g(n))$.

3.11 Prove properties (3) and (5) of Proposition 3.1.2:
a. $f(n) \in O(g(n)) \Leftrightarrow O(f(n)) \subseteq O(g(n))$.

b. $f(n) \in O(g(n)) \Leftrightarrow g(n) \in \Omega(f(n))$.

3.12 Prove property (4) of Proposition 3.1.2:

$$O(f(n)) = O(g(n)) \Leftrightarrow \Omega(f(n)) = \Omega(g(n)) \Leftrightarrow \Theta(f(n)) = \Theta(g(n)).$$

3.13 Prove each of the following:
a. $4n^3 + \sqrt{n} \sim 4n^3 - n^2 + 500$

b. $2^n + 50n^5 + 13n^2 + 42 \sim 2^n$

c. $(6n^2 + 50\sqrt{n})/(3\sqrt{n} + 5\ln n) \sim 2n^{3/2}$

d. $30n - 50 = O(n^2/23)$

e. $1000 \log_2 n = O(\sqrt{n})$

3.14 Suppose a and c are positive constants.

a. If f is a polynomial, show that $f(n + c) \sim f(n)$ and $f(cn) \in \Theta(f(n))$.

b. If $f(n) = a^n$, show that $f(n + c) \in \Theta(f(n))$ and $O(f(n)) \subset O(f(cn))$, $c > 1$.

c. If $f(n) = n!$, show that $O(f(n)) \subset O(f(n + c))$, c is a positive integer.

3.15 Let $P(n)$ be any polynomial of degree k whose leading coefficient is positive, and let a be any real number $a > 1$. Show that $P(n) = O(a^n)$.

3.16 Show that if $1 < a < b$, then $a^n = O(b^n)$.

3.17 Complete the proof of the ratio limit theorem (Proposition 3.1.4) by proving case 3:

$$L = \infty \Rightarrow O(g(n)) \subset O(f(n)), \text{ that is, } f \text{ has a } \textit{larger} \text{ order than } g.$$

3.18 The ratio limit theorem (Proposition 3.1.4) states that $\lim_{n \to \infty} f(n)/g(n) = 0$ implies that $O(f(n)) \subset O(g(n))$.

a. Show that a partial converse is true: If $O(f(n)) \subset O(g(n))$ and $\lim_{n \to \infty} f(n)/g(n)$ exists, then this limit must be zero.

b. Construct examples where $O(f(n)) \subset O(g(n))$ but $\lim_{n \to \infty} f(n)/g(n)$ does not exist.

c. Give examples similar to (b) for the other two cases of the ratio limit theorem.

3.19 Prove the following result from the definition of o and $\sim$. If $f(n)$ and $g(n)$ are functions such that $g(n) \in o(f(n))$, then

$$f(n) \pm g(n) \sim f(n).$$

3.20 The notions of Ω, Θ, and O can be viewed as binary relations on the set $\mathscr{F}$ of (eventually positive) functions $f: \mathbb{N} \to \mathbb{R}$. A (*binary*) *relation* R on a set S is any subset of the Cartesian product $S \times S$. For $x, y \in S$, we say that x is *related* to y, written $x R y$, if the ordered pair $(x, y) \in R$. Note that Θ determines a relation on the set $\mathscr{F}$ by defining $f \Theta g$ to mean $f(n) \in \Theta(g(n))$. In a similar way, Ω and O determine relations on $\mathscr{F}$.

A very important class of relations on a set S are the so-called equivalence relations. Equivalence relations on S correspond precisely to partitions of S into pairwise disjoint subsets (see Exercise 3.21).

DEFINITION

A relation R on S is said to be an *equivalence* relation if the following three properties are satisfied.

1. Reflexive property: xRx, $\forall\, x \in S$.

2. Symmetric property: $xRy \Rightarrow yRx$, $\forall\, x, y \in S$.

3. Transitive property: xRy and $yRz \Rightarrow xRz$, $\forall\, x, y, z \in S$.

   a. Show that the relation Θ is an equivalence relation of $\mathcal{F}$ (that is, verify all three properties of Proposition 3.1.1).

   b. Show that relations O and Ω are reflexive and transitive but not symmetric.

3.21 Given an equivalence relation R on a set S, each element $x \in S$ determines an *equivalence class*, denoted by $[x]$, consisting of all elements y such that xRy. It is easily proved that $[x] = [y]$ if and only if xRy. A finite or infinite collection of subsets of a set S is said to be a *partition* of S if the sets are pairwise disjoint and their union is S.

   a. Given an equivalence relation R on a set S, show that the set of equivalence classes is a partition of the set S.

   b. Conversely, given any partition of the set S, show there is a unique equivalence relation on S whose equivalence classes are precisely the subsets of the given partition (define xRy if and only if x and y lie in the same subset).

3.22   a. Show that the relation $\sim$ is actually an equivalence relation on $\mathcal{F}$.

   b. Show that $\sim$ is a stronger relation than Θ in the sense that $\sim$ refines Θ. Given two relations R_1 and R_2 on a set S, we say that R_2 *refines* R_1 if $xR_2y \Rightarrow xR_1y$. If both R_1 and R_2 are equivalence relations, and R_2 refines R_1, then each R_2-equivalence class is contained in an R_1-equivalence class. We say that the R_2-equivalence classes form a *refinement* of the R_1-equivalence classes.

3.23 Consider the relation K on $\mathcal{F}$ defined as follows:

$$fKg \iff \lim_{n \to \infty} \frac{f(n)}{g(n)} = L, \quad \text{where } 0 < L < \infty.$$

   a. Show that K is an equivalence relation.

   b. Show that K refines Θ.

   c. Show that K is refined by $\sim$.

3.24 Show that the functions $f(n) = n^3$ and $g(n) = n^4(n \bmod 2) + n^2$ are not comparable.

3.25 Find two strictly increasing functions $f, g \in \mathcal{F}$ whose orders are not comparable.

Section 3.2 Asymptotic Order Formulae for Three Important Series

3.26 Obtain a formula for the order of $S(n) = \sum_{i=1}^{n}(\log i)^2$.

3.27 Obtain an approximation for $\log n! = \sum_{i=1}^{n}(\log i)$ by using a technique similar to that used in Section 3.2.2 for approximating the harmonic series. (*Hint:* Use $\int_{1}^{n} \log x\, dx$.)

3.28 Show that $\lim_{n \to \infty} H(n) = \infty$.

3.29 Show directly from the definition of $S(n,k)$—that is, without using the recurrence relation in Formula (3.2.1)—that $S(n,k) \in \Theta(n^{k+1})$.

3.30 Show that $S(n, -k) = 1 + \left(\dfrac{1}{2}\right)^k + \left(\dfrac{1}{3}\right)^k + \cdots + \left(\dfrac{1}{n}\right)^k \in \Theta(1)$ for all integers $k \geq 2$.

3.31 Proposition 3.2.2 states that $S(n,k) = 1^k + 2^k + \cdots + n^k$ is a polynomial in n of degree $k + 1$ whose leading coefficient is $1/(k + 1)$. Using induction and Proposition 3.2.1, show that the coefficients of n^k and n^{k-1} in $S(n,k)$ are $1/2$ and $k/12$, respectively, for $k > 1$.

3.32 a. $S(n,k) = 1^k + 2^k + \cdots + n^k$ is a polynomial in n of degree $k + 1$ whose constant term is zero. Let $B(j,k)$ denote the coefficient of n^j in polynomial $S(n,k)$, $j = 1, \dots, k + 1$. Using the recurrence relation in Formula (3.2.1) for $S(n,k)$, obtain a recurrence relation for $B(j,k)$.

   b. Using the recurrence relation for $B(j,k)$ obtained in (a), give pseudocode for the procedure *SumOfPowers*, which outputs the (coefficients of) the polynomial $S(n,k)$.

   c. Modify the algorithm created in (b) to avoid truncation errors when dividing by large integers by storing the coefficients $B(j,k)$ as fractions in lowest form. These fractions can be stored as pairs of integers (*Numer,Denom*), where *Numer* is the numerator and *Denom* is the denominator. Obtain the lowest form of the fraction represented by (*Numer,Denom*) by employing Euclid's gcd algorithm.

3.33 Generalize the recurrence relation in Formula (3.2.1) for $S(n,k)$ to a recurrence relation for the sum of the kth powers of the first n terms in the arbitrary arithmetic progression

$$S(a,d,n,k) = a^k + (a + d)^k + \cdots + (a + (n - 1)d)^k.$$

Section 3.3 Recurrence Relations for Complexity

3.34 Derive and solve a recurrence relation for the best-case complexity $B(n)$ of *MergeSort*.

3.35 Solve the following recurrence relations:

a. $t(n) = 3t(n - 1) + n, \quad n \geq 1, \quad$ **init. cond.** $t(0) = 1.$

b. $t(n) = 4t(n - 1) + 5, \quad n \geq 1, \quad$ **init. cond.** $t(0) = 2.$

c. $t(n) = 2t(n/3) + n, \quad n \geq 1, \quad$ **init. cond.** $t(0) = 0.$

3.36 Determine the Θ-class of $t(n)$ where

$$t(n) = 2t(n - 1) + n^4 + 1, \textbf{ init. cond. } t(0) = 0.$$

3.37 A very natural question to ask related to MergeSort is whether we can do better by dividing the list into more than two parts. It turns out we cannot do any better, at least in the worst case. In this exercise, you will verify this fact mathematically. The following algorithm, *TriMergeSort*, a variant of *MergeSort*, splits a list into three equal parts instead of two. For convenience, assume that $n = 3^k$, for some nonnegative integer k.

```
procedure TriMergeSort(Low, High) recursive
Input:    Low, High (indices of a global array L[0:n-1], initially Low = 0 and
              High = n − 1 = 3^k − 1)
Output:   sublist L[Low:High] is sorted in nondecreasing order
    if High ≤ Low then return endif
    Third ← Low + ⌊(High − Low + 1 )/3⌋
    TwoThirds ← Low + 2⌊(High − Low + 1 )/3⌋
    TriMergeSort(Low, Third)
    TriMergeSort(Third + 1, TwoThirds)
    TriMergeSort(TwoThirds + 1, High)
    //merge sublists L[Low:Third] and L[Third:TwoThirds] of sizes n/3 and n/3
        Merge(Low, Third, TwoThirds)
    //merge sublists L[Low:TwoThirds] and L[TwoThirds:High] of sizes 2n/3 and n/3
        Merge(Low, TwoThirds, High)
end TriMergeSort
```

a. Give a recurrence relation for the worst-case complexity $W(n)$ of *TriMergeSort* for an input list of size n.

b. Solve the recurrence formula you have given in (a) to obtain an explicit formula for the worst-case complexity $W(n)$ of *TriMergeSort*.

c. Which is more efficient in the worst case, *MergeSort* or *TriMergeSort*? Discuss.

d. Repeat (a), (b), and (c) for the best-case complexity $B(n)$.

3.38 Design and analyze a variant of *TriMergeSort* that uses a single call to a merge procedure for merging three sorted sublists, where three pointers are used, one for each sublist.

3.39 In Section 3.3, we established a formula for the worst-case complexity $W(n)$ of *MergeSort* when n is a power of 2. Find an approximation to $W(n)$ for a general n, showing that $W(n) \in \Theta(n \log n)$.

Section 3.4 Mathematical Induction and Proving the Correctness of Algorithms

3.40 Prove by induction that

$$C(n,0) + C(n,1) + C(n,2) + \cdots + C(n,n) = 2^n.$$

3.41 Prove by induction that

$$C(n,0) - C(n,1) + \cdots + (-1)^i C(n,i) + \cdots + (-1)^n C(n,n) = 0.$$

3.42 Suppose you have a collection of n lines in the plane such that no two are parallel and no three meet in a point. Find a formula for the number of regions in the plane determined by these lines, and prove the formula using induction.

3.43 Prove *Merge* is correct.

3.44 Prove *QuickSort* is correct.

3.45 Prove *BubbleSort* is correct (see Exercise 2.36).

3.46 Prove *InsertionSort* is correct.

3.47 Prove *BinarySearch* is correct.

3.48 Prove *TriMergeSort* is correct (see Exercise 3.37).

3.49 There are many ways to generate all permutations of $\{1, \ldots, n\}$, but the following is certainly one of the most elegant. Prove that procedure

GeneratePermutations (below) passes all permutations of $\{i, \ldots, n\}$ to the procedure *OutputPerm*, so that it generates all permutations of $\{1, \ldots, n\}$ when called initially with $i = 1$.

```
procedure GeneratePermutations(i) recursive
Input:   i (integer 1≤i≤n), T[1:n] global array intialized to T[i] = i
Output: generates all permutations of {1, … , n} when called with i = 1
    if i = n then
        OutputPerm(T[1:n])
    else
        for j ← i to n do
            Swap (T[i], T[j])         // interchange T[i] and T[j]
            GeneratePermutations(i + 1)
            Swap (T[i], T[j])         // interchange T[i] and T[j]
        endfor
    endif
end GeneratePermutations
```

Section 3.5 Establishing Lower Bounds for Problems

3.50 Show that removing an inversion $(\pi(i), \pi(i + 1))$ by interchanging $\pi(i)$ and $\pi(i + 1)$ results in a decrease of exactly 1 in the total number of inversions in π.

3.51 Show that any comparison-based algorithm for merging two sorted lists of size $n/2$ to form a sorted list of size n cannot have complexity belonging to $O(n^{1-\varepsilon})$ for any $\varepsilon > 0$. (*Hint:* We have already seen that $\Omega(n \log n)$ is a lower bound for comparison-based sorting.)

3.52 a. For the algorithm *InsertionSort*, exhibit the permutations in each set of the partition C_p, $p = 1,2,3$ as described in the proof of Proposition 3.5.4.

b. Repeat part (a) for *MergeSort*.

Section 3.6 Hard Problems

3.53 a. Show that

$$(x + y) \bmod p = ((x \bmod p) + (y \bmod p)) \bmod p$$

$$(xy) \bmod p = ((x \bmod p)(y \bmod p)) \bmod p.$$

b. Give pseudocode for a modification *PowersRecMod* of *PowersRec* in which all calculations are carried out modulo p. The correctness of *PowersRecMod* follows from (a).

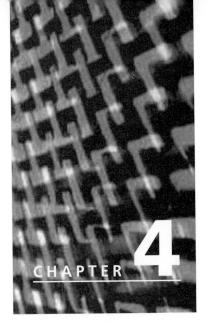

CHAPTER 4

TREES AND APPLICATIONS TO ALGORITHMS

I think that I shall never see / A poem lovely as a tree.

—Joyce Kilmer

Computer scientists, too, are enamored with trees. As defined in computer science and mathematics, trees sprout up everywhere in the subject of algorithms. Trees are often explicitly implemented in code for an algorithm or are implicitly present in the hierarchical logical organization of an algorithm.

You are no doubt familiar with tree-based hierarchical organizations such as family trees or organizational charts (see Figure 4.1). A table of contents in a book can be thought of as having a tree structure. The directory structure used by the operating system on your computer (UNIX, Windows, Mac OS, or otherwise) organizes files in a tree structure.

Trees play multiple roles in the design and analysis of algorithms and in computing in general. Storing data in a tree-based hierarchical structure can be very useful because it facilitates efficient access to the data. Imposing a tree structure on stored data often leads to logarithmic complexity of operations

FIGURE 4.1

A family tree

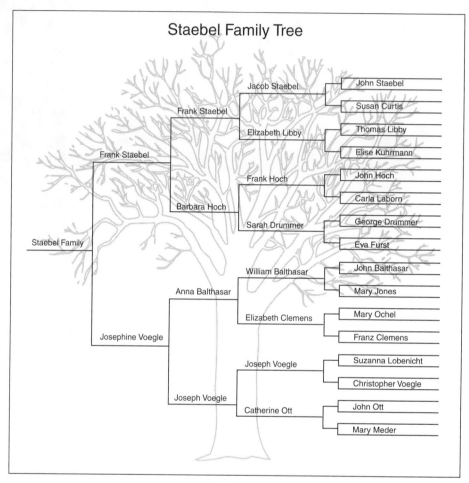

Staebel Family Tree

versus the linear behavior that would result in viewing the data as a linear structure. The tree structure can either be explicitly or implicitly implemented. For example, we will see in Section 4.6 how maintaining a priority queue using a tree-based structure known as a heap will allow addition and deletion of elements to be done in logarithmic time as opposed to the linear time that would result if the priority queue were maintained as a linear data structure. In this case, the tree structure is actually overlaid implicitly on the data that is stored contiguously in a linear array. As another example, the binary search algorithm for searching an ordered list stored contiguously in an array is based on the implicit binary search tree associated with the data (midpoint element being the root, its left and right children being the midpoints of the left and right subintervals, respectively, and so forth). In other cases, the data is stored in an explicitly created tree (typically using dynamically allocated storage). For example, balanced tree structures such as red-black trees and B-trees (see Chapter 21) are often explicitly built and maintained to facilitate rapid key location in a database. Internet searches and other textual pattern matching algorithms are usually based on storing pattern strings in explicitly constructed trees, such as suffix trees or tries (see Chapter 20).

We saw in Chapter 2 that trees are always implicitly present whenever the resolution of recursive algorithms is modeled. Examining the tree of recursive calls implicitly generated by the complete resolution of a recursive algorithm is often the technique used to measure the complexity of the algorithm. Comparison and decision trees modeling the action of algorithms are other ways in which trees are implicitly present in algorithm analysis. For example, a comparison tree modeling the action of a comparison-based algorithm for sorting a list of size n can be used to establish lower bounds for the complexity of the algorithm (see Chapter 25). These lower bounds follow from various mathematical properties of trees. Elementary properties of trees, such as depth, will be discussed in Section 4.6, whereas more sophisticated properties, such as leaf path length, are the subject of Section 4.8.

The topological structure of trees is frequently used as the basis for solving problems related to networks, such as the Internet, wired and wireless communication networks, computer networks, and so forth. For example, the fundamental problem of finding a minimal collection of links connecting the nodes in a network is solved by constructing a spanning tree of minimal cost (see Chapter 12). Another fundamental problem (also discussed in Chapter 12)—finding the shortest paths from a given node in a connected network to all other nodes—is solved by constructing a shortest-path spanning tree.

4.1 Definitions

There are a thousand hacking at the branches of evil to one who is striking at the root.

—Henry David Thoreau

In this section, we give the formal mathematical definition of trees and establish some of their elementary properties. Our trees are actually *rooted* trees, but we will usually simply refer to them as trees. We begin our discussion by defining a special class of trees known as binary trees. Every node in a binary tree has at most two children.

4.1.1 Binary Trees

There are many equivalent definitions of a binary tree, but the following recursive definition is certainly one of the most elegant.

DEFINITION 4.1.1 A binary tree T consists of a set of nodes that is either empty or has the following properties:

1. One of the nodes, say R, is designated the root node.
2. The remaining nodes (if any) are partitioned into two disjoint subsets, called the left subtree and the right subtree, respectively, each of which is a binary tree.

The roots of the left and right subtrees described in property (2) of the definition are called the left child and right child of R, respectively. Some examples of binary trees are given in Figure 4.2. A node is called a *leaf* if it has no children. Just as in family trees, we use genealogical notation such as *parent, grandchildren, great-grandchildren, sibling, descendant, ancestor*, and so forth.

The nodes of T can be partitioned into disjoint sets (levels) depending on their (genealogical) distance from the root R. In particular, the root R is at level 0. The *depth* (also called *height*) of T is the maximum distance from R to a leaf. The trees shown in Figures 4.2a and 4.2b have depths 3 and 4, respectively.

4.1.2 General Trees

The design of many algorithms requires more general trees than binary trees. General trees are often implicitly present in the logical organization of an algorithm. The following definition extends the concept of a rooted binary tree given by Definition 4.1.1 to a general rooted tree.

FIGURE 4.2

Sample binary trees of depths 3 and 4

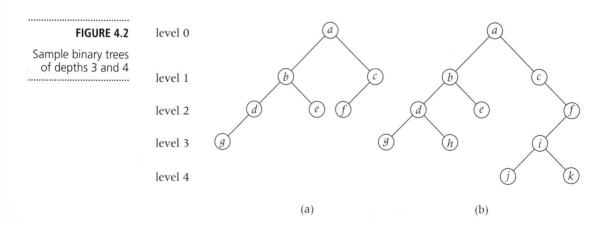

(a)   (b)

FIGURE 4.3

A sample tree
of depth 3

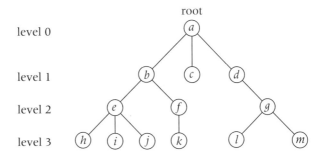

DEFINITION 4.1.2 A tree T consists of a set of nodes (also called vertices) that is either empty or has the following properties:

1. One of the nodes, say R, is designated the root node.
2. The remaining nodes (if any) are partitioned into j disjoint subsets $T_1, T_2, \ldots, T_j$, each of which is a tree (called a subtree).

Given the root R, the roots of the subtrees described in property (2) are called children of R. A node is called a leaf if it has no children. It should be noted that when applying property (2) to a subtree, the value of j will, in general, vary with the subtree. Just as for binary trees, we utilize genealogical terminology such as parent, grandchildren, great-grandchildren, sibling, descendant, ancestor, and so forth. We also have the notions of levels and depth of a tree. Figure 4.3 illustrates a tree of depth 3.

4.2 Mathematical Properties of Binary Trees

Often in this text, analyzing the complexity of a problem or algorithm depends on one or more of the mathematical properties of binary trees. In this section, we establish a number of these properties relating to depth, internal path length, and leaf path length.

Given a binary tree T, for ease of discussion, we denote the number of nodes, the number of leaf nodes, the number of internal nodes, and the depth by $n = n(T)$, $L = L(T)$, $I = I(T)$, and $d = d(T)$, respectively. Let n_i denote the number of nodes of T at level i, $i = 0, \ldots, d$. Because T is a binary tree, each node of T has at most two children, which yields the following recurrence relation:

$$n_i \leq 2n_{i-1}, \quad i = 1, \ldots, d, \quad \textbf{init. cond. } n_0 = 1. \tag{4.1.1}$$

Thus, a simple induction yields

$$n_i \le 2^i, \quad i = 0, \dots, D. \tag{4.1.2}$$

For a given level $i \in \{1, \dots, d\}$, we say that T is full at level i if $n_i = 2^i$.

4.2.1 Complete and Full Binary Trees

We can easily verify that if a binary tree T is full at level i, then it is full at every level j smaller than i. A binary tree T is *full* if it is full at every level. Equivalently, a binary tree is full if it is full at the last level. Note that a full binary tree exists only for those n satisfying

$$n = 1 + 2 + 2^2 + \cdots + 2^d = 2^{d+1} - 1. \tag{4.2.1}$$

We denote the full binary tree on n nodes by T_n, $n = 1,3,7,15$, and so on. The full binary tree T_{15} is shown in Figure 4.4a. Solving for d in Formula (4.2.1) yields the following formula for the depth of T_n

$$d = \log_2(n+1) - 1 = \lfloor \log_2 n \rfloor. \tag{4.2.2}$$

Full binary trees are special cases of complete binary trees, where n is 1 less than a power of 2. To define the *complete* binary tree T_n for a general n, we let k be the (unique) positive integer such that $2^k - 1 < n \le 2^{k+1} - 1$. Then, for n different from $2^{k+1} - 1$, T_n is defined as a *canonical subtree* of the full binary tree T_m, $m = 2^{k+1} - 1$ having the same depth and differing from T_n only at the last level. The $q = n - (2^k - 1)$ nodes of T_n on the last level occupy the leftmost q positions of T_m. More precisely, consider the following labeling of the nodes of T_m: Label the root node 0, and inductively, label the left and right children of node i as $2i + 1$ and $2i + 2$, respectively. Then the complete binary tree T_n on n nodes is the subtree of T_m consisting of those nodes labeled $0, 1, \dots, n - 1$ (see Figure 4.4b illustrating T_{10}).

The depth of T_n, $2^k - 1 < n \le 2^{k+1} - 1$, is the same as the depth k of the full tree on $2^{k+1} - 1$ nodes obtained by filling out the last level, and $k = \lfloor \log_2 n \rfloor$. Armed with these facts, we can find the depth of an arbitrary complete tree on n nodes using Proposition 4.2.1.

....
FIGURE 4.4

(a) Complete (full)
binary tree T_{15};
(b) complete
binary tree T_{10}
....

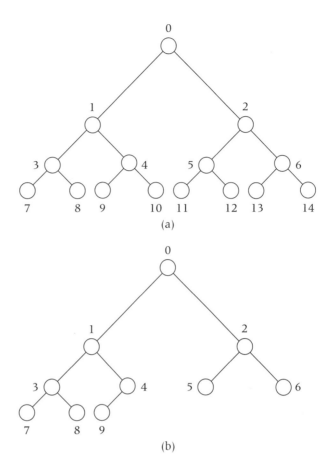

(a)

(b)

Proposition 4.2.1 The depth of the complete binary tree T_n for a general n is given by

$$d(T_n) = \lfloor \log_2 n \rfloor. \tag{4.2.3}$$

□

Because T_n is as full as possible for a binary tree on n nodes, it is not surprising that T_n has minimum depth for all binary trees on n nodes. The latter fact and other mathematical properties of binary trees are discussed in the next section.

REMARK

The terminology for complete and full binary trees varies in the literature. For example, sometimes a tree is termed *complete* that we have defined as *full,* and sometimes the term *left complete* is used to describe a tree we have defined as *complete.*

4.2.2 Logarithmic Lower Bound for the Depth of Binary Trees

Proposition 4.2.2 establishes the useful and intuitively clear result that the depth of a binary tree having n nodes is at least the depth of the complete binary tree T_n on n nodes.

Proposition 4.2.2 Suppose T is any binary tree having n nodes. Then T has depth of at least $\lfloor \log_2 n \rfloor$; that is,

$$D(T) \geq \lfloor \log_2 n \rfloor. \tag{4.2.4}$$

The lower bound $\lfloor \log_2 n \rfloor$ is achieved for the complete binary tree T_n.

PROOF
The argument follows a similar pattern to the argument that led to Formula (4.2.3), except we use inequalities in place of equalities. We leave the complete proof as an exercise. ∎

For $n = 2^k - 1$, then T_n is the only binary tree whose depth achieves the lower bound of $\lfloor \log_2 n \rfloor$. For a general n (different from $n = 2^k - 1$), there are many binary trees on n nodes that achieve the lower-bound depth of $\lfloor \log_2 n \rfloor$. In Figure 4.5, a tree having 16 nodes and depth 4 ($= \lfloor \log_2 n \rfloor$) is given, which is quite different from the complete tree T_{16}.

To establish various other mathematical properties of binary trees, we need to introduce the notion of a 2-tree.

4.2.3 2-Trees

A *2-tree* is a binary tree such that every node that is not a leaf has exactly two children. Any binary tree T can be canonically mapped to an associated 2-tree $\hat{T}$ having the same number of leaf nodes and no larger depth. The 2-tree $\hat{T}$ is obtained from T as follows: If a node of T has one child, then we contract the

FIGURE 4.5

A noncomplete tree
T with $n = 16$
nodes having depth
$= \lfloor \log_2 16 \rfloor = 4$

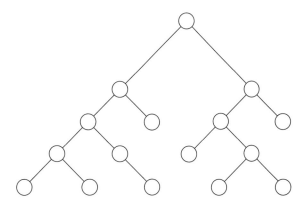

edge joining this node with its child (so that the node is identified with its child). This process is repeated until we end up at the 2-tree $\hat{T}$ (see Figure 4.6). Clearly, $L(T) = L(\hat{T})$, and $d(T) \geq d(\hat{T})$.

The Proposition 4.2.3 establishes a simple relationship between the number of internal nodes and the number of leaf nodes of a 2-tree.

Proposition 4.2.3 Suppose T is any 2-tree. Then the number of leaf nodes is 1 greater than the number of internal nodes of T; that is,

$$I(T) = L(T) - 1. \tag{4.2.5}$$

Equivalently, we have

$$n(T) = 2L(T) - 1. \tag{4.2.6}$$

$\square$

FIGURE 4.6

A binary tree T and
its associated
2-tree $\hat{T}$

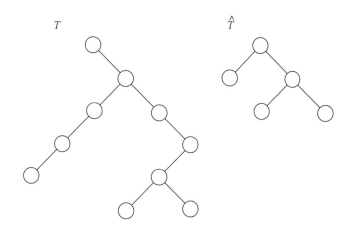

Proposition 4.2.3 is easily proved by induction. The proposition fails dramatically for binary trees in general, since an entirely skewed binary tree has only one leaf node.

Proposition 4.2.4 Suppose T is any binary tree. Then the depth of T satisfies

$$d(T) \geq \lceil \log_2 L(T) \rceil. \tag{4.2.7}$$

PROOF

Consider the 2-tree $\hat{T}$ associated with T. By Proposition 4.2.3, $n(\hat{T}) = 2L(\hat{T}) - 1$. Using Proposition 4.2.2 and the fact that $\lfloor \log_2(2n - 1) \rfloor = \lceil \log_2 n \rceil$ for any integer $n > 1$, we have

$$d(\hat{T}) \geq \lfloor \log_2(2L(\hat{T}) - 1) \rfloor = \lceil \log_2 L(\hat{T}) \rceil.$$

Because $L(T) = L(\hat{T})$ and $d(T) \geq d(\hat{T})$, it follows that

$$d(T) \geq d(\hat{T}) \geq \lceil \log_2 L(\hat{T}) \rceil = \lceil \log_2 L(T) \rceil. \qquad ■$$

Recall that a binary tree T is called full at level i if T contains the maximum number 2^i nodes at that level. A full binary tree T is full at every level i, $i = 0, \ldots, d(T)$. Proofs of the following two propositions are left to the exercises.

Proposition 4.2.5 Suppose T is a 2-tree. Then T is full at the second deepest level if and only if all the leaf nodes are contained in two levels ($d - 1$ and d). □

Proposition 4.2.6 If a 2-tree T is full at the second deepest level, then the depth $d(T)$ and the number of leaf nodes $L(T)$ are related by

$$d(T) = \lceil \log_2 L(T) \rceil. \tag{4.2.8}$$
□

4.2.4 Internal and Leaf Path Lengths of Binary Trees

Inputs to search algorithms that are based implicitly (such as *BinarySearch*) or explicitly on binary trees usually follow paths from the root to an internal or leaf node. Moreover, the number of basic operations performed by the algorithm is usually proportional to the length of such a path. In particular, determining the average complexity of such algorithms requires computing the sum of the lengths of all paths from the root to nodes in the tree, which motivates the following definitions. The *internal path length* of a binary tree T, $IPL(T)$, is defined as the sum of the lengths of the paths from the root to the internal nodes as the internal nodes vary over the entire tree. The *leaf path length, LPL(T)*, is defined similarly. Note that the length of a path from the root to a node at level i is i.

When the binary tree T is a 2-tree, then $LPL(T)$ is precisely $2I$ more than $IPL(T)$. This simple relationship between $IPL(T)$ and $LPL(T)$ for 2-trees is stated as Proposition 4.2.7; its proof is left as an exercise.

Proposition 4.2.7 Given any 2-tree T having I internal nodes,

$$IPL(T) = LPL(T) - 2I. \tag{4.2.9}$$

□

The following theorem establishes a useful lower bound for the leaf path length of a binary tree in terms of the number of leaf nodes.

Theorem 4.2.8 Given any binary tree T with L leaf nodes

$$LPL(T) \geq L\lfloor \log_2 L \rfloor + 2(L - 2^{\lfloor \log_2 L \rfloor}). \tag{4.2.10}$$

Moreover, Formula (4.2.10) is an inequality; it is an equality if and only if T is a 2-tree that is full at the second deepest level.

PROOF
We first verify that Formula (4.2.10) is an equality if T is a 2-tree that is full at the second deepest level. Suppose that $L = 2^k$, so that $\lfloor \log_2 L \rfloor = \log_2 L = k$. Then T is a full binary tree, and Formula (4.2.10) correctly yields the equality $LPL(T) = L\log_2 L$. Now suppose $2^{k-1} < L < 2^k$ for a suitable $k > 1$. By Proposition 4.2.4, T has depth $d = \lceil \log_2 L \rceil$. Because T is full at level $d - 1 = \lfloor \log_2 L \rfloor$, each of the L paths in T from the root to a leaf reach level $d - 1$. Hence, the total contribution to $LPL(T)$ from reaching level $d - 1$ is $L\lfloor \log_2 L \rfloor$, so that

$$LPL(T) = L\lfloor \log L \rfloor + \text{the number of nodes at level } d.$$

If x denotes the number of nodes at level $d - 1$ having two children (nonleaf nodes), then $2x$ equals the number of nodes at level d. The remaining $2^{d-1} - x$ nodes at level $d - 1$ are leaf nodes, so that $L = (2^{d-1} - x) + 2x$. Thus, we have $x = L - 2^{d-1}$, and $LPL(T) = L\lfloor \log_2 L \rfloor + 2(L - 2^{\lfloor \log_2 L \rfloor})$.

We now verify that inequality (4.2.10) holds for any binary tree. Clearly, if T is any binary tree with L leaf nodes, then its associated 2-tree $\hat{T}$ has L leaf nodes, and $LPL(\hat{T}) \leq LPL(T)$, so that we can assume without loss of generality that T is a 2-tree. Thus, to complete the proof of Theorem 4.2.8, it is sufficient to show that $LPL(T)$ is minimized for a 2-tree T having L leaf nodes that is full at the second deepest level.

Suppose T is a 2-tree of depth d that has L leaf nodes and is not full at level $d - 1$. We show that there then exists a 2-tree $\tilde{T}$ having L leaf nodes such that $LPL(\tilde{T}) < LPL(T)$. Because level $d - 1$ is not full, there exists a leaf node, say X, at some level $i \leq d - 2$. Let Y be any node at level $d - 1$ that is not a leaf node, and let C_1 and C_2 denote the children of Y. We construct $\tilde{T}$ from T by removing the leaf nodes C_1 and C_2 and adding two new leaf nodes $\tilde{C}_1$ and $\tilde{C}_2$ as the children of X (see Figure 4.7). Let $\mathscr{L}(T)$ and $\mathscr{L}(\tilde{T})$ denote the set of all leaf nodes of T and $\tilde{T}$, respectively. Then,

$$\mathscr{L}(\tilde{T}) = (\mathscr{L}(T) - \{C_1, C_2, X\}) \cup \{\tilde{C}_1, \tilde{C}_2, Y\}.$$

Because C_1, C_2, and X are at levels d, d, and i in T, respectively, and $\tilde{C}_1$, $\tilde{C}_2$, and Y are at levels $i + 1$, $i + 1$, and $d - 1$ in $\tilde{T}$, respectively, it follows that

$$\begin{aligned} LPL(\tilde{T}) &= LPL(T) - (2d + i) + (2(i + 1) + d - 1) \\ &= LPL(T) - d + i + 1 < LPL(T). \quad \blacksquare \end{aligned}$$

Corollary 4.2.9   If T is any binary tree with L leaf nodes, then

$$LPL(T) \geq \lceil L\log_2 L \rceil. \qquad\qquad (4.2.11)$$

Further, if T is a full binary tree, then inequality (4.2.11) is an equality.

PROOF
Inequality (4.2.11) follows immediately from inequality (4.2.10) of Theorem 4.2.8 by using the inequality

$$x\lfloor \log_2 x \rfloor + 2(x - 2^{\lfloor \log_2 x \rfloor}) \geq \lceil x\log_2 x \rceil, \quad \text{for any integer } x \geq 1.$$

Moreover, we have already observed in the proof of Theorem 4.2.8 that if T is a full binary tree, then $LPL(T) = L\log_2 L = \lceil L\log_2 L \rceil$.   ■

FIGURE 4.7

Construction of $\tilde{T}$
from T used in
the proof of
Theorem 4.2.8

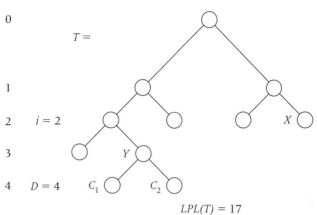

4.2.5 Number of Binary Trees

For any nonnegative integer n, let b_n denote the number of different binary trees on n nodes. The following theorem, which is proved in Appendix D, gives a simple formula for b_n.

Theorem 4.2.10   Let b_n denote the number of different binary trees on n nodes. Then,

$$b_n = \frac{1}{n+1}\binom{2n}{n}, \quad n \geq 1 \tag{4.2.12}$$

□

The value $b_n = \frac{1}{n+1}\binom{2n}{n}$, $n \geq 1$, occurs frequently in enumeration and is also known as the nth Catalan number. Formula (4.2.12), together with the lower bound estimate

$$\binom{2n}{n} \geq \frac{4^n}{(2n + 1)}, \quad n \geq 1$$

show that the number of binary trees on n nodes grows exponentially with n (see Exercise 4.14).

4.3 Implementation of Trees and Forests

4.3.1 Array Implementation of Complete Trees

The labeling of the nodes of the complete binary tree T_n illustrated in Figure 4.4 is particularly useful when the tree is implemented using an array $T[0:n - 1]$, where $T[i]$ corresponds to the ith node in the labeling $i = 0, \ldots, n - 1$. For example, in Section 4.6, we show how the heap ADT is implemented very effectively using the array implementation of T_n. Writing code for algorithms implementing the creation of a heap, and deletion and insertion operations, is greatly facilitated using the fact that the children of the ith node $T[i]$ are $T[2i + 1]$ and $T[2i + 2]$, and the parent of the ith node is $T[\lfloor (i - 1)/2 \rfloor]$.

4.3.2 Implementing General Binary Trees Using Dynamic Variables

Binary trees can be implemented using pointer and dynamic variables. The nodes of the tree are represented by a dynamic variable having the following structure:

```
BinaryTreeNode = record
    Info: InfoType
    LeftChild:→BinaryTreeNode
    RightChild:→BinaryTreeNode
end BinaryTreeNode
```

In addition to the dynamic variables representing the nodes of the binary tree, we have a pointer variable *Root* pointing to the root node. The implementation of the binary tree from Figure 4.2b using the pointer and dynamic variables is given in Figure 4.8.

4.3.3 Child-Sibling Representation of a General Tree

A child-sibling representation of a tree T can be implemented using pointer and dynamic variables, with the nodes of the tree represented by the following structure:

FIGURE 4.8

(a) Representation
of a node
of a binary tree;
(b) implementation
of a binary tree
using pointers and
dynamic variables

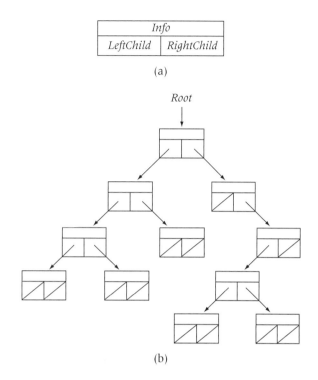

Info	
LeftChild	RightChild

(a)

(b)

```
TreeNode = record
    Info: InfoType
    LeftmostChild:→TreeNode
    NextSibling:→TreeNode
end TreeNode
```

As with binary trees, we keep a pointer variable *Root* that points to the root node of the tree. For example, the tree from Figure 4.3 is redrawn in Figure 4.9 using pointers and dynamic variables.

REMARK

This implementation of a general tree leads naturally to a transformation (known as the *Knuth transformation*) from a general tree to a binary tree. We simply think of the *LeftmostChild* as the left child of the node and the *NextSibling* as the right child. Indeed, Figure 4.9, showing the general tree implementation of the tree from Figure 4.3, is actually a binary tree.

FIGURE 4.9

(a) Representation of a node of a general tree; (b) child-sibling implementation of a tree using pointers and dynamic variables

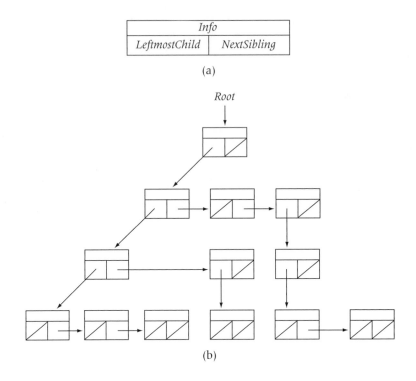

(a)

(b)

4.3.4 Parent Representation of Trees and Forests

Another representation of a general rooted tree, called the *parent representation*, keeps track of the parent of a node instead of its children. The parent representation has the advantage of efficiently generating the path in the tree from any given node of the tree to the root. However, the parent representation does not facilitate traversals of the tree.

The parent representation can actually be used to implement a slightly more general ADT known as a rooted forest. A *rooted forest* is a union F of pairwise disjoint rooted trees. A natural way to implement the parent representation of a rooted forest F uses an array $Parent[0:n - 1]$. For convenience, we assume that F has n nodes labeled $0, 1, \ldots, n - 1$. When referring to these nodes, we do not distinguish between a node and its label. For each $i \in \{0, 1, \ldots, n - 1\}$, $Parent[i]$ is -1 if i is a root of one of the trees in F; otherwise, $Parent[i]$ is the parent of node i. Information associated with the node i, $i = 0, 1, \ldots, n - 1$, can be stored in a second array $Info[0:n - 1]$. In Figure 4.10a, the values of the two arrays $Parent$ and $Info$ are given for the tree from Figure 4.3. The number beside each node of the tree in the diagram is the label of that node, and the character inside each node is the information stored in that node. In Figure 4.10b, the parent array representation of a sample forest is given.

The parent representation of a forest can also be implemented using pointers and dynamic variables. The nodes of the forest in this representation are given by the following structure:

ForestNode = **record**
    Info: InfoType
    Parent: →ForestNode
end *ForestNode*

The parent field of a node contains a pointer to the parent of that node if it has a parent. If the node corresponds to a root of one of the trees in the forest, then it contains the value **null**. The parent implementation of trees and forests has many important applications. Many of these applications exploit the fact that the parent implementation of a tree T allows efficient generation of the path P in T from any given node u of T to the root r. (The path in T from u to r is the sequence of nodes $u_0, u_1, \ldots, u_p$, where $u_0 = u$ and $u_p = r$, such that u_i is the parent of $u_{i-1}, i = 1, 2, \ldots, p$.) For example, in Figure 4.10a, we generate the path in the indicated tree T from vertex 7 to the root 3 as follows:

$$7, Parent[7] = 6, Parent[6] = 2, Parent[2] = 3$$

FIGURE 4.10

(a) Parent array implementation of a tree; (b) parent array implementation of a forest

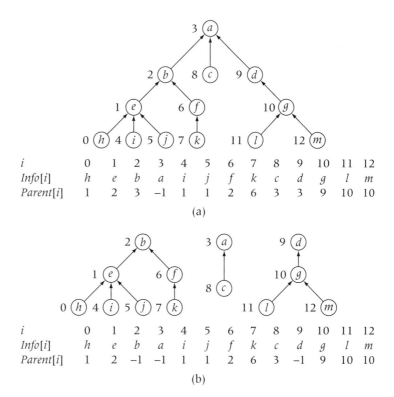

i	0	1	2	3	4	5	6	7	8	9	10	11	12
Info[i]	h	e	b	a	i	j	f	k	c	d	g	l	m
Parent[i]	1	2	3	−1	1	1	2	6	3	3	9	10	10

(a)

i	0	1	2	3	4	5	6	7	8	9	10	11	12
Info[i]	h	e	b	a	i	j	f	k	c	d	g	l	m
Parent[i]	1	2	−1	−1	1	1	2	6	3	−1	9	10	10

(b)

4.4 Tree Traversal

When a tree is implemented as a data structure in an algorithm, the nodes of the tree contain information (data) germane to the application in question. In many applications, it is necessary to access the fields in every node of the tree. During the execution of an algorithm, the current value of a variable (such as a pointer variable or index variable) that refers to a node in the tree makes the fields in that node accessible. A node is visited when it is accessed and some operation is performed on the information field(s) contained in the node. For example, visiting a node might consist of simply printing an information field. A tree is traversed if all its nodes are visited. The number of node accesses performed by a tree-traversal algorithm is used to measure the efficiency of the algorithm. (Normally during a traversal, a node is visited only once, but it can be accessed several times.)

4.4.1 Traversing Binary Trees

We discuss three standard traversals of a binary tree T: the preorder, inorder, and postorder traversals of T. Each traversal can be defined recursively, as illustrated by the following definition of preorder traversal:

DEFINITION 4.4.1   If T is not empty, the preorder traversal of T is defined recursively as consisting of the following steps:

1. Visit the root node R.
2. Perform a preorder traversal of the left subtree LT of the root.
3. Perform a preorder traversal of the right subtree RT of the root.

Note that no action is performed in the preorder traversal of an empty tree T. The inorder and postorder traversals of T differ from the preorder traversal only in the order in which the root is visited. In the inorder traversal, the root is visited after the left subtree tree has been traversed. In the postorder traversal the root is visited last (see Figure 4.11).

In Figure 4.11, the information in each node of the binary tree is a single alphabetical character. Assuming that visiting a node consists of simply printing the information stored in the node, then the following character strings are printed out when the tree is traversed in

preorder	*abdgheicfj*
inorder	*gdhbeiacjf*
postorder	*ghdiebjfca*

FIGURE 4.11

Here visiting a node consists of printing the single character information field. All three traversals have the same *path around the tree*, as indicated.

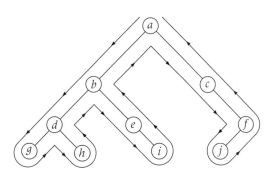

preorder: abdgheicfj   inorder: gdhbeiacjf   postorder: ghdiebjfca

All three traversals have the same "path around the tree," as shown in Figure 4.11. The difference between them is the order in which visits occur. Figure 4.12 illustrates the sequence of accesses and visits for the tree given in Figure 4.12 for each of the three traversals.

Preorder, inorder, and postorder traversals have many applications. For example, preorder and postorder traversals of algebraic expression trees generate *prefix* and *postfix* expressions, respectively (see Exercise 4.20). A postorder traversal can be used to free all the nodes in a dynamically allocated tree to delete the tree, whereas a preorder traversal in such a tree can be used to copy the tree. A preorder traversal of an appropriate binary tree can be used to generate a binary coding for a given alphabet for text compression purposes (see Chapter 7).

FIGURE 4.12

Accessing versus visiting for the binary tree given in Figure 4.11 for preorder, inorder, and postorder traversals

preorder traversal		inorder traversal		postorder traversal	
access		access		access	
a	visit	*a*		*a*	
b	visit	*b*		*b*	
d	visit	*d*		*d*	
g	visit	*g*	visit	*g*	visit
d		*d*	visit	*d*	
h	visit	*h*	visit	*h*	visit
d		*d*		*d*	visit
b		*b*	visit	*b*	
e	visit	*e*	visit	*e*	
i	visit	*i*	visit	*i*	visit
e		*e*		*e*	visit
b		*b*		*b*	visit
a		*a*	visit	*a*	
c	visit	*c*	visit	*c*	
f	visit	*f*		*f*	
j	visit	*j*	visit	*j*	visit
f		*f*	visit	*f*	visit
c		*c*		*c*	visit
a		*a*		*a*	visit

Inorder traversals are particularly useful in connection with binary search trees. In particular, an inorder traversal of a binary search tree visits the nodes in sorted order, which is the basis for the sorting algorithm treesort given in Section 4.5.6.

We now give a recursive procedure for a preorder traversal of the binary tree *T* implemented using pointers and dynamic variables, where the pointer variable *Root* points to the root of *T*. The procedure *Visit* performs some action with the data in *Info*, such as printing it out.

```
procedure Preorder(Root) recursive
Input:    Root (pointer to the root node of a binary tree T)
Output:  the preorder traversal of T
    if Root ≠ null then
        Visit(Root→Info)
        Preorder(Root→LeftChild)
        Preorder(Root→RightChild)
    endif
end Preorder
```

The procedures *Inorder* and *Postorder* have pseudocode identical to *Preorder* except for the order of the call to *Visit*.

Slightly different pseudocode for the tree traversals can be given when it is assumed that the tree *T* is not empty. To illustrate, we give pseudocode for the altered version of *Inorder*. By assuming that *Inorder2* is only invoked with nonempty trees, we avoid the need to check whether *Root* is **null** at the beginning of the code. Before attempting to traverse a subtree, we add a check to see whether the subtree is not empty. The depth of the recursion is reduced by one in the altered versions. However, it turns out that *Inorder* and *Inorder2* perform the same number of comparisons of a pointer variable to **null**.

```
procedure Inorder2(Root) recursive
Input:      Root (pointer to the root node of a tree T)   //T is assumed nonempty
Output:    the inorder traversal of T
    if Root→LeftChild ≠ null then
        Inorder2(Root→LeftChild)
    endif
    Visit(Root→Info)
    if Root→RightChild ≠ null then
        Inorder2(Root→RightChild)
    endif
end Inorder2
```

We now analyze the performance of *Inorder* (a similar analysis holds for *Preorder* and *Postorder*). The two main operations performed by *Inorder* are visiting a node (calls to *Visit*) and accessing a node. Because *Inorder* visits each node of *T* exactly once, the total number of node visits is *n*. During the performance of *Inorder*, each edge (line joining two nodes) in the tree *T* is traversed exactly twice, in opposite directions. For each edge traversal, the endpoint node (in the direction of the traversal) of the edge is accessed. Because the number of edges of a tree is one less than the number of nodes (see Chapter 11), *T* has $n - 1$ edges. It follows that *Inorder* performs $2(n - 1)$ node accesses, plus one additional initial access of the root. Therefore, the total number of node accesses performed by *Inorder* (or by *Preorder* or *Postorder*) is

$$1 + 2(n - 1) = 2n - 1.$$

Clearly, any algorithm that performs a traversal of a tree having *n* nodes must access each node at least once. Hence, any traversal algorithm must perform at least *n* node accesses. Because *Inorder* performs $2n - 1$ accesses, when we search for a better algorithm, we can only hope to narrow the gap between $2n - 1$ accesses and the lower bound of *n* accesses. *Inorder* can be modified to eliminate the reaccessing of nodes when returning to the inorder successor of a node *v* having no right child, where the inorder successor of *v* is the node visited immediately after *v* in the inorder traversal. We could eliminate the tail recursion, and use an explicit stack to simulate the remaining recursive call (in which case the inorder successor of a node with no right child is obtained by popping the stack). Alternatively, we could use the notion of an inorder threading, where a node with no right child contains instead a pointer to its inorder successor. These modifications of *Inorder* are developed in the exercises.

4.4.2 Traversing General Trees

We can generalize the three standard traversals of a binary tree to any tree. In fact, if a tree is implemented using the *LeftmostChild-NextSibling* representation, then these traversals simply reduce to the corresponding traversals of a binary tree. We can also define the preorder, inorder, and postorder traversals of a general tree *T* directly in terms of the recursive Definition 4.4.2.

DEFINITION 4.4.2 If *T* is not empty, the preorder traversal of *T* is defined recursively as follows:

1. Visit the root node *R*.
2. Perform successively a preorder traversal of $T_1, T_2, \ldots, T_j$.

FIGURE 4.13

Preorder, inorder, and postorder traversals of general T

preorder:	visit R	traverse T_1	traverse T_2 ...	traverse T_j
inorder:	traverse T_1	visit R	traverse T_2 ...	traverse T_j
postorder:	traverse T_1	traverse T_2 ...	traverse T_j	visit R

Again, the postorder traversal is identical to the preorder traversal except that steps 1 and 2 are interchanged. The definition of the inorder traversal of a general T is not as natural as it was for a binary tree because a visit can be performed in many intermediate orders. In Figure 4.13, we formulate an inorder traversal that visits a node immediately after traversing the leftmost subtree of the node.

Pseudocode for implementing preorder, inorder, and postorder traversals of general trees, as well as their generalizations to traversals of rooted forests, is developed in the exercises. As with binary trees, each of the standard traversals of general trees has its particular uses. For example, what amounts to a postorder traversal of a forest arises in an algorithm for determining the strongly connected components of the digraph (see Chapter 13). It turns out that a multivisit version of an inorder traversal is very useful in multiway search trees.

For general trees, visiting a node might occur more than once in the course of a traversal. For example, an inorder traversal might actually take the following form:

inorder: traverse T_1 visit$_1 R$ traverse T_2 visit$_2 R$ ... visit$_{j-1} R$ traverse T_j

where each visit of the node R, visit$_1 R$, visit$_2 R$, ... , visit$_{j-1} R$, results in a (possibly) different operation performed on the information fields in R. We call this type of traversal a multivisit inorder traversal. Multivisit inorder traversals can be used to visit the keys in a multiway search trees as defined in the next section.

4.5 Binary Search Trees

Given a totally ordered set S (the elements of S are called keys or identifiers), the *dictionary problem* is the well-known problem of designing an ADT to maintain a collection of items drawn from S. The classical dictionary problem restricts attention to the dictionary operations of inserting a key, deleting a key, and searching for a key, but we also might consider performing additional operations, such as finding the maximum or minimum elements or accessing the keys in sorted order.

In this section, we introduce the binary search tree ADT and show how it supports the dictionary operations. We assume that the entire binary search tree is kept in internal memory, which is a reasonable assumption if the number of keys to be maintained is not too large. For larger sets of keys (such as those typically in databases stored in external memory), other ADTs such as B-trees are more appropriate (see Chapter 21). However, as internal memory rapidly becomes larger and cheaper, binary trees held in internal memory and containing keys from database records held in external memory become more realistic.

Binary search trees are explicit generalizations of the implicit tree underlying the algorithm *BinarySearch*. The algorithm for inserting an element in a binary search tree is a variation of the searching strategy. Deletion is slightly more complicated, requiring in some cases a replacement of the deleted node by its inorder successor. We could also use the inorder predecessor for deletion, but for definiteness, we always use the inorder successor. A useful property of a binary search tree is that an inorder traversal visits the nodes in sorted order.

4.5.1 Definition and Examples of Binary Search Trees

A binary search tree T with respect to keys in the nodes of T can be defined recursively as follows:

DEFINITION 4.5.1   A binary tree T is called a binary search tree (with respect to a key field in each node) if T is empty or has root R and if its right and left subtrees RT and LT satisfy the following:

1. Each key in LT is not larger than the key in R.
2. Each key in RT is not smaller than the key in R.
3. Both LT and RT are binary search trees.

Figure 4.14 gives 6 of the 14 different binary search trees for the set of four keys (Ann, Joe, Pat, and Ray).

Given any set of n distinct keys (identifiers) and an arbitrary binary tree T on n nodes, there is a unique assignment of the keys to the nodes in T such that T becomes a binary search tree for the keys (see Exercise 4.30). Hence, the number of binary search trees containing a given set of n distinct keys equals the number

$$b_n = \frac{1}{n+1}\binom{2n}{n}$$ of binary trees on n nodes.

FIGURE 4.14

Sample binary
search trees for
the keys Ann, Joe,
Pat, and Ray

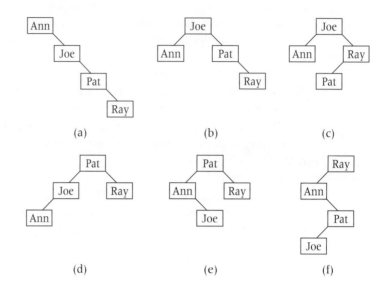

4.5.2 Searching a Binary Search Tree

A simple and efficient algorithm, *SearchBinSrchTree*, enables us to locate
information stored in binary search trees. For example, suppose we want to
determine which node in the tree (if any) has its key equal to a search element
X. When we initiate *SearchBinSrchTree,* it first compares *X* to the key contained in
the root. If *X* equals this key, we are done. Otherwise, if *X* is less than the key in
the root, the algorithm searches the left subtree and, if *X* is greater than the key
in the root, the algorithm searches the right subtree. *SearchBinSrchTree* returns
the pointer *Location* to the node where a search element *X* is found. If *X* is not
found in the tree, then *SearchBinSrchTree* sets *Location* to a node in the tree where
X can be inserted as a child and still maintain a search tree. In the following
pseudocode for *SearchBinSrchTree*, we assume that the nodes in the tree have the
structure described in Section 4.3.2.

```
procedure SearchBinSrchTree(Root, S, Location, Found)
Input:   Root (→BinaryTreeNode)      //points at root of a binary search tree
         X (KeyType)
Output:  Location (→BinaryTreeNode)  //points at occurrence of X, if any
         Found(Boolean)              //.false. if X not in tree, .true. otherwise
         Found ← .false.
         Location ← null
         Current ← Root
```

```
        while Current ≠ null .and. .not. Found do
            Location ← Current
            if X = Current→Key then
                Found ← .true.
            else
                if X < Current→Key then
                    Current ← Current→LeftChild
                else
                    Current ← Current→RightChild
                endif
            endif
        endwhile
    end SearchBinSrchTree
```

In Figure 4.15, we have not drawn the (implicit) leaf nodes corresponding to unsuccessful searches. The tree in Figure 4.14d is redrawn in Figure 4.15 with leaf nodes corresponding to unsuccessful searches added. For example, a search for 'Mary' would end up at the right child of 'Joe.' The latter node is where the key 'Mary' can be inserted and still maintain the binary search tree property.

FIGURE 4.15

Search tree with leaf nodes drawn representing unsuccessful searches

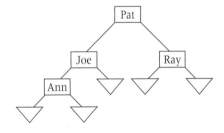

4.5.3 Inserting Nodes into Binary Search Trees

The following algorithm inserts a key X into a binary search tree T pointed to by *Root*. We assume that duplicate keys are not allowed in the tree (the case where duplicate keys are allowed is developed in the exercises). Hence, *InsertBinSrchTree* begins by calling *SearchBinSrchTree* to determine whether or not the key X is in the tree T. If X is not in the tree, then the output parameter *Location* of *SearchBinSrchTree* points to the node in the tree that is the appropriate parent node for the insertion of X. *InsertBinSrchTree* assumes that *Root* = **null** when it points to an empty tree.

```
procedure InsertBinSrchTree(Root, X)
Input:    Root (→BinaryTreeNode)          //points to root of binary search tree T
          X (KeyType)
Output:   Root (→BinaryTreeNode)          //points to root of the binary search tree
                                           obtained from T by inserting X
     if Root = null then                   //create a single-node tree containing X
          AllocateBinaryTreeNode(NodePtr)
          NodePtr→Key ← X
          Root ← NodePtr
     else
          SearchBinSrchTree(Root, X, Location, Found)
          if .not. Found then              //insert X into tree
               AllocateBinaryTreeNode(NodePtr)
               NodePtr→Key ← X
               if X < Location→Key then
                    Location→LeftChild ← NodePtr
               else
                    Location→RightChild ← NodePtr
               endif
          endif
     endif
end InsertBinSrchTree
```

A binary search tree can be created from a given set of keys by repeated invocations of *InsertBinSrchTree* with the keys as input parameters. We discuss this further in Section 4.5.6 in connection with the sorting algorithm treesort. Treesort is based on the fundamental property that inorder traversals of binary search trees visit the keys in increasing order.

4.5.4 Deleting Nodes from Binary Search Trees

There are three cases to consider when deleting a node v from a binary search tree:

1. v is a leaf node.
2. v is an internal node with a single child.
3. v is an internal node with two children.

In cases 1 and 2, we delete v by "splicing" an appropriate child of v to v's parent. In case 1, the appropriate child of v can be taken as either v's right or left child because they are both **null** (the pseudocode takes the right child). In case 2, the appropriate child of v is the single non-null child of v. The splicing out of v is illustrated in Figure 4.16, where we show the appropriate child of v as its right child.

FIGURE 4.16

Splicing out node *v*

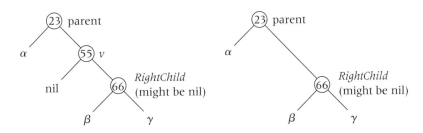

Case 3 is reduced to case 1 or 2 by replacing the values in the information and key fields in the node *v* by the values in corresponding fields of its inorder successor *w*, and then deleting *w* (which has at most one child). In particular, we do not alter the child pointer fields in *v* or its parent. Recall that the inorder successor of any node *v* having a right child can be found by moving to the right child and then traveling left as far as possible until a node *w* having no left child is encountered. Then *w* is the inorder successor of *v*. We leave it as an exercise to verify that the resulting tree is a binary search tree.

In Figure 4.17, we illustrate the three cases of node deletion. In each case, we assume that the deletion is from the binary search given in Figure 4.17a. We show the value of the key field in each node.

For cases 1 and 2, deleting a node *v* is done in constant time. In case 3, we must determine the inorder successor of *v*, which might require depth(*T*) node accesses and pointer comparisons.

FIGURE 4.17

Illustrations of the three cases of node deletion from a binary search tree. (a) Binary search tree before deletion of a node; (b) case 1 deletion: delete node *k*; (c) case 2 deletion: delete node *d*; (d) case 3 deletion: delete node *g*

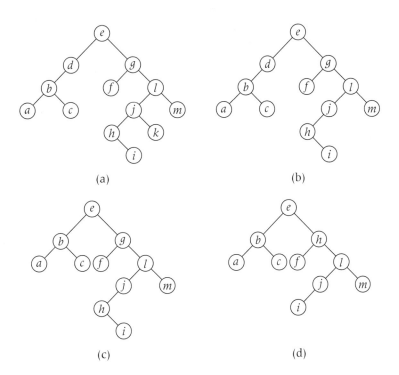

On input to *DeleteBinSrchTree*, the input-output parameters *Node* and *Parent* are pointers to the node *v* to be deleted and its parent, respectively. As output parameters, *Node* and *Parent* remain unchanged if *v* has at most one child, otherwise *Node* and *Parent* point to the inorder successor of *v* and its parent, respectively. If *Parent* = **null**, then the root node is deleted. In the following pseudocode for *DeleteBinSrchTree*, for convenience, we assume that the nodes in the tree have a parent field. We leave it as an exercise to rewrite the pseudocode for the case when no parent field exists.

```
procedure DeleteBinSrchTree(Root, Node)
Input:     Root(→BinSrchTreeNode)          //points to root of binary search tree T
              Node (→BinSrchTreeNode) //points to node v to be deleted
Output:    Root (→BinSrchTreeNode)  //points to root of binary search tree T'
                                                obtained from T by deleting v
if Node→LeftChild ≠ null .and. Node→RightChild ≠ null then
       Successor ← InorderSucc(Node)
       Node→Info ← Successor→Info
       Node→Key ← Successor→Key
       Node ← Successor
       Parent ← Node→ParentField
   endif
//Now Node points at node w to be deleted that has at most one child, so
//define the appropriate child x of w for splicing to w's parent. Note that x is
//null if w is a leaf.
       if Node→LeftChild ≠ null then          //determine appropriate child x of w
           ApproprChild ← Node→LeftChild         for splicing to parent of w
       else
           ApproprChild ← Node→RightChild
       endif
       if Parent = null then   //make x new root of tree
           Root ← ApproprChild
       else                                   //see which child of the parent
           if Parent→LeftChild = Node then //of w should be spliced to x
               Parent→LeftChild ← ApproprChild
           else
               Parent→RightChild ← ApproprChild
           endif
       endif
end DeleteBinSrchTree
```

The input parameter *Node* is typically determined by first calling *SearchBinSrchTree* to determine where a node having a given key is found. However, the pseudocode for *SearchBinSrchTree* does not determine *Parent*. We leave it as an exercise to alter *SearchBinSrchTree* so it determines the locations of both the search element and its parent.

4.5.5 Multiway Search Trees

Multiway search trees generalize binary search trees by allowing more than one key to be stored in a given node. Thus, multiway search trees allow multiway branching to occur at a given node, instead of the two-way branching allowed by binary trees. The keys in a given node of a multiway search tree are maintained as an ordered list. During a search of a multiway search tree, when a search element reaches a given node, a search of the keys in the node is performed. (The latter search is usually a linear search, but if the node contains a sufficiently large number of keys and the keys are maintained in an array, then a binary search might be used.) Either the search element equals one of the keys, or a branch is made to an appropriate child's subtree (which contains the key if it is in the tree at all), where the search continues. The following recursive definition places the fairly obvious restriction on the keys in a multiway search tree that must hold to support the natural generalization of the search strategy for binary search trees. In the definition, the value of j varies with the particular node in T.

DEFINITION 4.5.2 A multiway search tree T is either empty or consists of a root R containing j keys, $key_1 \leq key_2 \leq \ldots \leq key_j, j \geq 1$, and a collection of subtrees $T_1, T_2, \ldots, T_{j+1}$ having the following two properties:

1. For any $k_i \in T_i$, $1 \leq i \leq j + 1$, we have

$$k_1 \leq key_1 \leq k_2 \leq key_2 \leq \cdots \leq k_j \leq key_j \leq k_{j+1}.$$

2. Every T_i is a multiway search tree.

For a given fixed constant m, multiway search trees for which the maximum number of keys in a given node is bounded above by $m - 1$ are called m-way search trees. For example, a four-way search tree on 15 nodes is shown in Figure 4.18. Note that a binary search tree is a two-way search tree.

REMARKS

1. A commonly used multiway search tree is the B-tree (see Chapter 21). B-trees are subject to several additional restrictions, including bounds on the minimum and maximum number of keys allowed in each node. B-trees also satisfy the following more restrictive version of condition (2):

2. Either *every* T_i is empty or *every* T_i is a nonempty multiway search tree.

We adopt the more general condition (2) in our definition of multiway search trees so that multiway search trees generalize the notion of binary search trees.

FIGURE 4.18

A four-way search
tree on 15 nodes

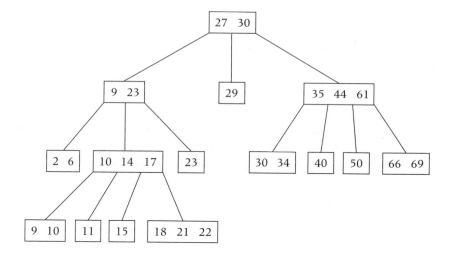

Figure 4.19 contains a high-level procedure determining a location in the multiway search tree T where the key k is found. In our high-level description, we do not specify how the tree T is implemented. The location of k consists of a pair (v,i), where v is a node of T in which k occurs, and i is a position of the occurrence of k in the ordered list of keys of v. If k does not occur in the tree, we set $i = 0$ and regard v as undefined. We initially perform step 1 in Figure 4.19 with a variable *Root* pointing at the root of T. Before repeating step 1, *Root* is redefined to point to the appropriate subtree being searched.

FIGURE 4.19

High-level
description of
procedure for
searching a
multiway search
tree

1. If k occurs in position i of the node v pointed to by *Root,* then return (v,i).
2. If we are at a leaf, then return $i = 0$.
3. Redefine *Root* to point at the root of subtree T_i and repeat step 1, where T_i is determined by one of the following three conditions:
   a. $i = 1$ and $k < key_1$,
   b. $1 < i < j$ and $key_{i-1} < key < key_1$,
   c. $i = j$ and $key > key_j$.

4.5.6 Treesort

The algorithm treesort is based on the following interesting key fact:

Key Fact

An inorder traversal of a binary search tree visits the nodes in increasing order of the keys.

You should convince yourself of the validity of this key fact (in Exercise 4.36, a formal proof uses mathematical induction). As a result of this fact, we can sort a given list $L[0:n - 1]$ by creating a binary search tree T whose keys are the elements of L and then performing an inorder traversal of T. In Exercise 4.33, we develop the algorithm *InsertBinSrchTree2* for inserting a key into a nonempty binary search tree with duplicate keys allowed. Given an input list $L[0:n - 1]$, the following procedure, *CreateBinSrchTree*, creates a binary search tree whose keys are the elements from L.

> **procedure** *CreateBinSrchTree(L[0:n − 1], Root)*
> **Input:**   *L[0:n − 1]* (a list of size *n*)
> **Output:** *Root(→BinaryTreeNode)*   //points to root of the binary search
>   //tree whose keys are the elements from *L*
>
>   *AllocateBinaryTreeNode(Root)*
>   *Root→Key ← L[0]*
>   **for** *i ← 0* **to** *n − 1* **do**
>   *InsertBinSrchTree2(Root, L[i])*
>   **endfor**
> **end** *CreateBinSrchTree*

In Figure 4.20, we show the binary search tree created by *CreateBinSrchTree* for a sample input list $L[0:15]$.

In the case where the list is already sorted, *CreateBinSrchTree* creates a completely skewed tree and has worst-case complexity given by

$$W(n) = 1 + 2 + \cdots + n - 1 = \frac{n(n - 1)}{2} \in \Theta(n^2).$$

However, in spite of the quadratic worst-case complexity of *CreateBinSrchTree*, it turns out that it has $\Theta(n\log n)$ average complexity. Because an inorder traversal of a tree is linear, treesort also has quadratic worst-case complexity and $\Theta(n\log n)$ average complexity.

Proposition 4.5.1 extends to multiway search trees the useful property that an inorder traversal of a binary search tree visits the nodes in sorted order. In our multivisit inorder traversal, if node v contains q keys, then $Visit(v,i)$ processes the ith key in the sequential ordering of the keys in the node, $i = 1, \ldots, q$.

Proposition 4.5.1   A multivisit inorder traversal of a multiway search tree visits the nodes in sorted order.   □

A formal proof of Proposition 4.5.1 is left to the exercises.

FIGURE 4.20

The binary search
tree created by
CreateBinSrchTree
for input list
$L[0:15]$ = (23, 10,
10, 10, 23, 12, 23,
11, 10, 50, 8, 10,
30, 5, 8, 23).
We show the list
element (key)
inside each
node and its index
in the original list
outside each node.

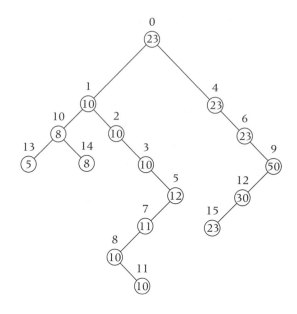

REMARK

Notice in Figure 4.20 that when encountering an existing key with the same value as a new key that we inserted in a tree , we always moved to the right. Of course, the binary search tree property would have also been maintained if we went to the left instead. We chose to use the *move-to-the-right rule* for a good reason: When creating a binary search tree by successively inserting a sequence of keys, an inorder traversal of the resulting search tree will visit duplicate keys in the order in which they were inserted. The latter property ensures that the procedure treesort is a stable sorting algorithm (see Exercise 4.37). It also facilitates visiting the set of nodes having a common key value.

4.6 Priority Queues and Heaps

A *priority queue* is a collection of elements, each of which has a priority value; and when an element is chosen for deletion from the collection, it is always the element of highest priority. (Note that a priority queue is *not* a queue—that is, it is not a FIFO list—but this ambiguity has become standard terminology.) One way to maintain a priority queue would be as a list ordered by priority values, with the highest-priority element at the end of the list. With this type of priority queue, deletion of the element would consist of a single list operation with $\Theta(1)$ complexity, and insertion of an element would have $\Theta(n)$ complexity in the worst case. Similarly, a priority queue could be maintained as a simple un-ordered list, in which case deletion would require a linear scan to find the element of highest priority; in this type of priority queue, deletion would have $\Theta(n)$ complexity in the worst case, and insertion would have $\Theta(1)$ complexity. It would be nice to find a data structure that would have, say, logarithmic complexity for both operations of deletion and insertion. The data structure known as a heap does the job.

4.6.1 Heap Implementation of a Priority Queue

The underlying structure of a heap is a complete binary tree whose root contains the highest-priority element.

DEFINITION 4.6.1 A *max-heap* (*min-heap*) *H* is a complete binary tree whose information fields contain values (keys) having the following *max-heap* (*min-heap*) *property*: Given any node *v* in *H*, the value of *v* is not smaller (not larger) than the value of any node in the subtree having *v* as a root.

For convenience, when we discuss max-heaps in this text, we sometimes simply use the word *heap* for *max-heap*. A completely analogous discussion would apply for *min-heaps* (see Figure 4.21).

> **Key Fact**
>
> Clearly, the max-heap property can be equivalently expressed by requiring that the value of each node *v* be no smaller than the value of its left child or right child (if they exist). This allows us to localize the heap property to each node. Thus, we can talk about the heap property holding or not holding at a given node.

FIGURE 4.21

(a) Max-heap;
(b) min-heap

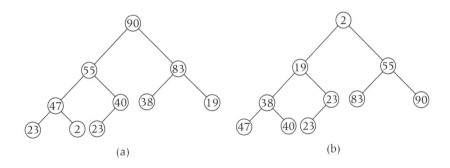

(a)   (b)

A very convenient implementation of a heap results from storing the n key values in an array $A[0:m - 1]$, where $m \geq n$. The convenience of the array implementation results from the ease in which we can reference the children of a node, as well as its parent. Indeed, given a node of index i, its left child has index $2i + 1$ and its right child has index $2i + 2$ (assuming that these children exist). Also, if $i > 0$, the parent of a node of index i is given by $\lfloor (i - 1)/2 \rfloor$.

Figure 4.22 shows the max-heap given in Figure 4.21 stored in an array $A[0:m - 1]$, $m \geq 10$.

FIGURE 4.22

Max-heap stored in array A [0: m−1], $m \geq 10$

A Index	0	1	2	3	4	5	6	7	8	9
Value	90	55	83	47	40	38	19	23	2	23

4.6.2 Inserting into a Heap

We now describe an algorithm for inserting a new element into an existing heap. We suppose that the existing heap occupies positions $A[0], \ldots, A[HeapSize - 1]$ within the array $A[0:m - 1]$. The idea is to initially place the new element in position $A[HeapSize]$ and let it "rise" along the unique path from $A[HeapSize]$ to the root until it finds a proper position. Letting $i = HeapSize$, we begin by comparing x to the value of the parent node $A[\lfloor (i - 1)/2 \rfloor]$. If x has a larger value than its parent, we move the parent down to position i and move x up to the previous position of its parent. The argument is then repeated until x has been moved up the path to a proper position. We illustrate this movement in Figure 4.23, where we insert the value $x = 70$ into the max-heap given in Figure 4.21.

The pseudocode for the insertion operation follows. Note that we do not need to make an assignment of x until we find a proper place for its insertion into the heap.

```
procedure InsertMaxHeap(A[0:m − 1], HeapSize, x)
Input:    A[0:m − 1] (an array containing a heap in positions 0, . . . , HeapSize − 1)
          HeapSize (the number of elements in the heap)
          x (a value to be inserted into heap)
Output:   A[0:m − 1] (array altered by addition of x and heap maintained)
          HeapSize (input HeapSize + 1)
      i ← HeapSize
      j ← ⌊(i − 1)/2⌋
                            //traverse path to root until proper
                            position for inserting x is found
```

FIGURE 4.23

Inserting the value
$x = 70$ into the
existing heap
$A[0:9]$

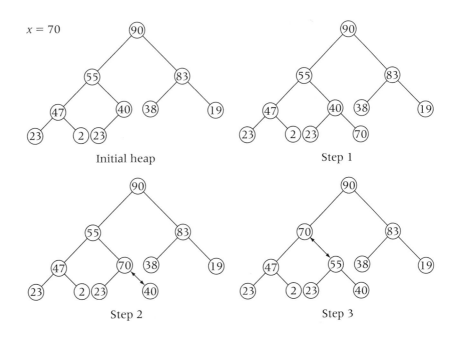

```
    while j ≥ 0 .and. A[j] < x do
        A[i] ← A[j]                    //move parent down one position in path
        i ← j                         //move x up one position in path
        j ←⌊(j − 1)/2⌋
    endwhile
    //i is now a proper position for x
    A[i] ← x
    HeapSize ← HeapSize + 1
end InsertMaxHeap
```

Using comparisons to an element in the heap as our basic operation, the worst-case complexity for *InsertMaxHeap* occurs when the inserted element must rise all the way to the root. Thus, *InsertMaxHeap* has $\Theta(\log n)$ worst-case complexity.

4.6.3 Deleting from a Heap

The other basic operation for a priority queue that we need to implement is removing the highest-priority element. For our heap implementation, this element is at the root. To remove the root, the bottom heap element $x = A[HeapSize - 1]$ is first elevated to the root and then allowed to "fall" down an appropriate path in the complete binary tree $A[0:HeapSize - 2]$ until it finds a proper position. Initially, x is compared to the larger of the two children $A[1]$ and $A[2]$. If x is smaller, the larger child is elevated to the root (made "king of the heap"), and x moves down to the position formerly occupied by the elevated child. The argument is then repeated until a proper position for x is found. We illustrate this operation in Figure 4.24 by removing the root from the max-heap given in Figure 4.23.

The adjustment operation illustrated in steps 1 through 3 in Figure 4.24 can be applied to the subtree rooted at any node having index i in a complete binary tree $A[0:n - 1]$, where the subtrees of $A[0:n - 1]$ with roots at the two children $2i + 1$ and $2i + 2$ are both heaps. In algorithm $AdjustMaxHeap$, $A[i]$ follows an appropriate path in the subtree with i as a root, thereby making a heap out of the subtree.

FIGURE 4.24

Removing the root
from a heap

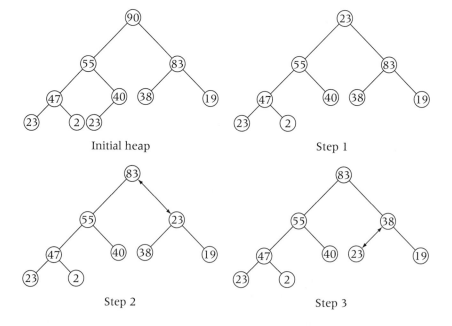

```
procedure AdjustMaxHeap(A[0:m − 1], n, i)
Input:    A[0:m − 1] (an array)
          n (consider A[0:n − 1] as complete binary tree, n ≤ m)
          i (index where subtrees of A[0:n − 1] rooted at 2i + 1and 2i + 2 are heaps)
Output:  A[0:m − 1]  (subtree of A[0:n − 1] rooted at A[i], adjusted so that it
                       becomes a heap)
   Temp ← A[i]
   //traverse down a path until a proper position for Temp = A[i] is found
   Found ← .false.     //Found signals when a proper position is found
   j ← 2*i + 1         //j is the path finder. At completion of loop,
                       //⌊(j −1)/2⌋ is a proper position for Temp = A[i]
   while j ≤ n .and. .not. Found do
      if j < n − 1.and. A[j] < A[j + 1] then //then move to right child j + 1
            j ← j + 1              //path finder updated to right child
      endif
      if Temp ≥ A[j] then
            Found ← .true.
      else
         A⌊(j − 1)/2⌋←A[j]    //move larger child up one position in path
         j ← 2*j + 1 //move path finder to next possible position for Temp
      endif
   endwhile
   A⌊(j − 1)/2⌋ ← Temp
end AdjustMaxHeap
```

Clearly, the worst-case complexity of *AdjustMaxHeap* occurs when the element $A[i]$ must fall all the way down to the bottom of the heap. Thus, when calling *AdjustMaxHeap* with the parameter i, in the worst case, we make $\log_2 n - \log_2 i$ comparisons.

The operation of removing the root from a heap is accomplished by the following pseudocode:

```
procedure RemoveMaxHeap(A[0:m − 1], HeapSize, x)
Input:     A[0:m − 1] (an array containing a heap in positions 0, . . . , HeapSize − 1)
           HeapSize (the number of elements in the heap)
Output:    A[0:m − 1] (array altered by removal of the root A[0] and heap maintained)
           x (assigned the value of the (original) root A[0])
           HeapSize (input HeapSize − 1)
   x ← A[0]
   HeapSize ← HeapSize − 1
   A[0] ← A[HeapSize]
   AdjustMaxHeap(A[0:m − 1], HeapSize, 0)
end RemoveMaxHeap
```

RemoveMaxHeap has $\Theta(\log n)$ worst-case complexity, so that we have implemented both the insertion of an element and the removal of the highest priority element with worst-case complexity $\Theta(\log n)$.

4.6.4 Creating a Heap

Given n values in the array $A[0:m - 1]$, how can we make $A[0:n - 1]$ into a heap? The most obvious answer is to sequentially invoke *InsertMaxHeap* $(A[0:m - 1],HeapSize,x)$ for $x = A[0], \ldots, A[n - 1]$. In fact, this method is well suited to applications where the heap is maintained dynamically, with new elements being added to an already existing heap.

procedure *CreateMaxHeap1* $(A[0:m - 1], n)$
Input: $A[0:m - 1]$ (an array)
             n (values in $A[0:n - 1]$ considered as complete binary tree, $n \leq m$)
Output: $A[0:m - 1]$ ($A[0:n - 1]$ made into a heap)
   HeapSize ← 0
   for j ← 0 **to** $n - 1$
      InsertMaxHeap$(A[0:m - 1], HeapSize, A[j])$
   endfor
end *CreateMaxHeap1*

Figure 4.25 shows the action of *CreateMaxHeap1* on the set of elements (10,5,20,30,25,7,40). We show the result after each iteration of the **for** loop.

Because the worst-case complexity of *InsertMaxHeap* belongs to $O(\log n)$, the worst-case complexity $W(n)$ of *CreateMaxHeap1* belongs to $O(n\log n)$. The worst case occurs when the elements are in increasing order, so that each element must rise to the root when it is inserted. We now show that $W(n)$ belongs to

FIGURE 4.25

Action of *MakeMaxHeap1* on the set of elements (10, 5, 20, 30, 25, 7, 40)

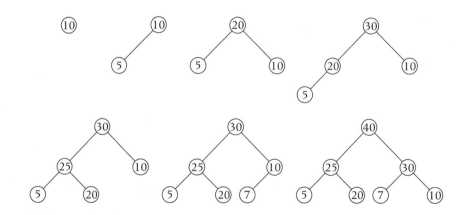

$\Omega(n\log n)$. Let $k = \lfloor \log_2 n \rfloor$ and recall that a complete binary tree on n elements has 2^i nodes at level i for $i = 0, \ldots, k - 1$. Because we make i comparisons for each node at level i, and applying identity (1.2.11), we have

$$W(n) > \sum_{i=0}^{k-1} i2^i = 2^k(k-2) + 2 \in \Omega(n\log n).$$

Hence, $W(n)$ belongs to $\Omega(n\log n) \cap O(n\log n) = \Theta(n\log n)$.

An alternative algorithm *CreateMaxHeap2* for creating a heap has worst-case complexity in $O(n)$. *CreateMaxHeap2* works by repeated calls to *AdjustMaxHeap*$(A[0:m-1],n,i)$. Recall that *AdjustMaxHeap*$(A[0:m-1],n,i)$ requires that the subtrees in $A[0:n-1]$ with roots $2i + 1$ and $2i + 2$ are already heaps. This will certainly be true if these two roots are leaf nodes of $A[0:n-1]$. Thus, we can make a heap by initially calling *AdjustMaxHeap*$(A[0:m-1],n,i)$ with $i = \lfloor (n-2)/2 \rfloor$ and then sequentially calling *AdjustMaxHeap*$(A[0:m-1],n,i)$ as i is decremented by 1 each time, until we finally reach the root.

```
procedure CreateMaxHeap2(A[0:m − 1], n)
Input:   A[0:m − 1] (an array)
              n (values in A[0:n − 1] considered as complete binary tree, n ≤ m)
Output:    A[0:m − 1] (A[0:n − 1] made into a heap)
   for i ← ⌊(n − )/2⌋ down to 0 do
     AdjustMaxHeap(A[0:m − 1], n, i )
   endfor
end CreateMaxHeap2
```

The action of *CreateMaxHeap2* is illustrated in Figure 4.26 on the set (10,5,20,30,25,7,40), which was the same set illustrated in Figure 4.25 for *CreateMaxHeap1*. Note that the heaps created are rather different, but both satisfy the heap property. In Figure 4.26, we show the array before and after each call to *AdjustMaxHeap*. We indicate in each "before" picture the particular subtree that is being made into a heap.

During the execution of the call to *AdjustMaxHeap*$(A[0:m-1],n,i)$, an element at level j will fall at most $k - j$ levels, where $k = \lfloor \log_2 n \rfloor$. Again, for $j < k$, there are exactly 2^j nodes at level j. We begin calling *AdjustMaxHeap*$(A[0:m-1],n,i)$ with $i = \lfloor (n-2)/2 \rfloor$, which is (the index of) a node at level $k - 1$. Hence, the worst-case complexity of *CreateMaxHeap2* satisfies

$$W(n) \le \sum_{i=0}^{k-1} 2^i(k - i) = \sum_{i=1}^{k} i2^{k-i} = 2^k \sum_{i=1}^{k} \frac{i}{2^i}.$$

FIGURE 4.26

Making a
max-heap using
MakeMaxHeap2

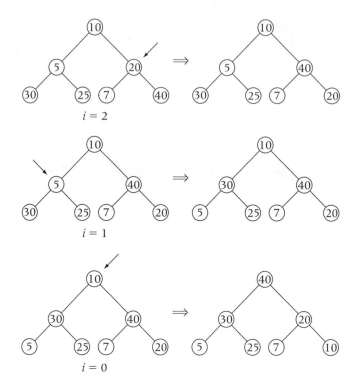

Applying identity (1.2.11) with $x = 1/2$, we obtain

$$W(n) \leq 2^k \left[2 - \frac{k + 2}{2^k} \right] = 2^{k+1} - (k + 2) \leq 2n \in O(n).$$

Because *CreateMaxHeap2* does $\lfloor n/2 \rfloor$ comparisons in the best case (when we
have a heap at the outset), we have shown that the best-case, worst-case, and
average complexities of *CreateMaxHeap2* all belong to $\Theta(n)$.

4.6.5 Sorting by Selection: Selectionsort Versus Heapsort

One of the simplest strategies for sorting a list $L[0:n - 1]$ of size n in increasing
order consists of the following steps: (1) Select the largest element in L and interchange it with $L[n - 1]$; (2) select the largest element in the sublist $L[0:n - 2]$
and interchange it with $L[n - 2]$; (3) in general, in the ith step, select the largest element in the sublist $L[0:n - i]$ and interchange it with $L[n - i], i = 1, \ldots, n - 1$.
Clearly, this strategy yields a sorted list. The most straightforward strategy for selecting the largest elements is to make a linear scan, as in the procedure *Max*. The
resulting algorithm is known as selectionsort. Clearly, selectionsort performs
$(n - 1) + (n - 2) + \cdots + 1 = n(n - 1)/2$ comparisons for any input list of size n,
so its worst-case, best-case, and average complexities are all in $\Theta(n^2)$.

The inefficiency of selectionsort results from the procedure used to select the largest elements. Our selection procedure amounted to regarding the list as a priority queue, where the priority is the value (key) of the list element. The algorithm heapsort emulates selectionsort except that the priority queue of list elements is maintained as a heap, thereby reducing the complexity from $\Theta(n^2)$ to $\Theta(n\log n)$.

Procedure *HeapSort* uses the algorithm *AdjustMaxHeap*. First, *CreateMaxHeap2* is called to create the heap $A[0:n - 1]$. Then the root is interchanged with the element at the bottom of the heap (position n) and *AdjustMaxHeap*($A[0:m - 1],n-1,1$) called. The new root is now interchanged with the element at position $n - 1$, and the process is continued. The pseudocode for *HeapSort* follows.

```
procedure HeapSort(A[0:n − 1])
Input:     A[0:n − 1] (a list of size n)
Output:    A[0:n − 1] sorted in increasing order
   CreateMaxHeap2(A[0:n − 1], n)
   for i ← 1 to n − 1 do
               //interchange A[0] with A[n − i]
       interchange (A[0], A[n − i])
       AdjustMaxHeap(A[0:n − 1], n − i + 1, 0)
   endfor
end HeapSort
```

The call to *CreateMaxHeap2* has best-case and worst-case complexities $\Theta(n)$, whereas the $n - 1$ calls to *AdjustMaxHeap* each have $\Theta(1)$ best-case and $\Theta(\log n)$ worst-case complexities. Thus, *HeapSort* has $\Theta(n)$ best-case complexity and $\Theta(n\log n)$ worst-case complexity. Because *HeapSort* is a comparison-based sorting algorithm, by lower-bound theory (see Chapter 25), it has $\Omega(n\log n)$ average complexity, which implies that *HeapSort* has $\Theta(n \log n)$ average complexity.

4.7   Implementing Disjoint Sets

Many algorithms, particularly graph algorithms, involve maintaining a (dynamically changing) equivalence relation on some universal (or base) set $S = \{s_1, s_2, \ldots, s_n\}$. For example, an efficient implementation of Kruskal's algorithm for finding a minimum-cost spanning tree in a weighted graph involves successively taking unions of vertex sets in different equivalence classes determined by trees in a forest. Because an equivalence relation on S determines a partition of S into disjoint subsets, the problem of maintaining equivalence relations reduces to the problem of maintaining disjoint sets. The two main operations associated with the disjoint set ADT are efficiently finding the set containing a given element and forming the union of two sets.

One method of maintaining disjoint sets would be to represent each subset $A \subseteq S$ by its characteristic vector $(v_1, v_2, \ldots, v_n)$, where $v_i = 0$ if $v_i \notin A$, and $v_i = 1$ if $v_i \in A$, $i = 1, 2, \ldots, n$. Given any collection C of k disjoint subsets $A_1, A_2, \ldots, A_k$ of the base set S, finding the set containing a given element s_i would amount to checking which of the k characteristic vectors contains a 1 in position i. For example, if we maintain a linked list of pointers to the k characteristic vectors, then this check has $\Omega(k)$ worst-case complexity, and requires $\Omega(kn)$ storage locations. Taking the union of two sets would amount to making a linear scan of the two characteristic vectors representing the two sets, resulting in linear complexity (again, assuming the above implementation of maintaining the characteristic vectors). Using trees, we now show how to achieve logarithmic behavior for both union and find operations, and also require only a one-dimensional integer array of length n to represent the disjoint sets.

4.7.1 Union and Find Algorithms

For disjoint sets, efficient implementations of the union and find operations are based on the parent array representation of a forest. Consider any collection C of k disjoint subsets $A_1, A_2 \ldots, A_k$ of the base set S, where for convenience we assume that $S = \{0, 1, \ldots, n - 1\}$. A rooted forest F represents the collection C of disjoint sets if it consists of k rooted trees $T_1, T_2, \ldots, T_k$ such that the vertex set of T_i is A_i, $i = 1, 2, \ldots, k$. Clearly, the k sets $A_1, A_2, \ldots, A_k$ are uniquely determined by the single array $Parent[0:n - 1]$ of the parent-array implementation of F. Further, once the array $Parent[0:n - 1]$ is given, the set A_i can be identified by the single element r_i, where r_i is the root of T_i, $i = 1, 2, \ldots, k$ (see Figure 4.27).

Given an element $x \in A_1 \cup A_2 \cup \ldots \cup A_k$, the following procedure, *Find1*, returns the root r of the tree in forest F containing x.

```
procedure Find1 (Parent[0:n − 1], x, r)
Input:    Parent[0:n − 1] (array representing disjoint subsets of S)
          x (an element of S)
Output:   r (the root of the tree corresponding to the subset containing x)
    r ← x
    while Parent[r] ≥ 0 do
        r ← Parent[r]
    endwhile
end Find1
```

The complexity of *Find1* is measured by the number of iterations of the **while** loop. Clearly, the complexity of *Find1* depends on the depths of the trees T_i in F. Thus, it is desirable to keep the depths of the trees in the forest relatively small.

FIGURE 4.27

Three sample forest
representations of
the collection $\mathscr{C}$

Disjoint collection of sets: $\mathscr{C} = \{\{0,2,4,8\},\{3,5,7,9,10\},\{1,6\},\{11\}\}$

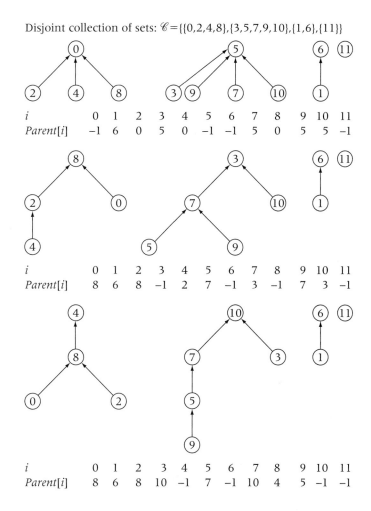

i	0	1	2	3	4	5	6	7	8	9	10	11
$Parent[i]$	−1	6	0	5	0	−1	−1	5	0	5	5	−1

i	0	1	2	3	4	5	6	7	8	9	10	11
$Parent[i]$	8	6	8	−1	2	7	−1	3	−1	7	3	−1

i	0	1	2	3	4	5	6	7	8	9	10	11
$Parent[i]$	8	6	8	10	−1	7	−1	10	4	5	−1	−1

Given $C = \{A_1, A_2, \ldots, A_k\}$, let C_{ij} denote the collection of $k - 1$ sets obtained from C by removing sets A_i and A_j and adding the set $A_i \cup A_j$. Consider the two forests F_{ij} and F_{ji}, where F_{ij} is obtained from F by setting $Parent(r_j) = r_i$, and F_{ji} is obtained from F by setting $Parent(r_i) = r_j$. Both forests represent the collection of sets C_{ij}. To help minimize the depth of the tree representing the union of A_i and A_j, we choose the forest F_{ij} if T_i has more vertices than T_j; otherwise, we choose the forest F_{ji}. This choice can be made instantly (in constant time) by dynamically keeping track of the number n_i of vertices in each tree T_i. An efficient way of keeping track of n_i without allocating additional memory locations is to dynamically store the negative of n_i in $Parent[r_i]$. The root vertices are still distinguishable from the other vertices because they index those locations of the array $Parent[0:n - 1]$ having negative values.

The following pseudocode for the algorithm *Union* computes the parent array implementation of the union of two sets based on the preceding discussion.

```
procedure Union(Parent[0:n − 1], r, s)
Input:     Parent[0:n − 1] (an array representing disjoint sets)
           r,s (roots of the trees representing two disjoint sets A, B)

Output:    Parent[0:n − 1] (an array representing disjoint sets after forming A ∪ B)
       sum ← Parent[r] + Parent[s]
       if      Parent[r] > Parent[s] then     //tree rooted at s has more vertices
               Parent[r] ← s                        than tree rooted at r
               Parent[s] ← sum
       else
               Parent[s] ← r
               Parent[r] ← sum
       endif
end Union
```

When implementing disjoint sets in a particular algorithm, the initial collection C of disjoint sets is usually the collection of all singleton subsets of the base set S. Figure 4.28 illustrates a sample sequence of calls to the procedure *Union*, starting with the collection of singleton subsets of the base set $S = \{0,1, \ldots , 8\}$.

Proposition 4.7.1 Let F be any forest resulting from some sequence of calls to *Union*, where the initial input forest consists of isolated vertices. Then the depth of any tree in F having j vertices is at most $\lfloor \log_2 j \rfloor$. □

We leave the proof of Proposition 4.7.1 as an exercise. It follows from Proposition 4.7.1 that if we start with a collection C consisting of singleton sets and perform a sequence of calls to *Union*, then the computing time of *Find1* for a given input x is $O(\log j)$, where j is the cardinality of the set containing x. Thus, the worst-case complexity in making an intermixed sequence of calls to *Union* and *Find1*, n calls to *Union*, and $m \geq n$ calls to *Find1*, is $O(m\log n)$.

4.7.2 Improved Union and Find Algorithms Using the Collapsing Rule

Even though the procedures *Union* and *Find1* are very efficient and might seem the best possible, there is still room for improvement. The improvement comes by modifying *Find1*(*Parent*[0:n − 1],x,r) as follows. After r is obtained, we can traverse the path from x to r again and set *Parent*[v] = r for each vertex v

FIGURE 4.28

Representative
forests and parent
arrays for a sample
sequence of calls to
procedure *Union*

Initial collection: {{0},{1},{2},{3},{4},{5},{6},{7},{8}}

i	0	1	2	3	4	5	6	7	8
$Parent[i]$	-1	-1	-1	-1	-1	-1	-1	-1	-1

Call *Union*[*Parent*[0:8],2,5] ⇒ {{0},{1},{2,5},{3},{4},{6},{7},{8}}

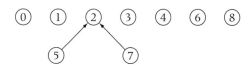

i	0	1	2	3	4	5	6	7	8
$Parent[i]$	-1	-1	-2	-1	-1	2	-1	-1	-1

Call *Union*[*Parent*[0:8],2,7] ⇒ {{0},{1},{2,5,7},{3},{4},{6},{8}}

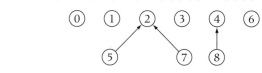

i	0	1	2	3	4	5	6	7	8
$Parent[i]$	-1	-1	-3	-1	-1	2	-1	2	-1

Call *Union*[*Parent*[0:8],4,8] ⇒ {{0},{1},{2,5,7},{3},{4,8},{6}}

i	0	1	2	3	4	5	6	7	8
$Parent[i]$	-1	-1	-3	-1	-2	2	-1	2	4

Call *Union*[*Parent*[0:8],0,4] ⇒ {{0,4,8},{1},{2,5,7},{3},{6}}

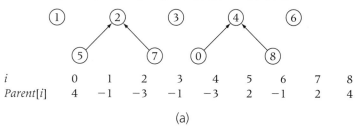

i	0	1	2	3	4	5	6	7	8
$Parent[i]$	4	-1	-3	-1	-3	2	-1	2	4

(a)

continued

FIGURE 4.28

Continued

Call *Union*[*Parent*[0:8],2,4] ⇒ {{0,2,4,5,7,8},{1},{3},{6}}

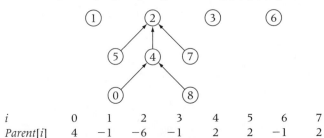

i	0	1	2	3	4	5	6	7	8
Parent[*i*]	4	−1	−6	−1	2	2	−1	2	4

Call *Union*[*Parent*[0:8],1,6] ⇒ {{0,2,4,5,7,8},{1,6},{3}}

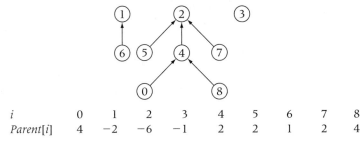

i	0	1	2	3	4	5	6	7	8
Parent[*i*]	4	−2	−6	−1	2	2	1	2	4

Call *Union*[*Parent*[0:8],1,2] ⇒ {{0,1,2,4,5,6,7,8},{3}}

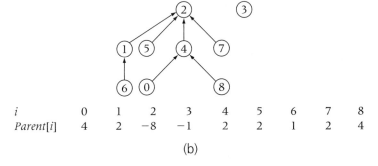

i	0	1	2	3	4	5	6	7	8
Parent[*i*]	4	2	−8	−1	2	2	1	2	4

(b)

encountered. This "collapsing" of the path basically doubles the computing time of *Find1*. However, it tends to reduce the depth of the trees in the forest so that an overall improvement is achieved in the efficiency of making an intermixed sequence of union and find operations. The following procedure, *Find2*, implements the collapsing rule.

procedure *Find2*(*Parent*[0:*n* − 1], *x, r*)
Input: *Parent*[0:*n* − 1] (an array representing disjoint subsets of *S*)
          x (an element of *S*)
Output: *r* (the root of the tree corresponding to subset containing *x*)
     r ← *x*
   while *Parent*[*r*] > 0 **do**
       r ← *Parent*[*r*]

```
        endwhile
        y ← x
        while y ≠ r do
            Temp ← Parent[y]
            Parent[y] ← r
            y ← Temp
        endwhile
    end Find2
```

Figure 4.29 illustrates the collapsing rule for a call to *Find2* with $x = 14$, for a sample input forest representing the sets

$$\{\{0,2,3,4,5,7,8,9,10,11,13,14,15\},\{1,6\},\{12\}\}.$$

FIGURE 4.29

Illustration of
collapsing rule for
sample call to
Find2

Forest representing collection $\{\{0,2,3,4,5,7,8,9,10,11,13,14,15\},\{1,6\},\{12\}\}$ before call to *Find2*:

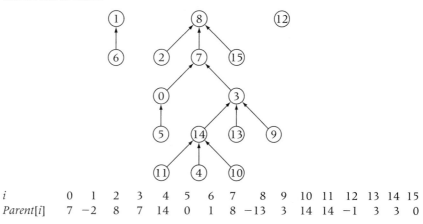

i	0	1	2	3	4	5	6	7	8	9	10	11	12	13	14	15
Parent[i]	7	−2	8	7	14	0	1	8	−13	3	14	14	−1	3	3	0

Forest representing collection $\{\{0,2,3,4,5,7,8,9,10,11,13,14,15\},\{1,6\},\{12\}\}$ after call to *Find2* with $x = 14$:

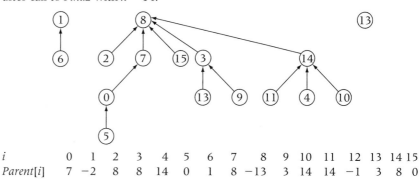

i	0	1	2	3	4	5	6	7	8	9	10	11	12	13	14	15
Parent[i]	7	−2	8	8	14	0	1	8	−13	3	14	14	−1	3	8	0

Tarjan has shown that the worst-case complexity in making an intermixed sequence of calls to *Union* and *Find2*, $n - 1$ calls to *Union* and $m \geq n$ calls to *Find2*, is $O(m\ \alpha(m,n))$, where $\alpha(m,n)$ is an extremely slow-growing function. In fact, it grows so slowly that, for all practical purposes, we can regard $\alpha(m,n)$ as a constant function of m and n. The function $\alpha(m,n)$ is related to a functional inverse of the extremely fast-growing Ackermann's function $A(m,n)$ given by the recurrence relation:

$$A(m, n) = A(m - 1, A(m, n - 1)), m \geq 1 \quad \text{and} \quad n \geq 2,$$
$$A(0, n) = 2n, A(m, 0) = 0, m \geq 1, A(m, 1) = 2, m \geq 1.$$

4.8 Closing Remarks

Further applications of trees will be found throughout the text. For example, in Chapter 7, we will describe the tree associated with Huffman coding for data compression. In Chapter 9, we will use dynamic programming to construct optimal binary search trees. In Chapter 10, we will discuss the state-space tree associated with backtracking and branch-and-bound algorithms. In Chapter 11, we will discuss the depth-first and breadth-first search trees in graphs and digraphs, and we will describe various algorithms for shortest-path trees in weighted graphs and digraphs. In Chapter 13, we will discuss the application of trees to routing tables in a network. In Chapter 21, we will discuss balanced search trees such as red-black trees and B-trees. In Chapter 25, we will use mathematical properties of trees to establish lower bounds for the complexity of algorithms.

References and Suggestions for Further Reading

Tarjan's original papers on maintaining disjoint sets:

Tarjan, R. E. "Efficiency of a Good but Not Linear Set Union Algorithm." *Journal of the ACM* 22 (1975): 215–225.

———. "A Class of Algorithms Which Require Nonlinear Time to Maintain Disjoint Sets." *Journal of Computer and Systems Sciences* 18 (1979): 110–127.

Williams, J. W. J. "Algorithm 232: Heapsort." *Communications of the ACM* 7 (June 1964): 347–348. The original work on heapsort.

Floyd, R. W. "Algorithm 245: Treesort 3." *Communications of the ACM* 7 (December 1964): 701. An improvement on Williams' heapsort algorithm.

EXERCISES   **Section 4.2** Mathematical Properties of Binary Trees

4.1 Show that if binary tree T is full at level i, then it is full at every level j smaller than i.

4.2 Show that the depth of the complete binary tree T_n for a general n is given by

$$D(T_n) = \lfloor \log_2 n \rfloor.$$

4.3 Using induction, prove Proposition 4.2.1.

4.4 Using induction, prove Proposition 4.2.2.

4.5 Using induction, give a direct proof of Proposition 4.2.3 without using the transformation to 2-trees.

4.6 Prove Proposition 4.2.4.

4.7 Prove Proposition 4.2.5.

4.8 Prove Proposition 4.2.6.

4.9 Prove Proposition 4.2.7.

4.10 Complete the verification of Theorem 4.2.8 by establishing the inequality

$$x \lfloor \log_2 x \rfloor + 2(x - 2^{\lfloor \log_2 x \rfloor}) \geq \lceil x \log_2 x \rceil, \quad \text{for any integer } x \geq 1.$$

4.11 Given a 2-tree T having L leaf nodes, let T_{left} and T_{right} denote the left and right subtrees (of the root) of T, respectively.

    a. Give a recurrence relation for $LPL(T)$ in terms of $LPL(T_{\text{left}})$, $LPL(T_{\text{right}})$, and L.

    b. Solve the recurrence relation in (a) to give an alternative proof of Corollary 4.2.9.

4.12 Show that the implicit search tree for *BinarySearch* is a 2-tree that is full at the second-deepest level.

4.13 A *k-ary tree* T is a rooted tree where every node has at most k children. A *k-tree* T is a k-ary tree where every nonleaf node has exactly k children. For each of the following, state and prove a generalization of the result for binary trees or 2-trees to k-ary trees or k-trees:

    a. Proposition 4.2.1

    b. Proposition 4.2.2

    c. Proposition 4.2.3

    d. Proposition 4.2.4

    e. Proposition 4.2.5

    f. Proposition 4.2.6

    g. Proposition 4.2.7

    h. Theorem 4.2.8

4.14 Prove by induction that

$$\binom{2n}{n} \geq \frac{4^n}{2n+1}, \quad n \geq 1,$$

and conclude that the nth Catalan number is

$$b_n = \frac{1}{n+1}\binom{2n}{n} \in \Omega(4^n/n^2).$$

4.15 Verify that the number b_n of different binary trees on n nodes satisfies the following recurrence relation:

$$b_n = \sum_{i=0}^{n-1} b_i b_{n-i-1} = b_0 b_{n-1} + b_1 b_{n-2} + \cdots + b_{n-1} b_0, \text{ init. cond. } b_0 = 1.$$

Section 4.3 Implementation of Trees and Forests

4.16 Write a program that inputs a tree using its parent array representation and converts the tree to its child-sibling representation.

Section 4.4 Tree Traversal

4.17 Consider the child-sibling implementation of a general tree using pointer and dynamic variables.

    a. Give pseudocode for a recursive procedure *TreePreorder* that performs a preorder traversal of the tree whose root node is pointed to by the pointer variable *Root*.

    b. In the case where T is a nonempty binary tree, show that the traversal of T generated by *TreePreorder* coincides with the traversal generated by the algorithm *Preorder* for binary trees.

c. Further, show that if T is any tree and T' is the binary tree obtained from T via the Knuth transformation, then the traversal of T generated by *TreePreorder* coincides with the traversal of T' generated by *Preorder*.

4.18 a. Show that a binary tree T can be reconstructed from its inorder and preorder traversal sequences.

b. Show that part (a) is not true in general for its postorder and preorder traversal sequences.

4.19 Give a recursive procedure for swapping the left and right children of every node in a binary tree.

4.20 Associated with each arithmetic expression E involving binary or unary operations is a binary expression tree T defined recursively as follows. The leaf nodes of T correspond to the operands in E, and the internal nodes correspond to the operators in E and are labeled accordingly. We may assume without loss of generality that E is fully bracketed. If $E = (E_1 \odot E_2)$ then the root node is labeled $\odot$, and the left and right subtrees of the root are expression trees for E_1 and E_2, respectively.

The reverse Polish (the postfix) form of expression E is defined recursively as follows. If F_1 and F_2 are reverse Polish expressions for E_1 and E_2 and $\odot$ is binary operator, then the reverse Polish expression of $E_1 \odot E_2$ is $F_1 F_2 \odot$. If $\odot$ is a unary operator, then the reverse Polish expression of $\odot E_1$ is $E_1 \odot$. For example, the reverse Polish expression for $(A + B)*(-C)$ is $AB + C - *$.

a. Given a string representing a fully bracketed arithmetic expression E involving the binary operators $+$, $-$, $*$, $/$ and the unary operator of minus, write a program that creates an expression tree for E.

b. Show that a postorder traversal of the expression tree for E yields the reverse Polish expression for E.

4.21 Give pseudocode for a version of the inorder successor function *Inorder-Succ* when there is a *Parent* field in each node.

4.22 a. Give pseudocode for a more efficient version of *Inorder*, *Inorder3*, that removes the tail recursive call, and uses an explicit stack to remove the other recursive call. Your version should eliminate the reaccessing of nodes performed by Inorder when going from a node with no right child to its inorder successor.

b. Give pseudocode for a simple modification of the algorithm *Inorder3* (see the previous exercise) that creates an inorder threading, where a node having no right child has its right child pointer changed from null to the inorder successor of the node.

4.23   Give pseudocode for an inorder traversal of an inorder threaded binary tree.

4.24   Give pseudocode for an inorder traversal of a binary tree that does not use an additional field for the parent pointer (or inorder threading), but instead simulates a parent pointer by dynamically reversing and resetting child pointers during the course of the traversal.

4.25   Show that a binary code allows for unambiguous (unique) decoding if and only if it is a binary prefix code.

4.26   Show that if T is any tree and T' is the binary tree obtained from T via the Knuth transformation, then the traversal of T generated by *TreeInorder* coincides with the traversal of T' generated by *Inorder*.

4.27   Give pseudocode for nonrecursive versions of

a. preorder traversal.

b. postorder traversal.

Section 4.5 Binary Search Trees

4.28   Give pseudocode for a recursive version of *InsertBinSrchTree*.

4.29   a. Give pseudocode for a procedure, *CreateBinSrchTree*, that creates a binary search tree by repeated calls to *InsertBinSrchTree*.

b. Show the binary search tree created by *CreateBinSrchTree* for the keys 22,11,0,72,27,55,23,108,1, inserted in that order.

c. Give three orderings for insertion of the keys in part (b) for which the binary search tree created by *CreateBinSrchTree* is a path; that is, each node has at most one child.

d. Give two orderings for insertion of the keys in part (b) for which the binary search tree created by *CreateBinSrchTree* is complete.

4.30   Given any set of n distinct keys (identifiers) and an *arbitrary* binary tree T on n nodes, show that there is a unique assignment of the keys to the nodes in T such that T becomes a binary search tree for the keys.

4.31   Show that a binary search tree without the (implicit) external leaf nodes added is full at the second deepest level if and only if the associated binary tree with the external leaf nodes added is full at the second deepest level.

4.32 Give pseudocode for an altered *SearchBinSrchTree* that determines the locations of both the search element and its parent.

4.33 a. Our pseudocode for inserting a key into a binary search tree assumed that the tree did not contain duplicate keys. Give pseudocode for an alternate version, *InsertBinSrchTree2,*that allows duplicate keys to be inserted. When inserting a duplicate key *X*, assume that you always move to the right child of a node already containing *X* (the move-to-the-right rule).

b. Show that when creating a binary search tree by successively inserting a sequence of keys using the move-to-the-right rule, an inorder traversal of the resulting search tree will visit duplicate keys in the order in which they were inserted. Moreover, when using *InsertBinSrchTree2* for a tree built with the move-to-the-right rule, show that the position in the tree of the first key inserted among a given set of duplicate keys is found. Thus, all keys having a given value can be found by executing *SearchBinSrchTree* to find the position of the first one that was inserted and then executing an inorder traversal of the right subtree of this position until a key having a different value is encountered.

4.34 Discuss an implementation of an *m*-way search tree using pointers and dynamic variables.

4.35 For the implementation of the *m*-way search tree given in the previous exercise, give pseudocode for the high-level searching procedure described in Figure 4.19.

4.36 Show by induction that an inorder traversal of a binary search tree visits the nodes in increasing order of the keys.

4.37 Prove that treesort is a stable sorting algorithm.

4.38 Given a permutation π of a set of keys, the algorithm *CreateBinSearchTree* creates a binary search tree T_π. Given T_π, show that π can be uniquely determined if and only if T_π is a path.

4.39 Show that the best-case and worst-case complexities of *CreateBinSrchTree* for a list of size *n* belong to $\Theta(n \log n)$ and $\Theta(n^2)$, respectively.

4.40 a. Show that an inorder traversal of a multiway search tree visits the keys in increasing order.

b. Design a sorting algorithm based on a multiway search tree that generalizes treesort.

c. Discuss how to guarantee that your sorting algorithm in (a) is stable.

Section 4.6 Priority Queues and Heaps

4.41   Demonstrate the action of *CreateMaxHeap1* on the set of elements (5,23,65,108,2,73,41,52,34); see Figure 4.12.

4.42   Demonstrate the action of *CreateMaxHeap2* (see Figure 4.13) on the same set of elements used in Exercise 4.18.

4.43   Another priority queue operation that is sometimes useful is *ChangePriority(Q,x,v)*, which changes the priority value of an element x in the queue Q to v (and maintains a priority queue). Give pseudocode for *ChangePriority* when the priority queue is implemented as a min-heap. *ChangePriority* should have worst-case complexity O($\log n$), where n is the number of elements in the min-heap.

4.44   The concept of a complete binary tree extends to the concept of a complete k-ary tree in the obvious way, $k \geq 2$.

    a. Show how a complete k-ary tree can be implemented efficiently using an array.

    b. Design and analyze a procedure for inserting an element into a k-ary heap implemented using an array.

    c. Design and analyze a procedure for deleting an element from a k-ary heap implemented using an array.

    d. Design and analyze a k-ary heapsort.

    e. Compare the result in (d) to that for an ordinary heap sort ($k = 2$).

Section 4.7 Implementing Disjoint Sets

4.45   Prove Proposition 4.7.1.

4.46   Suppose we have the following parent implementation of a forest representing a partition of a set of 17 elements:

i	0	1	2	3	4	5	6	7	8	9	10	11	12	13	14	15	16
Parent[i]	7	-3	8	7	14	0	1	8	-13	3	14	4	-1	3	3	0	1

    a. Sketch the trees in F.

    b. Show the state of *Parent*[0:16] after a call to *Union*(*Parent*[0:16],1,8)and sketch the trees in F.

    c. Given the state of *Parent*[0:16] in part (b), show the state of *Parent*[0:16] after an invocation of *Find2*(*Parent*[0:16],4), and sketch the trees in F.

CHAPTER 5

MORE ON SORTING ALGORITHMS

Computer scientists have long been interested in designing efficient sorting algorithms and have succeeded in devising highly efficient sequential and parallel sorting algorithms. The problem of sorting a list has a vast literature, with entire books devoted to the subject. We have already discussed some of the most well known sorting algorithms, including insertionsort, mergesort, quicksort, and heapsort. In this chapter we discuss another well-known and commonly used algorithm, Shellsort.

In addition to finding good general-purpose sorting algorithms, it is helpful to use efficient sorting algorithms when the lists have certain additional properties. For example, we have already discussed how insertionsort is efficient on lists that are in some sense close to being sorted. In fact, it is this property of insertionsort that is the basis of Shellsort. Bingosort, another algorithm we describe in this chapter, is useful when the list contains only a small number of distinct elements relative to the size of the list.

All the sorting algorithms we have seen so far, including insertionsort, selectionsort, mergesort, quicksort, treesort, and heapsort, are examples of comparison-based sorting algorithms. Comparison-based sorting algorithms make no assumption about the specific nature of the list elements, only that the elements can compared as to their relative order. When specific information is known about the list elements, we can sometimes design efficient algorithms that exploit this information. One of the most important examples is radixsort, discussed in Section 5.3, which assumes that the list elements are fixed length strings, such as strings representing decimal integers (padded, if necessary, with leading zeros to be of some fixed length).

All the previous sorting algorithms we have considered so far assume that the list is resident in high-speed internal memory (RAM). The last two algorithms we discuss in this chapter are examples of *external sorting* algorithms, where it is assumed that the list is stored in an external device such as a tape or disk.

5.1 Shellsort

When he designed Shellsort in 1959, Donald Shell's idea was to start out by sorting sublists of a list $L[0:n-1]$ of size n consisting of elements equally spaced but far apart. For example, if the successive elements in the sublists occupy positions k distance apart in the original list, then we have k sublists $S_0 = \{L[0], L[k], \dots\}$, $S_1 = \{L[1], L[1+k], \dots\}$, $\dots$, $S_{k-1} = \{L[k-1], L[2k-1], \dots\}$. The process of sorting these k sublists is called a *k-subsort* (note that a 1-subsort corresponds to a sorting of the entire list L). A list in which each of the sublists $S_0, S_1, \dots, S_{k-1}$ is sorted is called *k-subsorted* (also referred to in the literature as *k-ordered* or *k-sorted*). Each of the sublists $S_0, S_1, \dots, S_{k-1}$ contains at most $\lceil n/k \rceil$ list elements; thus, for a large k, sorting each sublist is fast using an algorithm like insertionsort. Although the list L itself is not sorted by the k-subsort, in some sense it is closer to being sorted. Shellsort works by performing a succession of k-subsorts with decreasing increments $k_0 > k_1 > \cdots > k_{m-1} = 1$.

To accomplish a k-subsort, rather than calling a sorting procedure for each sublist individually, we make a single call to the following variant of *InsertionSort*.

procedure *InsertionSubsort*($L[0:n-1], k$)
Input: $L[0:n-1]$ (a list of size n), k (a positive integer increment)
Output: $L[0:n-1]$ (k-subsorted in increasing order)
     for $i \leftarrow k$ **to** $n-1$ **do** //insert $L[i]$ in its proper position in the already
                 //sorted sublist $L[j], L[j+k], \dots, L[i-k]$ of S_j, $j = i$ **mod** k
        Current $\leftarrow L[i]$
        position $\leftarrow i - k$

```
        while position ≥ 1 .and. Current < L[position] do
                // Current must precede L[position]
            L[position + k] ← L[position]              // bump up L[position]
            position ← position − k
        endwhile
                // position + k is now the proper position for current = L[i]
        L[position+k] ← Current
    endfor
end InsertionSubsort
```

For $i = k, \ldots, n - 1$, *InsertionSubsort* parrots the code for *InsertionSort* by comparing $L[i]$ to $L[i − k]$, $L[i − 2k]$, and so on, until a proper place is found for its insertion in the already sorted sublist $L[j], L[j + k], \ldots, L[i − k]$ of S_j, $j = i \bmod k$. The pseudocode for *InsertionSubsort* shows how elegantly the work of sorting the sublists shifts from one sublist to another in a cyclic manner as *pass* varies from 1 to $n − k$ (see Figure 5.1). The shifting from S_j to S_{j+1} (where $S_k = S_0$) is an automatic consequence of the action of the pseudocode, and there is no need to explicitly implement the sublists. Note that the worst-case complexity of *InsertSubsort* is simply k times the worst-case complexity of *InsertionSort* with a list of size n/k, so that $W(n) = n^2/(2k) − n/2$.

The following pseudocode for *ShellSort* simply consists of successively calling *InsertionSubsort* with a given set of diminishing increments.

```
procedure ShellSort(L[0:n − 1], K[0:m − 1])
Input:    L[0:n − 1] (a list of size n)
                K[0:m − 1] (an array of diminishing increments K[0] > K[1] ··· >
                K[m − 1] = 1)
Output:   L[0:n − 1] (sorted in increasing order)
    for i ← 0 to m − 1 do
        InsertionSubsort(L[0:n − 1], K[i])
    endfor
end Shell Short
```

The final stage of *ShellSort* consists of performing *InsertionSort* on the entire list, so that it is unquestionably correct.

One might well question the efficiency of *ShellSort*, since the final step is a call to *InsertionSort* with the entire list. However, the following two facts are key to its efficiency.

FIGURE 5.1

Action of
InsertionSubsort
with k = 3 on list *L*:
23,11,5, 8,55,2,3

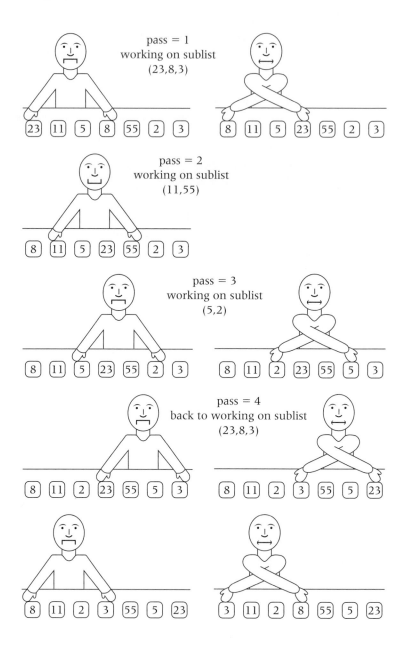

| Key Facts |

1. **Each *k*-subsorting brings the list closer to being sorted.**
2. ***InsertionSort,* and therefore *InsertionSubsort,* are efficient on lists that are close to being sorted. More precisely, suppose for each list element *L[i]* in a list *L[0:n − 1]* of size *n*, there are no more than *k* list elements *L[j]* such that *j < i* and *L[j] > L[i]*. Then *InsertionSort* makes at most (k + 1)(n − 1) comparisons to sort the list.**

The proof of Key Fact 2 is immediate, because when an element $L[i]$ is inserted, it has to move past at most k elements; that is, it makes at most $k + 1$ comparisons before it finds a proper position. Thus, for a fixed k, if a list of size n has this property, then *InsertionSort* performs on the order of kn comparisons so that it exhibits linear performance. Key Fact 1 is related to the following theorem, whose proof is left to the exercises.

Theorem 5.1.1   For any two integers k and l, suppose we perform an l-subsort on a list L that is already k-subsorted. Then L remains k-subsorted—that is, L becomes *both* k-subsorted *and* l-subsorted.   ■

To illustrate the efficiency of *ShellSort* as compared to *InsertionSort*, applying *InsertionSort* to the original list in Figure 5.2 results in 69 comparisons. On the other hand, applying *InsertionSort* as the 1-subsort in the last stage of Figure 5.2 results in only 19 comparisons.

FIGURE 5.2

Action of *ShellSort* showing results of calls to *InsertionSubsort* with increments 7, 2, 1

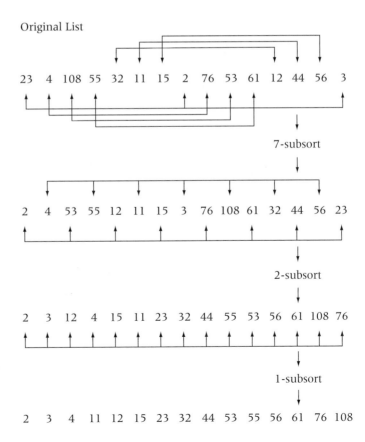

Original List

23   4   108   55   32   11   15   2   76   53   61   12   44   56   3

7-subsort

2   4   53   55   12   11   15   3   76   108   61   32   44   56   23

2-subsort

2   3   12   4   15   11   23   32   44   55   53   56   61   108   76

1-subsort

2   3   4   11   12   15   23   32   44   53   55   56   61   76   108

Even though Shellsort is a fairly simple algorithm and has been studied and used extensively by many researchers, its analysis is not yet complete. The number of comparisons for a given input of size n performed by Shellsort depends on what set of increments is used, and the general mathematical analysis is difficult. For a general n, it is not known what set of increments exhibits optimal behavior.

A number of results are known for special choices of the increments. An order of complexity improvement over insertionsort is already achieved when only two increments k and 1 are used for a suitable k. In fact, it has been shown in the two-increment case that the optimal average complexity has order $n^{5/3}$ and is achieved when k is approximately $1.72n^{1/3}$. It has also been shown that when the increments are of the form $2^j - 1$, for all such increments less than n, then Shellsort exhibits worst-case complexity in $O(n^{3/2})$. Since $2^{2j} - 1 = (2^j - 1)(2^j + 1)$, a large percentage of these increments divide one another, so we would expect to be able to do even better. Indeed, it has been shown that using increments of the form $2^i 3^j$ for all such increments less than n yields $\Theta(n(\log n)^2)$ worst-case complexity, which is within a logarithm factor of being optimal.

REMARK

Note that since insertionsubsort has $n^2/(2k) - n/2$ worst-case complexity, in order to achieve $\Theta(n(\log n)^2)$ worst-case complexity for Shellsort, the first increment used must be in $\Omega(n/\log n)$.

5.2 Bingosort

In all the algorithms we have studied so far, the input size was a function of a single variable n. However, as mentioned in Chapter 3, there are situations where the input size is most naturally a function of two or more variables. For example, suppose we consider the problem of finding efficient sorting algorithms for lists of size n with repeated elements. The input size is then a function of n and the number m of *distinct* elements in the list, where $1 \le m \le n$. This situation arises often in practice. For example, when sorting the records in a large mailing list by zip codes for bulk mailing, the number of distinct elements, m (zip codes), is usually small compared to the number of records, n. Bingosort is an example of a sorting algorithm that works well for input lists with many repeated elements.

We express the complexity of bingosort in terms of the two variables n and m. It turns out that when m is small compared with n, bingosort has average and worst-case complexities in $\Theta(mn)$ and best-case complexity in $\Theta(n + m^2)$. Hence, for $m < \log n$, bingosort outperforms comparison-based sorts such as mergesort and heapsort, which do not work any more efficiently on lists with repeated elements than they do on lists with distinct elements.

In bingosort, which is a variation of selectionsort, each distinct value in the list is considered to be a "bingo" value. Each pass of bingosort corresponds to "calling out" a bingo value. The bingo values are called out in increasing order. During a given pass, all the elements having the current bingo value are placed in their correct positions in the list.

The following pseudocode for *BingoSort* implements this process.

```
procedure BingoSort(L[0:n − 1])
Input:    L[0:n − 1] (a list of size n)
Output:   L[0:n − 1] (sorted in increasing order)
    // first determine the minimum and maximum values for a list element
    MaxMin3(L[0:n − 1], MaxValue, MinValue)
    Bingo ← MinValue            //initialize
    NextAvail ← 0
    NextBingo ← MaxValue
    while Bingo < MaxValue do //move up all list elements that equal Bingo
        StartPos ← NextAvail
        for i ← StartPos to n − 1 do
            if L[i] = Bingo then   //BINGO! Interchange L[i] and L[NextAvail]
                interchange(L[i], L[NextAvail])
                NextAvail ← NextAvail + 1   // update NextAvail
            else
                if L[i] < NextBingo then NextBingo ← L[i] endif
            endif
        endfor
        Bingo ← NextBingo        //initialize for next pass
        NextBingo ← MaxValue
    endwhile
end BingoSort
```

The action of *BingoSort* is illustrated in Figure 5.3 for a sample list of size 10.

FIGURE 5.3

Action of *BingoSort*
for list 23,10,15,
10,10,23,15,23,
23,10 after call to
MaxMin3

Pass 1	23	10	15	10	10	23	15	23	23	10
Start position 0	10	23	15	10	10	23	15	23	23	10
Bingo value 10	10	10	15	23	10	23	15	23	23	10
	10	10	10	23	15	23	15	23	23	10
	10	10	10	10	15	23	15	23	23	23
Pass 2										
Start position 4	10	10	10	10	15	23	15	23	23	23
Bingo value 15	10	10	10	10	15	15	23	23	23	23

The best case of *BingoSort* is achieved by a list in which $n - m + 1$ elements have the same minimum value, yielding $B(n,m) \in \Theta(n + m^2)$ as the best-case complexity (see Exercise 5.5). The worst case occurs for a list in which $n - m + 1$ elements have the same maximum value, yielding $W(n,m) \in \Theta(mn)$. When discussing the average complexity, it is natural to assume that each of the m distinct values occurs n/m times. Such a list generates $\Theta(mn)$ comparisons, so that the average complexity $A(n,m)$ belongs to $\Theta(mn)$ for *BingoSort* (see Exercise 5.6).

5.3 Radixsort

In this section we give an example of a sorting algorithm that is not a comparison-based algorithm but depends on the special nature of the list elements. In radix-sort, we assume that the list elements are strings of a given fixed length drawn from a given ordered alphabet, and that the ordering of the strings is the usual lexicographic ordering (that is, the one commonly used in practice). For example, we might be sorting personnel records based on Social Security numbers. Then the list elements are character strings of length 9 drawn from the ten character digits $0,1, \ldots ,9$. Alternatively, we might be sorting the records based on zip codes, so that the list elements are characters strings of length 5, again drawn from $0,1, \ldots ,9$.

One sorting method sometimes used when sorting by hand is to make a pass through the list and place the records in "buckets" based on the leading character in the string. For example, suppose we are sorting zip codes. Using ten buckets $B_0, B_1, \ldots ,B_9$, we would make a linear scan through the list, inserting the record in B_i whenever the zip code had the leading digit i, $i = 0, \ldots ,9$. The advantage of this method is that completing the sort simply requires us to sort the records within each bucket, a process that would proceed analogously except we would place each record in a sub-bucket based on its second leading digit. The disadvantage of this type of sort is the complication arising from the proliferation of buckets. However, in the case of binary strings, we can avoid this problem by developing a fairly elegant recursive procedure similar to *Quicksort* (see Exercise 5.16).

Another way to avoid proliferating buckets is to look first at the last (least significant) digit instead of the leading digit before placing a record in a bucket. We would then repeat the process by extracting the list from the buckets in the order $B_0, B_1, \ldots ,B_9$ and placing the records in these same ten buckets according to the second to the last digit. After five repetitions, the records would be sorted, as shown in Figure 5.4.

Original list:
45242   45230   45232   97432   74239   12335   43239   40122   98773   41123   61230

Pass 1	Bucket 0:	45230	61230			
Place in buckets	Bucket 2:	45242	45232	97432	41022	
based on fifth	Bucket 3:	98773	41123			
(least significant)	Bucket 5:	12335				
digit	Bucket 9:	74239	43239			

Extract list from buckets:
45230   61230   45242   45232   97432   40122   98773   41123   12335   74239   43239

Pass 2	Bucket 2:	40122	41123				
Place in buckets	Bucket 3:	45230	61230	45232	97432	12335	74239	43239
based on fourth digit	Bucket 4:	45242					
	Bucket 7:	98773					

Extract list from buckets:
40122   41123   45230   61230   45232   97432   12335   74239   43239   45242   98773

Pass 3	Bucket 1:	40122	41123			
Place in buckets	Bucket 2:	45230	61230	45232	74239	43239	45242
based on third digit	Bucket 3:	12335					
	Bucket 4:	97432					
	Bucket 7:	98773					

Extract list from buckets:
40122   41123   45230   61230   45232   74239   43239   45242   12335   97432   98773

Pass 4	Bucket 0:	40122		
Place in buckets	Bucket 1:	41123	61230	
based on second digit	Bucket 2:	12335		
	Bucket 3:	43239		
	Bucket 4:	74239		
	Bucket 5:	45230	45232	45242
	Bucket 7:	97432		
	Bucket 8:	98773		

Extract list from buckets:
40122   41123   61230   12335   43239   74239   45230   45232   45242   97432   98773

Pass 5	Bucket 1:	12335				
Place in buckets	Bucket 4:	40122	41123	43239	45230	45232	45242
based on first (most	Bucket 6:	61230					
significant) digit	Bucket 7:	74239					
	Bucket 9:	97432	98773				

Extract (sorted) list from buckets:
12335   40122   41123   43239   45230   45232   45242   61230   74239   97432   98773

FIGURE 5.4

Sorting a sample list of size $n = 11$, where each element is a five-digit numerical character string, so that there are ten buckets and five passes

We now give a high-level description of radixsort based on the procedure illustrated in Figure 5.4. In our high-level description of the procedure *RadixSort*, we assume the built-in function *Substring(string,i)*, which extracts the symbol in position i from *string*. We also assume high-level procedures *Enqueue(Q,X)*, which enqueues the element X into the queue Q, and *Dequeue(Q,Y)*, which dequeues Q and assigns the dequeued element to Y.

```
procedure RadixSort(L[0:n − 1], k)
Input:      L[0:n − 1] (a list of size n, where L[i] is a string of length k over an
                        alphabet s_0 < s_1 < ··· < s_m)
Output:   L[0:n − 1] (sorted in increasing order)
    for i ← k − 1 downto 0 do
        //place elements in queues B_0,B_1, . . . , B_m based on position i
        for j ← 0 to n − 1 do
            if Substring(L[j], i) = s_q then
                Enqueue(B_q, L[i])
            endif
        endfor
        //reassemble list L by successive dequeuing
        Ct ← 1
        for j ← 0 to m do
            while (.not. Empty(B_j)) do
                Dequeue(B_j, Y)
                L[Ct] ← Y
                Ct ← Ct + 1
            endwhile
        endfor
    endfor
end RadixSort
```

We leave the proof of the correctness of *RadixSort* as an exercise. Clearly, the best-case, worst-case, and average complexities of *RadixSort* are in $\Theta(kn)$. A convenient way to implement the queues used in *RadixSort* is to use linked lists. The action of the first pass of *RadixSort* is illustrated in Figure 5.5 with this implementation. We assume that the queues are pointed to by the elements in an array *Bucket*[0:9] of pointer variables. We also assume that we have an array *Rear*[0:9] of pointers, where *Rear*[i] points to the end of the queue whose first element is pointed to by *Bucket*[i], $i = 0, \ldots ,9$.

FIGURE 5.5

First pass of *RadixSort* for the sample list given in Figure 5.4, where the queues (buckets) are implemented using linked lists

Original list given in Figure 5.04:

45242 45230 45232 97432 74239 12335 43239 41022 98773 41123 61230

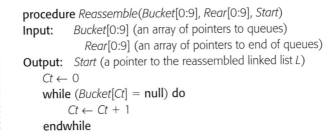

$Bucket[0] \rightarrow \boxed{45230} \rightarrow \boxed{61230} \leftarrow Rear[0]$

$Bucket[1] = null = Rear[1]$

$Bucket[2] \rightarrow \boxed{45242} \rightarrow \boxed{45232} \rightarrow \boxed{97432} \rightarrow \boxed{40122} \leftarrow Rear[2]$

$Bucket[3] \rightarrow \boxed{98773} \rightarrow \boxed{41123} \leftarrow Rear[3]$

$Bucket[4] = null = Rear[4]$

$Bucket[5] \rightarrow \boxed{12335} \leftarrow Rear[5]$

$Bucket[6] = null = Rear[6]$

$Bucket[7] = null = Rear[7]$

$Bucket[8] = null = Rear[8]$

$Bucket[9] \rightarrow \boxed{74239} \rightarrow \boxed{43239} \leftarrow Rear[9]$

Extract list from buckets:

$List \rightarrow \boxed{45230} \rightarrow \boxed{61230} \rightarrow \boxed{45242} \rightarrow \cdots \boxed{74239} \rightarrow \boxed{43239}$

Extracting the list from the buckets is a simple job of reassigning some pointers, as illustrated in Figure 5.6. Note that these pointer reassignments allow us to completely dequeue a given queue in one fell swoop! The reassembled list is a linked list pointed to by *Start*.

In general, *Start* points to the first nonempty queue; that is, $Start = Bucket[i]$, where i is the smallest integer such that $Bucket[i] \neq$ **null**. The reassembled linked list is then created by calling the following procedure, *Reassemble*. For convenience, we write the pseudocode for *Reassemble* under the assumption that our alphabet comprises the decimal digital characters.

```
procedure Reassemble(Bucket[0:9], Rear[0:9], Start)
Input:    Bucket[0:9] (an array of pointers to queues)
                 Rear[0:9] (an array of pointers to end of queues)
Output:   Start (a pointer to the reassembled linked list L)
     Ct ← 0
     while (Bucket[Ct] = null) do
          Ct ← Ct + 1
     endwhile
```

```
            Start ← Bucket[Ct]
            SaveCt ← Ct
            while(SaveCt < 9) do
                  Ct ← Ct + 1
                  while (Bucket[Ct] = null .and. Ct ≤ 9) do
                        Ct ← Ct + 1
                  endwhile
                  if Ct ≤ 9 then
                        Rear[SaveCt]→Next ← Bucket[Ct]
                        SaveCt ← Ct
                  endif
            endwhile
      end Reassemble
```

FIGURE 5.6

Extract list from buckets in the first pass of *RadixSort* for the sample list given in Figure 5.4, where the queues (buckets) and the reassembled list are implemented using linked lists

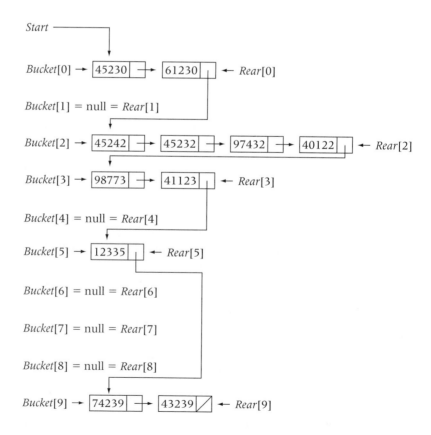

5.4 External Sorting

In all the sorting algorithms we have examined so far, we have made the assumption that the entire list fits into internal (main) memory. In practice, this may not be the case. Therefore, we now consider the problem of designing *external sorting* algorithms. External sorting algorithms (also called *out-of-core* sorting algorithms) assume that we can only fit a fixed number m of list elements into internal memory, where $m < n$. Thus, the list itself is originally assumed to reside in external memory, such as on a disk or tape.

Our external sorting algorithms assume that the input list originally resides in a single file on disk or tape. However, we allow the sorting algorithms the use of auxiliary external files. We assume that file access is sequential even when the file is on disk. The list elements are normally stored as records, with the sorting done on a given key field in each record. To access a given record in a sequential file, we must have read all the preceding records in the file. This means that if we have already passed a given record of a file and wish to access it again, we must reset the file to the beginning and sequentially read until the given record is located. In our external sorting algorithms, we want to minimize the number of times a field needs to be reset to the beginning. In particular, our external sorting algorithms always sequentially process all the records in a file before resetting the file. When designing a comparison-based external sorting algorithm, we would like to maintain order-optimal $\Theta(n\log n)$ worst-case complexity as measured using the number of comparisons made between keys. At the same time, we would like to minimize the number of times a record is accessed (read or written) in an external file.

One common approach to external sorting is based on a variation of *Merge-Sort*. To implement this variation, called *MultiMergeSort*, in the most straightforward fashion, we use four external files (either stored on disk or tape). During the first phase, blocks of size m are brought from the input file into internal memory (the size of the last block might be less than m). An efficient internal sorting algorithm is used to sort each block. The sorted blocks are written alternately to two external files (different from the input file). In the external files, a block of sorted records is called a *run*. Thus, after the initial sorting phase, two of the four files contain runs of size m. These two files are then the initial input files for phase 2.

Phase 2 consists of a number of merging passes. The merging of two sublists (runs) in different input files to an external output file is achieved using a slight modification of the algorithm *Merge* described in Chapter 2. The modified *Merge* compares list elements by reading them from their resident external input files into internal memory. (During the merge, we have at most two elements at a time in internal memory.) The merged list is written one element at a time to a suitable external output file, with the smaller of the two list elements in internal memory written to the output file and another element read in from the appropriate input file.

More precisely, at the start of each merge pass, we have two input files containing runs of a certain size, and the other two files are reset to empty for output. We then merge runs from the input files into runs twice as long and write the longer runs alternately to the two output files. The input-output roles of the four files keep alternating for the different merge passes. The merge passes continue until one of the files contains a single run of size n (that is, contains the sorted list), as illustrated in Figure 5.7.

FIGURE 5.7

Action of external sorting algorithm *MultiMergeSort* for a sample list *L* of size $n = 29$, where internal memory has size $m = 5$

Keys of original input list *L*

File *A*:
17 6 19 11 10 | 9 2 20 14 18 | 25 7 15 21 16 | 27 22 12 3 8 | 4 23 28 24 26 | 13 0 1 •

Phase 1

Blocks of size $m = 5$ (last block has size 3) are sequentially read from file *A* to internal memory, sorted using an efficient internal sorting algorithm, and alternately written to files *C* and *D*.

File *C*: 6 10 11 17 19 | 7 15 16 21 25 | 4 23 24 26 28 •
File *D*: 2 9 14 18 20 | 3 8 12 22 27 | 0 1 13 •

Phase 2–Merge Phase

Pass 1: Runs in input files *C* and *D* are merged and written to output files *A* and *B*

File *A*: 2 6 9 10 11 14 17 18 19 20 | 0 1 4 13 23 24 26 28 •
File *B*: 3 7 8 12 15 16 21 22 25 27 •

Pass 2: Runs in input files *A* and *B* are merged and written to output files C and D

File *C*: 2 3 6 7 8 9 10 11 12 14 15 16 17 18 19 20 21 22 25 27 •
File *D*: 0 1 4 13 23 24 26 28 •

Pass 3: Runs in input files *C* and *D* are merged and written to output file *A*, which now contains the sorted list *L*.

File *A*:
0 1 2 3 4 6 7 8 9 10 11 12 13 14 15 16 17 18 19 20 21 22 23 24 25 26 27 28 •

We now analyze the worst-case complexity $W(n)$ of *MultiMergeSort*. For convenience, we assume that n is a multiple of m. Let $W_1(n)$ and $W_2(n)$ denote the largest number of comparisons performed in the first and second phases of *MultiMergeSort*, respectively, so that $W(n) = W_1(n) + W_2(n)$. In the first phase, *MultiMergeSort* sequentially performs internal sorts on n/m lists, each of size m. Using an efficient internal sorting algorithm, each of these lists can be sorted using $\Theta(m \log m)$ comparisons. Thus,

$$W_1(n) \in \Theta\left(\frac{n}{m}(m \log m)\right) = \Theta(n \log m). \tag{5.4.1}$$

Let p denote the number of passes performed during the second (merge) phase of *MultiMergeSort*. Because the initial runs all have size m, and the size of the runs is doubled after each pass until a run of size n is obtained, we have $n = 2^p m$ (where, for convenience, we have assumed n/m is a power of 2). Hence,

$$p = \log_2\left(\frac{n}{m}\right). \tag{5.4.2}$$

With *Merge* performing at least k and less than $2k$ comparisons to merge two sublists of size k, it follows that the number of comparisons performed during each pass in the merge phase is at least $n/2$ and less than n. Thus, the total number of comparisons performed during the merge phase is at most $pn/2$ and less than pn, so that

$$\left(\frac{n}{2}\right)\log_2\left(\frac{n}{m}\right) \leq W_2(n) < n\log_2\left(\frac{n}{m}\right). \tag{5.4.3}$$

Combining Formulas (5.4.1) and (5.4.3), we obtain

$$W(n) = W_1(n) + W_2(n) \in \Theta\left(n \log m + n \log\left(\frac{n}{m}\right)\right) = \Theta(n \log n). \tag{5.4.4}$$

Thus, *MultiMergeSort* has order-optimal worst-case complexity.

We now count the number of times each element of the list L is accessed from an external file. Note that each element is written once to an external file for each time it is read from an external file. Clearly, each element is read from an external file once in phase 1 and p times in phase 2. Hence, the total number of times each element is read from an external file is given by $1 + p = 1 + \log_2(n/m) \in O(\log n)$. Note that this is also the number of times a given file needs to be reset for reading (or writing).

It is possible to design a more sophisticated version of *MultiMergeSort* that uses only three external files (see Exercise 5.13).

We could reduce the number of merge passes *MultiMergeSort* performs in the second phase if the initial runs constructed in the first phase were longer than *m*. To achieve this goal, we devise the algorithm *MultiMergeSortQ*, which uses a priority queue maintained in internal memory. The priority queue consists of list elements that have been tagged with a run number in a manner to be described shortly. When comparing two list elements, the list element with the lower run number has the higher priority. If two list elements have the same run number, then the list element with the smaller key has the higher priority.

MultiMergeSortQ begins by reading in the first *m* list elements (records) from the external input file. All *m* elements are given run number 1 because they are all part of the first run (written to the first external output file). A priority queue is constructed out of these *m* elements. Then *MultiMergeSortQ* begins creating runs by an alternating sequence of dequeuing and enqueuing until the input file is exhausted. Elements are enqueued from the input file after being tagged with a run number, which is computed as follows. Let *x* denote the current element to be dequeued and written to the output file as part of run *i*. Let *y* denote the element to be read from the input file, which will be enqueued after *x* has been dequeued. If the key of *y* is less than the key of *x*, then *y* cannot be part of the current run, so its run number is assigned the value *i* + 1. Otherwise, *y* can be included as part of the current run, and its run number is assigned the value *i*.

An internal variable *Run* keeps track of the number of the current run being written to an external output file. Before *x* is written, its run number is compared to *Run*. If the run number of *x* is 1 greater than *Run*, then we start a new run on the other output file and increment *Run* by 1. When the external input file is exhausted, we simply keep dequeuing *x* in the same fashion until the queue is empty. In Figure 5.8, we illustrate the initial run creating phase of *MultiMergeSortQ* with the same list as used in Figure 5.7. In Figure 5.8, we show the priority of a list element by the pair (run number, key). We show the contents of the priority queue at each stage, but do not show the data structure (such as a heap) we use to efficiently implement the priority queue.

The first run constructed by *MultiMergeSortQ* for the sample input list *L* of Figure 5.8 has length 12. This first run is more than twice as long as the first run (of length 5) constructed by *MultiMergeSort* for the same input list *L*. Also note that *MultiMergeSortQ* constructs a total of four runs in the first phase, as opposed to the six runs constructed by *MultiMergeSort*. Thus, in the second (merge) phase, *MultiMergeSortQ* performs only two passes, as opposed to the three passes performed by *MultiMergeSort*.

We leave the pseudocode of *MultiMergeSort* and *MultiMergeSortQ* as exercises.

FIGURE 5.8

Action of the run
creation stage of
MultiMergeSortQ

Original External Input List

17 6 19 11 10 9 2 20 14 18 25 7 15 21 16 27 22 12 3 8 4 23 28 24 26 13 0 1 •
Initial priority queue: (1,17) (1,6) (1,19) (1,11) (1,10)

File *C*		priority queue			
6	(1,17)	(1,9)	(1,19)	(1,11)	(1,10)
6 9	(1,17)	(2,2)	(1,19)	(1,11)	(1,10)
6 9 10	(1,17)	(2,2)	(1,19)	(1,11)	(1,20)
6 9 10 11	(1,17)	(2,2)	(1,19)	(1,14)	(1,20)
6 9 10 11 14	(1,17)	(2,2)	(1,19)	(1,18)	(1,20)
6 9 10 11 14 17	(1,25)	(2,2)	(1,19)	(1,18)	(1,20)
6 9 10 11 14 17 18	(1,25)	(2,2)	(1,19)	(2,7)	(1,20)
6 9 10 11 14 17 18 19	(1,25)	(2,2)	(2,15)	(2,7)	(1,20)
6 9 10 11 14 17 18 19 20	(1,25)	(2,2)	(2,15)	(2,7)	(1,21)
6 9 10 11 14 17 18 19 20 21	(1,25)	(2,2)	(2,15)	(2,7)	(2,16)
6 9 10 11 14 17 18 19 20 21 25	(1,27)	(2,2)	(2,15)	(2,7)	(2,16)
6 9 10 11 14 17 18 19 20 21 25 27	(2,22)	(2,2)	(2,15)	(2,7)	(2,16)

File *D*					
2	(2,22)	(2,12)	(2,15)	(2,7)	(2,16)
2 7	(2,22)	(2,12)	(2,15)	(3,3)	(2,16)
2 7 12	(2,22)	(3,8)	(2,15)	(3,3)	(2,16)
2 7 12 15	(2,22)	(3,8)	(3,4)	(3,3)	(2,16)
2 7 12 15 16	(2,22)	(3,8)	(3,4)	(3,3)	(2,23)
2 7 12 15 16 22	(2,28)	(3,8)	(3,4)	(3,3)	(2,23)
2 7 12 15 16 22 23	(2,28)	(3,8)	(3,4)	(3,3)	(2,24)
2 7 12 15 16 22 23 24	(2,28)	(3,8)	(3,4)	(3,3)	(3,26)
2 7 12 15 16 22 23 24 28	(3,13)	(3,8)	(3,4)	(3,3)	(3,26)

File *C*					
6 9 10 11 14 17 18 19 20 21 25 27 3	(3,13)	(3,8)	(3,4)	(4,0)	(3,26)
6 9 10 11 14 17 18 19 20 21 25 27 3 4	(3,13)	(3,8)	(4,1)	(4,0)	(3,26)
6 9 10 11 14 17 18 19 20 21 25 27 3 4 8		(3,13)	(4,1)	(4,0)	(3,26)
6 9 10 11 14 17 18 19 20 21 25 27 3 4 8 13			(4,1)	(4,0)	(3,26)
6 9 10 11 14 17 18 19 20 21 25 27 3 4 8 13 26				(4,1)	(4,0)

File *D*					
2 7 12 15 16 22 23 24 28 0					(4,1)
2 7 12 15 16 22 23 24 28 0 1					∅

5.5 Closing Remarks

In Chapter 3, we established a lower bound of $\Omega(n\log n)$ for the worst-case complexity of any comparison-based sorting algorithm. Because Shellsort has $O(n(\log n)^2)$ worst-case complexity for an appropriate choice of diminishing increments, we see that Shellsort is within a logarithm factor of being order optimal. In view of its simplicity and the fact that the implicit constants associated with the algorithm are small, Shellsort is often implemented in practice.

Although internal memory is growing rapidly with each new generation of computers, external memory (out-of-core) algorithms are necessary to deal with the massive data sets encountered in certain applications. Similar to the external sorting algorithms we have discussed, external memory algorithms are typically based on bringing chunks of data from external memory into internal memory, performing an internal algorithm on the chunks, and then writing the results back out to external memory. There is a vast literature on external memory algorithms, and a good survey of data structures and other issues associated with these algorithms can be found in the survey article by Vitter listed at the end of this chapter.

In Chapter 15, we will introduce parallel algorithms and architectures, and discuss some parallel sorting algorithms. One strategy for designing a parallel sorting algorithm is to look for inherent parallelism in a sequential algorithm. For example, in Chapter 15, we will discuss two classical parallel sorting algorithms that are modeled on parallelizing mergesort but replace the procedure *Merge* with parallel merging procedures to achieve satisfactory speedup. In Chapter 18, we will discuss sorting in the context of the message-passing distributed-computing paradigm.

References and Suggestions for Further Reading

Knuth, D. E. *The Art of Computer Programming*. Vol. 3, *Sorting and Searching*. 2nd ed. Reading, MA: Addison-Wesley, 1998. A comprehensive treatment of sorting algorithms and their history.

Shell, D. L. "A High-Speed Sorting Procedure." *Communications of the ACM* 2, no. 7 (July 1959): 30–32. The original paper on Shellsort.

Vitter, J. S. "External Memory Algorithms and Data Structures: Dealing with Massive Data." *ACM Computing Surveys* 33, no. 2 (June 2001): 209–271. A survey article on external memory algorithms, including external sorting.

Section 5.1 Shellsort

5.1   a. Demonstrate the action of *ShellSort* on the list (33,2,56,23,55,78,2, 98,61,108,14,60,56,77,5,3,1), with increments (5,3,1); see Figure 5.2.

b. Repeat (a) with increments (5,2,1).

5.2   a. Write a program that compares the number of comparisons made for a given input list $L[0:n-1]$ by *InsertionSort* and *ShellSort* with a given set of increments $K[0:m-1]$.

b. Run your program with the input list and sets of increments given in Exercise 5.1.

c. Repeat (b) for randomly generated lists of sizes 100, 1000, 10000.

5.3   Consider a permutation π of $\{1, \dots, n\}$. Prove (generalizing the result given in Exercise 3.49) that interchanging $\pi(i)$ and $\pi(i+k)$ results in a decrease of at most $2k-1$ in the total number of inversions.

5.4   Consider any comparison-based sorting algorithm, where each comparison involves elements that are at most k positions apart (that is, elements in positions indexed by i and $i+j$ for some $j \le k$). Use the result from Exercise 5.3 to show that the worst-case complexity $W(n)$ of such an algorithm is at least $(n^2/2 + n/2)/(2k-1)$. Note that this generalizes Proposition 3.5.2 of Chapter 3.

5.5   Use the result from Exercise 5.4 to show that *ShellSort* has $\Omega(n^2)$ worst-case complexity if the first increment $K[0]$ is a constant (with respect to n).

5.6   Prove Theorem 5.1.1.

Section 5.2 Bingosort

5.7   Trace the action of *BingoSort* for the list 2,1,1,5,1,2,4,4,4,7,1,1,1,3,3,5, 5,5,1,7,7,4.

5.8   Show that *BingoSort* is a stable sorting algorithm.

5.9   Show that if a list has m distinct elements, then after exactly $m-1$ passes of *BingoSort*, the list is sorted into increasing order and the algorithm terminates.

5.10   a. Analyze the best-case complexity $B(n,m)$ of *BingoSort*.

b. Analyze the worst-case complexity $W(n,m)$ of *BingoSort*.

5.11   Show that *BingoSort* performs $\Theta(nm)$ comparisons for an input list of size n having m distinct values, each of which occurs n/m times.

5.12   Empirically compare the number of comparisons performed by *BingoSort* versus *MergeSort* as follows:

   a. Implement *BingoSort* and *Mergesort* and compare the number of comparisons they perform by running both algorithms with various different input lists of sizes 100, 1000, 10000, where the lists consist of randomly chosen elements from a fixed set $\{1, ... ,m\}$, for various choices of $m < n$.

   b. For various runs with input lists of size $n = 100$ compute, for each input list, the number of comparisons performed by *Mergesort* and by *BingoSort* with inputs $m = 2,3, ...$, and output the largest ratio m/n for which *BingoSort* performs fewer comparisons than *Mergesort*. Repeat for lists of size 1000.

Section 5.3 Radixsort

5.13   Demonstrate the action of *RadixSort* for the following sample list, where each element is a seven-digit binary string (see Figure 5.4):

   1011101, 0100011, 1010110, 1111101, 0011101, 0000001, 1000000, 1010101

5.14   Demonstrate the first two passes of *RadixSort* for the sample list given in Exercise 5.13, where the buckets are implemented as linked queues (see Figures 5.5 and 5.6).

5.15   Prove the correctness of *RadixSort*.

5.16   Determine whether *RadixSort* is a stable sorting algorithm.

5.17   For binary strings stored in an array, design and analyze a recursive radix-sort based on partitioning the list into two sublists according to the most significant digit.

5.18   Write a program to empirically compare the computing times of *RadixSort* and *MergeSort* for randomly generated lists of positive integers less than some given k.

Section 5.4 External Sorting

5.19   a. Give pseudocode for *MultiMergeSort*.

   b. Give pseudocode for *MultiMergeSortQ*.

5.20   Design a version of *MultiMergeSort* where only three external files are used.

Additional Exercises

5.21   Although for large lists *InsertionSort* is, on average, much slower than *MergeSort*, it is faster for sufficiently small lists. A useful technique to improve the efficiency of a divide-and-conquer sorting algorithm such as *MergeSort* is to employ a sorting algorithm such as *Insertionsort* when the input size is not larger than some threshold t (a value of t between 8 and 16 usually works well).

   a. Write a program that computes the number of comparisons performed by *Mergesort* for a given input list and threshold t.

   b. Run for thresholds t from 1 to 20 for various randomly generated lists of sizes 100, 1000, 10000. Report on which threshold t you observe to be best, and how it compares to ordinary *MergeSort* ($t = 1$).

5.22   Repeat Exercise 5.21 for *Quicksort*.

5.23   A sloppy chef has delivered a stack of pancakes to a waiter, where the stack is all mixed up with respect to the size of the pancakes. The waiter wishes to rearrange the pancakes in order of their size, with the largest on the bottom. The waiter begins by selecting a pile of pancakes on the top of the stack and simply flips the pile over. He then keeps repeating this pancake-flipping operation until the pancakes are sorted.

   a. Show by induction that there always exists a set of flips that sorts any given stack of pancakes.

   b. Describe a pancake-flipping algorithm that performs at most $2n - 2$ flips in the worst case for n pancakes. Any pancake-flipping algorithm must perform at least $n - 1$ flips in the worst case for n pancakes (see the exercises in Chapter 25).

5.24   Suppose now that the pancakes in Exercise 5.23 have a burnt side, and the waiter wishes to have the pancakes stacked in order with the unburnt side up. Redo parts (a) and (b) with for this new problem.

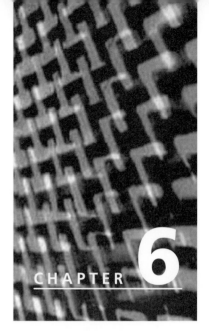

CHAPTER 6

PROBABILITY AND AVERAGE COMPLEXITY OF ALGORITHMS

When analyzing the complexity of an algorithm we intend to use repeatedly with varying inputs, the average complexity is often as important as the worst-case complexity. In this situation, we would tend to favor one algorithm over another based on average performance. For example, although quicksort has quadratic worst-case performance, we often use it in practice because it performs well on average.

Key Fact

The utility of an algorithm is not always captured by its worst-case performance, in which case it becomes important to determine its average complexity.

The average behavior of an algorithm only makes sense in the presence of a probability distribution on the inputs of size n. The particular probability distribution used will depend on the particular environment in which the algorithm is used and is often taken to be the uniform distribution (that is, all inputs equally likely). The average behavior of an algorithm is often difficult to analyze and requires advanced techniques from probability theory. In this text, we limit ourselves to a discussion of algorithms that we can analyze using the elementary probability techniques discussed in Appendix E [formulas from this appendix are referenced as (E.$i.j$)].

6.1 Expectation and Average Complexity

The definition of the average behavior of an algorithm given in Chapter 2 informally used some concepts from elementary probability theory. In this chapter, we use the formal mathematical concepts discussed in Appendix E to formulate precisely what is meant by the average complexity of an algorithm.

DEFINITION 6.1.1 **Average Complexity** Let $\mathscr{I}_n$ denote the set of all inputs of size n to a given algorithm. For $I \in \mathscr{I}_n$, let $\tau(I)$ denote the number of basic operations performed by the algorithm on input I. Given a probability distribution on $\mathscr{I}_n$, the *average complexity $A(n)$* of an algorithm is the expected value of τ; that is,

$$A(n) = E[\tau]. \qquad\qquad (6.1.1)$$

Key Fact

Average behavior depends on the probability distribution on $\mathscr{I}_n$.

Often there is a natural way to assign a probability distribution on $\mathscr{I}_n$. For example, when analyzing comparison-based sorting algorithms, we typically assume that each of the $n!$ permutations (orderings) of a list of size n is equally likely to be input to the algorithm. The average complexity of any comparison-based sorting algorithm is then the sum of the number of comparisons generated by each of the $n!$ permutations divided by $n!$. In practice, it is not feasible to examine each one of these $n!$ permutations individually, as $n!$ simply grows too fast. Fortunately, there are techniques that enable us to calculate this average without resorting to permutation-by-permutation analysis.

6.2 Techniques for Computing Average Complexity

Computing the average complexity of an algorithm frequently requires deep results from probability theory that are beyond the scope of this text. However, the relatively elementary techniques that follow suffice for our analysis of the average behavior of most of the algorithms we discuss in this text. To compute $A(n)$, we can apply one or some combination of the following formulations for $A(n)$ based on the characteristics of the algorithm we are analyzing. Each formulation assumes that $\mathcal{I}_n$ is finite.

Formulation I

$$A(n) = E[\tau] = \sum_{I \in \mathcal{I}_n} \tau(I)P(I). \qquad (6.2.1)$$

Formula (6.2.1) is simply Definition (E.3.5) of the expected value $E[X]$ with $X = \tau$, $s = I$, and $S = \mathcal{I}_n$. Because it is usually too cumbersome to examine each element in $\mathcal{I}_n$ individually, this formulation is rarely used directly.

Formulation II

Let p_i denote the probability that the algorithm performs exactly i basic operations; that is, $p_i = P(\tau = i)$. Then

$$A(n) = E[\tau] = \sum_{i=1}^{W(n)} ip_i. \qquad (6.2.2)$$

Formula (6.2.2) is a special case of Formula (E.3.7), with $X = \tau$ and $x = i$. Note that Formulas (6.2.1) and (6.2.2) are the same as the formulas (2.5.3) and (2.5.4), respectively, given in Chapter 2.

Formulation III

Let q_i denote the probability that the algorithm performs *at least i* basic operations; that is, $q_i = P\{\tau \geq i\}$. Then

$$A(n) = E[\tau] = \sum_{i=1}^{W(n)} q_i. \qquad (6.2.3)$$

Formula (6.2.3) follows easily from Formula (6.2.2) (see Exercise 6.19)

Formulation IV

Given that $\tau = \sum_{i=1}^{k} \tau_i$, then

$$A(n) = E[\tau] = \sum_{i=1}^{k} E[\tau_i]. \qquad (6.2.4)$$

Formula (6.2.4) is Formula (E.3.12) with $X = \tau$ and $X_i = \tau_i$.

Formulation V

Given that Y is a random variable defined in $\mathscr{I}_n$, then

$$A(n) = E[\tau] = \sum_{y} E[\tau \,|\, Y = y]P(Y = y), \qquad (6.2.5)$$

where the summation is taken over all y such that $P(Y = y) > 0$.

Formula (6.2.5) is Formula (E.4.6) with $X = \tau$.

Key Fact

To determine which of the formulations of $A(n)$ are best suited to a given algorithm, we usually use one or more of the following three techniques:

1. Partitioning the algorithm
2. Partitioning the input space
3. Recursion

Partitioning the algorithm refers to breaking down the steps in the algorithm into k stages. If τ_i denotes the random variable on $\mathscr{I}_n$ mapping each input onto the number of basic operations performed in stage i, $i = 1, \dots, k$, then $\tau = \sum_{i=1}^{k} \tau_i$, and Formulation IV applies. The partitioning is useful when each τ_i can be effectively computed when $i = 1, \dots, k$.

Partitioning the input space is appropriate when the inputs of size n to the algorithm can be partitioned into disjoint sets by using a naturally defined random variable Y and where the quantities $E[\tau \,|\, Y = y]$, $P(Y = y)$ occurring in

Formula (6.2.5) are effectively computable. Typically, Y involves mapping an input to some sort of integer constraint, such as the position in a list of size n where a maximum element occurs. Then $A(n)$ is computed using (6.2.5).

Often we can find a recurrence relation expressing $A(n)$ in terms of one or more of the values $A(m)$ with $m < n$. Of course, if the algorithm itself is written recursively, then the recurrence relation is usually easy to find. In general, finding a recurrence relation for $A(n)$ involves using the techniques of partitioning the algorithm or the input space.

6.3 Average Complexity of *LinearSearch*

In Chapter 2, we informally showed that the average complexity of *LinearSearch* is $n/2 + 1/2$, under the assumptions that the search element X is in the list $L[0:n-1]$ and the list consists of distinct elements, with each element equally likely to be X. We now calculate the average complexity of *LinearSearch* under these assumptions, but we assume that the search element X occurs in the list with probability p. Using the notation for conditional probability given in the Appendix E, this assumption becomes

$$P(X = L[i] \mid X \text{ is in the list } L) = 1/n, \quad i = 0, \dots, n - 1.$$

We will calculate $A(n)$ using Formula (6.2.2). For $1 \le i \le n$, p_i is equal to the probability that X is the ith list element $L[i-1]$. Hence, from Formula (E.2.3) we have

$$p_i = P(X = L[i-1] \mid X \text{ is in the list } L)P(X \text{ is in the list } L)$$
$$= \left(\frac{1}{n}\right)p = \frac{p}{n}, \quad i = 1, \dots, n - 1.$$

LinearSearch performs n comparisons when $X = L[n-1]$, or when X is not in the list L. Thus, $p_n = p/n + 1 - p$. Substituting these values of p_i into Formula (6.2.2) yields

$$A(n) = 1\left(\frac{p}{n}\right) + 2\left(\frac{p}{n}\right) + \cdots + (n-1)\left(\frac{p}{n}\right) + n\left(\frac{p}{n} + 1 - p\right)$$
$$= (1 + 2 + \cdots + n)\left(\frac{p}{n}\right) + n(1 - p) \qquad \textbf{(6.3.1)}$$
$$= \left(\frac{n(n+1)}{2}\right)\left(\frac{p}{n}\right) + n(1 - p) = \left(1 - \frac{p}{2}\right)n + \frac{p}{2}.$$

REMARK

If we set $p = 1$ in Formula (6.3.1), we obtain the formula $A(n) = (n + 1)/2$ derived in Chapter 2 for the average complexity of *LinearSearch* when X is assumed to be in the list.

6.3.1 Average Complexity of *LinearSearch* with Repeated Elements

We now determine the average behavior $A(n,m)$ of *LinearSearch* for lists $L[0:n - 1]$ of size n having m distinct elements drawn from a given fixed set $S = \{s_1, s_2, \dots, s_m\}$, where the search element $X \in S$. For purposes of computing $A(n,m)$, we assume that $L[i]$ has an equal probability $1/m$ of being any element in S, $i = 0, 1, \dots, n - 1$. Hence, the probability that X does not occur in position i is $(m - 1)/m$, $i = 0, 1, \dots, n - 1$. It follows that the probability that X is not in the list is $((m - 1)/m)^n$ and the probability that X is in the list is $1 - ((m - 1)/m)^n$.

Clearly, the p_i in Formula (6.2.2), $i = 1, 2, \dots, n - 1$, is the probability that the first occurrence of the search element X is in position i, and p_n is the probability that X does not occur in the first $n - 1$ positions. Thus, we have

$$p_i = \begin{cases} ((m - 1)/m)^{i-1}(1/m) & \text{if } 1 \le i \le n - 1, \\ ((m - 1)/m)^{n-1} & \text{if } i = n. \end{cases} \qquad \textbf{(6.3.2)}$$

Substituting Formula (6.3.2) into a suitably interpreted Formula (6.2.2) gives us

$$A(n,m) = \sum_{i=1}^{W(n)} i p_i = \left(\sum_{i=1}^{n-1} i \left(\frac{m - 1}{m} \right)^{i-1} \left(\frac{1}{m} \right) \right) + \left(\frac{m - 1}{m} \right)^{n-1}. \qquad \textbf{(6.3.3)}$$

We now employ Formula (B.2.11) from Appendix B, which states that

$$\sum_{i=1}^{n-1} i x^{i-1} = \frac{(n - 1)x^n - nx^{n-1} + 1}{(1 - x)^2}.$$

By replacing x by $(m - 1)/m$ in this formula and substituting the result in Formula (6.3.3), we obtain

$$A(n,m) = \left[(1/m) \frac{(n - 1)((m - 1)/m)^n - n((m - 1)/m)^{n-1} + 1}{m^{-2}} \right] + \left(\frac{m - 1}{m} \right)^{n-1}$$

$$= m\left(1 - \left(\frac{m - 1}{m} \right)^n \right) + \left(\frac{m - 1}{m} \right)^{n-1}.$$

If we hold m constant, then $((m-1)/m)^n$ approaches zero as n approaches ∞, so that $A(n,m) \sim m$. In particular, we have $A(n,m_{\text{fixed}}) \in \Theta(m_{\text{fixed}}) = \Theta(1)$, and thus $A(n,m_{\text{fixed}})$ has *constant* order. This behavior is very different from the linear average behavior $A(n)$ of *LinearSearch* for lists of *distinct* elements.

6.4 Average Complexity of *InsertionSort*

Because *InsertionSort* is a comparison-based algorithm, we can assume without loss of generality that inputs to *InsertionSort* are permutations of $\{1,2,\ldots,n\}$. We also assume that each permutation is equally likely to be the input to *Insertion-Sort*. Unlike our analysis of *LinearSearch*, we cannot compute $A(n) = E[\tau]$ directly by applying Formula (6.2.2). Instead, we partition the algorithm *InsertionSort* into $n-1$ stages. The ith stage consists of inserting the element $L[i]$ into its proper position in the sublist $L[0:i-1]$, where the latter sublist has already been sorted by the algorithm. Let τ_i denote the number of comparisons performed in stage i, so that $\tau = \tau_1 + \cdots + \tau_{n-1}$ and, by Formula (6.2.4),

$$A(n) = E[\tau] = E[\tau_1] + E[\tau_2] + \cdots + E[\tau_{n-1}]. \qquad \textbf{(6.4.1)}$$

We now calculate $E[\tau_i]$, $i = 1, \ldots, n-1$, using Formula (6.2.2). We have

$$E[\tau_i] = \sum_{j=1}^{i} j P(\tau_i = j). \qquad \textbf{(6.4.2)}$$

Our assumption of a uniform distribution on the input space implies that any position in $L[0:i]$ is equally likely to be the correct position for $L[i]$. Thus, the probability that $L[i]$ is the jth largest of the elements in $L[0:i]$ is equal to $1/(i+1)$. If $L[i]$ is the jth largest, where $j \leq i$, then exactly j comparisons are performed by *InsertionSort* when placing $L[i]$ in its correct position. If $L[i]$ is the $(i+1)^{\text{st}}$ largest (that is, the smallest), then exactly i comparisons are performed by *InsertionSort* when placing $L[i]$ in its correct position. It follows that

$$P(\tau_i = j) = \frac{1}{i+1}, \quad j = 1, \ldots, i-1,$$

$$P(\tau_i = i) = \frac{2}{i+1}, \quad i = 1, \ldots, n-1. \qquad \textbf{(6.4.3)}$$

Substituting Formula (6.4.3) into (6.4.2) and simplifying yields

$$E[\tau_i] = \left(\sum_{j=1}^{i} \frac{j}{i+1} \right) + \frac{i}{i+1} = \frac{i}{2} + 1 - \frac{1}{i+1}, \quad i = 1, \ldots, n-1. \quad \textbf{(6.4.4)}$$

Substituting Formula (6.4.4) into (6.4.1), we have

$$A(n) = \sum_{i=1}^{n-1} \left(\frac{i}{2} + 1 - \frac{1}{i+1} \right)$$

$$= (n-1)\frac{n}{4} + (n-1) - \left(\frac{1}{2} + \frac{1}{3} + \cdots + \frac{1}{n} \right)$$

$$= (n-1)\frac{n}{4} + n - H(n),$$

where $H(n)$ is the harmonic series $1 + 1/2 + \cdots + 1/n \sim \ln n$. In particular, $A(n) \in \Theta(n^2)$. Note that the average complexity of *InsertionSort* is about half that of its worst-case complexity, since the highest-order terms in the expressions for these complexities are $n^2/4$ and $n^2/2$, respectively.

6.5 Average Complexity of *QuickSort*

As with *InsertionSort*, we assume that input lists $L[0:n-1]$ to *QuickSort* are all permutations of $\{1,2, \dots n\}$, with each permutation being equally likely. We partition *QuickSort* into two stages, where the first stage is the call to *Partition* and the second stage is the two recursive calls with input lists consisting of the sublists on either side of the proper placement of the pivot element $L[0]$. Thus, $\tau = \tau_1 + \tau_2$, where τ_1 is the (constant) number $n + 1$ of comparisons performed by *Partition* and τ_2 is the number of comparisons performed by the recursive calls. Hence,

$$A(n) = E[\tau] = E[\tau_1] + E[\tau_2] = n + 1 + E[\tau_2]. \qquad \textbf{(6.5.1)}$$

We compute $E[\tau_2]$ using Formulation V by introducing the random variable Y that maps an input list $L[0:n-1]$ into the proper place for $L[0]$ as determined by a call to *Partition*. The uniform distribution assumption on the input space implies that

$$P(Y = i) = \frac{1}{n}, \quad i = 0, \dots, n-1. \qquad \textbf{(6.5.2)}$$

If $Y = i$, then the recursive calls to *QuickSort* are with the two sublists $L[0:i-1]$ and $L[i+1:n-1]$. Our assumption of a uniform distribution on the input space implies that the expected number of comparisons performed by *QuickSort* on the sublists $L[0:i-1]$ and $L[i+1:n-1]$ is given by $A(i)$ and $A(n-i-1)$, respectively. Hence,

$$E[\tau_2|Y = i] = A(i) + A(n-i-1), \quad i = 0, \dots, n-1. \qquad \textbf{(6.5.3)}$$

Combining Formulas (6.2.5), (6.5.1), (6.5.2), and (6.5.3), we have

$$
\begin{aligned}
A(n) &= (n + 1) + \sum_{i=0}^{n-1} E[\tau_2 | Y = i] P(Y = i) \\
&= (n + 1) + \sum_{i=0}^{n-1} (A(i) + A(n - i - 1))\left(\frac{1}{n}\right) \\
&= (n + 1) + \frac{2}{n}(A(0) + A(1) + \cdots + A(n - 1)),
\end{aligned}
\tag{6.5.4}
$$

init. cond. $A(0) = A(1) = 0$.

Recurrence relation (6.5.4) is an example of what is sometimes referred to as a *full history* recurrence relation, because it relates $A(n)$ to *all* of the previous values $A(i)$, $0 \le i \le n - 1$. Fortunately, with some algebraic manipulation, we can transform (6.5.4) into a simpler recurrence relation as follows. The trick is to first observe that

$$
nA(n) = n(n + 1) + 2(A(0) + A(1) + \cdots + A(n - 2) + A(n - 1)).
\tag{6.5.5}
$$

Substituting $n - 1$ for n in Formula (6.5.5) yields

$$
(n - 1)A(n - 1) = n(n - 1) + 2(A(0) + A(1) + \cdots + A(n - 2)).
\tag{6.5.6}
$$

By subtracting Formula (6.5.6) from (6.5.5), we obtain

$$
nA(n) - (n - 1)A(n - 1) = 2n + 2A(n - 1).
\tag{6.5.7}
$$

Rewriting Formula (6.5.7) by moving the term involving $A(n - 1)$ to the right-hand side and dividing both sides by $n(n + 1)$ yields

$$
\frac{A(n)}{n + 1} = \frac{A(n - 1)}{n} + \frac{2}{n + 1}.
\tag{6.5.8}
$$

Letting $t(n) = A(n)/(n + 1)$ changes Formula (6.5.8) to

$$
t(n) = t(n - 1) + \frac{2}{n + 1}.
\tag{6.5.9}
$$

Recurrence relation (6.5.9) directly unwinds to yield

$$
\begin{aligned}
t(n) &= 2\left(\frac{1}{3} + \frac{1}{4} + \cdots + \frac{1}{(n + 1)}\right) \\
&= 2H(n + 1) - 3,
\end{aligned}
\tag{6.5.10}
$$

where $H(n)$ is the harmonic series. Thus, $t(n) \sim 2\ln n$, so that the average complexity $A(n)$ of *QuickSort* satisfies

$$A(n) \sim 2n\ln n. \qquad \textbf{(6.5.11)}$$

In particular, *QuickSort* exhibits $O(n\log n)$ average behavior, which is order optimal for a comparison-based sorting algorithm.

6.6 Average Complexity of *MaxMin*2

We analyze the algorithm *MaxMin2* given in Chapter 2 as our third example. For convenience, we repeat the pseudocode for *MaxMin2* here.

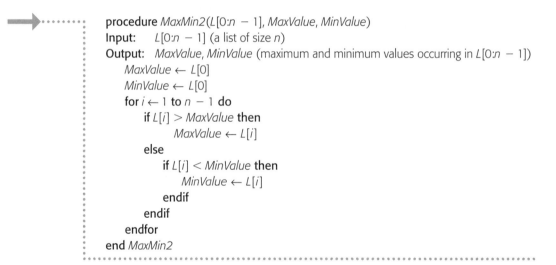

```
procedure MaxMin2(L[0:n − 1], MaxValue, MinValue)
Input:    L[0:n − 1] (a list of size n)
Output:   MaxValue, MinValue (maximum and minimum values occurring in L[0:n − 1])
    MaxValue ← L[0]
    MinValue ← L[0]
    for i ← 1 to n − 1 do
        if L[i] > MaxValue then
            MaxValue ← L[i]
        else
            if L[i] < MinValue then
                MinValue ← L[i]
            endif
        endif
    endfor
end MaxMin2
```

As observed in Chapter 2, the best-case complexity of *MaxMin2* is $n - 1$, and its worst-case complexity is $2(n - 1)$. Recall that the algorithm *MaxMin3* has best-case, worst-case, and average complexities all equal to $\lceil 3n/2 \rceil - 2$. Thus, to complete our comparison of *MaxMin2* and *MaxMin3*, we need to compute the average complexity of *MaxMin2*. Unfortunately, it turns out that the average complexity of *MaxMin2* is closer to its worst-case complexity than to its best-case complexity.

When analyzing the average complexity of *MaxMin2*, we again assume that the inputs are permutations of $\{1, 2, \dots, n\}$ and that each permutation is equally likely. Observe that $n - 1$ comparisons involving *MaxValue* are performed for any input permutation. An additional comparison involving *MinValue* is performed for each iteration of the loop in which *MaxValue* is not updated. If we let D

denote the random variable that maps the input permutation to the number of times that *MaxValue* is updated, then we have

$$\tau = n - 1 + (n - 1 - D) = 2n - 2 - D. \qquad \textbf{(6.6.1)}$$

Using Formula (6.6.1), the average complexity of *MaxMin2* is given by

$$A(n) = E[\tau] = 2n - 2 - E[D]. \qquad \textbf{(6.6.2)}$$

We compute the expected number of updates $E[D]$ by partitioning the input space using the random variable M that maps an input permutation π of $\{1, \dots, n\}$ to $\pi(n)$. Applying formula (6.2.5)), we obtain

$$E[D] = \sum_{i=1}^{n} E[D \mid M = i] P(M = i). \qquad \textbf{(6.6.3)}$$

The assumption of a uniform distribution on the input space implies that the maximum element is equally likely to occur in any position. Thus, we have

$$P(M = i) = \frac{1}{n}, \quad i = 1, \dots, n. \qquad \textbf{(6.6.4)}$$

Analogous with the notation $A(n)$ used for $E[\tau]$, the notation $\alpha(n)$ is used for $E[D]$ to facilitate the expression of a recurrence relation for $E[D]$. Clearly, we have

$$E[D \mid M = n] = \alpha(n - 1) + 1, \qquad \textbf{(6.6.5)}$$

because permutations of $\{1, \dots, n\}$ with $\pi(n) = n$ are in one-to-one correspondence with permutations of $\{1, \dots, n - 1\}$, and the maximum is updated for such permutations π exactly one more time than it was updated on $\pi(1), \dots, \pi(n - 1)$. On the other hand, for permutations π such that $\pi(n) = i \neq n$, we have

$$E[D \mid M = i] = \alpha(n - 1), \quad i \in \{1, \dots, n - 1\}, \qquad \textbf{(6.6.6)}$$

because the maximum is not updated on $\pi(n)$, and (for a fixed i) such permutations are again in one-to-one correspondence with permutations of $\{1, \dots, n - 1\}$. Hence, combining Formulas (6.6.3) through (6.6.6), we have

$$\alpha(n) = \left(\frac{1}{n}\right)(\alpha(n - 1) + 1) + ((n - 1)/n)\alpha(n - 1)$$
$$= \alpha(n - 1) + 1/n, \quad \textbf{init. cond. } \alpha(1) = 0. \qquad \textbf{(6.6.7)}$$

Recurrence relation (6.6.7) unwinds directly to yield

$$\alpha(n) = \frac{1}{2} + \frac{1}{3} + \cdots + \frac{1}{n} = H(n) - 1, \qquad \textbf{(6.6.8)}$$

where $H(n)$ is the harmonic series. By combining Formulas (6.6.2) and (6.6.8), we obtain the following formula for the average complexity $A(n)$ of *MaxMin2*:

$$A(n) = 2n - 2 - \alpha(n) = 2n - H(n) - 1. \qquad \textbf{(6.6.9)}$$

Because $H(n)$ is approximately equal to $\ln n$, $A(n)$ is approximately equal to $2n - \ln n - 1$. In particular, $A(n) \sim W(n)$ for *MaxMin2*.

6.7 Average Complexity of *BinarySearch* and *SearchBinSrchTree*

To compute the average complexity $A(n)$ of the algorithm *BinarySearch* given in Chapter 2, we choose the three-branch comparison of the **do case** statement as the basic operation. Let p denote the probability that the search element X is on the list. Given that X is on the list $L[0:n-1]$, we assume that it is equally likely to occur in any of the n positions. Given that the search element is not on the list, we assume that it is equally likely to occur in any of the following $n + 1$ intervals:

$$X < L[0], L[0] < X < L[1], \dots, L[n-2] < X < L[n-1], X > L[n-1].$$

In Figure 6.1, we show the implicit search tree T for *BinarySearch* with an input list $L[0:7]$ of size 8. Note that T is a 2-tree having n internal nodes (squares) corresponding to the elements of $L[0:n-1]$ and $n + 1$ leaf nodes (triangles) corresponding to these $n + 1$ intervals. Thus, the probability that X occurs on the list and is equal to any given element $L[i]$ is p/n, $i = 0, \dots, n-1$, and the probability that X occurs in any one of the $n + 1$ intervals is $(1 - p)/(n + 1)$.

Given a search element X, *BinarySearch* follows a path in the tree from the root to a node of T corresponding to X, or to a leaf node if X is not in the list. Thus, the average complexity $A(n)$ is given by

$$A(n) = \left(\frac{p}{n}\right)(IPL(T) + n) + \left(\frac{1-p}{n+1}\right)LPL(T). \qquad \textbf{(6.7.1)}$$

FIGURE 6.1

Implicit search tree
for *BinarySearch*
with an input list
L[0:7] of size 8. The
index of the list
element that is
compared to the
search element is
shown inside each
node. Leaf nodes
correspond to
unsuccessful
searches.

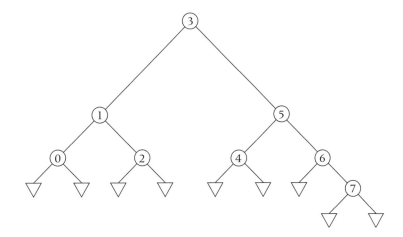

Employing Proposition 4.2.7 and substituting $LPL(T) - 2n$ for $IPL(T)$ in Formula (6.7.1), we obtain

$$A(n) = \left(\frac{p}{n}\right)(LPL(T) - n) + \left(\frac{1 - p}{n + 1}\right)LPL(T)$$

$$= \left(\frac{p}{n} + \frac{1 - p}{n + 1}\right)LPL(T) - p. \qquad \textbf{(6.7.2)}$$

The implicit search tree for *BinarySearch* is a 2-tree that is full at the second-deepest level (see Exercise 6.23). Hence, by Theorem 4.2.8,

$$LPL(T) = \lfloor L\log_2 L \rfloor + 2(L - 2^{\lfloor \log_2 L \rfloor})$$
$$\geq \lceil L\log_2 L \rceil = \lceil (n + 1)\log_2(n + 1) \rceil. \qquad \textbf{(6.7.3)}$$

Substituting the expression for $LPL(T)$ given in Formula (6.7.3) into (6.7.2), we obtain

$$A(n) \geq \left(\frac{p}{n} + \frac{1 - p}{n + 1}\right)\lceil (n + 1)\log_2(n + 1) \rceil - p. \qquad \textbf{(6.7.4)}$$

The lower-bound estimate for $A(n)$ in Formula (6.7.4) looks somewhat formidable, but it is easily seen to be asymptotic to the worst-case complexity; that is, $A(n) \sim W(n) = \lceil \log_2(n + 1) \rceil$. Furthermore, suppose we restrict attention to successful search, so that $p = 1$ in Formula (6.7.4). Then we have $A(n) \geq (1/n)\lceil (n + 1)\log_2(n + 1) \rceil - 1$. In other words, for large n, the average complexity of *BinarySearch* for successful searching is no more than 1 less than its worst-case complexity.

Another algorithm whose average behavior can be calculated using leaf path length is *SearchBinSrchTree* given in Chapter 4. The average complexity $A(n)$ of *SearchBinSrchTree* depends on the probability distribution on the set of input trees, as well as probabilities associated with the identifiers. The analysis of the average complexity $A(n)$ of *SearchBinSrchTree* over the set of all binary search trees is difficult. In any case, it is probably more interesting to analyze the average behavior $A(T,n)$ of *SearchBinSrchTree* for a given fixed tree T and a given set of probabilities associated with the identifiers.

Suppose, then, that T is a fixed input search tree (pointed at by *Root*), whose internal nodes correspond to a fixed set of n identifiers, or keys (K_0, K_1, ... , K_{n-1}). Note that T contains $n + 1$ implicit leaf nodes, corresponding to the $n + 1$ intervals

$$I_0{:}X < K_0, I_1{:}K_0 < X < K_1, \dots , I_{n-1}{:}K_{n-2} < X < K_{n-1}, I_n{:}X > K_{n-1}.$$

Given T, the average behavior $A(T,n)$ of *SearchBinSrchTree* (either version) depends on the probabilities $p_0, p_1, \dots , p_{n-1}$ assigned to the internal nodes, and the probabilities $q_0, q_1, \dots , q_n$ assigned to the implicit leaf nodes of the search tree. Assume now that all the p_i's are equal, and all the q_i's are equal. If p denotes the probability that X is one of the n keys $K_0, \dots , K_{n-1}$, then $p_i = p/n$ for all $i \in \{0, \dots , n - 1\}$ and $q_j = (1 - p)/(n + 1)$ for all $j \in \{0, \dots , n\}$. Under these assumptions, we can show that

$$A(T, n) = LPL(T)\frac{(1 + p/n)}{n + 1} - p. \qquad \textbf{(6.7.5)}$$

Applying Theorem 4.2.8 to Formula (6.7.5) yields the following theorem:

Theorem 6.7.1   Let T be any binary search tree (with external implicit leaf nodes added) for keys $K_0, \dots , K_{n-1}$, where $p_i = p/n$ for each $i \in \{0, \dots , n - 1\}$, and $q_j = (1 - p)/(n + 1)$ for each $j \in \{0, \dots , n\}$. Then,

$$A(T,n) \geq [(n + 1)\lfloor \log_2(n + 1)\rfloor + 2(n + 1 - 2^{\lfloor \log_2(n+1)\rfloor})]\left(\frac{1 + p/n}{n + 1}\right) - p$$

$$\geq \lceil \log_2(n + 1)\rceil\left(1 + \frac{p}{n}\right) - p \in \Omega(\log n). \qquad \textbf{(6.7.6)}$$

Moreover, the first inequality in Formula (6.7.6) is an equality if and only if T is a 2-tree that is full at the second deepest level.   ■

An important and natural problem is to determine an optimal search tree T in the sense that T minimizes $A(T,n)$ over all binary search trees containing n identifiers. Theorem 6.7.1 completely characterizes optimal binary search trees for the case where $p_i = p/n$ for each $i \in \{0, \dots, n-1\}$ and $q_j = (1-p)/(n+1)$ for each $j \in \{0, \dots, n\}$. That is, a binary search tree T is optimal for these probabilities if and only if it is full at the second deepest level. In Chapter 9, we will use the technique of dynamic programming to solve the more difficult problem of finding an optimal search tree for general probabilities p_i and q_j.

REMARK

A binary search tree without the implicit external leaf nodes added is full at the second deepest level if and only if the associated 2-tree with the external leaf nodes added is full at the second deepest level. Thus, Theorem 6.7.1 could be restated for binary search trees without the external leaf nodes added.

6.8   Searching a Link-Ordered List

Suppose we have a list $L[0{:}n-1]$ of records having multiple fields, and we wish to maintain a sorting of L with respect to more than one of these fields (keys). Maintaining multiple sortings is usually done using auxiliary tag arrays or link arrays. For a given key field, a tag array $Tag[0{:}n-1]$ has the property that the sorting of L is given by

$$L[Tag[0]], L[Tag[1]], \dots, L[Tag[n-1]].$$

In the linked-list implementation, we assume that a variable $Head$ contains the index of the smallest element in L with respect to the given key field. Then the link array $Link[0{:}n-1]$ has the property that the sorting of L is given by

$$L[Head], L[Link[Head]], L[Link[Link[Head]]], \dots, L[Link^{n-1}[Head]],$$

where $Link^m$ denotes the m-fold composition of $Link$ ($Link^0$ is the identity function). $Link[i] = -1$ indicates the end of the list. In Figure 6.2, we show a sample list $L[0{:}11]$ and its associated array $Link[0{:}11]$.

FIGURE 6.2

A list $L[0:11]$
maintained in order
using an auxiliary
array $Link[0:11]$

i	0	1	2	3	4	5	6	7	8	9	10	11
L	17	11	44	23	7	4	14	55	21	56	9	15
$Link$	8	6	4	7	10	4	11	9	3	-1	1	0

$Head = 5$

We now consider the problem of searching for an occurrence of a given element in L having a given key value X. The tag array $Tag[0:n-1]$ facilitates efficient searching using a binary search. Using the link array $Link[0:n-1]$, we cannot efficiently use a binary search because we have no way to directly determine the middle list element. Accessing the middle element $L[Link^{(n/2)-1}[Head]]$ requires $(n/2)-1$ accesses of the array $Link$. In fact, it can be shown that *any* algorithm for searching L requires n accesses to the array $Link$ in the worst case. We now describe an algorithm *ProbeLinSrch* for searching L whose average complexity belongs to $O(\sqrt{n})$.

The algorithm *ProbeLinSrch* uses an algorithm *LinkOrdLinSrch* for searching a link-ordered list. *LinkOrdLinSrch* is a variant of the straightforward analog of a linear search for link-ordered lists. *LinkOrdLinSrch* is based on the fact that if we use the array *Link* to make a search for the occurrence of X in L in sorted order, then we can terminate the search whenever we compare X to a list element that is larger than X. *LinkOrdLinSrch* returns the index of an occurrence of X in the list L, or it returns -1 if X is not in list L. For convenience in the following discussion, we identify the record $L[i]$ with its key field.

```
function LinkOrdLinSrch(L[0:n − 1], Link[0:n − 1], Head, X)
Input:      L[0:n − 1] (array of n list elements)
            Link[0:n − 1] (array pointing to sorted order of L[0:n − 1])
            Head (index of smallest element in L)
            X (search element)
Output:   Returns index of occurrence of X in L, or −1 if X is not in L
    i ← Head
    while X > L[i] do
        i ← Link[i]
        if i = −1 then return(−1) endif
    endwhile
    if X = L[i] then
        return(i )
    else
        return (−1)
    endif
end LinkOrdLinSrch
```

To analyze *LinkOrdLinSrch*, we note that the number of updates for the index variable i in *LinkOrdLinSrch* is at most 1 less than the number of comparisons of X with a list element in L. Thus, we choose comparisons of X to list elements as our basic operation. Clearly, the best-case and worst-case complexities of *LinkOrdLinSrch* are $B(n) = 2$ and $W(n) = n + 1$, respectively.

To compute the average complexity of *LinkOrdLinSrch*, we make the usual assumption that each list element is distinct. We also assume that each element is equally likely to be X and that X falls into each of the $n + 1$ "gaps": $X < L[Head]$, $L[Head] < X < L[Link[Head]]$, ... , $L[Link^{n-2}[Head]] < X < L[Link^{n-1}[Head]]$, $X > L[Link^{n-1}[Head]]$ with equal probability. Let $A_s(n)$ and $A_u(n)$ denote the expected number of comparisons for successful and unsuccessful searches, respectively. Then, if p denotes the probability that X occurs on the list, we have

$$A(n) = pA_s(n) + (1 - p)A_u(n). \qquad (6.8.1)$$

We can derive Formula (6.8.1) directly from the definition of conditional expectation, and it is actually a special case of (E.4.5)).

To compute $A_s(n)$, we assume that for each i between 1 and n, the probability that X occurs in position i is $1/n$, given that X is in the list. In addition, $i + 1$ comparisons of X to a list element are performed when $X = L[Link^{j-1}[Head]]$, $1 \leq i \leq n$. Hence,

$$A_s(n) = \frac{2 + 3 + \cdots + n + n + 1}{n} = \frac{1 + 2 + \cdots + n}{n} + 1$$
$$= \frac{n + 1}{2} + 1. \qquad (6.8.2)$$

To compute $A_u(n)$, we assume that for each i between 1 and $n + 1$, the probability that X occurs in the ith gap is $1/(n + 1)$, given that X is not in the list. In addition, we assume that $i + 1$ comparisons of X to a list element are performed when X is in the ith gap, $1 \leq i \leq n$, and n comparisons are made when $X > L[Link^{-1}[Head]]$. Hence,

$$A_u(n) = \frac{2 + 3 + \cdots + n + 1}{n + 1} + 1 - \frac{1}{n + 1}$$
$$= \frac{n + 2}{2} + 1 - \frac{2}{n + 1}. \qquad (6.8.3)$$

Using Formulas (6.8.2) and (6.8.3), we have $A_s(n) \sim n/2$ and $A_u(n) \sim n/2$. Thus, it follows from Formula (6.8.1) that $A(n) \sim n/2$.

ProbeLinSrch is a variant of *LinkOrdLinSrch* in which we first scan the list elements $L[0]$, ... , $L[\lfloor \sqrt{n} \rfloor - 1]$ for a better starting point than *Head*. Note that the index i is a feasible starting point for our search if $X \geq L[i]$. If there is no feasible starting point in index positions $0, \ldots, \lfloor\sqrt{n}\rfloor - 1$, then *ProbeLinSrch* invokes *LinkOrdLinSrch* with *Probe = Head*. Otherwise, *ProbeLinSrch* invokes *LinkOrdLinSrch* with *Probe* equal to the best feasible starting point found.

To illustrate, consider the lists $L[0:11]$ and $Link[0:11]$ shown in Figure 6.2. Given a search element X, we first determine the best feasible starting point *Probe* among $L[0], L[1], L[2] = L[\lfloor\sqrt{12}\rfloor - 1]$. For example, when X is 23, 3, or 46, then *Probe* is 0, 5, or 2, respectively.

```
function ProbeLinSrch(L[0:n − 1], Link[0:n − 1], Head, X)
Input:    L[0:n − 1] (an array of list elements)
          Link[0:n − 1] (an array pointing to sorted order of L[0:n − 1])
          Head (index of smallest element in L)
          X (search element)
Output:   returns index of occurrence of X in L, or −1 if X is not in L
     Probe ← Head
     Max ← L[Head]
          // look for the best feasible starting point (if any) between 0 and ⌊√n⌋ − 1
     for i = 0 to ⌊√n⌋ − 1 do
        Temp ← L[i]
        if Max < Temp .and. Temp ≤ X then
           Probe ← i
           Max ← Temp
        endif
     endfor
     return(LinkOrdLinSrch(L[0:n − 1], Link[0:n − 1], Probe, X))
end ProbeLinSrch
```

Clearly, the best-case and worst-case complexities of *ProbeLinSrch* are given by $B(n) = \lfloor\sqrt{n}\rfloor + 2$ and $W(n) = n + 1 + \lfloor\sqrt{n}\rfloor$, respectively. To determine the average complexity $A(n)$, it is useful to consider a generalization of *ProbeLinSrch* in which the first k list elements $L[0], \ldots, L[k-1]$ are probed for a feasible starting point. In the generalized version, k is an additional input parameter to *ProbeLinSrch*, and the ordinary version of *ProbeLinSrch* corresponds to the special case where $k = \lfloor\sqrt{n}\rfloor$. In the following discussion, we continue to refer to the generalized version as simply *ProbeLinSrch*.

We assume that the list elements are distinct and that the search element X is on the list. Further, we assume that X is equally likely to be any of the list elements. Let $x_i = L[Link^{i-1}[Head]]$ denote the ith-smallest list element, $i = 1, \ldots, n$.

Let Y denote the random variable that maps the input $(L[0:n-1],X)$ onto m where $X = x_m$. By Formula (6.2.5) we have

$$A(n) = \sum_{m=1}^{n} E[\tau | Y = m]P(Y = m) = \frac{1}{n}\sum_{m=1}^{n} E[\tau | Y = m]. \quad (6.8.4)$$

To compute $E[\tau | Y = m]$, note that *ProbeLinSrch* has three stages: Stage 1 consists of the **for** loop that determines the probe element, stage 2 consists of the **while** loop in *LinkOrdLinSrch*, and stage 3 consists of the final comparison made by *LinkOrdLinSrch*. For $m \in \{1, \dots ,n\}$, let β_m denote the random variable that maps an input X such that $X = x_m$ onto the number of comparisons performed by *LinkOrdLinSrch* during stage 2 with input X. Then we have

$$E[\tau | Y = m] = k + 1 + E[\beta_m], \quad m = 1, \dots ,n. \quad (6.8.5)$$

Given any $m \in \{1, \dots ,n\}$, we now calculate $E[\beta_m]$ using Formula (6.2.3). Let $q_i = q_i(m)$ denote the probability that *LinkOrdLinSrch* performs at least i comparisons during the second stage. Note that $q_i = 0$ when $i > m$ because the worst-case number of comparisons m occurs when a better start than *Head* was not found among $L[0], \dots , L[k-1]$ during stage 1. For $2 \leq i \leq m$, *LinkOrdLinSrch* performs less than i comparisons precisely when one of the elements $x_{m-i+2}, x_{m-i+3}, \dots , x_m$ belongs to $L[0], \dots , L[k-1]$. Thus, the probability q_i that at least i comparisons are performed is the probability that each of the list elements $L[0], \dots , L[k-1]$ belongs to the set of $n - i + 1$ complementary elements to $x_{m-i+2}, x_{m-i+3}, \dots , x_m$. Because the total number of ways to choose such a sequence $L[0], \dots , L[k-1]$ is $(n - i + 1)^{(k)}$ and the total number of ways to choose a sequence $L[0], \dots , L[k-1]$ from $x_1, x_2, \dots , x_n$ is $n^{(k)}$ (where $x^{(k)} = x(x-1)...(x-k+1)$), we have

$$q_i = \frac{(n - i + 1)^{(k)}}{n^{(k)}} \leq \frac{(n - i + 1)^k}{n^k}. \quad (6.8.6)$$

The inequality in (6.8.6) follows from Formula A.15 from Appendix A. Using Formula (6.2.3), we have

$$E[\beta_m] = \sum_{i=1}^{m} q_i \leq \sum_{i=1}^{m} \frac{(n - i + 1)^k}{n^k}$$

$$= \left(\frac{1}{n^k}\right)\sum_{i=n-m+1}^{n} i^k$$

$$= \left(\frac{1}{n^k}\right)\left[\left(\sum_{i=1}^{n} i^k\right) - \left(\sum_{i=1}^{n-m} i^k\right)\right] \quad (6.8.7)$$

$$\leq \left(\frac{1}{n^k}\right)\left(\sum_{i=1}^{n} i^k\right), \quad m = 1, \dots ,n.$$

As we showed in Chapter 3, $S(n,k) = \sum_{i=1}^{n} i^k$ is a polynomial in n of degree $k + 1$ with a leading coefficient of $1/(k + 1)$. Hence, Formula (6.8.7) implies

$$E[\beta_m] \leq \frac{n}{k + 1} + O(1), \quad m = 1, \dots, n. \qquad \textbf{(6.8.8)}$$

Substituting Formula (6.8.8) in (6.8.5), we have

$$E[\tau | Y = m] = k + 1 + E[\beta_m] \leq k + \frac{n}{k + 1} + O(1), \quad m = 1, \dots, n. \ \textbf{(6.8.9)}$$

Because the upper-bound estimate $k + n/(k + 1) + O(1)$ for $E[\tau | Y = m]$ given in Formula (6.8.9) is independent of m, substituting the estimate into (6.8.4) yields

$$A(n) \leq \frac{n}{k + 1} + k + O(1). \qquad \textbf{(6.8.10)}$$

Using calculus, it is easy to verify that $n/(k + 1) + k$ achieves a minimum value of $2\sqrt{n} - 1$ at the point $k = \sqrt{n} - 1$, which is approximately $\lfloor \sqrt{n} \rfloor$. Hence, using $k = \lfloor \sqrt{n} \rfloor$ in *ProbeLinSrch* gives us the following from (6.8.10):

$$A(n) \leq 2\sqrt{n} + O(1). \qquad \textbf{(6.8.11)}$$

Because $A(n) \geq B(n) = \lfloor \sqrt{n} \rfloor + 1$, Formula (6.8.11) implies that $A(n) \in \Theta(\sqrt{n})$.

REMARK

Choosing a value of k that minimizes $n/(k + 1) + k$ does not automatically guarantee that this k minimizes $A(n)$, because Formula (6.8.10) is an inequality rather than an equality. However, it does give us an idea of why $\lfloor \sqrt{n} \rfloor$ is the choice for k used in the design of *ProbeLinSrch*. Moreover, our estimate of $A(n)$ is pretty sharp, since $\sqrt{n} < A(n) < 2\sqrt{n} + O(1)$.

6.9 Closing Remarks

Probability theory is an important basic tool in the analysis of algorithms. Currently, the probabilistic analysis of algorithms is a very active area of research, as is introducing probabilistic techniques into the program logic of algorithms.

Algorithms that are not completely deterministic but use random choices as part of the program logic are called *probabilistic* algorithms (see Chapter 24). These algorithms use probabilistic techniques as a design strategy as opposed to merely an analysis tool.

References and Suggestions for Further Reading

For a more advanced treatment of probabilistic algorithm analysis, see the following:

Coffman, E. G., Jr., and G. Lueker. *Probabilistic Analysis of Packing and Partitioning Algorithms.* New York: Wiley, 1991.

Hofri, M. *Probabilistic Analysis of Algorithms.* New York: Springer-Verlag, 1987.

Section 6.1 Expectation and Average Complexity

For these exercises, we often refer to Appendix E for propositions and formulas.

6.1 Consider the sample space S corresponding to rolling two dice; that is, $S = \{(r_1, r_2) \mid r_1, r_2 \in \{1, \dots, 6\}\}$. Assume that the first die is fair but the second die is loaded, with probabilities 1/10, 1/10, 1/10, 1/10, 1/10, and 1/2 of rolling a 1, 2, 3, 4, 5, and 6, respectively.

a. Give a table showing the probability distribution for rolling these dice.

b. Compute the probability that at least one of the dice comes up 6.

c. Compute the conditional probability that the sum of the dice is 10 given that the loaded die does not come up 4.

6.2 Consider the random variable $X = r_1 + r_2$ defined on the sample space S given in Exercise 6.1.

a. Compute the density function $f(x) = P(X = x)$ and verify that it is a probability distribution on the sample $S_X = \{2, \dots, 12\}$.

b. Calculate the expectation $E[X]$.

6.3 Repeat Exercise 6.2 for the random variable $X = \max\{r_1, r_2\}$.

6.4 Let S be the sample space consisting of the positive integers. For a fixed p, $0 < p < 1$, show that the function $P(i) = (1 - p)^{i-1}p$ is a probability distribution on S.

6.5   Consider the sample space S corresponding to rolling three fair dice; that is, $S = (r_1, r_2, r_3) \mid r_1, r_2, r_3 \in \{1, \dots, 6\}\}$. Calculate the expectation $E[X]$ for each of the following random variables X:

a. $X = r_1 + r_2 + r_3$

b. $X = r_1 + r_2$

c. $X = \max \{r_1, r_2, r_3\}$

6.6   Give an alternative derivation of the expectation of a binomial distribution using Proposition E.3.2. (*Hint:* Let X_i be the random variable whose value is 1 if there was a success in the ith trial and 0 otherwise.)

6.7   Verify that the expectation of the geometric distribution (see Appendix E) with probability p of success is $1/p$.

6.8   Verify the following formula, which was used in the derivation of the variance of the geometric distribution with probability p of success:

$$\sum_{k=1}^{\infty} k^2 (1-p)^{k-1} p = \frac{2-p}{p^2}$$

6.9   Calculate the variance of the random variables given in Exercises 6.2 and 6.3.

6.10 Calculate the variance of the random variables given in Exercise 6.5.

6.11 a. Two random variables X and Y defined on a sample space S are *independent* if the events $X = x$ and $Y = y$ are independent for every x and y. Show that if $X_1, X_2, \dots, X_n$ are pairwise independent random variables, then

$$V(X_1 + X_2 + \cdots + X_n) = V(X_1) + V(X_2) + \cdots + V(X_n).$$

b. Employing the formula given in part (a), calculate the variance of the binomial distribution with p and n. (*Hint:* Let X_i be the random variable whose value is 1 if there was a success in the ith trial and 0 otherwise.)

6.12 Prove Proposition E.1.1.

6.13 Prove Propositions E.3.1 and E.3.2.

6.14 Verify that the probabilities given by Formula (E.3.3) satisfy the three axioms for a probability distribution on $\{0, 1, \dots, n\}$.

6.15 Verify that P_F defined by (E.4.1) satisfies the three axioms for a probability distribution on F.

6.16 Given a discrete random variable X, show that the probability density function $f(x) = P(X = x)$ determines a probability distribution on $S_X = \{x : f(x) \neq 0\}$.

6.17 Show that Formula (E.2.5) of Proposition E.2.1 reduces to Formula (E.3.7) when $X = Y$.

6.18 a. For events A and B, show that $P(A \cup B) = P(A) + P(B) - P(A \cap B)$

   b. State and prove a generalization of formula in part (a) to n sets $A_1, \dots, A_n$

Section 6.2 Techniques for Computing Average Complexity

6.19 Derive Formula (6.2.2) from Formula (6.2.1).

6.20 Derive Formula (6.2.3) from Formula (6.2.2).

Section 6.3 Average Complexity of *LinearSearch*

6.21 Calculate the average complexity $A(n)$ of *LinearSearch* assuming that *both* of the following two assumptions about the input list $L[0:n - 1]$ and search element X hold:

   The probability that X occurs in the list is 2/3.

   Given that X occurs in the list, X is twice as likely to occur in the first half of the list (positions 0 through $\lfloor n/2 \rfloor - 1$) as in the second half. Further, if X occurs in the first half of the list it is equally likely to occur in any position in the first half. A similar assumption is made about the second half.

Section 6.4 Average Complexity of *InsertionSort*

6.22 a. Give pseudocode for a recursive version *InsertionSortRec* of *InsertionSort*.

   b. Obtain a recurrence relation for the average complexity $A(n)$ of *InsertionSortRec*.

   c. Solve the recurrence relation obtained in (b), and compare it to the formula for $A(n)$ given in Section 6.4.

Section 6.5 Average Complexity of *QuickSort*

6.23 Suppose that we sort a list $L[0{:}n-1]$ by first determining an element of maximum value, placing it at position n, and then calling *QuickSort* with the (possibly altered) list $L[0{:}n-2]$. Analyze the average complexity of the resulting sorting algorithm, and compare it to *QuickSort*.

Section 6.6 Average Complexity of *MaxMin2*

6.24 Write a program to empirically test the average performance of *MaxMin2*, and compare this performance to *MaxMin3*.

Section 6.7 Average Complexity of *BinarySearch* and *SearchBinSrchTree*

6.25 Show that permutations $\pi{:}\{1,\dots,n\}{\to}\{1,\dots,n\}$ such that $\pi(n)=i\neq n$ are in one-to-one correspondence with permutations of $\{1,\dots,n-1\}$.

6.26 Show that the implicit search tree for *BinarySearch* is a 2-tree that is full at the second deepest level.

6.27 Derive Formula (6.7.5), which expresses $A(T,n)$ in terms of the leaf path length of T, and use it to prove Theorem 6.7.1

*6.28 Compute the average complexity $A(n)$ of *SearchBinSrchTree* over the set of all binary search trees T. Assume that each binary tree search T is equally likely to be the input tree to *SearchBinSrchTree*. Also assume that X is one of the keys in the search tree and that X has an equal chance of being any of the n keys.

Section 6.8 Searching a Link-Ordered List

6.29 Show that the algorithm for searching a link-ordered list of size n that simulates binary search would perform n index updates in the worst case.

6.30 Generalize Exercise 6.29 by showing that *any* comparison-based algorithm for searching a link-ordered list of size n requires n index updates in the worst case.

6.31 Show that Formula (6.8.1) can be derived directly from the definition of conditional expectation and is actually a special case of (E.4.5).

PART TWO

MAJOR DESIGN STRATEGIES

CHAPTER 7

THE GREEDY METHOD

The *greedy method* for solving optimization problems follows the philosophy of greedily maximizing (or minimizing) short-term gain and hoping for the best without regard to long-term consequences. Algorithms based on the greedy method are usually very simple, easy to code, and efficient. Unfortunately, as in real life, when we use the greedy method in an algorithm to solve a problem, we often end up with less-than-optimal results. However, the greedy method does yield optimal results for some important problems, such as computing optimal data compression codes, finding a shortest path between two nodes in a weighted digraph, and determining a minimum spanning tree in a weighted graph (we will discuss the latter two problems in Chapter 12). Moreover, in some important problems, the greedy method yields results that are not optimal but in some sense are good approximations to optimal results.

7.1 General Description

Because the subject is greed, it seems appropriate to illustrate the greedy method with a problem about money: making change. Suppose we have just purchased a sleeve of golf balls, and the salesperson wishes to give back exact change using the *fewest* number of coins. We assume that there is a sufficient amount of pennies, nickels, dimes, quarters, and half-dollars to make change in any manner whatsoever.

A greedy algorithm for making change uses as many coins of the largest denomination as possible, then uses as many coins of the next largest denomination, and so forth. For example, if the change was 74 cents, the greedy solution uses one half-dollar, two dimes, and four pennies, for a total of seven coins. It is easy to see that seven coins is the fewest number of coins that makes 74 cents in change. For any amount of change, the greedy method uses the fewest coins when all the previously mentioned denominations are used. However, when the mix of denominations is different, the greedy method of making change may not yield the fewest coins. For example, suppose we do not have any nickels. For 30 cents in change, the greedy method yields one quarter and five pennies, whereas three dimes does the job.

The coin-changing example serves as a good illustration of the general type of problem that might be amenable to the greedy method. These problems generally have the goal of maximizing or minimizing an associated *objective function* over all feasible solutions. In most cases, this objective function is a real-valued function defined on the subsets of a given base set S. For example, coin changing is a minimization problem, where the base set S is the set of denominations, a feasible solution is a set of coins making correct change, and the objective function is the number of coins used.

The greedy method might be applied to any problem whose solution can be viewed as the result of building up solutions to the problem via a sequence of partial solutions in the following manner. Partial solutions are built up by choosing the elements x_1, x_2, and so on from a set R, where R is initially equal to some base set S. Whenever the greedy method makes a choice x_i, then x_i is either added to the current partial solution or its addition is found to be infeasible and is rejected forever. In either case, x_i is removed from the set R.

In the following general paradigm for the greedy method, choices are made by invoking a suitably defined function *GreedySelect*(R). For example, *GreedySelect*(R) might be an element that optimizes (minimizes or maximizes) the change in the value of the objective function or some closely related function. When several equivalent choices exist, we assume *GreedySelect* chooses arbitrarily from the equivalent choices.

```
procedure Greedy(S, Solution)
Input:     S (base set)  //it is assumed that there is an associated objective
                         //function f defined on (possibly ordered) subsets of S
Output:   Solution (an ordered subset of S that potentially optimizes
                    the objective function f, or a message that Greedy
                    doesn't even produce a solution, optimal or not)
    PartialSolution ← ∅          //initialize the partial solution to be empty
    R ← S
    while PartialSolution is not a solution .and. R ≠ ∅ do
        x ← GreedySelect(R)
        R ← R\{x}
        if PartialSolution ∪ {x} is feasible then
            PartialSolution ← PartialSolution ∪ {x}
        endif
    endwhile
    if PartialSolution is a solution then
        Solution ← PartialSolution
    else
        write("Greedy fails to produce a solution")
    endif
end Greedy
```

In most applications of the greedy method, an associated weighting w of the elements of the base set S is given, and *GreedySelect*(R) merely chooses the smallest-weight or largest-weight element in R. To simplify our discussion, we assume that *GreedySelect* chooses the smallest-weight element. Choosing the smallest-weight element is facilitated by preconditioning the base set by sorting with respect to w or by maintaining the elements in the base set in a priority queue, where w determines the priority value of the elements.

Although the greedy method applied in a given situation might output a feasible solution, that solution might not be an *optimal* solution (recall the problem of making 30 cents change without nickels). Thus, proofs of optimality should always accompany solutions generated by greedy algorithms.

Key Fact

Making decisions based on optimizing short-term gain (using *GreedySelect*) may not lead to a solution that is optimal, so that you always need to prove that greedy solutions are indeed optimal.

In spite of its somewhat limited applicability, the greedy method solves a number of classic optimization problems. Moreover, when the greedy method does the job optimally, it generally leads to elegant and efficient code for solving the problem.

7.2 Optimal Sequential Storage Order

Suppose we are given objects $b_0, b_1, \ldots, b_{n-1}$ arranged sequentially in order $b_{\pi(0)}$, $b_{\pi(1)}, \ldots, b_{\pi(n-1)}$, where π is some permutation of $\{0, 1, \ldots, n-1\}$, such as files stored on a sequential access tape. We assume that there is a weight c_i associated with object b_i (for example, the length of a file) that represents the individual cost of processing b_i. We also assume that to process object $b_{\pi(i)}$, we must first process the objects $b_{\pi(0)}, b_{\pi(1)}, \ldots, b_{\pi(i-1)}$ that precede $b_{\pi(i)}$ in the sequential arrangement. For example, to read the ith file on a sequential tape (assuming that the tape is rewound to the beginning), we must first read the preceding $i - 1$ files on the tape. Thus, the total cost of processing $b_{\pi(i)}$ is $c_{\pi(0)} + c_{\pi(1)} + \cdots + c_{\pi(i)}$. In Figure 7.1, we illustrate this example with six files $b_0, b_1, \ldots, b_5$ of lengths 15, 6, 1, 22, 3, 10, respectively. A sample storage order of these files on a tape is given in Figure 7.1b. If we wish to read the file of length 22, we first have to read the files of length 1, 3, and 15 that precede this file on the tape. Thus, reading the file of length 22 results in reading files whose total length is $1 + 3 + 15 + 22 = 41$.

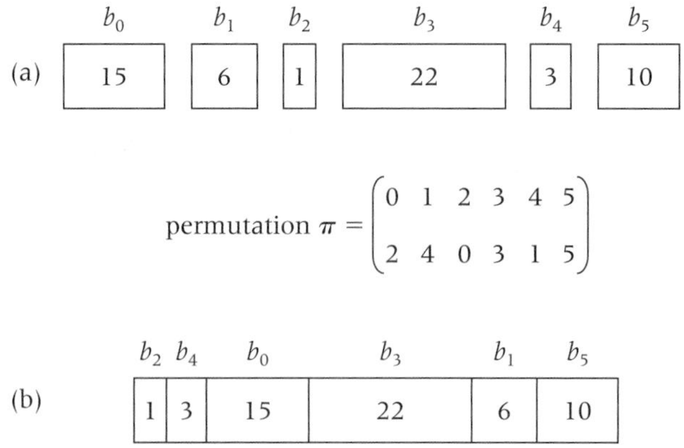

FIGURE 7.1

(a) Files of lengths 15,6,1,22,3,10; (b) a sample storage order of files on a sequential access tape corresponding to the permutation π

$$\text{permutation } \pi = \begin{pmatrix} 0 & 1 & 2 & 3 & 4 & 5 \\ 2 & 4 & 0 & 3 & 1 & 5 \end{pmatrix}$$

The *optimal sequential storage* problem for processing objects $b_0, b_1, \ldots, b_{n-1}$ is to find an arrangement (permutation) of the objects $b_{\pi(0)}, b_{\pi(1)}, \ldots, b_{\pi(n-1)}$ that minimizes the average time it takes to process an object. Let p_i denote the probability that the object b_i is to be processed, $i = 0, \ldots, n - 1$. Given these probabilities and a permutation π, clearly the average total cost of processing an object is given by

$$AveCost(\pi) = p_{\pi(0)}(c_{\pi(0)}) + p_{\pi(1)}(c_{\pi(0)} + c_{\pi(1)}) + \cdots + p_{\pi(n-1)}(c_{\pi(0)} + \cdots + c_{\pi(n-1)}). \quad \textbf{(7.2.1)}$$

We first consider the special case where each object is equally likely to be processed, so that $p_i = 1/n, i = 1, \ldots, n$. Then Formula (7.2.1) becomes

$$AveCost(\pi) = \frac{1}{n}\left[(c_{\pi(0)}) + (c_{\pi(0)} + c_{\pi(1)}) + \cdots + (c_{\pi(0)} + c_{\pi(1)} + \cdots + c_{\pi(n-1)})\right]$$

$$\textbf{(7.2.2)}$$

$$= \frac{1}{n}\sum_{i=0}^{n-1}(n - i)c_{\pi(i)}.$$

Looking at Formula (7.2.2), we see that the coefficients of $c_{\pi(i)}, i = 0, \ldots, n - 1$, decrease as i increases. Thus, it is intuitively obvious that $AveCost(\pi)$ is minimized when $c_{\pi(0)} \leq c_{\pi(1)} \leq \cdots \leq c_{\pi(n-1)}$, so that the greedy strategy we use is to select the objects in increasing order of their costs.

Now we consider the problem of minimizing $AveCost(\pi)$ as given by Formula (7.2.1) for a general set of probabilities $p_i, i = 1, \ldots, n$. Various greedy strategies come to mind. For example, we might use the same greedy strategy given previously, which gives the optimal solution when all the probabilities are equal. However, it is not hard to find examples where this strategy yields suboptimal results. We might also arrange the objects in decreasing order of probabilities (placing the objects most likely to be processed near the beginning), but again, it is not hard to find examples where this strategy fails. Alas, is there a greedy strategy that works? Yes, and we leave it as an exercise to show that arranging the objects in increasing order of the ratios c_i/p_i yields an optimal solution.

7.3 The Knapsack Problem

The *knapsack problem* involves n objects $b_0, b_1, \ldots, b_{n-1}$, and a knapsack of capacity C. We assume that each object b_i has a given positive weight (or volume) w_i and a given positive value v_i (or profit, cost, and so forth), $i = 0, \ldots, n - 1$. We place the objects or fractions of objects in the knapsack, taking care that the capacity of the knapsack is not exceeded. If a fraction f_i of object b_i is placed in the knapsack ($0 \leq f_i \leq 1$), then it contributes $f_i v_i$ to the total value in the knapsack.

The knapsack problem is to place objects or fractions of objects in the knapsack, without exceeding the capacity, so the total value of the objects in the knapsack is maximized. A more formal statement of the knapsack problem is

$$\text{maximize } \sum_{i=0}^{n-1} f_i v_i,$$

$$\text{subject to the constraints: } \sum_{i=0}^{n-1} f_i w_i \leq C, \qquad \textbf{(7.3.1)}$$

$$0 \leq f_i \leq 1, \quad i = 0, \dots, n-1.$$

As with the sequential storage order problem, several greedy methods are possible for solving the knapsack problem. For example, we might put as much as possible of the object with highest value into the knapsack, then as much as possible of the object of second highest value into the knapsack, and so forth until the knapsack is filled to capacity. Another greedy strategy would be to follow the same scheme but place the objects in the knapsack according to decreasing weights. But we can easily find examples where neither of these strategies yields optimal solutions. We will show that the strategy of putting the objects into the knapsack according to decreasing ratios (densities) v_i/w_i until the knapsack is full yields an optimal solution.

The following interpretation of the knapsack problem makes it clear that the ratio v_i/w_i is the critical issue. Suppose the (greedy) owner of a gourmet coffee shop wishes to mix a 10-pound bag of coffee using various types of coffee beans in such a way as to produce the coffee blend of maximum cost. The weights of the objects in the knapsack problem correspond to the quantity in pounds available of each type of coffee bean. The value of each quantity of coffee beans is the total cost of that quantity in dollars. In Figure 7.2, we list the types and amounts of coffee beans that are available.

Intuitively, we obtain the most expensive 10-pound bag of coffee if we first use as much as possible of the bean whose cost-per-pound ratio is the largest, then as much as possible of the bean whose cost-per-pound ratio is the second

	Type	Quantity Available in Pounds	Total Cost in Dollars for That Quantity
FIGURE 7.2	Colombian	8	32
Coffee shop	Jamaican	2	32
inventory	Java	4	25
	Bicentennial	1	10
	Mountain	2	9
	Roast	6	18
	Dark	10	55
	Special	50	100

Type	Cost/Pound	Fraction of Available Quantity Chosen	Quantity Chosen
Jamaican	16	1	2
Bicentennial	10	1	1
Java	6.25	1	4
Dark	5.5	0.3	3
Mountain	4.5	0	0
Colombian	4	0	0
Roast	3	0	0
Special	2	0	0

largest, and so on until we reach 10 pounds. Figure 7.3 lists the coffee beans in decreasing order of their cost-per-pound ratios and the quantity of each type of bean used as determined by this greedy method.

Generalizing the greedy strategy for making expensive coffee leads to a greedy algorithm for the knapsack problem. The algorithm *Knapsack* assumes as a precondition that the objects have been sorted in decreasing order of the ratios v_i/w_i, $i = 0, \ldots, n - 1$.

```
procedure Knapsack(V[0:n − 1], W[0:n − 1], C, F[0:n − 1])
Input:    V[0:n − 1] (an array of positive values)
          W[0:n − 1] (an array of positive weights)
          C (a positive capacity)
Output:  F[0:n − 1] (an array of nonnegative fractions)
     Sort the arrays V[0:n − 1] and W[0:n − 1] in decreasing order of densities, so that
          V[0]/W[0] ≥ V[1]/W[1] ≥ ⋯ ≥ V[n − 1]/W[n − 1]
     for i ← 0 to n − 1do
         F[i] ← 0
     endfor
     RemainCap ← C
     i ← 0
     if W[0] ≤ C then
         Fits ← .true.
     else
         Fits ← .false.
     endif
     while Fits .and. i ≤ n − 1 do
         F[i] ← 1
         RemainCap ← RemainCap − W[i]
         i ← i + 1
         if W[i] ≤ RemainCap then
             Fits ← .true.
         else
```

```
            Fits ← .false.
         endif
      endwhile
      if i ≤ n − 1 then F[i] ← RemainCap/W[i] endif
   end Knapsack
```

Clearly, procedure *Knapsack* generates an optimal solution when $\sum_{i=0}^{n-1} w_i \leq C$ because all the objects are then placed in the knapsack. Using a proof by contradiction, we now show that *Knapsack* generates an optimal solution when $\sum_{i=0}^{n-1} w_i > C$. By contrast, suppose the solution $F = (f_0, f_1, \ldots, f_{n-1})$ generated by *Knapsack* is suboptimal. Now consider an optimal solution $Y = (y_0, y_1, \ldots, y_{n-1})$, and let j denote the first index i such that $f_i \neq y_i$ so that $1 = f_i = y_i$, $0 \leq i \leq j - 1$. We choose Y such that j is maximized over all optimal solutions. Note that $\sum_{i=0}^{n-1} y_i w_i = C$ (otherwise, we could increase one of the y_i's and trivially increase the total value of the solution). Because of the greedy strategy used by *Knapsack*, we have $f_j > y_j$.

By altering Y, we now construct an optimal solution $Z = (z_0, z_1, \ldots, z_{n-1})$ that agrees with F in one more initial position. We set $z_i = f_i$, $0 \leq i \leq j$, and for $i > j$, the value of z_i is obtained by suitably decreasing y_i so that $\sum_{i=0}^{n-1} z_i w_i = C$. It follows that

$$(z_j - y_j) w_j = \sum_{i=j+1}^{n} (y_i - z_i) w_i. \tag{7.3.2}$$

Comparing the total values of the solutions Z and Y, we obtain

$$\sum_{i=0}^{n-1} z_i v_i - \sum_{i=0}^{n-1} y_i v_i = (z_j - y_j) v_j - \sum_{i=j+1}^{n-1} (y_i - z_i) v_i.$$

$$= (z_j - y_j) w_j v_j / w_j - \sum_{i=j+1}^{n-1} (y_i - z_i) w_i v_i / w_i$$

$$\geq \left[(z_j - y_j) w_j - \sum_{i=j+1}^{n-1} (y_i - z_i) w_i \right] v_j / w_j$$

(because $y_i \geq z_i$ and $v_0/w_0 \geq v_1/w_1 \geq \cdots \geq v_{n-1}/w_{n-1}$)

$= 0$ (because the number inside the square brackets is 0 by Formula (7.3.2)).

Thus, the value of Z is not less than the value of Y, so that Z is also an optimal solution. But Z agrees with F in the first j initial positions, which contradicts the assumption that Y is an optimal solution that agrees with F in the most initial positions.

Except for the $\Theta(n\log n)$ sorting step, the remainder of *Knapsack* has linear complexity in the worst case.

A natural variation of the knapsack problem, called the *0/1 knapsack problem*, does not allow fractional objects. More precisely, the 0/1 knapsack problem has the following formulation:

$$\text{maximize } \sum_{i=0}^{n-1} f_i v_i$$

$$\text{subject to the constraints: } \sum_{i=0}^{n-1} f_i w_i \leq C \tag{7.3.3}$$

$$f_i \in \{0,1\}, \quad i = 0, \dots, n - 1.$$

The greedy strategy of placing the objects in the knapsack in decreasing order of the ratios v_i/w_i, $i = 0, \dots, n - 1$, rejecting objects when their addition would overflow the knapsack, may yield a suboptimal solution to the 0/1 knapsack problem. While the knapsack problem is easily solved, the 0/1 knapsack problem is NP-hard. Note that we took the input size for the knapsack problems to be the number of objects n. This measure does not take into account the sizes of the weights and values of the objects. Assuming the capacity, weights, and values are positive integers, a more precise measure of the input size (in binary) would be the sum of the number of digits of each of these integers; that is

$$b = \lceil \log_2 C \rceil + \sum_{i=0}^{n-1} \lceil \log_2(w_i + 1) \rceil + \sum_{i=0}^{n-1} \lceil \log_2(v_i + 1) \rceil.$$

We chose n as the input size because it is simpler to analyze the algorithm in terms of n. Also, since $b \geq n$, any upper-bound formula for the complexity of the algorithm in terms of n applies when n is replaced with b. Sometimes it is useful to measure the input size in unary (base 1); for example, assuming the capacity, weights, and values are positive integers, the input size to the knapsack problems is measured in terms of $C + \sum_{i=0}^{n-1} w_i + \sum_{i=0}^{n-1} v_i$. Many NP-complete problems, such as the coin-changing and 0/1 knapsack problems, have polynomial complexity when measured by unary inputs. In Exercises 9.18 and 9.19 of Chapter 9, polynomial-time dynamic-programming solutions to coin-changing and 0/1 knapsack problems are developed when the input numbers are measured as unary integers.

 ## 7.4 Huffman Codes

With the emergence of the Internet, the need for data compression has become increasingly important. Transporting extremely large files across the Internet is commonplace today, and these files must be compressed to save time and storage resources. For example, standard data compression algorithms such as jpeg and gif are used to compress image files (such as photographs), and standard data compression algorithms are used for text and program files, such as those used to zip and unzip files. Even before the advent of the Internet, large text files needed to be compressed to minimize storage requirements. A classical data compression algorithm created by David A. Huffman in 1952 is based on a greedy strategy for constructing a code for a given alphabet of symbols. Huffman codes are useful not only for compressing text files but also as part of image or audio file compression techniques.

For a given *alphabet* of symbols $A = \{a_0, a_1, \ldots, a_{n-1}\}$, one approach to the problem of data compression involves encoding each symbol in the alphabet with a binary string. The alphabet A might be letters and punctuation symbols from the English language, the standard symbol set used by personal computers, *Discrete Cosine Transform (DCT)* coefficients in a jpeg compression of an image file, and so forth. We refer to the set of binary strings encoding the symbols in A as a *binary code* for A. For example, in the *ASCII* encoding system each symbol is represented by an 8-bit (1-byte) binary string. In our example, since each symbol in A is encoded with a fixed-length binary string, there is basically no compression being used. Using a fixed-length binary string to store symbols is convenient for computer implementation but does not optimize storage usage. By allowing variable-length binary strings for binary codes, we can save space when storing files (text, jpeg, mpeg, etc.) made up of symbols from our given alphabet.

Given a binary code for A, we obtain a binary encoding of any string consisting of symbols from A. We simply replace each symbol in the string with its binary encoding. For example, suppose $A = \{a,b,c\}$, and symbols a, b, and c are encoded as 1, 00, and 01, respectively. Then the binary encoding for the string '*cabbc*' is '011000001'.

To illustrate ambiguous codes, if a, b, and c are encoded as 0, 1, and 01, respectively, then the binary string '011' can be decoded as either '*abb*' or '*cb*'. Note that the binary string '0' is a prefix for the binary string '01'. It is easily verified that a binary code allows for unambiguous (unique) decoding if and only if no binary string in the code is a prefix of any other binary string in the code.

7.4.1 Binary Prefix Codes

A binary code having the property that no binary string in the code is a prefix of any other binary string in the code is called a *prefix code*. We can readily create a prefix code by using a 2-tree (recall from Chapter 4 that a 2-tree is a binary tree in which every nonleaf node has exactly two children). Suppose we have 2-tree T whose leaf nodes correspond to the n symbols in A. We first label each edge corresponding to a left child with a 0 and each edge corresponding to a right child with a 1. We then assign to each symbol a_i the binary string obtained by reading the labels on the edges when following a path from the root to the leaf node corresponding to a_i. The binary strings generated by a sample tree for the alphabet $A = \{a,b,c,d,e,f\}$ are shown in Figure 7.4.

For each node N of the 2-tree T, $B(N)$ denotes the binary string corresponding to following a path from the root to N in the manner we described earlier. Let L and R denote the left and right children of N, respectively. We can compute $B(L)$ and $B(R)$ from $B(N)$ by concatenating '0' and '1', respectively, to the end

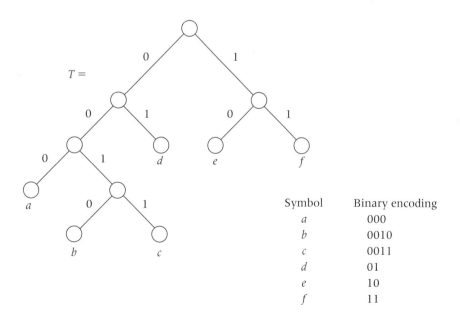

FIGURE 7.4

Encoding of alphabet $A = \{a,b,c,d,e,f\}$ generated by a sample 2-tree T

Symbol	Binary encoding
a	000
b	0010
c	0011
d	01
e	10
f	11

of $B(N)$; that is, $B(L) = B(N) + \text{'}0\text{'}$ and $B(R) = B(N) + \text{'}1\text{'}$ (where $+$ denotes the operation of concatenation).

We now give pseudocode for the algorithm *GenerateCode*, which uses this formula to compute the array *Code*, where *Code*[i] is the binary code for symbol a_i, $i = 0, \dots, n - 1$. *GenerateCode* computes $B(N)$ for each node by performing a preorder traversal of the 2-tree, where the generalized visit operation at node N involves computing $B(L)$ and $B(R)$ from $B(N)$ using the formula previously described. We assume that the 2-tree T is implemented using pointers and dynamic variables, where each node contains two pointer fields corresponding to the left and right children and two information fields *BinaryCode* and *Symbol-Index*. Before calling *GenerateCode*, we assume that the value of *SymbolIndex* for each leaf node has been initialized to contain the index i of the alphabet symbol a_i corresponding to the leaf node (*SymbolIndex* is left undefined for the internal nodes of T). The computed value $B(N)$ for each node N is stored in the variable *BinaryCode*. The root node's value of *BinaryCode* is initialized to the null string before calling *GenerateCode*.

```
procedure GenerateCode(Root, Code[0:n − 1]) recursive
Input:     Root (a pointer to root of 2-tree T)        //Root→BinaryCode is
                //initialized to the null string. The leaf node corresponding to a_i
                //has its SymbolIndex field initialized to i, i = 0, . . . , n − 1.
Output:   Code[0:n − 1] (array of binary strings, where Code[i] is the code for symbol a_i)
    if Root→LeftChild = null then            //a leaf is reached
        Code[Root→SymbolIndex] ← Root→BinaryCode
    else
        (Root→LeftChild)→BinaryCode ← Root→BinaryCode + '0'
        (Root→RightChild)→BinaryCode ← Root→BinaryCode + '1'
        GenerateCode(Root→LeftChild,Code)
        GenerateCode(Root→RightChild,Code)
    endif
end GenerateCode
```

The table *Code*[$0:n - 1$] of binary codes can be used to encode text consisting of strings of symbols from the alphabet A. Going the other direction, encoded text can be decoded using the 2-tree T in the obvious way.

7.4.2 The Huffman Algorithm

Now suppose we are encoding text composed of symbols from A, where the frequency of the occurrence of symbol a_i in such text is given by f_i, $i = 0, \dots, n - 1$. An important problem in data compression is to find an *optimal* binary prefix code—that is, a binary prefix code that minimizes the expected length of a *coded symbol*. Clearly, an optimal binary prefix code also minimizes the expected length of text generated using the symbols from A. The problem of finding optimal binary prefix codes is equivalent to the following problem for 2-trees. Each unambiguous binary code can be generated by traversing a suitable 2-tree T. We let λ_i denote the length of the path in T from the root to the leaf node corresponding to a_i, $i = 0, \dots, n - 1$. The expected length of the coded symbols determined by T is closely related to a generalization of the leaf path length called the *weighted leaf path length* $WLPL(T)$ *of* T, defined by

$$WLPL(T) = \sum_{i=0}^{n-1} \lambda_i f_i. \qquad \textbf{(7.4.1)}$$

Note that $WLPL(T)$ becomes $LPL(T)$ when all the f_i's equal 1. For example, given frequencies $(9,8,5,3,15,2)$ for the symbols (a,b,c,d,e,f), the weighted leaf path length for the binary tree T in Figure 7.5 is given by

$$WLPL(T) = (3)(9) + (4)(8) + (4)(5) + (2)(3) + (2)(15) + (2)(2) = 119. \ \textbf{(7.4.2)}$$

Since symbol a_i occurs with frequency f_i, the probability p_i, $i = 0, \dots, n - 1$, that symbol a_i occurs in a given text position is

$$p_i = \frac{f_i}{\sum\limits_{j=0}^{n-1} f_j}, \quad i = 0, \dots, n - 1.$$

Each binary digit in the binary string encoding a_i corresponds to an edge of the path in T from the root node to the leaf node containing a_i. Hence, the length of the binary string encoding a_i (in the binary code determined by T) equals λ_i, $i = 0, \dots, n - 1$, so that the expected length of a coded symbol is given by $WLPL(T)/\left(\sum_{i=0}^{n-1} f_i\right)$. Thus, the problem of finding an optimal binary prefix code is equivalent to finding a 2-tree having minimum $WLPL(T)$.

Given the set of frequencies $\{9,8,5,3,15,2\}$ for the set of symbols $\{a,b,c,d,e,f\}$, the 2-tree in Figure 7.5, which has a weighted leaf path length equal to 119, is not optimal. The binary tree given in Figure 7.5, which has a weighted leaf path length equal to 99, turns out to be an optimal 2-tree with respect to these frequencies.

We now describe Huffman's greedy algorithm for computing an optimal binary prefix code with respect to a given set of frequencies f_i, $i = 0, \dots, n - 1$. The procedure *HuffmanCode* computes a 2-tree T minimizing $WLPL(T)$ by constructing a sequence of forests as follows. At each stage in the algorithm, the

FIGURE 7.5

A tree having
minimum weighted
leaf path length
for alphabet
$A = \{a,b,c,d,e,f\}$
with respect to the
given frequencies

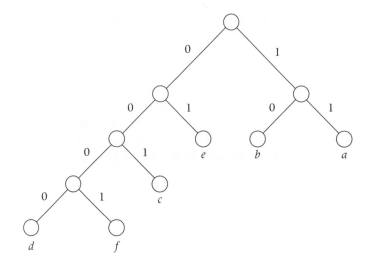

Symbol	Frequency	Encoding
a	9	11
b	8	10
c	5	001
d	3	0000
e	15	01
f	2	0001

$$WLPL(T) = (2)(9) + (2)(8) + (3)(5) + (4)(3) + (2)(15) + (4)(2) = 99$$

root of each tree in the forest is assigned a frequency. The initial forest F consists of the n single node trees corresponding to the n elements of A. At each stage, *HuffmanCode* finds two trees T_1 and T_2 whose roots R_1 and R_2 have the smallest and second smallest frequencies over all the trees in the current forest. A new (internal) node R is then added to the forest, together with two edges joining R to R_1 and R to R_2, so that a new tree is created with R as the root and T_1 and T_2 as the left and right subtrees of R. The frequency of the new root R is taken to be the sum of the frequencies of the old roots R_1 and R_2. The Huffman tree is constructed after $n - 1$ stages, involving the addition of $n - 1$ internal nodes.

The procedure *HuffmanCode* calls the procedure *GenerateCode* described earlier. We use high-level parameter descriptions in our calls to procedures implementing the various priority queue operations. For example, a call to *CreatePriorityQueue* with parameters *Leaf*[0:$n - 1$] and Q creates a priority queue Q of pointers to the leaf nodes. A call to *RemovePriorityQueue* with parameters Q and L removes the element at the front of the queue Q and assigns it to L.

Procedure *HuffmanCode*(*A*[0:*n* − 1], *Freq*[0:*n* − 1], *Code*[0:*n* − 1])
Input: *Freq*[0:*n* − 1]   (an array of nonnegative frequencies: *Freq*[*i*] = *f*ᵢ)
Output: *Code*[0:*n* − 1]   (an array of binary strings for Huffman code: *Code*[*i*] is the
                        binary string encoding symbol *aᵢ*, *i* = 0, . . . , *n* − 1)
   for *i* ← 0 **to** *n* − 1 **do**   //initialize leaf nodes
       AllocateHuffmanNode(*P*)
       P→*SymbolIndex* ← *i*
       P→*Frequency* ← *Freq*[*i*]
       P→*LeftChild* ← **null**
       P→*RightChild* ← **null**
       Leaf[*i*] ← *P*
   endfor
   CreatePriorityQueue(*Leaf*[0:*n* − 1], *Q*) //create priority queue of
                        //pointers to leaf nodes with *Frequency* as the key
   for *i* ← 1 **to** *n* − 1 **do**
       RemovePriorityQueue(*Q*, *L*)   //*L*, *R* point to root nodes of smallest and
       RemovePriorityQueue(*Q*, *R*)   //second-smallest frequency, respectively
       AllocateHuffmanNode(*Root*)
       Root→*LeftChild* ← *L*
       Root→*RightChild* ← *R*
       Root→*Frequency* ← (*L*→*Frequency*) + (*R* → *Frequency*)
       InsertPriorityQueue(*Q*, *Root*)
   endfor
   Root→*BinaryString* ← " //*BinaryString* of root initialized to null string
   GenerateCode(*Root*, *Code*[0:*n* − 1])
end *HuffmanCode*

The action of *HuffmanCode* is illustrated in Figure 7.6 for the same sample alphabet and set of frequencies as in Figure 7.5.

An efficient way to implement the priority queue *Q* is to use a min-heap (see Chapter 4). Then *CreatePriorityQueue* (*CreateMinHeap*), *RemovePriorityQueue* (*RemoveMinHeap*), and *InsertPriorityQueue* (*InsertMinHeap*) have worst-case complexities belonging to $O(n)$, $O(\log n)$, and $O(\log n)$, respectively. Hence, the worst-case complexity of *HuffmanCode* belongs to $O(n\log n)$.

The correctness of the algorithm *HuffmanCode* depends on the following proposition, whose proof is left to the exercises.

Proposition 7.4.1   Given a set of frequencies f_i, $i = 0, \ldots, n − 1$, the Huffman tree *T* constructed by *HuffmanCode* has minimal weighted *WLPL*(*T*) over all 2-trees whose edges are weighted by these frequencies.   □

FIGURE 7.6

Action of
HuffmanCode
for alphabet
A = {*a,b,c,d,e,f*}
with the same set
of frequencies as in
Figure 7.5

Initial forest

Stage 1

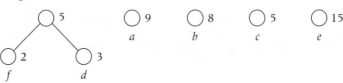

Stage 2

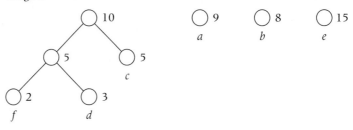

Stage 3

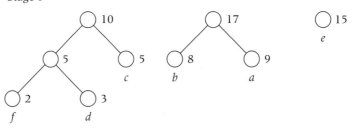

Stage 4

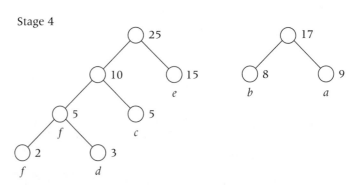

FIGURE 7.6

Continued

Stage 5: Huffman tree

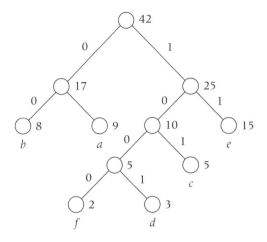

Symbol	Frequency	Encoding
a	9	01
b	8	00
c	5	101
d	3	1001
e	15	11
f	2	1000

$$WLPL(T) = (2)(9) + (2)(8) + (3)(5) + (4)(3) + (2)(15) + (4)(2) = 99$$

Finding a binary tree of minimum weighted leaf path length has other important applications besides Huffman codes. For example, the problem of finding optimal merge patterns is solved by constructing a binary tree having minimum weighted leaf path length, where the leaf nodes of the tree correspond to files or sublists and the weight of a leaf is the length of its associated file or sublist.

7.5 Closing Remarks

The greedy method is a powerful tool to use, when it applies, because solutions generated by this method are often elegant and very efficient. For example, we have seen that the Huffman code for data compression gave an elegant way to determine an optimal scheme for binary code compression. In subsequent chapters, we will solve some other important problems using the greedy method. For example, in Chapter 12, we use the greedy method to find minimum-cost spanning trees in weighted graphs and shortest paths in weighted graphs and digraphs. However, as we have seen, potential solutions generated by the greedy method must always be verified for correctness. Often, greedy decisions that are locally optimal do not result in solutions that are globally optimal.

Data compression is a very active area of research today, Because of limited bandwidth and the vast amount of visual and audio text files being transported over the Internet, data compression is absolutely necessary to handle these transmissions efficiently. Some data compression algorithms such as jpeg use not only the Huffman code algorithm but also transformations closely related to the Fast Fourier Transform, which we will discuss in Chapter 22.

References and Suggestions for Further Reading

Edmonds, J. "Matroids and the Greedy Algorithm." *Mathematical Programming* 1 (1971): 126–136. A classical paper relating the greedy strategy to the general theory of matroids, and where the term *greedy algorithm* was first introduced.

Huffman, D. A. "A Method for the Construction of Minimum Redundancy Codes." *Proceedings of the IRE* 40 (1952): 1098–1101. The original paper on Huffman codes.

Martello, S., and P. Toth. *Knapsack Problems: Algorithms and Computer Implementations*. Chichester, England: Wiley, 1990. A comprehensive treatment of the knapsack problem.

Section 7.1 General Description

7.1   Given the standard U.S. coins—pennies, nickels, dimes, quarters, and half-dollars—show that the greedy method of making change always yields a solution using the fewest coins.

7.2   For a given integer base $b > 2$, suppose you have an unlimited number of coins of each of the denominations $b^0, b^1, \ldots, b^{n-1}$. Show that the greedy method of making change for these denominations always yields a solution using the fewest coins.

Section 7.2 Optimal Sequential Storage Order

7.3   Design and analyze a greedy algorithm for the optimal sequential storage problem when m tapes are available.

7.4   For the sequential storage order problem, consider the general case of minimizing $AveCost(\pi)$, as given by Formula (7.2.1), where p_i denotes the probability that the object to be processed is b_i, $i = 0, \ldots, n-1$.

    a. Show that the greedy strategy used when all the probabilities are equal (that is, sorting the objects by increasing order of costs c_i) fails to give an optimal solution for a general set of probabilities p_i.

    b. Show that the greedy strategy of arranging the objects in decreasing order of probabilities also fails to give optimal solutions in general.

    c. Show that the greedy strategy of arranging the objects in increasing order of the ratios c_i/p_i yields an optimal solution.

Section 7.3 The Knapsack Problem

7.5   Solve the following instance of the knapsack problem for capacity $C = 30$:

i	0	1	2	3	4	5	6	7
v_i	60	50	40	30	20	10	5	1
w_i	30	100	10	10	8	8	1	1

7.6   For the knapsack problem with weights $w_0, w_1, \ldots, w_{n-1}$ and values $v_0, v_1, \ldots, v_{n-1}$, give a single example where both the greedy solution based on placing the objects in the knapsack in the order $w_0 \leq w_1 \leq \cdots \leq w_{n-1}$ as well as the greedy solution based on placing the objects in the knapsack in the order $v_0 \geq v_1 \geq \cdots \geq v_{n-1}$ yield suboptimal solutions.

7.7   a. Give an example where the greedy method described in Section 7.3 for the 0/1 knapsack problem yields a suboptimal solution.

    b. Show that the greedy method yields arbitrarily bad solutions; that is, given any $\varepsilon > 0$, find an example where the ratio of the greedy solution to the optimal solution is less than ε.

Section 7.4 Huffman Codes

7.8   Prove Proposition 7.4.1.

7.9   Trace the action of *HuffmanCode* for the letters (a,b,c,d,e,f,g,h) occurring with frequencies $(10,7,3,5,9,2,3,2)$.

7.10   Given the Huffman code tree shown in Figure 7.5 and Figure 7.6, decode the string '100111100001101111001'.

7.11   Suppose the Huffman tree has nodes with the structure

```
HuffmanTreeNode = record
    Symbol: character
    LeftChild:→HuffmanTreeNode
    RightChild:→HuffmanTreeNode
end HuffmanTreeNode
```

7.12 Given an arbitrary 2-tree T having n leaf nodes, find a set of frequencies such that T is a Huffman tree for these frequencies.

7.13 Write a program that computes a Huffman tree and associated Huffman code for a given text (where the set of symbols are those that occur in the text and the frequency of a symbol is its frequency in the text).

7.14 In the *optimal merge pattern problem*, you have n sorted files of lengths f_0, f_1, ... , f_{n-1}, which you wish to merge into a single file by a sequence of merges of pairs of files. To merge two files of lengths m_1 and m_2 takes $m_1 + m_2$ operations, and an optimal solution uses the minimum number of operations.

    a. Design a greedy algorithm to solve the optimal merge pattern problem.

    b. Show the action of the algorithm you have designed in part (a) for $n = 10$ and file lengths 2, 3, 4, 7, 10, 10, 14, 15, 16, 32.

Additional Exercises

7.15 Consider the following *task scheduling* problem: given n tasks T_1, ... , T_n, where task T_i has start time s_i and finish time f_i, $i = 1$, ... , n, assign these tasks to the fewest machines with the restriction that a new task can not be started on any machine until all tasks previously begun on the machine have been completed.

    a. Design and give pseudocode for an $O(n\log n)$ greedy algorithm for solving this problem based on ordering the tasks according to their start times.

    b. Verify that the algorithm you have designed in part (a) has $O(n\log n)$ complexity.

    c. Verify that the algorithm you have designed in part (a) finds an optimal solution; that is, schedules the tasks using the fewest machines.

7.16 Consider the problem of assigning n workers A_0, ... , A_{n-1} to n jobs B_0, ... , B_{n-1}, where each worker is qualified to perform any of the jobs, and where a (positive real) weight w_{ij} is associated with assigning worker A_i to job

B_j, $i, j \in \{0, \dots, n - 1\}$. An optimal assignment of workers to jobs is a set of n pairings $(A_0, B_{\pi(0)})$, $(A_1, B_{\pi(1)})$, $\dots$, $(A_{n-1}, B_{\pi(n-1)})$ for some permutation π of $\{0, \dots, n - 1\}$, such that the cost of the assignment given by $c(\pi) = w_{0\pi(0)} + w_{1\pi(1)} + \cdots + w_{n-1\pi(n-1)}$ is minimized. Show that each of the following three greedy strategies do not necessarily generate optimal solutions to this problem (an algorithm for obtaining an optimal solution is discussed in Chapter 14):

a. We initialize R to be the set of all jobs. For $i = 0, \dots, n - 1$, we choose a job B_j from R that minimizes w_{ij}, assign job B_j to worker A_i, and remove B_j from R.

b. We initialize R to be the set of all workers. For $j = 0, \dots, n - 1$, we choose a worker A_i from R that minimizes w_{ij}, assign job B_j to worker A_i and remove A_i from R.

c. We initialize R to be the set of all pairs (i,j), $i, j \in \{0, \dots, n - 1\}$. Until all the workers have been assigned jobs, we choose a pair (i,j) from R that minimizes w_{ij}, assign job B_j to worker A_i and remove all pairs (i,k) and (l,j) from R.

Exercises 7.17–.22 concern the *job sequencing with deadlines* problem. We are given jobs $J_0, \dots, J_{n-1}$ having positive integer deadlines $(d_0, \dots, d_{n-1})$. Associated with each job J_i is a profit p_i, where the profit is earned if and only if the job is completed by its deadline. We assume that each job takes one unit of time, and only one machine is available for processing the jobs. A subset S of the jobs is called *feasible* if there is a permutation of the jobs in S such that each job in S can be processed by the machine (in the order given by the permutation) by its deadline. The value of a feasible solution S is the sum of the profits of the jobs in S. The problem is to find a feasible solution having maximal value over all feasible solutions.

7.17 Given the deadlines $(d_0, d_1, d_2, d_3, d_4) = (2,1,1,2,2)$ and profits $(p_0, p_1, p_2, p_3, p_4) = (25, 20, 23, 21, 30)$, list all possible feasible solutions and their values, thereby determining the optimal solution.

7.18 For any set of jobs S, prove that S is feasible if and only if the jobs in S can be processed in increasing order of their deadlines.

7.19 Prove that the result stated in the previous exercise remains true even if the jobs have different processing times.

7.20 Consider the following greedy strategy: simply order the jobs by increasing deadline, and process as many jobs as possible in that order. Show that this strategy does not always generate an optimal solution.

7.21   Consider the following greedy strategy: Starting from the empty solution, amongst the remaining jobs pick the job having maximal profit such that adding the job maintains a feasible set. Continue until no more jobs can be added without creating an infeasible set.

a. Show that this greedy solution generates an optimal solution.

b. Design an algorithm implementing this greedy strategy. Your algorithm should maintain the jobs in the currently generated feasible set in increasing order of their deadlines, and use the result from Exercise 7.18 to check feasibility. Your algorithm should have $\Theta(n^2)$ complexity in the worst case.

7.22   Consider a different strategy for determining whether or not a job can be added using the greedy strategy in the previous exercise. When we are adding job J_i to a feasible set S, assign it to the time slot $[t - 1, t]$ where t is the largest integer such that $1 \le t \le d_i$ and the slot $[t - 1, t]$ has not already been used by a job in S. In other words, we put off processing J_i as long as possible.

a. Show that if there is no such free time slot available, then $S \cup J_i$ is infeasible.

b. Design an almost linear algorithm implementing this new feasibility check. HINT: use the union and find algorithms discussed in Chapter 4.

c. Write a program implementing your algorithm in part (b), and run for various inputs.

CHAPTER **8**

DIVIDE-AND-CONQUER

The *divide-and-conquer* paradigm is one of the most powerful design strategies available in the theory of algorithms. The paradigm can be described in general terms as follows. A problem input (instance) is divided according to some criteria into a set of smaller inputs to the same problem. The problem is then solved for each of these smaller inputs, either recursively by further division into smaller inputs or by invoking an ad hoc or a priori solution. Finally, the solution for the original input is obtained by expressing it in some form as a combination of the solution for these smaller inputs. Ad hoc solutions are often invoked when the input size is smaller than some preassigned *threshold* value. Examples of a priori solutions (solutions known in advance) include sorting single-element lists or multiplying single-digit binary numbers.

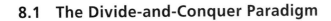

8.1 The Divide-and-Conquer Paradigm

The divide-and-conquer design strategy can be formalized as follows. Let *Known* denote the set of inputs to the problem whose solutions are known a priori or by ad hoc methods. The procedure *Divide_and_Conquer* calls two procedures, *Divide* and *Combine*. *Divide* has input parameter I and output parameters $I_1, \ldots, I_m$, where

m may depend on I. The inputs $I_1, \dots, I_m$ must be smaller or simpler inputs to the problem than I but are not required to always be a *division* of I into subinputs. *Combine* has input parameters $J_1, \dots, J_m$ and output parameter J. *Combine* is the procedure for obtaining a solution J to the problem with input I by combining the recursively obtained solutions $J_1, \dots, J_m$ to the problem with inputs $I_1, \dots, I_m$.

```
procedure Divide_and_Conquer(I, J) recursive
Input:    I (an input to the given problem)
Output:  J (a solution to the given problem corresponding to input I)
    if I ∈ Known then
        assign the a priori or ad hoc solution for I to J
    else
        Divide(I, I₁, . . . , Iₘ)   //m may depend on the input I
        for i ← 1 to m do
            Divide_and_Conquer(Iᵢ, Jᵢ)
        endfor
        Combine(J₁, . . . , Jₘ, J)
    endif
end Divide_and_Conquer
```

Often the work done by an algorithm based on *Divide_and_Conquer* resides solely in one of the two procedures *Divide* or *Combine*, but not both. For example, in the algorithm *QuickSort*, the divide step (a call to *Partition*) is the heart of the algorithm, and the combine step requires no work at all. On the other hand, in the algorithm *MergeSort*, the divide step is trivial and the combine step (a call to *Merge*) is the heart of the algorithm. Sometimes, both the divide and combine steps are difficult (see Figure 8.1).

For most divide-and-conquer algorithms, the number m of subproblems is a constant (independent of any particular input I). Divide-and-conquer algorithms in which m is a constant equal to 1 are referred to as *simplifications*. The binary search algorithm is an example of a simplification.

FIGURE 8.1

An example of a divide-and-conquer algorithm in which both the divide and combine steps are hard.

Reprinted by permission of Johnny Hart and Creators Syndicate, Inc.

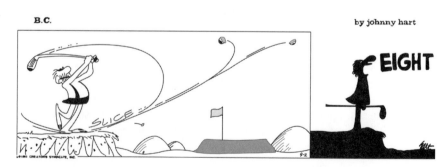

One useful technique to improve the efficiency of a divide-and-conquer algorithm is to employ a known ad hoc algorithm when the input size is smaller than some threshold. Of course, the ad hoc algorithm must be more efficient than the given divide-and-conquer algorithm for sufficiently small inputs.

For example, consider the sorting algorithm *MergeSort*, which has $\Theta(n\log n)$ average complexity. The sorting algorithm *InsertionSort*, which has $\Theta(n^2)$ average complexity, is much less efficient than *MergeSort* for large values of n. However, due to the constants involved, *InsertionSort* is more efficient than *MergeSort* for small values of n. Thus, we can improve the performance of *MergeSort* by calling *InsertionSort* for any input list whose size is not larger than a suitable threshold. Finding the optimal value for a threshold is often done empirically in practice. Empirical studies are needed because the best choice of a threshold depends on the constants associated with the implementation on a particular computer. For example, empirical studies have shown that for *MergeSort*, calling *InsertionSort* with a threshold of around $n = 16$ is usually optimal.

8.2 Symbolic Algebraic Operations on Polynomials

Algebraic manipulation of polynomials is an essential tool in many applications. Therefore, the need arises to design efficient algorithms to carry out basic arithmetic operations on polynomials, such as addition and multiplication, as efficiently as possible. Given a polynomial $P(x) = a_{m-1}x^{m-1} + \cdots + a_1x + a_0$, it is important to differentiate between the pointwise and the symbolic representation of $P(x)$. The *pointwise representation* of $P(x)$ is simply a function that maps an input point x to the output point $P(x)$. Thus, given two polynomials $P(x)$ and $Q(x)$, their *pointwise product* is the function *PtWiseMult*(P, Q) that maps an input point x to the output point $P(x) * Q(x)$.

The *symbolic representation* of a polynomial $P(x) = a_{m-1}x^{m-1} + \cdots + a_1x + a_0$ is its coefficient array $[a_0, a_1, \ldots, a_{m-1}]$. Thus, given two polynomials $P(x) = a_{m-1}x^{m-1} + \cdots + a_1x + a_0$ and $Q(x) = b_{n-1}x^{n-1} + \cdots + b_1x + b_0$, their symbolic product is the coefficient array $[c_0, c_1, \ldots, c_{m+n-2}]$ of the product polynomial $P(x)Q(x)$ given by

$$c_k = \sum_{i+j=k} a_ib_j, \ 0 \le i \le m-1, \ 0 \le j \le n-1, \ k = 0, \ldots, m+n-2. \quad \textbf{(8.2.1)}$$

For example, the symbolic product of $P(x) = 3x^2 + 2x - 5$ having coefficient array $[-5, 2, 3]$ and $Q(x) = x^3 - x + 4$ having coefficient array $[4, -1, 0, 1]$ is the polynomial $3x^5 + 2x^4 - 8x^3 + 10x^2 + 13x - 20$ having coefficient array $[-20, 13, 10, -8, 2, 3]$.

The symbolic representation of the product is particularly important for determining various properties of the product polynomial. For example, the function *PtWiseMult* does not lend itself to taking the derivative of the product polynomial, whereas it is a simple matter to compute the symbolic representation of the derivative of a polynomial that is represented symbolically. Similar comments hold for other operations on polynomials such as root finding, integration, and so forth. Throughout the remainder of this chapter, when discussing algebraic operations on polynomials, we implicitly assume that we are performing these operations symbolically.

8.2.1 Multiplication of Polynomials of the Same Input Size

An algorithm *DirectPolyMult* based on a straightforward calculation of Formula (8.2.1) has complexity $\Theta(mn)$ (where we choose multiplication of coefficients as our basic operation). We now describe a more efficient algorithm for polynomial multiplication based on the divide-and-conquer paradigm. We first assume that $m = n$. Setting $d = \lceil n/2 \rceil$, we divide the set of coefficients of the polynomials in half, with the higher-order coefficients $a_{n-1}, a_{n-2}, \dots, a_d$ in one set and the lower-order coefficients of $a_{d-1}, a_{d-2}, \dots, a_0$ in the other. Setting $P_1(x) = a_{d-1}x^{d-1} + a_{d-2}x^{d-2} + \cdots + a_1x + a_0$ and $P_2(x) = a_{n-1}x^{n-d-1} + a_{n-2}x^{n-d-2} + \cdots + a_{d+1}x + a_d$, we obtain

$$P(x) = x^d P_2(x) + P_1(x).$$

A similar division of the set of coefficients of $Q(x)$ yields polynomials $Q_1(x)$ and $Q_2(x)$ having input size of at most d such that

$$Q(x) = x^d Q_2(x) + Q_1(x).$$

A straightforward application of the distributive law yields

$$\begin{aligned} P(x)Q(x) &= x^{2d}P_2(x)Q_2(x) + x^d(P_1(x)Q_2(x) \\ &\quad + P_2(x)Q_1(x)) + P_1(x)Q_1(x). \end{aligned} \tag{8.2.2}$$

Note that polynomials $P_1(x)$ and $Q_1(x)$ both have input size d, and polynomials $P_2(x)$ and $Q_2(x)$ both have input size either d or $d-1$. When $P_2(x)$ and $Q_2(x)$ both have input size $d-1$, we add a leading coefficient of zero to each so they have input size d. Thus, the problem of multiplying $P(x)$ and $Q(x)$ has been reduced to the problem of taking four products of polynomials of input size $d = \lceil n/2 \rceil$ together with two multiplications by powers of x and three additions. It turns out that the resulting divide-and-conquer algorithm based on Formula (8.2.2) still has quadratic complexity. However, there is a clever way of combining the split polynomials that uses only *three* polynomial multiplications instead of four, based on the following simple identity:

$$P(x)Q(x) = x^{2d}P_2(x)Q_2(x) + x^d((P_1(x) + P_2(x))(Q_1(x) + \quad \text{(8.2.3)}$$
$$Q_2(x)) - P_1(x)Q_1(x) - P_2(x)Q_2(x)) + P_1(x)Q_1(x).$$

Formula (8.2.3) yields the divide-and-conquer algorithm *PolyMult1* for polynomial multiplication. *PolyMult1* calls a "split pea" procedure, *Split*$(P(x), P_1(x), P_2(x))$, which inputs a polynomial $P(x)$ (of input size n) and outputs the two polynomials $P_1(x)$ and $P_2(x)$. We write *PolyMult1* as a high-level recursive function whose inputs are the polynomials $P(x)$ and $Q(x)$ and whose output is the polynomial $P(x)Q(x)$. We will not be explicit about how the coefficients of the polynomials are maintained (linked lists, arrays, and so forth). We will also assume that we have well-defined procedures for multiplying a polynomial by x^i. For example, if the polynomial is maintained by an array of its coefficients, then this amounts to shifting indices by i and replacing the first i entries with zeros. We abuse the notation slightly by writing $x^iP(x)$ to mean the result of calling such a procedure. Also, for convenience we simply use the symbol $+$ to denote the addition of two polynomials.

```
function PolyMult1 (P, Q, n) recursive
Input:    P(x) = a_{n-1}x^{n-1} + ··· + a_1x + a_0, Q(x) = b_{n-1}x^{n-1} + ··· + b_1x + b_0
              (polynomials)
              n (a positive integer)
Output:  P(x)Q(x) (the product polynomial)
    if n = 1 then
        return(a_0b_0)
    else
        d ← ⌈n/2⌉
        Split(P(x), P_1(x), P_2(x))
        Split(Q(x), Q_1(x), Q_2(x))
        R(x) ← PolyMult1 (P_2(x), Q_2(x), d)
        S(x) ← PolyMult1 (P_1(x) + P_2(x), Q_1(x) + Q_2(x), d)
        T(x) ← PolyMult1 (P_1(x), Q_1(x), d)
        return(x^{2d}R(x) + x^d(S(x) − R(x) − T(x)) + T(x))
    endif
end PolyMult1
```

When analyzing *PolyMult1*, we choose coefficient multiplication as our basic operation and thus ignore the two multiplications by powers of x. However, the procedure referred to earlier for multiplying a polynomial by x^i has linear complexity and does not affect the order of complexity of *PolyMult1*. We also assume that n is a power of 2 because we can interpolate asymptotic behavior using Θ-scalability (see Appendix D). Since *PolyMult1* invokes itself three times with n replaced by $d = n/2$, the number of coefficient multiplications $T(n)$ performed by *PolyMult1* satisfies the following recurrence relation:

$$T(n) = 3T\left(\frac{n}{2}\right), \quad n > 1, \quad \textbf{init. cond. } T(1) = 1. \qquad \textbf{(8.2.4)}$$

It follows from a simple unwinding of Formula (8.2.4) that $T(n) \in \Theta(n^{\log_2 3})$ [see also the discussion following Formula (3.3.12) in Chapter 3]. Because $\log_2 3$ is approximately 1.59, we now have an algorithm for polynomial multiplication whose $\Theta(n^{\log_2 3})$ complexity is a significant improvement over the $\Theta(n^2)$ complexity of *DirectPolyMult*. In Chapter 22, we develop an even faster polynomial multiplication algorithm using the powerful tool known as the Fast Fourier Transform.

8.2.2 Multiplication of Polynomials of Different Input Sizes

In practice, we often encounter the problem of multiplying two polynomials $P(x)$ and $Q(x)$ of different input sizes m and n, respectively. If $m < n$, then we could merely augment $P(x)$ with $n - m$ leading zeros, but this would be quite inefficient if n is significantly larger than m. It is better to partition $Q(x)$ into blocks of size m. For convenience, we assume n is a multiple of m—that is, $n = km$ for some positive integer k. We let $Q_i(x)$ be the polynomial of degree m given by

$$Q_i(x) = b_{im-1}x^{m-1} + b_{im-2}x^{m-2} + \cdots + b_{(i-1)m+1}x + b_{(i-1)m}, \; i \in \{1, \ldots, k\}.$$

Clearly,

$$Q(x) = Q_k(x)x^{m(k-1)} + Q_{k-1}(x)x^{m(k-2)} + \cdots + Q_2(x)x^m + Q_1(x).$$

It follows immediately from the distributive law that

$$P(x)Q(x) = P(x)Q_k(x)x^{m(k-1)} + P(x)Q_{k-1}(x)x^{m(k-2)} + \cdots + P(x)Q_1(x).$$

Applying these ideas, we obtain the algorithm *PolyMult2* for multiplying two polynomials $P(x)$ and $Q(x)$. *PolyMult2* is efficient even if the degree $m - 1$ of $P(x)$ is much less than the degree $n - 1$ of $Q(x)$. If n is not a multiple of m, we compute the largest integer k such that $n > km$ and augment $P(x)$ with $n - km$ leading zeros.

function *PolyMult2(P(x), Q(x), m, n)*
Input: $P(x) = a_{m-1}x^{m-1} + \cdots + a_1 x + a_0$, $Q(x) = b_{n-1}x^{n-1} + \cdots + b_1 x + b_0$
           (polynomials)
           n, m (positive integers)   //$n = km$ for some integer k
Output: $P(x)Q(x)$ (the product polynomial)
     ProdPoly(x) ← 0 //initialize all coefficients of *ProdPoly(x)* to be 0
     for i ← 1 **to** k **do**
         $Q_i(x) = b_{im-1}x^{m-1} + b_{im-2}x^{m-2} + \cdots + B_{(i-1)m}$
     endfor
     for i ← 1 **to** k **do**
         ProdPoly(x) ← *ProdPoly(x)* + $x^{(i-1)m}$*PolyMult1 (P(x), Q_i(x), m)*
     endfor
     return(*ProdPoly(x)*)
end *PolyMult2*

The complexity of *PolyMult1* for multiplying two polynomials of degree $m - 1$ is $\Theta(m^{\log_2 3})$. Since *PolyMult2* invokes *PolyMult1* a total of $k = n/m$ times, each time with input polynomials of degree $m - 1$, it follows that the complexity of *PolyMult2* is

$$\Theta(km^{\log_2 3}) = \Theta\left(\frac{nm^{\log_2 3}}{m}\right) = \Theta(nm^{\log_2(3/2)}).$$

8.3   Multiplication of Large Integers

Computers typically assign a fixed number of bits for storing integer variables. Arithmetic operations such as addition and multiplication of integers are often carried out by moving the integer operands into *fixed-length* registers and then invoking arithmetic operations built into the hardware. However, for some important applications, such as those occurring in cryptography, the number of digits is too large to be handled directly by the hardware in this way. Such applications must perform these operations by storing the integers using an appropriate data structure (such as an array or a linked list) and then using algorithms to carry out the arithmetic operations. When analyzing the complexity of such algorithms, the size n of an integer A is taken to be the number of digits of A. Any base $b \geq 2$ can be chosen for representing an integer. We denote the ith least significant digit of U (base b) by u_i, $i = 0, 1, \ldots, n - 1$; that is,

$$U = \sum_{i=0}^{n-1} u_i b^i. \tag{8.3.1}$$

The classic grade-school algorithm for multiplying two integers U and V of size n clearly involves n^2 multiplications of digits. Viewing the right-hand side of Formula (8.3.1) as a polynomial in b leads us to a divide-and-conquer strategy for computing UV based on a formula analogous to Formula (8.2.3). Although similar to the multiplication of polynomials, addition and multiplication of large integers include the additional task of handling carry digits. The design details of the resulting $\Theta(n^{\log_2 3})$ algorithm *MultInt* are left to the exercises.

8.4 Multiplication of Matrices

Given two $n \times n$ matrices $A = (a_{ij})$ and $B = (b_{ij})$, $0 \le i, j \le n - 1$, recall that the product AB is defined to be the $n \times n$ matrix $C = (c_{ij})$, where

$$c_{ij} = \sum_{k=0}^{n-1} a_{ik} b_{kj}. \tag{8.4.1}$$

The straightforward algorithm based on this definition clearly performs n^3 (scalar) multiplications. In 1969 Strassen devised a divide-and-conquer algorithm for matrix multiplication of complexity $O(n^{\log_2 7})$ using certain algebraic identities for multiplying 2×2 matrices.

The classic method of multiplying 2×2 matrices performs 8 multiplications as follows:

$$AB = \begin{bmatrix} a_{00} & a_{01} \\ a_{01} & a_{11} \end{bmatrix} \begin{bmatrix} b_{00} & b_{01} \\ b_{01} & b_{11} \end{bmatrix} = \begin{bmatrix} a_{00}b_{00} + a_{01}b_{01} & a_{00}b_{01} + a_{01}b_{11} \\ a_{01}b_{00} + a_{11}b_{01} & a_{01}b_{01} + a_{11}b_{11} \end{bmatrix}. \tag{8.4.2}$$

Strassen discovered a way to carry out the same matrix product AB using only the following seven multiplications:

$$\begin{aligned}
m_1 &= (a_{00} + a_{11})(b_{00} + b_{11}) \\
m_2 &= (a_{10} + a_{11})b_{00} \\
m_3 &= a_{00}(b_{01} - b_{11}) \\
m_4 &= a_{11}(b_{10} - b_{00}) \\
m_5 &= (a_{00} + a_{01})(b_{11}) \\
m_6 &= (a_{10} - a_{00})(b_{00} + b_{01}) \\
m_7 &= (a_{01} - a_{11})(b_{10} + b_{11})
\end{aligned} \tag{8.4.3}$$

The matrix product AB is then given by

$$AB = \begin{bmatrix} m_1 + m_4 - m_5 + m_7 & m_3 + m_5 \\ m_2 + m_4 & m_1 + m_3 - m_2 + m_6 \end{bmatrix}. \tag{8.4.4}$$

Consider now the case of two $n \times n$ matrices where, for convenience, we assume that $n = 2^k$. We first partition the matrices A and B into four $(n/2) \times (n/2)$ submatrices, as follows:

$$A = \begin{bmatrix} A_{00} & A_{01} \\ A_{10} & A_{11} \end{bmatrix}, \quad B = \begin{bmatrix} B_{00} & B_{01} \\ B_{10} & B_{11} \end{bmatrix} \quad \text{(8.4.5)}$$

The product AB can be expressed in terms of eight matrix products as follows:

$$AB = \begin{bmatrix} A_{00}B_{00} + A_{01}B_{01} & A_{00}B_{01} + A_{01}B_{11} \\ A_{01}B_{00} + A_{11}B_{01} & A_{01}B_{01} + A_{11}B_{11} \end{bmatrix}. \quad \text{(8.4.6)}$$

Thus, in complete analogy with the 2×2 case, we can carry out the matrix product AB using only the following seven matrix multiplications:

$$
\begin{aligned}
M_1 &= (A_{00} + A_{11})(B_{00} + B_{11}) \\
M_2 &= (A_{10} + A_{11})B_{00} \\
M_3 &= A_{00}(B_{01} - B_{11}) \\
M_4 &= A_{11}(B_{10} - B_{00}) \\
M_5 &= (A_{00} + A_{01})(B_{11}) \\
M_6 &= (A_{10} - A_{00})(B_{00} + B_{01}) \\
M_7 &= (A_{01} - A_{11})(B_{10} + B_{11})
\end{aligned}
\quad \text{(8.4.7)}
$$

As in the case of 2×2 matrices, the matrix product AB is then given by

$$AB = \begin{bmatrix} M_1 + M_4 - M_5 + M_7 & M_3 + M_5 \\ M_2 + M_4 & M_1 + M_3 - M_2 + M_6 \end{bmatrix}. \quad \text{(8.4.8)}$$

Formulas (8.4.7) and (8.4.8) immediately yield Strassen's algorithm, a divide-and-conquer algorithm based on expressing the product of two $n \times n$ matrices in terms of seven products of $(n/2) \times (n/2)$ matrices. The complexity of Strassen's algorithm clearly satisfies the recurrence relation

$$T(n) = 7T\left(\frac{n}{2}\right), \quad n > 1, \quad \textbf{init. cond. } T(1) = 1. \quad \text{(8.4.9)}$$

By unwinding Formula (8.4.9), we see that $T(n) \in \Theta(n^{\log_2 7})$ [see also the discussion following Formula (3.3.12) in Chapter 3]. Because $\log_2 7$ is approximately 2.81, we now have an algorithm for matrix multiplication with complexity of $\Theta(n^{\log_2 7})$, which is a significant improvement over the $\Theta(n^3)$ complexity of the classical algorithm for matrix multiplication.

Strassen's identities (8.4.3) and (8.4.4) involve a total of 18 additions (or subtractions). Winograd discovered the following set of identities, which leads to a method of multiplying 2×2 matrices using only 15 additions or subtractions but still doing only seven multiplications:

$$
\begin{aligned}
m_1 &= (a_{10} + a_{11} - a_{00})(b_{11} - b_{01} + b_{00}) \\
m_2 &= a_{00}b_{00} \\
m_3 &= a_{01}b_{10} \\
m_4 &= (a_{00} - a_{10})(b_{11} - b_{01}) \\
m_5 &= (a_{10} + a_{11})(b_{01} - b_{00}) \\
m_6 &= (a_{01} - a_{10} + a_{00} - a_{11})b_{11} \\
m_7 &= a_{11}(b_{00} - b_{11} - b_{01} + b_{10})
\end{aligned}
\qquad \textbf{(8.4.10)}
$$

The matrix product AB is then given by

$$
AB = \begin{bmatrix} m_2 + m_3 & m_1 + m_2 + m_5 + m_6 \\ m_1 + m_2 + m_4 - m_7 & m_1 + m_2 + m_4 + m_5 \end{bmatrix}. \qquad \textbf{(8.4.11)}
$$

Although Formulas (8.4.10) and (8.4.11) involve a total of 24 additions or subtractions, it can be verified that a total of only 15 distinct additions or subtractions are needed. Thus, we obtain an improvement of three less additions or subtractions over Strassen's identities while keeping the number of multiplications at seven.

8.5   Selecting the kth Smallest Value in a List

Our next illustration of the divide-and-conquer paradigm is actually an instance of simplification. Given a list $L[0{:}n - 1]$ and an integer k, $1 \le k \le n$, we consider the problem of finding the kth smallest value in L. When $k = 1$ or $k = n$, this problem coincides with the problem of finding the minimum or maximum value in L, respectively. When n is odd and $k = (n + 1)/2$, we are finding the median value in L, whereas for n, even the median value is obtained by averaging the two values corresponding to $k = n/2$ and $t = n/2 + 1$. Since linear algorithms exist for finding the maximum or minimum value in L, we hope to find a linear algorithm for a general value of k. In fact, we first design a linear average-behavior algorithm *Select* for the general problem by using the procedure *Partition* that formed the basis of *QuickSort*, together with a strategy analogous to a binary search. Unfortunately, as did *QuickSort*, *Select* has quadratic worst-case performance. However, by modifying the algorithm, we can obtain a rather more complicated algorithm, *Select2*, having linear worst-case complexity. Because of its linear average performance and its simplicity compared with *Select2*, *Select* is more often used in practice.

8.5.1 The Algorithm Select

The kth smallest value in the list $L[0:n - 1]$ would appear in index position $t = k - 1$ if $L[0:n - 1]$ were sorted (in increasing order). It is convenient to use t as the input parameter to both *Select* and *Select2*. In particular, the output parameter is the value that would be in position t if $L[0:n - 1]$ were sorted.

Given $L[0:n - 1]$ and an index position t, suppose an initial call to the procedure *Partition* with $L[0:n - 1]$ returns the value $j = position$, so that in the rearranged list (which we still denote by L), $L[i] \leq L[j]$ for $0 \leq i < j$, $L[i] \geq L[j]$ for $j < i \leq n - 1$, and the pivot element $L[j]$ has the value of the original $L[0]$. Hence, in the rearranged list, the value in index position j is the value that would appear in this position if the original L were sorted (this was the basis of *QuickSort*). So we're done if $t = j$. Because each element in $L[0:j - 1]$ is not larger than each element in $L[j + 1:n - 1]$, it follows that if $t < j$, we are looking for the value that would appear in position t of $L[0:j - 1]$ if the latter sublist were sorted. Using similar reasoning, if $t > j$, then we are looking for the value that would appear in position t of $L[j + 1:n - 1]$ if the latter sublist were sorted. The recursive algorithm *Select* is based on these simple observations.

```
procedure Select(L[0:n − 1], low, high, t, x) recursive
Input:    L[0:n − 1] (an array of size n), low, high (indices of L[0:n − 1])
                t (a positive integer such that low ≤ t ≤ high)
Output:  x (the value that would appear in index position t if L[low:high] were sorted in
          increasing order)
    Partition(L[0:n − 1], low, high, position)
    case
        :t = position: x ← L[position]
        :t < position: Select(L[0:n − 1], low, position − 1, t, x)
        :t > position: Select(L[0:n − 1], position + 1, high, t, x)
    endcase
end Select
```

In Figure 8.2, we illustrate the action of *Select* for a sample list of size 7.

We now analyze *Select* for a list of size n, where we assume that $low = 0$ and $high = n - 1$. We use the list comparisons generated by calls to the procedure *Partition* as our basic operation. Let $W(n, t)$ and $A(n, t)$ denote the worst-case and average complexities of *Select* restricted to inputs where the parameter t is fixed. Hence,

$$W(n) = \max\{W(n, t) \mid 0 \leq t \leq n - 1\}, \qquad (8.5.1)$$

Original	index	0	1	2	3	4	5	6	7
List	list element	22	9	23	52	15	19	47	$+\infty$

call *Partition*(*L*[0:6],*position*)

Output	index	0	1	2	③	4	5	6	7
List	list element	15	9	19	22	52	23	47	$+\infty$

Output value of *position* = 3

call *Partition*(*L*[4:6],*position*)

Output	index	0	1	2	3	4	5	⑥	7
List	list element	15	9	19	22	47	23	52	$+\infty$

Output value of *position* = 6

call *Partition*(*L*[4:5],*position*)

Output	index	0	1	2	3	4	⑤	6	7
List	list element	15	9	19	22	23	47	52	$+\infty$

Output value of *position* = 5

call *Partition*(*L*[4:5],*position*)

Output	index	0	1	2	3	④	5	6	7
List	list element	15	9	19	22	23	47	52	$+\infty$

Output value of *position* = 4

x = 23

and assuming each *t* is equally likely,

$$A(n) = \frac{\sum_{t=0}^{n-1} A(n, t)}{n}. \tag{8.5.2}$$

Because *Partition* has complexity $n + 1$ for a list of size n, and because there exists an input list whose size is only narrowed by 1 with each call to *Partition*, we have

$$W(n, t) = (n + 1) + n + (n - 1) + \cdots + 2$$
$$= \frac{(n + 1)(n + 2)}{2} - 1 \in \Theta(n^2). \tag{8.5.3}$$

Thus, *Select* has the same quadratic worst-case behavior as *QuickSort*.

When analyzing the average performance of *Select*, we assume, as usual, that the inputs to *Select* are all permutations of $1, \ldots, n$, and that each permutation is equally likely. We now show by the strong form of induction on n that

$$A(n, t) \leq 4n, \quad \text{for all } n \text{ and all } t \in \{0, \ldots, n - 1\}. \quad \textbf{(8.5.4)}$$

Since $A(1, 0) = 2$, Formula (8.5.4) is true for $n = 1$ and $t = 0$. Assuming that (8.5.4) holds for all pairs m, t with $t \in \{0, \ldots, m - 1\}$ and $m < n$, we show that (8.5.4) also holds for n and all $t \in \{0, \ldots, n - 1\}$. Let t be any integer such that $0 \leq t \leq n - 1$. Our assumption that all permutations of $1, 2, \ldots, n$ are equally likely to be input to *Select* implies that after executing the call to *Partition* with $L[0{:}n - 1]$, each value $0, \ldots, n - 1$ is equally likely to be the output value of the parameter *position*. There are three cases to consider, depending on whether *position* is less than, equal to, or greater than t.

For convenience, let $i = position$. If $t = i$, then *Select* terminates after a single call to *Partition*, so that $n + 1$ comparisons are performed. If $t < i$, then *Select* calls itself recursively looking for x in the sublist $L[0{:}i - 1]$, so that the average number of comparisons done in this case is given by

$$n + 1 + A(i, t) \leq n + 1 + 4i \quad \text{(by induction hypothesis)}. \quad \textbf{(8.5.5)}$$

Finally, if $t > i$, then *Select* calls itself recursively looking for x in the sublist $L[i + 1{:}n - 1]$, so that the average number of comparisons performed in this case is given by

$$n + 1 + A(n - i - 1, t - i - 1) \leq n + 1 + 4(n - i - 1)$$
$$\text{(by induction hypothesis)}. \quad \textbf{(8.5.6)}$$

Using inequalities (8.5.5) and (8.5.6), we obtain

$$
\begin{aligned}
A(n, t) = \frac{1}{n}\Bigg[& n + 1 + \sum_{i=0}^{t-1} (n + 1 + A(n - i - 1, t - i - 1)) \\
& + \sum_{i=t+1}^{n-1} (n + 1 + A(i, t)) \Bigg] \\
= \frac{1}{n}\Bigg[& n(n + 1) + \sum_{i=0}^{t-1} A(n - i - 1, t - i - 1) \\
& + \sum_{i=t+1}^{n-1} A(i, t) \Bigg] \leq n + 1 + \frac{4}{n}\Bigg[\sum_{i=0}^{t-1} (n - i - 1) + \sum_{i=t+1}^{n-1} i \Bigg].
\end{aligned}
\quad \textbf{(8.5.7)}
$$

As a function of t, the right side of the inequality in Formula (8.5.7) is maximized when $t = \lceil (n - 1)/2 \rceil$. Now assume that n is odd (the proof when n is even is similar). Then using (8.5.7) and rewriting the term inside the last square bracket yields

$$
\begin{aligned}
A(n, t) \le A\left(n, \frac{n-1}{2}\right) &\le n + 1 + \frac{4}{n}\left[2\left(\sum_{i=1}^{n-1} i - \sum_{i=1}^{(n-1)/2} i\right)\right] \\
&= n + 1 + \frac{4}{n}\left[n(n-1) - \left(\frac{n-1}{2}\right)\left(\left(\frac{n-1}{2}\right) + 1\right)\right] \\
&\le n + 1 + \frac{4}{n}\left[n(n-1) - \frac{(n-1)^2}{4}\right] = n + 1 + \frac{4}{n}\left[(n-1)\left(n - \frac{n-1}{4}\right)\right] \\
&= n + 1 + \frac{4}{n}\left[(n-1)\left(\frac{3n+1}{4}\right)\right] = n + 1 + \frac{(n-1)(3n+1)}{n} \le 4n.
\end{aligned}
$$

This completes the inductive proof of (8.5.4).

It follows immediately from Formulas (8.5.2) and (8.5.4) that $A(n) \le 4n$. Because *Select* performs at least one call to *Partition* for any input, both $A(n, t)$ and $A(n)$ are at least $n + 1$, so that we have

$$n + 1 \le A(n),\ A(n, t) \le 4n, \text{ for all } n \text{ and all } t \in \{0, \dots, n-1\}. \quad \textbf{(8.5.8)}$$

Hence, $A(n), A(n, t) \in \Theta(n)$.

REMARK

We have shown $A(n, t) \le A(n, (n-1)/2) \le 4n$ and concluded that $A(n) \le 4n$. However, a similar induction argument can be used to show that $A(n, 0) \le 2(n + 1)$, which is a reduction by about half of our $4n$ upper bound. With $A(n)$ being the average of $A(n, t)$ over all $t \in \{0, \dots, n-1\}$, we might expect to obtain a better upper bound for $A(n)$. In fact, we can show that $A(n) \le 3n$, but we leave verification of this stronger inequality to an exercise.

8.5.2 A Version of *Select* with Linear Worst-Case Complexity

We now describe another version of *Select*, called *Select2*, which has linear worst-case complexity. The idea is to do a little more work choosing a pivot element before calling *Partition* so that the subsequent recursive calls (if any) are always with sublists whose size is reduced by a **fixed** ratio r. The following Proposition will then show that we should expect linear behavior in such a situation.

Proposition 8.5.1   Suppose r is a number such that $0 < r < 1$. Also, suppose that the worst case of a recursive algorithm satisfies the recurrence

$$W(n) = W(rn) + f(n), \text{ where } f(n) \in \Theta(n).$$

Then $W(n) \in \Theta(n)$, that is, $W(n)$ has linear complexity.

Proof

To prove Proposition 8.5.1, we unwind the recurrence as follows:

$$
\begin{aligned}
W(n) &= W(rn) + f(n) \\
&= W(r^2 n) + f(n)(1 + r) \\
&\ldots \text{ iterate until } r^k \leq 1/n \\
&\leq W(1) + f(n)(1 + r + r^2 + \cdots + r^k + \cdots) \\
&= W(1) + f(n)/(1 - r) \in \Theta(n).
\end{aligned}
$$
■

Note that in the algorithm *Select,* the first element in a list is always chosen as the pivot element in the call to *Partition*. This fixed choice of the pivot element leads to quadratic worst-case complexity because it is possible that the list is only narrowed down by 1 in our recursive calls to *Select*. What is needed is a choice of a pivot element that guarantees that the recursive calls will narrow the size of the list by a fixed ratio, which would lead to linear worst-case behavior by analogy with Proposition 8.5.1. Of course, choosing the median element in a list as a pivot element would narrow the list by about $1/2$. However, finding the median element is a special case of the problem at hand. We will settle for a pivot element *pm*, called a *pseudomedian*, which will be good enough to narrow the list by about $7/10$, so that the recursive call will have $W(7n/10)$ worst-case complexity. Because determining *pm* will turn out to have $W(n/5) + 6n/5$ complexity, we expect a recurrence relation of the form

$$
\begin{aligned}
W(n) &= W(7n/10) + W(n/5) + 6n/5 + n + 1 \\
&= W(7n/10) + W(2n/10) + 11n/5 + 1,
\end{aligned}
$$

which is not exactly of the form $W(n) = W(rn) + f(n)$ stated in Proposition 8.5.1, but it is close enough to still yield linear worst-case complexity.

To compute the pseudomedian *pm*, we assume for convenience that n is an odd multiple of 5, where $n = 5q$ and q is odd. We then break up the list $L[0:n-1]$ into $q = n/5$ sublists $L[0:4], L[5:9], \ldots, L[n-5:n-1]$, each of size 5, and determine the median of each sublist. The total number of comparisons required to determine these q medians $m_1, m_2, \ldots, m_q$ is $6n/5$, since the median of a five-element list can be found in six comparisons (see Exercise 8.20). The pseudomedian *pm* is the median of these q medians and is found by calling our recursive procedure *Select2* with the list of medians $m_1, m_2, \ldots, m_q$ and $k = (q + 1)/2$ (k is the median position of these medians). The worst-case complexity of finding *pm* is then $W(n/5) + 6n/5$. Now in the worst case, a recursive call to *Select2* is made with a list on one side or the other of *pm*. But as Figure 8.3 illustrates, *pm* must lie in the interval from $b(q)$ to $n - b(q) - 1$, where $b(q) = 3(q - 1)/2 + 2 =$ the number of points inside each of the indicated "pseudorectangles." In Figure 8.3, the five-element sublists are arranged (in our mind's eye) so that each sublist is sorted in increasing order (from left to right) and so that the medians are also sorted in increasing order (from top to bottom). This is done for analysis purposes only and is *not* done by the algorithm *Select2*. Each list element in the upper-left pseudorectangle is strictly smaller than *pm*, and each element in the lower-right pseudorectangle is strictly larger than *pm*.

FIGURE 8.3

The pseudomedian *pm* must lie in the interval from $b(q)$ to $n - 1 - b(q)$.

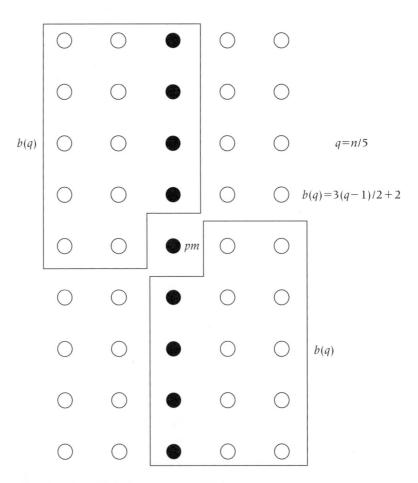

Hence, the size of the sublist searched in the recursive call is at most

$$r(q) = n - b(q) - 1 = 5q - [3((q - 1)/2) + 2] - 1 = 7q/2 - 3/2 < 7n/10.$$

Thus, it follows that $W(n)$ for *Select2* satisfies the recurrence

$$W(n) \leq W(7n/10) + W(2n/10) + 11n/5 + 1, \qquad \textbf{init. cond. } W(1) = 0.$$

A straightforward induction shows that $W(n) \leq 22n$ (see Exercise 8.21).

The following pseudocode for the recursive procedure *Select2* follows from our discussion and is similar to that for the procedure *Select*. However, in *Select2* the procedure *Partition* is replaced by the procedure *Partition2*, which uses the input parameter *Pivot* as the pivot element (by interchanging $L[low]$ with $L[Pivot]$ and then invoking *Partition*). Also, the procedure *MedianOfFive* returns in the output parameter $M[0:q - 1]$ the medians of the five-element sublists of $L[low:high]$.

```
procedure Select2(L[0:n − 1], low, high, t, x) recursive
Input:    L[0:n − 1] (an array of list elements), low, high (indices of L[0:n − 1])
                   t (a positive integer such that low ≤ t ≤ high)
Output:  x (the value that would appear in position t if L[low:high] were sorted in
               increasing order)
     if high − low + 1 ≤ 5 then
          use ad hoc method to find x
     endif
     q ← (high − low + 1)/5
     MedianOfFive(L[0:n − 1], low, high, M[0:q − 1])
     Select2(M[0:q − 1], 0, q − 1, (q − 1)/2, Pivot) //so that PseudoMedian = Pivot
     Partition2(L[0:n − 1], low, high, Pivot, position)
        case
            :t = position: x ← L[position]
            :t < position: Select2(L[0:n − 1], low, position − 1, t, x)
            :t > position: Select2(L[0:n − 1], position + 1, high, t, x)
        endcase
end Select2
```

8.6   Two Classical Problems in Computational Geometry

We now use the divide-and-conquer technique to solve two fundamental problems in computational geometry: the *closest-pair* problem and the *convex hull* problem. Although both problems can be posed for points in Euclidean

d-dimensional space for any $d \geq 1$, we limit our discussion of the solutions to these problems to the line and the plane ($d = 1$ and 2, respectively).

8.6.1 The Closest-Pair Problem

In the closest-pair problem, we are given n points $P_1, \ldots, P_n$ in Euclidean d-space, and we wish to determine a pair of points P_i and P_j such that the distance between P_i and P_j is minimized over all pairs of points drawn from $P_1, \ldots, P_n$. Of course, a brute-force quadratic complexity algorithm solving this problem is obtained by simply computing the distance between each of the $n(n - 1)/2$ pairs and recording the minimum value so computed. Actually, to avoid round-off problems associated with taking square roots, it would be best to work with the square of the distance, which we assume throughout the discussion (and which, by abuse of language and notation, we still refer to as simply the distance d).

Using divide-and-conquer, we now design an $O(n\log n)$ algorithm for the closest-pair problem. This turns out to be order optimal because there is a $\Omega(n\log n)$ lower bound for the problem. We describe the algorithm informally because the actual pseudocode, though straightforward, is somewhat messy to fully describe.

To motivate the solution to the problem in the plane, we first consider the problem for points on the real line. Of course, we can solve the problem on the line by sorting the points using an $O(n\log n)$ algorithm, and then simply making a linear scan of the sorted points. However, this method does not generalize to the plane. To find a method that does generalize, let m be the median value of the n points. Using the algorithm *Select2* described in Section 8.5 we can compute m in linear time. We divide the points $x_1, \ldots, x_n$ into two subsets of equal size, X_1 and X_2, with one subset comprising points less than or equal to the median, and other subset comprising the remaining points (a linear scan determines the division). Let d_1 and d_2 be the minimum distances between pairs of points in X_1 and X_2, respectively. Either $d = \min\{d_1, d_2\}$ is also the smallest distance between any pair drawn from $x_1, \ldots, x_n$ or there is a pair $x_i \in X_1$ and $x_j \in X_2$ having a strictly smaller distance than d. However, it is clear that the interval $(m - d, m]$ contains at most one point of X_1, and the interval $(m, m + d]$ contains at most one point of X_2. In linear time, we can determine if the only possible pair having closer distance than d actually exists. Thus, for $n = 2^k$, the complexity $W(n)$ of the algorithm satisfies the recurrence.

$$W(n) = 2W(n/2) + n, \qquad \textbf{init. cond. } W(1) = 0,$$

which unwinds to yield $W(n) \in O(n\log n)$.

The divide-and-conquer solution just described for points on the real line generalizes naturally to a divide-and-conquer solution in the plane by dividing the

n points $(x_1, y_1), \ldots, (x_n, y_n)$ into sets X_1 and X_2 on either side of line $x = m$, where m is the median of the x-coordinates of the points. The sets X_1 and X_2 can be determined with $O(n\log n)$ complexity by sorting the points by their x-coordinates. We then recursively find the minimum distances d_1 and d_2 between pairs of points in the sets X_1 and X_2, respectively. Again, either $d = \min\{d_1, d_2\}$ is also the smallest distance between any pair drawn from $(x_1, y_1), \ldots, (x_n, y_n)$, or there is a pair $(x_i, y_i) \in X_1$ and $(x_j, y_j) \in X_2$ having a strictly smaller distance than d. Also, if there is such a pair, then (x_i, y_i) lies in the strip S_1 determined by the lines $x = m - d$ and $x = d$, whereas (x_j, y_j) lies in the strip S_2 determined by the lines $x = d$ and $x = m + d$. However, unlike the case for the line, we can no longer be sure that there is at most a single pair of points to examine. Indeed, *all* the points $(x_1, y_1), \ldots, (x_n, y_n)$ might be in the strip $S = S_1 \cup S_2$ between the lines $x = m - d$ and $x = m + d$, so that we would have to examine a quadratic number of pairs, which is no better than the brute-force solution. However, the following proposition, whose proof we leave as an exercise, comes to our rescue.

Proposition 8.6.1 Consider a rectangle R in the plane of width d and height $2d$. There can only be at most six points in R such that the distance between each pair of these points is at least d. □

The following Key Fact follows from Proposition 8.6.1 and the definition of d.

Key Fact

For each point $(x, y) \in X_1 \cap S_1$, there are at most five points in $X_2 \cap S_2 \cap R$, where R is the rectangle with corner points $(x, y - d)$, $(x, y + d)$, $(x + d, y - d)$, $(x + d, y + d)$ (see Figure 8.4).

The Key Fact allows us to check less than $5n$ pairs to determine whether or not there is a pair $(x_i, y_i) \in X_1 \cap S_1$ and $(x_j, y_j) \in X_2 \cap S_2$ having distance less than d. To understand this, note that we can require our recursive calls determining X_1, d_1 and X_2, d_2 to return X_1 and X_2 sorted by their y-coordinates, which then can be merged using no more that $n - 1$ comparisons by the procedure *Merge* (discussed in Chapter 2). Thus, as we scan through the points in $X_1 \cap S_1$ in increasing order of their y-coordinates, a corresponding pointer can also scan the points in $X_2 \cap S_2$ in slightly oscillatory increasing order of their y-coordinates, checking at most $5n$ pairs. More precisely, suppose $P_1, \ldots, P_m$ (respectively, $Q_1, \ldots, Q_k$) are the points in $X_1 \cap S_1$ (respectively, in $X_2 \cap S_2$). We first scan $X_2 \cap S_2$ until we find a point (if any) such that d added to its y-coordinate is at least as large as P_1's y-coordinate. If we find such a point Q_i, then we leave a pointer Q at Q_i, and using Proposition 8.6.1, we need only check Q_i and the next four points $X_2 \cap S_2$ to determine if d needs updating. We then move to point P_2 and resume the scan of $X_2 \cap S_2$ starting at Q_j, this time looking for a point whose y-coordinate is at least as large as P_2's y-coordinate. We repeat this process until all of $X_1 \cap S_1$ is scanned, and less than $5n$ pairs of points will be examined for updates to the current smallest distance. Because we make at most $n - 1$ comparisons when merging X_1 and X_2, we see that the combine step in our divide-and-conquer algorithm performs less than $6n$ comparisons altogether. Hence, the worst case $W(n)$ of the algorithm satisfies

$$W(n) < 2W(n/2) + 6n, \qquad \textbf{init. cond. } W(1) = 0,$$

which shows that $W(n) \in O(n\log n)$.

When implementing this algorithm, there are various degenerate cases that have to be handled. For example, it might happen that some (or even all) of the points are on the line $x = m$. We leave the implementation details to the exercises.

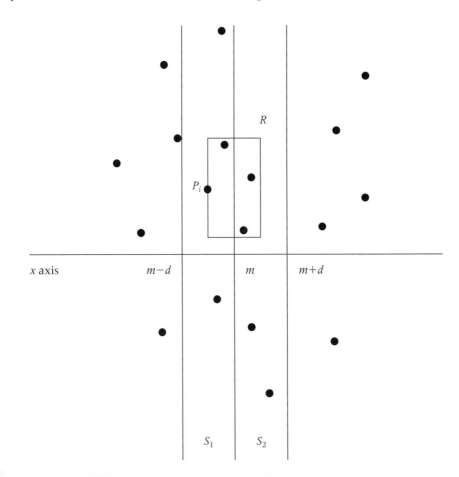

FIGURE 8.4

For $P_i \in X_1 \cap S_1$, rectangle R of width d and height $2d$ is shown where distances from P_i to points in $X_2 \cap S_2 \cap R$ need to be checked.

8.6.2 The Convex Hull Problem

Given any subset S of the Euclidean plane, S is called convex if, for each pair of points $P_1, P_2 \in S$, the line segment joining P_1 and P_2 lies entirely within the set S. Given a set of n points $(x_1, y_1), \dots, (x_n, y_n)$ in the plane, the *convex hull* of these points is the smallest convex set containing them. In other words, the convex hull of the points is contained in any convex set containing the points. There is a nice physical interpretation of the convex hull. Consider placing pegs (or golf tees) at each of the n points $(x_1, y_1), \dots, (x_n, y_n)$. Stretching a small rubber band around the entire set of points and releasing the band determines the boundary of the convex hull (see Figure 8.5).

Given the points $(x_1, y_1), \dots, (x_n, y_n)$ in the plane, the convex hull problem is to determine a subset of these points $P_1, \dots, P_k, P_{k+1} = P_1$ such that the boundary of the convex hull of the points $(x_1, y_1), \dots, (x_n, y_n)$ consists of the line segments joining P_i and P_{i+1}, $i = 1, \dots, k$. We assume that no three consecutive points in the (circular) list $P_1, \dots, P_k, P_{k+1} = P_1$ are collinear.

The divide-and-conquer algorithm for computing the convex hull that we now describe begins in the same way as the closest-pair algorithm; namely, we divide the n points $(x_1, y_1), \dots, (x_n, y_n)$ into sets X_1 and X_2 on either side of line $x = m$, where m is the median of the x-coordinates of the points. We then recursively determine the convex hulls $CH(X_1)$ and $CH(X_2)$ of X_1 and X_2, respectively. The initial condition for the recursion is a set of one, two, or three points, because the convex hull in these cases is a point, a line segment connecting the two points, and a triangle connecting the three points (unless they are collinear), respectively. It then becomes a question of how to merge the convex hulls $CH(X_1)$ and $CH(X_2)$ into the convex hull $CH(X_1 \cup X_2)$. The answer is to determine the upper and lower support line segments of $CH(X_1) \cup CH(X_2)$, as illustrated in Figure 8.6.

FIGURE 8.5

A small rubber band stretched and released around pegs at points in the plane determines the convex hull of these points.

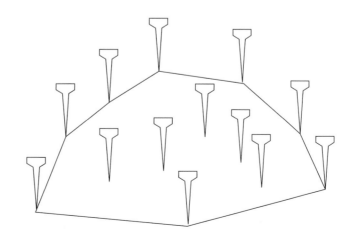

FIGURE 8.6

Upper and lower
support line
segments of
$CH(X_1) \cup CH(X_2)$.

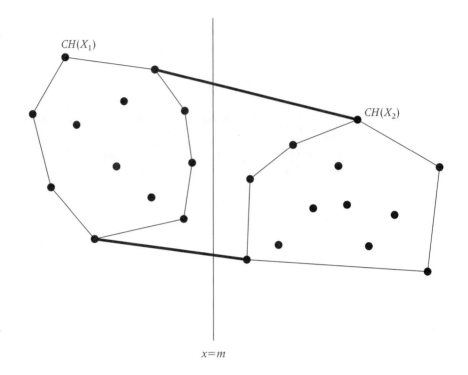

To determine the support line segments, we introduce the notion of a turn determined by an ordered triple of points (P_1, P_2, P_3) in the plane. We have a left turn, no turn, or right turn, respectively, as determined by the determinant shown in Figure 8.7. This determinant corresponds to twice the "signed area" determined by the triple of points (P_1, P_2, P_3).

We now use the notion of turns to determine the upper support line segment. Suppose $CH(X_1)$ is given by $P_1, \dots, P_k, P_{k+1} = P_1$ and $CH(X_2)$ is given by $Q_1, \dots, Q_m, Q_{m+1} = Q_1$, where both sequences are in clockwise order (that is, we make right turns as we pass through the sequences). Let P_i be the point in X_1 with the largest x-coordinate (if there are two such points, we take the point with the smaller y-coordinate). Consider the sequence of turns determined by $(P_i, Q_j, Q_{j+1}), j = 1, \dots, m$, where we set $Q_{m+1} = Q_1$ for convenience. Then the right-hand endpoint of the upper support line segment is the point Q_r, where the turns go from left turns or no turn to a right turn; that is, (P_i, Q_{r-1}, Q_r) is a left turn or no turn, and (P_i, Q_r, Q_{r+1}) is a right turn. Now consider the sequence of turns $(Q_r, P_j, P_{j-1}), j = 1, \dots, k$, where we set $P_0 = P_m$ for convenience (that is, we go around $CH(X_1)$ in counterclockwise order). Then the left-hand endpoint of the upper support line segment is the point P_s where the turns go from right turns or no turn to left turns. This determines the upper support segment. The lower support segment is obtained similarly.

FIGURE 8.7

The indicated
determinant
determines whether
the triple (P_1, P_2, P_3)
is a left turn, no
turn, or right turn;
that is, the turn
depends on
whether this
determinant is
positive, zero, or
negative,
respectively.

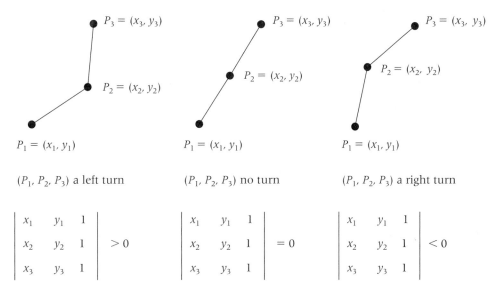

(P_1, P_2, P_3) a left turn

(P_1, P_2, P_3) no turn

(P_1, P_2, P_3) a right turn

$$\begin{vmatrix} x_1 & y_1 & 1 \\ x_2 & y_2 & 1 \\ x_3 & y_3 & 1 \end{vmatrix} > 0 \qquad \begin{vmatrix} x_1 & y_1 & 1 \\ x_2 & y_2 & 1 \\ x_3 & y_3 & 1 \end{vmatrix} = 0 \qquad \begin{vmatrix} x_1 & y_1 & 1 \\ x_2 & y_2 & 1 \\ x_3 & y_3 & 1 \end{vmatrix} < 0$$

Given the two support line segments, it is a simple matter to eliminate the points in $CH(X_1) \cup CH(X_2)$ that are not in $CH(X_1 \cup X_2)$ and to return the sequence of points in $CH(X_1 \cup X_2)$ in clockwise order. It is also easy to verify that the algorithm has $O(n\log n)$ complexity. As with the closest-pair problem, when implementing the convex hull algorithm, various degenerate cases have to be handled. We leave the implementation details to the exercises.

Other $O(n\log n)$ algorithms for determining the convex hull are not based on divide-and-conquer. Two of the most commonly used of these are the Graham scan and the Jarvis march. The references at the end of the chapter provide a discussion of these and other convex hull algorithms. We point out there is a $\Omega(n\log n)$ lower bound for the convex hull problem in the plane because sorting can be reduced to this problem (see Exercise 8.32). Hence, the divide-and-conquer algorithm and the algorithms of Graham and Jarvis all have optimal order of complexity.

8.7 Closing Remarks

Since Strassen's result for matrix multiplication appeared in 1969 researchers have been trying to improve the basic method. They look for identities that perform fewer multiplications when multiplying matrices of a certain fixed size m and then use this reduction as the basis of a divide-and-conquer algorithm. The algorithm uses decomposition into m^2 blocks of size n/m, where, for convenience, it is assumed that $n = m^k$ for some positive integer k. It has been shown that for 2×2 matrices, at least seven multiplications are *required*. Thus, divide-and-conquer algorithms, which use as their starting point a method of multiplying two $m \times m$ matrices using less than the number of multiplications used by Strassen's method, require that m be larger than 2.

Nearly ten years after Strassen discovered his identities, Pan found a way to multiply two 70×70 matrices that involves only 143,640 multiplications (compared with more than 150,000 multiplications used by Strassen's method), yielding an algorithm that performs $O(n^{2.795})$ multiplications. Improvements over Pan's algorithm have been discovered, and the best result currently known (due to Coppersmith and Winograd) can multiply two $n \times n$ matrices using $O(n^{2.376})$ multiplications. However, all these methods require n to be quite large before improvements over Strassen's method are significant. Moreover, they are very complicated due to the large number of identities required to achieve the savings in the number of multiplications. Hence, the currently known order of complexity improvements over Strassen's algorithm are mostly of theoretical rather than practical interest.

The subject of computational geometry has a vast literature and is an active area of research. We refer you to the references at the end of this chapter for further reading on this important topic.

References and Suggestions for Further Reading

References to matrix multiplication algorithms:

Gonnet, G. H. *Handbook of Algorithms and Data Structures.* Reading, MA: Addison-Wesley, 1984.

Wilf, H. S. *Algorithms and Complexity.* Englewood Cliffs, NJ: Prentice-Hall, 1986.

Books devoted to computational geometry:

O'Rourke, J. *Computational Geometry in C.* New York: Cambridge University Press, 1994.

Preparata, F. P., and M. I. Shamos. *Computational Geometry: An Introduction.* New York: Springer-Verlag, 1985.

Handbooks containing material on computational geometry:

Goodman, J. E., and J. O'Rourke., eds. *Handbook of Discrete and Computational Geometry, 2nd edition.* Boca Raton, FLCRC Press, 2004.

Pach, J., ed. *New Trends in Discrete and Computational Geometry.* Vol. 10 of *Algorithms and Combinatorics.* New York: Springer-Verlag, 1993.

Survey articles on computational geometry:

Aurenhammer, F. "Voronoi Diagrams: A Survey of a Fundamental Geometric Data Structure." *ACM Computing Surveys* 23 (September 1991): 345-405.

Lee, D. T., and F. P. Preparata. "Computational Geometry: A Survey." *IEEE Transactions on Computers* C-33 (1984): 1072-1101.

EXERCISES

Section 8.1 The Divide-and-Conquer Paradigm

8.1 Design and analyze a divide-and-conquer algorithm for finding the maximum element in a list $L[0:n-1]$.

8.2 Design and analyze a divide-and-conquer algorithm for finding the maximum and minimum elements in a list $L[0:n-1]$.

8.3 Suppose we have a list $L[0:n-1]$ representing the results of an election, so that $L[i]$ is the candidate voted for by person i, $i = 0, \ldots, n-1$. Design a linear algorithm to determine whether a candidate got a majority of the votes—that is, whether there exists a list element that occurs more than $n/2$ times in the list. Your algorithm should output a majority winner if one exists. *Note:* One way to solve this problem is to determine the median value in the list, because that value is the only candidate for the majority value. This solution can be done in linear time using *Select 2* from Section 8.5. You are to design a different algorithm to solve the problem.

8.4 Design a version of *QuickSort* that uses a threshold. Do some empirical testing to determine a good threshold value.

Section 8.2 Symbolic Algebraic Operations on Polynomials

8.5 Give pseudocode and analyze the procedure *DirectPolyMult*, which is based directly on Formula (8.2.1).

8.6 Repeat Exercise 8.5 for a version of *DirectPolyMult* in which the polynomials are implemented by storing the coefficients in

a. an array

b. a linked list

c. Consider the sparse case.

8.7 Give pseudocode for a version of *PolyMult1* in which the polynomials are implemented by storing the coefficients and the associated powers of the polynomials in a linked list.

8.8 When analyzing *PolyMult1*, we choose coefficient multiplication as our basic operation. This ignores the two multiplications by powers of x. Show how the procedure for multiplying a polynomial by x^i can be implemented with linear complexity. Taking this operation into account, verify that the order of complexity of *PolyMult1* remains unchanged.

8.9 Show that the divide-and-conquer algorithm for multiplying two polynomials based on the recurrence relation (8.2.2) has quadratic complexity.

Section 8.3 Multiplication of Large Integers

8.10 Design and analyze an algorithm *MultInt* for multiplying large integers.

8.11 a. Design an algorithm for adding two large integers implemented using arrays.

b. Repeat part (a) for linked list implementations.

8.12 Give pseudocode for the algorithm *MultInt* you designed in Exercise 8.10 for the following two implementations of large integers.

a. arrays

b. linked lists

Section 8.4 Multiplication of Matrices

8.13 Verify Formula (8.4.4).

8.14 Verify Formula (8.4.11).

8.15 Verify that the evaluation of Formulas (8.4.10) and (8.4.11) together require 15 distinct additions or subtractions, which is 3 less than what is performed when using Strassen's identities.

8.16 Give pseudocode for the procedure *Strassen*, which implements Strassen's matrix multiplication algorithm. Assume that the input matrices A and B are both $n \times n$ matrices, where n is a power of 2.

8.17 Demonstrate the action of the procedure *Strassen* in Exercise 8.16 for the following input matrices:

$$A = \begin{bmatrix} 2 & 0 & 1 & 1 \\ 3 & 0 & 0 & 4 \\ 3 & -4 & 5 & 7 \\ 0 & 1 & 2 & 3 \end{bmatrix} \quad B = \begin{bmatrix} 0 & 2 & 1 & 1 \\ 0 & 1 & 0 & -1 \\ 3 & 0 & 5 & 0 \\ 6 & 1 & 4 & 0 \end{bmatrix}$$

Section 8.5 Selecting the kth Smallest Value in a List

8.18   a. Show that for a list of size n, *Select* makes at most n calls to *Partition* when determining the kth smallest element.

   b. For a given n and $t = k - 1$, find a list exhibiting worst-case behavior — that is, for which the size of the sublist containing the kth smallest value of the original list is only reduced by one with each call to *Partition*.

8.19   Design and give pseudocode for an iterative version of the procedure *Select*.

8.20   Show that the median of five elements can be computed directly using six comparisons.

8.21   Consider the function $W(n)$ defined by the recurrence relation (8.5.9). Using induction, show that $W(n) \le 22n$.

8.22   Design and give pseudocode for an iterative version of the procedure *Select2*.

8.23   Design a version of *Select2* that works for lists $L[0:n - 1]$ where the elements are not necessarily distinct

8.24   Design a version of *Select2* that rearranges the list elements by directly comparing them to *PseudoMedian*.

8.25   Design an $O(\log k)$ divide-and-conquer algorithm for finding the kth smallest (largest) element in a list $L[0:2n - 1]$, where the sublists $L[0:n - 1]$ and $L[n, 2n - 1]$ are in nondecreasing order.

8.26   Design an algorithm *Partition2*($L[low:high]$, *Pivot*, *position*) that rearranges the input list about the element *Pivot* $\in L[low:high]$ so that each element to the left of *Pivot* is no larger than *Pivot*, and each element to the right is no smaller than *Pivot*. The final position of *Pivot* in the rearranged list should be returned in the parameter *position*.

Section 8.6 Two Classical Problems in Computational Geometry

8.27   Prove that a rectangle of width d and height $2d$ can contain at most six points whose pairwise distances are at least d.

8.28   Write a computer program implementing the closest-pair algorithm.

8.29   Verify that the divide-and-conquer algorithm for the convex hull problem discussed in Section 8.6. has $O(n\log n)$ complexity.

8.30 Show that the convex hull of a set of points $P_1, P_2, \ldots, P_n$ in the plane consists of the set of all points $\lambda_1 P_1 + \lambda_2 P_2 + \cdots + \lambda_n P_n$, where $\lambda_1, \lambda_2, \ldots, \lambda_n$ are all nonnegative real numbers such that $\lambda_1 + \lambda_2 + \cdots + \lambda_n = 1$.

8.31 Write a computer program implementing the divide-and-conquer algorithm for the convex hull problem discussed in Section 8.6.

8.32 Show that a lower bound in $\Omega(n\log n)$ exists for the convex hull problem in the plane. *Hint:* Let $x_1, \ldots, x_n$ be n real numbers. Consider the convex hull $P_1, \ldots, P_m$ of the n points $(x_1, x_1^2), \ldots, (x_n, x_n^2)$, listed in counterclockwise order, and where P_1 has a minimum x-coordinate. Show that $m = n$ and the x-coordinates of $P_1, \ldots, P_m$ (in that order) is a sorting of $x_1, \ldots, x_n$ in increasing order.

Section 8.7 Closing Remarks

8.33 Pan's divide-and-conquer matrix multiplication algorithm is based on a partitioning scheme that assumes n is a power of 70. The complexity $T(n)$ of Pan's divide-and-conquer algorithm satisfies the recurrence relation

$$T(n) = 143{,}640\,T(n/70), \quad n = 70^i, \quad i \geq 1, \qquad \textbf{init. cond. } T(1) = 1.$$

Show that this implies that $T(n)$ is approximately $n^{2.795}$.

CHAPTER 9

DYNAMIC PROGRAMMING

Dynamic programming is a design strategy that involves dynamically constructing a solution S to a given problem using solutions $S_1, S_2, \ldots, S_m$ to smaller (or simpler) instances of the problem. The solution S_i to a given smaller problem instance is itself built from the solutions to even smaller (or simpler) problem instances, and so forth. We start with the known solutions to the smallest (simplest) problem instances and build from there in a bottom-up fashion. To be able to reconstruct S from $S_1, S_2, \ldots, S_m$, we usually require some additional information. We let *Combine* denote the function that combines $S_1, S_2, \ldots, S_m$, using the additional information to obtain S, so that

$$S = Combine(S_1, S_2, \ldots, S_m).$$

Dynamic programming is similar to divide-and-conquer in the sense that it is based on a recursive division of a problem instance into smaller or simpler problem instances. However, whereas divide-and-conquer algorithms often use a top-down resolution method, dynamic programming algorithms invariably proceed by solving all the simplest problem instances before combining them into more complicated problem instances in a bottom-up fashion. Further, unlike many instances of divide-and-conquer, dynamic programming algorithms typically do not recalculate the solution to a given problem instance. Dynamic programming algorithms for optimization problems also can avoid generating suboptimal problem instances when the *Principle of Optimality* holds, thereby leading to increased efficiency.

9.1 Optimization Problems and the Principle of Optimality

The method of dynamic programming is most effective in solving optimization problems when the Principle of Optimality holds. Consider the set of all *feasible* solutions to an optimization problem; that is, all the solutions satisfying the constraints of the problem. An *optimal* solution S is a solution that optimizes (minimizes or maximizes) the objective function. If we wish to obtain an optimal solution S to the given problem instance, then we must optimize (minimize or maximize) over *all* solutions $S_1, S_2, \ldots, S_m$ such that $S = Combine(S_1, S_2, \ldots, S_m)$. For many problems, it is computationally infeasible to examine all feasible solutions because exponentially many possibilities exist. Fortunately, we can drastically reduce the number of problem instances that we need to consider if the Principle of Optimality holds.

DEFINITION 9.1.1 Given an optimization problem and an associated function *Combine*, the *Principle of Optimality* holds if the following is always true: If $S = Combine(S_1, S_2, \ldots, S_m)$ and S is an *optimal* solution to the problem instance, then $S_1, S_2, \ldots, S_m$, are *optimal* solutions to their associated problem instances.

> **Key Fact**
>
> **The efficiency of dynamic programming solutions based on a recurrence relation expressing the principle of optimality results from (1) the bottom-up resolution of the recurrence, thereby eliminating redundant recalculations, and (2) eliminating suboptimal solutions to subproblems as we build up optimal solutions to larger problems; that is, we use only optimal solution "building blocks" in constructing our optimal solution.**

We first illustrate the Principle of Optimality for the problem of finding a parenthesization of a matrix product of matrices $M_0, \ldots, M_{n-1}$ that minimizes the total number of (scalar) multiplications over all possible parenthesizations. If $(M_0 \cdots M_k)(M_{k+1} \cdots M_{n-1})$ is the "first-cut" set of parentheses (and the last product performed), then the matrix products $M_0 \cdots M_k$ and $M_{k+1} \cdots M_{n-1}$ must both be parenthesized in such a way as to minimize the number of multiplications required to carry out the respective products. As a second example, consider the problem of finding optimal binary search trees for a set of distinct keys. Recall that a binary search tree T for keys $K_0 < \cdots < K_{n-1}$ is a binary tree on n nodes, each containing a key such that the following property is satisfied: Given any node v in the tree, each key in the left subtree rooted at v is no larger than the key in v, and each key in the right subtree rooted at v is no smaller than the key in v (see Figure 4.17). If K_i is the key in the root, then the left subtree L of the root contains $K_0, \ldots, K_{i-1}$, and the right subtree R of the root contains $K_{i+1}, \ldots, K_{n-1}$. Given a binary search tree T for keys $K_0, \ldots, K_{n-1}$, let K_i denote the key associated with the root of T, and let L and R denote the left and right subtrees (of the root) of T, respectively. Again, it follows that L (solution S_1) is a binary search tree for keys $K_0, \ldots, K_{i-1}$, and R (solution S_2) is a binary search tree for keys $K_{i+1}, \ldots, K_{n-1}$. Given L and R, the function $Combine(L,R)$ merely reconstructs the tree T using K_i as the root. In the next section, we show that the Principle of Optimality holds for this problem by showing that if T is an optimal binary search tree, then so are L and R.

9.2 Optimal Parenthesization for Computing a Chained Matrix Product

Our first example of dynamic programming is an algorithm for the problem of parenthesizing a chained matrix product so as to minimize the number of multiplications performed when computing the product. When solving this problem, we will assume the straightforward method of matrix multiplication. If A and B are matrices of dimensions $p \times q$ and $q \times r$, then the matrix product AB involves pqr multiplications. Given a sequence (or chain) of matrices $M_0, M_1, \ldots, M_{n-1}$, consider the product $M_0 M_1 \cdots M_{n-1}$, where the matrix M_i has dimension $d_i \times d_{i+1}$, $i = 0, \ldots, n$, for a suitable sequence of positive integers d_0, $d_1, \ldots, d_n$. Because a matrix product is an associative operation, we can evaluate the chained product in one of many ways, depending on how we choose to parenthesize the expression. It turns out that the manner in which the expression is parenthesized can make a major difference in the total number of multiplications performed when computing the chained product. In this section, we consider the problem of finding an *optimal parenthesization*—that is, a parenthesization that minimizes the total number of multiplications performed using ordinary matrix products.

We illustrate the problem with an example that commonly occurs in multivariate calculus. Suppose A and B are $n \times n$ matrices, X is an $n \times 1$ column vector, and we wish to evaluate ABX. The product ABX can be parenthesized in two ways, $(AB)X$ and $A(BX)$, resulting in $n^3 + n^2$ and $2n^2$ multiplications, respectively. Thus, the two ways of parenthesizing make a rather dramatic difference in the number of multiplications performed; that is, order $\Theta(n^3)$ versus order $\Theta(n^2)$.

The following is a formal, recursive definition of a fully parenthesized chained matrix product and its associated first cut.

DEFINITION 9.2.1   Given the sequence of matrices $M_0, M_1, \ldots, M_{n-1}$, P is a *fully parenthesized* matrix product of $M_0, M_1, \ldots, M_{n-1}$ (which, for convenience, we simply call a *parenthesization of $M_0 M_1 \cdots M_{n-1}$*) if P satisfies

$$P = M_0, \quad n = 1,$$
$$P = (P_1 P_2), \quad n > 1,$$

where for some k, P_1 and P_2 are parenthesizations of the matrix products $M_0 M_1 \cdots M_k$ and $M_{k+1} M_{k+2} \cdots M_{n-1}$, respectively. We call P_1 and P_2 the *left* and *right* parenthesizations of P, respectively. We call the index k the *first-cut index* of P.

The table in Figure 9.1 shows all the parenthesizations of the matrices M_0, M_1, M_2, and M_3 having dimensions 20×10, 10×50, 50×5, and 5×30, respectively, with the optimal parenthesizations highlighted.

There is one-to-one correspondence between parenthesizations of $M_0 M_1 \cdots M_{n-1}$ and 2-trees having n leaf nodes. Given a parenthesization P of $M_0 M_1 \cdots M_{n-1}$, if $n = 1$, its associated 2-tree $T(P)$ consists of a single node corresponding to the matrix M_0; otherwise, $T(P)$ has left subtree $T(P_1)$ and right subtree $T(P_2)$, where P_1 and P_2 are the left and right parenthesizations of P. The 2-tree $T(P)$ is the *expression tree* for P (see Figure 9.2).

FIGURE 9.1

Number of multiplications performed for each full parenthesization shown for matrices M_0, M_1, M_2, and M_3 having dimensions 20×10, 10×50, 50×5, and 5×30, respectively. The optimal parenthesizations are shaded.

no. mult.	no. mult.	no. mult.	no. mult.
M_0	$(M_0 M_1)$ 10000	$(M_0(M_1 M_2))$ 3500	$(M_0(M_1(M_2 M_3)))$ 28500
		$((M_0 M_1)M_2)$ 15000	$(M_0((M_1 M_2)M_3))$ 10000
			$((M_0 M_1)(M_2 M_3))$ 47500
			$((M_0(M_1 M_2))M_3)$ 6500
			$(((M_0 M_1)M_2)M_3)$ 18000

FIGURE 9.2

Associated
expression 2-tree
for parenthesization
$(((M_0M_1)(M_2M_3))$
$(M_4M_5))$. The label
(i, j) inside each
node indicates
that the matrix
product associated
with the node
involves matrices
$M_i, M_{i+1}, \dots, M_j$.

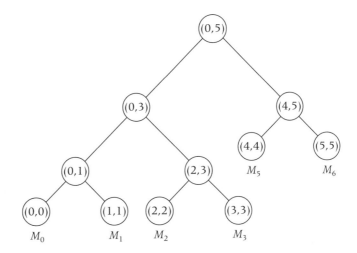

Thus, the number of parenthesizations p_n equals the number t_n of 2-trees having n leaf nodes, so that by Exercise 4.14 we have

$$p_n = \frac{1}{n}\binom{2n-2}{n-1} \geq \frac{4^{n-1}}{2n^2 - n} \in \Omega\left(\frac{4^n}{n^2}\right). \tag{9.2.1}$$

Hence, a brute-force algorithm that examines all possible parenthesizations is computationally infeasible.

We are led to consider a dynamic programming solution to our problem by noting that the Principle of Optimality holds for optimal parenthesizing. Indeed, if we consider any optimal parenthesization P for $M_0M_1 \cdots M_{n-1}$, clearly both the left and right parenthesizations P_1 and P_2 of P must be optimal for P to be optimal.

For $0 \leq i \leq j \leq n - 1$, let m_{ij} denote the number of multiplications performed using an optimal parenthesization of $M_iM_{i+1} \cdots M_j$. By the Principle of Optimality, we have the following recurrence for m_{ij} based on making an optimal choice for the first-cut index:

$$m_{ij} = \min_k\{m_{ik} + m_{k+1,j} + d_id_{k+1}d_{j+1} : 0 \leq i \leq k < j \leq n - 1\}$$
$$\textbf{init. cond. } m_{ii} = 0, i = 0, \dots, n - 1. \tag{9.2.2}$$

The value $m_{0,n-1}$ corresponds to the minimum number of multiplications performed when computing $M_0M_1 \cdots M_{n-1}$. We could base a divide-and-conquer algorithm *ParenthesizeRec* directly on a top-down implementation of the recurrence relation (9.2.2). Unfortunately, a great many recalculations are performed by *ParenthesizeRec*, and it ends up doing $\Omega(3^n)$ multiplications to compute the minimum number $m_{0,\,n-1}$ corresponding to an optimal parenthesization.

A straightforward dynamic programming algorithm proceeds by computing the values m_{ij}, $0 \le i \le j \le n - 1$, in a bottom-up fashion using (9.2.2), thereby avoiding recalculations. Note that the values m_{ij}, $0 \le i \le j \le n - 1$, occupy the upper-right triangular portion of an $n \times n$ table. Our bottom-up resolution proceeds throughout the upper-right triangular portion diagonal by diagonal, starting from the bottom diagonal consisting of the elements $m_{ii} = 0$, $i = 0, \dots, n - 1$. The qth diagonal consists of the elements $m_{i,\,i+q}$, $q = 0, \dots, n - 1$. Figure 9.3 illustrates the computation of m_{ij} for the example given in Figure 9.1. When computing m_{ij}, we also generate a table c_{ij} of indices k, where the minimum in (9.2.2) occurs; that is, c_{ij} is where the first cut in $M_i M_{i+1} \cdots M_j$ is made in an optimal parenthesization. The values c_{ij} can then be used to actually compute the matrix product according to the optimal parenthesization.

The following procedure, *OptimalParenthesization*, accepts as input the *dimension sequence* $d[0{:}n]$, where matrix M_i has dimension $d_i \times d_{i+1}$, $i = 0, \dots, n - 1$. Procedure *OptimalParenthesization* outputs the matrix $m[0{:}n - 1, 0{:}n - 1]$, where $m[i, j] = m_{ij}$, $0 \le i \le j \le n - 1$, is defined by recurrence (9.2.2). *OptimalParenthesization* also outputs the matrix *FirstCut*$[0{:}n - 1, 0{:}n - 1]$, where *FirstCut*$[i, j] = c_{ij}$, $0 \le i \le j \le n - 1$, which is the first-cut index in an optimal parenthesization for $M_i \cdots M_j$.

FIGURE 9.3

Table showing values m_{ij}, $0 \le i \le j \le 3$, computed diagonal by diagonal from $q = 0$ to $q = 3$ using the bottom-up resolution of (9.2.2) for matrices M_0, M_1, M_2, and M_3 having dimensions 20×10, 10×50, 50×5, and 5×30, respectively. The values of c_{ij} are shown underneath each m_{ij}, $0 \le i \le j \le 3$.

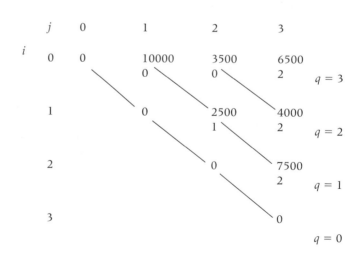

procedure *OptimalParenthesization*($d[0:n]$, $m[0:n - 1, 0:n - 1]$, *FirstCut*$[0:n - 1,$
    $0:n - 1]$)
Input: $d[0:n]$ (dimension sequence for matrices $M_0, M_1, \ldots, M_{n-1}$)
Output: $m[0:n - 1, 0:n - 1]$ ($m[i, j]$ = number of multiplications performed in an
                                optimal parenthesization for computing $M_i \cdots M_j$,
                                $0 \le i \le j \le n - 1$)
        FirstCut$[0:n - 1, 0:n - 1]$ (index of first cut in optimal parenthesization of
                                  $M_i \cdots M_j$, $0 \le i \le j \le n - 1$)
    for $i \leftarrow 0$ **to** $n - 1$ **do**   // initialize $M[i, i]$ to zero
        $m[i, i] \leftarrow 0$
    endfor
    for *diag* $\leftarrow 1$ **to** $n - 1$ **do**
        for $i \leftarrow 0$ **to** $n - 1 - $ *diag* **do**
            $j \leftarrow i + $ *diag*   // compute m_{ij} according to (9.2.2)
            Min $\leftarrow m[i + 1, j] + d[i]*d[i + 1]*d[j + 1]$
            TempCut $\leftarrow i$
            for $k \leftarrow i + 1$ **to** $j - 1$ **do**
                Temp $\leftarrow m[i, k] + m[k + 1, j] + d[i]*d[k + 1]*d[j + 1]$
                if *Temp* $<$ *Min* **then**
                    Min $\leftarrow$ *Temp*
                    TempCut $\leftarrow k$
                endif
            endfor
            $m[i, j] \leftarrow$ *Min*
            FirstCut$[i, j] \leftarrow$ *TempCut*
        endfor
    endfor
end *OptimalParenthesization*

A simple loop counting shows that the complexity of *OptimalParenthesization* is in $\Theta(n^3)$.

It is now straightforward to write pseudocode for a recursive function *ChainMatrixProd* for computing the chained matrix product $M_0 \cdots M_{n-1}$ using an optimal parenthesization. We assume that the matrices $M_0, \ldots, M_{n-1}$ and the matrix *FirstCut*$[0:n - 1, 0:n - 1]$ are global variables to the procedure *ChainMatrixProd*. The chained matrix product $M_0 \cdots M_{n-1}$ is computed by initially invoking the function *ChainMatrixProd* with $i = 0$ and $j = n - 1$. *ChainMatrixProd* invokes a function *MatrixProd*, which computes the matrix product of two input matrices.

```
function ChainMatrixProd(i, j) recursive
Input:    i, j (indices delimiting matrix chain M_i, . . . , M_j)
          M_0, . . . , M_{n-1} (global matrices)
          FirstCut[0:n − 1, 0:n − 1] (global matrix computed by
          OptimalParenthesization)
Output:   M_i · · · M_j (matrix chain)
    if j > i then
        X ← ChainMatrixProd(i, FirstCut[i, j])
        Y ← ChainMatrixProd(FirstCut[i, j] + 1, j)
        return(MatrixProd(X, Y))
    else
        return(M_i)
    endif
end ChainMatrixProd
```

For the example given in Figure 9.1, invoking *ChainMatrixProd* with M_0, M_1, M_2, M_3 computes the chained matrix product $M_0 M_1 M_2 M_3$ according to the parenthesization $((M_0(M_1 M_2))M_3)$.

9.3 Optimal Binary Search Trees

We now use dynamic programming and the Principle of Optimality to generate an algorithm for the problem of finding optimal binary search trees. Given a search tree T and a search element X, the following recursive strategy finds any occurrence of a key X. First, X is compared to the key K associated with the root. If X is found there, we are done. If X is not found, and if X is less than K, then we search the left subtree; otherwise, we search the right subtree.

Consider, for example, the binary search tree given in Figure 9.4 involving the four keys "Ann," "Joe," "Pat," and "Ray". The internal nodes correspond to the successful searches $X =$ "Ann," $X =$ "Joe," $X =$ "Pat," $X=$ "Ray," and the leaf nodes correspond to the unsuccessful searches $X <$ "Ann," "Ann" $< X <$ "Joe," "Joe" $< X <$ "Pat," "Pat" $< X <$ "Ray," "Ray" $< X$. Suppose, for example that $X =$ "Ann." Then *SearchBinSrchTree* makes three comparisons, first comparing X to "Pat," then comparing X to "Joe," and finally comparing X to "Ann." Now suppose that $X =$ "Pete." Then *SearchBinSrchTree* makes two comparisons, first comparing X to "Pat" and then comparing X to "Ray." *SearchBinSrchTree* implicitly branches to the left child of the node containing the key "Ray"—that is, to the leaf (implicit node) corresponding to the interval "Pat" $< X <$ "Ray." Let p_0, p_1, p_2, p_3 be the probability that $X =$ "Ann," $X =$ "Joe," $X =$ "Pat," $X =$ "Ray," respectively, and let q_0, q_1, q_2, q_3, q_4, denote the probability that $X <$ "Ann," "Ann" $< X <$ "Joe," "Joe" $< X <$ "Pat," "Pat" $< X <$ "Ray," "Ray" $< X$, respectively.

FIGURE 9.4

Search tree with
leaf nodes drawn
representing
unsuccessful
searches.

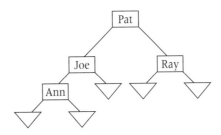

Then, the average number of comparisons made by *SearchBinSrchTree* for the tree
T of Figure 9.4 is given by

$$3p_0 + 2p_1 + p_2 + 2p_3 + 3q_0 + 3q_1 + 2q_2 + 2q_3 + 2q_4.$$

Now consider a general binary search tree *T* whose internal nodes correspond to a fixed set of *n* keys $K_0, K_1, \ldots, K_{n-1}$ with associated probabilities
$\mathbf{p} = (p_0, p_1, \ldots, p_{n-1})$, and whose $n + 1$ leaf (external) nodes correspond to the
$n + 1$ intervals $I_0: X < K_0, I_1: K_0 < X < K_1, \ldots, I_{n-1}: K_{n-2} < X < K_{n-1}, I_n: X >
K_{n-1}$ with associated probabilities $\mathbf{q} = (q_0, q_1, \ldots, q_n)$. (When implementing *T*,
the leaf nodes need not actually be included. However, when discussing the average behavior of *SearchBinSrchTree*, it is useful to include them.) We now derive
a formula for the average number of comparisons $A(T, n, \mathbf{p}, \mathbf{q})$ made by *Search-
BinSrchTree*. Let d_i denote the depth of the internal node corresponding to K_i,
$i = 0, \ldots, n - 1$. Similarly, let e_i denote the depth of the leaf node corresponding
to the interval I_i, $i = 0, 1, \ldots, n$. If $X = K_i$, then *SearchBinSrchTree* traverses the
path from the root to the internal node corresponding to K_i. Thus, it terminates
after performing $d_i + 1$ comparisons. On the other hand, if *X* lies in I_i, then
SearchBinSrchTree traverses the path from the root to the leaf node corresponding
to I_i and terminates after performing e_i comparisons. Thus, we have

$$A(T, n, \mathbf{p}, \mathbf{q}) = \sum_{i=0}^{n-1} p_i(d_i + 1) + \sum_{i=0}^{n} q_i e_i. \qquad (9.3.1)$$

We now consider the problem of determining an *optimal* binary search tree
T, optimal in the sense that *T* minimizes $A(T, n, \mathbf{p}, \mathbf{q})$ over all binary search trees
T. This problem is solved by a complete tree in the case where all the p_i's are
equal and all the q_i's are equal. Here we use dynamic programming to solve the
problem for general probabilities p_i and q_i. In fact, we solve the slightly more general problem, where we relax the condition that $p_0, \ldots, p_{n-1}$ and $q_0, \ldots, q_n$ are
probabilities by allowing them to be arbitrary nonnegative real numbers. One

could regard these numbers as frequencies, as we did when discussing Huffman codes in Chapter 7. That is, we solve the problem

$$\underset{T}{\text{minimize}}\ A(T, n, \mathbf{p}, \mathbf{q}) \qquad\qquad \textbf{(9.3.2)}$$

over all binary search trees T of size n, where $p_0, \dots, p_{n-1}$ and $q_0, \dots, q_n$ are given fixed nonnegative real numbers. For convenience, we sometimes refer to $A(T, n, \mathbf{p}, \mathbf{q})$ as the *cost* of T. We define $\sigma(\mathbf{p}, \mathbf{q})$ by

$$\sigma(\mathbf{p}, \mathbf{q}) = \sum_{i=0}^{n-1} p_i + \sum_{i=0}^{n} q_i. \qquad\qquad \textbf{(9.3.3)}$$

Note that we have removed the probability constraint that $\sigma(\mathbf{p}, \mathbf{q}) = 1$.

As with chained matrix products, we could obtain an optimal search tree by enumerating all binary search trees on the given identifiers and choosing the one with minimum $A(T, n, \mathbf{p}, \mathbf{q})$. However, the number of different binary search trees on n identifiers is the same as the number of binary trees on n nodes, which is given by the nth Catalan number

$$b_n + \frac{1}{n+1}\binom{2n}{n} \in \Omega\!\left(\frac{4^n}{n^2}\right).$$

Thus, a brute-force algorithm for determining an optimal binary search tree using simple enumeration is computationally infeasible. Fortunately, the Principle of Optimality holds for the optimal binary search tree problem, so we look for a solution using dynamic programming.

Let K_i denote the key associated with the root of T, and let L and R denote the left and right subtrees (of the root) of T, respectively. As we remarked earlier, L is a binary search tree for the keys $K_0, \dots, K_{i-1}$, and R is a binary search tree for the keys $K_{i+1}, \dots, K_{n-1}$. For convenience, let $A(T) = A(T, n, \mathbf{p}, \mathbf{q})$, $A(L) = A(L, i, p_0, \dots, p_{i-1}, q_0, \dots, q_i)$, and $A(R) = A(R, n-i-1, p_{i+1}, \dots, p_{n-1}, q_{i+1}, \dots, q_n)$. Clearly, each node of T that is different from the root corresponds to exactly one node in either L or R. Further, if N is a node in T corresponding to a node N' in L, then the depth of N in T is exactly one greater then the depth of N' in L. A similar result holds if N corresponds to a node in R. Thus, it follows immediately from Formula (9.3.1) that

$$A(T) = A(L) + A(R) + \sigma(\mathbf{p}, \mathbf{q}). \qquad\qquad \textbf{(9.3.4)}$$

We now employ recurrence relation (9.3.4) to show that the Principle of Optimality holds for the problem of finding an optimal search tree. Suppose that T is an optimal search tree; that is, T minimizes $A(T)$. We must show that L and R are also optimal search trees. Suppose there exists a binary search tree L' with $i - 1$ nodes involving the keys $K_0, \dots, K_{i-1}$ such that $A(L') < A(L)$. Clearly, the tree T' obtained from T by replacing L with L' is a binary search tree. Further, it follows from Formula (9.3.4) that $A(T') < A(T)$, contradicting the assumption that T is an optimal binary search tree. Hence, L is an optimal binary search tree. By symmetry, R is also an optimal binary search tree, which establishes that the Principle of Optimality holds for the optimal binary search tree problem.

Because the Principle of Optimality holds, when constructing an optimal search tree T, we need only consider binary search trees L and R, both of which are optimal. This observation, together with recurrence relation (9.3.4), is the basis of the following dynamic programming algorithm for constructing an optimal binary search tree. For $i, j \in \{0, \dots, n-1\}$, we let T_{ij} denote an *optimal* search tree involving the consecutive keys $K_i, K_{i+1}, \dots, K_j$, where T_{ij} is the null tree if $i > j$. Thus, if K_k is the root key, then the left subtree L is $T_{i,k-1}$, and the right subtree R is $T_{k+1,j}$ (see Figure 9.5). Moreover, $T = T_{0,n-1}$ is an optimal search tree involving all n keys. For convenience, we define $\sigma(i, j) = \sum_{k=i}^{j} p_k + \sum_{k=i}^{j+1} q_k$.

FIGURE 9.5

Principle of Optimality: If T_{ij} is optimal, then L and R must be optimal; that is, $L = T_{i,k-1}$ and $R = T_{k+1,j}$.

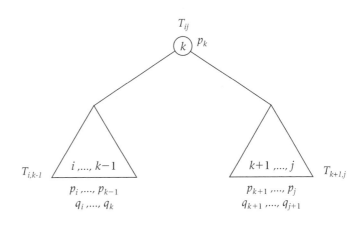

We define $A(T_{ij})$ by

$$A(T_{ij}) = A(T_{ij}, j - i + 1, p_i, p_{i+1}, \dots, p_j, q_i, q_{i+1}, \dots, q_{j+1}). \quad \textbf{(9.3.5)}$$

Because the keys are sorted in nondecreasing order, it follows from the Principle of Optimality and (9.3.4) that

$$A(T_{ij}) = \min_k \{A(T_{i,k-1}) + A(T_{k+1,j})\} + \sigma(i, j), \quad \textbf{(9.3.6)}$$

where the minimum is taken over all $k \in \{i, i + 1, \dots, j\}$.

Recurrence relation (9.3.6) yields an algorithm for computing an optimal search tree T. The algorithm begins by generating all single-node binary search trees, which are trivially optimal. Namely, $T_{00}, T_{11}, \dots, T_{n-1,n-1}$. Using (9.3.6), the algorithm can then generate optimal search trees $T_{01}, T_{12}, \dots, T_{n-2,n-1}$. In general, at the kth stage in the algorithm, recurrence relation (9.3.6) is applied to construct the optimal search trees $T_{0,k-1}, T_{1,k}, \dots, T_{n-k,n-1}$, using the previously generated optimal search trees as building blocks. Figure 9.6 illustrates the algorithm for a sample instance involving $n = 4$ keys. Note that there are two possible choices for T_{02} in Figure 9.6, each having a minimum cost of 1.1. The tree with the smaller root key was selected.

continued

FIGURE 9.6

Action of algorithm to find an optimal binary search tree using dynamic programing.

i	0	1	2	3	4
p_i	.15	.1	.2	.3	
q_i	.05	.05	0	.05	.1

$T_{00} = (0)$ $T_{11} = (1)$ $T_{22} = (2)$ $T_{33} = (3)$

$A(T_{00}) = .25$ $A(T_{11}) = .15$ $A(T_{22}) = .25$ $A(T_{33}) = .45$

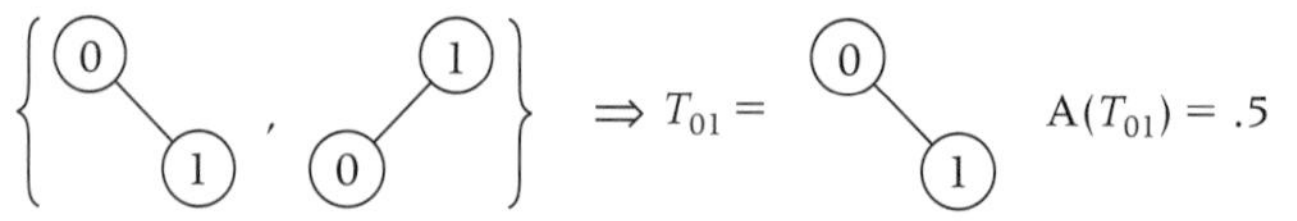

$\Rightarrow T_{01} =$ $A(T_{01}) = .5$

$\min \{0 + .15 = .15, .25 + 0 = .25\} + .35 = .5$

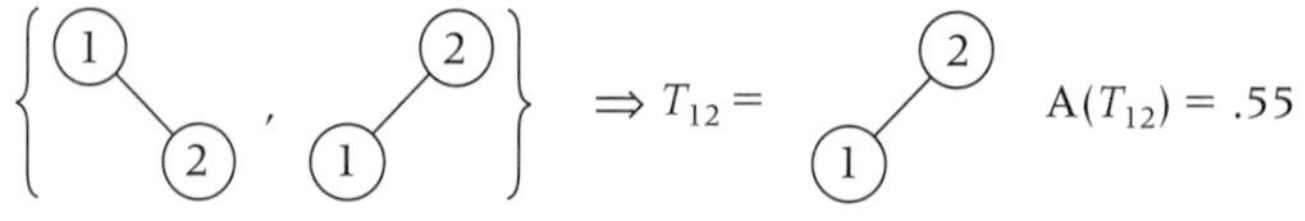

$\Rightarrow T_{12} =$ $A(T_{12}) = .55$

$\min \{0 + .25 = .25, .15 + 0 = .15\} + .4 = .55$

FIGURE 9.6

Continued

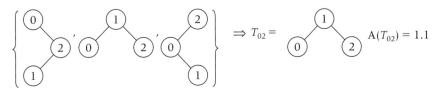

$$\min \{0 + .45 = .45, .25 + 0 = .25\} + .65 = .9$$

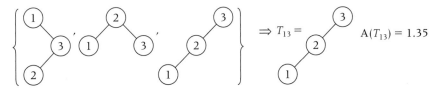

$$\min \{0 + .55 = .55, .25 + .25 = .5, .5 + 0 = .5\} + .6 = 1.1$$

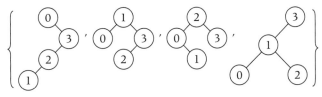

$$\min \{0 + .9 = .9, .15 + .45 = .6, .55 + 0 = .55\} + .8 = 1.35$$

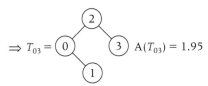

$$\min \{0 + 1.35 = 1.35, .25 + .9 = 1.15, .5 + .45 = .95, 1.1 + 0 = 1.1\} + 1 = 1.95$$

The following pseudocode for the algorithm *OptimalSearchTree* implements the preceding strategy. *OptimalSearchTree* computes the root, *Root*[i, j], of each tree T_{ij}, and the cost, $A[i, j]$, of T_{ij}. An optimal binary search tree T for all the keys (namely, $T_{0, n-1}$) can be easily constructed using recursion from the two-dimensional array *Root*[$0:n-1, 0:n-1$].

```
procedure OptimalSearchTree(P[0:n − 1], Q[0:n], Root[0:n − 1, 0:n − 1], A[0:n − 1,
         0:n − 1])
Input:   P[0:n − 1] (an array of probabilities associated with successful searches)
         Q[0:n] (an array of probabilities associated with unsuccessful searches)
Output:  Root[0:n − 1, 0:n − 1] (Root[i, j] is the key of the root node of T_{ij})
         A[0:n − 1, 0:n − 1] (A[i, j] is the cost A(T_{ij}) of T_{ij})
    for i ← 0 to n − 1 do
        Root[i, i] ← i
        Sigma[i, i] ← p[i] + q[i] + q[i + 1]
        A[i, i] ← Sigma[i, i]
    endfor
    for Pass ← 1 to n − 1 do // Pass is one less than the size of the optimal
                                trees T_{ij} being constructed in the given pass.
        for i ← 0 to n − 1 − Pass do
            j ← i + Pass
                            //Compute σ(p_i, . . . , p_j, q_i, . . ., q_{j+1})
            Sigma[i, j] ← Sigma[i, j − 1] + p[j] + q[j + 1]
            Root[i, j] ← i
            Min ← A[i + 1, j]
            for k ← i + 1 to j do
                Sum ← A[i, k − 1] + A[k + 1, j]
                if Sum < Min then
                    Min ← Sum
                    Root[i, j] ← k
                endif
            endfor
            A[i, j] ← Min + Sigma[i, j]
        endfor
    endfor
end OptimalSearchTree
```

In Figure 9.7, we illustrate the action of *OptimalSearchTree* for the optimal binary search tree just described. For convenience, we change all the probabilities to frequencies, which, in the case we are considering, result by multiplying each probability by 100 to change all the numbers to integers. As we have remarked, working with frequencies instead of probabilities can always be done. In fact, when we are constructing optimal subtrees, it is actually frequencies that we are dealing with instead of probabilities. The optimal subtrees T_{ij} are built starting from the base case T_{ii}, $i = 0, 1, 2, 3$. The figure shows how the tables are built during each pass for $A(T_{ij}) = A[i, j]$,

$Root(T_{ij}) = Root[i, j]$, and $Sigma[i, j] = p_i + \cdots + p_j + q_i + \cdots + q_{j+1} = Sigma[i, j-1] + p_j + q_{j+1}$.

FIGURE 9.7

Building arrays $A[i, j]$, $Root[i, j]$, $Sigma[i, j]$ from inputs $P[0{:}3] = (15,10,20,30)$ and $Q[0{:}4] = (5,5,0,5,10)$ to *OptimalSearchTree*.

i	0	1	2	3	4
p_i	15	10	20	30	
q_i	5	5	0	5	10

Pass 1

$A[i, j]$

i \ j	0	1	2	3
0	25	*	*	*
1		15	*	*
2			25	*
3				45

$Root[i, j]$

i \ j	0	1	2	3
0	0	*	*	*
1		1	*	*
2			2	*
3				4

$Sigma[i, j]$

i \ j	0	1	2	3
0	25	*	*	*
1		15	*	*
2			25	*
3				45

Pass 2

$A[i, j]$

i \ j	0	1	2	3
0	25	50	*	*
1		15	55	*
2			25	90
3				45

$Root[i, j]$

i \ j	0	1	2	3
0	1	1	*	*
1		2	3	*
2			3	4
3				4

$Sigma[i, j]$

i \ j	0	1	2	3
0	25	35	*	*
1		15	40	*
2			25	65
3				45

Pass 3

$A[i, j]$

i \ j	0	1	2	3
0	25	50	110	*
1		15	55	110
2			25	90
3				45

$Root[i, j]$

i \ j	0	1	2	3
0	1	1	2	*
1		2	3	4
2			3	4
3				4

$Sigma[i, j]$

i \ j	0	1	2	3
0	25	35	60	*
1		15	40	60
2			25	65
3				45

Pass 4

$A[i, j]$

i \ j	0	1	2	3
0	25	50	110	195
1		15	55	110
2			25	90
3				45

$Root[i, j]$

i \ j	0	1	2	3
0	1	1	2	3
1		2	3	4
2			3	4
3				4

$Sigma[i, j]$

i \ j	0	1	2	3
0	25	35	60	100
1		15	40	60
2			25	65
3				45

Because *OptimalSearchTree* does the same amount of work for any input $P[0{:}n-1]$ and $Q[0{:}n]$, the best-case, worst-case, and average complexities are equal. Clearly, the number of additions made in computing *Sum* has the same order as the total number of additions made by *OptimalSearchTree*. Therefore, we choose the addition made in computing *Sum* as the basic operation. Since *Pass* varies from 1 to $n-1$, i varies from 0 to $n-1-Pass$, and k varies from $i+1$ to

$i + Pass$, it follows that the total number of additions made in computing *Sum* is given by

$$\sum_{t=1}^{n-1}\sum_{i=0}^{n-1-t}\sum_{k=i+1}^{i+t} 1$$
$$= \sum_{t=1}^{n-1}(n-t)t$$
$$= n\sum_{t=1}^{n-1}t - \sum_{t=1}^{n-1}t^2$$
$$= n\left[(n-1)\frac{n}{2}\right] - \left[(n-1)n\frac{(2n-1)}{6}\right] \in \Theta(n^3).$$

9.4 Longest Common Subsequence

In this section, we consider the problem of determining how close two character strings are to one another. For example, a spell checker might compare a text string created on a word processor with pattern strings from a stored dictionary. If there is no exact match between the text string and any pattern string, then the spell checker offers several alternative pattern strings that are fairly close, in some sense, to the text string. As another example, a forensic scientist might compare two DNA strings to measure how close they match.

We can measure the closeness of two strings in several ways. In Chapter 20, we will consider one important measure called the *edit distance*, which is commonly used by search engines to find approximate matchings for a user-entered text string for which an exact match cannot be found. The edit distance is also used by spell checkers. Roughly speaking, the edit distance between two strings is the minimum number of changes that need to be made (adding, deleting, or changing characters) to transform one string to the other.

In this section, we consider another closeness measure, the longest common subsequence (LCS) contained in a text string and a particular pattern string. Computing either the LCS or the edit distance is an optimization problem that satisfies the Principle of Optimality and can be solved using dynamic programming. However, the solution to the LCS problem is easier to understand because it has a simpler recurrence relation, which we now describe.

Suppose $T = T_0 T_1 \cdots T_{n-1}$ is a text string that we want to compare to a pattern string $P = P_0 P_1 \cdots P_{m-1}$, where we assume that the characters in each string are drawn from some fixed alphabet A. A *subsequence* of T is a string of the form $T_{i_1} T_{i_2} \cdots T_{i_k}$, where $0 \le i_1 < i_2 < \cdots < i_k \le n - 1$. Note that a *substring* of T is a special case of a subsequence of T in which the subscripts making up the subsequence increase by one. For example, consider the pattern string "Cincinnati" and the text string "Cincinatti" (a common misspelling). You can easily check that the longest common subsequence of the pattern string and the text string has length 9 (just one less than the common length of both strings), whereas it takes two changes to transform the text string to the pattern string (so that the edit distance between the two strings is two).

We now describe a dynamic programming algorithm to determine the length of the longest common subsequence of T and P. For simplicity of notation, we assume that the strings are stored in arrays $T[0:n-1]$ and $P[0:m-1]$, respectively. For integers i and j, we define $LCS[i, j]$ to be the length of the longest common subsequence of the substrings $T[0:i-1]$ and $P[0:j-1]$ (so that $LCS[n, m]$ is the length of the longest common subsequence of T and P). For convenience, we set $LCS[i, j] = 0$ if $i = 0$ or $j = 0$ (corresponding to empty strings). Note that $LCS[1, 1] = 1$ if $T[0] = P[0]$; otherwise, $LCS[1, 1] = 0$. This initial condition is actually a special case of the following recurrence relation for $LCS[i, j]$:

$$LCS[i, j] = LCS[i-1, j-1] + 1 \quad \text{if } T[i-1] = P[j-1];$$
$$\text{otherwise, } LCS[i, j] = \max\{LCS[i, j-1], LCS[i-1, j]\}. \qquad \textbf{(9.4.1)}$$

To verify recurrence relation (9.4.1), note first that if $T[i-1] \neq P[j-1]$, then a longest common subsequence of $T[0:i-1]$ and $P[0:j-1]$ might end in $T[i-1]$ or $P[j-1]$, but certainly not both. In other words, if $T[i-1] \neq P[j-1]$, then a longest common subsequence of $T[0:i-1]$ and $P[0:j-1]$ must be drawn from either the pair $T[0:i-2]$ and $P[0:j-1]$ or from the pair $T[0:i-1]$ and $P[0:j-2]$. Moreover, such a longest common subsequence must be a longest common subsequence of the pair of substrings from which it is drawn (that is, the principle of optimality holds). This verifies that

$$LCS[i, j] = \max\{LCS[i, j-1], LCS[i-1, j]\} \text{ if } T[i-1] \neq P[j-1]. \textbf{(9.4.2)}$$

On the other hand, if $T[i-1] = P[j-1] = C$, then a longest common subsequence must end either at $T[i-1]$ in $T[0:i-1]$ or at $P[j-1]$ in $P[0, j-1]$, or both,; otherwise, by adding the common value C to a given subsequence, we would increase the length of the subsequence by 1. Also, if the last term of a longest common subsequence ends at an index $k < i-1$ in $T[0:i-1]$ (so that $T[k] = C$), then clearly we achieve an equivalent longest common subsequence by swapping $T[i-1]$ for $T[k]$ in the subsequence. By a similar argument involving $P[0:j-1]$, when $T[i-1] = P[j-1]$, we can assume without loss of generality that a longest common subsequence in $T[0:i-1]$ and $P[0:j-1]$ ends at $T[i-1]$ and $P[j-1]$. However, then removing these end points from the subsequence clearly must result in a longest common subsequence in $T[0{:}i-2]$ and $P[0{:}j-2]$, respectively (that is, the principle of optimality again holds). It follows that

$$LCS[i, j] = LCS[i - 1, j - 1] + 1 \text{ if } T[i - 1] = P[j - 1], \quad \textbf{(9.4.3)}$$

which, together with Formula (9.4.2), completes the verification of Formula (9.4.1).

The following algorithm is the straightforward row-by-row computation of the array $LCS[0{:}n, 0{:}m]$ based on the recurrence (9.4.1).

```
procedure LongestCommonSubseq(T[0:n − 1], P[0:m − 1], LCS[0:n, 0:m])
Input:    T[0:n − 1], P[0:m − 1] (strings)
Output:   LCS[0:n, 0:m] (array such that LCS[i, j] is length of the longest common
          subsequence of T[0:i − 1] and P[0:j − 1] )
    for i ← 0 to n do      // initialize for boundary conditions
        LCS[i, 0] ← 0
    endfor
    for j ← 0 to m do      // initialize for boundary conditions
        LCS[0, j] ← 0
    endfor
    for i ← 1 to n do      // compute the row index by i of LCS[0:n, 0:m]
        for j ← 1 to m do // compute LCS[i, j] using (9.4.1)
            if T[i − 1] = P[j − 1] then
                LCS[i, j] ← LCS[i − 1, j − 1] + 1
            else
                LCS[i, j] ← max(LCS[i, j − 1], LCS[i − 1, j])
            endif
        endfor
    endfor
end LongestCommonSubseq
```

Using the comparison of text characters as our basic operation, we see that *LongestCommonSubseq* has complexity in $O(nm)$, which is a rather dramatic improvement over the exponential complexity $\Theta(2^n m)$ brute-force algorithm that would examine each of the 2^n subsequences of $T[0{:}n-1]$ and determine the longest subsequence that also occurs in $P[0{:}m-1]$.

Figure 9.8 shows the array $LCS[0{:}8, 0{:}11]$ output by *LongestCommonSubseq* for $T[0{:}7] = $ "usbeeune" and $P[0{:}10] = $ "subsequence".

Note that *LongestCommonSubseq* determines the length of the longest common subsequence of $T[0{:}n-1]$ and $P[0{:}m-1]$ but does not output the actual subsequence itself. In the previous problem of finding the optimal paranthesization of a chained matrix product, in addition to knowing the minimum number of multiplications required, it was also important to determine the actual paranthesization that did the job. Thus, we needed to compute the array $FirstCut[0:n - 1, 0:n - 1]$ to be able to construct the optimal paranthesization. Similarly, in the optimal binary search tree problem, in addition to knowing the average search complexity of the optimal search tree, it was important to determine the optimal search tree itself. Thus, we kept track of the key $Root[i, j]$ in the root of the optimal binary search tree containing the keys $K_i < \cdots < K_j$. However, in the LCS problem, knowing the actual common subsequence is not as important as knowing its length. For example, in a process like spell checking, the subsequence is not as important as its length. Typically, to correct a misspelled word in the text, the spell checker displays a list of pattern strings that share subsequences exceeding a threshold length (depending on the length of the strings), as opposed to exhibiting common subsequences. Nevertheless, it is interesting that a longest common subsequence can be determined just from the array $LCS[0:n - 1, 0:m - 1]$ (and $T[0:n - 1]$ and $P[0:m - 1]$) without the need to maintain any additional information.

One way we can generate a longest common subsequence is to start at the bottom-right corner (n, m) of the array LCS and work our way backward through the array to build the subsequence in reverse order. The moves are dictated by looking at how we get the value assigned to a given position when we used (9.4.1) to build the array LCS. More precisely, if we are currently at position (i, j) in LCS, and $T[i - 1] = P[j - 1]$, then this common value is appended to the beginning of the string already generated (starting with the null string), and we move to position $(i - 1, j - 1)$ in LCS. On the other hand, if $T[i - 1] \neq P[j - 1]$, then we move to position $(i - 1, j)$ or $(i, j - 1)$, depending on whether $LCS[i - 1, j]$ is greater than $LCS[i, j - 1]$. When $LCS[i - 1, j]$ is equal to $LCS[i, j - 1]$, either move can be made. In the latter case, the two different choices might not only generate different longest common subsequences but also yield different longest common strings corresponding to these subsequences. For example, Figure 9.8a

FIGURE 9.8(a)

The matrix $LCS[0:8, 0:11]$ for the strings $T[0:7] =$ "usbeeune" and $P[0:10] =$ "subsequence", with the path in LCS generating the longest common string "sbeune" using the move-left rule.

		LCS	s 0 1	u 2	b 3	s 4	e 5	q 6	u 7	e 8	n 9	c 10	e 11
		0	0 0	0	0	0	0	0	0	0	0	0	0
u	1		0 0	1	1	1	1	1	1	1	1	1	1
s	2		0 1	1	1	2	2	2	2	2	2	2	2
b	3		0 1	1	2	2	2	2	2	2	2	2	2
e	4		0 1	1	2	2	3	3	3	3	3	3	3
e	5		0 1	1	2	2	3	3	3	3	3	3	3
u	6		0 1	2	2	2	3	3	4	4	4	4	4
n	7		0 1	2	2	2	3	3	4	4	5	5	5
e	8		0 1	2	2	2	3	3	4	5	5	5	6

FIGURE 9.8(b)

The path in the
matrix *LCS*
generating the
longest common
string "useune"
using the
move-up rule.

		s	u	b	s	e	q	u	e	n	c	e
LCS		0	1	2	3	4	5	6	7	8	9	10	11
	0	0	0	0	0	0	0	0	0	0	0	0	0
u	1	0	0	1	1	1	1	1	1	1	1	1	1
s	2	0	1	1	1	2	2	2	2	2	2	2	2
b	3	0	1	1	2	2	2	2	2	2	2	2	2
e	4	0	1	1	2	2	3	3	3	3	3	3	3
e	5	0	1	1	2	2	3	3	3	3	3	3	3
u	6	0	1	2	2	2	3	3	4	4	4	4	4
n	7	0	1	2	2	2	3	3	4	4	5	5	5
e	8	0	1	2	2	2	3	3	4	5	5	5	6

shows the path generated using the move-left rule, which requires us to move to position $(i - 1, j)$ when $T[i - 1] \neq P[j - 1]$, whereas Figure 9.8b shows the path resulting from always moving up to position $(i, j - 1)$. The darker shaded positions (i, j) in these paths correspond to where $T[i - 1] = P[j - 1]$. These two paths yield the longest common strings "sbeune" and "useune", respectively. When generating a path in *LCS*, we obtain a longest common subsequence when we reach a position where $i = 0$ or $j = 0$.

9.5 Closing Remarks

In subsequent chapters, we will use dynamic programming to solve a number of important problems. For example, in Chapter 12, we will discuss Floyd's dynamic programming solution to the all-pairs shortest-path problem in weighted directed graphs. In Chapter 20 we will use dynamic programming to solve the edit distance version of the approximate string matching problem. Dynamic programming, because it is based on a bottom-up resolution of recurrence relations, is usually amenable to straightforward level-by-level parallelization. However, this straightforward parallelization usually does not result in optimal speedup, and more clever parallel algorithms, sometimes based on finding recurrences better suited to parallelization, must be sought. We will see such an example in Chapter 16 for computing shortest paths.

References and Suggestions for Further Reading

Bellman, R. E. *Dynamic Programming.* Princeton, NJ: Princeton University Press, 1957. The first systematic study of dynamic programming.

Two other classic references on dynamic programming are:

Bellman, R. E., and S. E. Dreyfus. *Applied Dynamic Programming.* Princeton, NJ: Princeton University Press, 1962.

Nemhauser, G. *Introduction to Dynamic Programming.* New York: Wiley, 1966.

EXERCISES

Section 9.1 Optimization Problems and the Principle of Optimality

9.1 Suppose the matrix $C[0:n-1, 0:n-1]$ contains the cost of $C[i,j]$ of flying directly from airport i to airport j. Consider the problem of finding the cheapest flight from i to j where we may fly to as many intermediate airports as desired. Verify that the Principle of Optimality holds for the minimum-cost flight. Derive a recurrence relation based on the Principle of Optimality.

9.2 Does the Principle of Optimality hold for the costliest trips (no revisiting of airports, please)? Discuss.

9.3 Does the Principle of Optimality hold for coin changing? Discuss with various interpretations of the *Combine* function.

Section 9.2 Optimal Parenthesization for Computing a
 Chained Matrix Product

9.4 Given the matrix product $M_0 M_1 \cdots M_{n-1}$ and a 2-tree T with n leaves, show that there is a unique parenthesization P such that $T = T(P)$.

9.5 Give pseudocode for *ParenthesizeRec* and analyze its complexity.

9.6 Show that the complexity of *OptimalParenthesization* is in $\Theta(n^3)$.

9.7 Using *OptimalParenthesization*, find an optimal parenthesization for the chained product of five matrices with dimensions 6×7, 7×8, 8×3, 3×10, and 10×6.

9.8 Write a program implementing *OptimalParenthesization* and run it for some sample inputs.

Section 9.3 Optimal Binary Search Trees

9.9 Use dynamic programming to find an optimal binary search tree for the following probabilities, where we assume that the search key is in the search tree; that is, $q_i = 0, i = 0, \ldots, n$:

keys	i	0	1	2	3
probabilities	p_i	.4	.3	.2	.1

9.10 Use dynamic programming to find an optimal search tree for the following probabilities:

i	0	1	2	3	4	5
p_i	.2	.1	.2	.05	.05	
q_i	.05	0	.25	0	.1	0

9.11 a. Design and analyze a recursive algorithm that computes an optimal binary search tree T for all the keys from the two-dimensional array $Root[0:n-1, 0:n-1]$ generated by *OptimalSearchTree*.

   b. Show the action of your algorithm from part (a) for the instance given in Exercise 9.10.

9.12 a. Give a set of probabilities $p_0, \ldots, p_{n-1}$ (assume a successful search so that $q_0 = q_1 = \cdots = q_n = 0$), such that a completely right-skewed search tree T (the left child of every node is **null**) is an optimal search tree with respect to these probabilities.

   b. More generally, prove the following induction on n: If T is *any* given binary search tree with n nodes, then there exists a set of probabilities $p_0, \ldots, p_{n-1}$ such that T is the unique optimal binary search tree with respect to these probabilities.

Section 9.4 Longest Common Subsequence

9.13 Show the array $LCS[0:9, 0:10]$ that is built by *LongestCommonSubseq* for $T[0:8]$ = "alligator" and $P[0:9]$ = "algorithms".

9.14 By following various paths in the array $LCS[0:8, 0:11]$ given in Figure 9.8, find all the longest common subsequences of the strings "usbeeune" and "subsequence".

9.15 Design and analyze an algorithm that generates all longest common subsequences given the input array $LCS[0:n-1, 0:m-1]$.

9.16 Write a program that implements *LongestCommonSubseq*, and run it for some sample inputs.

Additional Problems

9.17 Consider a sequence of n distinct integers. Design and analyze a dynamic programming algorithm to find the length of the longest increasing subsequence. For example, consider the sequence:

45　23　9　3　99　108　76　12　77　16　18　4

The longest increasing subsequence is 3 12 16 18, having length 4.

9.18 The 0/1 knapsack problem is NP-hard when the input is measured in binary. However, when the input is measured in unary (see the discussion at the end of Section 7.3 of Chapter 7), dynamic programming can be used to find a polynomial-complexity solution. Design and analyze a dynamic programming solution to the 0/1 knapsack problem, with positive integer capacity and weights, which is quadratic in $C + n$, where C is the capacity and n is the number of objects. *Hint:* Let $V[i, j]$ denote the maximum value that can be placed in a knapsack of capacity j using objects drawn from $\{b_0, \ldots, b_{i-1}\}$. Use the principle of optimality to find a recurrence relation for $V[i, j]$.

9.19 Design and analyze a dynamic programming solution to the coin-changing problem under similar assumptions to that in the previous exercise.

9.20 Given n integers, the partition problem is to find a bipartition of the integers into two subsets having the same sum or determine that no such bipartition exists. Design and analyze a dynamic programming algorithm for solving the partition problem.

CHAPTER 10

BACKTRACKING AND BRANCH-AND-BOUND

Suppose you enter a maze of garden hedges, like that shown in Figure 10.1. To find the exit of the maze (or to determine that there is no exit), you need a guaranteed strategy. Does such a strategy exist? Yes. You simply walk along the trail with your left hand always touching the hedge. If you hit a dead end, you turn around and backtrack, still keeping your left hand touching the hedge. This left-hand backtracking strategy will always lead you to the exit, or return you to the entrance if there is no exit. It even works when you're blindfolded.

Of course, by symmetry, an algorithm for generating a path through a maze can also be based on the right-hand backtracking strategy. For the maze shown in Figure 10.1, the right-hand backtracking strategy generates a slightly shorter path. In general, however, neither backtracking strategy generates the shortest path. (In fact, Figure 10.1 provides an example.) Thus, although backtracking always gets you through the maze, some good heuristics might yield a shorter path (see Figure 10.2).

*Source: Jim Borgman,
© 1995 The Cincinnati
Enquirer. Reprinted with
permission. All rights
reserved.*

FIGURE 10.1

Garden maze and
path to exit
generated by the
left-hand
backtracking
algorithm.

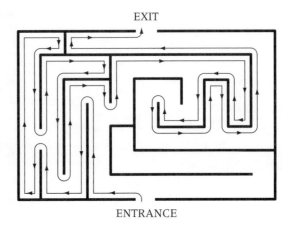

EXIT

ENTRANCE

FIGURE 10.2

The left-hand
backtracking
algorithm versus
heuristic search.

We can associate an implicit state-space T tree with the maze problem,
where a node (or state) in T corresponds to a *sequence of decisions* made leading to
a junction point in the maze. The children of a node correspond to the various
branches from that junction point, where we restrict the choice of branches to
those not leading to a junction already visited (this avoids cycles, yielding a finite
tree). The left-hand backtracking algorithm is based on performing a depth-first
search of the state-space tree.

10.1 State-Space Trees

The backtracking and branch-and-bound design strategies are applicable to any problem whose solution can be expressed as a sequence of decisions. Both backtracking and branch-and-bound are based on a search of an associated state-space tree that models all possible sequences of decisions. There may be several different ways to model decision sequences for a given problem, with each model leading to a different state-space tree. We assume in our model for the decision-making process that the decision x_k at stage k must be drawn from a finite set of choices. For each $k > 1$, the choices available for decision x_k may be limited by the choices that have already been made for $x_1, \dots, x_{k-1}$.

For a given problem instance, suppose n is the maximum number of decision stages that can occur. For $k \leq n$, we let P_k denote the set of all possible sequences of k decisions, represented by k-tuples $(x_1, x_2, \dots, x_k)$. Elements of P_k are called *problem states*, and problem states that correspond to solutions to the problem are called *goal states*.

Given a problem state $(x_1, \dots, x_{k-1}) \in P_{k-1}$, we let $D_k(x_1, \dots, x_{k-1})$ denote the *decision set* consisting of the set of all possible choices for decision x_k. Letting $\varnothing$ denote the null tuple ( ), note that $D_1(\varnothing)$ is the set of choices for x_1.

The decision sets $D_k(x_1, \dots, x_{k-1})$, $k = 1, \dots, n$, determine a decision tree T of depth n, called the *state-space tree*. The nodes of T at level k, $0 \leq k \leq n$, are the problem states $(x_1, \dots, x_k) \in P_k$ (P_0 consists of the null tuple). For $1 \leq k < n$, the children of $(x_1, \dots, x_{k-1})$ are the problem states $\{(x_1, \dots, x_k) \mid x_k \in D_k(x_1, \dots, x_{k-1})\}$.

A state-space tree that models a problem whose set of decision choices $D_k(x_1, \dots, x_{k-1})$ depends only on the input size is called *static*. A state-space tree in which D_k depends on not only the input size but also the particular input is called *dynamic*. For example, if we are solving the knapsack problem with objects $b_0, \dots, b_{n-1}$, a static state-space tree might be one in which the first decision is whether to include b_0, the second decision is whether to include b_1, and so forth (we are describing what we will call the static *fixed-tuple* state-space tree for the knapsack problem). On the other hand, based on some heuristic dependent on $b_0, \dots, b_{n-1}$, we might decide that our first decision is whether to include b_m, where m could be different from zero. Similar comments hold for other levels in the tree, leading to a dynamic state-space tree modeling the knapsack problem. In this chapter, we always use static state-space trees, but we do introduce a dynamic state-space tree in connection with the backtracking solution to the conjunctive normal form (CNF) satisfiability problem developed in the exercises.

10.1.1 An Example

Our first illustration of state-space trees is for the *sum of subsets problem*. An input to the sum of subsets problem is a multiset $A = \{a_0, \ldots, a_{n-1}\}$ of n positive integers, together with a positive integer *Sum*. A solution to the sum of subsets problem is a subset of elements $a_{i_1}, \ldots, a_{i_k}$ of A, $i_1 < \cdots < i_k$, such that $a_{i_1} + \cdots + a_{i_k} = Sum$.

The sum of subsets problem can be interpreted as the problem of making correct change, where a_i represents the denomination of the $(i + 1)^{st}$ coin, $i = 0, \ldots, n - 1$, and *Sum* represents the desired change. This differs from the version of the coin-changing problem discussed in Chapter 7, because here a limited number of coins of each denomination are available. For example, consider the multiset $A = \{25, 1, 1, 1, 5, 10, 1, 10, 25\}$. The denominations are 1, 5, 10, 25, which occur with multiplicities 4, 1, 2, 2, respectively.

There are two natural ways to model a decision sequence leading to a solution to the sum of subsets problem. In the first model, a problem state consists of choosing k elements $a_{i_1}, \ldots, a_{i_k}$ of A, $i_1 < \cdots < i_k$, in succession, for some $k \in \{1, \ldots, n\}$. The decision sequence can be represented by the k-tuple $(x_1, \ldots, x_k) = (i_1, \ldots, i_k)$, where x_j corresponds to the decision to choose element a_i at stage j, $1 \leq j \leq k$. For example, consider the instance $n = 5$, and suppose that we have decided to choose the second, fourth, and fifth elements. Then $x_1 = 1$, $x_2 = 3$, and $x_3 = 4$, so that the problem state associated with this decision sequence is the 3-tuple $(1, 3, 4)$.

Given that problem state $(x_1, \ldots, x_{k-1})$ has occurred (that is, the decision has been made to choose elements $a_{x_1}, \ldots, a_{x_{k-1}}$), then the available choices for decision x_k are $a_{x_{k-1}+1}, \ldots, a_n$, yielding

$$D_k(x_1, \ldots, x_{k-1}) = \{x_{k-1} + 1, x_{k-1} + 2, \ldots, n - 1\}, \quad 1 \leq k \leq n. \quad \textbf{(10.1.1)}$$

For example, suppose $n = 5$ and that problem state $(0, 2)$ has occurred. The only elements available for the third decision are a_3 and a_4, so that $D_3(0, 2) = \{3, 4\}$. Figure 10.3 illustrates the state-space tree T determined by $D_k(x_1, \ldots, x_{k-1})$ for the sum of subsets problem, where $n = 5$. The goal states (nodes) are not determined until a particular instance of the problem is specified. For example, for the instance $A = \{1, 4, 5, 10, 4\}$ and *Sum* = 9, the goal states are $(0, 2, 4)$, $(1, 2)$, and $(2, 4)$. On the other hand, for the same set A, if *Sum* = 10, then the goal states are $(0, 1, 2)$, (3), and $(0, 2, 4)$. State-space trees like this, in which the size of the goal states can vary for the same input size, are called *variable-tuple* state-space trees.

The second natural way to model the sum of subsets problem is an example of a *fixed-tuple* model, in which goal states can be considered as n-tuples. In this

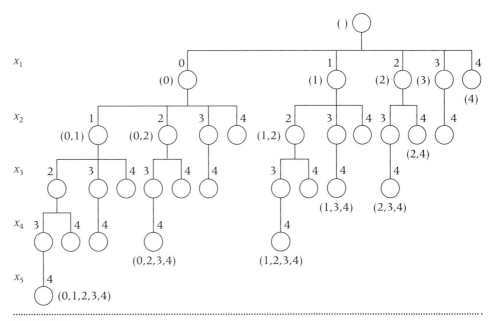

FIGURE 10.3

Variable-tuple state-space tree T modeling the decision set D_k given by Formula (10.1.1) for the sum of subsets problem with $n = 5$. Edges are labeled with the indices of the chosen elements. Index values of the problem states are shown outside some sample nodes.

model, the decision at stage k is whether to choose element a_{k-1}, $1 \le k \le n$. Thus, $D_k = \{0, 1\}$, where $x_k = 1$ if element a_{k-1} is chosen, and $x_k = 0$ otherwise. Thus, the state-space tree T associated with the decision sets $D_k(x_1, \ldots, x_{k-1})$ is the full binary tree on $2^{n+1} - 1$ nodes, with a left child of a node at level $k - 1$ corresponding to choosing a_{k-1} ($x_k = 1$) and a right child corresponding to omitting a_{k-1} ($x_k = 0$), so that

$$D_k(x_1, \ldots, x_{k-1}) = \{0, 1\}, \quad 1 \le k \le n. \tag{10.1.2}$$

Figure 10.4 shows the fixed-tuple state-space tree for the same sum of subsets problem illustrated in Figure 10.3. For the same instance $A = \{1, 4, 5, 10, 4\}$ and $Sum = 9$ considered earlier, the goal states are now represented by the 5-tuples (1, 1, 0, 0, 1), (0, 1, 1, 0, 0), and (0, 0, 1, 0, 1).

10.1.2 Searching State-space Trees

The state-space tree for most problems is large (exponential or worse in the input size). Thus, while a brute-force search of the entire state-space tree has the advantage of always finding a goal state if one exists, the search might not end in

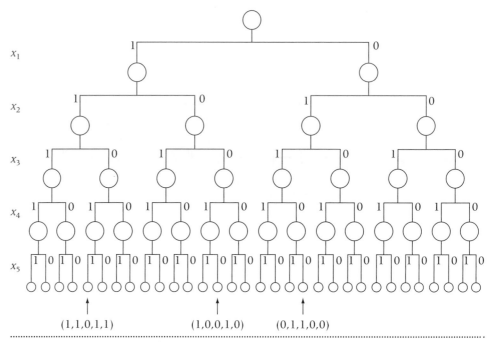

FIGURE 10.4

Fixed-tuple state-space tree T modeling the decision set D_k given by Formula (10.1.2) for the sum of subsets problem with $n = 5$. Edges ending at level k are labeled 1 or 0, depending on whether a_k was chosen or not. Labels of the path from the root to some sample leaf nodes shown.

a single lifetime, even for relatively small input sizes. However, we can often determine that there is no goal node in the subtree rooted at a given node X in the state-space tree. In this case, we say that X is *bounded*, and we can prune the state-space tree by eliminating the descendants of node X. Thus, when searching state-space trees, we look for good bounding functions. *Bounded* is a Boolean function such that if *Bounded*(X) is **.true.**, then there is no descendant of X that is a goal node. Good bounding functions can possibly limit the search to relatively small portions of the state-space tree.

> **Key Fact**
>
> **An algorithm that performs a potentially complete search of a state-space tree modeling a given problem will always find a goal state if one exists. However, the state-space tree usually grows exponentially with the input size to the problem, so unless good bounding functions can be found to limit the search, such an algorithm will usually be too inefficient in the worst case to be practical.**

In this chapter, we discuss two general-purpose design strategies based on searching the state-space tree associated with a given problem: *backtracking* and *branch-and-bound*. The state-space tree is usually implicit to backtracking algorithms, whereas branch-and-bound algorithms usually require the state-space tree to be explicitly implemented. Backtracking is based on a depth-first search of the state-space tree. When a node is accessed during a backtracking search, it becomes the current node being expanded (called the *E*-node), but immediately, its first child not yet visited becomes the new *E*-node. On the other hand, branch-and-bound algorithms are based on breadth-first searches of the state-space tree that generate all the children of the *E*-node when the node is first accessed. Thus, a node can be the *E*-node many times during a backtracking search, but a node is the *E*-node at most once during a branch-and-bound algorithm. There are various versions of branch-and-bound, differing only in the manner in which the next *E*-node is chosen. For example, the children might be placed on a queue (FIFO branch-and-bound), a stack (LIFO branch-and-bound), or a priority queue (least-cost branch-and-bound).

> **Key Fact**
>
> **Backtracking is based on a depth-first search of the state-space tree *T*, and only needs to explicitly maintain the current path (or problem state) at any given point in the search. Branch-and-bound is based on a breadth-first search and normally needs to explicitly maintain the entire portion already reached in the search (except for nodes that are bounded).**

As mentioned earlier, unless good bounding functions can be found, backtracking and branch-and-bound tend to be inefficient in the worst case. However, they can be applied in a wider variety of settings than the other major design strategies that we have discussed. Moreover, there are many practical and important problems for which the best solutions known are based on backtracking or branch-and-bound together with clever heuristics to bound the search. This is especially true for the NP-complete problems, such as the fundamental problem of determining the satisfiability of CNF Boolean expressions. The best-known solutions to CNF satisfiability are based on backtracking searches of dynamic state-space trees modeling the input as determined by clever heuristics and bounding strategies.

 ## 10.2 Backtracking

Before stating the general backtracking design strategy, we illustrate the method by applying it to the sum of subsets problem discussed in the previous section.

10.2.1 A Backtracking Algorithm for the Sum of Subsets Problem

Initially, we will not assume that the set $A = \{a_0, \ldots, a_{n-1}\}$ is ordered. (Later, we show that by sorting A in increasing order, we can obtain an improved bounding function.) We use the decision sequence formulation corresponding to the variable-tuple state-space tree, so that the decision sets $D_k(x_1, \ldots, x_{k-1})$ are given by Formula (10.1.1).

To motivate the definition of a bounding function for the problem states, we consider the instance of the sum of subsets problem where $n = 5$, $A = \{1, 4, 5, 10, 4\}$, and $Sum = 9$. The state-space tree for this instance, and the three goal states $(x_1, x_2, x_3) = (0, 1, 4)$, $(x_1, x_2) = (1, 2)$, and $(x_1, x_2) = (2, 4)$, are shown in Figure 10.5.

For example, consider the problem state $(0, 1, 2)$ in the state-space tree in Figure 10.5 corresponding to the choice of elements a_0, a_1, a_2. Note that $a_0 + a_1 + a_2 = 10 > Sum = 9$. Further, any extension of $(0, 1, 2)$ corresponds to a set of elements whose sum is even greater than 10. Thus, there is no path in the state-space tree from $(0, 1, 2)$ to a goal state. In other words, *"You can't get there from here!"* (See Figure 10.6.) We *bound* node $(0, 1, 2)$ because there is no need to examine any of its descendants.

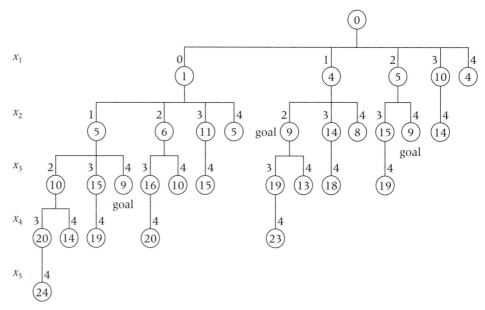

FIGURE 10.5

Variable-tuple state-space tree for sum of subsets problem with $A = \{1, 4, 5, 10, 4\}$ and $Sum = 9$. The value of the sum of the elements chosen is shown inside each node. Edges are labeled with the indices of the chosen elements.

FIGURE 10.6

A bounded node

Source: © 1996 by Sidney
Harris. Altered and
reprinted with
permission. All rights
reserved.

For the general problem state $(x_1, \ldots, x_k) \in P_k$, we define the bounding function *Bounded*$(x_1, \ldots, x_k)$ by

$$Bounded(x_1, \ldots, x_k) = \begin{cases} \textbf{.true.} & \text{if } s_{x_1} + \cdots + s_{x_k} \geq Sum, \\ \textbf{.false.} & \text{otherwise.} \end{cases} \quad \textbf{(10.2.1)}$$

Clearly, if the elements corresponding to $(x_1, \ldots, x_k)$ have a sum greater than or equal to *Sum*, then any extension of $(x_1, \ldots, x_k)$ corresponds to a set of elements whose sum is strictly greater than *Sum*. Thus, if *Bounded*$(x_1, \ldots, x_k) =$ **.true.**, then no descendant of $(x_1, \ldots, x_k)$ can be a goal state. For the problem instance $A = (1, 4, 5, 10, 4)$, Figure 10.7 shows the state-space tree T (from Figure 10.5) after it has been pruned at all the nodes bounded by Formula (10.2.1). The bounded nodes are labeled B, except the bounded nodes that are also goal nodes, which are so labeled. The unlabeled leaves correspond to nodes that were leaves in the original state-space T, before pruning.

The backtracking strategy performs a depth-first search of the state-space tree T, using an appropriate bounding function. By convention, when moving from an E-node to the next level of the state-space tree, we select the leftmost child not already visited. If no such child exists, or if the E-node is bounded, then we backtrack to the previous level. If only one solution to the problem is desired,

FIGURE 10.7

Pruned state-space tree for the sum of subsets problem with $A = \{1, 4, 5, 10, 4\}$ and $Sum = 9$. Edges are labeled with the indices of the chosen elements. Bounded nodes are labeled B.

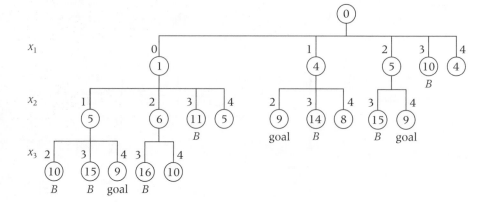

then the backtracking algorithm terminates once a goal state is found. Otherwise, the algorithm continues until all the nodes have been exhausted, outputting each goal state when it is reached.

We now give pseudocode for nonrecursive and recursive backtracking procedures for solving the sum of subsets problem. These procedures perform a depth-first search of the variable-tuple state-space tree T, using the bounding function given in Formula (10.2.1). The procedures output all goal nodes but can be trivially modified to terminate once the first goal state is found.

```
procedure SumOfSubsets(A[0:n − 1], Sum, X[0:n])
Input:    A[0:n − 1] (an array of positive integers)
          Sum (a positive integer)
          X[0:n] (an array of integers where X[1:n] stores variable-tuple problem states,
          and X[0] = −1 for convenience of pseudocode)
Output:   print all goal states; that is, print all (X[1], … , X[k]) such that
              A[X[1]] + ⋯ + A[X[k]] = Sum
          for i ← 0 to n do
              X[i] ← −1
          endfor
          PathSum ← 0
          k ← 1
          while k ≥ 1 do                    //E-node is (X[1], … , X[k − 1]). Initially
                                             // E-node = ( ) corresponding to root

              ChildSearch ← .true.
              while ChildSearch do           // searching for unbounded child of E-node
                  if X[k] = −1 then
                      X[k] ← X[k − 1] + 1    // visit first child of E-node
                  else
                      X[k] ← X[k] + 1        //visit next child of E-node
```

```
            endif
            if X[k] > n − 1 then                    // no more children of E-node
                ChildSearch ← .false.
            else
                PathSum ← PathSum + A[X[k]]
                if PathSum ≥ Sum then               //(X[1], ... , X[k]) is bounded
                    if PathSum = Sum then
                        Print(X[1], ... , X[k])      //print goal state
                        PathSum ← PathSum − A[X[k]]
                    endif
                else                                 //(X[1], ... , X[k]) is not bounded
                    ChildSearch ← .false.
                endif
            endif
        endwhile
        if X[k] > n − 1 then
            X[k] = 0            //backtrack to previous level; no more children of E-node
            k ← k − 1
        else
            k ← k + 1           //go one more level deep in state-space tree
        endif
    endwhile
end SumOfSubsets
```

The following recursive backtracking algorithm *SumOfSubsetsRec*(k) for the sum of subsets problem is called initially with $k = 0$. We assume that $A[0{:}n − 1]$, *Sum*, and $X[0{:}n − 1]$ are global variables. When calling *SumOfSubsetsRec* with input parameter k, it is assumed that $X[1], \ldots, X[k]$ have already been assigned values, so that $k = 0$ on the initial call.

```
procedure SumOfSubsetsRec(k) recursive
Input:    k (a nonnegative integer, 0 on initial call)
          A[0:n − 1] (global array of positive integers)
          Sum (global positive integer)
          X[0:n] (an array of integers, where X[1:n] stores variable-tuple problem states,
          X[1], ... , X[k] have already been assigned, and where X[0] = −1 for
          convenience of pseudocode)
          PathSum (global variable = A[X[1]] + ⋯ + A[X[k]])
Output:   print all descendant goal states of (X[1], ⋯ , X[k]); that is, print all (X[1], ... ,
          X[k], X[k + 1], ... , X[q]) such that A[X[1]] + ⋯ + A[X[k]] + A[X[k + 1]] +
          ⋯ + A[X[q]] = Sum
    k ← k + 1                               // move on to next level
```

```
    for Child ← X[k − 1] + 1 to n − 1 do
        X[k] ← Child
            PathSum ← PathSum + A[X[k]]
        if PathSum ≥ Sum then                    //(X[1], ... , X[k]) is bounded
            if PathSum = Sum then
                Print(X[1], ... , X[k])          // print goal state
                    PathSum ← PathSum − A[X[k]]
            endif
        else                                     //(X[1], ... , X[k]) is not bounded
            SumOfSubsetsRec(k)
        endif
    endfor
end SumOfSubsetsRec
```

If the elements $a_0, \ldots, a_{n-1}$ are first sorted in increasing order (the reverse of the ordering used by the greedy algorithm for the coin-changing problem), then the following bounding function can be used for the problem states $(x_1, \ldots, x_k)$. The bounding function (10.2.2) is stronger than that given by (10.2.1).

$$Bounded(x_1, \ldots, x_k) = \begin{cases} \textbf{.true.} & \text{if } a_{x_1} + \cdots + a_{x_k} + a_{x_k+1} > Sum, \\ \textbf{.false.} & \text{otherwise} \end{cases} \quad \textbf{(10.2.2)}$$

Because $a_0 \le a_1 \le \cdots \le a_{n-1}$, whenever the elements corresponding to problem state $(x_1, \ldots, x_k, x_k + 1)$ have a sum strictly greater than *Sum*, then the elements corresponding to any problem state $(x_1, \ldots, x_k, x_{k+1})$ also have a sum strictly greater than *Sum*. Thus, (10.2.2) is a valid bounding function. *SumOfSubsets* and *SumOfSubsetsRec* can be easily modified to use the bounding function given in 10.2.2

10.2.2 The General Backtracking Paradigm

The following general backtracking paradigm, *Backtrack*, follows the backtracking strategy we just described for the sum of subsets problem. *Backtrack* finds all solutions to a given problem by searching for all goal states in a state-space tree associated with the problem. *Backtrack* invokes a bounding function, *Bounded*, for the problem states. The definition of *Bounded* depends on the particular problem being solved. We assume that an implicit ordering exists for the elements of $D_k(x_1, \ldots, x_{k-1})$.

```
procedure Backtrack()
Input:      T (implicit state-space tree associated with the given problem)
            D_k (decision set, where D_k = Ø for k ≥ n)
            Bounded (bounding function)
Output:  all goal states
         k ← 1
           while k ≥ 1 do                          //E-node is (X[1], ... , X[k − 1]). Initially
                                                    //E-node = ( ) corresponding to root.

               Searching ← .true.
               while Searching do                   //searching for unbounded child
                   X[k] ← first of the remaining untried values from D_k(X[1], ... , X[k − 1]),
                          where this value is Ø if all values in D_k(X[1], ... , X[k − 1]) have
                          been tried
                   if X[k] ← Ø then
                       Searching ← .false.
                   else
                       if (X[1], ... , X[k]) is a goal state then
                           Print(X[1], ... , X[k])
                       endif
                       if .not. Bounded(X[1], ... , X[k]) then
                           Searching ← .false.
                       endif
                   endif
               endwhile
                   if X[k] = Ø then
                       Arrange for all values in D_k to be considered as untried
                       k ← k − 1                    //backtrack to previous level
                   else
                       k ← k + 1                    //move on to next level
                   endif
           endwhile
end Backtrack
```

The procedure *BacktrackRec* is the recursive version of the procedure *Back-track*. Since we are essentially performing a depth-first search of the state-space tree T starting at the root, *BacktrackRec(k)* is initially called with $k = 0$. Note how elegantly the recursion implements the backtracking process. We assume that $D_k(X[1], ... , X[k])$ is empty for $k \geq n$.

```
procedure BacktrackRec(k) recursive
Input:      T (implicit state-space tree associated with the given problem)
            k (a nonnegative integer, 0 in initial call)
            D_k (decision set, where D_k = Ø for k ≥ n)
```

$X[0:n]$ (global array where $X[1:n]$ maintains the problem states of T, and where the problem state $(X[1], \dots , X[k])$ has already been generated)

Bounded (bounding function)

Output: all goals that are descendants of $(X[1], \dots , X[k])$

$k \leftarrow k + 1$

for each $x_k \in D_k(X[1], \dots , X[k-1])$ **do**

$X[k] \leftarrow x_k$

if $(X[1], \dots , X[k])$ is a goal state **then**

Print$(X[1], \dots , X[k])$

endif

if .not. *Bounded*$(X[1], \dots , X[k])$ **then**

BacktrackRec(k)

endif

endfor

end *BacktrackRec*

REMARKS

1. Often, computing only one goal state is required. We can easily modify the procedures *Backtrack* and *BacktrackRec* to halt once the first goal state is reached.

2. Notice that in a slight variation from the pseudocode for procedures *Backtrack* and *BacktrackRec*, the *SumOfSubsets* and *SumOfSubsetsRec* pseudocode only checks for a goal state after determining that a problem state is bounded. Putting off this check for a goal state applies to any problem where all the goal states are bounded.

10.2.3 Tic-Tac-Toe

Consider the problem of finding a tie board (result of a "cat's game") in the familiar game of tic-tac-toe. Here we are trying to determine whether tie games are possible, not to devise a strategy for playing the game. (In Chapter 23, we consider the problem of designing strategies for various perfect-information games such as tic-tac-toe.)

The game of tic-tac-toe involves two players A and B, who alternately place Xs and Os into unoccupied positions on a board such as the one shown in Figure 10.8.

FIGURE 10.8

A 3 × 3 tic-tac-toe tie board

X	X	O
O	O	X
X	X	O

We assume that player A starts by placing an X in any position, and then player B places an O in any remaining position. The two players continue to alternately place Xs and Os on the board until either there are three Xs in a row (horizontally, vertically, or diagonally) so that A wins, there are three Os in a row so that B wins, or all nine positions are occupied with no three Os or three Xs in a row and the game is a tie (a cat's game).

We use backtracking to find a tie board — that is, a board corresponding to a tie game (see Figure 10.8). In fact, we solve the problem for an $n \times n$ board, where a *tie board* contains no "three in row" of either Xs or Os in any 3×3 subboard of contiguous positions in the $n \times n$ board. In our definition of a tie board, we do not assume that the number of Xs and the number of Os differ by at most 1. However, it is interesting that all tie boards in the $n \times n$ board have this property, so we don't need to check for it in our backtracking algorithm.

We refer to the cell in row i and column j of the $n \times n$ board as cell (i, j), $i, j \in \{1, \dots, n\}$. We also refer to cell (i, j) as the cell labeled k, where $k = n(i - 1) + j$; that is, k is a *row-major* labeling (see Figure 10.9). Row-major labeling of the cells is useful in defining the problem states P_k. However, when defining the bounding function, it is more convenient to use row-column labeling. The problem of finding a board filled with Xs and Os, containing no three in a row in either Xs or Os, can be expressed as a sequence of decisions in which the decision at stage k is whether to place an X or O in the cell labeled k. We set $x_k = 1$ if an X is placed

FIGURE 10.9

(a) Row-column labeling (i, j); (b) row-major labeling k; and (c) a 3×3 board configuration corresponding to the 7-tuple (1, 1, 0, 1, 0, 0, 1)

(1,1)	(1,2)	(1,3)
(2,1)	(2,2)	(2,3)
(3,1)	(3,2)	(3,3)

(a)

1	2	3
4	5	6
7	8	9

(b)

X	X	O
X	O	O
X		

(c)

in cell k in the kth stage; otherwise, $x_k = 0$. Thus, $D_k = \{0, 1\}$, and the problem states of size k, $1 \leq k \leq n$, are given by

$$P_k = \{(x_1, \ldots, x_k) \,|\, x_1, \ldots, x_k \in \{0, 1\}\}. \qquad \textbf{(10.2.3)}$$

The (fixed-tuple) state-space tree T for tic-tac-toe is identical to the fixed-tuple state-space tree for the sum of subsets problem; namely, T is the full binary tree on $2^{n+1} - 1$ nodes. Figure 10.9c shows the 3 $\times$ 3 board configuration corresponding to the 7-tuple $(1, 1, 0, 1, 0, 0, 1)$.

An obvious bounding function for tic-tac-toe is given by

$$Bounded(x_1, \ldots, x_k) = \begin{cases} \textbf{.true.} & \text{if board configuration corresponding} \\ & \text{to } (x_1, \ldots, x_k) \text{ contains 3 in a row,} \quad \textbf{(10.2.4)} \\ \textbf{.false.} & \text{otherwise.} \end{cases}$$

Note that $Bounded = \textbf{.true.}$ for the problem state $(1, 1, 0, 1, 0, 0, 1)$ in Figure 10.9. If the board configuration corresponding to the problem state $(x_1, \ldots, x_k)$ already contains three in a row (in either Xs or Os), then it obviously cannot be extended to a board configuration not containing three in a row. In particular, it cannot be extended to a goal state.

Before giving pseudocode for the algorithm *TicTacToe* solving the problem of finding an $n \times n$ generalized tie board configurations, we give pseudocode for the Boolean function *BoundedBoard* based on Formula (10.2.4). The board configuration is represented by the two-dimensional array $B[-1:n + 2, -1:n + 2]$, in which, for convenient implementation of *BoundedBoard* (and by abuse of notation), we assume the existence of "border" rows and columns indexed by -1, 0, $n + 1$, $n + 2$. The cells corresponding to these rows and columns are always empty; that is, $B[i, j] = $ "E" if either $i \in \{-1, 0, n + 1, n + 2\}$ or $j \in \{-1, 0, n + 1, n + 2\}$. We illustrate a bordered 4 $\times$ 4 board in Figure 10.10, together with an assignment of Xs and Os to the positions $k = 1, \ldots, 10$.

We assume that the two-dimensional array $B[-1:n + 2, -1:n + 2]$ is global to the function *BoundedBoard*. We refer to a set of three adjacent cells along a horizontal, vertical, or diagonal line as a *winning line*. Suppose the board configuration restricted to the cells labeled $1, 2, \ldots, k - 1$ in the row-major labeling of the 4 $\times$ 4 board contains no three in a row in either Xs or Os. Then, to determine whether the board configuration restricted to the cells labeled $1, 2, \ldots, k$ contains three in a row in either Xs or Os, we merely need to check all winning lines containing the cell labeled k. Four winning lines need to be checked: one horizontal, one vertical, and two diagonal. Figure 10.11 shows these lines for the cell in the board of Figure 10.10 whose row-major label is $k = 11$.

E	E	E	E	E	E	E	E
E	E	E	E	E	E	E	E
E	E	X	X	O	X	E	E
E	E	X	X	O	X	E	E
E	E	O	O	E	E	E	E
E	E	E	E	E	E	E	E
E	E	E	E	E	E	E	E
E	E	E	E	E	E	E	E

E	E	E	E	E	E	E	E
E	E	E	E	E	E	E	E
E	E	X	X	O	X	E	E
E	E	X	X	O	X	E	E
E	E	O	O	□	E	E	E
E	E	E	E	E	E	E	E
E	E	E	E	E	E	E	E
E	E	E	E	E	E	E	E

The following Boolean function *BoundedBoard*(*i*, *j*) returns the value **.true.** if and only if the board configuration corresponding to $B[-1:n + 2, -1:n + 2]$ contains all *X*s or *O*s in one of the four winning lines previously described.

```
function BoundedBoard(i, j)
Input:    B[−1:n + 2, −1:n + 2]          (global array corresponding to board
                                          configuration)
          i, j                           (integers between 1 and n, inclusive)
Output:   returns .true. if the board configuration involving the cells labeled 1, … ,
          k = n(i − 1) + j, contains three in a row in either Xs or Os along a line
          containing the cell labeled k.
     LineH ← (B[i, j] = B[i, j − 1]) .and. (B[i, j] = B[i, j − 2])
     LineV ← (B[i, j] = B[i − 1, j]) .and. (B[i, j] = B[i − 2, j])
     LineD1 ← (B[i, j] = B[i − 1, j − 1]) .and. (B[i, j] = B[i − 2, j − 2])
     LineD2 ← (B[i, j] = B[i − 1, j + 1]) .and. (B[i, j] = B[i − 2, j + 2])
     return(LineH .or. LineV .or. LineD1 .or. LineD2)
end BoundedBoard
```

We now give pseudocode for the algorithm *TicTacToe*. *TicTacToe* calls the procedures *Previous*(*i*, *j*) and *Next*(*i*, *j*), which accomplish the operations of backtracking to the previous cell ($k = k - 1$) and moving forward to the next cell ($k = k + 1$), respectively, in the row-major labeling. Thus, *Previous*(*i*, *j*) executes the statement

```
if j > 1 then
     j ← j − 1
else
     i ← i − 1
     j ← n
endif
```

and *Next*(*i*, *j*) executes the statement

```
if j < n then
     j ← j + 1
else
     i ← i + 1
     j ← 1
endif
```

```
procedure TicTacToe(n)
Input:    n (a positive integer representing size of board)
Output:   all generalized tie board configurations; that is, all board configurations not
          containing three in a row in either Xs or Os
    for i ← −1 to n + 2 do
        for j ← −1 to n + 2 do
            B[i, j] ← 'E';                    //initialize all positions on board to empty
        endfor
    endfor
    i ← 1                                     //k = 1
    j ← 1
    while i > 0 do
        if B[i, j] = 'O' then                 //backtrack: k = k − 1
            B[i, j] ← 'E'
            Previous(i, j)
        else
            if B[i, j] = 'E' then
                B[i, j] ← 'X'                 //visit left child of E-node
            else
                B[i, j] ← 'O'                 //visit right child of E-node
            endif
            if .not. BoundedBoard(i, j) then
                if (i = n) .and. (j = n) then
                    PrintBoard(Board[1:n, 1:n])    //print goal state
                else
                    Next(i, j)
                endif
            endif
        endif
    endwhile
end TicTacToe
```

We can write a recursive version, *TicTacToeRec(i, j)*, of *TicTacToe* as follows. *Tic-TacToeRec(i, j)* is initially called with $i = 0$ and $j = n$ ($k = 0$). The augmented board *Board* is initialized to "E."

```
procedure TicTacToeRec(i, j) recursive
Input:    i, j  (integers between 1 and n, inclusive, called initially with i = 0 and j = n)
          B[−1:n + 2, −1:n + 2]        (global array corresponding to board
              configuration, initialized to "E," and B[1, 1], ... , B[i, j] filled with Xs and
              Os with no three in a row)
Output:   all extensions of B[1, 1], ... , B[i, j] to goal states; that is, board configurations
          not containing three in a row in either Xs or Os
```

```
Next(i, j)                                          //k = k + 1
for Child ← 1 to 2 do
    if Child = 1 then
        B[i, j] ← 'X'
    else
        B[i, j] ← 'O'
    endif
    if .not. BoundedBoard(i, j) then
        if (i = n) .and. (j = n) then
            PrintBoard(Board[1:n, 1:n])             //print goal state
        else
            TicTacToeRec(i, j)
        endif
    endif
endfor
end TicTacToeRec
```

10.2.5 Solving Optimization Problems Using Backtracking

Backtracking is frequently used to solve optimization problems—that is, to optimize (maximize or minimize) an objective function f over all goal states for a given problem. For example, for a sum of subsets problem interpreted as a coin-changing problem, we want to make correct change using the fewest coins (the objective function f is the number of coins). To do so, we use the following generic backtracking paradigm for solving the problem of minimizing the objective function (the paradigm is easily altered to solve maximization problems). Given an objective function f, let f^* denote the minimum of f over all solution states. A solution state X such that $f(X) = f^*$ is a goal state. Note that for *any* solution state $X = (x_1, \dots, x_k)$, the value $f(X)$ is an upper bound for f^*. We maintain a variable UB, initialized to infinity. Additionally, at each stage of the backtracking algorithm, we maintain a solution state *CurrentBest* such that $UB = f(Current Best)$ is the minimum value of f over all solution states generated so far. For many problems, we can efficiently compute a function $LowerBound(x_1, \dots, x_k)$ that is not larger than the value of f on any solution state belonging to the subtree of the state-space tree rooted at $(x_1, \dots, x_k)$. We can then dynamically bound a problem state $(x_1, \dots, x_k)$ if $LowerBound(x_1, \dots, x_k) \geq UB$. For example, in the coin-changing problem modeled on the variable-tuple state-space tree, $LowerBound(x_1, \dots, x_k) = k$ if $(x_1, \dots, x_k)$ is a goal state; otherwise, $LowerBound(x_1, \dots, x_k) = k + 1$.

The generic backtracking paradigm for minimizing an objective function is based on the strategy just outlined. We describe the recursive version *Backtrack-*

MinRec of the paradigm, and leave the iterative version *BacktrackMin* as an exercise. The following high-level recursive procedure *BacktrackMinRec* is called initially with $k = 0$. During its resolution, *BacktrackMinRec* calls a function *StaticBounded*, which plays the same role as the function *Bounded* used for nonoptimization problems. For example, in the optimization version of the sum of subsets problem with input parameter *Sum*, a problem state is statically bounded if its sum was not smaller than *Sum*, whereas it is dynamically bounded if the cardinality of the subset corresponding to the problem state is at least as large as a previously generated solution state. In general, a problem state is either bounded dynamically ($LowerBound(x_1, \ldots, x_k) \geq UB$), or bounded statically ($Static\ Bounded(x_1, \ldots, x_k) = $ **.true.**).

```
procedure BacktrackMinRec(k, CurrentBest) recursive
Input:    T (implicit state-space tree associated with the given problem)
          D_k (decision set, with D_k = Ø for k ≥ n)
          f (objective function defined on problem states)
          k (a nonnegative integer, 0 on initial call)
          X[0:n] (global array where X[1:n] maintains the problem states of T, and where
          the problem state (X[1], … , X[k]) has already been generated)
          StaticBounded (a static bounding function on the problem states)
          LowerBound (a function defined on the problem states)
          CurrentBest (solution state extending (X[1], … , X[k]) with the current
          minimum value of f over all descendants of (X[1], … , X[k]) )
          UB (global variable, initialized to ∞)
Output:   CurrentBest (solution state extending (X[1], … , X[k]) with the minimum value
          of f over all descendants of (X[1], … , X[k]) )
     k ← k + 1
     for each X[k] ∈ D_k(X[1], … , X[k − 1]) do
          if (X[1], … , X[k]) is a solution state then
               if f(X[1], … , X[k]) < UB then
                    UB ← f(X[1], … , X[k])
                    CurrentBest ← (X[1], … , X[k])
               endif
          endif
          if LowerBound(X[1], … , X[k]) < UB .and.
               .not. StaticBounded(X[1], … , X[k]) then
               BacktrackMinRec(k, CurrentBest)
          endif
     endfor
end BacktrackMinRec
```

R E M A R K The paradigm *BacktrackMinRec* ends up returning the first optimal goal state that was encountered. (Of course, unlike nonoptimization problems solved using backtracking, the algorithm has no way of checking that it was an optimal goal state until all goal states have been examined or eliminated.) If all optimal goal states are desired, then *CurrentBest* must maintain *all* the goal states that have the current minimum value of *f*. For example, the sum of subsets problem illustrated in Figure 10.12 has two optimal goal states, represented by the tuples (1, 2) and (2, 4). Procedure *SumOfSubsetsMinRec* only outputs the goal state (1, 2).

The algorithm *BacktrackMinRec* is easily altered to apply to optimization problems where we wish to maximize the objective function *f*. For such problems, *LB* is the current maximum value of *f*, and *UpperBound*$(x_1, \ldots, x_k)$ is an upper bound for the maximum value of *f* over all solution states in the subtree of the state-space tree rooted at $(x_1, \ldots, x_k)$. Alternatively, a problem involving maximizing an objective function *f* can be canonically transformed into an equivalent problem of minimizing the associated objective function $g = M - f$, where *M* is a suitable constant. By replacing *f* by $M - f$ in a maximization problem, *BacktrackMinRec* can be applied directly to solve both minimization and maximization problems. Of course, *M* can be taken as zero, but for a given problem a nonzero value of *M* might yield a natural interpretation for *g*. For example, for the 0/1 knapsack problem, if *M* is taken as the sum of the values of all of the input objects, then $M - f$ is the sum of the values of the objects left out of the knapsack.

As our first illustration of the use of *BacktrackMinRec*, we show how it can be directly translated into a solution for the optimization version of the sum of subsets problem, where goal states are solution states having minimum cardinality. Thus, *UB* is the smallest cardinality of a solution state currently generated. Note that a problem state $(x_1, \ldots, x_k)$ corresponding to a subset of cardinality *k* can be dynamically bounded if *k* is not smaller than the current value of *UB*. Interpreting dynamic bounding in terms of the generic paradigm *BacktrackMinRec*, we see that *LowerBound*$(x_1, \ldots, x_k) = k + 1$ if $x_1 + \cdots + x_k < Sum$; otherwise, *LowerBound*$(x_1, \ldots, x_k) = k$.

procedure *SumOfSubsetsMinRec*(*k*, *CurrentBest*) **recursive**
Input: *k* (a nonnegative integer, 0 on initial call)
         A[0:*n* − 1] (global array of positive integers)
         Sum (global positive integer)
         X[0:*n*] (global array initialized to − 1s. It is assumed that *X*[1], ... , *X*[*k*]
         representing a partial solution is already defined) *CurrentBest* (solution state
         (*X*[1], ... , *X*[*m*]) extending (*X*[1], ... , *X*[*m*]) such that *m* is minimum over all
         currently examined solution states that are descendants of (*X*[1], ... , *X*[*k*]))

PathSum (global variable = $A[X[1]] + \cdots + A[X[k]]$)
UB (global variable, initialized to ∞)

Output: *CurrentBest* (solution state $(X[1], \ldots, X[m])$ such that m is a minimum over all solution states that are descendants of $(X[1], \ldots, X[k])$)

$k \leftarrow k + 1$ //go one level deeper in state-space tree
for *Child* $\leftarrow X[k - 1] + 1$ **to** n **do**
    $X[k] \leftarrow Child$
    Temp $\leftarrow$ *PathSum* $+A\ [X[k]]$
    if *Temp* $\geq$ *Sum* **then**   //$(X[1], \ldots, X[k])$ is statically bounded
        if *Temp* $=$ *Sum* **then**   //$(X[1], \ldots, X[k])$ is a solution state
            if $k <$ *UB* **then**
                UB $\leftarrow k$
                CurrentBest $\leftarrow (X[1], \ldots, X[k])$
            endif
        endif
    else   //$(X[1], \ldots, X[k])$ is not statically bounded
        if $k <$ *UB* **then**   //$(X[1], \ldots, X[k])$ is not dynamically bounded
            PathSum $\leftarrow$ *Temp*
            SumOfSubsetsMinRec(k, *CurrentBest*)
        endif
    endif
endfor
end *SumOfSubsetsMinRec*

The portion of the state-space tree generated by procedure *SumOfSubsets MinRec* is illustrated in Figure 10.12 for a sample set $A = \{1, 4, 5, 10, 4\}$ and *Sum* $= 9$.

SumOfSubsetsMinRec was written as a direct translation of *BacktrackMinRec*. However, since *BacktrackMinRec* is a generic paradigm, it is often the case that additional efficiencies might be possible when adapting it to a specific problem. Indeed, in the variable-tuple implementation of the optimization version of the sum of subsets problem, where a single optimal goal is to be output, when a goal state X is generated, there is no need to generate the remaining siblings of X because the subsets corresponding to these siblings cannot have smaller cardinality than the subset corresponding to X. To implement this improvement in the procedure *CoinChangingRec*, we need only break out of the **for** loop whenever a goal is generated (by simply adding a **break** statement after the assignment updating *CurrentBest*). For example, with this alteration, we would not generate the two siblings of the goal $(X[1] = 1, X[2] = 2)$ in Figure 10.12.

FIGURE 10.12

Portion of the
state-space tree
generated by
procedure
*SumOfSubsetsMin
Rec* for the set A =
{1, 4, 5, 10, 4} and
Sum = 9. Statically
bounded nodes are
labeled *SB*. Nodes
not statically
bounded but
dynamically
bounded are
labeled *DB*. Leaf
nodes in the entire
state-space tree are
unlabeled, unless
they are goals.
Solution states
resulting in updates
to *UB* and
CurrentBest are
labeled with
the updated value
of *UB*. At
termination,
*SumOfSubsetsMin
Rec* outputs the
final value
CurrentBest =
(1, 2).

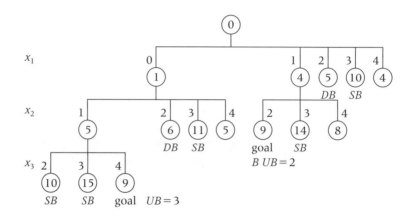

Our next example, the 0/1 knapsack problem, illustrates the transformation of maximization problems into minimization problems. In Chapter 7, an efficient greedy algorithm was given for solving the knapsack problem. The greedy method does not necessarily yield an optimal solution to the 0/1 knapsack problem. In fact, there is no known worst-case polynomial algorithm for solving the 0/1 knapsack problem. However, the greedy algorithm for the knapsack problem helps us to define a useful function *LowerBound* for dynamic bounding in the transformed minimization problem.

Since the 0/1 knapsack problem involves looking at subsets of a set of size n, we may solve the problem using backtracking by searching the same state-space tree as in the sum of subsets problem. Consider the variable-tuple state-space tree determined by (10.1.1) (see Figure 10.3). An obvious static bounding function for the problem state $(x_1, \ldots, x_k)$ is given by

$$\text{Static Bounded}(x_1, \ldots, x_k) = \begin{cases} \textbf{.true.} & \text{if } w_{x_1} + \cdots + w_{x_k} \geq C, \\ \textbf{.false.} & \text{otherwise.} \end{cases} \quad \textbf{(10.2.5)}$$

For $(x_1, \ldots, x_k)$ a problem state, let

$$Value(x_1, \ldots, x_k) = \sum_{i=1}^{k} v_{x_i}.$$

$$\quad \textbf{(10.2.6)}$$

$$Weight(x_1, \ldots, x_k) = \sum_{i=1}^{k} w_{x_i}.$$

For the 0/1 knapsack problem, the solution states consist of all tuples not statically bounded — that is, all tuples $(x_1, \ldots, x_k)$ such that $Weight(x_1, \ldots, x_k) \leq C$

goal states maximize the objective function *Value* over all solution states. The maximization problem is transformed into a minimization problem by letting

$$M = \sum_{i=0}^{n-1} v_i,$$

$$LeftOutVal(x_1, \dots, x_k) = M - Value(x_1, \dots, x_k) \qquad \textbf{(10.2.7)}$$

In other words, *LeftOutVal*$(x_1, \dots, x_k)$ is the total value of all the objects left out of the knapsack corresponding to solution state $(x_1, \dots, x_k)$. In the transformed problem, which we now consider, the objective is to minimize the objective function *LeftOutVal*. To dynamically bound problem states, we maintain a variable *UB*, which at each stage of the backtracking algorithm keeps track of the minimum value of *LeftOutVal*$(x_1, \dots, x_k)$ over all the solution states generated so far.

Consider a solution state $(x_1, \dots, x_k)$ corresponding to the partial filling of the knapsack with the subset of objects $B_k = \{b_{x_1}, \dots, b_{x_k}\}$. Suppose $(x_1, \dots, x_k)$ is not bounded by Formula (10.2.6), and let $C' = C - Weight(x_1, \dots, x_k)$ denote the remaining capacity of the knapsack. Let *LeftOutVal**$(x_1, \dots, x_k)$ denote the minimum value of *LeftOutVal* over all solution states in the state-space subtree rooted at $(x_1, \dots, x_k)$. In other words, *LeftOutVal**$(x_1, \dots, x_k)$ is the smallest value of *LeftOutVal* that can be achieved by placing additional objects in the knapsack from the remaining set of objects $B' = B \backslash B_k$. Clearly, if *LeftOutVal**$(x_1, \dots, x_k) \geq UB$, then $(x_1, \dots, x_k)$ can be dynamically bounded. Unfortunately, there is no known efficient method to compute *LeftOutVal**$(x_1, \dots, x_k)$. In fact, the general problem of computing *LeftOutVal**$(x_1, \dots, x_k)$ is equivalent to the original 0/1 knapsack problem.

Fortunately, we can efficiently compute a useful lower bound for *LeftOutVal**$(x_1, \dots, x_k)$ by applying the greedy algorithm *Knapsack*. For *B*, a given set of objects (with associated values and weights), and *C*, a given capacity for the knapsack, we let *Greedy*(C, B) denote the value of the optimal placement of objects in the knapsack, where fractions of objects are permitted (that is, the value of the knapsack generated by *Knapsack*). We define *LowerBound*$(x_1, \dots, x_k)$ by

$$LowerBound(x_1, \dots, x_k) = LeftOutVal(x_1, \dots, x_k) - Greedy(C', B'). \quad \textbf{(10.2.8)}$$

Clearly, we have

$$LeftOutVal^*(x_1, \dots, x_k) \geq LowerBound(x_1, \dots, x_k).$$

Thus, we can dynamically bound a problem state $(x_1, \dots, x_k)$ if *LowerBound* $(x_1, \dots, x_k) \geq UB$. Figure 10.13 shows the portion of the state-space tree *T* generated by backtracking for a sample instance of the 0/1 knapsack problem.

i	0	1	2	3	4
v_i	16	6	5	12	4
w_i	4	2	2	6	5
v_i/w_i	4	3	2.5	2	.8

, $C = 11$
$M = 43$

(43)

x_1
- $UB = 27$, 0, LoBd (27) $= 10$
- $UB = 15$, 1, LoBd (37) $= 19.2$ DB
- $UB = 15$, 2, LoBd (38) $= 23.6$ DB
- $UB = 15$, 3, LoBd (31) $= 27$ DB
- $UB = 15$, 4, LoBd (39) $= 39$ DB

x_2
- $UB = 21$, 1, LoBd (21) $= 10$
- 2, LoBd (22) $= 12$
- 3, $UB = 15$ LoBd (15) $= 14.2$ optimal goal node
- 4, $UB = 15$ LoBd (23) DB $= 23$

x_3
- $UB = 16$, 2, LoBd (16) $= 10$
- 3, ( ) SB
- 4, $UB = 16$ LoBd (17) DB $= 17$
- 3, ( ) SB
- 4, (18) SB SB
- 4, ( ) SB

x_4
- 3, ( ) SB
- 4, ( ) SB

$LoBd = LowerBound\ (x_1, \dots, x_k)$

FIGURE 10.13

Portion of the variable-tuple state-space tree T generated by the procedure *BacktrackMin* for a sample input to the 0/1 knapsack problem. Problem states that are statically bounded ($Weight(x_1, \dots, x_k) \geq C$) are labeled *SB*, whereas problem states not statically bounded but dynamically bounded (*LowerBound* $(x_1, \dots, x_k) \geq UB$) are labeled *DB*. *LeftOutVal*$(x_1, \dots, x_k)$ is shown inside each solution state. *LowerBound*$(x_1, \dots, x_k)$ and the current value of *UB* are shown outside each problem state where *UB* is updated, or where the problem state is dynamically bounded.

10.3 Branch-and-Bound

> *Cowards die many times before their deaths;*
> *The valiant never taste of death but once.*
> —Shakespeare, *Julius Caesar*, Act II, Scene II

As with backtracking algorithms, branch-and-bound algorithms are based on searches of an associated state-space tree for goal states. However, in a branch-and-bound algorithm, *all* the children of the *E*-node (the node currently being expanded) are generated before the next *E*-node is chosen. When the children are generated, they become *live* nodes and are stored in a suitable data structure, *LiveNodes*. *LiveNodes* is typically a queue, a stack, or a priority queue. Branch-and-bound algorithms using the latter three data structures are called *FIFO* (*first in, first out*) *branch-and-bound*, *LIFO* (*last in, first out*) *branch-and-bound*, and *least cost branch-and-bound*, respectively.

Immediately upon expansion, the current *E*-node becomes a *dead* node and a new *E*-node is selected from *LiveNodes*. Thus, branch-and-bound is quite different from backtracking, where we might backtrack to a given node many times, making it the *E*-node each time until all its children have finally been generated or the algorithm terminates. The nodes of the state-space tree at any given point in a branch-and-bound algorithm are therefore in one of the following four states: *E-node, live node, dead node,* or *not yet generated.*

As with backtracking, the efficiency of branch-and-bound depends on the utilization of good bounding functions. Such functions are used in attempting to determine solutions by restricting attention to small portions of the entire state-space tree. When expanding a given *E*-node, a child can be bounded if it can be shown that it cannot lead to a goal node.

We illustrate branch-and-bound by revisiting the sum of subsets problem, where the data structure *LiveNodes* is a queue. Such a branch-and-bound, called FIFO branch-and-bound, involves performing a breadth-first search of the state-space tree. Initially the queue of live nodes is empty. The algorithm begins by generating the root node of the state-space tree and enqueuing it in the queue *LiveNodes*. At each stage of the algorithm, a node is dequeued from *LiveNodes* to become the new *E*-node. All the children of the *E*-node are then generated. The children that are not bounded are enqueued (as they are generated from left to right). If only one goal state is desired, then the algorithm terminates after the first goal state is found. Otherwise, the algorithm terminates when *LiveNodes* is empty. Because of the nature of FIFO branch-and-bound, the first goal state found for the sum of subsets problems automatically has the smallest cardinality; that is, it solves the coin-changing problem.

Figure 10.14 illustrates FIFO branch-and-bound for the sum of subsets problem for the instance $A = (1, 11, 6, 2, 6, 8, 5)$ and $Sum = 10$. The action of the queue *LiveNodes* and the portion of the state-space tree generated in reaching the first goal state are given. For this instance of the sum of subsets problem, FIFO branch-and-bound generates fewer nodes of the state-space tree before reaching a goal state than are generated by backtracking.

Figure 10.15 illustrates LIFO branch-and-bound, where *LiveNodes* is a stack, for the same instance of the sum of subsets problem given in Figure 10.14. LIFO branch-and-bound is similar to backtracking, except that a move is made to the rightmost child of a node first instead of the leftmost. However, unlike backtracking, all the children of a node are generated before moving on.

LIFO branch-and-bound generates fewer nodes than does FIFO branch-and-bound for the input considered in Figure 10.14, but for other inputs, the opposite can be true. In general, since FIFO branch-and-bound is based on a breadth-first search of the state-space tree, it is more efficient than LIFO branch-and-bound when goal nodes are not very deep in the state-space tree.

FIGURE 10.14

Action of queue
LiveNodes and a
portion of
the variable-tuple
state-space tree
generated by FIFO
branch-and-bound
for the sum of
subsets problem
with $A = \{1, 11, 6,$
$2, 6, 8, 5\}$ and
Sum = 10. The sum
of the elements
chosen is shown
inside each node.

queue *LiveNodes*	
generate ()	enqueue ()
dequeue	*E*-node = ()
generate (0)	enqueue (0)
generate (1)	bounded
generate (2)	enqueue (2)
generate (3)	enqueue (3)
generate (4)	enqueue (4)
generate (5)	enqueue (5)
generate (6)	enqueue (6)
dequeue	*E*-node = (0)
generate (0,1)	bounded
generate (0,2)	enqueue (0,2)
generate (0,3)	enqueue (0,3)
generate (0,4)	enqueue (0,4)
generate (0,5)	enqueue (0,5)
generate (0,6)	enqueue (0,6)
dequeue	*E*-node = (2)
generate (2,3)	enqueue (2,3)
generate (2,4)	bounded
generate (2,5)	bounded
generate (2,6)	bounded
dequeue	*E*-node = (3)
generate (3,4)	enqueue (3,4)
generate (3,5)	goal node

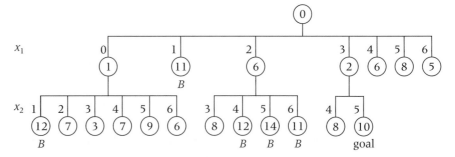

10.3.1 General Branch-and-Bound Paradigm

When we use backtracking, we do not explicitly implement the state-space tree.
However, in branch-and-bound algorithms, we must explicitly implement the
state-space tree and maintain the data structure storing the live nodes. In the
general branch-and-bound paradigm *BranchAndBound*, the state-space tree *T* is
implemented using the parent representation.

FIGURE 10.15

Action of queue
LiveNodes and
a portion of
the variable-tuple
state-space tree
generated by LIFO
branch-and-bound
for the sum of
subsets problem
with $A = \{1, 11, 6,$
$2, 6, 8, 5\}$ and
Sum = 10. The sum
of the elements
chosen is shown
inside each node.

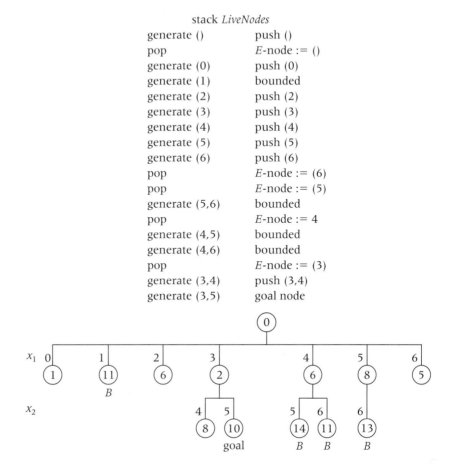

stack *LiveNodes*

generate ()	push ()
pop	E-node := ()
generate (0)	push (0)
generate (1)	bounded
generate (2)	push (2)
generate (3)	push (3)
generate (4)	push (4)
generate (5)	push (5)
generate (6)	push (6)
pop	E-node := (6)
pop	E-node := (5)
generate (5,6)	bounded
pop	E-node := 4
generate (4,5)	bounded
generate (4,6)	bounded
pop	E-node := (3)
generate (3,4)	push (3,4)
generate (3,5)	goal node

The nodes of T that are generated by paradigm *BranchAndBound* are represented as follows:

```
TreeNode = record
       Info:      InfoType
       Parent:    →TreeNode
   end
```

Only the value x_k need be stored in the information field *Info* of the node N corresponding to problem state $(x_1, \ldots, x_k)$. Given a pointer *PtrNode* to N, the entire tuple $(x_1, \ldots, x_k)$ is recovered by following the path in T from N to the root. For convenience, we denote $D_k(x_1, \ldots, x_{k-1})$ by $D_k(PtrNode)$, where *PtrNode* is a pointer to the problem state $(x_1, \ldots, x_{k-1})$.

The next E-node is chosen from the elements of *LiveNodes* by calling the procedure *Select*(*LiveNodes*, E-node, k), where E-node is a pointer to the E-node and k is the size of the E-node. The definition of procedure *Select* is dependent on the type of branch-and-bound being implemented. For example, *Select* may choose the next *E*-node from a queue *LiveNodes* (FIFO branch-and-bound), a stack *LiveNodes* (LIFO branch-and-bound), a priority queue *LiveNodes* (least cost branch-and-bound), and so forth.

Paradigm *BranchAndBound* adds a node to *LiveNodes*, by calling the procedure *Add(LiveNodes, PtrNode)*. *BranchAndBound* also invokes the Boolean functions *Answer(PtrNode)* and *Bound(PtrNode)*. *Answer(PtrNode)* assumes the value **.true.** if the node pointed to by *PtrNode* is a goal state. *Bound(PtrNode)* returns the value **.true.** if the node pointed to by *PtrNode* is bounded. Similar to backtracking, the definition of the bounding function depends on the particular problem being solved.

```
procedure BranchAndBound
Input:    function D_k(x_1, ... , x_{k-1}) determining state-space tree T associated with the
          given problem)
          Bounding function Bounded
Output:   All goal states to the given problem
    LiveNodes is initialized to be empty
    AllocateTreeNode(Root)
    Root→Parent ← null
    Add(LiveNodes, Root)                    //add root to list of live nodes
    while LiveNodes is not empty do
        Select(LiveNodes, E-node, k)        //select next E-node from live nodes
        for each X[k] ∈ D_k(E-node) do      //for each child of the E-node do
            AllocateTreeNode(Child)
            Child→Info ← X[k]
            Child→Parent ← E-node
            if Answer(Child) then           //if child is a goal node then
                Path(Child)                 //output path from child to root
            endif
            if .not. Bounded(Child) then
                Add(LiveNodes, Child)       //add child to list of live nodes
            endif
        endfor
    endwhile
end BranchAndBound
```

As with the general paradigm *Backtrack* there is a corresponding version of the general paradigm *BranchAndBound* for problems involving minimizing or maximizing objective functions. For example, the paradigm *BranchAndBoundMin* maintains in *CurrentBest* the solution state with the current minimum value of the objective function f, and the value $f(CurrentBest)$ is used to dynamically bound nodes. Again, this dynamic bounding is done using a suitable function, *LowerBound*, whose value at a given node X is a lower-bound estimate of the value of the objective function at all goal states in the subtree rooted at X. A node X can be (dynamically) bounded if $f(CurrentBest) \leq LowerBound(X)$. As with the 0/1 knapsack problem discussed earlier, the function $LowerBound(X)$ is often expressed in the form $f(X) + h(X)$, where $h(X)$ is a lower-bound estimate of the smallest incremental increase in f incurred in going from X to a descendant goal state. Sometimes $h(X)$ is a heuristic estimate that might not be provably a lower bound, but which nevertheless has been shown to work well in practice. *LiveNodes* is often maintained as a priority queue, where $LowerBound(X)$ is taken as the priority of a node X. The next E-node chosen by *Select* is the node in *LiveNodes* with the least value of *LowerBound*, and the strategy is called *least cost* branch-and-bound. A more detailed discussion of least cost branch-and-bound will be given in the Chapter 23, where it is shown to be a special case of a more general search strategy.

10.4 Closing Remarks

Both LIFO and FIFO branch-and-bound are blind searches of the state-space tree T in the sense that they search the nodes of T in the same order regardless of the input to the algorithm. Thus, they tend to be inefficient for searching the large state-space trees that often arise in practice. Using heuristics can help narrow the scope of otherwise blind searches. The least cost branch-and-bound strategy discussed above uses a heuristic cost function associated with the nodes of the state-space tree T, where the set of live nodes is maintained as a priority queue with respect to this cost function. In this way, the next node to become the E-node is the one that is the most promising to lead quickly to a goal.

Least cost branch-and-bound is closely related to the general heuristic search strategy called A*-search. A*-search can be applied to state-space digraphs (digraphs are discussed in Chapter 11), rather than just state-space trees. A*-search is one of the most commonly used search strategies in artificial intelligence. Both A*-search and least cost branch-and-bound are discussed in Chapter 23.

The backtracking and branch-and-bound strategies are well suited to parallelization because different portions of the state-space tree can be assigned to different processors for searching. In Chapter 18, we discuss a general parallel backtracking paradigm in the context of message-passing distributed computing; and in Appendix F, we give code for an MPI implementation for the optimization version of the sum of subsets problem.

References and Suggestions for Further Reading

Golumb, S., and L. Baumert. "Backtracking Programming." *Journal of the ACM* 12 (1965): 516–524. An early general description, and applications, of the backtracking method.

Walker, R. J. "An Enumerative Technique for a Class of Combinatorial Problems." *Proceedings of Symposia in Applied Mathematics.* Vol. X. Providence, RI: American Mathematical Society, 1960. The backtracking and branch-and-bound design strategies have been studied for a long time. (The name backtrack was coined by D. H. Lehmer in the 1950s.) Walker's article is one of the first accounts of the backtracking method.

For two early survey articles on the branch-and-bound paradigm, see:

Lawler, E. L., and D. W. Wood. "Branch-and-Bound Methods: A Survey." *Operations Research* 14 (1966): 699–719.

Mitten, L. "Branch-and-Bound Methods: General Formulation and Properties." *Operations Research* 18 (1970): 24–34.

EXERCISES

Section 10.1 State-Space Trees

10.1 Consider the backtracking solution to the following instance of the 0/1 knapsack problem. The capacity of knapsack = $C = 15$.

i	0	1	2	3	4	5	6
v_i	25	45	12	7	6	10	5
w_i	5	11	3	2	2	7	4

a. Give P_k, and $D_k(x_1, x_2, \ldots, x_{k-1})$.

b. Draw the variable-tuple state-space tree (first three levels).

10.2 Repeat Exercise 10.1 for the fixed-tuple state-space tree.

10.3 Show that the number of nodes of both the fixed-tuple and variable-tuple state-space trees for the sum of subsets problem are exponential in n.

Section 10.2 Backtracking

10.4 Modify the pseudocode for the procedure *SumOfSubsets* to use the bounding function given in 10.2.2

10.5   a. Give pseudocode for a nonrecursive backtracking procedure for solving the sum of subsets problem, based on the state-space tree given in Figure 10.4.

        b. Repeat part (a) for a recursive backtracking procedure.

10.6   a. Reformulate procedure *Backtrack* so it halts once the first goal is reached.

        b. Repeat part (a) for the procedure *BacktrackRec.*

10.7   Give pseudocode for versions of the procedures *Backtrack* and *BacktrackRec* that only check for a goal state after determining that a problem state is bounded. These modified algorithms only apply to problems in which all the goal states are bounded.

10.8   Give pseudocode for a nonrecursive version of the paradigm *BacktrackMin* for minimizing an objective function.

10.9   Show the portion of the state-space tree generated during backtracking for the instance of the 0/1 knapsack problem given in Exercise 10.1 using the bounding functions (10.2.5) and (10.2.8).

10.10   a. Give pseudocode for a backtracking algorithm that solves the 0/1 knapsack problem using the bounding functions (10.2.5) and (10.2.8).

        b. Write a program implementing your algorithm in part (a), and run the program for various inputs.

10.11   a. Write a program using backtracking that proves there are no tie boards for the $3 \times 3 \times 3$ tic-tac-toe game, even if we relax the condition that the number of Xs and the number of Os differ by one.

        b. Write a program using backtracking that outputs all tie boards for the $3 \times 3 \times 3$ board minus the center position (when playing the game of tic-tac-toe, no X or O is placed in the center position), where we relax the condition that the number of Xs is equal to the number of Os. Is there a tie board where the number of Xs equals the number of Os?

10.12   Two queens in the ordinary chessboard are *nonattacking* if they are not in the same row, column, or diagonal. A classical problem known as the *8-queens problem* is to place eight queens on the board so that each pair of queens is nonattacking. One solution to the 8-queens problem is shown in Figure 10.16.

FIGURE 10.16

A solution to the
8-queens problem

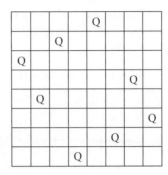

The *n-queens problem* is to place *n* queens on the $n \times n$ chessboard so that each pair of queens is nonattacking.

a. Design a backtracking algorithm that generates all solutions to the *n*-queens problem.

b. Write a program implementing your algorithm in part (a), and run your program with various values of *n*.

10.13 Another classical problem associated with chess is the *knight's tour* problem. A knight can make up to eight moves, as shown in Figure 10.17. Starting at an arbitrary position in the $n \times n$ board, a knight's tour is a sequence of $n^2 - 1$ moves such that every square of the board is visited once.

a. Design a backtracking algorithm that either produces a knight's tour or determines that no such tour exits.

b. Write a program implementing your algorithm in part (a), and run your program with various values of *n*.

FIGURE 10.17

The eight possible
moves for a knight
in the given
position

 = possible move

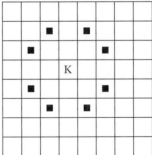

10.14 Let *Maze*[$0{:}n - 1, 0{:}n - 1$] be a 0/1 two-dimensional array.

a. Design a backtracking algorithm that either finds a path from *Maze*[0, 0] to *Maze*[$n - 1, n - 1$] or determines that no such path exists. Adjacent vertices in the path correspond to adjacent cells in the matrix. You are not allowed to move to a cell that contains a 1.

b. Write a program implementing your algorithm in part (a), and run your program with various values of n.

10.15 Write a program that uses backtracking to solve the game of Hi-Q. Hi-Q is a popular game that can be found in many toy stores. Thirty-two pieces are arranged on a board as shown in Figure 10.18, with the center position left empty. The goal is to remove all the pieces but one by jumping and have the last piece end up in the middle position. A piece is allowed to jump a neighbor in either a horizontal or vertical direction (diagonal jumps are not permitted). When a piece is jumped, it is removed from the board. Output the 32 board configurations showing the solution: the initial board config-uration and the board configuration after each jump is performed.

FIGURE 10.18

Initial board configuration for Hi-Q.

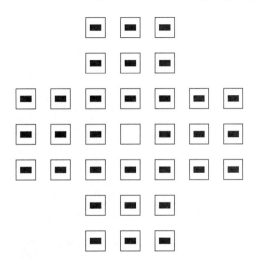

Section 10.3 Branch-and-Bound

10.16 Consider the optimization version of the sum of subsets problem for in-stance $\{a_0, \ldots, a_6\} = \{1, 11, 6, 2, 6, 8, 5\}$ and $Sum = 10$. Show that for this instance of the sum of subsets problem, FIFO branch-and-bound gener-ates fewer nodes of the state-space tree before reaching a goal state than backtracking does.

10.17 Give pseudocode for a version of the general procedure *BranchAndBound* that terminates as soon as a goal is found.

10.18 Give pseudocode for the procedure *Path(PtrNode)*.

10.19 Draw that portion of the variable-tuple state-space tree generated by FIFO branch-and-bound for the 0/1 knapsack problem given by the fol-lowing chart. Label the nodes with appropriate values of *UB*, *LoBd*, *SB*, *DB*, and indicate the optimal goal node, as in Figure 10.13. Trace the action of the queue *LiveNodes*, as illustrated in Figure 10.14.

i	0	1	2	3	4	Capacity $C = 12$
v_i	28	15	18	5.5	1	
w_i	8	5	6	4	1	

10.20 Repeat Exercise 10.19 for least cost branch-and-bound.

10.21 Repeat Exercise 10.19 using the fixed-tuple state-space tree.

10.22 Repeat Exercise 10.20 using the fixed-tuple state-space tree.

10.23 Given a set of Boolean variables $y_1, y_2, \ldots, y_m$, a CNF expression involving these variables is a conjunction of the form $C_1 \wedge C_2 \wedge \ldots \wedge C_n$, where each C_i is a disjunction of clauses of the form $z_{i,1} \vee z_{i,2} \vee \cdots \vee z_{i,n(i)}$, and where each $z_{i,j}$ (called a *literal*) is one of the Boolean variables y_1, $y_2, \ldots, y_m$ or its negation. The CNF SAT problem is to determine for a given CNF expression whether or not there is a truth assignment to the Boolean variables for which the CNF expression evaluates to **.true.** (that is, is *satisfied*). For a positive integer k, a k-CNF expression has the property that each clause contains exactly k literals. It turns out that the 2-CNF SAT problem has a polynomial solution (see Chapter 26), whereas the 3-CNF problem is already NP-complete. The best-known solutions to the CNF SAT problem involve fixed-tuple dynamic state-space trees and backtracking, together with such things as using clever heuristics to bound the search. In this exercise, we assume that each clause in a CNF expression is input as a string of integers, with positive integer i meaning that x_i occurs in the clause, and negative integer i meaning that the negative of x_i occurs in the clause. For example, 2, -5, 10 would represent the clause $y_2 \vee \overline{y_5} \vee y_{10}$.

a. Write a program that accepts a CNF expression as input and uses backtracking on a fixed-tuple static state-space tree to determine whether or not the CNF expression is satisfiable. The left (right) child of a node at level $k - 1$ corresponds to assigning **.true. (.false.)** to y_k, $k = 1, \ldots, n$.

b. Repeat part (a), but now use a dynamic state-space tree, where the kth decision (level) in the tree is to give a truth assignment to the Boolean variable that occurs (either positively or negatively) kth most often in the CNF expression (ties are decided using subscript ordering).

c. Repeat part (b), but now the decision at a given node in the tree is to assign a truth value to the variable that occurs most often in the clauses that have not already been satisfied by the previous assignments.

d. Run the programs written in parts (a), (b), and (c) with various input CNF expressions, and compare the results.

PART THREE

GRAPH AND NETWORK
ALGORITHMS

CHAPTER 11

GRAPHS AND DIGRAPHS

Many problems are naturally modeled using graphs and digraphs, and data structures implementing the graph or the digraph ADT are commonly used throughout computer science. The subject of graph algorithms is a very active area of research today. Graphs and digraphs also play an important role in the Internet and networks for communication, transportation, commodity flow, among others. The underlying structure of these networks is naturally modeled using a graph of a digraph.

Examples of network graphs abound. The interstate highway system can be modeled by a graph where the nodes represent cities (or junctions), and the edges represent highways linking the cities. The world wide web can be modeled with a directed graph, where the nodes correspond to Web pages, and a directed edge exists from Web page A to Web page B if Web page A includes a hyperlink reference (href) to Web page B. Graphs in parallel computing serve as models for interconnection networks. And we can use graphs to represent the overlay structure imposed on the Internet for a peer-to-peer network such as Gnutella (see Figure 11.1).

Besides their network applications, graphs and digraphs serve as natural models for a host of other applications. To cite an example from computer science, the logical flow of a computer program written in a high-level language is

FIGURE 11.1

A snapshot of a portion of the Gnutella peer-to-peer network.

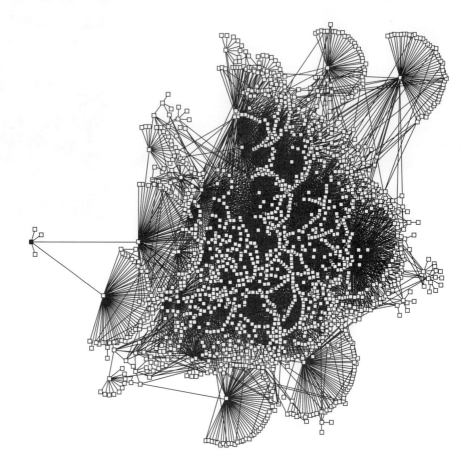

naturally modeled by a program digraph (flowchart). Optimizing compilers then use various properties of this digraph, such as strongly connected components and vertex coloring, to help achieve the goal of translating the high-level code into machine code that exhibits optimal performance.

In this chapter, we introduce several basic graph theory concepts. We also discuss the two basic search strategies, depth-first search and breadth-first search, and apply these strategies to such problems as topological sorting and finding shortest paths in graphs.

11.1 Graphs and Digraphs

In this section, we give a brief introduction to the theory of graphs and digraphs. We introduce basic terminology, prove several elementary results, and present two standard representations of graphs and digraphs.

11.1.1 Graphs

Formally, a *graph* $G = (V, E)$ is a set $V = V(G)$ called *vertices* (or *nodes*), together with a set $E = E(G)$ called *edges*, such that an edge is an *unordered* pair of vertices. An edge $\{u, u\}$ is called a *loop*. Unless otherwise stated, we restrict our attention to graphs without loops. For simplicity, we sometimes denote the edge $\{u, v\}$ by *uv*. Given an edge $e = uv$ in a graph $G = (V, E)$, we refer to vertices *u* and *v* as the *end vertices* of *e*, and we say that *e joins u* and *v*. Two vertices *u* and *v* are *adjacent* if they are the two end vertices of an edge in the graph (that is, $uv \in E$). The set of all vertices adjacent to *u* is the *neighborhood of u*. A vertex *v* and an edge *e* are *incident* if *e* contains vertex *v*—that is, if $e = vw$ for some vertex *w*. Two edges *e* and *f* are *adjacent* if they have an end vertex in common.

A graph can be represented pictorially by a drawing in the plane, where the vertices are represented by points in the plane and an edge $\{u, v\} \in E$ is represented by a continuous curve joining *u* and *v* (see Figure 11.2). Graphs such as that shown in Figure 11.2b allow the continuous curves to intersect at points (called *crossings*) other than vertices. It turns out that the graph shown in figure 11.2b cannot be drawn in the plane without at least one crossing, and such graphs are called *nonplanar graphs*.

Graphs such as that shown in Figure 11.2a, which can be drawn in the plane without crossings, are called *planar graphs*. Such a drawing is called an

FIGURE 11.2

(a) A planar graph, and (b) a nonplanar graph.

$V = \{0, 1, 2, 3, 4, 5, 6, 7, 8\}$
$E = \{\{0, 1\}, \{0, 2\}, \{1, 2\}, \{1, 3\}, \{1, 5\}, \{2, 3\}, \{3, 4\}, \{3, 5\}, \{6, 7\}, \{6, 8\}, \{7, 8\}\}$

$G =$

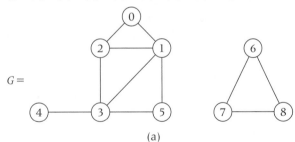

(a)

$V = \{0, 1, 2, A, B, C\}$
$E = \{\{0, A\}, \{0, B\}, \{0, C\}, \{1, A\}, \{1, B\}, \{1, C\}, \{2, A\}, \{2, B\}, \{2, C\}\}$

$G =$

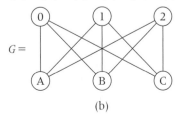

(b)

embedding of G in the plane. Planar graphs are particularly important in computer science. For example, they are useful in VLSI design and flow diagrams.

Two graphs $G = (V, E)$ and $G' = (V', E')$ are *isomorphic* if there exists a bijective mapping $\beta: V \to V'$ from the vertex set V of G onto the vertex set V' of G' such that adjacency relationships are preserved; that is, $\{u, w\} \in E$ if and only if $\{\beta(u), \beta(w)\} \in E'$. The mapping β is called an *isomorphism*. Deciding whether two graphs are isomorphic is, in general, a difficult problem. A graph is *complete* if every pair of distinct vertices is joined by an edge. Clearly, any two complete graphs having the same number of vertices are isomorphic. A complete graph on n vertices is denoted by K_n.

We denote the number of vertices and edges by $n = n(G)$ and $m = m(G)$, respectively, so that $n = |V|$ and $m = |E|$. The *degree* of a vertex $v \in V$, denoted by $d(v)$, is the number of edges incident with v. Let $\delta = \delta(G)$ and $\Delta = \Delta(G)$ denote the minimum and maximum degrees, respectively, over all the vertices in G, so that $\delta \le d(v) \le \Delta$ for all $v \in V$.

Proposition 11.1.1 is the useful formula derived by Euler that relates the number m of edges to the sum of the degrees of the vertices.

Proposition 11.1.1 The sum of the degrees over all the vertices of a graph G equals twice the number of edges; that is,

$$\sum_{v \in V} d(v) = 2m. \tag{11.1.1}$$

PROOF
Every edge is incident with exactly two vertices. Therefore, when summing the degrees over all the vertices, we count each edge exactly twice, once for each of its end vertices. ▪

A graph is *r-regular* if every vertex has degree r. A useful corollary of Proposition 11.1.1 is the following result relating the number of vertices and edges of an *r*-regular graph.

Corollary 11.1.2 If G is an *r*-regular graph with n vertices and m edges, then

$$m = rn/2. \tag{11.1.2}$$
□

Another corollary of Proposition 11.1.1 is obtained by taking both sides of formula (11.1.1) **mod** 2.

Corollary 11.1.3 For any graph G, the number of vertices of odd degree is even. □

A *path P of length p* ($p \geq 0$) joining vertices u and v is an alternating sequence of $p + 1$ vertices and p edges $u_0 e_1 u_1 e_2 \ldots e_p u_p$ such that $u = u_0$, $v = u_p$, where e_i joins u_{i-1} and u_i, $i = 1, 2, \ldots, p$. We call u_0 and u_p the *initial* and *terminal* vertices, respectively, and the remaining vertices in the path the *interior* vertices. Vertices in a path can be repeated, but edges must be distinct. Because the path P is completely defined by the sequence of vertices $u_0 u_1 \ldots u_p$, we often use this shorter sequence to denote P. If $u = v$, then the path is called a *closed path* or *circuit*. We call a path *simple* if the interior vertices in the path are all distinct and are different from the initial and terminal vertices. A *simple circuit* or *cycle* is a simple closed path. A path that contains every edge in the graph exactly once is called an *Eulerian path*. A circuit that contains every edge exactly once is called an *Eulerian circuit* or *Eulerian tour*. A simple path that contains every vertex in the graph is called a *Hamiltonian path*. A cycle that contains every vertex in the graph is called a *Hamiltonian cycle*.

Two vertices $u, v \in V$ are *connected* if there exists a path (of length 0 when $u = v$) that joins them. The relation *u is connected to v* is an equivalence relation on V. Each equivalence class C of vertices, together with all incident edges, is called a *(connected) component* of G. When G has only one component, then G is *connected*; otherwise, G is *disconnected*.

The *distance* between u and v, denoted by $d(u, v)$, is the length of a path from u to v that has the shortest (minimum) length among all such paths. By convention, if u and v are not connected, then $d(u, v) = \infty$. The *diameter* of G is the maximum distance between any two vertices. In Figure 11.3, the distance between every pair of vertices and the diameter is given for a sample graph G. We show the distances using a 6×6 *distance matrix*, whose ij^{th} entry is given by $d(i, j)$.

A *tree* is a connected graph without cycles. A rooted tree is simply a tree with one vertex designated as the root. Every tree is planar, meaning it can be drawn in the plane without crossings. The following propositions are not difficult, and their proofs are left as exercises.

FIGURE 11.3

Distances between
vertices for a
sample graph G on
six vertices.

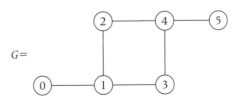

$G =$

Distance matrix of G

$$\begin{pmatrix} 0 & 1 & 2 & 2 & 3 & 4 \\ 1 & 0 & 1 & 1 & 2 & 3 \\ 2 & 1 & 0 & 2 & 1 & 2 \\ 2 & 1 & 2 & 0 & 1 & 2 \\ 3 & 2 & 1 & 1 & 0 & 1 \\ 4 & 3 & 2 & 2 & 1 & 0 \end{pmatrix}$$ Diameter $G = 4$

Proposition 11.1.4 A graph T is a tree if and only if there exists a unique path joining every pair of distinct vertices of T. □

Proposition 11.1.5 A connected graph T is a tree if and only if the number of edges of T is one less than the number of vertices. □

A *subgraph H* of G is a graph such that $V(H) \subseteq V(G)$ and $E(H) \subseteq E(G)$. A subgraph H that is a tree is a *subtree* of G, or simply a *tree* of G. A subgraph H of G is called a *spanning* subgraph if H contains all the vertices of G. When a subgraph H of G is a tree, we use the term *spanning tree* of G. Given a subset U of vertices of G, the subgraph $G[U]$ *induced by* U is the subgraph with vertex set U and edge set consisting of all edges in G having both end vertices in U. In Figure 11.4b, we show a subgraph and an induced subgraph on the same set of vertices U. Note that a component of a graph G is a connected induced subgraph of G that is not contained in a strictly larger connected subgraph (see Figure 11.4a).

FIGURE 11.4

(a) The components of G are the subgraphs, $G[A]$ and $G[B]$, induced by the vertex sets $A = \{0, 1, 2, 3, 4, 5, 6, 7\}$ and $B = \{8, 9, 10, 11\}$, respectively; (b) a subgraph spanning $U = \{2, 3, 4, 5, 6, 7\}$ and the induced subgraph $G[U]$

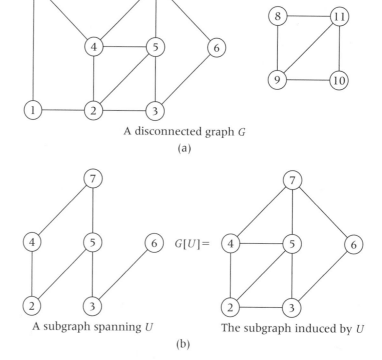

A disconnected graph G

(a)

$G[U] =$

A subgraph spanning U The subgraph induced by U

(b)

FIGURE 11.5

Two complete
bipartite graphs.

A graph is *bipartite* if there exists a bipartition of the vertex set V into two sets X and Y such that every edge has one end in X and the other in Y. The *complete bipartite* graph $K_{i,j}$ is the bipartite graph with $n = i + j$ vertices, i vertices belonging to X and j vertices belonging to Y, such that there is an edge joining every vertex $x \in X$ to every vertex $y \in Y$. The complete bipartite graph $K_{3,3}$ is shown in Figure 11.2b. Two other examples of complete bipartite graphs are given in Figure 11.5.

The graphs K_5 and $K_{3,3}$ are both nonplanar graphs. If you try drawing them in the plane without edge crossings, you will have trouble. In fact, K_5 and $K_{3,3}$ are in some sense the quintessential nonplanar graphs (see Theorem 11.1.6). A *subdivision S* of G is a graph obtained from G by replacing each edge e with a path joining the same two vertices as e (subdividing the edge e, as in Figure 11.6). Observe that G is a subdivision of itself (replace each edge with a path of length 1). Clearly, if G is nonplanar, then every subdivision of G is nonplanar. It is also clear that if G contains a nonplanar graph, then G is nonplanar. It follows that a graph is nonplanar if it contains a subgraph that is a subdivision of K_5 or $K_{3,3}$. The fact that the converse is also true is a surprising and deep result discovered by Kuratowski. We state Kuratowski's theorem without proof.

**Theorem 11.1.6
Kuratowski's
Theorem**
A graph G is nonplanar if and only if it contains a subgraph that is isomorphic to a subdivision of K_5 or $K_{3,3}$. □

The condition of being planar occurs in many computer applications, such as the design of very large-scale integration (VLSI) circuits. Moreover, planar graphs became of interest long before the advent of computers. For example, in 1750, Euler gave his famous polyhedron formula relating the number of vertices,

FIGURE 11.6

Subdividing a
graph.

$G =$ 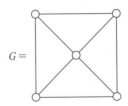 $S =$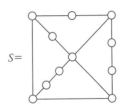

edges, and faces of a connected planar graph. As another example, a very famous mathematical question known as the four-color conjecture can be modeled using planar graphs. For centuries, mapmakers had known implicitly that they only needed four colors to color the countries in any map drawn on the globe so that no two neighboring countries (that is, countries sharing a common boundary consisting of more than an isolated point) get the same color (called a *proper* coloring). See Figure 11.7 for a four-coloring of the map of the 48 contiguous states. That four colors suffice for any map on the globe was stated by Guthrie in 1856 as a formal conjecture, which resisted proof for more than 100 years.

Given a map of any portion of the globe, there is a naturally associated planar graph whose vertices correspond to the countries, and where two vertices are adjacent if and only if the countries they represent are neighbors. It is easy to see that the graph associated with a map is planar. The map-coloring problem then transforms to the equivalent problem of coloring the vertices of a planar graph using no more than four colors so that no two adjacent vertices get the same color. Certainly the transformed problem has a rather elegant mathematical formulation unencumbered by geometrically complex boundary curves associated with maps. Moreover, because graphs can be input to a computer using simple data structures such as adjacency matrices, proofs involving exhaustive case checking are sometimes possible. In fact, it was that type of proof (together with deep mathematical insight) that Appel and Haken used in 1970 to settle the four-color conjecture in the affirmative. The proof consisted in showing that two contradictory conditions hold for planar graphs that are not four-colorable:

1. There is a certain finite set of planar graphs S, at least one of which would have to occur as a subgraph of any planar graph G that is not four-colorable (S is an *unavoidable* set).
2. If a graph G contains one of these subgraphs, then there would be another graph G' on fewer vertices that is also not four-colorable (each graph in S is *reducible*).

FIGURE 11.7

A proper four-coloring of the map of the United States using four shades of grey.

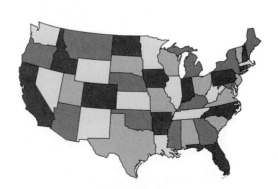

Clearly, these two conditions rule out the existence of planar graphs that are not four-colorable, because if such planar graphs existed, there would have to be one having a minimal number of vertices among all such graphs. Appel and Haken proved condition (1) mathematically but used a computer to check that each graph in S had the reducibility property given in condition (2). Since then, other proofs of the four-color conjecture have been given that follow a similar line of thinking but use a smaller set of unavoidable reducible graphs. However, exhaustive computer checking of cases remains a component of all known proofs of the four-color conjecture.

For an arbitrary graph G and an integer c, it is a difficult problem (in fact, it is NP-complete) to determine whether the vertices of G can be colored using no more than c colors such that no two adjacent vertices get the same color (called a *proper coloring* of G). The minimum number of colors needed to properly color the vertices of G is called the *chromatic number* of G. This invariant is discussed further in the exercises at the end of this chapter.

11.1.2 Graphs as Interconnection Networks

The underlying structure for an interconnection network model for parallel communication is a graph (see Chapter 15). The nodes of the graph correspond to the processors. Two nodes are joined with an edge (adjacent) whenever the corresponding two processors communicate directly with one another. In the interconnection network model, information is communicated between nonadjacent processors P and Q by relaying the information along a path in the network joining P and Q. The diameter is an upper bound on the number of communication steps needed to relay information between any two processors. A small diameter is clearly a desirable property of an interconnection network. Another desirable property is a small maximum degree because it makes the interconnection network model easier to build than does a large maximum degree.

The complete graph interconnection network K_n having n processors has diameter 1 (the distance between every pair of vertices is 1), but with each vertex having very high degree $(n - 1)$, the network is not practical to build. At the other extreme is the one-dimensional mesh M_p, $p = n$, which has maximum degree 2 and diameter $n - 1$ (the distance between processor P_0 and processor P_{p-1} is $n - 1$). The two-dimensional mesh $M_{q,q}$, $n = q^2$, has maximum degree 4 but has diameter $2(\sqrt{n} - 1)$, which is still quite large the maximum distance $2(q - 1)$ occurs between processors $P_{0,0}$ and $P_{q-1,q-1}$.

Other interconnection networks are based on graphs that compromise between extreme values of degree and diameter. One example is the hypercube interconnection network model. The k-dimensional hypercube H_k has 2^k nodes consisting of the set of all 0/1 k-tuples; that is, $V(H_k) = \{(x_1, \dots, x_k) \mid x_i \in \{0, 1\}, i = 1, \dots, k\}$. Two nodes in $V(H_k)$ are joined with an edge of H_k if and only if

FIGURE 11.8

Hypercubes H_i,
$i = 0, 1, 2, 3, 4$.

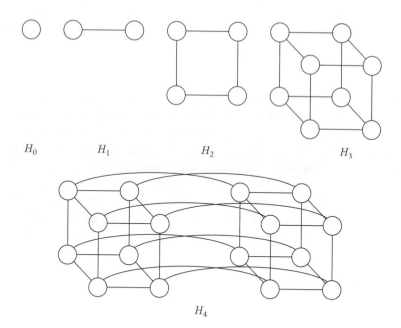

H_0 H_1 H_2 H_3

H_4

they differ in exactly one component. The hypercubes up to dimension 4 are shown in Figure 11.8. The hypercube of dimension k can be obtained by joining corresponding vertices in two copies of the hypercube of dimension $k - 1$.

The hypercube H_k of dimension k is k-regular and has diameter $k = \log_2 n$ (see Exercise 11.15). Thus, the maximum degree and diameter of H_k are both logarithmic in the number of vertices n.

11.1.3 Digraphs

Graphs with directed edges are natural models for many physical phenomena. For example, the pairings of the players in a tournament (for match-play golf, table tennis, or the like) can be represented by a graph, where the vertices correspond to the players, and two vertices A and B are joined with an edge if players A and B are to play each other. The winner of the match between each pair of players A and B can be recorded by "orienting" the edge joining A and B, so that it is directed from A to B if A defeats B. The resulting oriented graph is called a *directed graph* or *digraph*.

Formally, a *digraph* D is a set $V = V(D)$ of vertices together with a set $E = E(D)$ called *directed edges* (sometimes called *arcs*) such that a directed edge is an *ordered* pair of vertices. A digraph can be represented by a drawing in the plane in the same way that a graph can, except that we add an arrow to the curve representing each edge to indicate the orientation of that edge (see Figure 11.9).

FIGURE 11.9

Drawing a digraph.

$V = \{0,1,2,3,4,5,6\}$
$E = \{\{0,1\},\{1,0\},\{0,5\},\{3,1\},\{1,6\},\{2,3\},\{3,4\},\{3,6\},\{6,4\},\{5,4\},\{6,5\}\}$

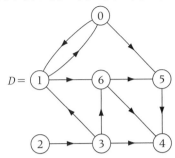

Because an unordered pair (a, b) is combinatorially equivalent to the two ordered pairs (a, b), (b, a), a digraph is actually a generalization of a graph. Associated with any given undirected graph $G = (V, E)$ is the combinatorial equivalent digraph $\hat{G} = (\hat{V}, \hat{E})$, where $V = \hat{V}$ and the ordered pairs (u, v), (v, u) are in $\hat{E}$ if and only if the unordered pair $\{u, v\}$ is in E (see Figure 11.10).

For simplicity, we sometimes denote the directed edge (u, v) by uv. We refer to u as the *tail* of e and refer to v as the *head* of e. The *out-degree* of a vertex $v \in V$, denoted by $d_{\text{out}}(v)$, is the number of edges having tail v. Similarly, the *in-degree* of a vertex $v \in V$, denoted by $d_{\text{in}}(v)$, is the number of edges having head v. It is easily verified that

$$\sum_{v \in V} d_{\text{out}}(v) = \sum_{v \in V} d_{\text{in}}(v) = m,$$

where m denotes the number of directed edges of D. The *out-neighborhood (in-neighborhood) of vertex u* is the set of all vertices v such that uv (vu) is a directed edge of D.

FIGURE 11.10

Graph G and its combinatorial equivalent digraph $\hat{G}$.

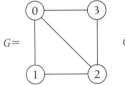 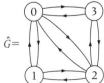

11.1.4 Implementing Graphs and Digraphs

Two standard implementations of a graph G are the adjacency matrix implementation and the adjacency lists implementation. For convenience, assume that the vertices of G are labeled $0, 1, \ldots, n-1$ (when referring to a vertex we do not distinguish between the label of the vertex and the vertex itself). The *adjacency matrix* of a graph G is the $n \times n$ symmetric matrix $A = (a_{ij})$ given by

$$a_{ij} = \begin{cases} 1 & \text{vertices } i \text{ and } j \text{ are adjacent in } G. \\ 0 & \text{otherwise,} \end{cases} \qquad i, j \in \{0, \ldots, n-1\}.$$

A sample graph G and its adjacency matrix are given in Figure 11.11.

FIGURE 11.11

Adjacency matrix of
a graph G.

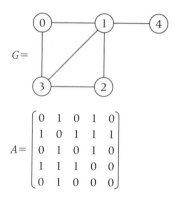

Implementing G using its adjacency matrix makes it easy to perform many standard operations on G, such as adding a new edge or deleting an existing edge. The adjacency matrix of G allocates n^2 memory locations no matter how many edges are in the graph. Thus, implementing G using its adjacency matrix is inefficient if the number of edges of G is small relative to the number of vertices. For example, if G is a tree with n vertices, then G has only $n-1$ edges. On the other hand, if $m \in \Theta(n^2)$, then the adjacency matrix representation is probably an efficient way to implement G.

Given a graph $G = (V, E)$, for $v \in V$, the *adjacency list of v* is the list consisting of all the vertices adjacent to v. The order in which the vertices are listed usually does not matter. The adjacency lists of G are generally implemented as linked lists, where pointers to the beginning of the linked lists are stored in *header nodes*. The header nodes can themselves be implemented using a linked list, or they can be stored in an array *Header*$[0{:}n-1]$. Figures 11.12a and 11.12b illustrate the adjacency lists implementation using linked lists for the graph given in Figure

FIGURE 11.12

Adjacency lists implementations for the sample graph *G* given in Figure 11.11.

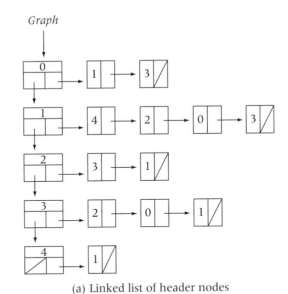

Graph
0
1
3
1
4
2
0
3
2
3
1
3
2
0
1
4
1
(a) Linked list of header nodes
Header[0]
1
3
Header[1]
4
2
0
3
Header[2]
3
1
Header[3]
2
0
1
Header[4]
1
(b) Array of header nodes

11.11, where the header nodes are implemented using a linked list and an array, respectively. We do not assume that the nodes in each adjacency list are maintained in increasing order of node labels.

Each node of the adjacency list of vertex i corresponds to an edge $\{i, j\}$ incident with i. In the adjacency lists implementation of a graph, where the header nodes belong to a linked list (see Figure 11.12a), it is convenient in practice to maintain a second pointer p in each list node defined as follows: If the list node belongs to the adjacency list of vertex i and corresponds to edge $\{i, j\}$ then p points to the header node of adjacency list j.

Both the adjacency matrix and adjacency lists implementations of graphs generalize naturally to digraphs. The *adjacency matrix* of a digraph D, whose vertices are labeled $0, 1, \ldots, n - 1$, is the $n \times n$ matrix $A = (a_{ij})$ defined by

$$a_{ij} = \begin{cases} 1 & \text{if there is an arc from } i \text{ and } j, \\ 0 & \text{otherwise,} \end{cases} \quad i, j \in \{0, \ldots, n - 1\}.$$

The adjacency matrix of a sample digraph D is given in Figure 11.13.

In Figures 11.14a and 11.14b, the adjacency lists implementations using a linked list of header nodes and an array of header nodes, respectively, are illustrated for the sample digraph given in Figure 11.13.

FIGURE 11.13

Adjacency matrix of
a digraph D.

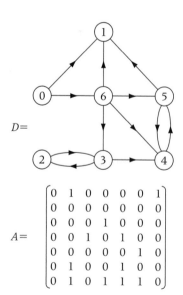

$$D=$$

$$A= \begin{bmatrix} 0 & 1 & 0 & 0 & 0 & 0 & 1 \\ 0 & 0 & 0 & 0 & 0 & 0 & 0 \\ 0 & 0 & 0 & 1 & 0 & 0 & 0 \\ 0 & 0 & 1 & 0 & 1 & 0 & 0 \\ 0 & 0 & 0 & 0 & 0 & 1 & 0 \\ 0 & 1 & 0 & 0 & 1 & 0 & 0 \\ 0 & 1 & 0 & 1 & 1 & 1 & 0 \end{bmatrix}$$

FIGURE 11.14

Adjacency lists
implementations of
the sample digraph
D given in Figure
11.13

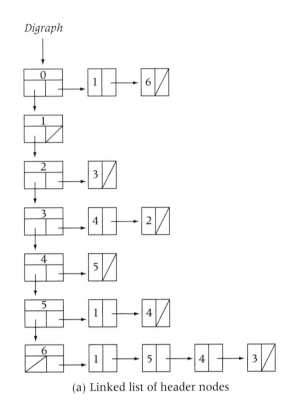

(a) Linked list of header nodes

continued

The adjacency matrix and adjacency lists representations of digraphs are generalizations of the adjacency matrix and adjacency lists representations of (undirected) graphs. To understand this, consider any undirected graph G and its combinatorially equivalent digraph $\hat{G}$ (see Figure 11.10). Clearly, the adjacency matrix and adjacency lists of G and $\hat{G}$ are identical.

FIGURE 11.14

Continued

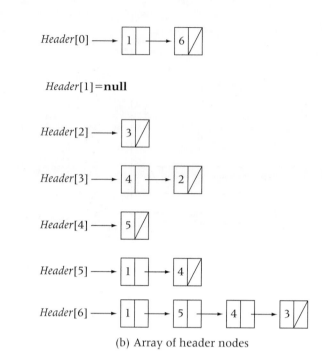

(b) Array of header nodes

 ## 11.2 Search and Traversal of Graphs and Digraphs

The solutions to many important problems require an examination (visit) of the nodes of a graph. Two standard search techniques are *depth-first search* and *breadth-first search*.

Depth-first search and breadth-first search differ in their exploring philosophies: Depth-first search always longs to see what's over the next hill (where pastures might be greener), whereas breadth-first search visits the immediate neighborhood thoroughly before moving on. After visiting a node, breadth-first search explores this node (visits all neighbors of the node that have not already been visited) before moving on. On the other hand, depth-first search immediately moves on to an unvisited neighbor, if one exists, after visiting a node. Whenever depth-first search is at an explored node, it "backtracks" until an unexplored node is encountered and then continues. This backtracking often returns to the same node many times before it is explored.

11.2.1 Depth-First Search

We first give the pseudocode *DFS* for a depth-first search. For simplicity, we assume that *G* has *n* vertices labeled $0, 1, \ldots, n - 1$; we use the symbol *v* to simultaneously denote a vertex and its label. We maintain an auxiliary array *Mark*$[0{:}n - 1]$ to keep track of the nodes that have been visited.

procedure *DFS*(*G*, *v*) recursive
Input: *G* (a graph with *n* vertices and *m* edges)
             v (a vertex)   //The array *Mark*$[0{:}n - 1]$ is global and
                                                      //initialized to 0s
Output: the depth-first search of *G* with starting vertex *v*
       Mark[*v*] ← 1
       call *Visit*(*v*)
       for each vertex *u* adjacent to *v* **do**
             if *Mark*[*u*] = 0 **then call** *DFS*(*G*, *u*) **endif**
       endfor
end *DFS*

The **for** loop in the *DFS* pseudocode does not explicitly describe the order in which the vertices are considered. This order is incidental to the nature of the search, and would, in general, depend on the particular implementation of the graph *G* (for example, adjacency matrix, adjacency lists, and so forth). Because we have labeled the vertices $0, 1, \ldots, n - 1$, we assume that the vertices are accessed by the **for** loop in increasing order of their labels (thereby making the order of visiting the nodes independent of the implementation). The graph in Figure 11.15 illustrates this convention.

FIGURE 11.15

DFS with *v* = 6 visits vertices of graph *G* in the order 6, 1, 0, 2, 3, 4, 5, 8, 7.

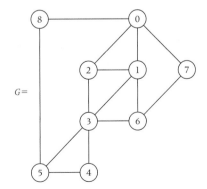

G =

For the graph G in Figure 11.15, *DFS* visits all the vertices of G. For a general graph G, *DFS* starts at vertex v and visits all the vertices in the (connected) component containing v.

To further illustrate the **for** loop in *DFS*, we show how this loop can be written in the two standard ways to implement a graph. First, suppose that G is implemented using its adjacency matrix $A[0{:}n-1, 0{:}n-1]$. We assume that the vertex v is labeled i. In this case, the **for** loop becomes

```
for j ← 0 to n − 1 do
    if (A[i, j] = 1) .and. (Mark[j] = 0) then
        call DFS(G, j)
    endif
endfor
```

On the other hand, suppose that G is implemented using adjacency lists. Recall that a typical version of this implementation has an array *Header*[0{:}n − 1] of header nodes, where *Header*[v] is a pointer to the adjacency list of v. A node in the adjacency list for v corresponding to vertex u contains a field *Vertex* containing the index (label) of u. It also contains a pointer *NextVertex* to the next vertex in the adjacency list. Under these assumptions, the **for** loop in *DFS* becomes

```
p ← Header[v]
while (p ≠ null) do
    if Mark[p→Vertex] = 0 then
        call DFS(G, p→Vertex)
    endif
    p ← p→NextVertex
endwhile
```

It is useful to write *DFS* as a nonrecursive procedure. For convenience, the nonrecursive version calls a procedure *Next* that determines the next unvisited node w adjacent to the node u just visited. If no such node w exists, then a Boolean parameter *found* is set to **.false..**

```
procedure DFS(G, v)
Input:    G (a graph with n vertices and m edges)
          v (a vertex)
Output:   the depth-first search of G starting from vertex v
          S a stack initialized as empty
          Mark[0:n − 1] a 0/1 array initialized to 0s
          Mark[v] ← 1
```

```
        call Visit(v)
        u ← v
        Next(u, w, found)
        while found .or. (.not. Empty(S))
            if found then              //go deeper
                Push(S, u)
                Mark[w] ← 1
                Visit(w)
                u ← w
            else
                Pop(S, u)     //backtrack
            endif
            Next(u, w, found)
        endwhile
    end DFS
```

Figure 11.16 illustrates the sequence of pushes, visits, and pops performed by *DFS* for the graph in Figure 11.15.

We analyze the complexity of *DFS* from the point of view of two basic operations: visiting a node and examining a node (by calls to *Next*) to see if it has been marked as visited. The worst-case complexity for both operations occurs when the graph is connected. If *G* is connected, then it is easily verified that every vertex is visited exactly once, so that we have a total of *n* node visits. Each edge *uw*

FIGURE 11.16

DFS with v = 6 and stack operations.

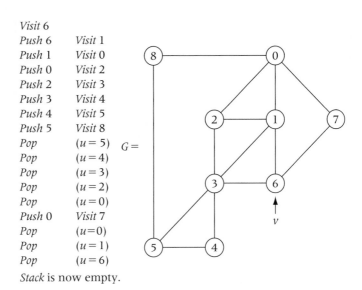

Visit 6	
Push 6	*Visit* 1
Push 1	*Visit* 0
Push 0	*Visit* 2
Push 2	*Visit* 3
Push 3	*Visit* 4
Push 4	*Visit* 5
Push 5	*Visit* 8
Pop	(u = 5)
Pop	(u = 4)
Pop	(u = 3)
Pop	(u = 2)
Pop	(u = 0)
Push 0	*Visit* 7
Pop	(u = 0)
Pop	(u = 1)
Pop	(u = 6)

G =

Stack is now empty.

in the graph gives rise to exactly two vertex examinations by *Next*, one with *u* as input parameter and one with *w* as input parameter. This shows that the worst-case complexity of *DFS* in terms of the number of vertices examined by *Next* is 2*m*. Therefore, the total number of basic operations of the two types performed by *DFS* in the worst case is $n + 2m \in O(n + m)$.

11.2.2 Depth-First Search Tree

A depth-first search with starting vertex *v* determines a tree, called the *depth-first search tree (DFS-tree) rooted at v*. During a depth-first search, whenever we move from a vertex *u* to an adjacent unvisited vertex *w*, we add the edge *uw* to the tree. This tree is naturally implemented using the parent array representation (denoted by *DFSTreeParent*[0:*n* − 1]), where *u* is the parent of *w*. For example, in the nonrecursive procedure *DFS*, we merely need to add the statement *DFSTreeParent*[*w*] ← *u* before pushing *u* on the stack, and add the array *DFSTreeParent*[0:*n* − 1] as a third parameter. We will refer to this augmented procedure as *DFSTree*.

The DFS-tree rooted at vertex 6 of the graph in Figure 11.16 is illustrated in Figure 11.17a, and the associated array *DFSTreeParent* is given in Figure 11.17b.

The array *DFSTreeParent*[0:*n* − 1] gives us the unique path from any given vertex *w* back to *v* in the depth-first search tree rooted at *v*. For example, suppose we wish to find the path in the depth-first search tree in Figure 11.17 from ver-

FIGURE 11.17

(a) The DFS-tree rooted at vertex 6 for the graph in Figure 11.16; (b) the associated array *DFSTreeParent*[0:8].

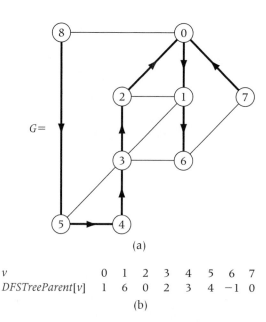

$G=$

(a)

v	0	1	2	3	4	5	6	7
DFSTreeParent[*v*]	1	6	0	2	3	4	−1	0

(b)

tex 8 to vertex 6. By simply starting at vertex 8 and following the pointers in the array *DFSTreeParent*[0:$n - 1$], we obtain the path

> 8, *DFSTreeParent*[8] = 5, *DFSTreeParent*[5] = 4, *DFSTreeParent*[4] = 3,
> *DFSTreeParent*[3] = 2, *DFSTreeParent*[2] = 0, *DFSTreeParent*[0] = 1,
> *DFSTreeParent*[1] = 6.

11.2.3 Depth-First Traversal

If the graph *G* is connected, then *DFS* visits *all* the vertices of *G* so that *DFS* performs a *traversal* of *G*. For a general graph *G*, the following simple algorithm based on repeated calls to *DFS* with different starting vertices performs a traversal of *G*.

```
procedure DFT(G)
Input:     G (a graph with n vertices and m edges)
Output:   the depth-first traversal of G
Mark[0:n − 1] a 0/1 array initialized to 0s
    for v ← 0 to n − 1 do
        if Mark[v] = 0 then
            DFS(G, v)
        endif
    endfor
end DFT
```

If we call the procedure *DFSTree* instead of *DFS*, then a forest of DFS-trees is generated (a DFS-tree rooted at *i* is generated for each *i* such that *i* is not visited when *v = i*). We refer to this forest as the *depth-first traversal forest* (*DFT-forest*) of *G*. In the procedure *DFTForest* that follows, the DFT-forest is implemented using an array *DFTForestParent*[0:$n - 1$].

```
procedure DFTForest(G, DFTForestParent[0:n − 1])
Input:     G (a graph with n vertices and m edges)
Output:   DFTForestParent[0:n − 1] (an array implementing the DFT forest of G)
    Mark[0:n − 1] a 0/1 array initialized to 0s
    for v ← 0 to n − 1 do
        DFTForestParent[v] ← 0
    endfor
    for v ← 0 to n − 1 do
        if Mark[v] = 0 then
            DFSTree(G, v, DFTForestParent[0:n − 1])
        endif
    endfor
end DFTForest
```

11.2.4 Breadth-First Search

Recall that the strategy underlying the breadth-first search is to visit all unvisited vertices adjacent to a given vertex before moving on. The breadth-first strategy is easily implemented by visiting these adjacent vertices and placing them on a queue. Then a vertex is removed from the queue, and the process repeated. A breadth-first search starts by inserting a vertex v onto an initially empty queue and continues until the queue is empty.

```
procedure BFS(G, v)
Input:   G (a graph with n vertices and m edges)
         v (vertex)                          //the array Mark[0:n − 1] is global and
                                             //initialized to 0s
Output:  the breadth-first search of G starting from vertex v
    Q    a queue initialized as empty
    call   Enqueue(Q, v)
    Mark[v] ← 1
    call Visit(v)
    while .not. Empty(Q) do
        Dequeue(Queue, u)
        for each vertex w adjacent to u do
            if Mark[w] = 0 then
                Enqueue(Q, w)
                Mark[w] ← 1
                Visit(w)
            endif
        endfor
    endwhile
end BFS
```

Clearly, *BFS* has the same $O(n + m)$ complexity as *DFS*. Figure 11.18 illustrates *BFS* starting at vertex 6 for the same graph as in Figure 11.16.

A breadth-first search with starting vertex v determines a tree spanning the component of the graph G containing v. As with *DFS*, a minor modification of the pseudocode for *BFS* generates this *breadth-first search tree* (*BFS-tree*) rooted at v. When enqueueing a nonvisited vertex w adjacent to u, we define the parent of w to be u. We denote the modified procedure by *BFSTree* and the parent array implementation by *BFSTreeParent*$[0:n − 1]$.

The breadth-first search tree rooted at vertex 6 and the associated array *TreeBFS* for the graph in Figure 11.18 is illustrated in Figure 11.19.

FIGURE 11.18

BFS with *v* = 6 visits
vertices of graph *G*
in the order 6, 1, 3,
7, 0, 2, 4, 5, 8.

Enqueue 6   *Visit 6*
Dequeue   (*u* = 6)
Enqueue 1   *Visit 1*
Enqueue 3   *Visit 3*
Enqueue 7   *Visit 7*
Dequeue   (*u* = 1)
Enqueue 0   *Visit 0*
Enqueue 2   *Visit 2*
Dequeue   (*u* = 3)
Enqueue 4   *Visit 4*
Enqueue 5   *Visit 5*
Dequeue   (*u* = 7)
Dequeue   (*u* = 0)
Enqueue 8   *Visit 8*
Dequeue   (*u* = 2)
Dequeue   (*u* = 4)
Dequeue   (*u* = 5)
Dequeue   (*u* = 8)
Queue is now empty.

$G =$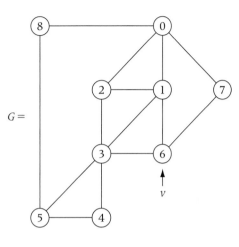

FIGURE 11.19

BFS-tree rooted at
vertex 6 and its
associated array
BFSTreeParent[0:8].

$G =$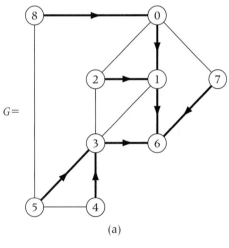

(a)

v	0	1	2	3	4	5	6	7
BFSTreeParent[*v*]	1	6	1	6	3	3	−1	6

(b)

Like a depth-first search, a breadth-first search can be used to determine whether the graph G is connected. Also, a *breadth-first traversal* of an arbitrary graph (connected or not) is obtained from the following algorithm:

```
procedure BFT(G)
Input:     G (a graph with n vertices and m edges)
Output:    the breadth-first traversal of G
    Mark[0:n − 1] a 0/1 array initialized to 0s
    for v ← 0 to n − 1 do
        if Mark[v] = 0 then
            BFS(G, v)
        endif
    endfor
end BFT
```

Similar to a depth-first traversal, a breadth-first traversal generates a breadth-first search forest as implemented by the parent array *BFSForest-Parent*$[0:n − 1]$.

11.2.5 Breadth-First Search Tree and Shortest Paths

The breadth-first search tree starting at vertex v is actually a *shortest-path tree* in the graph rooted at v; that is, it contains a shortest path from v to every vertex in the same component as v. We leave the proof of this shortest-path property as an exercise. The shortest-path property is in sharp contrast to the paths generated by a depth-first search. Indeed, we have seen that paths generated by a depth-first search with starting vertex v are often much longer than shortest paths to v, a fact well illustrated by the complete graph K_n on n vertices. Given any $v \in V(K_n)$, a breadth-first search generates shortest paths of length 1 from v to all other vertices. On the other hand, a depth-first search applied to K_n generates a depth-first search tree that is a path of length $n − 1$.

Clearly, any algorithm that finds a shortest-path tree must visit each vertex and examine each edge. Thus, a lower bound on the complexity of the shortest-path problem is $\Omega(n + m)$. Since the algorithm *BFSTree* has worst-case complexity $O(n + m)$, it is an (order) optimal algorithm.

11.2.6 Searching and Traversing Digraphs

Each search and traversal technique for a graph G generalizes naturally to a digraph D. It is convenient to define in-versions and out-versions of these searches and traversals (the out-version is equivalent to the in-version in

FIGURE 11.20

An in-tree and an
out-tree of a
digraph D

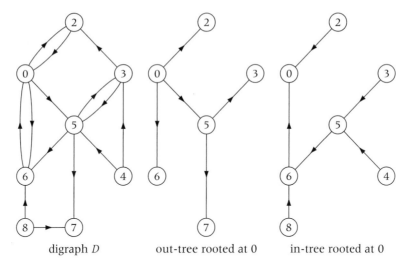

digraph D   out-tree rooted at 0   in-tree rooted at 0

the digraph with the edge orientations reversed). A *directed path from u to v* is
a sequence of vertices $u = w_0 w_1 \ldots w_p = v$, such that $w_i w_{i+1}$ is a directed edge of
D, $i = 0, \ldots, p - 1$. For convenience, we sometimes refer to a directed path
simply as a path. Given a vertex r in a digraph D, an *out-tree T rooted at r* is a
minimal subdigraph that contains a directed path from r to any other vertex
v in T. An *in-tree rooted at r* is defined analogously. Figure 11.20 illustrates an
example.

Corresponding to the algorithm *DFS* for graphs, we have the two algorithms
DFSIn, an in-directed depth-first search, and *DFSOut*, an out-directed depth-first
search. Similarly, corresponding to *DFSTree*, we have the algorithms *DFSInTree*
and *DFSOutTree*; and corresponding to *DFTForest*, we have *DFTInForest* and
DFTOutForest. Analogously, we have algorithms *BFSIn*, *BFSOut* and *BFSInTree*,
BFSOutTree, respectively, for a breadth-first search and similar algorithms for
breadth-first traversals of digraphs.

Figure 11.21a illustrates the sequence of pushes, visits, and pops performed
by *DFSOut* and *DFSIn* for a sample digraph D starting at vertex 1; and Figure
11.20b gives the DFS out-tree and DFS in-tree rooted at 1. Figure 11.21a illustrates the sequence of enqueues, visits, and dequeues performed by *BFSOut* and
BFSIn for the digraph D of Figure 11.21. Figure 11.22b gives the BFS out-tree
and BFS in-tree rooted at 1.

....
FIGURE 11.21

(a) *DFSOut* and
DFSIn with input *D*
and starting vertex
v = 1 visit vertices
in the order 1, 0, 2,
7, 6, 3 and 1, 6, 3,
4, 5, 7, 0, 2, 8,
respectively; (b) DFS
out-tree and in-tree
rooted at 1 and
their associated
arrays.
....

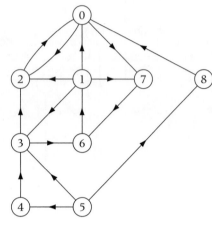

Visit 1		*Visit* 1	
Push 1	*Visit* 0	*Push* 1	*Visit* 6
Push 0	*Visit* 2	*Push* 6	*Visit* 3
Pop	(*u* = 0)	*Push* 3	*Visit* 4
Push 0	*Visit* 7	*Push* 4	*Visit* 5
Push 7	*Visit* 6	*Pop*	(*u* = 4)
Pop	(*u* = 7)	*Pop*	(*u* = 3)
Pop	(*u* = 0)	*Pop*	(*u* = 6)
Pop	(*u* = 1)	*Push* 6	*Visit* 7
Push 1	*Visit* 3	*Push* 7	*Visit* 0
Pop	(*u* = 3)	*Push* 0	*Visit* 2
Pop	(*u* = 1)	*Pop*	(*u* = 0)
		Push 0	*Visit* 8
Stack is now empty.		*Pop*	(*u* = 0)
		Pop	(*u* = 7)
		Pop	(*u* = 6)
		Pop	(*u* = 1)

Stack is now empty.

DFSOut starting at 1   *DFSIn* starting at 1   digraph *D*

(a)

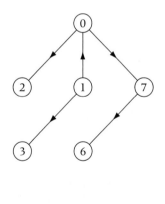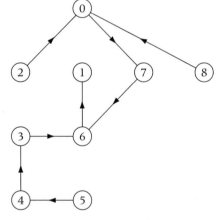

DFS out-tree rooted at 1   DFS in-tree rooted at 1

v	0	1	2	3	4	5	6	7	8
DFSOutTreeParent[*v*]	1	−1	0	1	−1	−1	7	0	−1
DFSInTreeParent[*v*]	7	−1	0	6	3	4	1	6	0

(b)

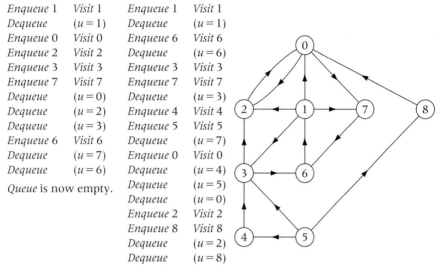

FIGURE 11.22

(a) *BFSOut* and *BFSIn* with input *D* and starting vertex *v* = 1 visit vertices in the order 1, 0, 2, 3, 7, 6 and 1, 6, 3, 7, 4, 5, 0, 2, 8, respectively; (b) BFS out-tree and in-tree rooted at 1 and their associated arrays.

Enqueue 1	*Visit* 1
Dequeue	(*u* = 1)
Enqueue 0	*Visit* 0
Enqueue 2	*Visit* 2
Enqueue 3	*Visit* 3
Enqueue 7	*Visit* 7
Dequeue	(*u* = 0)
Dequeue	(*u* = 2)
Dequeue	(*u* = 3)
Enqueue 6	*Visit* 6
Dequeue	(*u* = 7)
Dequeue	(*u* = 6)

Queue is now empty.

Enqueue 1	*Visit* 1
Dequeue	(*u* = 1)
Enqueue 6	*Visit* 6
Dequeue	(*u* = 6)
Enqueue 3	*Visit* 3
Enqueue 7	*Visit* 7
Dequeue	(*u* = 3)
Enqueue 4	*Visit* 4
Enqueue 5	*Visit* 5
Dequeue	(*u* = 7)
Enqueue 0	*Visit* 0
Dequeue	(*u* = 4)
Dequeue	(*u* = 5)
Dequeue	(*u* = 0)
Enqueue 2	*Visit* 2
Enqueue 8	*Visit* 8
Dequeue	(*u* = 2)
Dequeue	(*u* = 8)

Queue is now empty.

BFSOut starting at 1   *BFSIn* starting at 1   digraph *D*

(a)

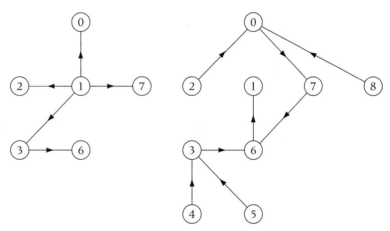

BFS out-tree rooted at 1   BFS in-tree rooted at 1

v	0	1	2	3	4	5	6	7	8
OutTreeBFS[*v*]	1	−1	1	1	−1	−1	3	1	−1
InTreeBFS[*v*]	7	−1	0	6	3	3	1	6	0

(b)

11.3 Topological Sorting

Suppose that we need to perform n tasks and that we must do certain tasks before others. For example, if we are building a house, the task of pouring the foundation must precede the task of laying down the first floor. However, for another pair of tasks, such as painting the kitchen and painting the bathroom, no particular order is required. The problem is to obtain a linear ordering of the tasks in such a way that if task u must be done before task v, then u occurs before v in the linear ordering.

The dependencies of the tasks can be naturally modeled using a directed acyclic graph (dag) D — that is, a directed graph without any directed cycles. The vertices of D correspond to the tasks, and a directed edge from u to v is in D if and only if task u must precede task v. A *topological sorting of D* is a listing of the vertices such that if uv is an edge of D, then u precedes v in the list. A *topological-sort labeling* of D is a labeling of the vertices in D with the labels $0, \ldots, n - 1$ such that for any edge uv in D, the label of u is smaller than the label of v.

A topological-sort labeling is obtained by performing an out-directed depth-first traversal, where we keep track of the order in which vertices become explored. A vertex becomes *explored* when the traversal accesses u having visited all vertices in the out-neighborhood of u (we assume here that a vertex is visited when it is first accessed by the traversal). The following proposition tells us immediately that a topological-sort labeling can be obtained by the reverse order in which the vertices become explored. That is, a vertex u is given topological-sort label $n - i$ if u is the ith vertex to become explored, $i = 1, \ldots, n$.

Proposition 11.3.1 Suppose uv is an arc in the dag D. Then v is explored before u in any out-directed depth-first traversal of D.

PROOF
We break the proof down into two cases.

Case 1. v is visited before u in the traversal.
In this case, note that there can not be a (directed) path from v to u in D; otherwise, D would contain a cycle. Hence, after visiting v, a depth-first search is done, and u is not visited in this part of the traversal. In other words, v will become explored before u is visited in the traversal.

Case 2. u is visited before v in the traversal.
In this case, when u is visited, there are unvisited vertices adjacent to u (namely, v), so that u will be pushed on the stack (either the explicit stack in

a nonrecursive encoding or the implicit activation record stack in a recursive encoding), and a depth-first search from u will commence as part of the traversal. Eventually, v will be visited in the depth-first search proceeding from u. When any vertex w is visited, if there are no unvisited vertices adjacent to w, then w becomes immediately explored. On the other hand, if there are unvisited vertices adjacent to w, then w is pushed on the stack. When a vertex w is popped from the stack, either w is immediately pushed again if there is an unvisited vertex adjacent to w, or w never is pushed again — that is, w becomes explored. This implies that anything on the stack when a vertex w is visited remains on the stack until w is explored; that is, all vertices on the stack when w is visited are explored after w. Because u is on the stack when v is visited, it follows that v is again explored before u. Note that in this case, we did not use the fact that D contains no cycles. ■

The following Key Fact follows immediately from Proposition 11.3.1 and is the basis of the procedure *Topological* that computes the topological-sort ordering.

Key Fact

Given a dag *D*, a topological-sort ordering results from the reverse order in which the vertices are explored.

The following procedure *TopologicalSort* computes the topological-sort ordering resulting from the reverse order in which the vertices are explored.

```
procedure: TopologicalSort(D, TopList[0:n − 1])
Input:    D (dag with vertex set V = {0, … , n − 1} and edge set E)
Output:   TopList[0:n − 1] (array containing a topologically sorted list of the vertices in D)
    Mark[0:n − 1] a 0/1 array initialized to 0s
    Counter ← n − 1
    for v ← 0 to do
        if Mark[n − 1] ← 0 then
            DFSOutTopLabel(D, v)
        endif
    endfor
    procedure DFSOutTopLabel(D, v) recursive
        Mark[v] ← 1
        for each w ∈ V such that vw ∈ E do
            if Mark[w] = 0 then
                DFSOutTopLabel(D, w)
            endif
        endfor
```

$TopList[Counter] \leftarrow v$
$Counter \leftarrow Counter - 1$
end *DFSOutTopLabel*
end *TopologicalSort*

The array *TopList*[0:*n* − 1] output by the procedure *TopologicalSort* is illustrated in Figure 11.23 for a sample dag *D*. Figure 11.23 shows the position in the list *TopList* outside each vertex.

FIGURE 11.23

A dag *D* and the array *TopList*[0:8] output by *TopologicalSort*

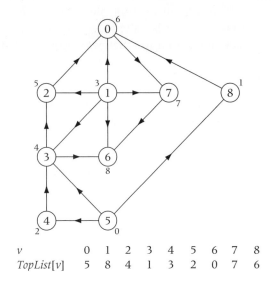

v	0	1	2	3	4	5	6	7	8
TopList[*v*]	5	8	4	1	3	2	0	7	6

11.4 Closing Remarks

In this chapter, we saw how breadth-first searches yield shortest paths in (unweighted) graphs and digraphs. The study of shortest-path algorithms has a long history, and many such algorithms can be found in the literature. In the next chapter, we will present algorithms for finding shortest paths in weighted graphs and digraphs based on the greedy method and dynamic programming.

The depth-first search has a host of applications. We saw how a labeling generated by a depth-first traversal yielded a topological sort of a dag. Other vertex labelings generated by depth-first searches are the basis of many classical graph algorithms (see Chapter 13). Among the useful properties of the depth-first search is a parenthesis structure associated with the first and last access of nodes (see Exercise 11.31).

References and Suggestions for Further Reading

There is a vast literature on the theory of graphs and numerous textbooks have been written on the subject.

Two recent books:

Chartrand, G., and L. Lesniak. *Graphs & Digraphs.* 4th ed. Boca Raton, FL: Chapman & Hall/CRC Press, 2004.

West, D. *Introduction to Graph Theory.* 2nd ed. Englewood Cliffs, NJ: Prentice Hall, 2001.

Jensen, T. R., and B. Toft. *Graph Coloring Problems.* New York: Wiley, 1995. A survey of graph coloring and related problems that includes a section on tie positions in the n^m tic-tac-toe game discussed in Chapter 10.

Gross, J. L., and J. Yellen, eds., *Handbook of Graph Theory*, Boca Raton, FL: Chapman & Hall/CRC Press, 2004. A recent comprehensive handbook on graph theory.

References and further readings for graph algorithms are included at the end of the next three chapters.

Section 11.1 Graphs and Digraphs

11.1   Show that for a digraph D having m directed edges, we have

$$\sum_{v \in V} d_{\text{out}}(v) = \sum_{v \in V} d_{\text{in}}(v) = m.$$

11.2   Prove Proposition 11.1.4.

11.3   Prove Proposition 11.1.5.

11.4   Design a greedy strategy for finding a proper coloring of a graph using $\Delta(G) + 1$ colors (where $\Delta(G)$ denotes the maximum degree of a vertex).

Exercises 11.5 through 11.8 involve finding proper vertex colorings of a graph using backtracking or branch-and-bound. If a graph has n vertices $\{0, 1, \dots, n - 1\}$, then we need at most n colors. Considering the vertices in the order, it is clear that we can restrict the color of vertex 0 to color 1. In the same way, we can restrict the color of vertex 1 to 1 or 2, and so forth. In other words, considering the vertices in the order $0, 1, \dots, n - 1$, you can limit the color choices for vertex i to colors $1, 2, \ldots, \max\{i+1, n\}$. You should use this "pruned" state-space tree in your answers.

11.5   Consider the following graph G.

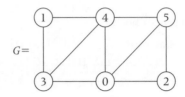

a. Determine the 3-coloring of G generated by a backtracking algorithm, and draw the portion of the state-space tree generated by the algorithm.

b. Determine the 3-coloring of G generated by a LIFO branch-and-bound algorithm, and draw the portion of the state-space tree generated by the algorithm.

11.6   Design a backtracking algorithm for finding a proper coloring of a graph using c colors (or determine that no such coloring exists).

11.7   Given a graph G, the *chromatic number* of G is the minimum number of colors required to properly color the vertices. Give pseudocode for a backtracking algorithm for computing the chromatic number of a input graph on n vertices. The algorithm should also output a coloring that uses the chromatic number of colors.

11.8   Give pseudocode for a LIFO branch-and-bound algorithm for computing the chromatic number of a graph of an input graph on n vertices. The algorithm should also output a coloring that uses the chromatic number of colors. Of course, your algorithm will certainly be horribly inefficient in the worst case. In your algorithm, you may assume *Push* and *Pop* routines for pushing and popping a stack. Use a suitable parent array implementation for the state-space tree of problem states.

11.9   Suppose a salesperson must visit n cities and that there is a cost associated with traveling from one city to another. Starting from a home city, the salesperson wishes to visit each of the other $n - 1$ cities once and return home in such an order that the total cost incurred is a minimum among all such tours (see Figure 11.24). The traveling salesman problem (TSP), which we discussed in Chapter 2, is to determine such a minimum cost tour.

The most straightforward algorithm is an *exhaustive search* that enumerates all $(n - 1)!$ tours and keeps track of the shortest tour generated. In this exercise, you will design a dynamic programming algorithm for the TSP having worst-case complexity in $\Theta(n2^n)$. Although certainly an im-

FIGURE 11.24

A minimum length tour of five cities among the 24 possible tours.

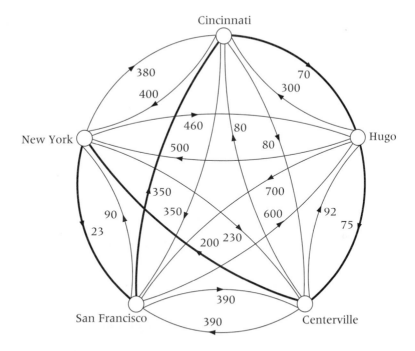

provement over $(n - 1)!$, this exponential complexity is disappointing. However, the TSP belongs to a class of problems (called NP-hard) for which it is believed that no polynomial-time algorithm exists for any problem in the class.

The TSP is equivalent to finding a minimum cost Hamiltonian cycle in a weighted digraph D. We may assume without loss of generality that D is the complete digraph $\hat{K}_n = (V, \hat{E})$, where $|V| = n$ and $\hat{E}$ consists of all pairs of distinct vertices (u, v), $u, v \in V$. Given a weighted digraph $D = (V, E)$, we merely extend the cost weighting c to $\hat{K}_n$ by setting $c(uv) = \infty$ for every (u, v) not in E. TSP for the (undirected) complete graph K_n with cost weighting c is a special case of the Traveling Salesman problem for the digraph $\hat{K}_n$: For each edge e of K_n assign both of the directed edges e^- and e^+ of $\hat{K}_n$ corresponding to e the weight $c(e)$.

Consider a Hamiltonian cycle H of $\hat{K}_n$, where without loss of generality we assume that vertex 0 is the initial and terminal vertex of H. Let i denote the first vertex visited by H after leaving vertex 0, and let H_i denote the subpath of H from vertex i to vertex 0, which passes through each vertex of $\hat{K}_n$ once (such a path is called a *Hamiltonian path*). If H is a minimum cost Hamiltonian cycle, then H_i must be a shortest path from i to 0 whose interior vertices consist of the set $V - \{0, i\}$. [A shortest path P joining two vertices i and j is a path that minimizes $Cost(P)$, where $Cost(P)$ is the sum of the costs over all the edges of P.] Now consider any subset U of V. For i, a vertex not in U, let $MinCost(i, U)$ denote the cost of a shortest (minimum cost) path P from i to 0 whose interior vertices consist of the set U. Note that since P is a shortest path, P must pass through each vertex of U exactly once. Note also that $MinCost(0, V - \{0\})$ is the minimum cost of a Hamiltonian cycle, that is, the cost of an optimal salesman tour.

a. Derive the following recurrence relation for $MinCost(i, U)$:

$$MinCost(i, U) = \min_{j \in U}\{c(i, j) + MinCost(j, U - \{j\})\}, \textbf{ init.cond.}$$
$$MinCost(i, \varnothing) = c(i, 0), \ 1 \le i \le n - 1$$

b. Give pseudocode for a dynamic programming algorithm *TravelingSalesman* based on the recurrence relation in part (a).

c. Verify that the worst-case complexity of your algorithm *TravelingSalesman* in part (b) is given by $W(n) = (n - 1)2^{n-2} \in \Omega(n2^n)$.

11.10 Design a backtracking algorithm that generates all Hamiltonian cycles in a digraph D.

11.11 Design a backtracking algorithm solving the TSP.

11.12 Design a LIFO branch-and-bound algorithm for the TSP.

11.13 Given a graph G, an *independent* set of vertices is a set of vertices no two of which are adjacent. Design a backtracking algorithm that outputs an independent set of vertices of largest size.

11.14 Prove by induction that the hypercube H_k of dimension k has

a. 2^k vertices

b. $k2^{k-1}$ edges

11.15 Consider the hypercube H_k of dimension k on $n = 2^k$ vertices.

a. Show that H_k is k-regular.

b. Show that H_k has diameter $k = \log_2 n$.

11.16 Give an alternative proof of the result in part (b) of Exercise 11.14 using part (a) of the previous two exercises and Corollary 11.1.2.

11.17 Prove by induction that the k-dimensional hypercube H_k has exactly $C(k, j)2^{k-j}$ different subhypercubes of dimension $j, j = 0, \dots, k$.

11.18 Give an example of each of the following graph types:

a. a 2-regular graph with diameter 8

b. a 3-regular graph with diameter 5

11.19 Suppose a 6-regular graph G has 20 more edges than vertices. How many vertices and edges does G have?

11.20 Does there exist a 5-regular graph with 44 edges? Explain.

11.21 a. Using Euler's degree formula and Proposition 11.1.5, prove Proposition 4.2.3, which states that the number of interior vertices in a 2-tree is one less than the number of leaf nodes.

b. Repeat part (a) for k-ary trees.

11.22 Design an $O(\log n)$ algorithm for summing n numbers on the k-dimensional hypercube H_k, where $n = 2^k$.

11.23 a. Prove that a graph G has an Eulerian path from a to b if and only if G is connected, every vertex different from a and b has even degree, and a and b have odd degree.

b. Prove that a graph G has an Eulerian cycle if and only if every vertex has even degree.

c. State and prove a necessary and sufficient condition for the existence of Eulerian paths and cycles in digraphs.

11.24 Give pseudocode for the standard ADT operations of adding and deleting an edge for a graph G for each of the following implementations:

a. an adjacency matrix

b. adjacency lists with an array of header nodes

c. adjacency lists with a linked list of header nodes

11.25 In the adjacency lists implementation of a graph, where the header nodes belong to a linked list (see Figure 11.12a), it is convenient in practice to maintain a second pointer p in each list node defined as follows: If the list node belongs to the adjacency list of vertex i and corresponds to edge i, j then p points to the header node of adjacency list j. Redo Exercise 11.24c with this enhanced implementation.

Section 11.2 Search and Traversal of Graphs and Digraphs

11.26 Consider the following graph.

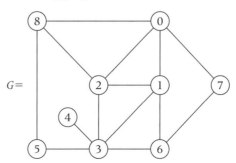

a. Starting at vertex 3, list the vertices in the order in which they are visited by a breadth-first search, and give the array *TreeBFS*[0:8] that gives a parent implementation of the breadth-first search spanning tree.

b. Repeat part (a) for a depth-first search, giving the *DFSTreeParent*[0:8].

11.27 a. Prove that a depth-first search with starting vertex *v* of a graph *G* visits every vertex of *G* if and only if *G* is connected.

b. More generally, prove that a depth-first search with starting vertex *v* of a graph *G* visits every vertex of the component of *G* containing *v*.

c. Repeat (a) and (b) for a breadth-first search.

11.28 Give complete pseudocode for *DFS* for the following implementations of a graph *G*, where the array *Current*[0:*n* − 1] is used by the procedure *Next*:

a. an adjacency matrix

b. adjacency lists with an array of header nodes

c. adjacency lists with a linked list of header nodes

11.29 Repeat Exercise 11.28 for *BFS*.

11.30 Prove that the breadth-first search out-tree rooted at vertex *v* is a shortest-path out-tree rooted at *v* in the digraph; that is, it contains a shortest path from *v* to every vertex accessible from *v*.

11.31 In a depth-first search, show that if we output a left parenthesis when a node is accessed for the first time and a right parenthesis when a node is accessed for the last time (that is, when backtracking from the node), the resulting parenthesization is proper; this is each left parenthesis is properly matched with a corresponding right parenthesis.

11.32 Consider an out-directed depth-first traversal of a directed graph *D*. A *back edge* is an edge *vu* not belonging to the depth-first search forest *F*, such that *u* and *v* belong to the same tree in *F* and *u* is an ancestor of *v*. Show that a directed graph *D* is a dag if and only if there are no back edges.

11.33 a. Design an algorithm for determining whether a digraph *D* is a dag.

b. Modify your algorithm in (a) to output a directed cycle if *D* is not a dag.

11.34 Design and analyze an algorithm that determines whether a graph is bipartite and identifies the bipartition of the vertices if it is bipartite for the following implementations of the graph:

a. an adjacency matrix

b. adjacency lists

11.35 The girth of a graph G is the length of the smallest cycle in G. Design and analyze an algorithm for determining the girth of G.

Section 11.3 Topological Sorting

11.36 Show the topological-sort labeling generated by *TopologicalSort* for the following dag:

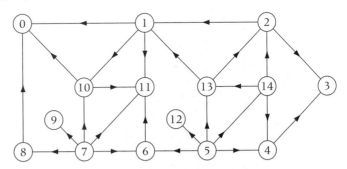

11.37 Design an algorithm that uses a topological labeling of the nodes of a dag to compute a longest path starting at vertex v, for each vertex v.

CHAPTER 12

MINIMUM SPANNING TREE AND SHORTEST-PATH ALGORITHMS

Two fundamental problems for weighted graphs with wide-ranging applications are the minimum spanning tree problem and the shortest-path problem. The problem of finding a minimum spanning tree in a weighted graph is particularly important in network applications. For example, the problem arises in the design of any physical network connecting n nodes, where the connections between nodes are subject to feasibility and weight constraints. Examples of such physical networks include communication networks, transportation networks, energy pipelines, and VLSI chips, among others. In all these examples, the weight of a minimum spanning tree provides a lower bound on the cost of building the network.

Finding shortest paths in weighted graphs and digraphs also has myriad applications to networks of various types. For example, in a computer or communication network, data is most efficiently transferred between nodes of the network along a shortest path between the nodes, where the weights on the edges represent communication latency. Another example is a digraph representing a network of airplane flights. The least costly flight (in terms of money, distance, or time) from one airport to another in the network is the shortest directed path from the departure airport to the arrival airport, where the edge weights are the appropriate costs.

In this chapter, we discuss various algorithms for solving the minimum spanning tree and shortest-path problems.

12.1 Minimum Spanning Tree

Given a spanning tree T in a graph G with a weighting w of the edges E, the *weight* of T, denoted *weight(T)*, is the sum of the w-weights of its edges. If T has minimum weight over all spanning trees of G, then we call T a *minimum spanning tree*.

In Figure 12.1, all the spanning trees of a weighted graph on four vertices are enumerated. The minimum spanning tree is then obtained by inspection.

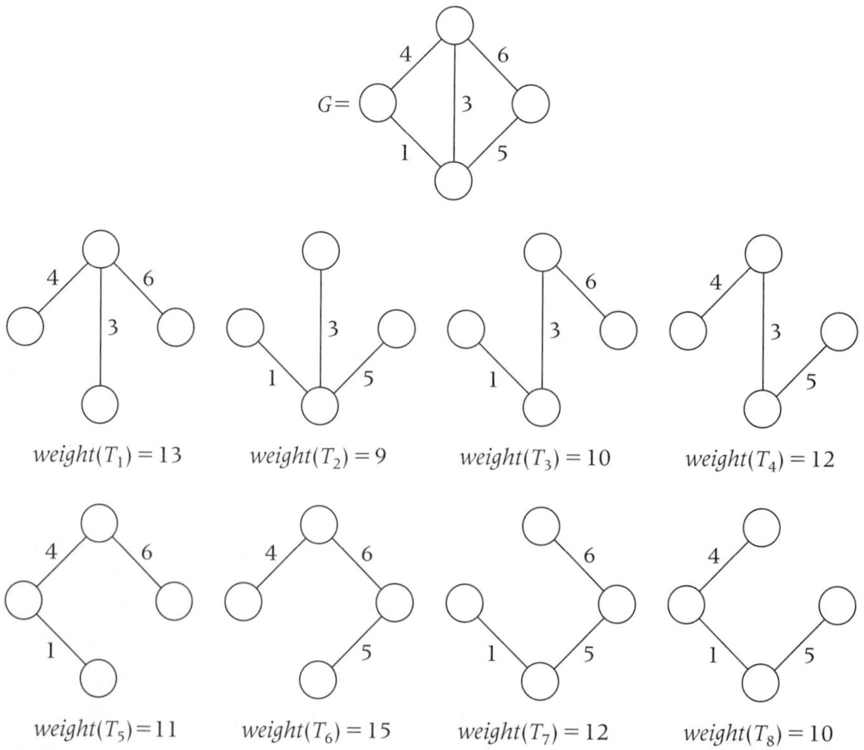

FIGURE 12.1

Enumeration of the spanning trees of G. The minimum spanning tree is T_2.

$$weight(T_1) = 13 \qquad weight(T_2) = 9 \qquad weight(T_3) = 10 \qquad weight(T_4) = 12$$

$$weight(T_5) = 11 \qquad weight(T_6) = 15 \qquad weight(T_7) = 12 \qquad weight(T_8) = 10$$

The number of spanning trees, even for relatively small graphs, is usually enormous, making an enumerative brute-force search infeasible. Indeed, Cayley proved that the complete graph K_n on n vertices contains

$$n^{n-2} \text{ spanning trees.}$$

Fortunately, efficient algorithms based on the greedy method do exist for finding minimum spanning trees. We discuss two of the more famous algorithms, Kruskal's and Prim's. These algorithms are similar in the sense that their selection functions always choose an edge of minimum weight among the remaining edges. However, Prim's algorithm selection function only considers edges incident to vertices already included in the tree. In particular, the partial solutions built by Prim's algorithm are trees, whereas the partial solutions built by Kruskal's algorithm are forests.

12.1.1 Kruskal's Algorithm

Given a connected graph $G = (V, E)$, with $|V| = n$ and $|E| = m$, and a weight function w defined on the edge set E, Kruskal's algorithm finds a minimum spanning tree T of G by constructing a sequence of n forests $F_0, F_1, \ldots, F_{n-1}$, where F_0 is the empty forest and F_i is obtained from F_{i-1} by adding a single edge e. The edge e is chosen so that it has minimum weight among all the edges not belonging to F_{i-1} and doesn't form a cycle when added to F_{i-1}. Kruskal's algorithm is illustrated for a sample graph in Figure 12.2.

REMARK

For convenience, we assume that the input graph G to Kruskal's algorithm is connected. However, Kruskal's algorithm is easily modified to accept *any* graph G (connected or disconnected) and to output a minimum (weight) forest, each of whose trees spans a (connected) component of G.

Using a proof by contradicton, we now show that the spanning tree K generated by Kruskal's algorithm is a minimum spanning tree. For convenience, we will assume that the edge weights are distinct (the proof can be slightly modified to hold for nondistinct edge weights; see Exercise 12.4). Let the edges of K be denoted by $x_1, x_2, \ldots, x_{n-1}$, listed in increasing order of their weights. Assume that K is not a minimum spanning tree, and let T be a minimum spanning tree with edges $y_1, y_2, \ldots, y_{n-1}$, listed in increasing order of their weights. Let j denote the first index i such that $x_i \neq y_i$, so that $x_i = y_i$, $1 \leq i \leq j - 1$. Since x_j was chosen by the greedy strategy, we have $w(x_j) < w(y_j)$.

FIGURE 12.2

Stages in Kruskal's
algorithm.

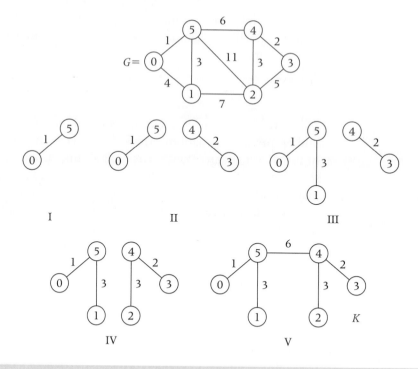

We now construct a spanning tree T' whose weight is smaller than T. Consider the subgraph H obtained by adding the edge x_j to T. It is easily verified that H contains a unique cycle C and that this cycle contains x_j. Since $y_i = x_i$, $i = 1, 2, \ldots, j - 1$, and the tree K does not contain C, it follows that C must contain the edge y_k for some index $k \geq j$. Let T' be the spanning tree obtained from H by deleting the edge y_k. Because $w(y_k) \geq w(y_j) > w(x_j)$, we have

$$weight(T') = weight(T) + w(x_j) - w(y_k) < weight(T),$$

contradicting our assumption that T is a minimum spanning tree. ■

The key implementation detail in Kruskal's algorithm is detecting whether the addition of a given edge e to the existing forest F creates a cycle. Observe that a cycle is formed by the edge $e = uv$ if and only if u and v belong to the same component (tree) in F. We can check whether u and v belong to the same component efficiently using the union and find algorithms for disjoint sets discussed in Chapter 4. In the current context, the collection of disjoint sets is the collection of vertex sets of each tree in forest F.

> **Key Fact**
>
> **When implementing Kruskal's algorithm, an edge *uv* can be added to the current forest if and only if *u* and *v* belong to different trees in the forest. To efficiently test this condition, we use the disjoint set ADT, where the disjoint sets correspond to vertex sets of the trees in the forest, and the forest is maintained using the procedures *Union* and *Find2* discussed in Chapter 4.**

In the following pseudocode for procedure *Kruskal*, the forest F is maintained using its set of edges.

```
procedure Kruskal(G, w, MCSTree)
Input:    G   (a connected graph with vertex set V of cardinality n
                and edge set E = {e_i = u_i v_i | i ∈ {1, ... , m}})
          w   (a weight function on E)
Output:  MCSTree (a minimum spanning tree)
    Sort the edges in nondecreasing order of weights w(e_1) ≤ ··· ≤ w(e_m)
    Forest ← ∅
    Size ← 0
    for i ← 0 to n − 1 do                    //initialize a disjoint collection of single vertices
        Parent[i] ← −1
    endfor
        j ← 0
    while Size ≤ n − 1 .and. j < m do
        j ← j + 1
        Find2(Parent[0:n − 1], u_j, r)      //e_j = u_j v_j
        Find2(Parent[0:n − 1], v_j, s)
        if r ≠ s then                        //add edge e_j to Forest
            Forest ← Forest ∪ {e_j}
            Size ← Size + 1
            Union(Parent[0:n − 1], r, s)    //combine sets containing u_j and v_j
        endif
    endwhile
    MCSTree ← Forest
end Kruskal
```

Since procedure *Kruskal* does $n - 1$ unions and at most m finds, it follows for the results given in Chapter 4 that checking for cycles has a worst-case complexity that is almost linear in m. In procedure *Kruskal*, we assume as a precondition that the edges were sorted in increasing order of their weights. Because presorting the edges can be done in time $O(m\log m) = O(m\log n)$, the overall order of the worst-case complexity is $\Theta(m\log n)$.

Instead of sorting the edges, we could more efficiently select the next minimum-weight edge by using a priority queue of edges of the graph, implemented, for example, with a min-heap. *CreatePriorityQueue (MakeMinHeap)* and *RemovePriority-Queue (RemoveMinHeap)* then have worst-case complexities belonging to $O(m)$ and $O(\log m) = O(\log n)$, respectively. Hence, the selection process remains $O(m \log n)$ in the worst case. However, improvement over procedure *Kruskal* occurs for inputs where the tree is completed early (that is, not many of the selected edges form cycles). For example, in the best case, the first $n - 1$ edges selected form a tree, yielding best-case complexity belonging to $O(m + n \log n)$.

12.1.2 Prim's Algorithm

Prim's algorithm for generating a minimum spanning tree differs from Kruskal's algorithm in that at each stage, it maintains a tree instead of a forest. The initial tree T_0 may be any single vertex r of the graph G. Prim's algorithm builds a sequence of n trees (rooted at r) $T_0, T_1, \dots, T_{n-1}$, where T_{i+1} is obtained from T_i by adding a single edge e_{i+1}, $i = 0, \dots, n - 2$. The edge e_{i+1} is selected (greedily) to be a minimum-weight edge among all edges having *exactly* one vertex in T_i. The set of all edges in G having exactly one vertex in T_i is denoted by $Cut(T_i)$. With this notation, at the ith step, Prim's algorithm chooses an edge e_i of minimum weight among all the edges in $Cut(T_i)$ (see Figure 12.3). Restricting our attention to edges in $Cut(T_i)$ is possible because of the following key fact.

FIGURE 12.3

Sample tree T_6 of Prim's algorithm.

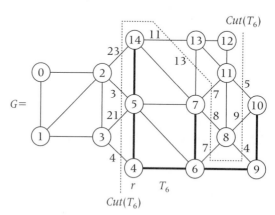

Sample tree T_6 of Prim's algorithm with $V(T_6) = \{4,5,6,7,9,10,14\}$ and $r = 4$.
$Cut(T) = \{\{3,4\},\{3,5\},\{2,5\},\{2,14\},\{13,14\},\{7,13\},\{7,11\},$
$\{7,8\},\{6,8\},\{8,9\},\{8,10\},\{10,11\}\}$.
At stage 6 Prim's algorithm adds edge $e_6 = \{2,5\}$ to T_6,
since $\{2,5\}$ has minimum weight 3 in $Cut(T_6)$.

Key Fact

Given any tree _T_ and edge _e_ in a graph _G_, _T_ ∪ _e_ is a tree if and only if _e_ ∈ _Cut_(_T_)

Proof that Prim's algorithm yields the minimum spanning tree is left to the exercises. Prim's algorithm is illustrated in Figure 12.4 using the same sample graph as in Figure 12.2.

FIGURE 12.4

Tree _T_ and _Cut_(_T_) at each stage in Prim's algorithm, with _r_ = 0.

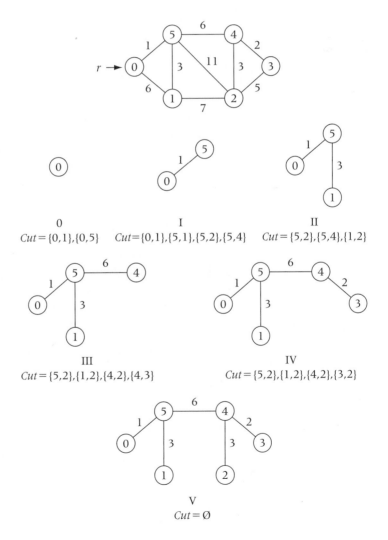

As with Kruskal's algorithm, the complexity of Prim's algorithm is dependent on specific implementation details. A straightforward implementation of Prim's algorithm based on explicitly implementing $Cut(T)$ at each stage is inefficient. A more efficient implementation of Prim's algorithm is based on the following observations. For convenience, we set $w(uv) = \infty$ (or some sufficiently large number) whenever u and v are nonadjacent vertices in G. For each vertex $v \in V(G) - V(T)$, we let $\eta_T(v)$ denote a vertex u of T that is "nearest" to v; that is, $w(uv)$ equals the minimum of $w(xv)$ over all $x \in V(T)$. For example, in Figure 12.3 with $T = T_6$, $V(G) - V(T)$ consists of the vertices $v = 3, 4, 9, 12, 14$, with $\eta_T(v) = 6, 5, 10, 11, 15$, respectively. Clearly, the following equality holds:

$$\min\{w(\{v,\eta_T(v)\})\,|\,v \in V(G) - V(T)\} = \min\{w(e)\,|\,e \in Cut(T)\}. \quad \textbf{(12.1.1)}$$

Thus, when implementing Prim's algorithm, we can maintain η_T at each stage rather than explicitly implementing $Cut(T)$.

When implementing Prim's algorithm, the tree T is dynamically maintained using an array $Parent[0:n - 1]$. The final state of $Parent[0:n - 1]$ yields the parent array implementation of a minimum spanning tree T. Guided by Formula (12.1.1), at any stage of the algorithm, a subarray of $Parent[0:n - 1]$ gives the parent array of the current tree T, whereas another subarray of $Parent[0:n - 1]$ maintains the nearest weight vertices $\eta_T(v)$. More precisely, $Parent[v]$ has the following dynamic interpretation. If $v \in V(T)$, then $Parent[v]$ is the parent of vertex v in T. If $v \notin V(T)$ but is adjacent to at least one vertex of T, then $Parent[v] = \eta_T(v)$. Otherwise, $Parent[v]$ is undefined. Initially, $Parent[r] = -1$.

In the following pseudocode for procedure $Prim$, we also maintain a local array $Nearest[0:n - 1]$, which is initialized to ∞ except for $Nearest[r]$, which is set to 0. At each stage, if $Parent[v]$ is defined, then $Nearest[v] = w(\{v, Parent[v]\})$; otherwise, $Nearest[v] = \infty$. The next vertex u to be added to the tree T is the one such that $Nearest[u]$ is minimized over all $u \notin V(T)$. The arrays $Parent[0:n - 1]$ and $Nearest[0:n - 1]$ are examined for possible alteration at each stage for each vertex v not belonging to T that is adjacent to u. If $w(uv) < Nearest[v]$, then we set $Parent[v] = u$ and $Nearest[v] = w(uv)$. Procedure $Prim$ also maintains a Boolean array $InTheTree$ to keep track of the vertices not in T.

```
procedure Prim(G, w, Parent[0:n − 1])
Input:    G (a connected graph with vertex set V and edge set E)
          w (a weight function on E)
Output:   Parent[0:n − 1] (parent array of a minimum spanning tree}
    for v ← 0 to n − 1 do
        Nearest[v] ← ∞
        InTheTree[v] ← .false.
    endfor
    Parent[r] ← − 1                          //root the tree at an arbitrary vertex r
    Nearest[r] ← 0
```

```
for Stage ← 1 to n − 1 do
    Select vertex u that minimizes Nearest[u] over all u such that InTheTree[u] =
    .false.
    InTheTree[u] ← .true.                      //add u to T
    for each vertex v such that uv ∈ E do      //update Nearest[v] and
        if .not. InTheTree[v] then             //Parent[v] for all v ∉ V(T)
            if w(uv) < Nearest[v] then         //that are adjacent to u
                Nearest[v] ← w(uv)
                Parent[v] ← u
            endif
        endif
    endfor
endfor
end Prim
```

The action of procedure *Prim* is illustrated in Figure 12.5 for the same graph given in Figure 12.4.

> **REMARK**
>
> Procedure *Prim* terminates after only $n − 1$ stages, even though there are n vertices in the final minimum spanning tree. The reason is simple: After stage $n − 1$ has been completed, *InTheTree*[0:$n − 1$] is **.false.** for only one vertex w. Thus, another iteration of the **for** loop controlled by *Stage* would result in no change to the arrays *Nearest*[0:$n − 1$] and *Parent*[0:$n − 1$]. In other words, the last vertex and edge in the minimum spanning tree come in for free.

Clearly, procedure *Prim* has $\Theta(n^2)$ complexity, where we choose the comparison used in updating *Nearest*[0:$n − 1$] in the inner **for** loop as the basic operation. The question arises as to whether procedure *Prim* is more or less efficient than procedure *Kruskal*, which has $\Theta(m \log m)$ worst-case complexity. The answer depends on the number of edges G has compared with the number of vertices. When the ratio m/n is large, then procedure *Prim* is more efficient, whereas when m/n is small, procedure *Kruskal* is better. For example, when the number of edges has the same order as the number of vertices (as for graphs whose vertex degrees are bounded above by some fixed constant), procedure *Kruskal* has $\Theta(n \log n)$ worst-case complexity, which is significantly better than the $\Theta(n^2)$ worst-case complexity of procedure *Prim*. At the other extreme, when the number of edges is quadratic in the number of vertices (such as for the complete graph K_n, so that $m = n(n − 1)/2$), procedure *Kruskal* has worst-case complexity $\Theta(n^2 \log n)$ compared with the $\Theta(n^2)$ worst-case complexity of procedure *Prim*.

....

FIGURE 12.5

Action of procedure
Prim for the same
graph given in
Figure 12.4.

....

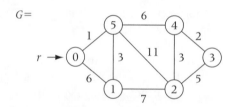

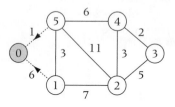

i	0	1	2	3	4	5
Nearest[i]	0	6	∞	∞	∞	1
Parent[i]	−1	0	−	−	−	0
InTheTree[i]	T	F	F	F	F	F

Weight = 0

Stage 1

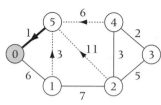

i	0	1	2	3	4	5
Nearest[i]	0	3	11	∞	6	1
Parent[i]	−1	5	5	−	5	0
InTheTree[i]	T	F	F	F	F	T

Weight = 1

Stage 2

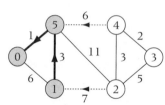

i	0	1	2	3	4	5
Nearest[i]	0	3	7	∞	6	1
Parent[i]	−1	5	1	−	5	0
InTheTree[i]	T	T	F	F	F	T

Weight = 4

Stage 3

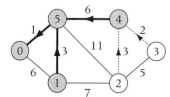

i	0	1	2	3	4	5
Nearest[i]	0	3	3	2	6	1
Parent[i]	−1	5	4	4	5	0
InTheTree[i]	T	T	F	F	T	T

Weight = 10

Stage 4

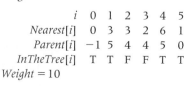

i	0	1	2	3	4	5
Nearest[i]	0	3	3	2	6	1
Parent[i]	−1	5	4	4	5	0
InTheTree[i]	T	T	F	T	T	T

Weight = 12

Stage 5

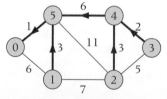

After stage 5, array *Parent* is now
complete, and implements a minimum
spanning tree with weight 15.

In procedure *Prim*, the operations performed on the array *Nearest* are essentially those associated with a priority queue. Thus, procedure *Prim* could be rewritten (procedure *Prim2*) using a priority queue Q of the vertices not in the current tree T. The priority of a vertex u is the weight of the edge joining u to its nearest neighbor $\eta_T(u)$ in T. After removing a vertex u from the priority queue and placing it in T, then we must reduce the priorities of each vertex v adjacent to u that is now "nearer" to the tree. If the priority queue Q is implemented as a min-heap, then both the operation of removing an element from Q and the operation of changing the priority value of an element in Q have $O(\log n)$ complexity. Because there are n removals of an element from Q and the number of times that the priority of an vertex v is lowered is no more than its degree, it follows that the worst-case complexity of *Prim2* belongs to $O(n\log n + 2m\log n) = O(m\log n)$. We leave the pseudocode for procedure *Prim2* as an exercise.

12.2 Shortest Paths in Graphs and Digraphs

In the previous chapter, we saw that a breadth-first search solves the problem of finding shortest paths from a given vertex r in a graph or digraph to every vertex v reachable from r, where the weight of a path is simply the number of edges in a path. In a network setting, this is often referred to as minimizing the number of *hops* from r to v. Often in applications, the important factor is not just the weight of a path as measured by the number of hops but the total weight obtained by summing the weights of its edges, where each edge e has been assigned a given weight $w(e)$. For example, a graph might model a network of cities, and the weight might be the distance or driving time between adjacent cities. As another example, a digraph might model a network of (direct) airplane flights, and the weight of a flight might be its cost or its flying time.

A natural and very important problem is to find a *shortest path* from r to a vertex v—that is, a path from r to v of minimum weight. Given a weighted graph or digraph, the *distance* from r to v is the weight of the shortest path from r to v.

Because a weighted graph is a special case of a weighted digraph, we consider the problem of finding shortest paths in a weighted digraph D. A *shortest-path (out) tree rooted at vertex r in D* is an out-tree that contains a shortest path from r to u for every vertex u for which there exists such a path. A *negative (directed) cycle* is a directed cycle in which the sum of the weights on the edges of the cycle is negative. If there exists a negative cycle, then we can obtain arbitrarily small weighted paths by repeatedly traversing the negative cycle. Thus, the notion of a shortest-path tree is not well defined in this case.

We will present three famous algorithms for finding shortest paths, due to Bellman and Ford, Dijkstra, and Floyd. The Bellman-Ford algorithm and Dijkstra's algorithm output a shortest path from an input vertex r to all other vertices reachable from r, whereas Floyd's algorithm generates shortest paths between *every* pair of vertices in the digraph.

Dijkstra's algorithm uses the greedy strategy, whereas Floyd's algorithm uses dynamic programming. We begin by discussing the Bellman-Ford algorithm, which is the oldest of the three and is not directly based on one of the major design strategies discussed in Part II.

12.2.1 The Bellman-Ford Algorithm

The Bellman-Ford algorithm is based on making successive scans through all the edges of the digraph, keeping track of the distance $Dist[v]$ from r to v using the best (smallest-weight) path from r to v generated so far. We initialize the array $Dist[0:n-1]$ by setting $Dist[r] = 0$, and $Dist[v] = \infty$ for $v \neq r$. We also keep track of the shortest paths generated so far using a parent array implementation $Parent[0:n-1]$ initialized by $Parent[r] = 0$, and $Parent[v] = \infty$ for $v \neq r$. The following key fact is the basis for the Bellman-Ford algorithm.

> **Key Fact**
>
> **During a given scan through the edges, when we examine the edge *uv*, *Dist[v]* is updated by checking whether or not a shorter path from *r* to *v* is obtained by replacing the current path by the path consisting of the current path from *r* to *u* together with the edge *uv*. This process of updating *Dist[v]* is called *relaxing* the edge *uv*.**

The relaxing of an edge is illustrated in Figure 12.6. In Figure 12.6a, we show the currently shortest path $P_{r,u}$ from r to u having weight $Dist[u]$, and the currently shortest path $P_{r,v}$ from r to v having weight $Dist[v]$, just before we consider the directed edge uv. In Figure 12.6b, by considering the edge uv, we have a second possible path from r to v—namely, the path $P'_{r,v}$ obtained by adding the edge uv to the path $P_{r,u}$.

The weight of $P'_{r,v}$ is the weight $Dist[u]$ of the path $P_{r,u}$ plus the weight $w(uv)$ of the edge uv. Hence, to see if we now have a shorter path from r to v, we simply need to check whether the weight of the path $P'_{r,v}$ is smaller than the weight of the path $P_{r,v}$; that is, we simply set

$$Dist[v] = \min\{\text{weight}(P_{r,v}), \text{weight}(P'_{r,v})\} = \min\{Dist[v], Dist[u] + w(uv)\}.$$

If we have found a shorter path—that is, if $\text{weight}(P'_{r,v}) < \text{weight}(P_{r,v})$—then we set $Dist[v] = \text{weight}(P'_{r,v}) = Dist[u] + w(uv)$, and $Parent[v] = u$. As usual, the path from r to v is given (in reverse order) by the sequence

$$v, Parent[v], Parent[Parent[v]], \ldots, Parent^k[v] = r.$$

FIGURE 12.6

Relaxing the edge
uv in the Bellman-
Ford algorithm.

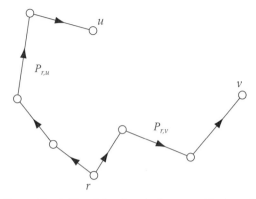

In Bellman–Ford Algorithm just before considering edge *uv*

(a)

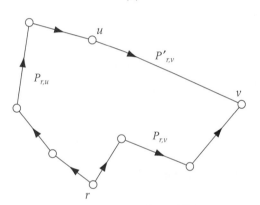

In Bellman–Ford Algorithm after considering edge *uv*.
We compare weight of $P_{r,v}$ with weight of $P'_{r,v}$
and update *Dist*[*v*] with smaller of the two

(b)

The current path from *r* to *v* may be updated many times during the same pass because *D* may have many edges *uv*. If *D* has no negative cycles, it turns out that shortest paths will have been computed after $n - 1$ scans. After completion of the first $n - 1$ scans, procedure *BellmanFord* makes a final scan of the edges to check for negative cycles. If there is any edge *uv* such that $Dist[v] > Dist[u] + w(uv)$, then a negative cycle exists. When *D* has a negative cycle—that is, a cycle such that the total weight of the directed paths making up the cycle is negative— then by repeatedly going around the cycle, we can make the weight of paths from *r* to vertices in this cycle as small as we desire.

The following pseudocode for the Bellman-Ford algorithm follows directly from our discussion.

```
procedure BellmanFord(D, r, w, Dist[0:n − 1], Parent[0:n − 1], NegativeCycle)
Input:     D (a digraph with vertex set V = {0, . . . , n − 1} and edge set E)
           w (a weight function on E)
           r (a vertex of D)
Output:    Parent[0:n − 1] (an array implementing a shortest-path tree rooted at r)
           Dist[0:n − 1] (an array of distances from r)
           NegativeCycle (a Boolean variable having the value .true. if and only if there
                          exists a negative cycle)
    for i ← 0 to n − 1 do                //initialize Dist[0:n − 1] and Parent[0:n − 1]
        Dist[i] ← ∞
        Parent[i] ← ∞
    endfor
    Dist[r] ← 0
    Parent[r] ← − 1
    for Pass ← 1 to n − 1 do             //update Dist[0:n − 1] and Parent[0:n − 1]
        for each edge uv ∈ E do          //by scanning all the edges
            if Dist[u] + w(uv) < Dist[v] then
                Parent[v] ← u
                Dist[v] ← Dist[u] + w(uv)
            endif
        endfor
    endfor
        NegativeCycle ← .false.          //check for negative cycles
    for each edge uv ∈ E do
        if Dist[v] > Dist[u] + w(uv) then
            NegativeCycle ← .true.
        endif
    endfor
end BellmanFord
```

In procedure *BellmanFord,* we do not specify the order in which the edges are scanned. In fact, any order will do. In Figure 12.7, during each pass, we scan the edges (u, v) in lexicographical order.

FIGURE 12.7

Action of procedure *BellmanFord* for a sample weighted digraph and root vertex $r = 6$, where edges (u, v) are scanned in lexicographical order.

Index	0	1	2	3	4	5	6	7	8		0	1	2	3	4	5	6	7	8
Pass																			
0	Dist:	∞	∞	∞	∞	∞	∞	0	∞	∞	Parent:	∞	∞	∞	∞	∞	∞	−1	∞	∞
1	Dist:	∞	3	∞	2	∞	∞	0	∞	∞	Parent:	∞	6	∞	6	∞	∞	−1	∞	∞
2	Dist:	1	3	1	2	5	9	0	5	6	Parent:	8	6	3	6	5	3	−1	1	5
3	Dist:	1	3	1	2	5	9	0	−3	6	Parent:	8	6	3	6	5	3	−1	0	5
4	Dist:	1	3	1	2	5	9	0	−3	6	Parent:	8	6	3	6	5	3	−1	0	5
5	Dist:	1	3	1	2	5	9	0	−3	6	Parent:	8	6	3	6	5	3	−1	0	5
6	Dist:	1	3	1	2	5	9	0	−3	6	Parent:	8	6	3	6	5	3	−1	0	5
7	Dist:	1	3	1	2	5	9	0	−3	6	Parent:	8	6	3	6	5	3	−1	0	5
8	Dist:	1	3	1	2	5	9	0	−3	6	Parent:	8	6	3	6	5	3	−1	0	5

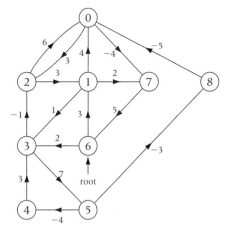

Because procedure *BellmanFord* examines each edge n times, it has best-case, average, and worst-case complexities belonging to $\Theta(nm)$. The best-case and average performance of procedure *BellmanFord* can be improved by adding a flag to test whether any changes to *Dist* occur during a given pass. If no change occurs in any particular pass, then the algorithm can terminate. For example, for the digraph illustrated in Figure 12.7, only four passes are required. By adding the flag, the performance of procedure *BellmanFord* can be drastically different for different orderings of passing through the edges. To see why, consider the three-vertex digraph shown in Figure 12.8 and notice the difference between *Dist*[v] after the first pass for the two different orderings of the edges. In fact, it is not hard to give an example of a weighted digraph D on n vertices and two orderings of the edges such that procedure *BellmanFord* performs only two passes in one ordering and the full n passes in the other ordering.

···················
FIGURE 12.8

First pass of
procedure
BellmanFord,
where edges are
considered in the
order *rv*, *uv*,
ru would yield
Dist[v] = 2, but the
order *ru*, *uv*, *rv*
would yield
Dist[v] = −1.
···················

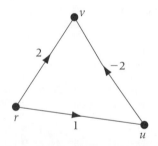

First pass of procedure *BellmanFord* where edges are
considered in the order *rv*, *uv*, *ru* would yield *Dist*[v] = 2
but the order *ru*, *uv*, *rv* would yield *Dist*[v] = − 1

Key Fact

The correctness of either version (flag or no flag) of procedure *BellmanFord* does not depend on the order in which the edges are scanned. However, with the flag added, the efficiency can vary drastically depending on the order in which the edges are scanned.

The correctness of procedure *BellmanFord* involves establishing the loop invariant stated in the following lemma.

Lemma 12.2.1

After completing k iterations of the *Pass* **for** loop, for each vertex v, $Dist[v]$ is no larger than the minimum weight $L_{v,k}$ of a path from r to v having at most k edges (where $L_{v,k} = \infty$ if no such path exists), $k = 0, \dots, n - 1$.

PROOF
We prove the lemma by induction on the number k of passes completed. Clearly, the lemma is true before any pass has been completed, so that the basis step is established. We can assume that after k passes have been completed, for each vertex v, $Dist[v]$ is no larger than the minimum weight $L_{v,k}$ of a path from r to v having at most k edges. Consider any vertex v for which there is a path from r to v having at most $k + 1$ edges (the lemma is trivially true if there is no such path), and let P be such a path of minimum weight $L_{v,k}$. Let uv be the terminal edge of P, and let Q be the subpath of P from r to u. Because Q has at most k edges, the weight of Q is at least $L_{u,k}$. Thus, the weight of P is at least $L_{u,k} + w(uv)$. But, by induction assumption, after the kth pass, $Dist[u]$ is at most $L_{u,k}$. Therefore, after the $(k + 1)$st pass, we have $Dist[v] \leq Dist[u] + w(uv) \leq L_{u,k} + w(uv) \leq$ weight of $P = L_{v,k}$. Thus, the loop invariant holds after $k + 1$ passes. ∎

When there are no negative cycles, a shortest path contains at most $n - 1$ edges. Hence, the correctness of *BellmanFord* when there are no negative cycles follows immediately from Lemma 12.2.1. We leave the correctness proof of *BellmanFord* when there are negative cycles as an exercise.

12.2.2 Dijkstra's Algorithm

Dijkstra's algorithm grows a shortest-path tree using the greedy method. Although Dijkstra's algorithm has superior worst-case performance to *Bellman-Ford*, it has the restriction that the edge weights must be nonnegative.

For undirected graphs, Dijkstra's algorithm follows a similar strategy to Prim's algorithm, differing only in the way the next edge is selected. At each stage in Dijkstra's algorithm, instead of selecting an edge of minimum weight in *Cut*(*T*), we select an edge $uv \in Cut(T)$, $u \in V(T)$, so that the path from r to v in the augmented tree $T \cup \{uv\}$ is shortest—that is, such that $Dist[u] + w(uv)$ is minimized over all edges $uv \in Cut(T)$, where $Dist[u]$ is the weight of a path from r to u in T. The following pseudocode is a high-level description of Dijkstra's algorithm.

```
procedure Dijkstra(G, a, w, T)
Input:   G (a graph with vertex set V = {0, . . . , n − 1} and edge set E)
         r (a vertex of G)
         w (a nonnegative weighting on E)
Output: T (a shortest-path tree rooted at r)
         Dist[0:n − 1] is an array initialized to ∞
         T is initialized to be the tree consisting of the single vertex r
         Dist[r] ← 0
         while Cut(T) ≠ ∅ do
             select an edge uv ∈ Cut(T) such that Dist[u] + w(uv) is minimized
             add vertex v and edge uv to T
         endwhile
end Dijkstra
```

Figure 12.9 shows the tree T at each stage of Dijkstra's algorithm for a sample weighted graph G. In this figure, the label on the outside of each vertex v already included in the growing tree T is the weight of the path from v to a in T.

Let T_i be the tree generated by procedure *Dijkstra* after i iterations of the **while** loop, $i = 0, 1, \ldots, t$, where t is the number of iterations of the loop ($t \leq n - 1$). For $v \in V(T_i)$, let $P_i^{(v)}$ denote the path from r to v in T_i, $i = 0, 1, \ldots, t$. We prove the correctness of procedure *Dijkstra* by establishing the following lemma.

FIGURE 12.9

Tree T and $Cut(T)$ at
each stage in
Dijkstra's algorithm

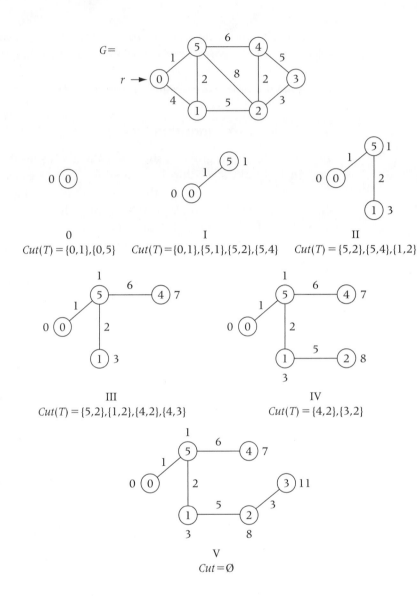

$$0$$
$$Cut(T) = \{0,1\}, \{0,5\}$$

$$I$$
$$Cut(T) = \{0,1\}, \{5,1\}, \{5,2\}, \{5,4\}$$

$$II$$
$$Cut(T) = \{5,2\}, \{5,4\}, \{1,2\}$$

$$III$$
$$Cut(T) = \{5,2\}, \{1,2\}, \{4,2\}, \{4,3\}$$

$$IV$$
$$Cut(T) = \{4,2\}, \{3,2\}$$

$$V$$
$$Cut = \emptyset$$

Lemma 12.2.2

For each vertex $v \in V(T_i)$, $P_i^{(v)}$ is a shortest path in G from r to v, $i = 0, 1, \ldots, t$.

PROOF

Basis step. Clearly, the lemma is true for $i = 0$ because T_0 consists of the single vertex r.

Induction step. Assume that the lemma holds for T_i. The tree T_{i+1} is obtained from T_i by adding a single edge uv that minimizes $Dist[u] + w(uv)$ over all edges $uv \in Cut(T_i)$, where $Dist[u]$ is the weight of $P_u^{(i)}$. By induction assumption, for all $x \in V(T_i)$, $P_x^{(i+1)} = P_x^{(i)}$ is a shortest path in G from r to x. It remains to show that $P_v^{(i+1)}$ is a shortest path in G from r to v. Consider any path Q in G from r to v. Because deleting the edges in $Cut(T_i)$ disconnects G with vertices r and v lying in different components, Q must contain edge xy from $Cut(T_i)$, $x \in V(T_i)$, such that the subpath Q_x of Q from r to x lies entirely in T_i. Then we have

$$
\begin{aligned}
weight(Q) &\geq weight(Q_x) + w(xy) && \text{(since the weight function} \\
& && \text{is nonnegative)} \\
&\geq weight(P_x^{(i)}) + w(xy) && \text{(since } P_x^{(i)} \text{ is a shortest path in } G \text{ from} \\
& && r \text{ to } x \text{ in } G) \\
&\geq weight(P_u^{(i)}) + w(uv) && \text{(by the greedy choice } Dijkstra \text{ makes)} \\
&= weight(P_u^{(i+1)})
\end{aligned}
$$

Since Q was chosen to be an arbitrary path in G from r to v, it follows that $P_u^{(i+1)}$ is a shortest path in G from r to v. This completes the induction step and the correctness proof of procedure *Dijkstra*. ■

As with Kruskal's and Prim's algorithms, the complexity of Dijkstra's algorithm depends on specific implementation details. We now implement the procedure *Dijkstra*, which is similar to the procedure *Prim* in that the tree T is dynamically grown using an array $Parent[0:n-1]$. We also maintain a Boolean array *InTheTree* to keep track of the vertices not in T. Again, rather than having to explicitly maintain the sets $Cut(T_i)$, we can efficiently select the next edge uv to be added to the tree by maintaining an array $Dist[0:n-1]$, where $Dist[v]$ is the distance from r to v in T and $Dist[v] = \infty$ if v is not in T. Upon completion of *Dijkstra*, the distance from the root r to all the vertices of G is contained in the array $Dist[0:n-1]$. At each intermediate stage $Dist[v]$ has the following dynamic interpretation. If $v \in V(T)$, then $Dist[v]$ is the weight of a path in T from r to v. If $v \notin V(T)$ and v is adjacent to a vertex of T, then $Dist[v]$ is the minimum value of $Dist[u] + w(uv)$ over all $uv \in Cut(T)$. If $v \notin V(T)$ and v is not adjacent to any vertex of T, then $Dist[v] = \infty$. $Dist[v]$ is initialized to ∞ for each vertex $v \neq r$ and $Dist[r]$ is initialized to 0. Each time a vertex u is added to the tree T, we need only update $Parent[v]$ and $Dist[v]$ for those vertices v that are adjacent to u and do not belong to the tree T. If $Dist[v] > Dist[u] + w(uv)$, then we set $Parent[v] = u$ and $Dist[v] = Dist[u] + w(uv)$.

```
procedure Dijkstra(G, w, r, Parent[0:n − 1], Dist)
Input:    G (a connected graph with vertex set V and edge set E)
          r (a vertex of G)
          w (a weight function on E)
Output:   Parent[0:n − 1] (parent array of a shortest-path tree)
          Dist[0:n − 1] (array of weights of shortest paths from r)
     for v ← 1 to n do              //initialize Dist[0:n − 1] and InTheTree[0:n − 1]
          Dist[v] ← ∞
          InTheTree[v] ← .false.
     endfor
     Dist[r] ← 0
     Parent[r] ← − 1
     for Stage ← 1 to n − 1 do
          Select vertex u that minimizes Dist[u] over all u such that InTheTree[u] = .false.
          InTheTree[u] ← .true.
          for each vertex v such that uv ∈ E do      //update Dist[v] and Parent[v] arrays
               if .not. InTheTree[v] then
                    if Dist[u] + w(uv) < Dist[v] then
                         Dist[v] ← Dist[u] + w(uv)
                         Parent[v] ← u
                    endif
               endif
          endfor
     endfor
end Dijkstra
```

REMARKS

1. As with procedure *Prim*, procedure *Dijkstra* terminates after only $n − 1$ stages, even though there are n vertices in the final shortest-path tree. Another iteration of the **for** loop controlled by *Stage* would result in no change to the arrays *Dist*[0:n − 1] and *Parent*[0:n − 1].

2. Although Prim's algorithm and Dijkstra's algorithm have some similarity and they both generate spanning trees, they solve different problems. Simple examples show that a shortest-path tree can fail to be a minimum spanning tree (see Exercise 12.18).

The shortest-path algorithms presented in this section for undirected graphs generalize naturally to digraphs. In fact, essentially unchanged code for procedure *Dijkstra* applies to digraphs. We merely have to be careful in the case of digraphs to note that uv corresponds to a directed edge $uv = (u, v)$ from u to v (as opposed to the undirected edge $uv = \{u, v\}$). We illustrate the action of Dijkstra's algorithm for a sample digraph in Figure 12.10, where the current value of $Dist[v]$ is shown outside each vertex v.

FIGURE 12.10

Action of procedure
Dijkstra for a
sample digraph *D*.

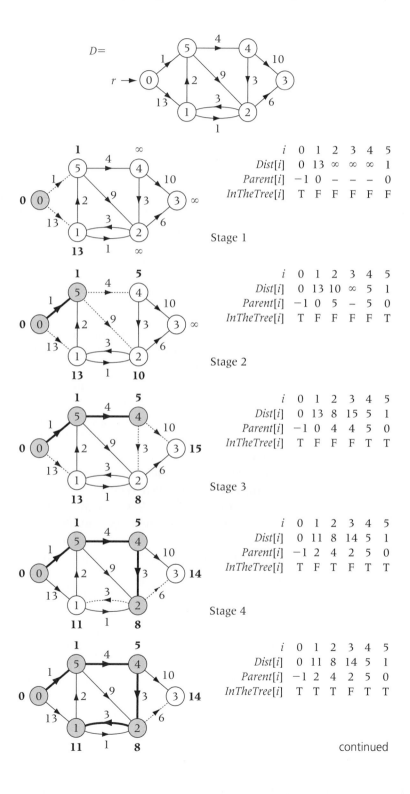

FIGURE 12.10

Action of procedure
Dijkstra for a
sample digraph *D*.

continued

FIGURE 12.10
Continued

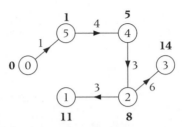

Resulting shortest path spanning out-tree rooted at vertex $r = 0$

As with procedure *Prim*, the worst-case complexity of procedure *Dijkstra* belongs to $\Theta(n^2)$ and to $\Theta(n\log n)$ if a priority queue is used. For either version, the worst-case complexity has smaller order than the $\Theta(mn)$ worst-case complexity of procedure *BellmanFord*.

12.2.3 Floyd's Algorithm

Both Dijkstra's and the Bellman-Ford shortest-path algorithms find paths from a single source vertex r to all other vertices of a weighted digraph $D = (V, E)$ and have complexities $\Theta(n^2)$ and $\Theta(nm)$, respectively. By repeated calls to either of these algorithms we obtain algorithms for a shortest path between every pair of vertices u and v, having complexities $\Theta(n^3)$ and $\Theta(n^2m)$, respectively. We now use dynamic programming to obtain a $\Theta(n^3)$ algorithm, Floyd's algorithm, for finding a shortest path between every pair of vertices of a weighted digraph D. Unlike the all-pairs shortest paths algorithm based on repeated applications of Dijkstra's algorithm, Floyd's algorithm works even if some of the edges have negative weights, provided there is no negative cycle (where the sum of the weights of the edges in the cycle is negative).

Consider a digraph D with vertex set $V = \{0, \ldots, n-1\}$ and edge set E, whose edges have been assigned a weighting w. Let P be a path joining two distinct vertices $i, j \in V$, and suppose v is an interior vertex of P (that is, any vertex of P different from either i or j). As discussed in Chapter 9, the Principle of Optimality holds, so the subpath P_1 from i to v is a shortest path from i to v, and the subpath P_2 from v to j is a shortest path from v to j.

For the nonnegative integer $k \leq n$, let V_k denote the subset of vertices $\{0, \ldots, k-1\}$ (by convention, $V_0 = \varnothing$). Let $S_k(i, j)$ denote the weight of a shortest path P from i to j, whose interior vertices (if any) all lie in V_k (if no such path P exists, then $S_k(i, j) = \infty$). By definition, $S_0(i, j)$ is the weight of a shortest path from i to j containing no interior vertices; thus, S_0 is equal to the *weight matrix W* defined as follows: $W(i, j) = w(e)$ if D contains an edge e from vertex i to vertex j, 0 if $i = j$, and ∞ otherwise. Note that $S_n(i, j)$ is the weight of a shortest path in G from i to j.

If k is not an interior vertex of P, then P is a shortest path from i to j whose interior vertices lie in V_{k-1}, so that $S_k(i,j) = S_{k-1}(i,j)$. On the other hand, if k is an interior vertex of P, then the interior vertices (if any) of the path P_1 from i to k and the interior vertices (if any) of the path P_2 from k to j all lie in V_{k-1}. Because P_1 is a shortest path from i to k and P_2 is a shortest path from k to j, we have $S_k(i,j) = S_{k-1}(i,k) + S_{k-1}(k,j)$. Thus, either $S_k(i,j) = S_{k-1}(i,j)$ or $S_k(i,j) = S_{k-1}(i,k) + S_{k-1}(k,j)$, depending on whether P contains vertex k. Since P is a shortest path from i to j, it follows that the weight of P is equal to the minimum of these two values, yielding the following recurrence relation for $S_k(i,j)$:

$$S_k(i,j) = \min\{S_{k-1}(i,j), S_{k-1}(i,k) + S_{k-1}(k,j)\}$$

init. cond. $\qquad S_0(i,j) = W(i,j) \text{ for all } i, j \in V.$ $\qquad$ **(12.2.1)**

Floyd's algorithm is based on recurrence relation (12.2.1). The matrix S_k keeps track of the weight of the shortest paths and not the shortest paths themselves. To keep track of the paths, we maintain another matrix $P_k(i,j)$ defined by

$$P_k(i,j) = \begin{cases} P_{k-1}(i,j) & \text{if } S_k(i,j) = S_{k-1}(i,j), \\ k & \text{otherwise} \end{cases}$$

init.cond. $\qquad P_0(i,j) = -1 \text{ for all } i, j \in V.$ $\qquad$ **(12.2.2)**

Floyd's algorithm is illustrated in Figure 12.11 for a sample digraph D and weight function w.

A shortest path from i to j in G can then be reconstructed from P_n as follows. If $P_n(i,j) = 0$, then a shortest path from i to j is directly along the edge (i,j); otherwise, if $P_n(i,j) = k$, then k is an interior vertex of a shortest path from i to j. Any other interior vertices in this shortest path can be obtained by recursively examining $P_n(i,k)$ and $P_n(k,j)$. For example, in Figure 12.11, a shortest path S from vertex 2 to vertex 4 can be reconstructed for the final matrix P_5 as follows. Because $P_5(2,4) = 1$, vertex 1 is an internal vertex of S. Now, $P_5(1,4) = -1$, so that there are no interior vertices of S between 1 and 4. Since $P_5(2,1) = 0$, vertex 0 is an interior vertex of S between 2 and 1. Now, $P_5(2,0) = -1$ and $P_5(0,1) = -1$, so that there are no interior vertices between 2 and 0 or between 0 and 1. Thus, a shortest path S from 2 to 4 is given by 2, 0, 1, 4.

FIGURE 12.11

Stages of Floyd's
algorithm for a
sample weighted
digraph D.

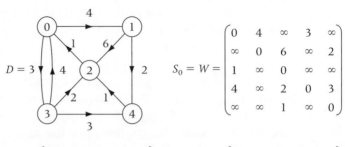

$$S_1 = \begin{pmatrix} 0 & 4 & \infty & 3 & \infty \\ \infty & 0 & 6 & \infty & 2 \\ 1 & 5 & 0 & 4 & \infty \\ 4 & 8 & 2 & 0 & 3 \\ \infty & \infty & 1 & \infty & 0 \end{pmatrix} \qquad P_1 = \begin{pmatrix} -1 & -1 & -1 & -1 & -1 \\ -1 & -1 & -1 & -1 & -1 \\ -1 & 0 & -1 & 0 & -1 \\ -1 & 0 & -1 & -1 & -1 \\ -1 & -1 & -1 & -1 & -1 \end{pmatrix}$$

$$S_2 = \begin{pmatrix} 0 & 4 & 10 & 3 & 6 \\ \infty & 0 & 6 & \infty & 2 \\ 1 & 5 & 0 & 4 & 7 \\ 4 & 8 & 2 & 0 & 3 \\ \infty & \infty & 1 & \infty & 0 \end{pmatrix} \qquad P_2 = \begin{pmatrix} -1 & -1 & 1 & -1 & 1 \\ -1 & -1 & -1 & -1 & -1 \\ -1 & 0 & -1 & 0 & 1 \\ -1 & 0 & -1 & -1 & -1 \\ -1 & -1 & -1 & -1 & -1 \end{pmatrix}$$

$$S_3 = \begin{pmatrix} 0 & 4 & 10 & 3 & 6 \\ 7 & 0 & 6 & 10 & 2 \\ 1 & 5 & 0 & 4 & 7 \\ 3 & 7 & 2 & 0 & 3 \\ 2 & 6 & 1 & 5 & 0 \end{pmatrix} \qquad P_3 = \begin{pmatrix} -1 & -1 & 1 & -1 & 1 \\ 2 & -1 & -1 & 2 & -1 \\ -1 & 0 & -1 & 0 & 1 \\ 2 & 2 & -1 & -1 & -1 \\ 2 & 2 & -1 & 2 & -1 \end{pmatrix}$$

$$S_4 = \begin{pmatrix} 0 & 4 & 5 & 3 & 6 \\ 7 & 0 & 6 & 10 & 2 \\ 1 & 5 & 0 & 4 & 7 \\ 3 & 7 & 2 & 0 & 3 \\ 2 & 6 & 1 & 5 & 0 \end{pmatrix} \qquad P_4 = \begin{pmatrix} -1 & -1 & 3 & -1 & 1 \\ 2 & -1 & -1 & 2 & -1 \\ -1 & 0 & -1 & 0 & 1 \\ 2 & 2 & -1 & -1 & -1 \\ 2 & 2 & -1 & 2 & -1 \end{pmatrix}$$

$$S_5 = \begin{pmatrix} 0 & 4 & 5 & 3 & 6 \\ 4 & 0 & 3 & 7 & 2 \\ 1 & 5 & 0 & 4 & 7 \\ 3 & 7 & 2 & 0 & 3 \\ 2 & 6 & 1 & 5 & 0 \end{pmatrix} \qquad P_5 = \begin{pmatrix} -1 & -1 & 3 & -1 & 1 \\ 4 & -1 & 4 & 4 & -1 \\ -1 & 0 & -1 & 0 & 1 \\ 2 & 2 & -1 & -1 & -1 \\ 2 & 2 & -1 & 2 & -1 \end{pmatrix}$$

We now give pseudocode for Floyd's algorithm.

```
procedure Floyd(W[0:n − 1, 0:n − 1], P[0:n − 1, 0:n − 1], S[0: n − 1, 0:n − 1])
Input:    W[0:n − 1, 0:n − 1] (weight matrix for a weighted digraph D)
Output:   P[0:n − 1, 0:n − 1] (matrix implementing shortest paths)
          S[0:n − 1, 0:n − 1] (distance matrix, where S[u, v] is the weight
          of a shortest path from u to v in G)
     for i ← 0 to n − 1 do                      //initialize P and S
         for j ← 0 to n − 1 do
             P[i, j] ← − 1
             S[i, j] ← W[i, j]
         endfor
     endfor
     for k ← 0 to n − 1 do            //update S and P using Formulas (12.2.1) and
                                          (12.2.2)}
         for i ← 0 to n − 1 do
             for j ← 0 to n − 1 do
                 if S[i, j] > S[i, k] + S[k, j] then
                     P[i, j] ← k
                     S[i, j] ← S[i, k] + S[k, j]
                 endif
             endfor
         endfor
     endfor
end Floyd
```

REMARK

An alternative way to maintain the shortest paths is to store in $P[i, j]$ the first vertex encountered on the current path from i to j (see Exercise 12.27).

12.3 Closing Remarks

The problem of finding a minimum spanning tree in an undirected graph G generalizes naturally to the problem of finding a minimum spanning in-tree (or out-tree) rooted at a given vertex r in a digraph D. Prim's algorithm extends to digraphs by replacing *Cut*(T) with *CutIn*(T) [or *CutOut*(T)] consisting of all edges of $Cut(T)$ having a head in T (or having a tail in T). Unfortunately, even though this greedy method yields a spanning in-tree (or out-tree) rooted at r, it doesn't always yield one of minimum weight. Algorithms for constructing minimum-weight in-trees (out-trees) can be found in the references.

An improvement to Prim's algorithm has been found that uses a Fibonacci heap and has $\Theta(m + n \log n)$ worst-case complexity. Probabilistic $\Theta(m)$ algorithms have been found for the minimum spanning tree problem.

We will design parallel algorithms for the minimum spanning tree and shortest-path problems in Chapter 16.

References and Suggestions for Further Reading

The following two excellent references contain the history of the minimum spanning tree problem:

Graham, R. L., and P. Hell. "On the History of the Minimum Spanning Tree Problem." *Annals of the History of Computing* 7 (1985): 43–57.

Tarjan, R. E. *Data Structures and Network Algorithms*. Philadelphia, PA: Society for Industrial and Applied Mathematics, 1983.

Gordon, M., and M. Minoux (trans. by S. Vajda). *Graphs and Algorithms*. New York: Wiley, 1984. This text contains algorithms for constructing minimum-weight spanning in-trees in digraphs and gives a comprehensive treatment of the shortest-path problem.

Wu, Y. W., and C. Kun-Mao. *Spanning Trees and Optimization Problems*. Boca Raton, FL: CRC Press, 2004. A book entirely devoted to spanning trees and their role in optimization problems.

The following references discuss generalizations of the minimum spanning algorithms to matroids:

Papadimitriou, C. H., and K. Steiglitz. *Combinatorial Optimization: Algorithms and Complexity*. Englewood Cliffs, NJ: Prentice-Hall, 1982.

Thulasiraman, K., and M. N. S. Swamy. *Graphs: Theory and Algorithms*. New York: Wiley, 1992.

EXERCISES

Section 12.1 Minimum Spanning Tree

12.1 Consider the following weighted graph G:

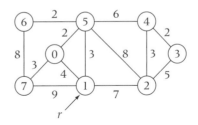

a. Trace the action of procedure *Kruskal* for G.

b. Trace the action of procedure *Prim* for G, with $r = 1$.

12.2 Give pseudocode for a version of procedure *Kruskal* that maintains the weighted edges of the graph in a priority queue.

12.3 Prove the following two propositions used in the proof of the correctness of Kruskal's algorithm.

a. Adding an edge to a tree creates a unique cycle.

b. Removing an edge from a cycle in a connected graph still leaves the resulting graph connected.

12.4 a. Show how the problem of finding a minimum spanning tree in a weighted graph with repeated edge weights can be transformed into an equivalent problem with distinct edge weights.

b. Show that the minimum spanning tree is unique when the edge weights are distinct.

12.5 Modify procedure *Kruskal* to accept *any* graph G (connected or disconnected) and to output a minimum-weight forest, each of whose trees is a minimum spanning tree for a component of G.

12.6 Prove that Prim's algorithm yields a minimum spanning tree.

12.7 Analyze the complexity of the variant of procedure *Prim* based on an explicit implementing of $Cut(T)$ at each stage of the algorithm. Compare its complexity with that of procedure *Prim*.

12.8 Give pseudocode for a procedure *Prim2* using a priority queue.

12.9 The problem of finding a minimum spanning tree in an undirected graph G generalizes naturally to the problem of finding a minimum spanning in-tree (or out-tree) rooted at a given vertex r in a strongly connected digraph D. Prim's algorithm directly generalizes to digraphs, with the modification that *Cut*(*T*) is replaced by *CutIn*(*T*) [or *CutOut*(*T*)] consisting of all edges of *Cut*(*T*) having a head in *T* (or a tail in *T*). Show that this greedy method doesn't always yield a spanning in-tree (or out-tree) rooted at *r*.

Section 12.2 Shortest Paths in Graphs and Digraphs

12.10 a. Redo the action of procedure *BellmanFord* shown in Figure 12.7 where $r = 1$.

b. Redo the action of procedure *BellmanFord* shown in Figure 12.7 where $r = 6$ and the weight of the edge (3,2) is changed to -2.

12.11 a. Design a modification of procedure *BellmanFord* that improves the best-case and average performance by terminating if no changes to *Dist* occur during a pass.

b. Analyze the best-case and worst-case complexity of your algorithm in part (a) in terms of the parameters *n* and *m*. Explicitly exhibit input digraphs achieving the best-case and worst-case complexities, respectively.

c. Repeat part (b) in terms of the single parameter *n*.

12.12 A high-level description of procedure *BellmanFord* is given in Section 12.2. Give a description of procedure *BellmanFord* for the following implementations of the digraph:

a. an adjacency matrix

b. adjacency lists

12.13 Show that if a weighted digraph contains no negative or zero cycles, then a shortest path contains at most $n - 1$ edges. Conclude the correctness proof of procedure *BellmanFord* when there are no negative cycles.

12.14 Give the correctness proof of procedure *BellmanFord* when there are negative cycles.

12.15 Modify procedure *BellmanFord* to output a negative cycle, when one exists.

12.16 Consider a version of procedure *BellmanFord* that checks each pass for any change in *Dist*[0:$n - 1$]. For this version, the order in which the edges are scanned can significantly affect the worst-case performance of the algorithm. Give an example of a weighted digraph and two orderings *A* and *B* of the edges such that if ordering A is used during each pass, procedure *BellmanFord* performs only two passes, but if ordering B is used during each pass, procedure *BellmanFord* performs n passes.

12.17 Trace the action of procedure *Dijkstra* for the following digraph with initial vertex $r = 2$:

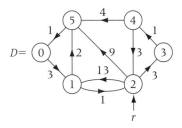

12.18 a. Trace the action of procedure *Dijkstra* for the graph G of Figure 12.5 with $r = 0$.

b. Note that the shortest-path tree generated in part (a) happens to coincide with the minimum spanning tree. Give an example of a weighted graph G with distinct weights and a vertex r such that the shortest-path[tree T generated by procedure *Dijkstra* is not a minimum spanning tree. In fact, find an example of a graph on n vertices where the shortest-path tree has only one edge in common with the minimum spanning tree.

12.19 Trace the action of procedure *Dijkstra* for the graph G of Exercise 12.1, with initial vertex $r = 1$.

12.20 Given a weighted graph G and vertices a, b, consider the following greedy strategy that attempts to grow a shortest path from a to b. Choose an edge e having the smallest weight among the remaining edges incident with the terminal vertex u of the path P previously generated such that e contains no vertex of P other than u. These greedy choices continue until either b is reached or no choice for e exists. Give an example where the path so grown

a. never reaches b

b. reaches b, but is not a shortest path from a to b

12.21 Prove that the tree generated by procedure *Dijkstra* spans all vertices in the component of the graph G containing a.

12.22 Give pseudocode for a version of Dijkstra's algorithm that uses a priority queue.

12.23 Show that Dijkstra's algorithm can fail when some of the weights are negative, even though no negative cycles exist. (In particular, why doesn't adding a sufficiently large positive constant to each edge always work?)

12.24 Show the action of Floyd's algorithm for the following graph:

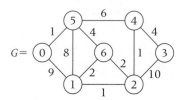

12.25 Given the following weighted digraph D, show the matrices $S_k[0:5, 0:5]$, $P_k[0:5, 0:5]$, $k = 0, \ldots, 5$ as computed by Floyd's algorithm. Describe how the matrix P_6 can be used, for example, to find the shortest path from vertex 1 to vertex 3.

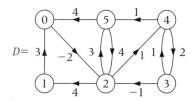

12.26 Give pseudocode for an algorithm that computes the shortest path from i to j from the matrix $P[0:n - 1, 0:n - 1]$ generated by Floyd's algorithm.

12.27 Alter procedure *Floyd* to store in $P[i, j]$ the first vertex encountered on the current path from i to j. Then repeat Exercise 12.26 for this altered matrix $P[0:n - 1, 0:n - 1]$.

12.28 Prove that Floyd's algorithm works even if some of the edges have negative weights provided there is no negative-weight cycle.

12.29 Show how Floyd's algorithm can be used to obtain longest paths between every pair of vertices in a dag.

CHAPTER **13**

GRAPH CONNECTIVITY AND FAULT-TOLERANCE OF NETWORKS

In many applications modeled using graphs and digraphs, it is important to determine whether certain connectivity properties hold. For example, in a communication or computer network, it is important to find an alternate path joining two nodes in the presence of node failures. In this chapter we present algorithms for some classical graph connectivity problems, such as finding the strongly connected components of a digraph, finding articulation points of a graph, and computing the open ear decomposition of a biconnected graph. We design $O(m + n)$ algorithms for these problems based on depth-first search numbering techniques introduced by Tarjan. We also discuss fault-tolerant routing schemes based on open ear decompositions and s-t orderings.

13.1 Strongly Connected Components

We can easily solve the problem of finding the components of an undirected graph G using depth-first traversal. The vertex set of each tree of a depth-first traversal forest is a component of G. Thus, we can compute the components of G in time $O(m + n)$ using *DFTForest* (see Chapter 11), where n and m denote the number of vertices and edges of G, respectively.

The notion of a strongly connected component in a digraph $D = (V, E)$ is a generalization of the notion of a component in a graph. Two vertices u and v in a digraph D are *strongly connected* if there is a directed path from u to v and a directed path from v to u. Clearly, the relation *strongly connected* is an equivalence relation on the set $V = V(D)$ of vertices of D. The subdigraphs induced by these equivalence classes are called *strongly connected components of D* (see Figure 13.1).

> **REMARK**
>
> Although the connected components of a graph partition the vertex set as well as the edge set, in general, the strongly connected components of a digraph only partition the vertex set. An edge can be in at most one strongly connected component, but it might not be in any.

FIGURE 13.1

Strongly connected components in a digraph D.

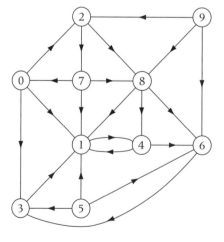

Digraph D

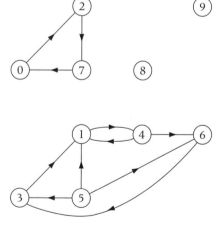

Strongly connected components

The depth-first search out-tree $T_{\text{out}, v}$ of digraph D rooted at v is an out-tree that contains a path from v to every vertex u for which there exists a path in D from v to u. The depth-first search in-tree $T_{\text{in}, v}$ of D rooted at v contains a path from u to v for every vertex u for which there exists a path in D from u to v. Thus, a vertex u belongs to the strongly connected component containing v if and only if u belongs to both $T_{\text{out}, v}$ and $T_{\text{in}, v}$. Computing $T_{\text{out}, v}$ and $T_{\text{in}, v}$ using *DFSOutTree* and *DFSInTree*, and then determining the vertices common to both, yields an $O(m + n)$ algorithm for finding the strongly connected component containing vertex v. Calling this algorithm for each vertex v yields an $O(n(m + n))$ algorithm for obtaining all the strongly connected components of D.

We now discuss a more efficient ($O(m + n)$) algorithm *StrongComponents* for obtaining the set of strongly connected components of a digraph, which is based on the notion of the postnumbering of the vertices of a digraph. For convenience, we assume that $V(D) = \{0, 1, \dots, n - 1\}$. The postnumbering of a digraph D is determined by performing an out-directed depth-first traversal of D. For definiteness in our illustrations, we assume that the depth-first traversal always chooses the smallest vertex whenever there is a choice. Recall that a vertex u of D becomes *explored* when the traversal accesses u, having visited all vertices in the out-neighborhood of u. The *postnumber* of u, denoted *PostNum(u)*, is the integer i, where u is the $(i + 1)^{\text{st}}$ vertex to be explored in an out-directed depth-first traversal of D, $i = 0, \dots, n - 1$ (see Figure 13.2a).

REMARK

Vertex u has postnumber i if u is the $(i + 1)^{\text{st}}$ vertex to be visited in a postorder traversal of the DFT out-forest, $i = 0, \dots, n - 1$.

Clearly, *PostNum* is a permutation of $0, 1, \dots, n - 1$. The inverse permutation of *PostNum*, which we denote by *PostNumInv*, can be computed in linear time. Note that *PostNumInv*(0), *PostNumInv*(1), ... , *PostNumInv*($n - 1$) lists the vertices in the order in which they have been explored. We can easily modify the depth-first traversal *DFTOut* to compute arrays *PostNum*[0:$n - 1$] and *PostNumInv* [0:$n - 1$], representing the permutations *PostNum* and *PostNumInv*, respectively. In Figure 13.2, we illustrate the values of the arrays *PostNum*[0:$n - 1$] and *PostNumInv*[0:$n - 1$] for a given digraph D.

The following two propositions are the basis for the algorithm *StrongComponents* for computing the strongly connected components of a digraph.

Proposition 13.1.1 Let C be the vertex set of a strongly connected component of a digraph D. Suppose u is a vertex such that $PostNum(u) < PostNum(r)$ for some vertex $r \in C$. If u is joined with an edge uv to some vertex v of C (not necessarily equal to r), then u belongs to C.

PROOF
We give a proof by contradiction. Assume that the hypothesis of the proposition holds, but u does not belong to C. It follows that there is no path from any vertex in C to u. Clearly, u does not become explored by the out-directed depth-first traversal until after v is accessed. Let x be the first vertex in C to be accessed by the out-directed depth-first traversal. Since C is the vertex set of a strongly connected component, it follows that every vertex of C different from x will be accessed and eventually explored before x becomes explored. Because there is no path from x to u, after having accessed x, the out-directed depth-first search will not access u until after x has been explored. Thus, every vertex in C is explored before u, so that every vertex in C has a smaller postnumber than u. However, this contradicts the fact that r has a greater postnumber than u. ■

Proposition 13.1.2 Given a digraph D, suppose we perform an in-directed depth-first traversal in which we scan the vertices in the order $PostNumInv[n - 1]$, $PostNumInv[n - 2]$, ... , $PostNumInv[0]$. Then the vertex sets of the in-trees $T_1, T_2, ... , T_k$ of the associated depth-first traversal in-forest coincide with the vertex sets that induce the strongly connected components of D. More precisely, given the tree T_i, let r_i denote the root vertex of T_i and let V_i denote the vertex set of T_i. Then the vertex set C of the strongly connected component containing r_i is precisely V_i, $i = 1, ... , k$.

PROOF
By proving that $C \supseteq V_i$, we show inductively that the vertices of V_i having depth d in T_i belong to C, $d = 0, ... , depth(T_i)$.

Basis step: Since r_i belongs to C, this result is true for $d = 0$.

Induction step: Assume that all vertices of T_i having depth d belong to C and consider a vertex u of T_i having depth $d + 1$. Because we choose r_i to be the vertex not in trees $T_1, ... , T_{i-1}$ having the largest postnumber, it follows that $PostNum(u) < PostNum(r_i)$. Further, since u has depth $d + 1$ in T_i, it is joined to some vertex v of T_i at depth d. By induction hypothesis, v belongs to C, so that Proposition 13.1.1 implies that u belongs to C. Thus, by induction, all the vertices of T_i belong to C. ■

The following algorithm, *StrongComponents*, finds the strongly connected components *D* in two stages. In the first stage, *StrongComponents* performs an out-directed depth-first traversal to compute the array *PostNumInv*[0:*n* − 1]. In the second stage, *StrongComponents* performs an in-directed depth-first traversal, where we scan in the order *PostNumInv*[*n* − 1], ... , *PostNumInv*[0]. In the pseudocode for *StrongComponents*, we use the array *InForest*[0:*n* − 1] to keep track of the depth-first traversal in-forest (see Figure 13.2). *StrongComponents* has the same order of complexity, $O(m + n)$, as the depth-first traversal.

```
procedure StrongComponents(D, PostNumInv[0:n − 1])
Input:     D (a digraph with n vertices and m edges)
              PostNumInv[0:n − 1] (PostNumInv[i] (the vertex u where PostNum[u] = i)
Output:   InForest[0:n − 1] (an array giving parent representation of the forest of in-
              trees T₁, T₂, . . . , Tₖ)
   Mark[0:n − 1]        //a 0–1 array
   InForest[0:n − 1]
   for v ← 0 to n − 1 do
      Mark[v] ← 0
      InForest[v] ← − 1
   endfor
   for i ← n − 1 downto 0 do          //perform an in-directed depth-first traversal
      v ← PostNumInv[i]               //according to reverse order of postnumbers
      if Mark[v] = 0 then
         DFSInTree(D, v, InForest)    //perform an in-directed depth-first search rooted
                                       //at vertex v and store associated depth-first in-tree
                                       //as part of InForest[0:n − 1]

      endif
   endfor
end StrongComponents
```

The action of *StrongComponents* is illustrated in Figure 13.2.

FIGURE 13.2

Arrays
PostNum[0:9],
PostNumInv[0:9],
and *InForest*[0:9] for
the digraph *D* given
in Figure 13.1.

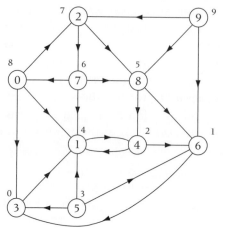
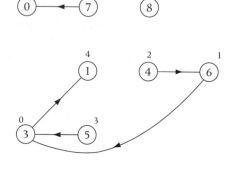

Digraph *D* with the post number
shown outside each node

In-forest generated by
StrongComponents

i	0	1	2	3	4	5	6	7	8	9
PostNum[i]	8	4	7	0	2	3	1	6	5	9
PostNumInv[i]	3	6	4	5	1	8	7	2	0	9
InForest[i]	−1	−1	7	1	6	3	3	0	−1	−1

 ## 13.2 Articulation Points and Biconnected Components

In many applications of graphs, it is useful to know that stronger connectivity
properties hold than merely being connected. For example, suppose *G* models a
communication network, where the vertices of *G* might correspond to people,
processors, computers, and so forth. Two vertices *u* and *v* in such a network are
joined with an edge whenever direct communication is possible between them.
A pair of vertices *u* and *v* that cannot communicate directly can communicate by
relaying the information along a *u–v* path—that is, a path joining *u* and *v*. In
practice, having more than one path connecting vertices *u* and *v* makes the communication network more tolerant of certain failures. For example, sometimes a
vertex in the network becomes "inoperable," meaning it can no longer relay information. This situation calls for finding communication paths that bypass the
inoperable vertex.

For some vertices in a graph, finding bypass paths might not be possible in all cases. For example, if deleting a certain vertex v disconnects the graph, then vertices u, w in two different components of $G - v$ can no longer communicate with one another because all paths connecting u and w in G must pass through v. In this section, we consider algorithms for identifying such troublesome vertices v, called articulation points.

Throughout this section, we assume that the graph G is connected. A vertex v of a connected graph G is an *articulation point* (also called a *cut vertex*) if the graph $G - v$ obtained from G by deleting vertex v and all incident edges is not connected. A *biconnected component* of G (also called a *block of G*) is a maximal subgraph B such that B has no articulation points (see Figure 13.3).

FIGURE 13.3

Articulation points
and biconnected
components of a
connected graph G.

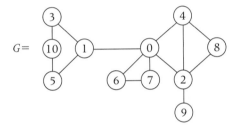

$G=$

Graph G with articulation points $\{0,1,2\}$

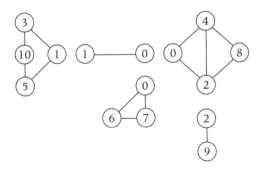

Biconnected components of G

There are many equivalent conditions for a graph to be biconnected. Six of these conditions are given in the following theorem.

Theorem 13.2.1 Let G be a connected graph with at least three vertices. Then the following statements are equivalent:

1. G is biconnected.
2. Every two vertices u and v belong to a common cycle. Equivalently, there exist two internal disjoint u–v paths.
3. Every vertex and edge belongs to a common cycle.
4. Every two edges belong to a common cycle.
5. Given two vertices u, v and an edge e, there is a u–v path containing e.
6. Given three distinct vertices u, v, w of G, there exists a u–v path containing w.
7. Given three distinct vertices u, v, w of G, there exists a u–v path not containing w. □

The proof of Theorem 13.2.1 is left to the exercises. Since a biconnected component is a maximal subgraph that is biconnected, the subgraph $G[U]$ induced by a set of vertices U is a biconnected component if and only if U is a maximal set such that $G[U]$ satisfies the conditions of Theorem 13.2.1.

We now consider the problem of finding the articulation points and the biconnected components of a connected graph G. First we design an algorithm for computing the articulation points, which we then use to compute the biconnected components. The algorithms we discuss for finding the articulation points of G are based on the DFS-tree T_v rooted at a vertex $v \in V(G)$. The following two easily verified propositions are useful in finding articulation points.

Proposition 13.2.2 Given a vertex r of a connected graph $G = (V, E)$, consider the DFS-tree T_r rooted at vertex r. Then for any edge $e \in E$, one end point of e is an ancestor of the other in T_r. More precisely, if $vw \in E$, and v is accessed before w in the depth-first search rooted at r, then v is an ancestor of w in T_r. □

Proposition 13.2.3 Given a vertex r of a connected graph $G = (V, E)$, consider the DFS-tree T_r rooted at vertex r. Then r is an articulation point in G if and only if r has two or more children in T_r. □

Using Proposition 13.2.3, computing T_r for each vertex r in the graph G yields an $O(nm)$ algorithm for determining the set of all articulation points.

We now discuss an $O(m)$ algorithm *ArticulationPoints* for computing the articulation points. As with the algorithm *StrongComponents*, *ArticulationPoints* is based on computing (two) numberings of the vertices based on a single depth-first search. The first numbering, *DFSNum*, is simply the order in which the vertices are (first) accessed by a depth-first search rooted at vertex r. The second numbering, *Lowest*, can be computed recursively at the same time as the depth-first search tree T_r rooted at vertex r (and associated numbering *DFSNum*) is determined. *Lowest* is defined in terms of the notion of a bypass edge.

Given a vertex u in T_r different from r, we show that u is an articulation point if and only if u has a child c in T_r that has no bypass edge defined as follows. Let $T_{r,c}$ denote the subtree of T_r having root vertex c, and let $P_{r,c}$ denote the path in T_r joining r to $parent(parent(c))$. A *bypass edge for* c is an edge $vw \in E$ such $v \in T_{r,c}$ and $w \in P_{r,c}$ (see Figure 13.4).

FIGURE 13.4

DFS-tree T_r, vertex c, subtree $T_{r,c}$, path $P_{r,c}$, and bypass edge vw for c.

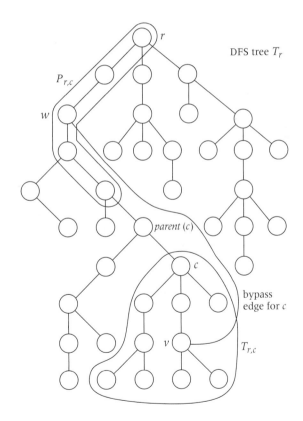

The following proposition and its corollary are easily verified.

Proposition 13.2.4   Given a vertex r of a connected graph $G = (V, E)$, consider the DFS-tree T_r rooted at vertex r. Then for any vertex c at depth at least two in T_r, there exists a path in G not containing *parent*(c) that joins c and r if and only if there exists a bypass edge for c.   □

Corollary 13.2.5   Given a vertex r of a connected graph $G = (V, E)$, consider the DFS-tree T_r rooted at vertex r. Then a vertex $v \neq r$ is an articulation point in G if and only if there exists a child c of v in T_r having no bypass edge for c.   □

An algorithm for finding the articulation points in G is based on Corollary 13.2.5 and the fact that the numbering *Lowest* gives a simple test for the existence of bypass edges. We define *Lowest*[c] to be the minimum DFS number of c and all vertices w for which there is a nontree edge vw, where v is either c or a descendent of c in T_r and w is an ancestor of c in T_r. Clearly, c has a bypass edge if and only if *Lowest*[c] < *DFSNum*(*parent*(c)). Therefore, by Corollary 13.2.5, we have the following proposition.

Proposition 13.2.6   Let u be any vertex of G different from the root of T_r. Then, u is an articulation point if and only if u has at least one child c such that

$$Lowest[c] \geq DFSNum(u). \qquad \textbf{(13.2.1)} \qquad □$$

For a given $v \in V(G)$, it is easily verified that *Lowest*[v] satisfies the following recurrence relation (see Exercise 13.11).

$$Lowest[v] = \min \begin{cases} \min \{Lowest[c] \,|\, c \text{ is a child of } v \text{ in } T_r\}, \\ \min \{DFSNum[w] \,|\, vw \in E, \, w \neq parent(v)\}, \\ DFSNum[v]. \end{cases} \qquad \textbf{(13.2.2)}$$

REMARKS

1. We assume that min{*DFSNum*[w] : $vw \in E$, $w \neq parent(v)$} = ∞ if no such w exists. Similarly, min{*Lowest*[c] | c is a child of v in T_r} = ∞ if v is a leaf node of T_r.
2. We can compute *Lowest* using a depth-first search. When computing *Lowest*[v] during such a search, if $vw \in E$, and $w \neq parent(v)$, then by Proposition 13.2.2, either w is an ancestor of v in T_r so that *DFSNum*[w] is defined, or $w \in T_{r,v}$ and *DFSNum*[w] will be defined during the recursive resolution of *Lowest*[c] for an appropriate child of v. This makes min{*DFSNum*[w] | $vw \in E$, $w \neq parent(v)$} well defined during our depth-first search.

FIGURE 13.5

Values of *DFSNum*
and *Lowest* for *G*
and the array
TreeDFS[0:10]
for T_0

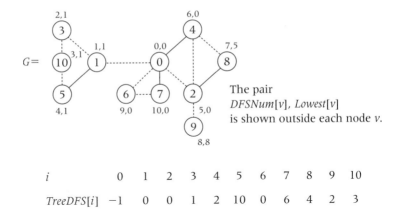

i	0	1	2	3	4	5	6	7	8	9	10
TreeDFS[*i*]	−1	0	0	1	2	10	0	6	4	2	3

Figure 13.5 illustrates the values of *DFSNum*[*v*] and *Lowest*[*v*] for the same graph as shown in Figure 13.3, where we use root vertex $r = 0$. The pair *DFSNum*[*v*], *Lowest*[*v*] is shown outside each node *v*, and the edges of the depth-first search tree *T* rooted at vertex 0 are shown as dotted.

We can compute the *Lowest* and *DFSNums* numberings by performing what amounts to a depth-first search as given by the following $O(m)$ recursive algorithm:

```
procedure DFSNumberings(G, v) recursive
Input:   G (a connected graph with n vertices and m edges)
         v (a vertex of G)    //v is root vertex r of DFS on initial call
         Mark[0:n − 1] (global array initialized to zeros)
         TreeDFS[0:n − 1] (global array initialized to zeros)
         DFSNum[0:n − 1] (global array)
         Lowest[0:n − 1] (global array)
         i (global integer initialized to −1)
Output:  the DFS and Lowest numberings of the vertices of G, and the parent
         implementation of the depth-first search tree TreeDFS(T_r) rooted at vertex r
   i ← i + 1
   Mark[v] ← 1
   DFSNum[v] ← i
   for each u adjacent to v do
       if Mark[u] = 0 then
           TreeDFS[u] ← v
           DFSNumberings(G, u)
       endif
   endfor
   Min1 ← {Lowest[c] for each child c of v}
   Min2 ← min {DFSNum[w] | v adjacent to w but w is not the parent of v}
   Lowest[v] ← min {DFSNum[v], Min1, Min2}
end DFSNumberings
```

R E M A R K

For simplicity, in our description of the output of *DFSNumberings*, we only described the output for the initial (nonrecursive) call to the procedure. The output from recursive calls also provides the proper updating of *Mark*, *DFSNum*, *TreeDFS*, and *Lowest*, thereby ensuring that the initial call returns the desired *DFS* and *Lowest* numberings of G.

With the aid of *DFSNumberings*, we now can present the algorithm *Articula-tionPoints*, which outputs the set of articulation points of a graph G. For simplicity of pseudocode, we assume that the root vertex for the depth-first search is $r = 0$.

```
procedure ArticulationPoints(G, Art)
Input:      G (a connected graph with n vertices and m edges)
Output:     Art (the set of articulation points)
    TreeDFS[0:n − 1], DFSNum[0:n − 1], Lowest[0:n − 1], and
    Mark[0:n − 1]  arrays of size n
    for v ← 0 to n − 1 do    //initialize Mark and TreeDFS
        Mark[v] ← 0
        TreeDFS[v] ← 0
    endfor
    i ← 0
    Art ← ∅
    DFSNumberings(G, 0)   //compute TreeDFS[u], DFSNum[u], Lowest[u]
                          //for each vertex u ∈ V use Proposition 13.2.3
                          //to test whether root r = 0 is an articulation point; that is,
                          //check to see if vertex 0 has more than one child in T₁
    Number ← 0
    c ← 1
    while Number < 2 .and. c ≤ n do
        if TreeDFS[c] = 1 then //c is a child of root vertex r = 1
            Number ← Number + 1
        endif
        c ← c + 1
    endwhile
    if Number = 2 then      //root vertex is an articulation point
        Art ← Art ∪ {0}
    endif
    //use Proposition 13.2.4 and Corollary 13.2.5 to determine nonroot articulation
    //points: whenever a child c has a parent v ≠ r such that Lowest[c] ≥ DFSNum[v],
    //then v is an articulation point
```

```
        for c ← 1 to n − 1 do
            v ← TreeDFS[c]
            if Lowest[c] ≥ DFSNum[v] .and. v ≠ 0 then
                Art ← Art ∪ {v}
            endif
        endfor
    end ArticulationPoints
```

ArticulationPoints outputs *Art* = {0, 1, 2} for the input graph *G* of Figure 13.6. Note that these are precisely the articulation points of *G*.

Algorithm *ArticulationPoints* uses the *Lowest* and *DFSNum* numberings to compute the articulation points of a connected graph *G*. We now describe how we can use these numberings to compute the biconnected components of *G*. The following key fact shows that we need to do more than just determine the articulation points.

Key Fact

Because vertices can belong to more than one biconnected component, simply knowing the articulation points in a graph _G_ may give very little information about the biconnected components. (Indeed, starting from any graph _H_, consider the graph _G_ obtained by adding a new vertex _v′_ for each vertex _v_ in _H_, together with an edge _vv′_. Then the articulation points of _G_ are simply the vertex set of _H_, which gives no information about the biconnected components of _G_ belonging to _H_.) However, each edge belongs to exactly one biconnected component, so that the biconnected components partition the edge set of _G_.

In addition to maintaining the usual stack of vertices associated with the depth-first search, we maintain a second stack of edges. Initially, this second stack is empty. When an edge *uv* is first examined during the depth-first search, we push *uv* on the second stack. Note that we also include edges *uv* where *v* has already been visited; that is, edges *uv* that do not belong to the depth-first search tree. When the depth-first search backtracks along a tree edge *uv* from *v* to *u*, where $Lowest[v] \geq DFSNum[u]$, we then perform a sequence of pops from the second stack until the edge *uv* is popped. It is easily verified (see Exercise 13.12) that the set of edges popped in this manner are precisely the edge set of a biconnected component of *G*. Because every edge of *G* is eventually scanned and pushed on the second stack, all the biconnected components are generated in this fashion.

We now describe of a nonrecursive algorithm for computing both the articulation points and the biconnected components by performing a single depth-first search. Again, two stacks are involved: a DFS-stack of vertices for implementing the depth-first search and a second stack of edges for computing the biconnected components. Initially both stacks are empty. When a vertex u is first visited, we compute the depth-first search number $DFSNum[u]$ (by incrementing the previously computed depth-first search number and assigning it to $DFSNum[u]$), and initialize $Lowest[u]$ to $DFSNum[u]$. When an edge uv is accessed during the depth-first search, we push uv onto the second stack of edges. If uv is not a tree edge, we replace $Lowest[v]$ by the minimum of $Lowest[v]$ and $DFSNum[v]$. When backtracking along a tree edge uv (that is, when v is popped from the DFS-stack having been being pushed on the stack when exploring u), we replace $Lowest[u]$ by the minimum of $Lowest[u]$ and $Lowest[v]$. If $Lowest[v] \geq DFSNum[u]$, then we pop all the edges down to and including edge uv from the second stack, generating the next biconnected component. We leave it as an exercise to verify the correctness of this algorithm.

13.3 Fault-Tolerant Routing Schemes

A fundamental network problem is to route data from a given node u in the network to another node v. We refer to u as the *source node* and v as the *destination node*. The condition of the network being connected ensures that a packet of data can be routed from u to v along a path from u to v. However, with many possible paths joining u and v, we need a routing scheme to move the packet along a specific path. One such scheme uses a routing table associated with the spanning tree T rooted at the destination node v. For each node u different from v, the routing table stores the parent node of u in T. A packet at any node u can then be rooted to v by successively moving to parent nodes until v is reached. To optimize the length of the path generated, often T is chosen to be a shortest-path tree. In the previous two chapters, we have discussed algorithms for computing such shortest-path trees. By associating a routing table (a spanning tree rooted at v) with each node v of the network, we can route packets from any source node u to any destination node v

In this section, we discuss a routing scheme that moves data successfully from any vertex u to a destination vertex v in the presence of a single vertex fault (not at u or v) in the network. The routing scheme we design is based on computing two independent spanning trees, T_1 and T_2, rooted at v.

DEFINITION 13.3.1 We say that two spanning trees, T_1 and T_2, rooted at a vertex v are *independent* if, for any vertex u, the path in T_1 from u to v and the path in T_2 from u to v have no interior vertices in common.

Note that if two spanning trees T_1 and T_2 rooted at a vertex v are independent and a single vertex w (different from u and v) fails, then the path from u to v in at least one of the trees avoids w. In this section, using the notion of an open ear decomposition, we design an algorithm for computing two independent trees rooted at v.

13.3.1 Open Ear Decompositions

The concept of an open ear decomposition, first introduced by Whitney, provides a useful characterization of biconnected graphs and has many algorithmic applications. Given any two adjacent vertices s and t, an *ear decomposition* of G is a sequence of paths $P_0, P_1, \ldots, P_{q-1}$, with P_0 consisting of the single edge st, and where P_i has only its end vertices in common with the subgraph G_i whose vertex set and edge set are the union of the vertex sets and edges sets, respectively, of the simple paths $P_0, P_1, \ldots, P_{i-1}$, $i = 1, \ldots, q$. Moreover, the set of paths partition the edges of G, so that $G = G_q$. The term *ear decomposition* derives from the image of P_i being an ear added to the graph G_i (see Figure 13.6). If the two end vertices of each path P_i are distinct—that is, if P_i is not a closed path—then we say that the ear decomposition is open.

FIGURE 13.6

An open ear
decomposition
$P_0, \ldots, P_6$.

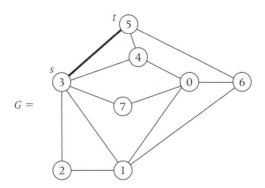

$G =$

P_0: 3,5 P_1: 3,2,1,6,5 P_2: 3,1 P_3: 1,0,6 P_4: 0,4,5 P_5: 3,4 P_6: 3,7,0

We now discuss an algorithm *OpenEarDecomposition* for computing an open ear decomposition of a biconnected graph G, starting with the edge st. We assume that the graph G is implemented using adjacency lists. Recall that the adjacency list for u consists of the set of vertices $u_1, u_2, \ldots, u_k$ adjacent to u, so that uu_1, $uu_2, \ldots, uu_k$ are the edges incident with u. Initially, the only restriction we place on these lists is that t occurs first in the adjacency list of s.

Algorithm *OpenEarDecomposition* is performed in three stages. In the first stage, we perform a depth-first search starting at vertex s (and first traversing edge st). Similar to the algorithm *ArticulationPoints*, we compute the DFS numbers *DFSNum*$[0:n-1]$ and the lowest numbers *Lowest*$[0:n-1]$ during this pass.

The second stage consists of a simple rearrangement of the adjacency lists so that, for each vertex u, the first edge uv is either an edge of the DFS-tree such that *Lowest*$[v] = $ *Lowest*$[u]$, or a nontree edge such that *DFSNum*$[v] = $ *Lowest*$[u]$. In the third stage, we perform a second depth-first search of G starting with edge st using the rearranged adjacency list resulting from the second stage. The sequence of edges generated by this second depth-first search can be partitioned into simple paths, where the first path is the edge st, and each subsequent path begins immediately after a nontree edge has been traversed and ends with a nontree edge. The set of paths generated in this way determines an open ear decomposition.

Pseudocode and the verification of the correctness of the algorithm *OpenEarDecomposition* are developed in the exercises. Because depth-first search has $O(m)$ worst-case complexity, it follows that *OpenEarDecomposition* has $O(m)$ worst-case complexity.

We have just shown how algorithm *EarDecomposition* constructs an open ear decomposition beginning with any edge st in a biconnected graph G. It is not difficult to verify that a graph G that has an open ear decomposition beginning with an edge st is biconnected (see Exercise 13.18). This yields the following classical characterization of biconnected graphs due to Whitney.

Theorem 13.3.1. A graph G is biconnected if and only if for any edge st of G there exists an ear decomposition beginning with ear st. ■

13.3.2 *s-t* Orderings and Independent Spanning Trees

We now show how to compute two independent trees. The first step is to compute an *s-t* ordering. An *s-t ordering* of a graph G is an ordering of the vertices such that s is first in the order, t is last, and every other vertex v has at least one vertex u in its neighborhood having a smaller *s-t* order and one having a larger *s-t* order.

Associated with an *s-t* ordering is the notion of an *s-t* orientation of the edges of G, defined as follows. An *orientation of G* assigns a direction to each edge. An *s-t orientation* (also called a *bipolar* orientation) of G is an orientation such that the resulting directed graph is acyclic, and s and t are the only source and sink vertices, respectively. (Recall that a *source vertex* is a vertex such that all incident edges are directed out of that vertex, and a *sink vertex* is a vertex such that all incident edges are directed into that vertex.) An *s-t* orientation can be obtained from an *s-t* ordering by directing each edge e from the end vertex of e having lower *s-t* order to the end having higher order. Conversely, given an *s-t* orientation, we obtain an *s-t* ordering by performing a topological sort of an associated acyclic digraph. It is easily verified that the topological ordering is an *s-t* ordering (see Exercise 13.19). Figure 13.7 illustrates an *s-t* orientation and an associated *s-t* ordering of a sample biconnected graph for the same graph as in Figure 13.6, where the $(i + 1)^{\text{st}}$ vertex in the *st*-ordering is labeled i, $i = 0, ..., n - 1$.

Given an open ear decomposition of a biconnected graph we can compute an *s-t* orientation, and thus an *s-t* ordering as follows. Given an ear $P_i = u_1$, $u_2, ... , u_p$, we orient the edges of P_i such that it forms a directed path from u_1 to u_p, in which case we say that it is directed out of u_1, or it forms a directed path from u_p to u_1, in which case we will say that it is directed into u_1. We begin by orienting the ears that have one end at s so that they are all directed out of s and push each of them on a stack. While the stack is not empty, we pop an ear P, and

FIGURE 13.7

An *s-t* orientation and an associated *s-t* ordering for the graph in Figure 13.6.

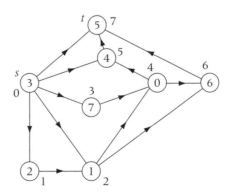

we scan P in the direction it is oriented performing the following operations. For each vertex u that is encountered, we orient the ears that are not already oriented and have one end at u so that they are all directed out of u, and we push each of these ears on the stack. It is easily verified that the resulting orientation is an s-t orientation. The s-t orientation of the graph in Figure 13.8 was obtained from the open ear decomposition given in Figure 13.7 using this algorithm. The algorithm just described constructs an s-t orientation from any open ear decomposition with st as the initial ear. Thus, it follows from Theorem 13.3.1 that a biconnected graph has an s-t orientation and s-t ordering for any given edge st. It is easily verified that the converse is true (see Exercise 13.21), yielding the following theorem.

Theorem 13.3.2. A graph G is biconnected if and only if for any edge st, there exists an s-t orientation (s-t ordering). ■

Given an s-t ordering, we can immediately generate two independent spanning trees rooted at s. For each vertex v different from s, we let $lower(v)$ be any vertex in the neighborhood of v that has lower s-t order; and for each vertex different from t, we let $higher(v)$ be any vertex in the neighborhood of v having higher s-t order, respectively. We construct a tree T_1 such that the parent of v is $lower(v)$ for each vertex different from s and t, and we construct a tree T_2 such that the parent of v is $higher(v)$ for each vertex different from s and t. In both trees, we make s the parent of t. Equivalently, given an s-t orientation we can generate two independent trees T_1 and T_2 rooted at s by choosing one vertex in the in-neighborhood and out-neighborhood, respectively, of each vertex v different from s and t and making it the parent of v. Again, in both trees, we make s the parent of t. Figure 13.8 illustrates two independent trees constructed using the method just described for the same graph and the same s-t orientation and s-t ordering given in Figure 13.7.

FIGURE 13.8

Two independent spanning trees constructed using the s-t orientation (s-t ordering) of the graph given in Figure 13.7. Part (a) shows the spanning tree T_1, and part (b) show the spanning tree T_2.

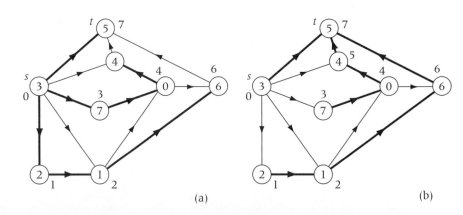

(a)　　　　　　　　(b)

We have just described an $O(m + n)$ algorithm *IndependentTrees* for computing two independent trees T_1 and T_2 rooted at a given vertex s of a biconnected graph G. We leave the design of pseudocode for the algorithm *IndependentTrees* as an exercise. It is easily verified that if a graph has two independent trees rooted at each vertex s, the graph is biconnected, which leads to the following theorem.

Theorem 13.3.3. A graph is biconnected if and only if it has two independent spanning trees rooted at any vertex v. □

▦ 13.4 Closing Remarks

Tarjan and Hopcroft in the early 1970s popularized the use of depth-first search in graph algorithms. The concept of biconnectivity generalizes to the concept of k-connectivity. A graph is said to be (vertex) k-connected if it remains connected after the removal of any set of $k - 1$ vertices and their incident edges. In the next chapter, we will consider the problem of determining k-connectivity from the point of view of network flow theory. In the present chapter, we have shown that a biconnected graph has two independent trees rooted at any vertex s. It is an open question whether a k-connected graph has k independent trees rooted at any vertex. The question has been answered affirmatively for $k = 3$.

References and Suggestions for Further Reading

Two references containing the early work of Tarjan and Hopcroft on various applications of depth-first search generated numberings:

Tarjan, R. E. *Data Structures and Network Algorithms*. Philadelphia, PA: Society for Industrial and Applied Mathematics, 1983.

Hopcroft, J. E., and R. E. Tarjan. "Efficient Algorithms for Graph Manipulation." *Communications of the ACM* 16, no. 6 (1973): 372–378.

Two early books on algorithmic graph theory:

Even, S. *Graph Algorithms*. Potomac, MD: Computer Science Press, 1979.

Gibbons, A. M. *Algorithmic Graph Theory*. Cambridge, England: Cambridge University Press, 1985.

Chartrand, G., and O. R. Oellerman. *Applied and Algorithmic Graph Theory*. New York: McGraw-Hill, 1993. A more recent book on graph algorithms.

Section 13.1 Strongly Connected Components

13.1 Without using the notion of postnumbering, design an $O(m + n)$ algorithm to test whether a digraph is strongly connected.

13.2 Let F be the depth-first out-forest of a digraph D consisting of trees $T_1, \ldots, T_k$, listed in the order they are generated by the out-directed depth-first traversal. Show that a vertex u has postnumber i if u is the $(i + 1)^{st}$ vertex to be visited in the *postorder traversal* of F, $i = 0, \ldots, n - 1$—that is, the traversal of F consisting of successive postorder traversals of T_j, $j = 1, \ldots, k$.

13.3 Give a linear-time algorithm for computing the array $PostNumInv[0:n - 1]$ from the array $PostNum[0:n - 1]$.

13.4 Modify the depth-first traversal procedure $DFTOut$ to compute arrays $PostNum[0:n - 1]$ and $PostNumInv[0:n - 1]$.

13.5 Show that an out-directed depth-first search starting at a vertex u of a digraph D visits all the vertices in the strongly connected component containing u.

Section 13.2 Articulation Points and Biconnected Components

13.6 Prove Theorem 13.2.1.

13.7 Prove Proposition 13.2.2.

13.8 Prove Proposition 13.2.3.

13.9 Prove Proposition 13.2.4.

13.10 Prove Proposition 13.2.6.

13.11 Verify recurrence relation (13.2.2).

13.12 Prove the correctness of the algorithm described for computing the biconnected components of a graph G given its articulation points.

13.13 Prove the correctness of the nonrecursive algorithm described for computing the articulation points and the biconnected components of a graph G.

13.14 Consider the following graph G:

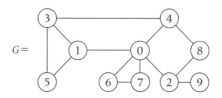

a. Using a depth-first search starting at vertex $r = 3$, compute the global arrays *TreeDFS*[0:9], *DFSNum*[0:9], and *Lowest*[0:9] output by *DFSNumberings*.

b. Demonstrate how the articulation points are obtained from the arrays computed in part (a).

13.15 Let G be graph that is not biconnected, and suppose B_1 and B_2 are any two biconnected components of G. Show that B_1 and B_2 have at most one vertex in common.

Section 13.3 Fault-Tolerant Routing Schemes

13.16 Consider the following example graph G and vertices s and t.

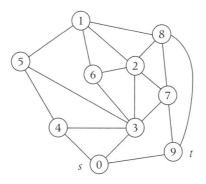

a. Demonstrate the action of the algorithm *OpenEarDecomposition* for computing an open ear decomposition of G with respect to the edge st. (Assume for definiteness that the adjacency lists are given in increasing order of vertex labels.)

b. Using the open ear decomposition you computed in part (a), demonstrate the action of the algorithm given in Section 13.3 for computing an s-t orientation.

c. Using the s-t orientation (s-t ordering) you computed in part (b), compute two independent trees rooted at vertex s.

13.17 Verify the correctness of the algorithm *OpenEarDecomposition*.

13.18 Verify that a graph G that has an open ear decomposition beginning with an edge st is biconnected.

13.19 Verify that a topological sorted ordering of an s-t oriented graph is an s-t ordering.

13.20 Verify the correctness of the algorithm for obtaining an s-t orientation from an open ear decomposition.

13.21 Show that a graph G is biconnected if for any edge st, G has an s-t orientation (s-t ordering).

13.22 Show that the trees T_1 and T_2 obtained from an s-t ordering of a biconnected graph G are independent.

13.23 Show that the trees T_1 and T_2 obtained from an s-t orientation of a biconnected graph G are independent.

13.24 Give pseudocode for the algorithm *IndependentTrees*.

CHAPTER 14

MATCHING AND NETWORK FLOW ALGORITHMS

Finding matchings and maximum flows in graphs and networks are two funda-mental problems with myriad practical applications. We begin this chapter with an algorithm for finding a perfect matching in a bipartite graph and a maximum-weighted perfect matching in a weighted complete bipartite graph. Some of the techniques we use to solving the matching problems, such as finding augment-ing paths when constructing a perfect matching in a bipartite graph, can be gen-eralized to apply to the maximum flow problem.

There are many natural interpretations of flows in networks, such as fluid flow through a network of pipelines, data flow through a computer network, traffic flow through a network of highways, current flow through an electrical network, and so forth. Usually, each edge in a network has a certain flow capac-ity (a *capacitated* network), and the problem arises of finding the maximum flow subject to the capacity constraints of the edges. One of the most celebrated the-orems about capacitated networks is the max-flow min-cut theorem of Ford and Fulkerson. In this chapter, we present this theorem and an associated algorithm for finding a maximum flow in a capacitated network. Finding a maximum flow is useful in solving the well-known marriage problem, which is equivalent to the problem of finding a perfect matching in a bipartite graph.

14.1 Perfect Matchings in Bipartite Graphs

An independent set of edges, or *matching,* in a graph G is a set of edges that are pairwise vertex disjoint. A matching that spans the vertices is called a *perfect matching.* In this section, we discuss an algorithm known as the Hungarian algorithm for finding a perfect matching or determining it does not exist. We also discuss the Kuhn-Munkres algorithm, which employs the Hungarian algorithm to find a maximum-weight perfect matching in an edge-weighted complete bipartite graph. We begin by discussing the marriage problem, which is a colorful interpretation of the problem of finding a perfect matching in a bipartite graph. In Chapter 24, we will give a probabilistic algorithm for determining whether or not a bipartite graph has a perfect matching.

14.1.1 The Marriage Problem

Suppose we have a set of n boys $b_1, b_2, \ldots, b_n$ and a set of n girls $g_1, g_2, \ldots g_n$, where each boy knows some of the girls. The classical *marriage problem* is to determine a necessary and sufficient condition so that each boy can marry a girl that he knows (no two boys can marry the same girl). More formally, the marriage problem is finding the conditions under which the permutation $\sigma: \{1, 2, \ldots, n\} \rightarrow \{1, 2, \ldots, n\}$ exists such that boy b_i knows girl $g_{\sigma(i)}$, $i = 1, 2, \ldots, n$. If such a permutation σ exists, then the corresponding set of matches $P_\sigma = \{\{b_i, g_{\sigma(i)}\| i = 1, 2, \ldots, n\}$ is called a perfect matching.

Let K_i denote the set of girls that boy b_i knows, $i = 1, \ldots, n$. For example, suppose that $n = 5$ and the sets K_i, $i = 1, \ldots, 5$, are given by

$$K_1 = \{g_1, g_2, g_4, g_5\}, K_2 = \{g_1, g_3\}, K_3 = \{g_2, g_3\}, K_4 = (g_3, g_4, g_5\}, K_5 = \{g_3\}.$$

Then, the following set of pairs determines a perfect matching:

$$\{b_1, g_4\}, \{b_2, g_1\}, \{b_3, g_2\}, \{b_4, g_5\}, \{b_5, g_3\}.$$

The marriage problem is naturally modeled using a bipartite graph G, where one set X of the vertex bipartition consists of the set of n boys and the other set Y consists of the set of n girls. A vertex b_i in X is joined to a vertex g_j in Y whenever the boy b_i knows the girl g_j (see Figure 14.1). The marriage problem then becomes determining a necessary and sufficient condition for a bipartite graph to contain a perfect matching—that is, a set of n edges no two of which have a vertex in common.

FIGURE 14.1

The bipartite graph G corresponding to sets
$K_1 = \{g_1, g_2, g_4, g_5\}$,
$K_2 = \{g_1, g_3\}$,
$K_3 = \{g_2, g_3\}$,
$K_4 = \{g_3, g_4, g_5\}$,
$K_5 = \{g_3\}$.
G contains the perfect matching
$\{b_1, g_4\}$, $\{b_2, g_1\}$,
$\{b_3, g_2\}$, $\{b_4, g_5\}$,
$\{b_5, g_3\}$.

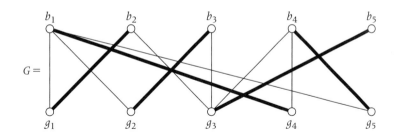

Suppose in the previous example that K_1 is replaced with the set

$$K_1' = \{g_1, g_2, g_3\}.$$

Because the four boys b_1, b_2, b_3, b_5 collectively know only the three girls g_1, g_2, g_3, a perfect matching cannot exist. More generally, if there exists a set of k boys who collectively know strictly less than k girls, then a perfect matching does not exit. Surprisingly, the converse is also true, by a theorem of Hall, which states that a solution to the marriage problem exists if and only if every set of k boys collectively knows at least k girls, $k \in \{1, 2, \ldots, n\}$.

We can restate Hall's theorem for bipartite graphs as follows: For S, a set of vertices of G, let $\Gamma(S)$ denote the set of all vertices that are adjacent to those in S; that is,

$$\Gamma(S) = \{v \in V | \text{there exists a vertex } u \text{ in } S \text{ such that } uv \in E\}. \tag{14.1.1}$$

Theorem 14.1.1   **Hall's Theorem**

A bipartite graph with vertex bipartition $V = X \cup Y$ contains a perfect matching if and only if, for every subset S of X,

$$|S| \leq |\Gamma(S)|. \tag{14.1.2}$$

PROOF

First, suppose that there exists a perfect matching M in G. For $u \in V$, let $M(u)$ denote the *mate* of u in M—that is, the unique vertex v such that $uv \in M$. For $S \subseteq X$, let

$$M(S) = \{M(x) | x \in S\}. \tag{14.1.3}$$

Clearly, $M(S) \subseteq \Gamma(S)$. Hence,

$$|\Gamma(S)| \geq |M(S)| = |S|. \qquad ■$$

We complete the proof of Theorem 14.1.1 in the next subsection by presenting a "matchmaker" algorithm, called Hungarian, which accepts an initial matching M (possibly empty) and repeatedly augments M until either a perfect matching is generated or a set $S \subseteq X$ is found such that $|\Gamma(S)| < |S|$.

14.1.2 The Hungarian Algorithm

The Hungarian algorithm uses the notion of an M-alternating path. Given a matching M, we say that a vertex v of G is M-*matched* if it is incident with an edge of M; otherwise, we say that v is M-*unmatched*. An M-*alternating path* is one where the edges alternately belong to $E(G) \setminus M$ and M. An M-*augmenting path* is an alternating path in which the initial and terminal vertices are both M-unmatched.

> **Key Fact**
>
> **Given an M-augmenting path P, the size of the matching M can be increased by 1 by removing the edges of M belonging to P, and adding to M the remaining edges of P.**

The larger matching described in this key fact can be expressed as the *symmetric difference* $M \oplus E(P)$ of M and the edges $E(P)$ of P; that is

$$M \oplus E(P) = (M \cup E(P)) \setminus (M \cap E(P)). \qquad \textbf{(14.1.4)}$$

The Hungarian algorithm searches for augmenting paths. To find an M-augmenting path in G, the algorithm grows a tree T, called an M-*alternating tree*, having the following properties:

1. The root r of T is an M-unmatched vertex belonging to X.
2. For each odd integer i less than the depth of T, each edge of T joining a vertex at level i to a vertex at level $i + 1$ belongs to M.
3. The leaf nodes of T all belong to X.

An M-alternating tree is illustrated in Figure 14.2. Clearly, all the paths in an M-alternating tree T are M-alternating paths, and X_T and Y_T denote the subset of vertices of X and Y, respectively, belonging to T.

FIGURE 14.2

An *M*-alternating
tree *T* rooted at
vertex *r*.

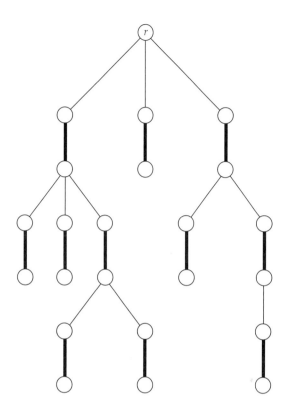

The proofs of the next three lemmas are straightforward and left as exercises.

Lemma 14.1.2 If M is a matching and P is an M-augmenting path, then $M \oplus E(P)$ is a matching of size one greater than M. □

Lemma 14.1.3 If T is an M-alternating tree, then

$$|X_T| = |Y_T| + 1. \qquad \textbf{(14.1.5)} \quad □$$

Lemma 14.1.4 Given an M-alternating tree T, if there exists a vertex $x \in X_T$ that is adjacent to an M-unmatched vertex y (not in T), then the path from the root r of T to x, together with the edge xy, determine an M-augmenting path. □

If all the vertices in X are M-matched, then M is a perfect matching. In this case, the Hungarian algorithm returns the perfect matching M and terminates. In the case where the vertices in X are not all matched, the Hungarian algorithm looks for an augmenting path by growing an M-alternating tree T. The tree T may be initialized to consist of the single vertex r, where r is chosen arbitrarily from the set of unmatched vertices in X. At each stage of growing the tree T, we encounter one of the following three cases:

1. $\Gamma(X_T) - Y_T$ is empty. (Action: algorithm terminates.)
   Then by Lemma 14.1.3, $|\Gamma(X_T)| = |Y_T| = |X_T| - 1$. The Hungarian algorithm then returns $S = X_T$ and terminates, because by Theorem 14.1.1, no perfect matching exists.
   In the next two cases, $\Gamma(X_T) - Y_T$ is nonempty, and we choose y to be any vertex in $\Gamma(X_T) - Y_T$ and x to be any vertex in X_T adjacent to y.

2. Vertex y is matched. (Action: T is augmented.)
   Then we augment T to obtain a new M-alternating tree by adding the edges xy and yz, where z is the mate of y in M.

3. Vertex y is unmatched. (Action: M is augmented.)
   Then an augmenting path P in T from r to x together with the edge xy has been found. We then replace M by the augmented matching $M \oplus E(P)$ containing one more edge.

In case 3, we either have found a perfect matching or we look for another augmenting path by growing another M-alternating tree rooted at a new unmatched vertex in X. Clearly, M can be augmented at most n times. Because at each stage the alternating tree T can be grown in time $O(n^2)$, the worst-case complexity of the following procedure *Hungarian* is $O(n^3)$. Pseudocode for *Hungarian* follows.

procedure *Hungarian*(G, M, S)
Input: G (a bipartite graph with vertex bipartition (X, Y))
             M (an initial matching, possibly empty)
Output: M (a perfect matching if one exists)
             S (a set of vertices with the property that $|\Gamma(S)| < |S|$ if no perfect matching exists)
      AugmentingM ← .**true.**
      while *AugmentingM* **do**
           if all the vertices in X are M-matched **then**   //M is a perfect matching
                AugmentingM ← .**false.**
           else   //Grow M-alternating tree T
                r ← any M-unmatched vertex in X
                T ← tree consisting of the single vertex r
                GrowingTree ← .**true.**

```
            while GrowingTree do
                if Γ(X_T) = Y_T then
                    S ← X_T                          // |Γ(S)| < |S|
                    GrowingTree ← .false.
                    AugmentingM ← .false.
                else
                    y ← any vertex in Γ(X_T) − Y_T
                    x ← any vertex in X_T adjacent to adjacent to y
                    if y is M-matched then            //augment T
                        z ← M(y)                     //z is the mate of y in M
                        T ← T ∪ xy ∪ yz
                    else                             //an M-augmenting path has been
                                                         found
                        P ← path in T from r to x together with the edge xy
                        M = M ⊕ E(P)                 //augment M
                        GrowingTree ← .false.
                    endif
                endif
            endwhile
        endif
    endwhile
end Hungarian
```

Figure 14.3 illustrates the action of procedure *Hungarian* for a sample bipartite graph. For definiteness, in Figure 14.3 we show the perfect matching generated by always choosing vertices in order of their vertex number. More precisely, the phrase "any ... vertex" occurring in three statements in the pseudocode for *Hungarian* is replaced by the phrase "the ... vertex of smallest index" when generating the perfect matching in Figure 14.3. We leave the intermediate steps in finding the augmenting paths as an exercise.

FIGURE 14.3

Action of procedure
Hungarian for a
sample bipartite
graph with initial
matching $\{x_1, y_1\}$,
$\{x_3, y_3\}$, $\{x_4, y_4\}$.
Vertices are
considered in the
order of their
indices.

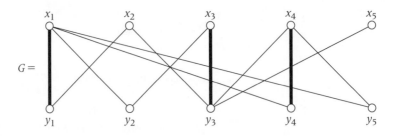

Sample bipartie graph G and initial matching $\{x_1, y_1\}$, $\{x_3, y_3\}$, $\{x_4, y_4\}$

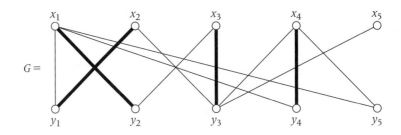

A first M-augmenting path P: $x_2 y_1 x_1 y_2$, found by *Hungarian* with
starting M-unmatched vertex x_2 yielding augmented
matching $M \oplus E(P) = \{x_1 y_2, x_2 y_1, x_3 y_3, x_4 y_4\}$

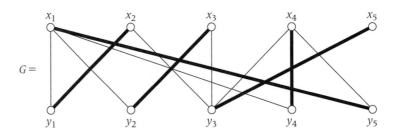

A second M-augmenting path P: $x_5 y_3 x_3 y_2 x_1 y_5$, found by *Hungarian* with
starting M-unmatched vertex x_5 yielding augmented perfect
matching $M \oplus E(P) = \{x_1 y_5, x_2 y_1, x_3 y_2, x_4 y_4, x_5 y_3\}$

14.1.3 Maximum Perfect Matching in a Weighted Bipartite Graph

Suppose n workers $x_1, x_2, \dots, x_n$ are to be assigned to n jobs $y_1, y_2, \dots, y_n$, where
each worker is qualified to perform any of the jobs. Associated with each
worker-job pair (x_i, y_j) is a weight ω_{ij} measuring how effectively worker x_i can

perform job y_j. The natural problem arises of finding assignments of workers to jobs so that the total effectiveness of each workers is optimized. This problem can be modeled using a weighted complete bipartite graph $G = (V, E)$, with vertex bipartition $X = \{x_1, \dots , x_n\}$ and $Y = \{y_1, \dots , y_n\}$. Each edge $x_i y_j$ of G is assigned the weight ω_{ij}, $i, j \in \{1, \dots , n\}$. Clearly, a perfect matching in G corresponds to an assignment of each worker to a job so that no two workers are assigned the same job. We define the *weight* of a perfect matching M, denoted by $\omega(M)$, to be the sum of the weights of its edges.

$$\omega(M) = \sum_{e \in M} \omega(e). \tag{14.1.6}$$

A *maximum perfect matching* is a perfect matching of maximum weight over all perfect matchings of G. Because G is complete, any permutation π of $\{1, 2, \dots , n\}$ determines a perfect matching $M_\pi = \{x_i y_{\pi(i)} \mid i \in \{1, \dots , n\}\}$ and conversely. Thus, a brute-force algorithm that enumerates all $n!$ perfect matchings and chooses one of maximum weight is hopelessly inefficient.

We now describe an $O(n^3)$ algorithm due to Kuhn and Munkres for finding a maximum perfect matching in a weighted complete bipartite graph. The Kuhn-Munkres algorithm uses the Hungarian algorithm, together with the notion of a feasible vertex weighting.

DEFINITION 14.1.1 A *feasible vertex weighting* is a mapping ϕ from V to the real numbers such that for each edge $xy \in E$ (each $x \in X$ and $y \in Y$),

$$\phi(x) + \phi(y) \geq \omega(xy). \tag{14.1.7}$$

Any sufficiently large ϕ is a feasible vertex weighting. For example, the following vertex weighting is feasible:

$$\phi(v) = \begin{cases} \max \quad \{\omega(vy) \mid vy \in E(G)\} & \text{if } v \in X, \\ 0 & \text{otherwise} \end{cases} \tag{14.1.8}$$

The following proposition is easily verified.

Proposition 14.1.5 Let ϕ be any feasible vertex weighting and M any perfect matching of G. Then,

$$\omega(M) \leq \sum_{v \in V} \phi(v). \tag{14.1.9} \quad \square$$

Given a vertex weighting ϕ, the *equality subgraph* $G_\phi = (V_\phi, E_\phi)$ is a subgraph of G such that $V_\phi = V(G)$ and E_ϕ consists of all the edges xy such that $\omega(xy) = \phi(x) + \phi(y)$. Note that it is possible for some of the vertices of G to be isolated vertices in G_ϕ.

proposition 14.1.6 Let ϕ be any feasible vertex weighting. If the equality subgraph G_ϕ contains a perfect matching M, then M is a maximum perfect matching in G. □

Observe that if M is a perfect matching in G_ϕ, then $\omega(M) = \Sigma_{v \in V}\phi(v)$. Hence, Proposition 14.1.6 follows from Proposition 14.1.5.

Starting with an initial feasible vertex weighting, such as the one given by Formula (14.1.8), the Kuhn-Munkres algorithm applies the Hungarian algorithm to the subgraph G_ϕ. If a perfect matching M_ϕ is found, then by Proposition 14.1.5, M_ϕ is a maximum perfect matching in G. On the other hand, suppose the Hungarian algorithm terminates by finding a matching M and an M-alternating tree T such that $\Gamma(X_T) - Y_T$ is empty. Then we have found a set $S = X_T$ such that $|\Gamma_\phi(S)| = |S| - 1 < |S|$. Instead of terminating at this point, we replace ϕ with a new feasible weighting ϕ' and continue the Hungarian algorithm in the equality graph $G_{\phi'}$ of ϕ'. The new feasible weighting ϕ' is constructed as follows. Set

$$\varepsilon = \min\{\phi(x) + \phi(y) - \omega(xy) \,|\, x \in S, y \in Y - \Gamma_\phi(S)\}. \quad \textbf{(14.1.10)}$$

For each $v \in V(G)$, the weighting ϕ' is defined by

$$\phi'(v) = \begin{cases} \phi(v) - \varepsilon & v \in S, \\ \phi(v) + \varepsilon & v \in \Gamma_\phi(S), \\ \phi(v) & \text{otherwise.} \end{cases} \quad \textbf{(14.1.11)}$$

It is easily verified that the vertex weighting ϕ' given by (14.1.11) is a feasible vertex weighting. Moreover, the following key fact allows us to continue growing the M-alternating tree T.

> **Key Fact**
>
> The equality subgraph $G_{\phi'}$ contains the *M*-alternating tree *T*. Further, $G_{\phi'}$ contains at least one edge $\{x, y\}$, where $x \in S$ and $y \in Y - \Gamma_{\phi'}(S)$. Since y is unmatched by *M*, the path in $G_{\phi'}$ consisting of the path in *T* from its root to x together with edge xy is an *M*-augmenting path.

Thus, by continuing the Hungarian algorithm in $G_{\phi'}$, the matching M will be augmented by at least one edge. After at most $n/2$ steps in which ϕ is replaced with ϕ', we obtain a perfect matching M and a feasible weighting ϕ^* such that M is contained in the equality subgraph G_{ϕ^*} of ϕ^*. By Proposition 14.1.6, such a perfect matching will necessarily be a maximum perfect matching in G.

In the following pseudocode for the Kuhn-Munkres algorithm, we call the procedure *Hungarian2*, which is identical to *Hungarian* except that the alternating tree T is added as an input/output parameter.

```
procedure KuhnMunkres(G, φ, M)
Input:    G (a weighted complete bipartite graph with vertex bipartition
                (X, Y), |X| = |Y| = n)
          φ (a positive edge weighting of G)
Output:   M (a maximum perfect matching)
          φ ← any feasible vertex weighting         //in particular, the one given by
                                                           Formula 14.1.8

          G_φ ← equality subgraph for φ
          M ← any matching in G_φ                   //in particular, M can be chosen to be
                                                           empty

          PerfectMatchingFound ← .false.
          while .not. PerfectMatchingFound do
              Hungarian2(G_φ, M, S, T)
              if M is a perfect matching then
                  PerfectMatchingFound ← .true.
              else
                  ε ← min {φ(x) + φ(y) − ω(xy) | x ∈ S, y ∈ Y − Γ_φ(S)}
                  for all x ∈ S do
                      φ(x) = φ(x) − ε
                  endfor
                  for all y ∈ Γ_φ(S) do
                      φ(y) = φ(y) + ε
                  endfor
              endif
          endwhile
end KuhnMunkres
```

We leave it as an exercise to show that the worst-case complexity of procedure *KuhnMunkres* is $O(n^3)$

14.2 Maximum Flows in Capacitated Networks

The problem of finding a maximum flow in a network from a source s to a sink t, where each link in the network has a given capacity, and the dual problem of finding a minimum cut in such a network, is a classical optimization problem with many applications. Our study of flows in networks begins by formally defining the notion of a flow in a digraph (an *uncapacitated* network) and establishing some elementary results about flows.

REMARK

The theory of flows in networks modeled on digraphs includes as an important special case flows modeled on graphs by associating with the graph its combinatorially equivalent (symmetric) digraph.

14.2.1 Flows in Digraphs

Let $D = (E, V)$ be a digraph with vertex set V and directed edge set E. A *real weighting* ω of the edges of D is a mapping from E to the set $\mathbb{R}$ of real numbers. We refer to $\omega(e)$ as the ω-*weight* of edge e. For $v \in V$, we let $\sigma_{in}(\omega, v)$ and $\sigma_{out}(\omega, v)$ denote the sum of the ω-weights over all the edges having head v and tail v, respectively, so that

$$\sigma_{in}(\omega, v) = \sum_{uv \in E} \omega(uv),$$

$$\sigma_{out}(\omega, v) = \sum_{vw \in E} \omega(vw).$$

By convention, $\sigma_{in}(\omega, v) = 0$ if there are no edges having head v. Similarly, $\sigma_{out}(\omega, v) = 0$ if there are no edges having tail v.

The following proposition is easily verified.

Proposition 14.2.1 Given any real weighting ω of the edges in a digraph D,

$$\sum_{v \in V} (\sigma_{in}(\omega, v) - \sigma_{out}(\omega, v)) = 0.$$

□

Now suppose we are given two vertices s and t such that there are no edges having head s or tail t. A *flow* f from s to t is a weighting of the edges such that

$$\sigma_{in}(f, v) = \sigma_{out}(f, v), \quad \forall v \in V \setminus \{s, t\}. \tag{14.2.1}$$

Given any vertex v in D, we refer to $\sigma_{in}(f, v)$ and $\sigma_{out}(f, v)$ as the *flow into v* and the *flow out of v*, respectively. Formula (14.2.1) is called a *flow conservation equation*. The *value of flow f*, denoted by $val(f)$, is defined to be the flow out of s. It follows easily from Proposition 14.2.1 that the flow out of s equals the flow into t. Hence,

$$val(f) = \sigma_{out}(f, s) = \sigma_{in}(f, t). \tag{14.2.2}$$

A *unit flow* is a flow f such that $val(f) = 1$. Figure 14.4 illustrates a flow f of value 55 on a sample digraph D.

The following proposition is easily verified.

Proposition 14.2.2 The set of all flows is closed under linear combinations; that is, for any flows f_1 and f_2 and real numbers λ_1 and λ_2, $\lambda_1 f_1 + \lambda_2 f_2$ is a flow. Moreover,

$$val(\lambda_1 f_1 + \lambda_2 f_2) = \lambda_1 val(f_1) + \lambda_2 val(f_2). \qquad \Box$$

FIGURE 14.4

A flow of value 55.

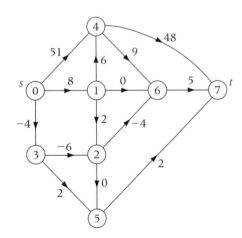

Now consider a directed path $P = se_1u_1e_2u_2 \ldots u_{p-1}e_pt$ from s to t (not necessarily a simple path). Associated with P is the flow χ_P from s to t given by

$$\chi_P(e) = \begin{cases} 1 & e \in E(P) \\ 0 & e \notin E(P), \end{cases} \quad \forall e \in E.$$

We call χ_P the *characteristic flow* of P. Note that the characteristic flow is a *unit flow*.

In the next section, we compute maximum flows in a capacitated network by using the notion of a semipath, which is a path where the orientation of the edges is ignored. More precisely, a *semipath* S from s to t is an alternating sequence of vertices and edges $se_1u_1e_2u_2 \ldots u_{p-1}e_pt$ such that either e_i has tail u_{i-1} and head u_i (e_i is a *forward edge of S*) or e_i has tail u_i and head u_{i-1} (e_i is *backward edge of S*), $i = 1, \ldots, p$, where $u_0 = s$ and $u_p = t$. Associated with semipath S is the flow χ_S, called the *characteristic flow* of S, given by

$$\chi_S(e) = \begin{cases} 1 & e \text{ is a forward edge of } S, \\ -1 & e \text{ is a backward edge of } S, \\ 0 & \text{otherwise,} \end{cases} \quad \forall e \in E. \qquad \textbf{(14.2.3)}$$

It is easily verified that χ_S is a unit flow.

14.2.2 Flows in Capacitated Networks

A *capacitated network* N (sometimes called a *transportation* or *flow* network) consists of the 4-tuple (D, s, t, c), where $D = (V, E)$ is a digraph; s and t are two distinguished vertices of D called the *source* and *sink*, respectively; and c is a positive real weighting of the edges, called the *capacity weighting* of D. We assume that all the edges incident with s are directed out of s, and all the edges incident with t are directed into t. We refer to $c(e)$ as the *capacity* of edge e.

A *flow f in a capacitated network* N is a flow in D from s to t such that for each $e \in E$, $f(e)$ is nonnegative and does not exceed the capacity of e; that is

$$0 \leq f(e) \leq c(e), \quad \forall e \in E.$$

Figure 14.5 shows a flow of value 23 in a sample capacitated network N on eight vertices. In Figure 14.5 and all subsequent figures, when illustrating a flow f, all edges e such that $f(e) = 0$ are omitted.

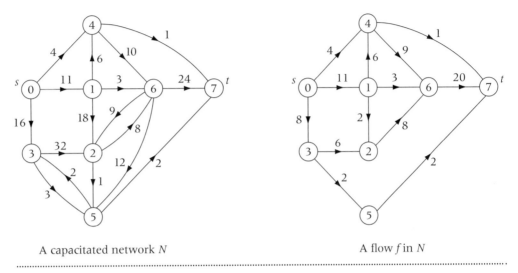

A capacitated network *N*   A flow *f* in *N*

FIGURE 14.5
A sample capacitated network *N* and a flow *f* having value *val*(*f*) = 23.

A *maximum* (*value*) *flow* is a flow *f* in *N* whose value is maximum over all flows in *N*. A naive attempt to finding a maximum flow might proceed as follows. First we find a path P_1 from *s* to *t* in *N* using an algorithm such as a breadth-first search. Let λ_1 denote the minimum capacity among all the edges of P_1. Then $f = \lambda_1 \chi_{P_1}$ is a flow in *N* having value λ_1. Next, we adjust the capacities of the edges of *N* by subtracting λ_1 from each edge belonging to P_1 and deleting all the edges of *N* whose capacity becomes zero. We then find a path P_2 (if one exists) in the new network. We now augment the flow *f* by $\lambda_2 \chi_{P_2}$, where λ_2 is the minimum capacity (in the new network) among all the edges of P_2. The current flow $f = \lambda_1 \chi_{P_1} + \lambda_2 \chi_{P_2}$ has value $\lambda_1 + \lambda_2$. Again, we subtract λ_2 from every edge belonging to P_2 and delete all the edges whose capacity becomes zero. Continuing in this way, we find paths $P_3, \ldots, P_k$ and associated real numbers $\lambda_3, \ldots, \lambda_k$, respectively, until no paths are left from *s* to *t* in the final network.

We illustrate the action of our naive attempt in Figure 14.6 for a sample capacitated network. Unfortunately, the final flow *f* attained has value 14, whereas the maximum flow shown in Figure 14.7 has value 24. However, any flow generated by our naive attempt does have a maximality property—namely, if *g* is any flow different from *f*, then $g(e) < f(e)$ for some edge *e*.

....

FIGURE 14.6

Action of naive attempt to find maximum flow for a sample capacitated network N, yielding flow $f = 10\chi_{P_1} + \chi_{P_2} + 3\chi_{P_3}$ having value 14. This flow is suboptimal because a maximum flow f^* shown in Figure 14.7 has value 24.

....

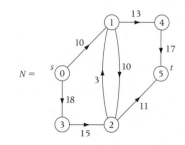

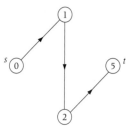

path P_1, $\lambda_1 = 10$

$f = 10\chi_{P_1}$

reduced N

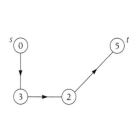

path P_2, $\lambda_2 = 1$

$f = 10\chi_{P_1} + \chi_{P_2}$

reduced N

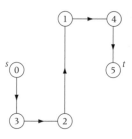

path P_3, $\lambda_3 = 3$

$f = 10\chi_{P_1} + \chi_{P_2} + 3\chi_{P_3}$

reduced N

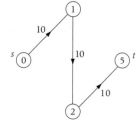

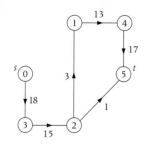

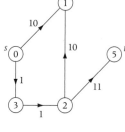

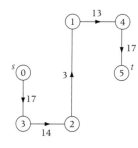

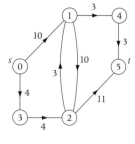

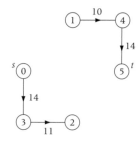

FIGURE 14.7

A maximum flow $f*$ having value 24 in the capacitated network N of Figure 14.5.

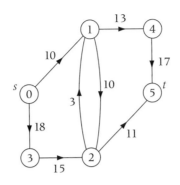

A capacitated network N

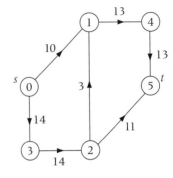

A maximum flow $f*$ on N

The flow f of Figure 14.6 generated by our naive algorithm is a dead end in our search for a maximum flow in the sense that we can no longer augment f by simply finding directed paths from s to t. The following key fact using the notion of a semipath allows us to continue to augment the flow f.

> **Key Fact**
>
> **Given a semipath with no forward edge used to capacity and nonzero flow in each backward edge, we can continue to augment f by adding flow to forward edges while removing flow from backward edges.**

14.2.3 Finding an Augmenting Semipath

The *residual capacity* with respect to a flow f is $c(e) - f(e)$. An edge e is f-*saturated* if the residual capacity is zero; otherwise, edge e is f-*unsaturated*. A semipath S is an f-*augmenting semipath* if every forward edge of S is f-unsaturated and $f(e) > 0$ for every backward edge e of S. For $e \in E(S)$, we let

$$c_f(S, e) = \begin{cases} c(e) - f(e) & e \text{ is a forward edge of } S, \\ f(e) & e \text{ is a backward edge of } S. \end{cases}$$

Let $c_f(S)$ denote the minimum value of $c_f(S, e)$ among all the edges of S; that is,

$$c_f(S) = \min\{c_f(S, e) \,|\, e \in E(S)\}.$$

Now consider the edge weighting $\hat{f}$ given by

$$\hat{f} = f + c_f(S)\chi_S, \tag{14.2.4}$$

where χ_S is the characteristic flow of S given by Formula (14.2.3). Thus, for each $e \in E(G)$,

$$\hat{f}(e) = \begin{cases} f(e) + c_f(S) & e \text{ is a forward edge of } S, \\ f(e) - c_f(S) & e \text{ is a backward edge of } S, \\ f(e) & \text{otherwise.} \end{cases}$$

Proposition 14.2.2 implies that the edge weighting $\hat{f}$ given by Formula (14.2.4) is a flow in the digraph D. Further, it is immediate from the definition of $c_f(S)$ that for all $e \in E$,

$$0 \le \hat{f}(e) \le c(e).$$

Hence, $\hat{f}$ is a flow in the capacitated network N. Further, since χ_S is a unit flow, it follows from Proposition 14.2.2 that

$$val(\hat{f}) = val(f) + c_f(S),$$

so that $\hat{f}$ has a strictly greater value than f.

A semipath S and the value $c_f(S)$ can be computed by finding a path from s to t in the *f-derived network* N_f constructed from the network N and the flow f. The network N_f is obtained by starting with vertex set V and adding edges as follows. For each edge uv of N that is *f*-unsaturated, we add an edge uv to N_f having weight $c(uv) - f(uv)$. For each edge uv of N such that $f(uv) > 0$, we add an edge vu to N_f having weight $f(uv)$. When uv and vu are both edges of N, it is possible for N_f to have two edges joining vertex u to vertex v. In our search for a maximum flow, allowing such pairs of edges does not present a problem. In fact, we can even eliminate the possibility of such pairs in N_f by replacing f with a new flow f obtained by subtracting min $\{f(uv), f(vu)\}$ from both $f(uv)$ and $f(vu)$ so that one of them becomes equal to zero. The latter operation does not affect the value of the flow f. Note that if $val(f) = 0$, then $N_f = N$. The *f*-derived network N_f for a sample network N and flow f is illustrated in Figure 14.8.

For P, a path from s to t in N_f, we define the weight $\mu(P)$ to be the minimum weight over all the edges of P; that is,

$$\mu(P) = \min\{w(e) \mid e \in E(P)\}.$$

The following proposition follows immediately from the definitions of N_f and the *f*-augmenting semipath S.

FIGURE 14.8

The f-derived
network N_f for a
sample network N
and flow f.

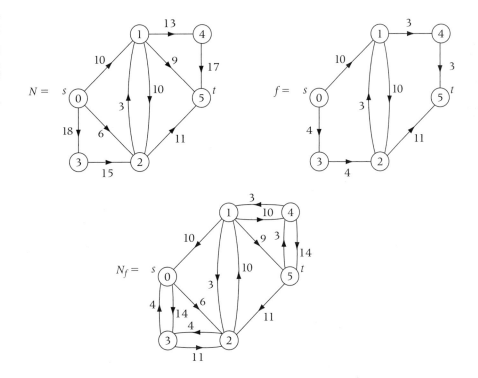

Proposition 14.2.3 If P is a path from s to t in N_f, then the corresponding semipath S in N is an f-augmenting semipath. Further,

$$c_f(S) = \mu(P).$$ □

It follows from Formula (14.2.4) that if there exists an f-augmenting semi-path S, then we can find a flow whose value is strictly greater than f. The Ford-Fulkerson algorithm is based on the fact that the converse is also true; that is, *if there is no f-augmenting semipath, then f is a maximum flow.* To prove this important result, we introduce the concept of a cut.

14.2.4 Bounding Flow Values by Capacities of Cuts

Consider a bipartition of the vertex set V into two disjoint sets X and Y. We denote this bipartition by (X, Y). The cut associated with the bipartition (X, Y), denoted $cut(X, Y)$, is defined by

$$cut(X, Y) = \{xy \in E \mid x \in X, y \in Y\}.$$

We say a set of edges Γ is a *cut* if $\Gamma = cut(X, Y)$ for some bipartition (X, Y) of V. For $u, v \in V$, if $u \in X$ and $v \in Y$, then we say that Γ *separates u and v*. Unless otherwise stated, we assume that Γ separates the source s from the sink t. The *capacity of* Γ, denoted by $cap(\Gamma)$, is the sum of the capacities of all the edges in Γ; that is,

$$cap(\Gamma) = \sum_{e \in \Gamma} c(e).$$

A *minimum capacity cut* (or simply *minimum cut*) is a cut Γ whose capacity is minimum over all cuts separating s and t.

Because deleting all the edges of a cut disconnects the source s from the sink t, intuitively we would expect that the value of any flow f is not greater than the capacity of any cut Γ. The following proposition affirms this intuition.

Proposition 14.2.4   Let f be any flow from s to t in N, and let $\Gamma = (X, Y)$ be any cut separating s and t. Then, the value of f is bounded above by the capacity of Γ; that is,

$$val(f) \le cap(\Gamma).$$

PROOF

Given a nonnegative weighting ω of E, we extend ω to a mapping of all $V \times V$ as follows:

$$\omega(u, v) = \begin{cases} \omega(uv) & uv \in E, \\ 0 & \text{otherwise.} \end{cases}$$

For $A, B \subseteq V$, let

$$\omega(A, B) = \sum_{a \in A} \sum_{b \in B} \omega(a, b). \tag{14.2.5}$$

In the notation of Formula (14.2.5), the flow conservation equation (14.2.1) can be rewritten as follows:

$$f(u, V) - f(V, u) = 0, \quad u \in V - \{s,t\}. \tag{14.2.6}$$

Formula (14.2.2) then becomes

$$f(s, V) = f(V, t) = val(f). \tag{14.2.7}$$

It follows immediately from Formulas (14.2.6) and (14.2.7) that

$$f(X, V) - f(V, X) = val(f).$$ **(14.2.8)**

Clearly, for U, which is any subset of V, we have

$$f(U, V) = f(U, X) + f(U, Y),$$
$$f(V, U) = f(X, U) + f(Y, U).$$ **(14.2.9)**

Substituting $U = X$ in both parts of Formula (14.2.9), subtracting the second part from the first, and employing Formula (14.2.8) yields

$$f(X, Y) - f(Y, X) = f(X, V) - f(V, X) = val(f).$$ **(14.2.10)**

Using Formula (14.2.10), we have

$$\begin{aligned}
val(f) &= f(X, Y) - f(Y, X) \\
&\leq f(X, Y) \\
&= \sum_{xy \in \Gamma} f(xy) \\
&\leq \sum_{xy \in \Gamma} c(xy) \quad \text{(since } f(e) \leq c(e) \text{ for all } e \in E) \\
&= cap(\Gamma).
\end{aligned}$$ ■

Corollary 14.2.5   If f is a flow from s to t and Γ is a cut separating s and t such that $val(f) = cap(\Gamma)$, then f is a maximum flow and Γ is a minimum cut.

PROOF
Let f' be any flow from s to t and let Γ' be any cut separating s and t. Then by Proposition 14.2.4, we have

$$\begin{aligned}
val(f') &\leq cap(\Gamma) = val(f), \\
cap(\Gamma') &\geq val(f) = cap(\Gamma).
\end{aligned}$$ ■

Corollary 14.2.5 states a condition guaranteeing that f is a maximum flow and Γ is a minimum cut, but it does not tell us whether such a flow f and cut Γ actually exist. In fact, a seminal result in flow theory is that such a flow f and cut Γ always exist.

Theorem 14.2.6	**Max-Flow Min-Cut Theorem**
	Let $N = (D, c, s, t)$ be a capacitated network. The maximum value of a flow from s to t equals the minimum capacity of a cut separating s and t. □

To prove Theorem 14.2.6, we use Corollary 14.2.5 to establish it is sufficient to exhibit a flow f and cut Γ such that $val(f) = cap(\Gamma)$. In the next subsection, we give an algorithm for computing such a flow f and cut Γ.

14.2.5 The Ford-Fulkerson Algorithm

The following procedure computes a maximum flow and minimum cut by repeatedly augmenting the current flow f using an f-augmenting semipath.

procedure *FordFulkerson*(N, f, Γ)
  Input: $N = (D, s, t, c)$ (a capacitated network)
  Output: f (maximum flow)
        Γ(minimum cut)
    $f \leftarrow 0$
    $N_f \leftarrow N$
    while there is a directed path from s to t in the f-derived network N_f **do**
      $P \leftarrow$ a path from s to t in N_f
      $S \leftarrow$ the f-augmenting semipath in N corresponding to path P in N_f
      $c_f(S) \leftarrow \mu(P)$ //$\mu(P)$ is the minimum weight over all the edges of P
      $f \leftarrow f + c_f(S)\chi_S$ //augment f
      update N_f
    endwhile
    $X \leftarrow$ set of vertices that are accessible from s in N_f //$s \in X$
    $Y \leftarrow$ set of vertices that are not accessible from s in N_f //$t \in Y$
    $\Gamma \leftarrow cut(X, Y)$
end *FordFulkerson*

The correctness of procedure *FordFulkerson* is established with the aid of the following two lemmas, whose proofs are left as exercises.

Lemma 14.2.7	Let f and (X, Y) be the flow and vertex bipartition, respectively, generated by procedure *FordFulkerson*. Then every edge xy of the cut $\Gamma = cut(X, Y)$ is saturated; that is,

$$f(xy) = c(xy).$$
□

Lemma 14.2.8   Let f and (X, Y) be the flow and vertex bipartition, respectively, generated by procedure *FordFulkerson*. Then for each edge $yx \in E(D)$, where $y \in Y$ and $x \in X$, we have

$$f(yx) = 0. \qquad \square$$

Lemmas 14.2.7 and 14.2.8 imply that

$$f(X, Y) = cap(\Gamma),$$
$$f(Y, X) = 0.$$

Thus, by Formula (14.2.10) we have

$$val(f) = f(X, Y) - f(Y, X) = cap(\Gamma).$$

By Corollary 14.2.5, f is a maximum flow and Γ is a minimum cut, which completes the correctness proof of procedure *FordFulkerson*.

The Ford-Fulkerson augmenting semipath algorithm is a general method for computing a maximum flow and minimum cut. In procedure *FordFulkerson*, we did not specify how the path P is generated in the derived network N_f at each stage. In general, there may be many such paths, and the efficiency of *Ford-Fulkerson* is dependent on which augmenting semipath S is chosen at each stage.

For a poor choice of augmenting semipaths S, procedure *FordFulkerson* may never terminate. However, in the case when the capacities on the edges are all integers, procedure *FordFulkerson* terminates after having performed at most $val(f)$ iterations of the **while** loop. Because each iteration can be performed in time $O(m)$, the worst-case complexity $W(n, m)$ of procedure *FordFulkerson* belongs to $O(m*val(f))$. Since $val(f)$ depends on the capacities of the edges, it can be arbitrarily large. It is not hard to find examples showing that for a poor choice of augmenting semipaths S, $W(n, m)$ can also be arbitrarily large.

Edmonds and Karp showed that a good choice for the augmenting semipath S at each stage of procedure *FordFulkerson* is the shortest one (with a minimum number of edges) over all such semipaths. At each stage, a shortest augmenting semipath S can be found by performing a breadth-first search of the f-derived network N_f to find a shortest path P from s to t. The Edmonds-Karp algorithm has worst-case complexity $W(n, m) \in O(nm^2)$. (The proof of this complexity result is beyond the scope of this book.) The Edmonds-Karp algorithm is illustrated in Figure 14.9 for a sample flow network N having eight vertices and 17 edges. The shortest path generated at each step is indicated with a dotted (as opposed to solid) line.

FIGURE 14.9

Action of the
Edmonds-Karp
algorithm for a
sample capacitated
network N.

Original flow network N with capacities c, and initial flow $f \equiv 0$:

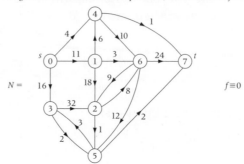

$N =$ $f \equiv 0$

Step 1:

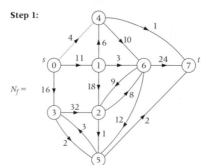

$N_f =$

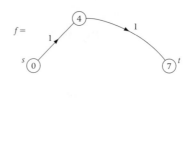

$f =$

Step 2:

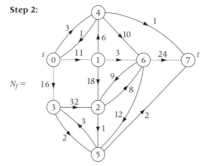

$N_f =$

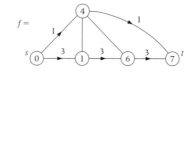

$f =$

Step 3:

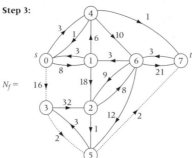

$N_f =$

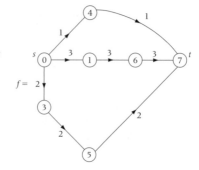

$f = 2$

FIGURE 14.9

Continued

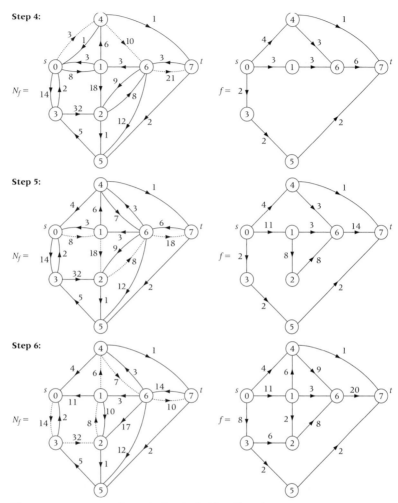

Step 4:

Step 5:

Step 6:

There are no more augmenting semipaths. The final flow f has value 23.

Step 7: Compute the f-derived network N_f and minimum cut $cut(X,Y)$.

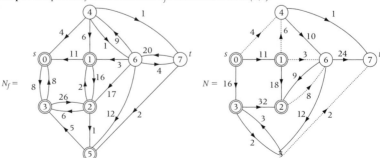

The set $X = \{1,2,3,4,6\}$ of vertices that are accessible in N_f from the source s (marked with ◯) and the set $Y = \{5,7,8\}$ of vertices that are not accessible from s determine a cut $\Gamma = cut(X,Y)$ of capacity $c(X,Y) = 4 + 6 + 3 + 8 + 2 = 23$. Hence, we have $val(f) = 23 = cap(\Gamma)$, so that f is a maximum flow Γ and is a minimum cut.

14.2.6 Maximum Flows in 0/1 Networks: Menger's Theorem

An *integer flow* in a digraph $D = (V, E)$ is a flow f such that $f(e)$ is an integer for every edge $e \in E$.

Proposition 14.2.9
Let $D = (V, E)$ be a digraph, and let f be any integer flow from s to t, where $s, t \in V$. Then there exists a set $\mathscr{P}$ of simple paths from s to t and positive integers $\{\lambda_p \mid P \in \mathscr{P}\}$ such that the number of paths containing edge e is at most $c(e)$ and

$$val(f) = \sum_{P \in \mathscr{P}} \lambda_p. \qquad \qquad \textbf{(14.2.11)} \;\square$$

We leave the proof of Proposition 14.2.9 as an exercise. A set of paths $\mathscr{P}$ and associated positive integers $\{\lambda_p \mid P \in \mathscr{P}\}$ satisfying Formula (14.2.11) can be computed in time $O(m * val(f))$.

A *0/1 flow* is an integer flow such that, for each edge e, $f(e)$ is either 0 or 1. The following result is an immediate corollary of Proposition 14.2.9.

Corollary 14.2.10
Let f be any 0/1 flow from u to v. Then there exists a set $\mathscr{P}$ of pairwise edge-disjoint paths from u to v such that

$$val(f) = |\mathscr{P}|. \qquad \qquad \square$$

When the capacities are all integers, $c_f(S)$ is an integer at each stage of the procedure *FordFulkerson*. Thus, for integer capacities, *FordFulkerson* generates a maximum integer flow f. In particular, if each edge has unit capacity, then a maximum 0/1 flow f is generated. By Corollary 14.2.10, if f is a 0/1 flow, then there exists a set $\mathscr{P}$ of pairwise edge-disjoint paths from u to v such that $val(f) = |\mathscr{P}|$. If $\mathscr{P}$ is a set of pairwise edge-disjoint paths from u to v, then $\Sigma_{P \in \mathscr{P}} \chi_P$ is a 0/1 flow. Thus, a set $\mathscr{P}$ of pairwise edge-disjoint paths from s to t has maximum cardinality over all such sets if and only if $\Sigma_{P \in \mathscr{P}} \chi_P$ is a maximum flow.

It follows that we can compute a maximum size set $\mathscr{P}$ of pairwise edge-disjoint paths from s to t in a given digraph D by first applying procedure *FordFulkerson* to the capacitated network $N = (D, c, s, t)$, where each edge e has capacity $c(e) = 1$ to obtain a maximum flow f, and then computing a set $\mathscr{P}$ of pairwise edge-disjoint paths from s to t such that $val(f) = |\mathscr{P}|$. Now consider the cut Γ generated by *FordFulkerson*. Because every edge has unit capacity, the capacity of Γ equals the size of (number of edges in) Γ. Since the capacity of Γ equals the value of f, it follows that the size of Γ equals the size of $\mathscr{P}$, which yields the classical theorem of Menger.

Theorem 14.2.11

Menger's Theorem for Digraphs

Let $D = (V, E)$ be a digraph. Then for $s, t \in V$, the maximum size of a set $\mathscr{P}$ of pairwise edge-disjoint paths from s to t equals the minimum size of a cut Γ separating s and t. □

The following corollary is the analog of Theorem 14.2.11 for graphs.

Corollary 14.2.12

Menger's Theorem for Undirected Graphs

Let $G = (V, E)$ be an undirected graph. Then for $s, t \in V$, the maximum size of a set $\mathscr{P}$ of pairwise edge-disjoint paths from s to t equals the minimum size of a cut Γ separating s and t. □

14.2.7 Maximum Size Matching

Procedure *FordFulkerson* can be applied to obtain a maximum size matching in a bipartite graph G. Let (X, Y) denote the associated bipartition of the vertex set V of G. Construct a digraph D as follows. The vertex set of D consists of the vertex set of G together with two new vertices s and t; that is,

$$V(D) = V(G) \cup \{s,t\}.$$

The edge set $E(D)$ of D consists of pairs xy such that $xy \in E(G)$, $x \in X$, and $y \in Y$, together with all pairs sx, $x \in X$, and all pairs yt, $y \in Y$; that is,

$$E(D) = \{xy | xy \in E(G), x \in X, y \in Y\} \cup \{sx | x \in X\} \cup \{yt | y \in Y\}.$$

Now consider the capacitated network $N = (D, c, s, t)$, where every edge e has capacity $c(e) = 1$. For f, a 0/1 flow from s to t, let $\mu(f)$ denote the set of all edges xy of G such that xy is an edge of D and $f(xy) = 1$. Clearly, $\mu(f)$ is a matching M in G, and $val(f)$ is equal to the size of M. Conversely, given any matching M of G there is a flow f in N such that $M = \mu(f)$. Let f^* be the flow generated by procedure *FordFulkerson*. Since f^* is a maximum-value flow in N, $\mu(f^*)$ is a maximum-size matching in G. The algorithm just described for finding a maximum-size matching is illustrated in Figure 14.10.

FIGURE 14.10

A maximum flow in an associated network where all edges have capacity 1 yielding a maximum matching in a bipartite graph G.

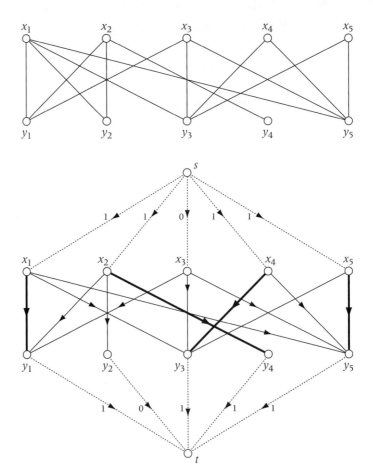

14.3 Closing Remarks

In addition to the Edmonds-Karp algorithm for finding a maximum flow, which uses the Ford-Fulkerson augmenting-path method, other efficient algorithms for finding maximum flows have been designed. These algorithms include the Dinac maximum flow algorithm and, more recently, the preflow push algorithm designed by Goldberg and Tarjan. The problem of finding a maximum flow from a single source s to a single sink t generalizes to the problem of finding a multicommodity flow from a set of sources to a set of sinks. The theory of multicommodity flows is an active research area, with applications to such areas as routing in communication networks and VLSI layout.

In this chapter, we discussed the Hungarian algorithm for finding a perfect matching in bipartite graph and the Kuhn-Munkres algorithm for finding a maximum-weight perfect matching in a weighted bipartite graph. We also showed how a maximum flow can be used to find a maximum-size matching in a bipartite graph. Algorithms for finding maximum flows and perfect matchings in general graphs can be found in the references.

In Chapter 24, we will present a parallel probabilistic algorithm for determining whether or not a bipartite graph contains a perfect matching.

References and Suggestions for Further Reading

Good references for network optimization algorithms, including flow and matching algorithms:

Ahuja, R. K. *Network Flows: Theory, Algorithms, and Applications.* Englewood Cliffs, NJ: Prentice-Hall, 1993.

Gordon, M., and M. Minoux. *Graphs and Algorithms* (trans. by S. Vajda). New York: Wiley, 1984.

Lawler, E. L. *Combinatorial Optimization: Networks and Matroids.* New York: Holt, Rinehart and Winston, 1976.

Papadimitriou, C. H., and K. Steiglitz. *Combinatorial Optimization: Algorithms and Complexity.* Englewood Cliffs, NJ: Prentice-Hall, 1982.

Tarjan, R. E. *Data Structures and Network Algorithms.* Philadelphia: Society for Industrial and Applied Mathematics, 1983.

Lovász, L., and M. D. Plummer. *Matching Theory.* Amsterdam: North Holland, 1986. A nice reference to results and algorithms on matchings.

Section 14.1 Perfect Matchings in Bipartite Graphs

14.1   Prove Lemma 14.1.2.

14.2   Prove Lemma 14.1.3.

14.3   Prove Lemma 14.1.4.

14.4   Show that at each stage of the procedure *Hungarian*, the alternating tree T can be grown in time $O(n^2)$, so the worst-case complexity of procedure *Hungarian* is $O(n^3)$.

14.5   Refine the pseudocode of the procedure *Hungarian* to include details for finding the augmenting paths.

14.6   Consider the following bipartite graph G:

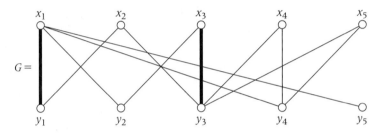

Starting with the given matching $M = \{x_1 y_1, x_3 y_3\}$, determine the perfect matching output by *Hungarian*. Show each augmenting path that is generated.

14.7   Prove Proposition 14.1.5.

14.8   Verify that the vertex weighting given by Formula (14.1.8) is a feasible vertex weighting.

14.9   a. Verify that the vertex weighting ϕ' given by Formula (14.1.11) is a feasible vertex weighting whose equality subgraph $G_{\phi'}$ contains the M-alternating tree T.

        b. Show that $G_{\phi'}$ contains at least one edge $\{x, y\}$, where $x \in S$ and $y \in Y - \Gamma_{\phi'}(S)$.

14.10   Show that the worst-case complexity of procedure *KuhnMunkres* is $O(n^3)$.

Section 14.2 Maximum Flows in Capacitated Networks

14.11 Let f be any flow from vertex s to vertex t in a digraph. Using Proposition 14.2.1, show that the flow out of s equals the flow into t.

14.12 Prove Proposition 14.2.2.

14.13 Verify that χ_s given by Formula (14.2.3) is a unit flow.

14.14 Verify that the final flow $f = \lambda_1 \chi_{P_1} + \cdots + \lambda_k \chi_{P_k}$ generated by the naive algorithm illustrated in Figure 14.5 is maximal in the sense that if g is any other flow, then $g(e) < f(e)$ for some edge e.

14.15 Prove Lemma 14.2.7.

14.16 Prove Lemma 14.2.8.

14.17 Show that for a poor choice of augmenting semipaths S, procedure *FordFulkerson* may never terminate.

14.18 Assuming that the capacities of the network are positive integers, show that for a poor choice of augmenting paths S, the worst-case complexity $W(n, m)$ of procedure *FordFulkerson* can also be arbitrarily large.

14.19 Using the Edmonds-Karp algorithm, find a maximum flow f and a minimum cut Γ in the following capacitated network N:

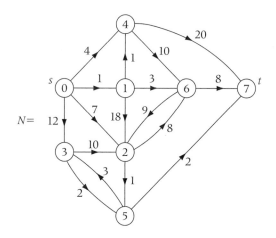

14.20 Design and analyze an algorithm for computing a set of paths P and associated positive integers $\{\lambda_p : P \in P\}$ satisfying (14.2.11).

14.21 Derive Menger's theorem for undirected graphs (Corollary 14.2.12) from Menger's theorem for digraphs (Theorem 14.2.11).

14.22 Using the Edmonds-Karp algorithm, find a maximum matching in the following bipartite graph G by computing a maximum flow in the associated capacitated network.

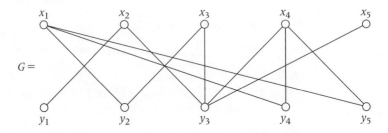

14.23 Derive Konig's theorem, which states that the size of a maximum matching in a bipartite graph G equals the size of a minimum cover (a *cover* is a set of vertices such that every edge of G is incident with at least one vertex in the cover) from Menger's theorem for digraphs (Theorem 14.2.11).

PART FOUR

PARALLEL AND DISTRIBUTED ALGORITHMS

CHAPTER 15

INTRODUCTION TO PARALLEL ALGORITHMS AND ARCHITECTURES

Many problems are most naturally modeled with parallelism. For example, in computational fluid dynamics, weather prediction, and image processing, data sampling is done with sensors (real or simulated) placed at points on a spatial grid. Clearly, it would be useful to have a different processor assigned to each sensor in the grid to input and process the data from the sensor and distribute results to other processors. Also, problems in engineering and the physical sciences often involve vector operations. With a processor assigned to each component in the vector, vector operations can take place in each component simultaneously (see Figure 15.1).

This chapter introduces parallel algorithms and architectures that use multiple processors to solve a given problem in parallel. We assume that the processors are under a central control and execute instructions in tightly synchronized lock-step fashion. In the more general paradigm of distributed algorithms

FIGURE 15.1

(a) Vector addition
on a serial machine,
one row done after
another; (b) vector
addition on a
parallel machine, all
rows done
simultaneously.

(a)

(b)

discussed in Chapters 18 and 19, processors are not necessarily centrally controlled and can execute instructions asynchronously without necessarily synchronizing these instructions with those of the other processors.

15.1 Approaches to the Design of Parallel Algorithms

Given the existence of massively parallel machines, a major challenge facing computer scientists today is to design algorithms that exploit the massively parallel paradigm. There are three main approaches to designing parallel algorithms:

1. Modify an existing sequential algorithm exploiting those parts of the algorithm that are naturally parallelizable.
2. Design a completely new parallel algorithm that may have no natural sequential analog.
3. For appropriate problems such as root finding, run the same sequential algorithm on many processors with different seeds until one processor reports "success." That is, all the processors start running a sequential algorithm with different initial conditions, and the first processor to achieve the desired result "wins the race."

All approaches must take the particular architecture of the parallel machine into consideration.

15.2 Architectural Constraints and the Design of Parallel Algorithms

When designing a parallel algorithm, a number of constraints must be taken into account that were not relevant to the design of a sequential algorithm. These constraints are imposed by the architecture of the particular parallel computer on which the algorithm is intended to be implemented.

1. Single instruction verses multiple instruction
2. The number and type of processors available
3. Shared memory (PRAM) model versus distributed memory (interconnection network) model
4. Communication constraints
   a. Read and write restrictions for the PRAM model
   b. Specification of the graph representing the direct connections that exist between processors in the interconnection network model
5. I/O constraints

We briefly elaborate on each of these constraints to give some notion of the underlying ideas.

15.2.1 Single Instruction Versus Multiple Instruction

A single-processor computer can only execute one instruction at a time. However, a parallel computer with p processors $P_0, \ldots, P_{p-1}$ can execute p instructions simultaneously, each processor operating on its own data. One model of parallel computation restricts the processors to each perform the *same* instruction (but possibly with different data) at the same time in a synchronized manner. This common instruction also contains information that can instruct a given processor to remain idle (masked out) during a given step. The common instruction to be executed is assumed to be sent to each processor by a front-end processor (*central control*) controlled by a global clock. In this book, we will not be concerned with the exact mechanism used by the central control processor to send the next instruction to be executed to each processor, nor will we consider the time taken by this instruction-broadcast when performing our complexity analysis. During each time interval of the global clock, all the processors synchronously perform the same operation: input or output data, perform computations on data, read from local memories, communicate between processors, and so forth. Parallel computers following this model are called SIMD (single-instruction, multiple-data) machines. Parallel computers that allow *different* instructions to be performed at the same time (on possibly different data) are called MIMD (multiple-instruction, multiple-data) machines. The single-processor computer can be viewed in this terminology as an SISD (single-instruction, single-data) machine. Since the SIMD model is simpler conceptually and easier to implement, we adopt the SIMD model here. Moreover, there is often a fairly straightforward translation of an algorithm written for an MIMD machine into an algorithm suitable for an SIMD machine. We give a few illustrations later in the chapter.

15.2.2 The Number and Type of Processors Available

In practice, computer manufacturers must consider whether to build a parallel computer using, say, tens or hundreds of powerful processors (so-called coarse-grain computers) or to build a parallel computer using thousands and thousands of relatively simple processors (fine-grain computers). We assume that the processors are powerful enough to execute all the normal instructions of a serial computer.

There are two approaches to designing parallel algorithms with respect to the number of processors available. The first approach is to design an algorithm where the number p of processors is an additional input parameter not dependent on the input size n. Many authors of texts on parallel algorithms adopt this approach because it is more directly applicable in practice. The second approach, which we adopt in this text, is to allow the number of processors used by the parallel algorithm to grow with the size of the input. Thus, p is not an input parameter to the algorithm but is a function $p(n)$ of the input size n. Of course, allowing $p(n)$ to grow with the input size is not realizable in practice, but it will give us an idea (from a theoretical point of view) as to how much parallelism could ideally be brought to bear on a given problem. Indeed, if we cannot achieve significantly faster execution time (compared with a sequential algorithm) for inputs of size n to a problem using as many processors as we want, then we certainly cannot achieve significantly faster execution time when we restrict the number of processors to a fixed number p independent of n.

Another motivation for allowing the number of processors for a parallel algorithm to grow with the input size is that by using a *division-of-labor technique,* an algorithm designed following the second approach can always be converted into an algorithm suitable for a fixed number of processors. For example, suppose an algorithm has been designed that uses $p(n) = n$ processors. Then for each parallel step of the original algorithm, the work in the converted algorithm is divided among the p processors into at most n/p sequential steps done by each processor. Of course, designing an algorithm with a fixed number p of processors taken into account from the outset might be a better approach than using the division-of-labor technique to convert an algorithm utilizing $p(n)$ processors. In fact, when we consider the subject of distributed algorithms, more specifically, in the message-passing paradigm, we will assume that the number of processors p is an input to the algorithm. The latter assumption is consistent with the rapidly emerging implementation of distributed algorithms, using such message passing libraries as MPI or PVM, which make explicit use of the number p of processors available for both communication and computation purposes (see Chapter 18). However, in the idealized world of parallel algorithms, we assume the luxury of having as many processors as we need.

15.2.3 Shared Memory: PRAMs

In a shared-memory model of a parallel computer, *all* processors have equal access to a single *shared* RAM memory (see Figure 15.2a). Parallel computers based on this model are referred to as parallel random access machines, or PRAMs, because they are based on parallel random access memory. In the PRAM, each processor has equal access to every memory location in the shared memory. Of course, the possibility of conflict arises if two processors attempt to read or write from the same memory location simultaneously. There are four models for dealing with such conflict (see Figure 15.2b): EREW (exclusive-read, exclusive-write:); CREW (concurrent-read, exclusive-write); ERCW (exclusive-read,

FIGURE 15.2

(a) A PRAM;
(b) read/write
possibilities for
PRAMs.

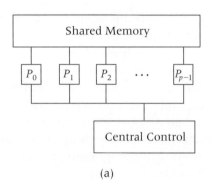

(a)

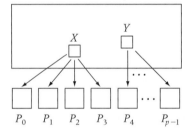

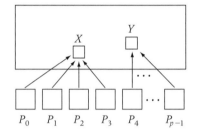

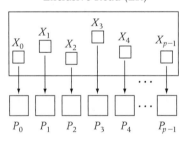

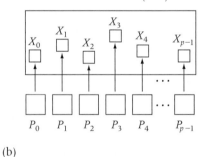

(b)

concurrent-write); and CRCW (concurrent-read, concurrent-write). Because the ERCW model is of little theoretical or practical interest, we do not include it in our discussion.

Algorithms for EREW PRAMs are assumed to be in error if a read or write conflict ever arises. CRCW PRAMs allow multiple processors to read from and write to the same memory location concurrently, resolving concurrent writes in various ways. A commonly used method only allows concurrent writes when all the processors are attempting to write the same value. Another method, used for numeric data, is to write the sum of all these values. Still other methods involve allowing a randomly chosen processor among contending processors to write its value, or always choosing the processor having the smallest index in some ordering of the processors.

The EREW model is the most realistic of the PRAM models to build in practice. Moreover, any algorithm designed for the EREW PRAM also runs without alteration on the other PRAM models. For this reason, when naming an algorithm designed for an EREW PRAM, we simply use the term *PRAM* in the name. Names for algorithms on the other models will explicitly mention the model, such as *CRCW* or *CREW*.

Given the current state of technology, even EREW PRAMs are difficult to build (although such efforts are currently under way). Nevertheless, PRAMs provide good models for theoretical results and for the initial design of a parallel algorithm unencumbered by processor communication details.

Next we illustrate some of the main design issues with an informal discussion of a parallel algorithm for searching a list $L[0:n-1]$ of size n for the occurrence of a search element X.

15.2.4 Example: Searching on a PRAM

A parallel search algorithm comes immediately to mind: in a single parallel step processor P_i compares X to $L[i]$, $0 \le i \le n-1$, as illustrated by the following pseudocode segment:

```
Index ← −1
for 0 ≤ i ≤ n − 1 do in parallel
    if X = L[i] then
        Index ← i
    endif
end in parallel
```

The question arises as to what assumptions about the model are required for the pseudocode segment to be correct? First, because X is being simultaneously read by n processors, the model must allow for concurrent reads (CR). Second, if X occurs more than once in the list, several processors will attempt to write different values to *Index* simultaneously; therefore, we need a PRAM model that allows for concurrent writes (CW). Third, we must assume a method of resolving the contention between concurrent writes, such as choosing the processor having the smallest index to be the winner. Thus, our solution assumes the CRCW PRAM.

Now suppose we have the more realistic EREW PRAM. For all processors to access the value of X simultaneously on the EREW PRAM, we need to allocate an auxiliary array, $Temp[0:n - 1]$, and assign the value of X to each array element $Temp[i]$, $0 \le i \le n - 1$. To do so, we assign X to $Temp[0]$ and then *broadcast* X to the other positions in the array as follows. For simplicity, we assume that $n = 2^k$ for some nonnegative integer k.

1. P_0 reads X and writes it to $Temp[0]$.
2. P_0 reads $Temp[0]$ and writes it to $Temp[1]$.
3. P_0 and P_1 read $Temp[0]$ and $Temp[1]$, respectively, and write X to $Temp[2]$ and $Temp[3]$, respectively, and so forth.

The broadcasting process continues these steps as illustrated in Figure 15.3, with $X = 5$ and $n = 16$. Clearly, after $\log_2 n$ steps, X is stored in all n memory locations of $Temp[0:n - 1]$. Figure 15.3 illustrates that even though the SIMD model restricts the processors to performing the same operation, some processors are allowed to remain idle in any given parallel step.

The following pseudocode accomplishes the broadcasting illustrated in Figure 15.3.

FIGURE 15.3

Broadcasting the value $X = 5$ in $\log_2 n$ steps.

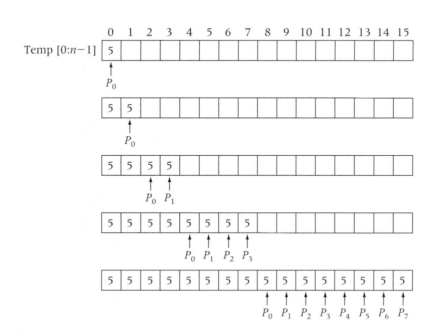

```
procedure BroadcastPRAM(A[0:n − 1], X)
Input:    A[0:n − 1] (an array of size n, n = 2^k)
          X (a value to be broadcast throughout A[0:n − 1])
Output:   A[0:n − 1] (array where A[i] = X, i = 0, ..., n − 1)
    A[0] ← X
    for i ← 1 to k do
        for 2^{i − 1} ≤ j ≤ 2^i − 1 do in parallel
            A[j] ← A[j − 2^{i − 1}]
        end in parallel
    endfor
end BroadcastPRAM
```

After X has been broadcast throughout $Temp[0:n − 1]$, then processor P_i, in parallel, compares $L[i]$ to $Temp[i] = X$ and writes i to $Temp[i]$ if $L[i] = X$; otherwise, it writes the value ∞ to $Temp[i]$ (see Figure 15.4). Here, ∞ is a constant equal to the largest value storable in an integer variable. Each processor can compute ∞ concurrently without having to access a common memory location. Pseudocode for this comparison step follows:

```
for 0 ≤ i ≤ n − 1 do in parallel
    if L[i] = Temp[i] then
        Temp[i] ← i
    else
        Temp[i] ← ∞
    endif
end in parallel
```

FIGURE 15.4

A single parallel comparison step between search elements and list elements.

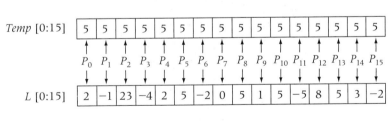

The array $Temp[0:n - 1]$ now contains the results of the search. However, we are still left with the problem of signaling a successful search. The first occurrence of X in L is the minimum entry in the array $Temp$. Fortunately, we have an efficient method known as *binary fan-in* (see Figure 15.5) we can use to find this minimum. For example, suppose we want to find the minimum of 16 numbers using eight processors. In the first parallel step, we divide these numbers into eight pairs and assign the pairs to eight processors for simultaneous computation of their minimums. In the next parallel step, we divide the eight minimums obtained in the first step into four pairs, assign them to four processors and simultaneously compute their minimums, and so forth. In the last step, one processor contains the desired minimum of all sixteen numbers. Thus, we have reduced the 15 sequential steps required by a single-processor machine to only four parallel steps, thereby achieving a speedup of 15/4 over the sequential algorithm.

FIGURE 15.5

Binary fan-in technique for computing the minimum value in $Temp[0:n - 1]$ in $\log_2 n$ parallel comparison steps.

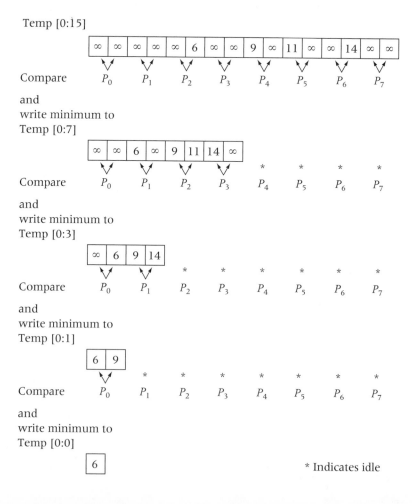

The following pseudocode for the function *MinPRAM* implements the binary fan-in method of computing the minimum value.

```
function MinPRAM(L[0:n − 1])
Model: EREW PRAM with p = n/2 processors
Input:    L[0:n − 1] (a list of size n, n = 2^k)
Output:   the minimum value of a list element in L
    for j ← 1 to log₂n do
        for 0 ≤ i ≤ n/2^j − 1 do in parallel
            if L[2*i − 1] > L[2*i] then
                L[i] ← L[2*i]
            else
                L[i] ← L[2*i − 1]
            endif
        end in parallel
    endfor
    return(L[0])
end MinPRAM
```

The binary fan-in technique requires $\log_2 n$ parallel steps to find the minimum of an n-element list. A powerful tool in parallel algorithms, the binary fan-in technique can be used for combining n elements with respect to any associative binary operation such as addition, multiplication, and so forth. The following pseudocode for *SearchPRAM* summarizes our discussion of searching a list in parallel.

```
procedure SearchPRAM(L[0:n − 1], X)
Model: EREW PRAM with p = n processors
Input:    L[0:n − 1] (a list of size n)        //n = 2^k
          X (a search element)
Output:   the smallest index where X occurs in L, or ∞ if X is not in L
    Broadcast(Temp[0:n − 1], X)
    for 0 ≤ i ≤ n − 1 do in parallel
        if L[i] = Temp[i] then
            Temp[i] ← i
        else
            Temp[i] ← ∞
        endif
    end in parallel
    return(MinPRAM(Temp[0:n − 1]))
end SearchPRAM
```

The basic operation for a sequential search algorithm is comparing a list element to the search element. To make all such comparisons in a single parallel step, as we want to do here, we must choose another basic operation that makes a meaningful statement concerning the complexity (number of parallel basic operations) of our search algorithm. We could use either the number of parallel assignments performed when broadcasting the search element or the number of parallel comparison steps in computing the index of a minimum value in $Temp[0:n-1]$ in the final phase. Either choice yields a complexity of $\log_2 n$.

<table>
<tr><td>**Key Fact**</td><td>**Sometimes a basic operation that is appropriate to use when analyzing a sequential algorithm for a problem is not appropriate to use when analyzing a parallel algorithm for the same problem.**</td></tr>
</table>

15.2.5 Distributed Memory: Interconnection Networks

The parallel computers being built today more closely follow the lines of the second main model for parallel computers, the interconnection network model. In this model, we assume that each processor has its own dedicated RAM memory and does not have access to a common shared memory. Because we are dealing with an SIMD machine, each variable in processor memory has an instantiation in *every* processor. This type of variable is called a *parallel* or *distributed* variable. Simply stated, if X is a distributed variable, then each processor in the network has a memory location reserved for its own version of X.

In the interconnection network model, we assume that each processor has enough local memory to carry out the task at hand. Nevertheless, we usually write a parallel algorithm so it only requires a constant (independent of the input size) number of distributed variables.

We emphasize that statements involving distributed variables might only be executed in a subset of the processors, with the other processors remaining idle (masked out). If X is a distributed variable, then in our pseudocode for such statements as interprocessor communication, we use the label prefix **P**:X to indicate the instantiation of X in processor P's local memory. We also assume that central control has a limited amount of local RAM memory for storing the instructions to be executed by the processors. As with PRAMs, we assume the SIMD computational model in which instructions are executed synchronously. The program resides in the central control processor, and instructions are sent one at time to each processor for parallel execution. A schematic drawing of an interconnection network model is shown in Figure 15.6.

In an interconnection network model, information is communicated between processors using messages sent along the network. Such messages pass along routes in the network where each link in a route is between directly connected (*adjacent*) processors. To avoid problems such as routing conflicts, unless

FIGURE 15.6

A schematic
diagram of an
interconnection
network with p
processors, showing
the distributed
variable X.

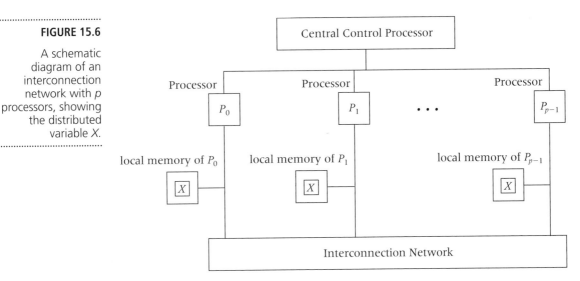

otherwise specified, we have designed all parallel algorithms in this book so that
in each step, communication in an interconnection network takes place only between adjacent processors.

To describe how communication takes place between adjacent processors P_i
and P_j, suppose the central control instructs processor P_j to assign to the variable
Y in its local memory the value of the variable X in the local memory of processor P_i. For our purposes, we view this as being accomplished as follows: Processor P_i reads the value of its local variable X and then sends this value along a link
in the interconnection network to processor P_j, which then writes it to its local
variable Y (see Figure 15.7). This communication is represented in our pseudocode by $\mathbf{P}_j{:}Y \Leftarrow \mathbf{P}_i{:}X$.

FIGURE 15.7

Communication from
processor P_i to
adjacent processor P_j.

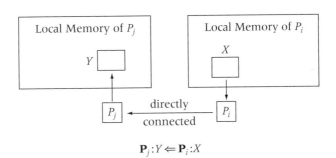

$$\mathbf{P}_j{:}Y \Leftarrow \mathbf{P}_i{:}X$$

FIGURE 15.8

(a) One-dimensional
mesh M_6; (b) two-
dimensional mesh
$M_{4,\,4}$.

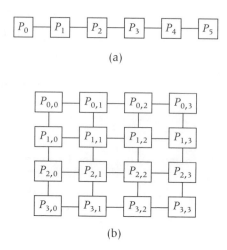

(a)

(b)

The most commonly used interconnection network models are *meshes* (*arrays*), *trees*, *hypercubes*, and some closely related networks. In this chapter, we limit our attention to networks related to meshes and trees. Other networks are introduced in later chapters as they arise naturally in applications.

The simplest interconnection network is the one-dimensional mesh M_p (linear array) with p processors $P_0, \dots, P_{p-1}$, which has P_i directly connected to P_j if and only if $|i - j| = 1$ (see Figure 15.8a). The square two-dimensional mesh $M_{q,q}$ with $p = q^2$ processors $P_{i,j}, i, j \in \{0, \dots, q - 1\}$ has $P_{i,j}$ directly connected with $P_{r,s}$ if and only if $i = r$ and $|j - s| = 1$ or $j = s$ and $|i - r| = 1$ (see Figure 15.8b). The k-dimensional mesh for $k \geq 3$ is defined similarly.

A tree interconnection network is a network whose processors and interconnections correspond to the nodes and edges in a tree. A particularly important example is the *complete binary tree network* on p nodes, $p = 2^k - 1$. We refer to this network as the *processor tree PT_p*. We can conveniently label the processors in PT_p using binary strings that represent a path from the root to a given processor. The root is labeled with the empty string (denoted by ε). Moving to the left adds a 0 to the end of the string, whereas moving to the right adds a 1 (see Figure 15.9).

The extreme version of an interconnection network is the complete graph K_p, where every processor is directly connected to every other processor (see Figure 15.10). Of course, this is a very convenient model for communication, but it is not practical to build.

FIGURE 15.9

Complete binary
tree interconnection
network PT_{15}

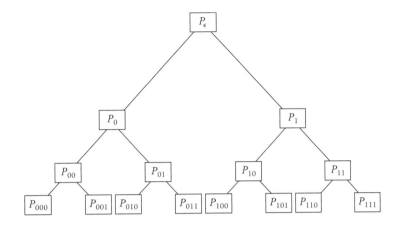

FIGURE 15.10

The complete graph
interconnection
network K_6

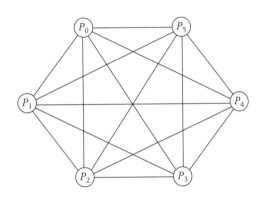

15.2.6 Three Basic Goodness Measures for Interconnection Networks

Given an interconnection network model M, we now discuss three basic goodness measures of M that are related to communication complexity within the network. For an arbitrary pair of processors P_i, P_j, in M, a given algorithm might require that sometime during this execution information initially in the local memories of P_i and P_j be combined (shared) in some way. If $dist(P_i, P_j)$ denotes the number of links in the shortest route connecting P_i and P_j, then the minimum number of communication steps required for information to be shared by P_i and P_j is $dist(P_i, P_j)/2$. This motivates the first goodness measure

$$diameter(M) = \max\{dist(P_i, P_j) | P_i, P_j \in M\}.$$

Clearly, it is desirable to keep the diameter of a network small, because the diameter serves as a lower bound for the communication complexity of algorithms implemented on the network that require information sharing between all the processors. One way to keep the diameter small is to have a large number of links incident with each processor. For example, the complete graph K_p has diameter 1 at the cost of having $p - 1$ links incident with each processor. Although K_p would be the most efficient interconnection network for algorithm design, it is the least feasible to build. With the current state of technology, only interconnection networks of relatively small degree are feasible. Our second goodness measure takes this physical limitation into account. The *degree* of a processor P is defined to be the number of links incident with P. The second goodness measure then is

$$maximum\text{-}degree(M) = \max \{degree(P)|P \in M\}.$$

The third goodness measure is somewhat subtler than the other two and relates to communication bottlenecks. Consider a bipartition of the processors of M into two sets X and Y. Clearly, any route joining a processor in X to a processor in Y must contain at least one link in the set $C(X, Y)$ of all links joining a processor in X to a processor in Y. If $C(X, Y)$ is small and X and Y are about equal in size, then algorithms requiring many processors in X to communicate with processors in Y will encounter congestion because of the large number of routings that will have to use the small number of links $C(X, Y)$. The size of the smallest such cut $C(X, Y)$ is called the *bisection width*. More precisely, the third goodness measure of M is given by

$$bisection\text{-}width(M) = \min\{|C(X, Y)| \mid abs(|X| - |Y|) \le 1\}.$$

Unfortunately, there is no interconnection network that optimizes all three goodness measures simultaneously. As Figure 15.11 shows, there are trade-offs among the three goodness measures. The hypercube (see Chapter 11) perhaps does the best job of compromising between all three goodness measures. Notice that in the table, we denote the hypercube with $p = 2^k$ processors as $H(p)$ to avoid confusion with the notation H_k used in Chapter 11. A verification of the goodness measures shown in Figure 15.11 is left to the exercises.

	Mode 1	Maximum Degree	Diameter	Bisection Width
FIGURE 15.11 Values of three basic goodness measures for sample interconnection models with p processors	K_p	$p - 1$	1	$p^2/4$
	M_p	2	$p - 1$	1
	$M_{\sqrt{p}, \sqrt{p}}$	4	$2\sqrt{p} - 2$	$\sqrt{p} + (p \bmod 2)$
	PT_p	3	$2\lfloor \log_2 p \rfloor$	1
	$H(p)$	$\log_2 p$	$\log_2 p$	$p/2$

15.2.7 Example: Searching on Meshes

To illustrate the difference between shared memory and distributed memory, we again consider the problem of searching for the occurrence of a search element X in a list $L[0:n - 1]$ but now on the one-dimensional mesh M_n. The issue now is that the communication constraints place a severe limitation on the efficiency of broadcasting X to each processor's local memory (assuming, for example, that X is initially stored in processor P_0's local memory). We cannot efficiently use the broadcast technique that was described earlier for the EREW PRAM, because it would involve communication between nonadjacent (that is, not directly connected) processors. In fact, it is easy to see that for the one-dimensional mesh, we can do no better than the sequential algorithm *LinearSearch*, which requires n comparison steps in the worst case.

Now consider the problem of searching on the two-dimensional mesh $M_{q,q}$. For convenience, we assume that the list has size $n = q^2$. Again, since the search element is a variable parameter (as opposed to a constant), it is not possible to initialize the distributed variable **P**:X with the value of the search element. Thus, we assume that the search element x is a front-end variable and that initially only $\mathbf{P}_{0,0}$:X is assigned the value x. We also assume that the list $L[0:n - 1]$ has been input to the distributed variable L in *row-major order*. That is, element $L[k]$ is assigned to processor $P_{i,j}$'s local instantiation of L, where

$$k = iq + j, k = 0, \dots, n - 1.$$

Each instantiation of the distributed variable *Index* is assigned the row-major value of its associated processor, which, unlike the assignment of the search element to the variable X, can be done in a single parallel step because it is a purely local computation (we assume that each processor $P_{i,j}$ knows its own index i, j). Figure 15.12 shows the initial states of the distributed variables.

As with the PRAM, we need to broadcast the value of the search element throughout the distributed variable X. The following simple two-phase procedure broadcasts the value of $x = \mathbf{P}_{0,0}$:X throughout the entire distributed variable $\mathbf{P}_{i,j}$:X, $0 \le i, j \le q - 1$, using $2q - 2$ parallel communication steps. In the first phase, x is broadcast across the first row in $q - 1$ steps, where in the $(i + 1)^{\text{st}}$ step, processor $P_{0, i}$ communicates x to its neighbor $P_{0, i + 1}$ on the right, $i = 0, \dots, q - 2$. In the second phase, x is broadcast down row-by-row in parallel, where in the $(i + 1)^{\text{st}}$ step, $P_{i, j}$ communicates x to its neighbor $P_{i + 1, j}$ below, $i = 0, \dots, q - 2$. The action of this broadcasting procedure is shown in Figure 15.13 for the search element $x = 5$.

FIGURE 15.12

Initial states of the distributed variables L, X, and Index after list L: 2, −1, 23, −4, 2, 5, −2, −2, 5, 1, 5, −5, 8, 5, 3, −2 is input using row-major order, and **P**$_{0,0}$:X has been assigned the value 5. The distributive variable Index initially is assigned the row-major valued of its associated processor.

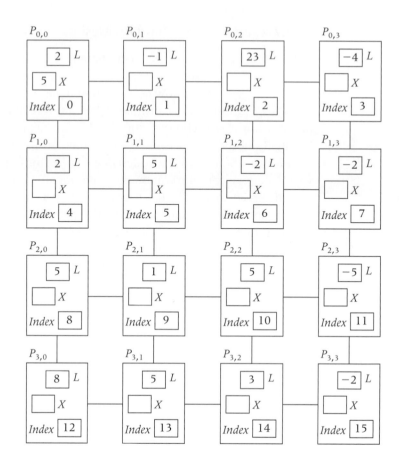

FIGURE 15.13

Broadcasting the value 5 throughout the distributed variable X on $M_{4,4}$.

Phase 1: Broadcast 5 across the first row

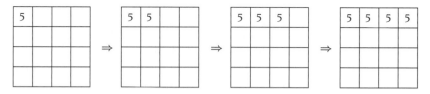

Phase 2: Broadcast 5 down from the ith row to the $(i + 1)$st row, $i = 1, \ldots, q - 1$

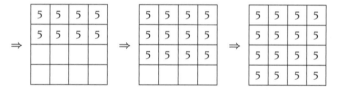

The following pseudocode implements the broadcast procedure illustrated in Figure 15.13.

```
procedure Broadcast2DMesh(P₀,₀:X, n)
Model: two-dimensional mesh Mq,q, with p = n = q² processors
Input:    P₀,₀:X (element to be broadcast)
Output:   P₀,₀:X is broadcast to each processor in Mq,q
    for i ← 0 to q − 2 do
    P₀,ᵢ₊₁:X ⇐ P₀,ᵢ:X              //propagate X to the right across first row
    endfor
        for i ← 0 to q − 2 do
            for Pᵢ,ⱼ, 0 ≤ j ≤ q − 1 do in parallel
            Pᵢ₊₁,ⱼ:X ⇐ Pᵢ,ⱼ:X      //propagate X down row-by-row
            end in parallel
        endfor
end Broadcast2DMesh
```

After the value of the search element has been broadcast to all n processors (so that each $\mathbf{P}_{i,j}$:X contains the value of the search element), in a single parallel comparison step, each processor $P_{i,j}$ compares $\mathbf{P}_{i,j}$:X to its list element $\mathbf{P}_{i,j}$:L and writes the value ∞ to $\mathbf{P}_{i,j}$:*Index* if the search element is not equal to the list element; otherwise, it writes its row-major index. The following is pseudocode for this parallel comparison step:

```
for Pᵢ,ⱼ, 0 ≤ i, j ≤ q − 1 do in parallel
    if Pᵢ,ⱼ:L ≠ Pᵢ,ⱼ:X then
    Pᵢ,ⱼ:Index ← ∞
    else
    Pᵢ,ⱼ:Index ← i*q + j
    endif
end in parallel
```

After the single parallel comparison step, the distributed *Index* contains the results of the search, but now do we return the result? It will be our convention that whenever a scalar-valued function defined on an interconnection network terminates, the value to be returned by the function resides in a particular processor's local instantiation of a suitable distributed variable. In our example, suppose we specify that $P_{0,0}$ should return the outcome of our search in its instantiation of the distributed variable *Index*. In other words, at the termination of our search algorithm, we want $\mathbf{P}_{0,0}$:*Index* to hold the smallest index i such that

$L[i] = X$, or ∞ if no such index exists. Thus, we want to return the minimum value in *Index*.

To compute the minimum value held in *Index*, we perform what amounts to a reverse-broadcast procedure. In phase 1, we compute column minimums in the obvious way. That is, we first compute the minimums of the elements in the qth row and their immediate neighbors above in the $(q - 1)^{\text{st}}$ row, leaving the results in the $(q - 1)^{\text{st}}$ row. Then we repeat the process for the new $(q - 1)^{\text{st}}$ row, then for the $(q - 2)^{\text{nd}}$ row, and so forth until the first row contains all the column minimums. In phase 2, we compute the minimum of the column minimums (that is, the minimum of the elements that are now in the first row) proceeding sequentially from right to left. The final result is in $\mathbf{P}_{0,0}$:*Index*. The algorithm is illustrated in Figure 15.14. Note that this reverse-broadcast algorithm works equally well for combining all the elements in *Index* with respect to any associative binary operation such as addition, multiplication, and so forth.

The following pseudocode for the function *Min2DMesh* implements the reverse-broadcast algorithm shown in Figure 15.14.

```
function Min2DMesh(X, n)
Model: two-dimensional mesh M_{q,q} with p = n = q² processors
Input:     X (a list of n real numbers x_0, x_1, . . . , x_{n-1})     range: P_{i,j}, 0 ≤ i, j ≤ q - 1
Output:    min {x_0, x_1, . . . , x_{n-1}}
    for Row ← q - 2 downto 0 do          //compute column minimums
        for P_{i,j}, i = Row .and. 0 ≤ j ≤ q - 1 do in parallel
                            //compute (i + 1)ˢᵗ row and iᵗʰ row minimums in parallel
            P_{i,j}:Temp ⇐ P_{i+1,j}:X          //communicate up from X to Temp
            X ← min {X, Temp}                   //compute min of P_{i,j}:X and P_{i,j}:Temp
        end in parallel
    endfor

                            //compute first row minimum sequentially
    for Column ← q - 2 downto 0 do
        for P_{i,j}, i = 0 .and. j = Column do in parallel
            P_{i,j}:Temp ⇐ P_{i,j+1}:X          //communicate left from X to Temp
            X ← min {X, Temp}                   //only P_{0,j} is active
        end in parallel
    endfor
    return(P_{0,0}:X)
end Min2DMesh
```

FIGURE 15.14

Computing the minimum on a two-dimensional mesh. Arrows indicate how the minimums are computed at each stage. The final result is in $P_{0,0}$.

Phase 1: Compute column minimums

$$
\begin{array}{ccccc}
\infty - \infty - \infty - \infty \\
| \quad | \quad | \quad | \\
\infty - 5 - \infty - \infty \\
| \quad | \quad | \quad | \\
8 - \infty - 10 - \infty \\
| \quad | \quad | \quad | \\
\infty - 13 - \infty - \infty
\end{array}
\Rightarrow
\begin{array}{ccccc}
\infty - \infty - \infty - \infty \\
| \quad | \quad | \quad | \\
\infty - 5 - \infty - \infty \\
\uparrow \quad \uparrow \quad \uparrow \quad \uparrow \\
8 - 13 - 10 - \infty \\
| \quad | \quad | \quad | \\
\infty - 13 - \infty - \infty
\end{array}
\Rightarrow
\begin{array}{ccccc}
\infty - \infty - \infty - \infty \\
\uparrow \quad \uparrow \quad \uparrow \quad \uparrow \\
8 - 5 - 10 - \infty \\
| \quad | \quad | \quad | \\
8 - 13 - 10 - \infty \\
| \quad | \quad | \quad | \\
\infty - 13 - \infty - \infty
\end{array}
\Rightarrow
\begin{array}{ccccc}
8 - 5 - 10 - \infty \\
| \quad | \quad | \quad | \\
8 - 5 - 10 - \infty \\
| \quad | \quad | \quad | \\
8 - 13 - 10 - \infty \\
| \quad | \quad | \quad | \\
\infty - 13 - \infty - \infty
\end{array}
$$

Phase 2: Compute first row minimum

$$
\Rightarrow
\begin{array}{ccccc}
8 - 5 \leftarrow 10 - \infty \\
| \quad | \quad | \quad | \\
8 - 5 - 10 - \infty \\
| \quad | \quad | \quad | \\
8 - 13 - 10 - \infty \\
| \quad | \quad | \quad | \\
\infty - 13 - \infty - \infty
\end{array}
\Rightarrow
\begin{array}{ccccc}
8 \leftarrow 5 - 10 - \infty \\
| \quad | \quad | \quad | \\
8 - 5 - 10 - \infty \\
| \quad | \quad | \quad | \\
8 - 13 - 10 - \infty \\
| \quad | \quad | \quad | \\
\infty - 13 - \infty - \infty
\end{array}
\Rightarrow
\begin{array}{ccccc}
5 - 5 - 10 - \infty \\
| \quad | \quad | \quad | \\
8 - 5 - 10 - \infty \\
| \quad | \quad | \quad | \\
8 - 13 - 10 - \infty \\
| \quad | \quad | \quad | \\
\infty - 13 - \infty - \infty
\end{array}
$$

Putting the preceding pieces together yields the following pseudocode for *Search2DMesh*. Note that we input the search element to the front-end variable *x* (as opposed to a distributed variable that has an instantiation in each processor).

```
function Search2DMesh(L, n, x)
Model: two-dimensional mesh M_{q,q} with p = n = q² processors
Input:    L (a list of n elements),        range: P_{i,j}, 0 ≤ i, j ≤ q − 1
          x (a search element),            front end variable
Output:   the smallest row-major index where x occurs in L, or ∞ if
          x is not in L
     P_{0,0}:X ← x
     Broadcast2DMesh(P_{0,0}:X, n)
     for 0 ≤ i, j ≤ q − 1 do in parallel
         if P_{i,j}:L ≠ P_{i,j}:X then
             P_{i,j}:Index ← ∞
         else
             P_{i,j}:Index ← i*q + j
         endif
     end in parallel
     return(Min2DMesh(Index, n))
end Search2DMesh
```

Similar to searching on a PRAM, our searching algorithm on $M_{q,q}$ performs a single parallel comparison between the search element and the elements of the list. Thus, the communication complexity is the appropriate measure of the complexity of our algorithm. The number of communication steps for both the broadcast phase and the reverse-broadcast phase is $2q - 2$. Hence, the complexity of our searching algorithm is $4q - 4 = 4\sqrt{n} - 4$, so we achieve a speedup of $n/(4\sqrt{n} - 4)$ over the sequential algorithm *LinearSearch*.

15.2.8 I/O Constraints

Any parallel machine must have some mechanism to read "outside world" data from external input devices into the processors' local memories, as well as to write data from these memories to external output devices. In this book, we adopt a high-level approach, leaving the exact nature of the I/O mechanism unspecified. As with serial (single-processor) computers, we simply assume that suitable parallel versions of **read** and **write** statements are available.

In fact, in the case of a PRAM, we typically assume that central control has already placed input data for algorithms into shared memory, using **read** or **write** statements infrequently. Also, in interconnection network models, we often assume that input data for algorithms has already been distributed to the local memory of the relevant processors without specifying the mechanism for accomplishing it. However, we use **read** and **write** statements more often for interconnection network models than for PRAMs because it is important to specify how data gets distributed to the processors' local memories in interconnection network models. Further, when a procedure is called or a function invoked in an interconnection network model, we are careful to specify which processors have meaningful data supplied to them on input or provide meaningful data on output. For example, if an algorithm for an interconnection network is supposed to sort a list $L[0:n-1]$, we are explicit about which processors receive the list on input, and we specify a linear ordering of the processors that contain the sorted list on output. Each local processor manages parameters, local and global variables, in a manner similar to single-processor serial computers.

15.3 Performance Measures of Parallel Algorithms

SIMD computers have the property that all the active processors (some may remain idle) perform the *same* operation (possibly on different data) during any parallel step. If this common operation is the basic operation, we refer to it as a *parallel basic operation*. The best-case, average, and worst-case complexities of a parallel algorithm are defined in terms of the number of parallel basic operations performed. For example, the worst-case complexity $W(n)$ of a parallel algorithm using $p(n)$ processors is defined to be the maximum number of parallel basic operations performed by the algorithm over all inputs of size n. We can define the best-case complexity $B(n)$ and the average complexity $A(n)$ of a parallel algorithm in a similar manner.

For parallel algorithms, the number of parallel basic operations performed usually depends only on the size n of the input; therefore, the best-case and average complexities are the same as the worst-case complexity.

One measure of the performance of a parallel algorithm results from comparing $W(n)$ to the smallest worst-case complexity $W^*(n)$ over all sequential algorithms for the problem. This leads to the following formal definition of the *speedup* $S(n)$ of the parallel algorithm.

DEFINITION 15.3.1 **Speedup of a Parallel Algorithm**

Let $W(n)$ denote the worst-case complexity of a parallel algorithm for solving a given problem, and let $W^*(n)$ denote the smallest worst-case complexity over all known sequential algorithms for solving the same problem. Then the *speedup* $S(n)$ of the parallel algorithm is defined by

$$S(n) = \frac{W^*(n)}{W(n)}. \qquad\qquad \textbf{(15.3.1)}$$

The definition of speedup does not explicitly depend on the number of processors used by the algorithm. Thus, the speedup in isolation is not a true measure of the efficiency of the parallel algorithm. Good speedup usually comes with the additional cost of using many processors. Consequently, when measuring the efficiency of a parallel algorithm, it is important to consider both the worst-case complexity $W(n)$ and the number of processors $p(n)$ used.

DEFINITION 15.3.2 **Cost of a Parallel Algorithm**

Let $W(n)$ denote the worst-case complexity of a parallel algorithm for solving a given problem using $p(n)$ processors. The *cost* $C(n)$ of the parallel algorithm is then defined as

$$C(n) = p(n) \times W(n). \qquad\qquad \textbf{(15.3.2)}$$

To judge the quality of a parallel algorithm, it is always useful to compare its cost to $W^*(n)$. A parallel algorithm is *cost optimal* if $C(n) = W^*(n)$. A parallel algorithm is considered *cost efficient* if its cost $C(n)$ is within a *polylogarithmic* factor of being cost optimal; a polylogarithmic function is a function belonging to $O(\log^k n)$.

There is a trade-off between using more processors to achieve better speedup and using fewer processors to achieve cost optimality. Indeed, a sequential algorithm having optimal worst-case complexity for a problem is, at the same time, cost optimal. The cost $C(n)$ equals the total number of basic operations performed by the algorithm only if each *parallel* basic operation consists of $p(n)$ basic operations—that is, only if none of the $p(n)$ processors used by the algorithm are idle when a parallel basic operation is performed. Thus, if the $p(n)$ processors are active and doing useful work, we can expect the ratio $W^*(n)/C(n)$ to be close to 1 (since the worst-case complexity of a sequential algorithm is measured in terms of the total number of basic operations). The ratio $W^*(n)/C(n)$, which indicates how effectively the processors are used, is known as the *efficiency $E(n)$*:

$$E(n) = \frac{W^*(n)}{C(n)}. \qquad \textbf{(15.3.3)}$$

It follows immediately from the definition of speedup that

$$E(n) = \frac{S(n)}{p(n)}. \qquad \textbf{(15.3.4)}$$

Note that $E(n) \leq 1$; otherwise, a faster sequential algorithm can be obtained from the parallel one. Moreover, a parallel algorithm is cost optimal if and only if $E(n) = 1$. Finding cost-optimal algorithms that also exhibit good speedup is usually difficult because of the trade-off mentioned earlier. Indeed, good speedup might come at the cost of using many processors, perhaps forcing more and more of the processors to remain idle as the algorithm progresses (see Figure 15.15).

We illustrate the performance measures by considering the algorithm *MinPRAM*. As shown earlier, *MinPRAM* has complexity $W(n) = \log_2 n$. Since the best sequential algorithm for finding the maximum of n elements has complexity $W^*(n) = n - 1$, *MinPRAM* has speedup $S(n) = \dfrac{n-1}{\log_2 n}$. Because *MinPRAM* uses $n/2$ processors, it has cost and efficiency given by

$$C(n) = \left(\frac{n}{2}\right)\log_2 n,$$

$$E(n) = \frac{2(n-1)}{n\log_2 n}.$$

However, *MinPRAM* is not cost optimal, because $C(n)$ is greater than $W^*(n)$.

FIGURE 15.15

© *Sidney Harris.*
Reprinted with
permission. All rights
reserved

"IT'S BECOMING MORE AND MORE HUMAN — USING ONLY 10% OF ITS BRAINPOWER."

To illustrate the importance of using factors other than speedup to measure performance, consider the problem of finding the minimum on a CRCW PRAM. Using $\binom{n}{2} = (n^2 - n)/2$ processors and the CRCW PRAM model, we can design an algorithm *MinCRCW* that finds the minimum value in a list $L[0:n - 1]$ of size n using a single parallel comparison step. However, the cost $(n^2 - n)/2$ of *MinCRCW* is even higher than the cost of *MinPRAM*. We use the CRCW PRAM model in which many processors can write concurrently to the same memory location only if they are writing the same value. For purposes of discussion, we denote the $\binom{n}{2} = (n^2 - n)/2$ processors used by *MinCRCW* by $P_{i,j}$, $i, j \in \{0, \dots, n - 1\}$, $i < j$. In one parallel step, a shared memory array $Win[0:n - 1]$ is initialized to the value 0. The array Win is used to store the results of "win-loss" comparisons of the elements in L. For each pair of numbers $L[i]$ and $L[j]$, $i < j$, $P_{i,j}$ reads $L[i]$ and $L[j]$, compares them, writes a 1 to $Win[i]$ if $L[i] > L[j]$, and writes a 1 to $Win[j]$ otherwise. It is clear that only one index k has the property that the corresponding array element $L[k]$ loses each of the $n - 1$ comparisons involving

$L[k]$. Thus, $Win[i] = 1$, $i \neq k$, and $Win[k] = 0$. The value of k is determined in one parallel step by assigning n processors the task of reading the array Win.

function *MinCRCW*($L[0{:}n - 1]$)
Model: CRCW PRAM with $p = (n^2 - n)/2$ **processors**
Input: $L[0{:}n - 1]$ (a list of size n)
Output: the minimum value of a list element in L
    for $0 \leq i \leq n - 1$ **do in parallel**
      $Win[i] \leftarrow 0$
    end in parallel
    for $0 \leq i, j \leq n - 1$ **.and.** $i < j$ **do in parallel**
                    //$P_{i,j}$ reads and compares $L[i]$ and $L[j]$
      if $L[i] > L[j]$ **then**
        $Win[i] \leftarrow 1$ //processors $P_{i,j}$ concurrently write 1 to $Win[i]$
      else
        $Win[j] \leftarrow 1$ //processors $P_{i,j}$ concurrently write 1 to $Win[j]$
      endif
    end in parallel
    for $0 \leq i \leq n - 1$ **do in parallel**
      if $Win[i] = 0$ **then** *IndexMin* $\leftarrow i$
      endif
    end in parallel
    return($L[IndexMin]$)
end *MinCRCW*

FIGURE 15.16

Action of *MinCRCW* for sample input list $L{:}95, 10, 6, 15$. *MinCRCW* uses six processors P_{01}, P_{02}, P_{03}, P_{12}, P_{13}, P_{23}.

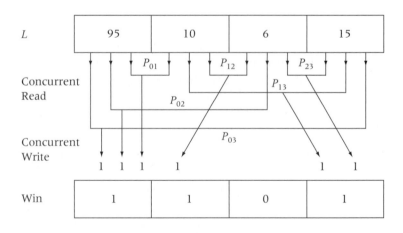

IndexMin $= 2$
$L[2] = 6$ is returned

FIGURE 15.17

Order formulae for the performance measures of algorithms discussed in this chapter.

Algorithm	Basic Operation	$p(n)$	$W(n)$	$S(n)$	$C(n)$	$E(n)$
SumPRAM	+	n	$\log n$	$n/\log n$	$n \log n$	$1/\log n$
MinPRAM	<	n	$\log n$	$n/\log n$	$n \log n$	$1/\log n$
SearchPRAM	<	n	$\log n$	$n/\log n$	$n \log n$	$1/\log n$
Sum2DMesh	+	n	$\sqrt{n}$	$\sqrt{n}$	$n^{3/2}$	$1/\sqrt{n}$
Min2DMesh	<	n	$\sqrt{n}$	$\sqrt{n}$	$n^{3/2}$	$1/\sqrt{n}$
Search2DMesh	<	n	$\sqrt{n}$	$\sqrt{n}$	$n^{3/2}$	$1/\sqrt{n}$
MinCRCW	+	n^2	1	n	n^2	$1/n$

The action of *MinCRCW* is illustrated for a sample list of size 4 in Figure 15.16.

MinCRCW has worst-case complexity $W(n) = 1$, because it only performs a single parallel comparison step. Thus, *MinCRCW* has speedup $S(n) = n - 1$. The drawback is seen in the large cost and low efficiency measures $C(n) = \dfrac{n^2 - n}{2}$ and $E(n) = \dfrac{2}{n}$, respectively. Figure 15.17 summarizes the analysis of most of the parallel algorithms discussed in this chapter. The figure shows the *order* of the number $p(n)$ of processors required, the worst-case complexity $W(n)$ (the average and best-case complexities are the same as the worst-case complexity for all the algorithms we have discussed so far), the speedup $S(n)$, the cost $C(n)$, and the processor efficiency $E(n)$.

15.3.1 Speedup and Amdahl's Law

Using p processors versus a single processor can yield significant speedup for certain problems. Ultimate speedup occurs for problems—called "embarrassingly parallel"—that involve independent operations requiring little or no communication between the processors. For example, adding two n-dimensional vectors $x = (x_0, x_1, \dots, x_{n-1})$ and $y = (y_0, y_1, \dots, y_{n-1})$, $p(n) = n$, can be done in a *single* parallel step. Simultaneously, processor P_i adds x_i and y_i for $i \in \{0, \dots, n-1\}$ (see Figure 15.1). This is a speedup by a factor of n over the n sequential steps required to do this vector addition on a single-processor machine. However, problems yielding such ultimate speedup are rare. Most problems have an inherently sequential component and therefore cannot be completely parallelized. Amdahl's law expresses an upper bound for the speedup achievable by any parallel algorithm for a given problem in terms of the inherently sequential component of the problem.

Observe that any parallel algorithm can be thought of as a parallelization of the associated sequential algorithm that performs the operations in each parallel operation sequentially. Now suppose that we are given a sequential algorithm that we wish to parallelize and that a fraction f of the basic operations must be performed sequentially for any input (no matter what the input size). If we have at most p processors, then the parallelization of the sequential algorithm has complexity at least $f + (1 - f)/p$ times the complexity of the sequential algorithm. Thus, for any input to the algorithm, the parallelized algorithm achieves a speedup of at most $1/[f + (1 - f)/p]$ over the sequential algorithm. This upper bound on the speedup S achieved for any input by parallelizing a sequential algorithm is known as Amdahl's law:

$$ S \le \frac{1}{f + (1 - f)/p} $$

In Amdahl's law, $S \le 1/f$ no matter how many processors we use. In particular, if f is as small as 0.05, we could only hope to achieve a speedup of 20 using an unlimited number of processors. Amdahl used his law to give a pessimistic view of the ultimate effectiveness of massively parallel computers and algorithms. However, in practice, it is often the case that f is not independent of the input size n and usually diminishes as the input size increases. Thus, good speedup can often be obtained even for problems that are far from embarrassingly parallel.

15.4 Parallel Sorting

In this section, we discuss sorting on PRAMs and interconnection networks. The design of parallel sorting algorithms is highly dependent on the particular parallel architecture under consideration. For example, using $(n^2 - n)/2$ processors on the CRCW PRAM with concurrent writes resolved by summing, we can sort a list of size n in constant time. On the other hand, the complexity of any sorting algorithm on the EREW PRAM is in $\Omega(\log n)$, and on the one-dimensional mesh is in $\Omega(n)$.

The fastest sequential comparison-based sorting algorithms have worst-case complexity $W^*(n) \in \Theta(n\log n)$ (see Chapter 25). In particular, a parallel sorting algorithm is order-cost optimal if its cost $C(n)$ belongs to $\Theta(n\log n)$.

15.4.1 Sorting on the CRCW and CREW PRAMs

A constant-time parallel sorting algorithm on the CRCW PRAM, *SortCRCW*, is based on an idea similar to that used to design *MinCRCW* in the previous section.

With *SortCRCW*, however, we assume a more powerful (and less realistic) model of resolving concurrent writes that *sums* the values to be concurrently written.

SortCRCW computes a proper position of $L[i]$ in the sorted order of L by determining the number of elements in the list L that are smaller than $L[i]$, $i = 0, \ldots,$ $n - 1$. *SortCRCW* uses $\binom{n}{2} = (n^2 - n)/2$ processors P_{ij} and an auxiliary array $Win[0:n - 1]$ in shared memory. $Win[i]$ contains the proper index position of $L[i]$ in the sorted list. The pseudocode for computing the values of $Win[0:n - 1]$ is identical to that used by *MinCRCW* for computing its array $Win[0:n - 1]$. Recall that in a single comparison step, every pair of list elements $L[i]$ and $L[j]$ are compared, $i < j$. The value 1 is written to $Win[i]$ if $L[i] > L[j]$; otherwise, the value 1 is written to $Win[j]$. The difference with *SortCRCW* is that concurrent writes are resolved by summing, so $Win[i]$ computes the total number of wins of $L[i]$, not simply whether or not $L[i]$ ever won.

```
procedure SortCRCW(L[0:n − 1])
Model: CRCW PRAM with p = (n² − n)/2 processors, write conflicts resolved by
           summing
Input:     L[0:n − 1] (an array of n list elements in shared memory)
Output:   L[0:n − 1] (L sorted in increasing order)
    for 0 ≤ i ≤ n − 1 do in parallel
        Win[i] ← 0
    end in parallel
    for 0 ≤ i, j ≤ n − 1 .and. i < j do in parallel
        if L[i] > L[j] then
                processors Pᵢⱼ concurrently write 1 to Win[i]
        else
                processors Pᵢⱼ concurrently write 1 to Win[j]
        endif
    end in parallel
    for 0 ≤ i ≤ n − 1 do in parallel
        L[Win[i]] ← L[i]
    end in parallel
end SortCRCW
```

In Figure 15.18, the action of *SortCRCW* in computing the array $Win[0:n - 1]$ is illustrated for a sample list of size 4.

Although *SortCRCW* sorts in constant time, it has two major drawbacks: the powerful concurrent write resolution model and the large number of processors used. Indeed, *SortCRCW* is far from cost optimal because it has cost $C(n) = (n^2 - n)/2 \in \Theta(n^2)$, whereas the optimal cost $W^*(n)$ is in $\Theta(n\log n)$.

FIGURE 15.18

Computation of
Win[0:3] by
SortCRCW from the
sample input list
L: 95, 10, 6, 15.
SortCRCW uses six
processors: P_{01}, P_{02},
P_{03}, P_{12}, P_{13}, P_{23}.

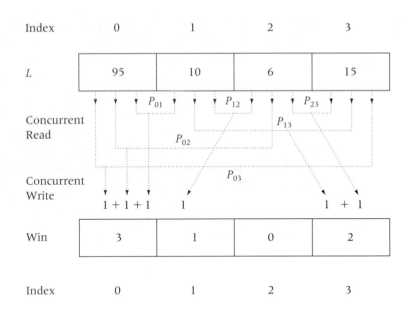

Addressing the first drawback, we can transform *SortCRCW* into the $\Theta(\log n)$ algorithm *SortCREW*, which would be suitable for the CREW PRAM, or the $\Theta(\log n)$ algorithm *SortPRAM*, which would be suitable for an EREW PRAM as follows. *SortCREW* uses an auxiliary two-dimensional array $Win[0{:}n-1;0{:}n-1]$ of n^2 shared-memory locations to record the results of the comparisons of $L[i]$ with $L[j]$. More precisely, P_{ij} writes the results of the comparison $L[i]$ with $L[j]$ to $Win[i, j]$ or $Win[j, i]$ instead of to $Win[i]$ or $Win[j]$ as in *SortCRCW*. Then the processors P_{ij} compute the index position of $L[i]$ by summing the numbers in the ith row of $Win[i, j]$. These sums can be simultaneously computed in $\log_2 n$ parallel steps using *SumPRAM*. Of course, in addition to the $\Theta(n^2)$ processors, *SortCREW* also requires n^2 auxiliary memory locations.

Transforming *SortCRCW* to *SortPRAM* on the EREW PRAM involves the same translation of the concurrent writes. *SortPRAM* translates concurrent reads using replication and broadcasting.

15.4.2 Even-Odd Mergesort on the EREW PRAM

SortPRAM is of limited practical interest because it uses a quadratic number of processors. A much more practical algorithm, *EvenOddMergeSortPRAM*, was discovered by K. E. Batcher in the 1960s. *EvenOddMergeSortPRAM* sorts a list of size n on the EREW PRAM using n processors, with complexity $\Theta(\log^2 n)$ and cost $\Theta(n \log^2 n)$. *EvenOddMergeSortPRAM* is within a logarithmic factor of both optimal complexity and optimal cost for a comparison-based parallel algorithm using n processors.

Before describing *EvenOddMergeSortPRAM*, we need to discuss how to exploit the inherent parallelism present in the sequential algorithm *MergeSort*. Recall that *MergeSort* is based on a divide-and-conquer strategy, which involves dividing the input list $L[0:n − 1]$ into two the sublists $L[0:n/2 − 1]$ and $L[n/2:n − 1]$, recursively sorting the two sublists, and then merging the resulting sorted sublists. The parallelization *MergeSortPRAM* of *MergeSort* is achieved by performing the two recursive calls concurrently. In the following pseudocode for *MergeSortPRAM*, we call a generic procedure *MergePRAM* for merging the sorted sublists $L[0:n/2 − 1]$ and $L[n/2:n − 1]$, where we assume, for convenience, that n is a power of 2. For simplicity, by abuse of notation, we also suppress the parameters *low* and *high* for the index ranges of sublists of $L[0:n − 1]$ that more correctly would accompany a parallelization of *MergeSort*. This abuse of notation will also be used for the sake of simplicity throughout this chapter in the discussion of other recursive parallel sorting algorithms.

```
procedure MergeSortPRAM(L[0:n − 1]) recursive
Model: EREW PRAM     //the number of processors needed depends on the
                     //implementation of MergePRAM
Input:    L[0:n − 1] (a list of size n = 2^k)
Output:   L[0:n − 1] (sorted list)
    if n ≥ 2 then        //concurrently make two recursive calls to MergeSortPRAM
                         //with input lists L[0:n/2 − 1] and L[n/2:n − 1]
        parallelcall MergeSortPRAM(L[0:n/2 − 1] | L[n/2:n − 1])
        MergePRAM(L[0:n − 1])
    endif
end MergeSortPRAM
```

We are now left with the problem of designing *MergePRAM*. Our first attempt could be to simply adapt the sequential procedure *Merge* used in the sequential algorithm *MergeSort* using $n/2$ processors. The problem with this approach is the lack of parallelism present in *Merge*. For example, in the resulting parallel algorithm *MergeSortPRAM*, when merging the 2^i sublists of size $n/2^i$ at level i of the tree of recursive calls (see Figure 15.19), only $2^{i − 1}$ processors are active, $i = 1, \ldots , k$. Since *Merge* performs $m − 1$ comparisons in the worst case when merging two sublists of size $m/2$, *MergeSortPRAM* performs $(n/2^{i − 1} − 1)$ parallel

FIGURE 15.19

The tree of recursive parallel calls to *MergeSortPRAM* for $n = 8$. Each node is labeled with the indices of its associated sublist.

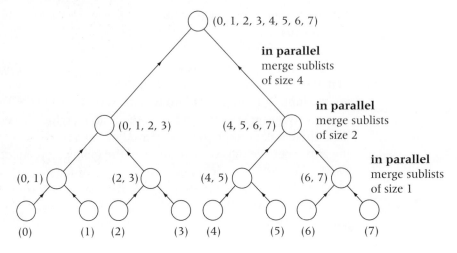

FIGURE 15.20

Resolution of parallel calls to *MergeSortPRAM* for the sample list $L[0:7] = (2, 7, 1, 6, 8, 3, 4, 5)$.

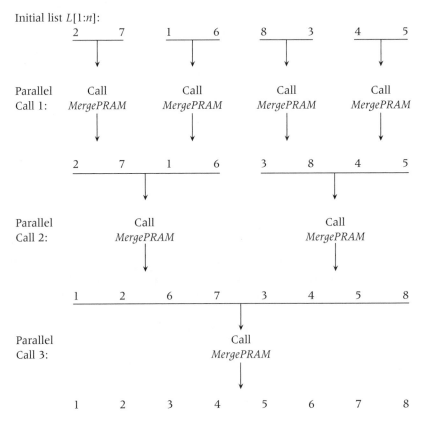

comparisons in the worst case when concurrently merging the 2^i sublists of size $n/2^i$, $i = 1, \dots, k$. Thus, the worst-case complexity $W(n)$ of *MergeSortPRAM* is given by

$$
\begin{aligned}
W(n) &= (n - 1) + \left(\frac{n}{2} - 1\right) + \cdots + \left(\frac{n}{2^{k-1}} - 1\right) \\
&= n\left(1 + \frac{1}{2} + \frac{1}{2^2} + \cdots + \frac{1}{2^{k-1}}\right) - k \\
&= n2\left(1 - \left(\frac{1}{2}\right)^k\right) - k \quad \text{(using the geometric series formula)} \\
&= 2n\left(1 - \frac{1}{n}\right) - \log_2 n \\
&= 2n - \log_2 n - 2 \in \Theta(n).
\end{aligned}
$$

The speedup $S(n)$ of *MergeSortPRAM* over the sequential algorithm *MergeSort* belongs to $\Theta(\log n)$, which is disappointingly low. Further, the cost $C(n) \in \Theta(n^2)$ achieved by *MergeSortPRAM* is high—optimal cost is of the order $\Theta(n\log n)$. To achieve significant speedup and low cost, we must design a sublinear parallel procedure for merging two lists.

More than 30 years ago, Batcher designed two $\Theta(\log n)$ parallel merging procedures that are still widely used today. We now discuss one of these merging procedures: *even-odd merge*.

Even-odd merge is similar to the sequential algorithm *ShellSort* (see Chapter 5) with increments 2 and 1. Consider a list $L[0:n-1]$ of size $n = 2^k$, $k \geq 1$, where $L[0:n/2 - 1]$ and $L[n/2:n - 1]$ are sorted. Recall that a 2-subsort of $L[0:n - 1]$ consists of independent sortings of the even-indexed and odd-indexed elements. *EvenOddMergePRAM* is based on the following proposition.

Proposition 15.2.1 For $n = 2^k$, $k \geq 1$, suppose $L[0:n/2 - 1]$ and $L[n/2:n - 1]$ are sorted sublists. Performing a 2-subsort on $L[0:n - 1]$ followed by an odd-even compare-exchange step results in a sorted list $L[0:n - 1]$. □

Figure 15.21 illustrates Proposition 15.2.1 for a sample list $L[0:15]$. The proof of Proposition 15.2.1 follows from the 0/1 sorting lemma given in the next section.

Batcher's odd-even merge proceeds by parallelizing both the 2-subsort step and the even-odd compare-exchange step illustrated in Figure 15.21. We need to assume that n is a power of 2, which always can be arranged by adding an appropriate number of elements to the end of the array. The 2-subsort is accomplished by first partitioning (pulling apart) $L[0:n - 1]$ into sublists $Even[0:n/2 - 1]$ and

FIGURE 15.21

Given a list $L[0:15]$, where sublists $L[0:7]$ and $L[8:15]$ are sorted, a 2-subsort followed by an odd-even compare-exchange step yields a sorted list.

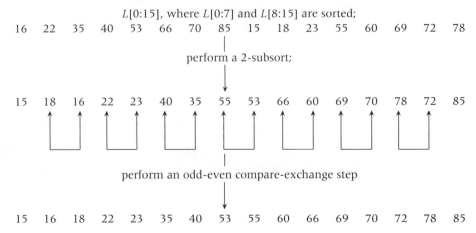

$L[0:15]$, where $L[0:7]$ and $L[8:15]$ are sorted;

16   22   35   40   53   66   70   85   15   18   23   55   60   69   72   78

perform a 2-subsort;

15   18   16   22   23   40   35   55   53   66   60   69   70   78   72   85

perform an odd-even compare-exchange step

15   16   18   22   23   35   40   53   55   60   66   69   70   72   78   85

$Odd[0:n/2 - 1]$ of elements having odd and even indices, recursively sorting these sublists, and then simply interleaving the two sorted sublists back together into $L[0:n - 1]$. The recursion is valid because the arrays Odd and $Even$ have the same property as the original list in that the first half and the second half of the list is sorted. After the 2-subsort is complete, a single parallel even-odd compare-exchange step yields a sorted list $L[0:n - 1]$.

Pseudocode for the following procedure *EvenOddMergePRAM* is based directly on the preceding discussion. Note the use of the syntax:

parallelcall *EvenOddMergePRAM(Even[0:n/2 – 1] | Odd[0:n/2 – 1])*

Recall from our pseudocode conventions that this statement uses n processors, half of which are used to execute the call *EvenOddMergePRAM(Even[0:n/2 – 1])*, and the other half are concurrently used to execute the call *EvenOddMergePRAM(Odd[0:n/2 – 1])*. The high-level action of *EvenOddMergePRAM* is illustrated in Figure 15.22 for a sample list $L[0:n - 1]$ of size 16.

```
procedure EvenOddMergePRAM(L[0:n – 1]) recursive
Model: EREW PRAM with p = n processors
Input:    L[0:n – 1] (list of size n = 2^k, where sublists L[0:n/2 – 1] and L[n/2:n – 1]
          are sorted)
Output:  L[0:n – 1] (sorted list)
    if n = 2 then
        if L[0] > L[1] then
            interchange(L[0], L[1])
        endif
    else
                    //separate list elements of even and odd indices
```

```
            evenoddsplit(L[0:n − 1], Even[0:n/2 − 1], Odd[0:n/2 − 1])
                            //recursively sort list elements of even and odd indices
            parallelcall EvenOddMergePRAM(Even[0:n/2 − 1] | Odd[0:n/2−1])
                            //Interleave computation to achieve a 2-subsort of L[0:n − 1])
            for 0 ≤ i ≤ n/2 − 1 do in parallel
                L[2∗i] ← Even[i]
                L[2∗i+1] ← Odd[i]
            end in parallel
                            //finish sort by a parallel odd-even compare and exchange
            for 1 ≤ i ≤ n/2 do in parallel
                if L[2∗i − 1] > L[2∗i] then
                    interchange(L[2∗i − 1], L[2∗i])
                endif
            end in parallel
        endif
    end EvenOddMergePRAM
```

FIGURE 15.22

The high-level action of *EvenOddMerge-PRAM(L[0:15])*. The final result of recursive calls to *EvenOddMerge-PRAM(Even[0:7])* and *EvenOddMerge-PRAM(Odd[0:7])* is shown but not the detailed resolution of these calls.

Original list $L[0:15]$

16 22 35 40 53 66 70 85 | 15 18 23 55 60 69 72 78

After separating elements of odd and even indices:

Even[0:7]   *Odd*[0:7]

16 35 53 70 | 15 23 60 72   22 40 66 85 | 18 55 69 78

After performing **parallelcall** *EvenOddMergePRAM(Even[0:n/2 − 1] | Odd[0:n/2 − 1])*:

Even[0:7]   *Odd*[0:7]

15 16 23 35 53 60 70 72   18 22 40 55 66 69 78 85

$L[0:15]$ after performing an interleave computation to achieve a 2-subsort:

15 18 16 22 23 40 35 55 53 66 60 69 70 78 72 85

$L[0:15]$ sorted after performing an even-odd compare-exchange step:

15 16 18 22 23 35 40 53 55 60 66 69 70 72 78 85

FIGURE 15.23

Action of
EvenOddMergePRAM
for the list
$L[0:7] = (-2, 17,$
$23, 55, 8,$
$10, 11, 79)$.

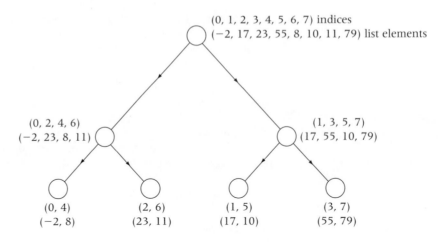

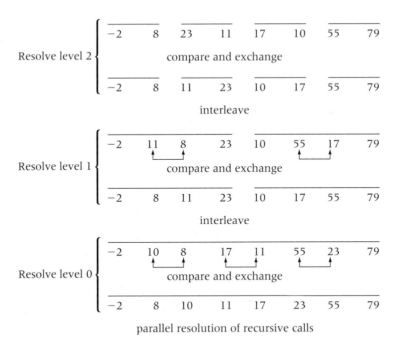

parallel resolution of recursive calls

Figure 15.23 shows the complete parallel resolution of the parallel recursive calls to *EvenOddMergePRAM* for a sample list of size 8. Note in Figure 15.23 that for a list of size 8, *EvenOddMergePRAM* performs $3 = \log_2 8$ parallel compare-exchange steps. In general, for a list of size $n = 2^k$, *EvenOddMergePRAM* performs $k = \log_2 n$ parallel compare-exchange steps.

In the general parallel sorting paradigm *MergeSortPRAM*, if *MergePRAM* is chosen to be *EvenOddMergePRAM*, then we obtain the parallel sorting algorithm *EvenOddMergeSortPRAM*. For the sake of completeness, we now give the pseudocode for *EvenOddMergeSortPRAM*.

```
procedure EvenOddMergeSortPRAM(L[0:n − 1]) recursive
Model: EREW PRAM (the number of processors needed depends on the
             implementation of MergePRAM)
Input:   L[0:n − 1] (a list of size n = 2ᵏ)
Output: L[0:n − 1] (sorted list)
    if n ≥ 2 then         //concurrently make two recursive calls to MergeSortPRAM
                          //with input lists L[0:n/2 − 1] and L[n/2:n − 1]
        parallelcall EvenOddMergeSortPRAM(L[0:n/2 − 1] | L[n/2:n − 1])
        call EvenOddMergePRAM(L[0:n − 1])
    endif
end EvenOddMergeSortPRAM
```

For an input list $L[0:n - 1]$ of size n, *EvenOddMergeSortPRAM* makes a total of $\log_2 n$ parallel calls, each involving concurrent calls to *EvenOddMergePRAM*. Further, each of the input sublists involved in the ith parallel call has size 2^{i-1}, $i = 1, \ldots, \log_2 n$. Because *EvenOddMergePRAM* performs $\log_2 2^i = i$ parallel comparisons for an input list of size 2^i, it follows that the total number of parallel comparisons performed by *EvenOddMergeSortPRAM* is given by

$$W(n) = 1 + 2 + \cdots + \log_2 n = \frac{(\log_2 n)^2}{2} + \frac{\log_2 n}{2} \in \Theta((\log n)^2).$$

EvenOddMergeSortPRAM uses $p(n) = n$ processors, so its cost is given by

$$C(n) = n\left(\frac{(\log_2 n)^2}{2} + \frac{\log_2 n}{2}\right) \in \Theta(n\log^2 n).$$

Hence, as previously stated, *OddEvenMergeSortPRAM* is within a logarithmic factor of being order-cost optimal.

15.4.3 The 0/1 Sorting Lemma

Certainly the most useful tool in proving that oblivious parallel sorting algorithms are correct is the 0/1 sorting lemma. A compare-exchange sorting algorithm is *oblivious* if, for all input lists of size n, it performs the same number of comparisons and the kth comparison made by the algorithm is always between elements in two list positions that only depend on k. Sequential oblivious sorting algorithms are rare. In fact, the only one that we have seen is the straightforward version of bubblesort that does *not* use a flag to terminate the algorithm after a pass in which no interchanges are made. Note, for example, for this version of bubblesort and $n = 4$, the six comparisons made are always between list elements in index positions 0 and 1, 1 and 2, 2 and 3, 0 and 1, 1 and 2, and 0 and 1, in that order, no matter what list of size 4 is considered. On the other hand, parallel sorting algorithms, such as *OddEvenMergeSortPRAM* discussed in the previous section, are usually oblivious. For such algorithms the 0/1 sorting lemma reduces correctness proofs to verifying correctness for the very special case of lists consisting of just 0s and 1s. The correctness proof for this special case is usually significantly easier than a proof that considers an arbitrary input list directly.

Lemma: 15.0.1

Sorting Lemma

Suppose an oblivious compare-exchange sorting algorithm is correct on all lists of size n consisting of 0s and 1s. Then it is correct on all lists of size n.

PROOF

We prove the 0/1 sorting lemma by induction on the number k of distinct values that occur in the list $L[0:n - 1]$. It is trivial when $k = 1$ (that is, all the elements in $L[0:n - 1]$ have the same value), so our basis step will start with $k = 2$.

Basis Step: $k = 2$. Suppose $L[0:n - 1]$ consists of just two distinct elements a and b, with $a < b$. Let $L'[0:n - 1]$ be the list obtained from $L[0:n - 1]$ by replacing every occurrence of a by 0 and every occurrence of b by 1. Then our oblivious compare-exchange algorithm will move a and b in exactly the same way as 0 and 1 move when we input the list $L'[0:n - 1]$. Because our algorithm correctly sorts $L'[0:n - 1]$, it must also sort $L[0:n - 1]$.

Induction Step: Assume that our algorithm correctly sorts all 0/1 lists and also sorts all lists having $j < k$ distinct values, where $k \geq 3$. Consider now a list $L[0:n - 1]$ having k distinct values. Let $L'[0:n - 1]$ be the list obtained from $L[0:n - 1]$ by amalgamating the largest and second largest values wherever they occur (for specificity, suppose we replace each occurrence of the second argest value by the largest value). For example, suppose $L[0:9]$ is the list containing exactly seven values:

i	0	1	2	3	4	5	6	7	8	9
$L[i]$	3	10	6	5	23	9	23	10	8	3

Then the list $L'[0:9]$ contains exactly six different values:

i	0	1	2	3	4	5	6	7	8	9
$L'[i]$	3	23	6	5	23	9	23	23	8	3

Since $L'[0:n-1]$ has exactly $k-1$ values, by induction hypothesis, our algorithm sorts $L'[0:n-1]$. However, note that the elements $L[0:n-1]$ that are not equal to the largest or second largest value move in exactly the same way when input to our algorithm as they do when $L'[0:n-1]$ is input to the algorithm. Indeed, our algorithm will make exactly the same compare-exchange operations involving these elements of $L'[0:n-1]$ as it did for these same elements of $L[0:n-1]$. Considering, for example, the list $L[0:9]$ previously shown, and assuming that our algorithm is correct for lists having at most six distinct elements, it would then follow that our algorithm would output the list in the following form:

i	0	1	2	3	4	5	6	7	8	9
$L[i]$	3	3	5	6	8	9	*	*	*	*

where * indicates where either 10 or 23 resides.

Now consider the list $L''[0:n-1]$ obtained from $L[0:n-1]$ by amalgamating all the list elements whose value is not equal to the largest value, so that $L''[0:n-1]$ has exactly two distinct values. Suppose for definiteness, that we amalgamate all these elements to the smallest value. Then, considering again the list $L[0:9]$ shown previously, $L''[0:9]$ is the following list:

i	0	1	2	3	4	5	6	7	8	9
$L''[i]$	3	3	3	3	23	3	23	3	3	3

Hence, by our basis step, $L''[0:n-1]$ is sorted when input to our oblivious algorithm. However, all the elements having the largest value in $L[0:n-1]$ move in exactly the same way when input to our algorithm as they do when $L''[0:n-1]$ is input to the algorithm. In other words, all the largest elements in $L[0:n-1]$ move to a correct position when $L[0:n-1]$ is input to our algorithm.

We have now shown that all elements in $L[0:n-1]$, except possibly those having the second largest value, move to correct positions when input to our algorithm. For example, applying this to our sample list, we now know that our algorithm outputs the list $L[0:n-1]$ in the form

i	0	1	2	3	4	5	6	7	8	9
$L[i]$	3	3	5	6	8	9	*	*	23	23

where * indicates the only places left for the two elements with value 10 to go; that is, the output list must be sorted. In general, because there is no place for the second largest elements to go except into correct positions, we conclude that the entire output list $L[0:n-1]$ is sorted, which finishes our inductive proof of the 0/1 sorting lemma.

Correctness Proof of *EvenOddMergeSortPRAM*. To illustrate the 0/1 sorting lemma, we first consider *EvenOddMergeSortPRAM*. The correctness of *EvenOddMergeSortPRAM* will obviously follow if we prove the correctness of *EvenOddMergePRAM*. We prove the correctness of *EvenOddMergePRAM* by induction on k, where the size of the list is $n = 2^k$. For $k = 2$, *EvenOddMergePRAM* is clearly correct. Assume, then, that *EvenOddMergePRAM* is correct for all 0/1 lists of size $n = 2^k$, and consider a 0/1 list of size 2^{k+1}. *EvenOddMergePRAM* first splits the input list into two sublists each of size 2^k consisting of the even-indexed and odd-indexed elements, respectively; the procedure then calls itself recursively with the latter two sublists. By induction hypothesis, the recursive calls result in sortings of the even-indexed and odd-indexed elements of the original list. Next, *EvenOddMergePRAM* interleaves the even-indexed list with the odd-indexed list, resulting in a 2-sorting of the original list. Finally, an odd-even compare-exchange step is performed.

The original list consisted of two sorted halves of the form

$$\underbrace{0, 0, 0, \dots, 0,}_{p \text{ times}} 1, 1, \dots, 1 \quad \text{and} \quad \underbrace{0, 0, 0, \dots, 0,}_{q \text{ times}} 1, 1, \dots, 1, \text{respectively.}$$

Thus, when these sublists are separated into even and odd indexed elements, there are exactly $\lceil p/2 \rceil + \lceil q/2 \rceil$ 0s in the even indexed list and $\lfloor p/2 \rfloor + \lfloor q/2 \rfloor$ 0s in the odd indexed list. There are three cases to consider, depending on the three possible values, 0, 1, and 2, of the difference $(\lceil p/2 \rceil + \lceil q/2 \rceil) - (\lfloor p/2 \rfloor + \lfloor q/2 \rfloor)$. It is easy to check that in the first two cases, the interleaved list is already sorted, so that the odd-even exchange step makes no exchanges. In the third case, the interleaved list is of the form

$$\underbrace{0, 0, 0, \dots, 0,}_{\lfloor p/2 \rfloor + \lfloor q/2 \rfloor \text{ times}} 0, 1, 0, 1, 1, \dots, 1.$$

Hence, the single out-of-place 1 is in an even position, and the odd-even compare-exchange step sorts the list. By induction, therefore, *EvenOddMergePRAM* correctly sorts all 0/1 lists of size $n = 2^k$. However, by the 0/1 sorting lemma, *EvenOddMergePRAM* (and hence *EvenOddMergeSortPRAM*) correctly sorts *all* lists of size n. ■

15.4.4 Sorting on the One-Dimensional Mesh

Any comparison-based parallel sorting algorithm on M_p, $p = p(n) = n$, must perform at least $n - 1$ communication steps to properly decide between the relative order of the elements in P_0 and P_{n-1}. Thus, we can achieve a speedup of at most $\log n$ on the one-dimensional mesh for comparison-based sorting. Although this result is disappointing, designing an optimal sorting algorithm for the one-dimensional mesh is useful to obtain a sorting algorithm on the two-dimensional mesh that exhibits better speedup.

Even-Odd Transposition Sort on a One-Dimensional Mesh. The next algorithm we consider is *EvenOddSort1DMesh*, which is not a straightforward parallelization of a standard sequential algorithm. The algorithm requires n iterations, where each iteration alternates between the following two parallel steps (see Figure 15.24):

1. *Even-odd exchange*: For all even i, $\mathbf{P}_i$:L is compared to $\mathbf{P}_{i+1}$:L, and their values are interchanged if $\mathbf{P}_i$:$L > \mathbf{P}_{i+1}$:L.
2. *Odd-even exchange*: For all odd i, $\mathbf{P}_i$:L is compared to $\mathbf{P}_{i+1}$:L, and their values are interchanged if $\mathbf{P}_i$:$L > \mathbf{P}_{i+1}$:L.

```
procedure EvenOddSort1DMesh(L, n)
Model:    one-dimensional mesh M_p with p = n processors
Input:    L (a list of size n),    range: P_i, 0 ≤ i ≤ n - 1
Output:   L sorted in nondecreasing order range: P_i, 0 ≤ i ≤ n - 1
    for Step ← 0 to n - 1 do
        if even(Step) then
            for P_i, 0 ≤ i ≤ n - 1 .and. even(i) do in parallel    //even-odd exchange
                P_i:Temp ⇐ P_{i+1}:L          //communicate left from L to Temp
                if P_i:L > P_i:Temp then       //exchange P_i:L and P_{i+1}:L
                    P_{i+1}:L ⇐ P_i:L
                    P_i:L ← P_i:Temp
                endif
            end in parallel
        else                                  //Step is odd
            for P_i, 0 ≤ i ≤ n - 1 .and. odd(i) do in parallel //odd-even exchange
                P_i:Temp ⇐ P_{i+1}:L          //communicate left from L to Temp
                if P_i:L > P_i:Temp then       //exchange P_i:L and P_{i+1}:L
                    P_{i+1}:L ⇐ P_i:L          //propagate L right
                    P_i:L ← P_i:Temp
                endif
            end in parallel
        endif
    endfor
end EvenOddSort1DMesh
```

FIGURE 15.24

Action of
EvenOddSort1DMesh
for sample list of
size 6.

Processors	P_0	P_1	P_2	P_3	P_4	P_5
List	4	2	0	5	1	3
Step 1	2___	__4	0 ___	__5	1 ___	__3
Step 2	2	0___	__4	1 ___	__5	3
Step 3	0___	__2	1 ___	__4	3 ___	__5
Step 4	0	1 ___	__2	3 ___	__4	5
Step 5	0___	__1	2 ___	__3	4 ___	__5
Step 6	0	1 ___	__2	3 ___	__4	5

Since *EvenOddSort1DMesh* is clearly an oblivious algorithm, we can use the 0/1 sorting lemma to prove its correctness. Actually, we will prove the correctness of both *OddEvenSort1DMesh* and *EvenOddSort1DMesh,* where *OddEven-Sort1DMesh* is the same as *EvenOddSort1DMesh,* except that the first exchange is an odd-even exchange (all the even-odd exchanges are replaced with odd-even exchanges and vice versa).

Theorem 15.4.1

Let L be a list of size n such that $L[i] \in \{0, 1\}$, $i = 0, 1, \dots, n - 1$. Then both *EvenOddSort1DMesh* and *OddEvenSort1DMesh* sort L. Hence, by the 0/1 sorting lemma, both *EvenOddSort1DMesh* and *OddEvenSort1DMesh* sort an arbitrary list of size n.

PROOF

We prove Theorem 15.4.1 by induction on the input size n. The theorem is trivially true for a list of size $n = 1$. Assume that the theorem is true for all lists of size $n = k - 1$, so that both *EvenOddSort1DMesh* and *OddEvenSort1DMesh* sort lists of size $k - 1$ satisfying the hypothesis of the theorem. Now let L be *any* list of size $n = k$ satisfying the hypothesis of the theorem.

We first consider *EvenOddSort1DMesh*. Clearly, during each iteration of *EvenOddSort1DMesh* the 0s either remain fixed or move one position closer to the beginning of the list. Similarly, the 1s either remain fixed or move one position closer to the end of the list. During any iteration of *EvenOddSort1DMesh,* the movement of the 1s in the sublist $L[1:n - 1]$ are unaffected, either directly or indirectly, by the movement of $L[0]$ (this is not necessarily true of the 0s). Also, an even-odd exchange (odd-even exchange) on L induces (with the obvious reindexing of $L[1:k - 1]$) an odd-even exchange (even-odd exchange) on the sublist $L[1:k - 1]$. Thus, the movement on the 1s belonging to $L[1:k - 1]$ during the first $k - 1$ iterations of *OddEvenSort1DMesh* applied to L is exactly the same as the movement of the 1s when *EvenOddSort1DMesh* is applied to the sublist $L[1:k - 1]$ (of size $k - 1$). It follows from the induction

hypothesis that after $k - 1$ iterations of *OddEvenSort1DMesh*, all the 1s originally in the sublist $L[1:n - 1]$ have moved to their proper position at the end
the list L.

During any iteration of *EvenOddSort1DMesh*, the movement of the 0s in the
sublist $L[0:k - 1]$ are unaffected, either directly or indirectly, by the movement
of $L[k - 1]$. Also, an even-odd exchange (odd-even exchange) on L induces an
even-odd exchange (odd-even exchange) on the sublist $L[0:k - 2]$. Thus, the
movement of the 0s belonging to $L[0:k - 2]$ during the first $k - 1$ iterations of
EvenOddSort1DMesh applied to the L is exactly the same as the movement
of the 0s when *EvenOddSort1DMesh* is applied to the sublist $L[0:k - 2]$. It
follows from our induction hypothesis that after $k - 1$ iterations of
EvenOddSort1DMesh, all the 0s originally in the sublist $L[0:k - 2]$ have moved
to their proper position at the beginning of the list L.

We have just shown that after $k - 1$ iterations of *OddEvenSort1DMesh*, all
the elements except possibly $L[0]$ and $L[k - 1]$ are in their correct positions.
Thus, after $k - 1$ iterations of *EvenOddSort1DMesh*, we have either a sorted list
or a list with the following properties: For some index j, the elements in positions $0, 1, \ldots, j - 1$ are all equal to 0, the element in position j equals 1, the element in position $j + 1$ equals 0, and the remaining elements are all equal to
1. We may assume that we have the latter list. Since the element in position j
is greater than the element in position $j + 1$ after iteration $k - 1$, it follows
that the elements in positions j and $j + 1$ were not compared during iteration
$k - 1$. Thus, they are compared and interchanged during iteration k, yielding
a sorted list. This shows that *EvenOddSort1DMesh* works correctly on L. Similar
arguments show that a sorted list is obtained when *OddEvenSort1DMesh* is
applied to L.

Because *EvenOddSort1DMesh* has worst-case complexity $W(n) = n$, it has
cost $C(n) = n^2$ and speedup $S(n) \in \Theta(\log n)$. Due to the communication complexity of the one-dimensional mesh, *EvenOddSort1DMesh* is actually an optimal comparison-based sorting algorithm on the one-dimensional mesh.
However, its speedup and cost are not very attractive. In the next section, we
design a sorting algorithm on the two-dimensional mesh that has better
speedup and cost. ■

15.4.5 Sorting on the Two-Dimensional Mesh

When we implement a sorting algorithm on an interconnection network model, we must specify a linear ordering of the range of processors that contain the sorted list. On the one-dimensional mesh M_n, we used the obvious linear ordering $P_0, P_1, \ldots, P_{n-1}$. For the two-dimensional mesh, it would be natural to consider row-major (or column-major) ordering. A moment's thought, however, reveals that neither row-major nor column-major ordering traverse the processors in a sequence where adjacent terms in the sequence are adjacent processors in the 2-dimensional mesh. This feature of these orderings make it unlikely that a natural (and communication-efficient) sorting algorithm could be designed that outputs the list sorted relative to either one of these orderings. An ordering that does give a sequencing of the processors such that adjacent processors in the sequence are also adjacent in the two-dimensional mesh is *snake ordering* (see Figure 15.25). The algorithm *Sort2DMesh* that we now design outputs the list sorted relative to snake ordering. *Sort2DMesh* is also referred to as shearsort.

In the snake order, processor $P_{i,j}$ is the $(k+1)^{\text{st}}$ processor in the order, where k is given by

$$k = \begin{cases} qi + j - 1 & \text{if } i \text{ is even}, \quad 0 \le i, j \le q - 1, \\ q(i + 1) - j - 1 & \text{if } i \text{ is odd}, \quad 0 \le i, j \le q - 1. \end{cases}$$

···

FIGURE 15.25

Snaking M_{16}
through $M_{4,4}$
···

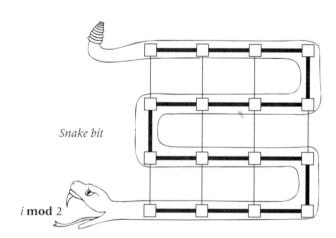

Snake bit

i **mod** 2

FIGURE 15.26

(a) The sample list
23, 6, 1, 5, 11, 13,
55, 19, −3, 12, −5,
−7, 9, 55, 28, −2
of size 16 stored in
the distributed
variable L on the
two-dimensional
mesh $M_{4,4}$

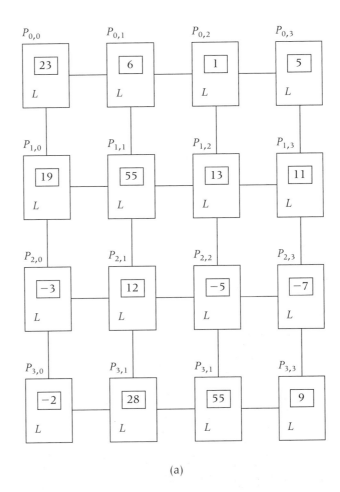

(a)

continued

In Figure 15.26a, we show a picture of a sample list of size 16 stored in the distributed variable L. In Figure 15.26b, the same list is shown after it is sorted relative to the snake ordering.

When describing our sorting algorithm *Sort2DMesh* on $M_{q,q}$, we assume for convenience that $n = q^2$. Note that each row and each column of $M_{q,q}$ corresponds to the one-dimensional mesh M_q. *Sort2DMesh* involves $\lceil \log_2 n \rceil + 1$ steps, where each odd step is a call to *EvenOddRowSort*, and each even step is a call to *EvenOddColumnSort*. As the names suggest, *EvenOddRowSort* concurrently sorts the list elements in row i for all $1 \le i \le q$, and *EvenOddColumnSort* concurrently sorts the list elements in column j for all $1 \le j \le q$. The sorting of row i (and column j) is achieved by emulating the sorting algorithm *EvenOddSort1DMesh* for

FIGURE 15.26

continued

(b) the same list stored in the distributed variable L after snake ordering.

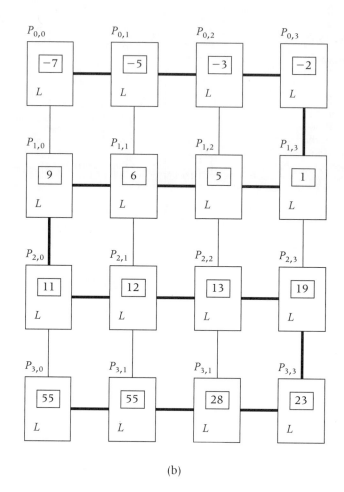

(b)

the one-dimensional mesh M_q. During each row-sorting step of *EvenOddRowSort*, if i is odd then row i is sorted in nondecreasing order, so that $\mathbf{P}_{i,1}:L \le \mathbf{P}_{i,2}:L, \le \dots \le \mathbf{P}_{i,q}:L$; otherwise, row i is sorted in nonincreasing order so that $\mathbf{P}_{i,1}:L \ge \mathbf{P}_{i,2}:L, \ge \dots \ge \mathbf{P}_{i,q}:L$. During each column-sorting step of *EvenOddColumnSort*, column j is sorted in nondecreasing order so that $\mathbf{P}_{1,j}:L \le \mathbf{P}_{2,j}:L \le \dots \le \mathbf{P}_{q,j}:L$. Figure 15.27 shows the action of *Sort2DMesh* for the same sample list used in Figure 15.26.

Procedure *Sort2DMesh* calls procedures *EvenOddRowSort* and *EvenOddColumn-Sort*; the pseudocode for these procedures is left as exercises.

FIGURE 15.27

Action of
Sort2DMesh for
input list 23, 6, 1,
5, 11, 13, 55, 19,
−3, 12, −5, −7, 9,
55, 28, −2 stored
in the distributed
variable *L* on the
two-dimensional
mesh $M_{4, 4}$.

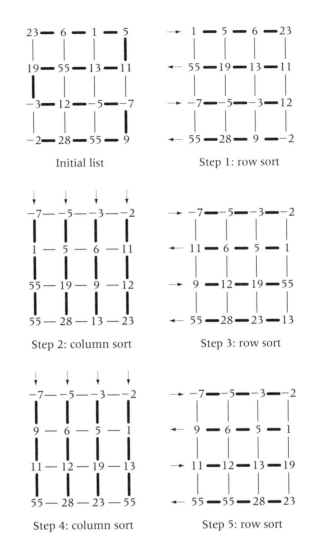

procedure *Sort2DMesh*(*L*, *n*)
Model: two-dimensional mesh $M_{q, q}$ **with** $p = n = q^2$ processors
Input: *L* (a list of size $n = q^2$)   range: $P_{i, j}$, $0 \leq i, j \leq q - 1$
Output: *L* (sorted in nondecreasing snake order)   range: $P_{i, j}$, $0 \leq i, j \leq q - 1$
   for *Step* ← 0 to $\lceil \log_2 n \rceil$ do
      if even(*Step*) then
         EvenOddRowSort(*L*, *n*)
      else
         EvenOddColumnSort(*L*, *n*)
      endif
   endfor
end *Sort2DMesh*

EvenOddRowSort and *EvenOddColumnSort* each perform $q = \sqrt{n}$ parallel comparison steps for an input list of size n; thus, *Sort2DMesh* performs $(\lceil \log_2 n \rceil + 1)$ $\sqrt{n}$ parallel comparison steps. This gives *Sort2DMesh* worst-case complexity $W(n) = (\lceil \log_2 n \rceil + 1) \sqrt{n}$ and cost $C(n) = n(\lceil \log_2 n \rceil + 1)\sqrt{n}$. *Sort2DMesh* has speedup $S(n) = n \log_2 n / [(\lceil \log_2 n \rceil + 1) \sqrt{n}]$, which is approximately $\sqrt{n}$. This speedup is much better than the $\log_2 n$ speedup achieved by *EvenOdd1DMesh*. Furthermore, the cost of *Sort2DMesh* is approximately $n^{3/2}\log_2 n$ versus the n^2 cost of *EvenOdd1DMesh*.

The snake order used in *Sort2DMesh* is not merely an artifact but is a fundamental design feature on which the correctness of the algorithm is based. For example, at first glance, one might conjecture that a sorting algorithm using row-major order would be obtained from *Sort2DMesh* by altering *EvenOddRowSort* to sort each row in increasing order from left to right. However, some lists in $M_{q,q}$ remain *unaltered* by this modified algorithm, even though the lists are not sorted in row-major order (see Exercise 15.14)

15.5 Closing Remarks

The wide variety of parallel architectures available presents the fundamental problem of determining the portability of an algorithm written for a specific architecture. In the case of PRAMs, algorithms designed for CRCW and CREW models with p processors can be simulated on the EREW PRAM with p processors at a cost of a multiplicative complexity factor of log p. For interconnection network models, the portability question is usually handled by establishing efficient ways to embed one interconnection network model into another. An embedding from an interconnection network model A into another model B yields a canonical translation of any algorithm written for A to one suitable for B. Embeddings between interconnection networks is a very active research area today.

A sequential algorithm is entirely impractical unless it has polynomial complexity $O(n^k)$ for some positive integer k. Sequential algorithms are sometimes called time efficient if they have polynomial worst-case complexity. A parallel algorithm on a PRAM is considered to be time efficient if it has *polylogarithmic* $(O((\log n)^k))$ worst-case complexity. A parallel algorithm for solving a given problem, which can be solved by a sequential algorithm in polynomial time (that is, one belonging to the class P), is said to be in the class NC if it has polylogarithmic complexity using a polynomial number of processors. The class NC,

FIGURE 15.28

Order of complexity
of some parallel
sorting algorithms

Algorithm	$p(n)$	$W(n)$	$S(n)$	$C(n)$	$E(n)$
SortCRCW	n^2	1	$n \log n$	n^2	$(\log n)/n$
SortCREW	n^2	$\log n$	n	$n^2 \log n$	$1/n$
EvenOddMergeSortPRAM	n	$(\log n)^2$	$n/\log n$	$n(\log n)^2$	$1/\log n$
InsertionSort1DMesh	n	n	$\log n$	n^2	$(\log n)/n$
EvenOddSort1DMesh	n	n	$\log n$	n^2	$(\log n)/n$
Sort2DMesh	n	$\sqrt{n} \log n$	$\sqrt{n}$	$n^{3/2} \log n$	$1/\sqrt{n}$

an abbreviation for Nick Pippenger's class, is important from a theoretical point of view, although assuming more than a linear number of processors is impractical for large n given the present state of technology. A fundamental unsolved question is whether P = NC (see Chapter 26).

Figure 15.28 summarizes the analysis of some of the parallel algorithms discussed in this chapter. Given is the *order* of the number $p(n)$ of processors required, the worst-case complexity $W(n)$ (the average and best-case complexities are the same as the worst-case complexity for all the algorithms we have discussed so far), the speedup $S(n)$, the cost $C(n)$, and the processor efficiency $E(n)$.

EvenOddMergeSortPRAM is within a logarithmic factor of being cost optimal. The problem of finding a depth $O(\log n)$ sorting network remained unsolved for about 20 years. (Of course, such a sorting network would yield a cost-optimal parallel sorting algorithm on an EREW PRAM using n processors.) Ajtai, Komlós, and Szemerédi discovered such a network, known as the AKS sorting network, which uses the notion of an *expander graph*. Unfortunately, the constants involved in the AKS sorting network are so large that it is only of theoretical interest. In 1986, a more practical parallel sorting algorithm was discovered by Cole for the EREW PRAM with n processors. However, Cole's sorting algorithm does not yield a sorting network.

References and Suggestions for Further Reading

A number of excellent graduate-level textbooks on parallel algorithms have appeared:

Akl, S. G. *The Design and Analysis of Parallel Algorithms.* Englewood Cliffs, NJ: Prentice Hall, 1991.

Cosnard, M, and D. Trystram. *Parallel Algorithms and Architectures.* Boston: PWS, 1991.

JaJa, J. *An Introduction to Parallel Algorithms.* Reading, MA: Addison-Wesley, 1992.

Lakshmivarahan, S., and S. K. Dhall. *Analysis and Design of Parallel Algorithms.* New York: McGraw-Hill, 1990.

Leighton, F. T. *Parallel Algorithms and Architectures.* San Mateo, CA: Morgan Kaufmann, 1992.

Quinn, M. J. Designing Efficient Algorithms for Parallel Computers. 2nd ed. New York: McGraw-Hill, 1994.

Smith, J. R. *The Design and Analysis of Parallel Algorithms.* New York: Oxford University Press, 1993.

Tchueste, M. *Parallel Computation on Regular Arrays.* Manchester, UK: Manchester University Press, 1991.

Wilkinson, B., and M. Allen. *Parallel Programming.* Upper Saddle River, NJ: Prentice Hall, 1999

Akl, S. G. *Parallel Sorting Algorithms.* Orlando, FL: Academic, 1985. An extensive treatment of parallel sorting in general.

Batcher, K. E. "Sorting networks and their applications." In *Proceedings of the AFIPS 1968 Spring Joint Computer Conference,* pp. 307–314. Montvale, NJ: AFIPS Press, 1968, pp. 307–314. Discusses the $\Theta(\log^2 n)$ merging procedures even-odd merge and bitonic merge.

Harris, T. J. "A survey of PRAM simulation techniques," *ACM Computing Surveys* 26 (1994): 187–206. A survey article discussing how parallel algorithms written for the PRAM can be simulated on more realistic machines.

Scherson, I., S. Sen, and A. Shamir. Shear-sort: A true two-dimensional sorting technique for VLSI networks *Proc. of 15th IEEE-ACM ICPP*, pp. 903–908, 1986. The original paper on shearsort.

Additional references to parallel algorithms will be given in later chapters.

EXERCISES

Section 15.2 Architectural Constraints and the Design of Parallel Algorithms

15.1   a. Generalize the concept of row-major order to the three-dimensional mesh $M_{q,q,q}$, and obtain a formula for l, where processor $P_{i,j,k}$ occurs lth in the respective orderings.

   b. Repeat (a) for the k-dimensional mesh $M_{q,q,\ldots,q}$ having q^k processors.

15.2 Argue that the bisection width of K_n is $n^2/4$ (where n is even).

15.3 Verify that PT_p has diameter $2\lfloor \log_2 p \rfloor$ and bisection width 1.

15.4 Consider the three-dimensional mesh $M_{q,q,q}$ with $n = q^3$ processors.

    a. Determine the maximum degree.

    b. Determine the diameter.

    c. Determine the bisection width.

15.5 Consider the altered two-dimensional mesh $\overline{M}_{q,q}$ where diagonal connections are added between processors.

    a. Determine the maximum degree of $\overline{M}_{q,q}$.

    b. Determine the diameter of $\overline{M}_{q,q}$.

    c. Determine the bisection width of $\overline{M}_{q,q}$.

15.6   a. Design a searching algorithm for the three-dimensional mesh $M_{q,q,q}$.

    b. Generalize your algorithm in (a) to the k-dimensional mesh.

15.7   a. Design an algorithm for summing n numbers on the three-dimensional mesh $M_{q,q,q}$, $n = q^3$.

    b. Design an algorithm from computing the dot product of two vectors on the three-dimensional mesh $M_{q,q,q}$, $n = q^3$.

    c. Generalize the algorithms in (a) and (b) to the k-dimensional mesh.

*15.8 Verify that the bisection width of mesh $M_{\sqrt{p}, \sqrt{p}}$ belongs to $O(\sqrt{p})$.

Section 15.3 Performance Measures of Parallel Algorithms

15.9 *SumPRAM* assumes that n is a power of two. When $2^{k-1} < n < 2^k$, we can augment the n numbers with $2^k - n$ zeros and invoke *SumPRAM* with the augmented list of 2^k numbers. This yields the desired sum in $k = \lceil \log_2 n \rceil$ parallel steps. Design a slightly more efficient algorithm that does not use this augmentation.

15.10 The processor tree PT_{n-1}. is ideally suited to execute binary fan-in algorithms, where the n values are initially input in pairs to the leaves, as illustrated below.

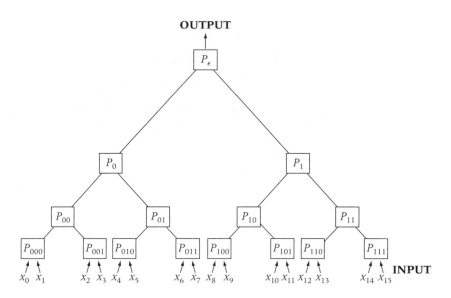

For this exercise, incorporate some simple binary string operations needed to describe interprocessor communication in pseudocode.

a. Give a pseudocode for an algorithm *MinPT* for finding the minimum of n numbers on the processor tree PT_{n-1}.

b. Suppose that you have m sets of n numbers, and you want find the minimum of each set on PT_{n-1}. The naive algorithm would be to simply call the algorithm *MinPT* designed in (a) m times. Analyze the complexity, speedup, and cost of this naive algorithm.

c. A more efficient algorithm for finding the minimums of m sets of n numbers uses pipelining. For example, in the algorithm *MinPT*, after the processors at a given level have computed their minimums and communicated the results up one level, they fall idle and remain so for the rest of the algorithm. However, they could be working on the other sets of numbers instead of remaining idle. Give pseudocode for this pipelined algorithm for finding the minimums of m sets of n numbers.

d. Analyze the complexity, speedup, and cost of your algorithm in (c).

15.11 a. Give the pseudocode for the algorithm *SearchPT* for searching on the processor tree PT_n containing a list in the leaves. *SearchPT* uses the algorithm *MinPT* described in Exercise 15.10 for computing the minimum value stored in the leaves.

b. Analyze the complexity, speedup, and cost of your algorithm in (a).

c. Repeat parts (a) and (b) for a pipelined version of *SearchPT*.

15.12 Suppose that you have m sets of n numbers to sum, and you have a PRAM with $n - 1$ processors (as opposed to the $n/2$ processors used by *SumPRAM*). Design an efficient algorithm using pipelining to compute the m sums. Analyze the complexity, speedup, and cost of your algorithm.

15.13 a. Give pseudocode for an algorithm *MaxIndexPRAM* for finding the index of a maximum element in a list $L[0:n - 1]$ of size n, where $n = 2^k$ for some nonnegative integer k. Analyze its performance.

b. Demonstrate the action of *MaxIndexPRAM* for the input list $L[0:n - 1]$ below, where L is augmented with the appropriate number of ∞'s so that its size is a power of 2.

k	0	1	2	3	4	5	6	7	8	9	10
$L[k]$	18	3	9	2	−11	4	1	−5	20	13	9

15.14 a. Give pseudocode for an algorithm *MaxIndex2DMesh* for finding the index of a maximum element in a list $L[0:n - 1]$ of size $n = m^2$, where the model is the two-dimensional mesh. Assume that L is stored in row-major order in the mesh. Assume also that processor $P_{i,j}$ can recognize its own indices i, j. Analyze the performance of your algorithm.

b. Demonstrate the action of *MaxIndex2DMesh* for the input list $L[0:n - 1]$ below, where L is augmented with the appropriate number of ∞'s so that its size is a perfect square.

k	0	1	2	3	4	5	6
$L[k]$	12	−1	13	−10	2	11	9

15.15 Verify the performance measure formulas given in Figure 15.28.

Section 15.4 Parallel Sorting

15.16 Using broadcasting in the simulation of concurrent reads and binary fan-in in the simulations of concurrent writes, transform *SortCRCW* to an $O(\log n)$ algorithm *SortPRAM* suitable for the EREW PRAM.

15.17 Give pseudocode for *SortCREW*.

15.18 Design and give pseudocode for a nonrecursive version of *MergeSort-PRAM*.

15.19 Consider the version of *MergeSortPRAM* for sorting a list $L[0:n-1], n = 2^k$, where *MergePRAM* is the sequential procedure *Merge*. An alternate technique for analyzing its complexities $B(n)$ and $W(n)$ is to use recurrence relations.

a. Obtain recurrence relations for $B(n)$ and $W(n)$.

b. Using the technique of repeated substitution solve the recurrence relations in part (a).

15.20 Repeat Exercise 15.19 for *OddEvenMergePRAM*.

15.21 Consider the problem of designing a parallel version of *QuickSort* for the PRAM.

a. Analyze the straightforward parallelization *QuickSortPRAM* that simply performs a recursive parallel call to *QuickSortPRAM*.

b. Design and analyze a more efficient version of *QuickSortPRAM* involving parallelizing *Partition*.

15.22 Demonstrate the action of *OddEvenSort1Dmesh* for the following list.

k	0	1	2	3	4	5	6	7	8	9	10
$L[k]$	18	3	9	2	−11	4	1	−5	19	13	9

15.23 Demonstrate the action of *EvenOddSort1Dmesh* for the list given in Exercise 15.22.

15.24 Demonstrate the action of *Sort2DMesh* for the following list (appropriately augmented):

$L[k]$	12	−1	13	−10	2	11	9

15.25 The median of a list of n elements can be computed by first sorting the elements and then finding the middle element if n is odd and the average of the two middle elements if n is even. Describe a function for computing the median on the two-dimensional mesh, where the sort is accomplished by calling *Sort2DMesh*. Have the median returned by processor P_{11}.

15.26 Show that the alteration of *Sort2DMesh* obtained by using row-major ordering instead of snake ordering (that is, by altering *OddEvenRowSort* to sort each row in increasing order from left to right) fails to yield a sorting algorithm. In fact, show that there are lists in $M_{q,q}$ that remain *unaltered* by this modified algorithm, even though the lists are not sorted in row-major order.

15.27 Adapt Batcher's odd-even merge to the two-dimensional mesh.

*15.28 Design and analyze parallel algorithms for the heap operations and *Heap-Sort* on the PRAM.

CHAPTER 16

PARALLEL DESIGN STRATEGIES

One commonly used parallel design strategy is to look for potential parallelism inherent in a sequential algorithm for the problem. For example, sequential design strategies such as divide-and-conquer and dynamic programming are amenable to straightforward parallelization by making parallel calls to solve subproblems. As shown in Chapter 15 with mergesort, this straightforward parallelization may not yield good speedup on its own without applying additional parallel techniques to remainder of the algorithm. Often the additional parallel techniques have no natural sequential analog and require an entirely new approach to achieve good parallelism.

In this chapter, we discuss three widely used tools in parallel algorithm design. The first tool, referred to as *parallel scan* or *parallel prefix,* is an efficient method for computing the prefix computations: $x_0 \oplus x_1 \oplus \cdots \oplus x_i, i = 0, \dots, n - 1$, where $\oplus$ is any associative operation on a set X. Parallel prefix has many important applications, including carry-lookahead addition, polynomial evaluation, various circuit design problems, solving linear recurrences, scheduling problems, and a variety of graph theoretic problems. Prefix computations are so often encountered that they have come to be regarded as primitive operations in parallel and distributed algorithms and have been implemented in the instruction set of some existing parallel machines. The MPI instruction set for distributed computation discussed in Chapter 18 also includes a parallel scan instruction.

The second tool, pointer jumping, is an efficient method of determining the root node of the tree containing a given node in a forest of trees implemented with parent pointers. The pointer-jumping technique has many important applications in the theory of parallel algorithms.

The third tool, efficient parallel algorithms for computing a matrix-vector product or a matrix-matrix product, arises often in scientific computations. In addition to playing a role in scientific computations, matrix algorithms are a useful algorithmic design tool, particularly in the design of graph algorithms. In this chapter, we discuss several algorithms for computing matrix-vector and matrix-matrix products on PRAMs and meshes.

16.1 Parallel Prefix Computations

Suppose we have a set X and a binary operation $\oplus$ defined on X. We assume that $\oplus$ is associative—that is, $(x \oplus y) \oplus z = x \oplus (y \oplus z)$ for all $x, y, z \in X$. Examples of such an operation include addition, multiplication, minimum of two elements, concatenation of strings, and so forth. For convenience, we simply refer to $\oplus$ as addition. We also assume the existence of an element 0 (called the identity element) having the property that $0 \oplus x = x \oplus 0 = x$ for all $x \in X$. Given elements $x_0, x_1, \ldots, x_{n-1}$ in X, let S_{ij} denote the sum $x_i \oplus x_{i+1} \oplus \cdots \oplus x_j$, $i \le j$. The sums $S_{0j} = x_0 \oplus x_1 \oplus \cdots \oplus x_j$, $j = 0, \ldots, n-1$ are called *prefix sums*. Although the problem of computing all the prefix sums might seem inherently sequential, in fact, it is highly parallelizable.

16.1.1 Parallel Prefix on a PRAM

The parallel binary fan-in method of computing $x_0 \oplus x_1 \oplus \cdots \oplus x_{n-1}$ (as used by *MinPRAM* to compute the minimum of $x_0, x_1, \ldots, x_{n-1}$) performs the following *binary fan-in sums*: $x_0 \oplus x_1, x_2 \oplus x_3, \ldots x_{n-2} \oplus x_{n-1}$, are computed in the first parallel step; $x_0 \oplus x_1 \oplus x_2 \oplus x_3, x_4 \oplus x_5 \oplus x_6 \oplus x_7, \ldots, x_{n-4} \oplus x_{n-3} \oplus x_{n-2} \oplus x_{n-1}$, are computed in the second parallel step; and so forth. Thus, the only prefix sums computed along the way are $x_0 \oplus x_1 \oplus \cdots \oplus x_{2^k-1}$, $k = 1, \ldots, \log_2 n$. In what follows, we let $S_{ij} = x_i \oplus x_{i+1} \oplus \cdots \oplus x_j$.

We now show how to compute all the prefix sums on the EREW PRAM using a *recursive doubling* scheme. We assume that the elements $x_0, x_1, \ldots, x_{n-1}$ reside in the array $X[0:n-1]$, where $X[i] = x_i$, $0 \le i \le n-1$. We begin by initializing *Prefix* to X in one parallel step. In the first parallel step after this initialization, P_i reads *Prefix*$[i-1]$ and *Prefix*$[i]$, computes *Prefix*$[i-1] \oplus$ *Prefix*$[i]$, and assigns the result to *Prefix*$[i]$, $1 \le i \le n-1$. (Note that we are not performing concurrent reads because P_i first reads *Prefix*$[i-1]$ and then reads *Prefix*$[i]$, $1 \le i \le n-1$.) Then, in

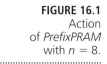

FIGURE 16.1
Action
of *PrefixPRAM*
with *n* = 8.

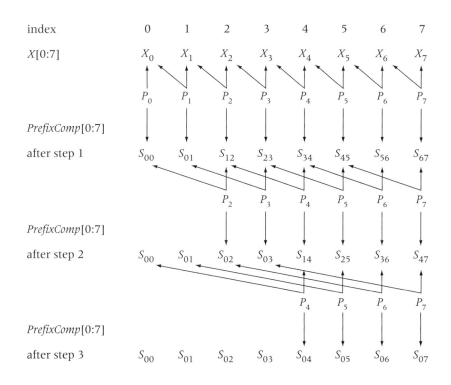

particular, *Prefix*[0] and *Prefix*[1] contain S_{00} and S_{01}, respectively. In the next parallel step, P_i reads *Prefix*[i − 2] and *Prefix*[i], computes *Prefix*[i − 2] $\oplus$ *Prefix*[i], and assigns the result to *Prefix*[i], $2 \le i \le n − 1$. Then *Prefix*[k] contains S_{0k}, k = 0, 1, 2, 3 (so that we have doubled the number of prefix sums computed). In general, for $1 \le j \le \log_2 n − 1$ and $2^{j−1} \le i \le n − 1$ at the jth parallel step, P_i reads *Prefix*[i − $2^{j−1}$] and *Prefix*[i], computes *Prefix*[i − $2^{j−1}$] $\oplus$ *Prefix*[i], and assigns the result to *Prefix*[i]. At the conclusion of the jth step, *Prefix*[k] contains S_{0k}, k = 0, ... , $2^j − 1$, so that all the prefix sums are computed after $\log_2 n$ steps (see Figure 16.1).

The following pseudocode for *PrefixPRAM* is based directly on the preceding discussion, and does not require that *n* be a power of 2.

```
procedure PrefixPRAM(X[0:n − 1], Prefix[0:n − 1])
Model: EREW PRAM with p = n processors
Input:   X[0:n − 1] (an array of elements x₀, x₂, ... , xₙ₋₁)
Output:  Prefix[0:n − 1] (Prefix[i] = x₀ ⊕ ··· ⊕ xᵢ, i = 0, ... , n − 1)
    for 0 ≤ i ≤ n − 1 do in parallel
        Prefix[i] ← X[i]
    end in parallel
    k ← 1
```

```
        while k < n do
            for k ≤ i ≤ n − 1 do in parallel
                Prefix[i] ← Prefix[i − k] ⊕ Prefix[i]
            end in parallel
            k ← k + k
        endwhile
    end PrefixPRAM
```

The proof of the correctness of *PrefixPRAM* is left as an exercise.

16.1.2 Parallel Prefix on the Complete Binary Tree

We now design a parallel algorithm for performing prefix computations on the processor tree PT_p, $p = 2^j − 1$, having p processors. Algorithms designed for PT_p are useful because there are efficient embeddings of PT_p in other standard interconnection networks, such as the hypercube. Hence, the parallel algorithm for performing prefix computations on T_p can be efficiently ported to these other networks.

The algorithm *PrefixPT* begins by assuming that the n operands x_0, x_1, ... , $x_{n−1}$ (n a power of 2) are input to the leaves of the complete binary tree $PT_{2n − 1}$. *PrefixPT* works in four phases. In phase 1, binary fan-in computations are performed starting at the leaves and working up to the processors P_0 and P_1 at level one. Phase 1 takes $(\log_2 n) − 1$ communication steps and $(\log_2 n) − 1$ binary operation steps. Phase 1 is illustrated in Figure 16.2a for eight operands.

During phase 2, for each pair of operands x_i, $x_{i + 1}$ in leaf nodes having the same parent, we replace the operand $x_{i + 1}$ in the right child by $x_i ⊕ x_{i + 1}$, $i = 0$, 2, ... , $n − 2$. Phase 2 takes two communication steps and a single binary operation step. During phase 3, each right child that is not a leaf node replaces its binary fan-in computation with that of its (left child) sibling, and the sibling replaces its binary fan-in computation with the identity element. Thus, phase 3 is done in two communication steps and one assignment step. The action of phases 2 and 3 are illustrated in Figure 16.2c for the addition operator.

In phase 4, binary fan-out computations are performed as follows. Starting with the processors at level one and working our way down level by level to the leaves, a given processor communicates its element to both its children, and then each child adds the parent value to its value.

Notice in Figure 16.2c (on page 510) that summing the numbers in the processors in the path from a node at level one to the $(i + 1)^{st}$ leaf node yields the $(i + 1)^{st}$ prefix sum, $i = 0, 1, ... , n − 1$. Phase 4 consists of $\log_2 n − 1$ steps, where in step i, each processor at level $i + 1$ combines its value with the value from its

FIGURE 16.2
Action of *PrefixPT*
for addition with
input numbers *a, b,*
c, d, e, f, g, h.

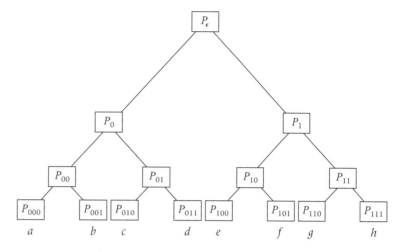

(a) Phase 1: Input the numbers in the leaves of PT_{2n-1}.

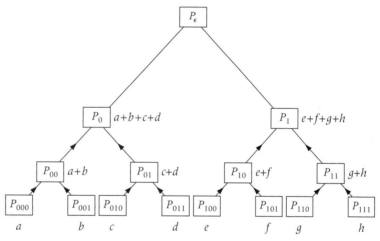

(b) Compute binary fan-in sums.

continued

parent. Because each such step requires two communication steps and one parallel binary operation step, phase 4 takes $2\log_2 n - 2$ communication steps and $\log_2 n - 1$ binary operation steps. At the end of phase 4, all the prefix computations reside in the leaf nodes. In particular, the prefix computation $x_0 \oplus x_2 \oplus \cdots \oplus x_{i-1}$ resides in the local memory of the $(i+1)^{\text{st}}$ leaf processor, $i = 0, 1, \ldots,$ $n - 1$. Phase 4 is illustrated in Figure 16.2d.

The correctness of *PrefixPT* can be verified using induction and is left as an exercise.

FIGURE 16.2

Continued

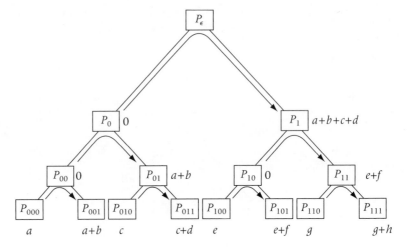

(c) Phase 2: For leaves, add sums in siblings and leave resulting sum in right child sibling. Phase 3: For non-root, non-leaf, left children, transfer binary fan-in sum to sibling then zero out own sum.

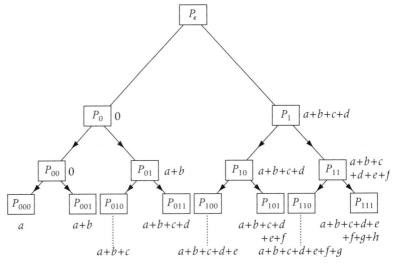

(d) Phase 4: Compute binary fan-out sums. Parallel prefix sums now reside in leaves.

16.1.3 Parallel Prefix on the Two-Dimensional Mesh

We now design *Prefix2DMesh* for performing prefix computations on the two-dimensional mesh $M_{q, q}$, $n = q^2$. We assume that the elements $x_0, x_1, \dots, x_{n-1}$ are stored in row-major order in the distributed variable *Prefix*.

Prefix2DMesh works in three phases. Phase 1 consists of $q - 1$ parallel steps, where in the jth step, column with index j of *Prefix* is added to column with index

$j + 1$. This is accomplished by communicating $\mathbf{P}_{ij}$:*Prefix* to processor $P_{i, j+1}$, and adding the result to $\mathbf{P}_{i, j+1}$:*Prefix*, $j = 0, \dots, q - 2$. Since the elements $x_0, x_2, \dots, x_{n-1}$ are stored in row-major order in the distributed variable *Prefix*, after the completion of phase 1, $\mathbf{P}_{i, j}$:*Prefix* has the value $S_{iq, iq + j}$ (see Figure 16.3a).

Phase 2 consists of $q - 1$ steps, where in the ith step $\mathbf{P}_{i-1, q-1}$:*Prefix* is communicated to processor $P_{i, q-1}$ and is then added to $\mathbf{P}_{i, q-1}$:*Prefix*, $i = 1, \dots, q - 1$ (see Figure 16.3b). Note in particular that at the completion of phase 2, the value of $\mathbf{P}_{i, q-1}$:*Prefix* is the desired prefix sum $S_{0, (i+1)q-1}$, $i = 0, \dots, q - 1$.

In phase 3, we add the value $\mathbf{P}_{i-1, q-1}$:*Prefix*, to $\mathbf{P}_{ij}$:*Prefix*, thereby obtaining the desired prefix sum $S_{0, iq + j}$ in $\mathbf{P}_{ij}$:*Prefix*, $1 \le i \le q - 1, 0 \le j \le q - 2$ (see Figure 16.3c). Phase 3 can be accomplished in $q - 1$ parallel steps.

16.1.4 Knapsack in Parallel

Recall from Chapter 7 that the knapsack problem is solved by first sorting the given n objects $b_0, b_1, \dots, b_{n-1}$ in increasing order of their weight per value ratios. Assuming that the objects do not all fit in at once, the knapsack is filled to

FIGURE 16.3
Tracing the action of the three phases of *Prefix2Mesh* for $n = 16$.

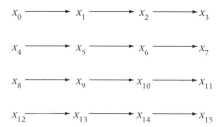

(a) Initial contents of *Prefix* and direction for performing the summing in phase 1.

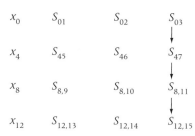

(b) Contents of *Prefix after* phase 1 and direction for performing the summing in phase 2.

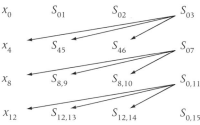

(c) Contents of *Prefix* after phase 2. Arrow from processor $P_{i-1, q-1}$ to P_{ij} indicates that P_{ij}:*Prefix* should be replaced with P_{ij}:*Prefix* $\oplus P_{i-1, q-1}$ *Prefix* in phase 3. This can be accomplished in q parallel steps.

(d) Contents of *Prefix* upon completion.

capacity by placing the first k objects in the knapsack and then a fraction $f = (C - (w_0 + \cdots + w_{k-1}))/w_k$ of the $(k + 1)^{st}$ object, where k is the largest index i such that $w_0 + \cdots + w_{i-1}$ is not greater than the capacity C of the knapsack. The sequential algorithm computes the prefix sums

$$w_0, \ w_0 + w_1, \ \dots, \ w_0 + \cdots + w_{i-1} \ .$$

until the knapsack capacity is exceeded.

The procedure *PrefixSumsPRAM*, which computes the partial weight sums $w_0 + \cdots + w_i$, $i = 0, \dots, n - 1$, yields a straightforward parallelization of the procedure *Knapsack* on the EREW PRAM. *PrefixSumsPRAM* is the version of *PrefixPRAM* in which the binary operation is addition. In the following pseudocode for *KnapsackPRAM*, the $(i + 1)^{st}$ partial sum $w_0 + \cdots + w_i$ is stored in index position i of the array *WeightSums*[0: $n - 1$] by a call to *PrefixSumsPRAM*. The solution array $F[0{:}n - 1]$ can be immediately computed from the array *WeightSums*[0: $n - 1$].

```
procedure KnapsackPRAM(Value[0:n − 1], Weight[0:n − 1], Capacity, F[0:n − 1])
Model:   EREW PRAM with n processors
Input:   Value[0:n − 1] (an array of positive real numbers)
         Weight[0:n − 1] (an array of positive real numbers)
         Capacity (a positive real number)
Output:  F[0:n − 1] (array of nonnegative fractions)
         Sort in parallel the arrays Value[0:n − 1] and Weight[0:n − 1] in decreasing
         order of ratios: Value[0]/Weight[0] ≥ Value[1]/Weight[1] ≥ · · · ≥
         Value[n − 1]/Weight[n − 1]
         PrefixSumsPRAM(Weight[0:n − 1],WeightSums[0: n − 1])
         for 0 ≤ i ≤ n − 1 do in parallel
             if WeightSums[i] ≤ Capacity then
                 F[i] ← 1
             else
                 if i > 0 .and. WeightSums[i − 1] > Capacity then
                     F[i] ← 0
                 else
                     F[i] ← (Capacity − WeightSums[i])/Weight[i]
                 endif
             endif
         end in parallel
end KnapsackPRAM
```

Since *PrefixSumsPRAM* has $\Theta(\log n)$ complexity, clearly *KnapsackPRAM* also has best-case, average, and worst-case $\Theta(\log n)$ complexity. We leave the pseudocode and analysis of the two-dimensional mesh version of *Knapsack* to the exercises.

16.1.5 Carry-Lookahead Addition

The familiar grade school algorithm for adding two numbers adds digits one at a time from right to left (least significant digit to the most significant digit), propagating the appropriate carry from each digit position to its immediate neighbor on the left. For binary integers $x = x_{n-1} \dots x_0$ and $y = y_{n-1} \dots y_0$, their sum $z = z_n \dots z_0$ is given by

$$z_i = (x_i + y_i + c_i) \mod 2, \quad 0 \le i \le n-1, c_0 = 0,$$
$$z_n = c_n, \quad (16.1.1)$$

where c_i is the carry, $i = 1, \dots, n$. Clearly, if all the carries c_i were known, then we could compute z on the EREW PRAM with n processors in just two parallel addition steps. But computing these carries seems like an essentially sequential problem, because c_2 depends on c_1, c_3 depends on c_2, and so forth. The following key fact gives us the surprising basis for an efficient parallel algorithm for adding two binary integers.

> **Key Fact**
>
> Given binary integers $x = x_{n-1} \dots x_0$ and $y = y_{n-1} \dots y_0$, the set of carries c_i, $i = 1, \dots, n$ corresponding to the sum $x + y$ can be computed in $\log_2 n$ steps using a suitable parallel prefix computation.

We now describe the parallel prefix computation referred to in the key fact. The operands in the computation are three possible states of the digit positions in the binary integers x and y. If both x_{i-1} and y_{i-1} are 0, then c_i is 0, and we say that the digit position i is in a *stop carry state*, denoted by s. If both x_{i-1} and y_{i-1} are 1, then c_i is 1, and we say that the digit position i is in a *generate carry state*, denoted by r. If $x_{i-1} \ne y_{i-1}$, then c_i equals the previous carry c_{i-1}, and we say that the digit position i is in a *propagate carry state*, denoted by p.

The carry states σ_{i-1} and σ_i of adjacent digit positions $i-1$ and i, respectively, can be combined using the following binary operation $\oplus$. The definition of $\oplus$ is motivated by Figure 16.4, where the computation of $\sigma_{i-1} \oplus \sigma_i$ is shown for the nine possible values of (σ_{i-1}, σ_i). (Although the ith digit position is to the left of the $(i-1)^{st}$ digit position, when performing the computation $\sigma_{i-1} \oplus \sigma_i$,

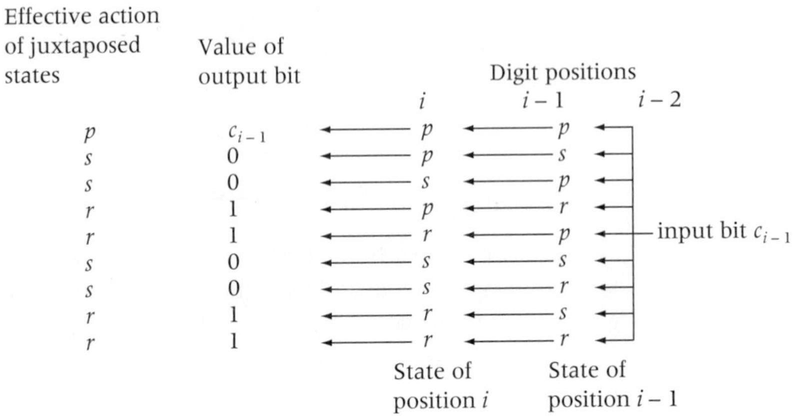

FIGURE 16.4
Ripple effect of carrying digit c_{i-1} through digit positions $i - 1$, i for the nine possible states s, t, p of these two positions.

FIGURE 16.5
Defining the binary operation $\oplus$ on $\{s, r, p\}$.

we have taken the carry state of the $(i - 1)^{st}$ digit position to be on the left.) The ripple effect illustrated in Figure 16.4 suggests defining the binary operation $\oplus$ on $\{s, r, p\}$ given in Figure 16.5.

The following proposition shows that the binary operation $\oplus$ on $\{s, r, p\}$ is amenable to parallel prefix computations.

Proposition 16.1.1 The binary operation $\oplus$ on $\{s, r, p\}$ is associative. □

We leave the proof of Proposition 16.1.1 as an exercise. The following proposition shows how prefix computations can be used to compute all the carries c_i, $1 \le i \le n$.

Proposition 16.1.2 Given n-digit binary integers x and y, let σ_i be the carry status of the ith digit of $x + y$, $0 \le i \le n$, so that $\sigma_0 = s$. Then $S_{0i} = \sigma_0 \oplus \sigma_1 \oplus \cdots \oplus \sigma_i$ is either r or s for each $i = 0, \ldots n$. Further,

$$c_i = \begin{cases} 0, & S_{0i} = s. \\ 1, & \text{otherwise.} \end{cases}$$

□

FIGURE 16.6
Using prefix computations and Proposition 16.1.2 to compute the binary sum of $x = 10101001$ and $y = 01101011$.

i	8	7	6	5	4	3	2	1	0
x_i		1	0	1	0	1	0	0	1
y_i		0	1	1	0	1	0	1	1
σ_i	p	p	r	s	r	s	p	r	s
S_{0i}	r	r	r	s	r	s	r	r	s
c_i	1	1	1	0	1	0	1	1	0
z_i	1	0	0	0	1	0	1	0	0

We leave the proof of Proposition 16.1.2 as an exercise. We illustrate Proposition 16.1.2 in Figure 16.6.

Propositions 16.1.1 and 16.1.2 yield an efficient algorithm for computing the sum of two n-digit binary integers x and y on the EREW PRAM with n processors. In the first parallel step, we compute the carry states σ_i, $1 \leq i \leq n$. We then use *PrefixPRAM* to compute the prefixes $S_{0i} = \sigma_0 \oplus \sigma_1 \oplus \cdots \oplus \sigma_i$, thereby determining all the carries c_i, $1 \leq i \leq n$. Finally, we compute $x + y$ (using 16.1.1) in two parallel addition steps. The complexity of this algorithm for computing $x + y$ on the EREW PRAM with n processors is in $\Theta(\log n)$.

Using *Prefix2DMesh*, we can compute $x + y$ on the two-dimensional mesh with n processors in time $O(\sqrt{n})$.

 ## 16.2 Pointer Jumping

Starting at any node in a linked list of nodes, we can move down the list using a sequential algorithm that uses the pointer at each node to move to the next node. After at most $n - 1$ pointer updates, we will reach the end of the list. On the EREW PRAM, there is a parallel algorithm that can start from any node and reach the end of the list in $\log_2 n$ parallel steps using the important technique of *pointer jumping*. Each node traces a "path" to the end of the list in parallel, but at each step, the path jumps over twice as many nodes as in the previous step (until it reaches the end). The pointer-jumping technique has many important applications in the theory of parallel algorithms.

16.2.1 Finding Roots in a Forest

The technique of pointer jumping generalizes immediately from linked lists to trees (or more generally, forests) maintained using the parent implementation. (Given any node in a forest maintained using parent pointers, a path from the node to the root of the tree containing it is simply a linked list.) To illustrate, we consider a rooted forest F on n nodes, where we denote the nodes by $0, 1, \ldots, n - 1$. We suppose that F is implemented using the parent array implementation *Parent*[0:*n* − 1] (see Chapter 4). To facilitate pointer jumping, we modify the implementation given in Chapter 4 slightly by setting *Parent*[*j*] = *j* when *j* is a root node rather than setting *Parent*[*j*] = −1 (see Figure 16.7).

Given a node *i* in the forest, where *R*[*i*] denotes the root of the tree in *F* containing the node *i*, *i* = 0, 1, ... , *n* − 1, we now consider the problem of designing a parallel algorithm for computing the entire array *R*[0:*n* − 1] on the CREW PRAM. Before presenting the parallel algorithm, we first consider the problem in a sequential setting. For a particular node *i* in *F*, clearly the optimal sequential algorithm for determining *R*[*i*] is to follow the path up the tree from *i* to *R*[*i*], as accomplished by the following pseudocode:

```
Current ← i
while Current ≠ Parent[Current] do
        Current ← Parent[Current]
endwhile
R[i] ← Current
```

If *i* is at level l_i in the tree, then this algorithm requires $l_i + 1$ assignments to *Current*. In particular, when *F* consists of a single tree and the tree is a path with *i* as a leaf, then the algorithm performs W(*n*) = *n* assignments to *Current*.

FIGURE 16.7
Parent array
implementation
of a forest.

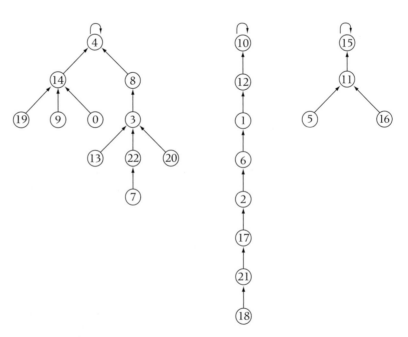

i	0	1	2	3	4	5	6	7	8	9	10	11	12	13	14	15	16	17	18	19	20	21	22
Parent [*i*]	14	12	6	8	4	11	1	22	4	14	10	15	10	3	4	15	11	2	21	14	3	17	3

To compute the entire array $R[0:n - 1]$, the most straightforward sequential algorithm that does the job simply repeats the previous pseudocode for each i between 1 and n. Unfortunately, the worst-case behavior of this algorithm belongs to $\Theta(n^2)$. A better sequential algorithm results from the observation that if j is any node along the path from i to $R[i]$, then $R[j] = R[i]$. Hence, we can stop our journey up the path from i to $R[i]$ whenever we encounter a node such that $R[j]$ has already been determined. Also, after determining $R[i]$, we can retrace the part of the path just traveled and assign $R[k] = R[i]$ for each node encountered. It turns out that the resulting algorithm has linear worst-case complexity. We leave the design and analysis of the improved sequential algorithm based on these observations to the exercises.

The key idea implemented in the design of an efficient parallel algorithm for computing $R[0:n - 1]$ on the CREW PRAM is the notion of *pointer jumping* mentioned earlier. At each step we double the number of levels we jump until we reach the root. The jumping is accomplished by replacing *Parent*[i] with *Parent*[*Parent*[i]] exactly $\log_2 n$ times (since *Parent*[i] = i, once we reach a root node we remain at the root). The following algorithm is illustrated in Figure 16.8.

FIGURE 16.8
Pointer jumping performed by *ForestRootCREW* for a sample path of length 16 from a node to a root of a tree in a forest.

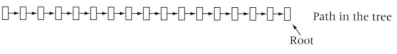

Path in the tree

Root

States of pointers in path after:

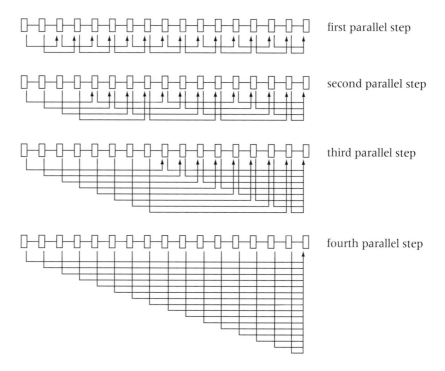

first parallel step

second parallel step

third parallel step

fourth parallel step

```
procedure ForestRootsCREW(Parent[0:n − 1], R[0:n − 1])
Model:    CREW PRAM with p = n processors
Input:    Parent[0:n − 1] (parent array of a forest F)
Output:   R[0:n − 1] (array such that R[i] is root of tree of F containing i, i = 0, 1, . . . ,
          n − 1)
             for 0 ≤ i ≤ n − 1 do in parallel
                 for j ← 1 to log₂n do
                     Parent[i] ← Parent[Parent[i]]
                 endfor
             end in parallel
             R[i] ← Parent[i]
end ForestRootsCREW
```

Clearly, *ForestRootsCREW* has complexity $W(n) \in \Theta(\log n)$, speedup $S(n) \in \Theta(n/\log n)$, and cost $C(n) \in \Theta(n\log n)$.

Procedure *ForestRootsCREW* can be adapted to the EREW PRAM at the expense of a logarithmic multiplicative increase in complexity. However, if all the trees in the forest *F* are paths, then *ForestRootsCREW* can be applied to the EREW PRAM without any slowdown. In the next subsection, we use *ForestRootsCREW* to find a polylogarithmic parallel algorithm for the minimum spanning problem.

16.2.2 Minimum Spanning Tree in Parallel

Kruskal's greedy algorithm for finding a minimum spanning tree is based on choosing the edge with smallest weight from the remaining edges and adding that edge to the forest unless a cycle is created. We now design a parallel greedy algorithm *MSTCREW* suitable for implementation on the CREW PRAM with $n^2/2$ processors having polylogarithmic complexity. For convenience, we take the vertex set *V* of the graph *G* to be the integers $0, 1, \ldots, n − 1$. Without loss of generality, we can assume that all edge weights are distinct Indeed, if the edge weights are not distinct, then we could replace the weight of each edge $e = \{i, j\}$ with a new weight consisting of the triple $(w(e), i, j)$ where $w(e)$ is the weight of edge *e*, and where the ordering of the triples is lexicographical. In this new weighting, the weights are distinct and the minimum spanning tree for the new weighting is also a minimum spanning tree for the original weighting (see Exercise 16.17). With distinct edge weights, the minimum spanning tree is unique. The first stage of *MSTCREW* involves choosing in parallel the smallest-weight edge at each vertex. Subsequent stages involve choosing in parallel the edge of smallest weight at each supervertex, where each supervertex has been identified by a leader and vertices in each supervertex find their leader using pointer jumping. The key idea behind *MSTCREW* is the following proposition, whose proof is left as an exercise.

Proposition 16.2.1 Consider a graph $G = (V, E)$ with distinct edge weights, and let U be any subset of V. The minimum-weight edge with one vertex in U and the other in $V \setminus U$ is in the minimum spanning tree.

For $v \in V$, we let $\mu(v)$ denote the edge of minimum weight incident with vertex v. Setting $U = \{v\}$ in Proposition 16.2.1, we obtain the following corollary.

Corollary 16.2.2 Consider a graph $G = (V, E)$ with distinct edge weights. For each vertex v, the edge $\mu(v)$ of minimum weight incident with vertex v is in the minimum spanning tree.

For convenience, we set $\mu(V) = \{\mu(i) | i \in V\}$. We assume that G is implemented using its *weighted* adjacency matrix $A = (a_{ij})$; that is, $a_{ij} = w(\{i, j\})$ if $\{i, j\} \in E$, and $a_{ij} = \infty$ otherwise. We can greedily choose edge $\mu(i)$ at each vertex $i \in V$ in approximately $\log_2 n$ parallel steps by allocating $n/2$ processors to vertex i and using the binary fan-in technique. Note that if $\{a, b\}$ is the minimum-weight edge in the graph G, then $\{a, b\} \in \mu(V)$ and $\mu(a) = \mu(b)$.

First suppose that for the remaining $n - 2$ vertices, no two vertices have the same minimum-weight incident edge, so that $\mu(V)$ contains $n - 1$ edges. Since the minimum spanning tree T has $n - 1$ edges and by Corollary 16.2.2 the $n - 1$ edges of $\mu(V)$ all belong to T, it follows that $\mu(V)$ is precisely the edge set of T.

Now suppose that $\mu(V)$ contains fewer than $n - 1$ edges. Then, $\mu(V)$ determines a spanning forest F_1 (the subscript on the forests generated by the algorithm indicate the iteration during which they are created), where each tree in F_1 contains a unique edge $\{i, j\}$ such that $\mu(i) = \mu(j)$. To see this, for each $i \in V$, mark edge $\mu(i)$ with an arrow having tail i (see Figure 16.9). Then the oriented edges determine a forest F_1, where each tree in F_1 contains exactly one doubly oriented edge.

We now define an equivalence relation on the set of vertices V, where two vertices are equivalent if they belong to the same tree in F_1. We call the equivalence classes *supervertices*. We let S_1 denote the set of all supervertices. Since each tree in F_1 contains at least one edge, F_1 contains at most $n/2$ trees. Thus, S_1 has at most half as many supervertices as G has vertices. For $s \in S_1$, $\mu(s)$ denotes the minimum-weight edge having exactly one vertex in s, and $\mu(S_1)$ denotes the set $\{\mu(s) | s \in S_1\}$. By Proposition 12.7.1, the edges in $\mu(S_1)$ belong to the minimum spanning tree. The mapping μ determines a forest F_2 among the supervertices (see Figure 16.10).

FIGURE 16.9
A sample weighted
graph and the
forest F_1
determined by the
mapping μ. Edges
marked with arrows
must belong to
the minimum
spanning tree.

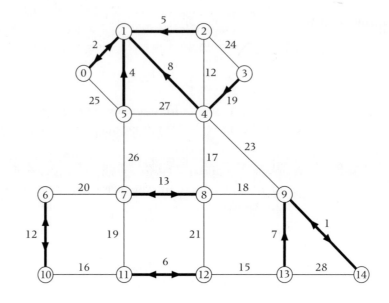

FIGURE 16.10
Forest F_2 among
supervertices $s \in S_1$
determined by the
mapping μ. Edges
that must be in the
minimum spanning
tree are marked in
bold, and edges in
$\mu(S_1)$ are marked
with arrows.

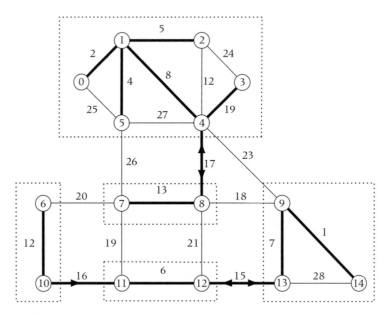

If $\mu(V) \cup \mu(S_1)$ contains $n - 1$ edges, then it must be the edge set of the minimum spanning tree. Otherwise, consider the equivalence relation on the set of vertices V such that two vertices are equivalent if they belong to supervertices that belong to the same tree in F_2, and let S_2 denote the set of all equivalence classes. Then the equivalence classes of S_2 constitute a new set of supervertices and a new set of edges $\mu(S_2)$ that belong to the minimum spanning tree (see Figure 16.11).

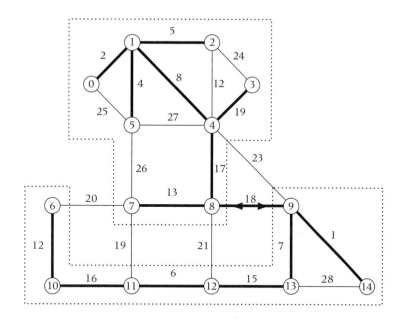

FIGURE 16.11
Forest (tree) F_3 is now two supervertices and an edge joining vertices 8 and 9. The algorithm has now generated the indicated minimum spanning tree.

If the forest F_3 determined by S_2 and μ is not a tree, the process is repeated. We thereby generate larger and larger supervertices, until after at most $\log_2 n$ steps we obtain a supervertex consisting of the entire vertex set V. We let $S_0, S_1, S_2, \ldots, S_k$ denote the sets of supervertices generated, where $S_0 = V$ and $S_k = \{V\}$. Since S_i has at most half as many supervertices as S_{i-1}, $i = 1, \ldots, k$, it follows that $k \le \log_2 n$. Further, by Proposition 16.2.1, $\mu(S_0) \cup \ldots \cup \mu(S_{k-1})$ are the edges of the minimum spanning tree. The high-level pseudocode for the algorithm *MSTPRAM* follows.

```
procedure MSTCREW(G, w, MSTree)
Model:   CREW PRAM with n²/2 processors
Input:   G (a connected graph with vertex set V = {0, ..., n − 1} and edge set E)
              w (a weighting of E using distinct weights)
Output:  MSTree (edges of a minimum spanning tree)
              MSTree ← Ø              //initialize MSTree to be empty
              S ← V                   //initialize S to be the set of n vertices of G
              while |S| > 1 do
                  for all s ∈ S do in parallel
                      Compute μ(s)
                  end in parallel
                  Compute forest F determined by μ(S) = {μ(s)|s ∈ S}
                  MSTree ← MSTree ∪ μ(S)
                  Compute the new set S of supervertices determined by F
              endwhile
end MSTCREW
```

To examine one key implementation detail of *MSTCREW*, consider the computation of $\mu(S)$ during iteration i of the **while loop**. As described earlier, during the first iteration $\mu(S)$ (where $S = V$) can be computed by concurrently using binary fan-in at each vertex. During the ith iteration, $i > 2$, $\mu(S)$ can be computed in approximately $2\log_2 n$ steps by two successive applications of the binary fan-in technique.

Another key implementation detail involves the method of maintaining the supervertices and can be solved as follows. Each supervertex s can be identified by a particular vertex $L(s)$, called the *leader*, that serves as a representative of s. At a given stage of the algorithm, the *leader* of a vertex v, denoted by $L(v)$, is the leader of the current supervertex containing v. Initially, $L(v) = v$ for every vertex $v \in V$. During each iteration of the **while** loop in *MSTCREW*, the leaders are updated as follows. Let S_{i-1} denote the set of supervertices at the beginning of the ith iteration, $i = 0, \dots, k - 1$, where k denotes the total number of iterations. Consider any supervertex s from S_i. An argument similar to one given earlier shows that the tree of forest F corresponding to s contains a unique ordered pair of supervertices (a, b), $a, b \in S_{i-1}$, such that $\mu(a) = \mu(b)$ and $L(a) < L(b)$. We define the leader $L(s)$ of s to be the leader $L(a)$ of a. Thus, for each vertex $v \in V$, the leader $L(v)$ of v is updated to equal $L(s)$, where s is the supervertex from S_i containing v. The leader $L(v)$ of each vertex can be updated in approximately $\log_2 n$ steps using pointer jumping.

We have shown that each iteration of the **while** loop in *MSTCREW* can be done in $O(\log n)$ parallel steps. Since the **while** loop performs at most $\log_2 n$ iterations, it follows that *MSTCREW* has complexity $W(n) \in O(\log^2 n)$ and cost $C(n) \in O(n^2 \log^2 n)$. Further, *MSTCREW* has speedup $S(n) \in \Omega(n^2/\log^2 n)$ over *Prim2*.

16.3 Matrix Operations in Parallel

In this section, we discuss a straightforward $O(\log n)$ parallel algorithm for computing the product of two matrices on the CREW PRAM. Using the binary powers method discussed in Chapters 1 and 2, we obtain an $O((\log n)^2)$ parallel algorithm for computing the powers of a matrix. The latter operation can be used to obtain NC algorithms (polylogarithmic computing time using a polynomial number of processors) for many important problems, where obtaining such algorithms without this tool could be rather difficult. For example, we show how to obtain an NC algorithm for computing shortest paths in weighted digraphs using matrix powers.

16.3.1 Matrix Multiplication on the CREW PRAM

Given a $p \times q$ matrix $A = (a_{ij})$ and a $q \times r$ matrix $B = (b_{ij})$, recall that the product AB is defined to be the $p \times r$ matrix $C = (c_{ij})$, where

$$c_{ij} = \sum_{k=0}^{q-1} a_{ik}b_{kj}, \quad 0 \le i \le p-1, 0 \le j \le r-1 \qquad \textbf{(16.3.1)}$$

An important special case of matrix multiplication is matrix-vector multiplication, which occurs when B is a column vector ($r = 1$).

The sequential algorithm based directly on Formula (16.3.1) performs pqr multiplications. We now describe the parallel algorithm *MatMultCREW*, which is the straightforward parallelization of this sequential algorithm to the CREW PRAM. We simply assign q processors the job of computing a given c_{ij}. The processors assigned to c_{ij} compute the q products $a_{ik}b_{kj}$ in a single parallel step, and then they perform the sum of these q products using the binary fan-in technique. Because this algorithm performs a *single* parallel multiplication, we choose addition as the basic operation when analyzing its performance. Therefore, in the case of square matrices ($p = q = r = n$), we see that the algorithm has $\Theta(\log n)$ complexity and uses n^3 processors; thus, it belongs to the class NC.

Adapting the procedure *MatMultCREW* to implementations on the EREW PRAM and to mesh interconnection networks is explored in the exercises.

Scientific computations often involve computing the powers of an $n \times n$ matrix A. We can compute the kth power A^k by applying the binary method discussed in Chapter 1, where the operation is matrix multiplication and we use *MatMultCREW* to compute the matrix multiplications. Then the total number of parallel multiplications and additions performed is $O(\log k)$ and $O((\log n)(\log k))$, respectively.

16.3.2 All-Pairs Shortest Paths in Parallel

We now show how matrix powers can be used to solve the all-pairs shortest paths problem for weighted digraphs.

Consider a digraph D with set $V = \{0, \dots n-1\}$ and edge set E. Using n^2 processors on the EREW PRAM, we can compute each iteration of Floyd's algorithm (see Chapter 12) in constant time. The resulting parallelization of Floyd's algorithm has complexity n and cost n^3. Although we obtain a parallel algorithm that is cost optimal (compared with Floyd's algorithm), our goal is to obtain a polylogarithmic parallel algorithm using a polynomial number of processors. We can achieve this goal by using a different recurrence relation that is more amenable to parallelization.

Given a weight function w for the edges, we let $A = (a_{ij})_{n \times n}$ be the matrix such that $a_{ij} = w(ij)$ if there is an edge from i to j, 0 if $i = j$, and ∞ otherwise. We define the matrix $A^{[q]} = (a_{ij}^{[q]})$ such that $A^{[q]}(i, j)$ is the length of a shortest path with respect to w, from vertex i to vertex j, and contains at most q edges, or ∞ if there is no such path, $i, j = 0, \dots, n - 1, q = 1, \dots, n - 1$. Note that $A^{[1]} = A$. Using the Principle of Optimality it follows that

$$a_{ij}^{[q]} = \min_{0 \leq k \leq n-1} (a_{ik}^{[q-1]} + a_{kj}^{[1]}), \quad \textbf{init.cond. } A^{[1]} = A. \qquad \textbf{(16.3.2)}$$

Since a shortest path is necessarily a simple path and the number of edges of any simple path in D is at most $n - 1$, it follows that the length d_{ij} of a shortest path in D from i to j (with respect to w) is the ij^{th} coefficient $a_{ij}^{[n-1]}$ of the matrix $A^{[n-1]}$.

Now we consider the problem of computing the qth power $A^q = (a_{ij}^{(q)})_{n \times n}$ of a matrix A. From the definition of matrix multiplication, we know that

$$a_{ij}^{(q)} = \sum_{0 \leq k \leq n-1} (a_{ik}^{(q-1)} * a_{kj}^{(1)}), \quad \textbf{init.cond. } A^1 = A. \qquad \textbf{(16.3.3)}$$

Note that recurrence relation (16.3.2) is identical to (16.3.3) except that the operation of addition is replaced with the operation min, and the operation of multiplication is replaced with the operation of addition. It follows that we can compute $A^{[q]}$ using an algorithm, such as *MatMultCREW* discussed earlier, for computing the qth power A^q of matrix A, with the operation of addition replaced with min and the operation of multiplication replaced with addition. Recall that the nth power of a matrix can be computed in time $O(\log^2 n)$ using n^3 processors on the CREW PRAM. Pseudocode for procedure *AllPairsShortestPathsCREW* based on the algorithm just described is left as an exercise.

16.4 Closing Remarks

In Chapter 20, we will adapt the procedure *MSTCREW* for the CREW PRAM to the distributed network setting. While *MatMultCREW* is an NC algorithm for computing the product AB of two $n \times n$ matrices, the cost of using n^3 processors is certainly prohibitive in practice. For large n, a less costly approach (in fact, cost optimal compared with ordinary matrix multiplication, which uses n^3 multiplications) would be to use n processors, where the $(j + 1)^{\text{st}}$ processor sequentially computes the product AB_j, for B_j equal to the $(j + 1)^{\text{st}}$ column vector of $B, j = 0, \dots, n - 1$. We will discuss the latter method in Chapter 18 in the context of distributed algorithms.

References and Suggestions for Further Reading

A book entirely devoted to applications of prefix computations in parallel computing:

Lakshmivarahan, S., and S. K. Dhall. *Parallel Computing Using the Prefix Problem.* New York: Oxford University Press, 1994.

Two books covering topics discussed in this chapter as well as material on network embeddings:

Leighton, F. T. *Parallel Algorithms and Architectures.* San Mateo, CA: Morgan Kaufmann, 1992.

Quinn, M. J. *Parallel Computing: Theory and Practice.* New York: McGraw-Hill, 1994.

Section 16.1 Parallel Prefix Computations

16.1 Prove the correctness of the algorithm *PrefixPRAM* on the EREW PRAM that performs the n prefix computations $x_0 \oplus x_1 \oplus \cdots \oplus x_i$, $i = 0, 1, \ldots, n - 1$. Analyze the complexity, speedup, and cost of your algorithm.

16.2 Give pseudocode for parallel prefix computations on the processor tree PT_n.

16.3 Give an inductive proof of the correctness of *PrefixPT*.

16.4 Prove Proposition 16.1.1.

16.5 Prove Proposition 16.1.2.

16.6 Design and analyze an algorithm for parallel prefix computations on a general binary tree (where the operands are input to leaves).

16.7 Design and analyze an algorithm for parallel prefix computations on the complete ternary tree.

16.8 Consider the problem of computing the prefix sums of sets of numbers. For example, for the sets $\{1, 45, 3\}, \{2, 5\}, \{1, 8, 90, 6\}, \{10, 20, 30\}$, the prefix sums are

$$1, 46, 48; 2, 7; 1, 9, 99, 105; 10, 30, 60.$$

We refer to these prefix sums as *segmented* prefix sums. Clearly, these segmented prefix sums can be computed by four separate calls to parallel prefix. However, it is interesting that they can be computed by a single call to parallel prefix. More generally, for any binary associative operation $\oplus$, we can compute *segmented (parallel) prefix* as a special case of parallel prefix. This is accomplished by introducing the symbol | and extending the set S of operands to the set $\overline{S}$ consisting of all operands of the form x and $|x$, where $x \in S$. We extend the binary operation $\oplus$ to the binary operation $\overline{\oplus}$ on the augmented set of symbols $\overline{S}$ shown in the figure below:

$\overline{\overline{\oplus}}$	y	$|y$
x	$x \oplus y$	x
$|x$	$|(x \oplus y)$	$|x$

a. Verify that the binary operation $\overline{\oplus}$ given by the preceding table is associative.

b. Show that performing the parallel prefix for the operation $\overline{\oplus}$, where $\oplus = +$, on the list

$$1, 45, 3, |\ 2, 5, |\ 1, 8, 90, 6, |\ 10, 20, 30$$

yields the segmented prefix sums.

c. Design an algorithm for computing segmented prefix using parallel prefix.

16.9 Design and analyze a parallel pancake-flipping sorting algorithm (see Exercise 5.23 of Chapter 5

16.10 Suppose the elements in an array $A[0:n-1]$ have two colors, red and blue. The *packing problem* is to rearrange the elements of the array so that all the red elements precede all the blue elements, while preserving the order of the elements in each color class.

a. Show how parallel prefix can be used to solve the packing problem.

b. Using part (a), design and analyze a parallelization of *RadixSort* for lists of binary elements.

c. Solve the packing problem for k colors, and use the result to design a parallelization of *RadixSort* for a general base k. Analyze your algorithm.

16.11 Design and analyze a parallelization of the version of *RadixSort* described in Exercise 5.17 of Chapter 5, which is based on proceeding from the most significant digit first. (*Hint:* Use the solution to the packing problem discussed in the previous exercise.)

Section 16.2 Pointer Jumping

16.12 Given a parent array representing a forest, give a linear worst-case sequential algorithm that determines an array $R[0:n-1]$, where $R[i]$ is the root of the tree containing element i, $i = 0, \ldots, n-1$.

16.13 Write an algorithm for the EREW PRAM to find the maximum element in a linked list.

16.14 Suppose we have a linked list implemented using two arrays $L[0:n-1]$ and $Next[0:n-1]$, where the variable $Start$ points to the index in $Next$ corresponding to the beginning of the linked list (assume that the end of the linked list is signaled by $Next[i] = -1$). The problem of computing the distance from each element in the list to the end of the list is called the *list-ranking problem*.

a. Design and analyze an $O(n)$ sequential algorithm for list ranking.

b. Using pointer jumping, design and analyze an $O(\log n)$ algorithm for list ranking on the EREW PRAM with n processors.

16.15 Design a list-ranking algorithm (see Exercise 16.14) that does not assume a variable $Start$ pointing to the beginning of the linked list is available.

16.16 Suppose we are maintaining a linked list using two arrays. Design an algorithm on the EREW PRAM that performs prefix computations on the linked list so that the ith prefix computation resides in the ith node of the linked list.

16.17 Let $G = (V, E)$ be a graph with vertex set $V = \{0, \ldots, n-1\}$ where each edge e has been assigned the weight $w(e)$, but where the edge weights with respect to w are not distinct. Consider the weighting obtained by replacing the weight of each edge $e = \{i, j\}$ with a new weight consisting of the triple $(w(e), i, j)$ where $w(e)$ is the weight of edge e, and where the ordering of the triples is lexicographical. Show that the edge weights are distinct with respect to this new weighting and that a minimum spanning tree for the new weighting is also a minimum spanning tree for the original weighting.

16.18 Trace the action of *MSTCREW* for the following weighted graph:

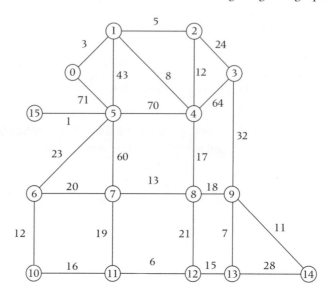

16.19 Adapt procedure *MSTCREW* to the EREW PRAM.

16.20 Design an algorithm on the CREW PRAM with $n^2/2$ processors to compute the components of a graph in time $O(\log^2 n)$. (*Hint:* Choose an appropriate edge weighting so that all weights are distinct, and then use a modification of *MSTCREW.*)

16.21 Design and analyze an $O(\log n)$ algorithm on the CREW PRAM with n processors for determining the depth of each node in a binary tree with n nodes.

*16.22 Repeat Exercise 16.20 for the EREW PRAM.

*16.23 Given a pair of real numbers a and b, the closed interval $[a, b]$ consists of all the real numbers that lie between a and b, inclusive; that is,

$$[a, b] = \{x \in \mathbb{R} \mid a \le x \le b\}.$$

Now, suppose you are given a set of n closed intervals $I_1 = [a_1, b_1], \dots,$ $I_n = [a_n, b_n]$. I_i and I_j have *strict intersection* if I_i and I_j have nonempty intersection but neither interval is contained in the other. Describe a polylogarithmic parallel algorithm on the CREW PRAM with n processors to determine whether any pair of intervals in the set $I_1, \dots, I_n$ have strict intersection. (*Hint:* Use sorting and pointer jumping.)

Section 16.3 Matrix Operations in Parallel

16.23 *MatVecProdCREW* used the CREW model of a PRAM as opposed to the EREW model. Design and analyze a version for the EREW PRAM.

16.24 Modify *MatMultCREW* so that it is suitable for the EREW PRAM.

16.25 Assuming that the ij^{th} entries of the $n \times n$ matrices A, B, C are stored in processor P_{ij}'s local memory on the two-dimensional mesh, various difficulties arise in managing the computation of $C = AB$.

a. Discuss these difficulties.

b. Design an algorithm for computing C on the *wraparound* two-dimensional mesh obtained from the ordinary mesh $M_{q, q}$ by joining processors $P_{i, 0}$ and $P_{i, q - 1}$ and processors $P_{0, i}$ and $P_{q - 1, i}$, $i = 0, \dots, q - 1$.

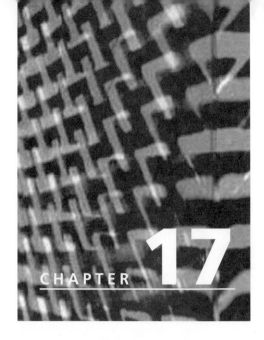

CHAPTER 17

INTERNET ALGORITHMS

The advent of the Internet and the World Wide Web has opened up a vast new frontier of information that is readily available to anyone with a computer and an Internet connection. However, for the Internet to revolutionize the way in which information is gathered and disseminated, it is essential that relevant information be made easily accessible. Search engines have played a central role in facilitating the Internet revolution by allowing users to efficiently locate relevant information on the Web for a given query (a set of relevant keywords). The speed at which commercial search engines (AltaVista, Google, Lycos, and Yahoo, among others) present a list of Web pages relevant to a given query is indeed impressive. In this chapter, we discuss search engines and algorithms for Web page ranking. Another fundamental Internet problem is the efficient delivery of content. In this chapter, we discuss the solution to this problem using Web caching and consistent hashing. We also discuss hashing in general, which is an important data structure used in many Web algorithms. Security is becoming increasingly important in sharing documents and message passing on the Web. We discuss a commonly used algorithm for encrypting messages called the RSA cryptosystem.

17.1 Search Engines

A search engine builds a database of Web documents, which it uses to answer queries. This database is created by using a *spider* (also called a *Web crawler* or *software robot*), which traverses and surveys the Web for information. In addition, some search engines use listings sent in by authors to build their databases. The spider starts with a set of initial *Web addresses* or *URLs* (*Uniform Resource Locators*) and uses the hyperlinks of these Web pages to access more Web pages. The hyperlinks of the newly accessed Web pages are in turn used to access more Web pages. This process continues until a desired amount of the Web has been accessed.

Because the database created by the search engine is huge, the information needs to be indexed for efficient retrieval. An index that is used to find relevant Web pages (URLs), given a term (word) or set of terms from a *lexicon* (vocabulary) of terms, is called a *reverse* or *inverted index*. An index that is used to find a term in a Web document is called a *forward index*. When you enter a query in the search engine Web site, the search engine uses the reverse index to retrieve URLs that contain the terms associated with the query. There are several methods for building an index. One of the most effective ways is to build a *hash table*, as discussed in Section 17.3.

In practice, many commonly used terms (keywords) have a vast number of Web pages associated with them. For example there are millions of Web pages that contain the keyword *algorithm*. Thus, a search engine must not only find Web pages for the query but also use relevancy algorithms to associate a *ranking* or *relevancy value* with the Web pages and list the top-ranked Web pages first. In the next section, we discuss two algorithms for ranking Web pages that are based on the hyperlink structure of the Web. These algorithms exploit the fact that human intelligence is involved in the creation of Web pages; therefore, the hyperlink structure can reveal a great deal of useful information about the relevancy of Web documents.

17.2 Ranking Web Pages

The first ranking algorithm we discuss, called *PageRank*, was developed in 1996 at Stanford by Larry Page and Sergey Brin, the cofounders of Google. PageRank assigns a measure of "prestige" or ranking to each Web page, independent of any query. It is defined using a digraph based on the hyperlink structure of the Web called the *Web digraph*. More formally, the Web digraph W is the digraph whose vertex set $V(W)$ consists of all Web pages (or in practice, a large collection of Web pages), and whose edge set $E(W)$ corresponds to the hyperlinks; that is, an edge is included from page p to page q whenever there is a hyperlink reference (href) in page p to page q.

The second algorithm, called *HITS* (Hyperlink Induced Topic Search), was developed by Jon Kleinberg at IBM in the same year. Unlike PageRank, HITS generates a ranking that is based on a particular query given by the user. Based on the query, HITS generates a subdigraph of the Web digraph called a *focused subdigraph*, which it uses to generate two weightings of the pages: an *authority weighting* and a *hub weighting*. These weightings are computed by using the mutual reinforcement relationship between authorities and hubs: A page has a high authority value, and can be identified as an *authoritative page*, if there are many pages with high hub values that link to that page. On the other hand, a page has high hub value, and can be identified as a *hub page*, if it includes many hyperlinks to authoritative pages.

17.2.1 PageRank

PageRank is an objective measure of people's subjective idea of the importance of the hyperlinks. The definition of PageRank has two distinct underlying motivations. The first motivation comes from the ranking academic citation literature, which existed long before the advent of the Web. The number of citations to a given publication gives some indication of the publication's importance and quality. The second motivation comes from performing a random walk on the Web digraph.

The number of Web pages q that include a hyperlink to p almost always gives a meaningful measure of the significance of Web page p. Thus, one possible ranking of the Web page p would be to compute the number of Web pages that belong to the in-neighborhood $N_{in}(p)$ of p in the Web digraph W—that is, the in-degree of p. However, intuitively, it makes sense to give more weight to Web pages q in $N_{in}(p)$ that have a high rank, so we define the rank of p to be the sum of the ranks of all q in the in-neighborhood of p. One drawback with this ranking is that it would allow pages q containing many hyperlinks to have too much influence on the ranking. Therefore, in defining the page rank, we divide by the number of hyperlinks that q contains, or equivalently by the out-degree $d_{out}(q)$ of q. This yields the following formula for assigning a rank $R[p]$ to a page p:

$$R[p] = \sum_{q \in N_{in}(p)} \frac{R[q]}{d_{out}(q)}. \tag{17.2.1}$$

The actual formula for PageRank given by Page and Brin incorporates a damping factor into the ranking function R. To simplify the discussion, we ignore the damping factor for now.

Formula (17.2.1) can be expressed using matrix notation as follows. Let B denote the matrix whose rows and columns are indexed by $V(W)$ such that

$$B[p, q] = \begin{cases} 1/d_{out}(p), pq \in E(W), \\ 0, \text{ otherwise.} \end{cases} \tag{17.2.2}$$

For convenience, we use R to also denote the column vector whose entry corresponding to p is $R[p]$. Then Formula (17.2.1) becomes

$$R = B^T R, \tag{17.2.3}$$

where B^T denotes the transpose of the matrix B. Thus, vector R is a so-called *stationary point* with respect to the linear transformation given by the matrix B^T.

Points in a vector space that remain stationary up to a scalar multiple with respect to a linear transformation are known as *eigenvectors*. The scalar multiple is called the *eigenvalue*. More precisely, an eigenvalue of a square matrix M over the real numbers is a real number λ such that $MX = \lambda X$ for some nonzero column vector X, called an eigenvector (see Appendix D). Thus, it follows from Formula (17.2.3) that R is an eigenvector for eigenvalue $\lambda = 1$. Further, it can be shown that 1 is the largest eigenvalue of B^T, called the *principal eigenvector* of B^T. There are numerical algorithms, beyond the scope of this book, for computing the principal eigenvector of a matrix. However, since the matrix B is so enormous, its size being the number of pages in the entire World Wide Web (or, in practice, a large portion of the Web), implementing such an algorithm on the matrix B would require a tremendous amount of computation.

We now describe a more practical algorithm that obtains a good approximation to R. This algorithm uses iteration and, starting with an initial vector R_0, successively generates vectors $R_0, R_1, \dots, R_i, \dots$. The initial vector R_0, can be taken to be any vector whose entries are positive and sum to 1. We then inductively compute R_i from R_{i-1} using the formula

$$R_i = B^T R_{i-1}, i = 1, 2, \dots . \tag{17.2.4}$$

Letting $R_i[p]$ denote the ranking function associated with R_i (that is, $R_i[p]$ is the value of the component of R_i corresponding to page p), the matrix equation (17.2.4) is equivalent to

$$R_i[p] = \sum_{q \in N_{in}(p)} \frac{R_{i-1}[q]}{d_{out}(q)}, i = 1, 2, \dots . \tag{17.2.5}$$

Using Formula (17.2.4) and iterating i times we obtain the formula

$$R_i = (B^T)^i R_0. \qquad\qquad (17.2.6)$$

The vector R_i will not necessarily converge to the principal eigenvector R unless the digraph W satisfies certain conditions. For example, it would need to be strongly-connected; otherwise, for some choices of R_0, $R_i[p]$ would equal 0 for all i, whereas for other choices, it would be nonzero for all i. In particular, suppose $R_0[p] = 1$ if $p = q$, and $R_0[p] = 0$ otherwise. Then if there is no path from q to p, we have $R_i[p] = 0$ for all i, whereas if there is a path, then $R_i[p]$ is nonzero for some i (exercise). However, it is not sufficient that W is strongly connected. We must assume the stronger condition that W is also *aperiodic*; that is, for each node p, there is a closed walk of length (number of edges) i containing p for all but a finite number of integers i, where a *walk* is defined similarly to a path, but where we allow both vertices and edges to be repeated. We state the following key fact whose proof is beyond the scope of this book.

Key Fact

> If the digraph *W* is strongly connected and aperiodic, then R_i will converge to the principal eigenvector *R* of B^T as *i* goes to infinity. Further, this convergence is independent of the choice of the initial vector R_0 whose entries are positive and sum to 1. Because we wish to find the ordering of pages determined by *R* rather than its actual value, it is enough to iterate sufficiently often (approximately 50 iterations usually is enough, even for millions of pages).

The PageRank $R[p]$ has an interesting interpretation in terms of random walks. Note that the sum of the entries in row p of B equals 1. Thus, B can be thought of as the matrix for a random walk (see Appendix E) on the digraph W, where $B[p][q]$ is the probability that a random walker at page p (or in our case, an "aimless surfer" of the Web) will follow the hyperlink from page p to page q. It is not difficult to show that the ith power matrix of the matrix B has the property that its pq^{th} entry $B^i[p][q]$ is the probability that an aimless surfer starting at page p reaches q in i steps by following a path of i hyperlinks (see Exercise 17.5). Equivalently, $(B^T)^i[p][q]$ is the probability that an aimless surfer starting at page q will reach p after i steps.

Because the entries of R_0 are positive and sum to 1, R_0 determines a probability distribution on the set of pages $V(W)$, where $R_0[q]$ is the probability that the aimless surfer begins surfing from page q. It follows from the previous result that $R_i = (B^T)^i R_0$ is then the probability that the surfer will end up at page p after i steps. In particular, choosing the probability distribution given by $R_0[q] = 1$ for a particular page q and $R_0[p] = 0$ for every other page p, $R_i[p]$ becomes the probability that the aimless surfer starting at the given page q will end up at p after i steps. As discussed earlier, if W is strongly connected and aperiodic, then the limit of R_i converges to R as i goes to infinity, independent of the choice of R_0 (The concept of aperiodic is defined more generally in a Markov chain. See Appendix D for more discussion on random walks and Markov chains.) It follows that we are free to choose any page q as the initial starting point for our aimless surfer, as long as we iterate enough times.

The aimless surfer interpretation gives us further intuition that PageRank is a meaningful ranking of Web pages. When randomly surfing the Web, we have a higher probability of ending up at a more significant page than a less significant one because more hyperlinks lead to significant pages.

To simplify our discussion of PageRank, we ignored the damping factor. However, in practice, to obtain better ranking results, a damping factor d, which is a value between 0 and 1, is included in the definition of PageRank.

DEFINITION 17.2.1 PageRank Let n denote the number of nodes of the Web digraph W. The PageRank $R[p]$ of a Web page p is given by

$$R[p] = (1 - d)/n + d \sum_{q \in N_{in}(p)} \frac{R[q]}{d_{out}(q)}, \qquad (17.2.7)$$

where d is the damping factor. Taking the damping factor d to be between 0.8 and 0.9 has been found to work well in practice.

Formula (17.2.1) is the special case of Formula (17.2.7), where the damping factor d is 1. The more general Formula (17.2.7) also has an interpretation in terms of an aimless surfer. The difference is that now the surfer at page q can either follow a hyperlink from page q to page p as before (with probability d/d_{out}), when such a hyperlink exists, or jump to a random page p with small probability [with probability $(1 - d)/n$]. Because the Web digraph is not strongly connected, this jumping allows the aimless surfer to potentially reach pages of the Web that he or she could not reach by simply following hyperlinks. Thus, the underlying graph becomes complete (and aperiodic). Similar to the algorithmic solution we discussed earlier for the case $d = 1$, the formula for PageRank given in Definition 17.2.1 can be solved using iteration. As before, the initial ranking R_0 can be any nonzero vector whose entries sum to 1. Based on Formula (17.2.7), we obtain the following iteration formula:

$$R_i[p] = d/n + (1 - d) \sum_{q \in N_{in}(p)} \frac{R_{i-1}[q]}{d_{out}(q)}, i = 1, 2, \ldots \qquad (17.2.8)$$

R E M A R K S

1. Page and Brin actually published two different versions of PageRank. In their original version, they defined PageRank by

$$R[p] = d + (1 - d) \sum_{q \in N_{in}(p)} \frac{R[q]}{d_{out}(q)}.$$

Although the two versions do not differ fundamentally, the version given by Formula (17.2.8) has the interesting idle surfer interpretation we just described.

2. Although PageRank is the centerpiece of Google's ranking mechanism, other criteria are also used, such as keywords, phrase matches, match proximity, and so forth. In fact, the rank of a page in the commercial version of PageRank used by Google can be increased by paying an appropriate fee.

Again, because we are more interested in the ranking (order) induced by the ranking function R than its exact value, we can stop iterating when R_i is close enough to R to induce the same ranking or close to the same ranking as R. For example, empirical experiments have shown that acceptable ranking functions R_i are achieved in 52 iterations for about 322 million hyperlinks.

Computing the page rank is a good way to prioritize the results of Web keyword searches. It has been shown that for most popular subjects, a simple text-matching search that is restricted to Web page titles performs well when PageRank is used to rank the results. However, the computation of PageRank is independent of any particularly query string Q. We now discuss the algorithm called *HITS*, which uses query string information to obtain an improved ranking.

17.2.2 *HITS* Algorithm

In the first phase of *HITS*, given a query Q, the algorithm computes a root set A consisting of the top-ranked Web pages for Q based on a "first approximation" ranking. This ranking can be obtained using textual information such as the frequency of occurrence of the query string on the page, whether the query string occurs in bold or in a large font size, PageRank, and so forth. The number of such Web pages chosen is based on a predetermined number r—say, $r = 200$. *HITS* then augments the root set A to obtain a base set B as follows. For each page p in the root set A, all the pages in its out-neighborhood in W and all the pages in its in-neighborhood are added to A. Because, in practice, the in-neighborhood could be huge, *HITS* limits the number of pages it chooses to some reasonable number of pages chosen in an arbitrarily fashion from the in-neighborhood of p. Also, we may wish to delete pages from popular sites, such as http://www. yahoo.com or http://www.google.com, which would tend to be the most

FIGURE 17.1

Expanding the root
set into a base set.

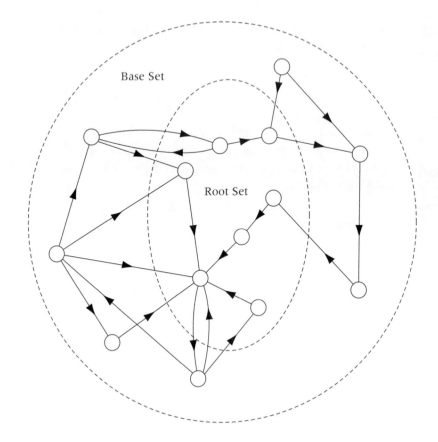

authoritative pages with respect to any query string they contain. The root set A
and its expansion to a base set B is illustrated in Figure 17.1. After computing the
base set B, *HITS* computes the induced subdigraph $W[B]$. However, hyperlinks
(edges) between pages within the same host are considered navigational or
nepotistic, rather than informational, so we remove them from $W[B]$ to obtain a
subdigraph that we call the *focused subdigraph for query Q*, and denote by F_Q.

Note that the focused subdigraph F_Q may include authoritative pages for the
query Q that do not contain even a single occurrence of the query string. For example, suppose hypothetically that Albert Einstein were still alive today and had
a Web page. Although Einstein's Web page may not contain any occurrences of
the string "genius," it is likely that at least one of the Web pages in the root set for
the query "genius" would contain a hyperlink to Einstein's Web page. Thus,
Einstein's Web page would be brought into the base set B and the focused subdigraph F_Q.

We define the hub value $h[p]$ of a page p to be the sum of the authority values over all pages q in its out-neighborhood $N_{out}(p)$ of the focused subdigraph F_Q and the authority value to be the sum of the hub values over all pages q in its in-neighborhood $N_{in}(p)$ of F_Q.

$$h[p] = \sum_{q \in N_{out}(p)} a[q], \qquad \qquad (17.2.9)$$

$$a[p] = \sum_{q \in N_{in}(p)} h[q]. \qquad \qquad (17.2.10)$$

Letting A denote the adjacency matrix of F_Q, and letting h and a denote the column vectors whose entries corresponding to page (vertex) p are $h[p]$ and $a[p]$, respectively, Formulas (17.2.9 and 17.2.10) become

$$a = A^T h, \qquad \qquad (17.2.11)$$

$$h = Aa. \qquad \qquad (17.2.12)$$

Combining Formulas (17.2.11) and (17.2.12), we obtain

$$a = A^T h = A^T(Aa) = A^T Aa, \qquad \qquad (17.2.13)$$

$$h = Aa = A(A^T h) = AA^T h. \qquad \qquad (17.2.14)$$

We normalize the vectors a and h by dividing by $\|a\| = \sum_{p \in V(F_Q)} a[p]$ and $\|h\| = \sum_{p \in V(F_Q)} h[p]$, respectively, so that $\|a\| = \|h\| = 1$.

We call $A^T A$ the *authority matrix* and AA^T the *hub matrix*. As with PageRank, a and h are the principal eigenvectors of the matrices $A^T A$ and AA^T, respectively, and we can iterate to obtain approximations a_i and h_i to a and h, respectively. The only difference is that we normalize a_i and h_i after each iteration. Initially, we choose a_0 and h_0 to both be the column vector $(1, 1, \dots, 1)^T$.

The following is a high-level description of the HITS algorithm.

procedure *HITS(Q, k, a, h)*
Input: *Q* (query string), *k* (number of iterations to be performed)
Output: *a* (authority ranking function), *h* (hub ranking function)
      Compute the focused subdigraph F_Q for the query *Q*
      Compute the adjacency matrix *A* of F_Q
      $a \leftarrow h \leftarrow (1, \dots, 1)^T$
        for *i* $\leftarrow$ 1 **to** *k* **do**

$$h \leftarrow Aa$$

Compute $\|h\| \leftarrow \sum_{p \in V(F_Q)} h[p]$

$$h \leftarrow h/ \|h\|$$

$$a \leftarrow A^T h$$

Compute $\|a\| \leftarrow \sum_{p \in V(F_Q)} a[p]$

$$a \leftarrow a/ \|a\|$$

endfor

end *HITS*

17.3 Hashing

To efficiently retrieve information from a database, such as the huge database of Web documents created by a search engine, it is useful to build an index. One of the most effective ways of building an index is to use a *hash function* and a *hash table* implemented using an array. The hash function maps the keys to some reasonably large interval of integral indices $\{0, 1, \ldots, n - 1\}$. Good choices of hash functions will avoid excessive "collisions" among the keys when they are mapped to the corresponding array *HashTable*$[0:n - 1]$. Operations performed on the hash table include inserting, deleting, and searching for keys. These operations are sometimes called *dictionary* operations. Other ADTs for implementing dictionary operations, such as balanced trees and B-trees, are given in Chapter 21.

Clearly, if we use an array for storing n keys whose index range is as large as the size of the ordered set S consisting of all possible keys, then we can reserve a unique position in the array for each key. In the so-called *direct-addressing scheme*, the ordered set S itself is used as the indexing for the array. For example, if S consists of integers between 0 and 99, and the actual keys in current use are 7, 23, 55, 61, and 80, then an array *DirAddr*$[0:99]$ supporting direct-addressing would have positions (slots) 7, 23, 55, 61, and 80 occupied with key values, and the remaining 95 slots would be unoccupied. If the keys are used to index records in a database file, then it would be assumed that the element in the ith slot of *DirAddr*$[0:99]$, $i = 0, \ldots, 99$, contains the address of the record having the key i in this file.

In a direct-addressing scheme, all the dictionary operations (inserting, deleting, and searching for a key) can be performed in constant time. Unfortunately, the direct-addressing scheme is not often feasible in practice because the size of S is simply too large. For example, suppose we have at most 10,000 records corresponding to students at UHash College, where the key is a student's 9-digit Social Security number. We would need to maintain an array of size 999,999,999 to have enough positions for every possible Social Security number, even though at most 10,000 of these positions would actually be used.

The idea behind hashing is to define an appropriate mapping h from the set S of all possible keys to a much smaller set S' consisting of consecutive integers. For example, in our UHash College example, suppose h maps each Social Security number s onto the number determined by the last four digits of s. Then h maps the set S of all Social Security numbers onto the much smaller set S' of integers between 0 and 9999, inclusive. The associated hash table can then be an array $H[0:9999]$, and a nine-digit Social Security number s would be stored in position $h(s)$ of the array H.

Although hashing has the advantage of saving memory, it has the drawback that multiple keys in S are mapped by h to the same integer in S'. For example, two or more students from UHash College may have Social Security numbers with the same last four digits. After the first student has been inserted in the hash table, the attempted insertion of a second student whose Social Security number has the same last four digits results in a *collision*. In the next two subsections, we discuss the two standard methods used to resolve collisions, *chaining* and *open addressing*. Of course, it is best to avoid collisions as much as possible by a good choice of hash function. In our UHash College example, the choice of hash function was not very good because it completely ignored the first five digits of the Social Security number. It would be better to use a hash function h that depends on all the digits of s, because there might be some bias present in the last four digits.

The word *hashing* derives form the fact that $h(s)$ is often obtained, as in our UHash College example, by chopping off or otherwise altering some aspect of the key value. Also, good hash functions should mix things up pretty well, thereby keeping collisions to a minimum.

17.3.1 Hash Functions

As just mentioned, a good hash function is one that minimizes the number of collisions. Of course, a good hash function should also be easily computable. The number of collisions is minimized if each key k from S is equally likely to be mapped by the hash function h to any given index (*slot*) in the hash table. In other words, if there are m slots $0, \ldots, m - 1$ in the hash table, and we independently draw keys from S according to a given probability distribution P, then the number of collisions is minimized if

$$P(h(k) = i) = \frac{1}{m}, \quad i = 0, 1, \ldots, m - 1. \tag{17.3.1}$$

A hash function satisfying Formula (17.3.1) is termed a *uniform hash function,* and such a hash function together with its associated hash table is called *uniform hashing.* Unfortunately, in most instances, the probability distribution P on S is not known. Even when P is known, uniform hash functions are difficult to obtain. However, heuristic techniques can be used to find hash functions that come close to satisfying the assumption of uniform hashing and therefore perform quite well in practice.

To simplify our discussion, from now on we assume that the keys are drawn from the set of integers. There is usually a natural way in which to satisfy this assumption in practice. For example, keys made up of alphabetical characters could be replaced by their ASCII (decimal) equivalents. Given integer keys, two standard hashing techniques are the division method and the multiplication method.

In the *division method,* h maps k onto $k \bmod m$, where m is the size of the hash table:

$$h(k) = k \bmod m. \qquad (17.3.2)$$

We must be careful in the choice of m so as not to bias the hash function. For example, if m is divisible by two, then h would have the bias that even (odd) integers would be hashed to even (odd) positions in the hash table (goodbye uniform hashing). Similar biases would exist if m has other nontrivial factors. For instance, considering again our UHash College example, note that the hash function was precisely Formula (17.3.2) with $m = 10^4$. To avoid these types of biases, a good choice of m is a prime not too close to an exact integer power.

In the *multiplication method,* we map the keys to slots in $H[0:m-1]$ by the formula

$$h(k) = \lfloor m(kA - \lfloor kA \rfloor) \rfloor, \qquad (17.3.3)$$

where A is a constant such that $0 < A < 1$. The term $(kA - \lfloor kA \rfloor)$ in Formula (17.3.3) is merely the fractional part of kA. While the method works for any choice of the constant A, for a particular set of keys, some choices of A will tend to yield a more uniform behavior for h than others. It turns out that the choice of A given by the inverse of the golden ratio $\phi^{-1} = (\sqrt{5} - 1)/2$ works well in many situations because of the especially uniform way that the points $0, \phi^{-1} - \lfloor \phi^{-1} \rfloor$, $2\phi^{-1} - \lfloor 2\phi^{-1} \rfloor$, $3\phi^{-1} - \lfloor 3\phi^{-1} \rfloor$, ... divide up the unit interval $[0, 1]$.

The choice of m in Formula (17.3.3) is guided, of course, by such things as the anticipated size of the set of keys to be stored in the hash table. Fortunately, the choice of m is not critical to the good behavior of the hashing function given by Formula (17.3.3). Thus, m is typically taken to be a power of two to make the implementation of $h(k)$ easier on most computers.

FIGURE 17.2

A chained hash function for student's social security numbers at UHash College, where the hash function *h* maps a social security number onto the number determined by its last four digits

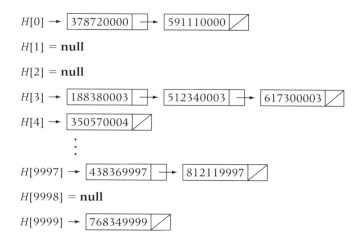

17.3.2 Collision Resolution by Chaining

In the method of collision resolution by *chaining*, the ith entry in the hash table $H[0:m-1]$, $i = 0, \ldots, m-1$, does not contain a key but instead contains a pointer to a linked list of keys, all of which satisfy $h(k) = i$. We illustrate collision resolution by chaining in Figure 17.2 for our UHash College example. Recall that the keys are nine-digit Social Security numbers, and $h(k)$ is the integer represented by the last four digits.

When searching for a given key, we first hash the key to the slot that points to the appropriate linked list (*chain*), and then we perform a search of this chain. When inserting a key, we hash the key to the appropriate slot and then insert the key in the corresponding linked list. Deletion of a key also amounts to simple deletion in the appropriate linked list.

Searching, insertion, and deletion each have worst-case behavior bounded by the longest chain pointed to by the hash table. Of course, in the worst case, all the keys hash to the same list, so that the dictionary operations are basically identical to that performed on an ordinary linked list (with the additional overhead of computing the hash function). Thus, the dictionary operations for hashing with chaining have linear worst-case complexity, which is certainly unattractive. However, as we will see, the average behavior of hashing with chaining is much better.

To discuss the average behavior of hashing with chaining, we need to make some assumptions and provide some notation. We focus on searching, since insertion and deletion have the same complexity as searching. Given a hash table

$H[0:m-1]$ of m slots containing n keys, we measure the average complexity of searching a hash table with chaining in terms of the *load factor* $\alpha = n/m$. The ratio α can be thought of as the average number of keys in a chain. However, it is only when our hash function h is close to uniform that each chain holds approximately α keys.

We now analyze the average behavior of both a successful search and an unsuccessful search of a hash table with chaining under the assumption that h is a uniform hash function. Let U_n and S_n denote the average number of key comparisons done in an unsuccessful search and a successful search, respectively. Note that U_n is nothing more than the average length of a chain. Moreover, since h is a uniform hash function, the average length of a chain is given by α. Hence, under our assumptions, the average complexity of unsuccessful search is given by

$$U_n = \alpha = \frac{n}{m}. \tag{17.3.4}$$

We now consider a successful search, where we assume that any key in the hash table is equally likely to be the search element. Under our assumptions of uniform hashing, the expected number of key comparisons made when searching for a given key is one more than that made when the key was inserted into the hash table. Thus, S_n is equal to 1 plus the average number of key comparisons made when inserting the ith key, $i = 1, \dots, n$. Since we have assumed uniform hashing and each key is equally likely, when the ith key was inserted, each chain had average length given by $(i-1)/m$. Thus, we have

$$\begin{aligned}
S_n &= \frac{1}{n}\sum_{i=1}^{n}\left(1 + \frac{i-1}{m}\right) = 1 + \frac{1}{nm}\sum_{i=1}^{n}(i-1) \\
&= 1 + \frac{1}{nm}\left(\frac{(n-1)n}{2}\right) \tag{17.3.5} \\
&= 1 + \frac{\alpha}{2} - \frac{1}{2m}.
\end{aligned}$$

From Formula (17.3.5), S_n is approximately equal to $1 + \alpha/2$ for large m, which is entirely reasonable since this is the average number of comparisons performed by a linear search on a list of size α.

What happens in the formulas for U_n and S_n as both m and n increase? If the number of slots m in the hash table is proportional to the number of keys n in the table, then $\alpha = n/m \in O(1)$. Then both successful search and unsuccessful search (and the other dictionary operations as well) can be done in constant time, on average. The dramatic improvement over the linear worst-case behavior is the reason that finding good hash functions is so important.

17.3.3 Collision Resolution with Open Addressing

The second major method of resolving collisions in hash tables is to use the technique of *open addressing*. When a collision is detected upon inserting a key, a search of the hash table is made to find the first available unoccupied slot in the hash table. The key is then inserted at this open position. In the open addressing scheme, we can never store more keys than available slots in the hash table. Thus, in contrast to the chaining scheme, the loading factor $\alpha = n/m$ for hashing with open addressing is never more than 1.

There are various methods of determining the first available open position for inserting a key. Each method generates a certain *probe sequence* that, starting from the slot given by the hash function, visits the other slots in the hash table in some determined order. We require that the probe sequence generate a permutation of the slots, to guarantee that all m slots are eventually reached by unsuccessful searches. We discuss two commonly used probing methods, *linear probing* and *double hashing*.

When inserting a key, we follow the appropriate probe sequence until the first unoccupied slot is found (if any). The key is then inserted at this first available slot. Searching for a key also works by executing the appropriate probe sequence until either the key is found, an unoccupied slot is encountered, or all m slots have been examined without finding the key. Both of the latter cases correspond to unsuccessful searches. The reason that encountering unoccupied slots signals an unsuccessful search is that each probe sequence is completely determined by the key and the specific probing method. In particular, if an unoccupied position is ever encountered when searching for a given key, the key is not in the table because it would have been already found or originally inserted at the unoccupied position.

The previous discussion highlights a problem that arises with open addressing. Namely, deletions confound subsequent searches. How do we tell whether an unoccupied slot was vacated by a previous deletion? Clearly, we must be able to recognize this; otherwise, searches might end prematurely and erroneously signal unsuccessful searches. One way around this dilemma is to keep a bit field around to signal whether or not a slot was ever occupied. While this solves the problem, it tends to generate long searches in the presence of many deletions. Thus, hashing with chaining is preferred over hashing with open addressing when there is the likelihood of a large number of deletions being performed.

slot	0	1	2	3	4	5	6	7	8	9	10	11	12	13	14	15	16	17	18	19	20	21	22
key	23			3	4	5	26	6	7	55							16	39	17				22

FIGURE 17.3

Contents of $H[0:22]$ after inserting 3, 4, 5, 26, 6, 7, 23, 16, 39, 17, 22, and 55 in initially empty table using the hash function $h(k) = k \bmod 23$ and open addressing with linear probing

Linear Probing. Perhaps the simplest probing method is *linear probing,* where starting from the slot given by the hash function, we perform a linear search of the table. We assume that the indices are stored circularly (that is, modulo m), so that the probe resumes at the beginning of the table after it reaches the end. Thus, for a given k, the linear probing sequence corresponding to k is given by

$$(h(k) + i) \bmod m, \quad i = 0, \dots, m - 1. \qquad \textbf{(17.3.6)}$$

In Figure 17.3, we show the contents of a hash table $H[0:22]$ after the insertion of the keys 3, 4, 5, 26, 6, 7, 23, 16, 39, 17, 22, and 55, where $h(k) = k \bmod 23$.

Unfortunately, while linear probing is easy to implement, it does not come very close to uniform hashing because long runs (called *primary clusters*) of occupied slots tend to build up even in relatively sparse tables. The reason for clustering is clear: An empty slot preceded by a nonempty slot is twice as likely to be filled by an insertion than is an empty slot preceded by an empty slot. In fact, if i slots are filled preceding a given open slot, then the empty slot has probability $(i + 1)/m$ of being filled by the next insertion, whereas it has probability of $1/m$ of being filled if its preceding slot is empty. (These calculations assume, as usual, that any slot is equally likely to be the hash value of the inserted key.)

Double Hashing. *Double hashing* gets its name from the fact that it uses two hash functions to generate its probing sequences. Given two hash functions h_1 and h_2, the double hash function generated by h_1 and h_2 has a probe sequence given by

$$(h_1(k) + ih_2(k)) \bmod m, \quad i = 0, \dots, m - 1, \qquad \textbf{(17.3.7)}$$

where it is required that $\gcd(h_2(k), m) = 1$.

slot	0	1	2	3	4	5	6	7	8	9	10	11	12	13	14	15	16	17	18	19	20	21	22
key	23			3	4	5	6	7		26			39		55		16	17					22

FIGURE 17.4

Contents of $H[0:22]$ after inserting 3, 4, 5, 26, 6, 7, 23, 16, 39, 17, 22, and 55 in initially empty table using the double hash function based on the hash functions $h_1(k) = k \bmod 23$ and $h_2(k) = 1 + (k \bmod 21)$ and open addressing

In particular, the double hash function has its initial value given by $h_1(k)$. The condition that $h_2(k)$ and m are relatively prime is needed to guarantee that the probe sequence generates a permutation of $0, \dots, m - 1$ (that is, all slots are reached). To ensure relative primality, we can define $h_2(k) = 1 + (k \bmod m')$, where m' is slightly smaller than m. Figure 17.4 illustrates a double hash function based on $h_1(k) = k \bmod 23$ and $h_2(k) = 1 + (k \bmod 21)$ for the same keys as in Figure 17.3.

Double hashing outperforms linear probing because it does not suffer from the problem of clustering. In practice, double hashing usually yields a rather good approximation to uniform hashing.

Average Behavior of Hashing with Open Addressing. When analyzing the average behavior of hashing with collision resolution by open addressing, a very strong form of uniform hashing is assumed. The strong form takes into account the entire probing sequence generated by the hash function, not just its initial value. A *strongly uniform hash function h* is a hash function with the property that each of the $m!$ permutations of $0, \dots, m - 1$ are equally likely to be the probe sequence generated by h for any key. In particular, a strongly uniform hash function is also a uniform hash function in our previous sense, because its initial value can be any of the slots $0, \dots, m - 1$ with equal probability.

Of course, strongly uniform hash functions are even harder to find than ordinary uniform hash functions. Double hashing is closer to being strongly uniform than linear probing. Linear probing generates a total of only m probe sequences because a linear probe is simply a cyclic shift of the identity permutation. On the other hand, double hashing generates m^2 probe sequences because each pair $(h_1(k), h_2(k))$ yields a distinct probe sequence.

The following theorem expresses the average behavior of unsuccessful and successful searches for hashing with collision resolution by open addressing. The proof of Theorem 17.3.1 is left to the exercises. Theorem 17.3.1 expresses the average behavior in terms of the loading factor $\alpha = n/m < 1$.

Theorem 17.3.1   Suppose we have an open-address hash table with a loading factor $\alpha = n/m < 1$ and a strongly uniform hashing function. Let U_n and S_n denote the expected number of probes in an unsuccessful and successful search, respectively. Then we have

$$U_n \leq \frac{1}{1 - \alpha}, \tag{17.3.8}$$

and

$$S_n \leq \frac{1}{\alpha}\left(1 + \log_2\left(\frac{1}{1 - \alpha}\right)\right). \tag{17.3.9}$$

■

Inserting an element has the same complexity as that for an unsuccessful search. Again, supposing that α is held relatively constant as m and n grow large, then Theorem 17.3.1 implies that both unsuccessful and successful searching can be done in constant time.

17.4 Caching, Content Delivery, and Consistent Hashing

In the first two sections of this chapter, we considered the fundamental problem of searching and retrieving information on the World Wide Web and the ranking of Web pages. In this section, we consider another fundamental problem, the efficient delivery of content on the Internet. We discuss an important strategy for solving this problem called *caching* and an efficient scheme for hashing content to caches called *consistent hashing*.

17.4.1 Web Caching

Web caching involves the storage of content at special servers called *caches*. Replicating information and storing it in caches alleviates a number of problems. First, it reduces network congestion by reducing the amount of redundant traffic that needs to cross the backbone of the Internet. Second, it reduces *latency*—the speed at which packets (data) need to travel to reach users. Third, caching reduces load and helps eliminate "hot spots"—locations where many users are trying to access data from the same server because content is distributed among multiple caches.

R E M A R K

Often in practice, the pictures on a Web site are cached but the text is not. The advantage of this is that the original site will have a high hit count, which is usually desired by the content provider.

The most straightforward approach to caching is to have a single large cache to serve each region, such as a city. This is called the *monolithic approach*. All users from a particular region—say, New York—would go to the cache to access content from various content provider sites (URLs) throughout the Internet. When the first client (user) from New York wishes to access content from a particular URL, the content will not be available in the New York cache, and the client will need to go directly to the original site. However, the content will then be cached locally in New York, so that subsequent clients from New York who request the same content can access it directly from the New York cache.

The monolithic approach has some disadvantages. For example, if a regional cache fails, then all the users in that region are cut off. Thus, a large fault-tolerant machine is needed for each region, which is expensive and not very practical to build and maintain. Another disadvantage is that each item must be replicated r times, where r is the number of regions for which at least one user in the region has requested the item. Although, a certain amount of replication is needed if the item is popular, in general, the amount needed for the monolithic approach far exceeds the amount needed simply to avoid hot spots. Thus, caches become congested.

Another approach, called the *distributed approach*, is to place many smaller caches distributed among local neighborhoods to serve the users in the neighborhood. Although this eliminates the need for a large, highly fault tolerant cache, it has the major disadvantage that the hit rate is low because the caches are receiving requests from a smaller population. This means that users have to go to original sites much of the time to obtain content. Clearly, it would be unfeasible to replicate each item in each cache every time there is a miss—that is, every time a user goes to the neighborhood cache and fails to find the item. Also, because individual caches are small, they can only hold a small portion of the data from content providers.

A hybrid approach, called *harvest caching*, combines the monolithic and distributed approaches. This approach involves a hierarchy of caches, where nodes closer to the root serve a larger region, and the leaf nodes correspond to the neighborhood caches. If there is no hit in a neighborhood cache, the parent cache can be searched for the item. This approach still has the disadvantage of the monolithic caching model in that it requires larger fault-tolerant machines for the regional caches.

In the next subsection we discuss a better approach using consistent hashing.

17.4.2 Consistent Hashing

Before discussing consistent hashing, we first consider the problem of using an ordinary hash function to map content to caches. We refer to the content objects to be cached as *items* and the caches as *buckets*. Let $\mathscr{I} = \{I_0, I_1, ..., I_{t-1}\}$ denote the set of items and $\mathscr{B} = \{B_0, ..., B_{k-1}\}$ the set of buckets. Suppose we use a linear hash function $h(i) = ai + b \pmod{k}$, where a and b are randomly chosen integers and i is a unique identifying integer associated with item $I \in \mathscr{I}$. Because a and b were chosen at random, we can expect that the load will be fairly evenly distributed among the buckets.

Using such a hash function has the advantage that no item needs to be replicated for clients to find it. Once an item is placed in a cache (bucket), subsequent clients go directly to the cache to access the item. However, this approach has a major drawback. In practice, the Internet is dynamic, with new caches constantly being added and caches going down or becoming full. Note that if we were to add a single new cache, the new hash function would become $h'(i) = ai + b \pmod{k+1}$. Thus, each item would now be mapped to a bucket that does not contain the item. Of course, when a client requests item *I* and it is not found in the cache (bucket) $h'(i)$, it can copied to $h'(i)$. However, in a worst-case scenario, after many additions of caches, it is possible that *I* might be replicated in every bucket.

We now describe a hash function, called a *consistent hash function*, with the property that, when a new bucket is added, exactly one of the old buckets has some ot its items reassigned to the new bucket and all other assignments of items remain the same. In particular, we discuss a consistent hash function called UC_{random}. UC_{random} is based on first independently and randomly mapping the items and the buckets to the unit circle. This mapping can be achieved using randomly selected hash functions h_{items} and $h_{buckets}$, which map the set of items and set of buckets, respectively, to the integers $0, 1, ..., N-1$ for some large number N, where $0, 1, ..., N-1$ are identified with N points evenly distributed around the unit circle.

Once the items and buckets are mapped to the unit circle, the UC_{random} hash function h then maps each item to the clockwise nearest bucket. A sample UC_{random} hash function h involving 8 buckets and 14 items is shown in Figure 17.5.

FIGURE 17.5

Example UC_{random} hash function for $k = 8$ buckets and $t = 14$ items.

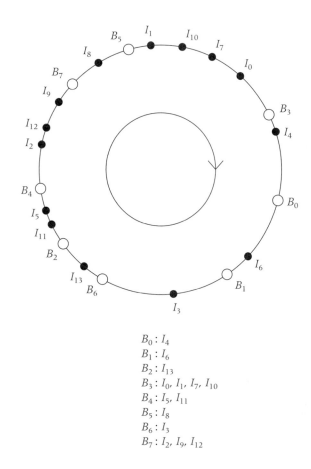

$B_0 : I_4$
$B_1 : I_6$
$B_2 : I_{13}$
$B_3 : I_0, I_1, I_7, I_{10}$
$B_4 : I_5, I_{11}$
$B_5 : I_8$
$B_6 : I_3$
$B_7 : I_2, I_9, I_{12}$

Note that if we were to add a new bucket B_8 between the points labeled I_{10} and I_7 in the unit circle in Figure 17.5, then only items I_1 and I_{10} would be reassigned to B_9. The assignment of all other items to buckets would remain the same.

The consistent hash function given in Figure 17.5 assumes that all the caches are available to every client that requests an item. However, in practice, caches may be down at certain times. Also, clients from different regions may be restricted in the caches they can access. Thus, when different clients request item I, they may have different *views* of the available caches. Consistent hashing can be naturally generalized to take this into account. Instead of simply mapping each item I to a bucket B, we map each item-view pair (I,V) to a bucket B where, $V \subseteq \mathcal{B}$. Such hash functions, which map $\mathcal{I} \times 2^{\mathcal{B}}$ to $\mathcal{B}$, are called *ranged hash functions*. The function UC_{random} can easily be extended to a ranged hash function by mapping each item I requested by a client to the clockwise nearest cache (bucket) in the client's view V. For the same random hashing of 8 buckets and 14 items to the unit circle given in Figure 17.5, Figure 17.6 shows the UC_{random} hash function for three different views.

FIGURE 17.6

UC_{random} hash function for three different views for the same hashing of 8 buckets and 14 items to the unit circle given in Figure 17.5.

$V = \{B_0, B_2, B_5, B_6\}$
$B_0: I_0, I_1, I_4, I_7, I_{10}$
$B_2: I_{13}$
$B_5: I_2, I_5, I_8, I_9, I_{11}, I_{12}$
$B_6: I_3, I_6$

$V = \{B_5, B_6\}$
$B_5: I_2, I_5, I_8, I_9, I_{11}, I_{12}, I_{13}$
$B_6: I_0, I_1, I_3, I_4, I_6, I_7, I_{10}$

$V = \{B_2, B_3, B_7\}$
$B_2: I_3, I_4, I_6, I_{13}$
$B_3: I_0, I_1, I_7, I_8, I_{10}$
$B_7: I_2, I_5, I_9, I_{11}, I_{12}$

The unit circle is equivalent to the unit interval [0,1] in the sense that we can take any point on the unit circle and map it to the point 0 of the unit interval and then map the point that is distance $2\pi x$ in the clockwise direction around the unit circle to the point x of unit interval, $0 \leq x < 1$. Thus, each bucket and item is assigned an integer value between 0 and 1. It follows that, given an item I, we can compute the bucket B it is mapped to by UC_{random} in $O(\log|V|)$ time by performing a binary search on the sorted list of buckets in the given view V to find the position where I would be inserted in the list.

It is possible that the random hash function maps buckets to the unit circle in a nonuniform way, making the distance to the nearest counterclockwise bucket for some buckets disproportionately large. Because such buckets "control" a larger proportion of the unit circle, the expected number of items that would be hashed by the UC_{random} to these buckets may be much greater than it would be to other buckets. Figure 17.7(a) shows such a nonuniform distribution involving eight buckets, where bucket B_3 controls a disproportionately large portion of the unit circle; and Figure 17.7(b) shows a sample mapping of 13 items to the same unit circle and the associated unbalanced assignment of these items to buckets by UC_{random}. To avoid such unfortunate distributions, we duplicate each bucket m times by randomly hashing each bucket to m different points on the unit circle. An item is still mapped to the nearest clockwise bucket, but the likelihood of a more balanced assignment of items to a bucket is improved. For the same mapping of items as in Figure 17.7(b), in Figure 17.7(c) a duplicate of each bucket is also mapped to the unit circle illustrating the case $m = 2$. Note the improved distribution of items to buckets.

An easily verified key fact about the UC_{random} hash function is the following monotonicity property.

Key Fact

If a bucket is added to a view, the only items reassigned are those assigned to the added bucket. More generally, given a UC_{random} hash function f, two views $V_1, V_2,$ where $V_1 \subset V_2,$ and an item $I, f(I, V_2) \in V_1,$ implies that $f(I, V_1) = f(I, V_2)$.

FIGURE 17.7

(a) Nonuniform distribution, where bucket B_3 controls a disproportionately large portion of the unit circle; (b) assignment of buckets to items for a sample mapping of 13 items to the unit circle

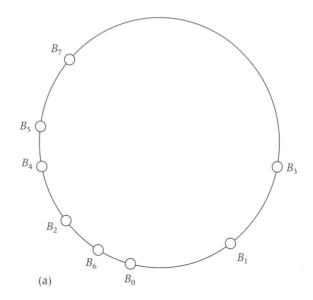

(a)

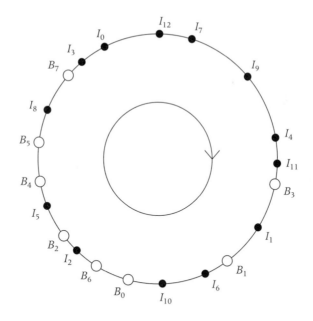

$B_0 : I_6, I_{10}$
$B_1 : I_1$
$B_2 : I_2$
$B_3 : I_0, I_3, I_4, I_7, I_9, I_{11}, I_{12}$
$B_4 : I_5$
$B_5 :$ empty
$B_6 :$ empty
$B_7 : I_8$

(b)

continued

FIGURE 17.7

Continued

(c) for the same
mapping of items as
in (a), a duplicate of
each bucket is also
mapped to the unit
circle illustrating the
case $m = 2$. Note
the improved
distribution of items
to buckets.

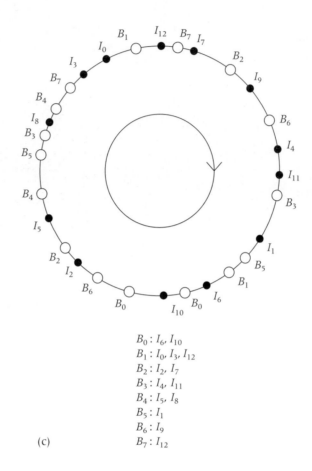

$B_0 : I_6, I_{10}$
$B_1 : I_0, I_3, I_{12}$
$B_2 : I_2, I_7$
$B_3 : I_4, I_{11}$
$B_4 : I_5, I_8$
$B_5 : I_1$
$B_6 : I_9$
$B_7 : I_{12}$

(c)

In addition to being monotone, the UC_{random} function has several other desirable properties. Three important goodness measures associated with hashing items to caches are spread, load, and balance. Consider a set of c clients with views $V_1, \dots, V_t$. Let $\mathscr{B}_t$ denote the union of the buckets over all these views; that is, $\mathscr{B}_t = V_1 \cup \dots \cup V_t$. Also, let b denote the number of such buckets; that is, $b = |\mathscr{B}_t|$. The *spread* of an item with respect to the set of views $V_1, \dots, V_t$ is the number of buckets from $\mathscr{B}_t$ containing the item. The *load* of a bucket $B \in \mathscr{B}_t$ is the number of items assigned to B over the set of views $V_1, \dots, V_t$. Given a view V, item I, and bucket $B \in V$, the *balance* is the probability that item I is mapped to B. It is desirable for the spread and load to be small and for the balance to be close to $1/|V|$ The following theorem (see the paper of Karger, et al. in the references), whose proof is beyond the scope of this book, shows that the spread and load are small for UC_{random}, and items are uniformly distributed among the buckets in any given view.

Theorem 17.4.1 Consider a set of t views $V_1, \ldots, V_t$, having the property that the number of buckets in each view contains at least a constant fraction of the buckets over all the views; that is, letting $\mathcal{B}_t = V_1 \cup \cdots \cup V_t$ and $b = |\mathcal{B}_t|$, suppose $|V_i| \geq b/c$, for some constant c, $i = 1, \ldots, t$. If m denotes the multiplicity with which each bucket is mapped to the unit circle by UC_{random} and r is a positive number representing a confidence factor, then the following three properties of UC_{random} hashing hold:

1. **Spread:** With probability at least $1 - 1/r$, any given item I is stored in $O(\log rt)$ buckets.
2. **Load:** Over all the views $V_1, \ldots, V_t$, with probability at least $1 - 1/r$, no bucket $B \in \mathcal{B}_t$ is assigned more that $O(\log rmt)$ times the average number of items assigned to the buckets in $\mathcal{B}_t$.
3. **Balance:** If $m \in \Omega(\log b)$, then for any fixed view V and item I, the probability that item I is mapped to a given bucket $B \in V$ is $O(1/|V|)$. □

▨ 17.5 Message Security Algorithms: RSA

To make messages sent over the Internet more secure, a cryptographic key can be used to encrypt the message. In Chapter 3, we discussed an algorithm for computing a cryptographic key known to only two parties, Alice and Bob. In this section, we consider the problem of computing both a public key E and secret (private) key D, where E is used to encrypt messages and D is be used to decrypt messages that have been encrypted using E. These keys need to be chosen so that it is computationally infeasible to derive D from E. Anyone with the public key E is able to encrypt a message, but only someone knowing D is able (in real time) to decrypt an encrypted message. Such a system is called a *public-key cryptosystem*. Many public-key cryptosystems have been designed. In this section, we discuss the popular RSA public key cryptosystem, named for its creators, Rivest, Shamir, and Adleman.

17.5.1 Modular Arithmetic

Before describing the RSA algorithm, we need to establish some concepts and results from modular arithmetic. The set $Z_n = \{0, \dots, n-1\}$ of integers (*residues*) mod n forms a commutative ring (see Appendix A), where the operations of addition and multiplication are defined the same as over the integers, but where the result of each operation is reduced mod n to an element in Z_n.

An element x of Z_n is *invertible* with respect to multiplication if there is an element y in Z_n, such that $xy \equiv 1 \pmod{n}$. We will refer to y as the *multiplicative inverse* of x. Integers x and n are *relatively prime* if and only if they have no divisor except 1 in common. Equivalently, x and n are relatively prime if and only if $\gcd(x, n) = 1$.

Proposition 17.5.1 An element x of Z_n is invertible with respect to multiplication if and only if it is relatively prime to n (that is, $\gcd(x, n) = 1$).

PROOF

Let $g = \gcd(x, n)$. It follows from Exercise 1.10 (see Chapter 1) that g can be expressed as an integer linear combination of x and n; that is, there exist integers s and t such that $sx + tn = g$. Further, g is the smallest integer with this property. Now suppose that x and n are relatively prime. Then $sx + tn = g = 1$, so that $sx \equiv 1 \pmod{n}$. It follows that $s \pmod{n}$ is the inverse of $x \pmod{n}$. Conversely, suppose that x is invertible, so that there exists an integer y such $xy \equiv 1 \pmod{n}$. Then we have that $xy - 1 = mn$ for some integer m, or equivalently, $xy - mn = 1 \pmod{n}$. However, since g is the smallest integer that is expressible as a linear combination of x and n, it follows that $g = 1$. ■

Let Z_n^* denote the subset of all nonnegative integers less than n that are relatively prime to n. For example, for the integers mod 15 shown in Figure 17.9, $Z_n^* = \{1, 2, 4, 7, 8, 11, 13, 14\}$. Then by Proposition 17.5.1, Z_n^* consists of all the elements from Z_n with a multiplicative inverse mod n. Given two integers x and y, the product xy is relatively prime with n if and only if both x and y are relatively prime with n. It follows that Z_n^* is closed under multiplication mod n. Thus, Z_n^* forms a group under multiplication mod n. The multiplication table for the group Z_{15}^* is shown in Figure 17.9. This table is obtained from the multiplication table for Z_{15} by deleting all rows and columns that do not contain a 1, which is precisely those rows and columns that are indexed by an integer having a divisor in common with 15.

FIGURE 17.8

The multiplication
table for the
group Z_{15}^*.

*	1	2	4	7	8	11	13	14
1	1	2	4	7	8	11	13	14
2	2	4	8	14	1	7	11	13
4	4	8	1	13	2	14	7	11
7	7	14	13	4	11	2	1	8
8	8	1	2	11	4	13	14	7
11	11	7	14	2	13	1	8	4
13	13	11	7	1	14	8	4	2
14	14	13	11	8	7	4	2	1

The inverse of an element x of Z_n^* can be computed efficiently using an extension of Euclid's algorithm (again, see Exercise 1.10) that computes integers g, s, and t for input integers a and b, where $g = \gcd(a, b)$ and $sa + tb = g$.

Let $\varphi(n)$ denote the number of elements less than n that are relatively prime to n, so that $\varphi(n)$ is the size of Z_n^*. The following useful theorem is due to Euler and generalizes an earlier result of Fermat known as Fermat's little theorem.

Theorem 17.5.2   Let x and n be relatively prime numbers. Then

$$x^{\varphi(n)} \equiv 1 \ (\text{mod } n). \tag{17.5.1}$$

PROOF

Because x and n are relatively prime numbers, it follows that $x \in Z_n^*$. Let a_1, $a_2, \ldots, a_{\varphi(n)}$ denote the elements of Z_n^*. Since x in invertible, $xa_1, xa_2, \ldots, xa_{\varphi(n)}$ is a permutation of the elements $a_1, a_2, \ldots, a_{\varphi(n)}$. Thus, we have that

$$(xa_1)(xa_2)\ldots(xa_{\varphi(n)}) = x^{\varphi(n)}a_1a_2 \ldots a_{\varphi(n)} = a_1a_2 \ldots a_{\varphi(n)} \ (\text{mod } n) \tag{17.5.2}$$

Since the product $a_1a_2 \ldots a_{\varphi(n)}$ is also in Z_n^*, it is invertible. Multiplying both sides of Formula (17.5.2) by the inverse of $a_1a_2 \ldots a_{\varphi(n)}$, we obtain Formula (17.5.1).   ■

Observing that $\varphi(n) = n - 1$ when n is a prime number, the following corollary known as Fermat's little theorem, follows immediately from Theorem 17.5.2.

Corollary 17.5.3   **Fermat's Little Theorem**

Let n be prime number and let x be any number that is not divisible by n. Then

$$x^{n-1} \equiv 1 \pmod{n}. \tag{17.5.3}$$

□

The following proposition will be useful in the design of the RSA algorithm.

Proposition 17.5.4   Let n be an integer that is the product of two prime numbers p and q. Then

$$\varphi(n) = (p - 1)(q - 1).$$

PROOF

The elements of Z_n that have a divisor different from 1 in common with n, excluding n itself, are the $q - 1$ multiples of p—namely, $p, 2p, \ldots, (q - 1)p$—and the $p - 1$ multiples of q—namely, $q, 2q, \ldots, (p - 1)q$. Thus, including pq, there are precisely $(p - 1) + (q - 1) + 1 = p + q - 1$ elements of Z_n that have a divisor different from 1 in common with n. Therefore, the number of elements of Z_n that do not have a divisor different from 1 in common with n—that is, the number of elements relatively prime to n—is given by $\varphi(n) = pq - (p + q - 1) = (p - 1)(q - 1)$. ■

As an illustration of Proposition 3.2.4, consider Z_{15}, whose addition and multiplication tables are illustrated in Figure 17.8. In this case, $p = 3$ and $q = 5$. As shown in Figure 17.8, the number of elements of Z_{15}^* is $(3 - 1)(5 - 1) = 8$.

The following theorem is the basis for the RSA algorithm described in the next subsection.

Theorem 17.5.5 Let $n = pq$, where p and q are two prime numbers; let e be an integer that is relatively prime with $\varphi(n)$; and let d be its multiplicative inverse mod $\varphi(n)$, that is, $ed \equiv 1 \pmod{\varphi(n)}$. Then for any integer m,

$$m^{ed} \equiv m \pmod{n}.$$

PROOF

Since $ed \equiv 1 \pmod{\varphi(n)}$, it follows that $ed = \varphi(n)k + 1$ for some integer k. First suppose that $\gcd(m, n) = 1$. Then applying Theorem 17.5.2, we have

$$\begin{aligned} m^{ed} &= m^{\varphi(n)k + 1} \\ &= (m^{\varphi(n)})^{k}m \\ &\equiv (1)^{k}m = m \pmod{n} \end{aligned}$$

Now consider the case when $\gcd(m, n) > 1$. If $\gcd(m, n) = n$, then n divides m and we have

$$m^{ed} \equiv 0^{ed} \equiv 0 \equiv m \pmod{n}.$$

Otherwise, since $n = pq$, either m is divisible by q but not p or n is divisible by p but not q. Assume without loss of generality that m is divisible by q but not p. Then by Fermat's little theorem (Corollary 17.5.3),

$$m^{p-1} \equiv 1 \pmod{p}. \tag{17.5.4}$$

Applying Formula (17.5.4), we obtain

$$\begin{aligned} m^{k\varphi(n)} &= m^{k(p-1)(q-1)} \\ &\equiv (m^{p-1})^{k(q-1)} \pmod{p} \\ &\equiv (1)^{k(q-1)} \equiv 1 \pmod{p}. \end{aligned}$$

It follows that

$$m^{k\varphi(n)} = jp + 1 \tag{17.5.5}$$

for some integer j. Multiplying both sides of Formula (17.5.5) by m, we obtain

$$m^{k\varphi(n)+1} = jpm + m. \tag{17.5.6}$$

However, because m is divisible by q, jpm is divisible by n. Therefore, we have

$$m^{k\varphi(n)+1} \equiv m \pmod{n}. \qquad ■$$

17.5.2 RSA Public-Key Cryptosystem

We now describe the RSA algorithm for computing a public and secret key for encrypting a message M and decrypting an encrypted message, respectively. Because a string can be represented as a binary sequence (for example, if the message is a string of ASCII characters, then each character in the string can be replaced with an 8-bit binary string representing its ASCII value), we can assume without loss of generality that M is an integer. We begin by choosing two large prime numbers p and q. To achieve security—that is, so that it is infeasible to compute the secret key from the public key—these primes must be about 100 digits long or longer. (The problem of designing efficient probabilistic algorithms for computing large prime numbers is discussed in Chapter 24.) We then compute the product $n = pq$.

We now choose a small odd integer e that is relatively prime with $\varphi(n)$, and take the *public key* to be the pair (e, n). The *secret key* is then chosen to be the pair (d, n), where d is the multiplicative inverse of e mod $\varphi(n)$. A message M is encrypted by taking it to the power e (mod n), and an encrypted message $C = M^e$ is decrypted by taking it to the power d (mod n). By Theorem 17.5.5, this is valid because $C^d = (M^e)^d = M^{ed} \equiv M$ (mod n). Using the modular exponential algorithm discussed in Chapter 3, both the encryption and decryption of messages can be performed efficiently. In fact, they require $O(b^3)$ bit operations, where b is the number of digits of n in its binary representation (see Exercise 17.17).

For the RSA cryptosystem to be unbreakable, d must not be computable from e in real time. It is generally believed that to compute d from e would require the factorization of n into its prime factors p and q. In practice, it is surprisingly difficult to factor large numbers (with hundreds of digits), even knowing that n is the product of two prime numbers p and q. Although the problem of factoring a number into prime factors has not been proved to be NP-hard, mathematicians and computer scientists alike have worked on the factorization problem for many years, and it is generally believed to be difficult. However, small numbers n can be efficiently factored, so we need to choose primes p and q that are about 100 digits long or longer to make the RSA cryptosystem unbreakable.

R E M A R K S

1. The message M before encryption is often called **plaintext** and after encryption is called **ciphertext**.

2. Encrypting a message using RSA may be too slow if the message is long. For such messages, RSA is often used in conjunction with a faster nonpublic-key cryptosystem, where encryption and decryption are done using the same key K. The idea is that Alice selects a key K at random and encrypts M using K to obtain the encrypted message (ciphertext) C. She then encrypts K using Bob's public RSA key $E = (e, n)$ to obtain $E(K) = K^e$ and transmits $(C, E(K))$ to Bob. K^e can be computed efficiently because K is small. After receiving the message, Bob then uses his secret RSA key $D(K) = (d, n)$ to decrypt $P(K)$, obtaining K, after which he uses K to decrypt C, obtaining the message M.

17.5.3 Digital Signatures and Authentication

Public-key cryptosystems, and in particular the RSA cryptosystem, have another very important application, the *authentication* of messages using *digital signatures*. Suppose that Alice wishes to send a message to Bob together with a digital signature, so Bob can verify that the message is actually from her and not a forgery from someone else. To do this, Alice encrypts M using her secret key D, yielding the digital signature $S = D(M)$. The RSA signature for M is $S = M^d \pmod{n}$. Alice then sends the pair (M, S) to Bob. Bob can authenticate the message M using the digital signature S and Alice's public key E by checking whether $M = E(S)$. In the case of the RSA signature, Bob checks whether $M = S^e \pmod{n}$.

17.6 Closing Remarks

In this chapter, we discussed two algorithms *PageRank* and *HITS* for ranking Web pages. Both algorithms are effective for *broad-based queries*, where there is an abundance of pages containing the query keyword. A user can make several other types of queries. One other type of query is called a *specific query*, which involves asking a question, such as "What is a search engine?" Another type is called a *similar-page query*, which involves finding Web pages similar to a given Web page or document. Different types of queries require different handling techniques. Designing efficient algorithms for these problems is an important and challenging area of research in Internet algorithms.

Search engines use hash functions extensively. In particular, they use perfect have functions to map URLs to an index. For a given set of input keys S contained in some universal set U of keys, a function $h : U \rightarrow \{0, 1, \dots, m - 1\}$ is called a *perfect hash function for S* if h is one-to-one on S. Thus, a perfect hash function avoids collisions altogether on S. If $|S| = n \leq m$, then clearly there are many perfect hash functions for S. The problem is to compute a perfect hash function efficiently for a given S, m, and U. Another requirement is that the perfect hash function should evaluate at any point in U in constant time. Quite a bit of research has been done on the problem of finding perfect hash functions. Most of the recent work in this direction involves probabilistic algorithms, which will be the topic of Chapter 24.

Various variants of the RSA public-key cryptosystem have been developed that speed up the decryption process. One such variant, which uses the Chinese remainder theorem, is explored in the exercises.

Other algorithms with applications to the Internet will be discussed in later chapters, such as string matching in Chapter 20, the FFT in Chapter 22, and multicasting and the Steiner tree in Chapter 27.

References and Suggestions for Further Reading

Chakrabarti, S. *Mining the Web, Discovering Knowledge from Hypertext Data*. San Francisco, CA: Morgan Kaufman Publishers, 2003. A book on mining the World Wide Web, including a discussion of the ranking and relevancy of Web pages.

Schmeh, K. *Cryptography and Public Key Infrastructure on the Internet*. West Sussex, England: John Wiley & Sons, 2003. A book on cryptography related to the Internet.

Karger D., E. Lehman, T. Leighton, M. Levin, D. Lewin, R. Panigrahy "Consistent Hashing and Random Trees: Distributed Caching Protocols for Relieving Hot Spots on the World Wide Web." *Proceedings of the 29th Annual ACM Symposium on Theory of Computing*, May 1997. Original paper on consistent hashing and the UC_{random} hash function.

Detailed discussions of hashing:

Aho, A. V., J. E. Hopcroft, and J. D. Ullman. *Data Structures and Algorithms*. Reading, MA: Addison-Wesley, 1983.

Gonnet, G. H. *Handbook of Algorithms and Data Structures*. Reading, MA: Addison-Wesley, 1984.

Knuth, D. E. *The Art of Computer Programming.* Vol. 3, *Sorting and Searching.* 2nd ed. Reading, MA: Addison-Wesley, 1998.

Majewski, B. S., N. C. Wormahld, G. Havas, and A. J. Czech. "Graphs, Hyper-graphs, and Hashing." *Proceedings of the 19th International Workshop on Graph-Theoretic Concepts in Computer Science (WG '93),* 1993. An excellent guide to perfect hashing schemes.

Section 17.2 Ranking Web Pages

17.1   a. Verify that matrix formula (17.2.3) is the same as Formula (17.2.1).

      b. Verify that Formula (17.2.6) follows from Formula (17.2.4).

17.2   a. Describe a digraph on n vertices, which is strongly connected but not aperiodic.

      b. Does R_i converge to the R as i goes to infinity for the digraph you have given in part (a), where $R_0 = (1,1, \dots ,1)$?

17.3   Suppose $R_0[p] = 1$ if $p = q$, and $R_0[q] = 0$ otherwise, for p and q two nodes of the digraph W. Show that, if there is no path from q to p, then $R_i[p] = 0$ for all i, whereas if there is a path, then $R_i[p]$ is nonzero for some i.

17.4   Write a program that computes R_i for input digraphs W, number of iterations i, damping factor d, and initial vector R_0. Test how quickly R_i converges R or whether it converges at all, for various choices of R_0 and damping factors d. In particular, test for the following input digraphs and damping factors d:

      a. Digraphs that are not strongly connected but not aperiodic, with $d = 0$.

      b. Digraphs that are aperiodic with $d = 0$.

      c. Digraphs with various nonzero values of d.

17.5   Show that the ith power matrix of the matrix B has the property that its pq^{th} entry $B^i[p][q]$ is the probability that an aimless surfer starting at page p reaches q in i steps.

17.6   Obtain a matrix formula for PageRank given by Formula (17.2.8), which generalizes Formula (17.2.4).

*17.7   Show that if the digraph W is aperiodic, then R_i will converge to the principal eigenvector R of B^T as i goes to infinity. Further, show that this convergence is independent of the choice of the initial vector R_0 whose entries are positive and sum to 1.

Section 17.3 Hashing

17.8　Show the contents of an open-address hash table $H[0:22]$ after the insertion of the keys 2, 11, 55, 23, 53, 9, 61, 46, 1, 3, 25, 19, 17, 34, 10, 38, and 48, where $h(k) = k \bmod 23$. Use linear probing to resolve collisions.

17.9　Repeat Exercise 17.8, using double hashing, with hash functions $h_1(k) = k \bmod 23$, and $h_2(k) = 1 + (k \bmod 21)$.

17.10　Consider the (not-so-good) hash function $h(i)$, which maps an integer i to its leading digit. Using the method of collision resolution by chaining, suppose the keys 23, 55, 123, 504, 211, 200, 88, 91, and 9 have been inserted in the hash table. Assuming each slot (leading digit) is equally likely for a given search k, determine the average behavior of a successful search.

17.11　Repeat Exercise 17.10 for an unsuccessful search.

17.12　Show that the probe sequence given by Formula (17.3.7) reaches all slots in the table if and only if $h_2(k)$ and m are relatively prime.

17.13　Prove Theorem 17.3.1.

Section 17.4 Caching, Content Delivery, and Consistent Hashing

17.14　Prove that the UC_{random} hash function h is monotone by showing that, given two views V_1, V_2, where $V_1 \subset V_2$, and an item I, $h(I, V_2) \in V_1$ implies that $h(I,V_1) = h(I,V_2)$.

17.15　Associate with each item $I \in \mathscr{I}$ a permutation π_I of the buckets, and consider the ranged hash function h that maps the item-view pair (I,V) onto the bucket $\pi_I(j)$, where j is the smallest index such that $\pi_I(j) \in V$.

　　a. Show that the function h is monotone.

　　b. Show that any monotone function can be constructed in this way.

Section 17.5 Message Security Algorithms: RSA

17.16 Give the multiplication table for the group Z_{23}^*.

17.17 Using the extended Euclid algorithm described in Exercise 1.10 (Chapter 1), compute the following:

a. Inverse of 3 mod 1097.

b. Inverse of 46 mod 1097.

c. Inverse of 127 mod 19888.

17.18 Consider the problem of dividing a by b. Show that, using the straightforward algorithm for long division, the quotient q and remainder r can be computed using $O(\log b + \log q \log b)$ bit operations.

17.19 Using the result from Exercise 17.18, show that RSA encryption and decryption of messages can be performed using $O(\beta^3)$ bit operations, where β is the number of binary digits of n.

17.20 Prove the following result, known as the Chinese remainder theorem: If $m_1, m_2, \ldots, m_k$ are k pairwise relatively prime and greater than or equal to 2, and $a_1, a_2, \ldots, a_k$ are any k integers, then there is a solution to the following simultaneous congruences:

$$x \equiv a_1 \pmod{m_1}$$

$$x \equiv a_2 \pmod{m_2}$$

$$\vdots$$

$$x \equiv a_k \pmod{m_k}.$$

In particular, $x = a_1 b_1 \dfrac{M}{m_1} + \cdots + a_k b_k \dfrac{M}{m_k}$, where $M = m_1 m_2 \cdots m_k$ and b_i is determined from $b_i \dfrac{M}{m_i} \equiv 1 \pmod{m_i}$, $i = 1, \ldots, k$.

17.21 Instead of directly decrypting the original message by computing $M \equiv C^d \pmod{n}$, as in the original RSA algorithm, we can achieve a speedup of about 4 by computing $M_p \equiv C^{d_p} \pmod{p}$ and $M_q \equiv C^{d_q} \pmod{q}$, where $d_p = d \pmod{p-1}$ and $d_q = d \pmod{q-1}$, and then computing $M = q(q^{-1} \bmod p) M_p + p(p^{-1} \bmod q) M_q$.

    a. Show that M satisfies the following two congruences:

$$M \equiv M_p \ (\mathrm{mod}\ p)$$

$$M \equiv M_q \ (\mathrm{mod}\ q)$$

    b. Applying the Chinese remainder theorem, show that M satisfies

$$M = q(q^{-1} \ \mathrm{mod}\ p)M_p + p(p^{-1} \ \mathrm{mod}\ q)M_q.$$

17.22 a. A speedup of about 9 can be achieved if n is the product of three primes $n = pqr$. Extend the result in Exercise 17.21 to for this case.

    b. Generalize the result in part (a) for n the product of k primes.

CHAPTER 18

DISTRIBUTED COMPUTATION ALGORITHMS

The subject of distributed algorithms is vast and includes parallel algorithms written for interconnection network models as special cases. While massively parallel machines implementing centrally controlled algorithms continue to be important (and this importance may grow as technology advances), recent trends in concurrent computing environments, such as networked workstations, grids, clusters, and the Internet, have emphasized the need for distributed algorithms that do not necessarily assume a central control. In its most general form, a *distributed algorithm* is implemented on a collection of possibly heterogeneous processors connected in some sort of network, and working on problems using various degrees of synchronization.

In recent years, the notions of a computational grid and grid computing have emerged. A *computational grid* can be defined as an infrastructure of multiple CPUs that is distributed over a local or wide area network and appears to an end user as one large computing resource. In general, there is no central control assumed in a computational grid, and the end-user may or may not directly control the computing resources in the grid. Examples of government-sponsored computational grids include the National Science Foundation's TeraGrid, NASA's Information Power Grid, and the Department of Energy's Science Grid. Open-source software packages like the Globus Toolkit are available to give the end-user a programming environment that uses a large computational grid. Commercial vendors are also rapidly entering the grid-computing scene with software packages that enable businesses to run their applications over private-sector computational grids.

In one model of grid computing, thousands of widely separated PCs or work-stations are connected via the Internet. The idle cycles of the processors forming this dynamically changing collection are captured and used to process data in a purely asynchronous fashion. An example of the use of this model of grid computing is the Searching for Extraterrestrial Intelligence (SETI) project, which captures the idle cycles of thousands of processors to analyze radio telescope data looking for signs of intelligent life in the universe. A contrasting model of grid computing consists of a set of homogeneous processors making up what is known as a *Beowulf cluster*, typically rack-mounted in a single physical location and connected by gigabit Ethernet or more specialized network systems such as *myrinet* (see Figure 18.1). As opposed to projects like the SETI project, in which standalone processors are available only when idle, processors in a Beowulf cluster are solely dedicated to working on problems hosted by the cluster.

FIGURE 18.1

Beowulf clusters in the Laboratory for Integrated Networked Computing (LINC) at the University of Cincinnati.

In this chapter, we introduce distributed algorithms by focusing on the special case of processors communicating with one another using message passing. The message-passing paradigm captures most of the relevant issues in the theory of distributed algorithms, at least from a high-level perspective. A communication step (sending or receiving a message) between processors is assumed to be far more time consuming than a computational step performed locally by a processor. Hence, as with our study of parallel algorithms on interconnection network models, we must consider communication complexity when analyzing the performance of a distributed algorithm. Moreover, it is now more difficult to measure communication complexity because the communication step in the message-passing environment might not include tight synchronization between the sending and receiving of a message. In any case, the following key fact always holds.

Good speedup in the distributed algorithm environment invariably requires computation steps to dominate communication steps.

In contrast to our treatment of parallel algorithms, we now assume that the input to our algorithm also includes the number of processors p, where p is independent of the input size n to the problem. Making the number of processors independent of the input size reflects today's commonly encountered application domain, where an algorithm is implemented on a Beowulf cluster using the Message Passing Interface (MPI) library of functions (see Appendix F). The MPI environment specifically requires the programmer to specify at the command line, the number of processes the program will use. It is possible to have a processor run more than one process, so we typically use the term *process* instead of *processor* in the remainder of this chapter. In fact, you can run an MPI job using $p > 1$ processes on a single processor, but, of course, no actual parallelism is then present. However, running on a single processor can be useful for debugging and testing, or for instructional purposes in environments where a multiple-processor cluster is not available.

18.1   SPMD Distributed-Computing Model

Of the many distributed-computing models we could consider, we focus our attention on a model that is somewhat complementary to the SIMD model of parallel computation. In particular, we do not assume that processes are executing instructions in a tightly synchronized lock-step fashion under the guidance of a central control process. We concentrate on distributed algorithms that are suitable for implementation on a network of possibly heterogeneous processes, typically executing asynchronously, and communicating with one another by message passing. With distributed algorithms, some synchronization might be required, but it must be explicitly implemented algorithmically, in contrast with the SIMD parallel model, in which tight synchronization is largely a consequence of the way single instructions are sent to all the processes by central control. In fact, we assume a *single-program, multiple-data* (SPMD) model of distributed computation, in which each process has a copy of the entire code to be executed.

Reflecting the SPMD model, our pseudocode for distributed algorithms looks just like sequential code, except we use some built-in functions to support message passing. (Our pseudocode resembles MPI code, and each of our pseudocode functions has a closely related MPI function.) However, each process has a unique ID, and parallelism is achieved by program logic that uses these IDs. Not only do the IDs allow processes to communicate with one another, but also each process ID can be used in the program to enable the process to execute a given block of code (or not) in a manner dependent on the ID. In our pseudocode, we assume that each process can determine its ID by calling the built-in function **myid**. Typically, the value of **myid** is assigned to the variable *myrank*, because MPI refers to process IDs as *ranks*.

Of course, as in the SIMD model, each process has its assigned portion of data from the input to the problem. With its large case construction, the SPMD model allows each process to execute entirely different code; however, in most of our examples, all processes execute identical code on their individual data portions (but not necessarily synchronously). The important exception is the *master-worker* scenario, in which one process is singled out as the master, executing code that supervises and coordinates the action of the other processes, called workers. Typically, all workers execute identical code (but on their local versions of the data, of course). Other common names for the master-worker model are *manager-worker*, *supervisor-worker*, and *master-slave*. Although the code is identical for each worker, workers usually execute their code relatively independently of one another, in a largely asynchronous manner.

18.2   Message Passing

We assume that the processes in our distributed computing model communicate with one another by message passing. Thus, the basic communication functions are **send** and **receive,** with appropriate parameter lists for identifying sender and receiver as well as the data to be transmitted. Actually, our **send** function has two variants, **Ssend** and **Bsend**. When message passing is synchronous (nonbuffered and blocking), a process executes an **Ssend** instruction, and further execution of its code is blocked until the corresponding **receive** has been acknowledged. On the other hand, when message passing is asynchronous (buffered and nonblocking), a process executes a **Bsend** instruction, and the message is stored in a buffer; the process is not blocked and can continue executing its code. The actions of **Ssend** and **Bsend** are further explained in subsections 18.2.1 and 18.2.5, respectively. In this section, we simply use **send** to denote both variants. For our purposes, and to keep things simple, we only use a blocking **receive** instruction, although MPI has a nonblocking version as well.

Assume that we have p processes with IDs $0, 1, \ldots, p - 1$ (thus, the processes $P_0, P_1, \ldots, P_{p-1}$ are indexed by their IDs in our discussions). We start the indexing with zero, in accordance with the MPI standard method of assigning ranks to processes. Recall that we assume that each process can determine its ID by invoking the **myid** built-in function. Our distributed pseudocode for (both variants of) the **send** instruction are of the form

   send(*data, dest, tag*)

where the parameter *data* is the data to be sent (which can be an array or a more complicated data structure), process P_{dest} is the destination (target) of the message, and *tag* contains information that may be used for such things as providing additional criteria for determining a match by a receive instruction, or to provide information on the action that should be taken on receiving the message. Although *tag* is always included in the parameter list of the **send** instruction, it might not contain any useful information, in which case it can be ignored by the receiving process.

Pseudocode for the **receive** instruction has the form

   receive(*data, src, tag, status*)

where the parameter *src* refers to the (source) process P_{src}, which should at some point issue a **send** instruction to match the **receive** instruction. The special wildcard variable ANY_SOURCE can be used as the second parameter, which (assuming the values of the *tag* parameters match) allows a **receive** instruction to match a **send** from any process (wildcards are not allowed in the **send** instruction). The third parameter *tag* plays a similar role to the *tag* parameter in the **send** instruction. Similar to ANY_SOURCE, a special wildcard variable ANY_TAG can be used for the *tag* parameter of the **receive** instruction to match the *tag* parameter of any **send** message. The last parameter is *status*, which is an output parameter pointing to a structure that contains two fields, *source* and *tag*. Then *status→source* is the ID of the process that was the source of the message received, and *status→tag* is the parameter *tag* of the message sent by the source process. The following key fact summarizes the matching situation between **send** and **receive** instructions when specific processes are used for the parameters *src* or *tag* in the **receive** instruction (as opposed to using ANY_SOURCE or ANY_TAG).

Key Fact

If a specific value *src* is used as the second parameter in a receive instruction, then a send message will not match this receive unless it comes from the process whose ID is *src*. In particular, the value *status→source* given by the fourth parameter *status* gives no additional information, because it will have the value *src* if the message is matched and received. Similarly, if a specific value *tag* is used as the third parameter in a receive instruction, then a send message will not match this receive unless the value of its parameter *tag* matches the value *tag* of the receive instruction. In particular, the value *status→tag* given by the fourth parameter *status* provides no additional information because it has the same value as *tag* of the source send message if the message is matched and received.

Although our pseudocode is consistent with the corresponding send and receive commands of the MPI library (C version)—MPI_Ssend, MPI_Bsend, and MPI_Recv—we simplified it to highlight the important high-level concepts. For example, MPI_Ssend has six parameters and MPI_Recv has seven. The translation from our pseudocode to MPI code is straightforward (see Appendix F). Each process can send a message directly to any other process without the need to worry about routing. In this sense, our distributed model is analogous to an interconnection network modeled on a complete graph. However, we need to consider certain issues of synchronization, and even the dreaded deadlock scenario discussed later is possible. Thus, we must go into some detail on the protocol of our **send** and **receive** functions and their variants.

18.2.1 Synchronous (Blocking) Message Passing

We will assume that our **Ssend** instruction is what is known as a *synchronous* or *blocking* send, which does not return until the matching **receive** instruction has actually received the corresponding message. In other words, code execution cannot proceed to the next instruction following an **Ssend** until the data has actually been received by the matching **receive**. Similarly, our **receive** instruction is blocking in the sense that it does not return until the message corresponding to the matching **send** has actually been received. Thus, these functions enforce highly synchronous message passing. More precisely, when an **Ssend** is executed, the target process is notified that it has a pending message. This "posting" of a pending message is done in the background and does not interrupt the execution sequence of the target process. If the posting of an **Ssend** message occurs before the matching **receive** is encountered by the target process, the source process must block (suspend) execution until the matching **receive** is executed by the target. When executing a **receive**, the target process checks to see if a matching **Ssend** has been posted. If not, the target must block (suspend) its execution sequence until such a posting has been made. Given such a posting, the target then acknowledges the posting to the source, and the source process then transfers the message to the target. This synchronization is illustrated in Figure 18.2, which shows how **Ssend** and **receive** functions must suspend their respective execution sequences until the message passing has been completed.

FIGURE 18.2

Synchronization of **Ssend** and **receive** functions.

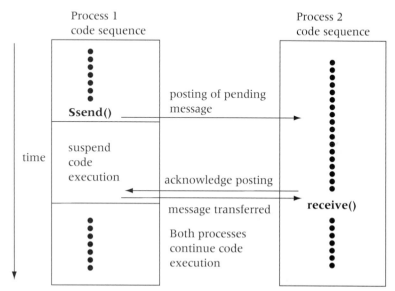

Source suspends when **Ssend()** occurs before matching **receive()** occurs

(a)

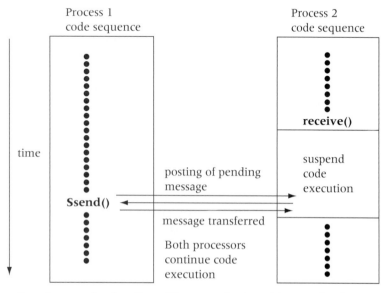

Target suspends when **Ssend()** occurs after matching **receive()** occurs

(b)

Actually, there may be several pending messages posted when a **receive** occurs. We assume that a posting list is maintained by the system, and this list is scanned by the system for a matching **send**. In case the parameter ANY_SOURCE is used by the **receive** function, the message corresponding to the first item in the posting list is received. Messages between two given processes are posted in the same order they are sent. However, for the messages posted from multiple processes, the order can be arbitrary.

18.2.2 Avoiding Deadlock

Because of the strict synchronization imposed by **Ssend** and **receive**, we must take care to avoid deadlock. For example, consider the following code sequence:

Process P_1 Process P_2
receive(z, 2, tag, status)   **receive**(w, 1, tag, status)
Ssend(x, 2, tag)   **Ssend**(y, 1, tag)

This is a deadlock situation because process P_1 waits for a matching **Ssend** from process P_2, and P_2 waits for a matching **Ssend** from P_1.

Similarly, the following code sequence also produces deadlock:

Process P_1 Process P_2
Ssend(x, 2, tag)   **Ssend**(y, 1, tag)
receive(z, 2, tag, status)   **receive**(w, 1, tag, status)

The obvious way to avoid this deadlock is to alternate the **Ssend** and **receive** between the two processes, as shown in the following code sequence:

Process P_1 Process P_2
Ssend(x, 2, tag)   **receive**(w, 1, tag, status)
receive(z, 2, tag,status)   **Ssend**(y, 1, tag)

This alternation between **Ssend** and **receive** is illustrated in the distributed-algorithm version of the even-odd transposition sort discussed in Section 18.3.

Key Fact

One way to avoid deadlock is to ensure the proper send-receive alternation. Another way is to use nonblocking versions of send and receive.

18.2.3 Compare-Exchange Operations

The comparison-based sequential and parallel algorithms that we have considered were all based on making comparisons between a pair of list elements and interchanging them if they were out of order. We now consider this same operation in the message-passing environment. The following pseudocode for *CompareExchange* compares data items a and b in processes P_i and P_j, respectively, and interchanges their values if $a > b$. Note that process P_i gets the smaller of the two values a and b, and P_j gets the larger.

```
procedure CompareExchange(a, b, i, j)
Model: message-passing distributed network
Input:     a, b (data elements in processes P_i and P_j, respectively)
Output:    a in process i gets the smaller of a and b, and b in process j gets the larger
    if myid = i then
        Ssend(a, j, tag)
        receive(temp, j, tag, status)        //store b in temp
        if a > temp then a ← temp endif
    endif
    if myid = j then
        receive(temp, i, tag, status)        //store a in temp
        Ssend(b, i, tag)
        if temp > b then b ← temp endif
    endif
end CompareExchange
```

In the pseudocode for *CompareExchange,* it is possible (and even likely for sorting algorithms) that the compare-exchange operation is actually between variables of the same local name a. In that case, we simplify the notation and write *CompareExchange*(a, i, j) instead of the more precise *CompareExchange*(a, a, i, j).

In our treatment of parallel sorting algorithms, we assumed that the number of processes grew with the input size. For example, for the even-odd transposition sort, we assumed that we had $p(n) = n$ processes. In the message-passing environment, recall that we focus on the more practical model, where we assume a fixed number p of processes independent of n. Thus, when considering message-passing versions of algorithms such as the even-odd transposition sort, it becomes a question of how we adapt the algorithm to the fixed number of processes. Certainly, the straightforward division-of-labor technique, where a single process simulates the work done by $m = n/p$ processes, is not very natural and requires very cumbersome code. A better way is to replace the compare-exchange operation between a pair of elements by a *compare-split* operation, where two sorted arrays, each of size m, in processes P_i and P_j are split in such a way that P_i gets the smallest m elements and P_j gets the largest m elements, and where each of the two split arrays is sorted. The following procedure, *Compare-Split,* accomplishes this operation and is the basis for adapting compare-exchange parallel algorithms to the message-passing environment with a fixed number p of processes. Again, since we are interested in using *CompareSplit* in sorting algorithms, we write a version that assumes that the sorted array is $a[0{:}m - 1]$ in both processes P_i and P_j. The version where the arrays are $a[0{:}m - 1]$ and $b[0{:}m - 1]$, respectively, is left as an exercise.

```
procedure CompareSplit(a[0:m − 1], i, j)
Model: message-passing distributed network
Input:    a[0:m − 1] (sorted arrays in processes Pᵢ and Pⱼ)
Output:   a[0:m − 1] is sorted in both processes, with Pᵢ's a[0:m − 1] getting the m
          smallest elements from both arrays, and Pⱼ's a[0:m − 1] getting the m largest
          elements
    if myid = i then
        Ssend(a[0:m − 1], j, tag)
        receive(tempa[0:m − 1], j, tag, status)  //receive Pⱼ's a[0:m − 1] in
                                                         tempa[0:m − 1]
        for k ← 0 to m − 1 do              //store copy of Pᵢ's a[0:m − 1] in
                                                  tempa[0:m − 1]

            temp[k] ← a[k]
        endfor
                                          // Pᵢ's a[0:m − 1] gets the m smallest
                                             elements

        q ← r ← 0
        for k ← 0 to m − 1 do
            if temp[q] ≤ tempa[r] then
                a[k] ← temp[q]
                q ← q + 1
            else
                a[k] ← tempa[r]
                r ← r + 1
            endif
        endfor
    endif
    if myid = j then
        receive(tempa[0:m − 1], i, tag, status)  //receive Pᵢ's a[0:m − 1] in
                                                         tempa[0:m − 1]
        Ssend(a[0:m − 1], i, tag)
        for k ← 0 to m − 1 do              //store copy of Pⱼ's a[0:m − 1] in
                                                  temp[0:m − 1]

            temp[k] ← a[k]
        endfor
```

// P'_j's $a[0{:}m-1]$ gets the m largest
elements

$q \leftarrow r \leftarrow m - 1$
for $k \leftarrow m - 1$ to 0 by -1 do
    if $temp[q] \geq tempa[r]$ then
        $a[k] \leftarrow temp[q]$
        $q \leftarrow q - 1$
    else
        $a[k] \leftarrow tempa[r]$
        $r \leftarrow r - 1$
    endif
  endfor
endif
end *CompareSplit*

Verifying the correctness of *CompareSplit* is straightforward and left as an exercise. Note that each of the processors P_i and P_j used by *CompareSplit* performs m list comparisons.

In sorting algorithms, a list of size n is typically stored in the array $a[0{:} n/p - 1]$ in each of the processes $P_0, P_1, \ldots, P_{p-1}$, where for convenience we will always assume that p divides n. When adapting an algorithm such as the even-odd transposition sort to p processes, we replace the compare-exchange steps by compare-split steps; otherwise, the adapted algorithm works essentially identically to the original.

18.2.4 Broadcast, Scatter, and Gather

In this subsection, we describe our built-in procedures for globally distributing data from one process to all the other processes, or gathering data from each process into a single process. These global operations are synchronous, meaning that all the processes must reach and execute the global operation before any of them can proceed to instructions following the global operation. For communication complexity purposes, we assume that each of our global built-in procedures takes a single communication step.

Broadcast. Often in a distributed algorithm it is necessary to broadcast data from one process to all the other processes. We assume a built-in function **broadcast**(a,i) for this task, where a is the data in process P_i to be broadcast. For simplicity, we assume that a is replicated to the local variable a in each process, as opposed to another variable b. We show the result of the **broadcast** operation in Figure 18.3, where we broadcast from P_0.

Each process must execute the **broadcast** instruction before any of the processes can continue; thus, **broadcast** enforces synchronization among the

FIGURE 18.3

Action of
broadcast(a,0).

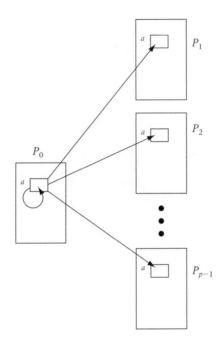

processes. In other words, each process must halt further execution until all the processes have encountered and executed the **broadcast** instruction. Of course, sometimes synchronization is not desirable, in which case we must explicitly code a **broadcast** instruction (see Section 18.5).

Scatter. The built-in **scatter** operation is similar to **broadcast**, except that each process gets a separate piece of the data. For example, in a sorting algorithm, we will typically assume that a list $L[0:n - 1]$ of size n is a local variable in the memory of process P_0, and process P_0 distributes (scatters) n/p elements of the list to each process. More precisely, process P_i receives the sublist $L[in/p: (i + 1)n/p - 1]$, $i = 0, 1, \ldots, p - 1$. We use the notation **scatter**($a[0:n - 1], b[0:n/p - 1], i$) for scattering the array $a[0:n - 1]$ throughout the processes and received by the array $b[0:n/p - 1]$ in each process. We show the result of the **scatter** operation in Figure 18.4, where we scatter from P_0.

Again, each process must execute the **scatter** instruction before any of the processes can continue.

Gather. The gather operation is basically the reverse operation of **scatter**, where now data in the local arrays $b[0:m - 1]$ in each process is gathered into a local array $a[0:pm - 1]$ in the memory of a single process P_i. More precisely, in the **gather**($b[0:m - 1], a[0:pm - 1], i$) operation, the subarray $a[mj: m(j + 1) - 1]$ of P_i receives the array $b[0:m - 1]$ from process P_j, $j = 0, 1, \ldots, p - 1$. We show the result of the **gather** operation in Figure 18.5, where we gather at P_0.

FIGURE 18.4

Action of
scatter(a[0:n − 1],
b[0:n/p − 1], 0).

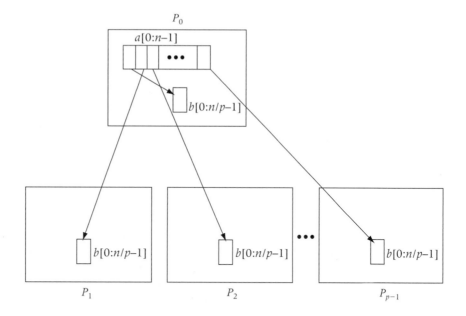

FIGURE 18.5

Action of
gather(b[0:m − 1],
a[0:pm − 1], 0).

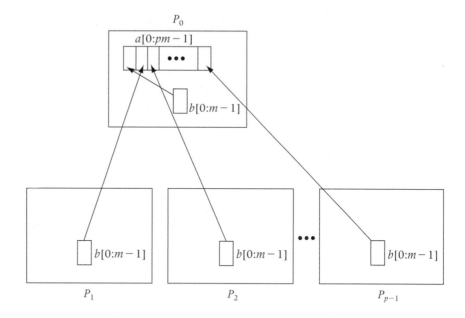

Once again, each process must execute the **gather** instruction before any of
the processes can continue. For example, after a sorting algorithm has sorted a
list of size n by splitting the list into sorted sublists of size n/p stored in each
process P_j, $j = 0, 1, \ldots, p − 1$, the sorted sublist might be gathered at process P_0
into a single sorted list. We illustrate this in Section 18.3, where the even-odd

transposition sort is implemented in a distributed network of processes communicating by message passing.

18.2.5 Asynchronous (Nonblocking) Message Passing

Blocking **send** and **receive** functions impose synchronization constraints that are not desirable in the case where the processes should be free to perform calculations in a highly asynchronous manner. For example, in the master-worker model discussed earlier, it might be quite desirable to allow a worker's processes to alternate between computation and communication phases without having to tightly synchronize their code with that of other workers.

To accomplish this alternation between communication and computation phases, we introduce two built-in functions, **Bsend** and **probe**. As mentioned earlier, the "B" in **Bsend** stands for "buffered," and the function corresponds to the MPI function MPI_Bsend. When a source process executes a **Bsend**, the message is placed in the source's *message buffer*, and the target process for the message receives a posting for the message, which is placed in the target's *posting list*. The posting identifies the source process so that when the posting is read, the target knows from which process message buffer to receive (retrieve) the message. The message is removed from the source's message buffer when the target receives it. Immediately after placing the message in the message buffer, **Bsend** returns and the source process can resume execution of the statement following the **Bsend** statement. We assume that this is "safe," in the sense that data sent in the **Bsend** operation can be altered before the message is received, because the corresponding message has been buffered.

From the target's point of view, a process can then check to see if it has any pending messages posted by executing the **probe** function, which returns the Boolean value **.true.** if the posting list contains a matching **send**, and **.false.** otherwise. The **probe** function has two parameters, *src* and *tag*, where *src* is the source process, and *tag* has the same meaning as in **send** and **receive**. Usually in this context *src* has the value ANY_SOURCE. This process is illustrated in Figure 18.6, which illustrates the outcome of executing a **probe** when a matching **Bsend** has been posted before the matching **receive** occurs. Figure 18.6 shows that **probe** is a nonblocking function (thus, it mirrors the MPI function MPI_Iprobe as opposed to the blocking MPI_Probe). Consequently, when the matching **receive** occurs before the corresponding **Bsend**, execution does not suspend until the **Bsend** is executed. We would expect that the execution would eventually loop back to the **probe** statement to receive the matching message. To illustrate how all available messages could be read before continuing further, Figure 18.6 shows the matching **receive** inside a **while** loop (which would itself be inside a loop for the reason just stated), as this is a common occurrence.

FIGURE 18.6

Action of **Bsend**.

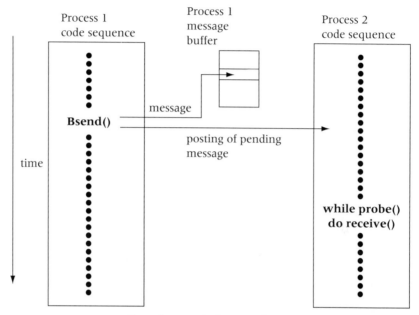

Process 1
code sequence

Process 1
message
buffer

Process 2
code sequence

Bsend()

message

posting of pending
message

while probe()
do receive()

time

Bsend occurs before matching **receive()**
(a)

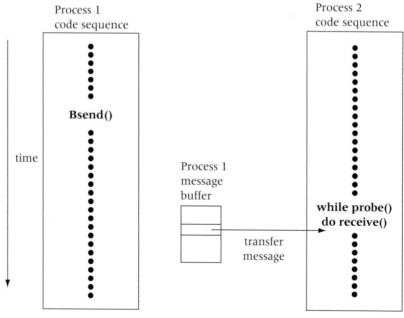

Process 1
code sequence

Process 2
code sequence

Bsend()

time

Process 1
message
buffer

while probe()
do receive()

transfer
message

Action of matching **receive()**
(b)

18.2.6 Computation/Communication Alternation

Bsend and **probe** support a distributed computing paradigm, where processes are assigned tasks and alternate between computation and communication phases. More precisely, after a process has completed a computation phase where a fixed amount of work (depending on problem parameters) is done, it can enter a **while probe do** loop to receive all its pending messages (note that new messages might be posted during the execution of this loop). The process can take appropriate action based on these messages before entering another computation phase. Moreover, when a process has completed its assigned task and becomes idle, it can then be given a new task, which might be a subtask assigned to another process (see Figure 18.7). In this way, good load balancing can possibly be achieved between communication and computation phases as well as for the distribution of the workload among processes. The flowchart in Figure 18.7 illustrates a generic alternating computation/communication cycle

FIGURE 18.7

Alternating computation/communication cycle performed by a process.

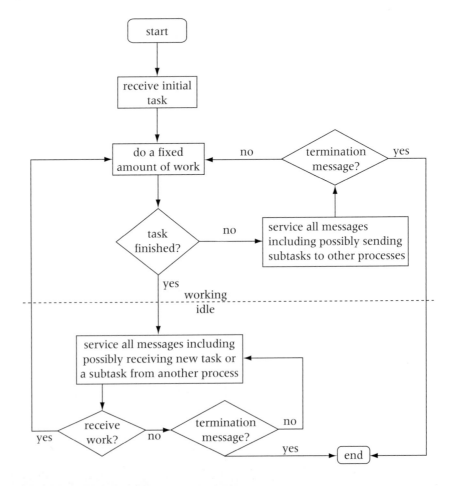

performed by a process. We have divided the flowchart into working and idle phases, where we consider a process working when it has not completed its computation task. Of course, as indicated in the figure, an "idle" process still participates in communication steps, such as broadcasting the best solution to an optimization problem found so far or a termination message.

The question remains how to implement the computation/communication cycle, including the execution of a termination condition by all processes. One method is to apply the master-worker paradigm discussed in Section 18.4 to a distributed depth-first search (backtracking), as discussed in Section 18.6.

18.3 Distributed Even-Odd Transposition Sort

The distributed even-odd transposition sort *EvenOddSort* illustrates the use of *CompareSplit* and **scatter** and **gather** instructions as well as the adaption of a parallel algorithm using n processes to a distributed message-passing algorithm using p processes. After scattering an input list $L[0{:}n - 1]$ in process P_0 to the processes P_0, $P_1, \dots, P_{p-1}$, *EvenOddSort* sorts each of the scattered sublists using an optimal sequential sorting algorithm (we have chosen *MergeSort*). Then p parallel compare-split steps are performed on the sublists: In an odd step, processes P_i and P_{i+1} participate in the compare-split step, $i = 1, 3, \dots$, and in an even step, $i = 0, 2, \dots$. In the final step, the sorted sublists are gathered back to process P_0.

```
procedure EvenOddSort(L[0:n − 1])
Model: message-passing distributed network of p processes
Input:    L[0:n − 1] (array in process P₀)
Output:   L[0:n − 1] is sorted in increasing order
    m ← n/p
    myrank ← myid
    scatter(L[0:n − 1], a[0:m − 1], 0)
    MergeSort(a[0:m − 1], 1, m)
    for k ← 0 to p − 1 do
        if even(k + myrank) then
            if myrank < p − 1 then
                CompareSplit(a[0:m − 1], myrank, myrank + 1)
            endif
        else            //odd(k + myrank)
            if myrank > 0 then
                CompareSplit(a[0:m − 1], myrank, myrank + 1)
            endif
        endif
    endfor
    gather(a[0:m − 1], L[0:n − 1], 0)
end EvenOddSort
```

The correctness of *EvenOddSort* follows from the correctness of *EvenOddSort1DMesh* (see Chapter 15) and is left as an exercise. Considering the complexity of *EvenOddSort*, note that the computational complexity of the call to *MergeSort* is in $\Theta((n/p)(\log n/p))$, and the computational complexity of the p parallel calls to *CompareSplit* is in $\Theta(n)$. Thus, for p small compared to n, we basically achieve the optimal speedup of p as well as the optimal cost. Because the communication complexity of *EvenOddSort* is in $\Theta(p)$, the sort is only attractive when p is small compared with n.

18.4 Embarrassingly Parallel Master-Worker Paradigm

As mentioned earlier, in the master-worker paradigm, one of the processes is designated as the master to coordinate the execution of a distributed algorithm by farming out tasks to the other processes, called workers. Also referred to as the *work pool* or *processor farm* approach, the master-worker paradigm has the following general code skeleton:

```
if myid = 0 then
        execute master code
else
        execute worker code
endif
```

In this section, we discuss the embarrassingly parallel master-worker paradigm, in which workers finish tasks completely independently of one another. In Section 18.6, we discuss the more complicated version, where workers cooperate in solving tasks by splitting their task with workers that become idle.

18.4.1 Embarrassingly Parallel Master-Worker Code Skeleton

In the embarrassingly parallel situation, the workers accept tasks sent by the master, execute the tasks, return the results to the master, accept further tasks, and so forth, until all tasks have been completed. There is no worker-to-worker communication, and each worker executes its code independently of the other workers, without any need to synchronize its computations with the other workers. When all tasks are completed, the master broadcasts a message indicating termination (thereby allowing for a graceful exit for all processes). Figure 18.8 depicts this version of the embarrassingly parallel master-worker paradigm.

The embarrassingly parallel master-worker pseudocode skeleton is as follows, where we use the blocking form of **send** and assume that we have n tasks, $task_1, \ldots, task_n$, and $p < n$ processes.

FIGURE 18.8

Embarrassingly
parallel master-
worker paradigm.

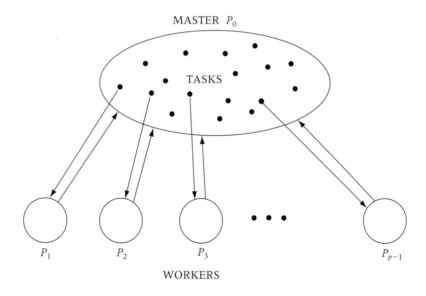

Master

for $i \leftarrow 1$ **to** $p - 1$ **do**
    Ssend($task_i$, i, tag)   //$task_i$ is a **null** task in the event that
                                                     there are more workers (processes)
                                                     than tasks

endfor
$numsent \leftarrow \min\{n, p - 1\}$ //number of tasks sent
$numrec \leftarrow 0$ //number of completed tasks received
while $numrec < n$ **do**
    receive($result$, ANY_SOURCE, tag, $status$)
    $SourceWorker \leftarrow status \rightarrow source$
    $numrec \leftarrow numrec + 1$
    if $numsent < n$ **then**
        $numsent \leftarrow numsent + 1$
        Ssend($task_{numsent}$, $SourceWorker$, tag) //send the next task back to the worker
                                               from whom the result was just received
    else
        Ssend($nulltask$, $SourceWorker$, tag)   //send the null task back to worker
    endif
endwhile
broadcast($termination$, 0)

Worker

```
receive(task, 0, tag, status)                    //receive a task from the master
while task ≠ nulltask do
    result ← CompleteTask(task)
    Ssend(result, 0, tag)                        //send result to master
    receive(task, 0, tag, status)                //receive a task from the master
endwhile
broadcast(termination, 0)
```

In our master code skeleton , sending the *nulltask* when there are no more tasks to be completed allows for synchronization of the **Ssend** and **receive** functions. The exact nature of the *nulltask* is problem dependent.

18.4.2 Matrix Multiplication

We illustrate the implementation of the embarrassingly parallel master-worker code skeleton with an algorithm for computing the product AB of two n-by-n matrices. We assume that process P_0, the master, originally holds A and B and broadcasts A to all of the other processes, the workers. Then the n columns B_i, $i = 0, 1, \ldots, n - 1$ of the matrix B are sent one at a time to the workers. When a worker receives a column B_i, it computes the matrix product AB_i, and returns the result to P_0. When P_0 receives a column-vector product from a worker, it sends the worker the next remaining column B_i (if any). The algorithm terminates after all the products AB_i are returned, $i = 0, 1, \ldots, n - 1$. We use the *tag* parameter to keep track of which column is being sent and received. When a worker receives a message from the master having $tag = n$, it knows that there is no more work to be done. The procedure *MatrixVectorProduct* called by each worker is the sequential algorithm for computing a matrix-vector product based directly on the definition. Also, the sequential procedure *GetColumn* called by each worker has the obvious meaning. The matrix $Null[0{:}n - 1]$ used in the algorithm can be filled with arbitrary values because it is only sent with $tag = n$, which is enough information for the receiving worker to know that it needs to take no further action. Of course, the worker could also check for the null matrix, but we wish to design the code to model the general code skeleton as closely as possible.

```
procedure MatrixProduct(A[0:n − 1, 0:n − 1], B[0:n − 1, 0:n − 1], C[0:n − 1, 0:n − 1])
Model:    message-passing distributed network of p processes
Input:    A[0:n − 1, 0:n − 1], B[0:n − 1, 0:n − 1] (n-by-n matrices of numbers in
          process P0)
Output:   C[0:n − 1, 0:n − 1] (the matrix product C = AB)
```

```
        broadcast(A[0:n − 1, 0:n − 1], 0)              //master broadcasts A to all workers
        if myid = 0 then                                //execute master code
            for i ← 1 to p − 1 do
                if i ≤ n then
                    Ssend(GetColumn(B[0:n − 1, 0:n − 1], i − 1), i, i − 1)
                                                        //send Pᵢ the iᵗʰ column of B
                else
                    Ssend(Null[0:n − 1], i, n)          //send Pᵢ a null vector
                endif
            endfor
            numsent ← min{n, p − 1}                     //a counter for the number of
                                                            columns sent

            numrec ← 0                                  //a counter for the number of matrix-
                                                            vector products received by the
                                                            master

            while numrec < n do
                receive(Column[0:n − 1], ANY_SOURCE, ANY_TAG, status)
                Col ← status→tag
                SourceWorker ← status→tag
                for i ← 0 to n − 1 do
                    C[i, Col] ← Column[i]
                endfor
                numrec ← numrec + 1
                if numsent < n then
                    numsent ← numsent + 1
                    Ssend(GetColumn(B[0:n − 1, 0:n − 1], numsent − 1), SourceWorker,
                    numsent − 1)
                                                        //send P_SourceWorker the column of B in
                                                            position numsent − 1

                else
                    Ssend(Null[0:n − 1], SourceWorker, n)
                endif
            endwhile
        else                                            //that is, myid ≠ 0, so execute
                                                            worker code
            receive(Column[0:n − 1], 0, ANY_TAG, status)
            Col ← status→tag
            while Col < n do
                Ssend(MatrixVectorProduct(A[0:n − 1, 0:n − 1], Column[0:n − 1]), 0, Col)
                receive(Column[0:n − 1], 0, ANY_TAG, status)
                Col ← status→tag
            endwhile
        endif
    end MatrixProduct
```

The straightforward sequential algorithm for multiplying two n-by-n matrices based directly on the definition of matrix multiplication performs n^3 multiplications. The distributed algorithm *MatrixProduct* performs $(n/(p - 1))n^2$ parallel multiplications (assuming $p < n$), thus achieving nearly optimal speedup over the straightforward sequential algorithm. Note that *MatrixProduct* performs $\max\{n, p - 1\}$ communication steps, so for large n (p fixed), the (cubic) computation complexity dominates the (linear) communication complexity.

By sending workers one column at a time, *MatrixProduct* has been designed to achieve good load balancing in a heterogeneous environment where the processing speed of the processes might vary considerably. However, when the processes are about equal in processing speed, an altered version—in which the columns of the matrix B are partitioned into n/p blocks and the master and each worker compute the corresponding block of columns of AB—would probably be preferred because the communication steps would be reduced from $\max\{n, p - 1\}$ to $p - 1$. The number of multiplications performed would be the same for both versions. We leave the pseudocode of the altered version as an exercise.

18.5 Shared-Task Master-Worker Paradigm

In the *shared-task* master-worker paradigm, after completing a task, a given worker might help another worker complete its assigned task. Moreover, in many problems such as searching a state-space tree, efficiency results from sharing information among the processes, such as the value of the best solution to an optimization problem found so far. During the execution of a distributed algorithm in this more complicated version, workers alternate between communication and computation phases, allowing the possibility of load balancing between these two phases to increase efficiency. The shared-task paradigm is illustrated in Figure 18.9.

Nonblocking buffered **send** and **receive** functions are required to enable workers to alternate between computation and communication phases. The master keeps track of the status of each worker by maintaining a state vector with an entry for each worker. Synchronization issues become critical in this paradigm. We assume that a worker can be in one of four states: *idle* (I), *working* (W), *refused helper* (R), or *sent as helper* (S).

After receiving an initial task from the master, each worker is in the working state W. When a worker A has finished its task, it sends a message to the master, which updates A's state to I. If there are unsent tasks remaining, the master sends one such task to worker A. If there are no unsent tasks remaining, the master selects a worker B that is in the working state (how B is chosen is problem dependent) and sends the worker a "help available" message indicating that a worker is available to help with B's task. The master then sets the status of A to S. When B reads such a "help available" message, it can either accept or reject help based

FIGURE 18.9

Shared-task master-
worker paradigm.

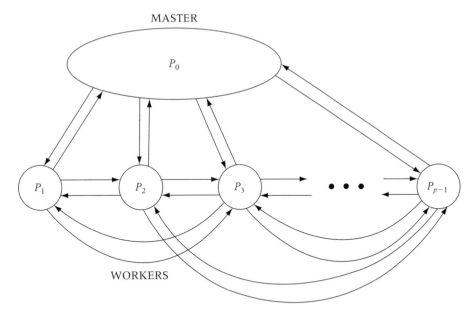

on several criteria. For example, B may refuse a helper because it does not have
sufficient work left to warrant splitting the task. In this case, B sends a message
back to the master refusing help, and the master updates the state of B to R to reflect this refusal, unless in the meantime B's state changes to I or S. The master
does not send any further helpers to B until B's state is updated to W.

If A's help is refused by B, then the master tries to send A as a helper to another
worker until A's help is either accepted or no processes are in state W. Finally, if B
accepts A's help, then B splits its task with A in some manner dependent on the
problem. We assume that the "help available" message contains the process ID of
A, so that B can send a message to A containing that portion of B's task that will be
now be A's responsibility. After receiving the latter message, A sends a message to
the master indicating it is working again, so A's status is updated to W. If no worker
accepts A's help, then A's state remains I. When the master determines that all
workers are idle, the program can be terminated.

To facilitate reactivation of idle processes, if worker A sends a message that it
is working again, then the master should check for idle workers and if found,
send one to help A. Note how this immediate sending of a helper to A has the
subsequent effect of cascading the reactivation of idle processes.

18.5.1 Generic Shared-Task Master-Worker Code Skeleton

We now describe the high-level pseudocode for our model of the shared-task
master-worker paradigm. In this model, we must explicitly design our own broadcast technique because the built-in **broadcast** function imposes a synchronization

that is incompatible with the independent alternating computation/communication cycles performed by the workers. The broadcast is initiated by the master and is sent to all the workers along an implicit broadcast tree. The master begins the broadcast by sending the message to process 1 and 2. Then, whenever a process $0 < i < p$ receives the broadcast message, it forwards it to processes $2i$ and $2i + 1$ (assuming $2i < p$ and $2i + 1 < p$). Occasionally—for example, when the master wants to broadcast the finished message—process $p - 1$ sends the message back to the master to complete the broadcast. After receiving this message, the master uses the built-in **broadcast** function to inform each process to gracefully exit. We use tags to indicate the nature of the messages. The following list summarizes the type of tags being used for the various types of messages.

Master-to-worker tags

H: informs the worker of the availability of a helper
T: sends the worker an initial task
F: tells the worker to broadcast the finished message (to worker 1 only)
U: tells worker 1 to broadcast some global information that will help the search, such as a newly found bound in an optimization problem

Worker-to-master tags:

R: rejects a helper
S: informs the master about a solution found
I: informs the master that it is idle
F: informs the master that the finished message has been received (process $p - 1$ only)
W: informs the master that it is working (again)
U: informs the master of information that might be of global use

Worker-to-worker tags:

T: sending a helper a subtask
F: tells the worker to broadcast the finished message
U: tells the worker to continue the broadcast of global information

The following high-level pseudocode for the shared-task master-worker paradigm uses these tags as well as the worker state vector described earlier. To keep the pseudocode relatively simple, we assume there are at least as many tasks as workers—that is, $p - 1 \le n$. We leave it as an exercise to explore the various ways to alter the pseudocode to allow for (and exploit) the possibility that $p - 1 > n$. We also assume that, in a nonoptimization problem, we wish to terminate if a solution is found rather than finding all solutions.

Master

Compute initial set of tasks $task_1, \ldots, task_n$
for $i \leftarrow 1$ **to** $p - 1$ **do**   //send each worker an initial task
    Bsend($task_i, i, T$)
endfor
initialize worker state vector to all Ws
SolutionFound $\leftarrow$ **.false.**
while .not. (each worker state = I **.or.** *SolutionFound*) **do**
        receive(*message*, ANY_SOURCE, ANY_TAG, *status*)
        SourceWorker $\leftarrow$ *status*→*source*
        case
           : *status*→*tag* = I: // informs the master that it is idle,
                                          change state of process
                                          SourceWorker to I
                if there are unsent initial tasks remaining **then**
                    extract next unsent initial task $task_{next}$
                    change state of process *SourceWorker* to W
                    Bsend($task_{next}$, *SourceWorker*, T)
                else
                    if some processes are in state W **then**
                        select a process *j* in state W
                        change state of process *SourceWorker* to S
                        helpermessage $\leftarrow$ *SourceWorker*
                        Bsend(*helpermessage*, *j*, H)
                    endif
                endif
           : *status*→*tag* = R: // rejects a helper
                if state of process *SourceWorker* is W **then**
                    change state of process *SourceWorker* to R
                endif
                    Helper $\leftarrow$ *message*
                if some processes are in state W **then**
                    select a process *j* in state W
                    helpermessage $\leftarrow$ *SourceWorker*
                    Bsend(*helpermessage*, *j*, H)
                else
                    change state of process *Helper* to I
                endif
           : *status*→*tag* = W: //informs the master that it is
                                              working, change state of process
                                          SourceWorker to W

```
                        if some processes are in state I then
                            select a process j in state I
                            change state of process j to S
                            helpermessage ← j
                            Bsend(helpermessage, SourceWorker, H)
                        endif
            : status→tag = S:                        //informs the master about a
                                                        solution found
                    if optimization problem and solution is better than
                        current best solution then
                        updatemessage ← message
                        Bsend(updatemessage, 1, U)      //initiate broadcast of update
                    else
                        if not an optimization problem then
                        SolutionFound ← .true.
                        break   //exit
                        endif
                    endif
            endcase
    endwhile
    Bsend(finishedmessage, 1, F)                     //initiate broadcast of finished
                                                        message
    receive(finishedmessage, p − 1 , F, status)      //broadcast of finished message
                                                        complete
    broadcast(termination, 0)
```

Worker

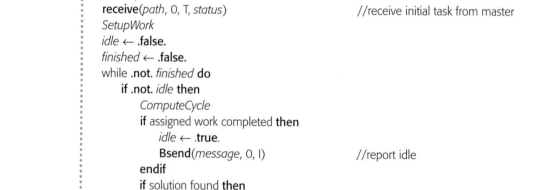

```
j ← myid
receive(path, 0, T, status)                          //receive initial task from master
SetupWork
idle ← .false.
finished ← .false.
while .not. finished do
    if .not. idle then
        ComputeCycle
        if assigned work completed then
            idle ← .true.
            Bsend(message, 0, I)                     //report idle
        endif
        if solution found then
            Bsend(solution, 0, S)                    //report solution
        endif
```

```
while (probe(ANY_SOURCE, ANY_TAG) .or. idle) .and. .not. finished do
receive(message, ANY_SOURCE, ANY_TAG, status)
case
    : status→tag = T:                         //an initial task
        SetupWork
        Bsend(workingmessage,0,W)
        idle ← .false.
    : status→tag = H:                         //helper available
        workptr ← null
        if .not. idle then
            workptr ← SplitWork               //SplitWork returns a pointer to a
                                                  subtask if help is accepted,
                                                  otherwise returns a null pointer

        endif
        if workptr ≠ null then                //helper accepted
            Helper ← process identified in helpmessage
            Embed workptr ← subtask info into subtaskmessage
            Bsend(subtaskmessage, Helper, T)
        else
            Bsend(refusemessage,0,R)     //helper refused
        endif
    : status→tag = U:                         //global information
        updatemessage ← message
        Update (updatemessage) //use global update info
            if 2 * j < p then
            Bsend(updatemessage, 2 * j, U)                //broadcast update
        endif
        if 2 * j + 1 < p then
            Bsend(updatemessage, 2 * j + 1, U)            //broadcast update
        endif
    : status→tag = F:                         //the finished message
        finished ← .true.
        if 2 * j < p then
            Bsend(finishedmessage, 2 * j, F)              //broadcast of finished
                                                              message

        endif
        if 2 * j + 1 < p then
            Bsend(finishedmessage, 2 * j + 1, F)          //broadcast of
                                                              finished message

        endif
```

```
            if j = p - 1 then
                Bsend(finishedmessage, 0, F)                    //broadcast of
                                                                  finished message

            endif
        endcase
    endwhile
endwhile
broadcast(termination, 0)
```

To adapt the pseudocode skeleton to a particular problem, we simply need to define the tasks; the functions *ComputeCycle*, *SetupWork*, *SplitWork*, and *Update*; and all the messages. In the next section, we illustrate how this is done in the case of the sum of subsets problem (optimization version).

18.6 Distributed Depth-First Search (Backtracking)

Both the embarrassingly parallel paradigm and the shared task master-worker paradigm are well suited to implementing a distributed algorithm for searching a state-space tree modeling an optimization or other search problem. Different processes simply use backtracking on different portions of the state-space tree. In this way, backtracking is combined with a form of branch-and-bound. For simplicity, we focus on problems modeled by the fixed-tuple binary state-space tree T (see Figure 10.4 in Chapter 10), but the ideas generalize naturally for more general state-space trees.

To illustrate, recall that in the case of the knapsack problem or the sum of subsets problem, given n sets $A_1, \ldots, A_n$, for a node at level i in the (static) fixed-tuple state-space tree T, a left child (labeled 1) corresponds to including A_i in the solution, whereas a right child (labeled 0) corresponds to leaving it out. As another example, for CNF satisfiability with Boolean variables $x_1, \ldots, x_n$, a left child (respectively, right child) at level i corresponds to assigning **.true.** (respectively, **.false.**) to x_i. In a dynamic state-space tree, the nodes at level i vary with the problem instance (and sometimes even vary within a level).

A dynamic tree is particularly useful in problems such as the CNF satisfiability problem, where various heuristics have been developed to determine which variable will be assigned a value next in the search. These heuristics attempt to speed up the search for a satisfying assignment (or show that none exists).

In the master-worker approach to searching a state-space tree T, each worker is assigned a different initial path (rooted at the root) in T and is responsible for searching the assigned path and the subtree rooted at the endpoint of the path. To guarantee that the entire tree T is searched (except, of course, for bounded subtrees), the master first generates an initial *covering set* of paths C,

FIGURE 18.10

The complete-tree
covering set for
$m = 6$ and $n = 32$
having six paths.

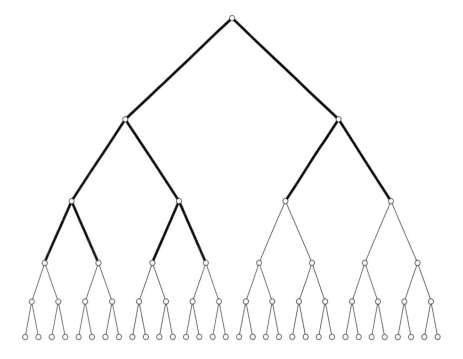

which is a set of paths such that every path in T from the root to a leaf has an initial segment consisting of a path in C. The simplest covering set, called a full-tree covering set, is the set of all 2^i paths starting at the root and ending at level i. Another simple covering set, called the complete-tree covering set, comprises the paths from the root of T to the leaves in the complete tree (see Chapter 4) on m leaves, which is the same as the previous covering set when $m = 2^i$. The example $m = 6$ is illustrated in Figure 18.10 for $n = 32$.

For simplicity, we always take our covering set to correspond to the paths in a complete tree; thus, for every path ending at a left child, the corresponding path ending at the right child sibling also belongs to the covering set.

18.6.1 Embarrassingly Parallel Backtracking

In the embarrassingly parallel version of backtracking, each path in a covering set is considered as a task, and the master simply sends out tasks in the manner illustrated in Figure 18.8. However, in optimization problems, the master can send along with the task information concerning the best solution found so far by any worker to help the worker bound the search of its current subtree.

Whether we use a complete-tree or a full-tree covering set depends on the problem. For example, if deep searches are anticipated, then one might choose the full-tree covering set so that the initial paths all end at a given level d (so that there are 2^d such paths) and where the number of processes p might be rather small compared with 2^d. In the latter case, there are slightly more initial tasks (subtrees) than processes. In practice, the choice of d would depend on p, the input size n, and perhaps some heuristics dependent on the problem. In other situations—for example, if there is some hope that solutions might be found at fairly shallow depths—a good choice would be the covering set consisting of the paths in T from the root to the leaves of the complete tree on $p - 1$ leaves, as illustrated in Figure 18.10, so that the number of initial tasks equals the number of workers.

No communication between workers is necessary in the embarrassingly parallel model. Moreover, because we are not using the alternating computation/communication cycle illustrated in Figure 18.7, there is no load balancing employed, nor have we arranged for termination as soon as possible whenever a solution is reported (for example, in CNF satisfiability or in the nonoptimization version of the sum of subsets problem). Thus, a process might continue working long after a solution has been found by another process. Although significant speedup can occur in this simplest of all versions for some inputs, we clearly need to work harder to find a version that will give us hope for good speedup on average.

One not-quite-so-embarrassing version would be to maintain the embarrassingly parallel paradigm, in which idle workers do not seek to help other workers with their tasks, but the alternating computation/communication cycle paradigm (implemented using **Bsend** and **probe**) is used at least to the extent that the master can inform a process to terminate soon after a solution has been by found by any process in a nonoptimization problem, or to inform a process of the best solution found so far soon after it is found to help bound the search in an optimization problem. The flowchart shown in Figure 18.7 still models this situation, but we would simply omit the two phrases referring to sending or receiving subtasks from other processes. Because we will be developing a more general parallel backtracking strategy, we do not give high-level pseudocode for either the embarrassingly parallel or the not-quite-so-embarrassingly parallel paradigms.

18.6.2 Shared-Task Parallel Backtracking

We now discuss adapting the shared-task master-worker pseudocode skeleton to searching a state-space tree using backtracking. The skeleton allows for covering sets in which the number of paths is greater than or equal to the number of processes (we ignore the case in which the number of paths is less than the number of processes because for problems of practical interest, we have an input size n such that $p < 2^n$). For simplicity, we assume that our covering sets are always associated with complete or full subtrees rooted at the root of the state-space tree T. The tasks in this context will be subtrees of T as determined by an initial path, together with the subtree rooted at the endpoint of the path.

The master will send each worker an initial path from the covering set, and the corresponding subtree of T will be the responsibility (task) of the worker. In particular, while searching its subtree, the worker will never backtrack past the endpoint of its initial path because that would mean encroaching on another worker's domain of responsibility. More generally, as the search continues, a worker keeps track of the point bt in its current path, which forms a *backtracking threshold* in the sense that the worker does not need to backtrack beyond bt (again, to avoid encroachment). The initial value of bt for each process is simply the endpoint of its initial path.

When a worker A accepts help from another worker B, the helper B takes responsibility for the subtree consisting of A's current path from the root to A's value of bt augmented by bt's right child x (recall that in a depth-first search, we visit the left child first, although there are exceptions to this in practice). Then B's value of bt is set to x, and A's new value of bt is computed by going to the left child of bt and then proceeding right as far as we can (see Figure 18.11).

The function *ComputeCycle* of the generic code skeleton in this context searches a given portion of the worker's assigned subtree. How much of the subtree is searched during a computation cycle can be set by the parameters needed to achieve good load balancing between computation and communication cycles, based on the particular problem. The function *SetupWork* in this context stores the initial path received as well as the value of bt. The function *SplitWork* in this context creates the message *subtaskmessage* containing the initial path to be sent to a helper and updates the worker's value of bt, as shown in Figure 18.11. We illustrate the implementation of this code in the next section for the optimization version of the sum of subsets problem discussed in Chapter 10 (where we used the variable tuple state-space tree).

18.6.3 Sum of Subsets Problem (Optimization Version)

Recall that in the sum of subsets problem, we are given a set of positive integers $a_0, a_1, \ldots, a_{n-1}$, and an integer *Sum*, and we wish to find a subset $a_{i_1}, a_{i_2}, \ldots, a_{i_m}$ such that $a_{i_1} + a_{i_2} + \cdots + a_{i_m} = Sum$. In the optimization problem, we wish to find such a subset of minimal cardinality. We store the integers $a_0, a_1, \ldots, a_{n-1}$, in an array $A[0:n-1]$ so that $A[i] = a_i, i = 0, \ldots, n-1$. A path of length m starting at the root in the state-space tree can then be represented by a subarray $X[0:m-1]$ of a 0/1 array $X[1:n]$. The subarray $X[0:m-1]$ corresponds to a characteristic vector representing a subset S of $a_0, a_1, \ldots, a_{m-1}$; that is, $a, \in S \Leftrightarrow X[i] = 1$, $i = 0, \ldots, m-1$. The sum of the elements in the subset S is then given by $A[0]*X[0] + A[1]*X[1] + \cdots + A[m-1]*X[m-1]$.

FIGURE 18.11

Splitting a path.

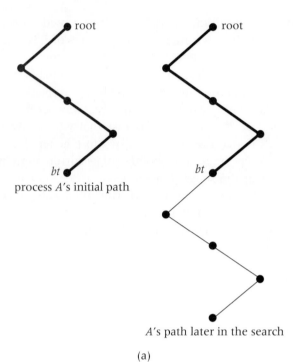

process *A*'s initial path

A's path later in the search

(a)

B's initial path sent by *A* for splitting *A*'s subtree and initial *bt* value

A's current path after accepting help from processor *B* and updated *bt* value

(b)

In the following pseudocode for the functions *SetupWork*, *SplitWork*, *ComputeCycle*, and *Update*, to keep the parameter lists reasonably short, we assume that we have the following global variables:

$A[0:n - 1]$ (an array of positive integers)
$X[0:n - 1]$ (a 0/1 array implementing paths in the state-space tree)
UB   (an upper bound for the minimum number of elements in an optimal
            solution; initially, we take $UB = n$)
btLevel   (the depth of the backtrack node *bt*, as discussed in the generic code skeleton)
k   (the current depth in the state-space tree)
Size   (the number of elements chosen = the number of 1s in current path)
rt   (the threshold for refusing help when insufficient work is left)
ComputeCycleLen (the number of nodes examined in the compute cycle)

procedure *SetupWork*$(P[0:n - 1], PathLen)$
Input: $P[0:n - 1]$ (array storing the initial path)
              PathLen (length of the initial path)
Output: Assigns appropriate values to the global variables $X[0:n - 1]$, *btLevel*, *Size*,
              and *k*
    for $i \leftarrow 0$ **to** $PathLen - 1$ **do**
        $X[i] \leftarrow P[i]$
    endfor
    $X[PathLen] \leftarrow 1$
    $btLevel \leftarrow PathLen$
    $k \leftarrow PathLen + 1$
    $Size \leftarrow 0$
    for $i \leftarrow 0$ **to** $k - 1$ **do**
        if $X[i] = 1$ **then**
            $Size \leftarrow Size + 1$
        endif
    endfor
end *SetupWork*

function *SplitWork*
Input: **global variables** *btLevel*, $X[0:n - 1]$, *rt*
Output: a pointer to a helper path $H[0:btHelperLevel - 1]$ if help accepted, a **null**
              pointer otherwise
    for $i \leftarrow 0$ **to** $btLevel - 1$ **do**
        $H[i] \leftarrow X[i]$
    endfor
    $i \leftarrow btLevel$

```
        while X[i] = 0 .and. i < k do
            H[i] ← X[i]
            i ← i + 1
        endwhile
        if n − i < rt then return(null) endif   //refuse help since not enough work left
        H[i] ← 0
        X[i] ← 1
        if k = i then
            k ← k + 1
            X[k] ← 1
            Size ← Size + 1
        endif
        k ← k + 1
        i ← i + 1
        btLevel ← i
        btHelperLevel ← i
        return(pointer to H[0:btHelperLevel − 1])
    end SplitWork
```

```
procedure ComputeCycle
Input:     global variables as indicated
Output:    examine number of nodes in state-space tree as determined by
           ComputeCycleLength
    iterations ← 0
    while   iterations < ComputeCycleLength .and.
            k > btLevel do
            iterations ← iterations + 1
            PathSum ← A[0]*X[0]
        for i ← 1 to k − 1 do
            PathSum ← PathSum + A[i]*X[i]
        endfor
        while k < n .and. PathSum < Sum
                .and. Size < UB − 1 do
            X[k] ← 1
            PathSum ← PathSum + A[k]
            Size ← Size + 1
            k ← k + 1
        endwhile
        if PathSum = Sum then          //solution found, embed solution X[0:k − 1]
                                       //            and Size in message solution
            UB = Size
        endif
```

$k \leftarrow k - 1$ //backtrack
if $X[k] = 1$ **then**
  $PathSum \leftarrow PathSum - A[k]$
endif
while $k \geq btLevel$ .and. $X[k] = 0$ **do**
  $k \leftarrow k - 1$
endwhile
if $k \geq btLevel$ **then**
  if $X[k] = 1$ **then** $Size \leftarrow Size - 1$ **endif**
  $X[k] \leftarrow 0$
  $k \leftarrow k + 1$
endif
endwhile
end *ComputeCycle*

procedure *Update(Size)*
Input: *Size*
Output: *UB* updated if *Size* < *UB*
 if *Size* < *UB* **then**
  $UB \leftarrow Size$
 endif
end *Update*

We leave the design of pseudocode for constructing the covering set (thereby constructing the initial tasks, $task_1, \ldots, task_n$) as an exercise.

18.7 Closing Remarks

The MPI function library and concomitant MPI programming have become the standard method of implementing parallel code on clusters of workstations—particularly, Beowulf clusters. The MPI standard now includes more than a hundred functions, but a relatively small number allow the programmer to implement a wide variety of programs. In Appendix F, we discuss some of the more important MPI functions (C version) used in most MPI programs and give MPI implementations of the pseudocode for matrix multiplication and sum of subsets. The References and Suggestions for Further Reading that follows lists several books on MPI, as well as cluster computing in general.

MPI-1 and the latest version, MPI-2, have many features not described in this text. For example, one of the features of MPI is the ability to form groups of processes with ranks defined within a group to support group-specific communication activities. Also, topologies such as meshes can be defined. Such topologies are very useful in programming scientific applications like fluid flow problems. Space limitations preclude a discussion of these additional features, and we refer the reader to the references for further details.

References and Suggestions for Further Reading

Two textbooks on parallel programming with MPI:

Pacheco, P. *Parallel Programming with MPI*. San Francisco: Morgan Kaufmann, 1997.

Quinn, M. *Parallel Programming in C with MPI and OpenMP*. New York: McGraw-Hill, 2003.

Good reference books on MPI:

Gropp, W., et al. *MPI—The Complete Reference*. 2 vols. 2nd ed. Cambridge, MA: MIT Press, 1998.

Gropp, W., E. Lusk, and A. Skjellum. *Using MPI—Portable Parallel Programming with the Message Passing Interface*. 2nd ed. Cambridge, MA, MIT Press, 1999.

Karniadakis, G., and R. Kirby II. *Parallel Scientific Computing in C++ and MPI : A Seamless Approach to Parallel Algorithms and Their Implementation*. Cambridge, England: Cambridge *University Press, 2003.*

A book on scientific programming with MPI.

Dongarra, J., I. Foster, G. Fox, W. Gropp, K. Kennedy, L. Torczon, and A. White. *The Sourcebook of Parallel Computation*. San Francisco: Morgan Kaufmann, 2003. Includes material on scientific programming in both the parallel and distributed settings.

Books on grid computing:

Berman F., G. Fox, and T. Hey (eds.). *Grid Computing: Making the Global Infrastructure a Reality*. New York: Wiley, 2003.

Foster I., and C. Kesselman. *The Grid 2: Blueprint for a New Computing Infrastructure*. San Francisco: Morgan Kaufmann, 1999.

EXERCISES

Section 18.2 Message Passing

18.1 Design pseudocode for a game of blackjack (also called 21) for two processes: Process 0 is the dealer and process 1 is a player.

18.2   The following pseudocode is intended to have process 0 receive a message from all processes. Discuss why it does not necessarily work correctly, and write a version that does work.

```
if myid = 0 then
    data ← 0
    while .not. data = p − 1 do
        recv(data, ANY_SOURCE, ANY_TAG, status)
    endwhile
else
    data ← myid
    send(data, 0, 0)
endif
```

18.3   State the conditions under which the following code will work:

```
if myid = 0 then
    Ssend(data, 1, 0)
else
    receive(data, 0, ANY_TAG, status)
endif
if myid = 0 then
    receive(data, 1, ANY_TAG, status)
else
    Ssend(data, 0, 0)
endif
```

18.4   Give pseudocode for *CompareSplit*($a[0:n − 1]$, $b[0:n − 1]$, i, j).

18.5   Verify the correctness of *CompareSplit*.

18.6   Design pseudocode for an asynchronous **scatter** function.

18.7   Design pseudocode for an asynchronous **gather** function.

18.8   Design pseudocode for a procedure that has each process generate a random integer, and process 0 prints the sum of all these numbers, under the following conditions:

a. Use only **send** and **receive** instructions.

b. Use **gather**.

18.9 Suppose all the processes have computed a value for their local variable x, and process 0 wants to receive all these values in the order of increasing process rank. Give a pseudocode segment that accomplishes this.

18.10 Design and analyze an algorithm for finding the maximum value in an array of size n.

18.11 Design and analyze an algorithm for finding the kth smallest element in an array of size n.

18.12 A classical algorithm called the Sieve of Eratosthenes searches for prime numbers. The algorithm starts with a list of natural numbers 2, ... ,n where none of them is marked. The algorithm then repeats the following two steps, until we reach n:

i. find the smallest unmarked k

ii. mark all multiples of k between k^2 and n

When the algorithm completes, all unmarked numbers between 2 and n are primes. Design pseudocode implementing this algorithm.

18.13 In Chapter 12, we discussed Floyd's algorithm, which solves the all-pairs shortest path problem. Design and analyze pseudocode for a distributed version of this algorithm.

Section 18.3 Distributed Even-Odd Transposition Sort

18.14 Prove the correctness of *EvenOddSort*.

18.15 Show that *EvenOddSort* is a stable sorting algorithm.

Section 18.4 Embarrassingly Parallel Master-Worker Paradigm

18.16 Design pseudocode for a version of *MatrixProduct* in which the matrix B is partitioned into n/p blocks of columns and each worker computes the corresponding block of columns of AB.

Section 18.5 Shared-Task Master-Worker Paradigm

18.17 In the general master-worker scenario discussed in Section 18.5.1, alter the pseudocode to exploit the possibility that $p - 1 > n$.

18.18 In the general master-worker scenario discussed in Section 18.5.1, due to timing issues, some messages might not be received by both master and worker processes. Discuss how this might happen and what changes to the master-worker pseudocode would be needed to avoid this situation.

Section 18.6 Distributed Depth-First Search (Backtracking)

18.19 In the parallel backtracking scenario, discuss the type of input that would yield superlinear speedup. Alternatively, what type of input might actually yield slowdown?

18.20 Design pseudocode for constructing a covering set in the sum of subsets problem.

18.21 Design a parallel backtracking solution to the n-queens problem (see Exercise 10.12 in Chapter 10).

Additional Exercises (MPI Programs)

18.22 Design an MPI program for *EvenOddSort*, and run the program with various inputs and numbers of processes. Estimate the number of processes necessary to yield significant speedup as a function of n.

18.23 Design an MPI program for the n-queens problem, and run the program with various inputs and numbers of processes. Estimate the number of processes necessary to yield significant speedup as a function of n.

18.24 Design an MPI program for Floyd's algorithm, and run the program with various inputs and numbers of processes. Estimate the number of processes necessary to yield significant speedup as a function of n.

18.25 Design an MPI program for implementing the Sieve of Eratosthenes (see Exercise 18.12), and run the program with various inputs and number of processes. Estimate the number of processes necessary to yield significant speedup as a function of n.

CHAPTER 19

DISTRIBUTED NETWORK ALGORITHMS

In our discussion of the SPMD model of distributed computing in the previous chapter, we assumed that each processor (process) knew the processor ID of every other processor and could send messages to any other processor without worrying about how the messages where actually routed by the system. In this chapter, our model is a network of processors, where a given processor only can send messages directly to its neighbors in the network, and where messages to other processors must be forwarded using flooding or other methods of broadcasting. Although each processor knows the ID of its neighbors, the number of processors and the global topology of the network are typically not known. Indeed, it becomes important to design distributed algorithms to determine global properties of the network topology, such as shortest paths, diameter, minimum spanning tree, and so forth.

Examples of distributed networks include local area networks, the Internet, ad hoc mobile computing networks, wireless communication networks, peer-to-peer networks, and so forth. For example, Figure 19.1 shows a snapshot of the topology of the backbone of the Gnutella peer-to-peer network. Such networks

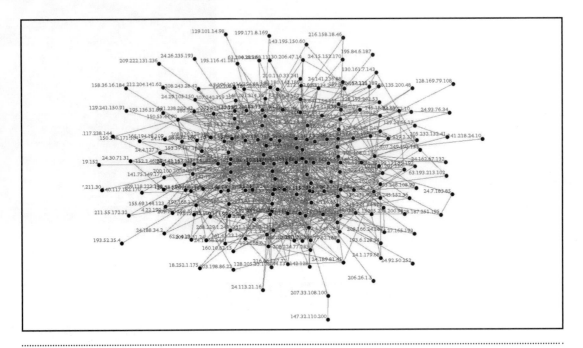

FIGURE 19.1

Snapshot of the topology of the backbone of the Gnutella peer-to-peer network.

are dynamic, in the sense that processors can join or leave the network at any given time. However, our model assumes that the network is fixed for the duration of the algorithm.

Unlike the interconnection network model discussed in Chapters 14 and 15, in which a central control processor sends the next instruction to be executed to each processor, here we do not assume any such central control. Similar to the situation for interconnection network models, we assume that the data for a problem is distributed over the network. However, we may not be able to bring this data efficiently to a single processor. For example, in a shortest-path problem for graphs, each processor might only know a limited, fixed portion of the graph throughout the entire execution of the algorithm (see Section 19.2). Indeed, the graph is usually taken to be the network itself, with nodes corresponding to processors and edges corresponding to direct communication channels between processors. In this interpretation, shortest paths actually determine routing tables for the network.

There are a number of models for distributed network computation, based on the assumptions made about how computation and communication are coordinated among processors. The simplest model is the synchronous network model, where execution proceeds in synchronous rounds. Although computation within a round is not necessarily performed in lockstep by all processors, we assume that the rounds themselves proceed in a lockstep fashion. Because we are focusing on high-level algorithms, we do not concern ourselves with the actual mechanism that might be used to achieve the synchronization of the rounds.

Similar to our conventions for interconnection network models, in our pseudocode for distributed network algorithms, we use the notation $v{:}X$ to represent v's local version of the distributed variable X. We also assume that each processor v has a unique identification number UID, which is stored in the distributed variable $v{:}UID$. In our pseudocode, we use a **forall-do-endforall** control structure to indicate that all processors execute the statements within the body of the structure.

When analyzing the performance of a synchronous algorithm, we use two complexity measures: the time complexity, which is the number of rounds executed, and the communication (message) complexity, which is the total number of messages sent. Typically, within each round, processors communicate with their neighbors and perform some local computations. The time complexity does not take into account the number of local computation steps performed by each processor, because the time is usually dominated by the message passing. Moreover, we assume a very general model of synchronization between the sending and receiving of messages between nodes and their neighbors in the network during a given round. For example, we often simply say that in a given round, nodes communicate a message to all (or some) of their neighbors and then proceed to process all the messages received from their neighbors.

Despite its being difficult to achieve directly in practice, the synchronous model is fundamental because the issues surrounding it are also encountered in more realistic models. Hence, dealing with these issues in the synchronous model gives insight into how to handle them in general, and solving problems on this model is a usually an intermediate step to solving them on more realistic models. Thus, we focus here on the synchronous model. However, the last section discusses how to adapt some of the algorithms developed in the synchronous model to the *asynchronous* model. In practice, the model is usually *partially synchronous*, where specific restrictions are placed on the timing of the execution, but execution does not proceed in simple lockstep.

We assume that the network of processors is represented by a connected graph $G = (V, E)$, with $|V| = n$ and $|E| = m$. Each node in V represents a processor, and the edges represent bidirectional communication channels between processors. We also assume that nodes store no global knowledge of the network other than knowledge about their local neighborhoods. Some of the algorithms we discuss, such as shortest-path algorithms, are designed for the more general model in which some communication channels might be one-way. In the more general case, we model the network using a directed graph D, which we assume is strongly connected.

Because we are not assuming a central control, it becomes important in many applications to identify a leader processor that can coordinate some computation in the distributed network. For example, we might want to simulate the master-worker paradigm discussed in the previous chapter, where the master is taken to be the processor identified as the leader. As another example, we might want to broadcast to or gather information from all the processors, and a source for the broadcast or target for the gather must be identified to allow these operations to proceed.

19.1 Leader Election

To illustrate how a leader can be chosen, we begin our discussion with one of the simplest distributed networks, a ring. The ring model has its origins in the token ring model of a local area network.

19.1.1 Leader Election in a Ring

In a ring model of n processors (see Figure 19.2), we assume that each processor knows its UID and that each processor has both clockwise and counterclockwise neighbor connections. We do not assume as a precondition that the processors know how many processors are in the ring.

FIGURE 19.2

A ring of 12
processors.

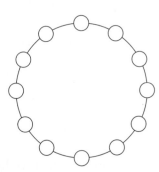

We determine the leader by identifying which processor has the maximum UID. In the first step of the algorithm, each processor sends its UID to its clockwise neighbor. On receiving a UID from its counterclockwise neighbor, a processor compares it with its own UID and, if the UID received is larger, sends this larger UID to its clockwise neighbor. These steps are repeated until one processor, P_{max}, receives its own UID and thus knows that its UID is maximum. In the second phase of the algorithm, P_{max} sends the "leader" message that contains its UID to its clockwise neighbor, which then sends the message to its clockwise neighbor, and so forth until the message has been passed around the entire ring. In the following pseudocode for the procedure *RingLeaderElection*, we assume that the input-output distributed variable *v:LeaderStatus* is initially *unknown*.

```
procedure RingLeaderElection(v:LeaderStatus)
Model: A ring network
Input:    v:LeaderStatus (initially unknown for each a node v)
Output:   v:LeaderStatus (leader node has status leader, all others have status not
          leader)
    forall v do
        send v:UID to clockwise neighbor
    endforall
    while not all v have received "leader" message do
        if u:UID received from counterclockwise neighborhood u then
            if v:UID < u:UID then
                send u:UID to clockwise neighbor
            else
                if v:UID = u:UID then
                    v:LeaderStatus ← leader
                    send "leader" message to clockwise neighbor
                endif
            endif
        endif
        if "leader" message has been received from counterclockwise neighbor then
            if v:LeaderStatus ≠ leader then
                v:LeaderStatus ← not leader
                send "leader" message to clockwise neighbor
            endif
        endif
    endwhile
end RingLeaderElection
```

As mentioned earlier, when analyzing the performance of distributed network algorithms, the time complexity is taken to be the number of rounds, and the communication complexity is taken to be the number of messages sent. It is easily verified that the time complexity and communication complexity of the leader election algorithm are $O(n)$ and $O(n^2)$, respectively.

19.1.2 Leader Election in a General Network

We now consider the problem of choosing a leader in a general network G. The strategy will be similar to a leader election in a ring. Again, the leader is found by determining the processor having the maximum UID. However, in the ring, as soon as a processor received back its own UID, it knew it was the leader. In the general setting, this simple test does not work, and we need more information. The additional information is the diameter d of the network. As discussed in the next section, another method for leader election can be designed even when the diameter of the network is not known.

The procedure *LeaderElection* uses the technique of *flooding* to compute the global maximum UID in d rounds. Flooding is the simplest technique for broadcasting information from one node to other nodes in the network. In each round, nodes simply send messages to all their neighbors. Each node v maintains a variable **v:MaxUID**, which is initially set to **v:UID** (v's own *UID*). On termination of the procedure, each **v:MaxUID** equals the maximum over all the UIDs in the network. During the ith round, $i = 1, \dots , d$, each node v sends **v:MaxUID** to all its neighbors. Each node v then compares **v:MaxUID** to the maximum of **u:MaxUID** over all nodes u in its neighborhood N_v, and updates **v:MaxUID** to this maximum if it is greater.

```
procedure LeaderElection(v:LeaderStatus, d)
Model: A distributed network G of diameter d
Input:    v:LeaderStatus (initially unknown for each a node v)
Output:   v:LeaderStatus (leader node has status leader, all others have status not
            leader)
    forall v do
        v:MaxUID ← v:UID
    endforall
    for Round ← 1 to d do
        forall v do
            send v:MaxUID to all neighbors in N_v
            for each u:MaxUID received do
                if v:MaxUID < u:MaxUID then
                    v:MaxUID ← u:MaxUID
                endif
            endfor
        endforall
    endfor
```

```
            forall v do
                if v:MaxUID = v:UID then
                    v:LeaderStatus ← Leader
                else
                    v:LeaderStatus ← Not Leader
                endif
            endforall
        end LeaderElection
```

The correctness of *LeaderElection* follows from the fact that after *k* rounds, all nodes within distance *k* of the node having the maximum UID have updated their value of *MaxUID* to this maximum. A formal induction proof is left to the exercises. Therefore, after *d* rounds, all nodes have updated their values of *MaxUID* to the maximum UID.

Since *LeaderElection* performs *d* rounds, it follows that the time complexity is $O(d)$. In each round, at most *m* messages are exchanged; thus, it follows that the communication complexity is $O(dm)$.

19.2 Broadcasting and Breadth-First Search

Broadcasting information from a source node (processor) *s* to all other nodes (processors) in the network and the reverse operation of gathering information (convergecast) from all the nodes to a source node are fundamental operations in a distributed network. In this section, we discuss how to accomplish these important operations.

19.2.1 Broadcasting Using Flooding

Recall that the simplest way to accomplish broadcasting is through the technique of flooding, where a node sends the information (message) to all its neighbors, who in turn send the information to all their neighbors, and so forth. In this way, the message is propagated throughout the network. In a dynamic network, such as a mobile ad hoc network or a peer-to-peer network, this flooding technique is the technique of choice. However, it has the disadvantage of creating congestion in the network. Also, unless we know the diameter of the network, we need to determine a method of detecting when all nodes in the network have received the message so we can stop the flooding. We solve the broadcasting problem in Section 19.2.4 by constructing a breadth-first search tree rooted at an arbitrary node in the network. The algorithm does not assume that the diameter is known. After a breadth-first search tree is constructed, then subsequent broadcasting can be accomplished efficiently using the tree. Also, by constructing (in parallel) breadth-first search trees rooted at every node, we can solve the leader election problem for a general network whose diameter we do not assume to know in advance.

19.2.2 Broadcasting in a Tree

As mentioned earlier, flooding tends to create congestion in the network. On the other hand, if we have a tree T rooted at a node s, then we can efficiently perform a broadcast from s to all other nodes in T (so that if T is a *spanning* tree, then the broadcast reaches all nodes in the network). If each node has a list of children in T, then we can broadcast information from s to all other nodes in T as follows. Node s simply sends the message to be broadcast to all its children, who, in turn, send the message on to all their children, and so forth, until the message has been propagated to all nodes in the tree. We illustrate the broadcast procedure in Figure 19.3, where the root initiates a broadcast throughout the tree T, and where the broadcast completes in three rounds. For simplicity, the UIDs in Figure 19.3 are four-digit integers.

Now suppose that each node has stored a list of nodes that are adjacent to it in T. Also, suppose that each node knows whether or not it is the root of T but has not stored its parent or a list of children. This situation arises in the minimum spanning tree algorithm discussed in Section 19.5. With this somewhat meager information, each node v can efficiently compute its parent and its list of children in the rooted tree containing v as follows. First, each nonroot node v with an adjacency list of size 1 (leaf node) records its unique neighbor u as its parent and sends a "your child" message to u. Subsequently, when a nonroot node has received a "your child" message from all its neighbors except for one, u, it records u as its parent and sends a "your child" message to u. The process continues until the root node has received a "your child" message from all its neighbors. Once the parent of each node and its list of children are determined, then, as before, efficient broadcasts can be performed.

Figure 19.4 illustrates this process using the same tree T as in Figure 19.3, except that now the nodes do not have lists of children or knowledge of their parents. The table shows which nodes received "your child" messages and from whom in each round.

19.2.3 Performing Global Computations Using Fan-In

Suppose that each node v in a tree T rooted at s in a distributed network stores a number in the distributed variable $v{:}X$. We assume that each node in T knows its parent, and has a list of its children. We wish to compute the sum of all the numbers and assign this sum to $s{:}Sum$. We begin by having each node v store its number $v{:}X$ in $v{:}Sum$. In each round a node v receives sums from some of its children

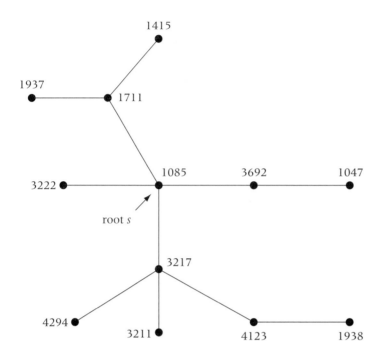

UID	Parent	Child List		Round 1	Round 2	Round 3
1047	3692	{}			*	
1085	none	{1711,3217,3222,3692}				
1415	1711	{}			*	
1711	1085	{1415,1937}		*		
1937	1711	{}			*	
1938	4123	{}				*
3211	3217	{}			*	
3217	1085	{3211,4123,4294}		*		
3222	1085	{}		*		
3692	1085	{1047}		*		
4123	3217	{1938}			*	
4294	3217	{}			*	
				* = receive broadcast		

FIGURE 19.3

Broadcast from root throughout tree *T* in three rounds when lists of children are known.

....
FIGURE 19.4

Table showing for
each node *v* and
each round *R* which
nodes send "your
child" message to *v*
during round *R*. The
lists of children are
completed after
three rounds.
....

	UIDs of Nodes Sending "Your Child" Messages		
UID	Round 1	Round 2	Round 3
1047			
1085	3222	1711, 3692	3217
1415			
1711	1415, 1937		
1937			
1938			
3211			
3217	3211, 4294	4123	
3222			
3692	1047		
4123	1938		
4294			

and adds these sums to **v**:*Sum*. When a node *v* has received sums from *all* of its children it sends **v**:*Sum* to its parent. Note that in the first round only the leafs send their sum to their parents, because they don't have any children. Once the root *s* has performed its summing operation, the algorithm is complete. When the algorithm is complete **v**:*Sum* contains the sum of all the numbers in the subtree rooted at *v*. In particular **s**:*Sum* contains the sum over all the numbers in the tree. If all the nodes need to know **s**:*Sum*, then *s* can merely initiate a broadcast of **s**:*Sum* to all the nodes in *T*. This method can be generalized to other operations, such as computing the maximum, or to simply gather data from all the nodes at the root. Note that if *T* is a spanning tree for a distributed network, then we are performing a global operation in the network. In the next subsection, we show how to construct such a (breadth-first) spanning tree.

Figure 19.5 illustrates the summing operation for the same tree as used in Figures 19.3 and 19.4, where the number initially stored in each node *v* is its de-

....
FIGURE 19.5

The value of
v:*DegreeSum* after
each round for each
node *v* in the tree *T*
given in Figure 19.3.
....

		Value of *v*:DegreeSum		
UID	**Degree**	Round 1	Round 2	Round 3
1047	1	1		
1085	4	5	13	22
1415	1	1		
1711	3	5		
1937	1	1		
1938	1	1		
3211	1	1		
3217	4	6	9	
3222	1	1		
3692	2	3		
4123	2	3		
4294	1	1		

gree stored in **v**:*DegreeSum*. As described in the previous paragraph, whenever a node *v* receives a summand from one of its children, it adds this summand to **v**:*DegreeSum*. Looking back to the table in Figure 19.4, we can see the children that are sending their value of **v**:*DegreeSum* to their parents in a given round. After a node has received summands from all its children, it sends **v**:*DegreeSum* to its parent. The table shows the value of **v**:*DegreeSum* at the end of each of the three rounds. The resulting value in **s**:*DegreeSum* is the sum of the degrees, so that the number of nodes in *T* is (**s**:*DegreeSum* + 2)/2.

19.2.4 A Distributed Algorithm for Constructing a Breadth-First Search Tree

We have just seen how we can perform efficient broadcasting and gathering of data in a distributed network if we have a spanning tree. We now design a procedure, *BFSDistributed,* that constructs a breadth-first search (spanning) tree T_s rooted at *s* in an arbitrary (connected) network. Initially in the procedure *BFSDistributed,* the status of each node is "not in tree." In round one, *s* changes its status to "in tree" and sends the message "join tree" to all its neighbors. In subsequent rounds, if an unmarked node receives the message "join tree," it changes its status to "in tree," chooses one of the nodes from which it has received the message to be its parent in the BFS-tree, sends the message "your child" to this parent, and sends the message "not your child" to all other neighbors. In the round immediately after it is marked, a given node sends the message "join tree" to all its unmarked neighbors. If the node has no unmarked neighbors, then it sends the message "terminated" to its parent. As soon as a node receives the message "terminated" from all its children, it sends the message "terminated" to its parent. Once the root node *s* receives the message "terminated" from all its neighbors, the procedure has finished. The following pseudocode for *BFSDistributed* is based directly on this discussion.

```
procedure BFSDistributed(s, v:Parent)
Model: A distributed network G
Input:    s (a node in G)
Output:   v:Parent (parent of node v in BFS-tree rooted at s)
     initially v:Status = not in tree for each node v
     s:Parent ← 0
     s:Status ← in tree
     s sends "join tree" message to all its neighbors
     forall v do
         if v:Status = not in tree .and. v has received "join tree" message then
             v chooses a node u that has sent "join tree" message
             v:Parent ← u
```

v sends "your child" message to *u* and "not your child" message to all other neighbors

v:Status ← in tree

v sends "join tree" message to all its neighbors

else

if *v* has received a child status message from all its neighbors **then**

if *v* has no children **then**   //*v* is a leaf node

v sends "terminated" message to its parent

else

if all children of *v* have sent a "terminated" message **then**

v sends "terminated" message to its parent

v takes no further action

endif

endif

endif

endif

endforall

end *BFSDistributed*

19.2.5 Leader Election in a General Distributed Network

We now reconsider the leader election problem in a general distributed network, which we solved in the previous section for the special case where the diameter of the network was known to each node. Here we solve the problem without making this assumption about the diameter. Each node *s* in the network independently computes a breadth-first search tree T_s rooted at *s*. Then each node *s* initiates a fan-in on its BFS-tree to compute the maximum of all the UIDs in the network. If its own UID equals this maximum, then it knows that it is the leader, and its identity is also known to all the other nodes.

19.3 Shortest Paths

Recall that BFS-tree T_s is a shortest-path tree rooted at *s*, where the length (weight) of the path is the number of edges in the path. A straightforward modification of procedure *BFSDistributed* also determines the (unweighted) distance from *s* to every other node (that is reachable from *s*). Also, *BFSDistributed* can be modified to work on the more general networks in which one-way communication might occur between nodes (so that the underlying graph is directed). In the directed model, it is not as straightforward to determine which out-neighbors are children in the out-directed BFS-tree. An out-neighbor might not be an in-neighbor and therefore must communicate along a directed path in the network (which is why we required that the network be strongly connected). The directed version of *BFSDistributed* is left to the exercises.

For the case in which each edge in the network is weighted, we give a distributed version of the Bellman-Ford algorithm (discussed in Chapter 14) for computing a shortest-path tree rooted at a given node s and weighted distances from s to all other vertices. Procedure *BellmanFordDistributed* assumes that each processor knows the number n of nodes in the network.

```
procedure BellmanFordDistributed(s, v:Dist, v:Parent)
Model: A distributed w-weighted, directed network D on n nodes
Input:    s (a node in a distributed weighted, directed network D)
Output:   v:Parent (parent of node v in shortest-path tree rooted at s)
          v:Dist (distance from s to node v)
     forall u distributed do
         v:Dist ← ∞
         v:Parent ← ∞
     endforall
     s:Dist ← 0
     s:Parent ← 0
     for Round 1 to n−1 do
         forall v do        // update v:Dist and v:Parent
             send v:Dist to all nodes in v's out-neighborhood N_out(v)
             after receiving u:Dist from all nodes u in v's in-neighborhood N_in(v)
                 v:Dist ← min{v:Dist, u:Dist + w(uv) for u ∈ N_in(v)}
         endforall
     endfor
end BellmanFordDistributed
```

The proof of the correctness of *BellmanFordDistributed* follows from the fact that after k rounds, v:*Dist* is no greater than the length of a shortest path from s to v using at most k edges. The inductive proof of this fact is similar to that given in Chapter 12 for the sequential version (see Exercise 19.9). Because *BellmanFordDistributed* performs $n - 1$ rounds and sends $(n - 1)m$ messages, it has $O(n)$ time complexity and $O(nm)$ communication complexity.

19.4 All-Pairs Shortest Paths

We now describe a distributed version of Floyd's algorithm. Recall from Chapter 12 that our sequential version of Floyd's algorithm proceeded in n stages, we labeled the nodes from 0 to $n - 1$, and in the kth stage the node k was allowed to be used as an internal node of a path between nodes i and j. In our distributed version, we assume some fixed ordering of the nodes (perhaps by their UIDs) but not necessarily from 0 to $n - 1$. The next node that we allow as an intermediate node is called the *pivot* node. Each node v maintains a table *v:Dist*, indexed by the nodes, where *v:DistTable[u]* is the (current) distance from v to u. Each node v also maintains a table *v:First*, where *v:FirstTable[u]* is the first node on a shortest path from v to u. The algorithm proceeds in n passes, each involving multiple rounds, where in each pass the next pivot node p broadcasts its distance table and first table to all other nodes, and then each node updates its distance and first table according to the usual formula.

```
procedure FloydDistributed(v:DistTable, v:FirstTable)
Model: A distributed w-weighted, directed network D on n nodes
Precondition: Every node knows the other nodes in D together with a fixed ordering of
              the nodes (used for table indexing and deciding next pivot)
Output:   v:DistTable (v:DistTable[u] is the distance from v to u)
          v: FirstTable (v:FirstTable[u] is the first node on a shortest path
          from v to u)
   forall v do //initialize distance tables v:DistTable
       forall u do
           if u in Nₒᵤₜ(v) then
               v:DistTable[u] ← w(vu)
               v:FirstTable[u] ← u
           else
               if u = v then
                   v:DistTable[u] ← 0
               else
                   v:DistTable[u] ← ∞
               endif
           endif
       endforall
   endforall
   for Pass ← 1 to n do
       let p denote the next node in the node ordering
       p broadcasts p:DistTable to all other nodes
       forall v do
           forall u
               if v:DistTable[u] > v:DistTable[p] + p:DistTable[u]
                   v:DistTable[u] ← v:DistTable[p] + p:DistTable[u]
                   v:FirstTable[u] ← v:FirstTable[p]
               endif
           endforall
       endforall
   endfor
end FloydDistributed
```

We leave the analysis of the time and communication complexities of *Floyd-Distributed* to the exercises.

19.5 Minimum Spanning Tree

We now design a distributed procedure *MSTDistributed* for computing a minimum spanning tree. *MSTDistributed* is an adaptation of the procedure *MSTCREW* developed in Chapter 16. As with *MSTCREW*, we assume as a precondition that all edge weights are distinct, so that the minimum spanning tree is unique. To ensure that the weights are distinct, the weight of each edge $e = uv$ could be replaced with a new weight consisting of the triple $(w(e),$ $\mathrm{UID}(u),\mathrm{UID}(v))$, where $\mathrm{UID}(u) < \mathrm{UID}(v)$, and where the ordering of the triple is lexicographical.

At each stage, *MSTDistributed* maintains a forest of trees, where initially each tree in the forest consists of a single node, and on termination of the algorithm, the forest is the (unique) minimum spanning tree. Recall that in the design of *MSTCREW*, we called the node (vertex) set of each tree in the forest a supervertex. To keep track of the trees (supervertices), each node v maintains an adjacency list of its tree neighborhood. Combining two trees by adding an edge xy becomes very simple using distributed adjacency lists—namely, x simply adds y to its adjacency list and vice versa. Also, because each node will know whether or not it is the root, using the distributed algorithm discussed in Section 19.2.2, each node can compute its list of children and its parent, thereby enabling effective communication within the tree.

Similar to the design of procedure *MSTCREW*, at each stage of the procedure and for each tree T in the current forest, *MSTDistributed* determines the minimum-weight edge xy, where x is in the tree and y is not. All such edges are then added to the current forest to create the forest in the next stage. The fact that all these minimum-weight edges belong to the unique minimum spanning tree follows from Proposition 16.2.1 (see Chapter 16). Determining a minimum-weight edge is possible because it turns out that each tree has a distinguished root (leader) node, and each node knows whether or not it is the root.

In the first stage of *MSTDistributed*, each node u computes the minimum-weight edge $\mu(u) = uv$ in its neighborhood N_u. Recall that directing edge $\mu(u)$ from u to v results in a forest, each tree in the forest contains exactly one bidirected edge (see Figure 16.11), and $\mu(u)$ is the parent of u in the tree containing u. The end node of the bidirected edge having the larger UID declares itself to be the root (leader) of the associated tree. Each node u adds $v = \mu(u)$ to its tree adjacency list and sends a message to v to add u to its tree adjacency list. Using the distributed process described in Section 19.2.2, each node uses its tree adjacency list to compute its parent and list of children in its tree. The root then initiates a broadcast of its UID to every node in the tree.

In subsequent stages, this process is repeated for the current set of trees (supervertices) as follows. Each node u determines the minimum-weight edge among all the edges uv, where v belongs to a different tree as determined by the leader UIDs, and informs the root node of its tree of this minimum weight edge (no message is sent if no such edge uv exists). After the root node has received these minimum-weight edges from all the nodes in its tree, it determines the minimum weight edge xy of these edges (the algorithm can terminate if the root receives no edges in the current round). The root then informs x that it is the node where this minimum occurs. After receiving this message from the root, node x then adds y to its tree adjacency list and sends a message to y to add x to its tree adjacency list. Again, each of the resulting trees has a unique bidirected edge among these added edges, and the roots in the new forest are taken to be the nodes with the largest UIDs in each bidirected edge. The root of each new tree then initiates a broadcast of its UID throughout its tree. The process is then repeated until we arrive at a single tree, which is then the minimum spanning tree. We leave the pseudocode for *MSTDistributed* as an exercise.

The correctness of *MSTDistributed* follows from Proposition 16.2.1. A formal correctness proof is left to the exercises. In going from one stage to the next, the number of trees in the current forest is at least halved; thus, there are $O(\log n)$ stages. Because each stage requires $O(n)$ rounds to compute and broadcast the minimum-weight edge in each tree, the time complexity is $O(n \log n)$. The messages passed in each stage occur within the forest, so there are at most $O(n)$ total messages passed during that stage, and the communication complexity is also $O(n \log n)$.

We illustrate the action of *MSTDistributed* in Figure 19.6, which uses the same graph used in Figure 16.11 (in Chapter 16) to design the parallel version. For simplicity, we assume in Figure 19.6 that the UID of a node is one more than its index, as shown in Figure 16.11. Each row in phase-1 portion of the table in Figure 19.6 shows the tree adjacency list for the given node v corresponding to that row, the initial forest of minimum-cost edges incident with each vertex, the list of children for the associated tree, and the leader of each tree in the forest. In subsequent phases, nodes added from minimum-cost edges between supervertices, lists of children, and the leaders of newly formed supervertices are shown after the completion of each phase.

UID	Phase 1 Tree Adjacency List	Phase 1 List of Children	Phase 1 Leader	Phase 2 Added Adjacency	Phase 2 List of Children	Phase 2 Leader	Phase 3 Added Adjacency	Phase 3 List of Children	Phase 3 Leader
1	{1}	{}	1		{}	8		{}	9
2	{0, 2, 4, 5}	{0, 2, 4, 5}	1		{0, 2, 5}	8		{0, 2, 5}	9
3	{1}	{}	1		{}	8		{}	9
4	{4}	{}	1		{}	8		{}	9
5	{1, 3}	{3}	1	8	{1, 3}	8		{1, 3}	9
6	{1}	{}	1		{}	8		{}	9
7	{10}	{}	10		{}	13		{}	9
8	{8}	{}	8		{}	8		{}	9
9	{7}	{7}	8	4	{4, 7}	8		{4, 7}	9
10	{13, 14}	{13}	14		{14}	13	9	{8, 13, 14}	9
11	{6}	{6}	10	11	{6}	13	8	{6}	9
12	{12}	{}	12	10	{10}	13		{10}	9
13	{11}	{11}	12	13	{11}	13		{11}	9
14	{9}	{}	14	12	{9, 12}	13		{12}	9
15	{9}	{9}	14		{}	13		{}	9

FIGURE 19.6

Action of *MSTDistributed* for the same graph as in Figure 16.11.

 ## 19.6 Asynchronous Model

In the asynchronous model, we can no longer assume that code execution proceeds in lockstep synchronous rounds, because processors are executing at various computation and communication speeds. We again assume that the network is modeled on a graph in which nodes represent processors and edges correspond to send/receive channels and in which the directed edge xy is for sending messages from x to y. Because the processes of sending and receiving messages are not tightly synchronized, we assume that each directed edge xy has a buffer **xy**:*SendBuffer* for messages sent from x to y. The buffer **xy**:*SendBuffer* is implemented as a queue. In our discussion of asynchronous algorithms, when x invokes the **send** function to send a message to y, it places the message in the **xy**:*SendBuffer*. Similarly, when y invokes the **receive** function to receive a message from x, it removes a message from **xy**:*SendBuffer*. These message-passing assumptions are analogous to the action of the nonblocking **send** and **receive** functions discussed in Chapter 18.

19.6.1 Asynchronous Leader Election in a Ring

As our first illustration of designing an asynchronous algorithm, we revisit the leader election in a ring. The asynchronous version is based on the same strategy as the synchronous version, except for the buffering of messages.

```
procedure RingLeaderElectionAsync(v:LeaderStatus)
Model: A ring network
Input:    v:LeaderStatus (initially unknown for each a node v)
Output:   v:LeaderStatus (leader node has status leader, all others have status not leader)
    Each node v sends v:UID to its clockwise neighbor
    Each vertex v performs the following operations until "leader" message is received
    receive message from uv:SendBuffer where u is v's counterclockwise neighbor
        if "UID" message then
            if v:UID < u:UID then
                send u:UID to v's clockwise neighbor
            else
                if v:UID = u:UID then
                v:LeaderStatus ← leader
                send "leader" message to clockwise neighbor
                endif
            endif
        else                                   //"leader" message has been received
            if v:LeaderStatus ≠ leader then
                v:LeaderStatus ← not leader
                send "leader" message to clockwise neighbor
            endif
        endif
end RingLeaderElection Async
```

19.6.2 Asynchronous Leader Election in a Tree

We now design an asynchronous algorithm for leader election in a tree. The strategy we use is similar to that used in Section 19.2.2. First, each leaf node u orients the (unique) edge uv it is joined to from u to v and sends this orientation information to v. Subsequently, when a given node v has received orientation messages from all but one of its neighbors w, it orients edge vw from v to w and sends this orientation information to w. Eventually, exactly two adjacent nodes x and y will have received an orientation message from all their neighbors; that is, there will be a unique bidirected edge xy (see Exercise 19.14). These two nodes decide a leader among themselves. For example, the node with the maximum UID is chosen as the leader. The leader then initiates a broadcast of its UID to all the other nodes using the orientation created in the first part of the algorithm.

19.6.3 Asynchronous Leader Election in a General Network

Now consider the problem of designing an asynchronous algorithm for the leader election problem in a general distributed network. The procedure *Leader-Election* we designed earlier assumed that each node knew diameter d of the network and thus knew to terminate after d rounds. In the asynchronous model, because we no longer proceed in synchronous rounds, we cannot use this condition. Thus, although we can adapt *LeaderElection* to work in an asynchronous setting using send buffers, we are still faced with the problem of implementing a termination condition. One method of solving this problem is to generate a spanning tree in a network and then apply the algorithm for leader election in the tree given in the previous subsection. In the next subsection, we see how to solve the latter problem by adapting the synchronous procedure *BFSDistributed*.

19.6.4 Asynchronous Broadcasting

A straightforward adaptation of *BFSDistributedAsync* that uses send buffers does not necessarily generate a BFS (shortest-path) tree. For example, suppose we perform *BFSDistributedAsync* on the triangle network x, y, z, rooted at x. The algorithm begins by performing a **send** to x and y. However, because of the asynchronous nature of the communication, z might have already received the message from **yz:***SendBuffer* before receiving it from **xz:***SendBuffer*. Therefore, the tree generated is the path xyz, whereas the shortest tree consists of the edges xy and xz.

To generate a shortest-path spanning tree, we modify the straightforward version *BFSDistributedAsync* by also maintaining a current distance $d(v)$ of each node v from the source s. Node s initiates the algorithm by sending its distance 0 to all its neighbors. Subsequently, each node v performs the following operations. For each received message from ***uv:****SendBuffer* where u is neighbor, v relaxes the edge uv; that is, if $d(u) + 1 < d(v)$, then v updates $d(v)$ to $d(u) + 1$ and *parent*(v) to u. After scanning the adjacent send buffers and relaxing all the edges thereby processed, node v sends the updated information to all its neighbors.

19.7 Closing Remarks

This chapter briefly introduced distributed network algorithms, limiting the discussion to some of the most basic problems in the area. We concentrated on the two models of synchronous and asynchronous message passing and developed pseudocode for (1) the synchronous model based on rounds and (2) the asynchronous model based on send buffers associated with the communication channels of the network. These two models capture many of the salient issues in distributed algorithms and provide the background needed to investigate distributed algorithms in more detail.

The theory of distributed algorithms is an ongoing, active area of research, fueled by the rapid expansion of distributed networks such as the Internet, ad hoc mobile computing networks, wireless communication networks, peer-to-peer networks, computation grids, and so forth. A variety of formal models for distributed algorithms have been developed. For example, one model is based on the notion of an input/output automaton, as described in the comprehensive text by Lynch mentioned in the references at the end of this chapter. In this model, processors are in various states and undergo state changes based on local computations and messages received from other processors or the environment.

We have assumed throughout this chapter that the network remains fixed throughout the execution of the algorithm. In particular, we have not considered that a communication link or processor might fail at some point in the algorithm. Designing distributed algorithms that can deal with such failures is an important area of distributed algorithms that is also covered in some of the references.

References and Suggestions for Further Reading

Three comprehensive textbooks on distributed algorithms:

Lynch, N. *Distributed Algorithms*. San Francisco: Morgan Kaufmann, 1997.

Peleg, D. *Distributed Computing: A Locally-Sensitive Approach*. Philadelphia: SIAM, 2000.

Tel, N. *Introduction to Distributed Algorithms*. 2nd ed. Cambridge, UK: Cambridge University Press, 2000.

Section 19.1 Leader Election

19.1   Verify that the time complexity and communication complexity of the procedure *RingLeaderElection* are $O(n)$ and $O(n^2)$, respectively.

19.2   In procedure *LeaderElection*, prove that after k rounds, all nodes within distance k of the node having the maximum UID have updated their value of *MaxUID* to that maximum.

19.3   Show how to improve the communication complexity of procedure *LeaderElection*.

Section 19.2 Broadcasting and Breadth-First Search

19.4   Create a table similar to that given in Figure 19.3 illustrating the broadcast procedure for the following rooted tree:

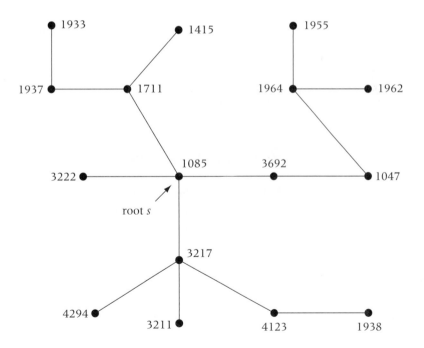

19.5   Repeat Exercise 19.4 for the tree T in which each node stores a list of nodes adjacent to it instead of storing the parent and list of children (see Figure 19.4).

19.6 Create a table (see Figure 19.5) showing the value of **v**:*DegreeSum* after each round for each node *v* in the tree illustrated in Exercise 19.4.

19.7 Show that the distributed variable **v**:*Parent* of procedure *BFSDistributed* actually determines a spanning tree by showing that no cycles are created.

Section 19.3 Shortest Paths

19.8 Design a directed version of *BFSDistributed*.

19.9 Show that in procedure *BellmanFordDistributed*, after k rounds, **v**:*Dist* is no greater than the length of the shortest path from s to v using at most k edges.

19.10 Analyze the time and communication complexities of *FloydDistributed*.

Section 19.5 Minimum Spanning Tree

19.11 Design pseudocode for procedure *MSTDistributed*.

19.12 Prove the correctness of *MSTDistributed*.

19.13 Show the action of *MSTDistributed* for the weighted graph given in Exercise 16.18 in Chapter 16. Create a table similar to Figure 19.6.

Section 19.6 Asynchronous Model

19.14 From our description of leader election in a tree, prove that eventually, exactly two adjacent nodes x and y will have received an orientation message from all their neighbors.

SPECIAL TOPICS

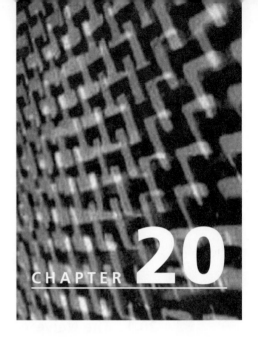

CHAPTER 20

STRING MATCHING AND DOCUMENT PROCESSING

Finding some or all occurrences of a given pattern string in a given text is an important and commonly encountered problem. For example, most word processing software packages have built-in search-and-replace functions and spell checkers, both of which depend on finding the occurrences of words in texts. On the Internet, string matching is used for locating Web pages containing a given query string. String matching and approximate string matching is also a key technique in bioinformatics, which entails searching gene sequences for patterns of interest.

In this chapter, we present three standard string-matching algorithms, due to Knuth, Morris, and Pratt (the KMP algorithm); Boyer and Moore (the BM algorithm); and Karp and Rabin (the KR algorithm). The KMP and BM algorithms preprocess the pattern string so that information gained during a search for a match of the pattern can be used to shift the pattern more than the one position shifted by a naive algorithm when a mismatch occurs. The KR algorithm shifts the pattern by only one position at a time, but it performs an efficient (constant-time) check at each new position.

Often it is useful to find an approximate match in a text to a given pattern string. An important measure of approximation is known as the edit distance between two strings, which is, roughly speaking, the minimum number of single-character alterations that will transform one string into another. We present a dynamic programming solution to computing the edit distance between strings.

We finish the chapter with a discussion of tries and suffix trees. When the text is fixed, preprocessing the text as opposed to the pattern string leads to efficient string-matching algorithms. This preprocessing is based on constructing a trie and a related suffix tree corresponding to the text. Tries can be used to create inverted indexes to strings in a large collection of data files, such as Web pages on the Internet.

■ 20.1 The Naive Algorithm

The string-matching problem can be formally described as follows. An *alphabet* is a set of characters or symbols $A = \{a_1, a_2, \ldots, a_k\}$. A *string* $S = S[0:n-1]$ of length n on A is a sequence of n characters (repetitions allowed) from A. Such a string $S = s_0 s_1, \ldots, s_{n-1}$ can be viewed as an array of characters $S[0:n-1]$ from A, so that the $(i+1)^{\text{st}}$ character s_i in the string is denoted by $S[i], i = 0, \ldots, n-1$. More generally, we denote the substring consisting of symbols in consecutive positions i through j of S by $S[i:j]$, $0 \le i \le j \le n-1$. The *null string*, denoted by ε, is the string that contains no symbols. We let A^* denote the set of all finite strings (including the null string ε) on A. The length of a string S, denoted $|S|$, is the number of characters in S. For $a \in A$, we let a^i denote the string of length i consisting of the single symbol a repeated i times.

Given a *pattern string* $P = P[0:m-1]$ of length m and *text string* $T = T[0:n-1]$ of length n, where $m \le n$, the string-matching problem is to determine whether P occurs in T. In our string-matching algorithms, we assume that we are looking for the first occurrence (if any) of the pattern string in the text string. The algorithms can be readily modified to return all occurrences of the pattern string.

A naive algorithm for finding the first occurrence of P in T is to position P at the start of T and simply shift the pattern P along T, one position at a time, until either a match is found or the string T is exhausted (that is, position $n - m + 1$ in T is reached without finding a match).

function *NaiveStringMatcher(P[0:m − 1], T[0:n − 1])*
Input: $P[0:m-1]$ (a pattern string of length m)
         $T[0:n-1]$ (a text string of length n)
Output: returns the position in T of the first occurrence of P, or -1 if P does not occur
         in T

```
    for s ← 0 to n − m do
        if T[s : s + m − 1] = P then
            return(s)
        endif
    endfor
    return(−1)
end NaiveStringMatcher
```

When measuring the complexity of procedure *NaiveStringMatcher*, it is natural to choose comparison of symbols as our basic operation. We can test whether $T[s: s + m − 1] = P$ by using a simple linear scan. Clearly, this scan requires a single comparison in the best case ($P[0] \neq T[s]$) and m comparisons in the worst case ($P[i] = T[s + i], i = 0, \ldots, m − 2$). Because the **for** loop of procedure *NaiveStringMatcher* is iterated $n − m + 1$ times, *NaiveStringMatcher* never performs more than $m(n − m + 1)$ comparisons. Moreover, $m(n − m + 1)$ comparisons are performed, for example, when $P[0:m − 1]$ and $T[0:n − 1]$ are the strings $0^{m−1}1$ and 0^n, respectively, over the alphabet $A = \{0, 1\}$. Thus, *NaiveStringMatcher* has worst-case complexity

$$W(m, n) = m(n − m + 1) \in O(nm).$$

The action of *NaiveStringMatcher* is illustrated for a sample pattern and text string in Figure 20.1.

FIGURE 20.1

Action of procedure *NaiveStringMatcher* for a sample pattern string $P[0:7]$ and a text string $T[0:22]$ on alphabet $A=\{0, 1, 2\}$. For each shift s, we show that portion of P that matches T, with the first mismatch shaded. A match is found beginning at the 11th character of T.

```
P       0 0 1 0 0 2 0 1
T       0 0 1 0 0 1 0 0 2 0 0 0 1 0 0 2 0 1 2 2 0 0
s = 0   0 0 1 0 0 2
s = 1     0 0
s = 2       0
s = 3         0 0 1 0 0 2 0 1
s = 4           0 0
s = 5               0
s = 6                 0 0 1
s = 7                   0 1
s = 8                     1
s = 9                       0 0 1
s = 10                          0 0 1 0 0 2 0 1
```

20.2 The Knuth-Morris-Pratt Algorithm

There is an obvious inefficiency in *NaiveStringMatcher*: At a given point we might have matched a good part of the pattern *P* with the text *T* until we found a mismatch, but we don't exploit this in any way. The KMP string-matching algorithm is based on a strategy of using information from partial matchings of *P* to not only skip over portions of the text that cannot contain a match but also to avoid checking characters in *T* that we already know match a prefix of *P*. The KMP algorithm achieves $O(n)$ worst-case complexity by preprocessing the string *P* to obtain information that can exploit partial matchings.

To illustrate, consider the pattern string *P* = "00100201" and text string *T* = "001001002000010020122000". Placing *P* at the beginning of *T*, note that a mismatch occurs at index position 5. The naive algorithm would then shift by one to *T*[1] and simply start all over again checking at the beginning of *P*. This completely ignores that we have already determined that *P*[0:4] = 00100 = *T*[0:4]. Indeed, by simply looking at *P*[0:4], we see that the first position in *T* where a match could possibly occur is at *i* = 3, because any shift of *P* by less than three will cause mismatches between the relevant prefix of *P*[0:3] = *T*[0:3] and suffix of *P*[1:4] = *T*[1:4] determined by the shift. Indeed, if we shift by one, we would be comparing the prefix 0010 of *P*[0:3] with the suffix 0100 of *P*[1:4]. Similarly, if we shift by two, we would be comparing the prefix 001 of *P*[0:3] with the suffix 100 of *P*[1:4]. Thus, we need to shift by three before we match the prefix 00 of *P*[0:3] with the suffix 00 of *P*[1:4]. Hence, from the mismatch that occurs at position *i* = 5, the next starting position where a match can occur is at position 5 − 2 = 3. Moreover, we do not need to check the first two characters in *P* because they already match the first two characters of *T* at this new position for *P*. Note that next position where a match can occur was obtained by subtracting the length of the largest prefix of *P*[0:3] that was also a suffix of *P*[l:4] from the position where the mismatch occurred.

More generally, suppose we have detected a mismatch at position *i* in *T*, where $T[i] \neq P[j]$, but we know that the previous *j* characters of *T* match with *P*[0:*j* − 1]. Also, suppose d_j is the length of the longest prefix of *P*[0:*j* − 2] that also occurs as a suffix of *P*[1:*j* − 1]. Then the next position where a match can occur is at position $i - d_j$. Moreover, to see whether we actually have a match starting at position $i - d_j$, we can avoid checking the characters that we already know agree with those in *T*—that is, the characters in the substring $T[s - d_j : i - 1]$. Hence, we need only check the characters in the substring $T[i : i + m - d_j - 1]$ with those in the substring $P[d_j : m - 1]$ to see if a match occurs (see Figures 20.2 and 20.3).

FIGURE 20.2

The state of T when $T[i] \neq P[j]$, but $T[i-j:i-1] = P[0:j-1]$ and d_j is the length of the longest prefix of $P[0:j-2]$ that agrees with a suffix of $P[1:j-1]$.

position $\quad i - j \qquad\quad i - d_j \qquad\qquad\qquad\qquad i - 1 \quad i$

$T \qquad \dots P[0]\ P[1] \dots P[j-d_j]\ P[j-d_j+1] \dots P[j-1]\ T[i] \neq P[j] \dots$

$\qquad\qquad\qquad\quad \| \qquad\qquad\quad \| \qquad\qquad\qquad \|$

$\qquad\qquad\qquad P[0] \qquad\quad P[1] \dots \qquad P[d_j-1]\ P[d_j] \dots$

FIGURE 20.3

Interpretation of Figure 20.2 for specfic P and T.

$T \qquad$ 0010010020001002012200 $\qquad\qquad$ 0010010020001002012200

$P \qquad$ 00100201 $\qquad\qquad\qquad\qquad\qquad$ 00100201

$\qquad$ mismatch at $i = j = 5$ $\qquad\qquad\qquad$ $5 - 2$ is next index where a match could occur (it doesn't occur there)

By preprocessing the string P, we can compute the array $Next[0:m-1]$, where $Next[j]$ is the length of longest prefix of $P[0:j-2]$ that agrees with a suffix of $P[1:j-1]$, $j = 2, \dots, m$. We set $Next[0] = Next[1] = 0$. For example, for the string $P = $ "00100201", we have the corresponding array $Next[0:7] = [0, 0, 1, 0, 1, 2, 0, 1]$. Then for this P and the T discussed earlier, Figure 20.3 shows the situation described in Figure 20.2 for $i = 5, j = 5$, and $d_j = 2$.

The following key fact summarizes our discussion and is the key to the efficiency of the KMP string matching algorithm.

> **Key Fact**
>
> Suppose in our scan of **T** looking for a match with **P** that we have a mismatch at position **s** in **T**, where $T[i] \neq P[j]$, but $P[0:j-1] = T[i-j:i-1]$. Setting $d_j = Next[j]$, the next position where a match of **P** can occur is at position $i - d_j$. Moreover, we need only check the substring $T[i:i+m-d_j-1]$ with the substring $P[d_j:m-1]$ to see if a match occurs there.

In the pseudocode *KMPStringMatcher*, we look for matches using a variable i that scans the text T from left to right one position at a time, and a second variable j that scans the pattern P in a slightly oscillatory manner, as dictated by the key fact (see Figure 20.4). The variable i never backs up, so that when a match occurs, it is actually at position $i - m + 1$ (in other words, s is the position of the last character in P corresponding to the matching). The pseudocode is elegant but somewhat subtle, because when a mismatch $P[j] \neq T[i]$ occurs, there is no need to explicitly place the pattern P at the next position $i - Next[j]$; we merely need to check $T[i : i + m - Next[j] - 1]$ against $P[Next[j] : m - 1]$ to see if a match of P occurs at $i - Next[j]$. We perform this check by continuing the scan of T by i and replacing j by $Next[j]$ before continuing the scan of P by j.

```
function KMPStringMatcher(P[0:m − 1], T[0:n − 1])
Input:    P[0:m − 1] (a pattern string of length m)
          T[0:n − 1] (a text string of length n)
Output:   returns the position in T of the first occurrence of P, or −1
          if P does not occur in T
     i ← 0                                    //i runs through text string T
     j ← 0                                    //j runs through pattern string P in manner
                                                 dictated by key fact
     CreateNext(P[0:m − 1], Next[0:m − 1])
     while i < n do
        if P[j] = T[i] then
             if j = m − 1 then                //match found at position i − m + 1
                 return(i − m + 1)
             endif
             i ← i + 1                        //continue scan of T
             j ← j + 1                        //continue scan of P
        else                                  //P[j] ≠ T[i]
             j ← Next[j]                      //continue looking for a match of P which
                                                 now could begin at position i − Next[j]
                                                 in T

             if j = 0 then
                 if T[i] ≠ P[0] then          //no match at position i
                     i ← i + 1
                 endif
             endif
        endif
     endwhile
     return(−1)
end KMPStringMatcher
```

In Figure 20.4, we illustrate the action of *KMPStringMatcher* for the pattern string P and text string T discussed earlier, by tracing the values of s and j for each iteration of the **while** loop. While *NaiveStringMatcher* used 37 comparisons to find a match, *KMPStringMatcher* only used 21 (not counting the comparisons made by *CreateNext* in preprocessing P).

FIGURE 20.4

(a) A trace of the values of i and j for each iteration of the **while** loop in *KMPString-Matcher* for $P = $ "00100201" and $T = $ "00100100200010 02012200". Positions marked with ! are where $T[i] \neq P[j]$ and j is reassigned with the value $Next[j]$. (b) The implicit shifting of P until a match is found.

iteration						!					!	!						
i	0	1	2	3	4	5	5	6	7	8	9	10	10	11	11	12	13	14 15 16 17
j	0	1	2	3	4	5	2	3	4	5	6	7	1	2	1	2	3	4 5 6 7

(a)

```
T        0 0 1 0 0 1 0 0 2 0 0 0 1 0 0 2 0 1 2 2 0 0
P        0 0 1 0 0 2 0 1
             0 0 1 0 0 2 0 1
                   0 0 1 0 0 2 0 1
                     0 0 1 0 0 2 0 1  match
```

(b)

KMPStringMatcher has linear complexity because of the following key fact.

Key Fact

The while loop in *KMPStringMatcher* is executed at most 2n times.

To verify the key fact, note that the loop executes n times when i is incremented within the loop. If i is not incremented in the loop, then the pattern P is implicitly shifted to position $i - Next[j]$, which is at least one more than the last implicit placement of P. Therefore, this implicit shift can happen at most n times, which verifies the key fact.

It remains to design the algorithm *CreateNext*. Again, there is a naive algorithm *NaiveCreateNext* that computes each value of $Next[i]$ from scratch, without using any of the information gleaned from computing $Next[k]$, $k < i$. It is easy to see that the worst case of *NaiveCreateNext* is in $\Omega(m^2)$. However, similar to the design of *KMPStringMatcher*, using information gleaned about $Next[i - 1]$ leads to a more efficient way to compute $Next[i]$ and yields an $O(m)$ algorithm. We leave the complexity analysis and correctness of *CreateNext* to the exercises.

function *CreateNext*($P[0:m - 1], Next[0:m - 1]$)
Input: $P[0:m - 1]$ (a pattern string of length m)
Output: $Next[0:m - 1]$ ($Next[i]$ is length of longest prefix of $P[0:i - 2]$ that is a suffix of $P[1:i - 1]$, $i = 0, \ldots, m - 1$)

```
          Next[0] ← Next[1] ← 0
          i ← 2
          j ← 0
          while i < m do
              if P[j] = P[i − 1] then
                  Next[i] ← j + 1
                  i ← i + 1
                  j ← j + 1
              else
                  if j > 0 then
                      j ← Next[j − 1]
                  else
                      Next[i] ← 0
                      i ← i + 1
                  endif
              endif
          endwhile
      end CreateNext
```

20.3 The Boyer-Moore String-Matching Algorithm

Similar to the KMP algorithm, the BM algorithm uses preprocessing of the pattern string to facilitate shifting the pattern string, but it is based on a right-to-left scan of the pattern string instead of the left-to-right scan made by the KMP algorithm. We present a simplified version of the BM algorithm that compares the rightmost character of the pattern with the character in the text corresponding to the current shift of the pattern and uses this comparison to determine the next pattern shift (if any). The full version of the BM algorithm is developed in the exercises.

In the BM algorithm, the pattern $P[0:m − 1]$ is first placed at the beginning of the text, and we check for a match by scanning the pattern from right-to-left. If we find a mismatch, then we have two cases to consider, depending on the character x of the text in index position $m − 1$ that is compared against the last character of P. If x does not occur in the first $m − 1$ positions of P, then clearly we can shift P by its entire length m to continue our search for a match. If x does occur in the first $m − 1$ positions of P, then we shift P so that the rightmost occurrence of x in $P[0:m − 1]$ is now at index position $m − 1$ in the text, and we repeat the process of scanning P from right-to-left at this new position. Again, if we find a mismatch, we shift the pattern again based on the text character that was aligned at the rightmost character of P. Also, in this simplified version, we ignore any information gleaned about partial matchings in our previous placement of P (this information *is* used in the full version of the BM algorithm).

The shifts associated with the two cases can be computed easily by preprocessing the pattern string P. In the following pseudocode for *CreateShift*, for convenience, we assume that the array *Shift* is indexed by the alphabet A from which the characters for the pattern P and text T are drawn.

procedure *CreateShift*($P[0:m - 1]$, *Shift*$[0: |A| - 1]$)
Input: $P[0:m - 1]$ (a pattern string)
Output: *Shift*$[0: |A| - 1]$ (the array of character-based shifts)
    for $i \leftarrow 0$ to $|A| - 1$ **do**   //initialize *Shift* to all m's.
      Shift$[i] = m$
    endfor
    for $i \leftarrow 0$ to $m - 2$ **do**   //compute shifts based on rightmost
                                  occurrence of $P[i]$ in $P[0:m - 1]$
      Shift$[P[i]] = m - i - 1$
    endfor
end *CreateShift*

For example, suppose $P[0:8]$ is the string "character". Then the values for the shifts of the characters e, t, c, a, r, h are 1, 2, 3, 4, 5, 7, respectively. The shift value for all other characters is 9. In Figure 20.5, we illustrate how the simplified BM algorithm uses these shifts to find a match of the pattern "character" in the text "BMmatcher_shift_character_example".

The worst-case performance of the simplfied BM algorithm is the same as that of the naive algorithm, $\Theta(nm)$ (see Exercise 20.8). However, it can be shown that its average behavior is linear in n and often works as well as the full version of the BM algorithm. The full version of the BM algorithm works identically to the simplified version when there is a mismatch between the rightmost character of the pattern and the text character corresponding to this rightmost character in the current shift of the pattern. If these two characters agree, however, the full version acts differently by exploiting the information gained by the matching of a suffix of P with the corresponding characters in the text for the given placement of P (see the discussion preceding Exercise 20.9).

FIGURE 20.5

Action of simplified BM algorithm, with positions where mismatches first occur in the right-to-left scan of the pattern indicated by !.

```
          !           !                 !
B M m a t c h e r _ s h i f t _ c h a r a c t e r _ e x a m p l e
c h a r a c t e r                           Shift ( r ) = 5
            c h a r a c t e r               Shift ( r ) = 9
                          c h a r a c t e r   Shift ( r ) = 2
                            c h a r a c t e r   match
```

20.4 The Karp-Rabin String-Matching Algorithm

In this section, we assume without loss of generality that our strings are chosen from the k-ary alphabet $A = \{0,1, \ldots, k - 1\}$. Each character of A can be thought of as a digit in radix-k notation, and each string $S \in A^*$ can be identified with the base k representation of an integer $\overline{S}$. For example, when $k = 10$, the string of numeric characters "6832355" can be identified with the integer 6832355. Given a pattern string $P[0:m - 1]$, we can compute the corresponding integer using m multiplications and m additions by employing Horner's rule.

$$\overline{P} = P[m - 1] + k(P[m - 2] + \atop k(P[m - 2] + k(P[m - 3] + \cdots + k(P[1] + kP[0]) \ldots)) \qquad \textbf{(20.4.1)}$$

Given a text string $T[0:n - 1]$ and an integer s, we find it convenient to denote the substring $T[s, s + m - 1]$ by T_s. A string-matching algorithm is obtained by using Horner's rule to successively compute $\overline{T_0}, \overline{T_1}, \overline{T_2}, \ldots$, where the computation continues until $\overline{P} = \overline{T_s}$ for some s (a match) or until we reach the end of the text T. Of course, this is no better than the naive string-matching algorithm. However, the following key fact is the basis of a linear algorithm.

Key Fact

Given the integers $\overline{T_{s-1}}$ and k^{m-1}, we can compute the integer $\overline{T_s}$ in constant time.

The key fact follows from the following recurrence relation:

$$\overline{T_s} = k(\overline{T_{s-1}} - k^{m-1}T[s]) + T[s + m] \quad s = 1, \ldots, n - m. \quad \textbf{(20.4.2)}$$

For example, if $k = 10$, $m = 7$, $\overline{T_{s-1}} = 7937245$, and $\overline{T_s} = 9372458$, then recurrence relation (20.4.2) becomes

$$\overline{T_s} = 10[7937245 - (1000000 \times 7)] + 8 = 9372458.$$

The constant $c = k^{m-1}$ in (20.4.2) can be computed in time $O(\log m)$ using the binary method for computing powers. Once c is computed, it does not need to be recomputed when Formula (20.4.2) is applied again. Thus, assuming that the arithmetic operations in (20.4.2) take constant time, each application of (20.4.2) takes constant time. Hence, the $n - m + 2$ integers $\overline{P}$ and $\overline{T_s}, s = 0, 1, \ldots, n - m$, can be computed in total time $O(n)$.

The problem with the preceding approach is that the integers $\overline{P}$ and $\overline{T}_s$, $s = 0, 1, \ldots, n - m$, may be too large to work with efficiently, and the assumption that Formula (20.4.2) can be performed in constant time becomes unreasonable. To get around this difficulty, we reduce these integers modulo q for some randomly chosen integer q. To avoid multiple-precision arithmetic, q is often chosen to be a random prime number such that kq fits within one computer word.

We now let

$$\overline{P}^{(q)} = \overline{P} \bmod q,$$
$$\overline{T}_s^{(q)} = \overline{T}_s \bmod q. \qquad\qquad \textbf{(20.4.3)}$$

The values $\overline{T}_s^{(q)}$ and $\overline{P}^{(q)}$ can be computed in time $O(n)$ using exactly the same algorithm described earlier for computing $\overline{T}_s$ and $\overline{P}$, except that all arithmetic operations are performed modulo q. Clearly, if $\overline{T}_s^{(q)} \neq \overline{P}^{(q)}$ then $T_s \neq P$. However, if $\overline{T}_s^{(q)} = \overline{P}^{(q)}$, we are not guaranteed that $P = T_s$. When a shift s has the property that $\overline{T}_s^{(q)} = \overline{P}^{(q)}$, but $T_s \neq P$ we have a *spurious match*. However, for sufficiently large q, the probability of a spurious match can be expected to be small. We check whether a match is spurious by explicitly checking whether $T_s = P$, and continuing our search for a match if $T_s \neq P$.

```
function KarpRabinStringMatcher(P[0:m − 1], T[0:n − 1], k, q)
Input:     P[0:m − 1] (a pattern string of length m)
           T[0:n − 1] (a text string of length n)
           k (A is the k-ary alphabet {0, 1, . . . , k − 1})
           q (a random prime number q such that kq fits in one computer word)
Output:    returns the position in T of the first occurrence of P, or −1 if P does not occur
           in T
     c ← k^(m − 1) mod q
     P̄^(q) ← 0
     T̄_s^(q) ← 0
     for i ← 1 to m do                          //apply Horner's rule to compute
                                                      P̄^(q) and T̄_s^(q)

           P̄^(q) ← (k∗P̄^(q) + P[i]) mod q
           T̄_0^(q) ← (k∗T̄_0^(q) + T[i]) mod q
     endfor
     for s ← 0 to n − m do
        if s > 0 then
              T̄_s^(q) ← (k∗(T̄_{s−1}^(q) − T[s]∗c) + T[s + m]) mod q
        endif
```

if $\overline{T}_s^{(q)} = \overline{P}^{(q)}$ **then**
    if $T_s = P$ **then**   //match is not spurious
        return(s)
    endif
endif
endfor
return(0)
end *KarpRabinStringMatcher*

Figure 20.6 illustrates the action of function *KarpRabinStringMatcher* for a sample pattern string $P[0{:}6]$ = "6832355", text string $T[0{:}20]$ = "895732102583 235544031", and prime modulus $q = 11$. To illustrate the calculations of $\overline{T}_s^{(11)}$ in Figure 20.6, we show how *KarpRabinStringMatcher* computes $\overline{T}_3^{(11)}$ from $\overline{T}_2^{(11)}$. Using Formula (20.4.2) and doing all arithmetic modulo $q = 11$, we have

$$\begin{aligned} 7321026 &\equiv 10(5732102 - 1000000 \times 5) + 6 \pmod{11} \\ &\equiv 10(2 - 1 \times 5) + 6 \pmod{11} \\ &\equiv 9 \pmod{11}. \end{aligned}$$

Because *KarpRabinStringMatcher* terminates after finding the first nonspurious match, the worst-case performance occurs for an input pair (P, T), where the pattern string P occurs precisely at the end ($s = n - m$) of the text string T. With q chosen at random, we can expect different behavior for different choices of q, so that we now consider the expected number $\tau_{\exp}(P, T)$ of string comparisons made by the algorithm. For $s \neq n - m$, we make the assumption that $\overline{T}_s^{(q)}$ takes on a particular value $i \in \{0, 1, \ldots, q - 1\}$ with equal probability $1/q$. Because a spurious match occurs only when $\overline{T}_s^{(q)} = \overline{P}^{(q)}$, $s = 0, \ldots, n - m - 1$, it follows that

$\overline{T}[0{:}20]$ 895732102683235544031
$\overline{P}[0{:}6]$ 6832355

s							$\overline{T}_s$										$\overline{T}_s^{(11)}$
0	8	9	5	7	3	2	1										10
1		9	5	7	3	2	1	0									9
2			5	7	3	2	1	0	2								2 Spurious match
3				7	3	2	1	0	2	6							9
4					3	2	1	0	2	6	8						6
5						2	1	0	2	6	8	3					0
6							1	0	2	6	8	3	2				4
7								0	2	6	8	3	2	3			0
8									2	6	8	3	2	3	5		5
9										6	8	3	2	3	5	5	2 Match: return (9)

FIGURE 20.6 Action of *KarpRabinStringMatcher* for a sample pattern string $P[0{:}6]$, text string $T[0{:}20]$, and prime modulus $q = 11$.

a spurious match occurs at shift s with probability $1/q$. Let r denote the expected number of spurious matches. A test for a spurious match involves m comparisons in the worst case, and $r + 1$ such tests are performed (including the test at shift $s = n - m$); thus, the expected performance $\tau_{\exp}(P, T)$ of *KarpRabinStringMatcher* for the input (P, T) is

$$\tau_{\exp}(P, T) = (r + 1)m + (n - m + 1). \qquad \textbf{(20.4.4)}$$

The value r is the expectation of the binomial distribution with $n - m$ trials (shifts), where success (a spurious match) occurs with probability $1/q$. Thus, from Formula (E.3.9) of Appendix E, we have

$$r = \frac{n - m}{q}. \qquad \textbf{(20.4.5)}$$

Substituting Formula (20.4.5) into Formula (20.4.4), we obtain

$$\tau_{\exp}(P, T) = \left(\frac{n - m}{q} + 1 \right)m + (n - m + 1). \qquad \textbf{(20.4.6)}$$

If we assume that q is bounded above by a fixed constant, then *KarpRabin-StringMatcher* achieves a worst-case complexity in $\Theta(nm)$, which is no better than the naive algorithm. However, in practice, it is reasonable to assume that q is much larger than m, in which case *KarpRabinStringMatcher* has complexity in $O(n)$. The Karp-Rabin string-matching algorithm has the additional feature that it is readily adapted to the problem of finding $m \times m$ patterns in $n \times n$ texts (see Exercise 20.16).

20.5 Approximate String Matching

In practice, there are often misspellings when creating a text, and it is useful when searching for a pattern string P in a text to find words that are approximately the same as P. In this section, we formulate a solution to this problem using dynamic programming. We have already discussed a solution to a similar problem in Chapter 9—namely, the problem of finding the longest common subsequence of two strings.

We first consider the problem of determining whether a pattern string $P[0:m - 1]$ is a k-approximation of a text string $T[0:n - 1]$. Later, we look at the problem of finding occurrences of substrings of T for which P is a k-approximation. The pattern string P is a k-*approximate matching* of the text string T if T can be converted to P using at most k operations involving one of the following

1. Changing a character of T (substitution)
2. Adding a character to T (insertion)
3. Removing a character of T (deletion)

For example, when P is the string "algorithm", one of the following might occur:

1. elgorithm → algorithm (*substitution* of e with a)
2. algorthm → algorithm *(insertion* of letter i)
3. lalgorithm → algorithm (*deletion* of letter l)

In this example, each string T differs from P by at most one character. Unfortunately, in practice, more serious mistakes are made, and the difference involves multiple characters. We define the *edit distance D(P, T)* between P and T to be the minimum number of operations of substitution, deletion, and insertion needed to convert T to P. For example, the strings "algorithm" and "logarithm" have edit distance 3.

$$logarithm \rightarrow alogarithm \rightarrow algarithm \rightarrow algorithm$$

Let $D[i, j]$ denote the edit distance between the substring $P[0:i-1]$ consisting of the first i characters of the pattern string P and $T[0:j-1]$ consisting of the first j characters of the text string T. If $P[i] = T[j]$, then $D[i, j] = D[i-1, j-1]$. Otherwise, consider an optimal intermixed sequence involving the three operations substitution, insertion, and deletion that converts $T[0:j-1]$ into $P[0:i-1]$. The number of such operations is the edit distance between these two substrings. Note that in transforming T to P, inserting a character into T is equivalent to deleting a character from P. For convenience, we will perform the equivalent operation of deleting characters from P rather than adding characters to T. We can assume without loss of generality that the sequence of operations involving the first $i-1$ characters of P and the first $j-1$ characters of T are operated on first. To obtain a recurrence relation for $D[i, j]$, we examine the last operation. If the last operation is substitution of $T[j]$ with $P[i]$ in T, then $D[i, j] = D[i-1, j-1] + 1$. If the last operation is the deletion of $P[i]$ from P, then $D[i, j] = D[i-1, j] + 1$. Finally, if the last operation is deletion of $T[j]$ from T, then $D[i, j] = D[i, j-1] + 1$ The edit distance is realized by computing the minimum of these three possibilities. Observing that the edit distance between a string of size i and the null string is i, we obtain the following recurrence relation for the edit distance:

$$D[i, j] = \begin{cases} D[i-1, j-1], & \text{if } P[i] = T[j], \\ \min\{D[i-1, j-1] + 1, D[i-1, j] + 1, D[i, j-1] + 1\}, & \text{otherwise.} \end{cases}$$
init. cond. $D[0, i] = D[i, 0] = i$.

$$(20.5.1)$$

The design of a dynamic programming algorithm based on this recurrence and its analysis is similar to that given for the longest common subsequence problem discussed in Chapter 9, and we leave it to the exercises. We also leave as an exercise designing an algorithm for finding the first occurrence or all occurrences of a substring of the text string T that is a k-approximation of the pattern string P.

20.6 Tries and Suffix Trees

By preprocessing the pattern string, the KMP and BM algorithms achieved improvement over the naive algorithm. Another approach that can be applied when the text is fixed is to preprocess the strings in the text using a data structure such as a tree. In this section, we discuss two important tree-based data structures, tries and suffix trees, for preprocessing the text to allow for very efficient pattern matching and information retrieval.

20.6.1 Standard Tries

Consider a collection C of strings from an alphabet A of size k, where no string in S is a prefix of any other string. We can then construct a tree T whose nodes are labeled with symbols from A, such that the strings in C correspond precisely to the paths in T from the root R to a leaf node as follows. We construct T such that the labels of the children of each node are unique and occur in increasing order as the children are scanned from left to right. Starting with the tree T consisting of a single root node R, we inductively incorporate a new string $S[0:p-1]$ from C into T as follows. If no child of the root R is labeled $S[0]$, then we simply add a new branch at the root consisting of a path of length p whose node at level $i+1$ is labeled $S[i]$, $i = 0, \dots,$ $p-1$. Otherwise, we follow a path from the root by first following the edge from the root to the unique child of the root labeled $S[0]$, then following the edge from that node to its child labeled $S[1]$, and so forth until we reach a node v at level i labeled $S[i-1]$ having no child (at level $i+1$) labeled $S[i]$. We then add a new branch at v consisting of a path of length $p - i - 1$, such that node in the path at level j (in the tree) is labeled $S[j-1]$, $j = i+1, \dots, p-1$. A tree T constructed in this way is called a *standard trie* for the string collection C. Figure 20.7 shows a standard trie for the sample string collection $C = \{$"internet", "interview", "internally", "algorithm", "all", "web", "world"$\}$.

The leaf nodes of the trie T can be used to store information about the string S corresponding to the leaf, such as the location in the text of P, the number of occurrences of P in the text, and so forth. The term *trie* comes from the word re*trie*val, because a trie can be used to retrieve information about P. In addition to pattern matching, tries can be used for word matching, where the pattern is matched only to substrings of the text corresponding to words. This is useful for creating a forward index of words in a web document.

....

FIGURE 20.7

Standard trie for the
collection of strings
C = {"internet",
"interview",
"internally",
"algorithm", "all",
"web", "world"}.

....

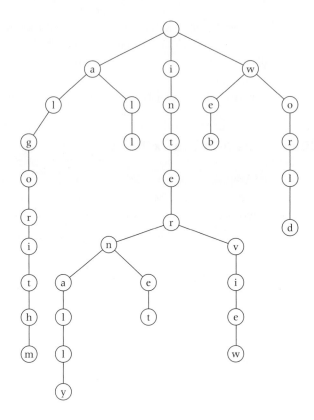

It is immediate that a standard trie T has the following three properties: (1) Each nonleaf node has at most k children, where k is the size of the alphabet A; (2) the number of leaf nodes equals the number of strings in S; and (3) the depth of T equals the length of the longest string in S. The following proposition about the space requirements for storing T is easily verified (see Exercise 20.22).

Proposition 20.6.1 Let T be a standard trie for a collection C of strings, and let s denote the total length over all the strings in C. Then the number of nodes $N(T)$ of T satisfies

$$N(T) \in O(s).$$

We can efficiently test whether a given pattern string $P[0:m-1]$ belongs to C by scanning the string P and successively following the child in the trie labeled with the current symbol that has been scanned until either no child of the current node has a label equal to the symbol or a leaf node labeled with the last symbol of P has been reached. Because we have made the assumption that no string in C is a prefix of any other string, it follows that the pattern string

$P[0:m-1]$ belongs to C if and only if a leaf node labeled with the last symbol in P is reached. Because each node has at most k children, this procedure has complexity $O(km)$. Thus, if the alphabet has constant size, the complexity of searching for P is linear in its length.

20.6.2 Compressed Tries

The $O(s)$ space requirement of a standard trie T can be reduced if there are nodes in T that have only one child. Consider any such node v, and let c denote its only child. Let x and y denote the labels of v and c, respectively, and let u denote the parent of v. Then the path generated by a string S from C that contains v must also contain c. Thus, without affecting our ability to match S, we can compress the trie by removing v, making c a child of u, and replacing the label y of c with the string xy. This operation can be repeated for other nodes having only one child, except that x and y may themselves be strings instead of just single symbols. After repeatly performing this compression operation until all internal nodes have at least two children, we obtain a tree labeled with strings, which we call the *compressed trie* for S. A compressed trie is also called a PATRICIA (practical algorithm to retrieve information coded in alphanumeric) tree . Note that the compressed trie for S can also be obtained by replacing every path $uu_1 \ldots u_k v$ from a node u to a node v in T whose internal nodes $u_1, u_2, \ldots, u_k$ are bivalent (have exactly one child), but whose end nodes u and v are not, with the edge uv and replacing the label y of v with the string $x_1 x_2 \ldots x_k y$, where x_i denotes the label of $u_i, i = 1, \ldots, k$. The compressed trie for the trie given in Figure 20.7 is shown in Figure 20.8.

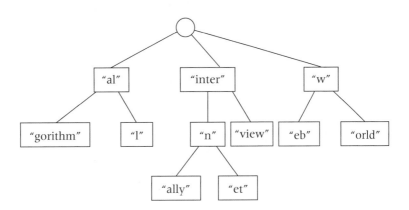

FIGURE 20.8

Compressed trie for the same string set C = {"internet", "interview", "internally", "algorithm", "all", "web", "world"} of Figure 20.7

The following proposition about the number of nodes of a compressed trie T is easily verified.

Proposition 20.6.2 Let T be a compressed trie for a collection C of c strings. Then the number of nodes $N(T)$ of T satisfies

$$N(T) \in O(c).$$

Comparing this result with Proposition 20.6.1, we see that compressing the standard trie has reduced the space requirements from $O(s)$ to $O(c)$. This becomes significant when the strings in C are long. A compressed trie can be created directly from the set of strings C without first constructing a standard trie for C and then compressing it. We leave as an exercise designing an algorithm for constructing a compressed trie directly from C. Using a slight modification of the technique used for a standard trie, we can search a compressed trie to efficiently test whether a given pattern string belongs to C (see Exercise 20.24).

20.6.3 Suffix Trees

A *suffix tree* (also called a *suffix trie*) with respect to a given text string T is a compressed trie for the string collection C consisting of all suffixes of T. This definition requires that no suffix be a prefix of any other suffix. For strings in which this occurs, we simply add a special symbol to the end of every suffix in C. Suffix trees are useful in practice because they can be used to determine whether a pattern string P is a substring of a given text string T. The suffix tree for the string $T =$ "babbage" is shown in Figure 20.9(a). Because the string label on each node corresponds to a substring $T[i:j]$ of T, it can be represented more compactly using just the pair (i, j). Figure 20.9(b) shows the more compact representation of the node labels for the suffix tree in part (a).

Given a pattern $P[0:m-1]$ in string P, it is easy to design an $O(km)$ algorithm that traces a path in the suffix tree corresponding to test T to determine whether P occurs as a substring of T. We leave the design of such an algorithm as an exercise.

FIGURE 20.9

(a) Suffix tree for string $T =$ "babbage".

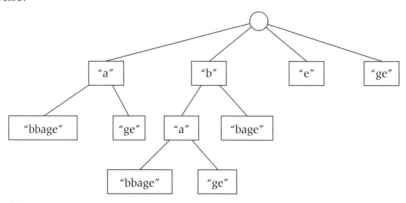

(a)

FIGURE 20.9

Continued.

(b) more compact representation of the node labels for the suffix tree in part (a).

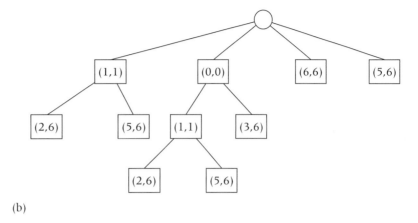

(b)

 ## 20.7 Closing Remarks

String and pattern matching have been areas of interest for a long time, and string algorithms have recently received increased attention because of their role in Web searching as well as in computational biology. In this chapter, we have introduced several of the most important string-matching algorithms, but the subject is vast. The interested reader should consult the references for more extended treatments of this important topic and its applications.

References and Suggestions for Further Reading

Books on string matching:

Aoe, J. *Computer Algorithms: String Pattern Matching Strategies*. Wiley-IEEE Computer Society Press, 1994.

Crochemore, M. *Text Algorithms*. New York: Oxford University Press, 1994.

Gusfield, D. *Algorithms on Strings, Trees, and Sequences: Computer Science and Computational Biology*. Cambridge: Cambridge University Press, 1997.

Navarro, G., and Raffinot, M. *Flexible Pattern Matching in Strings*. Cambridge: Cambridge University Press, 2002.

Stephen, G. A. *String Searching Algorithms*. London: World Scientific Publishing, 1994.

Chen, D., and Cheng, X., eds. *Pattern Recognition and String Matching*. Dordrecht, The Netherlands: Kluwer Academic Publishers, 2002. A collection of 28 articles contributed by experts on pattern recognition and string matching.

Survey articles on string matching:

Baeza-Yates, R. A. "Algorithms for String Matching: A Survey." *ACM SIGIR Forum* 23 (1989): 34–58.

Navarro, G. "A Guided Tour to Approximate String Matching." *ACM Computing Surveys* 33, no. 1 (2001): 31–88.

Section 20.2 The Knuth-Morris-Pratt Algorithm

20.1. Suppose $P[0:m-1]$ and $T[0:n-1]$ are the strings $0^{m-1}1$ and 0^n that were the worst-case strings of length m and n for *NaiveStringMatcher*.

    a. Show that $P[0:m-1]$ and $T[0:n-1]$ are best-case strings of length m and n for *KMPStringMatcher* for the case where P does not occur in T.

    b. Find worst-case strings $P[0:m-1]$ and $T[0:n-1]$, respectively, for *KMPStringMatcher*, and thereby determine $W(m,n)$ for *KMPStringMatcher*.

20.2 Compute the array *Next*[0:10] for the pattern string $P =$ "abracadabra".

20.3 Trace the action of *KMPStringMatcher* as in Figure 20.4 for the pattern string $P =$ "cincinnati" and the text string $T =$ "cincinatti_is_cincinnati_misspelled".

20.4 Verify the correctness of the algorithm *CreateNext*.

20.5 Show that *CreateNext* has $O(m)$ complexity.

20.6 Write programs implementing *NaiveStringMatcher* and *KMPStringMatcher*, and run them for various inputs for comparison.

Section 20.3 The Boyer-Moore String-Matching Algorithm

20.7 Design and analyze pseudocode for the simplified BM algorithm.

20.8 Show that the worst case of the simplified BM algorithm is as bad as the naive algorithm.

Exercises 20.9 through 20.14 involve the full version of the BM algorithm. As mentioned, when a mismatch occurs in the last position of the pattern string, the full version works the same way as the simplified version using the value *Shift*[*c*] to shift the pattern based on the mismatched text character *c*. The difference arises when we have matched the last $k > 0$ characters of the pattern string P, called a *good suffix* (of length k), before a mismatch occurs with a character *c* from the text. We then shift the pattern by the larger of the following two shifts, called the *bad character shift* s_1 and the *good suffix shift* s_2, respectively. The bad character shift s_1 is simply defined as $s_1 = \max\{Shift[c] - k, 1\}$. We can shift P by s_1 and not miss any matches, for reasons similar to those used when comparing against the last character in P.

The good suffix shift s_2 is also based on reasoning similar to that used to create the array *Shift*, but where we consider suffixes of *P* instead of a single character. More precisely, we look for the rightmost repeated occurrence of the good suffix of length *k* (if any) to shift this occurrence by the amount s_2 required to bring it to the end of the pattern. Of course, the character preceding this repeated occurrence (if any) must be different from the character preceding the good suffix; otherwise, a mismatch will occur again. Even when such a repeated occurrence of the good suffix does not happen, we might not be able to shift the pattern by its entire length *m* because we might miss a match that might occur when a suffix of length *j* of a good suffix of length *k*, $0 < j < k$, matches a prefix of length *j* of *P*. In the latter case, we shift by the amount required to bring the prefix to the end of the pattern *P*. For example, if $P = 011101001$, then the good suffix shifts for $k = 1, \ldots, 8$, which are given by $5, 3, 7, 7, 7, 7, 7, 7$, respectively.

20.9 Design and analyze pseudocode for an algorithm that creates the good-suffix shift values for a given input pattern $P[0{:}m - 1]$.

20.10 Compute the bad-character shifts and the good-suffix shifts for the following patterns:

a. $P = $ "01212121"

b. $P = $ "001200100"

20.11 Trace the action of the full version of the BM algorithm for the pattern $P = $ "amalgam" and text $T = $ "ada_gamely_amasses_amalgam_information".

20.12 Design and analyze pseudocode for the full version of the BM algorithm.

20.13 Write programs implementing the simplified and full versions of the BM algorithm, and compare their performance for various inputs.

20.14 Compare the performance of the programs written in the previous exercise to programs implementing *NaiveStringMatcher* and *KMPStringMatcher* (see Exercise 20.6) for various inputs.

Section 20.4 The Karp-Rabin String-Matching Algorithm

20.15 Trace the action of *KarpRabinStringMatcher* for the alphanumeric strings $P = $ "108" and $T = $ "002458108235" for the following values of *q*:

a. $q = 7$

b. $q = 11$

20.16   Adapt the Karp-Rabin string matching algorithm to the problem of finding $m \times m$ patterns $P[0{:}m-1, 0{:}m-1]$ in $n \times n$ texts $T[0{:}n-1, 0{:}n-1]$.

20.17   Verify recurrence relation (20.4.2).

20.18   Write a program implementing *KarpRabinStringMatcher*, and test its performance for various input strings and randomly generated modulus q.

Section 20.5   Approximate String Matching

20.19   a. Design and give pseudocode for a dynamic programming algorithm for approximate string matching based on recurrence relation (20.5.1).

   b. Analyze the approximate string algorithm that you gave in part (a).

20.20   a. Show how the k-approximate string-matching algorithm can be modified to find the first *substring* of the text string T that is a k-approximation of the pattern string P.

   b. Repeat part (a) for the problem of finding *all* occurrence of substrings of T that are k-approximations of P.

20.21   Show the $n \times m$ matrix $D[0{:}7, 0{:}10]$ that results from solving the recurrence relation (20.5.1) for the pattern string $P[0{:}7]$ = "patricia" and text string $P[0{:}8]$ = "patriarch".

Section 20.6   Tries and Suffix Trees

20.22   Prove Proposition 20.6.1.

20.23   Design an algorithm for constructing a compressed trie directly from a collection C of strings (without first constructing a standard trie and compressing).

20.24   Design an algorithm for searching a compressed trie to efficiently test whether a given pattern string belongs to the associated collection C.

20.25   Given a pattern $P[0{:}m-1]$ in string P, design and analyze an algorithm that traces a path in a suffix tree for text string T to determine whether P occurs as a substring of T.

CHAPTER **21**

BALANCED SEARCH TREES

The *dictionary operations* of inserting, deleting, or searching for keys stored in some type of data structure occur in a variety of applications. Database programs must support rapid location of customer records, word processing programs must contain search and replace operations, compilers must quickly recognize keywords, and so forth. Binary search trees, multiway search trees, and hash tables are commonly used to store keys. In this chapter, we discuss balanced search trees and their associated algorithms for efficiently implementing dictionary operations.

21.1 The Dictionary Problem

Given a totally ordered set S (elements of S will be called *keys* or *identifiers*), the *dictionary problem* is the problem of designing an ADT to maintain a collection of items drawn from S. The classic dictionary problem restricts attention to the dictionary operations of inserting a key, deleting a key, and searching for a key, but we also might consider performing additional operations, such as finding the maximum of minimum elements, accessing the keys in sorted order, and so forth. To do this, we need ADTs that perform dictionary operations efficiently.

In Chapter 17, we introduced the important ADT of hash functions and associated hash tables for performing dictionary operations. Other commonly used ADTs for the dictionary problem are balanced binary and multiway search trees. We have already discussed the dictionary operations for binary and multiway search trees in Chapter 4. Search trees not only support the dictionary operations, but they also support accessing keys in sorted order using inorder traversals. Unfortunately, they can become unbalanced by insertions and deletions, leading to linear worst-case behavior for the operations of inserting and searching for elements. By keeping the search trees balanced we can reduce the complexity of these operations to logarithmic complexity.

The ideally balanced binary tree on n nodes is the complete binary tree T_n, which has depth $\lfloor \log_2 n \rfloor$. Recall from Proposition 4.2.1 that T_n has minimum depth over all binary trees on n nodes. However, maintaining minimum-depth binary trees in the presence of dictionary operations is too costly. We need a compromise between a strong balance that guarantees minimum depth and an efficiently maintainable balance that is still strong enough to keep the depth logarithmic in the number of nodes.

Two well-known types of balanced binary search trees are AVL trees and red-black trees. Both AVL trees and red-black trees on n nodes have $O(\log n)$ depths. Insertion and deletion of elements in AVL trees and red-black trees begin just as for ordinary binary search trees. However, after inserting or deleting an element in an AVL tree or a red-black tree, rebalancing needs to be done to maintain their respective notions of balance.

A type of balanced multiway search tree known as a B-tree is commonly used to maintain the keys associated with records in a database stored on secondary (external) memory devices such as magnetic disks. Accessing and processing information in a node of a B-tree is similar to a disk access I/O operation—a much slower operation than accessing main (internal) memory. Algorithms for B-trees are designed to minimize node accesses (disk I/O operations). Because moves between adjacent levels in a B-tree require disk I/O operations, it is not unusual for B-trees to contain thousands of keys in each node to minimize the depth of the tree. Finding a key in a B-tree requires additional comparisons in each node, but comparisons are performed in internal memory and are orders of magnitude faster than disk I/O operations.

21.2   Rotations in Binary Search Trees

Rotations are the primary tool for restoring balance in balanced search trees after insertion or deletion of an element. Left and right rotations involving two nodes in a binary tree are illustrated in Figure 21.1. In the figure, α, β, and, γ represent subtrees. The following key fact is easy to verify by noting that the inorder traversal of either subtree shown in Figure 21.1 is $\alpha, A, \beta, B, \gamma$.

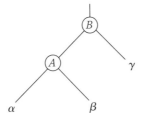
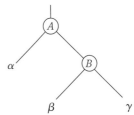

FIGURE 21.1

Left and right rotations involving nodes *A* and *B* in a binary tree T. The inorder traversal of T is preserved by either rotation.

Rotate (*B,A*) right
⇒

Rotate (*A,B*) left
⇐

Key Fact

Performing a left or right rotation in a binary tree does not alter the inorder traversal of the tree. In particular, rotations preserve the search tree property.

In our discussion of algorithms for maintaining binary search trees given in Chapter 4, we did not include a parent field in each node. Algorithms for balanced search trees typically contain parent pointers to facilitate insertion and deletion of nodes. We assume that the nodes in a balanced search tree have the following structure (*Info* may contain multiple fields):

BinSrchTreeNode = **record**
    Info: *InfoType*
    Key: *KeyType*
    LeftChild: →*BinSrchTreeNode*
    RightChild: →*BinSrchTreeNode*
    Parent: →*BinSrchTreeNode*
end *BinSrchTreeNode*

The following procedure, *RotateRight*, performs a right rotation of the nodes pointed to by *Node*, *Node* →*LeftChild* in a binary tree pointed to by *Root*. We leave the pseudocode for the symmetric case of a left rotation as an exercise.

procedure *RotateRight(Root, Node)*
Input: *Root* (→*BinaryTreeNode*)   //points at root of a binary tree *T*
           Node (→*BinaryTreeNode*)   //points at node where rotation takes place
Output: *Root* (→*BinaryTreeNode*)   //points at root of the binary search tree *T'*
                                  obtained by performing right rotation
        B ← *Node*   //simplify notation and tie to Figure 21.1
        A ← *Node*→*LeftChild*   //now move *A* up to *B*'s position

```
        if Root = B then
            Root ← A
        else
            if B = (B→Parent)→LeftChild then      //B is left child of its parent
                (B→Parent)→LeftChild ← A
            else
                (B→Parent)→RightChild ← A          //B is right child of its parent
            endif
        endif

                                                   //now make A's right subtree B's
                                                      left subtree

        B→LeftChild ← A→RightChild
        if A→RightChild ≠ null then
            (A→RightChild)→Parent ← B
        endif
                                                   //make B into A's right child
        A→RightChild ← B
        A→Parent ← B→Parent
        B→Parent ← A
    end RotateRight
```

In Figure 21.2, we show how two rotations are used to restore balance in an *AVL tree*, which is a binary search tree such that the depths of the left and right subtrees rooted at any node differ by at most 1. AVL trees are one of the earliest types of balanced search trees and are named after Adelson-Velskii and Landis, who introduced them in 1962.

Because algorithms implementing the dictionary operations for red-black trees (defined in the next section) are simpler than those for AVL trees, red-black trees are more commonly implemented today. Thus, we focus our attention on red-black trees.

FIGURE 21.2

Restoring balance
after inserting *k* in
an AVL tree.

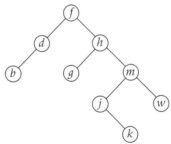

(a) Imbalance after inserting the node containing *k* in an AVL tree.

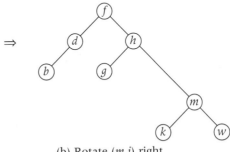

(b) Rotate (*m,j*) right

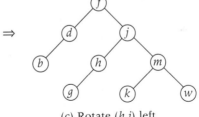

(c) Rotate (*h,j*) left

21.3 Red-Black Trees

About 10 years after the introduction of AVL trees, Bayer introduced what are now known as red-black trees (Bayer gave them the name symmetric binary B-trees). A red-black tree is balanced in the sense that no path from the root to a leaf is more than twice the length of any other such path. However, this balance is not part of the definition of a red-black tree but a consequence of the balance restrictions on node coloring. The color-balance restrictions for red-black trees are simpler to maintain than other balance restrictions, such as those for AVL trees, with correspondingly simpler algorithms for the dictionary operations.

21.3.1 Definition and Depth of Red-Black Trees

The color-balance restrictions of red-black trees are easier to state if we assume that augmented leaf nodes corresponding to unsuccessful searches are included as part of the tree. In particular, with augmented leaf nodes included, red-black trees are 2-trees. In the discussion that follows, we simply refer to the augmented leaf nodes of red-black trees as leaf nodes.

DEFINITION 21.3.1 A *red-black tree* is a binary search tree, augmented by (external) leaf nodes corresponding to an unsuccessful search, where each node has been assigned the color red or black subject to the following four properties:

1. Every leaf node is black.

2. If a node is red, then both its children are black.

3. Any two paths from a given node v down to a leaf node contain the same number of black nodes.

4. The root is black.

REMARKS

1. Including augmented leaf nodes in red-black trees makes properties 1 and 3 in Definition 21.3.1 have a powerful balancing effect. Indeed, if augmented leaf nodes were not included, then an all-black, completely skewed binary search tree would be a red-black tree.

2. Property 4, that the root is black, is for convenience. Clearly, if the other properties of a red-black tree are satisfied, and the root is colored red, then a red-black tree would result by recoloring the root to black.

We now consider the question of what degree of imbalance can exist in a red-black tree. The answer lies in the fact that for any node x in a red-black tree, the length of two paths from x to a leaf can differ only by at most a factor of 2. This fact is illustrated by the red-black tree in Figure 21.3, where any path from the root to a leaf in the left subtree is twice the length of a path from the root to a leaf in the right subtree (the example is easily generalized to an arbitrarily large number of nodes). In Figure 21.3, we have indicated the color outside each node.

Because the type of imbalance exhibited by the red-black tree in Figure 21.3 is maximal, we expect that the depth of a red-black tree on n internal nodes is at most about twice the depth ($\lfloor \log_2(n + 1) \rfloor$) of the most balanced binary tree on n internal nodes. The following proposition shows this to be the case, and this small depth property of red-black trees makes them candidates for good search trees.

Proposition 21.3.1 Let T be a red-black tree on n internal nodes. Then

$$\text{depth}(T) \leq 2\log_2(n + 1). \tag{21.3.1}$$

We establish Proposition 21.3.1 with the aid of Lemma 21.3.2. To state Lemma 21.3.2, for any red-black tree T, we let $b(T)$ denote the number of black nodes, excluding the root, on any path from the root of T to a leaf. Property 3 of Definition 21.3.1 shows that $b(T)$ is well defined.

FIGURE 21.3

A maximally imbalanced red-black tree on nine internal nodes.

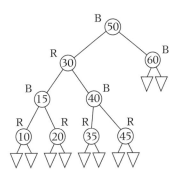

Lemma 21.3.2   Let T be a red-black tree. Then T has at least $2^{b(T)} - 1$ internal nodes.

PROOF

We prove Lemma 21.3.2 using induction on the number of internal nodes n in T.

Basis step: $n = 1$. Then $b(T) = 1$. Since T has $1 = 2^1 - 1$ internal nodes, the basis step is established.

Induction step: Assume that Lemma 21.3.2 has been verified for all red-black trees having fewer than $n > 1$ internal nodes. Note that the subtree rooted at any node v of a red-black tree is also a red-black tree. Hence, the left and right subtrees L and R, respectively, of the root of T are both red-black trees having fewer than n internal nodes. Since T is a 2-tree, both L and R are nonempty. Thus, by induction hypothesis, L and R both have at least $2^{b(R)} - 1$ internal nodes. Now the values of $b(L)$ and $b(R)$ are either $b(T)$ or $b(T) - 1$, depending on whether their roots are colored red or black, respectively. It follows that T has at least $2(2^{b(T)-1} - 1) + 1 = 2^{b(T)} - 1$ nodes, which establishes the induction step.   ■

PROOF OF PROPOSITION 21.3.1

Properties 1 and 2 of Definition 21.3.1 imply that at least half the nodes along any path from the root to a leaf, excluding the root, must be black. In other words, $b(T) \geq \text{depth}(T)/2$. Thus, using Lemma 21.3.2, we have

$$n \geq 2^{b(T)} - 1 \geq 2^{\text{depth}(T)/2} - 1. \qquad \textbf{(21.3.2)}$$

Proposition 21.3.1 now follows directly from Formula (21.3.2).   ■

21.3.2 Implementing Red-Black Trees

We assume that the nodes in a red-black tree have the following structure:

RedBlackTreeNode = **record**
  Info: *InfoType*
  Key: *KeyType*
  Color: *Boolean*   //0 = red, 1 = black
  LeftChild: →*RedBlackTreeNode*
  RightChild: →*RedBlackTreeNode*
  Parent: →*RedBlackTreeNode*
end *RedBlackTreeNode*

The augmented leaf nodes of the red-black tree are assumed to have the same structure as the nodes in the original tree, except that their information and key fields do not contain meaningful values. However, the parent fields of the augmented leaf nodes would be appropriately defined. In practice, allocating memory locations for each augmented leaf node simply wastes too much space. Instead, a single augmented node is added, called a *sentinel node.* All child pointers in the original tree that pointed to **null** augmented leaf nodes now hold the address of the sentinel node. Again, we assume the sentinel node has the same structure as the other nodes in the tree. In Figure 21.4, we show a red-black tree with a single sentinel node used for the augmented leaf nodes.

FIGURE 21.4

Red-black tree with
sentinel node.

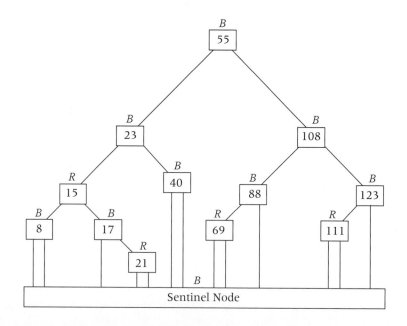

Using a sentinel node to handle **null** child pointers simplifies boundary conditions in algorithms that restore balance by suitably moving up the tree, sometimes starting from a **null** leaf. For convenience, in some figures that follow, we still represent **null** augmented nodes as separate nodes, as we did in Figure 21.3.

A search algorithm for a red-black tree is the same as that for an ordinary binary search tree. We now consider the operations of inserting and deleting nodes.

21.3.3 Inserting a Node into a Red-Black Tree

To insert a node into a red-black tree, we use the usual method of inserting into a binary search tree. We can use a call to the procedure *BinSrchTreeInsert* discussed in Chapter 4 (modified to maintain parent pointers), and we color the newly inserted node red. If the parent of the newly inserted node is black, we are done, because the tree is already a red-black tree. Otherwise, red-black property 2 is violated. (It is easy to see that the other properties of a red-black tree remain satisfied.) When inserting a node into a red-black tree, we see that a series of at most $\lfloor \log_2(n+1) \rfloor$ local neighborhood operations restore red-black tree property 2. Moreover, at most two rotations are required, the other operations being simple recolorings. The sequence of local neighborhood operations restoring property 2 does not generate any violation of the other red-black tree properties.

For any node v in a binary tree T, we define the *local neighborhood* of v to consist of v together with its parent, grandparent, and uncle. Each *correct-or-move-up* step in the eventual restoration of property 2 involves recoloring and (possibly) rotating the nodes in the local neighborhood of the current node. As implied by the name, a correct-or-move-up step accomplishes one of two things regarding the violation of property 2: the violation is either corrected or moved up two levels in the tree. During each correct-or-move-up step, no violations of the other two red-black properties are introduced. The current node is initially set to the newly inserted element.

For each correct-or-move-up step, there are six possible cases. Figure 21.5 illustrates cases 1, 2, and 3, which correspond to the parent of the current node being a red left child. The other three cases, cases $1'$, $2'$, and $3'$, are mirror images of these cases.

Case 1. The current node has a red uncle, and its parent node is a red left child. It doesn't matter whether the current node is a left or a right child (although for definiteness in Figure 21.5, we have shown the current node as a left child). We simply recolor the parent, grandparent, and uncle of the current node. If the great-grandparent of the current node is black, then the recoloring restores a red-black tree. Otherwise, the recoloring moves the violation of property 2 up two levels, and the current node is moved up to the grandparent. In both cases, the recoloring does not violate red-black property 3.

FIGURE 21.5

Case-by-case
actions leading to
restoration of a red-
black tree after
inserting a node.

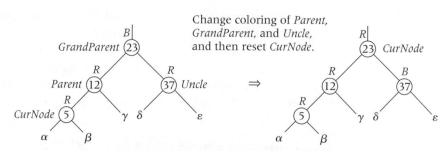

(a) Case 1: Parent of current node is a red left child.
Uncle of current node is also red.

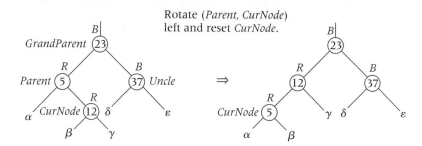

(b) Case 2: Parent of current node is red left child.
Uncle of current node is black. Current node is right child.

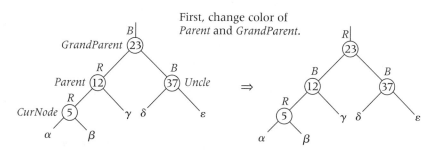

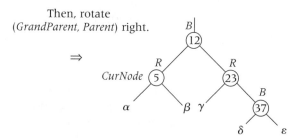

(c) Case 3: Parent of current node is red left child.
Current node is left child. Uncle of current node is black.

Case 2. The current node is a right child whose parent is a red left child and whose uncle is black. We perform a left rotation of (*Parent*, *CurNode*) and update the current node as in Figure 21.5, thereby transforming case 2 into case 3.

Case 3. The current node is a left child whose parent is a red left child and whose uncle is black. We recolor the parent and grandparent and then perform a right rotation of (*GrandParent*, *Parent*). These actions restore a red-black tree.

In Figure 21.6, we show the case transition diagram for correcting the violation of property 2 and restoring a red-black tree. Each arc in the case transition diagram represents a possible transition from one case to another. While case 1 (1′) can transition to anywhere, case 2 (2′) only transitions to case 3 (3′), and case 3 (3′) only transitions to the end—that is, to the restoration of a red-black tree.

On reaching case 2 (2′) and performing the relevant rotation and recoloring, we make the transition to case 3 (3′). On reaching case 3 (3′) and performing the relevant rotation and recoloring, a red-black tree is restored. Because case 1 (1′) does not involve a rotation, at most two rotations are ever needed in the process of restoring a red-black tree after inserting a node. However, notice in the case transition diagram that cases 1 and 1′ have self-loops possible, and a transition and loop are possible between case 1 and 1′. The action taken in both cases 1 and 1′ moves the violation of property 2 two levels up the tree. The frequency of this moving up of the violation is equal to at most one-half the depth of the tree; thus, these cases can be executed at most $\lfloor \log_2(n + 1) \rfloor$ times. All these considerations show that the insertion operation exhibits logarithmic performance.

An examination of each of the actions taken in the six cases shows that no other violations of the red-black tree properties are introduced other than the violation of property 2 that might still exist at the current node.

The following high-level pseudocode description of restoring a red-black tree after insertion is based directly on the transition diagram in Figure 21.6.

FIGURE 21.6

Case transition diagram for restoring a red-black tree after inserting a node.

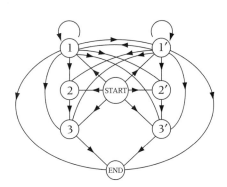

```
while (case 1 or 1' hold .and. property 2 is violated) do
    perform case 1 or 1' operations, whichever are appropriate
endwhile
if (property 2 is still violated .and. case 2 or 2') then
    perform case 2 or 2' operations, whichever are appropriate
endif
if (property 2 is still violated .and. case 3 or 3') then
    perform case 3 or 3' operations, whichever are appropriate
endif
```

By sequentially executing this pseudocode, we restore the red-black tree. Note that if we execute the first **if-then** statement, then we definitely execute body of the second **if-then** statement, but we don't need to explicitly take this into account in the pseudocode.

The pseudocode for the procedure *RedBlackTreeInsert* is a straightforward implementation of the previous high-level description. By definition, the red-black tree that calls *RedBlackTreeInsert* has a black root. During the course of the algorithm, the root may be colored red, but the last statement before the end of *RedBlackTreeInsert* restores its color to black. For readability, we use the terms *red* and *black* to correspond to the values 0 and 1, respectively, of the Boolean field *Color*. *RedBlackTreeInsert* calls the procedure *RBCorrect(ii)OrMoveUpL* when we encounter cases 1 through 3 and calls the procedure *RBCorrect(ii)OrMoveUpR* for the other three symmetric cases.

procedure *RedBlackTreeInsert(Root,X,Node)*

Input:	*Root* (→*RedBlackTreeNode*)	//points at black root of a red-black tree *T*
	X (*KeyType*)	//key to be inserted in *T*
Output:	*Root* (→*RedBlackTreeNode*)	//root of the red-black tree *T′* obtained by inserting *X*
	Node (→*RedBlackTreeNode*)	//points to node where *X* inserted
	BinSrchTreeInsert(Root, X, Node)	//ordinary search tree insertion, where *Node* now points to inserted node containing *X* Node→Color ← red

```
CurNode ← Node
while CurNode ≠ Root .and. (CurNode→Parent)→Color = red do
    Parent ← CurNode→Parent
    GrandParent ← (CurNode→Parent)→Parent
    if GrandParent→LeftChild = Parent then
        RBCorrect(ii )OrMoveUpL(Root, CurNode, Parent, GrandParent)
    else
        RBCorrect(ii )OrMoveUpR(Root, CurNode, Parent, GrandParent)
    endif
endwhile
Root→Color ← black
end RedBlackTreeInsert
```

We now give the pseudocode for *RBCorrect(ii)OrMoveUpL*. [The pseudocode for *RBCorrect(ii)OrMoveUpR* is obtained from *RBCorrect(ii)OrMoveUpL* by interchanging right and left.]

> **procedure** *RBCorrect(ii)OrMoveUpL(Root,CurNode,Parent,GrandParent)*
> **Input:**   *CurNode* (→*RedBlackTreeNode*)   //points at node of a tree *T*
>   //whose parent violates property 2
> **Output:** *CurNode* (→*RedBlackTreeNode*)   //*T* is restored to a red-black
>   //tree or *CurNode* is moved up
>   two levels}
>
>   *Uncle* ← *GrandParent*→*RightChild*
>   **if** *Uncle*→*Color* = red **then**   //case 1
>   *Parent*→*Color* ← black
>   *GrandParent*→*Color* ← red
>   *Uncle*→*Color* ← black
>   *CurNode* ← *GrandParent*   //move current node up two levels
>   **else**
>   **if** *Parent*→*RightChild* = *CurNode*   //case 2
>   *RotateLeft(Root,Parent)*
>   *CurNode* ← *CurNode*→*LeftChild*   //reset current node
>   **endif**
>   (*CurNode*→*Parent*)→*Color* ← black   //case 3
>   *GrandParent*→*Color* ← red
>   *RotateRight(Root,GrandParent)*
>   **endif**
> **end** *RBCorrect(ii)OrMoveUpL*

We illustrate the insertion of the sequence of keys 18, 16, and 55 into a red-black tree in Figure 21.7. For convenience in the figure, we have omitted pointers to the sentinel leaf node.

21.3.4 Deleting a Node from a Red-Black Tree

Deleting a node from a red-black tree is somewhat more complicated than inserting a node but has a similar flavor. We begin by calling *BinSrchTreeDelete* (modified to maintain parent pointers) to perform an ordinary deletion of node *v* from a binary search tree. Recall that when we delete an internal node *v* with two non-null children (a case 3 deletion in what follows), we replace the values in the information and key fields of *v* by the values in the information and key fields, respectively, of the inorder successor *w* of *v*. Then we delete *w*, which has at most one non-null child.

> **Key Fact**
>
> When deleting a node *v* with two non-null children, we replace only the *Key* and *Info* fields of *v* with that of *v*'s inorder successor *w*. In particular, we do *not* replace the value of the *Color* field of *v* by the value of the *Color* field of *w*. Thus, for a case 3 deletion, when we talk about the color of the deleted node, we mean the color of *w*, not *v*.

FIGURE 21.7

Inserting the
sequence of keys
18, 16, and 55 into
a red-black tree.

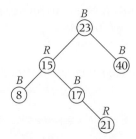

(a) Original red-black tree

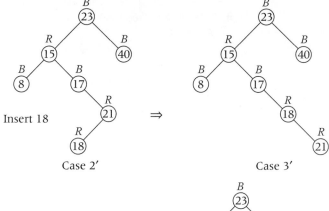

(b) Final red-black tree after inserting 18

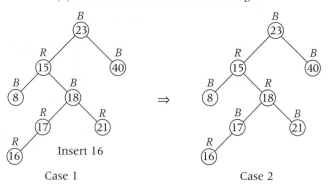

FIGURE 21.7

Continued

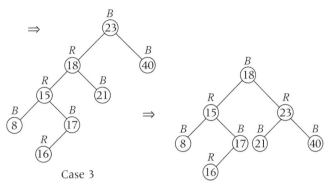

(c) Final red-black tree after inserting 16

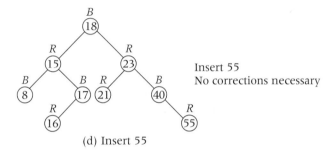

(d) Insert 55

The deletion of a node with at most one non-null child is accomplished by splicing it out (see Figure 4.19). If the deleted node is red, then we still have a red-black tree and nothing else need be done. If the deleted node is black and it has a red non-null child, then we restore the red-black tree by recoloring the non-null child black. Hence, we are left with the problem of restoring a red-black tree when the deleted node and its children are all black. In this case, property 3 is violated because any path that starts at a given node *y*, goes through the parent of the deleted node, and then goes on to the "spliced-in child" *CurNode* and down to a descendant leaf will have one too few black nodes than does a path from *y* to a leaf that doesn't go through *CurNode*. Also, any two paths from a node to a leaf that do not go through *CurNode* have the same number of black nodes. Thus, we can consider the violation of property 3 to be "rooted" at *CurNode*, the spliced-in child.

As before, we perform recolorings and rotations to restore a red-black tree, but our local neighborhood now consists of the current node, its parent, its sibling, and the left and right children of its sibling (denoted by *SLC* and *SRC*, respectively, in Figure 21.8). Recoloring and rotation either correct the violation of property 3 or move the violation up one level in the tree (at the same time not introducing any other violations of the red-black properties). There are ten cases to consider: five in which the current node is a left child, and five in which it is a

FIGURE 21.8

Cases in node
deletion determined
by colors of *Parent*,
Sibling, *SLC*, and
SRC, where R is red,
B is black, and * is
either red or black

Case	1	2a	2b	3	4	1′	2a′	2b′	3′	4′
Parent	B	B	R	*	*	B	B	R	*	*
Sibling	R	B	B	B	B	R	B	B	B	B
SLC	B	B	B	R	*	B	B	B	B	R
SRC	B	B	B	B	R	B	B	B	R	*

right child. The cases are determined by the local neighborhood (for deletion) of *CurNode*. The table in Figure 21.8 shows the colorings of these nodes that determine the relevant cases.

Figure 21.9 illustrates the five cases handled by *RBCorrect(iii)OrMoveUpL* (where the current node is a left child). We use the variable names *CurNode*, *Parent*, and *Sibling* to denote the nodes in a local neighborhood of the current node.

In case 1, *Sibling* is red, whereas in the other four cases, *Sibling* is black. Case 1 transforms into case 2b, case 3, or case 4. In case 2a, the violation is moved one level up the tree, and the loop is repeated (unless the current node becomes the root). In case 2b, the violation of property 3 is moved up one level, but a violation of property 2 is introduced there. However, the loop is terminated, leaving *CurNode* colored black and thus correcting the violation of both properties 2 and 3 in one fell swoop. Case 3 is transformed into case 4, where the violation of property 3 is corrected and the algorithm terminates. Figure 21.9 shows sample key values in the nodes so that the nodes can be traced during the action of *RBCorrect(iii)OrMoveUpL*.

It is important to verify in all ten cases that the transformations introduce no other violations of the red-black properties (except as noted for case 2b, which is then corrected), that each case except case 2a results in restoring a red-black tree, and that case 2a moves the root of the violation of property 3 one level up the tree. For example, Figure 21.9a shows that in case 1, any path starting at vertex v and going through either node 5, 17, or 55 on its way to a leaf node encounters the same number of black nodes before and after the transformation. Moreover, no other paths to leaf nodes are affected by the transformation, so the violation of property 3 remains rooted at node 5. Complete verifications of all ten cases are left as exercises.

Figure 21.10 is the case transition diagram for restoring a red-black tree after deletion of a node. Again, some looping may occur, this time involving cases 2a and 2a′. Action in these cases moves *CurNode* one level up the tree. Hence, these cases can be executed at most $2\lfloor \log_2(n + 1) \rfloor$ times before we reach the root (or leave case 2a and 2a′), and property 3 is restored.

FIGURE 21.9

Case-by-case
actions for storing a
red-black tree after
deleting a node.

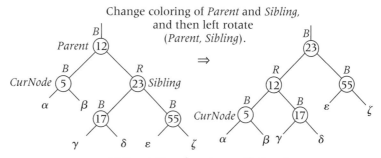

(a) Case 1: Transform to case 2b, 3, or 4

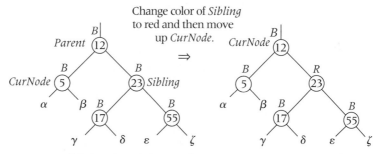

(b) Case 2a: Violation of property (iii) moves up one level

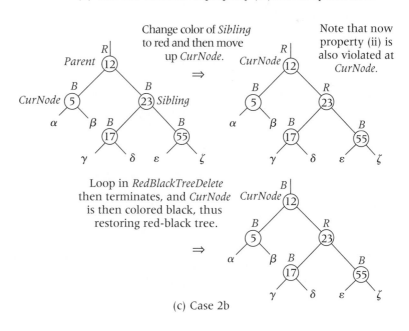

(c) Case 2b

continued

····································

FIGURE 21.9

Continued

····································

Change color of *Sibling* to red
and its left child to black, and then
right rotate (*Sibling, LeftChild*).

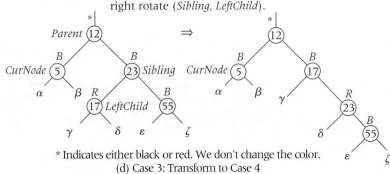

* Indicates either black or red. We don't change the color.
(d) Case 3: Transform to Case 4

Nodes colored c_1 and c_2 are either black or red.
These colors remain unchanged. Change color
of *Sibling*'s right child to black, color *Parent* black,
color *Sibling* c_1, and then left rotate (*Parent, Sibling*).
Finally, change *CurNode* to root of tree.

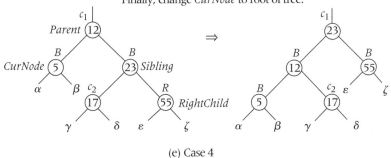

(e) Case 4

····································

FIGURE 21.10

Case transition
diagram for
restoring a red-
black tree after
deleting a node.

····································

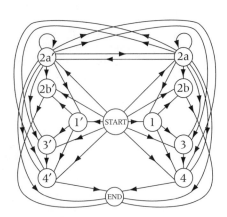

Note that you can transition anywhere from cases 2a or 2a'. If case 1 is entered, then we can transition to case 2b, 3, or 4, depending on whether the colors of *SLC* and *SRC* are B and B, R and B, or B and R, respectively. If case 1' is entered, then we can transition to case 2b', 3', or 4', depending on whether the colors of *SLC* and *SRC* are B and B, B and R, or R and B, respectively. Case 2b (2b') transitions to the end, case 3 (3') transitions to case 4 (4'), and case 4 (4') transitions to the end. Single rotations are done in cases 1, 3, and 4 (and their mirror images 1', 3', and 4') only, so that at most three rotations are ever done when restoring a red-black tree after deletion of a node. From these remarks, we see again that our algorithm for deleting a node from a red-black tree exhibits logarithmic performance.

The following high-level pseudocode description of restoring a red-black tree after node deletion is based directly on the case transition diagram in Figure 21.9.

```
while (property 3 is violated .and. case 2a or 2a' hold) do
    perform case 2a or 2a' operations, whichever are appropriate
endwhile
if (property 3 is violated .and. case 1 or 1') then
    perform case 1 or 1' operations, whichever are appropriate
endif
if (property 3 is violated .and. case 2b or 2b') then
    perform case 2b or 2b' operations, whichever are appropriate
    return (red-black tree is restored)
endif
if (property 3 is violated .and. case 3 or 3') then
    perform case 3 or 3' operations, whichever are appropriate
endif
if (property 3 is violated .and. case 4 or 4') then
    perform case 4 or 4' operations, whichever are appropriate
endif
```

Figure 21.11 illustrates the deletion of the sequence of nodes 88, 8, 55, and 61 from a red-black tree. Again, for convenience, we omit pointers to the sentinel leaf node *Sentinel*, except when the initial value of *CurNode* points at *Sentinel*, as in Figures 21.11c and 21.11d.

Note that we perform at most two rotations to correct the violation of property 3 and restore a red-black tree. When restoring the red-black properties after inserting or deleting a node, each time we call the correct-or-move-up algorithms, we perform a constant number of pointer and other field reassignments.

FIGURE 21.11

Deleting the
sequence of nodes
88, 8, 55, and 61
from a red-black
tree

(a) Original red-black tree

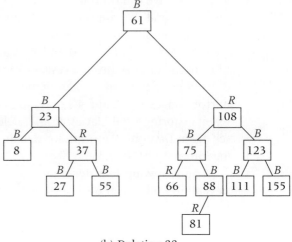

(b) Deleting 88

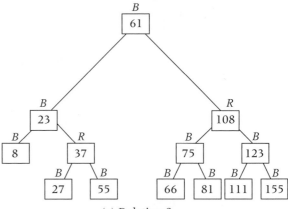

(c) Deleting 8

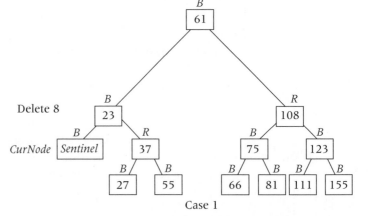

FIGURE 21.11

Continued

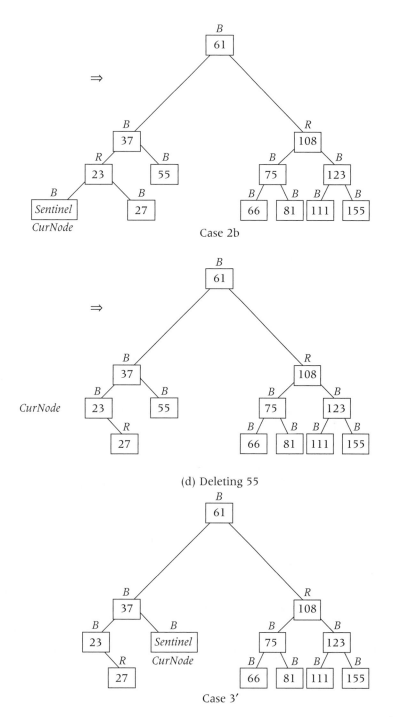

Case 2b

(d) Deleting 55

Case 3'

continued

FIGURE 21.11

Continued

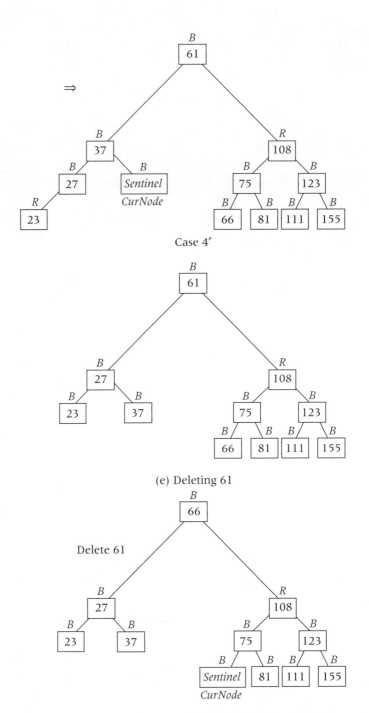

Case 4′

(e) Deleting 61

Delete 61

Case 2a: Replace 61 by its inorder successor 66, then delete original occurrence of 66

FIGURE 21.11

Continued

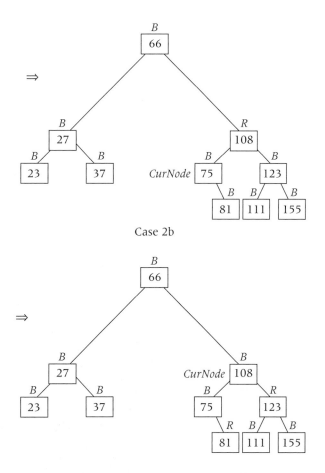

Case 2b

Thus, we have $O(\text{depth}(T)) = O(\log n)$ complexity for both inserting and deleting an element in a red-black tree T having n internal nodes. The pseudocode for deleting a node from a red-black tree is left as an exercise.

21.4 B-Trees

Introduced by Bayer and McCreight in the early 1970s, B-trees have been used extensively to implement the dictionary operations on database files stored on external storage devices (typically disks). Because accessing external memory through **read** and **write** operations is much more time consuming than accessing internal memory, we wish to keep external file accesses (**read**s or **write**s) to a minimum.

When using a B-tree as an index file for a database stored in external memory, we assume that each move from one level to another necessitates a **read** operation. More precisely, to access a node in a B-tree, we must **read** in all the keys in the node from external memory. We do not concern ourselves here with the memory management details associated with the paging in and paging out of various nodes.

To minimize the number of accesses to external memory performed by the dictionary operations, the depth of the B-tree is kept small using various balancing techniques, as well as by storing multiple keys in each node. Storing multiple keys in each node requires extra processing for dictionary operations in the nodes. However, because this processing is done in fast internal memory, the time taken for it is dominated by the time taken by reading from (and writing to) an external file.

The algorithms for maintaining B-trees are straightforward but somewhat cumbersome in their detail. We limit our discussion to defining B-trees and establishing some of their basic properties. We also illustrate and give high-level descriptions of insertion and deletion algorithms for B-trees.

21.4.1 Definition and Properties of B-Trees

The following definition imposes a very strict form of balance on B-trees. This balance, together with a restriction on the minimum number of keys contained in a node, is what makes B-trees have small depth compared with the number of keys contained in the tree (see Proposition 21.4.1).

DEFINITION 21.4.1 A *B-tree T* is a (rooted) tree satisfying the following properties:

1. *T* is a multiway search tree.

2. Every leaf of *T* is on the same level.

3. For some fixed integer $m \geq 2$, every node other than the root contains at least m keys and at most $2m$ keys. The root must contain at least one key and at most $2m$ keys.

4. An internal node containing t keys has $t + 1$ non-null children.

Each node in a B-tree has at most $2m + 1$ children; therefore, in the terminology of the previous section, B-trees are $(2m + 1)$-way search trees. For convenience, we refer to a $(2m + 1)$-way B-tree as a *B-tree of order m*. (Caution: Other names appear in the literature for B-trees of order m, such as B-trees of *minimum degree $2m + 1$*.) A node that contains the maximum number $2m$ of keys is called a *full* node. In Figure 21.12, we show a B-tree of order 2 containing 24 keys.

FIGURE 21.12

A B-tree of order 2 containing 24 keys.

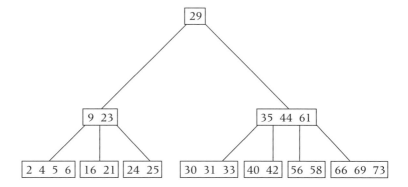

In practice, B-trees typically are of much higher order than the one shown in Figure 21.12, with orders of a thousand or more not uncommon. Because the number of nodes at level l is an exponential function of l, an enormous number of keys can be maintained by very shallow B-trees. Indeed, a B-tree of order 50 and depth 2 can store $100 + (101)(100) + (101^2)(100) = 1,030,301$ keys, which is more than enough for most databases maintained on personal computers. With the root node kept in internal memory, each of the 1,030,301 keys can be found by executing at most two **read** statements.

Proposition 21.4.1   Suppose T is a B-tree of order m and depth d. Then T contains at least $2(m + 1)^d - 1$ keys. Hence, if T contains n keys, then

$$\text{depth}(T) < \log_m \frac{n + 1}{2}. \tag{21.4.1}$$

PROOF
We establish the proposition by determining the minimum number $\mu(m,d)$ of keys contained in a B-tree of order m and depth d. Using properties 3 and 4 of Definition 21.4.1, $\mu(m,d)$ is obtained when the root has one key and every other node contains m keys. We then have

$$\mu(m,d) = 1 + m(2 + 2(m + 1) + 2(m + 1)^2 + \cdots + 2(m + 1)^{d-1})$$
$$= 1 + m\frac{((2m + 1)^d - 1)}{m} = 1 + 2((m + 1)^d - 1) \tag{21.4.2}$$
$$= 2(m + 1)^d - 1.$$

Formula (21.4.2) implies that if T is a B-tree of order m and depth d containing n keys, then

$$n \geq \mu(m,d) = 2(m + 1)^d - 1. \tag{21.4.3}$$

■

Our insertion and deletion procedures for B-trees require m to be an input parameter. Thus, in our analysis of the complexity of the algorithms for performing the dictionary operations on a B-tree, we give the worst-case complexity in terms of the base-m logarithm function $\log_m n$, rather than in terms of $\Theta(\log n)$ membership. There is another reason to measure complexity in terms of m: All base-m logarithms, $m > 1$, determine the same class $\Theta(\log n)$, so that a Θ-class measure is not sufficiently precise to distinguish between the performance, say, of balanced binary trees and B-trees.

21.4.2 Searching a B-Tree

Since B-trees are multiway search trees, the search strategy described in Section 2.6 applies. Letting *B-TreeSearch* denote the resulting algorithm, clearly the worst-case complexity occurs when the search key k is either in a leaf or not in the tree at all. In both cases, we perform depth(T) **read**s. Hence, Proposition 21.4.1 implies that *B-TreeSearch* performs at most $\log_m(n + 1)/2$ **read**s and $2m \log_m(n + 1)/2$ comparisons for a B-tree of order m on n keys.

The $2m\log_m(n + 1)/2$ comparisons performed by *B-TreeSearch* in the worst case is larger than the typical upper bound of $2\log(n + 1)$ comparisons performed by the dictionary operations on red-black trees on n keys. However, the $2\log_2(n + 1)$ worst-case depth for red-black trees is reduced to a $\log_m(n + 1)/2$ worst-case depth for B-trees. Trees of smaller depth reduce the corresponding number of time-consuming accesses to external memory.

21.4.3 Inserting a Key into a B-Tree

When inserting a key into a B-tree, we use a variation of our searching technique to descend down a path from the root of the B-tree to an appropriate leaf node for insertion. However, we might end up at a full leaf, and inserting the key there causes an overflow. There are two ways to remove the overflow at a node and thereby (eventually) restore a B-tree:

1. If the node has an immediately adjacent sibling that is not full, then send a key from the parent down to this sibling, and send a key up from the node to the parent.
2. If both immediately adjacent siblings are full, then split the node into two nodes by passing the median key up to the parent.

We always try to remove overflow using method 1 because it immediately restores the B-tree (see Figure 21.12). Using method 2 to remove overflow, the B-tree is immediately restored if the parent was not full; otherwise, an overflow occurs when passing the median key up to the parent (see Figure 21.13), and we must repeat the process at the parent. Continuing in this manner, we move up the tree until we eventually restore the B-tree. In the worst case, we work all the way back to the root. If the root is full, and if method 1 is not applicable, then the root is split and a new root is created containing the median key of the old root.

> **Key Fact**
>
> **Splitting the root increases the depth of the B-tree by 1 and is the only way that the depth of a B-tree increases. Thus, while binary search trees grow at the bottom, B-trees always grow at the top.**

We illustrate methods 1 and 2 of removing overflow in Figures 21.13 and 21.14, respectively. In both figures, the parent nodes are full. Hence, in Figure 21.14, the overflow gets passed up to the parent.

FIGURE 21.13

Removing overflow in a node using method 1 in a B-tree of order 2.

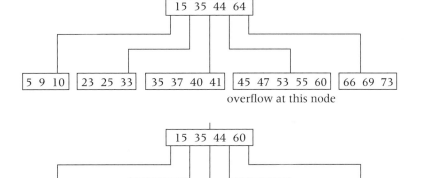

FIGURE 21.14

Removing overflow in a node using method 2 in a B-tree of order 2. In this example, an overflow is passed up to parent.

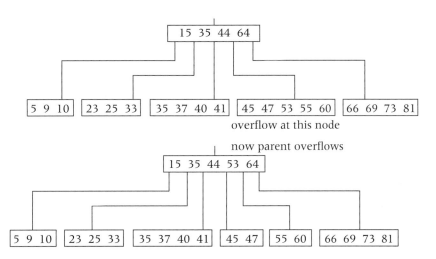

The example in Figure 21.14 is continued in Figure 21.15. In Figure 21.15a, the overflowed parent has an immediately adjacent sibling that is not full, so method 1 is used to restore a B-tree. In Figure 21.14b, because both immediately adjacent siblings to the overflowed parent are full, method 2 is used to remove overflow. We only show those nodes that are relevant to the overflow removal. Figure 21.16 shows the result of splitting the root node of a B-tree of order 2.

FIGURE 21.15

Continuation of example from Figure 21.14.

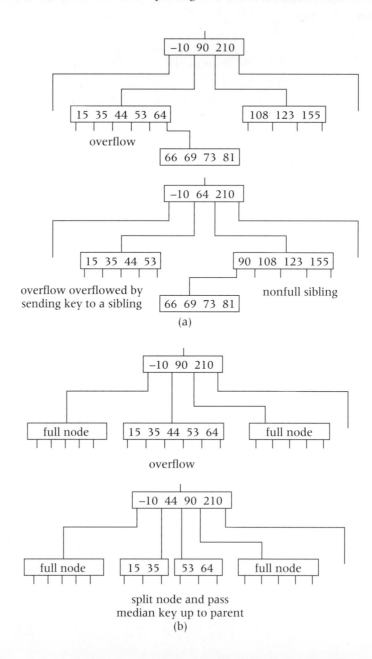

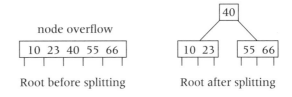

Figure 21.17 illustrates the process of inserting the sequence of keys into an initially empty B-tree of order 2. We only illustrate some of the intermediate steps in the total sequence of insertions. When using method 1, if both the immediate right and left siblings are not full, we assume that we send a key to the right child.

Using the techniques illustrated in Figures 21.13 through 21.17, it is relatively straightforward (but cumbersome in detail) to design a recursive algorithm for inserting a key in a B-tree. The recursion works as follows. If we are at a leaf node, we search the node for proper placement of the key. If the leaf node is not full, we insert the key. If the leaf node is full, then, if possible, we use method 1 to restore the B-tree. If we cannot use method 1, we split the node into two nodes, regarded as a left child and a right child of the median key that will be moved up to the parent node. The pointer to the original leaf node now points to the new left child leaf node, and we return the median key as well as a pointer to the newly created right child. The pointer to the right child is **null** if no splitting occurred.

If we are not at a leaf node, we search the node for the proper subtree in which to insert the key and recursively insert the key into this subtree. Again, if the root node of the subtree has to be split, then the recursive insertion returns a median key to be inserted at the current node, together with a pointer to the node that is to be the right child of this median key.

We now give pseudocode for the procedure *B-TreeInsert*(*Root*,*k*), which inserts a key *k* into the B-tree *T* of order *m* pointed at by *Root*. We assume that the nodes in the B-tree have the following structure:

```
B-TreeNode = record
    Key[0:2m − 1]:    KeyType        //an array of keys
    NumKeys:          Integer        //keeps track of current number of keys in
                                         node, Key[0], . . . , Key[NumKeys − 1]
    Child[0:2m]:      Child[i]→B-TreeNode, i = 0,1, . . . , NumKeys
                                     //an array of pointers to the children of
                                         the node
    Parent:           Parent→B-TreeNode  //a pointer to parent node
    Leaf:             Boolean        //a Boolean variable that is .true. if and
                                         only if the node is a leaf
end B-TreeNode
```

Insert 23, 98, 55, and 37 into initially empty B-Tree of order 2.

Result:

Insert 30: root overflow, so split root and make median key new root.

Result:

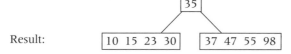

Insert 47, 35, and 15

Result:

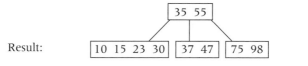

Insert 10: leaf overflow, so send key to sibling.

Result:

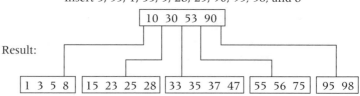

Insert 75: leaf overflow, sibling full, so split node.

Result:

Insert 3, 53, 1, 33, 5, 28, 25, 90, 95, 56, and 8

Result:

Insert 9: leaf overflow, so split leaf; root full, so split root.

Result:

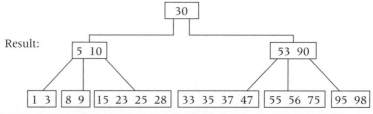

Because B-trees are multiway search trees, it follows that for each internal node, we have $k_0 \leq Key[0] \leq k_1 \leq Key[1] \leq \cdots \leq k_{\text{NumKeys}-1} \leq Key[NumKeys - 1] \leq k_{\text{NumKeys}}$, where k_i is any key in the subtree pointed at by $Child[i]$, $i = 0, 1, \ldots,$ *NumKeys*.

We assume a procedure *AllocateB-TreeNode*, which when called with output parameter *Node*, allocates (in internal memory) a memory location having the *B-TreeNode* record structure and an address placed in *Node*. In particular, all the algorithms for performing the dictionary operations on a B-tree T assume that T was initialized as an empty tree by executing the following statements:

AllocateB-TreeNode(Root)   //create an empty B-tree
Root→Leaf ← .true.
Root→NumKey ← 0
*parent ← **null***
write(*Root→B-TreeNode*)

The nonrecursive procedure *B-TreeInsert* calls the auxiliary recursive procedure *B-TreeInsertRec*, which does most of the work.

procedure *B-TreeInsert(Root, k, m)*
Input: *Root* (a pointer to root *r* of a B-tree *T*)
            k (a key to be inserted)
            m (order of *T*)
Output: *Root* (a pointer to *T* altered by inserting key *k*)
         B-TreeInsertRec(Root, k, m, RChild, MedianKey)
         if *RChild* ≠ **null then**   //root *r* was split: create new root
            B-TreeNewRoot(Root, RChild, MedianKey)
         endif
end *B-TreeInsert*

procedure *B-TreeInsertRec(Root, k, m, RChild, MedianKey)* **recursive**
Input: *Root* (a pointer to root node *s* of a subtree of a B-tree *T*)
            k (a key to be inserted)
            m (order of *T*)
Output: *T* altered by inserting key *k* in subtree
            RChild (a pointer to right child sibling of *s* if *s* is split, otherwise **null**)
            MedianKey (median key of keys in *s* ∪ *k* if *s* is split, otherwise undefined)
         NodeSearch(Root, k, Root→NumKeys, Index)
         if *Root→Leaf* **then**   //insert *k*
            InsertKeyInNode(Root, k, Root→NumKeys, Index, MedianKey, RChild)
         else
               B-TreeInsert(Root→Child[Index], k, m, RightChild, MedianKey)
               if *RChild* ≠ **null then**

```
          NodeSearch(Root, MedianKey, Root→NumKeys, Index)
          InsertKeyInNode(Root, MedianKey, Root→ NumKeys, Index, MedianKey,
            RChild)
      endif
    endif
  end B-TreeInsertRec
```

We leave the pseudocode for procedures *B-TreeNewRoot*, *NodeSearch*, and *InsertKeyInNode* as exercises.

The number of basic operations (**read**s and **write**s) performed by *B-TreeIn-sert* for a B-tree *T* is bounded above by 4(depth(*T*)). Hence, by Proposition 21.4.1, *B-TreeInsert* performs at most $4(\log_m (n + 1)/2)$ basic operations for a B-tree of order *m* on *n* nodes.

21.4.4 Deleting a Key from a B-Tree

When inserting a key into a B-tree of order 2*m*, we correct node overflows by sending keys to siblings or by splitting nodes. Because we only split full nodes, the minimum number *m* of keys in each node is always maintained. Deleting a key from a node containing *m* keys leaves the node one shy of having the mini-mum number of keys, so a correction must be done.

As with deletion in binary search trees, deleting a key *k* from an internal node involves finding the inorder successor *k** of *k* (*k** will be in a leaf), replacing *k* by *k**, and then deleting *k**. The inorder successor *k** is the leftmost key in the leftmost node of the right subtree rooted at *k*. If the node containing *k** has more than *m* keys, we merely delete *k** and are done. Otherwise, the deletion of *k** yields an underflow that we must remove in one of two ways:

1. If the node has an immediately adjacent sibling containing more than *m* keys, then we send a key from the sibling up to the parent and send a key from the parent down to the node.
2. If both immediate siblings have *m* keys, then we merge the node and an im-mediate sibling and send down a key from the parent, placing it between the keys in the merged siblings.

Note that performing method 1 results in the restoration of a B-tree. Per-forming method 2 with a parent having more than *m* keys also results in the restoration of a B-tree. However, when a parent has only *m* nodes, method 2 re-sults in underflow at the parent and must be repeated at the parent. In the worst case, this underflow will propagate all the way to the root. Performing method 2 on a root with a single key destroys the root, and a new root consisting of the two merged siblings results (see Figure 21.18).

We illustrate the actions of both methods in Figure 21.18 for a sample B-tree of order 2.

FIGURE 21.18

Two methods of
deleting a key from
a B-tree of order 2.

Case 1: Delete 88, send 77 from sibling to parent, and send 80 from parent to node

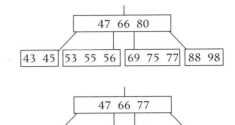

Result:

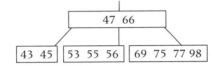

Case 2: Delete 80, merge node with sibling, and send down 77 from parent.

Result:

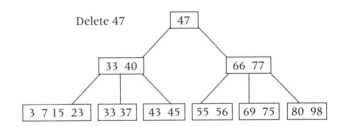

FIGURE 21.19

Deleting key
47 from a sample
B-tree of order 2.

Delete 47

Replace 47 by its inorder successor
55, then delete (the leaf
occurrence) of 55.

Underflow now
occurs at parent

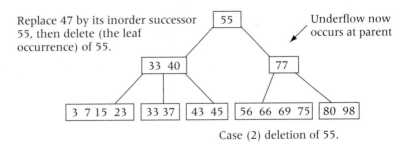

Case (2) deletion of 55.

Repeat case (2) at parent. Merged siblings now new root.

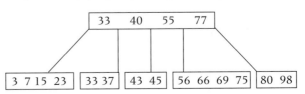

Figure 21.19 shows the action of deleting key 47 from a B-tree of order 2.

Designing the procedure *B-TreeDelete* based on the preceding discussion is straightforward but again somewhat cumbersome in detail. We leave the pseudocode for *B-TreeDelete* as an exercise. The number of basic operations (**read**s and **write**s) performed by *B-TreeDelete* for a B-tree T is bounded above by $4(\text{depth}(T)) < 4(\log_m(n + 1)/2)$.

21.5 Closing Remarks

B-trees are used so often in practice to index database files that it is of interest to try to improve their performance even more. For example, two common variants of B-trees are B^+-trees and B*-trees (discussed in the exercises). The references contain much more detail on B-trees and their variants.

References and Suggestions for Further Reading

Detailed discussions of balanced trees and B-trees can be found in the following:

Adelson-Velskii, G. M. and Y. M. Landis. "An Algorithm for the Organization of Information." *Doklady Akademii Nauk SSR* 146 (1962): 263–266. English translation in *Soviet Mathematics Doklady* 3 (1962): 1259–1263. The notion of balancing a search tree is due to Adelson-Velskii and Landis, who introduced AVL trees in this paper.

Aho, A. V., J. E. Hopcroft, and J. D. Ullman. *Data Structures and Algorithms.* Reading, MA: Addison-Wesley, 1983.

Bayer, R. "Symmetric Binary B-Trees: Data Structure and Maintenance Algorithms." *Acta Informatica* 1 (1972): 290–306. Bayer first introduced red-black trees under the name symmetric binary B-trees.

Bayer, R., and E. M. McCreight. "Organization and Maintenance of Large Ordered Indices." *Acta Informatica* 1 (1972): 173–189. The original reference to B-trees.

Comer, D. "The Ubiquitous B-tree." *ACM Computing Surveys* 11 (1979): 121–137. A nice survey of the topic of B-trees.

Gonnet, G. H. *Handbook of Algorithms and Data Structures.* Reading, MA: Addison-Wesley, 1984.

Knuth, D. E. *The Art of Computer Programming.* Vol. 3, *Sorting and Searching*, 2nd ed. Reading, MA: Addison-Wesley, 1998.

Section 21.2 Rotations of Binary Search Trees

21.1 Suppose we have keys $K_0 < K_1 < \cdots < K_{n-1}$ stored in a global array $K[0{:}n-1]$ (so that $K[i] = K_i$, $i = 0, \ldots, n-1$), and T is an abstract binary search tree for the keys. Also suppose that the global array $Root[0{:}n-1, 0{:}n-1]$ is such that $Root[i,j]$ is the index of the key in the root of the subtree of T containing the keys $K_i, K_{i+1}, \ldots, K_j$, $0 \le i \le j \le n-1$. (In particular, $Root[0, n-1]$ is the index of the key in the root of T.) Give pseudocode for a recursive function $CreateBinSrchTree(i,j)$ that creates the binary search tree containing the keys $K_i, K_{i+1}, \ldots, K_j$, $0 \le i \le j \le n-1$, and returns a pointer to the subtree. Note that calling $CreateBinSrchTree(0, n-1)$ should create the entire tree T. The nodes of the tree T are given the following structure:

```
BinSrchTreeNode = record
    Info:        InfoType
    Key:         KeyType
    LeftChild:   →BinSrchTreeNode
    RightChild:  →BinSrchTreeNode
    Parent:      →BinSrchTreeNode
end BinSrchTreeNode
```

$CreateBinSrchTree$ should call the procedure $AllocateNode(Q)$, which you can assume allocates space for the record shown above and returns, in the output parameter Q, a pointer to the allocated record.

21.2 Give pseudocode for an adaptation of $BinSrchTreeInsert$ for binary search trees with parent pointers and nodes having the structure given in Exercise 21.1.

21.3 Give pseudocode for an adaptation of $BinSrchTreeDelete$ for binary search trees with parent pointers and nodes having the structure given in Exercise 21.1.

21.4 Give pseudocode for a left rotation.

21.5 Recall that an AVL tree is a binary tree where the depths of the left and right subtrees of any node differ by at most 1. For an AVL tree T on n nodes, show that depth$(T) \in O(\log n)$.

21.6 Show that at most two rotations are needed to restore balance in an AVL tree after insertion of a node.

Section 21.3 Red-Black Trees

21.7 Prove that a red-black tree is balanced in the sense that no path from the root to a leaf has length more than twice that of any other such path.

21.8 Describe the five cases for *RBCorrect(iii)OrMoveUpR* that are symmetric to those for *RBCorrect(iii)OrMoveUpL*

21.9 Give pseudocode for *RBCorrect(iii)OrMoveUpL* and *RBCorrect(iii) OrMoveUpR.*

21.10 Verify that the ten transformations for restoring a red-black tree introduce no other violations of the red-black properties (except as noted for case 2b, which is then corrected), that each case except case 2a results in restoring a red-black tree, and that case 2a moves the root of the violation of property 3 one level up the tree.

21.11 Show the result of inserting the keys 9, 10, 5, 36, and 33 into the red-black tree illustrated in Figure 21.20.

FIGURE 21.20

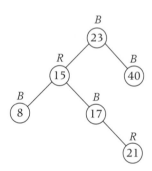

21.12 Show the result of deleting the keys 27, 108, 22, 122, and 61 from the red-black tree illustrated in Figure 21.21.

FIGURE 21.21

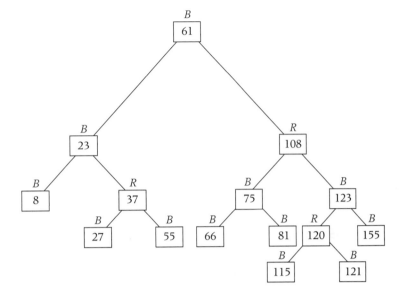

21.13 Note from Figure 21.9 that no deletion from a red-black tree can go through all five (unprimed) cases. Show that the red-black tree in the following figure that the deletion of node 10 ends the following sequence of case transitions: 2a ⇒ 1 ⇒ 3 ⇒ 4 ⇒. Show the resulting tree after the operations in each case are executed.

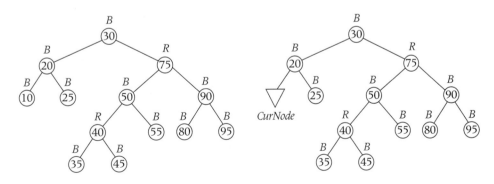

Original red-black tree

Delete node 10: violation of (iii) at CurNode

Case 2a then transforms to case 1

Section 21.4 B-Trees

21.14 Show that most of the keys in a B-tree are in leaf nodes.

21.15 Show that for any key *k* in a B-tree, if *k* is in an internal node, then both the inorder successor and the inorder predecessor of *k* are in leaf nodes.

21.16 Determine the minimum depth of a B-tree of order *m* containing *n* keys, $n \geq 1$.

21.17 Show the B-tree that results from using *B-TreeInsert* to insert the elements 1, 2, and 63 into the B-tree of order 2 illustrated in Figure 21.22.

FIGURE 21.22

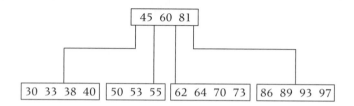

21.18 Show the B-tree that results from using *B-TreeDelete* to delete the elements 28, 29, 33, 30, 44, and 22 from the B-tree of order 2 in Figure 21.23.

FIGURE 21.23

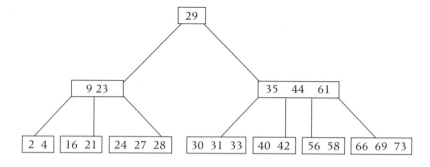

For exercises 21.19–21.25: Suppose that the nodes in a B-tree T of order m have the form described in Section 21.4, and that we have procedure *AllocateB-TreeNode*, which when called with output parameter *Node*, allocates (in internal memory) a memory location having the *B-TreeNode* record structure and whose address is placed in *Node*. In particular, we assume that the B-tree T was initialized as an empty tree by executing the following statements:

AllocateB-TreeNode(Root)   //create an empty B-tree
Root→Leaf ← **.true.**
Root→NumKeys ← 0
Parent ← **null**
write(*Root→B-TreeNode*)

21.19   Design and give pseudocode for a recursive algorithm *B-TreeSearch* that inputs a pointer to the root of a B-tree T and a search key k and outputs a pointer to a node v containing k (**null** if k is not in T), as well as the index in v's field *Key*[0:2m − 1] such that *Key*[*Index*] = k (−1 if k not in T).

21.20   Design and give pseudocode for the procedure *B-TreeNewRoot(Root,RChild, MedianKey)* called by procedure *B-TreeInsert*.

21.21   Design and give pseudocode for the procedure *NodeSearch(Root,k, Root→NumKeys, Index)* called by *B-TreeInsert*.

21.22   Design and give pseudocode for the procedure *InsertKeyInNode(Root,k, Root→NumKeys, Index, MedianKey, RChild)* called by *B-TreeInsert*.

21.23   Design and give pseudocode for a nonrecursive version of *B-TreeInsert* based on its bottom-up resolution.

21.24   Design and give pseudocode for a recursive procedure *B-TreeDelete*.

21.25   Design and give pseudocode for a nonrecursive version of *B-TreeDelete* based on its bottom-up resolution.

21.26   A B*-tree is a B-tree with the additional requirement that each node (except possibly the root) is at least two-thirds full. Algorithms for maintaining B*-trees avoid splitting nodes whenever possible. For example, when a key is inserted into a full node such that both immediate siblings are also full, the three full nodes are merged into two, and the data in the parent is appropriately adjusted. Design and analyze an algorithm for inserting into a B*-tree.

21.27 A B^+ tree is a B-tree where all keys in internal nodes are regarded as dummies (signposts to guide searches), as shown in Figure 21.24. Keys in internal nodes are duplicated in leaves. Note that if the leaves in a B^+-tree are linked together in increasing order of the keys, then traversals are easily accomplished. Design and analyze search and insertion algorithms for B^+-trees.

FIGURE 21.24

A B^+-tree of
order 2.

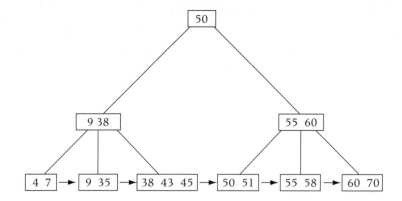

CHAPTER 22

THE FAST FOURIER TRANSFORM

One of the most celebrated divide-and-conquer algorithms is the Fast Fourier Transform (FFT) implementing the Discrete Fourier Transform (DFT). The Fast Fourier Transform algorithm has a wide range of important applications to such fields as signal processing and image processing, computerized axial tomography (CAT) scans, weather prediction and statistics, and coding theory. In fact, the FFT has been referred to as the "most important numerical algorithm in our life-time." In this chapter, we describe the FFT and show how it can be used to obtain an $O(n\log n)$ algorithm for polynomial multiplication. We begin by introducing the Discrete Fourier Transform, and then show how it can be computed by the $O(n\log n)$ divide-and-conquer algorithm FFT. Then we show how the FFT can be used to multiply two polynomials efficiently by transforming the problem to one of simply multiplying n numbers. We finish the chapter by a discussion of how the FFT can be implemented on the PRAM and on the Butterfly Interconnection Network.

22.1   The Discrete Fourier Transform

The Discrete Fourier Transform DFT_ω of a polynomial of degree n is defined relative to a *primitive n^{th} root of unity, ω*. A primitive n^{th} root of unity (over the field of complex numbers) is a complex number ω such that $\omega^n = 1$ and $\omega^k \neq 1$ for $0 < k < n$ (see Appendix A).

DEFINITION 22.1.1 Given a primitive n^{th} root of unity ω, the Discrete Fourier Transform DFT_ω transforms a polynomial $P(x) = a_{n-1}x^{n-1} + \cdots + a_1 x + a_0$ with *real* or *complex* coefficients into the polynomial $b_{n-1}x^{n-1} + \cdots + b_1 x + b_0$, where $b_i = P(\omega^i)$, $i = 0, 1, \ldots, n-1$. That is,

$$DFT_\omega(P(x)) = P(\omega^{n-1})x^{n-1} + \cdots + P(\omega)x + P(1). \qquad \textbf{(22.1.1)}$$

For convenience, we (equivalently) regard DFT_ω as transforming the coefficient array $\mathbf{a} = [a_0, a_1, \ldots, a_{n-1}]$ of the polynomial $P(x)$ into the coefficient array $\mathbf{b} = [b_0, b_1, \ldots, b_{n-1}]$ of the polynomial $DFT_\omega(P(x))$. Then $\mathbf{a}$ and $\mathbf{b}$ are related by the following matrix equation:

$$
\begin{bmatrix} b_0 \\ b_1 \\ \cdot \\ \cdot \\ \cdot \\ b_{n-1} \end{bmatrix}
=
\begin{bmatrix}
1 & 1 & 1 & \cdots & 1 \\
1 & \omega & \omega^2 & \cdots & \omega^{n-1} \\
\cdot & \cdot & \cdot & \cdots & \cdot \\
\cdot & \cdot & \cdot & \cdots & \cdot \\
\cdot & \cdot & \cdot & \cdots & \cdot \\
1 & \omega^{n-1} & (\omega^{n-1})^2 & \cdots & (\omega^{n-1})^{n-1}
\end{bmatrix}
\begin{bmatrix} a_0 \\ a_1 \\ \cdot \\ \cdot \\ \cdot \\ a_{n-1} \end{bmatrix}
\qquad \textbf{(22.1.2)}
$$

We denote the $n \times n$ matrix in Formula (22.1.2) by $F_\omega = (f_{ij})_{n \times n}$, so that

$$f_{ij} = \omega^{ij}, \quad i,j = 0, \ldots, n-1. \qquad \textbf{(22.1.3)}$$

22.2   The Fast Fourier Transform

A straightforward way to compute $DFT_\omega(P(x))$ is simply to evaluate $P(x)$ at the points $1, \omega, \ldots, \omega^{n-1}$ using Horner's rule, yielding an $O(n^2)$ algorithm. In fact, for evaluating $P(x)$ at any set of n points, repeated applications of Horner's rule is the best that we can do. However, the n points, $1, \omega, \ldots, \omega^{n-1}$, are very special beyond the mere fact that they are powers of a given number ω. The special nature of these points can be used to design an $O(n\log n)$ algorithm called the Fast

Fourier Transform for computing $DFT_\omega(P(x))$. Indeed, we now motivate the choice of points $1, \omega, \ldots, \omega^{n-1}$ by showing how a divide-and-conquer algorithm to evaluate $P(x)$ at n points might proceed if the n points have certain simple relationships with one another.

Suppose we choose the n points so that half the points are the negatives of the other half, as in the following:

$$z_0, z_1, \ldots, z_{n/2-1}, -z_0, -z_1, \ldots, -z_{n/2-1}. \qquad \textbf{(22.2.1)}$$

Evaluating a polynomial $P(x) = a_{n-1}x^{n-1} + \cdots + a_1x = a_0$ at such a set of points requires basically half the number of multiplications required for an arbitrary set of n points. To see this, we merely have to write $P(x)$ as the sum of two polynomials of degree $n/2 - 1$ by gathering up the even and odd powers of x:

$$P(x) = Even(x^2) + xOdd(x^2) \qquad \textbf{(22.2.2)}$$

where $Even(x) = a_{n-2}x^{n/2-1} + \cdots + a_2x + a_0$ and $Odd(x) = a_{n-1}x^{n/2-1} + \cdots + a_3x + a_1$. Now if we replace x by $-x$ in Formula (22.2.2), we obtain

$$P(-x) = Even(x^2) - xOdd(x^2). \qquad \textbf{(22.2.3)}$$

Thus, to evaluate $P(x)$ at the n points given by Formula (22.2.1), we need only evaluate the two polynomials $Even$ and Odd at the $n/2$ points $(z_0)^2, (z_1)^2, \ldots, (z_{n/2-1})^2$ and then perform the $n/2$ additions, $n/2$ subtractions, and n multiplications as described in Formulas (22.2.2) and (22.2.3). By dividing our evaluation problem into two problems of size $n/2$ and including a combine step of $O(n)$ complexity, we have made what looks like a promising start to a divide-and-conquer strategy that satisfies the familiar recurrence relation $t(n) = 2t(n/2) + O(n)$ and therefore yields an algorithm having $O(n\log n)$ complexity.

We can apply the same strategy to evaluate $Even$ and Odd at $(z_0)^2, (z_1)^2, \ldots, (z_{n/2-1})^2$ if we choose $z_0, z_1, \ldots, z_{n/2-1}$ to satisfy the relation

$$(z_{n/4+j})^2 = -(z_j)^2, \quad j = 0, \ldots, n/4 - 1. \qquad \textbf{(22.2.4)}$$

Formula (22.2.4) presents a *real* problem (not an *imaginary* problem, see Figure 22.1). More precisely, while we cannot find *real* (nonzero) numbers satisfying (22.2.4), there is no problem finding *complex* numbers that do the job. We merely have to take

$$z_{n/4+j} = iz_j, \quad j = 0, \ldots, \frac{n}{4} - 1, \quad i = \sqrt{-1}. \qquad \textbf{(22.2.5)}$$

FIGURE 22.1

Taking a number
that leads to
numbers satisfying
Formula (22.2.4).

If we carry the divide-and-conquer strategy to the next step, we are looking at the problem of evaluating degree $n/8 - 1$ polynomials at the $n/8$ points $(z_0)^8$, $(z_1)^8, \ldots, (z_{n/8 - 1})^8$. As before, the trick allowing us to use Formulas (22.1.2) and (22.1.3) works if we choose $z_{n/8 + j}, j = 0, \ldots, n/8 - 1$, so that

$$(z_{n/8+j})^4 = -(z_j)^4, \quad j = 0, \ldots, \frac{n}{8} - 1. \qquad \textbf{(22.2.6)}$$

Formula (22.2.6) is, in turn, satisfied if we set

$$z_{n/8+j} = \sqrt{i}(z_j), \quad j = 0, \ldots, \frac{n}{8} - 1. \qquad \textbf{(22.2.7)}$$

To see precisely where we are headed in the case of a general $n = 2^k$, we consider the case $n = 8$. The three steps just carried out for $n = 8$ determine the specially chosen eight points for rapid evaluation of polynomials of degree 7 or less. Figure 22.2 shows a table containing the eight points that have been chosen subject to Formulas (22.2.5), (22.2.6), and (22.2.7). For simplicity, we have added the additional condition that $z_0 = 1$.

Note that $\sqrt{i} \ (= e^{2\pi i/8} = (1 + i)/\sqrt{2})$ is a complex number ω such that $\omega^8 = 1$, whereas $\omega^j \neq 1$ for $0 < j < 8$. Hence, the points $z_0, z_1, z_2, z_3, z_4, z_5, z_6, z_7$ in Figure 22.2 are all distinct and are of the form $1, \omega, \omega^2, \omega^3, \omega^4, \omega^5, \omega^6, \omega^7$, where ω is a primitive eighth root of unity.

FIGURE 22.2

Table of special
points for
evaluating
polynomials of
degree ≤ 7.

z_0	z_1	z_2	z_3	z_4	z_5	z_6	z_7
1	$\sqrt{i}$	i	$i\sqrt{i}$	-1	$-\sqrt{i}$	$-i$	$-i\sqrt{i}$

Returning to the case of a general $n = 2^k$, if we continue choosing points by generalizing the constraints expressed by Formulas (22.2.4) and (22.2.6) in the obvious way, after $\log_2 n$ steps we arrive at the problem of evaluating constant polynomials at $(z_0)^n$, $\omega(z_0)^n$, where ω is a primitive n^{th} root of unity. Again, for simplicity, we take z_0 to be 1 and ω to be the complex number $e^{2\pi i/n}$. We can verify that the points that we have then generated by this divide-and-conquer strategy are $1, \omega, \omega^2, \omega^3, \ldots, \omega^{n-1}$. Following our previous discussion, an $O(n \log n)$ recursive algorithm *FFTRec* for evaluating $P(1), P(\omega), \ldots, P(\omega^{n-1})$ is then easily obtained.

When writing the pseudocode for the algorithm *FFTRec*, it is convenient to use the coefficient array $\mathbf{a} = [a_0, a_1, \ldots, a_{n-1}]$ to represent the polynomial $P(x) = a_{n-1}x^{n-1} + \cdots + a_1 x + a_0$. *FFTRec* evaluates $P(1), P(\omega), \ldots, P(\omega^{n-1})$ by first splitting $P(x)$ into the even- and odd-degree terms $Even(x) = a_{n-2}x^{n/2-1} + \cdots + a_2 x + a_0$ and $Odd(x) = a_{n-1}x^{n/2-1} + \cdots + a_3 x + a_1$. Then *FFTRec* recursively evaluates $Even(1), Even(\omega^2), \ldots, Even((\omega^2)^{(n/2)-1})$ and $Odd(1), Odd(\omega^2), \ldots, Odd((\omega^2)^{(n/2)-1})$. Finally, *FFTRec* uses Formulas (22.2.2) and (22.2.3) to evaluate $P(1), P(\omega), \ldots, P(\omega^{n-1})$.

For *FFTRec* to be a valid recursive procedure, we must verify that it is recursively invoked with the proper type of input. It is immediate that when n is a power of two, so is $n/2$. Moreover, it is easy to verify that when ω is a primitive n^{th} root of unity and n is a power of 2, then ω^2 is a primitive $(n/2)^{\text{th}}$ root of unity. Thus, $n/2$ and ω^2 are appropriate input parameters for a recursive invocation of *FFTRec*. In our pseudocode for *FFTRec* and other procedures in this chapter, we avoid using i for a loop index, to save possible confusion with $i = \sqrt{-1}$. However, we still find it convenient to use i for an integer when talking, for example, about the ith leaf node in the tree of recursive calls to *FFTRec*.

```
procedure FFTRec(a[0:n − 1], n, ω, b[0:n − 1]) recursive
Input:    a[0:n − 1] (an array of coefficients of the polynomial P(x) = a_{n−1}x^{n−1} +
                ··· + a_1x + a_0)
          n (a power of two)                    //n = 2^k
          ω (a primitive n^th root of unity)
Output:   b[0:n − 1] (an array of values b[j] = P(ω^j, j = 0, . . . , n − 1)
          if n = 1 then
              b[0] ← a[0]
          else
                                                 //divide into even-indexed and
                                                   odd-indexed coefficients

              for j ← 0 to n/2 − 1 do
                  Even[j] ← a[2*j]               //[a_0, a_2, . . . , a_{n−2}]
                  Odd[j] ← a[2*j + 1]            //[a_1, a_3, . . . , a_{n−1}]
              endfor
```

$$FFTRec(Even[0{:}n/2 - 1], n/2, \omega^2, e[0{:}n/2 - 1])$$
$$FFTRec(Odd[0{:}n/2 - 1], n/2, \omega^2, d[0{:}n/2 - 1])$$

//now combine according to
(22.1.5) and (22.1.6)

for $j \leftarrow 0$ **to** $n/2 - 1$ **do**
$\quad b[j] \leftarrow e[j] + \omega^j * d[j]$
$\quad b[j + n/2] \leftarrow e[j] - \omega^j * d[j]$
endfor
endif
end *FFTRec*

Figure 22.3 illustrates the tree of recursive calls to *FFTRec* resulting from an initial call with $n = 8$. As usual, the left (right) child of a node corresponds to the first (second) recursive call in the code. Each node in the tree lists the relevant **input** parameters for the given invocation. That is, we first list the input polynomial by listing its coefficient array, and we then list the current values of n and associated n^{th} root of unity for the given node.

Resolution of the tree of recursive calls made by *FFTRec* with $n = 8$ is shown in Figure 22.4.

....

FIGURE 22.3

Tree of recursive
calls to *FFTRec* with
$n = 8$.

....

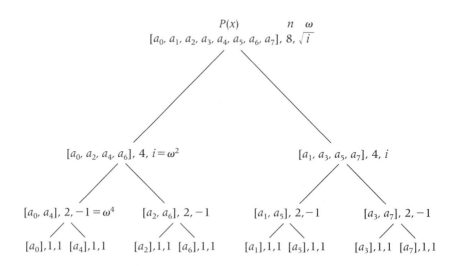

FIGURE 22.4

Resolutions of the
recursive calls made
by *FFTRec* with
$n = 8$.

$DFT_{\sqrt{i}}\ [a_0, a_1, a_2, a_3, a_4, a_5, a_6, a_7]$

$\quad = [a_0 + a_4 + a_2 + a_6 + 1(a_1 + a_5 + a_3 + a_7),$

$\qquad a_0 - a_4 + i(a_2 - a_6) + \sqrt{i}\,(a_1 - a_5 + i(a_3 - a_7)),$

$\qquad a_0 + a_4 - a_2 - a_6 + i(a_1 + a_5 - a_3 - a_7),$

$\qquad a_0 - a_4 - i(a_2 - a_6) + i\sqrt{i}\,(a_1 - a_5 - i(a_3 - a_7)),$

$\qquad a_0 + a_4 + a_2 + a_6 - 1(a_1 + a_5 + a_3 + a_7),$

$\qquad a_0 - a_4 + i(a_2 - a_6) - \sqrt{i}\,(a_1 - a_5 + i(a_3 - a_7)),$

$\qquad a_0 + a_4 - a_2 - a_6 - i(a_1 + a_5 - a_3 - a_7),$

$\qquad a_0 - a_4 - i(a_2 - a_6) - i\sqrt{i}\,(a_1 - a_5 - i(a_3 - a_7))]$

$DFT_i\ [a_0, a_2, a_4, a_6]$
$= [a_0 + a_4 + a_2 + a_6,\ a_0 - a_4 + i(a_2 - a_6),$
$\quad a_0 + a_4 - a_2 - a_6,\ a_0 - a_4 - i(a_2 - a_6)]$

$DFT_i\ [a_1, a_3, a_5, a_7]$
$= [a_1 + a_5 + a_3 + a_7,\ a_1 - a_5 + i(a_3 - a_7),$
$\quad a_1 + a_5 - a_3 - a_7,\ a_1 - a_5 - i(a_3 - a_7)]$

$DFT_{-1}\ [a_0, a_4]$
$= [a_0 + a_4,\ a_0 - a_4]$

$DFT_{-1}\ [a_2, a_6]$
$= [a_2 + a_6,\ a_2 - a_6]$

$DFT_{-1}\ [a_1, a_5]$
$= [a_1 + a_5,\ a_1 - a_5]$

$DFT_{-1}\ [a_3, a_7]$
$= [a_3 + a_7,\ a_3 - a_7]$

$[a_0]$ $\qquad [a_4]$ $\qquad [a_2]$ $\qquad [a_6]$ $\qquad [a_1]$ $\qquad [a_5]$ $\qquad [a_3]$ $\qquad [a_7]$

22.3 An Iterative Version of the Fast Fourier Transform

We can design an iterative version of *FFTRec* based on the bottom-up resolution
of the tree T of recursive calls shown in Figure 22.4. On examining Figure 22.4,
it is not immediately obvious for a general $n = 2^k$ which coefficient a_j corresponds to the ith leaf node, $i = 0, \ldots, n - 1$, in the tree of recursive calls for
FFTRec. Fortunately, there is a simple procedure for computing the permutation
$j = \pi_k(i)$ such that a_j is the coefficient corresponding to the ith leaf note of T.

Proposition 22.3.1 Suppose $n = 2^k$, and $\pi_k: \{0, \ldots, n - 1\} \Rightarrow \{0, \ldots, n - 1\}$ is the permutation such that a_j is the coefficient corresponding to the ith leaf node of T in the tree of recursive calls of *FFTRec* with input coefficient array $a[0:n - 1]$. Then the k-digit binary representation of $\pi_k(i)$ is obtained from the k-digit binary representation of i by simply reversing the digits, where leading zeros are included (if necessary).

To illustrate Proposition 22.3.1, suppose $k = 4$ ($n = 16$) and $i = 3$. The four-digit binary representation of 3 is 0011, so that $\pi_k(3) = 1100$ in binary (in decimal, $\pi_k(3) = 12$).

PROOF OF PROPOSITION 22.3.1

We prove Proposition 22.3.1 using induction on k.

Basis step: $k = 1$. Trivial.

Induction step: Assume that Proposition 22.3.1 is true for k. For $k + 1 = \log_2 n$, note that the leaves of the left subtree of the tree of recursive calls with input coefficients $a_0, a_1, \ldots, a_{2^{k+1}-1}$ and n^{th} root of unity ω consists of the coefficients $a_0, a_2, \ldots, a_{2^{k+1}-2}$. Moreover, this left subtree corresponds exactly to the tree of recursive calls of *FFTRec* with input coefficients $\tilde{a}_0, \tilde{a}_1, \ldots, \tilde{a}_{2^k-1}$ and $(n/2)^{\text{th}}$ root of unity ω^2, where

$$\tilde{a}_i = a_{2i}, \quad i = 0, \ldots, 2^k - 1. \tag{22.3.1}$$

It follows from (22.3.1) that

$$\pi_{k+1}(i) = 2\pi_k(i), \quad i = 0, \ldots, 2^k - 1. \tag{22.3.2}$$

By induction hypothesis to *FFTRec*, for input coefficients $\tilde{a}_i$, $i = 0, \ldots 2^k - 1$, the k-digit binary representation of $\pi_k(i)$ is obtained from the k-digit binary representation of i by simply reversing the digits. Using Formula (22.3.2), the $(k + 1)$-digit binary representation of $\pi_{k+1}(i)$ is obtained from $\pi_k(i)$ by adding a zero on the right. Since the $(k + 1)$-digit binary representation of i is obtained from the k-digit binary representation of i by adding a leading zero, we see that Proposition 22.3.1 holds for $\pi_{k+1}(i)$, $i = 0, \ldots, 2^k - 1$. The proof that Proposition 22.3.1 holds for $\pi_{k+1}(i)$, $i = 2^k, \ldots, 2^{k+1} - 1$ is similar (using the right subtree) and is left as an exercise. ■

The pseudocode for a procedure $ReverseBinPerm(R[0:n-1])$, which computes $R[i] = \pi_k(i)$, $i = 0, \ldots, n-1$, is easy to write. An iterative version of the FFT begins by loading an array $b[0:n-1]$ with the values $b[i] = a_{\pi_k(i)} = a[R[i]]$, $i = 0, \ldots, n-1$. The values $b[i]$ correspond to the leaves in the tree T of recursive calls to $FFTRec$, and the iterative version of the FFT proceeds by resolving these calls level-by-level in a bottom-up fashion. With the aid of Figure 22.4, you might want to proceed directly to the pseudocode for FFT given at the end of this subsection. However, it is instructive to describe the polynomial evaluations that take place at each level. The leaves are at level k in T and correspond to evaluating the constant polynomials $P_{0,i}(x) = a_{\pi_k(i)}$, $i = 0, \ldots, n-1$, at $(\omega^n)^0 = 1$. At level $k - j$, $j \in \{1, \ldots, k\}$, the iterative version of the FFT evaluates $n/2^j$ polynomials $P_{j,s}$, $s = 0, 2^j, \ldots, n - 2^j$ of degree $2^j - 1$ at the points $1, \omega^{n/2^j}, \ldots, (\omega^{n/2^j})^{2^{j-1}-1}$, $-1, -\omega^{n/2^j}, \ldots, -(\omega^{n/2^j})^{2^{j-1}-1}$. In this notation, the splitting of the polynomial $P_{j,s}$ into even and odd powers corresponds precisely to the two polynomials $P_{j-1,s}$ and $P_{j-1, s+2^{j-1}}$, respectively, at the next lower level in T. Hence, Formulas (22.2.2) and (22.2.3) become the following (see Figure 22.5):

$$P_{j,s}(x) = P_{j-1,s}(x^2) + xP_{j-1, s+2^{j-1}}(x^2), \qquad \textbf{(22.3.3)}$$

$$P_{j,s}(-x) = P_{j-1,s}(x^2) - xP_{j-1, s+2^{j-1}}(x^2), \qquad \textbf{(22.3.4)}$$

$$j = 1, \ldots, k, \quad s = 0, 2^j, \ldots, n - 2^j, \quad x = 1, \omega^{n/2^j}, \ldots, (\omega^{n/2^j})^{2^{j-1}-1}.$$

FIGURE 22.5

Level-by-level FFT computations for $n = 8$.

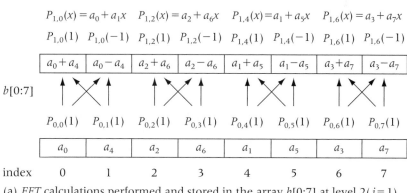

(a) *FFT* calculations performed and stored in the array $b[0:7]$ at level $2(j=1)$

continued

FIGURE 22.5

Continued

$P_{2,0}(1)$ $\quad P_{2,0}(i)$ $\quad P_{2,0}(-1)$ $\ P_{2,0}(-i)$ $\quad P_{2,4}(1)$ $\qquad P_{2,4}(i)$ $\quad P_{2,4}(-1)$ $\ P_{2,4}(-i)$

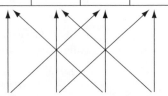

$b[0:7]$

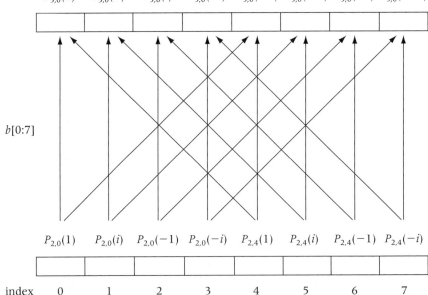

$P_{1,0}(1)$ $\quad P_{1,0}(-1)$ $\ P_{1,2}(1)$ $\quad P_{1,2}(-1)$ $\ P_{1,4}(1)$ $\quad P_{1,4}(-1)$ $\ P_{1,6}(1)$ $\quad P_{1,6}(-1)$

a_0+a_4	a_0-a_4	a_2+a_6	a_2-a_6	a_1+a_5	a_1-a_5	a_3+a_7	a_3-a_7

index $\quad$ 0 $\qquad$ 1 $\qquad$ 2 $\qquad$ 3 $\qquad$ 4 $\qquad$ 5 $\qquad$ 6 $\qquad$ 7

(b) *FFT* calculations performed and stored in the array $b[0:7]$ at level 1 ($j=2$)

$P_{3,0}(1)$ $\quad P_{3,0}(\omega)$ $\qquad P_{3,0}(i)$ $\quad P_{3,0}(\omega^3)$ $\ P_{3,0}(-1)$ $\ P_{3,0}(-\omega)$ $\ P_{3,0}(-i)$ $\ P_{3,0}(-\omega^3)$

$b[0:7]$

$P_{2,0}(1)$ $\quad P_{2,0}(i)$ $\quad P_{2,0}(-1)$ $\ P_{2,0}(-i)$ $\quad P_{2,4}(1)$ $\qquad P_{2,4}(i)$ $\quad P_{2,4}(-1)$ $\ P_{2,4}(-i)$

index $\quad$ 0 $\qquad$ 1 $\qquad$ 2 $\qquad$ 3 $\qquad$ 4 $\qquad$ 5 $\qquad$ 6 $\qquad$ 7

(c) *FFT* calculations performed in the array $b[0:7]$ at level 0 ($j=3$)

The iterative version of the FFT proceeds by computing Formulas (22.3.3) and (22.3.4) with three nested **for-do** loops: the outer loop is controlled by $j = 1, \ldots, k$; the middle loop is controlled by $s = 0, 2^j, \ldots, n - 2^j$; and the innermost loop is controlled by $x = 1, \omega^{n/2^j}, \ldots, (\omega^{n/2^j})^{2^{j-1}-1}$. The calculations at level $k - j$ begin with $b[0:n - 1]$ containing the previously calculated values.

$$b[s + m] = P_{j-1,s}((\omega^{n/2^{j-1}})^m), \tag{22.3.5}$$

$$s = 0, 2^{j-1}, \ldots, n - 2^{j-1}, \quad m = 0, 1, \ldots, 2^{j-1} - 1.$$

The values corresponding to level $k - j$ are then calculated by first using an auxiliary array $Temp[0:n - 1]$ to receive the results of calculations in the right sides of (22.3.3) and (22.3.4).

$$Temp[s + m] = b[s + m] + (\omega^{n/2^j})^m b[s + m + 2^{j-1}], \tag{22.3.6}$$

$$Temp[s + m + 2^{j-1}] = b[s + m] - (\omega^{n/2^j})^m b[s + m + 2^{j-1}], \tag{22.3.7}$$

$$j = 1, \ldots, k, \quad s = 0, 2^j, \ldots, n - 2^j, \quad m = 0, 1, \ldots, 2^j - 1$$

Formula (22.3.7) follows from (22.3.4) and the fact that $-b[s + m] = b[s + m + 2^{j-1}]$. Then the results in $Temp[0:n - 1]$ are copied back to $b[0:n - 1]$.

The level-by-level bottom-up calculations are illustrated in Figure 22.5, in which arrows show that the new value of $b[s + m]$ is determined from the previously calculated values of $b[s + m]$ and $b[s + m + 2^{j-1}]$. Due to space limitations, we only show the initial values of $b[0:7]$ and its values after one iteration. However, all the values at each level can be determined by examining Figure 22.4.

The pseudocode for the iterative *FFT* is based on the bottom-up strategy previously described.

```
procedure FFT(a[0:n − 1], n, ω, b[0:n − 1])
Input:    a[0:n − 1] (an array of coefficients of the polynomial P(x) = a_{n − 1}x^{n − 1} + ···
                 + a_1x + a_0)
          n (a positive integer)                    //n = 2^k
          ω (a primitive n^{th} root of unity)
Output:  b[0:n − 1] (an array of values b[j] = P(ω^j), j = 0, ··· , n − 1)
          ReverseBinPerm(R[0:n − 1])
          for j ← 0 to n − 1
               b[j] ← a[R[j]]
          endfor
          for j ← 1 to k do
               for s ← 0 to n − 2^j by 2^j do
                    for m ← 0 to 2^{j − 1} − 1
```

$$Temp[s + m] \leftarrow b[s + m] + (\omega^{n/2^j})^m * b[s + m + 2^{j-1}]$$
$$Temp[s + m + 2^{j-1}] \leftarrow b[s + m] - (\omega^{n/2^j})^m * b[s + m + 2^{j-1}]$$
     endfor
    endfor
    for $j \leftarrow 0$ **to** $n - 1$ **do**
     $b[j] \leftarrow Temp[j]$
    endfor
   endfor
  end *FFT*

22.4   Transforming the Problem Domain

In secondary school mathematics, you were introduced to the idea of transforming problems into equivalent problems that are simpler or easier to solve. For example, it is often convenient to deal with large numbers by transforming them using logarithms to a certain base—say, base 10. The problem of multiplying two large numbers a and b is then transformed into the simpler but equivalent problem of adding their logarithms and then using the inverse transformation (exponentiation) to compute the given product. The idea behind this transformation is captured by the commutative diagram shown in Figure 22.6.

The diagram given in Figure 22.6 is called commutative because the product ab can be computed either directly by following the top arrow or indirectly by following the three arrows along the sides and bottom of the diagram. The mathematical expression of this commutativity is simply the equation

$$ab = 10^{\log_{10}a + \log_{10}b}.$$

FIGURE 22.6

Commutative diagram for transforming multiplication using logarithms.

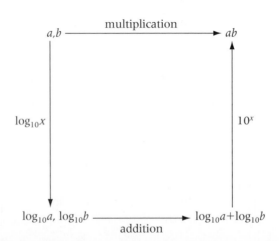

The utility of this transformation resides in the fact that addition can be carried out more quickly than multiplication. Making these transformations useful in practice is the objective of generating extensive tables of logarithms and antilogs.

The general idea behind transforming a given problem can be captured by the generic commutative diagram shown in Figure 22.7. For this transformation to be worthwhile, both the transformation to the new problem domain and its inverse must be done more efficiently than solving the problem in the original domain. Also, the problem in the transformed domain must be easier to solve than the problem in the original domain.

There is a host of important applications, such as signal and image processing, where the Discrete Fourier Transform can be used to transform the problem domain into an equivalent, but algorithmically simpler, problem domain. However, for this transformation to be effective, the DFT and its inverse need to be computed efficiently. As we will see, the inverse of a DFT is actually (except for a multiplicative factor) just another DFT. Fortunately, the FFT provides an efficient algorithm to compute DFTs and therefore efficiently transform the problem to the new domain and transform back to the original domain. The problem that we will use to illustrate DFT transformation of the domain is (symbolic) polynomial multiplication. This problem will be transformed into the simpler problem of multiplying n numbers.

FIGURE 22.7

Generic commutative diagram for transforming problems.

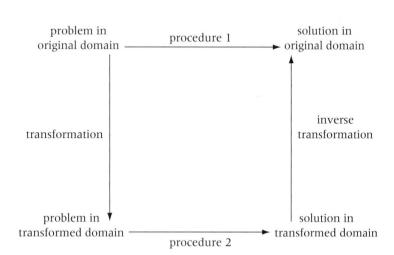

22.5 The Inverse Discrete Fourier Transform and Fast Polynomial Multiplication

We have mentioned that the FFT can be used to design an $O(n\log n)$ algorithm for polynomial multiplication. Of course, the FFT worked on polynomials whose input size was a power of 2. The product of two polynomials both of input size m is a polynomial of input size $n = 2m - 1$. Thus, for convenience in discussing polynomial multiplication, we assume that n is a power of 2 and that we are multiplying two polynomials of input size m, where $n = 2m - 1$. In practice, when multiplying any two polynomials, we can arrange for these conditions by adding leading terms with zero coefficients, if necessary.

Figure 22.8 shows how we can use DFT_ω to obtain the product polynomial $P(x)Q(x)$. We first apply DFT_ω to find the coefficient arrays $[P(1), P(\omega), \dots, P(\omega^{n-1})]$ and $[Q(1), Q(\omega), \dots, Q(\omega^{n-1})]$ of both $P(x)$ and $Q(x)$. Then we simply compute the coefficient array of the product polynomial $P(x)Q(x)$ by forming the n scalar products $P(1)Q(1), P(\omega)Q(\omega), \dots, P(\omega^{n-1})Q(\omega^{n-1})$. Thus, by following the left side and bottom of the commutative diagram in Figure 22.8, we have actually computed the DFT of the product polynomial $P(x)Q(x)$. Hence, to recover $P(x)Q(x)$, we need to be able to perform the inverse of the DFT. The inverse certainly exists, because it amounts to finding the polynomial interpolating the n points $(1, P(1)Q(1)), (\omega, P(\omega)Q(\omega)), \dots, (\omega^{n-1}, P(\omega^{n-1})Q(\omega^{n-1}))$.

The left side of the diagram in Figure 22.8 can be computed using *FFT* with $O(n\log n)$ complexity. The bottom of the diagram can be computed with $O(n)$ complexity. However, the most straightforward interpolation algorithms have

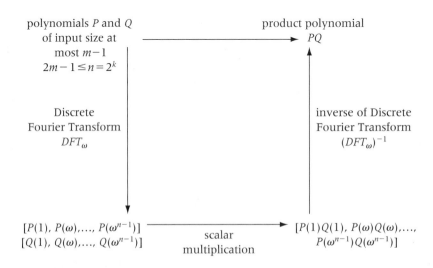

FIGURE 22.8

Commutative diagram for computing product of two polynomials using DFT_ω.

polynomials P and Q
of input size at
most $m-1$
$2m-1 \leq n = 2^k$

product polynomial
PQ

Discrete
Fourier Transform
DFT_ω

inverse of Discrete
Fourier Transform
$(DFT_\omega)^{-1}$

$[P(1), P(\omega),\dots, P(\omega^{n-1})]$
$[Q(1), Q(\omega),\dots, Q(\omega^{n-1})]$

scalar
multiplication

$[P(1)Q(1), P(\omega)Q(\omega),\dots,$
$P(\omega^{n-1})Q(\omega^{n-1})]$

complexity $O(n^2)$. Hence, to arrive at an $O(n\log n)$ algorithm for polynomial multiplication, we need to look for an $O(n\log n)$ algorithm to compute the inverse Discrete Fourier Transform DFT_ω^{-1}. Fortunately, we have the following useful key fact about the inverse DFT.

Key Fact

To compute the inverse of a Discrete Fourier Transform, we simply need to compute another Discrete Fourier Transform.

The key fact results from the following elegant formula for the inverse:

$$DFT_\omega^{-1} = \left(\frac{1}{n}\right)DFT_{\omega^{-1}}. \qquad (22.5.1)$$

To verify Formula (22.5.1), we can use the array and matrix notation discussed earlier for the Discrete Fourier Transform DFT_ω. Then Formula (22.5.1) is equivalent to verifying that the inverse of the matrix F_ω defined by (22.1.2) is given by the formula

$$F_\omega^{-1} = \left(\frac{1}{n}\right)F_{\omega^{-1}}. \qquad (22.5.2)$$

Equivalently, we must verify that

$$F_\omega^{-1} = \frac{1}{n}\begin{bmatrix} 1 & 1 & 1 & \cdots & 1 \\ 1 & \omega^{-1} & \omega^{-2} & \cdots & \omega^{-(n-1)} \\ \cdot & \cdot & \cdot & \cdots & \cdot \\ \cdot & \cdot & \cdot & \cdots & \cdot \\ \cdot & \cdot & \cdot & \cdots & \cdot \\ 1 & \omega^{-(n-1)} & (\omega^{-2})^{n-1} & \cdots & (\omega^{-(n-1)})^{n-1} \end{bmatrix} \qquad (22.5.3)$$

We leave the proof of Formula (22.5.3) to the exercises.

The commutative diagram in Figure 22.9 summarizes the application of *FFT* for $O(n\log n)$ polynomial multiplication. In the figure, we denote the application of *FFT* with input parameter ω by FFT_ω.

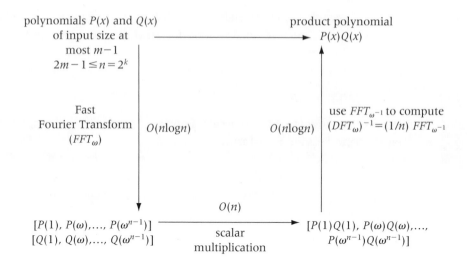

FIGURE 22.9

Commutative
diagram
summarizing
$O(n\log n)$
polynomial
multiplication
using FFT_ω.

We illustrate the actions of the commutative diagram in Figure 22.9 to compute the product of the polynomials $P(x) = x^3 - x + 2$ and $Q(x) = 2x^2 - 1$. The product polynomial has degree 5, so we take $n = 8$.

Then, $\omega = \sqrt{i} = (1 + i)/\sqrt{2}$.

Using FFT yields the evaluations

$$[P(1), P(\omega), \dots, P(\omega^7)] = [2, 2 - \omega + \omega^3, 2 - 2i, 2 + \omega - \omega^3, 2, 2 + \omega - \omega^3,$$
$$2 + 2i, 2 - \omega + \omega^3]$$
$$[Q(1), Q(\omega), \dots, Q(\omega^7)] = [1, \ 2i - 1, -3, -2i - 1, 1, 2i - 1, -3, -2i - 1].$$

Next we form the pointwise products $P(i)Q(i)$, $i = 1, \omega, \dots, \omega^7$ and acquire the coefficient array for $DFT_\omega(P(x)Q(x))$ given by

$$[2, 4i - 3\omega^3 - \omega - 2, 6i - 6, -4i - \omega^3 - 3\omega - 2, 2,$$
$$4i + 3 + \omega - 2, -6i - 6, -4i + \omega^3 + 3\omega - 2]. \quad \textbf{(22.5.4)}$$

To complete the illustration of computing the product polynomial $P(x)Q(x)$ using the commutative diagram, we use FFT to compute $(DFT_\omega)^{-1} = (1/8)DFT_{\omega^{-1}}$ for the polynomial (coefficient array) given by Formula (22.5.4). This yields the coefficient array $[-2, 1, 4, -3, 0, 2, 0, 0]$ of the product polynomial

$$P(x)Q(x) = 2x^5 - 3x^3 + 4x^2 + x - 2.$$

22.6 The Fast Fourier Transform in Parallel

In this section, we discuss how the FFT has a natural parallelization suitable for the EREW PRAM. We also introduce the butterfly interconnection network, which is particularly well suited for the implementation of parallel divide-and-conquer algorithms where a list (or coefficient array) is split into even- and odd-indexed elements.

22.6.1 The FFT on a PRAM

For the Fast Fourier Transform algorithm, both the divide and combine steps can be efficiently parallelized. *FFTRec* can be easily parallelized to obtain the following implementation of the Fast Fourier Transform on a PRAM.

> **procedure** *FFTRecPRAM*($a[0{:}n - 1]$, n, ω, $b[0{:}n - 1]$ **recursive**
> **Model:** EREW PRAM with $p = n$ processors
> **Input:** $a[0{:}n - 1]$ (an array of coefficients of the polynomial
> $P(x) = a_{n-1}x^{n-1} + \cdots + a_1x + a_0$)
> n (a power of two)   //$n = 2^k$
> ω (a primitive n^{th} root of unity)
> **Output:** $b[0{:}n - 1]$ (an array of values $b[j] = P(\omega^j), j = 0, \cdots, n - 1$)
>   **if** $n = 1$ **then**
> $b[0] \leftarrow a_0$//divide into even-indexed and odd-indexed coefficients
>   **else**
>   **for** $0 \leq j \leq n/2 - 1$ **do in parallel**
> $Even[j] \leftarrow a[2{*}j]$ //$[a_0, a_2, \cdots, a_{n-2}]$
> $Odd[j] \leftarrow a[2{*}j + 1]$ //$[a_1, a_3, \cdots, a_{n-1}]$
>   **end in parallel**
>   **parallelcall** *FFTRecPRAM*($Even[0{:}n./2 - 1]$, $n/2$, ω^2, $e[0{:}n/2 - 1]$) |
> $Odd[0{:}n/2 - 1]$, $n/2$, ω^2, $d[0{:}n/2 - 1]$)
>   **for** $0 \leq j \leq n/2 - 1$ **do in parallel**
> $b[j] \leftarrow e[j] + \omega^j {*} d[j]$
> $b[j + n/2] \leftarrow e[j] - \omega^j {*} d[j]$
>   **end in parallel**
>   **endif**
> **end** *FFTRecPRAM*

We can easily verify that *FFTRecPRAM* has complexity $W(n) \in \Theta(\log n)$. Thus, *FFTRecPRAM* has cost $C(n) \in \Theta(n\log n)$, which is optimal.

Note that a $\Theta(\log n)$ algorithm for computing DFT_ω can be based directly on its definition: Each of the n polynomial evaluations $f(1), f(\omega), \dots, f(\omega^{n-1})$ can be computed separately in $O(\log n)$ parallel steps on the PRAM. The drawback is that n^2 processors must be used, resulting in $\Theta(n^2 \log n)$ cost $C(n)$.

22.6.2 The FFT on the Butterfly Network

The *butterfly* interconnection network is particularly well-suited for implementation of divide-and-conquer algorithms, such as the Fast Fourier Transform and even-odd mergesort, where the divide step involves partitioning an array into even- and odd-indexed elements. The butterfly network B_k of dimension k contains $n = 2^k$ processors, $P_{j,0}, P_{j,1}, \dots, P_{j,n-1}$ at level j, $j = 0, \dots, k$, so that B_k contains $n(\log_2 n + 1)$ processors altogether. Only processors from adjacent levels are directly connected. For $0 \le j < n$, processor $P_{j,q}$ is directly connected to processors $P_{j+1,q}$ and $P_{j+1,r}$, where the binary representations of q and r differ only in the jth most significant bit. The butterfly network B_3 is shown in Figure 22.10.

FIGURE 22.10

Butterfly network B_3.

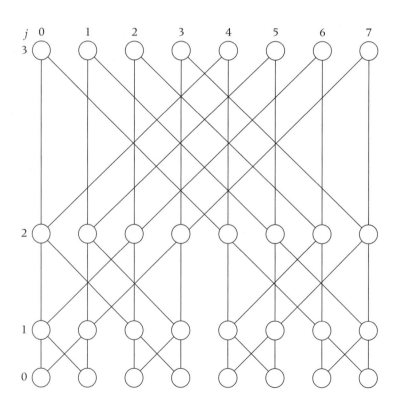

The butterfly network is doubly recursive in nature. By deleting the processors at the top level, the butterfly network of dimension k splits into two butterfly networks, each of dimension $k - 1$. The same phenomenon occurs by deleting the processors at the bottom level.

The connection between processors of B_k on adjacent levels are such that moving up a level in the bottom-up resolution of recursion based on splitting arrays into even- and odd-indexed elements can be accomplished using a single parallel communication step. For example, the bottom-up resolution of Figure 22.5 yields a Fast Fourier Transform algorithm *FFTButterfly* for the butterfly interconnection network. Clearly the complexity of *FFTButterfly* is the same as *FFTRecPRAM*. However, *FFTButterfly* uses $n(\log_2 n + 1)$ processors, so that it is off by a logarithmic factor n from being cost optimal.

For any given k, the degree of each node in the top and bottom levels of the butterfly network B_k is 2, and all other nodes have degree 4. The small-degree property of the butterfly network makes it attractive to build. Moreover, the communication complexity of the butterfly network is small because the maximum distance between any two nodes in B_k is $2k = 2(\log_2 n + 1)$.

As with the PRAM, DFT_ω can be computed on an interconnection network directly from its definition as a matrix-vector product. In particular, DFT_ω can be computed in $O(\log n)$ time on the two-dimensional mesh of trees. Again, the drawback is the cost because we would use $\Theta(n^2)$ processors.

22.7 Closing Remarks

A number of other transformations related to the Discrete Fourier Transform are often used in practice. For example, an important transform known as the Discrete Cosine Transformation (DCT) uses only cosines, instead of both sines and cosines as used by the DFT. For example, in combination with Huffman coding, the DCT is used in JPEG compression of graphics files.

References and Suggestions for Further Reading

Brigham, E. O. *The Fast Fourier Transform*. Englewood Cliffs, NJ: Prentice-Hall, 1974. A survey of various formulations of the Fast Fourier Transform algorithm.

Cooley, J. W., and J. W. Tukey. "An Algorithm for the Machine Calculation of Complex Fourier Series," *Mathematical Computation* 19 (1965): 297–301. The Fast Fourier Transform has a long history; the basic ideas were known as long as a century ago. However, this paper is credited with first showing how the Fast Fourier Transform can be effectively implemented in a computer.

Section 22.1 The Discrete Fourier Transform

22.1 Verify Formula (22.1.2).

22.2 Show that when ω is a primitive n^{th} root of unity and n is a power of 2, then ω^2 is a primitive $(n/2)^{\text{th}}$ root of unity.

Section 22.2 The Fast Fourier Transform

22.3 Give the tree of recursive calls to *FFTRec* for $n = 16$.

22.4 Write a program implementing *FFTRec*, and run the program for various inputs.

Section 22.3 An Iterative Version of the Fast Fourier Transform

22.5 For $i = 1, \dots, n = 2^k$, consider the permutation $\pi_k(i) = j$ such that a_j is the coefficient corresponding to the ith leaf node of the tree of recursive calls to *FFTRec*. Complete the inductive proof that the k-digit binary representation of $\pi_k(i)$ is obtained from the k-digit binary representation of i by simply reversing the digits, where leading zeros are included (if necessary).

22.6 Design and analyze the procedure *ReverseBinPerm*($R[0:n-1]$), which computes $R[i] = \pi_k(i), i = 0, \dots, n-1$.

22.7 Write a program implementing the iterative version of FFT, and run the program for various inputs.

Section 22.5 The Inverse Discrete Fourier Transform and Fast Polynomial Multiplication

22.8 Given the polynomials $P(x) = x^3 - x + 2$, $Q(x) = 2x^2 - 1$,

a. Show that going along the left side of the commutative diagram in Figure 22.8 and using *FFT* yields the evaluations following:

$$[P(1), P(\omega), \dots, P(\omega^7)] = [2, 2 - \omega + \omega^3, 2 - 2i, 2 + \omega - \omega^3,$$
$$2, 2 + \omega - \omega^3, 2 + 2i, 2 - \omega + \omega^3]$$
$$[Q(1), Q(\omega), \dots, Q(\omega^7)] = [1, 2i - 1, -3, -2i - 1, 1, 2i - 1, -3, -2i - 1].$$

b. Verify that the polynomial $P(x)Q(x)$ results from going along the right-hand side of the commutative diagram in Figure 22.12 by using *FFT* to compute $(DFT_\omega)^{-1} = (1/8)DFT_{\omega^{-1}}$.

Section 22.6 The Fast Fourier Transform in Parallel

22.9 Give pseudocode for the nonrecursive procedure *FFTPRAM* that is based on a direct parallelization of the nonrecursive procedure *FFT*.

22.10 Give pseudocode for the procedure *FFTButterfly*.

22.11 Determine the diameter, maximum degree, and bisection width of the butterfly network B_k.

22.12 a. Give pseudocode for an algorithm on the EREW PRAM implementing DFT_ω directly from its definition.

b. Repeat part (a) for the two-dimensional mesh of trees.

22.13 Design a version of odd-even merge sort for the butterfly network

Additional Exercises

22.14 Prove Proposition A.1 from Appendix A.

22.15 Prove Proposition A.2 from Appendix A.

22.16 Prove Proposition A.3 from Appendix A.

22.17 Given a complex number $z = x + iy$, its *complex conjugate* $\bar{z}$ is defined by $\bar{z} = x - iy$.

a. Give a geometric interpretation of $\bar{z}$.

b. Show that the complex conjugate has the following properties:

   i. $\overline{-z} = -\bar{z}$,

  ii. $\overline{z_1 + z_2} = \bar{z_1} + \bar{z_2}$,

 iii. $\overline{z_1 z_2} = \bar{z_1}\,\bar{z_2}$.

c. Use part (b) to show that the complex roots of a polynomial $P(x)$ with real coefficients occur in conjugate pairs; that is, if $P(z) = 0$, then $P(\bar{z}) = 0$.

22.18 Verify that the nth roots of z defined by (A.6.8) from Appendix A are all distinct.

CHAPTER 23

HEURISTIC SEARCH STRATEGIES: A*-SEARCH AND GAME TREES

> **heuristic:** *... providing aid or direction in the solution of a problem, but otherwise unjustified or incapable of justification. ... of or relating to exploratory problem-solving techniques that utilize self-learning techniques to improve performance.*
>
> **Webster's New Collegiate Dictionary**

Search strategies such as backtracking, LIFO and FIFO branch-and-bound, breadth-first search, and depth-first search are blind in the sense that they do not look ahead, beyond a local neighborhood, when expanding a node. In this chapter, we show how using heuristics can help narrow the scope of otherwise blind searches. We introduce a type of heuristic search strategy known as A*-search, which is widely used in artificial intelligence (AI). We then discuss strategies for playing two-person games. The alpha-beta heuristic for two-person games is based on assigning a heuristic value to positions reached by looking ahead a certain fixed number of moves. Then an estimate for the best move is obtained by working back to the current position using the so-called *minimax* strategy.

23.1 Artificial Intelligence: Production Systems

The subject of AI is concerned with designing algorithms that allow computers to emulate human behavior (see Figure 23.1). The major areas of AI include natural language processing, automatic programming and theorem proving, robotics, machine vision and pattern recognition, intelligent data retrieval, expert systems, and game playing. Certain activities that are child's play, such as using a natural language, present theoretically and computationally difficult problems that are beyond the reach of current technology. It is true that voice recognition computer programs are currently available that can properly interpret a limited set of spoken instructions. However, the time when we can carry out ordinary conversations with a computer, such as those between the spaceship crew and the computer Hal in the movie *2001: A Space Odyssey*, has yet to be fully realized.

Many problems in AI involve production systems. An AI production system is characterized by *system states* (also called *databases*), *production rules* that allow the system to change from one state to another, and a *control system* that manages the execution of the production rules and allows the system to evolve according to some desired scenario. For example, a system state might be the position of a robotic arm. A production rule allows the robotic arm to change its position. A control strategy is an algorithm that controls the movement of the arm from a given initial position to a final goal position. Here again, a two-year-old child can move his or her arms without much thinking, but designing an algorithm that allows a robot to accomplish the same thing is a complicated task.

Given any AI production system, there is a positive cost associated with the application of each production rule. A production system can be modeled as a positively weighted digraph, called a *state-space digraph,* where a node in the graph is the state of the system, and a directed edge from node v to node w is assigned the cost $Cost(v, w)$ of the production rule that transforms state v into state w. Given some initial state r (in which the root vertex is in the directed graph), we are interested in whether or not we can find a directed path from r to a goal state. A control system for the problem is then simply a search strategy for reaching a goal state starting from r. As usual, we wish to find control systems that perform searches efficiently.

FIGURE 23.1

© Sidney Harris.
*Reprinted with
permission. All rights
reserved.*

"IT FIGURES. IF THERE'S ARTIFICIAL INTELLIGENCE,
THERE'S BOUND TO BE ARTIFICIAL STUPIDITY."

23.2 8-Puzzle Game

We illustrate the ideas of an AI production system by the 8-puzzle game. The 8-puzzle game is a smaller version of the 15-puzzle game invented by Sam Lloyd in 1878. In the 8-puzzle game, there are eight tiles numbered 1 through 8 occupying eight of the nine cells in a 3×3 square board. The objective is to move from a given initial state in the board to a goal state. The only moves (production rules) allowed are to move a tile into an adjacent empty cell. It is convenient to characterize such a move as a movement of the empty cell. Thus, there are exactly four rules for moving the empty cell: move left, move right, move up, move down. Of course, the only states allowing all four rules to be applied are when the empty cell is in the center. When the empty cell is at a corner location in the board, then only two of the four rules can be applied. The remaining locations allow the application of three of the four rules.

We will let D be the state-space digraph whose vertex set consists of all possible board configurations in the 8-puzzle game. In D, a directed edge (v, w) exists if a move in the game transforms v into w. Note that if (v, w) is an edge, then (w, v) is also an edge. Thus, D can be considered a state-space graph, where the two directed edges (v, w) and (w, v) are replaced with the single undirected edge $\{v, w\}$. A portion of the state-space graph is shown in Figure 23.2. Suppose we use the breadth-first search control strategy to search for a path leading from the initial state to the goal state. We assume that our control strategy always generates the children of a node in the following order: move left, move right, move up, move down. In Figure 23.3, we have taken an initial position that is only four moves from the goal state. However, 28 states (not counting the initial state) are generated by breadth-first search.

FIGURE 23.2

A portion of the state-space graph for the 8-puzzle game.

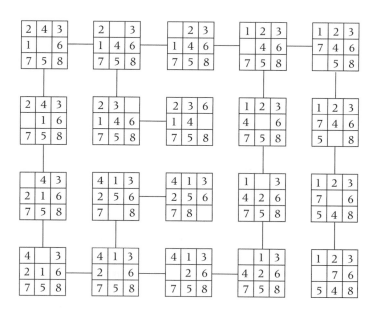

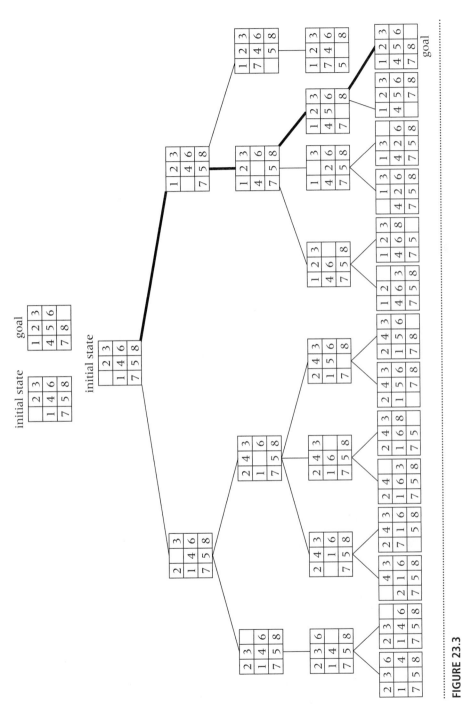

FIGURE 23.3

The states generated by the breadth-first search for a path from the given initial state to the goal state in the 8-puzzle game. The path to the goal is shown in bold.

In general, the number of nodes generated by a breadth-first search for the *n*-puzzle game is exponential in the minimum number of moves required to reach a goal. Thus, we must look for a better search strategy to solve the problem for initial states requiring many moves to reach the goal. We now describe such a strategy.

23.3 A*-Search

Given a root vertex *r* and a set of goal states in a state-space digraph, an A*-search is a strategy for finding a shortest path from *r* to a nearest goal. Such a path is called an *optimal path*. An A*-search finds an optimal path using a generalization of Dijkstra's algorithm. In the discussion of Dijkstra's algorithm in Chapter 12, we maintained an array $Dist[0:n-1]$. At each stage, the vertex *v* minimizing $Dist[v]$ over all vertices not in the tree was added to *T*. The values of $Dist[w]$ were then updated for all vertices *w* in the out-neighborhood of *v*. The operations performed on the array $Dist[0:n-1]$ were essentially those of a priority queue. To aid in the description of the A*-search strategy, we now give a high-level description of Dijkstra's algorithm based on maintaining a priority queue of vertices. We also modify Dijkstra's algorithm to terminate once a goal is dequeued.

We denote the priority of a vertex *v* in the queue by $g(v)$, where the smaller values of *g* have higher priority. At initialization, the root vertex *r* is enqueued with priority $g(r) = 0$. When a vertex *v* is enqueued, a parent pointer from *v* to *Parent(v)* is also stored. The parent pointers determine a tree. We call the subtree of the tree spanned by the vertices that have been dequeued the *dequeued tree T*. The tree *T* contains a shortest path in *D* from *r* to each vertex in *T*.

At each stage in the algorithm, a vertex *v* in the priority queue is dequeued, and the out-neighbors of *v* are examined. If an out-neighbor *w* of *v* is already in the tree *T*, then nothing is done to *w*. If the out-neighbor *w* has not been enqueued, then it is enqueued with priority $g(w) = g(v) + c(v, w)$, and a parent pointer from *w* to *v* is set. Finally, if the out-neighbor *w* is already on the queue, then the priority of vertex *w* is updated to $g(w) = \min\{g(w), g(v) + c(v, w)\}$. If $g(w)$ is changed to $g(v) + c(v, w)$, then the parent pointer of *w* is reset to point to *v*. The algorithm terminates once a goal is dequeued. The path in the final tree *T* from *r* to the goal is an optimal path. The action of the algorithm is shown in Figure 23.4 for a sample digraph.

Dijkstra's algorithm is too inefficient for most AI applications because the shortest-path tree can grow to be huge, even exponentially large. The reason for

FIGURE 23.4

The action of Dijkstra's algorithm is shown for a sample weighted digraph D. The distance g(v) is shown outside each node v. The vertices and the edges of the dequeued (shortest-path) tree are shaded. The priority queue at each stage consists of vertices w not in the dequeued tree, where the priority of w is g(w).

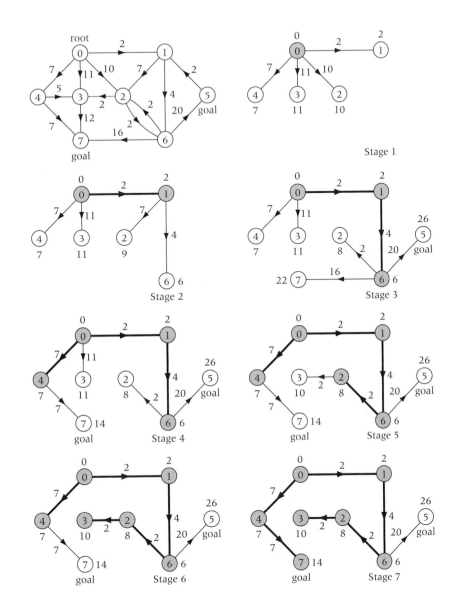

its inefficiency is that only local information is assumed when looking ahead to a goal. No global information is used that can help the shortest-path tree send out branches in a promising direction. In other words, in Dijkstra's algorithm, the shortest-path tree tends to grow fat (a "shotgun approach" to a goal) rather than grow skinny (a "beeline" approach to a goal).

23.3.1 Heuristics

When information beyond merely the costs of the edges in the digraph is available, Dijkstra's algorithm can be improved so that the shortest-path tree is less expansive and the search is more efficient. The idea is that the priority value $g(v)$ of a vertex v in the queue, which is the cumulative distance (cost) from the root r via the current path determined by the parent pointers, can be replaced by an overall estimate of the cost of the shortest path from r to a goal constrained to go through v. In Dijkstra's algorithm, the priority value of v is $g(v)$, but now we define the priority value of v to be the *cost function*

$$f(v) = g(v) + h(v), \qquad\qquad \textbf{(23.3.1)}$$

where $h(v)$ is some estimate of the cost of a shortest path from v to a goal vertex. Because the shortest path from v to a goal has not been found, the best that we can do is use a *heuristic* value for $h(v)$.

When no restriction is placed on the heuristic h in Formula (23.3.1), h is merely a heuristic for a greedy algorithm. When the vertices in the dequeued tree T are reexamined and their parent pointers updated when shorter paths for them are found, the algorithm based on (23.3.1) is called an *A-search*. There is no guarantee that the first path found to a goal is optimal using an A-search. When an A-search uses a heuristic $h(v)$ that is a lower bound of the cost of the shortest path from v to a goal, then the algorithm is called an *A*-search*. We assume that an A*-search terminates when it dequeues a goal, or when the queue is empty. The proof of the following theorem is left to the exercises.

Theorem 23.3.1   Given a positively weighted digraph G (finite or infinite), if a goal is reachable from a root vertex r, then an A*-search terminates by finding an optimal path from r to a goal.   □

In an A*-search, when a node v is dequeued, some of its neighbors may already be in the tree T. Unlike Dijkstra's algorithm, an A*-search must check these neighbors to see if shorter paths to them now exist via the vertex v just dequeued. If shorter paths are found, then T must be adjusted to account for them (see Figure 23.5).

Considerable computational cost may be incurred by an A*-search when adjusting the dequeued tree T. This computational cost can be avoided by placing a rather natural and mild restriction on the heuristic h used by A*-search. The heuristic value $h(v)$ is an estimate of the cost of going from v to the nearest goal.

FIGURE 23.5

The number shown
outside each node v
in T is the value
$g(v)$. This example
shows how the
dequeued tree T
can change during
an A*-search. Note
that the values of g
at vertices a, b and
c required updating.

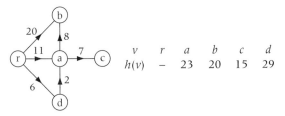

Portion of state space induced by vertices r, a, b, c, d,
and an associated function h

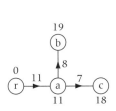 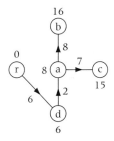

The dequeued tree T after vertices   The dequeued tree T after
r, a, b, c have been dequeued d has been dequeued

If the edge (v, w) exists, then one estimate is $c(v, w) + h(w)$. The restriction on a heuristic, called the *monotone restriction*, says that $h(v)$ should be at least as good as this estimate.

DEFINITION 23.3.1 A heuristic $h(v)$ for an A*-search for a given digraph with cost function c on the edges is said to satisfy the *monotone restriction*, if

$$h(v) \le c(v, w) + h(w), \quad \text{whenever the edge } (v, w) \text{ exists,}$$
$$h(v) = 0, \qquad\qquad\qquad \text{whenever } v \text{ is a goal.}$$

(23.3.2)

If h satisfies the monotone restriction, then we merely say that h is monotone.

If h is a monotone heuristic, then $h(v)$ is a lower bound of the cost of the shortest path from v to a goal. The following proposition states that an A*-search using a monotone heuristic does not need to update parent pointers of a vertex v already in the dequeued tree T, because the path in T from r to v is already a shortest path in D from r to v. The result is consistent with the fact that the A*-search algorithm reduces to Dijkstra's algorithm when $h(v) \equiv 0$ (and the identically zero function trivially satisfies the monotone restriction).

Proposition 23.3.2 Suppose an A*-search uses a monotone heuristic. Then the dequeued tree T is a shortest-path tree in the state-space digraph D. In particular, parent pointers for vertices in the dequeued tree T never need updating.

PROOF

For any vertex $v \in V$, let $g^*(v)$ denote the length of the shortest path in D from r to v (so that $g(v) \geq g^*(v)$ at every stage in the execution of an A*-search). We wish to show that $g(v) = g^*(v)$ at the time when v is dequeued. If $v = r$, then we have $g(v) = g^*(v) = 0$; thus, we can suppose that $v \neq r$. Let $P = v_0, v_1, \ldots, v_j$ be a shortest path in D from $r = v_0$ to $v = v_j$. Let vertex v_k be the last vertex in P such that $v_0, v_1, \ldots, v_k$ were all in the tree T when v was dequeued (v_k exists since $r = v_0 \in T$). Then v_{k+1} was in the queue Q at the time when v was dequeued. For any pair of consecutive vertices v_i, v_{i+1} in P, using the monotone restriction, we have

$$g^*(v_i) + h(v_i) \leq g^*(v_i) + h(v_{i+1}) + c(v_i, v_{i+1}). \tag{23.3.3}$$

Now v_i and v_{i+1} are in a shortest path in G, so that

$$g^*(v_{i+1}) = g^*(v_i) + c(v_i, v_{i+1}). \tag{23.3.4}$$

Substituting Formula (23.3.4) in Formula (23.3.3), we obtain

$$g^*(v_i) + h(v_i) \leq g^*(v_{i+1}) + h(v_{i+1}). \tag{23.3.5}$$

Iterating Formula (23.3.5) and using the transitivity of $\leq$ yields

$$g^*(v_{k+1}) + h(v_{k+1}) \leq g^*(v_j) + h(v_j) = g^*(v) + h(v). \tag{23.3.6}$$

Now v_{k+1} is on a shortest path P, and $v_0, v_1, \ldots, v_k$ all belong to T, so that $g(v_{k+1}) = g^*(v_{k+1})$. Hence, Formula (23.3.6) implies

$$f(v_{k+1}) = g(v_{k+1}) + h(v_{k+1}) \leq g^*(v) + h(v) + h(v) = f(v) \tag{23.3.7}$$

Thus, we must have had $g(v) = g^*(v)$ when v was dequeued; otherwise, $f(v_{k+1}) < f(v)$, and v would not have been dequeued in preference to v_{k+1}. ■

The following proposition helps explain the terminology *monotone restriction*. We leave the proof of Proposition 23.3.3 as an exercise.

Proposition 23.3.3 The *f*-values of the vertices dequeued by an A*-search using a monotone heuristic are nondecreasing. □

In any problem using an A*-search, the digraph and associated cost function are either implicitly or explicitly input to the algorithm. Here we give examples of both scenarios. When the digraph is very large, it is usually implicitly defined, and only the part of the digraph generated by the execution of the A*-search is made explicit. The following is a high-level description of A*-search using a monotone heuristic. At any given point in the execution of procedure *A*-SearchMH*, *T* is a subtree of *D* rooted at the root vertex *r* containing a path from *r* to each vertex that has been dequeued by the algorithm. Assuming that a path from *r* to a goal exists, Theorem 23.3.1 and Proposition 23.3.2 show that when *A*-SearchMH* terminates after dequeuing a goal, the corresponding path to the goal is optimal.

procedure *A*-SearchMH(D, c, r, GoalSet, h, T)*
Input:　*D* = (*V*, *E*) (a digraph, either implicitly or explicitly defined)
　　　　　c (a positive cost function on *E*)
　　　　　r (a root vertex in *D*)
　　　　　h (a heuristic function satisfying monotone restriction)
　　　　　GoalSet (a set of goal vertices in *D*)
Output:　a shortest-path out-tree *T* rooted at *r* containing an optimal path to a goal
　　　　　vertex, if one exists
　　　　　　Q (a priority queue of vertices, with *v* having priority value $f(v) = g(v) + h(v)$, where $g(v)$ is the cost of shortest path $P(v)$ from *r* to *v* currently
　　　　　　generated. *Q* also contains a parent pointer from *v* to *w* ∈ *T*, where edge
　　　　　　(*w*, *v*) belongs to $P(v)$)
　　　while *Q* is not empty **do**
　　　　　dequeue vertex *v* in *Q* with minimum priority value $f(v)$
　　　　　add vertex *v* to *T* using parent pointer
　　　　　if *v* ∈ *GoalSet* **then**
　　　　　　　return
　　　　　endif
　　　　　for all vertices *w* ∉ *T* and adjacent to *v* **do**
　　　　　　　if *w* ∉ *Q* **then**
　　　　　　　　　enqueue *w* with parent *v* and priority value $f(w) = g(w) + h(w)$
　　　　　　　　　where $g(w) = g(v) + c(v, w)$

```
                else
                    if f(w) ≥ g(v) + c(v, w) + h(w) then
                        reset parent pointer of w to v and update priority value of
                        w to f(w) = g(w) + h(w), where g(w) = g(v) + c(v, w)
                    endif
                endif
            endfor
        endwhile
        return "failure"
    end A*-SearchMH
```

The action of procedure A*-$SearchMH$ is illustrated in Figure 23.6 for a sample digraph D.

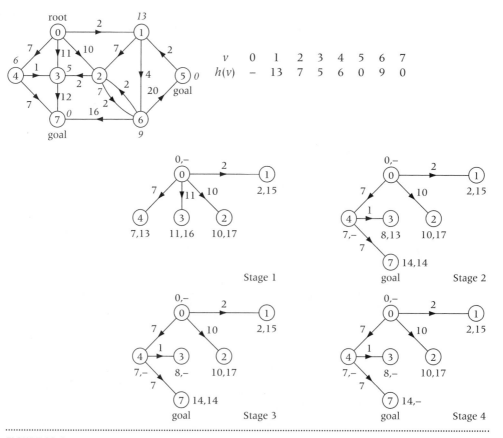

FIGURE 23.6

The action of A*-search with root vertex $r = 0$ and a monotone heuristic $h(v)$ is shown for the same weighted digraph D as in Figure 22.4.

We now illustrate procedure *A*-SearchMH* with two examples. First, we revisit the 8-puzzle problem. Then we consider the problem of finding shortest paths between cities in the United States using the freeway system. In the 8-puzzle problem, the state-space graph *G* is implicitly defined. In the freeway problem, the state-space graph is explicitly input to the algorithm.

23.3.2 A*-Search and the 8-Puzzle Game

Consider the heuristic

$$h(v) = \text{the number of tiles not in correct cell in the state } v.$$

It is easy to verify that $h(v)$ satisfies the monotone restriction. Using $h(v)$, Figure 23.7 shows the shortest-path tree generated by the A*-search for the same input as shown in Figure 23.3.

FIGURE 23.7

Shortest-path tree generated by the A*-search for the 8-puzzle game with the same initial state and goal state as in Figure 23.3.

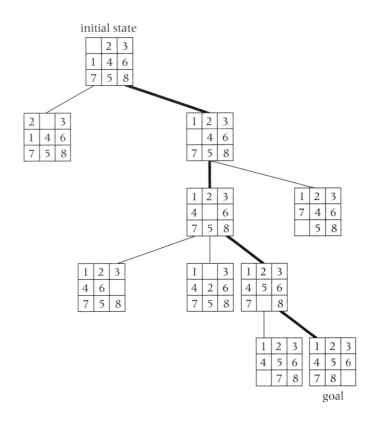

Note that the A*-search only generated 9 states compared to the 28 states generated by the breadth-first search for the same input. Other monotone heuristics exhibit even better behavior in general than the one used in Figure 23.7. For example, for any given state, the sum of the Manhattan distances (vertical steps plus horizontal steps) from the tiles to their proper positions in the goal state exhibits good performance.

23.3.3 Shortest Paths in the Freeway System

Our second example of an A*-search is for the problem of finding a shortest path on freeways between two cities in the continental United States (see Figure 23.8). The heuristic $h(v)$ we use will be a lower bound of the geographical (great-circle) distance between v and the destination city t. We assume that the distances between adjacent cities is available to the algorithm via a suitable adjacency cost matrix. The lower-bound estimate is computed using the longitude and latitude of each city, which we assume are both input to the algorithm as additional information. A lower bound of 50 miles is used for the longitude distance of one degree apart. A lower bound of 70 miles is used for the latitude distance of one degree apart. The square root of the sum of the squares of the longitude distance and the latitude distance between cities v and t is used as $h(v)$. The heuristic $h(v)$ is monotone because the cost (mileage on a freeway between adjacent cities) cannot be smaller than the geographical distance between them. Indeed, if the cost between adjacent cities v and w is $c(v, w)$, then $h(v)$, $h(w)$, and $c(v, w)$ form an almost planar triangle, and we have $h(v) \leq h(w) + c(v, w)$, which is the monotone restriction.

Figure 23.8 shows the graph of the United States as input to a Prolog program, as well as a shortest path from Cincinnati to Houston. Figure 23.9 shows the shortest-path tree generated by Dijkstra's algorithm ($h \equiv 0$), whereas Figure 23.10 shows the shortest-path tree generated by the A*-search. The number of vertices in the shortest path between Cincinnati and Houston is 9. The number

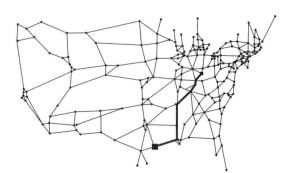

FIGURE 23.8

U.S. freeway system.

FIGURE 23.9

Shortest-path tree
generated by
Dijkstra's algorithm.

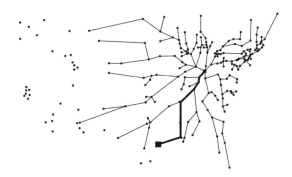

of vertices expanded when the heuristic is used is 34, compared with 213 vertices when expanded by Dijkstra's algorithm. Thus, the portion of the graph expanded using the A*-search is only 16 percent of that expanded using Dijkstra's algorithm for this example. The contrast between the trees grown in Figure 23.9 and in Figure 23.10 shows rather nicely the difference between the "shotgun" approach to a goal made by Dijkstra's algorithm versus the "beeline" approach made by A*-search.

The selection of a good heuristic is crucial to the success of an A*-search. The closer $h(v)$ is to the actual cost of the shortest path from v to a goal, the fewer nodes will be expanded during the A*-search. However, determining heuristics close to the actual cost is usually too expensive computationally, because determining close estimates is as hard as the original problem. It sometimes speeds the search to use a function for h that does not have the lower-bound property—that is, using an A-search instead of an A*-search. For example, there are better heuristics leading to A-searches for the 8-puzzle game than the monotone heuristic $h(v)$ that was the basis for our A*-search.

FIGURE 23.10

Shortest-path tree
generated by
A*-search.

23.4 Least-Cost Branch-and-Bound

Least-cost branch-and-bound is basically an A*-search applied to a state-space tree with the additional use of a bounding function. We use the same notation when describing the state-space tree T as we used in Chapter 10. Least-cost branch-and-bound applies to problems involving minimizing an objective function φ over each solution state in the state-space tree. The cost $c(v)$ of a given node $v = (x_1, \ldots, x_k)$ in the state-space tree is taken to be a lower-bound estimate for

$$\varphi^*(v) = \min\{\varphi(w)|w \in T_v \text{ and } w \text{ is a solution state}\}, \quad \textbf{(23.4.1)}$$

where T_v is the subtree of the state-space tree rooted at v, so that

$$c(v) \le \varphi^*(v). \quad \textbf{(23.4.2)}$$

Often, the cost function c has the same form as with an A*-search,

$$c(v) = g(v) + h(v), \quad \textbf{(23.4.3)}$$

where $g(v)$ is the cost associated with going from the root to the node v, and $h(v)$ is a heuristic lower-bound estimate of the incremental cost of going from v to a solution state v^* in T_v where φ is minimized (over T_v). Typically, $g(v)$ is $\varphi(v)$, where $\varphi(v)$ is an extension of the objective function φ to all problem states.

For example, in the coin-changing problem (see Chapter 7), $g(v)$ is the number of coins used in the problem state v. A natural heuristic $h(v)$ is obtained in a manner similar to the greedy method. Let $r(v)$ denote the remaining change required. We use as many of the largest-denomination coin as possible, then as many of the next-largest-denomination coin as possible, and continue in this manner as long as we do not exceed $r(v)$. The number of coins so obtained is our heuristic $h(v)$ used for the lower bound $c(v) = g(v) + h(v)$.

As a second example, consider the 0/1 knapsack problem formulated as a minimization problem (see Chapter 10). We then have

$$g(x_1, \ldots, x_k) = LeftOutValue(x_1, \ldots, x_k)$$

and

$$h(x_1, \ldots, x_k) = -Greedy(C', B'),$$

where $LeftOutValue(x_1, \ldots, x_k)$ is the sum of the values of the objects not in the set $\{b_{x_1}, \ldots, b_{x_k}\}$, B' is the set of objects $\{b_{x_k + 1}, \ldots, b_n\}$, $C' = C - (w_{x_1} + \ldots + w_{x_k})$, and $Greedy(C', B')$ is the value of the greedy solution to the (C', B') knapsack problem.

In least-cost branch-and-bound, the live nodes in the state-space tree are maintained as a priority queue with respect to the cost function c. In contrast to our method in A*-search, here we maintain a global variable UB, which is the smallest value of the objective function over all solution states already generated. Then a node v can be bounded if $c(v) \geq UB$; moreover, we have the following key fact.

Key Fact

Given a lower-bound cost function, if a node of least cost among the live nodes is bounded, then the algorithm can terminate, having already generated an optimal solution state (goal node).

The following paradigm for a least-cost branch-and-bound search strategy uses the same notation and implementation details for the state-space tree as in Chapter 10.

→ **procedure** *LeastCostBranchAndBound*
Input: function $D_k(x_1, \ldots, x_{k-1})$ (determining state-space tree T associated with the given problem)
objective function φ defined on the solution states of T
cost function $c(v)$ such that:
$c(v) \leq \varphi^*(v) = \min\{\varphi(w) \mid w \in T_v \text{ and } w \text{ is a solution state}\}$
Output: a solution state (goal) where φ is minimized
LiveNodes is initialized to be empty
AllocateTreeNode(Root)
Root→Parent ← **null**
AddPriorityQueue(LiveNodes, Root)   //add root to priority queue of live nodes
Goal ← *Root*   //initialize goal to root
UB ← ∞
Found ← .false.
while *LiveNodes* is not empty .and. .not. *Found* **do**
    Select(LiveNodes, E-node, k)   //select *E*-node of smallest cost from live nodes
        if $c(E\text{-}node) \geq UB$ **then**   //*Goal* points to optimal solution state
            Found ← .true.

```
                else
                    if E-node is a solution state and φ(E-Node) < UB then
                                                        //update UB
                        UB ← φ(E-Node)
                        Goal ← E-Node
                    endif
                    for each X[k] ∈ D_k(E-node) do          //for each child of the E-node do
                        if c(X[k]) < UB .and. .not. StaticBounded (X[1], . . . , X[k]) then
                            AllocateTreeNode(Child)
                            Child→Info ← X[k]
                            Child→Parent ← E-node
                            AddPriorityQueue(LiveNodes, Child)
                                                        //add child to list of live nodes
                        endif
                    endfor
                endif
            endwhile
            Path(Goal)                                  //output path from goal node to root
        end BranchAndBound
```

23.5 Game Trees

Since the invention of the electronic computer, there has been interest in computerized strategies for playing two-player games. For example, particular interest has been focused on designing computer programs to play chess. The first computer programs written for playing chess were not very sophisticated, partly because early computers were not powerful enough to store the vast amounts of information necessary to play a good game. Computer programs implemented on levels for such games as backgammon and computer programs for playing bridge, have exhibited excellent performance.

Computerized game-playing strategies are usually based on the efficient partial search of the enormous game tree modeling all possible legal moves for a given two-player game. The size of the game tree of all possible moves is generally much too large to admit complete searches. Thus, computerized game-playing strategies use heuristics to estimate the value of various moves based on looking down a limited number of levels in the game tree.

Game trees can become quite large even for simple games. For example, consider the game tree associated with tic-tac-toe on a 3×3 board (see Chapter 10). Suppose two players, A and B, are placing Xs and Os, respectively, and player A moves first. Player A has nine possible choices to place the first X. (Of course, using symmetries of the square, only three of these moves are nonequivalent. We

FIGURE 23.11

A portion of the
game tree for
tic-tac-toe on the
3 × 3 board.
Children of a single
node at level 1
are shown.

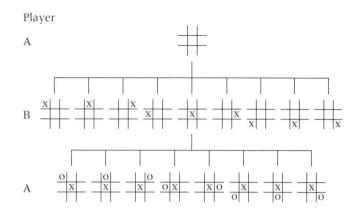

choose to ignore this reduction for the moment.) After player A moves, then
player B has eight possible choices for placing the first O. Continuing in this fashion, we see that the game tree has an upper bound of 9! = 362,880 nodes, although the actual number of nodes is smaller because the game terminates
whenever a player achieves three Xs or three Os in a row. Figure 23.11 shows all
the nodes at levels 0 and 1 of the game tree, but only that portion of the nodes at
level 2 corresponding to the eight possible moves from a particular single node at
level 1. Figure 23.12 shows all the nodes in the levels 0, 1, and 2 of the pruned
game tree that results by pruning symmetric board configurations.

Now consider the game tree modeling an arbitrary game between two players, A and B, who alternately make moves, with each player having complete

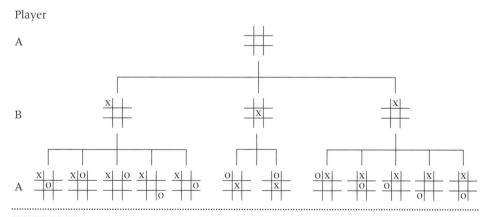

FIGURE 23.12

A portion of the game for tic-tac-toe on the 3 × 3 board pruned by symmetric board
configurations. All nodes at the first three levels are shown.

knowledge of the moves of the other (a *perfect information* game). The root of the game tree corresponds to the opening move in the game, which is assumed to be made by player A. Nodes at even levels in the game tree correspond to configurations where it is A's move and are called *A-nodes*. Nodes at odd levels correspond to configurations where it is B's move and are called *B-nodes*. The children of an A-node (respectively, B-node) correspond to all admissible moves available to player A (respectively, player B) from the node. Similar to the game tree for tic-tac-toe, for general games we assume a particular ordering of all admissible moves from a given node, so our game trees are always ordered trees. A leaf node in the game tree is called a *terminal* node and corresponds to the end of the game. In general, a terminal node corresponds to a win, loss, or tie for player A, although certain games such as nim cannot end in a tie.

Given a game tree, the value to player A is assigned to each terminal node (outcome of the game). We also assume that the game is a *zero-sum* game, so that the value to player B of a terminal node is the negative of its value to player A. *However, until further notice, when we speak of the value of a node it is always the value to player A.* We wish to design an algorithm that determines player A's optimal first move. In other words, we want to determine the move that player A should make so that the game will end at a terminal node of maximum value for player A, assuming that each player plays perfectly. Of course, if player B does not play perfectly, then the outcome for player A could be even better.

To analyze the entire game, it is enough to design a procedure to determine the optimal opening move. Indeed, after player A makes the opening move, we would simply repeat (from player B's point of view) the optimal strategy at the game subtree rooted at the node corresponding to this move, and so forth.

If the game tree is small enough to be completely traversed in a reasonable amount of time, then there is a simple *minimax procedure* for player A to determine the optimal opening move. We simply perform a postorder traversal of the game tree, in which a visit at an A-node corresponds to identifying a child of maximum value for a move from the A-node and assigning that value to the A-node. Similarly, a visit at a B-node corresponds to identifying a child of minimum value for a move from the B-node and assigning that value to the B-node.

Key Fact

The minimax strategy is nothing more than the definition of perfect play for the two players.

Note that postorder traversal is necessary because the value of each child of a node must be determined before the value of the node itself can be determined. When the postorder traversal is complete, the opening move, together with the value of the game to player A, will be determined.

We illustrate the minimax procedure for the game tree corresponding to a small instance of the game of nim. In the general game of nim, there are n piles of sticks, where the ith pile contains m_i sticks, $i = 1, \ldots, n$. Each player alternately chooses a nonempty pile and removes some or all of the sticks from this pile. There is usually a restriction made on how many sticks a player is allowed to remove in a given move. The last player to remove a stick loses. For large $m_1 + m_2 + \cdots + m_n$, the game tree modeling nim would be enormous. To keep things in sight, consider the instance $n = 2, m_1 = 3, m_2 = 2$. The game tree for this instance is shown in Figure 23.13, where the numbers inside each node correspond to the number of sticks left in each pile. Thus, terminal nodes correspond to 0, 0. We assign the value of $+1$ to a terminal A-node (A wins) and -1 to a terminal B-node (B wins). In Figure 23.14, we have done some pruning of the complete game tree to eliminate generating symmetric child configurations of the two nodes [1, 1] and [2, 2]. For example, in the complete game tree, the node [2, 2] generates the four nodes [0, 2], [1, 2], [2, 0], and [2, 1]. Using symmetry, we need only display the first two nodes in Figure 23.13 when drawing the (pruned) game tree.

FIGURE 23.13

Game tree for [3, 2] nim, pruned to eliminate symmetric children of [1, 1] and [2, 2]. Terminal node values are $+1$ when A wins and -1 when B wins.

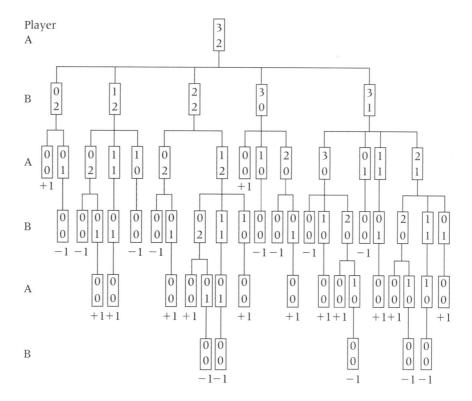

FIGURE 23.14

Values + = +1
and − = −1
assigned to each
node by the
minimax postorder
traversal of the
[3, 2] game of nim.

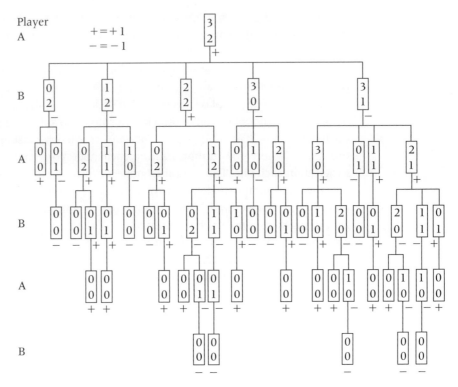

Figure 23.14 shows the results of a postorder traversal of the game tree in Figure 23.13, where visiting a node executes the minimax procedure described previously. In Figure 23.14, we show the value (to player A) of each node outside the node. Note that the [3, 2] game of nim is a win for player A. The complete traversal of the game tree shows that [2, 2] is a unique opening move that guarantees a win for player A. If a single winner strategy is desired, then the postorder traversal could be terminated as soon as it is determined that the root node has value +1 (with the opening move [2, 2]). Of course, similar termination can be done in any game where we simply have the values +1, 0, and −1 for win, tie, and loss, respectively.

A game in which a complete traversal of the game tree is feasible is usually too small to be interesting. Even the ordinary game of 3 × 3 tic-tac-toe has a rather large game tree. For games like chess, the game tree has been estimated to contain more than 10^{100} nodes. Thus, rather than attempting to traverse the entire game tree when determining an optimal move, in practice the minimax procedure is usually limited to looking ahead a fixed number of levels r in the game tree (*r-level search*). Terminal nodes encountered within r levels are assigned the value of the outcome of the game corresponding to this node. Nonterminal nodes at level r are assigned some estimate of the value of the node based on the best available knowledge, typically using some heuristic. Nodes that look more promising are given higher values. Of course, the better the estimate, the better the strategy generated by the r-level search.

Suppose we consider 3×3 tic-tac-toe with a two-level search. None of the nodes in the first two levels is a terminal node, so we need to come up with some estimate of the value of each node at level 2. A natural choice would be to assign to a given node (configuration of the board) the number of winning lines completable in Xs minus the number of winning lines completable by Os. For example, Figure 23.15 shows the value of each node at level 2 in the game tree (pruned by symmetries). The figure also shows the result of applying the two-level search (minimax procedure) to the game tree for 3×3 tic-tac-toe, which gives the values of -1, 1, and -2 to the nodes C_1, C_2, and C_3 at level 1, respectively, and gives the root node a value of 1.

We see from Figure 23.15 that player A's opening move would be to place an X in the center position. Then the minimax procedure is continued from the subtree rooted at the latter node. Unfortunately, continuing with the same two-level heuristic search method may lead to a loss for player A (see Exercise 23.24). The fairly obvious fix to this problem is to assign an appropriately large value to terminal positions when encountered in the search We simply give terminal nodes that are wins for player A (that is, three Xs in a row) any value greater than 8, which is the total number of winning lines for the 3×3 game. For example, we could assign the value 9 to terminal nodes that are wins for player A and -9 to terminal nodes that are wins for player B. Terminal nodes corresponding to tie games (cat's games) are assigned the value 0. With the values 9,

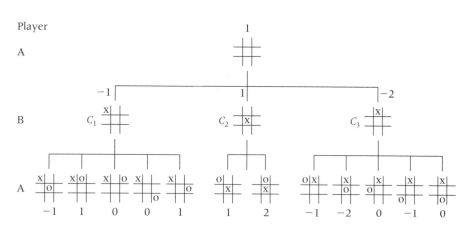

FIGURE 23.15

Value of each node at level 2 as computed using the number of winning lines completable by Xs minus the number of winning lines completable by Os. The values of nodes at levels 1 and 0 are computed using the minimax strategy.

0, and −9 so assigned to terminal nodes, a two-level search leads to a tie game. A tie game for the 3 × 3 board is the best that either player can hope for when both players play perfectly.

There is a heuristic strategy called *alpha-beta pruning* that can result in a significant reduction in the amount of nodes required to visit during an *n*-level search and still correctly compute the value of a given node. The easiest way to explain alpha-beta pruning is by example. Consider again the two-level search made in the game tree in Figure 23.15. After returning to the root from the middle child C_2, we know that player A can make a move to a node having value 1. Then we move to the third child C_3 of the root and begin visiting the children of C_3 (grandchildren of the root). The first child of C_3 has value −1, so we can immediately cut off our examination of the remaining children of C_3. The reason is simple: The value of C_3 is the minimum value of its children, so the value −1 of the first child of C_3 places an upper bound of −1 on the value of C_3. Because the lower bound on the value of the root is already known to be 1, the value of C_3 cannot possibly affect the value of the root. The cutoff just described is illustrated in Figure 23.16. A cutoff of the search of the grandchildren of an A-node (respectively, B-node) is called *alpha-cutoff* (respectively, *beta-cutoff*).

We formalize the notion of alpha-beta pruning as follows. A lower bound for the value of an A-node is called an *alpha value* of the A-node. Note that during an *r*-level search, an alpha value of a parent A-node is determined when we return to the A-node from its first child, and the alpha value can be updated, as appropriate, when we return from subsequent children. For example, after returning

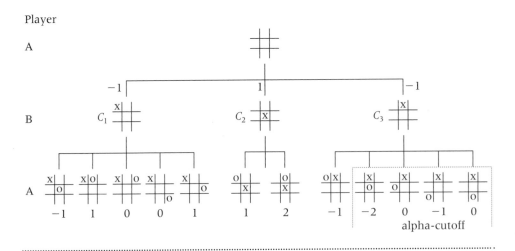

FIGURE 23.16

An alpha-cutoff.

to the root from child C_1 in Figure 23.16, we knew that -1 was an alpha value of the root. However, on returning to the root from the second child C_2, we could update the alpha value of the root to 1.

In general, suppose during an r-level search we are examining the children of the ith child of C_i, where the parent of C_i is an A-node X. If we encounter a child of C_i (grandchild of X) whose value is not larger than an alpha value of X, then we can cut off (alpha-cutoff) our search of the remaining children of C_i, because the value of C_i cannot affect the value of X.

An entirely symmetric discussion holds for B-nodes. Specifically, an upper bound for the value of a B-node is called a *beta value* of the B-node. Given any grandparent B-node Y, if during an r-level search we encounter a child (grandchild of Y) of the ith child D_i of Y whose value is not smaller than a beta value of Y, then we can cut off (beta-cutoff) our search of the remaining children of D_i, because the value of D_i cannot affect the value of Y.

Figure 23.17 illustrates a sample game tree and the effect of alpha-beta pruning for a complete search (that is, a three-level search) of the tree. To illustrate the dynamic nature of alpha and beta values, in Figure 23.17a, we show the indicated alpha and beta values of nodes just after returning to the node X from its second child. The value inside a given node is either the actual value of the node or an alpha or beta value as appropriate. Those nodes containing an alpha or a beta value are flagged as such. A value in a node that is shown as * means that the value is irrelevant because the node is never reached due to alpha-beta pruning. To emphasize the stage of the search in Figure 23.17a, no values are shown inside the nodes of the subtree rooted at the third child of X. In Figure 23.17b, values are supplied for the nodes in the latter subtree, where we show the results of the completed search.

When writing pseudocode implementing the minimax procedure, it is convenient to consider the value of a B-node to be the value to player B, not A. In other words, we simply change the signs of the values given to B-nodes in our previous discussion. These changes simplify the pseudocode by turning the minimax procedure into a max procedure. Note that in the max procedure, the value of either an A-node or a B-node is the maximum of the negatives of the values of their children. Thus, the identical max procedure is executed at an A-node or a B-node.

In the new scenario, our cutoff rule takes the same form whether we are examining the children of an A-node or those of a B-node. In either case, suppose LB is a lower bound for the value of the node v whose children are being evaluated, and suppose *ParentValue* is a lower bound for the value of the parent node. If we ever determine that $-LB \le ParentValue$, then we can cut off further examination of the children of v because the value of v cannot affect the value of the parent of v.

FIGURE 23.17

(a) The results of
the search just after
returning to X from
its second child C_2;
(b) the results of the
completed search.

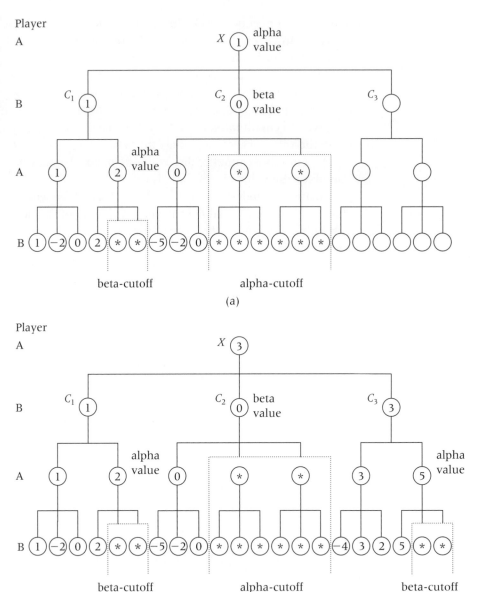

(a)

(b)

The following pseudocode for the recursive function *ABNodeValue* returns
the value of a node X in the game tree using a *NumLevels*-search, where the parameter *ParentValue* is a lower bound for the value of the parent of X. If X is a terminal node, or if *NumLevels* = 0, then we assume that X has been given an
appropriately defined value (denoted by *Val(X)*) as described earlier. Given a

node X and an integer r, the value of X would be calculated using an r-search by invoking *ABNodeValue* initially with arguments X, r, ∞.

```
function ABNodeValue(X, NumLevels, ParentValue) recursive
Input:     X (a node in the game tree having children C₁, C₂, . . . , Cₖ),
           NumLevels (number of levels to search)
           ParentValue (lower bound on the value of the parent of X)
Output:    returns the value of X
    if X is a terminal node .or. NumLevels = 0 then
        return(Val(X))
    else
        LB ← −NodeValue(C₁, NumLevels − 1, ∞) //initial lower bound for value of X
        for i ← 2 to k do
            if LB ≥ ParentValue then                    //cutoff
                return(LB)
            else
                LB ← max(LB, −NodeValue(Cᵢ , NumLevels − 1, −LB)
            endif
        endfor
    endif
    return(LB)
end ABNodeValue
```

When measuring the efficiency of *ABNodeValue*, the quantity of interest is the number of nodes cut off from the straight minimax r-search of the game tree that does not use the cutoff rule. Of course, not much can be said in general unless some assumptions are made about the regularity of the game tree. Even with strong regularity conditions imposed on the game tree, the analysis is difficult. We merely state one result in this direction. Perl has shown that for game trees in which each parent has the same number of children, and in which the terminal nodes are randomly ordered, *ABNodeValue* permits a search depth greater by a factor of 4/3 than that allowed by the straight minimax procedure in the same amount of time.

Alpha-beta pruning can be enhanced by adding an additional parameter *NodeValueLowBnd* into the algorithm *ABNodeValue*. *NodeValueLowBnd* is maintained as a lower bound on the value on the input parameter X. Additional pruning of the game tree results from the following key fact.

Key Fact

If the value of a grandchild of **X** is not larger than *NodeValueLowBnd*, then all remaining children of the grandchild can be pruned.

Whereas alpha-beta pruning only uses information from the parent, *NodeValueLowBnd* carries information deep into the tree, and the resulting evaluation of the game tree is called *deep* alpha-beta pruning. We leave the design of the recursive function for deep alpha-beta pruning as an exercise.

23.6 Closing Remarks

Seeking solutions to the 8-puzzle game or finding a shortest-length trip along a freeway system are examples of what has been called *single-agent* problems. In general, an A*-search is better suited for a large-scale problem in which the *entire solution* is sought in a reasonable length of time (and then saved for future reference) than for a real-time problem in which the first step (and each successive step) in the solution must be computed very quickly. For example, it might be acceptable for a computer to take weeks or even months to solve a highly important single-agent problem because its solution would then be known and usable in real time thereafter.

An ordinary A*-search as applied to a single-agent problem usually finds the entire path to a goal before even the first move from the starting position is definitely known. Hence, using an A*-search for a single-agent problem becomes too costly for a large-scale application where the optimal decisions along the way must be made quickly and in advance of the final solution. For example, you might be under a short time constraint to make each move in a game like the 8-puzzle game, rather than simply wanting to determine the *entire solution* in a larger but more reasonable length of time.

While most single-agent problems are not subject to intermediate real-time constraints, two-player games usually are. Chess, for example, usually restricts the amount of time a player has to make the next move. Moreover, the game tree for chess is so enormous that generating complete solutions is out of the question. To make real-time decisions, the alpha-beta heuristic is based on attempting to evaluate moves in a limited *search horizon*—that is, looking ahead a fixed number of moves.

For a single-agent problem, a heuristic search method called *real-time A*-search* combines the A*-search strategy with a limited look-ahead search horizon. A real-time A*-search uses an analog of minimax alpha-beta pruning called minimin *alpha pruning*. Alpha pruning drastically improves the efficiency of A*-search without affecting the decisions made. Like an A*-search, a real-time A*-search can find the entire solution to a fairly large-scale problem in a reasonable amount of time. However, a real-time A*-search has the advantage of generating the optimal moves along the way quickly and before the entire solution is known. Refer to the references for further information on the real-time A*-search.

Suppose that a perfect-information game involving alternate moves by two players A and B must end in a finite number of moves and a win for one of the two players. Then one of the two players must have a *winning strategy*—that is, a strategy that guarantees a win regardless of the moves made by the other player. The reason is simple: If neither player had a winning strategy, there would be a sequence of alternate moves made by A and B that never ends in a loss for either player. Because that sequence would not terminate, we would obtain a contradiction of the finiteness assumption of the game.

A two-person *positional* game is determined by a collection of sets A_i, $i = 1, \ldots, m$. The players alternately choose an element (which they keep) from $\cup_{i=1}^{n} A_i$. The first player to choose *all* the elements from one of the sets wins. Tic-tac-toe is an example of a positional game, where the sets A_i are the winning lines in the board. For positional games that cannot end in a tie, such as the $3 \times 3 \times 3$ game of tic-tac-toe, the first player always has a winning strategy. Indeed, we have just seen that one of the two players must have a winning strategy, so suppose it is the second player. Then the first player makes a random opening move, and thereafter assumes the role of the second player (basically ignoring the opening move). More precisely, when the first player moves, he chooses the move dictated by the second player's winning strategy, or moves randomly if he has previously made this move. Since having made an extra move in a positional game cannot possibly hurt, the first player is thus led to a win! This contradicts the assumption that the second player has a winning strategy and shows that the first player has a winning strategy. The same argument shows that if there is a winning strategy for a positional game, then it must belong to the first player.

For positional games that cannot end in a tie, the fact that the first player has a winning strategy does not mean that there is an efficient algorithm to generate the strategy. Also, for positional games that *can* end in a tie (given, perhaps, imperfect play), there still might exist a winning strategy for the first player. For example, tie positions exist for the $4 \times 4 \times 4$ game of tic-tac-toe (winning sets being four in a row). However, it was conjectured for a long time that the first player has a winning strategy in $4 \times 4 \times 4$ tic-tac-toe. This conjecture was finally established by Patashnik using clever bounding arguments that allowed a pruning of the enormous game tree for $4 \times 4 \times 4$ tic-tac-toe, reducing it to a size that was amendable to computer search.

References and Suggestions for Further Reading

Kanal, L., and V. Kumar, eds. *Search in Artificial Intelligence*. New York: Springer-Verlag, 1988. Contains numerous articles on search in artificial intelligence, including a discussion on the optimality of the A*-search.

Korf, R. E. "Real-Time Heuristic Search," *Artificial Intelligence* 42 (1990): 189–211. A paper devoted to the real-time A*-search.

Nilsson, N. J. *Principles of Artificial Intelligence.* Palo Alto, CA: Tioga, 1980. A detailed account of the A*-search, which was originally developed by Hart, Nilsson, and Raphael.

Pearl, J. *Heuristics: Intelligent Search Strategies for Computer Problem Solving.* Reading, MA: Addison-Wesley, 1984. A text devoted to heuristic searching.

Two books on artificial intelligence that contain extensive discussions of search strategies and game playing:

Rich, E., and K. Knight. Artificial Intelligence. 2nd ed. New York: McGraw-Hill, 1991.

Russell, S. J., and P. Norvig. Artificial Intelligence: A Modern Approach. Englewood Cliffs, NJ: Prentice Hall, 1995.

Patashnik, O. "Qubic: 4 3 4 3 4 Tic-Tac-Toe," Mathematics Magazine 53 (1980): 202–223. Survey discussion of n-dimensional tic-tac-toe, as well as the proof that the 4 3 4 3 4 is a first-player win.

Two papers containing detailed analyses of alpha-beta and deep alpha-beta pruning:

Baudet, G. "An Analysis of the Full Alpha-Beta Pruning Algorithm," Proceedings of the 10th Annual ACM Symposium on Theories of Computing, San Diego, CA: Association for Computing Machinery, 1978, pp. 296–313.

Knuth, D. "An Analysis of Alpha-Beta Cutoffs," Artificial Intelligence 6 (1975): 293–323.

Berlekamp, E. R., J. H. Conway, and R. K. Guy. Winning Ways, for Your Mathematical Plays. Vol. I, II. New York: Academic Press, 1982. Covers strategies for a host of games.

Section 23.2 8-Puzzle Game

23.1   Draw the first three levels of the state-space tree generated by a breadth-first search for the 8-puzzle game with the following initial and goal states:

	goal				initial state	
1	2	3		4	2	7
4	5	6		1		6
7	8			3	5	8

23.2 The $(n^2 - 1)$-puzzle is a generalization of the 8-puzzle to the $n \times n$ board. The goal position is where the tiles are in row-major order (with the empty space in the lower-right corner). For $k \in \{1, \dots, n^2\}$, let $L(k)$ denote the number of tiles t, $t < k$, such that the position of t comes after k in the row-major order in the initial arrangement (the empty space is considered as tile n^2). Show that a necessary and sufficient condition that the goal can be reached is that

$$\sum_{k=1}^{n^2} L(k) \equiv i + j (\bmod 2), \qquad \textbf{(23.3.4)}$$

where (i, j) is the position of the empty space in the initial arrangement.

Section 23.3 A*-Search

23.3 Show that if h is a monotone heuristic, then $h(v)$ is a lower bound of the cost of the shortest path from v to a (nearest) goal.

23.4 Prove Proposition 23.3.3.

23.5 Design an algorithm for an A*-search using a heuristic that is not necessarily monotone.

23.6 For the 8-puzzle game, consider the following heuristic:

$h(v)$ = the number of tiles not in correct cell in the state v.

Show that $h(v)$ satisfies the monotone restriction.

23.7 For the 8-puzzle game, consider the following heuristic:

$h(v)$ = the sum of the Manhattan distances
(vertical steps plus horizontal steps) from the
tiles to their proper positions in the goal state.

Show that h satisfies the monotone restriction.

23.8 For the 8-puzzle game, let h be the monotone heuristic defined in Exercise 23.6. For the following initial and goal states, draw the states generated by making the first three moves in the game using an A*-search with the priority function $f(v) = g(v) + h(v)$ [$g(v)$ is the number of moves made from the initial state to v]. When enqueuing states, assume that the (possible) moves of the empty tile are ordered as follows: move left, move right, move up, move down. Label each state v with its f-value.

goal		
1	2	3
4	5	6
7	8	

initial state		
4	2	7
1		6
3	5	8

23.9 Repeat Exercise 23.8 for the heuristic h defined in Exercise 23.7.

23.10 Write a program for the n-puzzle game using the Manhattan distance heuristic. Test your program for $n = 8$ and $n = 15$.

23.11 Can you find better heuristics (not necessarily lower bounds) for the n-puzzle game than the Manhattan distance heuristic? Test your heuristic empirically for $n = 8$ and $n = 15$.

23.12 Prove Theorem 23.3.1

Section 23.4 Least-Cost Branch-and-Bound

23.13 Show that the heuristic $h(v)$ given in Section 23.4 for the coin-changing problem is a lower bound for the minimum number of additional coins required to make correct change from the given problem state v.

23.14 Write a program implementing a least-cost branch-and-bound solution to the coin-changing problem.

23.15 Design a heuristic and a least-cost branch-and-bound algorithm for the variation of the coin-changing problem in which we have a limited number of coins of each denomination. Assume the number of coins of each denomination is input along with the denominations.

23.16 Draw the portion of the variable-tuple state-space tree generated by least-cost branch-and-bound for the instance of the 0/1 knapsack problem given in Figure 10.13 in Chapter 10, using the heuristic given in Section 23.4. Label each node with the value of $c(v)$ and the current value of UB.

23.17 Repeat Exercise 23.16 for the fixed-tuple state-space tree.

23.18 Write a program implementing a least-cost branch-and-bound solution to the 0/1 knapsack problem.

23.19 Given the complete digraph $\hat{K}_n$ with vertices $0, 1, \ldots, n - 1$ and a nonnegative cost matrix $C = (c_{ij})$ for its edges (we set $c_{ij} = \infty$ if $i = j$ or if the edge ij does not exist), a traveling salesman tour starting at vertex 0 corresponds to a sequence of vertices $0, i_1, i_2, \ldots, i_{n-1}, 0$, where $i_1, i_2, \ldots, i_{n-1}$ is a permutation of $1, \ldots, n - 1$. Consider a state-space tree T for the traveling salesman problem (finding a minimum-cost tour) where a node at level k in T corresponds to a simple path containing $k + 1$ vertices, starting with vertex 0. Thus, T has depth n, and leaf nodes correspond to a sequence of choices $i_1, i_2, \ldots, i_{n-1}$, determining the tour $0, i_1, i_2, \ldots, i_{n-1}, 0$.

We now describe a cost function $c(v)$ for a least-cost branch-and-bound algorithm for the traveling salesman problem. The definition of $c(v)$ is based on the notion of a reduced-cost matrix. A row (or column) of a nonnegative cost matrix is said to be *reduced* if it contains at least one zero. A nonnegative cost matrix is *reduced* if each row and column of the matrix is reduced (except for rows and columns whose elements are all equal to ∞). Given the cost matrix C, an associated reduced-cost matrix C_r is constructed as follows. First, reduce each row by subtracting the minimum entry in the row from each element in the row. In the resulting matrix, repeat this process for each column. We define $c(r)$ to be the total amount subtracted. The following example illustrates C_r for a sample C.

$$
C = \begin{pmatrix} \infty & 23 & 9 & 32 & 12 \\ 21 & \infty & 2 & 16 & 4 \\ 4 & 8 & \infty & 20 & 6 \\ 15 & 10 & 4 & \infty & 2 \\ 9 & 5 & 8 & 10 & \infty \end{pmatrix} \quad C_r = \begin{pmatrix} \infty & 14 & 0 & 18 & 3 \\ 19 & \infty & 0 & 9 & 2 \\ 0 & 4 & \infty & 11 & 2 \\ 13 & 8 & 2 & \infty & 0 \\ 4 & 0 & 3 & 0 & \infty \end{pmatrix} \quad c(r) = 27
$$

More generally, we define (inductively on the levels of T) a reduced-cost matrix for each nonleaf node by suitably reducing the cost matrix C_u associated with the parent node u of v. Suppose u corresponds to a path ending at vertex i, and v corresponds to adding the edge ij to this path. We then change all the entries in row i and column j of C_u to ∞, as well as the entry in the jth row and first column. We then perform the same subtracting operation on the resulting matrix as we did when computing C_r. Let s_v denote the total amount subtracted, and define $c(v) = c(u) + C_u(i, j) + s_v$.

For leaf nodes v, $c(v)$ is defined as the cost of the tour determined by v.

a. Show that $c(r)$ is a lower bound for the minimum cost of a tour.

b. More generally, show that $c(v) \leq \phi^*(v) = $ the minimum cost over all tours determined by the leaf nodes of the subtree of T rooted at v.

c. Part (b) shows that $c(v)$ is suitable for *LeastCostBranchAndBound*. Design and give pseudocode for *LeastCost BranchAndBound* implementing $c(v)$.

23.20 Draw the portion of the state-space tree T generated by the least-cost branch-and-bound discussed in the Exercise 23.19 for the cost matrix illustrated in that exercise. Label each node v with its cost value $c(v)$. Also, write out the reduced matrix associated with each node generated.

23.21 Discuss other state-space trees and associated cost functions $c(v)$ for the traveling salesman problem.

Section 23.5 Game Trees

23.22 Consider the two-person zero-sum game shown in the figure below. The values in the leaf nodes are values to player A. Use the minimax strategy (postorder traversal) to determine the value of the game to player A. Show clearly where alpha-cutoff and beta-cutoff occur, as well as (final) actual values, alpha values, and beta values of all nodes reached in the traversal.

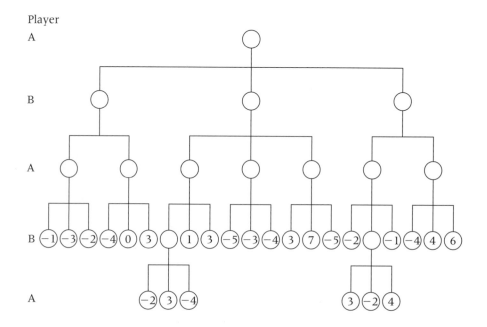

23.23 Rewrite the recursive function *NodeValue* as a recursive procedure that has the same input parameters, Y, *NumLevels*, *ParentValue*, but now returns in output parameters the value V of Y and the child C_i, whose value is $-V$.

23.24 Find a sequence of admissible moves for the two-level heuristic search illustrated in Figure 23.16 that leads to a loss for player A in 3×3 tic-tac-toe.

23.25 Show that by assigning the values 9, 0, and -9 to terminal nodes that are wins, ties, or losses, respectively, for player A, the two-level search illustrated in Figure 23.16 never leads to a loss for player A.

23.26 Because there are no tie positions in the $3 \times 3 \times 3$ tic-tac-toe game, the first player has a winning strategy. Find a winning strategy for the first player.

23.27 Design a recursive function *DABNodeValue*(*X*, *NumLevels*, *ParentValue*, *NodeValueLowBnd*) for deep alpha-beta pruning. The initial invocation of *DABNodeValue* should have *ParentValue* $= \infty$ and *NodeValueLowBnd* $= -\infty$.

23.28 Redo Exercise 23.22 for deep alpha-beta pruning. Indicate any pruned nodes that were not pruned by alpha-beta pruning.

CHAPTER 24

PROBABILISTIC AND RANDOMIZED ALGORITHMS

The algorithms that we have considered so far (with the exception of the Karp-Rabin string matcher) are *deterministic*; that is, they leave nothing to chance. Running a deterministic algorithm time after time with the same input produces identical results each time. On the other hand, a *probabilistic* algorithm contains steps that make random choices by invoking a random (or pseudorandom) number generator. Thus, they are subject to the laws of chance. In particular, a probabilistic algorithm can perform differently for two runs with the same input.

Probabilistic algorithms fall into four main design categories: randomizations of deterministic algorithms, Monte Carlo algorithms, Las Vegas algorithms, and numerical probabilistic algorithms. A randomization of a deterministic algorithm occurs when certain steps that made canonical choices are replaced by steps that make these choices in a random fashion. Randomization is done to break the connection between a particular input and worst-case behavior and thereby homogenize the expected behavior of inputs to the algorithm.

The expected behavior of a randomized algorithm over all inputs is no better than the average behavior of its associated deterministic algorithm and is usually a little worse due to the overhead of calls to a random number generator, among other factors. Monte Carlo algorithms often produce solutions very quickly but only guarantee correctness with high probability. A Las Vegas algorithm never outputs an incorrect solution but has some probability of reporting a failure to produce a solution. In practice, obtaining solutions with high probability is almost as satisfactory as the foolproof guarantee provided by a deterministic algorithm. For many important problems, such as prime testing, the most efficient algorithms currently known for their solutions are probabilistic.

Numerical probabilistic algorithms were among the first examples of introducing randomness into the design of algorithms. A classical example is the estimation of π obtained by throwing darts at a square and recording how many darts landed inside a circle inscribed in the square.

Probabilistic techniques have become very useful tools in the theory of parallel algorithms. The analog of the class NC for sequential algorithms is the class RNC for parallel algorithms. There are important examples of problems in RNC that are not known to be in NC.

24.1 Probabilistic Algorithms

Most of the probabilistic algorithms discussed in this chapter assume that we can make a random choice from a set of elements. For example, given integers m and n, $m < n$, we assume that a *random number generator* function *Random*(m, n) returns a random integer between m and n, with each integer being equally likely to be chosen. Moreover, successive calls to *Random* are independent of one another. When m and n are real numbers, we assume *Random*(m, n) returns a random real number between m and n. The distribution is uniform and independent on the interval (m, n).

In practice, random number generators are usually not available, and we must rely on *pseudorandom number generators*. A pseudorandom number generator is a deterministic procedure that from a given *seed* generates a sequence of numbers that closely resembles a sequence that might be obtained by successive calls to a genuine random number generator. However, given two identical seeds, a pseudorandom number generator generates identical sequences of numbers. Thus, most pseudorandom number generators implemented in programming languages use the system clock to generate a seed. While pseudorandom number generators closely simulate random number generators, we assume the existence of the latter in the design and analysis of our probabilistic algorithms.

The performance of a probabilistic algorithm depends not only on the input to the algorithm but also on the results of randomized choices. Because running the algorithm twice with the same input I can result in a different number of basic operations being performed, $\tau(I)$ is no longer well defined. Instead, what is relevant is the *expected* number, $\tau_{\exp}(I)$, of basic operations performed by the algorithm for input I with respect to the random choices made by the algorithm. As with any expectation, if we run the algorithm many times with *fixed input I*, then we can expect the algorithm to perform $\tau_{\exp}(I)$ basic operations on average. If the algorithm performs many random choices, then even for a single run we can expect the number of basic operations performed to be very close to $\tau_{\exp}(I)$. Analogous to the functions $B(n)$, $W(n)$, and $A(n)$ for the best-case, worst-case, and average complexities of a deterministic algorithm, we now have $B_{\exp}(n)$, $W_{\exp}(n)$, $A_{\exp}(n)$ for the expected best-case, worst-case, and average complexities of a probabilistic algorithm. These are defined by

$$B_{\exp}(n) = \min\{\tau_{\exp}(I) \,|\, I \in \mathscr{I}_n\}$$
$$W_{\exp}(n) = \max\{\tau_{\exp}(I) \,|\, I \in \mathscr{I}_n\}$$
$$A_{\exp}(n) = E(\tau_{\exp})$$

where $\mathscr{I}_n$ denotes the set of all inputs of size n to the algorithm.

In the next four sections, we design and analyze examples of each of the four main design strategies for probabilistic algorithms. In our analysis of Monte Carlo algorithms in Section 24.3, we actually consider $\tau_{\max}(I)$, which is defined as the maximum number of basic operations performed with input I, no matter what random choices are made in the algorithm. We then obtain the order of $W_{\max}(n) = \max\{\tau_{\max}(I) \mid I \in \mathscr{I}_n\}$, which also serves as an upper bound for $W_{\exp}(n)$.

24.2 Randomizing Deterministic Algorithms

Randomized algorithms arise from deterministic algorithms by introducing randomness in some of the steps of the algorithm. Situations arise where introducing randomness into an otherwise deterministic algorithm can alleviate, in a certain sense, unacceptably bad worst-case behavior. Randomized versions of deterministic algorithms tend to cause the expected behavior of *each* input to approach the average behavior of the deterministic algorithm so that $A_{\exp}(n)$ is approximately equal to $A(n)$. Thus, a randomized version of a deterministic algorithm has the most potential of being useful when the average complexity $A(n)$ of the deterministic algorithm is significantly smaller than the worst-case complexity $W(n)$. Then a suitable randomization usually results in a $W_{\exp}(n)$ that is also significantly smaller than $W(n)$.

The procedure *QuickSort* is a good example of when randomization is useful. Indeed, *QuickSort* has $\Theta(n\log n)$ average complexity but $\Theta(n^2)$ worst-case complexity. A randomization of *QuickSort* does not eliminate the possibility that an input performs $\Omega(n^2)$ basic operations, but it breaks the connection between an input and $\Omega(n^2)$ behavior. More precisely, the randomizations of *QuickSort* presented in this section have $\tau_{\exp}(I) = A(n)$ for any *any* input of size n, where $A(n)$ is the average behavior of an ordinary *QuickSort*. In particular, the randomized versions of *QuickSort* satisfy the ultimate homogenization condition:

$$B_{\exp}(n) = A_{\exp}(n) = W_{\exp}(n). \qquad \textbf{(24.2.1)}$$

Randomized algorithms satisfying the ultimate homogenization condition (24.2.1) have been dubbed *Sherwood algorithms* in honor of Robin Hood.

24.2.1 Randomizing *LinearSearch*

LinearSearch simply scans a list $L[0:n - 1]$ for the occurrence of a search element X from left to right (that is, in the order $L[0], L[1], \ldots , L[n - 1]$). Of course, it would make no difference to the efficiency of *LinearSearch* if we were to scan the list from right to left (that is, in the order $L[n - 1], L[n - 2], \ldots , L[0]$). For a successful search (X is in the list), we have $B(n) = 1$ and $W(n) = n$. If we make the additional assumption that each list element is distinct and equally likely to be X, then $A(n) = (n + 1)/2$.

A simple randomization yields $B_{\exp}(n) = A_{\exp}(n) = W_{\exp}(n) = (n + 1)/2$. We merely flip a fair coin once at the beginning to decide whether we scan from left to right or from right to left. To verify that $\tau_{\exp}(I) = (n + 1)/2$ for any input $I \in \mathscr{I}_n$, let $L[0:n - 1]$ be any input list and let k be the index in L of the occurrence of X. With probability $1/2$, the scan will be from left to right, resulting in k comparisons;, and with probability $1/2$ the scan will be from right to left, resulting in $n - k + 1$ comparisons. Thus, the expected number of comparisons performed by the algorithm to find X is given by

$$\frac{1}{2}(k) + \frac{1}{2}(n - k + 1) = \frac{n + 1}{2}.$$

Since L and X were any input I (where X is on the list), we have

$$\tau_{\exp}(I) = \frac{n + 1}{2}, \quad I \in \mathscr{I}_n. \qquad \textbf{(24.2.2)}$$

LinearSearch is the simplest example we can think of that illustrates the complete homogenization effect (24.2.1) of the behavior of its randomized versions. Running the algorithm over and over again with any given input *I* yields an expected number of comparisons equaling $(n + 1)/2$, independent of the input. However, only a single random decision was made at the beginning, so we cannot expect that the randomized version performs anything close to $\tau_{exp}(I)$ basic operations on a single run with input *I*. In fact, searching for the first element in the list has a 50-50 chance of making *n* comparisons. Thus, while the long-run behavior approaches $(n + 1)/2$, the variance of $\tau(I)$ is large for inputs *I* where the search element is near the beginning or the end of the list. We need to introduce more randomness into the algorithm so that the expected behavior *on a single running* is close to $(n + 1)/2$ for any input.

One way to introduce more randomness is to perform the search in two directions, using pointers *MoveRight* and *MoveLeft*, which initially point to the beginning and end of the list, respectively. Thus, initially *MoveRight* = 1 and *MoveLeft* = *n*. We then make a random choice (with equal probabilities) of *MoveRight* or *MoveLeft* and compare the search element *X* to *L*[*MoveRight*] or *L*[*MoveLeft*], depending on which one was chosen. If *X* is found, then we return the relevant value of *MoveRight* or *MoveLeft*. Otherwise, we increment *MoveRight* by one or decrement *MoveLeft* by one, depending on which one was chosen, and repeat the process. The process terminates when *X* is found (successful search) or when *MoveRight* becomes larger than *MoveLeft* (unsuccessful search). Since we have introduced randomness throughout the algorithm, we can expect a smaller variance $\tau(I)$ than our previous randomization of *LinearSearch*. We leave the coding and analysis of this probabilistic version of *LinearSearch* to the exercises.

24.2.2 Randomizing *ProbeLinSrch*

In Chapter 6, we designed a procedure *ProbeLinSrch* for searching a list $L[0{:}n - 1]$ that was maintained in sorted order using an auxiliary array $Link[0{:}n - 1]$. We assume that the variable *Head* contains the index of the smallest element in *L*. Thus, the sorted order of the list *L* is given by *L*[*Head*], *L*[*Link*[*Head*]], *L*[*Link*[*Link*[*Head*]]], ... , $L[Link^{n-1}[Head]]$, where $Link^m$ denotes the *m*-fold composition of *Link*. $Link[i] = -1$ indicates the end of the list.

Given a search element *X*, procedure *ProbeLinSrch* begins by determining the best place to start a link-ordered linear search from the first $\sqrt{n}$ elements in $L[0{:}n - 1]$. We saw in Chapter 6 that *ProbeLinSrch* has $\Theta(n)$ worst-case complexity but $\Theta(\sqrt{n})$ average complexity, so it is a good candidate for randomization. Moreover, the randomization of *ProbeLinSrch* is straightforward. Instead of determining the best start for a link-ordered linear search from *L*[0], *L*[1], ... , $L[\sqrt{n} - 1]$, the randomized version uses a random number generator to sample $\sqrt{n}$ points at random and determines the best start from those random choices.

The analysis that we gave of the average behavior of *ProbeLinSrch* also establishes that the randomized version has $\tau_{\text{exp}}(I) \in \Theta(\sqrt{n})$ for each $I = (L[0{:}n - 1], X)$, $X = L[0], L[1], \dots, L[n - 1]$.

24.2.3 Randomizing *QuickSort*

One way to randomize *QuickSort* is to make a random choice of a pivot element for the call to *Partition*. Another way to randomize *QuickSort* is to first randomly permute the elements in a given input list L and then input the permuted list L' to *QuickSort*. The latter method of randomization is an example of the general randomization technique known as *stochastic preconditioning*. Both methods of randomizing *QuickSort* accomplish the same thing; that is, the randomized versions of *QuickSort* perform the same expected number of comparisons for any input list of size n. Moreover, the expected number of comparisons performed by the randomized versions of *QuickSort* is the same as the average number of comparisons performed by the deterministic version of *QuickSort*. We now introduce some concepts and notation allowing a more precise description of the randomized versions of *QuickSort*.

QuickSort exhibits $\Theta(n^2)$ worst-case complexity, whereas its average complexity is in $\Theta(n\log n)$. Making a random choice for the pivot element in the call to *Partition* leads to *RandomizedQuickSort*, which exhibits completely homogenized behavior. When making a random choice for the pivot element in *RandomizedQuickSort*, we assume that each element in the relevant interval has an equal chance of being chosen. Our analysis for the average complexity $A(n)$ of *QuickSort* given in Chapter 6 was based on the assumption that each element of the input list $L[0{:}n - 1]$ is equally likely to be chosen as the pivot element. Thus, $\tau_{\text{exp}}(L) = A(n)$ for any input list L of size n, so that $W_{\text{exp}}(n) = A(n)$.

In a theoretical sense, we have not eliminated the worst-case $\Theta(n^2)$ behavior. Indeed, for any input list I of size n, there is a small chance that the random choice of the pivot element is always close to an endpoint of the relevant interval, thereby forcing the algorithm to perform $\Theta(n^2)$ comparisons. However, since *RandomizedQuickSort* makes many random choices of pivot elements (one choice for each internal node in its tree of recursive calls), performing $\Theta(n^2)$ comparisons has such a small chance of occurring that for all practical purposes it can be ignored, even for relatively small lists. Thus, in practice, we can expect the number of comparisons performed in any run of *RandomizedQuickSort* with any given input list L to be very close to $\tau_{\text{exp}}(L)$.

Procedure *RandomizedQuickSort* makes $O(n)$ calls to *Random*, where we assume each call takes unit time. Thus, the overhead due to calling *Random* is dominated by the $\Omega(n\log n)$ comparisons performed by *RandomizedQuickSort*.

We now design an algorithm *RandomQuickSort2* based on stochastic preconditioning. Given an input list $I = L[0{:}n - 1]$, *RandomizedQuickSort2* first calls the following procedure *Permute* with input list L and then calls *QuickSort*.

```
procedure Permute(L[0:n − 1])
Input:    L[0:n − 1] (an array of list elements)
Output:   L[0:n − 1] (an array of list elements randomly permuted)
    for i = 0 to n − 2 do
        j ← Random(i, n − 1)
        interchange(L[i], L[j])
    endfor
end Permute
```

Procedure *RandomQuickSort2* has the identical expected performance as *RandomizedQuickSort*.

24.3 Monte Carlo and Las Vegas Algorithms

A Monte Carlo algorithm is a probabilistic algorithm that has a certain probability of returning the correct answer whatever input is considered. On the other hand, a Las Vegas algorithm never returns an incorrect answer, but it might not return an answer at all (usually with very small probability). The most useful class of Monte Carlo algorithms are those that have a probability of returning the correct answer greater than some fixed positive constant for any input. Specifically, for a fixed real number p, $0 < p < 1$, a *p-correct Monte Carlo algorithm* is a probabilistic algorithm that returns the correct answer with probability not less than p, no matter what input is considered. Unfortunately, many times there is no efficient method available to test whether an answer returned by a Monte Carlo algorithm for a given input is correct.

24.3.1 Biased Monte Carlo Algorithms

A Monte Carlo algorithm for a decision problem is *false biased* if it is always correct when it returns the value **.false.** and only has some (hopefully small) probability of making a mistake when returning the value **.true.**. A similar definition holds for *true-biased* Monte Carlo algorithms. For convenience, throughout the remainder of this subsection, we restrict our attention to Monte Carlo algorithms that are false biased. Fundamental to the applicability of a Monte Carlo algorithm is the fact that the probability of returning the correct output increases with repeated trials. For example, given a false-biased Monte Carlo algorithm *MC*, consider the following algorithm *MCRepeat*. (In a particular application, we replace the generic name *MC* with the specific name of the Monte Carlo algorithm.)

```
function MCRepeat(k)
Input:    k (a positive integer)
Output:   .false. if MC returns .false. for any invocation, .true. otherwise
    for i ← 1 to k do
        if MC returns .false. then
            return(.false.)
        endif
    endfor
    return(.true.)
end MCRepeat
```

Key Fact

MCRepeat can ramp up the correctness of a *p*-correct Monte Carlo algorithm *MC* to a number as close to unity as desired.

The following proposition establishes the preceding key fact.

Proposition 24.3.1 Suppose that we have a p-correct false-biased Monte Carlo algorithm MC. Then the algorithm $MCRepeat(k)$ is a $(1 - (1 - p)^k)$-correct false-biased Monte Carlo algorithm.

PROOF
Clearly, repeating a false-biased algorithm results in a false-biased algorithm. For a given input I, let $q_k(I)$ denote the probability that $MCRepeat(k)$ outputs **.false.**. Let $p_k(I)$ denote the probability that $MCRepeat(k)$ outputs the correct answer for a given input I. Then, using the formula for conditional probability given in Chapter 6, we obtain

$$
\begin{aligned}
p_k(I) &= q_k(I)\text{Prob}(MCRepeat(k) \text{ is correct}|MCRepeat(k) \text{ outputs } \mathbf{.false.}) + \\
& \quad (1 - q_k(I))\text{Prob}(MCRepeat(k) \text{ is correct}|MCRepeat(k) \text{ outputs } \mathbf{.true.}) \\
&\geq q_k(I)(1) + (1 - q_k(I))(1 - (1 - p)^k) \\
&\geq q_k(I)(1 - (1 - p)^k) + (1 - q_k(I))(1 - (1 - p)^k) \\
&= (q_k(I) + (1 - q_k(I)))(1 - (1 - p)^k) = 1 - (1 - p)^k. \qquad \blacksquare
\end{aligned}
$$

To illustrate the use of Proposition 24.3.1, suppose we have a Monte Carlo false-biased algorithm MC for primality testing that is .75-correct. If MC is .75-correct, then even for k as small as 8, $MCRepeat(k)$ is .9999847-correct. Thus, we can be fairly confident that an integer n is prime if $MCRepeat(8)$ returns **.true.**

when we input n; otherwise, an event has occurred whose probability is not greater than .0000153.

REMARK

If we have an unbiased p-correct algorithm for a decision problem with $p \leq 1/2$, then repeating the algorithm does not ramp up the correctness. For unbiased p-correct Monte Carlo algorithms with $p > 1/2$, the correctness can be improved by repeating the algorithm a sufficient number of times and choosing the answer occurring most often.

24.3.2 A Monte Carlo Algorithm of Testing Polynomial Equality

Given symbolic polynomials (that is, represented by their coefficient arrays) $f(x)$, $g(x)$, and $h(x)$ of degrees $2n$, n, and n, respectively, we consider the problem of testing whether $f(x)$ is identically equal to $g(x)h(x)$, written $f(x) \equiv g(x)h(x)$. (We write $f(x) \not\equiv g(x)h(x)$ to indicate the negation of $f(x) \equiv g(x)h(x)$ if there exists at least one point x such that $f(x) \neq g(x)h(x)$.) In Chapter 22, we developed a deterministic $O(n\log n)$ algorithm *FFT* for computing the symbolic product of two polynomials, $g(x)$ and $h(x)$, each of degree n. Thus, an $O(n\log n)$ algorithm for testing whether or not $f(x) \equiv g(x)h(x)$ is obtained by computing $g(x)h(x)$ using *FFT* and comparing the coefficients of $g(x)h(x)$ to those of $f(x)$.

As our first illustration of a Monte Carlo algorithm, we now describe a simple false-biased (1/2)-correct Monte Carlo algorithm for testing $f(x) \equiv g(x)h(x)$ that has $O(n)$ complexity. The idea behind the algorithm is that a polynomial of degree n is completely determined by knowing its values at $n + 1$ points. Thus, two distinct polynomials of degree $2n$ could not agree at more than $2n$ integers drawn from $\{1, 2, \dots, 4n\}$. The following algorithm is therefore a false-biased (1/2)-correct Monte Carlo algorithm for testing whether $f(x) \equiv g(x)h(x)$.

```
function TestPolyEqual(f(x), g(x), h(x))
Input:    f(x), g(x), h(x) (symbolic polynomials of degrees 2n, n, and n, respectively)
Output:   .true. or .false. (always correct when .false. is output, and correct at least 50
            percent of the time when output is .true.)
    j ← Random(1, 4*n)
    if f(j) = g(j)*h(j) then
        return(.true.)
    else
        return(.false.)
    endif
end TestPolyEqual
```

The algorithm *TestPolyEqual* has $O(n)$ complexity since the evaluations of $f(j)$, $g(j)$, and $h(j)$ can be done with $2n$, n, and n multiplications, respectively, using the algorithm *HornerEval*. If $f(x) \not\equiv g(x)h(x)$, then we can have $f(j) = g(j)h(j)$ for at most $2n$ points $j \in \{1, 2, \ldots, 4n\}$. Hence, *TestPolyEqual* is a $(1/2)$-correct Monte Carlo algorithm. If we repeat *TestPolyEqual* 20 times, then according to Proposition 24.3.1, the probability of *TestPolyEqualRepeat*(20) making an error is less than one in a million no matter what instance is considered.

R E M A R K

By choosing a point from $\{1, 2, \ldots, mn\}$, we can make *TestPolyEqual* $(2/m)$-correct. We took $m = 4$ for convenience and to keep the domain of *Random* relatively small. Besides, 20 repetitions of *TestPolyEqual* gave us an algorithm whose correctness was very close to unity.

24.3.3 Primality Testing

A naive deterministic algorithm for testing whether an integer n is a prime is simply a test of whether any of the integers between 2 and $\lfloor \sqrt{n} \rfloor$ divides n. Recall that when measuring the complexity of number-theoretic algorithms having integer input n, we take the input size to be the number of digits in n (with respect to a convenient base). The number of digits in the decimal representation of n is given by $m = \lceil \log_{10}(n + 1) \rceil$. In the worst case (that is, when n is a prime), the function *PrimalityTest* executes the **for** loop $\lfloor \sqrt{n} \rfloor$ times. Since $\lfloor \sqrt{n} \rfloor \approx 10^{m/2}$, we see that the worst-case complexity of this naive algorithm is actually exponential in the input size m. Thus, the naive algorithm is of no practical use for integers having, say, more than 40 digits, because it would take millions of years for today's fastest computers to execute the algorithm in the worst case.

It was an open question for many years whether or not there was a polynomial deterministic algorithm for prime testing. Recently, M. Agrawal, N. Kayal, and N. Saxena have designed a 12th-degree polynomial algorithm for primality testing, which is of great theoretical interest but, because of the relatively high degree of the polynomial involved, is not practical for large n. We now describe a linear false-biased Monte Carlo algorithm for primality testing.

Recall Fermat's little theorem discussed in Chapter 17: Let n be a prime number and let a be any number that is not divisible by n; then,

$$a^{n-1} \equiv 1 \pmod{n}. \tag{24.3.1}$$

Based on the primality test given by Formula (24.3.1), which we refer to as the Fermat test, we have the following false-biased Monte Carlo algorithm: choose a base a at random from $\{2, \ldots , n - 1\}$ and return **.true.** (that is, the number is prime) if and only if $a^{n-1} \equiv 1 \pmod{n}$. Most composite numbers n fail the Fermat test for many integers a between 2 and $n - 1$. Thus, for such numbers, the Monte Carlo algorithm has a high probability of being correct. Unfortunately, there exist composite integers n for which $a^{n-1} \equiv 1 \pmod{n}$ for most $a < n$. In fact, there are composite numbers, called *Carmichael numbers*, for which Formula (24.3.1) holds for all $1 < a < n$. Thus, if we choose a Carmichael number as an input to our algorithm, it has no chance of being correct.

To obtain a stronger test, we look for a stronger condition satisfied by (odd) prime numbers. We observe that

$$a^{n-1} - 1 \equiv (a^{(n-1)/2} - 1)(a^{(n-1)/2} + 1).$$

Thus, if n is an odd prime, Fermat's little theorem tells us that

$$(a^{(n-1)/2} - 1)(a^{(n-1)/2} + 1) \equiv 0 \pmod{n}.$$

Also, since n is prime, it follows that one of the two terms must be divisible by n, so that

$$a^{(n-1)/2} \equiv \pm 1 \pmod{n}.$$

If $a^{(n-1)/2} \equiv 1$ and $(n-1)/2$ is even, then by the same reasoning, it follows that $a^{(n-1)/4} \equiv \pm 1$. Similarly, if $a^{(n-1)/4} \equiv 1$ and $(n-1)/4$ is even, it follows that $a^{(n-1)/8} \equiv \pm 1$, and so forth. Thus, we have either

$$a^{n-1} \equiv a^{(n-1)/2} \equiv \cdots \equiv a^{(n-1)/2^{j-1}} \equiv 1, a^{(n-1)/2^j} \equiv -1 \pmod{n},$$

for some j or

$$a^{n-1} \equiv a^{(n-1)/2} \equiv \cdots \equiv a^{(n-1)/2^{k-1}} \equiv a^{(n-1)/2^k} \equiv 1 \pmod{n},$$

where 2^k is the largest power of 2 that divides $n - 1$. Equivalently, letting m denote the largest odd number that divides $n - 1$, it follows that either $a^m \equiv 1$, $\pmod{n}$ or $a^{(n-1)/2^j} \equiv -1 \pmod{n}$ for some j, $0 \leq j \leq k$. Testing whether a number n satisfies these conditions is called the Miller-Rabin test. We have just shown that a prime number n satisfies this test. It turns out that an odd composite number n will pass the Miller-Rabin test for at most 25 percent of all possible bases a, $2 \le a \le n - 1$. Thus, the Miller-Rabin test yields a false-biased .75-correct Monte Carlo algorithm for primality testing. Pseudocode for *MillerRabinPrimalityTest* follows.

```
function MillerRabinPrimalityTest(n)
Input:    n (an odd positive integer)
Output:   .true. or .false. (always correct when .false. is returned, and correct at least
          75% when .true. is returned)
    a ← Random(2, n − 2)
    find positive integers k, m such that n − 1 = 2ᵏm, and m odd
    b ← aᵐ mod n                           //b ≡ aᵐ (mod n)
    for j ← 1 to k do
        if b ≠ 1 .and. b ≠ n − 1 then      //b ≢ ±1 (mod n)
            return(.false.)
        else
            if b = n − 1 then              //b ≡ −1 (mod n)
                return(.true.)
            endif
        endif
        b ← b*b mod n                      //b ≡ a²ʲm (mod n)
    endfor
    if b ≠ 1 then                          //aⁿ ⁻ ¹ ≢ 1 (mod n)
        return(.false.)
    else
        return(.true.)
    endif
end MillerRabinPrimalityTest
```

If the binary method for computing powers is used to compute a^m (mod n), algorithm *MillerRabinPrimalityTest* is linear in the input size (number of digits of n). Thus, repeating algorithm *MillerRabinPrimalityTest* yields an efficient primality-testing algorithm whose probability of error can be made quite small even for just a few repetitions.

The *primality testing problem*, and the related *factoring problem* of finding the prime factors of a composite number, play important roles in cryptography. For example, these two problems play complementary roles in the RSA cryptosystem discussed in Chapter 17, which is currently one of the most widely used methods for public-key cryptography and for digital signatures. The practicality of constructing RSA ciphers depends on (very high confidence) primality testing being efficient, whereas the security of the cipher depends on the fact that no known (probabilistic or otherwise) algorithm exists for efficiently factoring large numbers.

24.3.4 Minimum Cut in Graphs

Given a connected graph G, the *edge connectivity* of G is the minimum number of edges whose deletion disconnects G. Such a minimum set of edges is called a *minimum cut*. In Chapter 14, we used flows to solve the problem of finding a minimum cut separating two vertices s and t in a graph. We can obtain a (globally) minimum cut by computing a minimum cut separating s and t for a fixed vertex s and all vertices t, $t \neq s$. In this subsection, we present a probabilistic algorithm that is faster than the latter algorithm or any known deterministic algorithm based on network flows.

We first present a simple Monte Carlo algorithm *MCMinCut* based on a sequence of randomly chosen edge contractions. We will allow the input graph to our algorithm to have *multiedges*—that is, more than one edge joining the same pair of vertices. Given a graph G, the *contraction* of an edge uv is the operation of identifying vertices u and v and deleting all loops that are thereby created (see Figure 24.1). We denote the resulting graph by G/uv. Note that contraction may result in the creation of multiple edges. Performing a sequence of contractions resulting in a graph H determines a partition of vertices of G into *supervertices*, where each vertex v of H determines a supervertex consisting of all vertices of G that are identified with v.

The algorithm *MCMinCut* performs a sequence of $n - 2$ contractions, resulting in the sequence of graphs $G = G_0, G_1, \ldots, G_{n-2}$, where the edge e_i that is contracted at stage i, $i = 1, \ldots, n - 2$, is chosen uniformly and at random from the edges of G_{i-1}. The final graph G_{n-2} consists of two vertices a and b. *MCMinCut* then returns the cut $cut(A,B)$, where A and B are the supervertices of G corresponding to a and b (see Figure 24.2).

FIGURE 24.1

An edge
contraction in a
graph G.

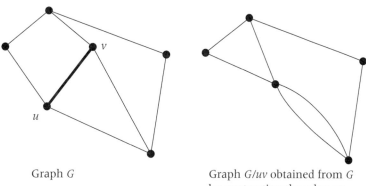

Graph G Graph G/uv obtained from G
by contracting the edge uv

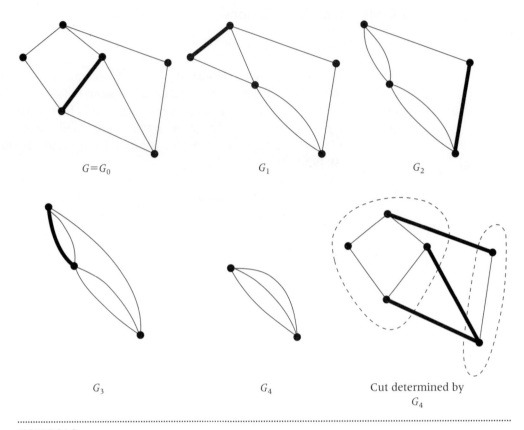

$G=G_0$ G_1 G_2

G_3 G_4 Cut determined by
                                G_4

FIGURE 24.2

Action of *MCMinCut* for a sample graph and random choice of edges. In each step, the edge involved in the contraction is shown in bold. The edges of G in the cut returned by *MCMinCut* are shown in bold in the last picture. Notice that the cut generated was not a minimum cut.

function *MCMinCut(G)*
Input: *G* (a connected graph on n vertices)
Output: *C* (a cut, minimum with probability $\geq 2/n^2$)
      $H \leftarrow G$
      for $i \leftarrow 1$ **to** $n - 2$ **do**//contract H until it is a two-vertex graph
         Choose an edge e of H at random
         $H \leftarrow H/e$ //contract edge e
      endfor
      $A, B \leftarrow$ supervertices of G corresponding to two vertices of H
      return *cut(A,B)*   //edges of two-vertex graph H correspond to cut in G
end *MCMinCut*

We now show that *MCMinCut* returns a minimum cut with probability at least $2/n^2$. In fact, we prove a stronger result—given any minimum cut C, *MCMinCut* returns C with probability at least $2/n^2$. Let E_i be the event of not picking an edge from C in the ith stage, $i = 1, \ldots, n - 2$. Then C is returned by the algorithm *MCMinCut* if and only if all the events $E_1, \ldots, E_{n-2}$ occur; that is, if the intersection event $\bigcap_{i=1}^{n-2} E_i$ occurs. The probability of the occurrence of this intersection event satisfies the following formula (see Exercise 24.4):

$$P\left(\bigcap_{i=1}^{n-2} E_i\right) = P(E_1)P(E_2|E_1) \ldots P\left(E_{n-2}\Big|\bigcap_{i=1}^{n-3} E_i\right). \qquad \textbf{(24.3.2)}$$

Let k denote the size of the minimum cut C. Since a single vertex v and its complement $V \setminus \{v\}$ determines a cut of degree $d(v)$, it follows that $d(v) \geq k$, for all vertices $v \in V$. Thus, by Euler's degree formula (see Chapter 11), we have $2m = \sum_{e \in E} d(v) \geq kn$, so that $m \geq kn/2$. Since e_1 is chosen from m possible edges, it follows that $P(E_1) \geq (m - k)/m = 1 - k/m \geq 1 - 2/n$. Now, let m_i denote the number of edges of G_i, $i = 1, \ldots, n - 1$. The size of a minimum cut in the graph G_{i-1} generated by performing the first $i - 1$ contractions is at least k, because of the following key fact.

Key Fact

Contracting edges does not decrease the size of a minimum cut of a graph.

Because G_{i-1} has $n - i + 1$ vertices, by applying Euler's degree formula, we know that G_{i-1} has at least $(n - i + 1)k/2$ edges; that is, $m_{i-1} \geq (n - i + 1)k/2$. Thus, the edge e_i is chosen uniformly and at random from at least $(n - i + 1)k/2$ edges. It follows that

$$P\left(E_i\Big|\bigcap_{j=1}^{i-1} E_j\right) = (m_{i-1} - k)/m_{i-1} = 1 - k/m_{i-1} \geq 1 - k/((n - i + 1)k/2)$$
$$= 1 - 2/(n - i + 1).$$

Substituting in Formula (24.3.2), we obtain

$$P\left(\bigcap_{i=1}^{n-2} E_i\right) \geq \prod_{i=1}^{n-2}\left(1 - \frac{2}{n - i + 1}\right) = \frac{2}{n(n-1)} > 2/n^2. \qquad \textbf{(24.3.3)}$$

Therefore, the probability that the algorithm *MCMinCut* returns the cut C is at least $2/n^2$.

By repeatedly calling algorithm *MCMinCut* at least $n^2/2$ times and maintaining the smallest cut found, we can ramp up the probability of correctness to at least

$$1 - \left(1 - \frac{2}{n^2}\right)^{n^2/2} > 1 - 1/e. \tag{24.3.4}$$

It is easy to see that *MCMinCut* is an $O(n^2)$ algorithm for an input graph that has no multiedges. Actually, the $O(n^2)$ complexity remains true even for input graphs with multiedges (see Exercise 24.5). Thus, running *MCMinCut* $n^2/2$ times to achieve $(1 - 1/e)$-correctness has $O(n^4)$ complexity.

We now describe an $O(n^2 \log n)$ Monte Carlo algorithm called *MCFastMinCut* that is $p(n)$-correct for $p(n) \in \Omega(1/\log n)$. *MCFastMinCut* independently performs two sequences of $n - r + 1$ edge contractions, where $r = \lceil 1 + n/\sqrt{2} \rceil$, to obtain r-vertex graphs H_1 and H_2. *MCFastMinCut* then performs two recursive calls with input graphs H_1 and H_2, respectively, to obtain cuts C_1 and C_2, respectively, returning the smaller of these two cuts.

```
function MCFastMinCut(G)
Input:    G (connected graph on n vertices)
Output:   C (a cut, minimum with probability p(n) ∈ Ω(1/log n))
    if n ≤ 6 then
        compute a minimum cut C by checking all possible cuts
    else
        r ← ⌈1 + n/√2⌉
        H₁ ← G
        for i ← 1 to n − r + 1 do      //contract H₁ until it is an r−vertex graph
            Choose an edge e of H₁ at random
            H₁ ← H₁/e                    //contract edge e
        endfor
    endif
        for i ← 1 to n − r + 1 do      //contract H₂ until it is an r−vertex graph
            Choose an edge e of H₂ at random
            H₂ ← H₂/e                    //contract edge e
        endfor
        C₁ ← MCFastMinCut(H₁)
        C₂ ← MCFastMinCut(H₂)
    if |C₁| < |C₂|
        C ← C₁
    else
        C ← C₂
    endif
    return C
end MCFastMinCut
```

We first analyze the complexity of *MCFastMinCut*. Note that the complexity of *MCFastMinCut* depends on the number of vertices n of G and not on the particular input graph of size n or random choices made in contracting edges. Because computing H_1 and H_2 requires time $O(n^2)$ and we are performing two recursive calls with graphs having $r = \lceil 1 + n/\sqrt{2} \rceil$ vertices, we obtain the following recurrence relation for the complexity $T(n)$ for $n > 6$:

$$T(n) = 2T(\lceil 1 + n/\sqrt{2} \rceil) + O(n^2). \qquad (24.3.5)$$

Solving the recurrence relation given in Formula (24.3.5) yields $T(n) \in O(n^2 \log n)$; we leave this as an exercise.

We now prove the following theorem about the probability that *MCFastMinCut* correctly returns a minimum cut for a graph on n vertices.

Theorem 24.3.2

Algorithm *MCFastMinCut* is $p(n)$-correct for $p(n) \in \Omega(1/\log n)$.

PROOF

Consider any minimum cut C in G. Let q_k denote the probability C lies in the subgraph H, where H is a subgraph on k vertices resulting from performing a sequence of $n - k + 1$ random edge contractions in the graph G. Using a similar argument to that used for *MCMinCut* for the special case where $k = 2$, it follows that

$$q_k = \frac{k(k-1)}{n(n-1)}. \qquad (24.3.6)$$

In particular, substituting $k = r$ into Formula (24.3.6) yields

$$q_r = \frac{r(r-1)}{n(n-1)} = \frac{\lceil 1 + n/\sqrt{2} \rceil (\lceil 1 + n/\sqrt{2} \rceil - 1)}{n(n-1)} \geq \frac{1}{2}. \qquad (24.3.7)$$

Thus, the probability that cut C lies in H_1 is at least $1/2$. It is immediate from the definition of $p(n)$ that the conditional probability that C_1 is a minimum cut in G, given that some minimum cut C from G lies in H_1, is at least $p(r)$. Thus, the probability that C_1 is a minimum cut of G is at least $p(r)/2$. Similarly, the probability that C_2 is a minimum cut is at least $p(r)/2$. It follows that the probability that neither C_1 nor C_2 are minimum cuts is at most $(1 - p(r)/2)^2$, so that the probability that one of C_1 and C_2 is a minimum cut is at least $1 - (1 - p(r)/2)^2$. Hence, we have

$$p(n) \geq 1 - \left(1 - \frac{p(r)}{2}\right)^2 = p(r) - \frac{p^2(r)}{4}$$

$$= p(\lceil 1 + n/\sqrt{2}\rceil) - \frac{p^2(\lceil 1 + n/\sqrt{2}\rceil)}{4}.$$

It follows that we can obtain an Ω-order formula for $p(n)$ by solving the recurrence relation

$$p(n) = p(\lceil 1 + n/\sqrt{2}\rceil) - \frac{p^2(\lceil 1 + n/\sqrt{2}\rceil)}{4},$$

$$\textbf{init. cond. } p(n) = 1, n \leq 6. \tag{24.3.8}$$

The initial condition in Formula (24.3.8) follows from the fact that *MCFastMin-Cut* always returns the correct answer for graphs having six or fewer vertices.

To make the recurrence relation given in (24.3.8) easier to solve we will substitute $(\sqrt{2})^k$ for n and approximate $p(\lceil 1 + (\sqrt{2})^{k-1}\rceil)$ with $p((\sqrt{2})^{k-1})$. We also replace the initial condition with the simpler condition $p(1) = 1$. This substitution and approximation will not affect the Ω-order of the formula we eventually derive for $p(n)$. We obtain

$$p((\sqrt{2})^k) = p((\sqrt{2})^{k-1}) - \frac{p^2((\sqrt{2})^{k-1})}{4}, \textbf{init. cond. } p(1) = 1. \tag{24.3.9}$$

Setting $t(k) = p((\sqrt{2})^k)$ and substituting in (24.3.9) yields the simpler recurrence relation

$$t(k) = t(k - 1) - \frac{t^2(k - 1)}{4}, \textbf{init. cond. } t(0) = 1. \tag{24.3.10}$$

To solve the recurrence relation (24.3.10), we transform it by setting $s(k) = (4/t(k)) - 1$, so that $t(k) = 4/(s(k) + 1)$. Substituting $t(k) = 4/(s(k) + 1)$ in (24.3.10) yields,

$$s(k) = s(k - 1) + 1 + \frac{1}{s(k - 1)}, \textbf{init. cond. } s(0) = 3. \tag{24.3.11}$$

It follows from Formula (24.3.11) that

$$1 + s(k - 1) \leq s(k) \leq 2 + s(k - 1),$$

which implies that $s(k) \in \Theta(k)$. Hence, $t(k) \in \Theta(1/k)$, so that $p(n) \in \Theta(1/\log n)$. ■

24.3.5 Las Vegas Algorithms

Unlike a Monte Carlo algorithm, a Las Vegas algorithm never returns an incorrect answer. However, a Las Vegas algorithm is subject to two types of disasters: It could run arbitrarily long without producing an answer, or it could make a random decision from which there is no recovery (a dead end). Usually, the Las Vegas algorithm signals the latter type of disaster and terminates, so that it can be restarted again from scratch. The probability that a dead end is reached on any given run is usually quite small; thus, running the algorithm several times significantly increases the probability that the algorithm successfully solves the given problem. Relative to the first type of disaster, running beyond a reasonable time usually has such a small probability of occurring that it can safely be ignored in practice. Thus, Las Vegas algorithms usually have a high probability of successfully finding the solution to a given problem.

> **REMARK**
>
> A Monte Carlo algorithm for which there is an efficient way to test whether the returned result is correct can be turned into a Las Vegas algorithm by simply repeating the algorithm in case an incorrect answer is returned.

To illustrate a Las Vegas algorithm, we consider the problem of searching a list with repeated elements. We assume that we are searching a list $L[0:n-1]$ where the search element X occurs *at least k times* in the list. For example, suppose we are sampling a large list of students for a student having a GPA of 3.3 or higher. If we know that at least one-tenth of the students have GPAs of 3.3 and higher, then $k \geq n/10$. Note that the worst-case complexity of solving this problem using *LinearSearch* is $n - k + 1$ and is achieved for an input list where X occupies precisely the last k positions in the list L. *LinearSearch* with stochastic preconditioning would not be useful here because it takes $n - 1$ calls to *Random* to randomly permute the list elements.

If k is sufficiently large with respect to n, say $k \geq n/d$ for some fixed constant $d > 0$, then we can expect to do much better than *LinearSearch* by the simple randomized searching algorithm *RandomSearch*. Rather than making a linear scan through the list, each iteration of the **while** loop in *RandomSearch* calls a random number generator *Random* to determine which list element to compare to X. In particular, *RandomSearch* might reexamine a list element more than once. Indeed, *RandomSearch* is subject to the first type of disaster; namely, it has the potential to run arbitrarily long for a fixed input size n. However, the expected number of iterations performed by *RandomSearch* in the worst case for an input of size *n* is relatively small.

```
function RandomSearch(L[0:n − 1], X)
Input:     L[0:n − 1] (an array of list elements), X (a search item, occurring at least k
           times in L)
Output:    returns index of an occurrence of X in L
    Found ← .false.
    while .not. Found do
        Choice ← Random(0, n − 1)
        if X = L[Choice] then Found ← .true. endif
    endwhile
    return(Choice)
end RandomSearch
```

The expected best-case complexity is $B_{\exp}(n) = 1$, since $\tau_{\exp}(I) = 1$ for an input $I = (L[0:n − 1], X)$ where each list element equals X. Now consider the expected worst-case complexity $W_{\exp}(n)$. Clearly, $W_{\exp}(n)$ is achieved by any input list in which X occurs exactly k times. For such an input list I_w, the search element X is found in any particular pass of the **while** loop with probability $p = k/n$. Therefore, the probability that exactly i passes are performed is given by $p_i = (1 − p)^{i−1}p, i = 1, 2, ...$ Thus,

$$W_{\exp}(n) = \tau_{\exp}(I_w) = \sum_{i=1}^{\infty} ip_i = \sum_{i=1}^{\infty} i(1 − p)^{i−1}p. \qquad \textbf{(24.3.12)}$$

Using Formula (A.3.5) from Appendix A, Formula (24.3.12) becomes

$$W_{\exp}(n) = \tau_{\exp}(I_w) = p\left(\frac{1}{1 − (1 − p)}\right)^2 = \frac{1}{p} = \frac{n}{k}. \qquad \textbf{(24.3.13)}$$

When k is a fixed percentage of the list elements, say $k \geq n/d$, for a fixed $d > 0$, then Formula (24.3.13) implies that $W_{\exp}(n) \leq d$, so that $W_{\exp}(n) \in O(1)$.

Given any integer i, the algorithm *RandomSearch* performs more than i iterations with probability $(1 − p)^i, p = k/n$. Although this probability approaches zero as i approaches infinity, *RandomSearch* has the diminishing potential to run arbitrarily long for a fixed input size n. However, in practice, the possibility of *RandomSearch* performing unacceptably more iterations than $W_{\exp}(n)$ is so remote that it can be safely ignored.

24.4 Probabilistic Numerical Algorithms

Historically, the first examples of probabilistic algorithms computed answers of a desired accuracy to numerical problems such as finding approximate values of definite integrals. Examples such as computing π by throwing darts, as discussed in the introduction to this chapter, were dubbed Monte Carlo algorithms or Monte Carlo simulations. By contrast, in this section, the term *Monte Carlo algorithm* is used to mean any probabilistic algorithm that approximates a numerical quantity by a random simulation process.

24.4.1 Numerical Integration

There are various deterministic algorithms for computing numerical approximations to the definite integral $\int_a^b f(x)\,dx$. For example, the interval $[a,b]$ is divided into n subintervals of equal length $\Delta x = (b - a)/n$ using points $x_0 = a, x_1 = a + \Delta x, x_2 = a + 2\Delta x, \dots, x_n = a = n\Delta x = b$. Then three standard approximations to $\int_a^b f(x)\,dx$ are given by

Left-Hand End Point Riemann Sum : $\Sigma_{i=1}^n f(x_{i-1})\,\Delta x = [\Sigma_{i=1}^n f(x_{i-1})](b - a)/n,$
Right-Hand End Point Riemann Sum : $\Sigma_{i=1}^n f(x_i)\,\Delta x = [\Sigma_{i=1}^n f(x_i)](b - a)/n,$

and the average of the preceding two Riemann sums,

Trapezoid Rule: $[f(x_0) + 2f(x_1) + 2f(x_2) + \cdots + 2f(x_{n-1}) + f(x_n)](b - a)/2n.$

In general, for a given number of iterations, the trapezoid rule achieves much better approximations to $\int_a^b f(x)\,dx$ than the probabilistic methods we are about to describe, but probabilistic methods become practical for integrating functions of four or more variables.

One probabilistic method, called *Monte Carlo integration*, is used for finding an approximation to $\int_a^b f(x)\,dx$ and relies on the interpretation of the integral as the signed area between the graph of f and the x axis. For purposes of discussion, we can assume without loss of generality that f is nonnegative on the interval $[a, b]$.

FIGURE 24.3

Throwing darts to approximate

$$\int_a^b f(x)\,dx$$

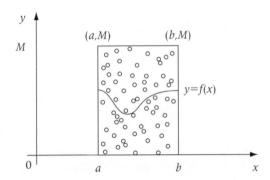

We also assume that M is an upper bound for the value of $f(x)$ as x varies over $[a,b]$. Referring to Figure 24.3, we have illustrated a random collection of points chosen from the rectangle R with corners $(a,0)$, (a,M), $(b,0)$, (b,M). We can think of the region between the graph of f and the x-axis as the target in the dartboard R, and the points illustrated in the figure as the result of throwing darts at R. If enough darts are thrown, we expect the ratio of the number of darts that hit the target to the total number of darts thrown to closely approximate the ratio of the area $\int_a^b f(x)\,dx$ of the target to the area $M(b-a)$ of the dartboard R.

The following Monte Carlo integration algorithm implements the dart-throwing technique.

function *ThrowDarts(f, a, b, M, n)*
Input: f (a function $f: [a, b] \rightarrow [0, +\infty)$)
           a, b (endpoints of an interval of real numbers)
           M (a real number such that $f(x) \le M$ for all $x \in [a, b]$)
           n (a positive integer equal to number of points sampled)

Output: approximation to $\int_a^b f(x)\,dx$

```
HitTarget ← 0
for Dart ← 1 to n do
    x ← Random(a, b)
    y ← Random(0, M)
    if y ≤ f(x) then
        HitTarget ← HitTarget + 1
    endif
endfor
return(M(b − a)*HitTarget/n)
end ThrowDarts
```

In practice, when f is computationally expensive to calculate, the direct test $y \leq f(x)$ can sometimes be replaced by an equivalent but easier-to-compute test. For example, consider the integral $\int_0^1 \sqrt{1 - x^2}\,dx$. Then the test $y \leq \sqrt{1 - x^2}$ is equivalent to the computationally easier test $x^2 + y^2 \leq 1$.

A second method of Monte Carlo integration to approximate $\int_a^b f(x)\,dx$ is simply to choose n points $x_1, x_2, \ldots, x_n$ at random in the interval (a, b) and multiply the arithmetic mean $(f(x_1) + f(x_2) + \cdots + f(x_n))/n$ of f evaluated at these points by the length of the interval $b - a$. Although the second method is more efficient than *ThrowDarts*, it is still less efficient than the trapezoid rule. The name *ApproxMeanValueIntegral* for the following Monte Carlo integration algorithm reflects the fact that the arithmetic mean of the values of f at n randomly selected points will approximate the value $f(x^*)$ in the mean value theorem for integrals, which states that $\int_a^b f(x)\,dx = (b - a)f(x^*)$ for some point x^* in (a, b).

```
function ApproxMeanValueIntegral(f, a, b, n)
Input:    f (a function f: [a, b]→(−∞, +∞))
          a, b (end points of an interval of real numbers)
          n (a positive integer equal to number of points sampled)
Output:   approximation to ∫ₐᵇ f(x) dx

    Sum ← 0
    for Count ← 1 to n do
        x ← Random(a, b)
        Sum ← Sum + f(x)
    endfor
    return((b − a)*Sum/n)
end ApproxMeanValueIntegral
```

For the same value of n, *ApproxMeanValueIntegral* generally gives a better approximation to $\int_a^b f(x)\,dx$ than does *ThrowDarts*. However, when $f(x)$ is expensive to calculate, *ThrowDarts* may be more efficient than *ApproxMeanValueIntegral*.

Monte Carlo integration starts to become computationally attractive for approximating multiple integrals in dimension greater than four. The reason is that deterministic approximations to k-fold multiple integrals are based on partitioning a rectangular parallelepiped $[a_1, b_1] \times [a_2, b_2] \times \cdots \times [a_k, b_k]$ by subdividing each interval $[a_i, b_i]$ into n subintervals of length $b_i - a_i$, $i = 1, \ldots, n$. For example, we then obtain an approximation to the multiple integral of $f(x_1, x_2, \ldots, x_n)$ over the original parallelepiped by summing the products of f evaluated at a suitable point in each of the n^k rectangular subparallelepipeds times the volume of the subparallelepipeds. Because the number of points used increases exponentially with the dimension, these deterministic approximation methods rapidly become computationally infeasible. On the other hand, the precision obtained by Monte Carlo integration using n points is generally not particularly sensitive to an increase in dimension.

To improve the precision of approximating multiple integrals, hybrid methods have been developed that are a mix of deterministic and probabilistic methods. Refer to the references for further discussion of Monte Carlo integrations in higher dimensions.

24.4.2 Estimating the Size of Sets

Monte Carlo integration algorithms find approximations to real numbers to within a desired accuracy. We finish our discussion of numeric probabilistic algorithms by noting that there are probabilistic algorithms that can be used to estimate the value of a (large) integer that otherwise would be difficult to compute. For example, suppose you wish to estimate the size of a finite set X that is too large to count by a simple enumeration of its elements. Suppose also (and this is a strong assumption) that there exists a method of randomly and uniformly drawing an element from the set X. Then a probabilistic estimate of the size of X is obtained by repeatedly drawing an element from X until the first repetition occurs. Laws of probability imply that this repetition has a good chance of occurring much earlier than might be guessed intuitively.

The classical example of choosing until a repetition occurs is the so-called *birthday paradox*. The birthday paradox is not really a paradox but rather the somewhat surprising answer to the question, "How many people do we need to randomly sample from a given population before the chance is better than 50-50 that two people share the same birthday?" At first glance, it might seem that we need to sample at least $188 = \lceil 365/2 \rceil$ randomly chosen people before we could bet even odds that two people share the same birthday. The surprise is that choosing 23 people suffices. The calculation proceeds as follows. First we randomly pick a person x_1 from the population. The chance that a second randomly chosen person x_2 from the remaining population has a different birthday from the first is $364/365$. Continuing in this fashion, the probability that the kth

randomly chosen person x_k has a birthday different from the previously chosen people $x_1, x_2, \ldots, x_{k-1}$ is given by

$P(k$ randomly drawn people all have different birthdays$) =$

$$\left(\frac{365}{365}\right)\left(\frac{364}{365}\right) \cdots \left(\frac{365 - k + 1}{365}\right). \qquad \textbf{(24.4.1)}$$

Formula (24.4.1) begins to be less than $1/2$ for $k \geq 23$.

REMARK

We assume in Formula (24.4.1) that each of the 365 days is equally likely to be a birthday for a random person. Actually, the distribution of birthdays over the entire populace is not quite uniform, and there is also the February 29th leap-year anomaly. The first consideration increases the probability for common birthdays, whereas the second consideration decreases the probability. However, these small effects are probably not enough to change the threshold value of $k = 23$.

Generalizing (and slightly altering) the birthday problem, suppose that we have a set X of n objects and we draw $k \leq n$ elements randomly from X. In contrast to the birthday problem, here we assume that our draws are with replacement. Then the number of ways we can obtain k distinct elements is $n(n - 1) \cdots (n - k + 1) = n!/(n - k)!$. Since there are n^k different ways to randomly draw (in order and with replacement) k elements from X, it follows that the probability that we obtain k distinct elements is given by

$$P(k \text{ elements drawn from } n \text{ are distinct}) = \frac{n!}{(n - k)!n^k}. \qquad \textbf{(24.4.2)}$$

By Stirling's formula, $n! \approx \sqrt{2\pi n}(n/e)^n$, we obtain

$$\frac{n!}{(n - k)!n^k} \approx e^{-k^2/2n}. \qquad \textbf{(24.4.3)}$$

Combining Formulas (24.4.2) and (24.4.3) yields the following theorem.

Theorem 24.4.1 Let k be the smallest integer such that the probability is greater than $1/2$ that we obtain at least one repetition in k random and uniform draws with replacement from a set of size n. Then, for large n,

$$k \approx \sqrt{2n \ln 2} \sqrt{n} \approx 1.177\sqrt{n}. \qquad \textbf{(24.4.4)}$$

■

The next theorem, whose proof is left as an exercise, gives the expected value of the number of draws required before the *first* repetition occurs.

Theorem 24.4.2 Suppose we randomly and uniformly draw elements with replacement from a set X of size n until a repetition occurs. Let ρ denote the random variable consisting of the number k of draws associated with each such event. Then, for large n, the expected value of ρ is given by

$$E(\rho) \approx \sqrt{\frac{\pi}{2}}\sqrt{n} \approx 1.253\sqrt{n}. \qquad \textbf{(24.4.5)}$$

□

Theorem 24.4.2 is the basis for the following probabilistic algorithm for estimating the size n of a finite set X.

```
function EstimateSize(X)
Input:    X (a finite set)
Output:   an estimate of the size of X
    k ← 1
    SetOfDraws ← Ø
    a ← Random(X)    //choose an element uniformly and at random from X
    while a ∉ SetOfDraws do
        k ← k + 1
        SetOfDraws ← SetOfDraws ∪ {a}
        a ← Random(X)
    endwhile
    return(2k²/π)
end EstimateSize
```

By Theorem 24.4.2, the expected number of repetitions of the **while** loop in *EstimateSize* belongs to $\Theta(\sqrt{n})$. Note that the space requirements for maintaining the set *SetOfDraws* also belongs to $\Theta(\sqrt{n})$. Thus, the expected complexity of *EstimateSize* belongs to $\Theta(\sqrt{n})$, assuming that the operations of checking set membership and adding elements to *SetOfDraws* can both be done at unit cost.

24.5 Probabilistic Parallel Algorithms

In this section, we discuss the obvious parallelization that exists for many of the probabilistic algorithms discussed earlier. We also describe probabilistic parallel algorithms for solving the well-known marriage problem and for determining a protocol for breaking communication deadlock in a completely symmetric network of processors.

24.5.1 Exploiting Obvious Parallelism

The procedure *MCRepeat(k)* for ramping up the correctness of a Monte Carlo algorithm simply repeats the algorithm k times. Since these repetitions are independent trials, there is the obvious parallelism for *MCRepeat(k)*: We simply assign k processors the job of running the algorithm in parallel and then communicate the results. Hence, the k repetitions of the sequential algorithm can be reduced to a single parallel running and a parallel communication step. For example, on the EREW PRAM, the communication step can be done in $O(\log k)$ time. A similar parallelization can be done for Las Vegas algorithms that are repeated to increase the certainty of correctness.

In the previous section, we saw that probabilistic numerical integration involves randomly choosing n points (throwing darts) in a $(k + 1)$-dimensional parallelepiped P in Euclidean space containing the region R corresponding to the value of a definite integral of a function of k variables. The resulting algorithm then estimates the value of the integral by computing the ratio of the number of darts that hit within R to the total number of darts n thrown and then multiplying this ratio by the volume of P. The parallelization of the process for estimating a definite integral reduces the problem to adding n numbers, each of which is 0 or 1.

On the EREW PRAM having n processors $P_i, i = 0, \ldots, n - 1$, the definite integral estimation can be done in $O(\log n)$ parallel steps (k is fixed). Indeed, each of the n processors would randomly choose a point in P (each processor making k calls to a random number generator). Then processor P_i writes a 0 or 1 to the memory location *HitOrMiss*[i] in the array *HitOrMiss*[$0:n - 1$], $i = 0, \ldots, n - 1$. An invocation of the function *SumPRAM* with input *HitOrMiss*[$0:n - 1$] then determines the number of points chosen within the region R, so that the definite integral can then be estimated as indicated earlier.

For interconnection network models, the processors each write the outcome of their choice of a point to a distributed variable *HitOrMiss*, and then the values in *HitOrMiss* are summed. Thus, the complexity of the parallelization reduces to the communication complexity of the network.

FIGURE 24.4

Bipartite graph
G and associated
matrix *R*.

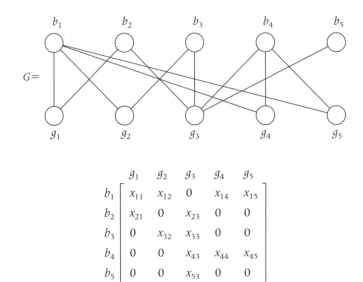

24.5.2 The Marriage Problem

The marriage problem, which we discussed in Chapter 14, is equivalent to the problem of determining the existence of a perfect matching in a bipartite graph $G = (V, E)$. To solve the problem we let the nodes be $b_1, \ldots, b_n$ on one side of the bipartition (boys) and $g_1, \ldots, g_n$ on the other side (girls). Then we associate the indeterminate weight x_{ij} with each edge $\{b_i, g_j\} \in E$, and we let $R = (r_{ij})$ be the $n \times n$ matrix such that $r_{ij} = x_{ij}$ if $\{b_i, g_j\}$ is an edge of G; otherwise, $r_{ij} = 0$. The matrix R for a sample bipartite graph G is shown in Figure 24.4. With S_n denoting the set of all permutations of $\{1, \ldots, n\}$, and given a permutation $\sigma \in S_n$, the set of pairs $P_\sigma = \{(b_i, g_{\sigma(i)}) \mid i = 1, 2, \ldots, n\}$ is a perfect matching of G if and only if $r_{i\sigma(i)}$ is nonzero for each $i \in \{1, \ldots, n\}$. We define $sign(P_\sigma) = sign(\sigma)$ We let $\mathscr{P}$ denote the set of all perfect matchings of G.

The following proposition gives a solution to the marriage problem and yields an associated parallel Monte Carlo algorithm for determining whether or not a bipartite graph has a perfect matching.

Proposition 24.5.1 The bipartite graph G contains a perfect matching if and only if the determinant of R is not the identically zero polynomial in the indeterminates x_{ij}. ■

Proposition 24.5.1 follows immediately from the following lemma.

Lemma 24.5.2

$$\det(R) = \sum_{P \in \mathcal{P}} sign(P) \prod_{\{b_i, g_j\} \in P} x_{ij}.$$

PROOF

Using the definition of the determinant and the connection between permutations of $\{1, \dots, n\}$ and perfect matchings, we obtain

$$\det(R) = \sum_{\sigma \in S_n} sign(\sigma) \prod_{i=1}^{n} r_{i\sigma(i)}$$

$$= \sum_{\sigma \in S_n} sign(P_\sigma) \prod_{(b_i, g_j) \in P_\sigma} r_{ij}$$

$$= \sum_{P \in \mathcal{P}} sign(P) \prod_{\{b_i, g_j\} \in P} x_{ij}.$$

■

Determining whether the determinant of R is identically zero by computing the coefficients of R as a polynomial in the indeterminates x_{ij} is computationally infeasible. However, the determinant of R can be computed efficiently for any particular assignment of values to the indeterminates. The following proposition provides the basis for an efficient Monte Carlo algorithm for determining whether or not the determinant of R is identically zero.

Proposition 24.5.3 Suppose $\det(R)$ is not the identically zero polynomial. For each edge $\{b_i, g_j\}$ of G, let R_w denote the matrix obtained from R by substituting the integer w_{ij} for x_{ij}, where the w_{ij}'s are chosen uniformly and independently from the set $\{1, 2, \dots, t\}$. Then, the probability that $\det(R_w)$ is zero is at most n/t.

PROOF

We prove the proposition by induction on n. Clearly, the proposition is true for $n = 1$, establishing the basis step. Assume the proposition is true for all $(n - 1) \times (n - 1)$ matrices R. Now consider an $n \times n$ matrix R whose determinant is not identically zero. Then, by Proposition 24.5.1, G contains a perfect matching P. For $\{b_i, g_j\}$ an edge of P, let R_{ij} and $(R_w)_{ij}$ denote the matrices obtained from R and R_w, respectively, by deleting the ith row and j^{th} column. Because the bipartite graph G_{ij} obtained from G by deleting vertices b_i, g_j, and all incident edges contains the perfect matching $P\backslash\{b_i, g_j\}$, $\det(R_{ij})$ is nonzero. Further, it follows from the definition of a determinant that for some integer k, we have

$$\det(R_w) = w_{ij}\det((R_w)_{ij}) + k.$$

By induction hypothesis, $\det((R_w)_{ij})$ is zero with probability at most $(n-1)/t$. Let q denote the probability that both $\det(R_w)$ and $\det((R_w)_{ij})$ are zero. Clearly, $q \leq (n-1)/t$. Now suppose $\det((R_w)_{ij})$ is nonzero. Because w_{ij} was chosen uniformly and independently from the set $\{1,2,\ldots,t\}$, the probability that w_{ij} equals $-k/\det((R_w)_{ij})$ is at most $1/t$. Equivalently, the probability that $\det(R_w)$ is zero, given that $\det((R_w)_{ij})$ is nonzero, is at most $1/t$. Hence, the probability that $\det(R_w)$ is zero is at most

$$q + \frac{1}{t} \leq \frac{n-1}{t} + \frac{1}{t} = \frac{n}{t}. \qquad \blacksquare$$

Proposition 24.5.3 yields the following Monte Carlo parallel algorithm *MC-Marriage* for solving the marriage problem. In the pseudocode for *MCMarriage*, we omit the particular parallel architecture and the number of processors, since the only portion of the code that requires this knowledge is the call to the function *Det* for computing the determinant of a matrix.

```
function MCMarriage(G, t)
Input:    G (a bipartite graph with vertex set V = {b₁, ... , bₙ} ∪ {g₁, ... , gₙ} and edge set E)
          t (a positive integer, t ≥ 2n)
Output:   .true. or .false. (always correct when .true. is returned and correct with
          probability at least 1 − n/t when .false. is returned)
      for 1 ≤ i, j ≤ n do in parallel
          if {bᵢ, gⱼ} ∈ E then
              R[i, j] ← Random(1, t)
          else
              R[i, j] ← 0
          endif
      end in parallel
      if Det(R) = 0 then
          return(.false.)
      else
          return(.true.)
      endif
end MCMarriage
```

Because the dominant operation of *MCMarriage* is computing the determinant of an $n \times n$ matrix, *MCMarriage* can be implemented in time $O(\log^2 n)$ using $O(n^4)$ processors on the EREW PRAM.

24.5.3 Randomized Protocols for Breaking Deterministic Deadlock

Suppose an American and a New Zealander are approaching one another on a narrow path. As they draw closer, the American moves to his right on the path to let the New Zealander pass. However, at that same instant, the New Zealander moves to her left on the path for the same purpose (recall that they drive on the left in New Zealand). Then they both decide simultaneously to move to the other side of the path, and so it goes. In real life, the resulting back and forth shuffle might continue for one or two more rounds before the deadlock is broken and they end up on opposite sides of the path (or until romance ensues).

While humans can decide on a protocol that resolves the path-passing deadlock with little more cost than a moment's embarrassment, situations arise in a communication network when processors executing completely deterministic protocols generate communication deadlocks requiring costly outside intervention by central control. The natural course of action in such cases is to introduce some type of randomness into the protocol. Indeed, randomized protocols are the basis of many communication protocols in use today.

We limit our discussion of randomized communication protocols to a simple problem of choosing a distinguished (leader) processor from a set of n processors connected in a simple ring (see Figure 24.5). (The problem can be generalized to other communication networks, but the ideas are similar.) We assume that each processor knows the number n of processors in the ring. However, unlike the leader election problem discussed in Chapter 19, here processors are not distinguished by an indexing scheme known to one another.

Suppose that each processor's local memory has been initialized with identical data. The processors are to decide on a leader by performing purely local calculations and communicating the results circularly around the ring. (Because the processors are not indexed, they cannot, for example, simply choose an integer j between 1 and n and say that the processor with index j is the leader.) Assuming that each processor executes the same deterministic algorithm with the same initial data, all the processors would communicate identical information

FIGURE 24.5

A ring of identical processors with $n = 12$.

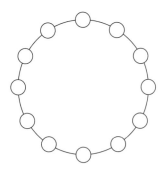

around the ring, and no processor could possibly be distinguished. To break the deadlock of symmetry, randomness is required.

One simple Las Vegas algorithm to chose a leader is based on the familiar "drawing straws" protocol. More precisely, the algorithm $DrawStraws(n, m)$ consists of having each of the n processors draw an integer at random from $\{1, \dots, m\}$ for some integer $m > 1$. Using $n - 1$ communication steps, the n choices are communicated to each processor in the ring and the maximum choice is determined. If the maximum was not drawn by more than one processor, then the leader is the processor that drew the maximum element. Otherwise, the algorithm $DrawStaws$ is repeated.

We choose bit communication as the basic operation when measuring the complexity of any algorithm for choosing a leader in our ring of processors. Thus, a single running of $DrawStraws(n, m)$ has complexity $(n - 1)\log_2 m$. If $\rho(n, m)$ denotes the expected number of repetitions of $DrawStraws(n,m)$ that are required for termination, we then have

$$\tau_{\exp}(n, m) = \rho(n, m)(n - 1)\log_2 m. \qquad \textbf{(24.5.1)}$$

Formula (24.5.1) shows the trade-off involved with making $\tau_{\exp}(n,m)$ small: To make $\rho(n, m)$ small, we must make m (and hence $\log_2 m$) large. In particular, the expected number of basic operations performed by the Las Vegas algorithm $RepeatDrawStraws(n, m)$ is not linear in n no matter what fixed value of m is used.

We now describe a Las Vegas algorithm (protocol) $RepeatDrawOne(n)$ for choosing a leader whose expected behavior is linear in n. The protocol involves repeatedly performing the operation $DrawOne$ until a leader is determined. During the operation $DrawOne$, each processor that is still a candidate for leader draws an integer at random from $\{1, \dots, NumCand\}$. Identification of the processors that drew the number 1 is communicated as follows. In the first communication step, if a processor drew a 1, then it communicates the bit 1 to its neighbor; otherwise, it communicates the bit 0. Noncandidate processors communicate bit 0 to their neighbors. After $n - 2$ additional communication steps, all the results are communicated to all the processors. In particular, each processor knows how many processors drew the number 1.

If no processor drew a 1, then $DrawOne$ is repeated under the same conditions ($NumCand$ remains unchanged). If a single processor drew a 1, this processor is the leader, and $RepeatDrawOne$ terminates. If more than one processor drew a 1, $NumCand$ is updated to the number of such processors. Then $DrawOne$ is repeated, with the processors that did not draw 1 dropping out of the contest for leader. Thus, each processor maintains a Boolean variable $Candidate$, which is initialized to **.true.** and is set to **.false.** when the processor is no longer a candidate for leader. Of course, the processors that are no longer candidates for leader still participate in the communication steps.

Letting $\tau_{exp}(n)$ be the expected number of parallel bit communication steps performed by *RepeatDrawOne* with input n and $\rho(n)$ be the expected number of calls to *DrawOne*, then we have

$$\tau_{exp}(n) = (n-1)\rho(n). \tag{24.5.2}$$

We now establish a recurrence relation for $\rho(n)$. The n choices made by the n processors during the first call to *DrawOne* can be thought of as performing n independent trials, where the probability of success (choosing a 1) is $1/n$ for each trial. Thus, if $p(n, i)$ denotes the probability of i successes (exactly i processors choose a 1), the binomial distribution yields

$$p(n,i) = \binom{n}{i}\left(\frac{1}{n}\right)^i\left(1 - \frac{1}{n}\right)^{n-i}. \tag{24.5.3}$$

The three basic (mutually disjoint) outcomes of the call to *DrawOne* described earlier correspond to $i = 0$ (repeat again from scratch), $i = 1$ (*Repeat DrawOne* terminates), and $2 \le i \le n$ (repeat again with i candidates for leader remaining). Because we call *DrawOne* at least once, we have

$$\rho(n) = 1 + p(n,0)\rho(n) + \sum_{i=2}^{n} p(n,i)\rho(i), \quad n \ge 2. \tag{24.5.4}$$

Solving for $\rho(n)$ in Formula (24.5.4) yields the following (full history) recurrence

$$\rho(n) = \frac{1 + \sum_{i=2}^{n-1} p(n,i)\rho(i)}{1 - p(n,0) - p(n,n)}, \quad n \ge 2, \text{ **init. cond.** } \rho(2) = 2. \tag{24.5.5}$$

Using Formula (24.5.5), it can be shown that $\rho(n) < e \approx 2.718, n \ge 2$ (see Exercise 24.21). Hence, the expected number of parallel bit communication steps performed by *RepeatDrawOne* is linear in the input size n.

24.6 Closing Remarks

R. Freivalds was one of the first researchers to popularize the use of Monte Carlo probabilistic algorithms, and the method we used to test the whether the polynomial $f(x)$ was identically equal to the product $g(x)h(x)$ is an example of what is known as the *Freivalds technique*.

Recall that a problem is in the class NC if there exists a parallel algorithm having polylogarithmic complexity for the problem on a PRAM with a polynomial number of processors. The randomized analog of this class, called RNC, is the class of algorithms for which there is a parallel Monte Carlo algorithm having polylogarithmic complexity for the problem on a PRAM with a polynomial number of processors. For a number of important and natural problems, NC algorithms are unknown but efficient RNC algorithms are fairly readily obtained. For example, there is no known NC algorithm for determining whether a multivariate polynomial $P(x_1, x_2, \ldots, x_m)$ of degree n is identically zero. On the other hand, an RNC algorithm for this problem can be readily given (see Exercise 24.22). In this chapter, we described an RNC parallel algorithm for determining the existence of a perfect matching in a bipartite graph. Finding an NC algorithm for this problem was open for many years and has only recently been solved.

In this chapter, we described some significant applications of the use of probability in the design of sequential and parallel algorithms. An important probabilistic method for optimization problems not covered in this chapter is *simulated annealing,* which is used for finding the global minimum of a cost function that might possess several local minima. Simulated annealing emulates phenomena occurring in nature—namely, the physical process occurring when a solid is slowly cooled. Another class of probabilistic algorithms that have been widely studied is genetic algorithms. The genetic algorithm design strategy is based on the laws of natural selection and survival of the fittest popularized by Darwin. We refer the student to the references for more on these probabilistic design strategies.

References and Suggestions for Further Reading

Motwani, R., and P. Raghavan. *Randomized Algorithms.* Cambridge, England, Cambridge University Press, 1995. An excellent text on probabilistic and randomized algorithnms.

Alon, N., J. Spencer, and P. Erdös. *The Probabilistic Method.* New York: Wiley, 1992. Covers many of the important applications of the probabilistic method introduced by Erdös and includes a chapter devoted to the derandomization of randomized algorithms.

Brassard, G., and P. Bratley. *Algorithmics: Theory and Practice.* Englewood Cliffs, NJ: Prentice-Hall, 1988. A nice treatment of probabilistic algorithms.

Gupta, R., S. Smolka, and S. Bhaskar. "On randomization in sequential and distributed algorithms," *ACM Computing Surveys* 25 (March 1994): 7–86. A comprehensive survey article on the use of probabilistic methods in sequential and parallel algorithms.

National Research Council. *Probability and Algorithms.* Washington, DC: National Academy Press, 1992. An outgrowth of a panel on probability and algorithms, sponsored by the National Research Council. Contains 12 independent articles that survey a number of topics on probabilistic algorithms, including simulated annealing.

Holland, J. *Adaptation in Natural and Artificial Systems.* Cambridge, MA, MIT Press, 1992. Written by the founder of the subject of genetic algorithms, this text is a revision of the 1975 version published by the University of Michigan.

There are many good books on genetic algorithms. Two of the more recent books:

Eiben, A., and J. Smith. *An Introduction to Evolutionary Computing.* Berlin: Springer-Verlag, 2003.

Koza, J., F. H. Bennett, D. Andre, and M. A. Keane. *Genetic Programming III: Darwinian Invention and Problem Solving.* San Francisco: Morgan Kaufmann, 1999.

EXERCISES

Section 24.2 Randomizing Deterministic Algorithms

24.1   For the randomized version of linear search in which we flip a coin (once) to determine the direction of the search, compute the variance of $\tau(I)$ for $I = (L[0{:}n - 1], X)$ where $X = L[i], 0 \leq i \leq n - 1$.

24.2   Consider the following deterministic algorithm:

```
function TwoWayLinearSearch(L[0:n − 1], X)
Input:     L[0:n − 1] (an array of list elements), X (a search item)
Output:    returns index of an occurrence of X in L, −1 if X not in list
    Left ← 0
    Right ← n − 1
    while Left ≤ Right do
        if X = L[Left] then return(Left) endif
        if X = L[Right] then return(Right) endif
        Left ← Left + 1
        Right ← Right − 1
    endwhile
    return(−1)
end TwoWayLinearSearch
```

a. Determine the best-case, worst-case, and average complexities of *TwoWayLinearSearch* under the assumptions that $L[0{:}n - 1]$ consists of distinct elements and X occurs on the list, with each list element equally likely to be X.

In parts (b),(c),(d), consider the randomized version of *TwoWayLinear-Search*, in which we flip a fair coin, and if it comes up heads, we compare X to $L[Left]$ and increment *Left* if $X \neq L[Left]$; otherwise (tails), we compare X to $L[Right]$ and decrement *Right* if $X \neq L[Right]$. The process is repeated as long as X is not found and *Left* ≤ *Right*.

b. Find an expression for $\tau_{exp}(I)$ for $I = (L[0: n - 1], X)$ where $X = L[0]$.

c. Compute the variance $\tau(I)$ for $I = (L[0: n - 1], X)$ where $X = L[0]$.

d. Compare the variances in part (d) with those from Exercise 24.1.

24.3 Show that the variance of $\tau(L)$ for any input list L to *RandomizedQuickSort* is small.

Section 24.3 Monte Carlo and Las Vegas Algorithms

24.4 Show that the probability of the occurrence of the intersection event

$\bigcap\limits_{i=1}^{n} E_i$ satisfies the following formula:

$$P\left(\bigcap_{i=1}^{n} E_i\right) = P(E_1)P(E_2|E_1) \ldots P\left(E_n | \bigcap_{i=1}^{n-1} E_i\right).$$

24.5 Show that *MCMinCut* has complexity $O(n^2)$, even for an input graph with multiedges.

24.6 Solve the recurrence relation given in Formula (24.3.5) to obtain

$$T(n) \in O(n^2 \log n).$$

24.7 Verify Formula (24.3.6).

24.8 Given that $s(k)$ satisfies

$$1 + s(k - 1) \leq s(k) \leq 2 + s(k - 1),$$

show that $s(k) \in \Theta(k)$.

24.9 Show that $s(k)$ defined by recurrence relation (24.3.11) satisfies

$$k < s(k) < k + H_{k-1} + 3,$$

where H_n denotes the harmonic series (see Chapter 3).

24.10 A *majority element x* in a list $L[0: n - 1]$ is an element that occurs more than $n/2$ times. Design and analyze a Monte Carlo algorithm for determining the majority element $L[0: n - 1]$ in a list, if one exists.

24.11 Consider the following Las Vegas algorithm for the n-queens problem.

procedure *QueensLasVegas*(*n, Column*[0: *n* − 1])
Input: *n* (an *n* × *n* chess board)
Output: *Column*[0: *n* − 1] (queen *i* is in row *i* and column *Column*[*i*] so that no two
          queens attack each other)
    AvailColumns ← {0, . . . , *n* − 1}
    R ← 0
    while *AvailColumns* ≠ ∅ .and. *R* ≤ *n* − 1 **do**
        choose a column *C* randomly and uniformly from *AvailColumns*
        Column[*R*] ← *C*   //place queen *R* in row *R* and column *C*
        R ← *R* + 1
        update *AvailColumns* to be the set of columns available for placing the $(R + 1)^{st}$
        queen in row *R* + 1 without creating a pair of attacking queens
    endwhile
end *QueensLasVegas*

    a. Write a program implementing *QueensLasVegas*.

    b. Run your program for $n = 8$. Empirically verify that the probability p for success is given by $p = 0.1293 \ldots$.

24.12 Give pseudocode for a version of *QueensLasVegas* that does not explicitly maintain the set *AvailColumns* of available columns.

24.13 Write a program similar to *QueensLasVegas* that places a number k of queens on the board in a random way and then uses backtracking to place the remaining queens (without changing the positions of the queens that were placed randomly). Test out your program for various values of k, and compare its performance to *QueensLasVegas*.

Section 24.4 Probabilistic Numerical Algorithms

24.14 Write a program to verify that the number of people we need to randomly sample from a given population before the chance is better than 50-50 that two people share the same birthday is 23, even for leap years.

24.15 When estimating the value of $\int_a^b f(x)\,dx$, show that we can assume without loss of generality that f is nonnegative on the interval $[a, b]$.

24.16 Show that Formula (24.4.1) begins to be less than 1/2 for $k \geq 24$.

24.17 Use Stirling's formula $n! \approx \sqrt{2\pi n}(n/e)^n$ to show that the value of Formula (24.4.2) can be approximated for large n by Formula (24.4.3):

$$\frac{n!}{(n-k)!n^k} \approx e^{-k^2/2n}.$$

24.18 Prove Theorem 24.4.2.

Section 24.5 Probabilistic Parallel Algorithms

24.19 Show that the expected number of basic operations performed by the Las Vegas algorithm *RepeatDrawStraws(n,m)* is not linear in n, no matter what fixed value of m is used.

24.20 Show that the expected number of calls to *DrawOne* made by algorithm *RepeatDrawOne* is smaller than 2.442.

24.21 Using Formula (24.5.5), show that $\rho(n) < e \approx 2.718, n \geq 2$, so that the expected number of basic operations performed by *RepeatDrawOne* is linear in the input size n.

24.22 Suppose that we are given an NC algorithm for evaluating a multivariate polynomial $P(x_1, x_2, \dots, x_m)$ of degree n over the real numbers. For example, $P(x_1, x_2, \dots, x_m)$ might be a determinant of matrix A whose entries involve the variables $x_1, x_2, \dots, x_m$. Design and analyze an RNC algorithm (a parallel Monte Carlo algorithm having logarithmic complexity in n and m, which uses a polynomial number of processors in n and m) for determining whether or not P is identically zero. Use the following lemma.

Lemma For any set of k real numbers $S = \{r_1, \dots, r_k\}$, the number of zeros in S^m of a multivariate polynomial $P(x_1, x_2, \dots, x_m)$ of degree n is at most $k^{m-1}n$. $\qquad\square$

CHAPTER 25

LOWER-BOUND THEORY

Given a problem and a specific algorithm for solving the problem, it is important to determine how close the algorithm comes to exhibiting optimal worst-case or average complexity for the *problem itself*. But how do we determine what optimal behavior *is* for the problem? Of course, the complexity of *any* algorithm that correctly solves the problem gives us *upper bounds* for the complexities of the problem. The object of this chapter is to discuss various techniques for determining good *lower-bound* estimates for the worst-case and average complexities of problems such as comparison-based searching and sorting.

 ## 25.1 Basic Terminology and Techniques

In Chapter 3, we found *sharp* lower-bound formulas for the worst-case complexity of the problem of adjacent-key comparison-based sorting and for the best-case, worst-case, and average complexities of the problem of finding the maximum value in a list. In other words, we found algorithms solving these problems that performed no more than the absolute minimum number of basic operations required to solve the given problems by *any* algorithm. There are relatively few problems for which sharp lower-bound formulas have been established. It is more realistic to search for lower-bound formulas for the order of complexity of a problem. An algorithm whose complexity has the same order as a lower bound for the problem is called *order optimal*. Even establishing order optimality is rare and usually can only be done in the context of suitably restricting the problem or type of algorithm allowed.

We discuss six basic techniques for determining lower bounds: simple counting arguments (based on a principle of minimal work), enumeration arguments, decision (comparison) tree arguments, adversary arguments, information theoretic arguments, and graph theoretic arguments.

25.1.1 Simple Counting Arguments

Simple counting arguments for establishing lower bounds are based on showing that any algorithm for solving a given problem must do a certain amount of minimal work to correctly output the solution for all inputs. This work is measured by associating a numeric quantity with the performance of a basic operation by the algorithm. For example, in Chapter 3 we used a simple counting argument to show that a comparison-based algorithm for finding a maximum element in an arbitrary list of size n must do at least $n - 1$ comparisons in the best case. Recall that we associated the notion of a loss (one unit of work) with each comparison made by the algorithm, and we simply counted the number of total losses that must occur if the algorithm is to correctly determine the maximum element. We showed that at least $n - 1$ units of work are required for any list of size n.

25.1.2 Enumeration Arguments

Enumeration arguments, which are useful for establishing lower bounds for the average complexity of a problem, are usually more complicated than simple counting arguments. The enumeration method depends on identifying a combinatorial or numeric entity associated with inputs of size n to the problem. Establishing a lower bound for average behavior then depends on showing that the average complexity $A(n)$ of *any* algorithm solving the problem is bounded below by the average number of the combinatorial entities per input. In Chapter 3, we calculated this average for adjacent-key comparison sorting by enumerating the total number of inversions over all permutations (inputs) of size n and then dividing by the number $n!$ of permutations of size n.

25.1.3 Decision Trees

A *decision tree* models the hierarchy of all possible branchings resulting from decisions made by an algorithm. The sequence of decisions and resultant branchings performed by the algorithm depends on the input and corresponds to a path from the root to a leaf in the decision tree. Suppose that the decision tree models the branching decisions made on the basis of performing basic operations such as comparing two elements in a list or multiplying two elements in a matrix. Then each internal node of the decision tree corresponds to the performance of one or more basic operations. Leaf nodes correspond to outputs of the algorithm (solutions to the problem). Nodes in the tree that are never reached by any input to the algorithm are pruned. Again, assuming that each internal node corresponds to the performance of at least one basic operation, then it is clear that the depth of the decision tree is a lower bound for the worst-case complexity of the algorithm. The decision tree method for obtaining lower bounds for the worst-case complexity of a problem consists of determining the minimum depth of a decision tree over all algorithms for solving the problem. Similarly, the decision tree method for obtaining lower bounds for the average complexity of a problem consists of determining the minimum leaf path length of a decision tree over all algorithms for solving the problem.

25.1.4 Adversary Arguments

Adversary arguments establish worst-case lower bounds by dynamically creating inputs to a given algorithm that force the algorithm to perform many basic operations. Adversary arguments work somewhat like playing a guessing game, where the decisions to be made by the algorithm are regarded as queries to an adversary, and the adversary answers these queries by providing as little information as possible. We only require that the adversary give answers that are consistent and truthful. Clever adversaries force any given algorithm to make many queries before the algorithm has enough information to output the solution. We assume that the algorithm uses a basic operation like comparing two list elements when querying the adversary. The adversary actually constructs a suitable input in response to the queries. Lower bounds for the worst-case complexity $W(n)$ are then obtained by counting the number of basic operations that the adversary forces the algorithm to perform.

25.1.5 Information Theoretic Arguments

Information theoretic arguments establish lower bounds by computing the limitations on information gained by a basic operation and then showing how much information is required before a given problem is solved. The familiar *rule of product* from elementary combinatorial theory provides the basis for many information theoretic arguments. The rule is applied as follows. Suppose that a basic operation provides b units of information. Then the upper bound for the cumulative amount of information that can be obtained from performing this basic operation n times in succession is b^n. For example, if the basic operation is a comparison, its outcome is either **.true.** or **.false.**, so that $b = 2$. Sorting algorithms must generate enough information to distinguish among the $n!$ permutations of a list of size n, which implies that the lower bound for the worst-case behavior of comparison-based sorting algorithms is $\lceil \log_2(n!) \rceil \in \Theta(n \log n)$.

25.1.6 Graph Theoretic Arguments

Graph theoretic arguments are often used to establish lower bounds for parallel algorithms. For example, on interconnection network models, the diameter and the bisection width of the network give lower bounds on the communication complexity (see Chapter 15). As another example, in Section 25.4, we obtain a lower bound for finding the maximum element in a list on the CRCW PRAM.

25.2 Decision Trees and Comparison Trees

Decision trees are an important and commonly used method of establishing lower bounds. In a decision tree modeling a comparison-based algorithm an internal node corresponds to a comparison made by the algorithm using one of the comparison operators $<$, $=$, or $>$. For convenience in pseudocode or drawing the decision tree, we also might use one of the respectively equivalent comparison operators $\geq$, $\neq$, or $\leq$. External leaf nodes correspond to outputs of the algorithm. We assume that any nodes in the decision tree that are never reached by any input to the algorithm are pruned. We will use the term *comparison tree* for such decision trees that are based on making a two-way branch, depending on the outcome of a comparison. On the other hand, nodes in decision trees in general may have more than two children. For example, a node corresponding to a **do case** decision may have as many children as the number of cases specified (see Figure 25.2a).

FIGURE 25.1

Comparison tree for *LinearSearch* with $n = 4$.

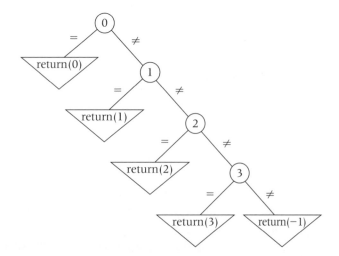

25.2.1 Examples

Figure 25.1 shows the comparison tree for *LinearSearch* with $n = 4$. Inside each internal node is the position in the list of the element being compared to the search element.

Figure 25.2a shows the *decision* tree that models *BinarySearch* with $n = 5$, whereas Figure 25.2b shows the *comparison* tree that models the same thing. The decision tree in Figure 25.2a is *not* a comparison tree because a three-way decision is made based on the **do case** statement in *BinarySearch*. Since we are basing our analysis of the complexity of comparison-based algorithms on two-way decisions resulting from comparisons, we must use the comparison tree given in Figure 25.2b, rather than the decision tree given in Figure 25.2a. In Figures 25.2a and 25.2b, the current values of *low* and *high* are shown outside each internal node. Inside each internal node is shown the current value of *mid*.

FIGURE 25.2

(a) The decision tree for *BinarySearch* with $n = 5$;

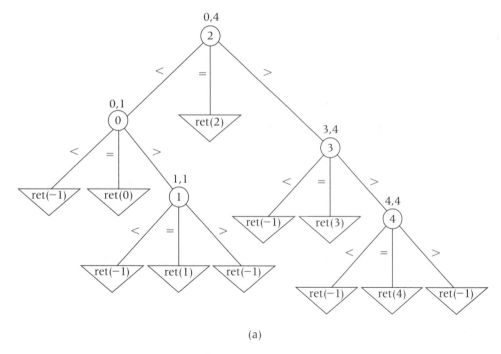

(a)

continued

FIGURE 25.2

Continued

(b) The comparison
tree for
BinarySearch with
n = 5.

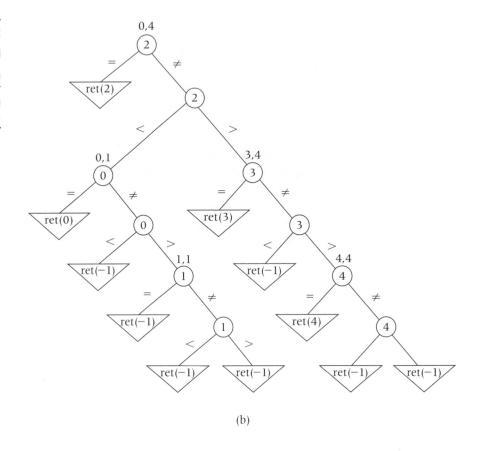

(b)

As a second illustration of comparison trees, we consider a variation of binary search, *BinarySearch2*, which makes an equality test only after the list has been narrowed to a single-element list.

```
function BinarySearch2(L[low:high], X) recursive
Input:    L[low:high]                    (a list of elements with indices between low
                                          and high, sorted in nondecreasing order)
          X (search item)                //We assume that the initial
                                          invocation of BinarySearch2 has
                                          low = 0 and high = n − 1 ≥ 0
Output:   Returns the index of an occurrence of X in the list, or −1 if X is not in the list
          if low = high then
              if X = L[low] then
                  return(low)
              else
                  return(−1)
              endif
          else
              mid ← ⌊(low + high + 1)/2⌋
```

```
        if X < L[mid] then
            return(BinarySearch2(L[low:mid − 1], X))
        else
            return(BinarySearch2(L[mid:high], X))
        endif
    endif
end BinarySearch2
```

It is easy to verify that if *low* < *high*, then *low* < *mid* ≤ *high*. Thus, each recursive invocation narrows the size of the sublist *L[low:high]* by at least 1, and eventually, *low* = *high* and the algorithm terminates. We leave the complete correctness proof of *BinarySearch2* as an exercise.

Figure 25.3 shows the comparison tree for *BinarySearch2*. The current values of *low* and *high*, respectively, are listed in the figure outside each internal node, and the current value of *mid* is shown inside each internal node whose children are not leaves. Leaf (output) nodes show the value returned based on the comparison of *X* to *L[low]*, where *low* is the current value corresponding to the parent node.

FIGURE 25.3

Comparison tree *T*
for *BinarySearch2*
with *n* = 5.

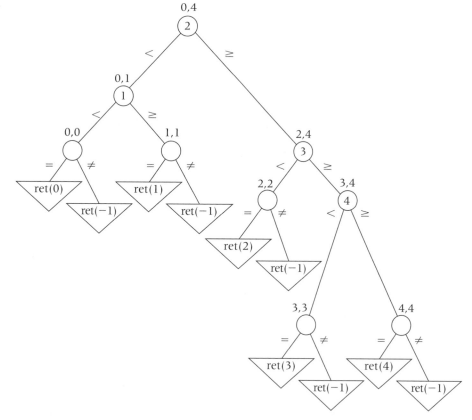

Clearly, for any search element X, the action of *BinarySearch2* corresponds to following a path in its comparison tree T from the root to a leaf node. Thus, the worst-case complexity of *BinarySearch2* equals the depth $D(T)$ of T. Also, the comparison tree T has $2n$ leaf nodes and is a 2-tree that is full at the second-deepest level (see Exercise 25.5). Thus, it follows from Proposition 4.2.6 that

$$W(n) = D(T) = \lceil \log_2 2n \rceil = \lceil \log_2 n \rceil + 1. \qquad \textbf{(25.2.1)}$$

Proposition 4.2.6 also implies that all the leaves of T are at levels $D(T) - 1$ and $D(T)$, so that the best-case complexity of *BinarySearch2* is at most 1 less than its worst-case complexity. Hence, it follows from (25.2.1) that

$$\lceil \log_2 n \rceil \le B(n) \le A(n) \le W(n) = \lceil \log_2 n \rceil + 1. \qquad \textbf{(25.2.2)}$$

25.2.2 Lower Bound for the Worst-Case Complexity of Comparison-Based Searching of Lists

Consider now the complexity of the *problem* of searching for the occurrence of a search element X in a list $L[0:n - 1]$. For arbitrary lists $L[0:n - 1]$, the worst-case complexity of the *problem* of searching for X in L using a comparison-based algorithm is n, since X must be compared to *every* list element for a list not containing X.

We now consider the problem of searching an ordered list of size n. A comparison tree T modeling a comparison-based algorithm for this problem must have at least $n + 1$ leaf nodes. Indeed, T must have n leaf nodes corresponding to outputting the n possible occurrences of the search element in the list, and T must also have at least one leaf node outputting -1 when the search element is not in the list. By Proposition 4.2.4, it follows that T has depth at least $\lceil \log_2 (n + 1) \rceil$.

This establishes the lower bound $\lceil \log_2 (n + 1) \rceil$ for comparison-based searching of an ordered list of size n, which we state as a theorem.

Theorem 25.2.1   A worst-case lower bound for the problem of searching an ordered list of size n using a comparison-based algorithm is given by

$$\lceil \log_2 (n + 1) \rceil. \qquad \textbf{(25.2.3)} \quad ■$$

Since *BinarySearch2* has $W(n) = \lceil \log_2 n \rceil + 1$, we see from Formula (25.2.3) that *BinarySearch2* comes within 1 of being an optimal worst-case algorithm for searching ordered lists. Thus, we have rather precisely determined the worst-case complexity of the problem of searching ordered lists using comparison-based algorithms.

25.2.3 Lower Bound for the Average Complexity of Comparison-Based Searching of Ordered Lists

We now establish a lower bound for the average complexity of searching an ordered list of distinct elements using a comparison-based algorithm. For simplicity, we assume that the search element X is on the list and is equally likely to occur in any position. Consider any algorithm for solving the problem, and let T be its associated comparison tree for a list of size n. Because the search element X can occur in any of the n positions in the list, every index from $\{0,1, \dots , n-1\}$ occurs as the output of some leaf node of T. We now prove that each index occurs as the output of exactly one leaf node. (Note that this property does not hold for all comparison-based algorithms for searching *arbitrary* lists.) Assume to the contrary that there exists an index i such that i is the output of two leaf nodes, say L_1 and L_2. Let N be the root of the smallest subtree of T containing both L_1 and L_2. Now N corresponds to a comparison of the search element X with a list element $L[j]$. The only way X can reach either L_1 or L_2 is for X to be equal to $L[i]$. Since L is ordered, the comparison of X to $L[j]$ corresponding to node N always has the same result, independent of the list. Therefore, X either always goes to the right child of N or to its left, independent of the list. Thus, $X = L[i]$ always ends at L_1 or L_2, so that either L_1 or L_2 can be pruned. Hence, T has exactly n leaf nodes, one for each index from $\{0, \dots , n-1\}$.

The number of comparisons made by the algorithm to reach a leaf (output) node equals the length of the path in T from the root to that leaf node. Thus, the average complexity $A(n)$ for a successful search is given by $LPL(T)/n$, where $LPL(T)$ denotes the leaf path length of T defined in Chapter 4. The following theorem follows from Theorem 4.2.8.

Theorem 25.2.2

A lower bound for the average complexity of the problem of successfully searching an ordered list of size n using a comparison-based algorithm, assuming that each list element has equal probability $1/n$ of being the search element, is

$$\lfloor \log_2 n \rfloor + \frac{2(n - 2^{\lfloor \log_2 n \rfloor})}{n} \in \Omega(\log n). \qquad (25.2.4) \qquad ■$$

The average complexity $A(n)$ of *BinarySearch2* (whether or not the search element is in the list) is no greater than $\lceil \log_2 n \rceil + 1$. Hence, *BinarySearch2* comes within 2 of having optimal average complexity.

25.2.4 Lower Bound for the Worst-Case Complexity of Comparison-Based Sorting Algorithms

In Chapter 3, we established a $\Omega(n\log n)$ lower bound for comparison-based sorting algorithms. We now establish this result using a comparison tree argument. As usual, we can assume that the inputs to the algorithm are the $n!$ permutations of $\{1,2, \dots , n\}$. Consider any comparison-based sorting algorithm, and let T be its associated comparison tree. We follow several conventions when drawing a comparison tree for modeling the action of the algorithm for an input list $x_1, x_2, \dots , x_n$. We label a node $x_i:x_j$, $i < j$, if the comparison being made by the algorithm is between x_i and x_j. Note that we are not labeling the node by the index positions that these elements currently occupy in the array containing these elements. We assume that the left (right) child of the labeled node corresponds to the action performed by the algorithm if $x_i \leq x_j$ ($x_i > x_j$). This action is either the next comparison made (internal node), or an output (leaf node).In Figure 25.4, the comparison tree for *ShellSort* is illustrated for $n = 3$ and the two increments $d_0 = 2$ and $d_1 = 1$. The current state of the list is shown outside each node. Note that the comparison tree has been pruned to remove nodes that are never reached by inputs to the algorithm.

FIGURE 25.4

Comparison tree for *ShellSort* with distinct elements x_1, x_2, x_3, and with two increments $d_0 = 2$ and $d_1 = 1$.

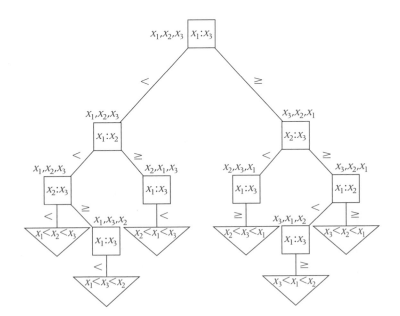

Figure 25.4 shows 3! = 6 leaf nodes corresponding to the six possible orderings of a three-element list x_1, x_2, x_3. In fact, the salient feature of the comparison tree corresponding to *any* comparison-based sorting algorithm is that for an input of size n, there must be *exactly* $n!$ leaf nodes. Each leaf node corresponds to one of the $n!$ possible orderings of a list of size n. Indeed, if there were less than $n!$ leaf nodes, then at least two distinct permutations of $\{1, 2, \ldots, n\}$ would have to follow identical paths from the root to the same leaf. In other words, the algorithm would perform identically on the two permutations and therefore could not possibly give the right output for both lists. On the other hand, there can't be more than $n!$ leaf nodes; otherwise, there would be a leaf node that is never reached by any of the $n!$ permutations, and this node would be pruned. By Proposition 4.2.4 of Chapter 4, any binary tree having $n!$ leaf nodes must have depth at least $\lceil \log_2 n! \rceil$. Thus, any comparison-based sorting algorithm must perform $\lceil \log_2 n! \rceil \in \Omega(n \log n)$ comparisons for some input of size n. We state this in the form of a theorem, where we use the result of Exercise 25.10 to estimate $\lceil \log_2 n! \rceil$.

Theorem 25.2.3   A lower bound for the worst-case complexity of any comparison-based sorting algorithm is $\lceil \log_2 n! \rceil = n \log_2 n - n / \log_e n + (1/2) / \log_2 n + O(1)$. In particular, the worst-case complexity belongs to $\Omega(n \log n)$.   ■

Of the sorting algorithms considered so far, it follows from Theorem 25.2.3 that *MergeSort* and *HeapSort* both exhibit order-optimal worst-case performance.

25.2.5 Lower Bound for the Average Complexity of Comparison-Based Sorting Algorithms

We now show that a lower bound for the average complexity of comparison-based sorting algorithms is $\lfloor \log_2 n! \rfloor$. (In particular, this lower bound for average complexity differs by at most 1 from the lower bound that we established for the worst-case complexity.) Our previous discussion shows that the decision tree for any comparison-based sorting algorithm must have $n!$ leaf nodes. Under our assumption for analyzing the average behavior of sorting algorithms, we assume that $\mathcal{I}_n$ consists of all permutations of $\{1, 2, \ldots, n\}$ and that each permutation is equally likely. Each permutation must follow some path in the comparison tree to a leaf, and our assumption implies that each leaf is equally likely to be a termination point of the algorithm. Because each internal node in the decision tree T corresponds to a comparison performed by the algorithm, it follows that the average number of comparisons performed by the algorithm is at least $LPL(T)/n!$. By Corollary 4.2.9 of Chapter 4, $LPL(T) \geq n! \lfloor \log_2 n! \rfloor$, so that the average number of comparisons is at least $\lfloor \log_2 n! \rfloor$. Again, we state this in the form of a theorem.

Theorem 25.2.4 A lower bound for the average complexity of any comparison-based sorting algorithm is $\lfloor \log_2 n! \rfloor$. In particular, the average complexity belongs to $\Omega(n \log n)$ ■

Of the comparison-based sorting algorithms considered so far, it follows from Theorem 25.2.4 that *MergeSort*, *HeapSort*, *TreeSort* and *QuickSort* all have order-optimal average complexity.

25.3 Adversary Arguments

Recall that adversary arguments work by dynamically constructing inputs to an algorithm that makes it work hard. Thus, adversary arguments establish lower bounds for *worst-case* complexity.

25.3.1 Lower Bound for Finding Maximum and Minimum Elements in a List

Our first example of an adversary argument determines a lower bound for worst-case complexity of any comparison-based algorithm for finding both the maximum and minimum elements in a list $L[0:n-1]$.

Theorem 25.3.1 Any comparison-based algorithm for finding both the maximum and minimum elements in an arbitrary list of size n must perform at least $\lceil 3n/2 \rceil - 2$ comparisons in the worst case.

PROOF

We use the simpler word *algorithm* for *comparison-based algorithm* in the proof. Because we are establishing a worst-case lower bound for the number of comparisons that any algorithm performs when determining the maximum and minimum elements for an *arbitrary* list $L[0:n-1]$, we can assume that $L[0:n-1]$ consists of distinct elements. When an algorithm compares two list elements $L[i]$ and $L[j]$, if $L[i] < L[j]$, then we say $L[i]$ lost the comparison and $L[j]$ won it, and vice versa if $L[i] > L[j]$.

With any algorithm, we associate a *state 4-tuple* modeling the performance of the algorithm as follows. As the algorithm works, we keep track of state 4-tuple $[\#U, \#W, \#L, \#WL]$, where $\#U$ denotes the number of list elements as yet unused in any comparison, $\#W$ denotes the number of elements that have won a comparison and never lost, $\#L$ denotes the number of elements that have lost a comparison and never won, and #*WL* denotes the number of elements that have both won a comparison and lost a comparison. Initially, we have the state 4-tuple [*n*,0,0,0]. An argument similar to the proof of Proposition 3.5.1 shows that an algorithm can correctly determine maximum and minimum elements in the list only after transforming this original state 4-tuple into the final state [0,1,1,*n* − 2].

We now design an adversary strategy that forces the algorithm to make at least $\lceil 3n/2 \rceil - 2$ comparisons before this final state is reached. In response to comparisons made by the algorithm, the adversary creates an input list dynamically. As the algorithm progresses, the adversary is allowed to change the values of list elements previously assigned, but such changes must be consistent with all win-loss comparisons that have occurred previously.

Key Fact

The critical property of the final list created by the adversary is that it can be input back into the algorithm and force the following two transition rules:
1. **Whenever #*U* changes, #*WL* does not, and vice versa.**
2. **Whenever #*WL* changes, it changes by 1.**

Note that if the transition rules are satisfied by the input list, then Theorem 25.3.1 is established. Indeed, it takes at least $\lceil n/2 \rceil$ comparisons to change #*U* from *n* to 0. By transition rule 1, these comparisons do not alter #*WL*. Hence, using transition rule 2, at least an additional *n* − 2 comparisons are required to change #*WL* from 0 to *n* − 2. It remains to show that the adversary can produce a list satisfying the transition rules.

At any point in the execution of the algorithm, a list element *X* can be in one of four states *U*, *W*, *L*, *WL*, depending on whether *X* has participated in no comparisons, has won every comparison, has lost every comparison, or has won at least one comparison and lost at least one comparison, respectively. Thus, when the algorithm compares two elements, these elements exhibit one of ten possible (unordered) pair states:

$$\{U,U\},\{U,W\},\{U,L\},\{U,WL\},\{W,W\},\{W,L\},\{W,WL\},\{L,L\},\{L,WL\},\{WL,WL\}.$$

We now show how the adversary creates a list satisfying the transition rules. For ease of discussion, we suppose that *X*,*Y* denotes the list elements being compared by the algorithm and that *X* has state S_1 in the pair state $\{S_1,S_2\}$. When the algorithm compares two list elements *X*,*Y* having the pair state $\{U,U\}$, the adversary makes a "whimsical" assignment of values to X and Y (that is, *any* choice will do subject only to the condition of maintaining a list of distinct elements). Similarly, when the algorithm compares two list elements X,Y having the pair state $\{U,WL\}$, the adversary makes a whimsical assignment of a value to X. Clearly, these two pair states cannot lead to a violation of transition rule 1 or 2 because #WL remains unchanged by a comparison of list elements having either of these states. We now consider those pair states that *can* lead to violations of the transition rules (that is, where #WL can change).

We first consider transition rule 1. Clearly, the only pair states that can lead to a violation of transition rule 1 are $\{U,W\}$ and $\{U,L\}$. Given, say, a comparison between two list elements X,Y in the pair state $\{U,W\}$, the adversary assigns a value to X that is smaller than Y. This forces the transition $[\#U,\#W,\#L,\#WL] \rightarrow [\#U - 1, \#W,\#L + 1,\#WL]$, which satisfies transition rule 1. Similarly, given a comparison between two list elements X,Y in the pair state $\{U,L\}$, the adversary assigns a value to X that is larger than Y. This completes the adversary strategy with respect to transition rule 1.

Now consider transition rule 2. Clearly, $\{W,L\}$ is the only pair state that can lead to a violation of transition rule 2 because comparisons between list elements having any other pair state can only change #WL by at *most* 1. Suppose, then, that the algorithm makes a comparison between the list elements X,Y having pair state $\{W,L\}$. Then the adversary makes X win, resulting in no change in the state 4-tuple; otherwise, #WL would change by 2. Note, however, that the adversary has to reassign the value of X in case the previous assignments resulted in the relation $X < Y$. If the latter is the case, the adversary merely reassigns a value to X making $X > Y$. This cannot be inconsistent with the results of previous comparisons involving X, because X always won such comparisons (now X is an even bigger winner). Moreover, reassigning the value for X does not affect the previous sequence of comparisons made by the algorithm because we are restricting attention to comparison-based algorithms. In particular, branching decisions made by such algorithms do not depend on the particular values of list elements, only their relative order.

The remaining pair states, $\{W,W\}$, $\{W,WL\}$, $\{L,L\}$, $\{L,WL\}$, $\{WL,WL\}$, cannot lead to violations of the transition rules. Thus, when the algorithm compares two list elements having any one of these states, the adversary makes no changes to the (already assigned) values of X and Y. We have thus shown that the adversary can, in response to comparisons made by the algorithm, create a list dynamically that satisfies the two transition rules. The final list that results can be put back into the algorithm, forcing it to perform $\lceil 3n/2 \rceil - 2$ comparisons. ■

R E M A R K

In forcing the transition rules to be satisfied, the adversary does not always give away as little information as possible. For example, when the algorithm compares two list elements X,Y having pair state $\{W,WL\}$, the adversary does not intervene. Thus, if $X < Y$, the state 4-tuple would undergo the transition $[\#U,\#W,\#L,\#WL] \rightarrow [\#U,\#W - 1,\#L,\#WL + 1]$. Although this does not violate either transition rule, the adversary could reassign a value to X, making $X > Y$. Then the state 4-tuple would undergo no change at all. This reflects the fact that a comparison involving the pair state $\{W,WL\}$ is wasted work when $X > Y$. However, for the purposes of the lower bound $\lceil 3n/2 \rceil - 2$, the adversary does not care. If the algorithm does even more work, so what? (Of course, if a larger lower bound could be found for *all* comparison-based algorithms, then the adversary *would* care! However, the algorithm *MaxMin3* described in Chapter 2 shows that such a larger lower bound cannot be found.)

Because algorithm *MaxMin3* (see Chapter 2) has worst-case complexity $\lceil 3n/2 \rceil - 2$, by Theorem 25.3.1 it is optimal, and the worst-case complexity of the problem of finding both the maximum and minimum elements in a list of size n is precisely $\lceil 3n/2 \rceil - 2$.

25.3.2 Lower Bound for Finding the Largest and Second-Largest Elements in a List

Our second example of an adversary argument is to find a lower bound for the problem of finding the largest and second-largest elements in a list. Again, we restrict attention to comparison-based algorithms, and we assume that the list contains distinct elements. The basic strategy of the adversary is to force any comparison-based algorithm to have the largest element participate in as many comparisons as possible. The reason for this strategy is clear from the following proposition.

Proposition 25.3.2 Suppose a comparison-based algorithm for finding the largest and second-largest elements in a list of size n compares the largest element to m other elements. Then the algorithm performs at least $m + n - 2$ comparisons altogether.

PROOF
Suppose for some list $L[0:n - 1]$ of distinct elements that a comparison-based algorithm determines $L[i],L[j]$ to get the largest and second-largest elements, respectively, and that it only makes at most $n - 3$ comparisons between elements, neither of which are $L[i]$. Using an argument similar to that used in

the proof of Proposition 3.5.1, there must be an element $L[k]$ different from $L[j]$ that never lost a comparison other than with $L[i]$. If we increase the value of $L[k]$ so that $L[j] < L[k] < L[i]$, clearly the algorithm works identically on the altered list, so that it would again declare $L[j]$ to be the second-largest—a contradiction. ■

The question now is, how large can the adversary force the m in Proposition 25.3.2 to be? The next proposition answers this question.

Proposition 25.3.3 Any comparison-based algorithm that determines the largest element in a list of n distinct elements (no matter what else it does) compares the largest element to $\lceil \log_2 n \rceil$ other list elements for a suitable list $L[0:n-1]$.

PROOF
Given any comparison-based algorithm that determines the largest element in a list, the adversary will dynamically construct a list that makes this largest element participate in $\lceil \log_2 n \rceil$ comparisons. Whenever a comparison is made between two list elements that have never lost, the adversary chooses the winner to be the one that has won the most previous comparisons (ties are decided arbitrarily). If a comparison is made between an element that has never lost and one that has lost, the adversary chooses the one that has never lost to be the winner. When choosing the winner, the adversary can clearly adjust a previously assigned value (if necessary) to achieve this strategy and remain consistent with previous win-loss comparisons.

We now show that the strategy just described forces the maximum to participate in $\lceil \log_2 n \rceil$ comparisons. We model the strategy as territorial takeover. We assume that initially each list element owns one unit of territory. The adversary adopts a simple "the rich get richer" strategy. Whenever a comparison is made between two list elements that have never lost a comparison, the winner always has at least as much territory as the loser, and the winner takes over all the territory formerly owned by the loser. The loser from that point on has no territory. The largest element in the list eventually will own all n units of territory. Because each element starts with one unit of territory and the winner of any comparison can at most double the amount of territory owned, the largest element has to participate in at least $\lceil \log_2 n \rceil$ comparisons. ■

Propositions 25.3.2 and 25.3.3 combine to yield the following theorem.

Theorem 25.3.4 A comparison-based algorithm for finding the largest and second-largest elements in a list of size n must perform at least $n + \lceil \log_2 n \rceil - 2$ comparisons. ■

The question arises as to whether there is an optimal algorithm for finding the largest and second-largest elements in a list of size n. The most obvious algorithm is to scan the list for the largest element using $n - 1$ comparisons and then scan the remaining elements for the second-largest using $n - 2$ comparisons, using $2n - 3$ comparisons altogether. However, $2n - 3$ is almost twice as large as the lower bound given in Theorem 25.3.4. The idea behind a better—in fact, optimal—algorithm is to model the algorithm as a match-play golf or table tennis tournament.

We regard the comparison of list elements as a golf or table tennis match between the elements (players). For simplicity, assume that $n = 2^k$. In the first round of the tournament, we pair the n players into $n/2$ matches. In the next round, the $n/2$ winners of the first round are paired into $n/4$ matches, and the $n/4$ winners advance into the third round. After $k = \log_2 n$ rounds, we obtain the winner of the tournament. We draw such a single-elimination tournament in Figure 25.5. Note that to arrange for n to be a power of two, we gave Player G a *bye* in the first round.

The algorithm based on this tournament method makes $n/2 + n/4 + \ldots + n/2^k = n(1/2 + 1/4 + \cdots + 1/2^k) = n - 1$ comparisons in determining the largest

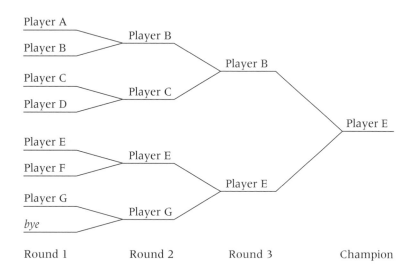

FIGURE 25.5

A single-elimination tournament.

element. The question remains as to how the algorithm can proceed to efficiently find the runner-up (second-largest). In actual golf or table tennis tournaments, it is customary to declare the runner-up to be the player who played the winner in the last round (Player B in Figure 25.5). However, sometimes that runner-up is not really the second-best player in the tournament. (Tournament organizers attempt to minimize the latter problem by avoiding early-round matches between highest-ranked, or so-called *top-seeded*, players. Just as we did in Figure 25.5, they use the method of seeding to facilitate tournament byes, so the highest-ranked players don't have to play in the first round or rounds. Byes allow the organizers to assume that the first round is between $n = 2^k$ players.)

Certainly, for the tournament method of determining the largest element in a list, we cannot assume that the list element that lost the last comparison made by the algorithm is the second-largest element in the list. However, the key observation here is that the second-largest element must have lost a comparison to the largest element in *some* round (not necessarily the last round). Thus, for example, in our tournament shown in Figure 25.5, the candidates for second-best are Player F, Player G, and Player B. More generally, if the algorithm maintains a dynamic list of losers for each element, then the second-largest element must be found among the largest element's final list of losers (although a linear number of loser-list updates are made, no additional comparisons are incurred). This final list contains $\log_2 n$ elements. A linear scan of these $\log_2 n$ elements (using $\log_2 n - 1$ comparisons) then determines the second-largest element in the list. Hence, the algorithm performs a total of $n + \log_2 n - 2$ comparisons and is an optimal algorithm.

25.3.3 Lower Bound for Finding the Median Element in a List

Our third example concerns the problem of determining the median element in a list $L[0:n - 1]$ using a comparison-based algorithm. We show that a lower bound for this problem is $3n/2 - 3/2$, where an adversary argument is used in the second part of the proof. We assume that the list consists of distinct elements. Also, for simplicity, we assume that n is odd, so that the median element M has the property that $(n - 1)/2$ elements are smaller (respectively, larger) than M (we leave the case of an even n to the exercises).

Given a comparison between two list elements X and Y, we say that this comparison is *one sided* if X and Y are on the same side of the median. Before describing the adversary strategy, we establish a lower bound on the number of *one-sided* comparisons that any comparison-based algorithm for determining the median must perform. By convention, any comparison involving the median is one sided. We *tag* any one-sided comparison with the comparand that is the farthest from the median (of the two comparands).

Proposition 25.3.5 Any comparison-based algorithm for finding the median element in a list $L[0:n − 1]$ performs a one-sided comparison tagged with X for each of the $n − 1$ list elements X different from the median.

PROOF

Suppose to the contrary that some input list $L[0:n − 1]$ to an algorithm has the property that there is at least one list element X not involved in any one-sided comparison that is tagged with X. We can assume without loss of generality that X is larger than the median M. Note that if X is compared to any list element Y that is larger than the median, then X is smaller than Y (otherwise X would tag a comparison). Let Z be the largest list element that is smaller than the median M. We now create a new list $L'[0:n − 1]$ as follows. We diminish X by a suitable amount to get X', which lies between Z and M, and we leave the remaining list elements unaltered. Clearly, all comparisons involving X' have exactly the same outcome as those involving X. Hence, the algorithm works the same on list L' as it does on L, so that M is also returned as the median element of L'. But this is a contradiction, since the number of elements larger than M in L' is 1 less than the number of elements larger than M in L. ■

A simple adversary strategy exists that forces any comparison-based algorithm for finding the median to perform at least $(n − 2)/2$ two-sided comparisons. Indeed, for definiteness, we assume that the adversary arbitrarily decides on the value M of the median element (but not its position). We call a comparison between list elements an *assigning comparison* if at least one of the comparands has not previously been involved in any comparison (so that the adversary must assign a value to each such comparand). The adversary ensures that each of the first $(n − 1)/2$ assigning comparisons performed by the algorithm are two-sided by simply assigning values to the previously unassigned comparand(s) that put the two comparands on opposite sides of the median. This is always possible because at most $n − 1$ distinct elements can be involved in the first $(n − 1)/2$ assigning comparisons, so that the adversary can put off assigning the median M until after the first $(n − 1)/2$ assigning comparisons have been performed. Thus, any comparison-based algorithm for finding the median can be forced to perform at least $(n − 1)/2$ two-sided comparisons in addition to the $n − 1$ one-sided comparisons guaranteed by Proposition 25.3.5. Hence we have established the following theorem.

| Theorem 25.3.6 | A comparison-based algorithm for finding the median element in a list of size n (n is odd) must perform at least $3n/2 - 3/2$ comparisons in the worst case. ■ |

The lower bound in Theorem 25.3.6 is not the best possible. In fact, a lower bound of slightly bigger than $2n$ has been established. An upper bound of $n\log_2 n$ for determining the median by a comparison-based algorithm is immediately obtained by sorting the list using an algorithm such as *MergeSort*. In Chapter 8, we described a linear comparison-based algorithm for the more general problem of determining the kth-smallest element in a list of size n for any k between 1 and n. Thus, the problem of determining the median element in a list has linear complexity.

25.4 Lower Bounds for Parallel Algorithms

All the lower bounds we have established for the complexity of problems solved by sequential algorithms made the implicit assumption that a single processor was used to make comparisons, perform arithmetic operations, and so forth. Thus, when we established lower bounds for the complexity of such problems as comparison-based sorting, we implicitly made the assumption that only one comparison could be made at any given step in the algorithm. When determining lower bounds for the complexity of problems solved by parallel algorithms, we must explicitly state the number of processors and the particular model and architecture that we are using. For example, consider the problem of finding the maximum value in a list of size n on the CREW PRAM using a comparison-based algorithm. If there are at most n processors available, then we obtain a lower bound of $\Omega(\log(\log n))$ parallel comparison steps for this problem. On the other hand, we obtain a lower bound $\Omega(\log n)$ for the same problem on the EREW PRAM with an unlimited number of processors.

As with sequential algorithms, a lower bound for a problem is sharp if there exists a parallel algorithm on the given architecture and number of processors whose complexity equals the lower bound. In the latter case, we have determined the complexity of the problem itself with respect to the given architecture and number of processors. As with sequential algorithms, we rarely are able to determine the exact complexity of a problem, or even its order.

Clearly, any lower bound for the complexity of a given problem on the EREW PRAM is a lower bound for the complexity of the problem on any particular interconnection network. Further, any lower bound for the complexity of a given problem on a particular PRAM model also is a lower bound for more restrictive PRAM models.

25.4.1 Lower Bound for Finding the Minimum on the EREW PRAM

The first lower-bound result that we obtain is for the problem of finding the minimum value in a list on the EREW PRAM.

Proposition 25.4.1 A lower bound for the complexity of the problem of finding the minimum value in a list $L[0:n − 1]$, using a comparison-based algorithm on the EREW PRAM with an unlimited number of processors, is $\lceil \log_2 n \rceil$.

PROOF

Our proof will use an adversary argument. We assume, without loss of generality, that $L[0:n − 1]$ is a list of distinct real numbers. In any parallel comparison step, when two distinct elements X and Y are compared, we say that X *wins* the comparison if $X < Y$; otherwise, X *loses.* At each stage of the algorithm, we let W denote the set of elements that have not yet lost a comparison. Initially, $|W| = n$. The algorithm does not terminate until the maximum element is the only element that has not lost a comparison.

A pair of elements from $L[0:n − 1]$ must first be read before they can be compared. Since the algorithm is being implemented on an EREW PRAM, no element can be read by more than one processor concurrently. Thus, during any single parallel comparison step, each element of the list is compared to at most one other element. It follows that after the first parallel comparison step, at least half the elements belong to W, so that $|W| \geq n/2$.

During the second parallel comparison step, for each comparison involving an element in W and an element not in W, the adversary arranges that the element from W wins. The adversary achieves this by replacing input list L with L', where L' is obtained from L by decreasing (if necessary) each element of L that lies in W so that (1) the relative order of the elements in W is preserved and (2) each element of W is strictly smaller than any element not in W. It follows that W can be reduced by at most half, so that $|W| \geq n/4$.

In general, using a similar adversary strategy, W is reduced by at most half after each parallel comparison is performed. A simple induction argument shows that $|W| \geq n/2^k$ after the first k parallel comparisons have been performed. Because the algorithm does not terminate before $W = 1$, it follows that the algorithm performs at least $\lceil \log_2 n \rceil$ comparisons. ■

Proposition 25.4.2 The worst-case complexity of the problem of finding the minimum value of an element in a list of size n, using a comparison-based algorithm on the EREW PRAM with an unlimited number of processors, is $\lceil \log_2 n \rceil$. Further, the same problem on the EREW PRAM using $\lceil n/2 \rceil$ processors also has complexity $\lceil \log_2 n \rceil$.

PROOF

The algorithm *MinPRAM* discussed in Chapter 15, suitably modified to handle input lists of any size n (not necessarily a power of two), has complexity $\lceil \log_2 n \rceil$ on the EREW PRAM using $\lceil n/2 \rceil$ processors. By Proposition 25.4.1, any algorithm for solving the problem on the EREW PRAM performs at least $\lceil \log_2 n \rceil$ parallel comparisons, no matter how many processors are used. Hence, the complexities of the problem of finding the minimum value in a list on an EREW PRAM using an unlimited number of processors, or using $\lceil n/2 \rceil$ processors, are both equal to $\lceil \log_2 n \rceil$. ■

25.4.2 Lower Bound for Comparison-Based Sorting on the EREW PRAM

Clearly, any lower bound for the worst-case complexity of the problem of finding the minimum element in a list is also a lower bound for the worst-case complexity of the problem of sorting a list. Hence, by Proposition 25.4.1, a lower bound for the worst-case complexity of the problem of comparison-based sorting of a list of size n on an EREW PRAM having an unlimited number of processors is $\lceil \log_2 n \rceil$. The $\lceil \log_2 n \rceil$ lower bound is order optimal because the algorithm *SortPRAM* (see Chapter 15) for sorting a list of size n on the EREW PRAM with $n(n - 1)/2$ processors has worst-case complexity $O(\log n)$. In fact, the $\lceil \log_2 n \rceil$ lower bound is order optimal even for the EREW PRAM with a linear number of processors because $O(\log n)$ algorithms for this model have been found.

25.4.3 Lower Bound for Finding the Minimum on the CRCW PRAM

Recall that algorithm *MinCRCW* finds the minimum element in a list using only a single parallel comparison step (see Chapter 15). Clearly, *MaxCRCW* is an optimal algorithm. However, because it uses $\Theta(n^2)$ processors, *MinCRCW* has cost $\Theta(n^2)$, which is far from the optimal cost of $\Theta(n)$. We now consider the problem of finding the maximum value of an element in a list on a CRCW PRAM using only n processors. We will obtain a worst-case complexity lower bound of $\Theta(\log(\log n))$ for the problem. This lower bound is sharp because there exists an algorithm *MinCRCW2* for finding the minimum element in a list of size n on a CRCW PRAM that has worst-case complexity $\Theta(\log(\log n))$; the design of *MaxCRCW2* is explored in the exercises.

Proposition 25.4.3 The worst-case complexity of the problem of finding the minimum element in a list of size n using a comparison-based algorithm on a CRCW PRAM with n processors is $\Theta(\log(\log n))$.

PROOF

The existence of the algorithm *MinCRCW2* establishes $O(\log(\log n))$ as an upper bound for the problem. To establish $\Omega(\log(\log n))$ as a lower bound to the problem, we employ the following graph theoretic result of Turan on the size of the largest independent set of vertices, where an *independent set of vertices* is a set of vertices with no edges between them. ∎

Theorem 25.4.4 The size $\beta(G)$ of the largest independent set of vertices in a graph $G = (V,E)$ satisfies

$$\beta(G) \geq |V|^2/(2|E| + |V|). \tag{25.4.2}$$

We use an adversary strategy to establish the lower bound for the problem, where we make the same assumptions as in the proof of Proposition 25.4.1. We let W_i denote the set of elements in $L[0{:}n-1]$ that have won every comparison after the ith parallel comparison step has been performed. We obtain a recurrence relation for $t(i) = |W_i|$ as follows. Initially, W_0 consists of all the elements in $L[0{:}n-1]$, so that $t(0) = n$. Since the minimum is determined only if $|W_i| = 1$, any parallel algorithm for solving the problem cannot terminate until $|W_i| = 1$. As in the proof of Proposition 25.4.1, at any step i, the adversary can arrange that all the elements in W_i are smaller than any element not in W_i. Therefore, an element from W_i can lose a comparison during the $(i + 1)^{\text{st}}$ parallel comparison step only if it is compared to another element from W_i. Consider the graph G_i having vertex set $V(G_i) = W_i$, whose edge set $E(G_i)$ consists of all pairs $\{u,v\}$ such that $u,v \in W_i$ and u and v are compared in the $(i + 1)^{\text{st}}$ parallel comparison step. Because only n processors are available, we have $|E(G_i)| \leq n$.

Now consider an independent set of vertices U_i of maximum size in G_i. Since U_i is an independent set, no pair of vertices in U_i is involved in a comparison during the $(i + 1)^{\text{st}}$ comparison step. Thus, by appropriately altering L so that all the elements of L in U_i are strictly smaller than any element not in U_i, the adversary arranges that all the elements in U_i win their comparisons in the $(i + 1)^{\text{st}}$ parallel comparison step, so that $|W_{i+1}| \geq |U_i|$. Using Formula (25.4.2), $|U_i| \geq |W_i|^2/(2n + |W_i|)$, so that $t(i) = |W_i|$ satisfies the recurrence relation

$$t(i + 1) \geq \frac{(t(i))^2}{2n + t(i)}, \text{ init. cond. } t(0) = n. \tag{25.4.3}$$

It follows from the definition of $t(i)$ that $t(i) \leq n$ for all i, so that

$$t(i + 1) \geq \frac{(t(i))^2}{3n}, \text{ init. cond. } t(0) = n. \qquad \textbf{(25.4.4)}$$

Iterating the inequality (25.4.4) yields

$$t(i) \geq \left(\frac{1}{3}\right)^{2^i} 3n. \qquad \textbf{(25.4.5)}$$

Because the algorithm cannot terminate before $t(i) = |W_i| = 1$, it follows from Formula (25.4.5) that in the worst case, the algorithm must perform $W(n) \geq i$ iterations, where i is large enough so that $(1/3)^{2^i} 3n \leq 1$. The latter inequality holds only if $n \leq 3^{2^i - 1}$, which implies that

$$W(n) \geq i \geq \log_2(1 + \log_3 n) \in \Omega(\log(\log n)). \qquad \textbf{(25.4.6)} \quad ■$$

25.5 Closing Remarks

In this chapter, we have only given a small sampling of the problems for which lower bounds have been successfully determined. However, lower-bound theory is a difficult subject in general, and we know relatively few instances of precise, or order-precise, lower bounds. Indeed, the most important problem in theoretical computer science today is to settle the lower-bound question for the wide class of problems known as the *NP-complete* problems. For example, the decision versions of many of the interesting problems in graph theory belong to this class (graph coloring, independent set, Hamiltonian paths, and so forth). The only known algorithms for solving these problems have super-polynomial complexity in the worst case. On the other hand, the only lower bounds known for the worst-case complexity of these problems are typically polynomial with relatively small degree. Thus, the gap between lower bounds and upper bounds for these problems is large indeed. Most computer scientists believe that NP-complete problems are truly computationally difficult in the worst case. In other words, they believe that worst-case lower bounds for these problems are actually super-polynomial in nature. However, reducing the upper bounds for worst-case complexity by finding an appropriate algorithm, or raising the lower bound through some mathematical argument, remains elusive in spite of years of effort by some of the best theoreticians in the field. We discuss these matters in more detail in Chapter 26.

References and Suggestions for Further Reading

Three books on computational complexity that contain discussions of lower-bound theory are:

Du, D. and K. Ko *Theory of Computational Complexity*, New York: Wiley-Interscience, 2000.

Sipser M., *Introduction to the Theory of Computation*, Boston, MA: PWS Publishing Company, 1997.

Papadimitriou, C.H., *Computational Complexity*, Reading, MA: Addison-Wesley, 1993.

EXERCISES

Section 25.1 Basic Terminology and Techniques

25.1   A sloppy chef has given a waiter a stack of pancakes of all different sizes. Before presenting the plate to the customer, the waiter wishes to re-arrange the pancakes in order of their size, with the largest on the bottom. He begins by selecting a pile of pancakes on the top of the stack and simply flips the pile over. He then keeps repeating this pancake-flipping operation until the pancakes are sorted.

    a. Show by induction that there always exists a set of flips that sorts any given stack of pancakes.

    b. Describe a pancake-flipping algorithm that performs at most $2n - 2$ flips in the worst case for n pancakes.

    c. Show that any pancake-flipping algorithm must perform at least $n - 1$ flips in the worst case for n pancakes.

    d. Suppose now that the pancakes have a burned side, and the waiter wishes to have the pancakes stacked in order with the unburned side up. Redo parts (a), (b), and (c) for this new problem.

25.2   Obtain and verify a lower bound for the worst-case complexity of adjacent-key comparison sorting restricted to lists in which every element is within k of its correct position in the list.

25.3   We have seen in Chapter 3 that *InsertionSort* has optimal worst-case complexity for adjacent key comparison sorts. Is it also optimal when the lists are restricted, as in the previous exercise?

Section 25.2 Decision Trees and Comparison Trees

25.4   Prove the correctness of *BinarySearch2*.

25.5   Show that the comparison tree for *BinarySearch2* for a list of size n is a 2-tree with $2n$ leaf nodes, which is full at the second-deepest level.

25.6   a. Design an algorithm *TernarySearch* that is analogous to *BinarySearch* but is based on dividing the list into three sublists instead of two.

   b. Draw the comparison tree for *TernarySearch* for a list of size 25.

   c. Does *TernarySearch* have order-optimal worst-case complexity?

   d. Does *TernarySearch* have order-optimal average complexity?

25.7   Repeat Exercise 25.5 for the analog *TernarySearch2* of *BinarySearch2*.

25.8   Construct an example of a comparison-based algorithm for searching an arbitrary list $L[0:n - 1]$ such that an index in L can occur more than once as an output leaf of the associated comparison tree.

25.9   Suppose $L[0:n - 1]$ is a sorted list of integers. Exercise 2.26 (see Chapter 2) asked for an algorithm that finds an index i such that $L[i] = i$, or returns -1 if no such index exists. Show that a lower bound for the complexity of any algorithm for solving this problem is $\Omega(\log n)$.

25.10   Stirling's approximation formula for $n!$ states that

$$n! \sim \sqrt{2\pi n}(n/e)^n e^{1/(12n)}.$$

Using this formula show that

$$\lceil \log_2 n! \rceil = n\log_2 n - \frac{n}{\ln 2} + \left(\frac{1}{2}\right)\log_2 n + O(1).$$

25.11   Given a list of integers $L[0:n - 1]$, where adjacent elements in the list differ by at most 1 and $L[0] < L[n - 1]$, do the following:

   a. Design and analyze an algorithm that finds an index j such that $L[j] = X$ for a given search element X, where $L[0] \leq X \leq L[n - 1]$.

   b. Determine the lower bound for the worst-case complexity of the problem in part (a). Is your algorithm in part (a) optimal?

Sections 25.3 Adversary Arguments

25.12 Complete the proof of Proposition 25.3.2 by showing that if the algorithm makes at most $n - 3$ comparisons between elements that are not the largest element $L[i]$ and second-largest element $L[j]$, then there exists an element different from both $L[i]$ and $L[j]$ that never lost a comparison other than with $L[i]$.

25.13 Give pseudocode for the tournament-based algorithm described in Section 25.3.2 for finding the largest and second-largest element in a list.

25.14 Extend Theorem 25.3.6 to the case in which n is even.

25.15 Show that *Merge* is an optimal sequential algorithm in the worst case for merging two ordered sublists of size $n/2$.

Section 25.4 Lower Bounds for Parallel Algorithms

25.16 Design a parallel algorithm *MinCRCW2* for finding the minimum element in a list of size n on a CRCW PRAM with n processors that has worst-case complexity belonging to $\Theta(\log(\log n))$. (*Hint:* First make $n/2$ comparisons so that $n/2$ winners are determined. Then in successive iterations, divide up the winners into appropriately sized groups and use *MinCRCW* on these groups.)

CHAPTER 26

NP-COMPLETE PROBLEMS

It is a curious phenomenon that the worst-case complexities of known sequential algorithms for most of the commonly encountered problems in computer science fall into the following two categories:

1. Bounded above by low degree polynomials.
2. Bounded below by super-polynomial functions. (A function f is *super-polynomial* if $f \in \Omega(n^k)$ for *all* integers $k \geq 1$.)

Problems in graph theory illustrate this situation well. For example, we have seen $O(n^2)$ and $O(n^3)$ algorithms, respectively, for the problems of finding minimum-cost spanning trees and finding the shortest paths between every pair of vertices in weighted graphs, whereas the best-known algorithms for the Hamiltonian cycle problem and the graph-coloring problem have super-polynomial complexity. On the other hand, no one has been able to show that super-polynomial lower bounds for these problems exist. Problems such as the Hamiltonian cycle and graph-coloring problems (or more precisely, their decision versions, as defined in the next section) belong to a large class of fundamental decision problems called *NP-complete problems*. It turns out that if any NP-complete problem is solvable by a polynomial (time) algorithm, then they all are so solvable. It has long been conjectured that no polynomial algorithm exists for any of the NP-complete problems. This conjecture is arguably the most important open question in theoretical computer science.

In this chapter, we give a brief introduction to the class of NP-complete problems. Our treatment is somewhat intuitive and informal. In particular, we do not establish the formal machinery necessary to prove the famous result of Cook that NP-complete problems exist; rather, we refer the interested student to the references for a completely rigorous treatment.

We also expand our earlier discussion of the class NC and introduce the notion of P-completeness. P-completeness can be viewed as the analog for parallel computation of NP-completeness for sequential computation.

26.1 The Classes P and NP

We consider a problem to be *tractable* if it can be solved by a worst-case polynomial (time) algorithm. Problems having super-polynomial worst-case complexity are considered *intractable*. Throughout this chapter, when we use the term *computing time* (or *complexity*) we always mean the worst-case computing time (complexity).

Super-polynomial algorithms are computationally infeasible to implement in the worst case. Even though we have called a problem tractable if it can be solved by a polynomial algorithm, such an algorithm may still be computationally infeasible if it has complexity $\Omega(n^k)$ where k is large. For example, an algorithm having complexity n^{64} will not finish in our lifetime even for $n = 2$. Nevertheless, it is standard in the theory of algorithms to regard problems solved by polynomial algorithms as tractable, and it becomes important to identify those problems. Besides, if a polynomial algorithm has been shown to exist for a problem (even one of high degree), then there may be hope that a more practical polynomial algorithm of relatively small degree can be found for the problem.

In the theory of complexity, it is convenient and useful to restrict attention to decision problems—that is, problems whose solutions simply output "yes" or "no" (0 or 1). Let P denote the class of decision problems that are solvable by algorithms having polynomial (worst-case) complexity.

26.1.1 Input Size

When considering membership in P, we must be very careful about how input size is measured (recall our discussion of primality testing in Chapter 24). For example, when considering a decision problem having input parameters that are numeric quantities, the size of these numeric quantities is taken into account when measuring input size. We usually use the number of digits in the binary representation of the sum of the appropriate sizes of these numeric quantities. For example, consider an input $(w_0, w_1, \dots, w_{n-1})$, $(v_0, v_1, \dots, v_{n-1})$ and C to the

0/1 knapsack problem. If we let $m = \sum_{i=0}^{n-1}(w_i + v_i)$ and d denote the number of digits of m, then the size of this input is $n + d \in \Theta(n + \log m)$.

26.1.2 Optimization Problems and Their Decision Versions

Decision problems occur naturally in many contexts. For example, an important decision problem in graph theory is to determine whether a clique of size k occurs in a given input graph. In mathematical logic, a fundamental decision problem is whether the Boolean variables in a given Boolean formula can be assigned truth values that make the entire formula true. In addition to such decision problems that are of interest in their own right, optimization problems usually give rise to associated decision problems. Moreover, restricting attention to the decision version of an optimization problem sometimes can be done without loss of generality (up to polynomial factors). In other words, the decision version of an optimization problem may have the property that a polynomial solution to the optimization problem exists if and only if a polynomial solution to the associated decision problem exists (the "only if" part is always true).

To illustrate, consider the optimization problem of determining the chromatic number $\chi = \chi(G)$ of a graph G on n vertices—that is, finding the minimum number of colors necessary to properly color the vertices of a graph G such that no two adjacent vertices get the same color. Given an integer k, the associated decision problem asks whether a proper k-coloring of G exists. Clearly, a solution to the optimization problem immediately implies a solution to the decision problem: A proper k-coloring exists if and only if $k \geq \chi(G)$. On the other hand, a polynomial solution to the decision problem also implies a polynomial solution to the original problem: Simply call the decision problem for $k = 1, 2, \ldots$ until a "yes" is returned (which will happen after at most n calls).

As another example, consider the 0/1 knapsack problem with input weights $w_0, w_1, \ldots, w_{n-1}$, values $v_0, v_1, \ldots, v_{n-1}$, and capacity C. The decision version of this problem adds an integer input parameter k and asks whether a collection of the objects can be placed in the knapsack whose total value is at least k. Here again, it is obvious that the ordinary version of the 0/1 knapsack problem yields a solution of the decision version with no extra work. However, in the case of noninteger (rational) weights and values, there is no obvious polynomial number of decision problems whose answers yield the optimal solution to the 0/1 knapsack problem. The situation improves if we restrict attention to the case of *integer* weights and values. Then each possible solution has an integer value, with the largest possible value equal to $m = v_0 + v_1 + \ldots + v_{n-1}$. Unlike the graph-coloring problem, we cannot simply call the decision problem for $k = m, m - 1, \ldots$ until a "yes" is returned, since this will take an exponential number (with respect to input size) of calls in general. However, using a binary search strategy, by making $\log_2 m$ calls to the decision problem for suitable values of k, we can determine the optimal solution in polynomial time (see Exercise 26.1).

R E M A R K

It is not known in general whether a polynomial solution to the 0/1 knapsack decision problem implies a polynomial solution to the 0/1 knapsack optimization problem.

26.1.3 The Class NP

The class NP (nondeterministic polynomial) consists of decision problems for which yes instances can be solved in polynomial time by a nondeterministic algorithm. Formal treatments of the class NP and nondeterministic algorithms are usually given in terms of Turing machines and formal languages. We proceed less formally and base our discussion on the intuitive notion of "guessing and verifying." In this context, we give the following high-level pseudocode for a generic nondeterministic polynomial algorithm *NPAlgorithm*. Step 1 in *NPAlgorithm* is the nondeterministic step, and step 2 is the deterministic step.

```
function NPAlgorithm(A, I)
Input:    A (a decision problem), I (an instance of problem A)
Output:   "yes" or "don't know"
          1. In polynomial time, guess a candidate certificate C for the problem A.
          2. In polynomial time, use C to deterministically verify that I is a yes instance.
             if a yes instance is verified in step 2 then
                 return ("yes")
             else
                 return("don't know")
             endif
end NPAlgorithm
```

NPAlgorithm is considered correct if, whenever *I* is a yes instance, then a certificate can be produced in step 1 (by "perfect" guessing) that verifies that *I* is a yes instance, whereas if *I* is a no instance, then "don't know" is always returned. Be careful to note that a given running of *NPAlgorithm* might return "don't know" even on a yes instance. The correctness requirement says that if *I* is a yes instance, then a verification certificate *can be* produced in step 2, assuming the appropriate guess is made.

For example, if the decision problem is whether a graph can be properly colored using at most *k* colors for a given input graph *G*, a nondeterministic algorithm would simply guess a color from $\{1, 2, \dots, k\}$ for each vertex. Perfect guessing would produce a proper *k*-coloring for a graph *G* if it exists, and this coloring would then be a certificate that can be used to deterministically verify that G is a yes instance.

A decision problem is in the class NP if it can be solved by a nondeterministic algorithm. In the k-coloring problem, clearly a certificate coloring can be verified to be a proper coloring in polynomial time.

Note that $P \subseteq NP$, because if A is a polynomial algorithm for a decision problem, then a nondeterministic algorithm for the problem is obtained by guessing any succinct (that is, computable in polynomial time) certificate S for a given input I and then using A to solve the problem instance I, completely ignoring S.

26.1.4 Some Sample Problems in NP

We illustrate the definition of NP with some sample problems in NP. In each example, it is obvious that a certificate can be produced and verified for a yes instance in polynomial time. A *clique* Q of size k in a graph G is a subset of k vertices that are pair-wise adjacent.

Clique.   Given the graph $G = (V, E)$ and the integer k, does there exist a clique of size k in G?

A nondeterministic algorithm guesses a candidate solution by choosing a set of k vertices. The verification that the set of vertices is distinct and forms a clique can be done in polynomial time.

Sum of Subsets.   Given the input integers $\{a_0, a_1, \dots, a_{n-1}\}$, and the target sum C, is there a subset of the integers whose sum equals C?

The nondeterministic algorithm guesses a candidate solution by choosing a subset of the integers $\{a_{i_1}, a_{i_2}, \dots, a_{i_m}\}$. The verification that $a_{i_1} + a_{i_2} + \cdots + a_{i_m} = C$ can be done in polynomial time.

Hamiltonian Cycle.   Given the graph $G = (V, E)$, does G have a Hamiltonian cycle?

A nondeterministic algorithm guesses a Hamiltonian cycle by choosing a sequence of vertices $v_0, v_1, \dots, v_{n-1}, v_0$. Verification that the sequence of vertices is a Hamiltonian cycle can be done in polynomial time.

Showing that the problems in this section were in NP was relatively easy. However, for some problems, membership in NP is quite difficult to establish. A notable example is prime testing, which asks whether a given integer n is prime. Note that a yes instance means that the answer is no to the question of whether n has factors, and the nonexistence of factors has no obvious certificate. However, it was shown by Pratt that a succinct certificate can be produced by a nondeterministic algorithm that can be verified in polynomial time (see Exercise 26.2). In 2002, it was shown that primality testing is actually in P.

The question of whether P = NP can be viewed as asking whether adding nondeterminism allows us to solve a class of problems in polynomial time that may not otherwise be solvable in polynomial time. It seems reasonable that adding the luxury of making good guesses should really help, and most computer scientists believe that P ≠ NP. For example, the question of whether or not a search element occurs in a list of size n can be solved in constant time by a nondeterministic algorithm, whereas any deterministic algorithm solving this problem has linear worst-case complexity. Reinforcement of the belief that P ≠ NP can be found in the fact that there are thousands of varied problems in NP that have resisted all attempts to find polynomial solutions.

26.2 Reducibility

One reason that polynomial complexity is such a convenient measure is that polynomials have nice closure properties. For example, the composition $f(x) = g(h(x))$ of two polynomials g and h is yet another polynomial; in other words, a polynomial of a polynomial is a polynomial. Another example is the property that the sum (or difference or product) of a polynomial and a polynomial is a polynomial. These closure properties of polynomials allow a convenient description of when a given decision problem A is not harder to solve than another decision problem B; namely, the solution to B should yield the solution to A with at most a polynomial factor of additional work. We make this precise in the following definition.

DEFINITION 26.2.1 Given two decision problems A and B, we say that A is polynomially *reducible* to B, denoted $A \propto B$, if there is a mapping f from the inputs to problem A to the inputs to problem B, such that the following conditions apply:

1. The mapping f can be computed in polynomial time (that is, a polynomial algorithm exists that, for input I to problem A, outputs the input $f(I)$ to problem B).
2. The answer to a given input I to problem A is yes if, and only if, the answer to the input $f(I)$ to problem B is yes.

In particular, condition (1) of Definition 26.2.1 implies that there exists a polynomial $p(n)$ such that $|f(I)| \in O(p(|I|))$, for any input I to algorithm A, where $|I|$ denotes the size of I.

The following two propositions are easy consequences of the closure properties of polynomials.

Proposition 26.2.1 The relation $\propto$ is transitive; that is, if $A \propto B$ and $B \propto C$ then $A \propto C$. □

Proposition 26.2.2 If $A \propto B$ and B has polynomial complexity, then so does A. □

We now illustrate the notion of reducibility by several examples. Further examples are given in Section 26.4.

Example 26.2.1: Hamiltonian Cycles $\propto$ Traveling Salesman. Given the graph $G = (V, E)$, $|V| = n$, define the following weighting w on K_n on the complete graph on n vertices: $w(e) = 1$ if $e \in E$; otherwise, $w(e) = 2$. Clearly, w can be computed in polynomial time. We now map G to the instance $f(G) = (K_n, w, k = n)$ of Traveling Salesman (so that $p(n) = n^2$). Thus, G has a Hamiltonian cycle if and only if K_n with weighting w has a tour of cost no more than n.

Example 26.2.2: Clique $\propto$ Vertex Cover $\propto$ Independent Set $\propto$ Clique. A *vertex cover* C in a graph G is a set of vertices with the property that every edge in G is incident to at least one vertex in C. The vertex cover problem asks whether a graph G has a vertex cover of size k. An *independent set* of vertices in a graph G is a set of vertices no two of which are adjacent. The independent set problem asks whether a graph G has a vertex cover of size k. Since the relation $\propto$ is transitive, Example 26.2.2 says that the three problems, clique, vertex cover, and independent set, are each polynomially reducible to one another. Given the graph $G = (V, E)$, recall that the complement $\overline{G} = (V, \overline{E})$ is the graph with the same vertex set V, such that $e \in \overline{E}$ if and only if $e \notin E$. Given G, clearly the complement $\overline{G}$ can be computed in polynomial time. The polynomial reductions are consequences of the following proposition, whose proof is left as an exercise.

Proposition 26.2.3 Given the graph $G = (V, E)$, then the following three conditions are mutually equivalent conditions on a subset of vertices $U \subseteq V$.

1. U is a clique.
2. U is an independent set of vertices in the complement $\overline{G} = (V, \overline{E})$.
3. The set $V - U$ is a vertex cover in the complement $\overline{G} = (V, \overline{E})$. □

The reducibility illustrated in the previous examples was easy to show and not very surprising because the problems involved were highly related. In Section 26.4, we give examples of disparate problems A and B where $A \propto B$.

The following definition makes precise the notion of two problems being polynomially equivalent to one another.

DEFINITION 26.2.2 Two decision problems A and B are *polynomially equivalent* to one another if $A \propto B$ and $B \propto A$.

Since the relation $\propto$ is clearly reflexive, it follows from Proposition 26.2.1 that the relation of polynomial equivalence is an equivalence relation on the set of decision problems.

26.3 NP-Complete Problems: Cook's Theorem

S. A. Cook raised a fundamental question: Is there a problem in NP that is as hard (up to polynomial factors) as every other problem in NP? In other words, is there a problem C in NP such that if A is *any* problem in NP, then $A \propto C$? If such a problem exists, then it is called *NP-complete*. (Note that all NP-complete problems are automatically polynomially equivalent to one another.) In one of the most celebrated results in theoretical computer science, Cook showed in 1971 that the satisfiability problem for Boolean expressions (as defined presently) is NP-complete. About the same time, Levin showed that a certain tiling problem was NP-complete. The following proposition follows easily from the transitivity of the relation $\propto$.

Proposition 26.3.1 Suppose A is in NP, and B is NP-complete. If $B \propto A$, then A is NP-complete. □

In the time since Cook's result appeared, hundreds of NP-complete problems have been identified. Despite considerable effort, no polynomial algorithm has been found for any NP-complete problem. This lack of success reinforces the belief that P $\neq$ NP. The following corollary of Proposition 26.3.1 shows that it is unlikely that a polynomial algorithm for any NP-complete problem will ever be found.

Corollary 26.3.2 If any NP-complete problem A also belongs to P, then P $=$ NP. □

A problem A (not necessarily a decision problem) is *NP-hard* if it is as hard to solve as any problem in NP. More precisely, A is NP-hard if a polynomial-time solution for A would imply P = NP. For example, if the decision version of an optimization problem is NP-complete, then the optimization problem itself is NP-hard. Note that the NP-complete problems are precisely those problems in NP that are NP-hard.

To describe Cook's result, we need to recall some terms from first-order logic (see also Exercise 10.23 in Chapter 10). As with our pseudocode conventions, a Boolean (logical) variable is a variable that can only take on two values, true (T) or false (F). Given a Boolean variable x, we denote by $\bar{x}$ the variable that has the value T if and only if x has the value F. Boolean variables can be combined using logical operators *and* (denoted by $\wedge$ and called *conjunction*), *or* (denoted by $\vee$ and called *disjunction*), *not* (denoted by $\neg$ and called *negation*), and parenthesization, to form Boolean expressions (formulas). A *literal* in a Boolean formula is of the form x or $\bar{x}$, where x is a Boolean variable. Note that $\neg x$ has the same truth value as $\bar{x}$. A Boolean formula is said to be in *conjunctive normal form* (CNF) if it has the form $C_1 \wedge C_2 \wedge \cdots \wedge C_m$, where each clause C_i is a disjunction of $n(i)$ literals, $i = 1, \ldots, m$.

A Boolean formula is called *satisfiable* if there is an assignment of truth values to the literals occurring in the formula that makes the formula evaluate to true. For example, the CNF formula

$$(x_2 \vee \bar{x}_3) \wedge (x_1 \vee \bar{x}_2) \wedge (x_1 \vee x_3) \wedge (\bar{x}_1 \vee x_3)$$

is satisfiable (by setting $x_1 = x_2 = x_3 = T$), whereas the CNF formula

$$(x_2 \vee x_3) \wedge (\bar{x}_1 \vee \bar{x}_2) \wedge (x_1 \vee \bar{x}_2) \wedge (x_1 \vee \bar{x}_3) \wedge (\bar{x}_1 \vee x_2 \vee \bar{x}_3)$$

is not satisfiable.

The *CNF satisfiability* problem (CNF SAT) is the problem of determining whether a given CNF formula is satisfiable. CNF SAT is a fundamental problem in mathematical logic and computer science, with numerous applications.

The input size of a CNF formula can be defined as the total number of literals (counting repetitions) occurring in the formula. Clearly, CNF SAT $\in$ NP, because a linear scan of the formula determines whether a candidate assignment to the literals occurring in the formula results in the formula evaluating to true. CNF SAT was the first example shown to be NP-complete.

Theorem 26.3.3 **COOK'S THEOREM**
CNF SAT is NP-complete. □

Given any decision problem A in NP, there is a nondeterministic algorithm that produces a candidate solution for A that can be checked in polynomial time. Cook proved Theorem 26.3.3 by constructing a CNF formula that, roughly speaking, modeled the action of the nondeterministic algorithm. The length of the formula constructed by Cook is polynomial in the size of an instance I of A and is satisfiable if and only if the problem A is true for I.

26.4 Some Sample NP-Complete Problems

As soon as it was established that CNF SAT is NP-complete, the door was opened to show that a host of other NP-complete problems exist. Proposition 26.3.1 gives a recipe for proving that a problem A is NP-complete, which we state as a key fact.

> **Key Fact**
>
> **Two steps are required to show that a problem A is NP complete:**
> 1. **Show that A is in NP.**
> 2. **Find any NP-complete problem B such that B $\propto$ A.**

Condition 1 is usually easy to show, so that condition 2 becomes the issue. However, as we have already seen, there are cases where condition 1 is difficult to verify.

Thousands of classical and practical problems have been shown to be NP-complete. If we are working on a problem that we think might be NP-complete, we can check the vast list of NP-complete problems for one that might resemble our problem. The following subsections provide a short sample list of NP-complete problems. We have already shown that the clique problem and the sum of subsets problems are in NP. For each of the other examples, we leave it as an exercise to show the problem is in NP. For each of the sample problems in this section, we give a reduction that shows the problem is NP-complete.

Example 26.4.1: 3-CNF SAT. An instance of the 3-CNF SAT problem is a CNF Boolean formula in which every clause contains *exactly* three literals. Because general CNF SAT is in NP, 3-CNF SAT is also in NP. Surprisingly, 3-CNF SAT is NP-complete, even though 2-CNF SAT (in which each clause consists of two literals) is in P (see Exercise 26.9).

We show that CNF SAT $\propto$ 3-CNF SAT by showing how any CNF formula $I = C_1 \wedge C_2 \wedge \cdots \wedge C_m$ can be mapped onto a 3-CNF formula $f(I)$ with no more than $12\,|I|$ literals, such that I is satisfiable if and only if $f(I)$ is satisfiable. More precisely, we construct $f(I)$ by replacing each clause $C_i = i = 1, \ldots, m$, by conjunctions of three-literal clauses according to the following three cases.

1. C_i has exactly three literals.
2. C_i has more than three literals.
3. C_i has less than three literals.

In case 1, we leave C_i unaltered. In case 2, suppose C_i contains $k > 3$ literals $x_1, x_2, \ldots, x_k$, so that $C_i = x_1 \vee x_2 \vee \cdots \vee x_k$. We then replace C_i by the $k - 2$ clauses

$$(x_1 \vee x_2 \vee y_1) \wedge (\bar{y}_1 \vee x_3 \vee y_2) \wedge (\bar{y}_2 \vee x_4 \vee y_3) \wedge \cdots$$
$$\wedge (\bar{y}_{k-3} \vee x_{k-1} \vee x_k),$$

where $y_1, y_2, \ldots, y_{k-3}$ are new Boolean variables. We leave it as an exercise to show that C_i is satisfiable if, and only if, the conjunction of the $k - 2$ clauses replacing C_i is satisfiable.

Now consider case 3. If C_i consists of a single literal x, then we can replace x by $(x \vee y \vee z) \wedge (x \vee y \vee \bar{z}) \wedge (x \vee \bar{y} \vee z) \wedge (x \vee \bar{y} \vee \bar{z})$, where y and z are new Boolean variables. If C_i consists of the two-literal clause $x_1 \vee x_2$, then we replace C_i by $(x_1 \vee x_2 \vee y) \wedge (x_1 \vee x_2 \vee \bar{y})$, where y is a new Boolean variable. In both cases, it follows easily that C_i is satisfiable if and only if the conjunction of the clauses replacing it is satisfiable.

Example 26.4.2: Clique. This example establishes a connection between Boolean formulas and graph theoretic problems, thereby extending the realm of NP-complete problems into the latter domain. We show that CNF SAT $\propto$ Clique. Consider any CNF formula $I = C_1 \wedge C_2 \wedge \cdots \wedge C_m$. Writing clause C_i as $y_1 \vee \cdots \vee y_j \vee \overline{y_{j+1}} \vee \cdots \vee \overline{y_k}$ (the j and k depend on i), where $y_1, \ldots, y_j \in \{x_1, \ldots, x_n\}$ and $\overline{y_{j+1}}, \ldots, \overline{y_k} \in \{\bar{x}_1, \ldots, \bar{x}_n\}$, let $V_i = \{(y_1, i), \ldots, (y_j, i), (\overline{y_{j+1}}, i), \ldots, (\overline{y_k}, i)\}$, $i = 1, \ldots, m$. We map I to the graph $G = f(I)$ as follows. The vertex set V of G is the union of the V_i's, $i = 1, \ldots m$. We define two vertices (a, i) and (b, j) to be adjacent if and only if $i \neq j$ and the literal a is not the negative of the literal b. For example, if $(x_1, 3)$, $(x_5, 7)$, $(\bar{x}_8, 2)$, $(x_2, 4)$, $(\bar{x}_3, 1)$, $(\bar{x}_8, 1)$, $(x_6, 2)$, and $(\bar{x}_6, 5)$ are vertices of G, then $\{(x_1, 3), (x_5, 7)\}$ and $\{(\bar{x}_8, 2), (x_2, 4)\}$ are edges of G but $\{(\bar{x}_3, 1), (\bar{x}_8, 1)\}$ and $\{(x_6, 2), (\bar{x}_6, 5)\}$ are not. Note that G can be constructed in polynomial time.

CLAIM

I is satisfiable if and only if G has a clique of size m.

PROOF

Suppose that G has a clique W of size m. By definition of adjacency in G, it follows that, for each clause C_i in I, there is exactly one vertex in W of the form (a, i). If a is the positive literal x_q, then assign x_q the value T. If a is the negative literal $\overline{x_q}$, then assign $\overline{x_q}$ the value T (that is, x_q is F). These assignments are well defined because, by definition of adjacency in G, none of the literals (in the second component) of a vertex is the negative of another. Moreover, these assignments make each of the clauses C_i evaluate to T, so that I evaluates as true.

Now suppose that I is satisfiable. Let $Z = \{z_1, \ldots, z_n\}$ denote the n literals from $\{x_1, \ldots, x_n\} \cup \{\overline{x_1}, \ldots, \overline{x_n}\}$ that have the value T. Since each clause C_i must have the value T, $i = 1, \ldots, m$, C_i contains at least one literal z_i from Z. However, by the definition of G, (z_i, i) is a vertex of G. Further, the set of vertices $\{(z_i, i) \mid i \in \{1, \ldots, m\}\}$ forms a clique of size m. ■

Example 26.4.3: Vertex Cover and Independent Set. That these problems are both NP-complete follows from Example 26.4.2 and Proposition 26.2.3.

Example 26.4.4: Three-Dimensional Matching. Recall that the perfect-matching problem in a bipartite graph interprets the classical marriage problem, which asks whether marriages can be arranged between a set of n boys and a set of n girls so that each boy marries a girl that he knows, and no girl marries more than one boy. The three-dimensional matching problem generalizes the marriage problem by adding n houses to the mix. Not only do we want to arrange marriages, but we also wish to match each married couple with a house from a specified subcollection of the houses available to the couple, and we want to ensure that no two couples share the same house. Adding houses turns a problem solved by an $O(n^3)$ algorithm into an NP-complete problem.

More formally, given three sets H, B, and G (houses, boys, and girls, respectively), each having the same cardinality $|H|$, and a subset $M \subseteq H \times B \times G$, the three-dimensional matching problem asks whether there is a subset (matching) $M' \subseteq M$ of cardinality $|M'| = |H|$ such that none of the triples in M' agree in any coordinate. We refer to the triples in M' as *households*. The three-dimensional matching problem is in NP because a nondeterministic algorithm guesses a set of $|H|$ triples, and the verification that no two triples agree in any coordinate can be done in polynomial time. We now show that the three-dimensional matching problem is NP-complete by showing that CNF SAT reduces to it.

Suppose $I = C_1 \wedge C_2 \wedge \cdots \wedge C_m$ is any instance of CNF SAT, and suppose I contains the Boolean variables $x_1, x_2, \ldots, x_n$. We will construct an instance of the three-dimensional matching problem $H, B, G, M \subseteq H \times B \times G$, where $|H| = |B| = |G| = 2mn$, such that a matching $M' \subseteq M$ exists if and only if I is satisfiable. H consists of m copies of the literals $\{x_1, x_2, \ldots, x_n\}$, $\{\bar{x}_1, \bar{x}_2, \ldots, \bar{x}_n\}$. We use subscripts and superscripts to denote the elements in H, where subscripts reference literals, and superscripts reference clauses in I; that is

$$H = \{x_i^{(j)}, \bar{x}_i^{(j)} \mid 1 \le i \le n, 1 \le j \le m\}.$$

We now create sets B and G of $2mn$ boys and $2mn$ girls, respectively. The sets B and G will be divided into three classes, and marriages are restricted to taking place only between boys and girls in the same class. Thus, the division of the boys and girls induces a division of M into three classes of households, which we call truth-setting, satisfaction-testing, and remaining households, respectively. As the names imply, truth-setting households force an assignment of truth values to the Boolean variables $x_1, x_2, \ldots, x_n$, whereas satisfaction-testing households determine whether this truth assignment makes the formula I true. The remaining households in M are made up of a set of additional couples created merely to occupy the remaining houses not covered by the households in the first two classes. We now describe the division of the boys and girls into three classes together with the resulting three classes of households.

Truth-Setting Households. The truth-setting households are divided into n components T_i, $i = 1, \ldots, n$, where each component holds m households. For each i, $1 \le i \le n$, we create a set of m boys and m girls

$$B_{T_i} = \{b_i^{(1)}, b_i^{(2)}, \ldots, b_i^{(m)}\}, \; G_{T_i} = \{g_i^{(1)}, g_i^{(2)}, \ldots, g_i^{(m)}\}, i = 1, \ldots, n.$$

Marriages are restricted, so that a boy in the ith component B_{T_i} must marry a girl in the ith component G_{T_i}. The marriages are further restricted within each component T_i to take place between people who are adjacent when arranged in a circle, as in Figure 26.1.

FIGURE 26.1

In each component, marriages must take place between adjacent people in the given circle arrangement, as illustrated for $m = 3$.

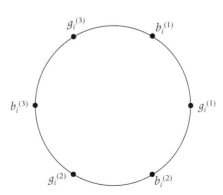

In particular, there are only two marriage schemes possible in T_i: a clockwise scheme, $\{b_i^{(1)}, g_i^{(1)}\}, \{b_i^{(2)}, g_i^{(2)}\}, \ldots, \{b_i^{(m)}, g_i^{(m)}\}$, and a counterclockwise scheme, $\{b_i^{(1)}, g_i^{(m)}\}, \{b_i^{(m)}, g_i^{(m-1)}\}, \{b_i^{(m-1)}, g_i^{(m-2)}\}, \ldots, \{b_i^{(2)}, g_i^{(1)}\}$.

In each component T_i, only one house is made available to a given couple. If girl $g_i^{(j)}$ marries boy $b_i^{(j)}$, then she must live in house $\bar{x}_i^{(j)}$. Otherwise (girl $g_i^{(j)}$ marries boy $b_i^{(j+1)}$, where we set $b_i^{(m+1)} = b_i^{(1)}$), she must live in house $x_i^{(j)}$. The housing restrictions are illustrated in Figure 26.2, which helps explain the "truth-setting" nomenclature. We see from Figure 26.2 that any matching M' must intersect the households in the ith component T_i in precisely one of two ways: Either $M' \cap T_i$ consists of the set $T_i(t)$ of shaded households, or $M' \cap T_i$ consists of the set $T_i(f)$ of unshaded households. Thus, the component T_i forces a matching M' to set a truth value for x_i, $i = 1, \ldots, n$, where $M' \cap T_i = T_i(t)$ is considered as setting x_i to T, whereas $M' \cap T_i = T_i(f)$ is considered as setting x_i to F.

In summary, the truth-setting households in M consist of n components T_i, $i = 1, \ldots, n$, where each T_i is the union of two sets of triples:

$$T_i(t) = \{(\bar{x}_i^{(j)}, b_i^{(j)}, g_i^{(j)}) \mid 1 \le i \le n, 1 \le j \le m\},$$
$$T_i(f) = \{(x_i^{(j)}, b_i^{(j+1)}, g_i^{(j)}) \mid 1 \le i \le n, 1 \le j < m\} \cup (x_i^{(m)}, b_i^{(1)}, g_i^{(m)}).$$

FIGURE 26.2

The household of T_i corresponding to $m = 3$. Any matching must intersect T_i precisely in either the shaded households $T_i(t)$ or the unshaded households $T_i(f)$.

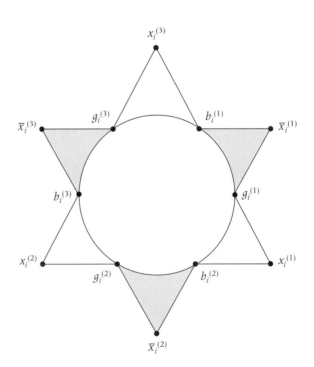

Moreover, no household in M other than T_i contains a boy $b_i^{(j)}$ or a girl $g_i^{(j)}$, $1 \leq i \leq n$, $1 \leq j \leq m$.

Satisfaction-Testing Households. We now create m boys $s_b^{(j)}$ and m girls $s_g^{(j)}$, respectively, $j = 1, \ldots, m$, and match them by prearranged marriages $\{\{s_b^{(j)}, s_g^{(j)}\} \mid j = 1, \ldots, m\}$. Moreover, the only houses available to couple $\{s_b^{(j)}, s_g^{(j)}\}$ are literals (x_i or $\bar{x}_i$) that appear in clause C_j. Thus, the satisfaction-testing households in M consist of the triples:

$$S_j = \{(x_i^{(j)}, s_b^{(j)}, s_g^{(j)}) \mid x_i \in C_j, i = 1, \ldots, n\} \bigcup \{(\bar{x}_i^{(j)}, s_b^{(j)}, s_g^{(j)}) \mid \bar{x}_i \in C_j, i = 1, \ldots, n\}.$$

No other households in M contain a boy $s_b^{(j)}$ or a girl $s_g^{(j)}$, $j = 1, \ldots, m$. Hence, any matching $M' \subseteq M$ must contain exactly one household from each S_j, $j = 1, \ldots, m$. Moreover, if the household chosen in S_j uses a house corresponding to the variable x_i, then that house must not be included in $M' \cap T_i$. In other words, we must choose a house whose truth setting for x_i as determined by M' satisfies clause C_j. *Thus, a matching $M' \subseteq M$ cannot exist unless I is satisfiable.*

Remaining Households. Any matching M' uses nm houses to accommodate the truth-setting households and m houses to accommodate the satisfaction-testing households. Thus, there are $m(n - 1)$ houses not covered by the truth-setting or satisfaction-testing households, making up a *partial-matching M'*. We create a set of $m(n - 1)$ boys $r_b^{(j)}$ and $m(n - 1)$ girls $r_g^{(j)}$, respectively, $j = 1, \ldots, m(n - 1)$, so that they can occupy the remaining $m(n - 1)$ houses not covered by such a partial-matching M' and thereby extend M' to a matching. These boys and girls are matched by prearranged marriages consisting of couples $\{\{r_b^{(j)}, r_g^{(j)}\} \mid j = 1, \ldots, m(n - 1)\}$. While these couples had no choice in their marriages, the set M places no housing restrictions on them. Thus, the remaining households R in M consist of the following triples:

$$R = \{(x_i^{(j)}, r_b^{(k)}, r_g^{(k)}) \mid i = 1, \ldots, n, j = 1, \ldots, m, k = 1, \ldots, m(n - 1)\}$$
$$\bigcup \{(\bar{x}_i^{(j)}, r_b^{(k)}, r_g^{(k)}) \mid i = 1, \ldots, n, j = 1, \ldots, m, k = 1, \ldots, m(n - 1)\}.$$

Given the instance I of CNF SAT, the set $H \times B \times G$ and the subset of households $M \subseteq H \times B \times G$ can clearly be constructed in polynomial time. We have already noted that a matching $M' \subseteq M$ cannot exist unless I is satisfiable. We complete the proof that CNF SAT $\propto$ three-dimensional matching by showing that if I is satisfiable, then a matching $M' \subseteq M$ exists. Consider a truth assignment to the variables $x_1, x_2, \ldots, x_n$ that makes I true. For each clause C_j, we choose a literal I_j occurring in C_j having the value T. Such a choice must be possible since I is assumed true with the given truth assignment. We then set

$$M' = \left(\bigcup_{x_j = T} T_i(t) \right) \cup \left(\bigcup_{x_i = T} T_i(f) \right) \cup \left(\bigcup_{j=1}^{m} \{(l_j, s_b^{(j)}, s_g^{(j)})\} \right) \cup R',$$

where R' is a suitably constructed collection of remaining households that includes all the couples $\{r_b^{(k)}, r_g^{(k)}\}$, $k = 1, \dots, m(n-1)$ and all the remaining houses not covered by the truth-setting or satisfaction-testing households in M'. We leave it as an exercise to verify that R' can be constructed and that the resulting set M' is a matching.

Example 26.4.5: 3-Exact Cover. Given a family $F = \{S_1, S_2, \dots, S_n\}$ of n subsets of $S = \{x_1, x_2, \dots, x_{3m}\}$, each of cardinality three, the *3-exact cover* problem asks if there is a subfamily $\{S_{i_1}, S_{i_2}, \dots, S_{i_m}\}$ of m subsets of F that covers S; that is, $S = \bigcup_{j=1}^{m} S_{i_j}$. The 3-exact cover problem is in NP because a nondeterministic algorithm guesses a subfamily and the verification that the subfamily covers S can be done in linear time. (We can use characteristic bit vectors of length $3m$ to represent subsets of F.)

Note that Three-Dimensional Matching $\propto$ 3-Exact Cover. In fact, Three-Dimensional Matching is actually just a special case of 3-Exact Cover where we ignore the ordering of the subsets. More precisely, we simply associate the instance $M \subseteq H \times B \times G$ of the three-dimensional matching problem with the instance $S = H \cup B \cup G$ and $F = \{\{h, b, g\} \mid (h, b, g) \in M\}$ of the 3-exact cover problem.

Example 26.4.6: Sum of Subsets. We now show that 3-Exact Cover $\propto$ Sum of Subsets. Given an instance $F = \{S_1, S_2, \dots, S_n\}$, $S = \{x_1, x_2, \dots, x_{3m}\}$ of 3-Exact Cover, as noted previously we can consider the sets in F as represented by their characteristic bit vectors of length $3m$. For example, if $m = 3$ and $S_1 = \{x_2, x_3, x_8\}$, then S_1 is represented by $(0, 1, 1, 0, 0, 0, 0, 1, 0)$. We map an instance of 3-Exact Cover to an instance of Sum of Subsets by interpreting each characteristic vector as an integer in the base-$(n + 1)$ system. Thus, for each $S_j \in F$, we associate with S_j the integer $a_{j-1} = \sum_{x_i \in S_j} (n + 1)^{i-1}$. We let C be the integer corresponding to the bit vector of all 1s; that is, $C = \sum_{i=0}^{3m-1} (n + 1)^i$. We leave it as an exercise to show that F, S is a yes instance of 3-Exact Cover if and only if $a_0, a_1, \dots, a_{n-1}$ and target sum C is a yes instance of Sum of Subsets.

Example 26.4.7: Graph Coloring. We now show that 3-CNF SAT $\propto$ Graph Coloring. Suppose $I = C_1 \wedge C_2 \wedge \cdots \wedge C_m$ is an instance of 3-CNF SAT involving the

Boolean variables $\{x_1, x_2, \ldots, x_n\}$. We can assume that $n \geq 4$, because otherwise the satisfiability of I can be checked in polynomial time. We construct an instance $G = (V, E), k = n + 1$, of Graph Coloring as follows.

$$V = \{x_1, x_2, \ldots, x_n\} \cup \{\overline{x}_1, \overline{x}_2, \ldots, \overline{x}_n\} \cup \{y_1, y_2, \ldots, y_n\} \cup \{c_1, c_2, \ldots, c_m\},$$

$$E = \{x_i \overline{x}_i | 1 \leq i \leq n\} \cup \{y_i y_j | 1 \leq i < j \leq n\} \cup \{x_i y_j | 1 \leq i \neq j \leq n\}$$
$$\cup \{\overline{x}_i y_j | 1 \leq i \neq j \leq n\} \cup \{x_i c_j | x_i \notin C_j, 1 \leq i \leq n, 1 \leq j \leq m\}$$
$$\cup \{\overline{x}_i c_j | \overline{x}_i \notin C_j, 1 \leq i \leq n, 1 \leq j \leq m\}.$$

Clearly, G can be constructed from I in polynomial time. We leave it as an exercise to show that I is satisfiable if and only if the graph G is $(n + 1)$-colorable.

26.5 The Class co-NP

Given a decision problem Π, the complementary problem $\overline{\Pi}$ is the decision problem with the same instances, but an instance I of the problem Π is true if and only if I is false for $\overline{\Pi}$. For example, suppose Π is the decision problem, "Does a graph G contain a Hamiltonian cycle?" The complementary decision problem $\overline{\Pi}$ asks, "Is there *no* Hamiltonian cycle in G?" A certificate for a Hamiltonian cycle is easy to verify, but what would a certificate be for the complementary problem? One would be an enumeration of all possible Hamiltonian cycles, but there are far too many candidates to check in polynomial time. In fact, it is believed that the non-Hamiltonian problem does not belong to NP.

Clearly, the complement $\overline{\Pi}$ of a problem in P also belongs to P. Indeed, a polynomial algorithm for Π also serves as a polynomial algorithm for $\overline{\Pi}$ by outputting "yes" for an instance I of $\overline{\Pi}$ if and only if the algorithm outputs "no" for instance I of problem Π. However, the same argument does not work for problems in NP. Given a problem $\Pi \in NP$, a yes instance for Π corresponds to a no instance for $\overline{\Pi}$, and we cannot be assured of the existence of certificates that can be verified in polynomial time for no instances of problems in NP.

The class *co-NP* comprises problems that are complements of problems in NP. As an example, consider again the problem of prime testing, which asks whether a given integer n is prime. Prime testing is in co-NP because its complement belongs to NP. A nondeterministic algorithm merely guesses a factor, and it can be checked in polynomial time whether the factor divides n evenly. Recall that it has recently been shown that prime testing is actually in P.

A natural question is whether co-NP $\neq$ NP. Most computer scientists believe the answer is yes and conjecture that any NP-complete problem provides the answer. The following theorem motivates this belief.

FIGURE 26.3

Conjectured relationships between P, NP, and co-NP.

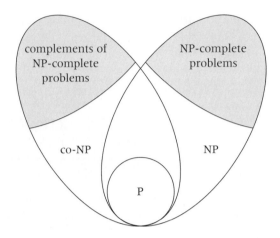

FIGURE 26.3

Conjectured relationships between P, NP, and co-NP.

Theorem 26.5.1 Let Π be any NP-complete problem. If the complement $\overline{\Pi}$ belongs to NP, then NP = co-NP. □

We leave the proof of Theorem 26.5.1 as an exercise.

The Venn diagram in Figure 26.3 shows the conjectured relationships between P, NP, and co-NP. However, there still is the (very unlikely) possibility that P = NP, in which case the whole diagram would collapse to P.

26.6 The Classes NC and P-Complete

We considered a sequential algorithm to be good (tractable) if it has polynomial worst-case complexity. Analogously, we consider a parallel algorithm on a PRAM to be good if it uses a polynomial number of processors and has polylogarithmic worst-case complexity. The class of problems solvable by such an algorithm is called the class NC. (Because any algorithm using P processors on an EREW PRAM or CREW PRAM can be simulated on the CRCW PRAM using p processors with at most logarithmic slowdown, the definition of the class NC is independent of the model of PRAM chosen.) In this section, we introduce the notion of P-completeness with respect to NC, which can be viewed as the analog for parallel computation of NP-completeness.

DEFINITION 26.6.1 Given two decision problems A and B, we say that A is *NC-reducible* to B if there is a mapping f from instances of A to instances of B such that the following two conditions apply:

1. The mapping f can be computed in polylogarithmic time using a polynomial number of processors on a PRAM.
2. The answer to a given instance I of problem A is yes if and only if the answer to instance $f(I)$ of B is yes.

Using the fact that the composition of two polynomials is a polynomial, it follows that if B is in NC then A is also in NC. We say that a problem B is *P-hard* if for any problem A in P, A is NC-reducible to B. We say that a problem B is *P-complete* if it belong to P and is P-hard. The P-complete problems can be viewed as the "hardest" problems in P with respect to the class NC because they have the following property: If a P-complete problem B is in NC, then every problem in P is in NC. The question of whether there exists a P-complete problem that is in NC—that is, whether NC = P—is an important open problem, comparable to the problem of whether P = NP for sequential computation.

It is not obvious that P-complete problems exist, but it turns out that many natural problems are P-complete. In this section, we give several examples of such problems.

26.6.1 Straight-Line Code Problem for Boolean Expressions

Just as the satisfiability of CNF Boolean expressions is a fundamental NP-complete problem, the satisfiability of a certain form of a set of Boolean equations is a fundamental P-complete problem. Consider the following set of Boolean equations:

$$x_1 = B_0$$
$$x_2 = B_1(x_1)$$
$$x_3 = B_2(x_1, x_2)$$

$$\cdot$$
$$\cdot$$
$$\cdot$$

$$x_n = B_{n-1}(x_1, \dots, x_{n-1}),$$

where B_0 is a constant and $B_i(x_1, \dots, x_{i-1})$ is a Boolean expression involving only the Boolean variables $x_1, \dots, x_{i-1}, i = 2, \dots, n$. Regarding = as the assignment operator, we call these equations *straight-line code*. The problem of computing the value of $x_i, i = 1, \dots, n$, is called the *straight-line code (SLC) problem*.

Clearly, the straightforward sequential algorithm for solving the SLC problem, which successively evaluates x_i, $i = 1, \ldots, n$, has linear computing time, where the input size is the total number m of symbols over all n equations (a symbol is counted k times if it occurs in k equations). Thus, the SLC problem is in P.

The SLC problem can be formulated as a decision problem, in which we ask the question, "Given $i \in \{1, \ldots, n\}$, does x_i have the value T?" We can obtain a solution to the SLC problem by solving this decision problem concurrently for each x_i, $i = 1, \ldots, n$. The SLC problem is our first example of a P-complete problem. The proof that the SLC problem is P-complete is beyond the scope of this book. In the remainder of this section, we illustrate NC reductions from the SLC problem to several other problems in P, thereby showing that they too are P-complete.

26.6.2 Straight-Line Code Without Disjunction

Straight-line code without disjunction (SLCWD) is a straight-line code in which the operation of disjunction is not used. We now describe an NC reduction of the SLC problem to the SLCWD problem, thereby showing that the SLCWD problem is P-complete. We employ the following useful identities, known as DeMorgan's laws, where $\neg$ represents the unary operation of negation.

Proposition 26.6.1 **DeMorgan's Laws**

For $x, y \in \{T, F\}$, the following laws apply:

1. $\neg (x \vee y) = \neg x \wedge \neg y$,
2. $\neg(x \wedge y) = \neg x \vee \neg y$. □

Using the fact that $\neg(\neg x) = x$ and DeMorgan's law 1 we have

$$x \vee y = \neg(\neg x \wedge \neg y).$$

We now consider the transformation f that maps an instance I of the SLC problem to the instance $f(I)$ of the SLCWD problem, where $f(I)$ is constructed from I by concurrently replacing each occurrence of $x \vee y$, where x and y are Boolean expressions, with $\neg (\neg x \wedge \neg y)$. Each such replacement involves changing $\vee$ to $\wedge$ and inserting three NOT operations and a left and right parenthesis in the appropriate place. We leave it as an exercise to design an NC algorithm for computing $f(I)$ from I. Figure 26.4 illustrates this transformation for a sample instance of the SLC problem. Since $f(I)$ can be computed in polylogarithmic time using a polynomial number of processors, the SLC problem is NC-reducible to the SLCWD problem, thereby proving that the SLCWD problem is P-complete.

FIGURE 26.4

The NC reduction transformation f from the general SLC problem to the SLCWD problem shown for a sample instance I of the SLC problem

$$x_1 = T$$
$$x_2 = \neg x_1$$
$$x_3 = \neg x_1 \wedge (x_1 \vee x_2)$$
$$x_4 = (x_3 \wedge \neg(x_1 \vee x_2)) \vee (x_1 \wedge \neg x_3)$$

Instance I of the general SLC problem

$$x_1 = T$$
$$x_2 = \neg x_1$$
$$x_3 = \neg x_1 \wedge (\neg(\neg x_1 \wedge x_2))$$
$$x_4 = \neg(\neg(x_3 \wedge \neg(\neg(\neg x_1 \wedge \neg x_2))) \wedge \neg(x_1 \wedge \neg x_3))$$

Instance $f(I)$ of the SLCWD problem

26.6.3 NOR Straight-Line Code

The operation NOR is defined by

$$x \text{ NOR } y = \neg(x_j \vee x_k)$$

NOR straight-line code is straight-line code where all assignments are of the following two forms:

$$x_i = T,$$
$$x_i = x_j \text{ NOR } x_k, \quad j, k < i. \tag{26.6.1}$$

We now show that the problem of solving NOR straight-line code (the NOR SLC problem) is P-complete. We first describe a transformation g from an instance I of the general SLC problem to a set of equations involving only NOR operations and assignments to T, but not necessarily of the form given in Formula (26.6.1). We construct $g(I)$ from I by concurrently performing the following replacement operations:

1. F is replaced with T NOR T.
2. $\neg x$ is replaced with x NOR x. (26.6.2)
3. $x \wedge y$ is replaced with $(x \text{ NOR } x) \text{ NOR } (y \text{ NOR } y)$.

In these operations, x and y are Boolean expressions. We leave it as an exercise to describe an NC transformation h that converts $g(I)$ into an instance of the NOR SLC problem by replacing each equation with a set of equations of the form given in Formula (26.6.1). The transformation $f(I) = h(g(I))$ yields an NC reduction from the general SLC problem to the NOR SLC problem, showing that the NOR SLC problem is P-complete.

26.6.4 Lexicographically First Maximal Independent Set

Let $G = (V, E)$ be a graph with vertex set $V = \{1, \ldots, n\}$ and edge set E of size m. A *maximal independent set* is an independent set U (no two vertices of U are adjacent) such that $U \cup \{v\}$ is not an independent set for any vertex $v \in V$. The *lexicographical ordering* of 2^V (the *power set* of V, consisting of all subsets of V) is a linear ordering such that a subset $A < B$ if either $A \subset B$ or the minimum element in $A \backslash B$ is smaller than the minimum element in $B \backslash A$. For example,

$$\{2, 4, 5\} < \{2, 4, 5, 9\} < \{3\} < \{5, 7\}.$$

The *lexicographically first maximal independent set* (LFMIS) is the maximal independent set U whose lexicographical order is smallest among all the maximal independent sets of G. The lexicographically first maximal independent set is illustrated for a sample graph in Figure 26.5.

....

FIGURE 26.5

Lexicographically
first maximal
independent set of
G is $\{1, 5, 6, 9, 10\}$.
....

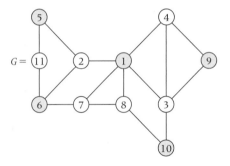

In this subsection, we show that the LFMIS problem is P-complete. (As with the SLC problem, the LFMIS problem can be formulated as a decision problem, where we ask the question, "Given a vertex $i \in V$, does i belong to the lexicographically first maximal independent set?")

First, we show that the LFMIS problem is in P by designing a polynomial-time procedure *SequentialLFMIS* for computing the lexicographically first maximal independent set U. Procedure *SequentialLFMIS* maintains a set R of remaining vertices where R is initially the set V of all vertices. At each stage, procedure *SequentialLFMIS* (1) chooses the smallest vertex u from R, (2) adds u to U, and (3) removes vertex u and all vertices adjacent to u from R. Procedure *SequentialLFMIS* terminates when R is empty. We leave the pseudocode for procedure *SequentialLFMIS* as an exercise. It is easily verified that *SequentialLFMIS* has complexity $\Theta(m + n)$, where m denotes the number of edges of G.

We now show how to NC-reduce an instance I of the NOR SLC problem to an instance $f(I)$ of the LFMIS problem. Instance $f(I)$ is a graph $G = (V, E)$ with vertex set $V = \{1, 2, \ldots, n\}$, where vertex i corresponds to variable x_i of I, $i = 1, 2, \ldots, n$. For each assignment $x_i = x_j$ NOR x_k of I there is an edge $\{i, j\}$ and an edge $\{i, k\}$. It is easily verified that G can be computed in polylogarithmic time on a PRAM using a polynomial number of processors. It can also be verified that a node i of G belongs to the lexicographically first maximal independent set if and only if the value of x_i is T in I. In Figure 26.6, the NC transformation f is shown for a sample instance I of the NOR SLC problem.

FIGURE 26.6

The transformation from a sample instance I of the NOR SLC problem to the instance $G = f(I)$ of the LFMIS problem.

Sample instance I of NOR SLC problem

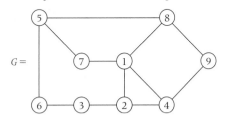

$G =$

Graph $G = f(I)$ of the LFMIS problem

26.7   Closing Remarks

Cobham introduced the class P in 1964. Edmonds, who independently proposed the class P in 1965, also introduced the class NP and conjectured that P ≠ NP. Cook, who introduced the notion of NP-completeness in 1971, showed that CNF SAT and 3-CNF SAT are NP-complete. Shortly thereafter, Levin independently discovered the notion and also proved the existence of NP-complete problems. Karp popularized the notion of NP-completeness by establishing that a wide variety of important and practical problems are NP-complete.

Our discussions of the notions of NP, NP-completeness, and P-completeness were somewhat informal in the sense that we did not establish a formal model of computation such as a Turing machine. The interested student can find formal treatments in the references.

References and Suggestions for Further Reading

Garey, M., and D. Johnson. *Computers and Intractability: A Guide to the Theory of NP-Completeness.* New York: W. H. Freeman, 1979. This classic reference to the theory of NP-completeness contains a list of hundreds of important NP-complete problems.

Books containing extensive discussions of NP-completeness:

Horowitz, E., and S. Sahni. *Fundamentals of Computer Algorithms.* Potomac, MD: Computer Science Press, 1978.

Papadimitriou, C., and K. Steiglitz. *Combinatorial Optimization: Algorithms and Complexity.* Englewood Cliffs, NJ: Prentice-Hall, 1982.

Greenlaw, R., H. J. Hoover, and W. L. Ruzzo. *Limits to Parallel Computation: P-Completeness Theory.* New York: Oxford University Press, 1995. A recent text devoted to P-completeness.

EXERCISES

Sections 26.1 and 26.2 The Classes P and NP and Reducibility

26.1 Suppose that the weights and values of the objects in the 0/1 knapsack problem are all integers. Show that the 0/1 knapsack problem and its associated decision version are polynomially equivalent. (*Hint*: Use a binary search technique.)

26.2 Given an integer n, it was shown by Pratt that n is prime if and only if there exists an integer a such that

i. $a^{n-1} \equiv 1 \pmod{n}$

ii. $a^{(n-1)/p} \not\equiv 1 \pmod{n}$ for all prime divisors p of $n-1$

Based on this result, show that the prime-testing problem is in NP.

26.3 Prove a result for the traveling salesman problem analogous to that of Exercise 26.1.

26.4 Prove Proposition 26.2.1.

26.5 Prove Proposition 26.2.2.

26.6 Prove Proposition 26.2.3.

Sections 26.3 and 26.4 NP-Complete Problems

26.7 Verify that each of the NP-complete problems in Section 26.4 belong to NP.

26.8 Prove Proposition 26.3.1

26.9 Show that 2-CNF SAT is in P.

26.10 This exercise refers to the mapping f from CNF SAT to 3-CNF SAT described in Example 26.4.1.

    a. Show that the input size of $f(I)$ is at most 12 times the input size of I for any instance I of CNF SAT.

    b. Show in cases 2 and 3, each clause C_i of I is satisfiable if and only if the conjunction of the clauses replacing C_i is satisfiable.

26.11 In Example 26.4.4, verify that the set R' of remaining households can be constructed and that the resulting set M' is a matching.

26.12 Show that the instance F, S of the 3-exact cover problem is a yes instance if and only if the instance $a_1, a_2, \ldots, a_n$ and C constructed in Example 26.4.6 is a yes instance of the sum of subsets problem.

26.13 Show that the problem of determining whether a graph G is bipartite (has a proper 2-coloring) is in P.

26.14 In Example 26.4.7, show that the graph G constructed from the instance I of 3-CNF SAT is $(n + 1)$-colorable if and only if I is satisfiable.

26.15 Given a multiset $S = \{s_1, s_2, \ldots, s_n\}$ of positive integers, the *partition problem* asks whether S can be partitioned into two subsets having the same sum. Show that the partition problem is NP-complete. (*Hint*: Show that sum of subsets $\propto$ partition.)

26.16 Show that the 0/1 knapsack problem is NP-complete. (*Hint*: Show that partition $\propto$ 0/1 knapsack [partition is defined in Exercise 26.15].)

26.17 Suppose we have a set of n objects $\{x_1, x_2, \ldots, x_n\}$ of sizes $\{s_1, s_2, \ldots, s_n\}$, where $1 < s_i < 1, i = 1, \ldots, n$. The *bin-packing* optimization problem is to place the objects into bins of unit size using the minimum number of bins. Each bin can contain any subset of objects whose total size does not exceed one. The decision version asks for a given integer k whether we can pack the objects using no more than k bins. Show that the bin problem is NP-complete. (*Hint*: Show that sum of subsets $\propto$ bin packing.)

Section 26.5 The Class co-NP

26.18 Prove Theorem 26.5.1.

Section 26.6 The Classes NC and P-Complete

26.19 Prove Proposition 26.6.1 (DeMorgan's Laws).

26.20 Use induction to prove the following generalization of DeMorgan's laws. For $x_1, x_2, \ldots, x_k \in \{T, F\}$,

a. $\neg(x_1 \wedge x_2 \wedge \cdots \wedge x_k) = \neg x_1 \vee \neg x_2 \vee \cdots \vee \neg x_k$.

b. $\neg(x_1 \vee x_2 \vee \cdots \vee x_k) = \neg x_1 \wedge \neg x_2 \wedge \cdots \wedge \neg x_k$.

26.21 Let f be the transformation that maps an instance I of the SLC problem to the instance $f(I)$ of the SLCWD problem, where $f(I)$ is constructed from I by concurrently replacing each occurrence of $x \vee y$, where x and y are Boolean expressions, with $\neg(\neg x \wedge \neg y)$. Design an NC algorithm for computing $f(I)$ from I.

26.22 a. Design an NC algorithm for performing the replacement operations given in Formula (26.6.2) to obtain $g(I)$ from an instance I of the SLCWD problem.

b. Design an NC algorithm for converting $g(I)$ to an instance I of the NOR SLC problem.

26.23 a. Give pseudocode for the procedure *SequentialLFMIS* for computing the lexicographically first maximal independent set of a graph G.

b. Analyze the complexity of procedure *SequentialLFMIS*.

26.24 a. Design an NC algorithm for performing the reduction from an instance I of the NOR SLC problem to the instance $G = f(I)$ of the LFMIS problem shown in Figure 26.5.

b. Show that x_i has the value T in instance I of the NOR SLC problem if and only if vertex i is in the lexicographically maximal independent set in $G = f(I)$.

CHAPTER 27

APPROXIMATION ALGORITHMS

Many problems encountered in computer science and engineering are NP-hard; that is, they have no known polynomial solutions in the worst-case. For such problems, we can seek (but not always find) algorithms that work well on average. Another approach, particularly for optimization problems, is to find efficient algorithms for computing an "approximation" to the solution for instances of the given problem—for example, a solution whose value is within a constant multiplicative factor of the optimal solution.

There are various ways to measure the degree of approximation of a solution to the optimal solution. We focus here on approximations that are within multiplicative factors of the optimal solution. More precisely, let $C^*(n)$ denote the value of an optimal solution to a given optimization problem for an input of size n (we assume $C^*(n) > 0$). If the problem is a maximization problem, then for a given real-valued positive function $\rho(n)$, we say that a solution $C(n)$ is a $\rho(n)$-*approximation* to $C^*(n)$ if

$$\frac{C^*(n)}{C(n)} \le \rho(n), \quad n = 1, 2, \dots .$$

If the problem is a minimization problem, then $C(n)$ is a $\rho(n)$-*approximation* to $C^*(n)$ if

$$\frac{C(n)}{C^*(n)} \leq \rho(n), \quad n = 1, 2, \dots .$$

When $\rho(n)$ is a constant k, we say that we have a *k-approximation* to the optimal solution $C^*(n)$. For example, if we have an algorithm whose output is a 2-approximation to $C^*(n)$, then the solution it produces is never more than twice as bad as the optimal solution. For many NP-hard optimization problems, it is possible to find polynomial algorithms that are k-approximations to the optimal solutions. For other NP-hard optimization problems, such as the traveling salesman problem (TSP), it can be shown that polynomial-time k-approximations for any constant k to the optimal solutions cannot exist unless P = NP. However, in this chapter, for the case of the TSP in which distances satisfy the triangle inequality, we discuss an $O(n^2)$ algorithm for a 2-approximation. We also present approximation algorithms for the bin packing, Steiner tree, and facility location problems.

27.1 The Traveling Salesman Problem

We consider the restricted version of the TSP, where we have the undirected complete graph K_n in which the weights on the edges satisfy the triangle inequality. Given a positive weighting ω on the complete graph K_n, we say that ω satisfies the triangle inequality if for any three vertices u, v, w we have

$$\omega(uv) \leq \omega(uw) + \omega(wv), \quad u, v, w \in V(K_n).$$

When the triangle inequality holds for the edge weighting, the following simple $O(n^2)$ algorithm generates a tour whose length is no more than twice that of an optimal tour. Starting at an arbitrary initial vertex r, we generate a minimum spanning tree T rooted at r. T can be generated by Prim's algorithm in time $O(n^2)$. Then we perform a preorder traversal of T, where the vertices are visited (first accessed) in the order $v_0 = r, v_1, \dots v_{n-1}$. Consider the tour with edges

$$v_0 v_1, v_1 v_2, \dots , v_{n-2} v_{n-1}, v_{n-1} v_n, \quad v_0 = v_n = r. \qquad \textbf{(27.1.1)}$$

Proposition 27.1.1   If the weighting ω satisfies the triangle inequality, then given any spanning tree T, the cost of the tour given by Formula (27.1.1) is no more than twice the cost of T.

PROOF

Consider the (vertex) access sequence generated by a preorder traversal of T. The associated (vertex) visit sequence is a subsequence of the access sequence, and (when the starting vertex is added at the end) generates a Hamiltonian cycle [the tour given by Formula (27.1.1)]. Consecutive (in the visit sequence) vertices v and w of an edge in this tour also occur in the access sequence, but where there are possibly some additional intermediate vertices occurring in the access sequence between v and w. The triangle inequality shows that the weight of the edge vw is not greater than the sum of the weights of the edges traversed in the preorder traversal as it goes from v to w. Hence, the cost of the tour is certainly no more than the sum of the weights of the edges having endpoints given by consecutive vertices in the access sequence. Because an edge T is traversed exactly twice (once in each "direction") during a preorder traversal, it follows that the latter sum is exactly twice the cost of T, which proves Proposition 27.1.1.   ■

Corollary 27.1.2   If the weighting ω satisfies the triangle inequality, then the cost of the tour given by Formula (27.1.1) for a minimum spanning tree T is less than twice the cost of an optimal tour.

PROOF

If we delete any edge from an optimal tour, then we obtain a spanning tree whose cost is not less than the cost of minimum spanning tree T.   ■

We illustrate the tour given by Formula (27.1.1) in Figure 27.1 for a sample minimum spanning tree. We leave it as an exercise to find the optimal tour.

FIGURE 27.1

Cost of the tour
generated by the
preorder traversal
of the minimum
spanning tree T is
less than twice the
optimal tour for
the TSP.

$$\begin{pmatrix} 0 & 19 & 14 & 16 & 17 & 13 & 18 & 20 \\ 19 & 0 & 17 & 12 & 11 & 19 & 15 & 15 \\ 14 & 17 & 0 & 18 & 16 & 12 & 16 & 16 \\ 16 & 12 & 18 & 0 & 10 & 20 & 11 & 20 \\ 17 & 11 & 16 & 10 & 0 & 16 & 10 & 14 \\ 13 & 19 & 12 & 20 & 16 & 0 & 18 & 15 \\ 18 & 15 & 16 & 11 & 10 & 18 & 0 & 17 \\ 20 & 15 & 16 & 20 & 14 & 15 & 17 & 0 \end{pmatrix}$$

Cost matrix $C = (c_{ij})$ satisfying triangle inequality,
where c_{ij} is the cost of edge $\{i,j\}$ in K_8

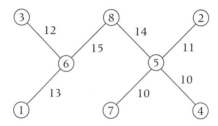

A minimum spanning tree T in weighted graph K_8 having preorder traversal

1 6 3 8 5 2 4 7

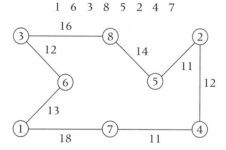

Tour generated by preorder traversal of T

27.2 Bin Packing

Suppose we have a set of n objects $a_1, a_2, \ldots, a_n$ of sizes $f_1, f_2, \ldots, f_n$, respectively,
where $0 < f_i < 1$, $i = 1, \ldots, n$. The *bin-packing* optimization problem is to place
(pack) the objects into bins $B_1, \ldots, B_m$ having unit size using the minimum number $m \le n$ of bins. Each bin can contain any subset of objects whose total size
does not exceed 1. If m^* denotes the minimum number of bins in an optimal so-
lution, then it is easy to see that $m^* \ge \lceil F \rceil$, where $F = \sum_{i=1}^{n} f_i$ (see Exercise 27.6).
The decision version asks, for a given integer k, whether we can pack the objects

using no more than k bins. It can be seen that that bin-packing problem is NP-complete even for $k = 2$ by showing that sum of subsets reduces to bin packing (see Exercise 26.17 in Chapter 26). In this section, we discuss two strategies, next fit and decreasing first fit, that yield a 2-approximation and (an almost) 1.5-approximation, respectively.

27.2.1 Next Fit

The *next-fit* strategy for solving the bin-packing problem proceeds by successively placing the objects $a_1, a_2, \ldots, a_n$ into the bins as follows. A bin is considered *open* if the next object can be placed in the bin; otherwise, it is considered *closed*. We begin by placing a_1 into B_1. In general, when placing the next object a_i, if B_j is the last bin used and a_i fits into B_j, we place it there and continue; otherwise, we close B_j and place a_i into B_{j+1}.

We now consider now many bins are used by the next-fit strategy. Let m denote the number of bins used by the next-fit algorithm, and let s_i denote the sum of the sizes over all the objects that have been placed in the ith bin B_i by the algorithm. Clearly, $F = \sum_{i=1}^{m} s_i$. It follows from the design of the next-fit algorithm that no object placed in bin B_i, $i = 2, \ldots, m$ could be added to the objects that were placed in bin B_{i-1}, without exceeding the capacity of B_{i-1}, (otherwise, the object should have been added to B_{i-1} before it was closed). Thus, we have

$$s_2 \geq 1 - s_1,$$
$$s_3 \geq 1 - s_2, \tag{27.2.1}$$
$$\ldots$$
$$s_m \geq 1 - s_{m-1}.$$

Observing that the values on the left side of Formula (27.2.1) sum to $F - s_1$ and the values on the right side sum to $m - (F - s_1)$, we have that $F - s_1 \geq m - 1 - (F - s_m)$, or, equivalently,

$$m \leq 2F + (1 - s_1 - s_m). \tag{27.2.2}$$

Because m is an integer, it follows from Formula (27.2.2) that

$$m \leq \lceil 2F \rceil \leq 2\lceil F \rceil \leq 2m^*. \tag{27.2.3}$$

The inequalities in Formula (27.2.3) show that the number m of bins used by the next-fit algorithm is at most double the number m^* of bins used by an optimal algorithm, so that the next-fit algorithm is a 2-approximation.

27.2.2 First Fit

The *first-fit* heuristic is similar to next fit except that the next object a_i is placed in the first available bin that has enough remaining capacity to fit in the object. Unlike next fit, we assume that all the bins are open. It can be shown (see Exercise 27.10) that if m denotes the number of bins used by a first-fit solution, then

$$m \leq 1.7\,m^* + 2. \tag{27.2.4}$$

However, in the *first-fit decreasing* version of the algorithm, where the objects are first sorted in decreasing order of size—that is, $f_1 \geq f_2 \geq \cdots \geq f_n$—we do better than Formula (27.2.4), obtaining

$$m \leq 1.5\,m^* + 1. \tag{27.2.5}$$

To verify inequality (27.2.5), we partition the objects into the following four sets:

$$A = \left\{ a_i : f_i > \frac{2}{3} \right\}$$

$$B = \left\{ a_i : \frac{1}{2} < f_i \leq \frac{2}{3} \right\}$$

$$C = \left\{ a_i : \frac{1}{3} < f_i \leq \frac{1}{2} \right\}$$

$$D = \left\{ a_i : f_i \leq \frac{1}{3} \right\}$$

There are two cases to consider.

Case 1. *D is nonempty, and one bin contains all the objects in D.* It follows from the design of the algorithm that all the items must be contained in the last bin B_m. Further, all bins except B_m must have used more than two-thirds of their capacities—that is $s_i > 2/3$, $i = 1, \ldots, m - 1$—otherwise, all the objects in bin B_m would fit in whichever of these bins had two-thirds or less capacity, and the algorithm would never have put the objects into B_m. It follows that

$$F = \sum_{i=1}^{m} s_i \geq \sum_{i=1}^{m-1} s_i \geq \frac{2}{3}(m - 1).$$

Therefore, we have

$$m \leq 1.5F + 1 \leq 1.5\lceil F \rceil + 1 \leq 1.5m^* + 1.$$

Case 2. *No bin contains all the objects in D, or D is empty.* In this case, we can remove all the items from D without changing the number of bins. Thus, case 2 can be reduced to the special case of the bin-packing problem in which all the objects belong to A, B, or C—that is, have size of at least one-third. However, for this special case, it is not difficult to show that the first-fit decreasing algorithm actually produces an optimal solution (see Exercise 27.11).

27.3 The Steiner Tree Problem

The Steiner tree problem generalizes both the minimum spanning tree and the shortest-path problems for undirected graphs, as discussed in Chapter 12. The Steiner tree problem has important applications to establishing efficient network communication between a group S of nodes. Let $G = (V, E)$ be a graph on node (vertex) set V and edge set E representing a network, and suppose W is a positive real weighting of the edges. Given a subset S of k nodes in the graph G, a *Steiner tree* for S is a minimum-weight subtree of G that contains all the nodes in S (see Figure 27.2). Note that a Steiner tree for $S = V$ is a minimum spanning tree, and a Steiner tree for $S = \{u, v\}$ is a shortest path joining u and v. Given S and an integer k, the problem of determining whether there exists a tree having k edges that contains the nodes of S is NP-complete (see Exercise 27.15), so that the Steiner tree problem is NP-hard. However, in this section, we describe a 2-approximation algorithm for the Steiner tree problem. In fact, the algorithm we describe is slightly better than a 2-approximation, yielding a tree whose weight is at most $2 - 2/k$ times the weight of a Steiner tree.

Given S, in the first stage of constructing a 2-approximation for a Steiner tree T^* for S, we compute the matrix D of weighted distances between every pair of vertices u and v in S. The matrix D can be computed in time $O(kn^2)$ by applying Dijkstra's shortest-path algorithm (see Chapter 12) k times, once for each node in S as the root. Now consider the complete graph $H = (S, E_H)$ on S, where each

FIGURE 27.2

A Steiner tree for S
= {1, 3, 4, 7}.

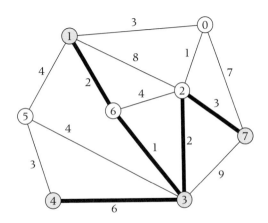

edge $\{u, v\} \in E_H$ is weighted with the distance $D(u, v)$. Note that the distance matrix D is the weighted adjacency matrix of a weighted graph H.

In the second stage, we compute a minimum spanning tree T_H in the graph H, which can be done in time $O(k^2)$ using a minimum spanning tree algorithm such as Prim's algorithm (see Chapter 12). In the third stage, we construct a tree T_G in G by joining a pair of nodes x and y from S with a shortest path from x to y, whenever $\{x, y\}$ is an edge of T_H. More precisely, let $\{x_1, y_1\}, \dots , \{x_{k-1}, y_{k-1}\}$ denote the edges of T_H and let $P_1, \dots , P_{k-1}$ be shortest paths from x_i to y_i, $i = 1, \dots , k - 1$ (we can compute these shortest paths in stage 1 when computing the distance matrix D). We initialize T_G to be the path P_1, and successively use P_i to extend T_G, $i = 2, \dots , k - 1$, as follows. First, we assume that P_i contains at least two nodes that belong to the current T_G, and we let a and b denote the first and last such nodes encountered, respectively, when traversing P_i from x_i to y_i. We then add the subpaths of P_i from x_i to a and from b to y_i to T_G (adding only nodes and edges that are not already in T_G). On the other hand, if P_i contains at most one node from T_G, then we add the entire path P_i to T_G.

We will show later that tree T_G gives us the promised 2-approximation to T^*. However, we can potentially obtain further improvement by computing a minimum spanning tree T' in the graph induced by the node set of T_G in G, and then pruning T' to remove any nodes and edges that do not lie on a path in the tree joining two nodes from S.

Theorem 27.3.1 The weight of T_G is no greater that $2 - 2/k$ the weight of T^*.

PROOF

Consider a closed walk W around the tree T^*—that is, a sequence of nodes and edges $v_0\ e_1\ v_1 \dots v_{2n-2}\ e_{2n-2}\ v_{2n-1} = v_0$, where $e_i = \{v_{i-1}, v_i\}$, $i = 1, \dots , 2n - 2$ such that every edge is traversed twice, once in each direction (see Figure 27.3). Let $s_1, s_2, \dots , s_k$ denote the nodes from S listed in the order that they are first encountered by W. Then W decomposes in k subwalks $W_1, \dots , W_k$, where W_i is the subwalk joining s_i and s_{i+1}, $i = 1, \dots , k$, where $s_{k+1} = s_1$. Because each edge is traversed by W exactly twice, letting $\omega(W_i)$ denote the sum of the weights over all the edge of W_i with an edge counted twice if it is traversed twice by W_i gives us

$$\sum_{i=1}^{k} \omega(W_i) = \omega(W) = 2\omega(T^*). \tag{27.3.1}$$

Figure 27.4 shows the decomposition of W into five walks for a sample tree T^* and set S of size 5.

FIGURE 27.3

Walk W around the tree T^*

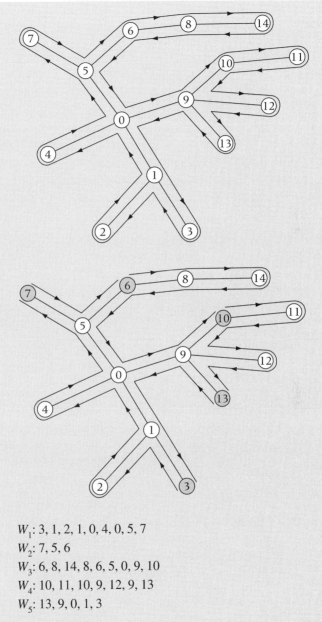

FIGURE 27.3

Walk W around the tree T^*

FIGURE 27.4

Decomposition of walk W around the same tree T^* given in Figure 27.3 into five subwalks for set $S = \{3, 6, 7, 10, 13\}$.

W_1: 3, 1, 2, 1, 0, 4, 0, 5, 7
W_2: 7, 5, 6
W_3: 6, 8, 14, 8, 6, 5, 0, 9, 10
W_4: 10, 11, 10, 9, 12, 9, 13
W_5: 13, 9, 0, 1, 3

Now we remove the walk, say W_j, having the largest weight. The weight of W_j must be at least as great as the average weight of the paths $W_1, \dots, W_k$, so that using Formula (27.3.1) gives us

$$\omega(W_j) \ge \left(\sum_{i=1}^{k} \omega(W_i) \right) / k = 2\omega(W^*)/k, \qquad \textbf{(27.3.2)}$$

and hence

$$\sum_{i \in \{1, \, \ldots, \, k\} - \{j\}} \omega(W_i) = (2 - 2/k)\omega(T^*). \qquad \text{(27.3.3)}$$

Because the weight of W_i is at least as great as distance $D(s_i, s_{i+1})$ (length of a shortest path) from s_i to s_{i+1}, it follows that

$$\sum_{i \in \{1, \, \ldots, \, k\} - \{j\}} D(s_i, s_{i+1}) = (2 - 2/k)\omega(T^*). \qquad \text{(27.3.4)}$$

Since the set of edges $\{\{s_i, s_{i+1}\} \mid i \in \{1, \ldots k\} - \{j\}\}$ determines a spanning tree in H, it follows that

$$\sum_{i \in \{1, \, \ldots, \, k\} - \{j\}} D(s_i, s_{i-1}) \geq D(T_H) \geq \omega(T_G). \qquad \text{(27.3.5)}$$

Combining Formulas (27.3.4) and (27.3.5) yields

$$\omega(T_G) \leq (2 - 2/k)\omega(T^*). \qquad \blacksquare$$

27.4   The Facility Location Problem

Consider a network represented by a graph $G = (V, E)$, together with a real-valued distance function $d(u, v)$ defined for each pair of vertices $u, v \in V$, satisfying the *triangle inequality*; that is, $d(x, y) + d(y, z) \leq d(x, y)$ for every triple of vertices x, y, z. For example, $d(u, v)$ could be the weight of a shortest path from u to v with respect to some real weighting of the edges of G, where there are no negative cycles.

The *facility* or *server* location problem is the problem of locating k facilities (servers) at k vertices of the graph, so that the farthest distance r from any vertex of the graph to the nearest facility (server) is minimized. We call the set of vertices C that satisfies this minimization condition a *k-center* of the graph G, and we call the associated minimum value r_k^* of r the *k-radius* of G. More formally, we define the distance $d(U, v)$ from a subset of vertices U to a vertex v to be the minimum distance from a vertex $u \in U$ to v, and define $r(U)$ by

$$r(U) = \max \{d(U, v) \mid v \in V\}$$

In Figure 27.5, $d(x, y)$, $d(v, y)$ and $r(U)$ are shown for a sample graph G and sample set U of size 3, where the distance $d(x, y)$ is taken to be the length of a shortest path from x to y in G. The *k-radius* of G is given by

$$r_k^* = \min \{r(U) \mid U \subseteq V, \mid U \mid = k\},$$

and a *k-center* is a subset C of vertices of cardinality k such that $r(C) = r_k^*$.

FIGURE 27.5

(a) Sample graph G and distances $d(x, y)$; (b) $d(U, v)$ and $r(U)$ for $U = \{0, 1, 8\}$.

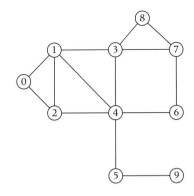

$d(i,j)$

i / j	0	1	2	3	4	5	6	7	8	9
0	0	1	1	2	2	3	3	3	3	4
1	1	0	1	1	1	2	2	2	2	3
2	1	1	0	2	1	2	2	3	3	3
3	2	1	2	0	1	2	2	1	1	3
4	2	1	1	1	0	1	1	2	2	2
5	3	2	2	2	1	0	2	3	3	1
6	3	2	2	2	1	2	0	1	2	3
7	3	2	2	1	2	3	1	0	1	4
8	3	2	3	1	2	3	2	1	0	4
9	4	3	3	3	2	1	3	4	4	0

(a)

$U=\{0,1,8\}$

i	0	1	2	3	4	5	6	7	8	9
$D(U,i)$	0	0	1	1	1	2	2	1	0	3

$r(U) = 3$

(b)

FIGURE 27.6

A 3-center C with radius $r(C) = r_3^* = 1$ for the same graph as in Figure 27.5.

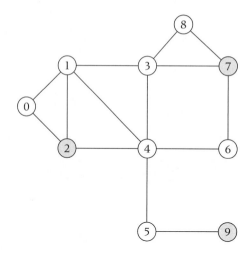

In Figure 27.6, a 3-center with radius $r_3^* = 1$ is shown for the same graph as in Figure 27.5. In the case where the k-radius $r_3^* = 1$, a k-center C is a *dominating set*—that is, a subset of vertices of a given size k such that every vertex not in the set is adjacent at least one vertex in the set. The decision version of the dominating-set problem—Does there exist a dominating set of size k?—is a well-known NP-complete problem (see Exercise 27.17). Thus, the problem of determining r_3^* is NP-hard. It is interesting that the problem of obtaining an approximation that is better than a 2-approximation for the facility location problem is also NP-hard; that is, the problem of finding a k-approximation to r_3^* for $k < 2$ is NP-hard (see Exercise 27.18).

The following theorem shows how we can use a greedy heuristic to obtain a 2-approximation to the k-center problem.

Theorem 27.4.1
Let the set A be constructed by starting with any vertex a_1 and iterating as follows. For $1 < i \leq k$, assuming that $\{a_1, \ldots, a_{i-1}\}$ has been chosen, then add to A a vertex a_i such that that $d(A, a_i)$ is maximized. Then, A is a 2-approximation to a k-center.

PROOF
Let $C = \{c_1, \ldots, c_k\}$ be a k-center. For each vertex c_i in the center C, let R_i denote the subset of all vertices whose distance from c_i is at most r_k^*, and let $R = \{R_1, \ldots, R_k\}$. Because C is a k-center, every node v must lie in at least one subset from R. First suppose that each node of A lies in a unique subset from R, and consider any node v of G. Let R_j denote the subset of R that v belongs to and let a_p denote the node from A that lies in R_j. Then, applying the triangle inequality, we have

$$d(A, v) \leq d(a_p, v) \leq d(a_p, c_j) + d(c_j, v) \leq 2r_k^*.$$

On the other hand, suppose that two nodes of A, say a_p and a_q, where $p < q$, lie in the same subset of R, say R_j. Choose the smallest index q with this property; that is, $a_1, a_2, \ldots, a_{p-1}$ each lie in different subsets of R, but a_p lies in the same subset as a_q. Now consider any vertex v. Since a_q was chosen using the greedy method, we have

$$d(\{a_1, \ldots, a_{q-1}\}, v) \le d(\{a_1, \ldots, a_{q-1}\}, a_q). \tag{27.4.1}$$

Because $a_p \in \{a_1, \ldots, a_{q-1}\}$, it follows from the definition of $d(U, v)$ that

$$d(\{a_1, \ldots, a_{q-1}\}, a_q) \le d(a_p, a_q) \tag{27.4.2}$$

Again, applying the triangle inequality we have

$$d(a_p, a_q) \le d(a_p, c_j) + d(c_j, a_q) \le 2r_k^*. \tag{27.4.3}$$

Combining Formulas (27.4.1), (27.4.2) and (27.4.3), we have

$$d(A, v) \le d(\{a_1, \ldots, a_{q-1}\}, v) \le d(\{a_1, \ldots, a_{q-1}\}, a_q) \le d(a_p, a_q) \le 2r_k^*. \quad ■$$

Theorem 27.4.1 yields a greedy 2-approximation algorithm for the facility location problem. The approximation 3-center A generated by this greedy algorithm for the same graph as in Figure 27.6 is shown in Figure 27.7. Note that $r(A) = 2$, which is twice the actual 3-radius $r_3^* = 1$.

FIGURE 27.7

Approximation 3-center $A = \{0, 7, 9\}$ generated by a greedy algorithm based on Theorem 27.4.1 in the order 0, 9, 7 for same graph as in Figure 27.6. Note that $r(A) = 2$, which is twice the actual 3-radius $r_3^* = 1$.

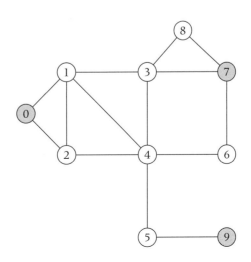

27.5 Closing Remarks

Although we have seen that an $O(n^2)$ 2-approximation algorithm for the TSP exists under the assumption that the triangle inequality holds, the problem of finding a k-approximation algorithm for the TSP, for any constant k, is NP-hard if we do not make this assumption (see Exercise 27.3). In this chapter, we discussed a 2-approximation algorithm for the Steiner tree problem. Using more-sophisticated arguments, Robins and Zelikovski designed a 1.55-approximate algorithm to the Steiner tree problem.

Because NP-hard problems arise in so many practical situations, much research has been devoted to finding approximation algorithms for these problems. We refer the reader to the references for further discussion of this important research area.

References and Suggestions for Further Reading

Three books on approximation algorithms:

Ausiello, G., P. Crescenzi, G. Gambosi, V. Kann, A. Marchetti-Spaccamela, M. Protasi. *Complexity and Approximation: Combinatorial Optimization Problems and Their Approximability Properties*. New York: Springer-Verlag, 1999.

Hochbaum, D. (ed.). *Approximation Algorithms for NP-Hard Problems.* Boston: PWS, 1997.

Vazirani, V. V. *Approximation Algorithms*. Berlin: Springer-Verlag, 2001.

Coffman, E.G., M. R. Garey, and D.S. Johnson. "Approximation Algorithms for Bin Packing—An Updated Survey." In *Algorithm Design for Computer System Design*, edited by G. Ausiello, M. Lucertini, and P. Serafini, 46—93. New York: Springer-Verlag, 1984. A survey paper on approximation algorithms for bin packing.

EXERCISES

Section 27.1 The Traveling Salesman Problem

27.1   Find an optimal tour for the instance of the TSP given in Figure 27.1, and compare your tour with the tour shown in Figure 27.1 generated by the 2-approximation algorithm.

27.2   Show that the 2-approximation algorithm provided by the minimum spanning tree argument does not yield a ρ-approximation for any $\rho < 2$; that is, for every n, give a weighting of K_n satisfying the triangle inequality such that the tour generated by the approximation algorithm is strictly greater than ρ times the optimal tour.

27.3 Show that if a polynomial algorithm A exists yielding a ρ-approximation for the general TSP problem, then a polynomial algorithm exists for the Hamiltonian cycle decision problem. [*Hints*: Let $G = (V, E)$ be any instance of the Hamiltonian cycle decision problem. Consider the instance of the TSP on the complete graph $G' = (V, E')$ with the following weighting: $\omega(u, v) = 1$ if $uv \in E$, otherwise $\omega(u, v) = \rho|V| + 1$. Show that G' has a tour of cost $\leq \rho|V|$ if, and only if, G has a Hamiltonian cycle.]

27.4 Show the action of the 2-approximation algorithm for the TSP given in Section 27.1 for ten nodes, where the weighted adjacency matrix of K_{10} is given by the matrix in Figure 27.5(a).

27.5 Write a program implementing the 2-approximation algorithm for the TSP given in Section 27.1.

Section 27.2 Bin Packing

27.6 Let m^* denote the minimum number of bins in an optimal solution to the bin-packing problem. Show that $m^* \geq \lceil F \rceil$, where $F = \sum_{i=1}^{n} f_i$.

27.7 Show the action of the next-fit heuristic for the following instances of the bin-packing problem:

a. $(f_1, f_2, \ldots, f_9) = (.1, .6, .4, .1, .7, .4, .15, .35, .9)$.

b. $(f_1, f_2, \ldots, f_{11}) = (.5, .3, .4, .9, .7, .4, .15, .35, .05, .95, .1)$.

27.8 Repeat Exercise 27.7 for first fit.

27.9 Repeat Exercise 27.7 for first fit decreasing.

27.10 Verify Formula (27.2.4).

27.11 Complete the argument for case 2 of the verification of inequality (27.2.5) as follows:

a. Show that case 2 can be reduced to the special case of the bin-packing problem in which all the objects belong to A, B, or C—that is, have size of at least one-third.

b. Show that if all the objects have size of at least one-third, then the first-fit decreasing algorithm produces an optimal solution.

27.12 Write a program implementing and comparing the next-fit, first-fit, and first-fit decreasing heuristics.

Section 27.3 The Steiner Tree Problem

27.13 Show the action of the 2-approximation algorithm for finding an approximation to the Steiner tree problem given in Section 27.3 for the set S in the following weighted graph, where the nodes of S are shaded.

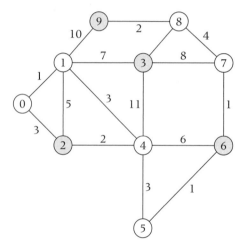

27.14 Write a program implementing the 2-approximation algorithm for the Steiner tree problem given in Section 27.3.

27.15 Given a graph $G = (V, E)$, a subset S of V, and a positive real number k, show that the problem of determining whether there exists a tree with k edges containing the nodes of S is NP-complete.

Section 27.4 The Facility Location Problem

27.16 For the value of k specified in each part, show the action of the greedy 2-approximation algorithm given in Section 27.4 for computing an approximation to a k-center in the graph G below, where $d(i, j)$ is the length of a shortest path from i to j.

a. $k = 2$.

b. $k = 3$.

c. $k = 6$.

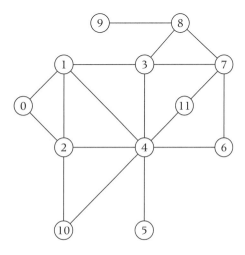

27.17 Show that the dominating-set problem is NP-complete. (*Hint*: Show that Vertex Cover ∝ Dominating Set.)

27.18 The decision version of the facility location problem is to determine whether the k-radius r_k^* is at most b for any given integer b. Show that the problem of finding a ρ-approximation to the facility location problem for any given $\rho < 2$ is NP-complete by a reduction from the dominating-set problem.

Additional Exercise

27.19 Consider the following algorithm for the vertex cover problem:

```
procedure  VertexCoverApprox(G, Cover)
Input:    G (a graph with vertex set V and edge set E)
Output:   Cover (a vertex cover containing no more than twice the number of vertices
          in a minimum vertex cover)
          Cover ← ∅
          RemainEdges ← E
          while RemainEdges ≠ ∅ do
              choose any edge uv ∈ RemainEdges
              Cover ← Cover ∪ {uv}
              remove from RemainEdges all edges incident with either u or v
          endwhile
end VertexCoverApprox
```

Show that *VertexCoverApprox* is a 2-approximation algorithm.

MATHEMATICAL NOTATION AND BACKGROUND

Designing and analyzing algorithms require familiarity with certain concepts from mathematics, such as functions, sets, various summation formulas, and so forth. In this appendix, we review some of these commonly used concepts and establish appropriate notation. Various other mathematical concepts are briefly discussed, including complex numbers, and modular arithmetic.

A.1 Basic Mathematical and Built-in Functions

Certain functions occur frequently in the design and analysis of algorithms and are usually implemented as built-in functions in most high-level languages. Two of the most commonly used functions are the ceiling $\lceil x \rceil$, defined to be the smallest integer greater than or equal to x, and the floor $\lfloor x \rfloor$, defined to be the largest integer smaller than or equal to x. For example, $\lceil 1.23 \rceil = 2$, and $\lfloor 1.23 \rfloor = 1$. For a positive x, $\lfloor x \rfloor$ is obtained from x by truncating its decimal part. Note that $x - 1 < \lfloor x \rfloor \le x$, and $x \le \lceil x \rceil < x + 1$.

When $\lceil x \rceil$ and $\lfloor x \rfloor$ are invoked in our pseudocode as built-in functions, we often retain the mathematical notation for such invocations rather than using names such as **ceiling**(x) and **floor**(x), respectively. On the other hand, for other functions, such as $\sqrt{x}$, we usually use names, such as **sqrt**. Following is a list of names and definitions for some of the more commonly used built-in functions in our pseudocode:

sqrt$(x) = \sqrt{x}$, x is a nonnegative real number.

abs $(x) = |x| = \begin{cases} x & x \geq 0 \\ -x & \text{otherwise,} \end{cases}$ x is a real number.

$a \bmod b = a - b \lfloor a/b \rfloor$, a and b are integers, $b \neq 0$.

odd$(n) = $ **.true.** if and only if $n \bmod 2 = 1$, n an integer.

even$(n) = $ **.true.** if and only if $n \bmod 2 = 0$, n an integer.

Note that for positive integers a and b, $a \bmod b$ is the remainder when a is divided by b.

Another important function in algorithms is the logarithm function. Given a base $b > 1$, the logarithm of x to the base b, denoted by $\log_b x$, is defined to be the functional inverse of the exponential function b^x. In other words, $\log_b x$, $x > 0$, is defined to be the power to which the base b must be raised to equal x, so that

$$b^{\log_b x} = x. \qquad \text{(A.1.1)}$$

We illustrate the functional inverse relationship of 2^x and $\log_2 x$ in Figure A.1. Note that their graphs are the reflections of one another about the line $y = x$. Since 2^x grows very rapidly, it follows that $\log_2 x$ grows very slowly.

FIGURE A.1

Graphs of $y = \log_2 x$, $y = x$, and $y = 2^x$

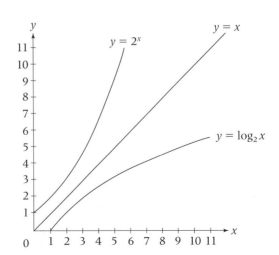

FIGURE A.2

Table of values of
$y = x$, $y = \log_2 x$,
and $y = 2^x$.

x	$\log_2 x$	2^x
1	0	2
2	1	4
4	2	16
8	3	256
16	4	65,536
48	5.58496	562,949,953,421,312
562,949,953,421,312	48	eeeeeeeenormous

The differences between logarithmic growth ($y = \log_2 x$), linear growth ($y = x$), and exponential growth ($y = 2^x$) are dramatic (see Figure A.2). We obtained the first few entries for x in Figure A.2 by doubling the previous value. Note that doubling the input to the function $\log_2 x$ only increases its output by one. On the other hand, doubling the input to the function 2^x results in squaring its output. This is indeed a dramatic difference.

The exponential function b^x has the following fundamental properties:

$$b^{x+y} = b^x b^y, \qquad \textbf{(A.1.2)}$$

$$(b^x)^y = (b^y)^x = b^{xy}. \qquad \textbf{(A.1.3)}$$

The following two properties of $\log_b x$ corresponding to (A.1.2) and (A.1.3) are immediately obtained by raising both sides to the power b and using (A.1.1).

$$\log_b xy = \log_b x + \log_b y, \qquad \textbf{(A.1.4)}$$

$$\log_b x^y = y \log_b x. \qquad \textbf{(A.1.5)}$$

The following useful formula allows us to change from one base to another:

$$\log_a x = \frac{\log_b x}{\log_b a}. \qquad \textbf{(A.1.6)}$$

The most commonly used bases are 2, e, and 10. When the base is e, the logarithm is referred to as the *natural* logarithm and is denoted by $\ln x$.

A.2 Modular Arithmetic

Modular arithmetic is often used in cryptography to compute a cryptograpic key. In particular, it is used in Chapter 17 in the design of the RSA public-key cryptosystem. The operations of addition and multiplication for the set

$Z_n = \{0, \dots, n - 1\}$ of integers (*residues*) modulo n are defined the same as over the integers, but the result x of each operation is reduced by replacing x with the remainder r when x is divided by n. We denote this remainder by $x \bmod n$. We write

$$x \equiv y \ (\text{mod } n)$$

if $x - y$ is divisible by n—that is, if both x and y have the same remainder on dividing by n. It is easily verified that Z_n satisfies the following commutative ring properties:

Addition is commutative and associative, and every element has an inverse, so that Z_n is a commutative (Abelian) group under addition:

1. $x + y \equiv y + x \ (\text{mod } n)$
2. $(x + y) + z \equiv x + (y + z) \ (\text{mod } n)$
3. $x + (- x) \equiv 0 \ (\text{mod } n)$

Multiplication is commutative and associative:

4. $xy \equiv yx \ (\text{mod } n)$
5. $(xy)z \equiv x(yz) \ (\text{mod } n)$

Multiplication distributes over addition:

6. $x(y + z) \equiv xy + xz \ (\text{mod } n)$

In the case when n is prime, Z_n is also a commutative group under multiplication, so that it determines a field known as the Galois field of integers modulo n, denoted by $\text{GF}(n)$.

It is easily verified that the relation R on the set Z of all integers, given by xRy if and only if $x \equiv y \ (\text{mod } n)$, is an equivalence relation, and an element x from $Z_n = \{0, \dots, n - 1\}$ can be identified with the equivalence class $[x] = \{\dots, x - 2n, x - n, x, x + n, x + 2n, \dots \}$ of all integers y such that $x \equiv y \ (\text{mod } n)$.

A.3   Some Summation Formulas

Summations involving arithmetic and geometric progressions occur frequently in the analysis of algorithms. Given real numbers a and d and a positive integer n, the sum of the first n terms of the arithmetic progression with leading term a and difference d is given by

$$a + (a + d) + (a + 2d) + \cdots + (a + (n - 1)d) = \frac{n(2a + (n - 1)d)}{2}. \textbf{(A.3.1)}$$

Formula (A.3.1) is easily proved by adding the progression to a copy of itself, but where we add the ith term in the original progression to the $(n - i + 1)^{\text{st}}$ term in the copy. Then each of the resulting n summands equals $(2a + (n - 1)d)$. In algorithm analysis, Formula (A.3.1) occurs most often with $a = d = 1$, in which case it reduces to

$$1 + 2 + \cdots + n = \frac{n(n + 1)}{2}. \qquad \text{(A.3.2)}$$

Given a real number x and a positive integer n, the sum of the first n terms of the geometric progression $1, x, x^2, \ldots, x^p, \ldots$ is given by

$$1 + x + x^2 + \cdots + x^{n-1} = (x^n - 1)/(x - 1). \qquad \text{(A.3.3)}$$

Formula (A.3.3) follows easily by multiplying both sides by $x - 1$ and simplifying the left side. An important special case in the analysis of algorithms occurs when $x = 2$. Then (A.3.3) reduces to

$$1 + 2 + 2^2 + \cdots + 2^{n-1} = 2^n - 1. \qquad \text{(A.3.4)}$$

Another way of interpreting Formula (A.3.4) is to note that the base-two expansion of the number $2^n - 1$ consists of a sequence of n 1s.

A formula that is useful when analyzing the average behavior of algorithms is obtained by replacing n by $n + 1$ in Formula (A.3.3) and then differentiating both sides of the equation, yielding

$$1 + 2x + 3x^2 + \cdots + nx^{n-1} = \frac{nx^{n+1} - (n + 1)x^n + 1}{(x - 1)^2}. \qquad \text{(A.3.5)}$$

For x a real number, $-1 < x < 1$, taking the limit of both sides of Formulas (A.3.3) and (A.3.5) as n approaches infinity yields the following two useful power series formulas:

$$\sum_{n=0}^{\infty} x^n = \frac{1}{1 - x} \qquad \text{(A.3.6)}$$

$$\sum_{n=0}^{\infty} (n + 1)x^n = \frac{1}{(1 - x)^2} \qquad \text{(A.3.7)}$$

Of course, Formula (A.3.7) can also be obtained from Formula (A.3.6) by differentiating both sides of the equation.

A.4 Binomial Coefficients

We now consider two combinatorial quantities that arise often in counting arguments and in probability computations. Suppose we have a finite set S having n elements. For any k between 0 and n, the number of ways to make an *ordered* choice of k elements from S is given by the product

$$n^{(k)} = n(n-1)\ldots(n-k+1). \qquad \textbf{(A.4.1)}$$

In particular, note that $n! = n^{(n)}$. The following inequality is useful:

$$\frac{n^{(k)}}{m^{(k)}} \le \left(\frac{n}{m}\right)^k, \quad 0 < k \le n < m. \qquad \textbf{(A.4.2)}$$

Let $C(n, k)$ denote the number of ways to make an *unordered* choice of k elements from S. It then follows that

$$C(n, k) = \frac{n^{(k)}}{k!}, \quad \text{for } k = 0, \ldots, n, \qquad \textbf{(A.4.3)}$$

because $n^{(k)}$ stood for the number of ordered choices of k elements, and there are $k!$ different orderings of these k elements. Hence, using Formulas (A.4.1) and (A.4.3), we have

$$C(n, k) = \frac{n(n-1)\ldots(n-k+1)}{k!} = \frac{n!}{(n-k)!k!} \quad \text{for } k = 0, \ldots n. \; \textbf{(A.4.4)}$$

We refer to $C(n, k)$ as "n choose k." We often use the alternative notation $\binom{n}{k}$ for $C(n, k)$. As an illustration, consider the set $S = \{a, b, c, d\}$. There are 12 ways to choose an ordered subset of two elements from S, namely,

$$ab, ba, ac, ca, ad, da, bc, cb, bd, db, cd, dc,$$

but only $12/2! = 6$ ways to choose an unordered two-element subset, namely,

$$\{a, b\}, \{a, c\}, \{a, d\}, \{b, c\}, \{b, d\}, \{c, d\}.$$

Thus, $4^{(2)} = 12$, and $C(4, 2) = \binom{4}{2} = 6$.

The number $C(n, k) = \dbinom{n}{k}$ is also called a *binomial coefficient* because of its appearance in the binomial expansion

$$(a + x)^n = \sum_{i=0}^{n} \binom{n}{i} a^{n-i} x^i$$

$$= \binom{n}{0} a^n x^0 + \binom{n}{1} a^{n-1} x^1 + \binom{n}{2} a^{n-2} x^2 + \cdots + \binom{n}{i} a^{n-i} x^i + \cdots + \binom{n}{n} a^0 x^n. \quad \textbf{(A.4.5)}$$

Taking the partial derivative of both sides of Formula (A.4.5) with respect to x and then multiplying by x yields the following useful identity:

$$nx(a + x)^{n-1} = \sum_{i=0}^{n} \binom{n}{i} a^{n-1} x^i i \quad \textbf{(A.4.6)}$$

The binomial coefficients give us yet another interpretation of the formula $1 + 2 + \cdots + n = n(n + 1)/2$. Combining Formulas (A.3.2) and (A.4.4) yields

$$1 + 2 + \cdots + n = \binom{n + 1}{2}. \quad \textbf{(A.4.7)}$$

A direct verification of Formula (A.4.7) can be given as follows. Let $\{1, 2, \ldots , n + 1\}$ be the $(n + 1)$-element set. Then there are n ways to choose a two-element subset containing 1, $n - 1$ ways to choose a two-element subset containing 2 but not 1, $n - 2$ ways to choose a two-element subset containing 3 but not 1 and 2, and so forth.

The binomial expansion (A.4.5) has the following important generalization (due to Newton) to the case where $a = 1$ and $|x| < 1$ and n is an arbitrary real number c:

$$(1 + x)^c = \sum_{i=0}^{\infty} \binom{c}{i} x^i, \quad \textbf{(A.4.8)}$$

where the generalized binomial coefficient is defined by

$$\binom{c}{k} = c(c - 1)\ldots(c - k + 1)/k!. \quad \textbf{(A.4.9)}$$

Formula (A.4.8) is often called the binomial theorem. A problem arises when attempting to implement an algorithm for $C(n, k)$ based directly on Formula (A.4.4): the rapid growth of the factorial function $k!$. For example, many compilers store integer variables using four bytes of storage, so that the largest integer that can be stored without overflow is $2^{31} - 1 = 2,147,483,648$. This value is already exceeded by 13!. One way around this is to calculate $C(n,k)$ as the product of the k fractions $\dfrac{n(n-1)}{1 \quad 2} \cdots \dfrac{(n-k+1)}{k}$. This calculation avoids integer overflow but has the disadvantage of using real arithmetic and introducing round-off errors if we simply compute and multiply the fractions. However, if at the ith stage we multiply the previous result by the numerator $(n-i)$ and then divide by the denominator $i + 1, i = 1, \ldots, k-1$, we avoid round-off errors. In applications where you desire a table of all the binomial coefficients $C(j, k)$ for $j = 1, \ldots, n, k = 0, \ldots, j$, it is best to use Pascal's recurrence relation given by

$$C(n, k) = C(n - 1, k - 1) + C(n - 1, k), \quad \textbf{init. cond. } C(n, 0) = C(n, n) = 1. \quad \textbf{(A.4.10)}$$

To verify recurrence relation (A.4.10), consider a set of n elements $S = \{s_1, s_2, \ldots, s_n\}$. The initial conditions in (A.4.10) are true because the only subset having zero elements is the empty set, and the only subset having n elements is S itself. To prove the recurrence relation, consider the element s_1. The subsets of S having k elements fall into two disjoint classes: those that contain s_1 and those that do not. If s_1 is in a subset of size k, then the remaining $k - 1$ elements of the subset must be chosen from the $n - 1$ elements in the subset $S\backslash\{s_1\}$. The number of such choices is $C(n - 1, k - 1)$. On the other hand, if s_1 is not in a subset of size k, then all k elements of this subset must be chosen from $S\backslash\{s_1\}$. The number of such choices is $C(n - 1, k)$. Thus, the total number of ways to choose a subset of k elements is the sum of $C(n - 1, k - 1)$ and $C(n - 1,k)$, which establishes the recurrence relation (A.4.10).

In Figure A.3, we show the famous *Pascal's triangle*, where each successive row in the triangle is obtained from the row above by using the recurrence relation

FIGURE A.3

Pascal's triangle generated by $C(n,k) = C(n - 1, k - 1) + C(n - 1, k)$, **init. cond.** $C(n, 0) = C(n, n) = 1$.

$k = 0$	1	2	3	4	5	6	7	8	9	.	.	.
$n = 0$	1											
1	1	1										
2	1	2	1									
3	1	3	3	1								
4	1	4	6	4	1							
5	1	5	10	10	5	1						
6	1	6	15	20	15	6	1					
7	1	7	21	35	35	21	7	1				
8	1	8	28	56	70	56	28	8	1			
9	1	9	36	84	126	126	84	36	9	1		

(A.4.10). The initial conditions yield the 1s forming two sides of the (infinite) triangle. The famous philosopher and mathematician Blaise Pascal exploited various properties of this triangle in a paper appearing in 1654. However, the triangle itself was already known to the Chinese as early as the 11th century.

A.5 Sets

Various definitions and notations from the elementary theory of sets are needed in our discussion of asymptotic behavior given in Chapter 3. Notations from set theory are also required in our discussion of elementary probability theory given in Chapter 6 and Appendix E. In addition to using sets in the mathematical analysis of algorithms, there are many important algorithms that implement **union** and **find** operations for disjoint sets.

Whenever we talk about a set, we assume that the set is contained in a certain *universal set U*. The set U is always clear from context (all edges in a graph, all real-valued functions defined on the nonnegative integers, all outcomes of an experiment, etc.). The set of real numbers and the set of nonnegative integers occur often, and we denote them by $\mathbb{R}$ and $\mathbb{N}$, respectively.

Given a set A, we indicate that x is a member of (belongs to) A by $x \in A$. We write $x \notin A$ when x is not a member of (does not belong to) A. The set having no members, called the *empty set*, is denoted by $\emptyset$. Given two sets A and B, we say that A is a *subset* of B, denoted by $A \subseteq B$, if every member of A is also a member of B; we also say that *A is contained in B*. If $A \subseteq B$ and $A \neq B$, then we say that A is a *proper subset* of B, denoted by $A \subset B$; we also say that A is *strictly* contained in B. The *union* of A and B, denoted by $A \cup B$, is the set of all elements that are members of either A or B (or both). The *intersection* of A and B, denoted by $A \cap B$, is the set of all elements that are members of both A and B. The sets A and B are called *disjoint* if $A \cap B = \emptyset$. The *difference* between A and B, denoted by $A \backslash B$, is the set of all members of A that are not members of B. The *complement* of A, denoted by A^c, is the set of all members of the universal set U that are not members of A, that is $A^c = U \backslash A$. The *Cartesian product* $A \times B$ is the set of all ordered pairs $\{(a, b) : a \in A, b \in B\}$.

Figure A.4 gives *Venn diagrams* illustrating subset, union, intersection, difference, and complement.

FIGURE A.4

Venn diagrams for
set operations.

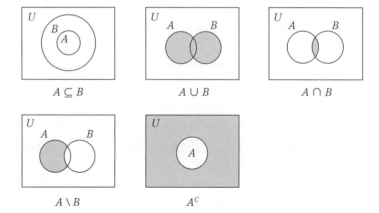

$A \subseteq B$ $A \cup B$ $A \cap B$

$A \setminus B$ A^C

A.6 Complex Numbers

Often when solving problems in which inputs and outputs are real numbers, it is useful in intermediate stages to use the complex numbers. For example, in Chapter 22, we develop a fast algorithm for computing the symbolic product of two input polynomials with *real* coefficients (so that the output product polynomial also has *real* coefficients) by using the Fast Fourier Transform (FFT) to evaluate the polynomials at the set of nth roots of unity. We now quickly review the necessary theory of complex numbers required by the FFT and similar algorithms.

The use of counting numbers is part of the earliest written historical record. However, the use of negative numbers occurs much later. There are understandable reasons for the relatively late appearance of negative numbers, but their introduction apparently caused little controversy. This was not the case, however, when numbers such as $\sqrt{-1}$ were introduced. Mathematicians wanted to solve simple equations that had no solutions in the real numbers, such as $x^2 + 1 = 0$. Thus, the so-called *complex numbers* of the form $a + ib$ were introduced, where $i = \sqrt{-1}$ stood for a number whose square was -1. To make the introduction of i more acceptable, it was called an *imaginary number*. More generally, ib is referred to as the *imaginary part* of the complex number $a + ib$, and a is called the *real part*.

The early apologies made for $i = \sqrt{-1}$ are somewhat amusing nowadays because the complex numbers $a + ib$ can be formally introduced simply as pairs (a, b) of real numbers [so that $a + ib$ corresponds to (a, b)], together with arithmetic operations of addition, subtraction, multiplication (denoted by juxtaposition), and reciprocation defined as follows:

DEFINITION A.6.1   Arithmetic Operations

1. $(a, b) \pm (c, d) = (a \pm c, b \pm d)$,
2. $(a, b)(c, d) = (ac - bd, ad + bc)$,
3. $(a, b)^{-1} = (a/(a^2 + b^2), -b/(a^2 + b^2))$.

The right sides of definitions 1, 2, and 3 use the usual arithmetic operations on real numbers, and the left sides define the corresponding operation (using the same symbols) on the complex numbers. Using definition 3, division is defined as $(a, b)/(c, d) = (a, b)(c, d)^{-1}$. Definitions 2 and 3 seem somewhat unmotivated, but they arise naturally, as explained shortly. Note that the real number a can be identified with the complex number as $(a, 0)$. When definitions 1, 2, and 3 are restricted to the pairs $(a, 0)$ as a varies over the real numbers, they coincide with the ordinary arithmetic rules for real numbers. Thus, we have naturally extended the real numbers to the larger set of complex numbers. Moreover, $(0, 1)^2 = (-1, 0)$, so that we have indeed found $\sqrt{-1}$, which we denote by i. Of course, $-i = (0, -1)$ also squares to -1, so we now have two complex numbers whose square is -1, whereas the real numbers have none.

Under our identification of b with $(b, 0)$ [and using i to denote $(0, 1)$], we can think of ib as the product of $(0, 1)$ with $(b, 0)$; that is, ib corresponds to $(0, b)$. In the same way, the addition $(a, 0) + (0, b)$ can be written as $a + ib$, and the multiplication $(c, 0)(a, b) = (ca, cb)$ can be viewed as $c(a + ib) = ca + icb$. With similar identifications, we see how definition 2 arises naturally from the distributive and commutative laws.

$$(a, b)(c, d) \text{ corresponds to } (a + ib)(c + id)$$
$$= ac + iad + ibc + i^2bd$$
$$= ac - bd + i(ad + bc)$$

which corresponds to $(ac - bd, ad + bc)$.

Definition 3 for reciprocals takes its motivation from

$$\frac{1}{a + ib} \frac{a - ib}{a - ib} = \frac{a - ib}{a^2 + b^2}.$$

Just as we consider the real numbers as corresponding to points on a straight line, we think of the complex numbers as corresponding to points in a plane. Thus, we identify the complex numbers $z = x + iy$ with points (two-dimensional vectors) (x, y) in the xy plane, with the reals x identified with the points $(x, 0)$ on the x-axis. The *modulus of* $z = x + iy$, denoted by $|z|$, is defined to be the distance from (x, y) to the origin $(0, 0)$; that is,

$$|z| = (x^2 + y^2)^{1/2}.$$

Note that the modulus of a point on the x-axis corresponds to the absolute value of the point.

Using the analogy with polar coordinates in the plane, given the complex number $z = x + iy$, it is useful to write z as

$$z = |z| \left(\frac{z}{|z|} \right), \tag{A.6.1}$$

where $\dfrac{z}{|z|}$ is a point on the unit circle. Hence, $\dfrac{z}{|z|}$ can be written as $\cos(\theta) + i\sin(\theta)$ for an appropriate angle θ between the vector determined by z and the x axis (see Figure A.5), so that Formula (A.6.1) becomes

$$z = |z| \left(\cos(\theta) + i \sin(\theta) \right). \tag{A.6.2}$$

In the representation (A.6.2), the angle θ is referred to as an *argument* of z. If $0 \le \theta < 2\pi$, then θ is called the *principal argument* of z.

FIGURE A.5

Modulus I z I and principle argument θ of a sample complex number z.

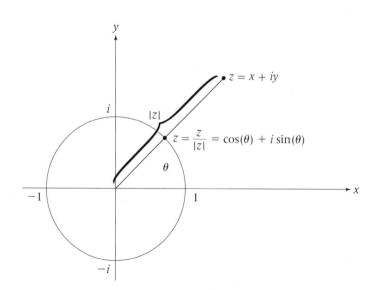

Using the exponential function e^z, we rewrite Formula (A.6.2) as follows. In analogy with the Taylor's expansion for e^x for real x, the Taylor's expansion for e^z for complex z is given by

$$e^z = 1 + z + \frac{z^2}{2!} + \cdots + \frac{z^n}{n!} + \cdots . \qquad \text{(A.6.3)}$$

Substituting $z = i\theta$ into Formula (A.6.3) yields

$$e^{i\theta} = 1 + i\theta - \frac{\theta^2}{2!} - \frac{i\theta^3}{3!} + \frac{\theta^4}{4!} + \frac{i\theta^5}{5!} - \frac{\theta^6}{6!} - \frac{i\theta^7}{7!} + \cdots$$

$$= \cos(\theta) + i\sin(\theta). \qquad \text{(A.6.4)}$$

Setting $r = |z|$ and substituting Formula (A.6.4) into (A.6.2) yields

$$z = re^{i\theta}, \quad r = |z|, \frac{z}{|z|} = \cos(\theta) + i\sin(\theta). \qquad \text{(A.6.5)}$$

REMARK

Substituting $\theta = \pi$ into Formula (A.6.5) yields Euler's formula

$$e^{i\pi} + 1 = 0,$$

a remarkable formula indeed because it relates the fundamental mathematical constants e, i, π, 1, and 0 in such a simple way.

The expression (A.6.5) for z yields a nice geometric interpretation (see Figure A.6) for the product of two complex numbers $z_1 = r_1 e^{i\theta_1}$, $z_2 = r_2 e^{i\theta_2}$:

$$z_1 z_2 = (r_1 e^{i\theta_1})(r_1 e^{i\theta_2})$$

$$= r_1 r_2 e^{i(\theta_1 + \theta_2)}. \qquad \text{(A.6.6)}$$

From the generalization of (A.6.6) to the product of n complex numbers, we have the following multiplication rule for obtaining the modulus and argument of the product of n complex numbers.

DEFINITION A.6.2 Multiplication Rule for n Complex Numbers

Multiply the moduli and add the arguments.

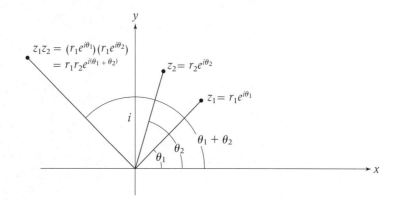

An important special case of the multiplication rule is a formula for the nth power of a complex number $z = re^{i\theta}$, known as DeMoivre's formula:

$$(re^{i\theta})^n = r^n e^{in\theta}. \tag{A.6.7}$$

Given the complex number $z \neq 0$, Formula (A.6.7) yields a formula for the n different complex numbers whose n^{th} powers equal z (that is, the nth roots of z):

$$z^{1/n} = \{ r^{1/n}(e^{i((\theta + 2\pi k)/n)}) \,|\, z = re^{i\theta}, 0 \leq \theta < 2\pi, k = 0,1, \dots, n-1 \} \tag{A.6.8}$$

It is easily verified that the nth roots of z defined by Formula (A.6.8) are all distinct. When $z = 1$, Formula (A.6.8) yields the set of nth *roots of unity*. These points all lie on the unit circle and are equally spaced, starting at 1 (see Figure A.7). Moreover, they are all powers of the single n^{th} root $e^{2\pi i/n}$, which is a primitive n^{th} root of unity. More generally, a primitive n^{th} root of unity ω is a complex number such that $\omega^n = 1$, but $\omega^k \neq 1$ for $k = 1, \dots, n-1$.

The following useful propositions are easily verified.

Proposition A.6.1

Let ω be a primitive nth root of unity, and let k be an integer such that $0 < k < n$. Then

$$1 + \omega^k + (\omega^k)^2 + \cdots + (\omega^k)^{n-1} = 0.$$

Proposition A.6.2

If ω is a primitive n^{th} root of unity, then ω^2 is a primitive $(n/2)^{\text{th}}$ root of unity.

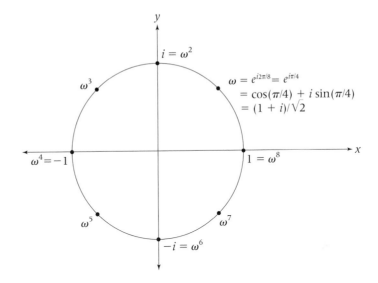

Proposition A.6.3

If ω is a primitive n^{th} root of unity and k is a positive integer, then $\omega^k = 1$ if and only if n divides k.

▦ A.7 Mathematical Induction

Mathematical induction is the most commonly used technique for establishing the correctness of an algorithm. Correctness proofs often proceed by establishing loop invariants with the aid of mathematical induction. Mathematical induction is also useful in both the analysis of algorithms and as an algorithm design tool.

Often we would like to establish the validity of a proposition or formula concerning the set of positive integers such as

$$1^2 + 2^2 + \cdots + n^2 = \frac{n(n + 1)(2n + 1)}{6}$$ is true for each positive integer n.

This formula can be easily verified for any particular small n by directly computing and comparing both sides of the equation. For example, if $n = 5$, we get $1^2 + 2^2 + 3^2 + 4^2 + 5^2 = 1 + 4 + 9 + 16 + 25 = 55 = 5(6)(11)/6$. The question is, how do we verify that the formula is true for *all* positive integers n? More generally, suppose we have a sequence of propositions $P(1), P(2), \ldots, P(n), \ldots$ indexed by the

positive integers, and we wish to establish the truth of each one of these propositions. For example, the preceding formula is the sequence of propositions

$$P(n): 1^2 + 2^2 + \cdots + n^2 = \frac{n(n+1)(2n+1)}{6}.$$

Another example might be

$$P(n): EvenOddSort1dMesh \text{ sorts a list of size } n.$$

Given such a sequence, we clearly cannot prove each proposition one at a
time; that would take forever. Thus, we use the Principle of Mathematical Induction, a very powerful method by which the truth of such a sequence of
propositions $P(1), P(2), \ldots, P(n), \ldots$ can be established.

A.7.1 Principle of Mathematical Induction

We first state the principle of mathematical induction in its usual form. We then
state the principle in various alternative (basically equivalent) forms, which are
often used in algorithm analysis.

DEFINITION A.7.1   Principle of Mathematical Induction

Suppose we have a sequence of propositions $P(1), P(2), \ldots, P(n), \ldots$ for
which the following two steps have been established:

Basis step: $P(1)$ is true

Induction (or implication) step: *If* $P(k)$ *is true for any given* k, *then* $P(k + 1)$
must also be true.
Then $P(n)$ is true for all positive integers n.

The validity of the Principle of Mathematical Induction can be seen as follows. Since $P(1)$ is true, the induction step shows that $P(2)$ is true. But the truth
of $P(2)$ in turn implies that $P(3)$ is true, and so forth. The induction step allows
this process to continue indefinitely. The truth of $P(n)$ for all n rests ultimately on
the following property of the positive integers: Every nonempty subset of the
positive integers has a smallest element. The assumption that $P(k)$ is false for
some k then leads to a contradiction. Indeed, if the set $\{k \mid P(k) \text{ is false}\}$ is non-

empty, then it has a smallest element L. But $l > 1$, so that $P(l - 1)$ is true. Letting $n = l - 1$, our induction step implies that $P(n + 1) = P(l)$ is true, which is a contradiction.

As our first illustration of the use of mathematical induction, we now establish that the formula $1^2 + 2^2 + \cdots + n^2 = n(n + 1)(2n + 1)/6$ is true for all n. We proceed as follows:

Basis step: $1^2 = 1 = 1(1 + 1)\dfrac{1(1 + 1)(2 + 1)}{6}$ ($P(1)$ is true).

Induction step: Assume that $P(k)$ is true for a given k, so that $1^2 + 2^2 + \cdots + k^2 = k(k + 1)(2k + 1)/6$. We must show that it would follow that $P(k + 1)$ is true—namely, that $1^2 + 2^2 + \cdots + (k + 1)^2 = (k + 1)(k + 2)(2k + 3)/6$. We have

$$1^2 + 2^2 + \cdots + k^2 + (k + 1)^2 = (1^2 + 2^2 + \cdots + k^2) + (k + 1)^2$$

$$= k(k + 1)\frac{(2k + 1)}{6} + (k + 1)^2 \text{ (since } P(k) \text{ is assumed true)}$$

$$= \frac{(k + 1)[k(2k + 1) + 6(k + 1)]}{6} = \frac{(k + 1)(2k^2 + 7k + 6)}{6}$$

$$= \frac{(k + 1)(k + 2)(2k + 3)}{6},$$

and therefore $P(k + 1)$ is true.

We have thus proved the induction step, and by the Principle of Mathematical Induction, the proposition $1^2 + 2^2 + \cdots + n^2 = n(n + 1)(2n + 1)/6$ is true for all positive integers n.

A.7.2 Variations of the Principle of Mathematical Induction

The following three variations of the Principle of Mathematical Induction are frequently encountered in the analysis of algorithms. In practice, a combination of these variants might be used.

1. Often the sequence of propositions starts with an index different from 1, such as 0. Then the basis step starts with this initial index. The induction step remains the same, and the two steps together establish the truth of the propositions $P(n)$ for all n greater than or equal to this initial index.

2. Sometimes the propositions are only finite in number, $P(1), \ldots, P(l)$. Then the induction step is modified to require that $k < l$. Of course, the conclusion then drawn is that $P(1), \ldots, P(l)$ are all true if the basis and induction steps are valid.

3. The Principle of Mathematical Induction can also be stated in the following so-called *strong form*, where the induction step is as follows:

> ***Induction step (strong form):*** For any positive integer k, *if $P(j)$ is true for all* positive integers $j \leq k$, *then $P(k + 1)$ must also be true.*

The strong form of induction is very useful in establishing the correctness of recursive algorithms, because for an input of size n, the recursive calls often involve smaller input sizes than $n - 1$. For example, to prove that an inorder traversal of a binary search tree on n nodes visits the keys in increasing order, which is the basis of the treesort algorithm given in Chapter 4, the strong form of induction is needed because the left and right subtrees can have any number of nodes between 0 and $n - 1$.

LINEAR DATA STRUCTURES

Many algorithms discussed in this text use a list as one of the primary abstract data types. Among the operations associated with a list are insertion, deletion, and accessing a particular element in the list. For convenience, when describing algorithms, we often implement the list ADT as an array. However, in practice there are a number of situations where a linked list implementation would improve performance.

B.1 Implementing the List ADT: Arrays Versus Linked Lists

The array implementation of a list has the important advantage of allowing quick and *direct* access to any element of the list. However, there are some disadvantages in using an array. For example, inserting an element at index position i of a list stored in positions $0, \dots, n - 1$ of an array requires $n - i$ array assignments. Deleting an element also requires many array assignments.

Another disadvantage relates to inefficient use of space. A particular list may occupy only a small portion of an array that has been declared to handle much larger lists. A linked list avoids these disadvantages at the expense of direct access.

FIGURE B.1

A linked list.

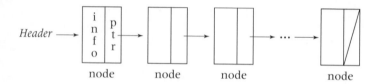

A linked list is a set of nodes, where each node contains an information field and a pointer field. The information field contains data whose type depends on the application, and the pointer field contains a *pointer* that specifies the location of the next node in the linked list. In addition to the pointers contained in each node, there is a pointer to the beginning of the linked list (see Figure B.1).

Most high-level languages support pointers and dynamic variables; therefore, except for additional space used by the pointers, we can implement lists without wasted storage. Nodes can be allocated and disposed of as needed. The nodes of a linked list can then be stored in dynamic variables, which are records of the following type:

> *ListNode* = **record**
> > *Info*: *InfoType*
> > *Next*: →*ListNode*
> > **end**

InfoType represents a generic type, which could be an integer, a real, a string, or even a record containing many information fields.

Given a pointer to an appropriate position in the list, insertion and deletion of elements in a linked list are particularly efficient because only two pointers need to be altered. For example, suppose *Place* is a pointer to a node of the linked list, and *NewNode* is a pointer to a node not in the linked list. The node pointed to by *NewNode* can be inserted into the linked list immediately after the node pointed to by *Place* and the linked list maintained as follows:

> *NewNode*→*Next* ← *Place*→*Next*
> *Place*→*Next* ← *NewNode*

If *Place* points to the first node of the linked list, then we would replace *Place* by *Header* in the pseudocode. The action of this pseudocode is illustrated in Figure B.2.

FIGURE B.2

Inserting an element into a linked list using only two pointer assignments.

Before insertion:

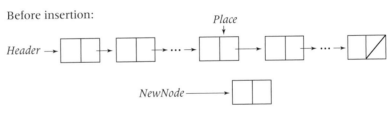

After insertion:

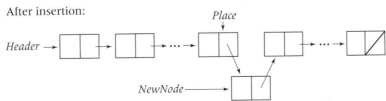

B.2 Stack ADT

A *stack* is a list in which all insertions and deletions are made at one end, called the *top*. Because the last element inserted is the first element removed, a stack is also commonly referred to as a LIFO (last in, first out) list. The operation of inserting an element into the stack is called *push*, and the operation of removing an element is called *pop*. Stacks pop up everywhere in the field of computer science. In addition to their use in algorithm design, stacks are used by computer systems to maintain parameters, local variables, return addresses, and so forth for function invocations and procedure calls.

Because a stack is a list, it can be implemented using an array or a linked list. In the array implementation, we use an array $Stack[0:MaxSize - 1]$ and the auxiliary variable Top to hold the index of the array element that is at the top of the stack. An empty stack corresponds to $Top = -1$, whereas a full stack corresponds to $Top = MaxSize - 1$. Checking whether a stack is empty or full, respectively, is an additional operation of the stack ADT.

Pushing (inserting) an element x on the stack can be performed using the following unrefined pseudocode:

```
if Top = MaxSize − 1 then          //Stack is full
        take appropriate action on stack full condition
else
        Top ← Top + 1
        Stack[Top] ← x
endif
```

Popping the stack and assigning the popped element to *x* is accomplished by the following unrefined pseudocode:

```
if Top = − 1 then                                    //Stack is empty
    take appropriate action on stack empty condition
else
    x ← Stack[Top]
    Top ← Top − 1
endif
```

B.3   Queue ADT

A *queue* is a list in which all insertions are made at one end of the list, called the *rear*, and all deletions are made at the other end, called the *front*. In a queue, the first element inserted is the first element removed; thus, a queue is also referred to as a FIFO (first in, first out) list. Queues occur frequently and in a variety of settings in computer science. Examples in the systems area include queues of tasks waiting for a shared printer, queued access to disk storage, jobs waiting for CPU access in a time-sharing environment, and so forth. Queues are also used in simulations and as data structures in algorithms such as breadth-first search of graphs, branch-and-bound searching of state-space trees, message queues in a distributed network, and so forth.

Since a queue is a list, it can be implemented by using an array or a linked list. Consider an array implementation *Queue*[0:*MaxSize* − 1] that mimics, for example, a queue of people waiting in a checkout line. When an element is dequeued, all the remaining elements are bumped up one position in the array, so that the element in the front of the queue always has index 0 (*Queue*[0]). A variable *Rear* contains the index of the element at the rear of the queue and is simply incremented by 1 when enqueueing an element. However, dequeueing is very inefficient because it involves *Rear* − 1 index updates (and a decrementing of *Rear* by 1).

A more efficient (but still troublesome) array implementation is to use *Front* and *Rear* as variables containing indices of the elements at the front and one past the rear of the queue, respectively. Both *Front* and *Rear* might be initialized to 0. We increment *Rear* by 1 for enqueueing and increment *Front* by 1 for dequeueing. The condition *Front* = *Rear* signals that the queue is empty, whereas *Rear* = *MaxSize* signals that the queue is full. As long as we never perform more than *MaxSize* enqueues, everything is fine. Otherwise, an obvious problem can arise: We might end up with the queue being signaled as full when it is practically empty. For example, starting from an initially empty queue ($Front = Rear = 0$), an alternating sequence of *MaxSize* enqueues and *MaxSize* − 1 dequeues results in *Front* = *MaxSize* and *Rear* = *MaxSize*. An attempt to enqueue an element results in the queue being signaled as full even though the array contains a single element!

An array implementation of a queue that avoids the problems arising in the previous two implementations is the *circular array,* which is an array with indices viewed in a circular fashion. This implementation of a queue is developed in Exercise 2.14 in Chapter 2. Another efficient way to implement a queue is to use a linked list.

B.4 Removing Recursion

Recursion is used throughout the text in the design of algorithms. However, while recursion is a power design tool, often it is useful to redesign a recursive algorithm to minimize the overhead resulting from recursive calls and to eliminate redundant computations that often accompany multiple-reference recursion. In this section, we show how to remove tail recursion, and then discuss how to use stacks to eliminate recursive calls by simulating the action that a compiler takes to handle recursive calls (or, more generally, any function call).

B.4.1 Removing Tail Recursion

A recursive procedure or function is *tail recursive* when the last executable statement in the pseudocode is a simple recursive reference. Such a recursive reference (called *tail recursion*) can be removed by (1) redefining parameters or assigning the parameter expressions involved in the recursive call to suitable local variables, and (2) making an unconditional branch to the first executable statement in the code. The reason that this action obviates the need for actually making the recursive call is that on resolving such a recursive reference, the return is to the end of the code. Hence, the code either terminates or immediately resolves the previous recursive reference. In other words, no useful work would result from saving the current activation record on the implicit stack modeling the recursion.

When removing tail recursion, the unconditional branch to the first executable statement in the code is typically implemented by introducing a **while** loop that continues to execute until the initial conditions of the recursion are satisfied. A final statement (or statements) after the **while** loop then returns the appropriate function value or assigns appropriate values to output parameters (or performs a suitable operation) as determined by the initial conditions. Removing tail recursion is usually desirable if for no other reason than to save the overhead of the recursive calls.

To illustrate how to remove tail recursion, we consider the famous Towers of Hanoi puzzle. You are probably familiar with this example, as it is usually discussed when recursion is first introduced in beginning computer science courses. Although it is certainly not a practical example, we discuss it here because it serves to illustrate the general technique of removing recursion. In Chapter 2, we illustrate the removal of tail recursion with a rather more practical example, namely, quicksort. In Chapter 4, we remove the tail recursion of an inorder traversal of a binary tree.

Suppose we have three pegs A, B, C with n disks. The n disks are of different diameters and are initially placed on peg A so that a larger disk is always below a smaller disk (see Figure B.3). The object is to move all n disks to peg C using peg B as an auxiliary. A move consists of removing a single disk at the top of a peg and moving it to another peg. However, a given disk may never be placed on top of a smaller one. An elegant solution to the puzzle can be described easily using recursion.

The problem is immediately solved for $n = 1$: Simply move the disk on peg A to peg C. Although it is not clear how an explicit solution to the puzzle might be obtained for general n, we can easily state a solution for the n disks in terms of a solution for the $n - 1$ disks:

1. Move the top $n - 1$ disks from A to B, using C as an auxiliary.
2. Move the remaining disk from A to C.
3. Move the $n - 1$ disks from B to C, using A as an auxiliary.

The following pseudocode for the multiple-reference recursive procedure *Towers* amounts to nothing more than a direct translation of these three steps. The only trick is to be careful to use the appropriate arguments in the two recursive calls. The original call to *Towers* is with three character arguments 'A', 'B', 'C', and integer argument n.

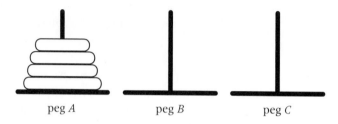

FIGURE B.3

The Towers of Hanoi puzzle.

peg A peg B peg C

procedure *Towers(First, Auxiliary, Last, n)* **recursive**
Input: *First, Auxiliary, Last* (names of three pegs), *n* (a positive integer)
Output: a solution to the Towers of Hanoi puzzle
    if $n = 1$ **then**
        write ("Move disk", 1, "from peg", *First*, "to peg", *Last*)
    else
        Towers(First, Last, Auxiliary, n − 1)
        write ("Move disk", *n*, "from peg", *First*, "to peg", *Last*)
        Towers(Auxiliary, First, Last, n − 1)
    endif
end *Towers*

Removing the tail recursion from *Towers* results in the following pseudocode for *Towers2*:

procedure *Towers2(First, Auxiliary, Last, n)* **recursive**
Input: *First, Auxiliary, Last* (names of three pegs)
Output: a solution to the Towers of Hanoi puzzle
    while $n > 1$ **do**
        Towers2(First, Last, Auxiliary, n − 1)
        write ("Move disk", *n*, "from peg", *First*, "to peg", *Last*)
        interchange(*Auxiliary, First*)
        $n \leftarrow n - 1$
    endwhile
    write ("Move disk", 1, "from peg", *First*, "to peg", *Last*)
end *Towers2*

B.5 Removing Explicit Recursion by Simulation

Whenever a recursive function or procedure is executed, an implicit stack of unresolved activation records is maintained. Executing a recursive reference results in pushing the current activation record on the stack and starting another execution of the recursive function or procedure with a new activation record that includes the new values for the input parameters as specified in the recursive reference. The stacked activation record typically contains (among other things, such as the state of the registers) the values that all local variables had when the recursive reference was executed, as well as the return address of he first executable statement in the code following the recursive reference. When a given recursive reference is resolved by executing a return statement, the stack is popped, execution continues at the statement determined by the popped return address, and the now current activation record is restored from the popped values. If the recursive reference has out or inout parameters, then the appropriate values for these parameters must be assigned to the corresponding values on the top of the stack before the stack is popped. Also, if we are dealing with a recursive function, then arrangements must be made to return the value to an appropriate variable in the now current activation record.

By simulating this stacking and unstacking of the activation records using an explicit stack, we can translate a recursive function or procedure into an equivalent nonrecursive version. Roughly speaking, recursive invocations or calls are simulated by pushing all parameters and local variables on a stack, together with a return address for the first executable statement following the recursive reference. Then parameters are recomputed according to the expressions in the recursive call, and a branch is made to the beginning of the pseudocode. Returns are simulated by popping the stack and assigning parameters and local variables the appropriate popped values. Then a branch is made to the statement determined by the return address that was popped off the stack (or otherwise determined), and execution is continued.

We illustrate this simulation by translating *Towers*. We use *Towers* instead of *Towers2* because tracing its action shows that tail recursion generates useless pushing and popping of activation records. In the pseudocode for *Towers3*, we introduce statement numbers and use the **goto** statement to facilitate the direct simulation of recursion.

Of course, the **goto** statement has been discredited, as its use often leads to "spaghetti" code that is hard to follow. We use it here because it most closely reflects the simple translation of the recursion.

```
procedure Towers3(First, Auxiliary, Last, n) recursive
Input:    First, Auxiliary, Last (names of three pegs), n (a positive integer)
Output:                      a solution to the Towers of Hanoi puzzle
    stack S
1 if n = 1 then
        write ("Move disk", 1, "from peg", First, "to peg", Last)
    else
        Push(S, First, Auxiliary, Last, n − 1, 2)
        interchange(Auxiliary, Last)
        goto 1
2       write ("Move disk", n, "from peg", First, "to peg", Last)
        Push(S, First, Auxiliary, Last, n − 1, 3)
        interchange(First, Auxiliary)
        goto 1
    endif
```

```
3 if .not. Empty(S) then
        Pop(S, First, Auxiliary, Last, RetAddr)
        goto RetAddr
    endif
end Towers3
```

Note that whenever we push the stack *S* with *RetAddr* = 3 corresponding to the tail recursive call, when the activation record corresponding to this push is popped, we either terminate the code or simply execute another pop of the stack. This reinforces the fact that this tail recursion should be removed. The result of this removal leads to *Towers4*. Since *Towers4* is now single-reference recursion, there is only one place to return from a recursive call (statement 2 in our case), so that we do not need to stack the return address. This is generally true for single-reference recursion.

```
procedure Towers4(First, Auxiliary, Last, n) recursive
Input:    First, Auxiliary, Last (names of three pegs), n (a positive integer)
Output:   a solution to the Towers of Hanoi puzzle
    stack S
1   if n = 1 then
        write ("Move disk", 1, "from peg", First, "to peg", Last)
    else
        Push(S, First, Auxiliary, Last, n − 1)
        interchange(Auxiliary, Last)
        goto 1
2       write ("Move disk", n, "from peg", First, "to peg", Last)
        interchange(First, Auxiliary)
        goto 1
    endif
    if .not. Empty(S) then
        Pop(S, First, Auxiliary, Last)
        goto 2
    endif
end Towers4
```

Towers4 can be rewritten in a manner that conforms to modern structured programming practices (in particular, without **goto**s). Our informal discussion of the simulation of recursion using an explicit stack can be made completely formal and general. A completely general canonical description of the stack simulation that uses a set of formal rules for translating out the recursion in a line-by-line fashion can be found in the references.

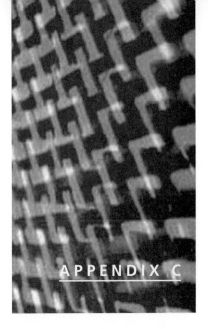

INTERPOLATING ASYMPTOTIC BEHAVIOR

Interpolating asymptotic behavior is a useful tool in algorithm analysis, especially when solving recurrence relations. Suppose we have two functions $f(n)$, $g(n) \in \mathscr{T}$, and we know that $f(s(n)) \in \Theta(g(s(n)))$, where $s(0) < s(1) < s(2) < \ldots$. For example, in the analysis of binary search given in Chapter 3, we showed that $W(n)$ is equal to $1 + \log_2 n$ for $n = 1, 2, 2^2, \ldots$ (this result does not hold for all n). Thus, setting $f(n) = W(n)$, $g(n) = \log_2 n$ for $s(k) = 2^k$, we find that $f(s(n)) \in \Theta(g(s(n)))$. Using the fact that $W(n)$ is an increasing function, we were able to show that $W(n) \in \Theta(\log n)$. Given general functions $f(n)$ and $g(n)$, where $f(s(n)) \in \Theta(g(s(n)))$, we seek conditions on $f(n)$ and $g(n)$ that imply $f(n) \in \Theta(g(n))$.

For our purposes it is sufficient to restrict $s(n)$ to powers of a base b (usually $b = 2$); namely, $s(n) = b^n$, $n \in \mathbb{N}$. For such a sequence $s(n)$ there are simple conditions on $f(n)$ and $g(n)$ that yield our desired interpolation result. The first condition on $f(n)$ and $g(n)$ is that they be eventually nondecreasing. A function $h(n)$ is *eventually nondecreasing* if there exists an integer n_0 such that $h(n) \leq h(m)$, whenever $m \geq n \geq n_0$. Most of the time, the functions $W(n)$, $B(n)$, and $A(n)$, which measure the complexity of an algorithm, are eventually nondecreasing because the number of basic operations performed usually increases as the input size n increases. A second condition that we place on $g(n)$ is that

$$g(cn) \in \Theta(g(n)), \quad \text{for all positive constants (integers) } c. \quad \textbf{(C.1)}$$

Proposition C.1   If $g(n) \in \mathscr{F}$ has the property that $g(cn) \in \Theta(g(n))$, then $f(cn) \in \Theta(g(n)) = \Theta(f(n))$ for all $f(n) \in \Theta(g(n))$.

Proposition C.1 implies that the class $\Theta(g(n))$ is invariant under any "change of scale" of the input n to any representative of $\Theta(g(n))$. We refer to such a Θ-class as *scale invariant*, and we refer to any function in the class as Θ-*invariant under scaling*. Functions that are Θ-invariant under scaling include logarithm functions and polynomials but not exponential functions. Also, sums and products of functions that are Θ-invariant under scaling are themselves Θ-invariant under scaling.

Proposition C.2   Suppose $g(n) \in \mathscr{F}$ is eventually nondecreasing and Θ-invariant under scaling. Further, suppose $f(n) \in \mathscr{F}$ is eventually nondecreasing and $f(b^n) \in X(g(b^n))$, $n \in \mathbb{N}$, where X is one of the classes Θ, Ω, O, and $b > 1$. Then $f(n) \in X(g(n))$.

PROOF

First we consider the case $X = O$. Clearly, any positive integer n is either a power of b or lies between two powers of b. That is, given any positive integer n, there exists a positive integer $k(n)$ (dependent on n) such that $b^{k(n)-1} \leq n < b^{k(n)}$. Since $f(n)$ is eventually nondecreasing, there exists a positive integer constant N (independent of n) such that

$$f(b^{k(n)-1}) \leq f(n) \leq f(b^{k(n)}), \quad \forall n \geq N. \quad \textbf{(C.2)}$$

Now $f(b^n) \in O(g(b^n))$. Thus, there exist positive constants d and m_0 such that

$$f(b^m) \leq dg(b^m), \quad \forall m \geq m_0. \quad \textbf{(C.3)}$$

Because g is Θ-invariant under scaling, it follows that there exist positive constants d' and m_0' such that

$$g(b^m) = g(bb^{m-1}) \leq d' \, g(b^{m-1}), \quad \forall m \geq m_0'. \tag{C.4}$$

We now choose $m = n(k)$, so that $b^{m-1} \leq n < b^m$. Since g is eventually non-decreasing, it follows that there exists a positive constant N' such that

$$g(b^{m-1}) \leq g(n), \quad \forall n \geq N'. \tag{C.5}$$

It follows from Formulas (C.2), (C.3), (C.4), and (C.5) that there exists a positive constant n_0 such that

$$f(n) \leq f(b^m) \leq dg(b^m) \leq dd'g(b^{m-1}) \leq dd'g(n), \quad \forall n \geq n_0. \tag{C.6}$$

Hence, $f(n) \in O(g(n))$, which proves Proposition C. 2 for the case $X = O$. A similar proof yields the case $X = \Omega$. The case $X = \Theta$ then follows immediately from the cases $X = O$ and $X = \Theta$.

RANDOM WALKS IN DIGRAPHS

In this appendix, we give a brief description of some concepts involving random walks and Markov chains that we use in our discussion of Web page ranking in Chapter 17. A *walk* W of length p in a graph G from u to v, also called a u-v walk, is an alternating sequence of vertices and edges $v_0, e_1, v_1, e_2, v_2, \ldots, e_p, v_p$, where $v_0 = u$ and $v_p = v$, such that each $e_i = \{v_i, v_{i+1}\}$ is an edge of G, $i = 0, 1, \ldots, p$. Vertices v_0 and v_p are the initial and terminal vertices of W, respectively, and vertices $v_1, \ldots, v_p$ are the internal vertices of W. A u-v walk in a directed graph D is defined analogously except that $e_i = (v_i, v_{i+1})$ is a directed edge.

 ## D.1 Enumerating Walks

The number $w_{ij}(k)$ of walks from v_i to v_j of length k can be computed using the adjacency matrix as follows. We assume that the node set of the digraph D is $V = \{0, 1, \ldots, n - 1\}$.

Theorem D.1.1

The number $w_{ij}(k)$ of walks from i to j of length k in a digraph D equals the ij^{th} entry of the kth power of the adjacency matrix A of D; that is,

$$w_{ij}(k) = A^k(i,j), i, j = 0, \ldots, n-1.$$

PROOF

We prove Theorem D.1.1 using mathematical induction on k. The theorem is true for $k = 0$ because the only walks of length 0 are the trivial walks with no internal vertices whose initial and terminal vertices are the same, establishing the basis step. Now assume the theorem is true for walks of length $k - 1$; that is, $w_{ij}(k-1) = A^{k-1}(i,j)$. It follows from the definition of a walk that

$$
\begin{aligned}
w_{ij}(k) &= \sum_{il \in E} w_{lj}(k-1) \\
&= \sum_{l=0}^{n-1} A(i,l) w_{lj}(k-1)
\end{aligned}
$$

Thus, by induction hypothesis, we have

$$w_{ij}(k) = \sum_{l=0}^{n-1} A(i,l) A^{k-1}(l,j) = A^k(i,j). \qquad ◼$$

Theorem D.1.1 can be generalized as follows to the case in which we associate a real weight p_{ij} with each edge (i,j).

Theorem D.1.2

Let D be a digraph and let p be a weighting of the edges over the real numbers. Suppose $w_{ij}(k)$ is the sum over all walks W of length k of the product of the p-weights on the edges of W. Then, $w_{ij}(k)$ equals the ij^{th} entry of the kth power of the p-weighted adjacency matrix A_p of D. $\qquad \square$

D.2 Markov Chains and Random Walks

A Markov chain represents a physical system that at any time can be in one of the states $S_0, S_1, \ldots, S_{n-1}$ and that changes its state only at the times $t_1, t_2, \ldots, t_k, \ldots$. The probability of transition of the system into some state S_j at time b,

$t_k < b < t_{k+1}$ depends only on what the state of the system was at time a, $t_{k-1} < a < t_k$ and is unaffected by anything that might become known about its state at an earlier time. Given that the system is in state S_i, we let p_{ij} denote the probability that the next transition is to state S_j. The Markov chain can be represented by the p-weighted digraph D on vertex set $V = \{0, 1, \dots, n-1\}$, where vertex i represents state S_i, $i = 0, \dots, n-1$, and where D has an edge (i, j) of weight p_{ij} whenever $p_{ij} > 0$ (note that we allow D to have a loops representing transitions to the same state). Letting $p_{ij}(k)$ denote the probability of moving from state i to state j after k transitions, it is easily verified that $p_{ij}(k) = w_{ij}(k)$. Thus, by Theorem D.1.2, $p_{ij}(k)$ can be computed as the ij^{th} entry of the kth power of the matrix A_p.

A Markov chain can be interpreted as a random walk in the digraph D, or an idle surfer in the case when D is the Web digraph W (see Chapter 17), where p_{ij} is the probability that a walker (idle surfer) at state i will move to state j in the next step. An important special case is when the transition probabilities for any node i are all same, so that

$$p_{ij} = \begin{cases} 1/d_{out}(i) & if \ (i, j) \in E(D) \\ 0, & \text{otherwise} \end{cases},$$

where $d_{\text{out}}(i)$ denotes the out-degree of vertex i.

We say that the Markov chain is *irreducible* if D is strongly connected and that it is *aperiodic* if for any state i the greatest common divisor over all the numbers k such that $p_{ii}(k) > 0$ is 1; that is, $\gcd \{k \mid p_{ii}(k) > 0\} = 1$.

It is easily verified that the latter condition is equivalent to the condition that, for any node i, there is a closed walk of length k containing i for all but a finite number of integers k.

D.3 Eigenvalues and Eigenvectors

Let M be an $n \times n$ matrix over the real numbers. An *eigenvalue* of a M is a real number λ such that

$$MX = \lambda X \qquad\qquad \textbf{(D.3.1)}$$

for some nonzero column vector X. The vector X is called an eigenvector associated with eigenvalue λ. There may be multiple linearly independent eigenvectors associated with the same eigenvalue. For example, if M is the identity matrix, then every vector is an eigenvector for eigenvalue 1. Subtracting λX from both sides of Formula (D.3.1), we obtain

$$(M - \lambda I) X = 0.$$

If follows that the matrix $M - \lambda I$ is singular, so that its determinant is zero; that is

$$\det(M - \lambda I) = 0. \qquad \qquad \textbf{(D.3.2)}$$

All the eigenvalues of M are determined by Formula (D.3.2). Note that the eigenvalues of M are the same as its transpose M^{T}. Further, since $A_p J = J$, where J is the column vector consisting entirely of 1s, 1 is an eigenvalue of A_p. If M is the matrix A_p associated with a Markov chain, then it can be shown that all the eigenvalues are less than or equal to 1, so that 1 is the largest eigenvalue of A_p. It follows that 1 is the largest eigenvalue of A_p^{T}, and there is an eigenvector vector X (written as a column vector) such that

$$A_p^{\mathrm{T}} X = X.$$

If the Markov chain associated with A_p is irreducible and aperiodic, then it can be shown that X is unique. We refer to this unique vector as the *principle eigenvector* or *stationary distribution* of A_p. Further X can be approximated by iterating the formula

$$X_i = A_p X_{i-1}, i = 1, 2, \dots ,$$

where the initial column vector X_0 can be taken to be any vector whose entries sum to 1. If the Markov chain associated with the matrix A_p is irreducible and aperiodic, then, for any column vector X_0 of positive real numbers whose entries sum to 1, the limit of X_i as i goes to infinity is the principle eigenvector or stationary distribution X of A_p.

ELEMENTARY PROBABILITY THEORY

The definition of the average behavior of an algorithm requires concepts from elementary probability theory that are reviewed in this appendix. We formally define such notions as a probability distribution on a sample space, conditional probability, and the expectation of a random variable. These notions allow us to define the average behavior of an algorithm in a general setting. Various properties of expectation are established that are useful tools in average behavior calculations. In Chapter 6, we use these notions from probability theory to analyze the average behavior of algorithms, and in Chapter 24, probabilistic techniques are embedded into the algorithms themselves.

E.1 Sample Spaces and Probability Distributions

We now formalize the notions of sample space, event, probability distribution, random variable, and expected value. Consider an experiment such as tossing two dice, flipping a coin, playing a card game such as poker, playing the lottery, and so forth. The sample space of the experiment, denoted by S, is the set of all possible outcomes of the experiment. For example, tossing two dice has 36 possible outcomes, since each die can come in six ways independently of the other die. When playing poker, the sample space consists of $C(52,5) = 52!/(5!47!)$ possible five-card hands. A sample space is called *discrete* if it is finite, or countably infinite (that is, in one-to-one correspondence with the positive integers). For our purposes, it suffices to restrict attention to discrete sample spaces.

When analyzing the average complexity of a given algorithm, we consider as our sample space the set $\mathcal{I}_n$ of all possible inputs of size n to the algorithm. For most of the algorithms we consider, the sample space $\mathcal{I}_n$ is either finite or can be transformed to a finite sample space without changing the average complexity. For example, for comparison-based sorting algorithms, we let $\mathcal{I}_n$ be the set of all permutations of $\{1, 2, \dots , n\}$, because any list of size n (of comparable elements) is ordered in the same way as a permutation of $\{1, 2, \dots , n\}$; hence, the algorithm works identically on the list and on the corresponding permutation.

An *event* in the sample space S is a subset of outcomes from S. If E is a singleton subset $\{s\}$, where $s \in S$, then E is a *simple event*. For convenience, we sometimes denote the single element subset $\{s\}$ simply by s. A probability distribution arises by assigning a probability $P(E)$ to each event E in S. We first consider the case where S is finite and any outcome in S has an equal chance of occurring. Then, any particular outcome from S occurs with probability $1/|S|$ (where $|S|$ denotes the cardinality of S). Given an event E in S, the probability that E occurs, denoted by $P(E)$, is the probability that the outcome of the experiment lies in E. Clearly, if E is a simple event, then $P(E) = 1/|S|$. More generally, since E contains $|E|$ outcomes out of a total of $|S|$ possible outcomes, the probability of event E is given by

$$P(E) = \frac{|E|}{|S|}.$$ **(E.1.1)**

Formula (E.1.1) defines the probability $P(E)$ of an event E, under the special assumptions that S is finite and each outcome is equally likely to occur. The mapping P defined by $P(s) = 1/|S|$ for all $s \in S$ is called the *uniform probability distribution* on the sample space S. For example, when tossing two *fair* dice, then each of the 36 simple events have probability 1/36 of occurring. For example, if E is the event that the sum of the dice is 7, then $P(E) = |E|/|S| = 6/36$. In drawing 5 cards from an ordinary deck of 52 playing cards, suppose E_1 is the event that the 5 cards form a *straight* (that is, 5 cards in successive denomination, such as 8, 9, 10, jack, queen, where the cards can have any mix of suits). Note that $|E_1| = 9 * 4^5 = 9,216$ because there are nine ways to choose the smallest denomination in the straight, and then 4^5 ways to choose the 5 cards making up the straight having the given smallest denomination. Hence, assuming the uniform distribution on S, $P(E_1) = |E_1|/|S| = 9,216/C(52, 5)$.

Now suppose E_2 is the event that we draw 5 cards that are all from the same suit, called a *flush*. Then $|E_2| = 4 * C(13, 5) = 1,287$ because there are four ways to choose the suit, and then there are $C(13, 5)$ ways to choose 5 cards from the given suit. Hence, again assuming the uniform distribution on S, we have $P(E_2) = 1{,}287/C(52, 5)$. Because $P(E_2) < P(E_1)$, a flush is less likely to occur and thus "beats" a straight. The ability to calculate such things as winning positions in games of chance like poker was the original impetus of probability theory.

We now give the three basic axioms of probability theory that characterize the probability $P(E)$ of an event occurring in sample spaces S (finite or infinite), where simple events (outcomes) are not necessarily equally likely. For example, if we have loaded dice, then we cannot use Formula (E.1.1) to calculate the probability of events resulting from those dice. We need the axioms of probability to handle this more general situation.

Two events E and F are said to be *mutually exclusive* if they have no outcomes in common—that is, if $E \cap F = \varnothing$. More generally, a given sequence $E_1, E_2, \ldots$ of events in S is said to be *mutually exclusive* if $E_i \cap E_j = \varnothing$ for every pair of distinct events E_i and E_j in the sequence. A *probability distribution* P on the sample space S is a mapping from the events in S to the real numbers satisfying the following three axioms:

1. $0 \le P(E) \le 1$
2. $P(S) = 1$.
3. For any sequence $E_1, E_2, \ldots$ of mutually exclusive events in S,

$$P\left(\bigcup_{i=1}^{\infty} E_i \right) = \sum_{i=1}^{\infty} P(E_i).$$

A probability distribution is called *discrete* if it is defined on a discrete sample space.

Proposition E.1.1 Suppose P is defined for the simple events in a discrete sample space S and satisfies the following two conditions:

1. $0 \le P(\{s\}) \le 1$, for $s \in S$.
2. $\displaystyle\sum_{s \in S} P(\{s\}) = 1$.

Further, suppose that, for any given event E in S, we define $P(E)$ by

$$P(E) = P\left(\bigcup_{s \in E} \{s\} \right) = \sum_{s \in E} P(\{s\}). \tag{E.1.2}$$

Then P satisfies the three axioms for a probability distribution on S. □

We illustrate Proposition E.1.1 by considering the experiment of rolling a single loaded die D. The sample space for this experiment is the set $S = \{1, 2, 3, 4, 5, 6\}$. Assume, for example, that the die is loaded and that the simple events $\{1\}, \{2\}, \{3\}, \{4\}, \{5\}, \{6\}$ occur with probabilities $1/10$, $1/10$, $1/10$, $1/5$, $1/5$, $3/10$, respectively. (Such an assignment of probabilities to the simple events might be arrived at by rolling the die a large number of times and recording the results.) We then apply Formula (E.1.2) to arrive at a probability distribution on S. Now suppose we wish to compute the probability of the occurrence of the event E that the number showing on the die is odd. Applying (E.1.2), we obtain

$$P(E) = P(\{1\}) + P(\{3\}) + P(\{5\}) = \frac{1}{10} + \frac{1}{10} + \frac{1}{5} = \frac{2}{5}.$$

E.2 Conditional Probability

Conditional probabilities often play a role when we analyze the average behavior of algorithms. To motivate the notion of conditional probability, suppose that we roll two fair dice D_1 and D_2, and the first die comes up 2. We now want to determine the probability that the sum of the two dice is at most 5. In other words, we want to compute the *conditional probability* that the sum of the dice is at most 5, *given* that the first die came up 2. Let E denote the event that the sum of the two dice is at most 5, and let F denote the event that the first die is a 2. We can easily check that E contains ten outcomes and F contains six outcomes, so that $P(E) = 10/26 = 5/18$ and $P(F) = 6/36 = 1/6$. Let $P(E|F)$ denote the conditional probability the E occurs given that F has occurred. The condition that D_1 comes up 2 amounts to restricting the sample space to $F = \{(2, i) \mid i \in \{1, \ldots, 6\}\}$, where (x, y) denotes the numbers showing on D_1 and D_2, respectively. This restricted sample space has six simple events. Of these six simple events, only the three events in $E \cap F = \{(2,1), (2,2), (2,3)\}$ yield a sum that is at most 5. Thus,

$$P(E|F) = \frac{|E \cap F|}{|F|} = \frac{3}{6} = \frac{1}{2}. \tag{E.2.1}$$

Because $\dfrac{|E \cap F|}{|F|} = \dfrac{|E \cap F|/|S|}{|F|/|S|} = \dfrac{P(E \cap F)}{P(F)}$, we can express $P(E|F)$ in terms of the probabilities of the events $E \cap F$ and F as follows:

$$P(E|F) = \frac{P(E \cap F)}{P(F)}. \tag{E.2.2}$$

Substituting $P(E \cap F) = 3/36 = 1/12$ and $P(F) = 1/6$ into Formula (E.2.2) also yields $P(E|F) = 1/2$.

For an arbitrary (discrete) sample space S and events E, F, the formula $P(E|F) = \dfrac{|E \cap F|}{|F|}$ can only be used when we are considering the uniform distribution on S. However, Formula (E.2.2) can be used as the general definition of the conditional probability $P(E|F)$. Formula (E.2.2) is often rewritten as follows, expressing $P(E \cap F)$ in terms of $P(E|F)$ and $P(F)$:

$$P(E \cap F) = P(E|F)P(F). \qquad \text{(E.2.3)}$$

Events E and F are said to be *independent* if $P(E|F) = P(E)$. Equivalently, E and F are independent if

$$P(E \cap F) = P(E)P(F). \qquad \text{(E.2.4)}$$

The following useful proposition generalizes Formula (E.2.4).

Proposition E.2.1

Suppose $F_1, F_2, \ldots, F_n$ are mutually exclusive events in S, and $S = \bigcup\limits_{i=1}^{n} F_i$. Let E be any event in S. Then we have

$$P(E) = P(F_1)P(E|F_1) + P(F_2)P(E|F_2) + \cdots + P(F_n)P(E|F_n). \qquad \text{(E.2.5)}$$

■

Formula (E.2.5) is easily proved by noting that $E = (E \cap F_1) \cup (E \cap F_2) \cup \ldots \cup (E \cap F_n)$, and then applying axiom 3 and Formula (E.2.3).

An important special case of Formula (E.2.5) occurs when $n = 2$, $F_1 = F$, and $F_2 = F^c = S \backslash F$. First note that axioms 2 and 3 imply that

$$P(F^c) = 1 - P(F). \qquad \text{(E.2.6)}$$

Using (E.2.5) and (E.2.6) we have

$$P(E) = P(F)P(E|F) + (1 - P(F))P(E|F^c). \qquad \text{(E.2.7)}$$

E.3 Random Variables and Expectation

A *random variable X* on a (discrete) sample space S is simply a mapping from S to the set $\mathbb{R}$ of real numbers. For example, consider the sample space S corresponding to the experiment of rolling two dice. The most relevant random variable X defined on S maps a simple event (r_1, r_2) (r_i = the number that came up for D_i, $i = 1, 2$) to the sum $r_1 + r_2, r_1, r_2 \in \{1, \dots, 6\}$. For algorithm analysis, our sample space will be $S = \mathcal{I}_n$ = all inputs of size n to the algorithm, and the most relevant random variable defined on $\mathcal{I}_n$ will be $X = \tau$, where for each $I \in \mathcal{I}_n$, $\tau(I)$ = the number of basic operations performed when I is the input to algorithm.

Given a random variable X, for x a real number, let

$$P(X = x) \qquad\qquad \textbf{(E.3.1)}$$

denote the probability of the occurrence of the event $E = \{s \in S | X(s) = x\}$. The function $f(x) = P(X = x)$ is called the *probability density function of X*. Consider the sample space S_X consisting of all real numbers x such that $f(x) \neq 0$. It is easily verified that $f(x)$ determines a probability distribution of S_X, which we refer to as the *distribution of the random variable X*.

For example, consider the random variable X mapping the outcome of the tossing of two fair dice to the sum of the two dice. Then the probability density function X is given by

$$P(X = i) = \frac{6 - |7 - i|}{36}, \quad i = 2, \dots, 12. \qquad \textbf{(E.3.2)}$$

As a second rather more important example in probability theory, consider a trial that can have one of two outcomes, success or failure, and the probability of success is p. For example, the trial might be flipping a coin, where we consider the coin coming up heads as success. A fair coin would have $p = 1/2$. Suppose now that n independent trials are performed (called *Bernoulli trials*), so that we obtain a sample space consisting of all 2^n possible outcomes of the n trials. Since the trials are independent, any outcome with i successes and $n - i$ failures occurs with probability $p^i(1 - p)^{n-i}$. Given n and p, the *binomial random variable X* is defined to be the number of successes associated with a given outcome. Since there are $\binom{n}{i}$ events with i successes, the probability density function of X is given by

$$P(X = i) = \binom{n}{i}(1 - p)^{n-i}p^i, \quad i = 0, \dots, n. \qquad \textbf{(E.3.3)}$$

The distribution on {0, 1, ... , n} determined by (E.3.3) is called a *binomial distribution*.

As a third example, which we mention for completeness in view of its importance in probability theory, we now consider another distribution involving Bernoulli trials but this time for an infinite sample space S. Corresponding to each positive integer i, we obtain a simple event in S by running i trials, where the first $i - 1$ trials result in failure, and the last trial results in success. The probability distribution on S is $P(s) = (1 - p)^{i-1}p$, where s is the simple event consisting of i trials. The random variable X defined on S maps s to the number of trials associated with s. Hence,

$$P(X = i) = (1 - p)^{i-1}p, \quad i = 1, 2, ... \qquad \textbf{(E.3.4)}$$

The probability distribution on {1,2, ... } determined by Formula (E.3.4) is called a *geometric distribution*.

In the following discussion of random variables, we assume that the sample space S is finite. One of the most important concepts in probability theory is the expectation $E[X]$ of a random variable X on a finite sample space S. The *mean* or *expectation* of X is defined by

$$E[X] = \sum_{s \in S} X(s)P(s). \qquad \textbf{(E.3.5)}$$

In the special case where we are dealing with the uniform distribution on S, Formula (E.3.5) becomes

$$E[X] = \left(\sum_{s \in S} X(s) \right)/|S|, \qquad \textbf{(E.3.6)}$$

a result that is entirely reasonable because it simply amounts to the ordinary average of the values of the random variable X.

Collecting terms having a common value of X, Formula (E.3.5) becomes equivalent to

$$E[X] = \sum_{x} x\, P(X = x), \qquad \textbf{(E.3.7)}$$

where the summation is over all real numbers x such that $P(X = x) > 0$. For example, suppose X is the random variable corresponding to the sum of two tossed fair dice. Substituting the values for $P(X = i)$ from Formula (E.3.2) into Formula (E.3.7) yields

$$E[X] = \sum_{i=2}^{12} iP(X = i) = \sum_{i=2}^{12} i\frac{(6 - |7 - i|)}{36} = 7.$$

As another example, suppose X is the binomial random variable corresponding to a given n and p. Substituting the values for $P(X = i)$ from Formula (E.3.3) into Formula (E.3.7) yields

$$E[X] = \sum_{i=0}^{n} \binom{n}{i}(1 - p)^{n-i} p^i i. \tag{E.3.8}$$

Applying identity (A.3.5) of Appendix A with $a = 1 - p$ and $x = p$ to the right side of Formula (E.3.8), we obtain

$$E[X] = np. \tag{E.3.9}$$

Formula (E.3.9) is intuitively obvious because we are performing n trials where the success of each trial is p. Another intuitively obvious result is that the expectation of the geometric distribution with probability p for success is given by

$$E[X] = \frac{1}{p}. \tag{E.3.10}$$

A random variable X on the sample space S is a *constant* if it maps every element in S onto the same real number c (denoted $X \equiv c$). It follows immediately from the definition of expectation that $E[X \equiv c] = c$.

The following two useful propositions are easily proved.

Proposition E.3.1   Let X be a random variable on S. Then for any constant c,

$$E[cX] = cE[X]. \tag{E.3.11} \quad \square$$

Proposition E.3.2   If $X_1, X_2, \ldots, X_n$ are n random variables on the sample space S, and $X = X_1 + X_2 + \cdots + X_n$, then

$$E[X] = E[X_1] + E[X_2] + \cdots + E[X_n]. \tag{E.3.12} \quad \square$$

In addition to computing the expectation $E[X]$ of a random variable, it is useful to measure how much X deviates, on average, from $E[X]$. A small deviation indicates that X assumes, with high probability, only values close to its expectation, whereas a large deviation indicates that X assumes values far off $E[X]$ with relatively high probabilities. The deviation of X from $E[X]$ is formally defined in terms of the *variance* as follows:

$$V[X] = E[(X - E[X])^2].$$ (E.3.13)

The *standard deviation* $\sigma[X]$ of X is defined to be the square root of the variance of X; that is,

$$\sigma[X] = \sqrt{V[X]}.$$ (E.3.14)

Note that $E[X]$ can be viewed as a constant random variable on the sample space S, mapping every outcome in S to the same value $c = E[X]$. Another formulation of the variance of X is obtained from (E.3.13) by employing Formulas (E.3.11) and (E.3.12):

$$\begin{aligned}
V[X] = E[(X - E[X])^2] &= E[(X - c)^2] \\
&= E[X^2 - 2cX + c^2] \\
&= E[X^2] - E[2cX] + E[c^2] \\
&= E[X^2] - 2cE[X] + c^2 \\
&= E[X^2] - c^2.
\end{aligned}$$

Hence, we have the following proposition.

Proposition E.3.3 Let X be a random variable on a sample space S. Then,

$$V[X] = E[X^2] - (E[X])^2.$$ ■

As an illustration of Proposition E.3.3, we calculate the variance of the geometric distribution. Clearly, the probability density function for the random variable X^2 is given by

$$P(X^2 = i) = \begin{cases} (1 - p)^{k-1}p & i = k^2 \text{ for some positive integer } k \\ 0 & \text{otherwise.} \end{cases}$$ (E.3.15)

Substituting (E.3.15) in Formula (E.3.7), we obtain

$$E[X^2] = \sum_{i=1}^{\infty} iP(X^2 = i)$$
$$= \sum_{k=1}^{\infty} k^2(1-p)^{k-1}p$$
$$= \frac{2-p}{p^2}$$

Thus, by Proposition E.3.3 and Formula (E.3.10), we have

$$V[X] = E[X^2] - (E[X])^2$$
$$= \frac{2-p}{p^2} - \frac{1}{p^2}$$
$$= \frac{1-p}{p^2}.$$

Because of their importance in data analysis, and for the sake of completeness, we included the foregoing discussion of variance and standard deviation, but we make only limited use of these two concepts in the text.

E.4 Conditional Expectation: Partitioning the Sample Space

Formulas (E.3.5), (E.3.6), and (E.3.7) for $E[X]$ are sometimes difficult to apply directly. In such cases there is often a natural partitioning of the sample space S into disjoint sets $F_1, F_2, \dots, F_m$ that facilitates the evaluation of $E[X]$ using a generalization of Formula (E.3.7) and the notion of conditional expectation, which we now define.

Given a sample space S with probability distribution P and a subset $F \subseteq S$, let P_F be the function defined on F by

$$P_F(s) = P(s|F) = P(s)/P(F), \quad s \in F. \tag{E.4.1}$$

It is immediate that P_F defined by Formula (E.4.1) satisfies the three axioms for a probability distribution on F. If P is the uniform distribution on S, then the following proposition is also immediate because $P_F(s) = P(s)/P(F) = (1/|S|)/(|F|/|S|) = 1/|F|, s \in F$.

Proposition E.4.1   Given a sample space S, suppose P is the uniform distribution on S—that is, $P(s) = 1/|S|, s \in S$—and suppose $F \subseteq S$ is any subset of S. Then P_F is the uniform distribution on F; that is,

$$P_F(s) = 1/|F|, s \in F. \qquad \square$$

If X is a random variable defined on S, let X_F denote the random variable defined on F by restricting X to F; that is, $X_F(s) = X(s)$, $s \in F$. (The notation $X|F$ is also commonly used for X_F.) We then define the *conditional expectation* $E[X|F]$ to be $E[X_F]$. Using Formulas (E.3.5) and (E.4.1), we have

$$E[X|F] = \sum_{s \in F} X_F(s) P_F(s) = \sum_{s \in F} X(s) P(s|F) = \left(\sum_{s \in F} X(s) P(s) \right) / P(F). \qquad \textbf{(E.4.2)}$$

Equivalently, using Formula (E.3.7), we have

$$E[X|F] = \sum_x x P(X = x|F), \qquad \textbf{(E.4.3)}$$

where the sum is taken over all x such that $P(X = x|F) > 0$.

To illustrate, consider the sample space S consisting of all possible outcomes of rolling two fair dice, and let X denote the random variable that maps the outcome (r_1, r_2) onto $r_1 + r_2$, $r_1 r_2 \in \{1, \dots, 6\}$. Suppose F is the event that die D_1 comes up 2, so that F consists of the six outcome pairs $(2, r_2)$, $r_2 \in \{1, \dots, 6\}$. By Proposition E.4.1, P_F is the uniform distribution on F, so that

$$P_F((2, r_2)) = P((2, r_2)|F) = \frac{1}{6}, r_2 \in \{1, \dots, 6\}. \qquad \textbf{(E.4.4)}$$

Substituting Formula (E.4.4) into (E.4.2), we obtain

$$E[X|F] = \sum_{s \in F} X(s) P(s|F) = \left(\frac{1}{6} \right) \sum_{r_2 \in \{1, \dots, 6\}} (2 + r_2)$$

$$= \left(\frac{1}{6} \right) (3 + 4 + 5 + 6 + 7 + 8) = 5.5.$$

The next proposition gives us a convenient method to compute $E[X]$ whenever the sample space S is partitioned into m disjoint subsets F_i, $i = 1, 2, \dots, m$, and where $P(F_i)$ and $E[X|F_i]$ are all readily computable.

Proposition E.4.2 Let X be a random variable on the discrete sample space S. Suppose that we are given a partition $S = \bigcup_{i=1}^{m} F_i$ of S into disjoint subsets F_i, $i = 1, \dots, m$. Then we have

$$E[X] = \sum_{i=1}^{m} E[X \mid F_i] P(F_i). \tag{E.4.5}$$

PROOF

We have

$$E[X] = \sum_{s} X(s) P(s) = \sum_{i=1}^{m} \left(\sum_{s \in F_i} X(s) P(s) \right) = \sum_{i=1}^{m} \left(\sum_{s \in F_i} X(s) P(s) / P(F_i) \right) P(F_i)$$

$$= \sum_{i=1}^{m} E[X \mid F_i] P(F_i). \qquad \blacksquare$$

A partition of a sample space S is often described using a naturally arising second random variable Y (and vice versa). Indeed, given a mapping $Y : S \to \{1, 2, \dots, m\}$, we obtain a partition of S into m disjoint subsets by defining $F_i = Y^{-1}(i) = \{s \in S \mid Y(s) = i\}$, $i \in \{1, 2, \dots, m\}$. Conversely, given $S = F_1 \cup F_2 \cup \dots \cup F_m$ into m disjoint subsets, defining $Y : S \to \{1, 2, \dots, m\}$ by $Y(s) = i \Leftrightarrow s \in F_i$ then yields $F_i = Y^{-1}(i) = \{s \in S \mid Y(s) = i\}$, $i \in \{1, 2, \dots, m\}$. Thus, partitions of S into m sets are in one-to-one correspondence with mappings (random variables) $Y : S \to \{1, 2, \dots, m\}$. In terms of a second random variable $Y : S \to \{1, 2, \dots, m\}$, Proposition E.4.2 becomes equivalently stated as the following proposition.

Proposition E.4.3 Let X be a random variable on the sample space S, and suppose $Y : S \to \{1, 2, \dots, m\}$ is a second random variable on S. Then,

$$E[X] = \sum_{i=1}^{m} E[X \mid Y = i] P(Y = i). \tag{E.4.6}$$

We finish this appendix with an illustration of the use of Formula (E.4.6) to obtain an interesting result about a very simple algorithm—namely, making a linear scan of a list to find the maximum value. The body of the pseudocode for determining the maximum value in a list $L[0{:}n-1]$ is as follows:

```
max ← L[0]
for i = 1 to n − 1 do
    if L[i] > max then max ← L[i] endif
endfor
```

Because $n-1$ comparisons are made by the algorithm for any list $L[0{:}n-1]$, what possibly could be interesting about such a simple piece of code? The interesting question is, what is the average number of times $t(n)$ that *max* is updated? As usual with comparison-based algorithms, when discussing questions concerning average behavior, we assume that our sample space $S = \mathcal{I}_n$ is all permutations of $\{1, 2, \dots, n\}$, and that we have the uniform distribution on S. Let $X : S \to \{0, 1, 2, \dots, n-1\}$ be the random variable defined by $X(\pi) = $ the number of times *max* is updated for input π, so that $t(n) = E[X]$. Consider the second random variable $Y : S \to \{1, 2, \dots, n\}$, defined by $Y(\pi) = \pi(n)$ for $\pi \in S$. Clearly, $P(Y = i) = 1/n, i = 1, 2, \dots, n$. Hence, using Formula (E.4.6) with $m = n$, we have

$$t(n) = E[X] = \sum_{i=1}^{m} E[X|Y=i]P(Y=i) = \frac{1}{n}\sum_{i=1}^{m} E[X|Y=i]. \qquad \textbf{(E.4.7)}$$

To illustrate Formula (E.4.7), consider $n = 3$. Then

$$Y^{-1}(1) = \{231,321\}, \ Y^{-1}(2) = \{132,312\}, \text{ and } Y^{-1}(3) = \{123,213\}.$$

Moreover, by Proposition E.4.1, $P_{Y^{-1}(i)}$ is the uniform distribution on $Y^{-1}(i)$, $i = 1,2,3$, so that Formula (E.4.7) becomes

$$E[X|Y=1] = X(231)*1/2 + X(321)*1/2 = 1*1/2 + 0*1/2 = 1/2,$$
$$E[X|Y=2] = X(132)*1/2 + X(312)*1/2 = 1*1/2 + 0*1/2 = 1/2, \qquad \textbf{(E.4.8)}$$
$$E[X|Y=3] = X(123)*1/2 + X(213)*1/2 = 2*1/2 + 1*1/2 = 3/2.$$

Thus, using Formulas (E.4.7) and (E.4.8), we have

$$E[X] = \frac{1}{3}\sum_{i=1}^{m} E[X|Y=i] = (1/2)*(1/3) + (1/2)*(1/3) + (3/2)(1/3) = 5/6.$$

Of course, since n is only 3, we can compute $E[X]$ by a direct enumeration to get

$$E[X] = (X(231) + X(321) + X(132) + X(312) + X(123) + X(213))/6$$
$$= (1 + 0 + 1 + 0 + 2 + 1)/6 = 5/6,$$

which agrees with our computation of $E[X]$ using Formula (E.4.7). However, the direct method of computing $E[X]$ for a general n is clearly unfeasible, so we must rely on the use of Formula (E.4.7). In fact, what we will get is a recurrence relation for $t(n) = E[X]$. Indeed, it is clear that $E[X|Y = n] = t(n - 1) + 1$, because *max* will be updated at the last iteration of the **for** loop when $\pi(n) = n$ and an average of $t(n - 1)$ times in the previous iterations (since the previous iterations will be dealing with arbitrary permutations of $\{1, 2, \ldots, n - 1\}$). Similarly, $E[X|Y = i \neq n] = t(n - 1)$, because *max* will not be updated in the last iteration of the **for** loop when $\pi(n) = i \neq n$ and an average of $t(n-1)$ times in the previous iterations (since the previous iterations will be dealing with arbitrary permutations of $\{1, 2, \ldots, n\}\backslash\pi(n)$). Plugging these results into Formula (E.4.7) yields the recurrence

$$t(n) = (1/n)(nt(n - 1) + 1) = t(n - 1) + 1/n, \textbf{ init. cond. } t(1) = 0. \textbf{ (E.4.9)}$$

Unwinding the recurrence (E.4.9) gives $t(n) = H_n - 1$, where H_n is the harmonic series $H_n = 1 + \_ + \ldots + 1/n$. Now H_n is closely approximated by $\ln n$ (see Chapter 3), so that the average number of times that *max* is updated is also closely approximated by $\ln n$, an unexpected result to be sure. We use this result in Chapter 2 when we look for an optimal algorithm for determining both the maximum and the minimum values in a list of size n.

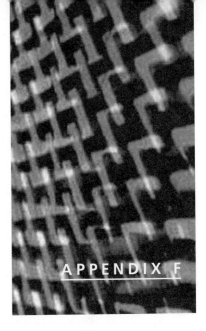

EXAMPLES OF MESSAGE-PASSING INTERFACE CODE

In this appendix, we give a very brief introduction to writing message-passing interface (MPI) code for executing programs on a Beowulf cluster. We limit our discussion to the MPICH C-version of MPI. Good documentation for MPICH can be found at the official MPICH Web site, http://www.mcs.anl.gov/mpi. Also, the references listed at the end of Chapter 18 describe the MPI programming environment in much more detail.

The MPI library consists of more than 100 executable functions, with new routines and functionality being added continually. However, there is a rather small subset of MPI that suffices for many applications. We first describe six MPI functions that are normally part of every MPI program. We then describe a few more functions sufficient to implement two of the programs described in Chapter 18.

F.1 Some Basic MPI Function Descriptions (C Version)

The following six functions are normally part of every MPI program:

```
MPI_Init
MPI_Comm_rank
MPI_Comm_size
MPI_Send (or one of its variants)
MPI_Recv (or one of its variants)
MPI_Finalize
```

The first three functions usually occur near the beginning of each MPI program. Each of these MPI functions returns an integer that equals the constant MPI_SUCCESS if no error is encountered and is a differing value otherwise. To keep things simple, we have suppressed this error-trapping capability of the MPI functions in what follows. For functions that have analogs in our pseudocode, we include the corresponding pseudocode function and its parameters. For example, in our pseudocode send and receive instructions, we amalgamate the first three parameters of the MPI **send** and **receive** functions, which contain the location, number of units, and type of the message data, respectively, into a single parameter *data*. Also, because we do not use a communicator other than MPI_COMM_WORLD, we suppress the communicator parameter in our pseudocode.

```
MPI_Init(int *argc, char ***argv) //initializes the MPI
                                            environment
MPI_Comm_rank(MPI_Comm comm, int *rank)
```

INPUT: comm   (We always use the calling argument MPI_COMM_WORLD for this parameter, which means that all of the processes are considered as a single group. MPI allows for processes to be assembled in subgroups, with ranks defined relative to the subgroup, in which case this parameter is used to specify a particular subgroup. We do not use this additional functionality, so that here and in what follows, the parameter comm is always called with argument MPI_COMM_WORLD.)

OUTPUT: rank   (Output parameter rank is assigned the rank of the process, so that $0 \leq \text{rank} \leq p - 1$, where we have p processes.)

PSEUDOCODE: *myid*

```
MPI_Comm_size(MPI_COMM comm, int *size)
```

INPUT: comm   (We will always use the argument MPI_COMM_WORLD for this parameter.)

OUTPUT: size   (Output parameter size is assigned the total number of processes.)

PSEUDOCODE: assumed to be global variable *p*

Our pseudocode functions Ssend and Bsend are analogous to the MPI functions MPI_Ssend and MPI_Bsend. These versions support synchronous and asynchronous communication, respectively. In our pseudocode for these functions, for simplicity, we amalgamate the first three parameters of MPI_SSend and MPI_BSend into a single parameter, *data*. The MPI_Bsend has the same parameters as MPI_Ssend, but with the additional requirement that a buffer must be specifically attached to the MPI_Bsend by the programmer (using the MPI_Buffer_attach statement). We limit our discussion in what follows to MPI_Ssend.

```
MPI_Ssend(void *senddata, int count, MPI_Datatype datatype,
int dest, int tag, MPI_Comm comm)
```

INPUT: senddata (the memory location where the start of the data to be sent is located)

count (how many items of data are to be sent)

datatype (the type of the data to be sent, that is, MPI_INT, MPI_FLOAT, MPI_CHAR, and so forth)

dest (the rank, or ID, of the process that is to receive the data)

tag (used for matching a **recieve** or other information)

comm (We will always use the argument MPI_COMM_WORLD for this parameter.)

OUTPUT: Basic synchronous send to process dest.

PSEUDOCODE: Ssend *(data, dest, tag)*

We will use the blocking receive function MPI_Recv, which has the form

```
MPI_Recv(void *recvdata, int count, MPI_Datatype datatype,
int source, int tag, MPI_Comm comm, MPI_Status *status)
```

INPUT: recvdata (the memory location where the start of the data to be received is located)

count (how many items of data are to be received; not necessarily the same as the value of count in the associated send function)

datatype (the type of the data to be sent—that is, MPI_INT, MPI_FLOAT, MPI_CHAR, and so forth)

source (the rank, or ID, of the process that is the source of the data to be received. Unlike MPI_Ssend, source can be the wildcard MPI_ANY_SOURCE, thereby allowing the message to be received from any process.)

tag (used for matching **send** or other information)

comm (We will always use the argument MPI_COMM_WORLD for this parameter.)

status (The seventh parameter status, not present in MPI_Ssend, is used to retrieve the source, tag, and count of the message actually received. The parameter status is a structure of type MPI_Status, and the message's values of source and tag are stored in status.MPI_SOURCE and status.MPI_TAG, respectively.)

OUTPUT: Basic synchronous (blocking) receive from process source.

PSEUDOCODE: receive *(data, source, tag, status)*

The following MPI command typically occurs at the end of code and should be executed by each process:

```
MPI_Finalize(void)
```

We also need two other MPI functions for broadcasting data to and gathering data from each process. Each process must execute these functions, so proper synchronization must be explicitly present in the code; otherwise, such things as deadlock may occur.

```
MPI_Bcast(void *bcastdata, int count, MPI_Datatype, int root,
MPI_Comm comm)
```

INPUT: The parameters have the usual meaning, with root having the rank of the
               process that initiates the broadcast.

OUTPUT: count items of data starting at the address of bcastdata in process root are
               broadcast to all other processes (and received at the start of bcastdata in
               each process).

PSEUDOCODE: **broadcast** *(data, root)*

```
MPI_Gather(void *senddata, int sendcount, MPI_Datatype
senddatatype, void *recvdata, int recvcount, MPI_Datatype
recvdatatype, int root, MPI_Comm comm)
```

INPUT: The parameters have the usual meaning, with root having the rank of the
               process where the data is gathered.

OUTPUT: sendcount items of data starting at the address of senddata in each process
               are gathered starting at the address of recvdata in process root. We always
               assume that sendcount = recvcount, and senddatatype = recvdatatype.

PSEUDOCODE: **gather** *(senddata, recvdata, root)*

```
MPI_Scatter(void *senddata, int sendcount, MPI_Datatype
senddatatype, void *recvdata, int recvcount, MPI_Datatype
recvdatatype, int root, MPI_Comm comm)
```

INPUT: The parameters have the usual meaning, with root having the rank of the
               process where the data is gathered.

OUTPUT: sendcount items of data starting at the address of senddata in the root
               process are scattered to all other processes starting at the address of
               recvdata. We always assume that sendcount = recvcount, and
               senddatatype = recvdatatype.

PSEUDOCODE: **scatter** *(senddata, recvdata, root)*

F.2   MPI Version of *EvenOddSort*

The following is a complete MPI program illustrating the MPI version of *Even-OddSort* given in Chapter 18. We assume that we are sorting an array of integers, so that our CompareSplit function is written for arrays of integers.

```c
#include <stdio.h>
#include <stdlib.h>
#include <mpi.h>

int compare(const void *x, const void *y)
{  //prepare C built-in qsort for sorting integers in
   //increasing order
   return(*(int*)x - *(int*)y);
}

void CompareSplit(int *a,int m,int i,int j)
{
   int k,q,r,myrank,*tempa,*temp;
   MPI_Status status;
   tempa = (int *) malloc(m*sizeof(int));
   temp = (int *) malloc(m*sizeof(int));
   MPI_Comm_rank(MPI_COMM_WORLD,&myrank);
   if(myrank == i) {
      MPI_Ssend(a,m,MPI_INT,j,0,MPI_COMM_WORLD);
      MPI_Recv(tempa,m,MPI_INT,j,0,MPI_COMM_WORLD,&status);
      for(k = 0; k < m; k++) {
         temp[k] = a[k];
      }  //a gets the m smallest elements
      q = 0; r = 0;
      for(k = 0; k < m; k++) {
         if(temp[q] < tempa[r]) {
            a[k] = temp[q];
            q = q + 1;
         } else {
            a[k] = tempa[r];
            r = r + 1;
         }
      }
   }
   if(myrank == j) {
      MPI_Recv(tempa,m,MPI_INT,i,0,MPI_COMM_WORLD,&status);
      MPI_Ssend(a,m,MPI_INT,i,0,MPI_COMM_WORLD);
      for(k = 0; k < m; k++) {
         temp[k] = a[k];
      }
      q = m - 1; r = m - 1;
      for(k = m - 1; k >= 0; k--) {
         if(temp[q] >= tempa[r]) {
            a[k] = temp[q];
            q = q - 1;
         } else {
            a[k] = tempa[r];
            r = r - 1;
         }
      }
   }
```

```
        }
        free(tempa);
        free(temp);
    }

    void EvenOddSort(int *L, int n)
    {
        int m, myrank, p, k, *a;
        MPI_Comm_size(MPI_COMM_WORLD,&p);
        m = n/p;
        MPI_Comm_rank(MPI_COMM_WORLD,&myrank);
        a = (int *) malloc(m*sizeof(int));
        MPI_Scatter(L,m,MPI_INT,a,m,MPI_INT,0,MPI_COMM_WORLD);
        qsort(a,m,sizeof(int),compare);   //qsort is actually
                               //mergesort on some implementations
        for(k = 0; k <= p - 1; k++) {
            if((k + myrank) % 2 == 0) {
                if(myrank < p - 1) {
                    CompareSplit(a,m,myrank,myrank + 1);
                }
            } else {//odd(k + myrank)
                if(myrank > 0) {
                    CompareSplit(a,m,myrank - 1,myrank);
                }
            }
        }
        MPI_Gather(a,m,MPI_INT,L,m,MPI_INT,0,MPI_COMM_WORLD);
        free(a);
    }

    #define M 10000                 // chunk of data per process

    int main(int argc, char *argv[])
    {
        int size, rank, *arr=NULL, n, i;
        MPI_Init(&argc, &argv);
        MPI_Comm_rank(MPI_COMM_WORLD, &rank);
        if(rank == 0) {
            MPI_Comm_size(MPI_COMM_WORLD, &size);
            n = size*M; // ensures that n is divisible by size
            arr=(int *) malloc(n*sizeof(int));
            for(i=0;i<n;i++) arr[i] = random()%20000;
        }
        MPI_Bcast(&n, 1, MPI_INT, 0, MPI_COMM_WORLD);
        EvenOddSort(arr, n);
        if(rank == 0) {
            free(arr);
        }
        MPI_Finalize();
    }
```

If the above source module were compiled and saved under the name sortmpi (such as using a command % mpicc sortmpi.c -o sortmpi), then the following is typical of a command that, when issued at the command prompt, will run the program with, say, 16 processes:

```
% mpirun -np 16 sortmpi
```

F.3 MPI Version of *MatrixProduct*

We now give MPI code for computing a matrix product as described by the procedure *MatrixProduct* given in Chapter 18. We assume that the matrices have floating point entries. To closely model the high-level pseudocode, we write MatrixProduct in a form that requires the variable *N* to be defined globally.

```
Void MatrixProduct(float A[N][N], float B[N][N], float C[N][N])
{
    float colvector[N],Column[N];
    int numsent,numrec,Col,i,p,myid,SourceWorker;
    MPI_Status status;
    MPI_Bcast(A,N*N,MPI_FLOAT,0,MPI_COMM_WORLD);
                                        //master broadcasts A to
                                        //all workers
    MPI_Comm_size(MPI_COMM_WORLD,&p);
    MPI_Comm_rank(MPI_COMM_WORLD,&myid);
    if (myid == 0) {            //execute master code
        for (i=1; i < p; i++) {
            if (i <= N) {
                GetColumn(B,i,Column);    //assign ith column of B
                                          // to colvector
                MPI_Ssend(Column,N,MPI_FLOAT,i,i,MPI_COMM_WORLD);
                                          //send P_i the ith column of B
            } else {                      //send P_i a null vector (TAG=0)
                MPI_Ssend(NULL,0,MPI_FLOAT,i,
                    0,MPI_COMM_WORLD);
            }
        }                                 // end for
        numsent = N<(p-1)?N:(p-1);        //a counter for the
                                          //number of
                                          //(non-null) columns sent
        numrec = 0;                       //a counter for the
                                          //number of matrix-vector
                                          //products received by
                                          //the master
        while (numrec < N) {
```

```
            MPI_Recv(Column,N,MPI_FLOAT,MPI_ANY_SOURCE,
               MPI_ANY_TAG,MPI_COMM_WORLD,&status);
            Col = status.MPI_TAG;
            SourceWorker = status.MPI_SOURCE;
            SetColumn(C, Col, Column);
            numrec = numrec + 1;
            if (numsent < N) {
               numsent = numsent + 1;
               GetColumn(B,numsent,colvector);
               MPI_Ssend(colvector,N,MPI_FLOAT,SourceWorker,
                  numsent,MPI_COMM_WORLD);
                              //send P_SourceWorker the column of B
                              //in position numsent
            } else {
               MPI_Ssend(NULL,0,MPI_FLOAT,SourceWorker, 0,
                     MPI_COMM_WORLD);
            }
            }
      } else {                            //execute worker code
         MPI_Recv(Column,N,MPI_FLOAT,0,MPI_ANY_TAG,
                     MPI_COMM_WORLD,&status);
         Col = status.MPI_TAG;
         while (Col > 0) {
            MatVectProd(A, Column, colvector);
         MPI_Ssend(colvector,N,MPI_FLOAT,0,Col,MPI_COMM_WORLD);
            MPI_Recv(Column,N,MPI_FLOAT,0,MPI_ANY_TAG,
                     MPI_COMM_WORLD,&status);
            Col = status.MPI_TAG;
         }
      }
   }
```

REMARK

It is possible to gain experience with MPI programming even with a single-processor machine. For example, there is an open-source downloadable Windows version of MPI available from Argonne National Laboratories (http://www.mcs.anl.gov/mpi/mpich). Even on a single-processor machine, you can ask for as many processes as you want, but of course, the single processor must perform all the processes. Clearly, you won't obtain any speedup! However, nearly identical code submitted on a single processor machine will work on a Beowulf cluster of multiple processors. Moreover, a single-processor MPI environment is not only useful for educational purposes but is also useful for debugging and testing purposes.

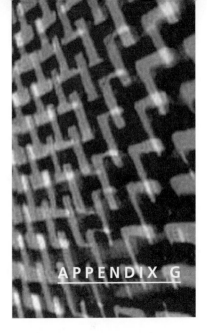

PSEUDOCODE CONVENTIONS

G.1   Pseudocode Conventions for Sequential Algorithms

We include pseudocode for most of the algorithms that we discuss in this book. Our sequential pseudocode is a hybrid of several high-level languages. To delineate blocks, we use matching keywords such as **if-endif**, **for-endfor**, **while-endwhile**, **case-endcase**, and so forth.

Our algorithms are always implemented as subprograms, which come in two flavors, functions and procedures. In the case of a function, we include a **return** statement for returning the value of the function. Information is passed to and from functions and procedures by argument-parameter correspondence or by global variables. We always make explicit which parameters are input parameters, and which are output parameters. For procedures, a parameter can be an input parameter, an output parameter, or both. However, we assume that all parameters for a function are strictly input parameters. We assume that all input parameters to procedures and functions (that are not also output parameters) are passed by value, so that the corresponding argument is not changed even if the input parameter is altered by the procedure or function, thereby avoiding unwanted side effects.

The opening syntax for a procedure has the following form, where information enclosed in pointed brackets $<>$ is supplied by the code designer (the pointed brackets themselves are not written in the pseudocode).

procedure *<Name>(<List of parameters>)*
Input: *<parameter 1> (<description>)*

.

.

.

   <parameter k> (<description>)
Output: *<parameter k + 1> (<description>)*

.

.

.

   <parameter m> (<description>)

The opening syntax for a function is similar, except that the **Output** statement describes the value returned. We indicate arrays by using square brackets for index ranges, where we begin indexing at zero so that our pseudocode is more easily translated into C, C++, or Java code.

For brevity of notation, when we include an array $A[0 : n - 1]$ in the parameter list of a function or procedure, we are passing not only the array but the variable n as well. Comments in the body of the pseudocode begin with // and continue to the rest of the line. Occasionally, comments that extend over more than one line do not use // on continuation lines if these lines do not contain code. Comments are distinct from the descriptions of parameters in **Input** or **Output** statements that are enclosed in round brackets (descriptions). To keep the pseudocode clean and easy to read, we avoid including extensive commentary in the pseudocode itself. Instead, we save our commentary for the text describing the algorithm.

For brevity of code, we usually do not explicitly declare local variables because their role is usually clear from their context. Also, in most cases, we are not explicit about the variable type (integer, real, character, and so forth) because either the variable type is obvious from the context or the algorithm in question does not depend on the particular variable type being used (as in comparison-based sorting, searching, and so forth). We do, however, indicate which variables are global.

We now describe the form of our pseudocode constructs for branching and looping. We do not describe the action of these constructs here because they are standard and found in any modern book on programming.

We use two branching constructs in our pseudocode, **if-endif**, and **case-endcase.** The **if-endif** construct has the following form:

```
if <Boolean expression> then
    <statement 1>
            .
            .
            .
    <statement k>
else
    <statement k + 1>
            .
            .
            .
    <statement m>
endif
```

The **else** clause is omitted when an alternative action is not to be executed if the Boolean expression is false. When there is only one statement in the body of the *if* clause, and there is no *else* clause, then we often write the construct on one line as follows:

```
if <boolean expression> then <statement> endif
```

The **case endcase** construct with *n* branches has the form:

```
case
    :<Boolean expression 1>:
        <statement>
            .
            .
            .
        <statement>
    :<Boolean expression 2>:
        <statement>
            .
            .
            .
        <statement>
            .
            .
            .
```

```
        :<Boolean expression n − 1>:
            <statement>
                .
                .
                .
            <statement>

        :otherwise:
            <statement>
                .
                .
                .
            <statement>
    endcase
```

The **otherwise** clause is omitted if no action is required when all the Boolean expressions are false. We assume that the Boolean expressions are evaluated in order, and for convenience, we assume (as opposed to C, C++, Java) that we branch out of the construct after executing the statements associated with the first Boolean expression having the value **true**, or after executing the code associated with the **otherwise** clause (if included) when all the Boolean expressions are false. Similar to our **if-endif** construct, when the code associated with one of the case clauses consists of a single statement, then we write the statement on the same line the clause itself.

We adopt the following priority rules when evaluating arithmetic or Boolean expressions. We list them from highest priority to lowest, with operations on the same level having equal priority. Priority between two operations at the same level proceeds left to right (we avoid using the exponentiation operator **).

1. Remove parentheses (from inside out, if nested)
2. Multiplication and division: $*$ and $/$
3. Addition and subtraction: $+$ and $-$
4. Relational operations: $<, >, \geq, \leq, =$, and $\neq$
5. Boolean connectives: **.not., .and., .or.**

Thus, the Boolean expression:

$$(x + y) * z \geq y − 1 \text{ .or. } z < 3 \text{ .and. .not. } x/z > s \text{ .or. } x = 5$$

is equivalent to the more fully parenthesized version:

$$(((x + y) * z \geq y − 1) \text{ .or. } (z < 3 \text{ .and. } (\text{.not. } (x/z > s)))) \text{ .or. } (x = 5)$$

We assume the following short-circuit convention for the evaluation of a compound Boolean expression of the form A **.and.** B, where A and B are Boolean expressions. If A has the value **.false.**, then the expression A **.and.** B automatically has the value **.false.**, without evaluating B (which might not be defined). An analogous convention holds for compound expressions of the form A **.or.** B, where B is evaluated if and only if A is false.

We use the following three loop control constructions in our pseudocode:

for <*variable*> ← <initial> **to** (downto) <final> **do**
    <*statement* 1>
      .
      .
      .
    <*statement k*>
endfor

while <*Boolean expression*> **do**
    <*statement* 1>
      .
      .
      .
    <*statement k*>
endwhile

repeat
    <*statement* 1>
      .
      .
      .
    <*statement k*>
until <*Boolean expression*>

We use ← for assignment versus = for logical comparison. We also use mathematical notation for the other logical comparison operators such as $\le$, $\le$, $\ne$, and so forth. For pointers, we use the notation $P\rightarrow$ to indicate the contents of the dynamic variable pointed to by the pointer P. For example, suppose the nodes of a linked list are stored in dynamic variables, which are records of the following type:

Node = **record**
    Info: *Infotype*
    Next: →*Node*
end *Node*

If P is a pointer variable containing the address of a dynamic variable having the record type Node, then $P{\rightarrow}Info$ denotes the contents of the information field of the node, and $P{\rightarrow}Next$ denotes the contents of the pointer field of the node.

When writing pseudocode for sequential algorithms, we assume that we have a sequential (serial) computer having a single processor capable of executing all the standard arithmetical operations, logical branching instructions, assignment statements, and so forth. We assume an internal random access memory (RAM), with each memory location being accessible with equal speed. Since our main concern is with high-level design strategies, most of our algorithms assume that we have sufficient RAM to store all the variables used by the algorithm. Thus, we do not make much use of external memory devices accessed by read and write statements. In practice, however, it is sometimes necessary to design algorithms that input or output data from and to external devices such as disks and tapes, often in an "on-line" fashion. An important example is provided by B-trees that contain keys from externally stored databases, where the complexity of the algorithms for searching, inserting, and deletion are dominated by the read and write operations required.

We use a number of built-in mathematical functions in our pseudocode for algorithms. A discussion of these built-in functions is included in Appendix A. We also assume that there is a built-in procedure **interchange**(A,B), which interchanges the values of A and B.

G.2 Pseudocode Conventions for Parallel Algorithms

A number of issues arise when designing pseudocode for parallel algorithms that are not present for sequential algorithms. In particular, we need to know whether the pseudocode is designed for a shared-memory parallel computer (various types of PRAMs) or for an interconnection network model. In the latter case, we must explicitly arrange for communication between adjacent processors and decide on pseudocode corresponding to this communication.

G.2.1 Pseudocode Conventions for PRAMs

Similar to sequential algorithms, with both PRAMs and interconnection network models, we always make explicit which parameters are input parameters and which are output parameters. Again, to avoid side effects, we assume that all input parameters (that are not also output parameters) are passed *by value*; that is, the corresponding argument is not changed even if the input parameter is altered by the parallel procedure or function. All parameters of a parallel function are assumed to be input parameters.

Because PRAMs have a single shared memory, the pseudocode for PRAMs is an extension of the pseudocode for sequential algorithms. The major new elements are the **in parallel** statement, the **parallelcall** statement, and various opening syntax specifications.

Opening Syntax. The opening syntax for a procedure written for a PRAM has the following form, which is identical to that for a sequential procedure except for the addition of the model specification and the number $p = p(n)$ of processors used.

> **procedure** <Name>(<List of parameters>)
> **Model:** <Model name> **with** p = <function of n> **processors**
> **Input:**   <Description of input variables>
> **Output:** <Description of output variables>

The opening syntax for a function written for the PRAM is similar, except that the **Output** statement describes the value returned. The name of the procedure usually begins with a reference to the problem being solved, followed by a reference to the model of PRAM. In the procedure name, we simply use the term PRAM for EREW PRAM. However, we use the full term EREW PRAM for <Model name>.

> **function** SumPRAM(X[1:n])
> **Model:** EREW PRAM **with** $p = n/2$ **processors**
> **Input:**   X[0:n − 1] (array of numbers $x_0, x_1, \ldots, x_{n-1}$) //n = 2^k
> **Output:** $x_0 + x_1 + \cdots + x_{n-1}$

In Parallel Statement. In addition to the usual instructions for serial machines, we have an in parallel statement, which allows operations to be performed on more than one component of an array simultaneously.

> **for** <Boolean expression involving array indices> **do in parallel**
>   <statement 1>
>   <statement 2>
>
>   .
>   .
>   .
>   <statement k>
> **end in parallel**

The **for** clause is a Boolean expression involving array indices. Only those array elements whose indices satisfy the Boolean expression participate in the instructions contained in the body of the **in parallel** statement. These instructions can be any statements from the sequential pseudocode that apply to arrays (however, we do have to be careful not to violate the SIMD model, as discussed in Chapter 15). All these statements are performed simultaneously by a set of active processors. We do not specify in our pseudocode those processors that are active; we only need to be careful that there are enough processors around to do the job.

Since we have assumed that each processor in a PRAM is as powerful as in a serial machine, the built-in functions and procedures **odd**, **even**, **interchange**, **sin**, **read**, **write**, and so forth that were assumed for serial machines are also assumed capable of execution by each processor in parallel.

We assume the existence of the built-in parallel procedures **split**($L[0:n-1]$, $A[0:n/2-1]$, $B[0:n/2-1]$), which splits the list $L[0:n-1]$ into two sublists $A[0:n/2-1] = L[0:n/2-1]$ and $B[0:n/2-1] = L[n/2:n-1]$, and **even-oddsplit**($L[0:n-1]$, $A[0:n/2-1]$, $B[0:n/2-1]$), which split the list $L[0:n-1]$ into two sublists $A[0:n/2-1]$ and $B[0:n/2-1]$ consisting of the even-indexed elements and odd-indexed elements of $L[0:n-1]$, respectively.

We also allow parallel procedures and functions to be executed in parallel.

Parallelcall. On many occasions, particularly in the presence of recursion, the parameters of a parallel call to a function or a procedure are not conveniently indexed. For example, in the recursive merging procedure *EvenOddMerge PRAM*($L[0:n-1]$) given in Chapter 15, simultaneous recursive calls are made with two lists *Even*$[0:n/2-1]$, *Odd*$[0:n/2-1]$. If we renamed these lists $A[0,0:n/2-1]$ and $A[1,0:n/2-1]$, we could do a parallel call to *EvenOddMergePRAM* with the help of A, as follows:

```
for 0 ≤ i ≤ 1 do in parallel
    call EvenOddMergePRAM(A[i, 0:n/2 − 1])
end in parallel
```

However, the renaming and associated assignments of *Even* and *Odd* are cumbersome and distract from the high-level description of the algorithm. Therefore, to accomplish the parallel call, we introduce the more compact pseudocode convention

parallelcall *EvenOddMergePRAM*(*Even*$[0:n/2-1]$ | *Odd*$[0:n/2-1]$),

where we use the symbol | to separate the parameters corresponding to each simultaneous call to *EvenOddMergePRAM*.

G.2.2 Pseudocode Conventions for Interconnection Network Models

Pseudocode for algorithms designed for interconnection networks is more complex than that for PRAMs because it must include statements to describe communication between processors, specification of processors handling I/O, central control variables versus distributed variables, and so forth.

Opening Syntax. Each procedure for an interconnection network model begins with opening syntax similar to that for the PRAM. Parameters in the parameter list of a procedure or function on an interconnection network model include distributed variables. Therefore, for each distributed variable parameter, it is important to describe the set of processors that contain meaningful information on input for that parameter. Thus, our input statement not only describes the high-level nature of the parameter but also includes a range clause specifying the range of indices of processors containing meaningful input data for the parameter. Those parameters for which no range is given in the input statement are so-called *front-end* or *central control* variables that are in the local memory of the front-end processor (central control). The front-end variable parameters are usually used to specify ranges of indices in the input and output statements. The output statement contains similar specifications for all output parameters.

procedure <Name>(<List of parameters>)
Model: *<Model name>* **with** p = *<function of n>* **processors**

Input: *<Description of input parameter 1>* **range:** *<processor range 1>*
          •
          •
          •

        <Description of input parameter i> **range:** *<processor range i>*
Output: *<Description of output parameter 1>* **range:** *<processor range 1>*
          •
          •
          •

        <Description of output parameter j> **range:** *<processor range j>*

All variables occurring in a procedure other than parameters are either additional front-end variables used for counters and loop control or distributed variables. The difference between front-end variables and distributed variables should always be clear from the context.

The opening syntax for a function on an interconnection network is similar to that for functions defined in PRAMs. As an example, we give the opening syntax for the function *Search2DMesh* described in Chapter 15.

→ **function** *Search2DMesh(L,n,x)*
Model: two-dimensional mesh $M_{q,q}$ **with** $p = n = q^2$ **processors**
Input: *L* (a list of *n* elements),   **range:** $P_{i,j}$, $0 \le i, j \le q - 1$
           x (a search element),   front-end variable
Output: the smallest index where *x* occurs in *L*, or ∞ if *x* **is not in** *L*

In Parallel Statement. The in parallel statement is similar to that for a PRAM, ex-cept that the for clause contains a Boolean expression involving processor in-dices instead of array indices. The processor index might be a single index, as in the one-dimensional mesh; a pair of indices, as in the two-dimensional mesh; a bit string, as in the hypercube; and so forth. It is implicit in all our in parallel statements that a processor recognizes its own index. (In practice, this might be accomplished using a distributed variable *ID* in the read-only local memory of each processor. Then for each processor *P*, **P**:*ID* would contain the index of processor *P*.) Each processor whose index does not satisfy the Boolean expres-sion in the for clause is *idle* (masked out). The active processors simultaneously execute the instructions in the body of the in parallel statement, while the re-maining processors are idle. The general syntax for the in parallel statement is as follows:

→ **for** *<processor P>,<Boolean expression involving index of P>* **do in parallel**
     <statement 1>
     <statement 2>
         •
         •
         •
     <statement k>
end in parallel

Note that the **in parallel** statement is counted as representing *k* parallel steps.

For interconnection networks, we consider two main types of functions: those that are simply parallel invocations of sequential functions and those that require communication between processors. The first type of function can be either built in or user defined. A parallel invocation of a sequential function works within each processor's local memory and does not require communica-tion between processors. For example, consider a parallel invocation of the built-in function **sin** on the one-dimensional mesh M_p. Then the statement

```
for P_i, 0 ≤ i ≤ n − 1 do in parallel
    B ← sin(A)
end in parallel
```

where A and B are distributed variables, assigns $\mathbf{sin}(\mathbf{P}_i{:}A)$ to $\mathbf{P}_i{:}B$, $i = 0, \dots, n-1$.

As another example of a parallel invocation of a sequential function, the statement

```
for P_i, 0 ≤ i ≤ n − 1 do in parallel
    C ← EuclidGCD(A, B)
end in parallel
```

where A, B, and C are distributed variables, assigns $EuclidGCD(\mathbf{P}_i{:}A, \mathbf{P}_i{:}B)$ to $\mathbf{P}_i{:}C$, $i = 0, \dots, n-1$. Note that the number of steps performed by $EuclidGCD(\mathbf{P}_i{:}A, \mathbf{P}_i{:}B)$ can vary greatly depending on the value of i. Strictly speaking, this would violate the SIMD model. However, by allowing processors to remain idle until all processors have completed their execution of $EuclidGCD$, we can reconcile it with the SIMD model.

The second type of function, which requires communication between processors, is restricted to functions that return a scalar. When such a function terminates, it is assumed that the value to be returned by the function resides in a particular processor's local instantiation of a suitable distributed variable. For example, suppose the scalar value to be returned by a function implemented on a two-dimensional mesh resides in $\mathbf{P}_{0,0}{:}X$. Then the **return** statement is given by

```
return(P_{0,0}:X)
```

REMARK

The **return** statement is only used for convenience and must not be interpreted as returning a value to central control that is directly accessible to all the processors. The returned value is resident in a suitable output register of $P_{0,0}$ only. If other processors require this returned value, then it must be broadcast.

Interprocessor Communication Statement. In Chapter 15 in our discussion of the interconnection network model we introduce the pseudocode $\mathbf{P}_j{:}Y \Leftarrow \mathbf{P}_i{:}X$ for communicating processor P_i's local variable X to an adjacent processor P_j's local

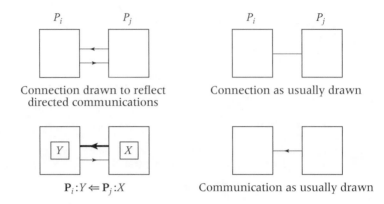

P_i P_j

Connection drawn to reflect
directed communications

P_i P_j

Connection as usually drawn

Y X

$\mathbf{P}_i : Y \Leftarrow \mathbf{P}_j : X$

Communication as usually drawn

variable Y (see Figure 15.7). The communication process $P_j : Y \Leftarrow P_i : X$ can be viewed as consisting of the following steps. Processor P_i fetches the value of X from its local memory and stores it to an output register. Then the content of this output register is communicated to an input register of the adjacent processor P_j. Finally, P_j writes the value in this input register to the local variable Y. We assume that these steps constitute a single communication step taking unit time.

It is customary to indicate that processors P_i and P_j are adjacent by drawing a single (undirected) edge between them. However, it would perhaps be more realistic to have two directed edges drawn between them to indicate the fact that communication is always directed (see Figure G.1).

The general form of the interprocessor communication statement is

<target processor : target variable> $\Leftarrow$ *<source processor : source variable>*

Typically, the interprocessor communication statement is embedded in the body of an **in parallel** statement, and the **for** clause includes a Boolean expression involving source processor indices that determine the set of active source processors. Any active source and corresponding target processor *must be adjacent* in the interconnection network. We illustrate a sample parallel interprocessor communication statement in Figure G.2.

We only allow communication in one direction in a single parallel step to maintain a strict SIMD model. For example, in the one-dimensional mesh, we do not allow some of the active source processors to communicate to the left while others communicate to the right in the same parallel communication step.

If the communication involves the same distributed variable, we use the term *propagate* instead of *communicate*. Propagating a distributed variable is illustrated in Figure G.3.

FIGURE G.2

Action of parallel
communication
step

for P_i, $2 \leq i \leq 2k$ .and. even(i) **do in parallel**
    $\mathbf{P}_{i-1}{:}B \Leftarrow \mathbf{P}_i{:}A$ {communicate left from A to B}
end in parallel

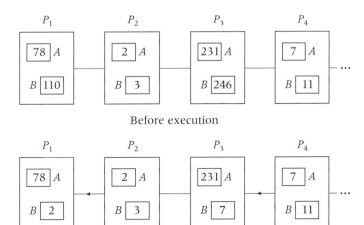

FIGURE G.3

Action of parallel
communication
with processors
being both source
and target

for P_i, $1 \leq i \leq n - 1$ **do in parallel**
    $\mathbf{P}_{i+1}{:}A \Leftarrow \mathbf{P}_i{:}A$ {propagate A to the right}
end in parallel

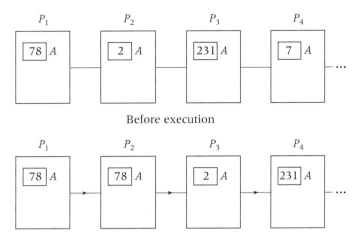

In Figure G.3, there are processors that are both target and source during a single communication step, which is reasonable in view of the systolic nature of a communication step. At the beginning of a communication step, each active source processor initiates the process of sending (pulsing) data from its local memory to the relevant adjacent processor. At the end of the communication step (that is, after unit time), the target processor receives (and assigns) this data. Thus, it is both a natural and a common feature of many parallel algorithms to have the same processor send information at the beginning of the communication step and receive information at the end of the step. However, we *do not permit* any processor to be the target or source of more than one processor during a single communication step.

Interprocessor communication as illustrated in Figure G.3 is counted as a single (parallel) communication step. The total number of communication steps performed by a parallel algorithm is called the *communication complexity* of the algorithm. By requiring communication to take place between adjacent processors only, we can usually conclude that the time complexity (as measured by counting the number of parallel basic operations performed) of a parallel algorithm is proportional to the communication complexity.

Read/Write Statements. We assume two parallel I/O statements: read for input and write for output. Suppose, for example, that we have a list of n values stored sequentially in the input device. These n values might be read into a one-dimensional mesh M_p by the following statement:

```
for P_i, 0 ≤ i ≤ n − 1 do in parallel
    read(P_i:L)
end in parallel
```

This **in parallel** statement simultaneously reads the $(i + 1)^{st}$ value in the external input device into the variable $\mathbf{P}_i:L$ in the local memory of processor P_i, $i \in \{0, \ldots, n - 1\}$.

BIBLIOGRAPHY

Adelson-Velskii, G. M., and Y. M. Landis. "An Algorithm for the Organization of Information." *Doklady Akademii Nauk SSR* 146 (1962): 263–266. English translation in *Soviet Mathematics Doklady* 3 (1962): 1259–1263.

Aggarwal, A., and J. S. Vitter. "The Input/Output Complexity of Sorting and Related Problems." *Communications of the ACM* 31 (September 1988): 1116–1127.

Aho, A. V., J. E. Hopcroft, and J. D. Ullman. *Data Structures and Algorithms.* Reading, MA: Addison-Wesley, 1983.

Ahuja, R. K., T. L. Magnanti, and J. B. Orlin. *Network Flows: Theory, Algorithms, and Applications.* Englewood Cliffs, NJ: Prentice-Hall, 1993.

Ahuja, R. K., K. Mehlhorn, J. B. Orlin, and R. E. Tarjan. "Faster Algorithms for the Shortest Path Problem." *Journal of the ACM* 37 (1990): 213–223.

Ahuja, R. K., J. B. Orlin, and R. E. Tarjan. "Improved Time Bounds for the Maximum Flow Problem." *SIAM Journal on Computing* 18, no. 5 (1989): 939–954.

Ajtai, M., J. Komlos, and E. Szemeredi. "Sorting in $c\log n$ Parallel Steps." *Combinatorica* 3 (1983): 1–19.

Akl, S. G. *The Design and Analysis of Parallel Algorithms.* Englewood Cliffs, NJ: Prentice-Hall, 1991.

———. *Parallel Sorting Algorithms.* Orlando, FL: Academic Press, 1985.

Akra, M., and L. Bazzi. "On the Solution of Linear Recurrence Equations." *Computational Optimization and Applications* 10, no. 2 (1998): 195–210.

Alon, N. "Generating Pseudo-Random Permutations and Maximum Flow Algorithms." *Information Processing Letters* 35 (1990): 201–204.

Alon, N., J. Spencer, and P. Erdös. *The Probabilistic Method.* New York: Wiley, 1992.

Annexstein, F., and K. A. Berman. "Directional Routing via Generalized st-Numberings." *SIAM Journal of Discrete Mathematics* 13, no. 2 (2000): 268–279.

Aoe, J. *Computer Algorithms: String Pattern Matching Strategies.* Los Alamitos, CA: Wiley-IEEE Computer Society Press, 1994.

Appel, K., and W. Haken. "Every Planar Map Is Four-Colorable." *Bulletin of the American Mathematical Society* 82 (1976): 711–712.

Arora, S. "The Approximability of NP-Hard Problems." In *Proceedings of the 30th Annual ACM Symposium on Theory of Computing*, 1998, pp. 337–348.

———. "Polynomial Time Approximation Schemes for Euclidean Traveling Salesman and Other Geometric Problems." *Journal of the ACM* 45, no. 5 (1998): 753–782.

Atallah, M.,ed. *Algorithms and Theory of Computation Handbook.* Boca Raton, FL: CRC Press, 1998.

Aurenhammer, F. "Voronoi Diagrams: A Survey of a Fundamental Geometric Data Structure." *ACM Computing Surveys* 23 (September 1991): 345–405.

Ausiello, G., P. Crescenzi, G. Gambosi, V. Kann, A. Marchetti-Spaccamela, and M. Protasi. *Complexity and Approximation: Combinatorial Optimization Problems and Their Approximability Properties.* New York: Springer-Verlag, 1999.

Baase, S., and A. Van Gelder. *Computer Algorithms: Introduction to the Design and Analysis.* 3rd ed. Reading, MA: Addison-Wesley, 2000.

Bach, E., and J. Shallit. *Algorithmic Number Theory.* Vol. I of *Efficient Algorithms.* Cambridge, MA: MIT Press, 1996.

Baeza-Yates, R. A. "Algorithms for String Matching: A Survey." *ACM SIGIR Forum* 23 (1989): 34–58.

Batcher, K. E. "Sorting Networks and Their Applications." In *Proceedings of the AFIPS 1968 Spring Joint Computer Conference*, pp. 307–314. Montvale, NJ: AFIPS Press, 1968.

Baudet, G. "An Analysis of the Full Alpha-Beta Pruning Algorithm." In *Proceedings of the 10th Annual ACM Symposium on Theory of Computing*, 1978, pp. 296–313.

Bayer, R. "Symmetric Binary B-Trees: Data Structure and Maintenance Algorithms." *Acta Informatica* 1 (1972): 290–306.

Bayer, R., and E. M. McCreight. "Organization and Maintenance of Large Ordered Indices." *Acta Informatica* 1 (1972): 173–189.

Bellman, R. E. *Dynamic Programming.* Princeton, NJ: Princeton University Press, 1957.

———. "On a Routing Problem." *Quarterly of Applied Mathematics* 16, no. 1 (1958): 87– 90, 1958.

Bellman, R. E., and S. E. Dreyfus. *Applied Dynamic Programming.* Princeton, NJ: Princeton University Press, 1962.

Bent, S. W., and J. W. John. "Finding the Median Requires 2*n* Comparisons." In *Proceedings of the 17th Annual ACM Symposium on Theory of Computing,* 1985, pp. 213–216.

Bentley, J. L. *Programming Pearls.* Reading, MA: Addison-Wesley, 1986.

———. *Writing Efficient Programs.* Englewood Cliffs, NJ: Prentice-Hall, 1982.

Bentley, J. L., D. Haken, and J. B. Saxe. "A General Method for Solving Divide-and-Conquer Recurrences." *SIGACT News* 12, no. 3 (1980): 36–44.

Berlekamp, E. R., J. H. Conway, and R. K. Guy. *Winning Ways for Your Mathematical Plays.* Vols. I and II. New York: Academic Press, 1982.

Berlinski, D. *The Advent of the Algorithm.* New York: Harcourt, 2000.

Berman, F., G. Fox, and T. Hey, eds. *Grid Computing: Making the Global Infrastructure a Reality.* New York: Wiley, 2003.

Berman, K. A., and J. L. Paul. "4-Color Theorem for Surfaces of Genus g." *Proceedings of the American Mathematics Society* 105 (1989): 513–522.

———. "Verifiable Broadcasting and Gossiping in Communication Networks." *Discrete Applied Mathematics* 118 (2002): 293–298.

Blum, M., R. W. Floyd, V. Pratt, R. L. Rivest, and R. E. Tarjan. "Time Bounds for Selection." *Journal of Computer and System Sciences* 7 (1973): 448–461.

Bollobas, B. *Random Graphs.* London: Academic Press, 1985.

Bondy, J. A., and U. S. R. Murty. *Graph Theory with Applications.* London: Macmillan, , 1976.

Boyer, C. B., I. Asimov, and U. C. Merzbach. *A History of Mathematics.* New York: Wiley, 1991.

Brassard, G. "Crusade for a Better Notation," *SIGACT News* 17, no.1 (1985): 60–64.

Brassard, G., and P. Bratley. *Algorithmics: Theory and Practice.* Englewood Cliffs, NJ: Prentice-Hall, 1988.

———. *Fundamentals of Algorithmics.* Englewood Cliffs, NJ: Prentice-Hall, 1996.

Brent, R. P. "An Improved Monte Carlo Factorization Algorithm." *BIT* 20, no. 2 (1980): 176–184.

Brigham, E. O. *The Fast Fourier Transform.* Englewood Cliffs, NJ: Prentice-Hall, 1974.

Carrano, F. M., and J. J. Pritchard. *Data Abstraction and Problem Solving with C++, Walls and Mirrors.* 3rd ed. Boston: Addison-Wesley, 2002.

Chabert, J. L., ed. *A History of Algorithms from the Pebble to the Microchip.* Translated by Chris Weeks. Berlin: Springer, 1999.

Chakrabarti, S. *Mining the Web, Discovering Knowledge from Hypertext Data.* San Francisco: Morgan Kaufmans, 2003.

Chartrand, G., and L. Lesniak. *Graphs & Digraphs.* 4th ed. Boca Raton, FL: Chapman & Hall/CRC Press, 2004.

Chartrand, G., and O. R. Oellerman. *Applied and Algorithmic Graph Theory*. New York: McGraw-Hill, 1993.

Chazelle, B. "A Minimum Spanning Tree Algorithm with Inverse-Ackermann Type Complexity." *Journal of the ACM* 47, no. 6 (2000): 1028–1047.

Chen, D., and X. Cheng, eds. *Pattern Recognition and String Matching*. Dordrecht, The Netherlands: Kluwer Academic, 2002.

Cherkassky, B. V., and A. V. Goldberg. "On Implementing the Push-Relabel Method for the Maximum Flow Problem." *Algorithmica* 19, no. 4 (1997): 390–410.

Cherkassky, B. V., A. V. Goldberg, and C. Silverstein. "Buckets, Heaps, Lists and Monotone Priority Queues." *SIAM Journal on Computing* 28, no. 4 (1999): 1326–1346.

Chvatal, V. "A Greedy Heuristic for the Set-Covering Problem." *Mathematical Operations Research* 4 (1979): 233–235.

Coffman, E. G., Jr., and G. Lueker. *Probabilistic Analysis of Packing and Partitioning Algorithms*. New York: Wiley, 1991.

Coffman, E. G., Jr., M. R. Garey, and D. S. Johnson. "Approximation Algorithms for Bin Packing?An Updated Survey." In *Algorithm Design for Computer System Design*, edited by G. Ausiello, M. Lucertini, and P. Serafini, pp. 49–106New York: Springer-Verlag, 1984.

Comer, D. "The Ubiquitous B-Tree." *ACM Computing Surveys* 11 (1979): 121–137.

Cook, S. A. "The Complexity of Theorem-Proving Procedures." In *Proceedings of the Third Annual ACM Symposium on the Theory of Computing*, 1971, pp. 151–158.

Cooley, J. W., and J. W. Tukey. "An Algorithm for the Machine Calculation of Complex Fourier Series." *Mathematical Computation* 19 (1965): 297–301.

Coppersmith, D., and S. Winograd. "Matrix Multiplication via Arithmetic Progressions." In *Proceedings of the 19th Annual ACM Symposium on Theory of Computing*, 1987, pp. 1–6.

Cormen, T. H., C. E. Leiserson, R. L. Rivest, and C. Stein. *Introduction to Algorithms*. 2nd ed. Cambridge, MA: MIT Press, 2001.

Cosnard, M., and D. Trystram. *Parallel Algorithms and Architectures*. Boston: PWS, 1991.

Crochemore, M. *Text Algorithms*. New York: Oxford University Press, 1994.

De Bruijn, N. G. *Asymptotic Methods in Analysis*. Amsterdam: North Holland, 1961.

Dietzfelbinger, D., A. Karlin, K. Mehlhorn, F. M. auf der Heide, H. Rohnert, and R. E. Tarjan. "Dynamic Perfect Hashing: Upper and Lower Bounds." *SIAM Journal on Computing* 23, no. 4 (1994): 738–761.

Diffie, W., and M. E. Hellman. "New Directions in Cryptography." *IEEE Transactions on Information Theory* 22, no. 6 (1976): 644–654.

Dijkstra, E. W. "A Note on Two Problems in Connection with Graphs." *Numerische Mathematik* 1 (1959): 269–271.

Dixon, J. D. "Factorization and Primality Tests." *American Mathematical Monthly* 91, no. 6 (1984): 333–352.

Dongarra, J., I. Foster, G. Fox, W. Gropp, K. Kennedy, L. Torczon, and A. White. *The Sourcebook of Parallel Computation*. San Francisco: Morgan Kaufmann, 2003.

Dor, D., and U. Zwick. "Selecting the Median." In *Proceedings of the Sixth Annual ACM-SIAM Symposium on Discrete Algorithms*, 1995, pp. 28–37.

Driscoll, J. R., H. N. Gabow, R. Shrairaman, and R. E. Tarjan. "Relaxed Heaps: An Alternative to Fibonacci Heaps with Applications to Parallel Computation." *Communications of the ACM* 31 (1998): 1343–1354.

Du, D., and K. Ko. *Theory of Computational Complexity*. New York: Wiley-Interscience, 2000.

Edelsbrunner, H. *Algorithms in Combinatorial Geometry*. Vol. 10 of *EATCS Monographs on Theoretical Computer Science*. Berlin: Springer-Verlag, 1987.

Edmonds, J. "Matroids and the Greedy Algorithm." *Mathematical Programming* 1 (1971): 126–136.

———. "Paths, Trees, and Flowers." *Canadian Journal of Mathematics* 17 (1965): 449–467.

Edmonds J., and R. M. Karp. "Theoretical Improvements in the Algorithmic Efficiency for Network Flow Problems." *Journal of the ACM* 19 (1972): 248–264.

Eiben, A., and J. Smith. *An Introduction to Evolutionary Computing*. Berlin: Springer-Verlag, 2003.

Even, S. *Graph Algorithms*. Potomac, MD: Computer Science Press, 1979.

Floyd, R. W. "Algorithm 97: Shortest Path." *Communications of the ACM* 5, no. 6 (1962): 345.

———. "Algorithm 245: Treesort 3." *Communications of the ACM* 7, no. 12 (1964): 701.

Ford, L. R., Jr., and D. R. Fulkerson. *Flows in Networks*. Princeton, NJ: Princeton University Press, 1962.

Foster, I., and C. Kesselman. *The Grid 2: Blueprint for a New Computing Infrastructure*. San Francisco: Morgan Kaufmann, 1999.

Fredman, M. L., and M. E. Saks. "The Cell Probe Complexity of Dynamic Data Structures." In *Proceedings of the Twenty-First Annual ACM Symposium on Theory of Computing*, 1989, pp. 345–354.

Fredman, M. L., and R. E. Tarjan. "Fibonacci Heaps and Their Uses in Improved Network Optimization Algorithms." *Journal of the ACM* 34, no. 3 (1987): 596–615.

Gabow, H. N. "Path-Based Depth-First Search for Strong and Biconnected Components." *Information Processing Letters* 74 (2000): 107–114.

Gabow, H. N., and R. E. Tarjan. "A Linear-Time Algorithm for a Special Case of Disjoint Set Union." *SIAM Journal on Computing* 30, no. 2 (1985): 209–221.

Gabow, H. N., Z. Galil, T. Spencer, and R. E. Tarjan. "Efficient Algorithms for Finding Minimum Spanning Trees in Undirected and Directed Graphs." *Combinatorica* 6, no. 2 (1986): 109?122.

Galil, Z., and O. Margalit. "All Pairs Shortest Distances for Graphs with Small Integer Length Edges." *Information and Computation* 134, no. 2 (1997): 103–139.

———. "All Pairs Shortest Paths for Graphs with Small Integer Length Edges." *Journal of Computer and System Sciences* 54, no. 2 (1997): 243–254

Garey, M. R., and D. Johnson. *Computers and Intractability: A Guide to the Theory of NP-Completeness.* New York: W. H. Freeman, 1979.

Garey, M. R., R. L. Graham, and J. D. Ullman. "Worst-Case Analysis of Memory Allocation Algorithms." In *Proceedings of the Fourth Annual ACM Symposium on Theory of Computing*, 1972, pp. 143–150.

Gibbons, A. M. *Algorithmic Graph Theory.* Cambridge, England: Cambridge University Press, 1985.

Goemans, M. X., and D. P. Williamson. "Improved Approximation Algorithms for Maximum Cut and Satisfiability Problems Using Semidefinite Programming." *Journal of the ACM* 42, no. 6 (1995): 1115–1145.

———. "The Primal-Dual Method for Approximation Algorithms and Its Application to Network Design Problems." In *Approximation Algorithms for NP-Hard Problems*, edited by Dorit Hochbaum, pp. 144–191. Boston: PWS, 1997.

Goldberg, A. V. "Scaling Algorithms for the Shortest Paths Problem." *SIAM Journal on Computing* 24, no. 3 (1995): 494–504.

Goldberg, A. V., and S. Rao. "Beyond the Flow Decomposition Barrier." *Journal of the ACM* 45 (1998): 783–797.

Goldberg, A. V., and R. E. Tarjan. "A New Approach to the Maximum Flow Problem." *Journal of the ACM* 35 (1988): 921–940.

Goldberg, A. V., E. Tardos, and R. E. Tarjan. "Network Flow Algorithms." In *Paths, Flows, and VLSI-Layout*, edited by B. Korte, L. Lovasz, H. J. Promel, and A. Schrijver, pp. 101–164. New York: Springer-Verlag, 1990.

Golumb, S., and L. Baumert. "Backtracking Programming." *Journal of the ACM* 12 (1965): 516–524.

Gonnet, G. H. *Handbook of Algorithms and Data Structures.* Reading, MA: Addison-Wesley, 1984.

Gonnet, G. H., and Baeza-Yates, R. *Handbook of Algorithms and Data Structures in Pascal and C.* 2nd ed. Reading, MA: Addison-Wesley, 1991.

Goodman, J. E., and J. O'Rourke, eds. *Handbook of Discrete and Computational Geometry.* 2nd ed. Boca Raton, FL: CRC Press, 2004.

Goodrich, M. T., and Tamassia, R. *Algorithm Design, Foundations, Analysis, and Internet Examples,* New York, NY: John-Wiley & Sons, 2002.

Gordon, M., and M. Minoux. *Graphs and Algorithms.* Translated by S. Vajda. New York: Wiley, 1984.

Graham, R. L. "Bounds for Certain Multiprocessor Anomalies." *Bell Systems Technical Journal* 45 (1966): 1563–1581.

———. "An Efficient Algorithm for Determining the Convex Hull of a Finite Planar Set." *Information Processing Letters* 1 (1972): 132–133.

Graham, R. L., and P. Hell. "On the History of the Minimum Spanning Tree Problem." *Annals of the History of Computing* 7 (1985): 43–57.

Graham, R. L., D. E. Knuth, and O. Patashnik. *Concrete Mathematics: A Foundation for Computer Science.* 2nd ed. Reading, MA: Addison-Wesley, 1994.

Greenlaw, R., H. J. Hoover, and W. L. Ruzzo. *Limits to Parallel Computation: P-Completeness Theory*. New York: Oxford University Press, 1995.

Gropp, W., et al. *MPI—The Complete Reference*. 2 vols. 2nd ed. Cambridge, MA: MIT Press, 1998.

Gropp, W., E. Lusk, and A. Skjellum. *Using MPI—Portable Parallel Programming with the Message Passing Interface*. 2nd ed. Cambridge, MA: MIT Press, 1999.

Gross, J. L., and J. Yellen, eds. *Handbook of Graph Theory*. Boca Raton, FL: Chapman & Hall/CRC Press, 2004.

Grotschel, M., L. Lovász, and A. Schrijver. *Geometric Algorithms and Combinatorial Optimization*. New York: Springer-Verlag, 1988.

Gries, D. *The Science of Programming*. New York: Springer-Verlag, 1981.

Gupta, R., S. Smolka, and S. Bhaskar. "On Randomization in Sequential and Distributed Algorithms." *ACM Computing Surveys* 25 (March 1994): 7–86.

Gusfield, D. *Algorithms on Strings, Trees, and Sequences: Computer Science and Computational Biology*. Cambridge, England: Cambridge University Press, 1997.

Harary, F. *Graph Theory*. Reading, MA: Addison-Wesley, 1969.

Harel, D. *Algorithmics: The Spirit of Computing*. 2nd ed. Reading, MA: Addison Wesley, 1992.

Harfst, G. C., and E. M. Reingold. "A Potential-Based Amortized Analysis of the Union-Find Data Structure." *SIGACT News* 31, no. 3 (2000): 86–95.

Harris, T. J. "A Survey of PRAM Simulation Techniques." *ACM Computing Surveys* 26 (1994): 187–206.

Hartmanis, J and R. E. Stearns. "On the Computational Complexity of Algorithms." *Transactions of the American Mathematical Society* 117 (1965): 285–306.

Heideman, M. T., D. H. Johnson, and C. S. Burrus. "Gauss and the History of the Fast Fourier Transform." *IEEE ASSP Magazine* (1984): 14–21.

Hoare, C. A. R. "Quicksort." *Computer Journal* 5 (1962): 10–15. Reprinted in *Great Papers in Computer Science*, edited by Phillip Laplante, pp. 31–39. Minneapolis/St. Paul: West Publishing, 1996.

Hochbaum, D. S. *Approximation Algorithms for NP-Hard Problems*. Monterey, CA: Brooks/Cole, 1996.

———. "Efficient Bounds for the Stable Set, Vertex Cover and Set Packing Problems." *Discrete Applied Mathematics* 6 (1983): 243–254.

Hofri, M. *Probabilistic Analysis of Algorithms*. New York: Springer-Verlag, 1987.

Holland, J. *Adaptation in Natural and Artificial Systems*. Cambridge, MA: MIT Press, 1992.

Hopcroft, J. E., and R. E. Tarjan. "Efficient Algorithms for Graph Manipulation." *Communications of the ACM* 16, no. 6 (1973): 372–378.

Hopcroft, J. E. and J. D. Ullman. "Set Merging Algorithms." *SIAM Journal on Computing* 2, no. 4 (1973): 294–303.

Horowitz, E., and S. Sahni. *Fundamentals of Computer Algorithms*. Potomac, MD: Computer Science Press, 1978.

Horowitz, E., S. Sahni, and S. Rajasekaran. *Computer Algorithms*. New York: Computer Science Press, 1998.

Horspool, R. N. "Practical Fast Searching in Strings." *Software-Practice and Experience* 10 (1980): 501–506.

Hu, T. C., and M. T. Shing. "Computations of Matrix Chain Products, Part I." *SIAM Journal on Computing* 11, no. 2 (1982): 362–373.

———. "Computations of Matrix Chain Products, Part II." *SIAM Journal on Computing* 13, no. 2 (1984): 228–251.

Huffman, D. A. "A Method for the Construction of Minimum Redundancy Codes." *Proceedings of the Institute of Radio Engineers* 40 (1952): 1098–1101.

Ibarra, O. H., and C. E. Kim. "Fast Approximation Algorithms for the Knapsack and Sum of Subset Problems." *Journal of the ACM* 9 (1975): 463–468.

JaJa, J. *An Introduction to Parallel Algorithms*. Reading, MA: Addison-Wesley, 1992.

Jarvis, R. A. "On the Identification of the Convex Hull of a Finite Set of Points in the Plane." *Information Processing Letters* 2 (1973): 18–21.

Jensen, T. R., and B. Toft. *Graph Coloring Problems*. New York: Wiley, 1995.

Johnson, D. S. "Approximation Algorithms for Combinatorial Problems." *Journal of Computer and System Sciences* 9 (1974): 256–278.

Johnsonbaugh, R., and M. Schaefer. *Algorithms*. Upper Saddle River, NJ: Pearson Prentice-Hall, 2004.

Kanal, L., and V. Kumar, eds. *Search in Artificial Intelligence*. New York: Springer-Verlag, 1988.

Karger, D. R., P. Klein, and R. E. Tarjan. "A Randomized Linear-Time Algorithm to Find Minimum Spanning Trees." *Journal of the ACM* 42 (1995): 321–328.

Karger, D., E. Lehman, T. Leighton, M. Levin, D. Lewin, and R. Panigrahy. "Consistent Hashing and Random Trees: Distributed Caching Protocols for Relieving Hot Spots on the World Wide Web." In *Proceedings of the 29th Annual ACM Symposium on Theory of Computing*, 1997, pp. 654-663..

Karmarkar, N. "A New Polynomial-Time Algorithm for Linear Programming." *Combinatorica* 4 (1984): 373–395.

Karniadakis, G., and R. Kirby, II. *Parallel Scientific Computing in C++ and MPI: A Seamless Approach to Parallel Algorithms and Their Implementation*. Cambridge, England: Cambridge University Press, 2003.

Karp, R. M. "An Introduction to Randomized Algorithms." *Discrete Applied Mathematics* 34 (1991): 165–201.

———. "Reducibility Among Combinatorical Problems of Computer Computaions." In *Complexity of Computer Computations*, edited by E. Miller and J. W. Thatcher, pp. 88–104. New York: Plenum Press, 1972.

Karp, R. M., and M. O. Rabin. *Efficient Randomized Pattern-Matching Algorithms*. Technical Report TR-31-81. Cambridge, MA: Harvard University, Aiken Computation Laboratory, 1981.

King, V., S. Rao, and R. E. Tarjan. "A Faster Deterministic Maximum Flow Algorithm." *Journal of Algorithms* 17 (1994): 447–474.

Kingston, J. H. *Algorithms and Data Structures: Design, Correctness, Analysis*. Reading, MA: AddisonWesley, 1997.

Klein, P. N., and N. E. Young. "Approximation Algorithms." In *Algorithms and Theory of Computation Handbook*, edited by M. J. Atallah, pp. 34-1–34-19. Boca Raton, FL: CRC Press, 1999.

Knuth, D. "An Analysis of Alpha-Beta Cutoffs." *Artificial Intelligence* 6 (1975): 293–323.

Knuth, D. E. *The Art of Computer Programming*. Vol. 1: *Fundamental Algorithms*. 3rd ed. Reading, MA: Addison-Wesley, 1997.

———. *The Art of Computer Programming*. Vol. 2: *Seminumerical Algorithms*. 3rd ed. Reading, MA: Addison-Wesley, 1998.

———. *The Art of Computer Programming*. Vol. 3: *Sorting and Searching*. 2nd ed. Reading, MA: Addison-Wesley, 1998.

———. "Big Omicron and Big Omega and Big Theta." *SIGACT News* 8, no. 2 (April–June 1976): 18–24.

———. "Optimum Binary Search Trees." *Acta Informatica* 1 (1971): 14–25.

Knuth, D. E., J. H. Morris, Jr., and V. R. Pratt. "Fast Pattern Matching in Strings." *SIAM Journal on Computing* 6, no. 1 (1977): 323–350.

Korf, R. E. "Real-Time Heuristic Search," *Artificial Intelligence* 42 (1990): 189–211.

Kouril, M., and J. Paul. "A Parallel Backtracking Framework (BkFr) for Single and Multiple Clusters." In *Proceedings of ACM CF'04 (Computer Frontiers)*, 2004, pp. 302-312

Koza, J., F. H. Bennett, D. Andre, and M. A. Keane. *Genetic Programming III: Darwinian Invention and Problem Solving*. San Francisco: Morgan Kaufmann, 1999.

Kozen, D. C. *The Design and Analysis of Algorithms*. New York: Springer-Verlag, 1992.

Kruse, R. L. *Data Structures and Program Design*. Englewood Cliffs, NJ: Prentice-Hall, 1984.

Kruskal, J. B., Jr. "On the Shortest Spanning Subtree of a Graph and the Traveling Salesman Problem." *Proceedings of the American Mathematical Society* 7 (1956): 48–50.

Lakshmivarahan, S., and S. K. Dhall. *Analysis and Design of Parallel Algorithms*. New York: McGraw-Hill, 1990.

———. *Parallel Computing Using the Prefix Problem*. New York: Oxford University Press, 1994.

Lawler, E. L. *Combinatorial Optimization: Networks and Matroids*. New York: Holt, Rinehart and Winston, 1976.

Lawler, E. L., and D. W. Wood. "Branch-and-Bound Methods: A Survey." *Operations Research* 14 (1966): 699–719.

Lawler, E. L., J. K. Lenstra, A. H. G. R. Kan, and D. B. Schmoys, eds. *The Traveling Salesman Problem*. New York: Wiley, 1985.

Lee, D. T., and F. P. Preparata. "Computational Geometry: A Survey." *IEEE Transactions on Computers* C-33 (1984): 1072–1101.

Leighton, F. T. *Parallel Algorithms and Architectures*. San Mateo, CA: Morgan Kaufmann, 1992.

Levin, L. A. "Universal Sorting Problems." *Problemy Peredachi Informatsii* 9, no. 3 (1973): 115–116. English translation in *Problems of Information Transmission* 9 (1973): 265–266.

Levitin, A. *The Design and Analysis of Algorithms.* New York: Addison-Wesley, 1993.

Lewis, H. R., and C. H. Papadimitriou. *Elements of the Theory of Computation.* 2nd ed. Upper Saddle River, NJ: Prentice-Hall, 1998.

Lovász, L. "On the Ratio of Optimal Integral and Fractional Covers." *Discrete Mathematics* 13 (1975): 383–390.

Lovász, L., and M. D. Plummer. *Matching Theory.* Amsterdam: North Holland, 1986.

Lynch, N. *Distributed Algorithms.* San Francisco: Morgan Kaufmann, 1997.

Majewski, B. S., N. C. Wormahld, G. Havas, and A. J. Czech. "Graphs, Hypergraphs, and Hashing." In *Proceedings of the 19th International Workshop on Graph-Theoretic Concepts in Computer Science,* 1993, pp. 153-165.

Manber, U. *Introduction to Algorithms: A Creative Approach.* Reading, MA: Addison-Wesley, 1989.

Marchetti-Spaccamela, A. *Complexity and Approximation: Combinatorial Optimization Problems and Their Approximability Properties.* New York: Springer-Verlag, 1999.

Martello, S., and P. Toth. *Knapsack Problems: Algorithms and Computer Implementations.* Chichester, England: Wiley, 1990.

Mehlhorn, K. *Data Structures and Algorithms 1: Sorting and Searching.* Vol. I of *EATCS Monographs on Theoretical Computer Science.* Heidelberg, Germany: Springer-Verlag, 1984.

———. *Data Structures and Algorithms 2: Graph Algorithms and NP-Completeness.* Vol. 2 of *EATCS Monographs on Theoretical Computer Science.* Heidelberg, Germany: Springer-Verlag, 1984.

———. *Data Structures and Algorithms 3: Multi-dimensional Searching and Computational Geometry.* Vol. 3 of *EATCS Monographs on Theoretical Computer Science.* Heidelberg, Germany: Springer-Verlag, 1984.

Menezes, A. J., P. C. van Oorschot, and S. A. Vanstone. *Handbook of Applied Cryptography.* Boca Raton, FL: CRC Press, 1997.

Miller, G. L. "Riemann's Hypothesis and Tests for Primality." *Journal of Computer and System Sciences* 13, no. 3 (1976): 300–317.

Mitten, L. "Branch-and-Bound Methods: General Formulation and Properties." *Operations Research* 18 (1970): 24–34.

Moore, E. F. "The Shortest Path Through a Maze." In *Proceedings of the International Symposium on the Theory of Switching,* pp. 285–292. Cambridge, MA: Harvard University Press, 1959.

Motwani, R., and P. Raghavan. *Randomized Algorithms.* Cambridge, England: Cambridge University Press, 1995.

Motwani, R., J. Naor, and P. Raghavan. "Randomized Approximation Algorithms in Combinatorial Optimization." In *Approximation Algorithms for NP-Hard Problems,* edited by Dorit Hochbaum, pp. 447–481. Boston: PWS, 1997.

National Research Council. *Probability and Algorithms.* Washington, DC: National Academy Press, 1992.

Navarro, G. "A Guided Tour to Approximate String Matching." *ACM Computing Surveys* 33, no. 1 (2001): 31–88.

Navarro, G., and M. Raffinot. *Flexible Pattern Matching in Strings*. Cambridge, England: Cambridge University Press, 2002.

Nemhauser, G. *Introduction to Dynamic Programming*. New York: Wiley, 1966.

Nilsson, N. J. *Principles of Artificial Intelligence*. Palo Alto, CA: Tioga, 1980.

O'Rourke, J. *Computational Geometry in C*. New York: Cambridge University Press, 1994.

Pach, J., ed. *New Trends in Discrete and Computational Geometry*. Vol. 10 of *Algorithms and Combinatorics*. New York: Springer-Verlag, 1993.

Pacheco, P. *Parallel Programming with MPI*. San Francisco: Morgan Kaufmann, 1997.

Papadimitriou, C. H. *Computational Complexity*. Reading, MA: Addison-Wesley, 1993.

Papadimitriou, C. H., and K. Steiglitz. *Combinatorial Optimization: Algorithms and Complexity*. Englewood Cliffs, NJ: Prentice-Hall, 1982.

Patashnik, O. "Qubic: 4¥4¥4 Tic-Tac-Toe." *Mathematics Magazine* 53 (1980): 202–223.

Pearl, J. *Heuristics: Intelligent Search Strategies for Computer Problem Solving*. Reading, MA: Addison-Wesley, 1984.

Peleg, D. *Distributed Computing: A Locally-Sensitive Approach*. Philadelphia: Society for Industrial and Applied Mathematics, 2000.

Pollack, S. E. "The Development of Computer Science." In *Studies in Computer Science*, edited by S. Pollack, Washington, DC: Mathematical Association of America, 1982.

Pomerance, C. "On the Distribution of Pseudoprimes." *Mathematics of Computation* 37, no. 156 (1981): 587–593.

———, ed. *Proceedings of the AMS Symposia in Applied Mathematics: Computational Number Theory and Cryptography*. Providence, RI: American Mathematical Society, 1990.

Pratt, W. K. *Digital Image Processing*. 2nd ed. New York: Wiley, 1991.

Preparata, F. P., and M. I. Shamos. *Computational Geometry: An Introduction*. New York: Springer-Verlag, 1985.

Prim, R. C. "Shortest Connection Networks and Some Generalizations." *Bell System Technical Journal* 36, no. 1 (1957): 1389–1401.

Purdom, P. W., Jr., and C. Brown. *The Analysis of Algorithms*. New York: Holt, Rinehart and Winston, 1985.

Quinn, M. J. *Designing Efficient Algorithms for Parallel Computers*. 2nd ed. New York: McGraw-Hill, 1994.

———. *Parallel Computing: Theory and Practice*. New York: McGraw-Hill, 1994.

———. *Parallel Programming in C with MPI and OpenMP*. New York: McGraw-Hill, 2003.

Rabin, M. O. "Probabilistic Algorithm for Testing Primality." *Journal of Number Theory* 12, no. 1 (1980): 128–138.

Reingold, E. M., J. Nievergelt, and N. Deo. *Combinatorial Algorithms: Theory and Practice*. Englewood Cliffs, NJ: Prentice-Hall, 1977.

Rich, E., and K. Knight. *Artificial Intelligence*. 2nd ed. New York: McGraw-Hill, 1991.

Rivest, R. L., A. Shamir, and L. Adleman. "A Method for Obtaining Digital Signatures and Public-Key Cryptosystems." *Communications of the ACM* 21, no. 2 (1978): 120–126.

Rosenkrantz, D. J., R. E. Stearns, and P. M. Lewis. "An Analysis of Several Heuristics for the Traveling Salesman Problem." *SIAM Journal on Computing* 6 (1977): 563–581.

Russell, S. J., and P. Norvig. *Artificial Intelligence: A Modern Approach*. Englewood Cliffs, NJ: Prentice-Hall, 1995.

Scherson, I., S. Sen, and A. Shamir. "Shear-Sort: A True Two-Dimensional Sorting Technique for VLSI Networks." In *Proceedings of the 15th IEEE-ACM ICPP (Institute for Certification of Computing Professional)*, 1986, pp. 903–908.

Schmeh, K. *Cryptography and Public Key Infrastructure on the Internet*. West Sussex , England: Wiley, 2003.

Schonhage, A., M. Paterson, and N. Pippenger. "Finding the Median." *Journal of Computer and System Sciences* 13, no. 2 (1976): 184–199.

Schrijver, A. "Paths and Flows—A Historical Survey." *CWI Quarterly* 6 (1993): 169–183.

Sedgewick, R. *Algorithms*. 2nd ed. Reading, MA: Addison-Wesley, 1988.

Sharir, M. "A Strong-Connectivity Algorithm and Its Application in Data Flow Analysis." *Computers and Mathematics with Applications* 7, no. 1 (1981): 67–72.

Shell, D. L. "A High-Speed Sorting Procedure." *Communications of the ACM* 2, no. 7 (July 1959): 30–32.

Shmoys, D. B. "Computing Near-Optimal Solutions to Combinatorial Optimization Problems." In *Combinatorial Optimization*, edited by W. Cook, L. Lovász, and P. Seymour. Vol. 20 of *DIMACS Series in Discrete Mathematics and Theoretical Computer Science*. Providence, RI: American Mathematical Society, 1995.

Sipser, M. *Introduction to the Theory of Computation*. Boston: PWS, 1997.

Skiena, S. S. *Algorithm Design Manual*. New York: Springer-Verlag, 1998.

Sleator, D. D., and R. E. Tarjan. "A Data Structure for Dynamic Trees." *Journal of Computer and System Sciences* 26, no. 3 (1983): 362–391.

———. "Self-Adjusting Binary Search Trees." *Journal of the ACM* 32, no. 3 (1985): 652–686.

Smith, J. R. *The Design and Analysis of Parallel Algorithms*. New York: Oxford University Press, 1993.

Spencer, J. *Ten Lectures on the Probabilistic Method*. Regional Conference Series on Applied Mathematics 52. Philadelphia: Society for Industrial and Applied Mathematics, 1987.

Stephen, G. A. *String Searching Algorithms*. London: World Scientific Publishing, 1994.

Strassen, V. "Gaussian Elimination Is Not Optimal." *Numerische Mathematik* 14, no. 3 (1969): 354–356.

Tarjan, R. E. "Algorithm Design." *Communications of the ACM* 30, no. 3 (1987): 204–212.

———. "Amortized Computational Complexity." *SIAM Journal on Applied and Discrete Mathematics* 14 (November 1985): 862–874.

———. "A Class of Algorithms Which Require Nonlinear Time to Maintain Disjoint Sets." *Journal of Computer and Systems Sciences* 18 (1979): 110–127.

———. *Data Structures and Network Algorithms*. Philadelphia: Society for Industrial and Applied Mathematics, 1983.

———. "Depth First Search and Linear Graph Algorithms." *SIAM Journal on Computing* 1, no. 2 (1972): 146–160.

———. "Efficiency of a Good but Not Linear Set Union Algorithm." *Journal of the ACM* 22 (1975): 215–225.

Tarjan, R. E., and J. van Leeuwen. "Worst-Case Analysis of Set Union Algorithms." *Journal of the ACM* 31, no. 2 (1984): 245–281.

Tchueste, M. *Parallel Computation on Regular Arrays*. Manchester, England: Manchester University Press, 1991.

Tel, N. *Introduction to Distributed Algorithms*. 2nd ed. Cambridge, England: Cambridge University Press, 2000.

Thulasiraman, K., and M. N. S. Swamy. *Graphs: Theory and Algorithms*. New York: Wiley, 1992.

Van Leeuwen, J., ed. *Algorithms and Complexity*. Vol. A in *Handbook of Theoretical Computer Science*. Cambridge, MA: Elsevier Science and MIT Press, 1990.

Van Loan, C. *Computational Frameworks for the Fast Fourier Transform*. Philadelphia: Society for Industrial and Applied Mathematics, 1992.

Vazirani, V. V. *Approximation Algorithms*. New York: Springer-Verlag, 2001.

Verma, R. M. "General Techniques for Analyzing Recursive Algorithms with Applications." *SIAM Journal on Computing* 26, no. 2 (1997): 568–581.

Vitter, J. S. "External Memory Algorithms and Data Structures: Dealing with Massive Data." *ACM Computing Surveys* 33, no. 2 (June 2001): 209–271.

Walker, R. J. "An Enumerative Technique for a Class of Combinatorial Problems." In *Proceedings of Symposia in Applied Mathematics* 10 (1960): 91–94

Warshall, S. "A Theorem on Boolean Matrices." *Journal of the ACM*. 9, no. 1 (1962): 11–12.

Weiss, M. A. *Data Structures and Algorithm Analysis in Java*. Reading, MA: Addison-Wesley, 1999.

West, D. *Introduction to Graph Theory*. 2nd ed. Englewood Cliffs, NJ: Prentice-Hall, 2001.

Wilf, H. S. *Algorithms and Complexity*. Englewood Cliffs, NJ: Prentice-Hall, 1986.

Wilkinson, B., and M. Allen. *Parallel Programming*. Upper Saddle River, NJ: Prentice-Hall, 1999.

Williams, J. W. J. "Algorithm 232: Heapsort." *Communications of the ACM* 7 (June 1964): 347–348.

Wu, Y. W., and C. Kun-Mao. *Spanning Trees and Optimization Problems*. Boca Raton, FL: CRC Press, 2004.

INDEX

*Page numbers in italic represent diagrams/figures/psuedocode.